Nineteenth-Century Literature Criticism

Guide to Gale Literary Criticism Series

When you need to review criticism of literary works, these are the Gale series to use:

If the author's death date is:	You should turn to:
After Dec. 31, 1959 (or author is still living)	***CONTEMPORARY LITERARY CRITICISM*** for example: Jorge Luis Borges, Anthony Burgess, William Faulkner, Mary Gordon, Ernest Hemingway, Iris Murdoch
1900 through 1959	***TWENTIETH-CENTURY LITERARY CRITICISM*** for example: Willa Cather, F. Scott Fitzgerald, Henry James, Mark Twain, Virginia Woolf
1800 through 1899	***NINETEENTH-CENTURY LITERATURE CRITICISM*** for example: Emily Dickinson, Fedor Dostoevski, Gerard Manley Hopkins, George Sand
1400 through 1799	***LITERATURE CRITICISM FROM 1400 TO 1800 (excluding Shakespeare)*** for example: Anne Bradstreet, Pierre Corneille, Daniel Defoe, Alexander Pope, Jonathan Swift, Phillis Wheatley ***SHAKESPEAREAN CRITICISM*** Shakespeare's plays and poetry
Antiquity through 1399	***CLASSICAL AND MEDIEVAL LITERATURE CRITICISM*** for example: Dante, Plato, Homer, Sophocles, Vergil, the Beowulf poet *(Volume 1 forthcoming)*

Gale also publishes related criticism series:

CHILDREN'S LITERATURE REVIEW

This ongoing series covers authors of all eras. Presents criticism on authors and author/illustrators who write for the preschool through high school audience.

CONTEMPORARY ISSUES CRITICISM

This two volume set presents criticism on contemporary authors writing on current issues. Topics covered include the social sciences, philosophy, economics, natural science, law, and related areas.

ISSN 0732-1864

Volume 13

Nineteenth-Century Literature Criticism

Excerpts from Criticism of the
Works of Novelists, Poets, Playwrights,
Short Story Writers, Philosophers, and Other
Creative Writers Who Died between 1800
and 1900, from the First Published Critical
Appraisals to Current Evaluations

Cherie D. Abbey
Editor

Jelena Obradovic Kronick
Janet Mullane
Associate Editors

Gale Research Company
Book Tower
Detroit, Michigan 48226

STAFF

Cherie D. Abbey, *Editor*

Jelena Obradovic Kronick, Janet Mullane, *Associate Editors*

Gail Ann Schulte, Robert Thomas Wilson, *Senior Assistant Editors*

Rachel Carlson, Mary Nelson-Pulice, *Assistant Editors*

Sheila Fitzgerald, Phyllis Carmel Mendelson, Emily B. Tennyson,
Anna C. Wallbillich, *Contributing Editors*
Melissa Reiff Hug, Patricia Askie Mackmiller, *Contributing Assistant Editors*

Lizbeth A. Purdy, *Production Supervisor*
Denise Michlewicz Broderick, *Production Coordinator*
Eric Berger, *Assistant Production Coordinator*
Kathleen M. Cook, Maureen Duffy, Sheila J. Nasea, *Editorial Assistants*

Victoria B. Cariappa, *Research Coordinator*
Maureen R. Richards, *Assistant Research Coordinator*
Daniel Kurt Gilbert, Kent Graham, Michele R. O'Connell,
Keith E. Schooley, Filomena Sgambati, Vincenza G. Tranchida,
Mary D. Wise, *Research Assistants*

Linda Marcella Pugliese, *Manuscript Coordinator*
Donna Craft, *Assistant Manuscript Coordinator*
Maureen A. Puhl, Rosetta Irene Simms, *Manuscript Assistants*

Jeanne A. Gough, *Permissions Supervisor*
Janice M. Mach, *Permissions Coordinator, Text*
Patricia A. Seefelt, *Permissions Coordinator, Illustrations*
Susan D. Battista, *Assistant Permissions Coordinator*
Margaret A. Chamberlain, Sandra C. Davis, Kathy Grell,
Josephine M. Keene, Mary M. Matuz, *Senior Permissions Assistants*
H. Diane Cooper, Colleen M. Crane, Mabel C. Gurney, *Permissions Assistants*
Margaret A. Carson, Helen Hernandez, Anita Williams, *Permissions Clerks*

Frederick G. Ruffner, *Publisher*
Dedria Bryfonski, *Editorial Director*
Ellen Crowley, *Associate Editorial Director*
Christine Nasso, *Director, Literature Division*
Laurie Lanzen Harris, *Senior Editor, Literary Criticism Series*
Dennis Poupard, *Managing Editor, Literary Criticism Series*

Copyright © 1986 by Gale Research Company

Library of Congress Catalog Card Number 81-6943
ISBN 0-8103-5813-1
ISSN 0732-1864

Computerized photocomposition by
Typographics, Incorporated
Kansas City, Missouri

Printed in the United States

Contents

Preface

The nineteenth century was a time of tremendous growth in human endeavor: in science, in social history, and particularly in literature. The era saw the development of the novel, witnessed radical changes from classicism to romanticism to realism, and contained intellectual and artistic ideas that continue to inspire authors of our own century. The importance of the writers of the nineteenth century is twofold, for they provide insight into their own time as well as into the universal nature of human experience.

The literary criticism of an era can also give us insight into the moral and intellectual atmosphere of the past, because the criteria by which a work of art is judged reflect current philosophical and social attitudes. Literary criticism takes many forms: the traditional essay, the book or play review, even the parodic poem. Criticism can also be of several types: normative, descriptive, interpretive, textual, appreciative, generic. Collectively, the range of critical response helps us to understand a work of art, an author, an era.

The Scope of the Work

The success of two of Gale's current literary series, *Contemporary Literary Criticism (CLC)* and *Twentieth-Century Literary Criticism (TCLC),* which excerpt criticism of creative writing from the twentieth century, suggested an equivalent need among students and teachers of literature of the nineteenth century. Moreover, since the analysis of this literature spans almost two hundred years, a vast amount of critical material confronts the student.

Nineteenth-Century Literature Criticism (NCLC) presents significant passages from published criticism on authors who died between 1800 and 1900. The author list for each volume of *NCLC* is carefully compiled to represent a variety of genres and nationalities and to cover authors who are currently regarded as the most important writers of their era as well as those whose contribution to literature and literary history is significant. The truly great writers are rare, and in the intervals between them lesser but genuine artists, as well as writers who enjoyed immense popularity in their own time and in their own countries, are important to the study of nineteenth-century literature. The length of each author entry is intended to reflect the amount of attention the author has received from critics writing in English and from foreign critics in translation. Articles and books that have not been translated into English are excluded. However, since many of the major foreign studies have been translated into English and are excerpted in *NCLC,* author entries reflect the viewpoints of many nationalities. Each author entry represents a historical overview of critical reaction to the author's work: early criticism is presented to indicate initial responses and later selections represent any rise or decline in the author's literary reputation. We have also attempted to identify and include excerpts from the seminal essays on each author as well as modern perspectives. Thus, *NCLC* is designed to serve as an introduction for the student of nineteenth-century literature to the authors of that period and to the most significant commentators on these authors.

NCLC entries are intended to be definitive overviews. In order to devote more attention to each writer, approximately fifteen authors are included in each 600-page volume compared with about fifty authors in a *CLC* volume of similar size. Because of the great quantity of critical material available on many authors, and because of the resurgence of criticism generated by such events as an author's centennial or anniversary celebration, the republication of an author's works, or publication of a newly translated work or volume of letters, an author may appear more than once. Usually, a few author entries in each volume of *NCLC* are devoted to single works by major authors who have appeared previously in the series. Only those individual works that have been the subject of extensive criticism and are widely studied in literature courses are selected for this in-depth treatment. Jane Austen's *Pride and Prejudice* and George Eliot's *Middlemarch* are the subjects of such entries in *NCLC,* Volume 13.

The Organization of the Book

An author section consists of the following elements: author heading, biographical and critical introduction, principal works, excerpts of criticism (each preceded by explanatory notes and followed by a bibliographical citation), and an additional bibliography.

- The *author heading* consists of the author's full name, followed by birth and death dates. The unbracketed portion of the name denotes the form under which the author most commonly wrote. If an author wrote consistently under a pseudonym, the pseudonym will be listed in the author heading and the real name given in parentheses on the first line of the biographical and critical introduction. Also located at the beginning of the introduction are any name variations under which an author wrote, including transliterated forms for authors whose languages use nonroman alphabets. Uncertainty as to a birth or death date is indicated by a question mark.

- A *portrait* of the author is included when available. Many entries also feature illustrations of materials pertinent to an author's career, including manuscript pages, letters, book illustrations, and representations of important people, places, and events in an author's life.

- The *biographical and critical introduction* contains background information that elucidates the author's creative output. When applicable, biographical and critical introductions are followed by references to additional entries on the author in past volumes of *NCLC* and in other literary reference series published by Gale Research Company. These include *Dictionary of Literary Biography, Children's Literature Review,* and *Something about the Author.*

- The list of *principal works* is chronological by date of first book publication and identifies genres. In those instances where the first publication was in other than the English language, the title and date of the first English-language edition are given in brackets. Unless otherwise indicated, dramas are dated by the first performance, rather than first publication.

- *Criticism* is arranged chronologically in each author section to provide a perspective on any changes in critical evaluation over the years. In the text of each author entry, titles by the author are printed in boldface type. This allows the reader to ascertain without difficulty the works being discussed. For purposes of easier identification, the critic's name and the publication date of the essay are given at the beginning of each piece of criticism. Unsigned criticism is preceded by the title of the journal in which it appeared. For an anonymous essay later attributed to a critic, the critic's name appears in brackets at the beginning of the excerpt and in the bibliographical citation.

- Essays are prefaced with *explanatory notes* as an additional aid to students using *NCLC.* The explanatory notes provide several types of useful information, including the reputation of the critic, the importance of a work of criticism, a synopsis of the essay, the specific approach of the critic (biographical, psychoanalytic, structuralist, etc.), and the growth of critical controversy or changes in critical trends regarding an author's work. In some cases, these notes include cross-references to related criticism in the author's entry or in the additional bibliography. Dates in parentheses within the explanatory notes refer to other essays in the author entry.

- A complete *bibliographical citation* designed to facilitate the location of the original essay or book follows each piece of criticism. An asterisk (*) at the end of the citation indicates that the essay is on more than one author.

- The *additional bibliography* appearing at the end of each author entry suggests further reading on the author. In some cases it includes essays for which the editors could not obtain reprint rights. An asterisk (*) at the end of a citation indicates that the essay is on more than one author.

An appendix lists the sources from which material in the volume is reprinted. It does not, however, list every book or periodical consulted for the volume.

Cumulative Indexes

Each volume of *NCLC* includes a cumulative index listing all the authors who have appeared in *Contemporary Literary Criticism, Twentieth-Century Literary Criticism, Nineteenth-Century Literature Criticism,* and *Literature Criticism from 1400 to 1800,* along with cross-references to the Gale series *Children's Literature Review, Authors in the News, Contemporary Authors, Contemporary Authors Autobiography Series, Dictionary of Literary Biography, Something about the Author,* and *Yesterday's Authors of Books for Children.* Users will welcome this cumulated author index as a useful tool for locating an author within the various series. The index, which lists birth and death dates when available, will be particularly valuable for those authors who are identified with a certain period but whose death date causes them to be placed in another, or for those authors whose careers span two periods. For example, Fedor Dostoevski is found in *NCLC,* yet Leo Tolstoy, another major nineteenth-century Russian novelist, is found in *TCLC.*

NCLC also includes a cumulative nationality index to authors. Authors are listed alphabetically by nationality, followed by the volume numbers in which they appear.

A cumulative index to critics is another useful feature of *NCLC*. Under each critic's name are listed the authors on whom the critic has written and the volume and page where the criticism appears.

Acknowledgments

No work of this scope can be accomplished without the cooperation of many people. The editors especially wish to thank the copyright holders of the excerpts included in this volume, the permissions managers of the book and magazine publishing companies for assisting us in securing reprint rights, and the staffs of the Detroit Public Library, University of Michigan Library, and Wayne State University Library for making their resources available to us. We are also grateful to Anthony J. Bogucki for his assistance with copyright research.

Suggestions Are Welcome

The editors welcome the comments and suggestions of readers to expand the coverage and enhance the usefulness of the series.

Authors to Appear in Future Volumes

About, Edmond Francois 1828-1885
Aguilo I. Fuster, Maria 1825-1897
Aksakov, Konstantin 1817-1860
Aleardi, Aleadro 1812-1878
Alecsandri, Vasile 1821-1890
Alencar, Jose 1829-1877
Alfieri, Vittorio 1749-1803
Allingham, William 1824-1889
Almquist, Carl Jonas Love 1793-1866
Alorne, Leonor de Almeida 1750-1839
Alsop, Richard 1761-1815
Altimirano, Ignacio Manuel 1834-1893
Alvarenga, Manuel Inacio da Silva
    1749-1814
Alvares de Azevedo, Manuel Antonio
    1831-1852
Anzengruber, Ludwig 1839-1889
Arany, Janos 1817-1882
Arene, Paul 1843-1893
Aribau, Bonaventura Carlos 1798-1862
Arjona de Cubas, Manuel Maria de
    1771-1820
Arnault, Antoine Vincent 1766-1834
Arneth, Alfred von 1819-1897
Arnim, Bettina von 1785-1859
Arnold, Thomas 1795-1842
Arriaza y Superviela, Juan Bautista
    1770-1837
Asbjornsen, Peter Christian 1812-1885
Ascasubi, Hilario 1807-1875
Atterbom, Per Daniel Amadeus
    1790-1855
Aubanel, Theodore 1829-1886
Auerbach, Berthold 1812-1882
Augier, Guillaume V.E. 1820-1889
Azeglio, Massimo D' 1798-1866
Azevedo, Guilherme de 1839-1882
Bakin (pseud. of Takizawa Okikani)
    1767-1848
Bakunin, Mikhail Aleksandrovich
    1814-1876
Baratynski, Jewgenij Abramovich
    1800-1844
Barnes, William 1801-1886
Batyushkov, Konstantin 1778-1855
Beattie, James 1735-1803
Beckford, William 1760-1844
Becquer, Gustavo Adolfo 1836-1870
Bentham, Jeremy 1748-1832
Beranger, Jean-Pierre de 1780-1857
Berchet, Ciovanni 1783-1851
Berzsenyi, Daniel 1776-1836
Black, William 1841-1898
Blair, Hugh 1718-1800
Blicher, Steen Steensen 1782-1848
Bocage, Manuel Maria Barbosa du
    1765-1805

Boratynsky, Yevgeny 1800-1844
Borel, Petrus 1809-1859
Boreman, Yokutiel 1825-1890
Borne, Ludwig 1786-1837
Botev, Hristo 1778-1842
Brinckman, John 1814-1870
Bronte, Emily 1812-1848
Brown, Charles Brockden 1777-1810
Browning, Robert 1812-1889
Buchner, Georg 1813-1837
Campbell, James Edwin 1867-1895
Campbell, Thomas 1777-1844
Carlyle, Thomas 1795-1881
Castelo Branco, Camilo 1825-1890
Castro Alves, Antonio de 1847-1871
Channing, William Ellery 1780-1842
Chatterje, Bankin Chanda 1838-1894
Chivers, Thomas Holly 1807?-1858
Claudius, Matthais 1740-1815
Clough, Arthur Hugh 1819-1861
Cobbett, William 1762-1835
Colenso, John William 1814-1883
Coleridge, Hartley 1796-1849
Collett, Camilla 1813-1895
Comte, Auguste 1798-1857
Conrad, Robert T. 1810-1858
Conscience, Hendrik 1812-1883
Cooke, Philip Pendleton 1816-1850
Corbiere, Edouard 1845-1875
Crabbe, George 1754-1832
Cruz E Sousa, Joao da 1861-1898
Desbordes-Valmore, Marceline
    1786-1859
Deschamps, Emile 1791-1871
Deus, Joao de 1830-1896
Dickinson, Emily 1830-1886
Dinis, Julio 1839-1871
Dinsmoor, Robert 1757-1836
Du Maurier, George 1834-1896
Echeverria, Esteban 1805-1851
Eminescy, Mihai 1850-1889
Engels, Friedrich 1820-1895
Espronceda, Jose 1808-1842
Ettinger, Solomon 1799-1855
Euchel, Issac 1756-1804
Ferguson, Samuel 1810-1886
Fernandez de Lizardi, Jose Joaquin
    1776-1827
Fernandez de Moratin, Leandro
    1760-1828
Fet, Afanasy 1820-1892
Feuillet, Octave 1821-1890
Fontane, Theodor 1819-1898
Freiligrath, Hermann Ferdinand
    1810-1876
Freytag, Gustav 1816-1895
Gaboriau, Emile 1835-1873

Ganivet, Angel 1865-1898
Garrett, Almeida 1799-1854
Garshin, Vsevolod Mikhaylovich
    1855-1888
Gezelle, Guido 1830-1899
Ghalib, Asadullah Khan 1797-1869
Godwin, William 1756-1836
Goldschmidt, Meir Aron 1819-1887
Goncalves Dias, Antonio 1823-1864
Griboyedov, Aleksander Sergeyevich
    1795-1829
Grigor'yev, Appolon Aleksandrovich
    1822-1864
Groth, Klaus 1819-1899
Grun, Anastasius (pseud. of Anton
    Alexander Graf von Auersperg)
    1806-1876
Guerrazzi, Francesco Domenico
    1804-1873
Gutierrez Najera, Manuel 1859-1895
Gutzkow, Karl Ferdinand 1811-1878
Ha-Kohen, Shalom 1772-1845
Halleck, Fitz-Greene 1790-1867
Harris, George Washington 1814-1869
Hayne, Paul Hamilton 1830-1886
Hazlitt, William 1778-1830
Hebbel, Christian Friedrich 1813-1863
Hebel, Johann Peter 1760-1826
Hegel, Georg Wilhelm Friedrich
    1770-1831
Heiberg, Johann Ludvig 1813-1863
Herculano, Alexandre 1810-1866
Hernandez, Jose 1834-1886
Hertz, Henrik 1798-1870
Herwegh, Georg 1817-1875
Hoffman, Charles Fenno 1806-1884
Holderlin, Friedrich 1770-1843
Holmes, Oliver Wendell 1809-1894
Hood, Thomas 1799-1845
Hooper, Johnson Jones 1815-1863
Hopkins, Gerard Manley 1844-1889
Horton, George Moses 1798-1880
Howitt, William 1792-1879
Hughes, Thomas 1822-1896
Imlay, Gilbert 1754?-1828?
Irwin, Thomas Caulfield 1823-1892
Issacs, Jorge 1837-1895
Jacobsen, Jens Peter 1847-1885
Jippensha, Ikku 1765-1831
Kant, Immanuel 1724-1804
Karr, Jean Baptiste Alphonse 1808-1890
Keble, John 1792-1866
Khomyakov, Alexey S. 1804-1860
Kierkegaard, Soren 1813-1855
Kinglake, Alexander W. 1809-1891
Kingsley, Charles 1819-1875
Kivi, Alexis 1834-1872

Koltsov, Alexey Vasilyevich 1809-1842
Kotzebue, August von 1761-1819
Kraszewski, Josef Ignacy 1812-1887
Kreutzwald, Friedrich Reinhold
    1803-1882
Krochmal, Nahman 1785-1840
Krudener, Valeria Barbara Julia de
    Wietinghoff 1766-1824
Lampman, Archibald 1861-1899
Landon, Letitia Elizabeth 1802-1838
Landor, Walter Savage 1775-1864
Larra y Sanchez de Castro, Mariano
    1809-1837
Lebensohn, Micah Joseph 1828-1852
Leconte de Lisle, Charles-Marie-Rene
    1818-1894
Lenau, Nikolaus 1802-1850
Leontyev, Konstantin 1831-1891
Leopardi, Giacoma 1798-1837
Leskov, Nikolai 1831-1895
Lever, Charles James 1806-1872
Levisohn, Solomon 1789-1822
Lewes, George Henry 1817-1878
Leyden, John 1775-1811
Lobensohn, Micah Gregory 1775-1810
Longstreet, Augustus Baldwin 1790-1870
Lopez de Ayola y Herrera, Adelardo
    1819-1871
Lover, Samuel 1797-1868
Luzzato, Samuel David 1800-1865
Macedo, Joaquim Manuel de 1820-1882
Macha, Karel Hynek 1810-1836
Mackenzie, Henry 1745-1831
Malmon, Solomon 1754-1800
Mangan, James Clarence 1803-1849
Manzoni, Alessandro 1785-1873
Mapu, Abraham 1808-1868
Marii, Jose 1853-1895
Markovic, Svetozar 1846-1875
Martinez de La Rosa, Francisco
    1787-1862
Mathews, Cornelius 1817-1889
McCulloch, Thomas 1776-1843
Merriman, Brian 1747-1805
Meyer, Conrad Ferdinand 1825-1898
Montgomery, James 1771-1854
Moodie, Susanna 1803-1885
Morton, Sarah Wentworth 1759-1846
Muller, Friedrich 1749-1825
Murger, Henri 1822-1861
Neruda, Jan 1834-1891

Nestroy, Johann 1801-1862
Newman, John Henry 1801-1890
Niccolini, Giambattista 1782-1861
Nievo, Ippolito 1831-1861
Nodier, Charles 1780-1844
Obradovic, Dositej 1742-1811
Oehlenschlager, Adam 1779-1850
O'Neddy, Philothee (pseud. of
    Theophile Dondey) 1811-1875
O'Shaughnessy, Arthur William
    Edgar 1844-1881
Ostrovsky, Alexander 1823-1886
Paine, Thomas 1737-1809
Peacock, Thomas Love 1785-1866
Perk, Jacques 1859-1881
Pisemsky, Alexey F. 1820-1881
Pompeia, Raul D'Avila 1863-1895
Popovic, Jovan Sterija 1806-1856
Praed, Winthrop Mackworth 1802-1839
Prati, Giovanni 1814-1884
Preseren, France 1800-1849
Pringle, Thomas 1789-1834
Procter, Adelaide Ann 1825-1864
Procter, Bryan Waller 1787-1874
Pye, Henry James 1745-1813
Quental, Antero Tarquinio de 1842-1891
Quinet, Edgar 1803-1875
Quintana, Manuel Jose 1772-1857
Radishchev, Aleksander 1749-1802
Raftery, Anthony 1784-1835
Raimund, Ferdinand 1790-1836
Reid, Mayne 1818-1883
Renan, Ernest 1823-1892
Reuter, Fritz 1810-1874
Rogers, Samuel 1763-1855
Ruckert, Friedrich 1788-1866
Runeberg, Johan 1804-1877
Rydberg, Viktor 1828-1895
Saavedra y Ramirez de Boquedano,
    Angel de 1791-1865
Sacher-Mosoch, Leopold von 1836-1895
Saltykov-Shchedrin, Mikhail 1826-1892
Satanov, Isaac 1732-1805
Schiller, Johann Friedrich 1759-1805
Schlegel, August 1767-1845
Schlegel, Karl 1772-1829
Scott, Sir Walter 1771-1832
Scribe, Augustin Eugene 1791-1861
Sedgwick, Catherine Maria 1789-1867
Senoa, August 1838-1881
Shelley, Mary W. 1797-1851

Shelley, Percy Bysshe 1792-1822
Shulman, Kalman 1819-1899
Sigourney, Lydia Howard Huntley
    1791-1856
Silva, Jose Asuncion 1865-1896
Slaveykov, Petko 1828-1895
Slowacki, Juliusz 1809-1848
Smith, Richard Penn 1799-1854
Smolenskin, Peretz 1842-1885
Stagnelius, Erik Johan 1793-1823
Staring, Antonie Christiaan
    Wynand 1767-1840
Stendhal (pseud. of Henri Beyle)
    1783-1842
Stifter, Adalbert 1805-1868
Stone, John Augustus 1801-1834
Taine, Hippolyte 1828-1893
Taunay, Alfredo d'Ecragnole 1843-1899
Taylor, Bayard 1825-1878
Tennyson, Alfred, Lord 1809-1892
Terry, Lucy (Lucy Terry Prince)
    1730-1821
Thompson, Daniel Pierce 1795-1868
Thompson, Samuel 1766-1816
Thomson, James 1834-1882
Tiedge, Christoph August 1752-1841
Timrod, Henry 1828-1867
Tommaseo, Nicolo 1802-1874
Tompa, Mihaly 1817-1888
Topelius, Zachris 1818-1898
Turgenev, Ivan 1818-1883
Tyutchev, Fedor I. 1803-1873
Uhland, Ludvig 1787-1862
Valaoritis, Aristotelis 1824-1879
Valles, Jules 1832-1885
Verde, Cesario 1855-1886
Vigny, Alfred Victor de 1797-1863
Villaverde, Cirilio 1812-1894
Vinje, Aasmund Olavsson 1818-1870
Vorosmarty, Mihaly 1800-1855
Weisse, Christian Felix 1726-1804
Welhaven, Johan S. 1807-1873
Werner, Zacharius 1768-1823
Wescott, Edward Noyes 1846-1898
Wessely, Nattali Herz 1725-1805
Whitman, Sarah Helen 1803-1878
Wieland, Christoph Martin 1733-1813
Woolson, Constance Fenimore
    1840-1894
Zhukovsky, Vasily 1783-1852

William Harrison Ainsworth

1805-1882

(Also wrote under pseudonyms of Cheviot Ticheburn and Thomas Hall) English novelist, editor, balladist, short story writer, and poet.

Ainsworth was a minor but celebrated Victorian novelist who helped popularize historical and criminal fiction in the nineteenth century. In the 1830s and 1840s he was a well-known writer, producing such popular crime romances as *Rookwood* and *Jack Sheppard* in addition to numerous historical novels. The widespread appeal of his early works gave Ainsworth celebrity status and immediate entrance into social and literary circles; his friendships with authors and artists, including Charles Lamb, William Makepeace Thackeray, Charles Dickens, John Forster, Benjamin Disraeli, and George Cruikshank, as well as his lavish dinners and weekend retreats, established him as the most noted literary host of his time. Thus although his works are rarely read today, Ainsworth is remembered as an influential editor and active member of nineteenth-century London literary society.

Ainsworth was born and raised in Manchester, England. As a youth he exhibited his precocious writing ability in contributions to numerous literary magazines that he signed with fanciful pseudonyms or names borrowed from schoolmates. His first published volume, *Poems,* was issued under the name Cheviot Ticheburn and dedicated to Charles Lamb, an author the seventeen-year-old admired greatly. Ainsworth wanted to pursue a literary career, but obeyed the wishes of his family and studied law, first in Manchester and later in London. Though he began practicing law, his involvement in literature continued. In 1826, Ainsworth married Anne Frances Ebers, but they separated in 1835 for unknown reasons, and Fanny died only three years later. At the time of his marriage, Ainsworth joined the publishing business of his father-in-law, John Ebers, and continued with the concern for four years. His career as a novelist began during this time also: he produced *Sir John Chiverton* in collaboration with J. P. Aston, a school friend, in 1826. The novel, which Sir Walter Scott described as imitative of his historical romance style, received little attention.

The 1830s proved to be a decade of varied achievements for Ainsworth: he practiced law, published and edited the works of others, and composed his three best-known novels. Because his publishing venture with Ebers was not a financial success, Ainsworth left the business in 1830 to return to his law practice. At the same time, he established a number of friendships in the literary world, becoming a member of the Fraserians, the group that founded *Fraser's Magazine* and included Thackeray, Thomas Carlyle, Samuel Taylor Coleridge, and Robert Southey. Ainsworth also began work on his first significant novel, *Rookwood.* This unique tale, a combination of the fantastic history of a cursed noble line and the adventures of the highway robber, Dick Turpin, was an immediate success. Critics point out, however, that the author's dandified appearance and many literary friends contributed as much to his fame as the universally acclaimed episode of Turpin's escape to York on his black mare, Bess. Stage adaptations, complete with musical productions of Ainsworth's flash songs—comic, slang ballads recounting criminal feats—added to the *Rookwood* rage. *Rook-*

wood was followed three years later by *Crichton.* This imaginative history, set in the court of Henri III of France, recounts the life and adventures of the sixteenth-century Scottish poet and scholar, James Crichton. Although some critics who had enjoyed *Rookwood*'s engrossing narrative faulted the extensive digressive documentation used to support the historical material in *Crichton,* popular response was predominantly favorable: all 1,250 copies of the initial printing of *Crichton* were sold in one day.

With his next novel, *Jack Sheppard,* Ainsworth adopted the serial form of publication. After assuming the editorship of *Bentley's Miscellany* from Dickens in 1839, Ainsworth serialized his latest novel as Dickens had done with *Oliver Twist.* The two works appeared simultaneously in the magazine for several issues and were often linked as examples of "the Newgate school of fiction." This term, which originated with Edward Bulwer-Lytton's *Paul Clifford,* was used to describe works that dealt sympathetically with a criminal hero. While such romances were avidly read, many critics objected to the genre on moral grounds. Ainsworth's *Jack Sheppard,* a chronicle of the notorious thief's prison escapes, readily falls into the Newgate category, though Ainsworth envisioned it as a "Hogarthian novel," patterned after the didactic works of the eighteenth-century painter William Hogarth. The tale, which contrasts idleness and industry in the characters of the thief Jack and his virtuous counterpart, Thames Darrell, was highly popular. Controversy marred Ainsworth's triumph, however, when Courvoisier, a French servant convicted of murdering his elderly master, testified in court that he was motivated by a reading of Ainsworth's latest novel. The publicity surrounding the trial fueled moral objections to the Newgate novels, and the subsequent attacks on *Jack Sheppard* were so severe that Ainsworth abandoned plans for a third novel on the Newgate pattern, turning instead to historical fiction.

During the 1840s, Ainsworth attempted, with varying success, to combine magazine editing and proprietorship with novel writing. His first historical romances, published in segments as *Jack Sheppard* had been, were well received. In *The Tower of London* and *Old Saint Paul's: A Tale of the Plague and the Fire,* Ainsworth centered the action of the novels around these monumental buildings. His antiquarian knowledge (particularly of sixteenth- and seventeenth-century England) imbued these novels with the flavor of life in an earlier age as Ainsworth guided the reader through scenes and settings of historical importance.

Following an argument with Richard Bentley in 1841, Ainsworth left *Bentley's* to start *Ainsworth's Magazine.* He continued to serialize his novels in *Ainsworth's* and later in the *New Monthly Magazine,* which he purchased in 1845. Yet most critics agree that the novels Ainsworth wrote from 1842 onward declined in quality, probably because the author's many editorial responsibilities left him little time for writing. As an editor, however, Ainsworth continued to influence the literature of his time. He was highly respected for the courtesy and consideration he showed to his magazine contributors, and he introduced many fledgling writers and illustrators to the major literary figures of his day during the famed gatherings at his home of Kensal Lodge. Among those in Ainsworth's debt was Dickens; while still an unknown journalist, he had first met George Cruikshank, the illustrator of *Oliver Twist,* and John Forster, his friend and future biographer, and John Macrone, his publisher, at Kensal Lodge.

Financial hardships and decreased social activity marked Ainsworth's later years. In 1854, he acquired *Bentley's Miscellany* and discontinued *Ainsworth's Magazine* to eliminate competition between the periodicals. He suffered heavy financial losses, however, in the following years: as the novels' sales diminished, the magazines faltered, and Ainsworth was forced to sell family property to cover business debts. In 1856, he was awarded a small government pension as a retired author, but continued nevertheless to write prolifically, often at the rate of a novel each year. No longer popular, he published his later novels in cheap paperback editions or in *Bow Bells,* a penny weekly. Having outlived most of his friends, he became almost reclusive in his later years. But Ainsworth was not completely forgotten: less than four months before his death in 1882, the seventy-six year old author was named the "Lancashire novelist" at a banquet given in his honor by the mayor of Manchester, his home town.

With few exceptions, Ainsworth's novels readily fall into two categories: the Newgate novels, notable for their criminal heroes, and the historical romances, characterized by Ainsworth's unusual mix of antiquarian detail and improbable, dramatic action. Although the two Newgate novels, *Rookwood* and *Jack Sheppard,* were widely read in the 1830s and 1840s despite adamant critical condemnation of their immorality, they fell into obscurity later in the nineteenth century. Early in the twen-

tieth century they were regarded merely as wholesome, old fashioned adventures lacking in literary merit and were relegated to children's reading lists. In the 1960s, Keith Hollingsworth refined that view in his study of Newgate fiction, calling Ainsworth's *Jack Sheppard* "the highpoint of the Newgate novel as entertainment." The historical romances, less popular and less entertaining than the Newgate tales, received minimal critical attention in the nineteenth century. Although a few reviewers praised Ainsworth's historical accuracy and imaginative rendering of the past, most dismissed him as an inferior imitator of Scott. Recently, such commentators as Llewellyn Ligocki and George J. Worth have reassessed Ainsworth's contribution to historical fiction, pointing to his innovative approach: unlike Scott, who used fictional characters, Ainsworth portrayed actual historical personages caught up in the events of their day. While critics generally concur that both his criminal and historical novels lack insightful characterization and polished style, they praise the fast-paced narration and keen story-telling ability that enliven his best works.

Though Ainsworth is not ranked as a first-rate author by modern scholars, his works and the early critical reactions to them are valued as evidence of the social and literary climate during his era. One of England's most popular authors early in his career, his books were translated into German, French, Dutch, and Russian, his ballads were sung throughout England, and his tales were dramatized in numerous theatrical productions. Nonetheless, his reputation began its steady decline during his lifetime, and Ainsworth was overlooked by most commentators throughout the first half of the twentieth century. In recent years, a small group of scholars has given attention to his novels, focusing particularly on the historical romances. To the student of Victorian literature, Ainsworth is mainly of historical interest, remembered as a popular novelist, the editor of several periodicals, and an influential member of the literary circles of his time.

(See also *Something about the Author,* Vol. 24 and *Dictionary of Literary Biography,* Vol. 21: *Victorian Novelists before 1885.*)

*PRINCIPAL WORKS

Poems [as Cheviot Ticheburn]   (poetry)   1822
December Tales [with others]   (juvenilia)   1823
Sir John Chiverton [with J. P. Aston]   (novel)   1826
Rookwood   (novel)   1834; also published in revised form
    as *Rookwood,* 1837
Crichton   (novel)   1837
Jack Sheppard   (novel)   1839
The Tower of London   (novel)   1840
Guy Fawkes; or, The Gunpowder Treason   (novel)   1841
Old Saint Paul's: A Tale of the Plague and the Fire
    (novel)   1841
The Miser's Daughter   (novel)   1842
Windsor Castle   (novel)   1843
The Lancashire Witches: A Romance of Pendle Forest
    (novel)   1849
Ballads: Romantic, Fantastical, and Humorous   (ballads)
    1855
***Mervyn Clitheroe*   (novel)   1858
Ovingdean Grange: A Tale of the South Downs   (novel)
    1860
Auriol; or, The Elixer of Life   (novel)   1865
Boscobel; or, The Royal Oak: A Tale of the Year 1651
    (novel)   1872

*The Good Old Times: The Story of the Manchester Rebels of
    '45* (novel) 1873
The Leaguer of Lathom: A Tale of Civil War in Lancashire
    (novel) 1876
Beau Nash; or, Bath in the Eighteenth Century (novel)
    1879
Stanley Brereton (novel) 1881
The Novels of William Harrison Ainsworth. 20 vols.
    (novels) 1901-02

*Most of Ainsworth's novels were originally published serially in
 periodicals.

**Segments of this work were originally published as *The Life and
 Adventures of Mervyn Clitheroe* from 1851 to 1852.

SIR WALTER SCOTT (journal dates 1826)

[*Scott was a Scottish novelist, poet, historian, biographer, and
critic of the Romantic period who is best known for his historical
novels, which were great popular successes. In the journal entries
from which the following excerpt is taken, Scott compares* Sir
John Chiverton, *attributed to Ainsworth, and* Brambletye House,
*by Horace Smith, with his own writings. Though subsequent critics
often cite this comparison in describing Ainsworth as an imitator
of Scott, there is some question of Ainsworth's role in producing*
Sir John Chiverton; *some sources suggest that Ainsworth merely
edited and published the work of his friend, J. P. Aston.*]

[October 17, 1826]

Read over **Sir John Chiverton** and *Brambletye House*— novels
in what I may surely claim as the stile

> Which I was born to introduce—
> Refined it first, and showd its use.

They are both clever books; one in imitation of the days of
chivalry; the other (by Horace Smith, one of the authors of the
Rejected Addresses) dated in the time of the Civil Wars, and
introducing historical characters. I read both with great interest
during the journey. (p. 247)

• • • • •

[October 18, 1826]

I take up again my remarks on imitations. I am sure I mean
the gentlemen no wrong by calling them so, and heartily wish
they had followd a better model; but it serves to show me *veluti
in speculo* my own errors, or, if you will, those of the *stile*.
One advantage, I think, I still have over all of them. They may
do their fooling with better grace; but I, like Sir Andrew Ague-
cheek, do it more natural. They have to read old books and
consult antiquarian collections to get their information; I write
because I have long since read such works, and possess, thanks
to a strong memory, the information which they have to seek
for. This leads to a dragging-in historical details by head and
shoulders, so that the interest of the main piece is lost in minute
descriptions of events which do not affect its progress. . . . [In]
my better efforts, while I conducted my story through the
agency of historical personages and by connecting it with historical incidents, I have endeavoured to weave them pretty
closely together, and in future I will study this more. Must not
let the background eclipse the principal figures—the frame
overpower the picture. (pp. 248-49)

Sir Walter Scott, in journal entries of October 17 &
October 18, 1826, in his The Journal of Sir Walter
Scott, edited by John Guthrie Tait, revised edition,
Oliver and Boyd, 1950, pp. 247-49.*

THE ATHENAEUM (essay date 1834)

[*In the following anonymous review of* Rookwood, *the critic lightly
chastises Ainsworth for his extravagant plot and melodramatic
expression.*]

Though, for our own amusement, we should not select that
class of books to which **Rookwood** belongs, yet we know that
there are many readers who delight in the semi-supernatural,
the almost impossible, and the decidedly improbable; therefore,
we shall give a fair report of the mode in which the work is
executed, without any fastidious reference to our own peculiar,
and, as we take it, more refined taste. . . .

Rookwood then, is a thorough romance, though it possesses a
most unromantic chronology, being coeval with the days of
the celebrated Dick Turpin, some of whose exploits it spiritedly
relates, and whose name it may perhaps call forth to an ephemeral resuscitation. In breadth of delineation, and in depth of
colouring, it is most complete; its villains are most villanously
villanous, and its terrors are most terribly terrible. . . .

There seems to be very little, if any, attempt at delineation of
character, or minuteness of moral painting, which in a romance
would, perhaps, be as much out of keeping, as miniature drawing in scene-painting. Recklessness is the general characteristic
of the chàracters, and the author, as if mindful of what Solomon
said concerning the wickedness of woman, makes Lady Rookwood the sublimest brute of the whole party. . . . Amidst much
that is horrible and appalling, tragic and romantic, there is
some good delineation of probabilities and realities. The . . .
portrait of Dick Turpin's horse is finely done, and will be read
with interest by those who can scarcely tell a horse from an
ass. . . . (p. 323)

[Turpin's celebrated ride from London to York, is set forth]
with a minuteness and elaborateness, which stimulate rather
than weary the reader. . . .

The great fault of this story is, that the horrible is strained to
an excess that makes it ludicrous. Authors should take care
that they do not over-stimulate their readers, for when the
excitement runs into extravagance, it is not merely a failure,
but a positive nuisance—we may forget a feeble work, but we
remember, against the writer, all acts of outrageousness. (p. 324)

A review of "Rookwood: A Romance," in The Athenaeum, No. 340, May 3, 1834, pp. 323-24.

THE EXAMINER (essay date 1834)

[*This critic objects to the Gothic elements and slang in* Rookwood.
*Yet while disparaging the book, the reviewer admits that certain
portions display "power and spirit."*]

[*Rookwood*] is a graft of the Newgate calendar on the stock of
the old romance. For horror, the author makes a free use of
coffins, corpses, and skeleton hands. He riots in the abundance
of a charnel house, and seems to think that the very sublimity
of the terrible is attained by descending into crammed vaults,
and parading funeral trains, and now and then exposing a dead
body. There is also the customary allowance of thunder and
lightning, and second sight, and omens; and of course we have

a machine of the *Merrilies* sort, a sexton, with terrible eyes, and an unearthly laugh, and frightful scorn. Combined with horrors of this mouldy kind, all turning on the idea of death, there are the characters, achievements, and loathsome slang of highwaymen. Turpin, whom the writer is pleased with loving familiarity to call Dick, is the hero of the tale. Doubtless, we shall soon see Thurtell presented in sublime guise, and the drive to Gill's Hill described with all pomp and circumstance. There are people who may like this sort of thing, but we are not of the number. Indeed we have found it extremely difficult to read the book; and, to confess the truth, without making leaps far exceeding those of Turpin in his ride to York, we could not have scampered through it. The author has, we suspect, been misled by the example and success of "Paul Clifford," but in "Paul Clifford" the thieves and their dialect serve for illustration, while in *Rookwood,* the highwayman and his slang are presented as if in themselves they had some claim to admiration. Who cares to know that "wedge" in the thieves' tongue signifies silver, and "rag" money, and "dibs" cash?— if it be known from this authority; for the probability is that the lingo is misapplied, or that, if the language of thieves, it is the language of the present time, and not appropriate to cut-throats of the time of Turpin . . . , and who can have pleasure of any sort in reading such stuff as this? . . .

While we give our opinion of the book—admitting that with faults peculiarly distasteful to us, it has passages of power and spirit—we think it just to state that it has its admirers among persons whose judgment cannot be denied weight. . . .

> *A review of "Rookwood: A Romance," in* The Examiner, *No. 1372, May 18, 1834, p. 308.*

FRASER'S MAGAZINE (essay date 1834)

[*Fraser's Magazine for Town and Country, established in 1830, was principally Tory and conservative in its leanings. From its foundation, Ainsworth was a member of the Fraserians, a group that included Thackeray, Carlyle, and Count D'Orsay, among other literary celebrities. The critic from* Fraser's *here favors Ainsworth's* Rookwood *over Bulwer Lytton's* Paul Clifford, *praising Ainsworth's unflagging narrative, forceful characterizations, and innate ability to write the comic, slang ballads known as "flash songs."*]

The best and most conclusive thing that can be said about [*Rookwood*] is, that it has "created a *sensation.*" . . . Mr. Ainsworth has produced a romance of no ordinary kind. (p. 724)

We are not sure that we should have mentioned the name of Mr. Bulwer on the present occasion, had not the editor of the *Examiner* and the critic in the *Spectator* both instituted a comparison between the "*flash*" scenes in *Rookwood* and those in *Paul Clifford,*—the former giving the preference to Bulwer, the latter decidedly, and we think justly, declaring, that "there is more of reality about the low scenes of *Rookwood* than there is in those of *Paul Clifford.*" The fact is simply this, that with Mr. Ainsworth all is natural, free, and joyous; with Mr. Bulwer all is forced, constrained, and cold. Ainsworth is always thinking of—or rather *with*—his hero; Bulwer is always thinking of himself. Bulwer's *slang* has been culled and arranged with the greatest assiduity, but we are unmoved,

> For *soul* is wanting there.

The cant phrases used by Ainsworth may, for any thing we know, have cost him as much labour in the selection as his celebrated namesake bestowed on the well-known magazine

of words; but, be this as it may, when reading his flash scenes you think nothing about the phrase-lexicon; so far from this, you are absolutely *bored* by the foot-notes of explanation. Full of the spirit of the scene so vividly described, you catch the import of a word or phrase, however strange, by a sort of intuitive consciousness that you are "up, down, and fly" to the songster's meaning. This we take to be the triumph of such descriptions. . . .

The story of *Rookwood* is a legend of enchaining interest. (p. 725)

The course of the narrative, like that of Dick Turpin's ride, never for a moment flags. The principal characters are sustained with a force and energy, which shine forth in admirable contrast with the gentle beauty of the author's descriptions of

> The outward shows of sky and earth,
> Of hill and valley—

or of the depth and delicacy of that love which

> Dwells in deep retreats,

sanctifying the "undistinguishable throng" of woman's hopes and fears. We are greatly deceived if *Rookwood* be not destined to have a run of the true Turpin style.

We cannot conclude our notice of this work without pointing out what we conceive to be its principal, because its most original feature. We know of nothing—and if there be any thing of the kind extant, we shall be delighted to meet with it—we know of nothing at all to be compared with the "High Toby" songs of Mr. Ainsworth. We should imagine no man of any pretensions to knowledge in such matters would mention the elaborate nonsense put into the mouth of "Gentleman George," and all the rest of them, in *Paul Clifford.* There is really no comparison. The humorous is not Mr. Bulwer's *forte;* and without the keenest relish for humour, no man can produce a flash song. Stringing together the words used by "the family" may be done easily enough—and, indeed, has been done, and that not unfrequently. Mr. Bulwer has done this. But Mr. Ainsworth has done more. He has breathed the spirit of the reckless rogues into the language of his songs. To some, as to the editor of the *Examiner,* this matter may appear unimportant. But even they will not deny, that he who does any thing as well as it possibly can be done, is deserving of high praise; and this praise must, we think, be given to the author of *Rookwood* as regards this matter of the songs. . . . (pp. 735-36)

That there is "good stuff" in this author is evident; and we hope to see him soon again. (p. 738)

> *"High-Ways and Low-Ways; or, Ainsworth's Dictionary, with Notes by Turpin," in* Fraser's Magazine, *Vol. IX, No. LIV, June, 1834, pp. 724-38.*

[WILLIAM MAGINN] (essay date 1836)

[*One of the most prominent journalists in England during the first half of the nineteenth century, Maginn wrote prolifically for a variety of English periodicals. His articles range from burlesques in verse to literary criticism and contain a rich blend of farcical humor, classical allusions, and political commentary. Maginn here praises the publication of a third edition of* Rookwood *with additional ballads and odes.*]

We [at *Fraser's*] were among the first to predict the rapid and successful career of Mr. Ainsworth as a novelist [see excerpt from *Fraser's Magazine* dated 1834]; when Turpin first did ride abroad, we were there to see, to admire, and to applaud: at this stage of his popularity, now that he has kicked up such a cloud of Olympic dust, . . . our encouraging cheer is drowned in the general shout of acclamation. Yet needs must we confess, that our REGINA takes still a *quasi*-maternal interest in this young author. . . . We recur, therefore, with manifest complacency, to our original opinions in this gentleman's favour. We knew well what we spoke of; and it has given us much more gratification than surprise thus to find the public ratifying our verdict and verifying our vaticination, by demanding, in a voice of thunder, a third edition of his romance. (p. 488)

For our part, we expect to hear of new editions in the eastern as well as the western hemisphere: we anticipate Tartar translations and Arab commentaries. We see no reason why this romance should not be read as eagerly on the plains of Mesopotamia as on the banks of the Potomack. The Cossacks on the river Don have, no doubt, already sent their orders to No. 3 St. James's Square. Fortunate author! (p. 489)

When first the romance of *Rookwood* burst on an admiring world, and claimed for its author a place in the foremost rank of contemporary novel-writers, the lyrical poetry with which the work abounded challenged for him a name among the most distinguished modern votaries of the muse. The *songs* formed a leading and substantive merit of the book, and were found to be so successful, that Mr. Ainsworth, awaking one day, recognised in himself a poet. He has shewn a due appreciation of the public's approval. More than a dozen additional ballads and odes adorn the pages of this new edition; and we must say that they decidedly are of the right sort, full of glowing enthusiasm, and redolent of inspiration. We know not whether he has yet determined what school of poetry he intends to patronise—whether the *lake* or *leg of mutton school;* should he consult us, *we* think that he has a decided vocation for the *"sepulchral:"* his immortal ballad of "the Sexton," which still haunts our imagination; it revealed in him the existence of a power akin to that of Ezekiel, and was, in sooth, as glorious a vision of dry bones as we can recollect just now. Southey has chosen a domicile on the margin of his favourite lakes, to enact the *genius loci;* it is not without reason that Ainsworth has latterly selected a rural residence close by the grand necropolis on the Harrow Road: if "the cemetery company's directors" have any brains, they will vote him 500*l*. a-year, and create him laureate of the grave-yard, with the grass of the enclosed grounds in fee-simple to his Pegasus for ever. (pp. 490-91)

[Whoever has read the] ballad of "the Lime-tree Branch" will not refuse to join with us in pronouncing Mr. Ainsworth a finished proficient on the old national lyre, and highly deserving of a bough of bay, *laureá donandus Apollinari*. His tones are, in sooth, most musical, most melancholy; yet he never appears to more advantage than when he relapses into his favourite subjects, the exploits of the highway brotherhood—*"le département des ponts et chaussées."* Footpad poetry, or, as Horace calls it, *sermo pedestris*, would seem to have for him ineffable charms. Every great poet has a pet topic. (p. 492)

[We] bid thee good night, Dick Turpin. Keep thy powder dry, my lad; let all thy movements be regular; but let not thy intellect get rusty by too much rustication. The world is impatiently awaiting thy next appearance in the character of "the Admirable Crichton." (p. 493)

[William Maginn], *"Another Caw from the 'Rookwood'—Turpin out Again,"* in Fraser's Magazine, *Vol. XIII, No. LXXVI, April, 1836, pp. 488-93.*

[FRANCIS MAHONY]   (essay date 1836)

[*Despite his admitted doubts about Ainsworth's ability to write historical fiction, Mahony here lauds the characterizations, songs, and translations in* Crichton.]

We looked for the appearance of [*Crichton*], this long announced and much talked-of work, with something more of curiosity than is usual with us, at our advanced period of literary life. And for the following reasons: In the first place, it appeared to us that the "Admirable Crichton's" scanty history could not be turned to effective account, or it would long since have been handled by some one or other; and, in the next place, with all respect for the author of *Rookwood,* judging him by his past performances we were not of opinion that, if the thing was to be done, he was precisely the man to do it. With the reluctance natural to those who are forced to resign pre-conceived notions "on compulsion," we are bound to confess, that in both surmises we were wrong. For, in the volumes before us, we have the history of Crichton, scanty as it is, made subservient to most striking effects, both as regards the hero himself, and the ever-interesting period in which he flourished: and this we find done by the writer, whose aptitude for the work we had doubted—the author of *Rookwood.* Yet, in justice to our discrimination, we may observe, that wiser heads than ours (if any such there be) might have miscalculated quite as much in this matter. We, and other readers, who had scampered away to York with this author, at a rate from the effect of which we have scarcely yet recovered; who, under his guidance, had sermonised and solemnised in sepulchral vaults and feudal towers; and, furthermore, played truant in gipsy-haunts and way-side taverns; we were not unnaturally at a loss to conjecture what such a vivid and rattling narrator could possibly make out of the character and excellences of Crichton, "admirable" as the young Scotchman is, on all hands, admitted to have been. Well, our misgivings were, as we have intimated, all wrong! (p. 733)

Mr. Ainsworth thinks it necessary to apologise . . . for having avoided that obvious and exclusive delineation of Crichton, which is suggested by the mere mention of his name—*i.c.*—his scholastic eminence. Had the author been writing a book for the edification or instruction of the learned world, . . . then, indeed, he might have indulged misgivings, had his work been deficient in "Dry-as-dust" distinction. But forasmuch as Ainsworth has written for the "reading world"—a very different set from the "learned" world—as, at all events, his book will be thumbed by light readers among the males, and fingered by fair skimmers among those whose

> Eyes
> Rain influence and adjudge the prize—

he has acted like a man of taste in bringing into strong light the more courtly and universally captivating features of his hero's character. (p. 734)

At the opening of book the second we are introduced to [the celebrated character Queen Catherine of Medicis], and others of the gay, intriguing, and heartless court of Henry III. Ainsworth sketches the principal personages of this period, so rich in recollections, with a free, vigorous, and, at the same time, graceful hand. . . . [Often] as the same persons have, in one way or other, been handled, it will be found that our author has invested them with the charm of novelty. (p. 737)

There are many lyrics scattered through the volume, all sustaining the author's acknowledged reputation as a song-writer.

In the work before us there are none of those mystic lays which puzzled the uninitiated in **Rookwood** as much as they delighted the knowing ones. In **Crichton** the songs are all intelligible to ''chiefs and ladies bright.'' . . . (p. 746)

[*Francis Mahony*], *in a review of ''Crichton,'' in* Fraser's Magazine, *Vol. XIV, No. LXXIV, December, 1836, pp. 733-47.*

THE MONTHLY REVIEW, LONDON   (essay date 1837)

[*In the following excerpt, the anonymous critic eulogizes Ainsworth's* Crichton, *citing the author's scholarly research of his subject, his imaginative representation, his skilled characterization of Catherine de Medicis, and his translations and unique lyrics.*]

Probably the first remark that every critical reader of this admirable romantic novel makes, refers to the learning which it displays; and the second observation ought to regard the success, the bold freedom, the perfect ease with which the author embodies in his work the spirit of the times, and personates the characters represented. It is impossible, we think, to peruse [**Crichton**] without frequently being so strongly carried back into the sixteenth century, and so deeply convinced of the reality of the events described, as to believe that Mr. Ainsworth must have been an immediate witness of what he details, and a hearty actor in many of the incidents; so completely has he identified his representative characters with all that history has bequeathed us concerning one of the most stirring epochs in the annals of nations, and concerning some of the most celebrated names on record; and so firmly does he seem to stand, as it were, in the shoes of all the illustrious personages introduced.

To have accomplished all this in the case of such characters, and of such a period as he has chosen, required no ordinary skill and attainments. Of late years there have been hundreds of novels and romances, which have usurped a claim to the dignity and authority of *historical*, without possessing one shred of a title to the character, farther than might consist in the adoption of certain proper names, the assumption of a particular era, and the arbitrary use of a few obsolete forms of speech, without the betrayal of one idea, or circumstance of action that can point to the genius of the characters or the periods supposed. But whoever bestows an hour's attention upon **Crichton** . . . cannot fail to perceive that the author is not only gifted with a lively fancy, and a creative imagination, so as both to paint faithfully and invent with a master's confidence, but that he has studied with an antiquarian's care and relish every thing pertaining to his theme. To all this is added great scholarship, as we have already intimated, a highly polished taste and style, and that *con amore* relationship to his subject which enables him to be the accomplished, the spirited, and enthusiastic artist that he is. In short, **Crichton** will become one of our standard novels, because it combines deep learning, accurate representation, and beautiful writing, in the production of a splendid, and an arresting story. It must be added, that the reader cannot rise from its perusal as from a display of merely gorgeous pictures, but will experience something like those valuable and gratifying results which partake of mental enlargement and moral instruction.

We think it will not escape the reflections of any one who turns his attention to the number and variety of English novels and romances belonging to the modern school, that no small degree of ingenuity must have been exerted, and no small share of

anxious theme or subject-hunting encountered by the authors of many of them. Is it not strange, that, in such a dilemma, toil of research, and occasion for squeamishness of taste, no one should have forestalled Mr. Ainsworth in reference to his present hero? This neglect, we may presume, however, did not arise so much from oversight, as from a conviction that must have been entertained by every modest writer, of *mediocre* powers and acquirements, viz., that nothing but surpassing ability and rare attainments could deal with a hero, who, from a few recorded achievements, and a traditional renown had obtained the highest possible honour and glory which the imagination can accord to humanity. He who was proverbially ''admirable,'' how could he acquire a higher fame or a more affectionate wonder? But we deem it fortunate that he has been so long neglected, that he might at last fall into the hands of Mr. Ainsworth; for, however graceful and exalted, **Crichton** may formerly have appeared to the wholesale and indiscriminate admirer, he is here made to stand out above all others, the greatest among the great, with a distinct personality, and to take a prominent share in some of the most interesting, stirring, and dazzling scenes recorded in history, so as to become decked with new and more extraordinary attributes; and to have possessed not only more astonishing, but more diversified gifts than we had ever dreamt of, even in his case. This, the author has legitimately done, by overstepping that confined boundary, which would merely represent his hero as an unparalleled scholar, or the *beau ideal* of all that is graceful in personal appearance and elegant accomplishments. He has, accordingly made his Crichton a courtier, and the observed of all observers, amongst the gayest and most exalted of the age in which he lived. His gallantry, his honour, his intuitive royalty of thought and action, are altogether matchless. (pp. 53-5)

Mr. Ainsworth has, perhaps, not shown his powers to greater advantage than in the translations and the lyrics with which he has strewn and gemmed these volumes. (p. 66)

The action and the excitement of the story gather importance and more densely crowd every page as we proceed in the third volume. . . . [The scene in which Catherine solicits Crichton's help contains a dialogue] that cannot, perhaps, be surpassed in point of absorbing interest and dramatic power, in the whole range of English fiction. (p. 67)

We are sure that though we were to exhaust the whole vocabulary of eulogistic language, a stronger or happier recommendation could not be composed in behalf of this novel, than the dialogue [of the novel itself]. . . . The whole work, however, deserves careful study, were it for nothing else than the successful manner in which the author has fathomed and developed the character of Catherine, dramatised the passions, the pleasure, and the hate that distinguished the court of Henri III., and painted the complexion of the times, when chivalry though about to expire, presented many of its most picturesque features. It was the period when every thing that confers on life its chief blessings and most enduring embellishments—such as learning, commerce, science, and freedom of thought—was about to elevate the nations of Europe; so that, whether we consider the era, the scene, or the actors in the story, Mr. Ainsworth has been remarkably felicitous in his choice and execution. We shall soon have it turned to good account for our theatres. (p. 69)

A review of ''Crichton,'' in The Monthly Review, *London, Vol. 1, No. 1, January, 1837, pp. 53-69.*

A sketch of the author of Rookwood *at twenty-nine.*

WILLIAM HARRISON AINSWORTH (essay date 1837?)

[*In the following excerpt from his preface to* Rookwood, *Ainsworth describes the experiences and settings that shaped his romance. While he admits that his purpose was to entertain and to revitalize the romance genre, he maintains that a moral may be gleaned from the novel. This edition of Ainsworth's preface is dated December 15, 1849, but contemporary critics indicate that it appeared in earlier editions.*]

During a visit to Chesterfield, in the autumn of the year 1831, I first conceived the notion of writing this story. Wishing to describe, somewhat minutely, the trim gardens, the picturesque domains, the rook-haunted groves, the gloomy chambers, and gloomier galleries, of an ancient Hall with which I was acquainted, I resolved to attempt a story in the bygone style of Mrs. Radcliffe (which had always inexpressible charms for me), substituting an old English squire, an old English manorial residence, and an old English highwayman, for the Italian marchese, the castle, and the brigand of the great mistress of Romance.

While revolving this subject, I happened, one evening, to enter the spacious cemetery attached to the church with the queer, twisted steeple, which, like the uplifted tail of the renowned Dragon of Wantley, to whom "houses and churches were as capons and turkeys," seems to menace the good town of Chesterfield with destruction. Here an incident occurred, on the

opening of a vault, which it is needless to relate, but which supplied me with a hint for the commencement of my romance, as well as for the ballad entitled **"The Coffin."** Upon this hint I immediately acted; and the earlier chapters of the book, together with the description of the ancestral mansion of the Rookwoods, were completed before I quitted Chesterfield. (p. 3)

The Ride to York was completed in one day and one night. This feat—for a feat it was, being the composition of a hundred ordinary novel pages in less than twenty-four hours—was achieved at "The Elms"—a house I then occupied at Kilburn. Well do I remember the fever into which I was thrown during the time of composition. My pen literally scoured over the pages. So thoroughly did I identify myself with the flying highwayman, that, once started, I found it impossible to halt. Animated by kindred enthusiasm, I cleared every obstacle in my path with as much facility as Turpin disposed of the impediments that beset his flight. In his company, I mounted the hill-side, dashed through the bustling village, swept over the desolate heath, threaded the silent street, plunged into the eddying stream, and kept an onward course, without pause, without hindrance, without fatigue. With him I shouted, sang, laughed, exulted, wept. Nor did I retire to rest till, in imagination, I heard the bell of York Minster toll forth the knell of poor Black Bess. (pp. 3-4)

It has been well observed by Barry Cornwall, "that the songs which occur in dramas are more natural than those which proceed from the author in person." With equal force does the reasoning apply to the romance, which may be termed the drama of the closet. It would seem strange, on the first view, that an author should be more at home in an assumed character than his own. But experience shows the position to be correct. Conscious he is no longer individually associated with his work, the writer proceeds with all the freedom of irresponsibility. His idiosyncrasy is merged in that of the personages he represents. He thinks with their thoughts; sees with their eyes; speaks with their tongues. His strains are such as he himself (*per se*) would not—perhaps could not—have originated. In this light he may be said to bring to his subject not one mind, but several; he becomes not one poet, but many; for each actor in his drama has a share, and an important share, in the lyrical *estro* to which he gives birth. This it is which has imparted any verve, variety, or dramatic character they possess, to the ballads contained in this production. Turpin I look upon as the real songster of "Black Bess"; to Jerry Juniper I am unquestionably indebted for a flash melody which, without his hint, would never have been written; while to the Sexton I owe the solitary gleam of light I have been enabled to throw upon the horrors and mystery of the churchyard.

As I have casually alluded to the flash song of Jerry Juniper, I may, perhaps, be allowed to make a few observations upon this branch of versification. It is somewhat curious, with a dialect so racy, idiomatic, and plastic as our own cant, that its metrical capabilities should have been so little essayed. The French have numerous *chansons d'argot*, ranging from the time of Charles Bourdigné and Villon down to that of Vidocq and Victor Hugo, the last of whom has enlivened the horrors of his *Dernier Jour d'un Condamné* by a festive song of this class. The Spaniards possess a large collection of *Romances de Germania*, by various authors, amongst whom Quevedo holds a distinguished place. We, on the contrary, have scarcely any slang songs of merit. With a race of depredators so melodious and convivial as our highwaymen, this is the more to be wondered at. Had they no bards amongst their bands? Was there no minstrel at hand to record their exploits? (pp. 4-5)

And here, as the candidates are so few, and their pretensions so humble,

> I can't help putting in my claim for praise.

I venture to affirm that I have done something more than has been accomplished by my predecessors, or contemporaries, with the significant language under consideration. I have written a purely flash song; of which the great and peculiar merit consists in its being utterly incomprehensible to the uninformed understanding, while its meaning must be perfectly clear and perspicuous to the practised *patterer* of *Romany*, or *Pedlar's French*. I have, moreover, been the first to introduce and naturalize amongst us a measure which, though common enough in the Argotic minstrelsy of France, has been hitherto utterly unknown to our *pedestrian* poetry. (p. 6)

Turpin was the hero of my boyhood. I had always a strange passion for highwaymen, and have listened by the hour to their exploits, as narrated by my father, and especially to those of "Dauntless Dick," that "chief minion of the moon." One of Turpin's adventures in particular, the ride to Hough Green, which took deep hold of my fancy, I have recorded in song. When a boy, I have often lingered by the side of the deep old road where this robbery was committed, to cast wistful glances into its mysterious windings; and when night deepened the shadows of the trees, have urged my horse on his journey, from a vague apprehension of a visit from the ghostly highwayman. And then there was the Bollin, with its shelvy banks, which Turpin cleared at a bound; the broad meadows over which he winged his flight; the pleasant bowling-green of the pleasant old inn at Hough, where he produced his watch to the Cheshire squires, with whom he was upon terms of intimacy; all brought something of the gallant robber to mind. No wonder, in after years, in selecting a highwayman for a character in a tale, I should choose my old favourite, Dick Turpin. (pp. 6-7)

If the design of Romance be, what it has been held, the exposition of a useful truth by means of an interesting story, I fear I have but imperfectly fulfilled the office imposed upon me; having, as I will freely confess, had, throughout, an eye rather to the reader's amusement than his edification. One wholesome moral, however, may, I trust, be gathered from the perusal of this Tale; namely, that, without due governance of the passions, high aspirations and generous emotions will little avail their possessor. The impersonations of the Tempter, the Tempted, and the Better Influence, may be respectively discovered, by those who care to cull the honey from the flower, in the Sexton, in Luke, and in Sybil.

The chief object I had in view in making the present essay, was to see how far the infusion of a warmer and more genial current into the veins of old Romance would succeed in reviving her fluttering and feeble pulses. The attempt has succeeded beyond my most sanguine expectation. Romance, if I am not mistaken, is destined shortly to undergo an important change. Modified by the German and French writers—by Hoffmann, Tieck, Hugo, Dumas, Balzac, and Paul Lacroix *(le Bibliophile Jacob)*—the structure commenced in our own land by Horace Walpole, Monk Lewis, Mrs. Radcliffe, and Maturin, but left imperfect and inharmonious, requires, now that the rubbish which choked up its approach is removed, only the hand of the skilful architect to its entire renovation and perfection.

And now, having said my say, I must bid you, worthy reader, farewell. Beseeching you, in the words of old Rabelais, "to interpret all my sayings and doings in the perfectest sense. Reverence the cheese-like brain that feeds you with all these jolly maggots; and do what lies in you to keep me always merry. Be frolic now, my lads! Cheer up your hearts, and joyfully read the rest, with all ease of your body, and comfort of your reins." (pp. 7-8)

> *William Harrison Ainsworth, in a preface to his* Rookwood, *edited by Ernest Rhys, E. P. Dutton & Co., 1931, pp. 3-8.*

THE EDINBURGH REVIEW (essay date 1837)

> [*Ainsworth was uniquely successful in combining supernatural elements with a realistic setting in* Rookwood, *this critic believes; in* Crichton, *however, he is guilty of exaggeration and absurdity. Despite the imperfections in Ainsworth's first historical romance, this critic thinks highly of his skill.*]

[Mr Ainsworth] has certainly produced in his *Rookwood* a work indicating very considerable powers and resources. The experiment was a bold one; but its success is evinced by the fact that the edition which lies before us is the fourth, and that it has been thought worthy of being illustrated by the graphic powers of Cruickshank—who has given to the picture of Turpin's flight to York, already described by Mr Ainsworth with no ordinary vivacity in words, the additional attraction of some excellent and characteristic illustrations. What Mr Ainsworth has ventured to do, and successfully, was to revive the almost exploded interest afforded by the supernatural; and to preserve this, too, not in connexion with days long gone by, but side by side with the sober realities of 1737,—with the convivialities of Yorkshire squires and country attorneys, with the humours of justices of the peace, and the feats of Dick Turpin the highwayman. . . . The mere announcement of such juxtaposition as takes place in *Rookwood,* will satisfy any one that it is not a romance on the ordinary plan; and will probably enable them also to conjecture that its claims to the title of romance, in the highest sense of the word, are at least doubtful. The writer himself observes in his introduction [see excerpt dated 1837], that 'the chief object he had in view was to see how far the infusions of a warmer and more genial current into the veins of old romance would succeed in reviving her fluttering and feeble pulses.' He has raised her pulse certainly, but it is by the common expedient of administering a dram. It is by pitching every thing upon a key above nature and truth—and playing up to it—no doubt with much vigour and execution, but still, with an obvious straining, at times, on his own part, and with a corresponding sensation of occasional anxiety and discomfort on the part of the audience. (pp. 193-94)

Properly speaking, then, it is questionable whether the term Romance be justly applicable to a production like *Rookwood,* which, from its very nature, is so essentially fantastic. To character, it makes little pretension: its stronghold on the imagination arises entirely from the interest of incident, and the mingling with all the human incidents of the story a strong under current of the supernatural, in the supposed agency of an awful, avenging, and unavoidable destiny. But viewing it in this light, as what our German neighbours call a *nacht-stuck,* or night piece—a graft of Victor Hugo on Theodore Hoffmann, with here and there some grisly exhibition of *diablerie à-la-Callot*—it is unquestionably a work of remarkable interest, and of very considerable ability. Strange as it may seem, the author has contrived to present the terrors of burial vaults, and the blood-stained mysteries of family crime, side by side with the most familiar scenes of the every day life of the eighteenth century,—without exciting the slightest feeling of the ludicrous; nay more, with a character of earnestness and solemnity with which *a priori* we should have hardly thought that such subjects could have been invested. The truth is, the reader is never allowed to pause for an instant to think at all—he is hurried on with breathless haste, and with vivid curiosity, from the charnel-house to the blood-stained family secrets of the old hall,—to the gipsy's encampment, to the haunts of highwaymen, to the pursuit from London to York, and through a series of the strangest encounters, discoveries, plots and counterplots, murders and disclosures; so that in truth he arrives at the end of the volume before he has time to ask himself the question— Is this a romance, or a melodrama compounded of the Castle Spectre and the Newgate Calendar?

We have a very sincere admiration of the ability displayed by Mr Ainsworth in this supernatural *capriccio;* but not a high opinion, we must confess, of the class of romance 'to which he restricts himself.' The interest of such performances ceases with the first reading. When the mystery is solved, and the first breathless anxiety of the hair-breadth 'scapes, and moving accidents in which they deal is over, we revert to them no more. Our first feeling then certainly was one of regret that Mr Ainsworth had not chosen a subject more susceptible of a natural and not overstrained human interest; accompanied by a wish that, if the success of his first publication should induce him again to appear before the public, he might choose a theme somewhat more suited to ordinary sympathies. More mature consideration induced us, however, to doubt whether in that case his success might be so probable: and whether the qualities of his mind did not, after all, harmonize less with the more compact and symmetrical form which a proper historical romance would require, than with that 'Gothic imagery of darker shade' which forms the moving principle of *Rookwood.* (pp. 195-96)

In *Crichton,* Mr Ainsworth has aspired to the honour of framing a regular historical romance. He has set about his task evidently with great pains; has read a great deal of contemporary history; has familiarized himself with the manners of the time; is well versed in its scandal and intrigues; and he has woven the result of his reading and meditations into a series of scenes, certainly rapid, graphic, and imposing in their movement, of which the admirable Crichton is the hero, during his early residence at the Court of France. And yet the romance is an unsatisfactory one; for it is bottomed on the same false principle of exaggeration, which, though it might be tolerated in an avowed extravagance like *Rookwood,*—which, by its very nature, seemed in some measure emancipated from the rules of ordinary composition,—is totally inadmissible in a genuine romance, of which a well-known historical character is the subject. This is the mistake which prevails throughout; we have exaggeration of characters and passions, exaggeration of humours, exaggeration of incidents. The very idea of repose seems never to occur to Mr Ainsworth; he is as restless as Ahasuerus himself. Rapid change is the principle of the whole romance; at one instant Crichton has the king's authority to arrest Gonzaga; the next he is met by some other person bearing the queen's authority to arrest *him;* at one moment all-powerful, the next plunged into a prison, contending with assassins, or fighting with lions or bulls;—in short, the gleam of daggers is so incessant, the danger so constant, and yet the escapes so uniform and so constantly achieved by Crichton's own resources, either of body or mind, that we cease at last to feel agitated about him, considering him as possessing a charmed life.

It seems pretty plain that, to have exhibited Crichton's character with effect, it should have been the object of the writer rather to diminish than increase that halo of the marvellous which hangs about the history of the Scottish cavalier; at any rate, not to have gone beyond the materials furnished by the (somewhat doubtful) chronicles of the times. But here he is represented as running, in the course of three days, through more dangers, and greater feats of daring and strength, than are ascribed to him by all his biographers, authentic or fabulous. . . . It is obvious, indeed, that Victor Hugo has contributed not a few ideas to *Crichton.* Most of the chapters are prefaced by mottoes from his works (and those, too, among the worst of his publications—*Le Roi s'Amuse,* and *Lucrece Borgia*), denoting the most careful study of his manner, and an evident preference of his wild and startling conceptions over the calmer delineations of our own great masters. It is not possible to read the opening chapters, where the students without the university are impatiently waiting the issue of the contest between Crichton and the doctors,—at the same time jesting and quarrelling among themselves,—without thinking of the similar scenes in *Notre Dame,* where the multitude are waiting the representation of the mystery, and the students are represented as distinguishing themselves pretty much in the same manner as in the scene just mentioned. (pp. 197-99)

[Of Chicot, the courtjester,] we hear a great deal too much— and great as was the license permitted to court fools, we cannot but think his endless impertinence would never have been tolerated by the personages to whom it is here supposed to be addressed. Mr Ainsworth seems to have laboured this character with considerable assiduity,—particularly as it afforded him the means of introducing much of the odd and out-of-the-way reading, which in the course of his preparation for this romance he seems to have amassed. A good deal of this erudition we could willingly have dispensed with. . . . The parade of antiquarian expression is frequently most tedious; so much so, that many of the descriptions are scarcely intelligible. What, for instance, are we to make of the following technicalities where the author is describing the appearance of Joyeuse on horseback, and speaking of

> The ease with which he ever and anon compelled him to perform the balotades croupades, and other graces of the high manège, alluded to in the following alliterative verses:—
>
> > Vite virade,
> > Pompante pannade,
> > Saut soulevant,
> > Prompte peterrade.

> While the female portion of the assemblage marvelled at the exceeding beauty of feature, disclosed by the open visor of his casque, and the manly symmetry of the limbs, defined by his light and curiously-fashioned breastplate, "brassards, cuissards, jamb, and selleret." The housings of his steed were of white damask, diapered with gold, and bordered with minever. His chamfrin was decorated, like that of Gonzaga, with a superb *houpe de plumes,* and similarly accoutred. From the crest of the knight depended a lambrequin of slashed silk; and his surcoat was woven with his blazon, a lion rampant azure, armed, and langued gules.

(pp. 202-03)

We have stated fairly our impression as to the manifold faults of *Crichton;* all of which, however, have their origin in that tendency to exaggerate, to which we alluded in the outset. Mr Ainsworth will not trust to nature; he must dazzle and confound; or hold the mind in suspense by scenes of peril and terror. This, however, is no uncommon fault in a young writer; and we are not without hopes that Mr Ainsworth will, at no distant period, come to entertain sounder views as to the true principles on which a romance should be constructed. He already has many of the best qualities of a romance writer; he requires rather the due balance and regulation of what he possesses than the addition of any thing new. Had we not, with all its imperfections, thought highly of *Crichton,* we should have passed it over with the single observation that it was interesting and dramatic; but entertaining the opinion that it is the work of a man of genius, we have thought it right fairly and candidly to indicate what appears to us to be their origin, in the hope that in his future productions he may give more scope to his judgment, and less to the caprices of imagination. (p. 204)

> *"Recent English Romances," in* The Edinburgh Review, *Vol. LXV, No. CXXXI, April, 1837, pp. 180-204.**

AMERICAN QUARTERLY REVIEW   (essay date 1837)

[*While admitting that the subject of* Crichton *is interesting, the author of the following excerpt contends that Ainsworth does not sufficiently condemn the criminal characters and the licentious court setting, thus violating "the rules of critical propriety and accuracy."*]

[*Crichton*] possesses throughout a quality which is essential to the success of every book of its class—we mean interest; and it is one which often makes us overlook many and great defects. Without it, the best arranged and most regularly protracted story drags heavily on; and, with it, even loosely constructed and unfinished narratives absorb the attention. The latter is the case with *Crichton.* It violates many of the rules of critical propriety and accuracy; and the fate of the most interesting personage in the book is wholly involved in obscurity. We merely know that she is brutally injured and degraded, without being informed whether the only relief, in her case desirable—death—came to her succour. The outrage offered to her was by no means essential to the story, and is, besides, of a most revolting character; and its introduction, therefore, bespeaks but little consideration for the taste of Mr. Ainsworth; while the conclusion of the tale, without the exhibition or even intimation of any punishment upon her destroyer, is a heavy accusation against its moral.

Indeed, a charge of this description would be sustained by numerous proofs, aside from this merely negative testimony. The scene of the romance is laid in an epoch and at a court infamous for its licentiousness; and the hero revels in all its fulness, is guilty, indeed, of one of the deepest crimes, without incurring, in the estimate of the author, the slightest reproach or criminality. It may be said that such was the custom of the age—the tone of society; and, perhaps, early education and the influences of fashion might, in individual cases, have lessened the enormity of their transgression; but the vices of no era, and of no class of persons, should be held up as pictures to the youthful mind, in our day, without a decided and unqualified reprobation at the hand of the author.

There is something in the stirring incidents of the story—the descriptions of a magnificent and licentious court—the devel-

opment of state intrigues, and the motley crowd of priests, warriors, students, women, jesters, and rabble—which reminds the reader of the better days of Scott; but that great writer never laid himself open to the imputation against which our author has not been sufficiently careful to guard; for, while he delighted the fancy, he was ever cautious not to weaken or to warp the moral sense.

Mr. Ainsworth was happy in his choice of a subject. There was enough generally known of Crichton to render any production, of which he was the hero, sure to excite curiosity. There was enough, and more than enough, in his extraordinary and romantic career to gratify the most eager craving. That our author has failed to satisfy expectation, we are fain to assert. Had he taken up the life of his hero from infancy, and brought it down to his early death—for his career, though replete with matter for admiration, filled but a span—and devoted the powers of description and of imagination which he undoubtedly possesses, to the exhibition of the character and performances of this wonder of his age, we are confident that his work would have been more likely than it now is to survive the brief period which is usually allotted as the term of its existence to the "last Romance." (pp. 250-51)

> *A review of "Crichton," in* American Quarterly Review, *Vol. 22, No. XLIII, September, 1837, pp. 250-51.*

THE LITERARY GAZETTE, LONDON   (essay date 1839)

[*Unlike most contemporary critics, this reviewer claims that Ainsworth gave his tale of criminal life,* Jack Sheppard, *a positive moral effect in addition to its interesting plot, skilled descriptions, and artful construction.*]

Upon looking at [*Jack Sheppard*], several questions suggest themselves before pronouncing critical sentence upon the work. First, Is it necessary that every publication should be framed for the express purpose of pointing a moral? Secondly, Does *Jack Sheppard* succeed or fail in this object? And, thirdly, Do such subjects offer fair materials to exercise the talent of authors, and afford public gratification, without injury, to the public mind? To the first inquiry we think we are bound to concede, that, much as we value moral inculcation, to adhere to it as a *sine quá non* would be to exclude a multitude of amusing, playful, imaginative, and innocent productions, which have ever been the enjoyment of cultivated society. To the second the reply would be, that, so long as human nature is human nature, and there is guilt as well as virtue, it may be as expedient to explore the lower and darker recesses of villainy as to develope the stilted crimes of tragedy in high places. Nay, as the former immediately affect and come in contact with the vast majority of our fellow-creatures, it is the more expedient to put the ignorant many on their guard against the seductions of common vice and the invasions of bold brutality. The main point, therefore, comes, after all, to be the treatment of the theme. Are we made to feel a deeper concern for the scoundrel and murderer than for the wronged and good?—is criminality made prosperous, and honour and honesty (alas! too often suffering in the real world) held up to disregard and odium?— is there no justice manifested in apportioning punishment and misery to the evil-doer, as the consequence of evil deeds, and awarding consolation, if not happiness, to the virtuous? If such were the gist of any plot and narrative, however striking for the talent with which they were contrived and wrought, we should at once condemn the book, and lament that an author capable of such things should have betrayed the cause, for the promotion of which Providence had gifted him with superior intelligence and endowments. But we find none of these offences in *Jack Sheppard*.... [We think Mr. Ainsworth has elected his ruffian victim, Jack Sheppard, to demonstrate] that depravity, however covered by bravado, is sure to entail compunction and punishment; and that unequal as are the fates of the bad and the good, the preponderance of suffering rests with the former, and the balance of even earthly comfort with the latter class. Our author has curiously, though incidentally, supported this view, by supposing that Hogarth took the hint of his vigorous and impressive lesson of Industry and Idleness (in the two apprentices) from seeing Jack Sheppard previous to his execution, when his portrait was painted by Sir James Thornhill: May not we also guess that something of Mr. Ainsworth's story might have been suggested by Hogarth's Pictures? . . .

In fine, Jack Sheppard is

> To all an example,
> To no one a pattern,

and an ignominious death is the just reward of an atrocious life. The touches of remorse and repentance with which it has pleased Mr. Ainsworth to invest his closing career, are worthy of much commendation, not only as finishing the humanity of his conception, but as doing homage to the invincible principles of conscience and retribution. Of the literary ability with which he has executed his design, we need say nothing, as it has been every where acknowledged; and for intense description and fearful interest, there are portions of this production which it would not be easy to surpass in our own or any other language. (p. 657)

> *A review of "Jack Sheppard: A Romance," in* The Literary Gazette, *London, No. 1187, October 19, 1839, pp. 657-58.*

THE ATHENAEUM   (essay date 1839)

[*This critic asserts that in his desire to be read, Ainsworth catered to the coarse and vulgar tastes of the public, producing* Jack Sheppard, *"a bad book," improbable and melodramatic.*]

If we consider Mr. Ainsworth in the usual light of a mere caterer for the public appetite, and as devoting his talents to the production of a popular work either at his own or his publisher's suggestion, we must freely admit [*Jack Sheppard*] to be on a level with the usual specimens of the class, and at least as good as the occasion required. It is not his fault that he has fallen upon evil days, and that, like other tradesmen, he must subordinate his own tastes to those of his customers. If, therefore, in the remarks which we are about to make, we appear to bear hard on the publication in question, we do not intend thereby to dispute the author's power of producing better things, or even to reproach him too severely with his submission to the necessity of pandering to the prevalent corruption of intellect,—a reproach by the bye, to which we all, in our desire to be read, render ourselves in some degree liable.

Jack Sheppard, then, is a bad book, and what is worse, it is of a class of bad books, got up for a bad public.... In the ... [engraved illustrations] are embodied all the inherent coarseness and vulgarity of the subject; and all the horrible and (it is not too strong to say) unnatural excitement, which a public, too prudish to relish humour, and too *blasé* to endure true pathos, requires to keep alive attention and to awaken a sen-

sation.... To relieve the tedium of an endless repetition of adventures, ... and to raise the work above the level of dry extract from the Newgate Calendar, and the newspapers of the day, the hero is involved in a melo-dramatic story of motiveless crime, and impossible folly, connected with personages of high degree; and an attempt is made to invest Sheppard with good qualities, which are incompatible with his character and position. But the sacrifice of probability and of moral propriety is vain. We never escape from the staple: crime is the one source of every interesting situation; and, if we cannot exactly say, that horse-pistols are the sources of horse-laughs, we may safely assert, that the only proofs the *dramatis personae* exhibit of possessing brains, is the constant liability under which they live and move and have their being, of having them knocked or blown out. In the elaboration of a work of this description, little is required beyond mere technical authorship. The invention and the excitement are furnished to the author's hand. The characters, actions, thoughts and expressions, dictated beforehand, are all of the lowest and the most monotonous kind. It is not man, it is not nature that are wanted; but a corrupted, stunted, and deformed degradation of both; not an universality, but a special and an exceptional combination. To throw away on such a composition either feeling or humour, would be not merely a waste of time, but a disappointment to the reader. Such things would not merely be superfluous, but out of place. (p. 803)

> *A review of "Jack Sheppard: A Romance," in* The Athenaeum, *No. 626, October 26, 1839, pp. 803-05.*

[JOHN FORSTER]   (essay date 1839)

[*Forster was an English biographer, critic, and journalist. In the following excerpt, he deplores the lack of morality in* Jack Sheppard *and claims that "public morality and public decency have rarely been* more *endangered" than by this popular tale.*]

We notice this "romance" with very great reluctance, because we have thought the author capable of better things. It is however in every sense of the word so bad, and has been recommended to circulation by such disreputable means that the silence we meant to preserve upon the subject would be almost as great a compromise with truth as the morals of the book or the puffs of the bookseller.

Bad as we think the morals, we think the puffs more dangerous. Our silence would never have been broken if the book had been suffered to rest on its own merits. Little danger might then have been anticipated....

[Since] *Tom and Jerry* crowded the theatres with thieves and the streets with brawlers, or since the doings and the histories of Messrs Moffat and Haggard hurried their various victims to the gallows, public morality and public decency have rarely been *more* endangered than by the trumpeted exploits of Jack Sheppard. All the original insignificance of the thing is lost, in the pernicious influences that are set at work around it.

For these reasons we think it necessary to speak out, and exhibit the real character and tendencies of the book before us.

For it is not the title, even though it be *Jack Sheppard,* that should warn good taste from such a book. It is the uses to which it is applied. It is not the subject we shrink from; the treatment is the paramount objection. We meet with a succession of swindlers and thieves in *Gil Blas;* we shake hands with highwaymen and housebreakers all round in the *Beggars' Opera;* we pack cards with La Ruse or pick pockets with Jonathan in Fielding's *Mr Wild the Great;* we follow vice from its least beginnings to its grossest ends in the plates of Hogarth; but for all that our morals stand none the looser. . . . The low was indeed set forth, with all the graces of literature or of art, by our Fieldings, our Hogarths, and our Gays, but only to pull down the false pretensions of the high. . . . *The vulgarity of vice was the object at which they drove, and not its false pretensions to heroism or its vile cravings for sympathy.* . . .

Nothing could have been more vile [than Mr Ainsworth's treatment of his subject, Jack Sheppard]. At the commencement of the book, indeed, are a few spirited scenes—the description of the great storm of 1703 for example—and some hope seems to be held out that the nominal hero may be wisely reserved throughout as a mere background to that sort of picture of romance, for a correct rendering whereof Mr Ainsworth has indisputable requisites. Soon, however, is this illusion dissipated, and crime—bare, rascally, unmitigated, ferocious crime— becomes the idea constantly thrust before us. From that instant all of what with courtesy we will call the interest of the book may be said to hang upon the gallows, and the reader finds himself suddenly launched on one undeviating and very dirty road to that pleasing and elevated object. The sentiments of the work are pretty constant to two great principles. The one is a slavish adulation of high birth and the more vulgar incidents thereto belonging. The other is a strong sense of the moral capabilities, nice emotions, and sensitive affections, which belong to thieves and murderers. . . .

Such being the general style and tendency of this ''romance,'' it is needless to say that it is devoid of anything like skilful delineation of character. How can anything natural be formed out of materials so grossly out of nature? Yet will the reader scarcely be prepared for such hideous combinations of absurdity, as are designed by the author of *Jack Sheppard* for portraits of human beings! (p. 691)

Thank Heaven! I'm not basely born! [Jack says when he learns his mother is a baron's sister.] This sentiment of the housebreaker now becomes the clue to all he does and to all he repents having done. The knowledge of his mother's high alliance inspires him with sudden respect for her, and he incontinently goes off to pay her the visit in Bedlam. He now feels that if he had only known of his high birth he'd not have been a housebreaker. And this, if there is any moral in it, is the moral of the book! Very different that, from our dear friends Fielding and Gay! . . . It is a nice evidence, perhaps, of the author's finely graduated respect for rank, that after all Thames Darrell is made out to have been, by the father's side, better born than Jack. Indeed, he turns out to be a marquis! Thus the entire victory of Miss Wood, in getting Thames instead of Jack, is more decisively shown. She has not only a man of superior virtue, but a man of infinitely superior quality. . . .

[An] appearance of the baronet's housebreaking nephew which is worth noting takes place, after another of his escapes, at the supper table of Mr Kneebone. This appearance is in consequence of a promise made to the latter, and another point of very strong morality with Mr Sheppard is, never to break his word. *''I never yet broke an engagement. Though a thief, Jack Sheppard is a man of his word!''*—are sentiments many times repeated and referred to in the work. Thus it is arranged with delicate skill in every case, that whenever the condemned felon is arrested after one of his escapes, he is sure to be caught at some pious office of charity, friendship, or filial devotion, or else by reason of his too scrupulously keeping his word. Thus all our sympathies are of necessity requested to go back with

him to his cruel confinement, and we are to be quite uneasy till he escapes again. . . .

[Jack would have left England to seek an honorable fortune abroad] but for the unlucky accident of his mother's funeral! He has already perilled his life in getting his mother's dead body into a hackney coach, that Thames Darrell may give it decent burial; but he determines to hazard everything again to attend the burial, and what eye can refuse to weep when the stern Jonathan seizes at such a time, and in such a place, the devoted son?''

> ''Let me see the earth thrown over her,'' implored Jack ''and take me where you please.''
>
> ''No,'' thundered Wild.
>
> ''Allow him that small grace,'' cried Wood.
>
> ''No, I tell you,'' rejoined Jonathan, shouldering his way out of the crowd.
>
> ''My mother—my poor mother!'' exclaimed Jack.
>
> But, in spite of his outcries and resistance, he was dragged along by Jonathan and his janizaries.

Need we go farther than this in exposure of this so called ''romance''? . . . The heroics of Gay's Macheath, of Fielding's Jonathan Wild-the-Great, are mock heroics. Modest nature— the tender, the true, the beautiful—is never implicated in them, but only looks laughing on. The heroics of *Jack Sheppard* are real, and nature, moved with unspeakable disgust, turns blushing and degraded away.

But there is a climax still!—The lowest deep contains a lower!— So thoroughly has the writer identified *his* sympathies at least with the crime of his hero as a trifling peccadillo, and indeed with thieves and murderers in general as naughty but yet amusing people, that the *fatal rope* which has awaited them from the first page of his book to the last, seems now in the nature of an unworthy if not unrighteous thing. The idea of Mr Sheppard, the heir presumptive to the baronetcy, dying by hempseed! The nice imaginations of the book cannot tolerate it. Instinctively the author supposes, as it were, that such a thing would only outrage the sympathies he has most largely interested, and give offence, especial and even personal offence, to modern admirers of the hero. The gentility of a bullet is therefore called in aid, and ''thus died Jack Sheppard.''

> ''I died no felon's death!
> A warrior's weapon freed a warrior's soul!'' . . .

But let no simple reader for an instant suppose that he died so! The real Jack Sheppard, be assured, danced upon nothing and turned him round with the best that have ever been notorious for that remarkable feat, and verily do we believe that of all who have at any time ''died suddenly'' at Tyburn, none deserved his fate more richly. No man ever sucked the moisture of the last consolatory orange, or felt the nip of the last fatal noose, or strove to fix his listless eyes on the ghastly prayerbook, for whom, in our opinion, the Tyburn tree was more aptly kept than Jack Sheppard. He was of the very refuse of the rope. None more base have ever favoured an anxious and curious public with sight of themselves in nightcap on a public platform, and never may a ''more audacious dog'', to use the language of a Newgate Ordinary, '' hope to stretch a halter.''

It is recorded that, shortly after his execution, a sermon of allusion to his last extraordinary escape (at which we more than suspect the turnkeys connived) was preached by a notorious person in the city, and from this we venture, in concluding this article, to take one ingenious passage. Thus it ran.

> Let me exhort ye then to open the locks of your hearts with the nail of repentance; burst asunder the fetters of your beloved lusts; mount the chimney of hope; take from thence the bar of good resolution, break through the stone wall of despair, and all the strongholds in the dark entry of the valley of the shadow of death; raise yourselves to the leads of divine meditation; fix the blanket of faith with the spike of the Church; let yourselves down to the turner's house of resignation, and descend the stairs of humility; so shall ye come to the door of deliverance from the prison of iniquity, and escape the clutches of that old executioner the Devil, who goeth about like a roaring lion, seeking whom he may devour.

Now, parodying this parody, let us exhort Mr Ainsworth to open the locks of his brain with the nail of common sense and nature, to burst asunder the fetters of his beloved bookseller, mount the chimney of manly aspiration, take from thence the bar of good resolution, break through the frail wall of purchased puff, and all the strongholds in the dark entry of the valley of New Burlington street, and raise himself to the leads of "divine meditation." Then will he be content to fix such another wet blanket as the present book on the sharp spike of a sense of its utter unworthiness; let it gently down to the trunkmaker's house of resignation; and descend the stairs of humility. And so shall he come to the door of deliverance from the panderers of the moment, and escape the clutches of that old executioner he wots of, who goeth about like a slinking wolf, seeking whom he may devour.

When this is so, and his talents are engaged in no unworthy work, we shall rejoice again to welcome him, heartily as of old. (p. 693)

> *[John Forster], in a review of "Jack Sheppard: A Romance," in* The Examiner, *No. 1657, November 3, 1839, pp. 691-93.*

THE MONTHLY CHRONICLE (essay date 1840)

[*According to this critic, such sensational novels as* Jack Sheppard *stimulate the baser human propensities.*]

The glare and glitter attendant on a high station, or the misery and crime too often darkening the lowest, are considered indispensable to the creation of a powerful interest. The tawdry frivolity of the one, and the coarseness and violence of the other class, are derived from congenial sources; and such novels as "Almacks" and *Jack Shepherd* have their springs of interest equally in our mere animal propensities: the desire of the sensual indulgences procurable by wealth and rank, and the fear and horror with which we listen to a tale of blood and physical suffering, are equally remote from intellectual pleasure. Such stimulants as these ought to be most sparingly employed, and never but in the strictest subordination to some higher object; yet these are the staple commodities with a vast majority of our novel writers. (pp. 35-6)

"Novel Writing and Newspaper Criticism," in The Monthly Chronicle, *Vol. V, No. 1, January, 1840, pp. 33-8.**

[WILLIAM THACKERAY] (essay date 1840)

[*A famed Victorian author, Thackeray is best known for his satiric sketches and novels of upper- and middle-class English life. Here, Thackeray finds Ainsworth's eloquence and power of description misplaced in the "gallows school of literature" that* Jack Sheppard *represents. For further commentary by Thackeray on* Jack Sheppard, *see excerpt dated September, 1840.*]

With a very great regard for Ainsworth . . . , and a full sense of the talent and research which he brings to bear upon every subject which he touches, we must say that we like not this gallows school of literature. (p. 227)

[We regret to find Ainsworth] "pampering the vanity which perpetuates the determination to crime," by investing the low ruffians of the *Newgate Calendar,* and their profligate companions, with all the interest and the graces of romance. It is said that the popularity of Charles Moor, in Schiller's *Robbers,* induced young men of rank in Germany to turn highway robbers—the story, we believe, is apocryphal, though it may have some foundation in fact; but there is no doubt that the popular exhibition of Jack Sheppard, metamorphosed from a vulgar ruffian into a melodramatic hero, with all the melodramatic virtues and splendours about him, in Mr. Ainsworth's novel, and its manifold theatrical adaptations, will tend to fill many a juvenile aspirant for riot and notoriety with ideas highly conducive to the progress of so ennobling a profession as that of housebreaking. . . .

The avowedly fictitious part of Ainsworth's novel—that relating to the adventures of Sir Rowland Trenchard and his sister—is not very probable in its construction; but it is agreeably written, and contains many passages of high interest. The antiquarian portion, if we can apply such an epithet to dates of little more than a century's standing—is carefully got up; and many scenes and chapters display considerable power. (p. 228)

In order to make his romance interesting, Ainsworth has engrafted upon it a wonderfully fine story of Sir Rowland Trenchard, Thames Darrell, the Marquess of Chatillon, and so forth,—marvellous, and terrible to read. By itself it would be a good rawhead and bloody-bones tale enough; and, beyond question, it is here and there powerfully written; but, in connexion with the deeds and exploits of a drunken London housebreaker, it comes in so queerly as to be sometimes ineffably laughable. The conceit of making Jack Sheppard the son of a woman of high family, and connected by blood with a house of long descent, is rather droll. Jack was a blackguard, blood, bone, and sinew; and any refining does his character perfect injustice. The plain history of his case, if rightly taken, is infinitely more sad than all the heroics and lamentations of Mr. Ainsworth. To impute to our old friend Jonathan any revengeful ideas, any notions not exactly quadrating with his profession of thief-taker,—feelings, in short, of any kind but those arising from considerations of money-making, by training and selling victims to the gallows, is quite contrary to *nature,*—that is, to such natures as his. If saving Jack Sheppard's life would have put a shilling in Wild's pocket beyond the blood-money, *plus* the fame, *i.e.* the means of making more money, by augmenting his reputation as an active officer, Jonathan would have saved Jack with as much readiness as he hanged him. It

The Fraserians, from a drawing by Daniel Maclise.

is a pity to see the hero of Fielding and the prototype of Peachum swelling into fits of passion,—talking, like meaner knaves, of being actuated by vows in heaven,—snivelling over recollections of bygone love,—in fact, doing in reality what in the hands of other artists, who knew something of what they were about, he is made to burlesque. (pp. 236-37)

It would be hard to expect Mr. Ainsworth to turn his novel into a book of example for the imitation or the avoidance of the dealers in criminal law. Yet we cannot help thinking, that by keeping close to the true story, as he chose it at all, he might not only have pointed a better moral, but have more adorned his tale. (p. 238)

The Mrs. Sheppard of the romance would never have reared its hero according to the most approved maxims of *The Child's Guide to the Gallows*. If she had been actuated by the deep remorse, and agitated by the never-ending grief, in which we find her decked out by Mr. Ainsworth, she would have found some means of keeping him from the contamination of the villanous company which was his undoing. Much of strict education and moral culture might not have been in her power; but where there is a will there is a way; and the woman of acute feelings, reformed conduct, and generous instincts, if not accurate principles, *must* have communicated some touch of her nature to her son. It is utterly out of drawing, as the painters say, to find Jack Sheppard the child of such a mother; and we feel it equally difficult to reconcile his romantic, delicate, devoted, filial affection, with the rest of his habitual conduct. (p. 239)

If Jack's mother cannot be supposed to be any thing like what Ainsworth has made her, just as little can we suppose Jack himself to be the fine hero he has depicted. He had great dexterity in the blackguard business which he had adopted; and

his breakings out of prison, if he accomplished them, as on his last appearance at the Old Bailey he said he did, "without any other help than that of Providence," are almost as wonderful as those of Baron Trenck: but there his merits end. He was a poor fool, permitted by the thieftakers to render himself notorious by bootless swaggering, in order to enhance their own merit in taking him. It is probable that some of his more audacious pranks were played, not only under the connivance of the police authorities, but with their direct collusion. [In the novel] . . . he puts himself in many an attitude of bold defiance, and speaks words not only brave but eloquent, and well worthy of the Sea-Captain himself, or any other of the most renowned heroes of regular blank verse. Commend us the rather to the real Jack himself. (pp. 240-41)

The other characters in the novel we shall pass without notice, except a word or two as to that of Jonathan Wild. Sir Walter Scott objects to Fielding, for having in his famous history ascribed a train of fictitious adventures to a real character. How much more deservedly, then, would he have objected to Ainsworth! The latter, it must be admitted, has Scott's own example to plead for making rather free with historical facts and personages; but it is too much to make Wild a downright assassin. He had, no doubt, much to answer for; but his execution was as criminal as any of his own criminal acts. (p. 241)

Mr. Ainsworth has, with much power, and eloquence, and interest, executed the task he has chosen, we readily admit. We trust that he will choose a loftier and purer subject the next time; and that in his *Tower of London*, which he has so well begun, he will

> purge off the baser stains,
> And soar aloft among the swans of Thames.

> (p. 245)

[William Thackeray], "William Ainsworth and 'Jack Sheppard'," in Fraser's Magazine, Vol. XXI, No. CXXII, February, 1840, pp. 227-45.

[ALBANY FONBLANQUE]   (essay date 1840)

[*Reporting on the Courvoisier trial, Fonblanque highlights the murderer's allegations that Ainsworth's* Jack Sheppard *motivated the crime.*]

[In his confession, Courvoisier] ascribes his crimes to the perusal of that detestable book, *Jack Sheppard;* and certainly it is a publication calculated to familiarise the mind with cruelties, and to serve as the cut-throat's manual, or the midnight assassin's *vade mecum,* in which character we now expect to see it advertised.

Curious it is that the very words used by Courvoisier, in describing the way in which he committed the murder, "I drew the knife across his throat," are to be found in the horrid book alluded to, in Blueskin's murder of Mrs. Wood. The passage is this:—

> Seizing her by the hair, he pulled back her head, *and drew the knife with all his force across her throat.* There was a dreadful stifled groan, and she fell heavily upon the landing. . . .

If ever there was a publication that deserved to be burnt by the hands of the common hangman it is *Jack Sheppard.* (p. 402)

*[Albany Fonblanque], "Mr. Phillips's Defence of Courvoisier," in The Examiner, No. 1691, June 28, 1840, pp. 401-02.**

W. HARRISON AINSWORTH   (letter date 1840)

[*In the following letter, Ainsworth disputes the* Examiner's *claim that Courvoisier was motivated to commit murder by reading* Jack Sheppard *(see excerpt above).*]

A statement to the effect that the assassin Courvoisier, in one of his reputed confessions, had asserted that the idea of murdering Lord William Russell was first suggested to him by a perusal of the romance of *Jack Sheppard,* and that he wished 'he had never seen the book,' having appeared in the *Morning Chronicle,* I have taken means to ascertain the correctness of the report, and find it utterly without foundation. The wretched man declared he had neither read the work in question, nor made any such statement. A collection of lives of noted malefactors (probably the *Newgate Calendar* had, indeed, fallen in his way), but the account of *Jack Sheppard,* in this series, had not particularly attracted his attention. I am the more anxious to contradict this false and injurious statement, because a writer in the *Examiner* of Sunday week, without inquiring into the truth of the matter, has made it the groundwork of a most virulent and libellous attack upon my romance.

W. Harrison Ainsworth, in a letter to the editor of "The Morning Chronicle" on July 4, 1840, in The Examiner, No. 1693, July 12, 1840, p. 434.

WILLIAM EVANS   (letter date 1840)

[*Evans, the sheriff of London, maintains that Courvoisier did indeed testify that* Jack Sheppard *inspired him to murder.*]

I observe in your journal of this morning a letter signed 'W. Harrison Ainsworth,' denying that Courvoisier had asserted that the idea of murdering his master was first suggested to him by a perusal of the romance of *Jack Sheppard.* I think it my duty to state distinctly, that Courvoisier did assert to me that 'the idea of murdering his master was first suggested to him by a perusal of the book called *Jack Sheppard,* and that the said book was lent to him by a valet of the Duke of Bedford.'

William Evans, in a letter to the editor of "The Times" on July 7, 1840, in The Examiner, No. 1693, July 12, 1840, p. 434.

THE EXAMINER   (essay date 1840)

[*The* Examiner, *though acquitting Ainsworth of immoral intent in writing* Jack Sheppard, *condemns the novel for inciting violent tendencies.*]

If the statement of Mr Ainsworth had remained uncontradicted, it would not have altered our opinion of the character and tendencies of *Jack Sheppard.* Had the book disgraced the time of Hogarth, the perusal of it would probably have made the first step in the great master's illustration of the Progress of Cruelty. As the passions are all excitable through the imagination, we look upon this book as calculated to create a lust for cruelty in minds having any predisposition to the vice. Its tendencies are to familiarise the imagination with deeds of blood, and to hold up to admiration the savage criminals acting in them. There is often in effects what never entered into intention, and we acquit the author of having intended or foreseen the encouragement of cruelty, but the admiration of the criminal is the studied purpose of the book.

"Courvoisier and Jack Sheppard," in The Examiner, No. 1693, July 12, 1840, p. 434.

W. M. THACKERAY   (essay date 1840)

[*In an essay on the novelist Henry Fielding, from which the following excerpt is taken, Thackeray berates Ainsworth's* Jack Sheppard *as absurd, unreal, and immoral. Thackeray's comments first appeared in the* Times *on September 2, 1840. For further commentary by Thackeray on* Jack Sheppard, *see excerpt dated February, 1840.*]

Vice is never to be mistaken for virtue in Fielding's honest downright books; it goes by its name, and invariably gets its punishment. See the consequences of honesty! Many a squeamish lady of our time would fling down one of these romances with horror, but would go through every page of Mr. Ainsworth's *Jack Sheppard* with perfect comfort to herself. Ainsworth dared not paint his hero as the scoundrel he knew him to be; he must keep his brutalities in the background, else the public morals will be outraged, and so he produces a book quite absurd and unreal, and infinitely more immoral than anything Fielding ever wrote. *Jack Sheppard* is immoral actually because it is decorous. The Spartans, who used to show drunken slaves to their children, took care, no doubt, that the slaves should be really and truly drunk. Sham drunkenness, which never passed the limits of propriety, but only went so far as to be amusing, would be rather an object to excite youth to intoxication than to deter him from it, and some late novels have always struck us in the same light. (p. 239)

W. M. Thackeray, "Fielding's Works," in his The Complete Works of W. M. Thackeray: Literary Es-

says, Essays on Art, *Thomas Y. Crowell Company, Publishers, 1904, pp. 231-42.**

R. H. HORNE   (essay date 1844)

[*Horne dismisses Ainsworth's historical novels as generally dull and plotless.*]

With regard to the Newgate narrative of *Jack Sheppard* and the extraordinarily extensive notoriety it obtained for the writer, upon the residuum of which he founded his popularity, so much just severity has already been administered from criticism and from the opinion of the intellectual portion of the public, and its position has been so fully settled, that we are glad to pass over it without farther animadversion.

The present popularity of Mr. Ainsworth could not have risen out of its own materials. His so-called historical romance of *Windsor Castle* is not to be regarded as a work of literature open to serious criticism. It is a picture book, and full of very pretty pictures. Also full of catalogues of numberless suits of clothes. It would be difficult to open it any where without the eye falling on such words as cloth of gold, silver tissue, green jerkin, white plumes. (pp. 218-19)

The book is also full of processions, banquets, royal hunting parties, courtiers, lords, and jesters, who are indeed "very dull fools." . . . As to plot or story it does not pretend to any.

Old St. Paul's, a tale of the Plague and the Fire, is a diluted imitation of some parts of De Foe's "Plague in London," varied with libertine adventures of Lord Rochester and his associates. It is generally dull, except when it is revolting. There are descriptions of nurses who poison or smother their patients, wretched prisoners roasted alive in their cells, and one felon who thrusts his arms through the red-hot bars,— "literally" is added, by way of apology. (pp. 220-21)

> *R. H. Horne, "William Harrison Ainsworth," in his A New Spirit of the Age, Vol. II, Smith, Elder and Co., 1844, pp. 215-22.*

J. HAIN FRISWELL   (essay date 1870)

[*In the following excerpt, Friswell castigates Ainsworth. The Newgate novels, with their corrupted values and immoral admiration of criminals, sent impressionable boys to prison, the critic contends, while the historical tales are stilted, dull, and nonsensical.*]

Let us start with an opinion, fearlessly expressed as it is earnestly felt, that the existence of this writer is an event to be deplored; and the fact that he is able to assume that he is a Man of Letters who has been of service to his country, and that he has received from the hands of a Prime Minister, himself a Man of Letters, the reward of £100 a-year pension for literary services, is a disgrace to this bewildered and Philistine nation. (p. 257)

It is really time that the English people should speak their mind as to their public servants, the authors. They stand in the stead of the prophets of old; they form the minds of the young; they set the bias of the mind towards virtue or vice, towards unholy greed, a cold lust of selfish gain, or a generous and manly life of duty, honesty, forbearance, and holiness.

Now, Mr. Harrison Ainsworth has not done the latter. He is, perhaps, not so much to be blamed, poor man, being a person of small attainments and not a very strong intellect, as the

times in which he was born. . . . [In] that very lively age people required a literature that teemed with adventure and had "go" in it. (pp. 258-59)

He began by writing highwaymen romances, and he has only just at present . . . concluded a story of *Claude Duval, a Tale of the Days of Charles the Second,* in that widely-circulated journal, *Bow Bells.* Let us add that he writes evidently with more decency and less open applause of robbery and brutality for one penny, than he did when one paid half-a-crown for his rubbish. His Claude Duval is not the Knight of the Road after all. The highwayman's name is merely taken as a "draw" by the vulgar novelist. He knows that little thieves and incipient burglars will be taken in by the name. He knows that in the purlieus of the New Cut, in the wynds of Glasgow, in the slums of Manchester and Birmingham, the name of Claude Duval is a name of might. He therefore takes it, but he wishes to be virtuous as well; he is as modest as a lady of a certain fame and occupation is at a christening—a great deal more modest than virtue itself. Claude Duval shot by the Duke of Buckingham!—(Ha, ha! what says Dame History to *that?*)—in single combat in Windsor Park, is attended in his duello by a female page dressed as a man, "with a wild shriek that betrayed her sex"—oh, you foolish old copyist, are not discarded women-pages of Sir Philip Sidney and of Shakspeare yet done with? (pp. 259-60)

Now this is mean in the extreme. Here is this old and accomplished author, who has drawn his brilliant existence, as the sun draws exhalations from a swamp, from the *Newgate Calendar;* who has sent so many boys to prison that Government has forbidden his plays to be acted with one hand and has pensioned him with the other. . . . (p. 261)

[He] took in Jack Sheppard and Cruikshank the artist, and aided by that very vulgar but wonderful draughtsman, he made an efficient story of the burglar's or housebreaker's life. He might have done this and kept to the truth, or have pointed a moral. He did neither. He gave Jack a kind of apotheosis; he made all his villains on the side of the law, and all his rogues and slatternly strumpets, washings of the kennel and gatherings from the stews, whom he termed fair and charming women, law-breakers, but to be admired by the reader! (p. 263)

[In *Ainsworth's Magazine* he] wrote certain stilted nonsense— *The Tower of London, Old St. Paul's, The Miser's Daughter,* and so forth. Of these not one could hold the public without its illustrations. . . .

Previous to this the poor scribe, whose historical novels were a mere list of the frippery of the wardrobe, had written another thieves' romance out of a penny chapbook, of which he has such a great idea that he has given the public the most touching scene to weep over. It is the death of Dick's mare, "Black Bess." (p. 264)

Knell of poor Black Bess! that never existed, that was never ridden to York, save in the brain of some half-starved author of a penny chapbook! And if this author had the common sense to have followed Fielding, he might, if he chose, have falsified history without making vice alluring. But such is the perverse blindness of such genius as inspires Bulwer and Ainsworth, that they represent the lazy loafer—who took to the road in fear and trembling, when he could no longer live on the wages of sin his poor female companion brought him—as a puissant knight-errant; and the mercers, travellers, and bagmen as so many cowards, who trembled at the sight of them. (p. 265)

Mr. Ainsworth and Lord Lytton have corrupted our boys by the hundred-fold. One has a peerage, the other a pension, for his services! We are rewarded for buying, they for writing this trash.

The author of *Jack Sheppard* may be, and possibly is, a very amiable gentleman, but he has no right to be allowed to escape scot-free from the result of his teachings. It is difficult for the candid mind to comprehend why the popular favour is extended to robbers and burglars, unless it be man envying the rich;— poor people love and admire those who rob and despoil the rich. (p. 269)

Mr. Ainsworth is, we believe, as Lord Lytton is, we know, a wealthy man through this literature; but if every farthing each has received from his books, pensions and all, were a hundred-pound note, and employed in building reformatories for boy-thieves, the unhappy man could not undo the evil his perverted taste, vulgar admiration, and his fatal itch of writing to pander to the savage instincts of the thief and robber, has caused, and will yet cause, in years to come. (p. 270)

> *J. Hain Friswell, "Mr. Harrison Ainsworth," in his* Modern Men of Letters Honestly Criticised, *Hodder and Stoughton, 1870, pp. 257-70.*

ONCE A WEEK (essay date 1872)

[*This critic believes that Ainsworth's sympathetic treatment of criminal characters has a negative moral effect on the reader and that "English literature would have been the gainer" had Ainsworth never written his novels.*]

It is as the biographer of such gentlemen as Mr. Jack Sheppard, of bad fame, that our author must lay claim to immortality; and it is in this field of labour that he is most at home. He has himself placed on record the state of his feelings after he had disposed of Mr. Turpin's apocryphal steed, "Black Bess" [see excerpt by Ainsworth dated 1837]. "Well do I remember," says the author, "the fever into which I was thrown during the time of composition. My pen literally scoured over the pages. So thoroughly did I identify myself with the flying highway-man, that, once started, I found it impossible to halt. . . . In his (Turpin's) company I mounted the hillside, dashed through the bustling village, swept over the desolate heath, threaded the silent street, plunged into the eddying stream. . . . With him I shouted, sang, laughed, exulted, wept; nor did I retire to rest till in imagination I heard the bell of York Minster toll forth the knell of poor Black Bess."

This is poetic frenzy with a vengeance; and nobody will be disposed to deny that whatever else the novelist lacked, it certainly was not sympathy for his creations.

The moral tendency of his writings, and the effect they were likely to produce on the youthful or untrained mind, have often been the subject of criticism. Of these, we think there can be no doubt, the effect must be bad. While we wish Mr. Ainsworth no harm, we wish the cause of morality in fiction well; and we cannot help thinking that if the "fever into which he was thrown" by the recital of the lawless adventures of a high-wayman had carried off his passion for writing novels, English literature would have been the gainer. (p. 473)

> *"W. H. Ainsworth," in* Once a Week, *n.s. Vol. X, No. 257, November 30, 1872, pp. 472-73.*

GEORGE AUGUSTUS SALA (essay date 1895)

[*Sala, the editor of* Temple Bar: A London Magazine for Town and Country Readers *from 1860 to 1863, highly praises Ainsworth's "word-painting" of Turpin's ride to York in* Rookwood.]

[Edward Lytton Bulwer was] beaten on his own ground by another writer of fiction very much his inferior in genius, but who was nevertheless endowed with a considerable amount of melodramatic power, and who had acquired a conspicuous faculty for dramatic description. This was young Mr. William Harrison Ainsworth, who first essayed felonious fiction in his interesting but unequal romance *Rookwood,* in which one of the leading characters was the notoriously coarse and crapulous highwayman and horsethief, Dick Turpin. Turpin's ride to York, as a piece of word-painting, has been rarely, if ever, surpassed in the prose of the Victorian era. (p. 86)

In *Jack Sheppard* he out-Newgated Bulwer's Newgate epics. Every student of criminal annals knows that John Sheppard, footpad and housebreaker, was a vulgar, squalid, illiterate, drunken scamp, whose only talent was one for breaking out of gaol. Ainsworth made him a dashing young blood of illicitly noble descent, who dressed sumptuously and lived luxuriously; but even had the novelist refrained from converting this vulgar gaol-bird into a hero of romance, there was quite enough in the vigorous description of his escapes from Newgate, and the extraordinarily able illustrations thereof by George Cruikshank, to delight and enchant a public which had already been captivated by the murder and housebreaking scenes in "Oliver Twist." . . . (pp. 86-7)

> *George Augustus Sala, "Newgate Novels and an Apology," in his* The Life and Adventures of George Augustus Sala, *Vol. I, Charles Scribner's Sons, 1895, pp. 80-8.**

GEORGE SAINTSBURY (essay date 1896)

[*Saintsbury was an English literary historian and critic of the late nineteenth and early twentieth centuries. A prolific writer, he composed several histories of English and European literature as well as numerous critical works on individual authors, styles, and periods. Saintsbury maintains that although Ainsworth excelled in presenting interesting incidents, his works are poor from a literary standpoint.*]

[Harrison Ainsworth] had a real knack of arresting and keeping the interest of those readers who read for mere excitement: he was decidedly skilful at gleaning from memoirs and other documents scraps of decoration suitable for his purpose, he could in his better days string incidents together with a very decided knack, and, till latterly, his books rarely languished. But his writing was very poor in strictly literary merit, his style was at best bustling prose melodrama, and his characters were scarcely ever alive. (p. 139)

> *George Saintsbury, "The New Fiction," in his* A History of Nineteenth Century Literature (1780-1895), *1896. Reprint by The Macmillan Company, 1923, pp. 125-65.**

BEVERLY STARK (essay date 1903)

[*Two years before the centenary of Ainsworth's birth, Stark finds his "old-fashioned and old-formed tales" enjoyably entertaining, but far from the first rank of novels by Eugène Sue, Victor Hugo, and Alexandre Dumas.*]

Kensal Manor House, where Ainsworth entertained his literary friends.

Whatever place may be assigned to Thackeray as a literary critic, his use of burlesque in dealing with the kind of fiction which he did not admire made him infinitely more dangerous to the reputation that was not solidly and soundly established than the most savage and truculent literary "bludgeoners" of his day.... There was much in Dickens, notably in *Oliver Twist*, with which Thackeray was never in sympathy, though he deemed it best never to say very much on that score.

But with William Harrison Ainsworth he had no such compunctions, and in the indictment of *Jack Sheppard* contained in the article on Fielding which Thackeray contributed to the *Times* [see excerpt dated 1840], in which he said "Ainsworth dared not paint his hero as the scoundrel he knew him to be. He must keep his brutalities in the background, else the public morals will be outraged, and so he produces a book quite absurd and unreal, and infinitely more immoral than anything Fielding ever wrote. *Jack Sheppard* is immoral actually because it is decorous;" in his arraignment of the style of the same book, in the article on George Cruikshank which appeared in the *Westminster Review* in 1840; and in *Catherine*, Ainsworth received his most severe critical rebuffs. When we recall that the sales of *Jack Sheppard* exceeded those of *Oliver Twist*, which appeared about the same time, and that Thackeray, conscious of his own great powers, was daily wincing under underappreciation and repulse, some of the irritation of the future author of *Vanity Fair* may be understood. But if Ainsworth was overrated by the public for which he wrote, a succeeding generation, by its utter neglect, has evened the account, and as two years hence we shall be noting his centenary with more or less interest, it is very much worth while to take up the new

edition of his works which has just been brought out, and to derive a fresh pleasure from the old-fashioned and old-formed tales. (pp. 568-70)

[Ainsworth was] one of the most prolific of English writers, and his industry and fertility of invention is shown by the forty novels which bear his name....

[Despite some critics' claims that Ainsworth modelled his novels on the works of Eugène Sue, Victor Hugo, and Alexandre Dumas, to] the present writer Ainsworth is not in the least like Hugo or Dumas, although, as the chronological order of his novels will show, he did much to popularise English history as Dumas popularised French history. But he lacked Dumas's brilliancy, just as he lacked Hugo's sweep. He was nearest to Sue. He had some of the Frenchman's talent and resource for the handling of scenes designed to inspire sheer terror, and he also surpassed Sue in the fault of overdoing these scenes. Judged by the broadest standards, Ainsworth can never by any possibility be admitted near to the first rank. But as a writer of exciting romance he deserved the success which he won; and a reaction that would take us back for a month of pleasant evenings among the people and the rookeries of his old London would be by no means an unhealthy one. (p. 570)

Beverly Stark, "William Harrison Ainsworth," in The Bookman, *New York, Vol. XVI, No. 6, February, 1903, pp. 568-70.*

FRANCIS GRIBBLE   (essay date 1905)

[*Gribble finds that Ainsworth's greatest limitations were, ironically, the secrets to his success. The novelist, incapable of pro-*

fundity, was a case of arrested development, the critic notes, yet the boyish quality of his work, combined with his adult knowledge of history, makes the novels appealing to both young boys and "the eternal boy who lingers . . . in the breast of every man." Likewise, Ainsworth's failure to create psychologically realistic characters pleased his readers, for it allowed them to project themselves into the situations provided by the author.]

Harrison Ainsworth has been the friend of almost every critic's boyhood, so that one is glad to "judge him by the standards of his time," or make any other reasonable concession which may excuse him a portion of the responsibility for his limitations. His work is at once very good and very bad; but one of the reasons why it is just what it is may doubtless be found in the fact that he began to write before novelists in general—at any rate in England—had begun to take themselves seriously, or to view their art as anything more than a means of popular entertainment. The greater writers of his generation—the example of Dickens may serve—grew up to higher aims. From *Oliver Twist* to *A Tale of Two Cities* there is a great evolution, not only of the technique, but also of the point of view. There has been a similar, if a less complete, evolution between *Paul Clifford* and *Kenelm Chillingly*. But there is no corresponding development between *Jack Sheppard*—which was more popular than either *Paul Clifford* or *Oliver Twist*—and any of Harrison Ainsworth's later novels that the reader likes to name. Whereas Dickens and Bulwer Lytton evolved, Harrison Ainsworth went on as he began. Or perhaps one should rather say that, beginning as a precocious schoolboy, he grew up, not into an artist, but into an old fogey, confined by his limitations to the last, and also to the last unconscious of them.

He had, of course, his personal limitations: a lack, in the first place, of any sense of humour, and, in the second place, of any true perception of beauty; but these were defects which rather directed than obstructed his success. (p. 533)

The first fact that helps us to "place" Harrison Ainsworth is the fact that, in all his long series of writings, he never achieved or even attempted [to interpret life or show humankind in relation to the world and the universe]. Not only did he never attempt it on purpose; he never even came near to attempting it by accident. Everything is a matter of course for him—even the supernatural. His "feeling about the infinite" amounts to no more than a general interest—not always a very intelligent interest—in ghosts and haunted houses. He is neither concerned to explain the ghosts away, nor to view them as links between the invisible and visible worlds. They are merely a part of his stock in trade, like his foundlings and his changelings. Like the foundlings and the changelings, they help to furnish incidents; so, finding them useful, he uses them and asks no questions. For a novel to him is a string of incidents and nothing more—unless it be perhaps a lecture on English history; and it is almost idle to attempt to criticise his work from any other point of view. Yet the fact remains that his work was once very popular, and, within its limitations, is quite good. Perhaps, building an epigram on a familiar model, we may say that he was the greatest of the commonplace and the most commonplace of the great.

His life was absolutely commonplace. . . . [The] only fact about him that impressed his contemporaries seems to have been that he was vain of his personal appearance. (p. 534)

[The] appearance of this peculiar vein of vanity in the blameless life of a respectable family man speaks as eloquently of his limitations as of his ideals. It imperiously suggests the suburbs and the second rate. It carries instinctive conviction that when this blameless vain man takes to literature, he will tread its paths with an exceedingly flat foot. And this is just what Harrison Ainsworth does. His foot on the paths of literature is sometimes sure and firm, it is occasionally even swift; but it is always flat—fit only for progress on the lower levels.

This depreciation may seem excessive—may seem to prove too much—may even appear to be confuted by the fact that Harrison Ainsworth succeeded, and kept his success for a long time, and to a certain extent, so far as the "general reader" is concerned keeps it still. But that is hardly so; and depreciation may fairly go a good deal further before the critic pulls himself up, and turns round to face the question: How then did Harrison Ainsworth come to succeed? What was his secret?

As has already been said, he had no humour. What passes for such is the clumsiest knockabout farce: two scullions fighting a duel with bags of flour on the table of the royal kitchen at Windsor Castle, and that sort of thing. He never drew a character worthy to be remembered, like D'Artagnan and Private Mulvaney, apart from any particular exploit. Dick Turpin assuredly is not such a character; he is not distinguishable from any other rascal with a taste for disguises who might ride to York. Solomon Eagle, perhaps, is better; but even he is not so much a character as an opportune apparition. So let characterisation go. A still graver charge that can be made and sustained is of clumsiness in the telling of his stories. There can be few clumsier stories in the world than *Windsor Castle*. In the first place it is hardly a story at all, but only a disjointed series of historical tableaux. In the second place the author actually stands still in the midst of his story, such as it is, to relate the history of the Castle from the earliest times, and give particulars of its measurements and its cost. In the third place, he actually interrupts this superfluous description to inform the reader that he himself has been to Windsor, and seen Queen Victoria walking on the slopes, that her Majesty was "taking rapid walking exercise with the prince upon the south side of the garden terrace," and that "a thousand kindling aspirations were awakened by the sight." Nothing, one would say, could be more fatuous. It would be impossible to find a critic anywhere to approve. Yet, in spite of the fatuity, Harrison Ainsworth was conspicuously successful. He had his secret; and that secret largely resided in his personality, which it is so easy to cover with derision.

That personality, it is true, is not in the least interesting in itself. . . . But his personality was none the less a cause which produced effects, as causes will; effects profitable to Harrison Ainsworth to the extent, at one time, of about £2,000 a year. It is a personality, therefore, which we must endeavour to seize and define.

We have already said that Harrison Ainsworth was a clever boy who grew up to be, not an artist, but an old fogey. The definition, however, can be made more precise. He became a particular kind of old fogey, and he began by being a particular kind of clever boy; and, to a certain extent, though not altogether, the terms of his boyhood and his fogeyhood ran concurrently. The truest way of putting it is perhaps to say that he was, with half his nature, the sort of boy who improvises blood-curdling tales in the dormitory at the dead of night, and with the other half a Fellow of the Society of Antiquaries. His reputation rests upon his earlier work, in which the boy was the predominant partner—upon such books as *Rookwood, Jack Sheppard, Old Saint Paul's*, and *The Tower of London*. The later books by comparison are tedious. That is really all that need be said; and it only remains to prove the statement.

The proof, in fact, must needs leap to the eyes of all who read. The first thing that one instinctively exclaims in reading is: "This is a boy's book." But there follows the second exclamation, not less instinctive: "This is a very different kind of boys' book from those of Ballantyne and Henty." They, and W. H. G. Kingston, were persons of adult, though limited, intelligence, consciously stooping to what they conceived to be the boy's point of view, confining their purview to subjects in which they thought it good for him to be interested, mingling instruction with entertainment, avoiding crime, avoiding even love, as if it were the unclean thing. (pp. 535-37)

Boys, beyond question, are interested in fur-trading, and marooning, and fighting, and scalp-hunting, and running away to sea; but they are interested in other things as well. Crime and its detection always interest them—they often want to be detectives. Love interests them—they do not usually think the better of a story because it is without a heroine. Of course they do not understand such matters. Of course they approach them fumblingly and unintelligently. But they do approach them, alike in the stories which they tell each other in the dormitories, and in the stories which they laboriously write for those manuscript magazines which pass from hand to hand in the schoolroom; not comprehending the things of which they speak and write, not swept by the passion of the most passionate situation, but vaguely perceiving that such interests make life richer and fuller, and are essential to it as a drama and a spectacle. And that is just the Harrison Ainsworth point of view. The voice is never that of the grown man unbending to entertain the boys. It is the voice of the boy himself, endowed indeed with the knowledge of the Fellow of the Society of Antiquaries, but handling his material with all a boy's limitations—realising, that is to say, his situations, but not realising the emotions on which they depend.

Perhaps the chief boyish traits are the lack of humour already referred to, and the surfeit of simple melodramatic surprises. A boy's humour, as we all know, is rather exuberant than subtle. The joke which he thoroughly enjoys is the joke of sitting down on wet paint, or rather of seeing someone else sit down on it. Harrison Ainsworth's jokes are all of that rough-and-tumble order, typified by the duel with flour bags in the kitchen; while his wit consists of puns, which are also a notable part of the jocular apparatus of youth. A boy's notion, again, of dramatic surprise in fiction is that somebody shall pull off a wig and turn out to be somebody else; and Harrison Ainsworth works that machinery with an untiring hand, and, if not with supreme skill, at least with skill sufficient to deceive the inexperienced. You always have to read his books to the end before you can be quite certain of the true identity of any character presented in their pages. For, if they are not wandering through the world in disguise, they have probably been changed at birth or stolen by the gipsies in early childhood. You soon discover that Jack Palmer is in reality Dick Turpin in *Rookwood;* but you are startled at a later stage to learn that the Sexton is really the younger brother of a baronet, lying low and vowing vengeance. The many disguises of the Earl of Rochester and Major Pillichody in *Old Saint Paul's* are penetrated almost as fast as they are assumed; but the secret of the identity of Nizza Macascree with Lady Isabella Argentine is reserved until the last. The disguises of Jonathan Wild are not of a nature to delude; but on the top of them comes the mystery of the birth of Thames Darrell, who is really the Marquis de Châtillon, and the disclosure that the mother of Jack Sheppard is really "heiress to the Trenchard property, one of the largest estates in Lancashire."

In so far as Harrison Ainsworth's stories can be said to have plots at all, these disguises and concealed identities constitute the machinery that works then; but, strictly speaking, they are plotless. It is not merely that, in the severely historical works, like *The Tower of London* and *Windsor Castle,* the plot is covered up by the tableaus taken from Hollinshed's and other chronicles. Even in the novels in which history is kept more or less in the background we find no plot in the sense of the gradual push of forces towards an inevitable close, but only a series of exciting incidents, not linked as causes and effects, but strung together like beads upon a thread. The impression always is that the story was not thought out but improvised: that the author, at certain given moments, reflected, and said to himself:—"What shall happen next? It must be something startling, or the reader will go to sleep. Oh, yes. I have it. Suppose Mrs. Sheppard was really, &c. . . . That will keep them awake." And so the surprise is sprung, and is the more surprising because the author has not himself contemplated it or prepared for it, or led up to it, but has merely had a happy thought at the eleventh hour.

This air of extemporisation, not less than these disguises and these deceptions, suggests the dormitory. So do the machine-made ghosts, and the habit of handling the supernatural with no eye to anything but stage effects. But it is perhaps in the prose style that the suggestion is strongest and most striking. One has only to open one of the novels at random, and copy out a few sentences to make this point. For instance:—

> "The important secret remained locked in my breast, but I resolved to be avenged. I swore I would bring your husband to the gallows. . . ."

> "Consent to become my wife, and do not compel me to have recourse to violence to effect my purpose, and I will spare your son."

> "It is my death warrant," said he, gloomily. And so it proved; two days afterwards his doom was accomplished. . . .

> Gathering together his remaining strength, he dragged himself towards the niche wherein his brother, Sir Reginald Rookwood, was deposited, and placing his hand upon the coffin, solemnly exclaimed, "My curse—my dying curse—be upon thee evermore!" Falling with his face upon the coffin, Alan instantly expired. In this attitude his remains were discovered.

(pp. 537-39)

One could multiply such extracts indefinitely. There is no need to search for them, for they bloom upon every page; and if the diction with its flat fall from the high falutin' to the conventional is not that of the story-teller of the dormitory, then the story-teller of the dormitory has no diction of his own. Nor is it a diction which he learned from Harrison Ainsworth, though Harrison Ainsworth's influence may have perfected and confirmed him in it. It is the diction which is natural to the young when they are fumbling after style. All story-tellers began by writing like that if they began early enough; and Harrison Ainsworth never arrived at writing otherwise. His case is one of arrested development. He grew in knowledge of history; and it is inconceivable that he did not also grow in knowledge of the world. But the knowledge of the world which we are bound to assume him to have acquired never found its way into his books. The treatment of the subjects, far more than the subjects themselves, divorces literature from life. The conventions of Surrey side melodrama lord it in his pages. They are not redeemed, as Bulwer Lytton's use of the melodramatic conventions is sometimes redeemed, by the influence of the habit of contact with great affairs. The emotions, therefore, are to every critical reader, if not to every adult reader, as unreal as the situations and the characters.

For the critical reader, indeed, Harrison Ainsworth has one merit only, though he possesses that merit in an eminent degree. He can use incident—can compel incident, in fact, into vivid cinematographic pictures. However unreal the figures composing it, the pictures themselves, if we confine ourselves to the best examples, are real and effective. The picture of the burning of the Hot Gospeller in *The Tower of London* is hideously real. There has never been in fiction a picture at once so graphic and so well-sustained as that of the Great Plague in *Old Saint Paul's*. The story of Dick Turpin's ride to York is one of the finest stories ever written of a ride for life. The story of Jack Sheppard's escape from Newgate is the finest of all prison-breaking stories. It does not matter that Jack Sheppard, and Dick Turpin, and Leonard Holt, and Amabel, and the Hot Gospeller are the merest cardboard puppets. The picture is the thing—that and the press of incident. These appeal, in the first instance, to all boys, and, in the second instance, to the eternal boy who lingers, however deeply buried, in the breast of every man. They are related as the boy himself would try to relate them—from the boy's point of view, and with the boy's methods, but with the grown man's greater knowledge and technical skill. That is Harrison Ainsworth's secret.

We must remember, moreover, that the unreality of which the critical reader is conscious goes unperceived by a large public. A large public, in fact, does not ask for reality as the critic understands it. It is not merely that it is well content to be confined with him within the four walls of the finite, careless of the more subtle meanings of life and of the relation of man to the universe, letting its heart go out far more readily to the ''raconteur'' than to the interpreter. Instinctively it restricts the functions of the story-teller far more than this, feeling that psychology only gives the reader unnecessary trouble, and that elaborate characterisation only fetters the free play of his fancy.

Such readers like, of course, the externals of characterisation: red noses, cadaverous cheeks, strange oaths, gigantic or dwarfed stature, a Scottish or Irish accent. These things are convenient labels serving as aids to memory. And characters must also, of course, be broadly distinguished for them as young or old, virtuous or vicious, beautiful or ugly, attractive or unprepossessing. But that is all they want. Any deeper characterisation—any attempt to fill a book with definite individuals doing the things which it was inevitable for them to do, being what they are—is resented. It challenges intellectual combativeness instead of reposing the mind. A reader of the sort indicated does not want to be set wondering whether such and such a person—a person probably of a type outside his experience— would or would not act in such and such a way. He or she— perhaps more often she than he—prefers simply to be told that such and such things happened, and to imagine himself or herself, and his or her friends or enemies, playing their appropriate parts in the situation which the novelist provides. The boy likes to imagine himself breaking out of Newgate in Jack Sheppard's place. The tradesman's daughter likes to credit Amabel Bloundel with her own emotions—whatever she supposes that these would be—if some modern Earl of Rochester were to obtain access to her bedroom by a ladder and ask her to step round to Saint Paul's and get married. This particular

emotional debauch, however, would be impossible if Amabel Bloundel or Jack Sheppard were too definitely individualised; and consequently for such readers the reality of the drama largely depends upon the unreality of the *dramatis personae*. That is how their point of view differs from that of the critic. They ask the writer not for psychology but for situations. It is essential to their enjoyment of the feast of fiction that they should provide the psychology themselves. Harrison Ainsworth lets them do so—that is his second secret.

It is a secret, not a trick. The thing is not deliberately done, but happens. Harrison Ainsworth undoubtedly supposed himself to be realising his characters as clearly as he realised his tableaus. One can divine that from the care with which he describes their personal appearance. He writes as if he considered the whole art of characterisation to consist in saying that such a man had red hair and bandy legs, and that such a young woman had teeth like pearls and lips like coral. It was the common delusion of the English novelists of his age. Even Dickens began with it, though his genius carried him beyond it. But it was a delusion which helped Harrison Ainsworth instead of hindering him. He was incapable of psychology, and if he had attempted it he would have stumbled clumsily. Avoiding it, he walked, as has been said, with a foot that was sure and firm, and sometimes swift, though flat. A limited man, writing for limited people, he never taxed their intelligence with intellectual subtleties, but merely shook the kaleidoscope, leaving them to do the rest. They did it, and were pleased with the result.

A writer so limited could not, of course, exert an influence or found a school. He might be imitated, since he was obviously supplying a commodity in great demand; but he could not hand on a torch, because he carried none. Smaller men might copy him, but greater men could not learn from him. The history of his followers must be a history not of growth but of declension. That is what the critical reader of Harrison Ainsworth's novels would expect, and that is what he finds. The true successor of the creator of *Jack Sheppard* is the creator of *Jack Harkaway*. In the evolution of the novel that is the highest place that can be assigned to him. That is the penalty which he was bound to pay in the end for being commonplace—for dealing not with ideas but with events—for seeing life as a picture without any particular meaning. But among commonplace men he ranks very high indeed; for he had the gift of expressing himself, whereas most commonplace men have not. He was a *raconteur,* and he was well-informed and well read, if not precisely learned. So that the epigram suggested at the beginning of this article may be justified, and he may be classed definitely as the greatest of the commonplace and the most commonplace of the great. (pp. 539-42)

Francis Gribble, ''Harrison Ainsworth,'' in The Fortnightly Review, *Vol. LXXXIII, No. CCCCLIX, March 1, 1905, pp. 533-42.*

ADRIAN HOFFMAN JOLINE (essay date 1910)

[*Joline attributes Ainsworth's early success to his sensitivity to contemporary concerns and attitudes. While the author excels in description and rendering historical detail, according to Joline, he falls short of enduring literary fame, for he fails to analyze motive and develop character.*]

Reviewers, critics and students of literature are inclined to resent the assertion with respect to a writer once eminent, that he is substantially forgotten. But it is safe to say that if we regard the millions of readers in this country whose literary nutriment is made up chiefly of works of fiction or of biography of the lighter sort, as "the reading public of America", the name of William Harrison Ainsworth is by no means familiar in the United States. There are many book-owners who keep his "Works" upon their shelves, and know the backs of the volumes, and some of the omniverous have doubtless read *Jack Sheppard, Crichton, The Tower of London,* and perhaps *Rookwood;* yet thousands who are well acquainted with their Scott, their Dickens and their Thackeray would be sorely puzzled if they were asked to tell us who Ainsworth was, and exactly when he lived, or to give a synopsis of the plot of a single one of his numerous stories; and he has been dead not quite thirty years. (p. 83)

One would scarcely believe that there was a time when he was esteemed to be a worthy rival of Charles Dickens, and when in the eyes of the critics and of the public he far outshone Edward Lytton Bulwer. (p. 84)

It was something of an honor for a lad of seventeen to receive the praise of Charles Lamb, who appears to have discovered one of his young correspondent's besetting sins—redundancy [see Additional Bibliography]. (pp. 86-7)

It has been said that he was inspired by Mrs. Radcliffe, whose gloomy mysteries, weird scenes, and supernatural machinery once made her a favorite with fiction-lovers, and that he sought to adapt old legends to English soil. Others have ascribed his impulse to the influence of the French dramatic romancers, Eugène Sue, Victor Hugo, and Alexandre Dumas. I question whether he owed his inspiration to any particular source, although all these writers may have affected his temperament. Perhaps he unconsciously divined the needs of the reading public, of which his editorial experience may have taught him much. The inane, fashionable novel had become tiresome. Moreover, it was a time, in the early thirties, when the nation of England was absorbed in the growth of her material prosperity, and when a country is engrossed in commerce and manufactures, in the production of wealth, tales of adventure seem necessary to stimulate flagging imagination. (pp. 89-90)

It was not until . . . dramatic productions [of *Jack Sheppard*] appeared that the sedate and fastidious began the outcry against the so-called criminal school of romance. . . . The author and the novel were bitterly attacked. The main ground of denunciation seems to have been the belief that the lower orders might be aroused to emulate the brilliant robber, all of which is sheer nonsense. (p. 96)

[We] have no proof that the awful novel caused any marked increase of crime. The real utility and value of stories like *Jack Sheppard* may well be questioned, for they surely do not belong to the highest and best in literature, but that any one became a thief or a highway robber because of them is yet to be demonstrated. (p. 97)

It is doubtless true that there is a demand for [Ainsworth's] tales among the less cultivated English readers, but it can not, I think, be maintained successfully that the author has a permanent and enduring literary fame. Perhaps I am influenced in my opinion by the American lack of acquaintance with Ainsworth and his works. (p. 116)

Ainsworth had no power to portray character or to analyze motives; his genius was purely descriptive. He had a strong literary bent, and he was a man of letters in the true sense. He did not possess the spark which gives immortality, but he toiled

faithfully and his work was well done even if he did not reach the standard of the greatest of his contemporaries. (p. 122)

Adrian Hoffman Joline, "William Harrison Ainsworth," in his At the Library Table, *The Gorham Press, 1910, pp. 83-123.*

HUGH WALKER   (essay date 1910)

[*In the following excerpt, Walker dismisses Ainsworth as an imitative and altogether insignificant novelist.*]

[Ainsworth] was a follower of Scott who had no real understanding of his master's method. In his best-known works, *The Tower of London* . . . , *Old St. Paul's* . . . and *Windsor Castle* . . . he is led by Victor Hugo into the error of making a place rather than a person the centre of the story. As Ainsworth has neither Hugo's inspiration nor his force, the result is confusion through the introduction of a mass of irrelevant detail. These novels are wearisome, and the praise they have won has been due rather to a sense that they must be useful in building up the mind of youth, than to any real belief in their merit as novels. Their educational value may, however, be doubted; while it can hardly be questioned that the acts of cruelty and the horrible deaths with which they abound pander to a depraved taste and are likely to vitiate the mind that is not repelled by them.

An unwholesome element of a different sort is noticeable in the other class of Ainsworth's novels, those studies of criminality which we find in *Rookwood* . . . and in *Jack Sheppard.* . . . In these Ainsworth was following the lead of Bulwer in his *Paul Clifford* and *Eugene Aram.* Ainsworth's contributions to this school of criminal romance, though poor on the whole, are not without passages of merit. The celebrated ride to York, in particular, is, despite its impossibilities and absurdities, a very spirited performance. . . . In either department his literary merit is extremely slight, and there is little probability that he will ever again enjoy the vogue which was once his. (p. 621)

Hugh Walker, "After Scott," in his The Literature of the Victorian Era, *Cambridge: at the University Press, 1910, pp. 612-59.**

FRANK SWINNERTON   (essay date 1931)

[*In this excerpt from his introduction to* Rookwood, *Swinnerton praises Ainsworth's vigorous writing style and vivid descriptions. Despite imperfections of literary style, according to Swinnerton, Ainsworth's work is consistently interesting and occasionally rises to excellence, as in his depiction of Dick Turpin's ride to York.*]

Turpin is the hero of *Rookwood.* He is the author's chief (though not his only) creation. And, since Turpin was a real figure of the eighteenth century, he has been a cause of perplexity to all commentators upon Ainsworth's work. For one thing, the lives of highwaymen were not recorded, in olden times, with the particularity which is nowadays seen to be their due. They soon became legendary. And, just as the same fairy story turns up surprisingly in several languages, so, in legends of heroes, the same exploits occur. . . . But whatever foundation Ainsworth may have had for the story, the Ride to York has been a feat of Turpin's since *Rookwood* was published; and so it must be claimed for Ainsworth that he has very circumstantially persuaded the modern world of the supremacy of his hero.

It is upon the Ride to York that the fame of *Rookwood* rests; but there is far more in the book than the Ride to York. For one thing, it is extraordinarily interesting to read throughout. There is power in the opening scene—even in the opening words, which instantly seize the attention. There is great vigour in the description of Luke's flight and struggle with the keeper. The conversations between Dr. Polycarp Small, Dr. Titus Tyrconnel, Mr. Codicil Coates, and "Jack Palmer" are very lively and dramatic in the eighteenth-century fashion. The natural descriptions are all very sincere and expressive. And at all times, here and there, astonishing excellences arise. It must be admitted that the story has faults, but among these faults dulness is not to be included. It is the first demand that a reader makes of any romance, that it should ensnare his interest, and keep it ever engaged until the end.

The faults are those of bad literary style and melodrama. As a writer, Ainsworth, especially when he wanted to be grave, was given to using two long words where one short one would have been an improvement. He was rhetorical. Having learned a great deal from Marlowe's mighty line, he pitched his note high; and the penalty of pitching one's note high, if one has no upper register, is that the result embarrasses all listeners. Ainsworth's grand manner is dreadful. (pp. xi-xii)

And, as to melodrama, the reader need turn no farther than the opening chapter, where the mysterious (and as it proves disguised) sexton tells the deadly secret of the Rookwood family to a surviving Rookwood. . . . [The] whole scene, though powerful, is written as if for the transpontine stage.

Some will think it a serious fault that *Rookwood* suffers from confusion of plot; but the confusion is more apparent than real. The whole story follows a trusted convention, and the uncertainties are those of episode rather than those of outline. Luke, who has a grievance at the beginning of the book, since he has been cheated of his inheritance, has to suffer a sea change in the gipsy encampment, because it is essential that he should sacrifice his true love to his ambition. He is thrown over by the author, and becomes a savage fellow, demented, and almost villainous. His step-brother, the speaker in the grand manner . . . , is a stick. The bride is a fainting dummy. Her brother is a mere recurrent figure. The two mothers in the book have more energy, and Lady Rookwood, although she makes one laugh by her changes of front, has a wickedness and a kind of swelling impudence which is impressive. The old sexton, who begins well, is by the end of the book a discredited carcase. His last scene, however, is frightful enough, and shows the author's enthusiasm to be unabated. Wherever these persons lose their vitality it is because shortage of invention has led Ainsworth to twist a character to suit his plot. That is why his successes lie with the ignoble.

It would be difficult, in my opinion, to overpraise the character of Turpin. He is at all times and in all places a rascal. He does not become a gentleman: his honour is that of a thief. We like him, and we relish his performances; but we know he is a rogue, and we (as it were) button our pockets at his approach just as we open our hearts. This is exactly what Ainsworth intended. . . . I have no doubt at all that the Ride to York, which has "made" history, is one of the achievements of romantic fiction. It is as good as its reputation, though less sweeping in its tempo than those with modern ideas of speed may expect.

The success of *Rookwood* upon its first publication was outstanding. The book was read everywhere. It made the author

a literary lion. He never seems to us to be quite an interesting man, in spite of the assurances we have that he was extremely popular in the world; but there is every sign that with his early books, and particularly with *Rookwood* and *Jack Sheppard,* he jumped into importance thereafter. (pp. xii-xiii)

His long life during which he produced a great quantity of historical fiction, tended to make him seem the familiar purveyor of a commodity, and thus to diminish his stature as a literary giant. For this reason he has had less attention from critics than he perhaps deserves. His talent is not negligible. He is a master of black-and-white. He has strong descriptive powers. Except when he is stilted or rhetorical, he writes with vividness. And he is continuously interesting, even when he is grotesque, so vigorous is his own zest and so rapid his manipulation of a fluent pen. (pp. xiii-xiv)

Frank Swinnerton, in an introduction to Rookwood *by William Harrison Ainsworth, E. P. Dutton & Co., 1931, pp. vii-xiv.*

MALCOLM ELWIN (essay date 1934)

[*In the following excerpt, Elwin maintains that Ainsworth has been unjustly neglected in the twentieth century. While he finds that Ainsworth "contributed little or nothing to the development of the novel," Elwin praises the pageantry of* Windsor Castle, The Tower of London, *and* Old Saint Paul's.]

Of all the Victorian novelists, his literary life is among the most important and the most interesting. With regard to his writings, he certainly contributed little or nothing to the development of the novel. *The Miser's Daughter* alone presents an appearance of symmetry in structure. Like Dickens, he had

George Cruikshank's depiction of Dick Turpin's escape on Black Bess, from an early edition of Rookwood.

the vaguest notion of a plot; he strung together incident after incident and imported fresh personalities as his story progressed, till, at the end, he was sometimes concerned with a set of characters scarcely connected with those figuring in the beginning. This lack of form in the mid-Victorian novel is undoubtedly due to the fashion for serial stories; nearly every novel of note—and almost all Ainsworth's, except *Rookwood* and *Crichton*—was introduced by instalments in magazines or in separate monthly parts.

His faults as a craftsman are manifold and easy to seek.... His stilted style of dialogue for instance, is frequently feeble and unnatural.... The interjection 'Ha!' is a favourite expression with Ainsworth's villains; it begins or concludes the exclamations of them all, from Herne the Hunter to Sir Giles Mompesson.

His characters, too, are almost always sterile or stereotyped. Like Scott, he considered his hero must perforce be an insufferable prig; one does not wonder that Leonard Holt and Humphry Chetham failed to inspire passion in the ladies of their choice, while it is a matter for regret that Winifred Wood preferred Thames Darrell to the depraved but pleasantly human Jack Sheppard. His heroines are uniformly colourless. All of them, at whatever epoch they are supposed to have flourished—Eleanor Rookwood in the plain-spoken age of Lady Mary Wortley Montagu, Amabel Bloundel in the day of Pepys, Viviana Radcliffe in the exciting times of the Gunpowder Plot—are vapourish Victorian misses, wilting beneath the discomfort of existence in circumstances remote from their natural surroundings and conscious of dreadful indecency at being deprived of their crinolines by their inconsiderate creator. If Turpin and Sheppard are excepted, along with numerous minor characters like Coates the attorney, John Habergeon, Sergeant Scales, Mrs. Wood, and Blaize Shotterel, it is difficult to dispute Professor Saintsbury's assertion that Ainsworth's characters are 'scarcely ever alive' (see excerpt dated 1896).

But it must not be forgotten that he always painted on a crowded canvas. He was never concerned simply with the portrayal of a single person or even of a particular family. His art was in pageantry rather than portraiture, resembling rather that of Dumas than of Scott. In *Windsor Castle,* we have a glimpse of Anne Boleyn as a lovely woman of emphatic personality, an instinctive and incorrigible coquette, and the possessor of that arrogant dignity which distinguished her daughter. Here was an admirable subject for dramatic treatment. But Ainsworth had neither time nor space to spare on one individual character. Into the compass of a single novel he had to compress a history of Windsor Castle, an account of the legend of Herne the Hunter, the fall of Wolsey, the divorce of Catherine of Aragon, the romance of Surrey and the fair Geraldine, and the execution of Anne herself. In the preface to *The Tower of London,* he describes the design of this romance:

> Desirous of exhibiting the Tower in its triple light of a Palace, a Prison, and a Fortress, the Author has shaped his story with reference to that end; and he has endeavoured to contrive such a series of incidents as should naturally introduce every relic of the whole pile—towers, chapels, halls, chambers, gateways, arches, and drawbridges—so that no part of it should remain un-illustrated.

Is there matter for wonder that the compact and cohesive plot considered a *sine qua non* by our modern novelists is absent in Ainsworth? As Blanchard said of *The Tower,* 'it is curious to observe how this purpose is worked out in entire consistency with an unbroken and uninterrupted narrative'.

For this reason, several of his novels—particularly *The Tower of London* and *Old St. Paul's,* in spite of the absurd antics of the hero of the latter—have undoubtedly the quality of durability. No writer could hope to surpass either as romantic histories of their particular subjects. *Rookwood, Jack Sheppard,* and *Crichton* are of a different class; they are historical romances instead of romantic histories and must take their chance as such. All three possess too many fine qualities to be forgotten, and few that have once read them would hesitate to read them again in preference, for instance, to *The Fortunes of Nigel* or *Rob Roy.* Whether *Ovingdean Grange* and *Boscobel* may be preferred to *Woodstock* is less certain, but there is no reason why the public which delights in the romances of Stanley Weyman and Mr. Rabael Sabatini would not enjoy them. Some day there will be a revival of interest in Ainsworth, as there has been in Trollope. Collectors will be hot on the trail of the paper-covered copies of *Tower Hill* and *Talbot Harland,* and enthusiasts will voraciously devour the forty odd novels. The general reader's life is too short for this, but he will not regret having read a considered selection. (pp. 172-76)

Malcolm Elwin, "Wallflower the Fourth: Harrison Ainsworth," in his Victorian Wallflowers: A Panoramic Survey of the Popular Literary Periodicals, *Jonathan Cape, 1934, pp. 154-76.*

BRYAN BEVAN   (essay date 1955)

[*In this discussion of Ainsworth's best-known novels, Bevan notes that Ainsworth does not offer subtle analysis or deep characterizations, but does excel as a storyteller. In the critic's evaluation, the historical novels are a skilled blend of fact and fiction, sustained by Ainsworth's superb descriptions and striking scenes of terror.*]

[*Rookwood*], with its imaginative account of Dick Turpin's ride to York along the Great North Road on his immortal mare Black Bess, illustrates Ainsworth's superb gifts as a descriptive writer. All the more remarkable because historically there is little evidence the ride to York ever took place. When we read about the pathetic death of Black Bess it is difficult to remember that the mare was the product of Ainsworth's rich creative imagination. Cuckfield Place in Sussex is the real model for Rookwood Hall, as described by Ainsworth. With its dark mysterious closets, its gloomy galleries and haunted chambers, it was a most congenial subject for him. (p. 97)

[*Jack Sheppard*] is one of the many examples of Ainsworth's skilful blending of fact with fancy.... The description of the Great Storm of 1723 in London with its power of suggesting terror and the fear of the supernatural, is one of the finest passages in Ainsworth. (p. 98)

[*Crichton*] is a masterly work with its vivid picture of the intrigues which permeated the vicious Court of Henri III. Ainsworth positively luxuriates in his detailed descriptions of the costumes and jewels of the period. Whilst visiting Paris Ainsworth had closely studied the setting for his story. As in many of his books there is the characteristic attraction to ghosts and the occult. The most sinister character is the malevolent Catherine de Medici, plotting her Machiavellian schemes, helped by her confederate the astrologer Ruggieri.

In order to write *Old Saint Paul's*—one of the most dramatic and terrible accounts of the Plague and Great Fire of London ever written—Ainsworth steeped himself in the history of the period. He particularly studied Daniel Defoe's *Journal of the Plague Year*. The book is a wonderfully vivid picture of Old London with its narrow, winding streets and high-pointed gables. As we read it we are back again in 1665 and hear once again the thunderous voice of Solomon Eagle (his real name was Eccles)—that crazy prophet of doom—denouncing the city and the wickedness of the Court. We see with horror the red crosses marked outside the houses of those smitten with the plague, irrevocably awaiting the death-cart. What strange streak of heredity in Ainsworth's nature was responsible for his ghoulish delight in the macabre and grotesque? From his father he certainly inherited his interest in criminal history and the lore of highwaymen. But his morbid interest in the supernatural, which so fascinated him, was more probably inherited from his mother's ancestors.

It was always Ainsworth's ambition to be known as *The Lancashire Novelist*. Many of his works have a Lancashire setting. Undoubtedly the best of these is *The Lancashire Witches*, with its dramatic account of the capture of Abbot Paslew, an ill-fated leader of the Pilgrimage of Grace. It contains also superb descriptions of the wild, lonely Pendle Forest Country in East Lancashire. It was Crossley, who first suggested to Ainsworth the idea of using Pott's *Wonderful Discoverie of Witches in the countie of Lancaster*—published in 1613—as the basis for a romance. It is the most important account of a Witch Trial in the seventeenth-century. Ainsworth also made use of Nicholas Assheton's Journal. All the Witches mentioned in Pott's account—such as Mother Demdike, Mother Chattox and Alice Nutter, come vividly to life again in Ainsworth's work. But he was a novelist, not an historian. Consequently he takes a certain amount of author's licence. (p. 99)

His strength as a novelist rests in his marvellous gifts as a story-teller. He was a truly creative writer, but he needed historical fact on which to exercise his fertile imagination. Subtle analysis or delineation of character and motive are not prominent. Nevertheless, as we become engrossed in his novels, we too, like Macaulay, "are lost in amazement that his wonderful novels have not an abiding place in every house." (p. 100)

Bryan Bevan, "Harrison Ainsworth," in Contemporary Review, *Vol. CLXXXVIII, No. 1076, August, 1955, pp. 96-100.*

KEITH HOLLINGSWORTH   (essay date 1963)

[*Naming* Jack Sheppard "*the highpoint of the Newgate novel as entertainment," Hollingsworth cites social and psychological reasons for the immense popularity of Ainsworth's novel during the nineteenth century.*]

Rookwood is a story by Mrs. Radcliffe transplanted. Ainsworth's own expression of the obvious debt occurs in the preface he wrote for the novel [see excerpt by Ainsworth dated 1837]. . . . There is probably no single item of originality in all the profusion of Gothic elements. The ancient hall, the family curse, the gruesome burial vaults, the secret marriage, and all the rest had long been in the common domain. (pp. 98-9)

The English robber whom Ainsworth chose to entangle incongruously in his Gothic tale was Dick Turpin, executed in 1739. (p. 99)

Although Turpin appears in a considerable part of *Rookwood,* he has no inherent connection with the plot. By stealing a marriage certificate he introduces a minor complication, but this seems a triviality—merely one of the weary quantity of arranged motions that the puppets must go through. But in spite of his being forced within the pages of the book, Turpin's presence does all that anything could do to lighten them. Unreal as he is, he is far more lively than any of the other figures of the tale. . . .

Turpin takes possession of a large section of the book when he sets out to escape pursuit and rides his fine mare, Black Bess, from London to York. . . . The account of the ride impressed contemporary readers more than the stale Gothic omens, and they were right. The style is less turgid in this passage than elsewhere. . . . (p. 101)

[In *Jack Sheppard,* as] in *Rookwood,* Ainsworth produced a standard romance—though not this time a Gothic one—in which a figure from criminal history might be involved. His instincts as an entertainer were very keen, his sense of the public taste good, and his craftsmanship improved to the point of excellence. *Jack Sheppard,* as a result, became a sensational success, more popular than *Oliver Twist,* and the high point of the Newgate novel as entertainment. It also became, though only five years had elapsed since *Rookwood,* a high point of controversy. (pp. 131-32)

[The Jack Sheppard of history, a petty thief,] was a huge sensation in his own time; he had many visitors in prison, the newspapers were full of him, and pamphlets were numerous. . . . [William Hogarth may] have seen Sheppard then. In his pictures of the industrious and the idle apprentices, done much later, in 1747, Jack Idle has a bodily resemblance to Sheppard. . . . (p. 134)

[Ainsworth's romance renewed and increased Sheppard's] reputation which had lasted more than a century. The influence of Hogarth, already commented on, worked very directly here; for Ainsworth from the beginning thought of his project as "a sort of Hogarthian novel," and set about obtaining information which would make his backgrounds historically accurate. He has the two apprentices: Jack, who gives way to temptation, and Thames Darrell, a boy of about the same age, whose early virtue obviously will continue and will be rewarded. We have, then, two careers to follow, the fictional one of Darrell and the real one of Sheppard, woven into the plot more intricately than Turpin's in *Rookwood.* Ainsworth keeps Sheppard as close to history as he can while carrying out his aim of involving him in the Darrell romance. (pp. 134, 136)

The Thames Darrell story is plotted with that ingenuity which was then so much enjoyed and which now seems so tiresome. Arranged in three sequences, dated 1703, 1715, and 1724, the action is so concentrated that the author must sometimes follow more than one set of persons through events of the same few hours. The invention is unflagging, the coincidences extraordinary. (p. 136)

Ainsworth's narrative technique has many virtues, perhaps because of his attention to the theatre. Except for the planned passages of description, such as a whole chapter at the appropriate point about Old Newgate, he carries the story swiftly. It always moves. His theatrical talent does not, however, extend to the writing of realistic dialogue: "I don't ask you to liberate me," says Thames Darrell, "but will you convey a message for me?" The stage clichés come naturally to Ainsworth. "Hell-hounds!" Jack says to Wild and his men, "Release me!" And Mrs. Sheppard has this line to speak: "'Begone, wretch!' cried the mother, stung beyond endurance by his taunts, 'or I will drive you hence with my curses.'"

The character of Sheppard all through the story is adroitly made acceptable and even admirable. (p. 137)

The novel contains no propaganda. Ainsworth holds the attitude of a nineteenth-century humanitarian—he causes Mrs. Sheppard to speak feelingly of "how much misery has to do with crime"—but his story is not aimed at reforming the law or the prisons. . . . He could indeed claim that, like Hogarth, he had shown a bad end for the idle apprentice; the criminal goes to the gallows. But he likes to think of his story as being in the tradition of the *Beggar's Opera* and of the Spanish chronicles of roguery.

In avoiding the earnest tone of the reformer, *Jack Sheppard* forms an obvious contrast with *Oliver Twist*. The difference— the more noticeable because the two books show so many likenesses—is partly responsible for the censure to be incurred by Ainsworth. One pair of scenes will illustrate the point. Dickens had his gang of young boys being taught to pick pockets; Ainsworth has a flash-ken, where Jack and other boys are introduced to a life of depravity. But Ainsworth puts foremost the sexual element that Dickens carefully avoided: Jack is lured on to crime by the blandishments of Edgeworth Bess and Poll Maggot. The author, somewhat casually, calls their plan "odious," and goes on with his lively description. (p. 138)

Sheppard was not simply a sensation in fiction, but an extra-literary popular phenomenon. The theatres were chiefly responsible. . . . On December 1 and 2, Thackeray commented on the Sheppard craze in a letter to his mother:

> I have not read this latter romance [*Jack Sheppard*] but one or two extracts are good: it is acted at *four* theatres, and they say that at the Cobourg [sic] people are waiting about the lobbies, selling Shepherd-bags—a bag containing a few pick-locks that is, a screw driver, and iron lever, one or two young gentlemen have already confessed how much they were indebted to Jack Sheppard who gave them ideas of pocket-picking and thieving which they never would have had but for the play. Such facts must greatly delight an author who aims at popularity.

Exactly why there was so much enthusiasm for Jack Sheppard is a matter for wonder. Ainsworth's novel had, it is true, the elements to make a popular success: a spotless hero and an underdog to sympathize with, both pitted against a fearful villain; a glimpse of aristocracy, a suggestion of sex, hairbreadth adventures and plenty of virtuous emotions. The theatre appealed even more directly. Bess and Poll were *there,* and very pretty, too. Jack was *seen* . . . prostrate with grief upon his mother's grave. The whole house wept—and later watched with horrified delight when a crowd set fire to the house of Jonathan Wild. The theatre also added some songs and even a bit of dancing. But spectacle and sex and sentiment, as well as music, were standard in the theatre. Why did *this* combination arouse a unique response?

The reasons, surely, were psychological and social; they lay in the readiness of public feeling at the time. It was not that a plebeian hero was wanted. In certain persons, perhaps, a sense of injustice already present might flow into sympathetic identification with young Jack; but, despite some Chartist feeling in the populace, this was not the temper of the Sheppard enthusiasm, which was fundamentally gay. Frowning Newgate, the grim hangman, and the gallows represented old oppressions, maintained by the law of the rulers; and humanitarian feeling had made the middle class quite as uneasy about them as the class without property had ever been. If Jack himself was not quite everybody's darling, Sheppardism was not merely a working-class epidemic. Jack was not felt to be an enemy of society; he was a boy who scaled prison walls to be free and who set himself against the villain Wild, tolerated by the oppressors. The owners of Newgate had been forced to yield some of their power in 1832; the death-dealing laws had been swept away in the half-dozen years just preceding this novel and these plays; hangings had become few, the gallows less obtrusive; policemen walked the streets of a safer London. Prison reform was respectable. The crudest terrors of Newgate, well enough remembered, could be thought of as safely in the past. Freedom and opportunity were in the air. A vast public could, at such a moment, permit itself to idolize a young thief— could see him as a victim of the old system or as a rebel against it, or could merely be entertained by a daring scamp who loved his mother—without suffering a really inhibiting concern about the gravity of the issue. This general high-spirited extravagance would not have been possible twenty years earlier; its *raison d'être* would have been lacking twenty years later. Ainsworth provided his novel at the right time. The Sheppard mania which followed was an uncalculated, uncalculating paean to the end of the bad old days and the arrival of a time like morning. (p. 141)

> Keith Hollingsworth, "The First Newgate Novels, 1830-34" and "The Newgate Novel and the Moral Argument, 1837-40," in his The Newgate Novel, 1830-1847: Bulwer, Ainsworth, Dickens, & Thackeray, Wayne State University Press, 1963, pp. 65-110, 111-66.*

GEORGE J. WORTH (essay date 1969)

[*Worth uses the response of nineteenth-century critics to* Jack Sheppard *as proof of the limitations of didactic criticism in evaluating a crime novel, noting that most overlooked Ainsworth's innovative structure and misunderstood his preoccupation with violence.*]

It is easy to see why [*Jack Sheppard*] won such favor with a large reading audience. Appearing at the end of the decade during which what Keith Hollingsworth has called "the Newgate novel" was at the height of its vogue [see excerpt dated 1963], *Jack Sheppard* was the exciting story of a notorious early eighteenth-century thief and prison breaker, taking him from his infancy to his death by hanging at Tyburn, replete with colorful characters, vivid descriptions, and sensational incidents, and narrated with great *brio* and a fair degree of skill. Some contemporaneous criticism, at least, was very much alive to these obvious virtues in *Jack Sheppard*. Without going into detail, and relying on copious quotation rather than on close analysis, the *Literary World*, for example, praised Ainsworth's "admirable minuteness," his "descriptive powers," his "considerable research for materials," and his "judicious employment of them." The *Literary Gazette,* after disclaiming any need to discuss "the literary ability with which he has executed his design . . . as it has been every where acknowledged," asserted that "for intense description and fearful interest, there are portions of this production which it would not be easy to surpass in our own or any other language" [see excerpt dated 1839].

But these virtues, of verisimilitude and visceral appeal, were the only ones which reviewers acknowledged. Nothing of any depth or value was said in print of the two aspects of Ainsworth's novel which most forcibly strike the modern reader: the author's structural skill and his perception of the darker side of human nature.

Structurally, Ainsworth was confronted with some serious problems in giving a fictionalized account of the career of Jack Sheppard. How does one tell such a story without turning it into a monotonous series of escapades? How does one present the criminal title character in such a way as to retain some semblance of sympathy for him? How does one select the episodes to be treated, blanket coverage of the twenty-two years of his life being an impossibility?

Ainsworth went a long way toward solving these problems by the introduction into his narrative of two additional characters, one historical and one invented, Jonathan Wild and Thames Darrell. From the beginning, the thief and thief-taker Jonathan Wild hovers over Jack like an evil destiny. A disappointed suitor of Jack's mother, Wild corrupts and sends to the gallows first her husband and ultimately Jack himself. Thames Darrell, Jack's foil, is his fellow apprentice in the carpenter shop of Mr. Wood of Wych Street. Like Jack the son of a father who has died violently and of a mother who has been abused and persecuted, and like Jack too in being the object of Wild's cruelty, Thames nevertheless chooses the path of virtue and is rewarded in the end by the hand of the beautiful Winifred, his master's daughter. The stories of the two young men are closely intertwined, each lad helping us to see the other in a better, more human light; and Thames ultimately prospers through the help of Jack and his lieutenant, the cutthroat Blueskin. No reviewer had anything useful whatever to say about Thames and the uses to which Ainsworth put him; as for Jonathan Wild, though at least one critic praised the set-piece description of his house. Ainsworth's treatment of him was unfavorably compared with Fielding's [see excerpts by Thackeray dated 1840], and little more than that was said about it. (pp. 52-3)

John Forster, reviewing *Jack Sheppard* in the *Examiner,* complained, among numerous other things, about the violence and improbability of the action involving Jonathan Wild [see excerpt dated 1839], and the critic for the *Athenaeum* dismissed the novel as "a melo-dramatic story of motiveless crime" [see excerpts dated 1839]. Such typical comments as these miss a very important point: though there are violence, melodrama, and even improbability galore in *Jack Sheppard,* they are not in the novel for the sake of cheap effect but as aspects of a world view which is perhaps more comprehensible to a twentieth-century reader than to a reviewer accustomed to the placid domestic realism of much English fiction in the late 1830's and 1840's. Malignity, cruelty, and violence are always key elements in Ainsworth's view of human nature and not mere devices, in such other characteristic novels as *The Tower of London, Guy Fawkes,* and *Old Saint Paul's* as well as in *Jack Sheppard.* Important characters in all these novels are driven by an inordinate and inexplicable greed for power, and, far from being mustache-twirling stage villains, they tend to be dispassionate and ironical in their ruthlessness. Because men do not live together in a benign society effectively ruled by

reason, suffering and chaos are everyday aspects of the human lot in Ainsworth's fiction.

Driven by a will to power that defies rational explanation, Jonathan Wild is determined to control the criminal underworld of London and to ruin Jack Sheppard: to ruin him, moreover, in a protracted way that will be especially painful to all concerned. Wild's violent instincts are turned against everyone who is in some way inconvenient to him. When, for instance, Thames Darrell's evil uncle, from whom Wild has extorted large sums of money, ceases to be useful to him, Wild and a grimy associate unhesitatingly put him to a horrible death, which is fully described by Ainsworth. Nothing in the early Victorian reviewer's experience prepared him to take a character like Jonathan Wild, as depicted by Ainsworth, seriously: the only frame of reference which came ready to hand, other than the obviously inappropriate one of the novel of domestic realism, was that of contemporary melodrama, but this was inadequate for other reasons. The Gothic novel of an earlier generation, or the theater of cruelty (and the daily newspaper headlines) of the mid-twentieth century, would have furnished much more relevant analogues. There are hidden abysses in human nature of which the author of *Jack Sheppard* and—presumably, in view of the novel's popularity—his readers had instinctive knowledge; but, his reviewers refused to accept their existence. (pp. 55-6)

George J. Worth, "Early Victorian Criticism of the Novel and Its Limitations: 'Jack Sheppard', a Test Case," in The Nineteenth-Century Writer and His Audience: Selected Problems in Theory, Form, and Content, *edited by Harold Orel and George J. Worth, University of Kansas Publications, 1969, pp. 51-60.*

LLEWELLYN LIGOCKI (lecture date 1972)

[*Ainsworth's novels are historically reliable, Ligocki contends, and when the novelist deviates from his factual sources, it is done deliberately for artistic effect. In addition, the violence and sensationalism some criticize in the novels are factual and intrinsic elements of the historical period. For further commentary by Ligocki, see excerpts dated 1973 and 1975.*]

A close reading of Ainsworth's historical sources demonstrates that Ainsworth's history is extremely reliable in both generalities and particulars; his alterations, usually minor, serve only to adumbrate his concept of history as cycle. Thus, even though he is a novelist and not a historian, the faithful revelation of the past is central to his work. He examines history carefully in order to present truths about life and in order to demonstrate how history reveals these truths.

By looking at the critical misunderstanding of two central facets of history in *The Tower of London,* Ainsworth's most important novel, we can see the unfairness of critics' gratuitous denial of Ainsworth's achievement. Perhaps most interesting and instructive to the student of the historical novel and its critical reputation in nineteenth-century England is that the critics who reprove Ainsworth for his mishandling of history frequently point to the wrong places when they try to show his "capriciousness" in action. Instead of seeing Ainsworth's genuine alterations, they incorrectly view some of his most historical characters and scenes as having been fabricated. (pp. 23-4)

Ainsworth's treatment of violence has also been singled out for castigation, as though the so-called sensationalism in his novels were of his own making and not a part of the age he attempts to depict. . . . [While such] comments reflect Ainsworth's preoccupation with violence, they misconstrue his motives. In fact, their failure to comprehend Ainsworth's need to depict Tudor violence itself demonstrates how important it was for Ainsworth to present it as a pervading influence. The "sensationalism," particularly surrounding the torture of criminals and traitors, depicts accurately a facet of the Tudor era. The modern reader may have difficulty in accepting that the tortures of the day are presented faithfully and without exaggeration by Ainsworth. He gives them, however, exactly as he finds them, no matter how unbelievably cruel they may seem. It is central to our understanding of the novel and of the period that we know precisely, as the Tudors did, what losing a political struggle or being discovered in treachery actually meant. The meaning of action itself in a political setting relates to this fear of potential physical harm or death. (p. 25)

[Ainsworth's departures from his sources] serve to support the thematic function of his use of torture—a consequence which actually helps to depict the Tudor period as Ainsworth shows it. Tortures show the cruelty and ruthlessness of the politically ambitious of the age, who exacted by physical harm the desired confessions even from those who had nothing to confess. Such "justice" is unnatural to Ainsworth. Thus, for him to pass lightly over the tortures because of some false notion of propriety would be to distort the reality he is trying to recreate. The frankness of the modern novel in its treatment of sex and violence offers a parallel. Ainsworth should not be criticized for being true to the Tudor age, for showing the dark sides of the characters he is trying to reveal. (p. 26)

The fact that the historical novel was more a popular form than an art form [in the nineteenth century] is no justification for critics to conclude, without examining the evidence, that minor nineteenth-century historical novelists misused history in general or in specifics. One should take care not to accept all such criticism unquestioningly, for it is just such uncritical assumptions that have led to unfair assessments of Ainsworth's achievement as a historical novelist. (pp. 26-7)

Llewellyn Ligocki, "Ainsworth's Historical Accuracy Reconsidered," in Albion, Vol. 4, No. 1, Spring, 1972, pp. 23-8.

GEORGE J. WORTH (essay date 1972)

[*In his study of Ainsworth, Worth examines the author's use of structure, history, supernatural elements, violence, character, and authorial voice. In the excerpt below, Worth discusses the last two topics and concludes that although Ainsworth's works may appear cliché-ridden to modern readers, they nevertheless contain valuable insights into certain aspects of human nature.*]

Not even the most sympathetic reader of Ainsworth's novels would deny the element of truth in Malcolm Elwin's charge that Ainsworth's characters are "almost always sterile or stereotyped" [see excerpt dated 1934]. We have only to recall his invincible heroes, like Crichton; his virtuous heroines, like Lady Jane Dudley; his hard-luck protagonists, like Thames Darrell—figures, all of them, who either come through adversity unruffled and unblemished or—less often—serenely die the death of the just and the pure. On the other end of the moral scale, there are the many deep-dyed villains whose evil natures are tempered by no saving touch of humanity. Between these extremes, there are hundreds of characters who are little more than names, descriptions, attributes—characters who are quickly forgotten. (p. 90)

Ainsworth's handling of character is unquestionably inept in several respects. He is, for instance, excessively fond of complicating characterization by the use of mistaken identities: someone behaves in a manner inappropriate to his station, and it is ultimately discovered that his real station is quite different from what it appears to be. Alan Rookwood in *Rookwood*, the Princess of Condé and Ginevra Malatesta in *Crichton*, Constance Sheppard in *Jack Sheppard*, Angela Mountjoy in *The Tower of London*, Lady Isabella Argentine in *Old Saint Paul's*, Mabel Lyndwood in *Windsor Castle*, Alizon in *The Lancashire Witches*, and Lady Amicia Wilburton in *Mervyn Clitheroe* are among the most prominent examples. Sometimes these false identities are deliberately assumed; in other instances, they stem from mysteries of parentage of which the characters involved are themselves unaware. In either case, Ainsworth resorts to this tired device so frequently that its use takes on the aspect of an obsession. (p. 91)

Ainsworth's characters don and doff disguises with the greatest of ease and with a high degree of effectiveness. Perhaps the extreme example of this facility occurs in *Tower Hill*, when Francis Dereham so contorts his features and alters his posture as to assume a new identity, that of Hugh Tilney, secretary to Catherine Howard. He plays this role without the benefit of makeup or costume. (p. 92)

[Ainsworth's] treatment of certain characters often seems to vacillate. In these cases, we are not concerned with the complexity of human behavior, which does tend to vary considerably from moment to moment in all but the most dully stable of us, but with certain contradictions and ambiguities which leave Ainsworth open to the charge of negligence or even forgetfulness. Some examples are helpful in establishing this point.

In *Guy Fawkes,* it is difficult to be certain about the motivation of one of the chief conspirators, Robert Catesby. Catesby is in love with Viviana Radcliffe, the daughter of a rich Catholic landowner in Lancashire. She, however, is strongly attracted to Fawkes. Catesby is jealous of Fawkes for this reason, and he is furious with Fawkes because Fawkes has broken up a forced marriage between Catesby and Viviana by giving Viviana proofs that Catesby already has a wife. Humiliated and frustrated, Catesby vigorously swears to withdraw from the gunpowder plot; at his next appearance, nevertheless, he resumes his role of arch-conspirator and never again either mentions or shows his animosity to Fawkes.

A more serious problem in a less spectacular novel has to do with the characterization of old Scarve, the miser, in *The Miser's Daughter.* Ainsworth's preface makes it appear that the novel is going to be some sort of pious moral tract: "To expose the folly and wickedness of accumulating wealth for no other purpose than to hoard it up, and to exhibit the utter misery of a being who should thus surrender himself to the dominion of Mammon, is the chief object of these pages." Avarice, obviously, is a subject with endless possibilities for the imaginative writer; and a Molière or a Balzac can show it manifesting itself in many ways in the same individual. But with Ainsworth, miserliness is a matter of now one thing, now another, with no unity or coherence in our response to the character concerned. It is difficult to know whether to despise Scarve, feel sorry for him, or laugh at him. At different times we do all three, and his gruesome death—"unattended, in a cellar, half entombed in the hole digged as a hiding-place for a portion of his wealth" . . .—is out of keeping with the matter-of-fact

An illustration from Crichton.

mood of the rest of the novel, even though it does underscore the theme enunciated in the preface.

Scarve, at least, is a reasonably consistent character: it is the situations into which he is thrust, and the ways in which he is made to react to them, that vary. Quite another problem occurs in the characterization of Increase Micklegift, the Puritan minister in *Ovingdean Grange,* who cannot seem to decide with which party in the English Civil War to throw in his lot: basically, of course, his allegiance is to the Roundheads, but he loves Dulcia Beard, the daughter of the Royalist clergyman whom he has displaced, and he hates the Puritan officer Stelfax, whom he rightly regards as his rival for Dulcia's affections. Had it been possible, or worth Ainsworth's while, to give anything like full treatment to this unhappy man, his dilemma might have been made entirely credible and even effective; as it is, the reader finds it difficult to accept Micklegift's vacillation.

A similar problem arises in *The Constable de Bourbon.* Is the protagonist of that novel, set in France, Italy, and Spain in the 1520s, a wronged nobleman or is he a contemptible traitor? There is evidence on both sides, and Ainsworth—with a huge canvas to cover—does not really paint a clear enough picture of Bourbon to provide us with an answer.

Equally hard to explain is the sudden repentance of Felix Fairlie, the villain of *The Spendthrift.* The scheming corrupter of the protagonist for most of the novel, Fairlie suffers a seizure near the end after hearing of his daughter's death, and undergoes a ''total revulsion'': ''he was just as eager to repair the wrongs he had committed as he had lately been to uphold them.'' . . . The fact that his dramatic conversion is totally unnecessary makes it even harder to accept: Fairlie's complicated plottings have brought him to the point where his exposure and the undoing of his villainous deeds are imminent anyway.

Some of Ainsworth's inconsistent characters, it should be added in all fairness, are rather more effectively done than Catesby, Scarve, Micklegift, Bourbon, and Fairlie; in *The Lancashire Witches,* Nicholas Assheton, the Puritan squire who engages in some un-Puritanical diversions and who combines superstition and common sense in a remarkable way, comes off quite well—as does, in the same novel, James I, who is by turns magnanimous and petty, royally stern and appealingly human.

In the main, however, Ainsworth was unquestionably prone to take the easy way out in his characterizations, and he was not above an occasional blunder. But it would be doing him an injustice simply to leave the matter at that. At his best, he was capable of bringing to his treatment of character the same sort of imaginative intensity which marked his handling of dramatic or visual scenes; and, even though he did not succeed in creating a whole gallery of unforgettable portraits, he certainly managed to fashion some compelling figures. (pp. 92-4)

No one could claim that Ainsworth ranks with Shakespeare or Dickens as a prolific inventor of remarkable characters, or with Jane Austen or Thackeray as a psychologist. No one could quarrel with the assertion that his characters, on the whole, are stock figures, either frozen immobile in fixed postures or given to wildly inconsistent alterations. It seems undeniable, however, that Ainsworth at his best can energize his characters by thrusting them into inherently dramatic situations, that he can infuse them with the vitality that marks so much of his writing, that he is at his best in depicting the desperate, the power-mad, and the malign—that he can, in short, wring from even the most reluctant reader a response, however grudging, to the actions and the passions of his people. (pp. 100-01)

• • • • •

No writer in the century and a half which marked the golden age of the English novel was less reticent than . . . Ainsworth about intruding his own personality and his own views. Everywhere in his novels we hear what we soon come to recognize as his distinctive voices. This observation is certainly and obviously true of his expository passages; but it is even noticeable to the reader moderately familiar with Ainsworth's work in scenes which are rendered dramatically.

As we might expect from a writer who deals so extensively with architectural or topographical settings, Ainsworth frequently assumes the role of guide, pointing out—much as some kinds of handbook would—the distinctive features of the physical background which he is attempting to establish. (p. 102)

There are countless set pieces in Ainsworth's historical novels describing in minute detail not only the physical appearance of his characters but also their dress and every aspect of the ceremonial occasions in which they participated, such as processions, pageants, and especially (Ainsworth must have been exceedingly fond of the pleasures of dining and drinking well) banquets. Aside from their frequency, length, and specificity, two things are striking about these passages: the enormous amount of social-historical research that must have gone into them, and (usually) their tendency to slow down the action of the novels in which they are included. Even in the best intentioned reader, fully alive to Ainsworth's rich descriptive power, the temptation to skip or skim such passages occasionally becomes overwhelming. (p. 104)

Less obviously related to the kind of fiction he characteristically wrote is Ainsworth's repeated insistence on explicitly judging the figures in his novels: not with tongue-in-cheek irony, like that displayed by Thackeray and Trollope on similar occasions, not with the compassionate penetration of a George Eliot, but tersely, straightforwardly, in terms of black and white moral criteria. As we have seen, Ainsworth suggests quite clearly, in a number of ways, what we are to think of the more important characters in his novels; about the lesser ones, there can usually be no doubt whatever, because he flatly tells us.

Regarding Henry VIII, for example, we are given our signals at the very beginning of *The Constable of the Tower:* "Rapacious and cruel, and lavish as rapacious, his greediness was insatiable. . . . Crafty as well as resolute, he framed laws merely to deride and break them." Because the author must resort to this kind of shorthand here, and because his judgment of Henry is that which is commonly held, Ainsworth is on quite safe ground in this case; less acceptable, however, is his frequent interruption of the narrative in order to censure or to excuse the actions of his characters. In the same novel, when Catherine Parr finally yields to Sir Thomas Seymour's passionate suit and agrees to marry him, Ainsworth instructs us how we are to react: "She knew the character of the man who sought her hand. Yet she agreed to a sudden and secret marriage with him. Her love overmastered her discretion. Some excuse may be found for her in the resistless manner and extraordinary personal attractions of her suitor. Few of her sex would have come off scathless from the ordeal to which she was subjected." . . . (pp. 108-09)

Ainsworth the guide, Ainsworth the chronicler, Ainsworth the judge, Ainsworth the moralist—all these roles which our author is fond of assuming quickly become familiar as we get to know his work. Certain quirks of style and diction, too, soon come to strike us as distinctively Ainsworthian.

He is inordinately given to the dangling modifier. . . . His characters are forever "making the best of their way" somewhere or, when wounded, exhausted, or badly frightened, finding

that "their limbs refuse their office." Exclamatory expressions abound, with "Soh!" perhaps the most frequent and certainly the tersest. Ainsworth also can be precious and arch: in *Old Court,* which reads in places as if Ainsworth had enrolled in the silver-fork school, the romantic affliction of a young officer is described in these words: "the blind god had winged his keenest shaft up to the feather in the gallant captain's heart" . . . ; a pair of youthful lovers on horseback are "enamoured equestrians" . . . ; and so on. When he attempts to be lyrical, he often succeeds only in sounding strained, resembling nothing so much as one of Thackeray's parodies of his contemporaries' excesses:

> Animate nature was just beginning to feel the quickening influence of the God of Day. The garrulous occupants of the higher trees made the welkin ring with their cawing as they flew past in quest of their morning meal; lesser birds twittered amongst the boughs; the mavis burst from the holm-tree to dispute the first worm upon the grass plot with the intrusive starling; pigeons were circling around the house, or alighting on the roof; lowings of oxen and other noises resounded from the farm-yard; and the tinkling of the sheep-bell was heard on the adjacent down, where might be seen the fleecy company, just released from the fold, in charge of the shepherd, and looking as grey as the turf on which they browsed. (*Ovingdean Grange*. . . .)

(pp. 110-11)

In addition to such verbosity, inflation, and circumlocution, Ainsworth's language is often marked by the mock antiquity of Wardour Street English. In a historical novel like *The Constable of the Tower* we come upon chapter titles such as this: "How the Right High and Renowned King Henry the Eighth waxed grievously Sick, and was like to Die" . . . ; and upon speeches like "'Tis horrible to think that a foul and murtherous caitiff should disfigure a god-like frame like yours, and sever such a head from such a frame! No—no—it cannot—shall not be" . . . or "Vindictive wretch! thou hast well deserved thy fate! . . . Remove the body to Mauger's vault yonder—beneath the Bloody Tower. . . . And let these sanguinary stains be effaced. . . . Now, bring on the prisoner. To the palace!" . . .

Ainsworth's efforts at historical verisimilitude in his dialogue are frequently painful. A sixteenth-century French king speaks to his jester, who has just sung a particularly clever song:

> "Gramercy . . . thou hast fairly earned thy hippocras, were it only for the justice rendered to the lovely Esclairmonde, who, as thou truly sayest, outshines all. But, by our lady, messeigneurs, we must not neglect the service of Bacchus for that of Apollo. Samson, thy choicest Cyprus—a health!" (*Crichton*. . .).

And a seventeenth-century Puritan fumes with moral outrage (which, Ainsworth suggests, was perpetual among Cromwell's adherents in the Civil War):

> "What! thou perfidious and dissembling Episcopalian, hast thou entrapped our leader, a mighty man of valour like Amasiah, the captain of Jehoshaphat, and fastened him within yon closet? Give me the key thereof instantly, or I will smite thee with the edge of the sword, even

as the false priests of Baal were put to death
by the soldiers of Jehu'' (*Ovingdean Grange*. . .).

(p. 111)

Clearly, Ainsworth had no intention of disappearing from his narratives. Nor, having decided to obtrude himself, was he capable of the irony, the wit, the profundity, the subtlety, or the humor which the sophisticated modern reader tends to look for in authorial commentary. He was, rather, straightforward and matter-of-fact—traits which were probably welcome and helpful to his large nineteenth-century audience. In his dramatic scenes, too, he eschewed psychological nuances and fidelity to everyday habits of speech, drawing instead in big, bold, obvious strokes. The voices of Harrison Ainsworth address us as from the podium or across the flickering footlights; but, if we abandon some of our modern prejudices about the proper language of fiction and surrender ourselves to the spell which he attempts to cast, these voices often reach us with surprising clarity and power.

·····

What, then, is the twentieth-century reader to make of the novels of Harrison Ainsworth? If that reader looks to Ainsworth for well-wrought plots and memorable characterizations, he is likely to suffer disappointment. If he seeks subtlety of technique and finely shaded nuances in the fiction he admires, he will not find them in Ainsworth. If he has little patience with the stock conventions of the classical English novel, he will be repelled by a great deal in Ainsworth's cliché-ridden books.

He may, however, discover some surprising compensations in these dusty volumes. As what used to be called, rather condescendingly, "escape" literature, they are unsurpassed, capturing in each novel a crowded, swarming, teeming, self-contained world. Whereas the contemporary novelist is likely to offer his reader a thin, pale, chilled, slightly acrid fictional broth, Ainsworth sets down before him a steaming, bubbling, thick and hearty stew, redolent of exotic seasonings and full of strange, unexpected chunks and morsels.

But the modern reader who comes to Ainsworth to scoff and who then stays to lose himself in his fictional world may learn something else before he returns to the real world. Hopelessly antiquated though much of Ainsworth is, he nonetheless knew a good deal about some aspects of human nature which we often prefer to forget. Man's craving for power—latent in all of us, an obsession in some—has been better understood by only a handful of novelists. How power is won; and, once won, how it is exercised are subjects to which Ainsworth returns again and again: how one man—or, less often, a faction—comes to dominate a court and a whole country. Conversely, he also shows how loss of power over oneself and others can bring a man to ruin: a very painful sort of ruin, generally, because Ainsworth is under no illusion about the mercy and charity which we are wont to extend to our fellows.

If Ainsworth's world is full of surface pomp and pageantry and a sense of continuity and tradition which runs rather deeper, it is nevertheless cruel and violent at the core—a truth, quite possibly, which makes it all the more imperative to retain what we can of ceremony and convention and what little there may be of human compassion. More than the general run of nineteenth-century novelists and more than even many writers of our own day, Ainsworth was aware of the irrational side of human nature and of the drives, the hopes and fears, to which it gives rise. The modern reader—recognizing the shrewdness of this insight, and eventually coming to appreciate the skill

with which Ainsworth renders his world view—may well concede that much in Ainsworth engages the highest powers which he is capable of bringing to the fiction he reads. (pp. 114-16)

George J. Worth, in his William Harrison Ainsworth, *Twayne Publishers, Inc., 1972, 134 p.*

LLEWELLYN LIGOCKI (essay date 1973)

[According to Ligocki, Scott's casual comment naming Ainsworth as an imitator (see excerpt dated 1826) has misled critics, for Ainsworth's approach differed significantly from the pattern set by Scott. Whereas Scott examined the effect of historical events on fictional characters, Ainsworth directly depicted historical incidents and people. For further commentary by Ligocki, see excerpts dated 1972 and 1975.]

Sir Walter Scott's position as the first important writer of historical fiction has created difficulties in assessing the achievements of some of the less important historical novelists who immediately followed him. His preeminence has invited critics to label the followers, sometimes indiscriminately, as servile imitators. Although it is fair to say that these novelists exploited a genre made popular by Scott, it is not always fair to charge these novelists with direct imitation. Certainly this is the case with William Harrison Ainsworth, author of *The Tower of London, Old Saint Paul's, Windsor Castle,* and almost forty other novels. Ironically, a casual statement by Scott himself initiated the criticism that Ainsworth was merely his imitator; critics have carelessly extended and misapplied Scott's statement. Now the label stands, even though its origin has long been forgotten. (p. 443)

[In contrast to] careless critics, those few who study Ainsworth in some detail discover that he departed in important respects from Scott's practices. . . . The two writers differ in the most basic ways. Whereas Scott used the major events and characters of history as background and treated the consequences of historical events on the lives of unhistorical characters, Ainsworth generally centered on the historical events and characters themselves. This difference in methodology reflects a dissimilarity in aesthetic viewpoint. Scott's general habit was to use the historical record as a means of establishing the worlds in which his own characters existed; Ainsworth, on the other hand, used history itself as the subject to be explored. The point is not that Ainsworth is as skillful in realizing history as Scott is, but that he went about the task differently. . . . [One of Scott's strengths] is that he does not bind himself to characters and events that are in large part matters of historical record—such as Henry VIII's marriages, Lady Jane Grey's deposition by Mary, and Guy Fawkes and the Gunpowder Plot, all of which are absolutely central in Ainsworth's novels. Yet for all that, Scott's relative success in re-creating history does not remove the basic difference between his approach and Ainsworth's: he explored time and place indirectly, while Ainsworth did it directly. (p. 445)

[Contrary] to Ainsworth's slavish imitation of Scott, his real debt is only to Scott's bringing the historical novel into currency as a genre. He accepted the inherited form, then used it in his own way. The label "imitator" does nothing but prevent Ainsworth's novels from getting an independent reading. (p. 446)

Llewellyn Ligocki, "The Imitators and the Imitated: Scott, Ainsworth, and the Critics," in The Papers of the Bibliographical Society of America, *Vol. 67, fourth quarter, 1973, pp. 443-46.**

LLEWELLYN LIGOCKI (essay date 1975)

[Though Ligocki judges Ainsworth's technical skills unequal to his vision, he defends the novelist-historian's use of the past as a means of presenting universal truths. For further commentary by Ligocki, see excerpts dated 1972 and 1973.]

In Ainsworth's novels one often has difficulty dissociating the "history" from the "fiction" precisely because the two are interrelated; Ainsworth uses history purposefully in order to give us a commentary on history, not a work of history. So important was the historical novel as a vehicle for his artistic statement that he continued to write such novels long after they went out of fashion in the middle of the nineteenth century. Virtually all of his novels, moreover, concentrate on important historical events and personages; he does not relegate these events and characters to the background. It should not be surprising to discover, therefore, that Ainsworth does not treat history capriciously, or that history is not incidental to his purposes. He attempts to derive his judgments about life from what he sees as historical truth.

One can learn much about Ainsworth's attitudes to history and fiction by examining his fiction in the context of the historical materials that he used as quarry. Ainsworth himself, by adopting as narrator the persona of the historian, invites us to consider history as the ostensible frame of reference for judging the characters and events. His practice in his well-known *The Tower of London* is representative of the way in which he consciously exploits history and the artistic role of the historian in his fiction. Rather than obscuring his historical spadework and background reading as Scott might have done, Ainsworth calls attention to it. In the Preface he cites many (although not all) of his sources and discusses his conscious desire to rehabilitate the image of Mary Tudor. In the body of the novel,

An illustration by Cruikshank from Jack Sheppard.

also, he refers explicitly to historians and other commentators. (pp. 196-97)

[Although Ainsworth is not a mere romancer,] neither is he a scholarly historian, intent mainly upon establishing for his countrymen a well-documented work of history under the guise of the novel. Falling between the two categories, Ainsworth uses his wide and rather careful reading of a great number of historical sources as the basis for a generalized literary commentary on the meaning of history: man cannot avoid the relentless and cyclical world of process, of which man is both agent and victim. History is Ainsworth's world-view by another name; it functions, in *The Tower of London* and Ainsworth's other historical novels, as myth. Hence, it is more important for Ainsworth to seem factual than for him necessarily to be factual. His pose as historian serves primarily as a literary tool in that it helps to establish his authority to make large-scale pronouncements on reality; and it places in context the particular pattern that he sees in reality. Thus, Ainsworth's overriding goal seems to be that of maintaining literary consistency while remaining as close to the historical record as his literary purpose will allow. Generally—though not completely—accurate, he is mainly interested in demonstrating imaginatively his concept of history. The somewhat elaborate historical machinery, including his narrative stance, functions as part of his literary design.

The theme of *The Tower of London* demands that Ainsworth establish clearly for the reader that he is dealing with the materials of history and that it is in historical perspective that the action in the novel must be seen. He attempts to make us aware that the rising and falling fortunes of Lady Jane Grey and those surrounding her are part of a historical—and therefore universal—fabric of which these particular actions are only a part. The characters and events in the novel gain importance as they demonstrate the operation of time. But these ultimately thematic considerations are reinforced by Ainsworth's use of history in his narrative strategy.

Ainsworth goes to some length in *The Tower of London* to develop his pervasive but not generally obtrusive stance as historian even to the point of exaggerating his scholarship. . . .

Ainsworth implicitly exaggerates his historical research in order to enhance our conception of the narrator's authority. And as long as the reader does not suspect what Ainsworth is up to, the technique increases our trust that the narrator has examined carefully the historical materials available to him; the probability is increased, further, that we will accept the conclusions he draws on the materials as well. (p. 198)

In most cases Ainsworth either mentions [his] sources or he uses so convincingly the details garnered from them that the reader cannot but be aware that in some way the history in the novel functions as part of the total design. . . .

[A study of] Ainsworth's general use of his sources allows us to draw some important conclusions about Ainsworth's craft as a novelist. The first relates to his selection and use of the novelist-historian as persona, a usage that differentiates Ainsworth from a number of popular Victorian novelists who merely wrote historical novels. Ainsworth's conscious exploitation of the role of historian and his use of history as the supreme common denominator is an astute perception of a chief preoccupation of his age. Scarcely an important writer from Wordsworth through Arnold failed to use the past literally or figuratively in his works. In both popular and academic circles history became a central concern. Thus, in an age in which

Englishmen increasingly looked to history as a way of seeing the present and as a possible measure of certitude and stability, Ainsworth found the appropriate voice for speaking to his readers. His subject matter, too, was timely: an effective context for treating man's place in time's panorama. Hence, the relationship between form and content, strategy and statement, is quite intimate.

Another conclusion to be drawn about Ainsworth's craft relates to his conscious control of his materials. His wide reading of many historical sources indicates beyond a doubt that he knew well the history of the period about which he was writing and that he knew even most of the major historical issues and points of contention among the historians. We must, then, judge any apparent irregularities in his handling of history within the framework of his wide reading and try to determine the manner in which they seem to relate to his design.

To be sure, Ainsworth's technical skill in amalgamating the historical materials does not always match his vision; some of the exposition, in particular, seems occasionally a bit undigested.... Furthermore, compromises for the purpose of his essentially popular audience lead at times to jarringly melodramatic scenes or to gratuitous love-plots. Yet on the whole the historical machinery operates smoothly and purposively, demonstrating to the careful reader the firm but not obtrusive hand of the author. (p. 200)

> Llewellyn Ligocki, "William Harrison Ainsworth as Novelist-Historian," in Research Studies, Vol. 43, No. 3, September, 1975, pp. 196-200.

J. A. SUTHERLAND   (essay date 1976)

[*Sutherland contends that Ainsworth's inability to break away from his trademark historical romances—demonstrated by the failure of his semi-autobiographical novel* Mervyn Clitheroe—*led to the drastic decline in his popularity.*]

For a while Ainsworth's star was higher than Dickens's. But he broke no new ground in his prime. It is as if Dickens had written in his first five years as a novelist: *Pickwick Papers, Nicholas Nickleby, Peter Pickleton, The Bagwig Club, The Picklington Papers, The Adventures of Harry Hogstock,* etc. . . . [The] danger of this kind of stereotype repetitiousness was that a novelist stunted his development and became so closely associated with one brand of fiction that it was impracticable for him to change. In 1851 Ainsworth had a demonstration of this when he brought out **Mervyn Clitheroe,** something quite different from the run of his earlier fiction, an autobiographical work, lacking the historical setting and adventure plot which were by now his trademarks. Ainsworth himself regarded this 'mere transcript' of his early schooldays as a risky experiment. . . . His 'story of modern life' was found unexciting by those who had expected something Ainsworthian and issue was suspended after only four parts had been published by Chapman and Hall. So, in 1853, Ainsworth returned to the old groove with **The Star Chamber.**

Mervyn Clitheroe may be seen as a crucial moment in Ainsworth's career, the moment when he failed to break out of the limiting format of the historical romance. (pp. 153-54)

With sixty years, Ainsworth can claim the longest novel-writing career of the century. But it is made up almost entirely of the same historical romances, with the same grandiose action, rousing titles and thin veneer of scholarship. When times and tastes changed, as they inevitably did, he was left beached,

his talents exhausted and capable of nothing but increasingly feeble reiteration. (pp. 154-55)

Hilary St Ives was a pathetic attempt to produce a novel set in the present day, a transparent imitation of Collins's *Moonstone* and *Armadale.* It failed miserably. Years of habit had confirmed Ainsworth as the kind of novelist with only one novel in him—his modern characters were always prone to explete 'Zounds' when surprised and give the impression that they would be happier in armour than tweeds. It was now too late to desert historical fiction for sensational. (p. 159)

> J. A. Sutherland, "Lever and Ainsworth: Missing the First Rank," in his Victorian Novelists and Publishers, The University of Chicago Press, 1976, pp. 152-65.*

RICHARD MAXWELL   (essay date 1978)

[*Maxwell notes that* Revelations of London (*published as* Auriol) *and* Old Saint Paul's *reflect Ainsworth's fascination with French literature, notably Hugo's* Notre Dame de Paris *and Sue's* Les mystères de Paris.]

One of the first writers in England to work with the pattern established by *Nôtre-Dame* was William Harrison Ainsworth. In 1841, Ainsworth published **Old Saint Paul's,** which is like a marginal gloss on the earlier book. Writing for the popular and respectable *Sunday Times,* he simplified Hugo's plot and ideas, sometimes to the point of absurdity. Frollo and Quasimodo, both essential to *Nôtre-Dame,* disappear completely. Instead of one heroine there are two, so that the conflicting erotic energies which converge on Hugo's Esmeralda are broken up and dissipated. Most important, Hugo's elaborate theory of history . . . is reduced to a hymn in praise of the rising middle classes (as opposed to wicked courtiers). What remains of the French novel is a picked-over skeleton; the reader may recognize certain structures, but the flesh, the meaning, is largely gone.

Old Saint Paul's embodies Ainsworth's preoccupations at the zenith of his career. He looks to French fiction, Hugo especially, for models. He does not, as yet, display any special understanding of these models. In fact, the only evidence that he ever understood them is a serial he began work on a few years later which he called **Revelations of London.** . . .

[In **Revelations of London** different] historical periods are related not by simple juxtaposition but through the device of the man who lives forever. Ainsworth has found a plot which allows him to write about 1599 and then about 1830, with occasional retrospections. (p. 158)

Ainsworth's **Revelations,** despite its long gestation period, is conspicuously an imitation [of Sue's *Les mystères de Paris*]. English revelations are set against French mysteries; the fascinations which produced **Old Saint Paul's** have taken another and perhaps more promising form.

The opening chapter of **Revelations** fulfills this promise. A pair of criminals prowls through some sinister riverfront areas of London. Like Sue's malefactors, these two have more or less colorful nicknames: the Sandman and the Tinker. Also as in the French tradition, they are soon to become involved with a dandified young man who is involved in intrigues all over the city. A third striking feature is the landscape itself. The Sandman and the Tinker arrive finally in an abandoned and ruinous neighborhood, an area off Vauxhall Road which has been used as a dumping ground by riverside industry, including a ship-breaking yard. What is important here is a combination of fantasy and precise topographical description. While the landscape is no doubt authentic, it is being used for a special purpose. The novelist delights in mixing past and present, the debris of myth and technology heaped together with political and pastoral icons. . . . (p. 159)

That initial picture embodies one plight of the modern city whose past is being swept away while its present and future seem to lack coherent form. When Ainsworth tries to develop this theme in terms of plot, he reaches a point of deadlock. His hero, Auriol, gets into increasingly difficult straits, chasing about London attempting to deal with Satan and a group of subsidiary villains. The heroine is harder pressed—she is eventually murdered and her soul captured for Hell. A few minor characters wander about in catacombs underneath the city, but not to much effect. Ainsworth—and this is a unique incident in his career—has written himself into a corner. Many years later (1865) he completed the tale in a few hasty chapters so that it might be issued in book form. But the ending, as it stands, resolves nothing. (p. 160)

Neither protagonist nor author can resolve the dialectic of past and present as it bears on the life of the city. Indeed, after 1845 Ainsworth himself became increasingly a relic from the past. His attempt to come to terms with romantic French fiction (Hugo and then Sue) had been a failure. He was more and more looked on as a hopeless hack grinding out lifeless historical novels, an aimless eccentric without a place in the modern world. . . . (p. 161)

> Richard Maxwell, "City Life and the Novel: Hugo, Ainsworth, Dickens," in Comparative Literature, *Vol. XXX, No. 2, Spring, 1978, pp. 157-71.*

ANDREW SANDERS   (essay date 1979)

[*According to Sanders, Ainsworth's historical novels are clumsy, anachronistic, disjointed, and melodramatic escape literature in which the author trivializes historical events to further his sensational plots.*]

Harrison Ainsworth's novels have much to answer for in having given historical fiction a bad name, but they in fact tend to ignore Scott's precedent in an attempt to restore and re-embellish the Gothic fiction of the early century. Despite his considerable initial success, Ainsworth proved to be incapable of development or of sustaining his achievement; he ransacked English history for likely plots, and often he ended up with unlikely ones; he looked to sensationalism to sell his novels, and he pleased neither his early critics nor a later and more critical audience. By the 1850s Ainsworth had already outwritten the fashion for the kind of romance he had hoped to rejuvenate. (p. 17)

Ainsworth had a deep and romantic attraction to the England of the Tudors and Stuarts, and he wrote popular books about the period for an audience which shared his passion. Ainsworth wrote quickly and spiritedly, and, for the first decade of his literary career at least, he maintained a phenomenal and often inexplicable success. He was a best-seller in an age which enjoyed the benefits of industrialism for the production and distribution of literature, but which nevertheless affected a sentimental attachment to a time and place wihout machines. His novels catered [to] a taste for easily assimilated historical romance, even though, like his audience, Ainsworth held an

A caricature of the aging author.

equivocal view of the relevance of the study of history. On the one hand, he was content to be a Victorian Englishman and to have escaped the plagues, racks and bigotry of the past; on the other, he was drawn to history in search of an imaginative release from the drabness and relative stability of life in the nineteenth century. Ainsworth was a product of the declining era of Romanticism, and of the Romantic tendency to long for an escape from modern reality; paradoxically, he happily accepted a concept of social progress and was both amused and shocked by the narrowness of his ancestors' world. He had, in fact, no real idea about history, simply a delight in being surrounded by its trappings. The relatively scholarly taste for history, for Gothic architecture and for tradition which marks the 1840s, was a product of intellectual advance, as well as a reaction against it; the study of the past revealed the advantages of living in the present, but it also suggested that society had fallen away from a more vivid pattern of conduct. To an alert mind the culture of the early Gothic Revival presented a dilemma. At its best the age produced Carlyle's *Past and Present,* Ruskin's *Seven Lamps of Architecture,* and the designs and polemics of Pugin; its shabbier, escapist side is represented by Ainsworth's novels. It is revealing to remember that Ainsworth, who was so proud of his Mancunian origins and education, should habitually have described his home town not as Cottonopolis, but in its placid, pre-industrial aspect.

The expansion of popular antiquarianism in the first quarter of the nineteenth century influenced both Ainsworth's choice of subjects and the very form of his novels. It seems to have encouraged his tendency to see his novels as, in part, archaeological hand-books. Five of his stories published between 1840 and 1854 were given titles drawn from important national monuments, and, in the cases of *The Tower of London, Old Saint Paul's* and *Windsor Castle,* he selected settings with very complex historical and architectural associations. When he builds a novel around a castle, a cathedral or a palace, he regards it as a novelist's duty to tell the story of the building as much as that of his characters. (pp. 32-3)

It would be unfair to suggest that Ainsworth was simply pinning stories to guide-books, for he was genuinely committed to the idea of a novel which would resurrect the style and technique of Gothic fiction, injected with a revivifying dose of instruction. His didacticism is of a peculiarly unimaginative kind, however, for he was not so much concerned with moral teaching as with the value of facts and dates. Above all, his novels reveal that, unlike most other Victorian writers, he had learnt very little indeed from Sir Walter Scott. (p. 33)

Scott was perhaps fortunate not to have lived to witness Ainsworth's . . . popular success and esteem. The Waverley novels had proved that history could be the proper, and profitable, matter of fiction, but they had also shown that successful historical fiction was best rooted in a detailed investigation of character and environment. Ainsworth signally failed to grasp the full impact of Scott's achievement and, though his literary career outstretches those of Dickens, Thackeray and George Eliot (his last novel appeared in 1881), he seems to have remained unconscious of, and oblivious to, most contemporary developments in the novel. . . . Even his steadily popular *The Lancashire Witches* . . . , with its attempt to reproduce the dialect and customs of a province, shows little evidence of his having learnt, as George Eliot or Hardy certainly had, from the example of Scott's regional novels. To its detriment, Ainsworth's work only barely relates the meaning and impact of an historical crisis to the experience of the individual, and the novelist seems happy with simply telling an involved, and often incredible story about people who happen to be historical. (p. 34)

[His] novels somehow bypass Scott's achievement, and return to the less investigatory, less fluid modes of his predecessors; they reject social and psychological analysis in favour of a revived stress on fantastic action, on the supernatural, and on the superficial glamour of costume drama.

This determined preference for the 'Mrs Radcliffe school' perhaps explains the somewhat cavalier approach to historical fact and interpretation in Ainsworth's work. Most of his books have a vigorous and straightforward plot, but characters, both fictional and factual, tend to conform to stereotypes, and to be repeated from novel to novel. Plots are moulded around historical crises which oblige the novelist to follow a line of development faithful to his sources, but his sub-plots, which are often more involved, show more of a desire for variety than for a complement to the main story. Against a background of historical intrigue, he habitually plays groups of comic, low characters, and a melodramatic story of the wooing of a beautiful young heroine by a virtuous and generally aristocratic hero. The hero is pitched against a clearly defined villain, but it seems a matter of chance whether or not he will actually involve himself in the historical events on which the novel ostensibly turns. In most of the novels plots are tripartite, and Ainsworth seems to be more concerned to balance his historical, comic and amatory interest than he is to maintain a focus on a single, influential group of characters. Rarely are we led to feel that history impinges upon any but the statesmen playing an aristocratic game.

Any serious attempt to investigate the social impact of historical events is further diffused by Ainsworth's re-introduction of the clichés of Gothic fiction into his novels. Characters gesture or orate, and speeches tend to be little more than declamations revealing intentions, not motives. He avoids psychological development in character as though he regards it as an impediment to the movement of his story. At their best, however, the novels have fast-moving and visually effective plots which chiefly lack the advantages which tighter structuring might have given. They are rarely sufficiently tense, for Ainsworth contorts action in order to provide for the unexpected *frisson,* the hair-breadth escape, or the supernatural manifestation, and thereby detracts from any sustained interest in a situation. Walls are threaded with secret passages; panels and trap-doors fly open; the living are confused with the dead, the dead with the unearthly. Characters appear or disappear to suit the novelist's convenience in delivering them into or from difficulties. Where it is appropriate, and often where it is inappropriate, rituals are performed, or unspecified horrors suggested. . . . At the ends of the novels, the virtuous are rewarded by benign monarchs, the villains have their villainy proved, or, if unpunished, we are assured by the narrator that history, as well as the novel, shows them to have been in the wrong. At their worst, but by no means uncommonly, the novels end as arbitrarily as they began. Ainsworth does not lack gusto; he is simply deficient in a controlling artistic intelligence.

Despite his pretensions to scholarship and to didacticism, Ainsworth takes considerable liberties with the facts of history in his novels, and in this he reveals the gulf that separates him from the more serious of Scott's successors. . . . History is moulded to suit the requirements of sensationalism, despite the damage done to credibility. Often Ainsworth forgets to tie up all the ends of his plots, leaving elements unresolved, or unbalanced after a concluding marriage or a disaster. He will attempt to bring his fictional story to a happy end, while offering no solution to the vaster historical problem which he purports to be describing at the centre of the novel.

Many of his important historical characters are presented with a destructive ambiguity simply because he has not thought out the implications of his plots with sufficient thoroughness. In some cases, like those of Guy Fawkes or Mary Tudor, he attempts to challenge a conventional view of the character, but instead of offering a re-interpretation of action and motive, he develops one line of approach before abruptly switching to another. In *Old Saint Paul's,* Charles II and the Earl of Rochester appear at first as reckless and immoral; by the end of the story they have inexplicably assumed both dignity and decisiveness through their behaviour during the Great Fire of London. In *Guy Fawkes,* Ainsworth ambitiously set out to make a case for the Jacobean recusants, but he succeeds only in confusing the political issue still further. Fawkes emerges as an enigma, with a tormented conscience, moral scruples and a wife, while Frs Oldcorne and Garnet put the novelist in the equivocal position of exploiting a case against persecution *and* justifying a traditional English suspicion of Jesuits. In all his novels, Ainsworth's kings are fickle, arrogant, and ill-advised but, he tells us, unfailingly regal and nearly always justifiable.

This ambiguity is equally evident in his treatment of ordinary citizens. In his stories, unlike Scott's, the common people are allowed to express the novelist's prejudices without appearing to have evolved any kind of understanding of what is happening to them. They are rarely more than spectators observing events which they have no power to influence. Voices emerge from a crowd, or a yokel is engaged in comic dialogue. The crowd, especially in the novels about the Tudor period, is unthinkingly legitimist and monarchist in its sentiments; it admires bluff King Hal for his bluffness, and Good Queen Bess for her goodness; it accepts Mary Tudor's claim to the throne and suspects Lady Jane Grey's; it distrusts Anne Boleyn, but respects Henry VIII's marital whims as evidence of his capacity to rule. 'I love my king,' proclaims the host of the Garter Inn in *Windsor Castle,* 'and if he wishes to have a divorce, I hope his holiness the Pope will grant him one, that's all.' When a butcher in the Inn declares that the king is tyrannical, he is denounced as a traitor and is arrested without a murmur of protest from the other guests. In *The Tower of London,* the 'low' characters swim with the religious current of the Court; there is little room for subtlety, and no sense at all of a society which is corporately involved in, and affected by, the complex political and religious situation. The intrigues of the great are played against a background of common assent and acceptance. When Ainsworth does attempt to describe popular uprisings, as he does at the beginning of *The Lancashire Witches,* he prefers to concentrate upon figures of popular authority. Readers, like the crowd, are generally required to assent to the *status quo,* and however much Ainsworth attempts to challenge conventional judgements of events or characters, he always balances his challenge against an equally telling restatement of the convention. History is observed as a series of rights and wrongs, and all that the novelist does is to suggest that, on occasions, certainties can contain areas of doubt within them without actually ceasing to be certainties. (pp. 35-8)

[Ainsworth announced that *The Tower of London*] would be so contrived as to 'naturally introduce every relic of the whole pile—its towers, chapels, halls, chambers, gateways, arches and drawbridges'. Nevertheless, the final effect is of a nervous indigestion resultant from an overindulgent desire to prove that facts are palatable if they are dressed and served to the author's taste. . . .

Although the novel is freer of the discursive descriptions of the fabric which intrude into the central parts of *Windsor Castle, The Tower of London* never escapes having to function partly as a guidebook. The author's didactic voice interferes and interrupts the flow of the story; we are told what happened in the reign of Edward III, or what will happen in the reign of James I, rather than simply the significance of events in the period of the novel's setting. At best, Ainsworth is inconsistent, at worst, he seems quite unconscious of being anachronistic. (p. 39)

In seeking to make his novel comprehensive, Ainsworth brings together as many elements as he can, regardless of their effect on the unity of his work. *The Tower of London* is various and elaborate, but it is clumsily put together and disorganised where it most needs artistic control. The novel is built around abrupt contrasts. The fortunes of characters rise and fall, and, despite the probable accuracy of this as an impression of Tudor politics, readers are left with what seems to be an arbitrary succession of events, fictional as well as historical. . . . [The] novel is too overcrowded with characters and incidents to allow an effective balance of moods to succeed. The contrasts jar because they do not form a part of an organic whole. . . . Above all he does not tell us in the novel why the rebellion has taken place and what its significance is for the Queen and for the country. Here, as so often elsewhere, we are unable to take the play of emotions seriously because there is no firm basis for the emotions.

The confusion at the core of *The Tower of London* derives not simply from Ainsworth's failure to work out his plot with sufficient care, but also from the fact that he cannot sustain interest in the broad spectrum of his characters. He mixes the fictional and the historical indiscriminately, but, unlike the best Victorian historical novelists, he derives no strength from what he does, nor any fresh insight into the development of the events he describes. The antics of the comic characters—Xit, the dwarf, and the giant yeoman warders—are intended to be amusing parallels to the intrigues of the Court, and to be foils to the black comedy of the jailors, Nightgall and Wolfytt, and the headsman, Mauger, but they merely work as a digression. The novel's chief defect in characterisation is found not in the low characters, but in the neutral and fictional hero and heroine, Cuthbert and Angela, and, more significantly, in the historical characters involved in the struggle for the royal succession. (pp. 40-1)

Because the novel concentrates so many characters and events into one place at one time, Ainsworth seems to find it impossible to vary the pace and speed of events, and to concentrate on one important group of characters more than the rest. The history is muddled in the interests of the romance, but the romance is never able, as it does in Scott or Dickens for example, to unmuddle the history.

The Tower of London is pre-eminently about Lady Jane Grey, but Lady Jane is so confused in a jumble of other interests that we never have a sufficiently clear view of her or her problem. The novel opens with her entry to the Tower as claimant to the throne, and it ends with her execution as a threat to the legitimate sovereign. Jane is the only important historical figure whose story is followed to a conclusion or a resolution. All the other major figures, Ainsworth reminds us during the novel, to the detriment of his fiction, have destinies which expand beyond the scope of his chosen framework. The invented characters are given their appropriate marital partners, but they will have little chance of influencing the future history of England if their careers in the story are anything to go by. Mary and Elizabeth Tudor have their reigns before them, the bishops have persecution or martyrdom, the ambassadors and courtiers new schemes, but they are left in suspension as the novel closes with Lady Jane's death. The novel may have set out to investigate a national crisis, and the Tower's part in it, but leaves the problem only partially solved, and the small solution it offers is ambiguous. Throughout the story we are required to assent to the justice of Mary Tudor's claim to the throne, and to acknowledge the folly of Jane's usurpation; Mary is a worthy woman and a just ruler, despite the narrowness of her religious opinions. At the same time, however, we are asked to sympathise with Jane's hope of replacing an illiberal Catholic regime with a progressive Protestant one. Ainsworth relies on the fact that his reader will accept the premiss that Protestantism will rightly succeed in the end, despite the evidence of the events of the novel, and that Jane's cause will be vindicated by history. In matters of politics Mary is right and Jane wrong; in matters of religion the reverse position holds. Ainsworth plays the one against the other, without appearing to sense that, for a Tudor monarch as much as for a Tudor citizen, the two positions might have been one. He also seems oblivious to the fact that his own extended view of Tudor England, and its effect on periods which succeeded it, is not shared by any of his characters. He sees them merely as puppets with predetermined roles, rather than as men and women working out their destinies with horizons limited by their ignorance of the future.

Throughout his novel Ainsworth portrays Lady Jane Grey as noble, self-assured, pious and guileless, but trapped by the schemes of politicians. Her loyalty to her family and her faith, and the pressures exerted by them, lead to her ultimate destruction. Unfortunately the novelist never manages to persuade us that Jane's dilemma is tragic. Any attempt at establishing a personality for her is inevitably hampered by the clutter of plot in which she is embedded, and by Ainsworth's own imaginative limitations. He has not planned an ambitious psychological study of an historical figure . . . , but in choosing so conspicuous and morally justified a heroine, he leads us to expect a more investigatory novel than he gives us. The status of the central figure is diminished by a general lack of precision in understanding either Jane's private world or her public one. In the middle sections of the novel she even seems to fade from view while the novelist concentrates on other strands in his plot. At the end of his novel, her imprisonment, trial and execution are really little more than a pendant to a story which has effectively concluded elsewhere in the marriages of Mary Tudor, Cuthbert Cholmondeley and Xit.

Jane is presented as the champion of Protestant rectitude and consequently in the mainstream of the development of English culture. Even though he gives no details of the nature of her theological arguments (one should be grateful that Ainsworth does not make the attempt), the novelist shows her Catholic opponents to be retrogressive, unscrupulous, and bigoted. When Jane is offered pardon for herself and her husband in exchange for her submission to Rome, the offer is presented as blackmail, and she predictably rejects it. Ainsworth adds weight to Jane's moral stand by making all the virtuous characters in the novel sympathetic to it, and leaving no room for spiritual, political, or psychological subtlety. In their last interview the Queen offers Lady Jane a final chance of saving her life by accepting conversion:

> 'Your highness will not impose these fatal conditions upon me?' cried Jane, distractedly.
>
> 'On no other will I accede,' replied Mary, peremptorily. 'Nay, I have gone too far already. But my strong sympathy for you as a wife, and my zeal for my religion, are my inducements. Embrace our faith, and I pardon your husband.'
>
> 'I cannot,' replied Jane, in accents of despair; 'I will die for him, but I cannot destroy my soul alive.'
>
> 'Then you shall perish altogether,' replied Mary, fiercely. . . .

It is a typical enough piece of dialogue from the novel, with the adverbs pointing the melodrama rather than suggesting emotion or conviction. The language deflates the passion which Ainsworth wants us to read into the scene, and the characters seem to be doing little more than assuming poses in a *tableau* representing defined rights and wrongs.

All the important conflicts are presented as clumsily. If Jane Grey's tragedy is never given a sufficiently forceful expression, the study of Mary Tudor is too deeply ambiguous for it ever to persuade us that the Queen may have been wronged by generations of Protestant historians. In his Preface, however, Ainsworth leads us to expect that he truly wishes to challenge the conventions:

> To those, who conceive that the Author has treated the character of Queen Mary with too great leniency, he can only affirm that he has written according to his conviction of the truth. Mary's worst fault as a woman—her sole fault as a sovereign—was bigotry: and it is time that the cloud, which prejudice has cast over her, should be dispersed.

The very use of the term 'bigotry' here suggests that the pretence of open-mindedness cannot long withstand the pressure of a traditional view of Mary, who, as Dickens reminded his readers in *Barnaby Rudge,* did more harm in her grave than she ever did on the throne. Religious and historical prejudices are predetermined. Jane, though no persecutrix, is every bit as 'bigoted' in her opinions as Mary; both are unmovable, but Jane is admirable for her stand, while Mary is open to the strongest criticism. In nearly all her actions in the novel Mary is seen to justify the antagonistic attitudes of historians, while the book as a whole, with its asides and assumptions as to the virtues of Jane and Elizabeth, serves to reaffirm the convention.

Ainsworth's portrait of Mary as Queen closely follows the pattern, to be found elsewhere in his novels, of what he believes to be proper in a sovereign. Arbitrary decisions are approved of as evidence of a monarchic will to rule, but royal immovability is relieved by the sort of bluff sense of humour which the novelist takes to be indicative of superior understanding. Mary is most honoured, and best obeyed, by the novel's apolitical yeomen-of-the-guard, servants, and faithful citizens, and from them we gather that open criticism of a monarch is tantamount to treason. The limits to Mary's humanity may be contrasted to Jane's learned simplicity, and to Elizabeth's dignity and political acumen, but she is never explicitly criticised for her actions. . . . [Ambiguity] works against Ainsworth's attempt to offer an historical judgement; within the novel Mary is respected for her decisions, outside it we are told that posterity has proved her wrong. The two options are allowed to co-exist without any resolution or balance being offered through the narrative.

In spite of, or perhaps because of, their intellectual slightness, a few of Ainsworth's early novels have remained popular well into the twentieth century. A taste for them may well have been restimulated by their closest parallels as entertainments, the simplified images of European history projected by Hollywood in the 1930s. (pp. 41-5)

In Ainsworth's work the common complaint that the English historical novel is outside the mainstream of fiction might seem to be justified. In *The Tower of London,* he had dealt with a period which contained within it a conflict of ideas which was to influence the subsequent history of Britain, but he had taken historical events and trivialised them as a source for a sensational plot. . . . [His] novels were destructive of the real potential of historical fiction. (pp. 45-6)

> *Andrew Sanders, "Introduction" and "A Gothic Revival: William Harrison Ainsworth's 'The Tower of London',"* in his *The Victorian Historical Novel, 1840-1880, St. Martin's Press, 1979, pp. 1-31, 32-46.* *

ADDITIONAL BIBLIOGRAPHY

Crossley, James. "William Harrison Ainsworth." Introduction to *Ballads . . . ,* by William Harrison Ainsworth, pp. xiii-xxiii. London: George Routledge and Sons, 1872.

An early biographical sketch originally published in the *Manchester School Register*.

Duller, Mr. [pseudonym of Francis Mahony; also wrote under pseudonym of Father Prout]. ''The Cruel Murder of Old Father Prout by a Barber's Apprentice.'' *Bentley's Miscellany* XI (1842): 467-72.

A lengthy doggerel poem in which Ainsworth is portrayed as a barber's apprentice who bores customers with tales of Newgate, which he scribbles on curling papers.

Ellis, S. M. *William Harrison Ainsworth and His Friends*. 2 vols. London: John Lane The Bodley Head, 1911.

The standard biography.

Evans, John. ''The Early Life of William Harrison Ainsworth.'' *The Manchester Quarterly* I, No. II (April 1882): 136-55.

Traces Ainsworth's early literary career. Evans suggests that *Mervyn Clitheroe* is based on the author's experiences as a schoolboy.

Green, Roger Lancelyn. ''Stories of Adventure.'' In his *Tellers of Tales: British Authors of Children's Books from 1800-1964*, rev. ed., pp. 74-84. New York: Franklin Watts, 1965.*

Includes Ainsworth's novels in a discussion of adventure fiction popular with young readers. Green contends that the elements of gore, horror, intrigue and the supernatural in Ainsworth's works appeal to children but render the novels unreadable to adults.

Hill, Jonathan E. ''Cruikshank, Ainsworth, and Tableau Illustration.'' *Victorian Studies* 23, No. 4 (Summer 1980): 429-59.*

Discusses the collaboration between author and artist. According to Hill, the phenomenal success of Ainsworth's novels was due, in part, to Cruikshank's illustrations, which were often adapted as stage sets for dramatizations of the books.

Lamb, Charles. Letter to William Harrison Ainsworth, May 7, 1822. In *The Lambs: Their Lives, Their Friends, and Their Correspondence*, by William Carew Hazlitt, pp. 195-96. London: Elkin Mathews, 1897.

A letter in which Lamb thanks Ainsworth for dedicating *Poems* to him. Lamb calls the work ''prettily told, the language often finely poetical,'' but notes that Ainsworth is occasionally careless and redundant.

Mason, Leo. ''William Harrison Ainsworth.'' *The Dickensian* XXXV, No. 251 (Summer 1939): 155-61.*

A comparison of Ainsworth and Dickens. Mason observes that though the novelists were equally popular in the late 1830's, Dickens's genius has endured while Ainsworth's reputation has waned.

Pitcher, Edward W.R. ''Poe's Borrowings from Ainsworth's 'The Falls of Ohiopyle'.'' *American Notes and Queries* XIX, No. 1 (September 1980): 4-6.*

Compares Ainsworth's short story from *December Tales* with passages from Poe's *Narrative of Arthur Gordon Pym*. Pitcher theorizes that early reading of Ainsworth's Gothic tales influenced Poe, who unconsciously adapted both their subject matter and phrasing for his own writing.

Simmons, James C. ''Of Kettledrums and Trumpets: The Early Victorian Followers of Scott.'' *Studies in Scottish Literature* VI, No. 1 (July 1968): 47-59.*

Pronounces Ainsworth an imitator of Scott who combined all the weaknesses and none of the strengths of the earlier novelist.

Jane Austen

1775-1817

English novelist.

The following entry presents criticism of Austen's novel *Pride and Prejudice* (1813). For additional information on Austen's career and *Pride and Prejudice*, see *NCLC*, Vol. 1.

A perennial favorite of readers and critics alike, *Pride and Prejudice* is often regarded as Austen's consummate achievement and one of English literature's greatest novels. Utilizing an outwardly limited range of subject matter and emotional expression, she created a work celebrated for its wit, artistic economy, polished style, and insightful understanding of the subtle motivations that shape human interactions. In Elizabeth Bennet, Austen brought to life one of the most vibrant, intelligent, and popular heroines in the English novel. *Pride and Prejudice* also abounds with other characters—from the proud and taciturn Fitzwilliam Darcy to a small gallery of comic personalities, including Mr. Collins, Mrs. Bennet, and Lady Catherine de Bourgh—that have proved memorable to generations of readers. Modern critics have praised both the artfully conceived dramatic structure of the novel and its almost classical sense of restraint and proportion. While some writers have faulted the limitations of the novel's world view, many consider *Pride and Prejudice* one of the most perfectly realized masterpieces of prose fiction published during the nineteenth century.

Austen began writing while she was still living at her childhood home at Steventon Rectory in Hampshire, England. Her life at Steventon, though sheltered from the world at large, gave her an intimate knowledge of a segment of English society— the landed gentry—that was to provide the materials for most of her fiction, and by 1787 Austen had already begun to produce stories, dramas, and short novels. In 1795 she commenced writing *Elinor and Marianne*, an early version of her first published novel, *Sense and Sensibility*. One year later, she started *First Impressions*, the work that eventually evolved into *Pride and Prejudice*. When Austen finished *First Impressions* in 1797, her father submitted it to a London publisher. Although rejected, the story remained a popular favorite among the circle of relations and acquaintances with whom Austen shared her writings. Scholars have suggested that she was still working intermittently on *First Impressions* when she moved to Bath in 1801 and continued to do so prior to 1805 when, following the deaths of both her father and a close friend, she appears to have given up writing for almost five years. In 1809, after a difficult period of traveling and staying with various relatives, Austen settled once again in Hampshire at Chawton Cottage, a location close to her former home at Steventon. There she resumed writing and in 1809-10 began revising the manuscript of *Sense and Sensibility* for publication. By the time that work appeared in 1811, Austen was recasting *First Impressions* into *Pride and Prejudice* in its present form. On January 28, 1813, *Pride and Prejudice* was published anonymously in London.

The precise relationship between *First Impressions* and *Pride and Prejudice* has never been discovered since no copy of the earlier manuscript is known to exist. Scholars, however, have

speculated on various possibilities, including the theory that *First Impressions*, like *Elinor and Marianne*, may have originally been written in epistolary form. Critics and biographers have also debated both the extent to which Austen revised *First Impressions* and the dates when she may have done so, with largely inconclusive results. While some researchers argue that the novel was substantially rewritten in either 1797-1804 or 1810-12, others suggest that the text as it is known today was largely complete in 1797, with only minor revisions by Austen at a later date. Critics generally agree, however, that she was forced to abandon the title "First Impressions" after a work with the same name was published in 1800. Most commentators believe that the author then borrowed the phrase "pride and prejudice" from a passage in Fanny Burney's novel *Cecilia* for the new title.

The plot of *Pride and Prejudice* revolves around a series of misunderstandings between Elizabeth, a lively young middle-class woman with a satirical temperament, and Darcy, an unconsciously arrogant and enormously wealthy upper-class young man who becomes her suitor. Initially offended by Darcy's apparently haughty manner, Elizabeth determines "to be uncommonly clever in taking so decided a dislike to him." Darcy, however, finds himself reluctantly drawn to Elizabeth despite the "inferiority of her connections" and the "want of propriety'' displayed by her son-in-law-hunting mother, officer-chasing younger sisters, and kind but indolent and cynical father. Elizabeth is taken entirely by surprise when Darcy proposes. Her prejudice against him and the sense that he is lowering himself, which he communicates during his proposal, cause her to summarily reject his offer of marriage. The two part for a time, but not before Darcy has written a letter explaining his past conduct and absolving himself of most of the offenses with which Elizabeth charged him. The remainder of the novel traces the series of events that eventually leads to their reconciliation. When Darcy renews his offer of marriage, he does so with the knowledge that his pride had made him arrogant and insensitive, and Elizabeth accepts him fully aware that her precipitous judgment had led her to mistake his real character. In their union both find happiness and a better understanding of themselves.

The critical history of *Pride and Prejudice* is in most respects indistinguishable from that of Austen's writings as a whole, despite the novel's long-standing popularity with readers and the tendency of critics to rank it (with *Emma* and *Mansfield Park*) as the author's finest work. During Austen's lifetime, both her anonymous mode of publication and quiet life prevented her from being widely known: approximately fifteen early reviews of her works have been uncovered, including only three on *Pride and Prejudice*. B. C. Southam has pointed out, however, that while the critical press granted limited attention to the work when it first appeared, in light of the harsh treatment granted most novels, *Pride and Prejudice* was ''remarkably well-received,'' with anonymous articles in the *British Critic* (see *NCLC*, Vol. 1) and the *Critical Review* praising Austen's characterization and her portrayal of domestic life. Additional early commentary exists in the diaries and letters of such prominent contemporary readers as Mary Russell Mitford and Henry Crabb Robinson, both of whom expressed admiration for the work's characters, realism, and freedom from the trappings of Gothic fiction. After the initial reviews of the novel, however, little substantial criticism appeared during the first half of the nineteenth century. Influential articles on Austen by Sir Walter Scott in 1815 and Archbishop Richard Whateley in 1821 (see *NCLC*, Vol. 1) derive their importance primarily from their analysis of the general qualities of her fiction rather than from their insight into individual novels. Scott recorded in a journal entry on *Pride and Prejudice* his respect for Austen's ability to render ''commonplace things and characters interesting'' (see *NCLC*, Vol. 1). Apart from such private commentary, however, recent scholarship indicates that less than a dozen articles devoted to Austen were published in the period from 1820 to 1850, none of them giving more than cursory attention to *Pride and Prejudice*.

Standing in marked contrast to Scott, Charlotte Brontë was one of a number of prominent mid-nineteenth-century authors who harshly criticized the ''commonplace'' aspects of *Pride and Prejudice*. Writing to the critic George Henry Lewes, Brontë acknowledged the accuracy and perfect realism of the novel, but faulted its narrow range of materials and lack of ''*poetry*,'' imperfections that in her view excluded Austen from the ranks of ''great'' authors. Literary historians interpret Brontë's remarks as exemplifying a widespread Victorian distaste for the outwardly restricted subject matter and avoidance of passionate emotion that characterize Austen's writings; her comments also anticipate one of the major focuses of critical writing on *Pride and Prejudice* (and Austen's works in general) during the late-nineteenth and twentieth centuries.

One of the most vocal advocates of Austen's writings during the nineteenth century, Lewes was also one of the first writers to discuss at length the nature of the critical problem that Brontë had articulated. Lewes, as well as most subsequent Austen critics, focused on the question of Austen's avowed perfection of style and structure in *Pride and Prejudice* versus the seemingly inescapable limitations of the fictional world she portrayed. Some critics have maintained that despite its masterful execution and aesthetic integrity *Pride and Prejudice* cannot be considered a great novel because it fails to address such all-important subjects as death, religion, and human sexuality. Yet others have argued both that the novel's artistic brilliance raises it above questions of subject matter and that beneath its comic exterior it does in fact confront the ''larger'' issues of life. Although Lewes's series of articles and observations on Austen was oriented chiefly toward an appreciation of her works as a whole, he summed up what many nineteenth-century critics saw as the greatest strengths of *Pride and Prejudice*: its seamless structure and artistic precision.

The publication in 1870 of the first major biography of Austen, by her nephew James Edward Austen-Leigh, inspired a number of important articles on the novelist by such critics as Margaret Oliphant and Richard Simpson. Modern scholars, however, have come to see the attempts of Austen's family and her legions of staunch admirers (christened ''The Janeites'' by Rudyard Kipling) to portray her as a benign and pious ''spinster aunt'' as ultimately inhibiting the progress of serious Austen criticism. Southam has contended that despite occasional outbursts of interpretive acumen in the late Victorian era, the majority of criticism presented only ''a sentimental portrait of Jane Austen as a kind of Sunday writer, an amateur genius, a gentlewoman who surprised her family and herself with the success of her books.'' Thus, while both Austen's life and works received increasing attention at the end of the nineteenth century—including a lengthy discussion of characterization, narrative perspective, and satire in *Pride and Prejudice* by George Saintsbury—it remained for twentieth-century critics to explore in depth such facets of the novel as its structure, language, irony, and sociological background.

Despite groundbreaking essays on Austen by A. C. Bradley and Reginald Farrer in the first two decades of the twentieth century (see *NCLC*, Vol. 1), R. W. Chapman's seminal edition of the novels in 1923, and the early feminist perspective on *Pride and Prejudice* by Virginia Woolf in 1929, a number of scholars have asserted that modern Austen criticism began with the publication in 1939 of Mary Lascelles's *Jane Austen and Her Art*, the first comprehensive study of the author and her works. In her analysis of *Pride and Prejudice*, Lascelles explored its carefully detailed and deliberately plotted structure, contesting the notion that Austen was an unconscious, ''natural'' artist and paving the way for the proliferation of articles and books on Austen's art that began in the 1940s, gathered momentum in the 1950s, and flourished in recent years.

Among the most influential commentaries published on *Pride and Prejudice* in the 1940s was that of Samuel Kliger, who posited that the novel derived its structure from a series of variations on the popular eighteenth-century theme of nature versus art. According to Kliger, Elizabeth and Darcy's union can be seen as an ideal balancing of the art-nature dialectic. The structure of the novel has also been illuminated in the last three decades in notable studies by such critics as Dorothy Van Ghent, Mark Schorer, A. Walton Litz, and Norman Page. The language and dynamic dialogue of *Pride and Prejudice* have been discussed by various critics, among them Van Ghent, Page, and Howard S. Babb. During the 1950s, Reuben Arthur Brower (see *NCLC*, Vol. 1) and Marvin Mudrick contributed significantly to critical understanding of the complex patterns of irony and wit in *Pride and Prejudice*, demonstrating Austen's previously unheralded sophistication as a satirist. Mudrick is considered perhaps the most important critic to further develop an approach that was first fully elaborated by D. W. Harding in 1940 (see *NCLC*, Vol. 1). Harding, Mudrick, and others suggested that there was a darker side to Austen's irony and humor beneath the veneer that she described in the case of *Pride and Prejudice* as "too light and bright and sparkling." In Mudrick's view, Austen's use of irony is the primary characteristic of her fiction, one that reveals her often ambivalent perspective on the social values of her world. A number of writers have attempted to analyze *Pride and Prejudice* within the context of its contemporary social, political, and literary climate. Martha Satz, for example, maintained that *Pride and Prejudice* represents a fundamentally conservative world view, and Schorer asserted that the novel reflects the contemporary conflict between feudalism and mercantilism in English society.

Although the perfection versus limitations controversy figures prominently in recent critical assessments of *Pride and Prejudice,* such commentators as Brigid Brophy have argued that beneath the novel's deceptively superficial surface lies a profound comprehension of the social, economic, and sexual forces that influence men and women—one which critics have still to explore and adequately understand. Recent surveys of Austen scholarship suggest that the study of her works has not yet fully matured in the manner of authors of similar importance, a situation that augurs well for the continued critical appreciation and elevation in stature of *Pride and Prejudice*. The novel remains a rare example of an acknowledged classic of English literature whose interest for scholars is closely paralleled by its enormous popularity.

JANE AUSTEN (letter dates 1813)

[*In the following excerpts from letters written to her sister, Austen describes the experience of receiving a published copy of* Pride and Prejudice *(her "own darling child"). Austen suggests that the novel might have benefited from the inclusion of occasional passages of serious or contemplative prose that would contrast with its light and generally animated style.*]

[January 29, 1813]

I want to tell you that I have got my own darling child from London. . . . Miss Benn dined with us on the very day of the books [*sic*] coming & in the evening we set fairly at it, and read half the first vol. to her, prefacing that, having intelligence from Henry that such a work would soon appear, we had desired him to send it whenever it came out, and I believe it passed with her unsuspected. She was amused, poor soul! *That* she could not help, you know, with two such people to lead the way, but she really does seem to admire Elizabeth. I must confess that I think her as delightful a creature as ever appeared in print, and how I shall be able to tolerate those who do not like *her* at least I do not know. There are a few typical errors;

and a 'said he,' or a 'said she,' would sometimes make the dialogue more immediately clear; but

> I do not write for such dull elves
> As have not a great deal of ingenuity themselves.

The second volume is shorter than I could wish, but the difference is not so much in reality as in look, there being a larger proportion of narrative in that part. I have lop't and crop't so successfully, however, that I imagine it must be rather shorter than *S. & S.* altogether. (pp. 297-99)

• • • • •

[February 4, 1813]

Your letter was truly welcome, and I am much obliged to you all for your praise; it came at a right time, for I had had some fits of disgust. Our second evening's reading to Miss Benn had not pleased me so well, but I believe something must be attributed to my mother's too rapid way of getting on: and though she perfectly understands the characters herself, she cannot speak as they ought. Upon the whole, however, I am quite vain enough and well satisfied enough. The work is rather too light, and bright, and sparkling; it wants shade; it wants to be stretched out here and there with a long chapter of sense, if it could be had; if not, of solemn specious nonsense, about something unconnected with the story; an essay on writing, a critique on Walter Scott, or the history of Buonaparté, or anything that would form a contrast, and bring the reader with increased delight to the playfulness and epigrammatism of the general style. I doubt your quite agreeing with me here. I know your starched notions. (pp. 299-300)

> *Jane Austen, in letters to Cassandra Austen on January 29 and February 4, 1813, in her* Jane Austen's Letters to Her Sister Cassandra and Others, *edited by R. W. Chapman, second edition, Oxford University Press, 1952, pp. 296-99, 299-301.*

THE CRITICAL REVIEW (essay date 1813)

[*In the following excerpt, the anonymous critic praises characterization in* Pride and Prejudice *as well as the novel's scenes of domestic life.*]

Instead of the whole interest of the tale hanging upon one or two characters, as is generally the case in novels, the fair author of [*Pride and Prejudice*] introduces us, at once, to a whole family, every individual of which excites the interest, and very agreeably divides the attention of the reader. (pp. 318-19)

On the character of Elizabeth, the main interest of the novel depends; and the fair author has shewn considerable ingenuity in the mode of bringing about the final *eclaircissment* between her and Darcy. Elizabeth's sense and conduct are of a superior order to those of the common heroines of novels. From her independence of character, which is kept within the proper line of decorum, and her well-timed sprightliness, she teaches the man of Family-Pride to know himself. (p. 323)

An excellent lesson may be learned from the elopement of Lydia—the work also shows the folly of letting young girls have their own way, and the danger which they incur in associating with the officers, who may be quartered in or near their residence. The character of Wickham is very well portrayed;—we fancy, that our authoress had Joseph Surface before her eyes when she sketched it; as well as the lively Beatrice, when she drew the portrait of Elizabeth. Many such silly women as Mrs. Bennet may be found; and numerous parsons like Mr. Collins, who are every thing to every body; and servile in the extreme to their superiors. Mr. Collins is indeed a notable object.

The sentiments, which are dispersed over the work, do great credit to the *sense* and *sensibility* of the authoress. The line she draws between the prudent and the mercenary in matrimonial concerns, may be useful to our fair readers. . . . (pp. 323-24)

[This performance] rises very superior to any novel we have lately met with in the delineation of domestic scenes. Nor is there one character which appears flat, or obtrudes itself upon the notice of the reader with troublesome impertinence. There is not one person in the drama with whom we could readily dispense;—they have all their proper places; and fill their several stations, with great credit to themselves, and much satisfaction to the reader. (p. 324)

> *A review of "Pride and Prejudice," in* The Critical Review, *n.s. Vol. III, No. III, March, 1813, pp. 318-24.*

ANNE ISABELLA MILBANKE (letter date 1813)

[*Milbanke was a mathematician and heiress who later became the wife of the English Romantic poet George Gordon, Lord Byron. In the following excerpt from a letter to her mother, she praises various aspects of* Pride and Prejudice.]

I have finished the Novel called **Pride and Prejudice,** which I think a very superior work. It depends not on any of the common resources of Novel writers, no drownings, nor conflagrations, nor runaway horses, nor lapdogs & parrots, nor chambermaids & milliners, nor rencontres and disguises. I really think it the *most probable* fiction I have ever read. It is not a crying book, but the interest is very strong, especially for Mr Darcy. The characters which are not amiable are diverting, and all of them are consistently supported. I wish much to know who is the author or *ess* as I am told.

> *Anne Isabella Milbanke, in an extract from a letter to her mother on May 1, 1813, in* Lord Byron's Wife *by Malcolm Elwin, 1962. Reprint by John Murray, 1974, p. 159.*

JANE AUSTEN (letter date 1813)

[*According to biographers, Austen was fond of speculating about her characters and endowing them with a life outside the novels. In the following excerpt, she writes fancifully about searching for portraits of Jane and Elizabeth Bennet at several art exhibitions she attended in London.*]

Henry & I went to the Exhibition in Spring Gardens. It is not thought a good collection, but I was very well pleased—particularly . . . with a small portrait of Mrs. Bingley, excessively like her. I went in hopes of seeing one of her Sister, but there was no Mrs. Darcy;—perhaps however, I may find her in the Great Exhibition which we shall go to, if we have time;—I have no chance of her in the collection of Sir Joshua Reynolds's Paintings which is now shewing in Pall Mall, & which we are also to visit.—Mrs. Bingley's is exactly herself, size, shaped face, features & sweetness; there never was a greater likeness. She is dressed in a white gown, with green ornaments, which convinces me of what I had always supposed, that green was

a favourite colour with her. I dare say Mrs. D. will be in Yellow. (pp. 309-10)

. . . . .

We have been both to the Exhibition & Sir J. Reynolds',— and I am disappointed, for there was nothing like Mrs. D. at either. I can only imagine that Mr. D. prizes any Picture of her too much to like it should be exposed to the public eye.— I can imagine he [would] have that sort of feeling—that mixture of Love, Pride & Delicacy. (p. 312)

> *Jane Austen, in a letter to Cassandra Austen on May 24, 1813, in her* Jane Austen's Letters to Her Sister Cassandra and Others, *edited by R. W. Chapman, second edition, Oxford University Press, 1952, pp. 309-13.*

M[ARY] R[USSELL] MITFORD (letter date 1814)

[*Mitford was an English sketch writer, dramatist, poet, novelist, and critic whose legacy to English literature includes some of the nineteenth century's most enduring sketches of country life. In a letter to a friend, she comments on Elizabeth's character.*]

The want of elegance is almost the only want in Miss Austen. I have not read her **Mansfield Park;** but it is impossible not to feel in every line of **Pride and Prejudice,** in every word of "Elizabeth," the entire want of taste which could produce so pert, so worldly a heroine as the beloved of such a man as Darcy. Wickham is equally bad. Oh! they were just fit for each other, and I can not forgive that delightful Darcy for parting them. Darcy should have married Jane. He is, of all the admirable characters, the best designed and the best sustained. I quite agree with you in preferring Miss Austen to Miss Edgeworth. If the former had a little more taste, a little more perception of the graceful, as well as of the humorous, I know not indeed any one to whom I should not prefer her. There is none of the hardness, the cold selfishness of Miss Edgeworth about her writings; she is in a much better humor with the world; she preaches no sermons; she wants nothing but the *beau-idéal* of the female character to be a perfect novel writer; and perhaps even that *beau-idéal* would only be missed by such a *petite maîtresse* in books as myself, who would never admit a muse into my library till she had been taught to dance by the Graces. (p. 231)

> *M[ary] R[ussell] Mitford, in a letter to Sir William Elford on December 20, 1814, in her* The Life of Mary Russell Mitford, Told by Herself in Letters to Her Friends, *Vol. I, edited by Rev. A. G. K. L'Estrange, Harper & Brothers, Publishers, 1870, pp. 229-32.**

WILLIAM GIFFORD (letter date 1815)

[*Gifford was an English critic and poet who served as editor of the conservative* Quarterly Review *from 1809 to 1824. In the excerpt below, he expresses admiration for* Pride and Prejudice.]

I have for the first time looked into **Pride and Prejudice;** and it is really a very pretty thing. No dark passages; no secret chambers; no wind-howlings in long galleries; no drops of blood upon a rusty dagger—things that should now be left to ladies' maids and sentimental washerwomen.

> *William Gifford, in an extract from a letter to John Murray in 1815, in* A Publisher and His Friends: Memoir and Correspondence of the Late John Mur-

ray, Vol. I *by Samuel Smiles, Charles Scribner's Sons, 1891, p. 282.*

HENRY CRABB ROBINSON   (diary date 1819)

[*A nineteenth-century English journalist, Robinson is remembered for his voluminous correspondence and diaries, which chronicle London's social and intellectual history. In the following excerpt, he describes reading* Pride and Prejudice *late into the night and praises the novel's dialogue and characters.*]

I sat up till two, as I did last night, to finish *Pride and Prejudice.* This novel I consider as one of the most excellent of the works of our female novelists. Its merit lies in the characters, and in the perfectly colloquial style of the dialogue. Mrs. Bennet, the foolish mother, who cannot conceal her projects to get rid of her daughters, is capitally drawn. There is a thick-headed servile parson, also a masterly sketch. His stupid letters and her ridiculous speeches are as delightful as wit. The two daughters are well contrasted—the gentle and candid Jane and the lively but prejudiced Elizabeth, are both good portraits, and the development of the passion between Elizabeth and the proud Darcy, who at first hate each other, is executed with skill and effect.

> *Henry Crabb Robinson, in a diary entry of January 12, 1819, in his* Henry Crabb Robinson on Books and Their Writers, Vol. I, *edited by Edith J. Morley, J. M. Dent and Sons Limited, 1938, p. 227.*

ATKINSON'S CASKET   (essay date 1832)

[*In the following excerpt from a review of the first American edition of* Pride and Prejudice *(published under the title* Elizabeth Bennet; or, Pride and Prejudice*), the anonymous critic praises Austen's realistic and perceptive portrayal of society as well as her avoidance of "sickly sentimentality."*]

[*Elizabeth Bennet; or, Pride and Prejudice*] possesses merits of more than an ordinary character. The writer, Miss Austin [*sic*], appears to have observed life under various aspects, surveyed the influence of the different ranks of society upon each other, and viewed the whole in their social condition, with a clear philosophic eye; and has happily presented her observations in a manner as creditable to herself, as they will prove useful and entertaining to her readers. Her family pictures are admirably drawn; her domestic pictures are pleasing and rational, and her several characters are exhibited with a fidelity and truth, worthy the highest commendation.

Miss Austin has, with the British public, heretofore held a high rank in the literary world, and we are sure that her reputation will suffer no diminution from the work before us. She displays life as it is to be found every day; and her book is not rendered disgusting by any sickly sentimentality, with which this class of writings unfortunately too much abounds.

The plot of this novel is simple, natural and intelligible. The characters are few, and the whole structure of the novel [is] such as to insure it a ready passport to public favor, and a large share of popularity. (p. 470)

> *A. C. D., in a review of "Elizabeth Bennet; or, Pride and Prejudice," in* Atkinson's Casket, *Vol. VII, No. 10, October, 1832, pp. 470-73.*

C. BELL [PSEUDONYM OF CHARLOTTE BRONTË]   (letter date 1848)

[*Brontë was an English novelist and poet whose vivid, skillfully constructed novels, including* Jane Eyre: An Autobiography, *broke the nineteenth-century fictional stereotype of women as submissive, dependent, beautiful, and ignorant. In the passage below, written in reaction to a review of recent novels in which the critic George Henry Lewes had praised Austen, Brontë insists that* Pride and Prejudice *lacks life and depth of subject matter.*]

Why do you like Miss Austen so very much? I am puzzled on that point. What induced you to say that you would have rather written *Pride and Prejudice* or *Tom Jones,* than any of the Waverley Novels?

I had not seen *Pride and Prejudice* till I read that sentence of yours, and then I got the book. And what did I find? An accurate daguerreotyped portrait of a commonplace face; a carefully fenced, highly cultivated garden, with neat borders and delicate flowers; but no glance of a bright, vivid physiognomy, no open country, no fresh air, no blue hill, no bonny beck. I should hardly like to live with her ladies and gentlemen, in their elegant but confined houses. These observations will probably irritate you, but I shall run the risk.

Now I can understand admiration of George Sand; for though I never saw any of her works which I admired throughout (even *Consuelo,* which is the best, or the best that I have read, appears to me to couple strange extravagance with wondrous excellence), yet she has a grasp of mind which, if I cannot fully comprehend, I can very deeply respect: she is sagacious and profound; Miss Austen is only shrewd and observant. (p. 387)

> *C. Bell [pseudonym of Charlotte Brontë], in a letter to George Henry Lewes on January 12, 1848, in* The Brontës: Life and Letters, Vol. I *by Clement Shorter, Hodder and Stoughton, 1908, pp. 386-87.**

[GEORGE HENRY LEWES]   (essay date 1860)

[*Lewes was one of the most versatile men of letters in the Victorian era. Critics often cite his influence on the novelist George Eliot, to whom he was a companion and mentor, as his principal contribution to English letters, but they also credit him with critical acumen in his literary commentary, most notably in his dramatic criticism. In the excerpt below, Lewes praises the construction and artistic economy of* Pride and Prejudice.]

Pride and Prejudice is a finely-constructed work, and shows what a fine artistic sense Miss Austen had. The ease and naturalness of the evolution of the story are so perfect, that only very critical readers are aware of its skill in selection. Take it to pieces, examine the characters, scenes, and dialogues, in relation to each other and to the story, and you will find that there is nothing superfluous—that all this variety is secretly tending to one centre; that all this ease of nature, which looks so like the ordinary life of every day, is subordinate to the principles of Economy and Selection; and that nothing is dragged in, nothing is superfluous. Then turn to *Tom Jones,* and remember that while scarcely any one has insisted on Miss Austen's construction, every one insists on the excellence of Fielding. (p. 335)

> [*George Henry Lewes], "A Word about 'Tom Jones'," in* Blackwood's Magazine, *Vol. LXXXVII, No. DXXXIII, March, 1860, pp. 331-41.**

[MARGARET OLIPHANT]   (essay date 1870)

[*Oliphant was a prolific nineteenth-century Scottish novelist, biographer, critic, and historian who contributed regularly to* Blackwood's Edinburgh Magazine. *Here, she discusses Austen's portrayal of the characters of Mr. Collins, Elizabeth, and Darcy, contending that the novelist's "secondary characters, in their various and vivid originality, carried the day over her first." For additional commentary by Oliphant on* Pride and Prejudice, *see the excerpt listed under* Blackwood's Edinburgh Magazine *in NCLC, Vol. 1.*]

[The background of *Pride and Prejudice*] is all so common—never rising above the level of ordinary life, leaving nothing (so think the uninstructed) to imagination or invention at all—and yet what other hand has ever been able to detach such a group from the obscure level of their ordinary fate? Mr. Collins, for instance, who is the heir of Mr. Bennet's entailed estate, and who, with a certain quaint sense of justice which enhances his self-importance, comes prepared to propose to one of the daughters, whom he is obliged to deprive of their inheritance. We give so much explanation, with a certain shame at the very possibility that Mr. Collins should want a formal introduction to any portion of the British public; but yet it is true that the young ones are not so well up in the relationships of the Bennets as we could wish them to be. The sublime and undisturbed complacence of his arrival, when he compliments Mrs. Bennet on having so fine a family of daughters, "and added that he did not doubt her seeing them all in time well disposed of in marriage," is inimitable. . . . When he receives Elizabeth's refusal to marry him with undisturbed complacency, attributing it to "your wish of increasing my love by suspense, according to the usual practice of elegant females," the situation rises to one of the most genuine comedy, and our only regret is that Mr. Collins's adventures have never been adapted for the stage.

Miss Austen does not even let her victim escape her when he is married and has left the central scene. She pursues him to his home with the smile growing a little broader in her eyes. "Elizabeth was prepared to see him in all his glory; and she could not help fancying that in displaying the good proportions of his room, its aspect and its furniture, he addressed himself particularly to her, as if wishing to make her feel what she had lost in refusing him." His pompous assurance that "he has no hesitation in saying" that his goddess and patroness, Lady Catherine, will include his cousin in her invitations—his triumph when the party is asked to dinner—the pride with which he takes his seat at the foot of the table by her ladyship's command, looking "as if he felt that life could furnish nothing greater"—the "delighted alacrity" with which he carved and ate and praised—his game at cards with his august patroness after dinner, in which "he was employed in agreeing to everything her ladyship said, thanking her for every fish he won, and apologising if he thought he won too many,"—are all so many touches which add perfection to the picture; and when we take our parting glance of Mr. Collins, watching the country road from his "book-room," and hastening to inform his wife and her friends every time Miss De Burgh drives by in her phaeton, we feel that the power of consistent remorseless ridicule can no further go. There is not a moment's faltering, nor the ghost of an inclination on the part of the author to depart from her wonderful conception. He stands before us tall and grave and pompous, wrapt in a cloud of solemn vanity, servility, stupidity, and spitefulness, but without the faintest gleam of self-consciousness or suspicion of the ridiculous figure he cuts; and his author, with no pity in her heart, walks round and round him, giving here and there a skilful touch to bring

out the picture. It is amazing in its unity and completeness—a picture perhaps unrivalled, certainly unsurpassed, in its way. It is, we repeat, cruel in its perfection.

Whether it is not too cruel to make the wife of this delightful Mr. Collins share so completely in his creator's estimate of him is a different matter. "When Mr. Collins could be forgotten there was really a great air of comfort throughout, and by Charlotte's evident enjoyment of it Elizabeth supposed he must be often forgotten"—the unflinching narrative goes on. "The room in which the ladies sat was backward, and Elizabeth at first had rather wondered that Charlotte should not prefer the dining-parlour for common use—it was a better-sized room and had a pleasanter aspect; but she soon saw that her friend had an excellent reason for what she did, for Mr. Collins would undoubtedly have been much less in his own apartment had they sat in one equally lively; and she gave Charlotte credit for the arrangement." This is rather diabolical, it must be owned, and there is a calmness of acquiescence in the excellent Charlotte's arrangements which it takes all the reader's fortitude to stomach. It is possible that the very youth of the author may have produced this final stroke of unexampled consistency; for youth is always more or less cruel, and is slow to acknowledge that even the most stupid and arrogant of mortals has his rights.

Mr. Collins, however, is one of the most distinct and original portraits in the great gallery of fiction, and we accept him gladly as a real contribution to our knowledge of humankind; not a contribution certainly which will make us more in love with our fellow-creatures, but yet so lifelike, so perfect and complete, touched with so fine a wit and so keen a perception of the ridiculous, that the picture once seen remains a permanent possession. And when we are told that the Bennet family, with all its humours—the father who is so good and sensible, and yet such an unmitigated bear; the mother whom he despises and ridicules without hesitation, even to his heroine-daughters who accept his sarcastic comments as the most natural thing in the world; the stupid pompous Mary, the loud and noisy, heartless and shameless Lydia—are all drawn with an equally fine and delicate touch, we have not a word to say against it. We acknowledge its truth, and yet we rebel against this pitiless perfection of art. It shocks us as much as it could possibly have shocked Mr. Darcy, to allow that these should be the immediate surroundings of the young woman whom we are called upon to take to our hearts. We blush for the daughter who blushes for her mother. We hate the lover who points out to her, even in self-defence, the vulgarities and follies of her family. A heroine must be superior, it is true, but not so superior as this; and it detracts ever so much from the high qualities of Elizabeth when we see how very ready she is to be moved by a sense of the inferiority of her mother and sisters, how ashamed she is of their ways, and how thankful to think that her home will be at a distance from theirs.

Curiously enough, it would seem that Miss Austen herself felt for this same Elizabeth, and for her alone, the enthusiasm of a parent for a child. . . . "I must confess that I think her as delightful a creature as ever appeared in print, and how I shall be able to tolerate those who do not like *her* at least I do not know" [see excerpt dated January, 1813]. In a later letter she adds—"Fanny's praise is very gratifying. My hopes were tolerably strong of her, but nothing like a certainty. Her liking Darcy and Elizabeth is enough; she might hate all the others if she would." This is as curious a piece of revelation as we know, and proves that the young woman who had just given so original a work to the world was in reality quite unaware of its real power, and had set her heart upon her hero and heroine like any schoolgirl. Our beloved Mr. Collins, upon whom the spectator would be tempted to think a great deal of pains and some proportionate anxiety must have been expended, evidently goes for very little with his maker. It is her lovers she is thinking of, a commonplace pair enough, while we are full of her inimitable fools, who are not at all commonplace. This curious fact disorders our head a little, and makes us ponder and wonder whether our author is in reality the gentle cynic we have concluded her to be, or if she has produced all these marvels of selfish folly unawares, without knowing what she was doing, or meaning anything by it. Genius, however, goes a great deal deeper than conscious meaning, and has its own way, whatever may be the intentions of its owner; and we but smile at the novelist's strange delusion as we set aside Elizabeth and Darcy, the one a young woman very much addicted to making speeches, very pert often, fond of having the last word, and prone to hasty judgments, with really nothing but her prettiness and a certain sharp smartness of talk to recommend her; and the other a very ordinary young man, quite like hosts of other young men, with that appearance of outward pride and *hauteur* which is so captivating to the youthful feminine imagination, though it must be admitted that he possesses an extraordinary amount of candour and real humility of mind under this exterior. It is curious to realise what a shock it must have given to the feelings of the young novelist when she found how little her favourite pair had to do with the success of their own story, and how entirely her secondary characters, in their various and vivid originality, carried the day over her first. (pp. 299-302)

> [Margaret Oliphant], "Miss Austen and Miss Mitford," in Blackwood's Edinburgh Magazine, Vol. CVII, No. DCLIII, March, 1870, pp. 290-313.*

GEORGE SAINTSBURY (essay date 1894)

[*Saintsbury was an English literary historian and critic of the late nineteenth and early twentieth centuries. A prolific writer, Saintsbury composed several histories of English and European literature as well as numerous critical works on individual authors, styles, and periods. Here, he argues that* Pride and Prejudice *is Austen's masterpiece as he explores the novel's structure, major and minor characters, and humor. Saintsbury also compares Austen's satirical skills with those of Joseph Addison and Jonathan Swift. This essay was first published as an introduction to an 1894 edition of* Pride and Prejudice.]

Walt Whitman has somewhere a fine and just distinction between "loving by allowance" and "loving with personal love". This distinction applies to books as well as to men and women; and in the case of the not very numerous authors who are the objects of the personal affection, it brings a curious consequence with it. There is much more difference as to their best work than in the case of those others who are loved "by allowance", by convention, and because it is felt to be the right and proper thing to love them. And in the sect—fairly large and yet unusually choice—of Austenians or Janites, there would probably be found partisans of the claim to primacy of almost every one of the novels. (p. 194)

I, for my part, declare for *Pride and Prejudice* unhesitatingly. It seems to me the most perfect, the most characteristic, the most eminently quintessential of its author's works; and for this contention, in such narrow space as is permitted to me, I propose here to show cause.

In the first place, the book ... was in its first shape written very early, somewhere about 1796, when Miss Austen was barely twenty-one; though it was revised and finished at Chawton some fifteen years later, and was not published till 1813, only four years before her death. I do not know whether, in this combination of the fresh and vigorous projection of youth and the critical revision of middle life, there may be traced the distinct superiority in point of construction which, as it seems to me, it possesses over all the others. The plot, though not elaborate, is almost regular enough for Fielding; hardly a character, hardly an incident, could be retrenched without loss to the story. The elopement of Lydia and Wickham is not, like that of Crawford and Mrs. Rushworth, a *coup de théâtre;* it connects itself in the strictest way with the course of the story earlier, and brings about the *dénouement* with complete propriety. All the minor passages—the loves of Jane and Bingley, the advent of Mr. Collins, the visit to Hunsford, the Derbyshire tour—fit in after the same unostentatious but masterly fashion. There is no attempt at the hide-and-seek, in-and-out business, which in the transactions between Frank Churchill and Jane Fairfax contributes no doubt a good deal to the intrigue of **Emma,** but contributes it in a fashion which I do not think the best feature of that otherwise admirable book. Although Miss Austen always liked something of the misunderstanding kind, which afforded her opportunities for the display of the peculiar and incomparable talent to be noticed presently, she has been satisfied here with the perfectly natural occasions provided by the false account of Darcy's conduct given by Wickham, and by the awkwardness (arising with equal naturalness) from the gradual transformation of Elizabeth's own feelings from positive aversion to actual love. I do not know whether the all-grasping hand of the playwright has ever been laid upon *Pride and Prejudice;* and I dare say that, if it were, the situations would prove not startling or garish enough for the footlights, the character scheme too subtle and delicate for pit and gallery. But if the attempt were made, it would certainly not be hampered by any of those loosenesses of construction which, sometimes disguised by the conveniences of which the novelist can avail himself, appear at once on the stage.

I think, however, though the thought will doubtless seem heretical to more than one school of critics, that construction is not the highest merit, the choicest gift, of the novelist. It sets off his other gifts and graces most advantageously to the critical eye; and the want of it will sometimes mar those graces—appreciably, though not quite consciously—to eyes by no means ultra-critical. But a very badly built novel which excelled in pathetic or humorous character, or which displayed consummate command of dialogue—perhaps the rarest of all faculties—would be an infinitely better thing than a faultless plot acted and told by puppets with pebbles in their mouths. And despite the ability which Miss Austen has shown in working out the story, I for one should put *Pride and Prejudice* far lower if it did not contain what seem to me the very masterpieces of Miss Austen's humour and of her faculty of character-creation—masterpieces who may indeed admit John Thorpe, the Eltons, Mrs. Norris, and one or two others to their company, but who, in one instance certainly, and perhaps in others, are still superior to them.

The characteristics of Miss Austen's humour are so subtle and delicate that they are, perhaps, at all times easier to apprehend than to express, and at any particular time likely to be differently apprehended by different persons. To me this humour seems to possess a greater affinity, on the whole, to that of Addison than to any other of the numerous species of this great

British genus. The differences of scheme, of time, of subject, of literary convention, are, of course, obvious enough; the difference of sex does not, perhaps, count for much, for there was a distinctly feminine element in "Mr. Spectator", and in Jane Austen's genius there was, though nothing mannish, much that was masculine. But the likeness of quality consists in a great number of common subdivisions of quality—demureness, extreme minuteness of touch, avoidance of loud tones and glaring effects. Also there is in both a certain not inhuman or unamiable cruelty. It is the custom with those who judge grossly to contrast the good nature of Addison with the savagery of Swift, the mildness of Miss Austen with the boisterousness of Fielding and Smollett, even with the ferocious practical jokes that her immediate predecessor, Miss Burney, allowed without very much protest. Yet both in Mr. Addison and in Miss Austen there is, though a restrained and well-mannered, an insatiable and ruthless delight in roasting and cutting up a fool. . . .

[Some] (I think unreasonably) have found "cynicism" in touches of Miss Austen's . . . , such as her satire of Mrs. Musgrove's self-deceiving regrets over her son. But this word "cynical" is one of the most misused in the English language, especially when, by a glaring and gratuitous falsification of its original sense, it is applied, not to rough and snarling invective, but to gentle and oblique satire. If cynicism means the perception of "the other side", the sense of "the accepted hells beneath", the consciousness that motives are nearly always mixed, and that to seem is not identical with to be—if this be cynicism, then every man and woman who is not a fool, who does not care to live in a fool's paradise, who has knowledge of nature and the world and life, is a cynic. And in that sense Miss Austen certainly was one. She may even have been one in the further sense that, like her own Mr. Bennet, she took an epicurean delight in dissecting, in displaying, in setting at work her fools and her mean persons. I think she did take this delight, and I do not think at all the worse of her for it as a woman, while she was immensely the better for it as an artist.

In respect of her art generally, Mr. Goldwin Smith has truly observed that "metaphor has been exhausted in depicting the perfection of it, combined with the narrowness of her field"; and he has justly added that we need not go beyond her own comparison to the art of a miniature painter. To make this latter observation quite exact we must not use the term miniature in its restricted sense, and must think rather of Memling at one end of the history of painting and Meissonier at the other, than of Cosway or any of his kind. And I am not so certain that I should myself use the word "narrow" in connection with her. If her world is a microcosm, the cosmic quality of it is at least as eminent as the littleness. She does not touch what she did not feel herself called to paint; I am not so sure that she could not have painted what she did not feel herself called to touch. (pp. 195-200)

[If] her knowledge was not very extended, she knew two things which only genius knows. The one was humanity, and the other was art. On the first head she could not make a mistake; her men, though limited, are true, and her women are, in the old sense, "absolute". As to art, if she has never tried idealism, her realism is real to a degree which makes the false realism of our own day look merely dead-alive. Take almost any Frenchman, except the late M. de Maupassant, and watch him laboriously piling up strokes in the hope of giving a complete impression. You get none; you are lucky if, discarding two-thirds of what he gives, you can shape a real impression out of the rest. But with Miss Austen the myriad, trivial, unforced

strokes build up the picture like magic. Nothing is false: nothing is superfluous. When (to take the present book only) Mr. Collins changed his mind from Jane to Elizabeth "while Mrs. Bennet was stirring the fire" (and we know *how* Mrs. Bennet would have stirred the fire), when Mr. Darcy "brought his coffee-cup back *himself*", the touch in each case is like that of Swift—"taller by the breadth of my nail"—which impressed the half-reluctant Thackeray with just and outspoken admiration. Indeed, fantastic as it may seem, I should put Miss Austen as near to Swift in some ways as I have put her to Addison in others.

This Swiftian quality appears in the present novel as it appears nowhere else, in the character of the immortal, the ineffable Mr. Collins. Mr. Collins is really *great;* far greater than anything Addison ever did, almost great enough for Fielding or for Swift himself. It has been said that no one ever was like him. But in the first place, *he* was like him; he is there—alive, imperishable, more real than hundreds of prime ministers and archbishops, of "metals, semi-metals, and distinguished philosophers". In the second place, it is rash, I think, to conclude that an actual Mr. Collins was impossible or non-existent at the end of the eighteenth century. It is very interesting that we possess, in this same gallery, what may be called a spoiled first draught, or an unsuccessful study of him, in John Dashwood. The formality, the under-breeding, the meanness, are there; but the portrait is only half alive, and is felt to be even a little unnatural. Mr. Collins is perfectly natural, and perfectly alive. In fact, for all the "miniature", there is something gigantic in the way in which a certain side, and more than one, of humanity, and especially eighteenth-century humanity, its Philistinism, its well-meaning but hide-bound morality, its formal pettiness, its grovelling respect for rank, its materialism, its selfishness, receives exhibition. I will not admit that one speech or one action of this inestimable man is incapable of being reconciled with reality, and I should not wonder if many of these words and actions are historically true.

But the greatness of Mr. Collins could not have been so satisfactorily exhibited if his creatress had not adjusted so artfully to him the figures of Mr. Bennet and of Lady Catherine de Bourgh. The latter, like Mr. Collins himself, has been charged with exaggeration. There is, perhaps, a very faint shade of colour for the charge; but it seems to me very faint indeed. Even now I do not think that it would be impossible to find persons, especially female persons, not necessarily of noble birth, as overbearing, as self-centred, as neglectful of good manners, as Lady Catherine. A hundred years ago, an earl's daughter, the Lady Powerful (if not exactly Bountiful) of an out-of-the-way country parish, rich, long out of marital authority, and so forth, had opportunities of developing these agreeable characteristics which seldom present themselves now. As for Mr. Bennet, Miss Austen and Mr. Darcy and even Miss Elizabeth herself were, I am inclined to think, rather hard on him for the "impropriety" of his conduct. His wife was evidently, and must always have been, a quite irreclaimable fool; and unless he had shot her or himself there was no way out of it for a man of sense and spirit but the ironic. From no other point of view is he open to any reproach, except for an excusable and not unnatural helplessness at the crisis of the elopement; and his utterances are the most acutely delightful in the consciously humorous kind—in the kind that we laugh with, not at—that even Miss Austen has put into the mouth of any of her characters. It is difficult to know whether he is most agreeable when talking to his wife or when putting Mr. Collins through his paces; but the general sense of the world has probably been right in preferring to the first rank his consolation to the former when she maunders over the entail, "My dear, do not give way to such gloomy thoughts. Let us hope for better things. Let us flatter ourselves that *I* may be the survivor"; and his inquiry to his colossal cousin as to the compliments which Mr. Collins has just related as made by himself to Lady Catherine, "May I ask whether these pleasing attentions proceed from the impulse of the moment, or are the result of previous study?" These are the things which give Miss Austen's readers the pleasant shocks, the delightful thrills, which are felt by the readers of Swift, of Fielding, and we may here add, of Thackeray, as they are felt by the readers of no other English author of fiction outside of these four.

The goodness of the minor characters in **Pride and Prejudice** has been already alluded to, and it makes a detailed dwelling on their beauties difficult in any space, and impossible in this. Mrs. Bennet we have glanced at, and it is not easy to say whether she is more exquisitely amusing or more horribly true. Much the same may be said of Kitty and Lydia; but it is not every author, even of genius, who would have differentiated with such unerring skill the effects of folly and vulgarity of intellect and disposition working upon the common weaknesses of woman at such different ages. With Mary, Miss Austen has taken rather less pains, though she has been even more unkind to her; not merely in the text, but, as we learn from those interesting traditional appendices which Mr. Austen Leigh has given us, in dooming her privately to marry "one of Mr. Philips's clerks". The habits of first copying and then retailing moral sentiments, of playing and singing too long in public, are, no doubt, grievous and criminal; but perhaps poor Mary was rather the scapegoat of the sins of blue-stockings in that Fordyce-belectured generation. It is at any rate difficult not to extend to her a share of the respect and affection (affection and respect of a peculiar kind, doubtless) with which one regards Mr. Collins, when she draws the moral of Lydia's fall. I sometimes wish that the exigencies of the story had permitted Miss Austen to unite these personages, and thus at once achieve a notable mating and soothe poor Mrs. Bennet's anguish over the entail.

The Bingleys and the Gardiners and the Lucases, Miss Darcy and Miss de Bourgh, Jane, Wickham, and the rest, must pass without special comment, further than the remark that Charlotte Lucas (her egregious papa, though delightful, is just a little on the thither side of the line between comedy and farce) is a wonderfully clever study in drab of one kind, and that Wickham (though something of Miss Austen's hesitation of touch in dealing with young men appears) is a not much less notable sketch in drab of another. Only genius could have made Charlotte what she is, yet not disagreeable; Wickham what he is, without investing him either with a cheap Don Juanish attractiveness or a disgusting rascality. But the hero and the heroine are not thus to be dismissed.

Darcy has always seemed to me by far the best and most interesting of Miss Austen's heroes; the only possible competitor being Henry Tilney, whose part is so slight and simple that it hardly enters into comparison. It has sometimes, I believe, been urged that his pride is unnatural at first in its expression and later in its yielding, while his falling in love at all is not extremely probable. Here again I cannot go with the objectors. Darcy's own account of the way in which his pride had been pampered is perfectly rational and sufficient; and nothing could be, psychologically speaking, a *causa verior* for its sudden restoration to healthy conditions than the shock of

Elizabeth's scornful refusal acting on a nature *ex hypothesi* generous. Nothing in even our author is finer and more delicately touched than the change of his demeanour at the sudden meeting in the grounds of Pemberley. Had he been a bad prig or a bad coxcomb, he might have been still smarting under his rejection, or suspicious that the girl had come husband-hunting. His being neither is exactly consistent with the probable feelings of a man spoilt in the common sense, but not really injured in disposition, and thoroughly in love. As for his being in love, Elizabeth has given as just an exposition of the causes of that phenomenon as Darcy has of the conditions of his unregenerate state, only she has of course not counted in what was due to her own personal charm.

The secret of that charm many men and not a few women, from Miss Austen herself downwards, have felt, and like most charms it is a thing rather to be felt than to be explained. Elizabeth of course belongs to the *allegro* or *allegra* division of the army of Venus. Miss Austen was always provokingly chary of description in regard to her beauties; and except the fine eyes, and a hint or two that she had at any rate sometimes a bright complexion, and was not very tall, we hear nothing about her looks. But her chief difference from other heroines of the lively type seems to lie first in her being distinctly clever—almost strong-minded, in the better sense of that objectionable word—and secondly in her being entirely destitute of ill-nature for all her propensity to tease and the sharpness of her tongue. Elizabeth can give at least as good as she gets when she is attacked; but she never "scratches", and she never attacks first. Some of the merest obsoletenesses of phrase and manner give one or two of her early speeches a slight pertness, but that is nothing, and when she comes to serious business, as in the great proposal scene with Darcy (which is, as it should be, the climax of the interest of the book), and in the final ladies' battle with Lady Catherine, she is unexceptionable. Then, too, she is a perfectly natural girl. She does not disguise from herself or anybody that she resents Darcy's first ill-mannered personality with as personal a feeling. (By the way, the reproach that the ill-manners of this speech are overdone is certainly unjust; for things of the same kind, expressed no doubt less stiltedly but more coarsely, might have been heard in more than one ball-room during this very year from persons who ought to have been no worse bred than Darcy.) And she lets the injury done to Jane and the contempt shown to the rest of her family aggravate this resentment in the healthiest way in the world.

Still, all this does not explain her charm, which, taking beauty as a common form of all heroines, may perhaps consist in the addition to her playfulness, her wit, her affectionate and natural disposition, of a certain fearlessness very uncommon in heroines of her type and age. Nearly all of them would have been in speechless awe of the magnificent Darcy; nearly all of them would have palpitated and fluttered at the idea of proposals, even naughty ones, from the fascinating Wickham. Elizabeth, with nothing offensive, nothing *viraginous,* nothing of the "New Woman" about her, has by nature what the best modern (not "new") women have by education and experience, a perfect freedom from the idea that all men may bully her if they choose, and that most will run away with her if they can. Though not in the least "impudent and mannish grown", she has no mere sensibility, no nasty niceness, about her. The form of passion common and likely to seem natural in Miss Austen's day was so invariably connected with the display of one or the other, or both of these qualities, that she has not made Elizabeth outwardly passionate. But I, at least, have not the slightest doubt that she would have married Darcy just as willingly without Pemberley as with it, and anybody who can read between lines will not find the lovers' conversations in the final chapters so frigid as they might have looked to the Della Cruscans of their own day, and perhaps do look to the Della Cruscans of this.

And, after all, what is the good of seeking for the reason of charm?—it is there. There were better sense in the sad mechanic exercise of determining the reason of its absence where it is not. In the novels of the last hundred years there are vast numbers of young ladies with whom it might be a pleasure to fall in love; there are at least five with whom, as it seems to me, no man of taste and spirit can help doing so. Their names are, in chronological order, Elizabeth Bennet, Diana Vernon, Argemone Lavington, Beatrix Esmond, and Barbara Grant. I should have been most in love with Beatrix and Argemone; I should, I think, for mere occasional companionship, have preferred Diana and Barbara. But to live with and to marry, I do not know that any one of the four can come into competition with Elizabeth. (pp. 201-09)

George Saintsbury, "Miss Austen: 'Pride and Prejudice'," in his Prefaces and Essays, *Macmillan and Co., Limited,* 1933, pp. 194-209.

MARK TWAIN [AS REPORTED BY ALBERT BIGELOW PAINE] (conversation date 1900-07)

[*Twain, considered one of the most important shapers of modern American literature, broke with the genteel traditions of the nineteenth century by endowing his characters and narratives with natural speech patterns and colloquial language and by writing of subjects hitherto considered beneath serious art. Twain's antipathy toward Austen and her works is evidenced in the following remarks on* Pride and Prejudice. *The conversation from which this comment is drawn is thought to have taken place between 1900 and 1907.*]

When I take up one of Jane Austen's books, . . . such as *Pride and Prejudice,* I feel like a barkeeper entering the kingdom of heaven. I know what his sensation would be and his private comments. He would not find the place to his taste, and he would probably say so.

Mark Twain [*as reported by Albert Bigelow Paine*], in a conversation between 1900-1907, in Mark Twain, a Biography: The Personal and Literary Life of Samuel Langhorne Clemens, *Vol. III by Albert Bigelow Paine, Harper & Brothers Publishers, 1912, p. 1500.*

A. C. BRADLEY (essay date 1911)

[*Bradley was a renowned English Shakespearean scholar and influential literary critic. In the excerpt below, he compares* Pride and Prejudice *and* Mansfield Park, *describing them as the finest works in the Austen canon and discussing such topics as humor, the reader's sympathy with various characters, and the question of Elizabeth Bennet's alleged "impertinence." For additional commentary by Bradley on* Pride and Prejudice, *see* NCLC, *Vol. 1.*]

Among [admirers of Austen] there is a disposition to regard *Pride and Prejudice* and *Mansfield Park* as rivals for the first place, and to quarrel over them with some heat. There is something a little absurd about a competition of this kind, but I fancy the authoress would have enjoyed listening to it, and at any rate it may be made the vehicle of comparison and criti-

cism. *Pride and Prejudice,* I imagine, is the most popular of all the novels, and many of its champions seem hardly to understand why *Mansfield Park* should be much admired. (p. 25)

Mansfield Park allows less scope to Jane Austen's humour than most, perhaps than any, of her other novels. One of her nieces remembered how aunt Jane, when on a visit to her brother, 'would sit quietly working beside the fire in the library, saying nothing for a good while, and then would suddenly burst out laughing, jump up, and run across the room to a table where pens and paper were lying, write something down, and then come back to the fire and go on quietly working as before'. I doubt if this happened very frequently during the composition of *Mansfield Park.* There is often ironic humour in the presentment of the story and in the exhibition of Edmund's feelings. Both the Crawfords have themselves a pleasant vein of humour. We smile at Dr. Grant, at Mrs. Rushworth and her son; broadly at Mr. Yates, with wry faces at Mrs. Norris. But we 'burst out laughing' only when we meet Lady Bertram. This again may be inevitable, and, because in keeping, may even be alleged as a merit; but is it not difficult to describe as Jane Austen's 'best novel' one in which, for however good a reason, Jane Austen's humour fails to have full play? (pp. 27-8)

[One may also ask]: Is there anybody in *Mansfield Park* for whom we care much, not as a study, but as a person? I put this as a question, because undoubtedly there is one person, Fanny Price, for whom Jane Austen *means* us to care a great deal. 'My Fanny' she calls her, in the novel itself, and I do not think any other person in her works receives such a compliment. But—I speak for myself because I am speaking for many others—though I know, not only from this, but from the whole tone of the narrative, what I am expected to feel for Fanny, and though I try to feel it, I make but a moderate success of the business. I pity, approve, respect, and admire her, but I neither desire her company nor am greatly concerned about her destiny, and she makes me impatient at moments when I doubt if she was meant to. Now if this is all my own fault, it is not the fault of *Mansfield Park;* and there is a strong general probability, no doubt, that those who feel as a great writer meant them to feel, are in the right. But then in this matter I am one of a large and respectable band, and I am not convinced that we are wrong. In reading of Elizabeth Bennet, on the other hand, it is impossible for me to doubt either the author's intentions or my own feelings. I was meant to fall in love with her, and I do. Besides, I like her father and her elder sister better than any one in *Mansfield Park,* and I prefer both Darcy and Bingley to the Rev. Edmund Bertram. On this side, therefore, as well as on the side of humour, I must put *Pride and Prejudice* first: and this side, surely, is very important. It is a great merit, that is, in a story that, besides admiring the characters as studies, you care for some of them as persons, and care very much for at least one.

Here, however, we have to meet a serious objection. For we shall be told that we are wrong in finding Elizabeth so delightful as we do; because she has, in addition to that fault on which the plot depends, a very unattractive defect: she is pert or impertinent. And I must try to deal with this charge.

First of all we may remark that it is connected with something—arises, I should say, from a misunderstanding of something—which is a main source of her attractiveness. She has, in a very high degree, that spirit which is lacking in Elinor, Fanny, and Anne. She has more of it than Catherine, an quite as much of it as Emma; and as she also has what they have not, the humour of Jane Austen herself, and as she is free from certain defects which are essential to Emma's story, she delights us. That is what all her friends say: we *delight* in her. Well, obviously, such a person might easily say things which could be misconstrued as impertinent even if they were not so. And accordingly this accusation appears in the novel itself. It is brought against Elizabeth by Miss Bingley, and playfully it is brought by Elizabeth herself when she asks her lover if he admired her for her impertinence, and is answered: 'for the liveliness of your mind I did'. I think his version the true one.

Next we must observe that when Jane Austen put that charge into the mouth of Miss Bingley, Elizabeth's tasteless and spiteful rival, she was implicitly denying it; and that she herself cannot have meant her heroine to be pert or impertinent. Her feeling for Elizabeth, which appears in the letters as well as in the novel, was of a very special kind. She had a tenderness, we saw, for Fanny Price. So she had, one feels as one reads, for Anne Elliot. Yet she wrote to a niece who was eager to see *Persuasion:* 'You will not like it, so you need not be impatient. You may, perhaps, like the heroine, as she is almost too good for me.' Of Emma she said: 'I am going to take a heroine whom no one but myself will much like.' But she wrote of Elizabeth—not in the glow of her first creation, but long after, in 1813, when the novel was about to appear: 'I must confess that I think her as delightful a creature as ever appeared in print, and how I shall be able to tolerate those who do not like *her* at least I do not know' [see excerpt dated January, 1813]. These are precisely the sentiments, the enthusiastic and resentful sentiments, of those for whom I speak. But who will believe that an impertinent girl could have been for Jane Austen as delightful a creature as ever appeared in print?

Still, she may possibly have made Elizabeth impertinent without meaning to do so. And to prove the contrary is beyond human power. But I will ask, To *whom* is Elizabeth impertinent? Surely no one can object to, or fail to exult in, her answers to Lady Catherine de Bourgh, that bullying old snob. After repeated and anxious search I can find no colour for the charge except in one or two of her speeches to Darcy, especially in the scene where they are partners in a dance. Certainly, in one of these speeches, the words, if we take them alone, do sound impertinent; but they sound so, I maintain, only because we take them alone. And that is the origin of the misunderstanding. That which, said seriously, is impertinent, need not be so if playfully said. We forget that these words form part of a conversation which, on Elizabeth's side, is throughout playful in tone. We forget to imagine the smile about her lips, and the dancing light in her eyes. And we forget what we were expressly told before, when she gave Darcy a defiant answer and rather expected him to be affronted: 'there was a mixture of sweetness and archness in her manner which made it difficult for her to affront anybody.'

And now, to return for a moment to the question, 'Which is the best novel, *Mansfield Park* or *Pride and Prejudice*?' I cannot answer it, any more than I can say which is Shakespeare's best drama. Each of the two has qualities in which it surpasses the other. Those in which *Mansfield Park* are superior are probably the more fundamental, and I could not think of asserting that *Pride and Prejudice* is the better novel, though I prefer it. But I do not merely prefer it; it seems to me to show us more of Jane Austen's genius. We could feel surer, from reading it, that the author would some day be able to write *Mansfield Park,* than, from reading *Mansfield Park,* that the author would ever be able to write *Pride and Prejudice.* (pp. 28-32)

A. C. Bradley, ''Jane Austen,'' *in* Essays and Studies, *Vol. II, 1911, pp. 7-36.*

SIR WALTER RALEIGH   (letter date 1917)

[*A renowned lecturer and literary critic, Raleigh's approach to literature, in both his lectures and in such works as* The English Novel *and* Shakespeare, *was that of a highly perceptive, urbane commentator whose literary exegesis served to facilitate the non-specialist's understanding of English literature through concise textual analysis. In the following excerpt from a letter to the noted Austen editor, critic, and biographer R. W. Chapman, Raleigh comments on Austen's understanding of life and on her knowledge of her limitations in* Pride and Prejudice.]

I have been reading *Pride and Prejudice* in bed. (It's a comfort to have it done right, with a proper text.) So I thought I would tell you. Of course it's very swell. She knows a lot; and I believe she knows what she doesn't know. At least, I shouldn't like to believe that she thought she knew anything about married people or young men. Her married people are merely a bore or a comfort to the young—nothing to each other. Her young men, my Gawd! I will take only Darcy and Bingley. Of course they have no profession—they have money. But there is no scrap of evidence, no indication, that they can *do* anything, shoot a partridge, or add up figures, or swim or brush their hair. They never talk of anything except young women, a subject taboo among decent young men. (I find that women mostly don't know that men never talk intimately about them. Jane didn't know this.) Well, Darcy and Bingley have only one interest in life—getting married, and marrying their friends one to another.

It is incredible, immense, yet it deludes you while you read.

As for the young women, they are marvellous and incomparable, so that Jane is a swell all the same. But her young men would be black-balled in any Club. . . . (p. 471)

Sir Walter Raleigh, in a letter to R. W. Chapman on October 23, 1917, in his The Letters of Sir Walter Raleigh (1879-1922), *Vol. II, edited by Lady Raleigh, Macmillan Publishing Company, 1926, pp. 471-72.**

VIRGINIA WOOLF   (essay date 1929)

[*A British novelist, essayist, and short story writer, Woolf is considered one of the most prominent literary figures of the twentieth century and an important practitioner of the stream-of-consciousness novel. In the following excerpt, she comments upon the experience of reading* Pride and Prejudice, *comparing the work with Charles Dickens's novel* Bleak House *and discussing such topics as Austen's characterization, range of subject matter, and narrative viewpoint.*]

The novels which make us live imaginatively, with the whole of the body as well as the mind, produce in us the physical sensations of heat and cold, noise and silence, one reason perhaps why we desire change and why our reactions to them vary so much at different times. Only, of course, the change must not be violent. It is rather that we need a new scene; a return to human faces; a sense of walls and towns about us, with their lights and their characters after the silence of the wind-blown heath.

After reading the romances of Scott and Stevenson and Mrs. Radcliffe, our eyes seem stretched, their sight a little blurred, as if they had been gazing into the distance and it would be a relief to turn for contrast to a strongly marked human face, to characters of extravagant force and character in keeping with our romantic mood. Such figures are most easily to be found in Dickens, of course, and particularly in *Bleak House* where, as Dickens said, "I have purposely dwelt upon the romantic side of familiar things." (p. 269)

In Dickens the characters are impressive in themselves but not in their personal relations. Often, indeed, when they talk to each other they are vapid in the extreme or sentimental beyond belief. One thinks of them as independent, existing forever, unchanged, like monoliths looking up into the sky. So it is that we begin to want something smaller, more intense, more intricate. Dickens has, himself, given us a taste of the pleasure we derive from looking curiously and intently into another character. He has made us instinctively reduce the size of the scene in proportion to the figure of a normal man, and now we seek this intensification, this reduction, carried out more perfectly and more completely, we shall find, in the novels of Jane Austen.

At once, when we open *Pride and Prejudice,* we are aware that the sentence has taken on a different character. Dickens, of course, at full stride is as free-paced and far-stretched as possible. But in comparison with this nervous style, how large-limbed and how loose. The sentence here runs like a knife, in and out, cutting a shape clear. It is done in a drawing-room. It is done by the use of dialogue. Half a dozen people come together after dinner and begin, as they so well might, to discuss letter-writing. Mr. Darcy writes slowly and "studies too much for words of four syllables". Mr. Bingley, on the other hand (for it is necessary that we should get to know them both and they can be quickest shown if they are opposed) "leaves out half his words and blots the rest". But such is only the first rough shaping that gives the outline of the face. We go on to define and distinguish. Bingley, says Darcy, is really boasting when he calls himself a careless letter-writer because he thinks the defect interesting. It was a boast when he told Mrs. Bennet that if he left Netherfield he would be gone in five minutes. And this little passage of analysis on Darcy's part, besides proving his astuteness and his cool observant temper, rouses Bingley to show us a vivacious picture of Darcy at home. "I don't know a more awful object than Darcy, on particular occasions, and in particular places; at his own house especially, and of a Sunday evening, when he has nothing to do."

So, by means of perfectly natural question and answer, everyone is defined and, as they talk, they become not only more clearly seen, but each stroke of the dialogue brings them together or moves them apart, so that the group is no longer casual but interlocked. The talk is not mere talk; it has an emotional intensity which gives it more than brilliance. Light, landscape—everything that lies outside the drawing-room is arranged to illumine it. Distances are made exact; arrangements accurate. It is one mile from Meryton; it is Sunday and not Monday. We want all suspicions and questions laid at rest. It is necessary that the characters should lie before us in as clear and quiet a light as possible since every flicker and tremor is to be observed. Nothing happens, as things so often happen in Dickens, for its own oddity or curiosity but with relation to something else. No avenues of suggestion are opened up, no doors are suddenly flung wide; the ropes which tighten the structure, since they are all rooted in the heart, are so held firmly and tightly. For, in order to develop personal relations to the utmost, it is important to keep out of the range of the abstract, the impersonal; and to suggest that there is anything

that lies outside men and women would be to cast the shadow of doubt upon the comedy of their relationships and its sufficiency. So with edged phrases where often one word, set against the current of the phrase, serves to fledge it (thus: "and whenever any of the cottagers were disposed to be quarrelsome, discontented, or *too poor*") we got down to the depths, for deep they are, for all their clarity.

But personal relations have limits, as Jane Austen seems to realize by stressing their comedy. Everything, she seems to say, has, if we could discover it, a reasonable summing up; and it is extremely amusing and interesting to see the efforts of people to upset the reasonable order, defeated as they invariably are. But if, complaining of the lack of poetry or the lack of tragedy, we are about to frame the familiar statement that this is a world which is too small to satisfy us, a prosaic world, a world of inches and blades of grass, we are brought to a pause by another impression which requires a moment further of analysis. Among all the elements which play upon us in reading fiction there has always been, though in different degrees, some voice, accent or temperament clearly heard, though behind the scenes of the book. "Trollope, the novelist, a big, blustering, spectacled, loud-voiced hunting man"; Scott, the ruined country gentleman, whose very pigs trotted after him, so gracious was the sound of his voice—both come to us with the gesture of hosts, welcoming us, and we fall under the spell of their charm or the interest of their characters.

We cannot say this of Jane Austen, and her absence has the effect of making us detached from her work and of giving it, for all its sparkle and animation, a certain aloofness and completeness. Her genius compelled her to absent herself. So truthful, so clear, so sane a vision would not tolerate distraction, even if it came from her own claims, nor allow the actual experience of a transitory woman to color what should be unstained by personality. For this reason, then, though we may be less swayed by her, we are less dissatisfied. It may be the very idiosyncrasy of a writer that tires us of him. Jane Austen, who has so little that is peculiar, does not tire us, nor does she breed in us a desire for those writers whose method and style differ altogether from hers. Thus, instead of being urged as the last page is finished to start in search of something that contrasts and completes, we pause when we have read *Pride and Prejudice.*

The pause is the result of a satisfaction which turns our minds back upon what we have just read, rather than forward to something fresh. Satisfaction is, by its nature, removed from analysis, for the quality which satisfies us is the sum of many different parts, so that if we begin praising *Pride and Prejudice* for the qualities that compose it—its wit, its truth, its profound comic power—we shall still not praise it for the quality which is the sum of all these. At this point, then, the mind, brought to bay, escapes the dilemma and has recourse to images. We compare *Pride and Prejudice* to something else because, since satisfaction can be defined no further, all the mind can do is to make a likeness of the thing and, by giving it another shape, cherish the illusion that it is explaining it, whereas it is, in fact, only looking at it afresh. To say that *Pride and Prejudice* is like a shell, a gem, a crystal, whatever image we may choose, is to see the same thing under a different guise. Yet, perhaps, if we compare *Pride and Prejudice* to something concrete, it is because we are trying to express the sense we have in other novels imperfectly, here with distinctness, of a quality which is not in the story but above it, not in the things themselves but in their arrangement.

Pride and Prejudice, one says, has form; *Bleak House* has not. The eye (so active always in fiction) gives its own interpretation of impressions that the mind has been receiving in different terms. The mind has been conscious in *Pride and Prejudice* that things are said, for all their naturalness, with a purpose; one emotion has been contrasted with another; one scene has been short, the next long; so that all the time, instead of reading at random, without control, snatching at this and that, stressing one thing or another, as the mood takes us, we have been aware of check and stimulus, of spectral architecture built up behind the animation and variety of the scene. It is a quality so precise it is not to be found either in what is said or in what is done; that is, it escapes analysis. It is a quality, too, that is much at the mercy of fiction. Its control is invariably weak there, much weaker than in poetry or in drama because fiction runs so close to life the two are always coming into collision. That this architectural quality can be possessed by a novelist, Jane Austen proves. And she proves, too, that far from chilling the interest or withdrawing the attention from the characters, it seems on the contrary to focus it and add an extra pleasure to the book, a significance. It makes it seem that here is something good in itself, quite apart from our personal feelings.

Not to seek contrast but to start afresh—this is the impulse which urges us on after finishing *Pride and Prejudice.* We must make a fresh start altogether. Personal relations, we recall, have limits. In order to keep their edges sharp, the mysterious, the unknown, the accidental, the strange subside; their intervention would be confusing and distressing. The writer adopts an ironic attitude to her creatures, because she has denied them so many adventures and experiences. A suitable marriage is, after all, the upshot of all this coming together and drawing apart. A world which so often ends in a suitable marriage is not a world to wring one's hands over. On the contrary, it is a world about which we can be sarcastic; into which we can peer endlessly, as we fit the jagged pieces one into another. Thus, it is possible to ask not that her world shall be improved or altered (that our satisfaction forbids) but that another shall be struck off, whose constitution shall be different and shall allow of the other relations. People's relations shall be with God or nature. They shall think. They shall sit, like Dorothea Casaubon in *Middlemarch,* drawing plans for other people's houses; they shall suffer like Gissing's characters in solitude; they shall be alone. *Pride and Prejudice,* because it has such integrity of its own, never for an instant encroaches on other provinces and, thus, leaves them more clearly defined. (pp. 271-73)

> *Virginia Woolf, "Phases of Fiction, Part 2," in* The Bookman, *New York, Vol. LXIX, No. 3, May, 1929, pp. 269-79.**

VIRGINIA WOOLF   (essay date 1929)

[*In the following excerpt from* A Room of One's Own, *her influential work on the difficulties faced by women writers, Woolf comments on the social and physical restrictions of the environment in which Austen wrote* Pride and Prejudice, *asserting that the novelist's "gift and her circumstances matched each other completely."*]

Without boasting or giving pain to the opposite sex, one may say that *Pride and Prejudice* is a good book. At any rate, one would not have been ashamed to have been caught in the act of writing *Pride and Prejudice.* Yet Jane Austen was glad that a hinge creaked, so that she might hide her manuscript before any one came in. To Jane Austen there was something dis-

creditable in writing *Pride and Prejudice.* And, I wondered, would *Pride and Prejudice* have been a better novel if Jane Austen had not thought it necessary to hide her manuscript from visitors? I read a page or two to see; but I could not find any signs that her circumstances had harmed her work in the slightest. That, perhaps, was the chief miracle about it. Here was a woman about the year 1800 writing without hate, without bitterness, without fear, without protest, without preaching. That was how Shakespeare wrote, I thought, looking at *Antony and Cleopatra;* and when people compare Shakespeare and Jane Austen, they may mean that the minds of both had consumed all impediments; and for that reason we do not know Jane Austen and we do not know Shakespeare, and for that reason Jane Austen pervades every word that she wrote, and so does Shakespeare. If Jane Austen suffered in any way from her circumstances it was in the narrowness of life that was imposed upon her. It was impossible for a woman to go about alone. She never travelled; she never drove through London in an omnibus or had luncheon in a shop by herself. But perhaps it was the nature of Jane Austen not to want what she had not. Her gift and her circumstances matched each other completely. (pp. 116-18)

> *Virginia Woolf, in a chapter in her* A Room of One's Own, Harcourt Brace Jovanovich, 1929, *pp. 100-36.**

ELIZABETH JENKINS   (essay date 1938)

[*In the following excerpt from* Jane Austen, *Jenkins's highly regarded biographical and critical study of the novelist, the critic comments on characterization, realism, structure, and comic irony in* Pride and Prejudice. *The characters discussed by the critic include Jane and Elizabeth Bennet, Darcy, Wickham, and Mr. Bennet.*]

The depth, the perspective of impression conveyed by *Pride and Prejudice* is so intense that when one re-reads the book one is astonished by its brevity. The people in the story are so distinctly present to one's mind that one searches in vain for the actual passage of description that made them so.

There is none; and in this lies the most characteristic aspect of Jane Austen's art, and the one most difficult to discuss and understand. What Macaulay said of Milton might with more aptness be said of her: 'There would seem at first sight to be no more in his words than in other words. But they are words of enchantment. No sooner are they pronounced, than the past is present, and the distant, near . . . . Change the structure of the sentence . . . and the whole effect is destroyed. The spell loses its power, and he who should hope to conjure with it would find himself as much mistaken as Cassim in the Arabian tale, when he stood saying Open Wheat, Open Barley, to the door which obeyed no sound but Open Sesame.' (pp. 154-55)

The structure of *Pride and Prejudice* explains what [Austen meant by saying to her niece] Anna Austen that two or three families in a small area was the very thing to work upon and just the situation she liked herself. She did not mean it to be inferred that a pleasant round of gossip and intrigue and an absence of anything of external interest were all that she herself felt fitted to cope with; but that, for her method of establishing conviction, it was essential to keep the threads of the story converging upon a single point and to show the various characters, not only as she saw them, or as two of them saw each other, but as each of them appeared to his or her acquaintance as a whole.

In *Pride and Prejudice* this interlacing of the characters forms, as it were, the steel structure upon which the work, with its amazing buoyancy, is sprung. Every important fact in the story is shown to be the inevitable consequence of something that has gone before. The fact that Bingley, pliable as he was, should be deterred by Darcy from his courtship of Jane Bennet is at first surprising; and Darcy's explanation is that Bingley was very modest, and really believed Darcy's representation of Jane's indifference; which, added Darcy, he genuinely believed himself. He saw that Jane liked Bingley, but he did not believe her to be in love, and therefore liable to be injured except in a worldly sense by Bingley's withdrawal. We then remember what Charlotte Lucas had said, very early in Jane and Bingley's acquaintance, when Elizabeth had remarked to her that though Jane was falling in love with Bingley, her serenity and self-control were such that Elizabeth did not think anyone else would be able to notice it. (p. 156)

The suddenly brought about marriage of Charlotte and Mr. Collins, which is in its way one of the most interesting things in the book, is led up to before the reader has any suspicion of what is to happen. At the Netherfield Ball, before Mr. Collins has made his famous proposal to Elizabeth, he exacerbates her almost beyond endurance by his pertinacious attentions; as she has refused to dance with him, she is not able, in the etiquette of the day, to accept another partner; therefore she has to sit and endure Mr. Collins, who says he had rather sit by her than dance with anybody else. Her only moments of relief are when Charlotte Lucas comes to them and kindly diverts some of Mr. Collins' conversation to herself.

The difference between the meretricious, dishonest Wickham and his father, who had been the trusted steward and lifelong friend of old Mr. Darcy, is explained in a single statement. The elder Wickham had had an extravagant wife.

The celestial brightness of *Pride and Prejudice* is unequalled even in Jane Austen's other work; after a life of much disappointment and grief, in which some people would have seen nothing but tedium and emptiness, she stepped forth as an author, breathing gaiety and youth, robed in dazzling light. The penetration, the experience, the development of a mature mind, are latent in every line of the construction, in every act and thought; but the whole field of the novel glitters as with sunrise upon morning dew. The impression cannot be wholly analysed and accounted for, but it is worth while noting that in this book there are no people who are thrown in upon themselves by an unsympathetic atmosphere, like Fanny Price; no one who is labouring under a painful secret like Jane Fairfax; no one whose natural frame of mind is one of stormy light and shade, like Marianne Dashwood; no one whose life has been radically altered by a killing past of unhappiness like Anne Elliot; there is disappointment in the book, and agitation, and acute distress, but the characters are all, even Wickham's, of an open kind, despite their individual variety.

Much of the novel's charm is created by the relationship of the two sisters; the idea that we have here something of the relationship of Jane and Cassandra is inescapable, particularly in such a passage as: 'I was uncomfortable enough—I was very uncomfortable—I may say, unhappy. And with no one to speak to of what I felt, no Jane to comfort me, and say that I had not been so very weak and vain and nonsensical as I knew I had! Oh, how I wanted you!' Cassandra Austen is to us something of a sybil; she is a veiled presence whose face we never see. Her sister is always talking to her; and we listen to her sister's voice and watch the changing expression of her face,

but we never see the person to whom Jane is turned. . . . In acknowledging one of her letters, Jane declared her to be 'one of the finest comic writers of the age.' Would Cassandra but read her own letters through five times, she might get some of the pleasure out of them that her sister did. Jane sent delighted thanks for the 'exquisite piece of workmanship' which had been brought into Henry's breakfast-room among the other letters.

Now a letter from Jane Bennet would never have ranked as an exquisite piece of workmanship. A partial sister could not have described her as one of the first comic writers of the age. If she had been, Mr. Bingley would not have fallen in love with her. (pp. 157-58)

'Mild' and 'steady' are words used in describing her; her very beauty was of the reposeful cast; she was not so light nor so used to running as Elizabeth; she was the sooner out of breath when they pursued Mr. Bennet across the paddock. In every respect she forms the ideal contrast to her mercurial sister, whose face, Miss Bingley said, was too thin, and whose eyes enchanted Mr. Darcy with 'their shape and colour, and the eye-lashes, so remarkably fine.'

Of the young men, Bingley and Wickham sustain the sense of gaiety and open good humour which is a part of the novel's atmosphere. Bingley is simple, modest, easily led; but with a disposition to be pleased. (p. 159)

The character of Wickham, though so base, is not of a kind to cloud the brilliant surface of the mirror. A curious degree of sexual attraction often goes with a lively, unreliable disposition, which may either be somewhat superficial but perfectly well-meaning, or, driven by circumstances which it has not the strength to withstand, become that of a scoundrel. Wickham was well on the way to being a scoundrel; but his sexual fascination was so great that Elizabeth Bennet, who was normally of a very critical turn of mind, saw at first absolutely nothing in him but what made him seem the most charming man she had ever met. Even Mrs. Gardiner thought him delightful and only warned Elizabeth against him because he was not in the position to support a wife. (p. 160)

Elizabeth Bennet has perhaps received more admiration than any other heroine in English literature. Stevenson's saying, that when she opened her mouth he wanted to go down on his knees, is particularly interesting because it is the comment of a man on a woman's idea of a charming woman. Not less significant is Professor Bradley's: 'I am meant to fall in love with her, and I do' [see excerpt dated 1911]. She is unique. The only girl between whom and herself there is any hint of resemblance is Benedict's Beatrice. The wit, the prejudice against a lover, the warm and generous indignation against the ill usage of a cousin or a sister, remind us, something, one of the other. She attacks the mind in two ways:

> . . . when she moves you see
> Like water from a crystal over-filled,
> Fresh beauty tremble out of her, and lave
> Her fair sides to the ground.

She is also completely human. Glorious as she is, and beloved of her creator, she is kept thoroughly in her place. She was captivated by Wickham, in which she showed herself no whit superior to the rest of female Meryton. She also toyed with the idea of a fancy for Colonel Fitzwilliam, who was much attracted by her. 'But Colonel Fitzwilliam had made it clear that he had no intentions at all, and, agreeable as he was, she did not mean to be unhappy about him.' Above all there is her prejudice against Darcy, and though their first encounter was markedly unfortunate, she built on it every dislike it could be made to bear; her eager condemnation of him and her no less eager remorse when she found that she had been mistaken, are equally lovable.

The serious side of her nature is perhaps nowhere better indicated than in the chapter where Charlotte Lucas secures and accepts Mr. Collins' proposal and then has to tell Elizabeth that she has done so. (pp. 160-61)

It is a scene between two young women, both of them normal, pleasant and good; the conversation is of the briefest; in it the more remarkable of the two speaks only twice, and less than a dozen words in all; but what a world of thought and feeling, experience and philosophy it conjures up! (pp. 161-62)

The character of Fitzwilliam Darcy has been said to have no counterpart in modern society. The error is a strange one. Darcy's uniting gentle birth with such wealth is indeed an anachronism. To-day death duties would have felled the Pemberley woods and the estate passed into the hands of ales and stout. But Darcy's essential character is independent of circumstances. He had the awkwardness and stiffness of a man who mixes little with society and only on his own terms, but it was also the awkwardness and stiffness that is found with Darcy's physical type, immediately recognizable among the reserved and inarticulate English of to-day. That his behaviour in the early part of the book is owing to a series of external circumstances rather than to his essential character is very carefully shown, and we have a further proof of how easy it was to misunderstand him: when he and Elizabeth were becoming reconciled to each other at Lambton, and Elizabeth had suddenly to give him the news of Lydia's elopement, he was quite silent and took an abrupt departure. She thought his behaviour owing to his redoubled disgust at her family; it was really consternation at a state of affairs for which, as one who had failed to expose Wickham to society, he thought himself partially responsible.

That his character was actually quite different from what it appeared to be on the surface is of course revealed by his behaviour once the shock of Elizabeth's abuse has made him realize how it struck other people. It is a piece of extremely subtle characterization that when Elizabeth first met Lady Catherine, she thought that she and Mr. Darcy were alike, and after she had fallen in love with Darcy, she wondered how she could ever have imagined a resemblance. We do not, however, doubt that the resemblance was there. It was a family likeness, accentuated on the one hand by a harsh and arrogant nature and on the other by a shy and uncommunicative one. This view of Darcy is borne out by the drawing of his sister. Georgiana Darcy was a very well-meaning girl, but she was so extremely shy that society was an agony to her; and though for her brother's sake she was longing to please Elizabeth and Mrs. Gardiner, it was all that her gentle, pleasant governess could do to guide her through the occasion of their call as became the lady of Pemberley.

That some of his real nature had been, if unconsciously, perceived by Elizabeth before their reconciliation is proved by one of Jane Austen's rare and very beautiful touches of sensibility. It occurs when Elizabeth and her party are being taken round Pemberley by the housekeeper and arrive at the picture-gallery. 'In the gallery were many family portraits, but they could have little to fix the attention of a stranger. Elizabeth walked on in quest of the only face whose features would be known to her. At last it arrested her—and she beheld a striking resemblance of Mr. Darcy, with such a smile over the face, as she remembered to have sometimes seen when he looked at her.'

It is true that in an attempt to see whether Darcy's character would stand the test of time, it is necessary to see how it would appear were he denuded of his wealth; but from the point of view of his position in the work of art that presents him to us, the background of Pemberley, that Derbyshire landscape with its trees in the variegated beauty and the stillness of summer, is truly harmonious. (pp. 162-63)

There is such intense psychological interest in Jane Austen's work that it is possible, strange as it may seem, to forget for a moment that they are primarily creations of comedy; not only are they so in the broader sense, by which one implies that in the development of the plot a character which begins with a mistaken attitude to life is brought back to the angle of normality, and reformed in the process, but Jane Austen's own attitude to the various characters is largely satirical, in however mildly luminous a degree; there is none of her figures whom she treats in a consistently serious manner. Most important of all, she has comic portraits whose effect is that of 'straight' comedy, though their foundation is of the most brilliant and subtle excellence. Mr. Bennet is one of the most remarkable figures in the whole range of English comedy. Dean Swift is one of the few English masters of irony; it is not perhaps too much to say that Mr. Bennet is another. Of every other one of Jane Austen's male characters we may say that they are men as they appear to women; and that they are so is no reflection upon her powers. Man's aspect as he appears to women is after all as important, neither more nor less, as his aspect as he appears to men. But Mr. Bennet is the unique exception; he might have been drawn by a man, except that it is difficult to think of a man who could have drawn him so well. It is relatively easy to be witty at somebody else's expense; but to create the character of a genuinely witty man is, one would say, for a woman, next door to impossible. Male characters of unconscious humour, women, with their capacity for acute observation, achieve very well. George Eliot was highly successful in this genre, so was Fanny Burney; even Emily Brontë relaxed her sternness over the delineation of old Joseph; Jane Austen herself is of course inimitable; but Mr. Bennet was something extraordinary even for her. To detach his remarks from their context is to deprive them of half their subtlety and force: as, for instance, his reply to the endless maunderings of Mrs. Bennet on the subject of the entail in Mr. Collins's favour. '"How anyone could have the conscience to entail away an estate from one's own daughters, I cannot understand, and all for the sake of Mr. Collins, too! Why should *he* have it more than anybody else?"'

'"I leave it to yourself to determine," said Mr. Bennet.'

One can appreciate the full aroma of that only after having read the twenty-three chapters that precede it.

Of Mrs. Bennet and Mr. Collins, those two creations of unconscious humour, the only method of doing justice to them would be to repeat every word uttered by either; but it is one of the remarkable aspects of Jane Austen's comedy that though such characters are brilliantly funny, one can at the same time see them in relation to every aspect of ordinary life. (pp. 164-65)

The distinguishing of novelists as 'subjective' and 'objective' is essentially misleading, since a purely objective presentation

*A sketch of Austen's childhood home, Steventon Rectory.
Courtesy of the Jane Austen Memorial Trust.*

of a character is, to a human being, an impossibility; but the
degree to which novelists appear to be either is sometimes very
marked. In the last four of Jane Austen's works we are insen-
sibly drawn in to believing that her rendering of the characters
of Mrs. Bennet and Mrs. Norris and Miss Bates and Mary
Musgrave gives us the actual scientific truth about those characters. It is impossible, almost, to have any other opinion of
them than that held by Jane Austen herself. She makes none
of those violent assaults upon our prejudice and our imagination
which the writer makes who is eminently subjective; she seems
to leave us quite free to form our own judgement on the most
mature of her masterpieces, but really the guiding is there,
only it is so firm and skilful that we have not the opportunity
to perceive it, excepting just now and again. (pp. 165-66)

> *Elizabeth Jenkins, in her* Jane Austen: A Biography,
> *1938. Reprint by Victor Gollancz Ltd., 1968, 286 p.*

MARY LASCELLES (essay date 1939)

[Lascelles's Jane Austen and Her Art, *from which the following
excerpt is drawn, was the first comprehensive treatment of the
novelist's works and is still considered a valuable study. Here,
Lascelles discusses how three minor and apparently one-dimensional characters—Mr. Collins, Mrs. Bennet, and Lady Catherine—play important parts in the plot of* Pride and Prejudice.
*Later in the excerpt, the critic posits that the pattern of the novel
is "formed by diverging and converging lines" tracing the series
of hostile interactions between Elizabeth and Darcy that eventually lead to their reconciliation. For additional commentary by
Lascelles on* Pride and Prejudice, *see NCLC, Vol. 1.]*

'I cannot . . . conceive,' Henry James says, 'in any novel worth
discussing at all, of a passage of description that is not in its
intention narrative, a passage of dialogue that is not in its
intention descriptive, a touch of truth of any sort that does not
partake of the nature of incident, or an incident that derives
its interest from any other source than the general and only
source of the success of a work of art—that of being illustrative.' And, having dealt severely with the critics who like
compartments and labels, he asseverates: 'I cannot see what is
meant by talking as if there were a part of a novel which is
the story and part of it which for mystical reasons is not.'

This conviction of the integrity of a good novel—this impression that it must be unprofitable to study 'plot' and 'characters'
separately—is strongly borne out by a study of Jane Austen's

narrative art, and by particular observation of the course of its
development. Whether we approach it in the first place by way
of her presentation of character, or of her construction of plot,
we shall discover the need—more urgent as we draw towards
the later novels—of reaching some central vantage-point, from
which the 'old-fashioned distinction between the novel of character and the novel of incident' (as Henry James calls it) is
seen to be insignificant. For, 'What' (he demands) 'is character
but the determination of incident? What is incident but the
illustration of character?'

It is not often that this can be said of those fictitious characters
whose internal mechanism is of the simplest kind—characters
to which comedy has always been hospitable. They are often
curiously intractable—likely, when they are compelled to serve
the main interests of the story, to do or suffer injury. If they
have been introduced for the sake of suggesting some contrast,
they will either give it an unintended turn—throw queer lights
on the figure to which they are to act as foil . . .—or else lose
all characteristics but those that serve for this contrast. (pp.
146-47)

[One] would hardly expect usefulness of Mr. Collins, a creature
born of his author's youthful fancy in its most hilarious mood.
'Can he be a sensible man, sir?' Elizabeth asks her father, after
hearing him read the letter in which their cousin introduces
himself; and Mr. Bennet answers: 'No, my dear; I think not.
I have great hopes of finding him quite the reverse.' Indeed,
he is a being of some exquisitely non-sensible world, of another
element than ours, one to which he is 'native and endued'.
Whether he bestows his favour upon Elizabeth, pleased to
contemplate the notion of her wit 'tempered with silence', or
whether he withdraws it—yet gravely explains that she is not
excepted from his good wishes for the health of her family—
he does not strain probability, as Sir William Lucas strains
it by the simplicity of *his* machinery; he transcends it. And so it
is not enough to exclaim, 'No one would speak so'; and one
is still too moderate if one protests, 'No one would even think
so'; for Mr. Collins is the *quintessence* of a character, in Lamb's
sense of the word when he defined quintessence as an apple-
pie made all of quinces. He does and says not those things
which such a man would say and do, nor even those which he
would wish to say and do, but those towards which the whole
bias of his nature bends him, and from which no thought of
consequences, no faintest sense of their possible impact upon
other people, deters him. And is such a creature as this to be
put into the shafts and draw a plot? Mr. Elton [in *Emma*], his
nearest relation, might, and does, perform such a service, for
he, with all his comic exuberance, is a being of our familiar
element; but can it be exacted of Mr. Collins? It is, and with
capital effect. As well as making his own contribution to the
story, by the comedy he plays out with Elizabeth and her family
and neighbours, he has to draw and hold together Longbourn
and Hunsford; to bring Hunsford within range of our imagination awhile before we can be taken there (and incidentally
to confirm Elizabeth's ill opinion of every one connected with
Darcy), to draw Elizabeth to Hunsford when the time is ripe,
and eventually to send Lady Catherine post-haste to Longbourn
on her catastrophic visit. It is worth stopping to notice how
unobtrusively this last incident is suggested: Lady Catherine,
questioned by Mrs. Bennet, mentions that she saw Mr. and
Mrs. Collins 'the night before last'. To Elizabeth, she opens
her attack by saying: 'A report of a most alarming nature,
reached me two days ago'—the report of her engagement to
Darcy. We are left to infer a connexion between these two
references; and then, after a sufficient interval for the carriage

of a letter, comes Mr. Collins's warning to Elizabeth against 'a precipitate closure with the gentleman's proposals': 'We have reason to imagine that his aunt, lady Catherine de Bourgh, does not look on the match with a friendly eye.... After mentioning the likelihood of this marriage to her ladyship last night', he has felt it his duty to offer this warning. Such are the care and ingenuity that Jane Austen expends even on the broadly comic characters of her early invention. (pp. 149-50)

The problem which Mrs. Bennet presents is a little different; she is not the sort of character that is likely to embarrass its creator by uncontrollable vitality ...; Mrs. Bennet was 'a woman of mean understanding, little information, and uncertain temper. When she was discontented she fancied herself nervous. The business of her life was to get her daughters married; its solace was visiting and news.' That, summing up for us the impressions of her that we have gained from her first appearance, seems to dispose of Mrs. Bennet, to set her where she must remain throughout the story. But we are to have a good deal of her company, for her post is at the centre of the action; and she must not become a dead weight. Mr. E. M. Forster, when he divides the characters of fiction into 'round' and 'flat', brings his argument to a head in this sentence: 'The test of a round character is whether it is capable of surprising in a convincing way. If it never surprises, it is flat. If it does not convince, it is a flat pretending to be round.' But it seems to me that this analysis does not allow for such a character as Mrs. Bennet, of whose comic essence it is that she should be incapable of any but her habitual, and therefore inapposite, reaction to life in all its variety. She must indeed surprise us—in order to keep our response to her alive—but may surprise us only by the inexhaustible variety of expression devised for her unvarying reaction to circumstance. And it is in devising this variety of form for what is substantially invariable—for a Mrs. Bennet who is to be left as she was found 'occasionally nervous and invariably silly'—that Jane Austen displays her virtuosity, giving her creature the entail on Longbourn, a theme of specious importance, to play her variations upon. We hear of it first when Mr. Collins offers himself as a visitor, and Mr. Bennet reminds his wife that this cousin 'when I am dead, may turn you all out of this house as soon as he pleases'. '''Oh my dear,'' cried his wife, ''I cannot bear to hear that mentioned. Pray do not talk of that odious man. I do think it is the hardest thing in the world, that your estate should be entailed away from your own children; and I am sure if I had been you, I should have tried long ago to do something or other about it.''

'Jane and Elizabeth attempted to explain to her the nature of an entail. They had often attempted it before, but it was a subject on which Mrs. Bennet was beyond the reach of reason...' There we are, in the thick of it, knowing what is to be Mrs. Bennet's inevitable response to this subject, ignorant how its mode will be varied—though the close of this very passage promises something:

'... She continued to rail bitterly against the cruelty of settling an estate away from a family of five daughters, in favour of a man whom nobody cared anything about.'

Mr. Collins, on arrival, is offered a sufficiently surprising variation on this theme: '... Such things I know are all chance in this world. There is no knowing how estates will go when once they come to be entailed'—and contributes something to it himself by his proposal of marrying one of his cousins in reparation. And when this falls through—and, worse still, he marries some one else—Mrs. Bennet returns to her favourite subject with fresh energy: 'How any one could have the conscience to entail away an estate from one's own daughters I cannot understand; and all for the sake of Mr. Collins too!— Why should *he* have it more than anybody else?'

And yet she still has something in reserve for us: when Elizabeth returns from visiting Mr. and Mrs. Collins her mother asks her whether they do not 'often talk of having Longbourn when your father is dead.... Well, if they can be easy with an estate that is not lawfully their own, so much the better. *I* should be ashamed of having one that was only entailed on me.' And so she leaves us with the assurance that, as she had been talking of this subject before the story began, so she will continue after its close, with ever fresh turns of absurdity, happily corresponding with the busy futility of her actions. (pp. 151-53)

Lady Catherine's part in the story of *Pride and Prejudice* is ... precisely planned, but the fun of it is independent of burlesque; for the execution of this plan is so consistent with the comic essence of her character, that not only her appearances but the very anticipation of them (since she is portentously anticipated) compose themselves into a pattern of comedy. The story is shaped by the original misunderstanding and eventual good understanding between Darcy and Elizabeth; and it is Lady Catherine's office to assist at the first, unwittingly, and at the second against her will: her active interference in their affairs— itself finely in character—is the determining circumstance in their coming to understand one another's feelings and their own. Its effect on Elizabeth is direct and obvious; but what a pleasantly ironic invention it is that Darcy, who has alienated Elizabeth by interfering with her sister's affairs, and is by no means ready to repent his interference, should be roused to indignation and action when Lady Catherine tries to interfere with *his*. Her 'unjustifiable endeavours', as he calls them, to separate him from Elizabeth, send him straight to Longbourn; and so, as Elizabeth remarks: 'Lady Catherine has been of infinite use, which ought to make her happy, for she loves to be of use.' And with that most appropriate valedictory the pattern of her part in the story is completed, as though with a flourish. (pp. 154-55)

[The pattern of *Pride and Prejudice* shows a] delight in the symmetry of correspondence and antithesis.... This pattern is formed by diverging and converging lines, by the movement of two people who are impelled apart until they reach a climax of mutual hostility, and thereafter bend their courses towards mutual understanding and amity. It is a pattern very common in fiction, but by no means easy to describe plausibly.

Of the two courses, Jane Austen traces but one by means of a continuous line; that line, however, is firm and fluent. Elizabeth's chief impetus is due to Wickham; but there is hardly a character in the story who contributes no momentum to it, nor any pressure from without to which she does not respond characteristically. Her misunderstanding of Darcy is thus much less simple, much less like the given condition of an invented problem, than Marianne's misunderstanding of Willoughby, or of Elinor [in *Sense and Sensibility*]. Her initial impulse towards this misunderstanding comes, of course, from Darcy himself, in that piece of flamboyant rudeness which I suspect of being a little out of keeping; but from this point on all follows plausibly. Darcy's more characteristic reference to his own implacability prepares her to believe just what she is going to hear of him so soon as Wickham addresses her. And how insinuating that address is! There had been a suspicion of burlesque about Willoughby's mode of entrance into the story—

something that recalls the ironic apology for the absence of the hero in the opening of *Northanger Abbey;* chance has disposed it too smoothly to his advantage. Wickham owes no more to chance than that first silent encounter with Darcy that stirs Elizabeth's wakeful curiosity; it is his adroitness that transforms curiosity into sympathetic indignation. What provincial young lady, brought up among the small mysteries and intrigues of Mrs. Bennet's world, would not be flattered into sympathy by his relation of his own story (so nicely corresponding with that of many heroes in popular fiction), or would criticize him for telling or herself for listening to such a private history? Or what young lady of Elizabeth's self-assurance would suspect that she was not to remain its only hearer? Henceforward his adversaries—and even indifferent spectators—play into his hands: Miss Bingley's insolent interference rouses Elizabeth's pride and clouds her judgement; Charlotte Lucas causes her to mistake her own prejudice for generous sentiment; Mr. Collins, by associating Darcy in her mind with the idol of his worship, strengthens every ill impression; Lady Catherine herself, by answering to Wickham's description, confirms part of his story, and by her proprietary praise of Darcy fixes some of its implications; and Colonel Fitzwilliam, by his indiscreet half-confidence, ensures that Elizabeth shall see Darcy's action towards her sister in the harshest light.

Meanwhile, Darcy's ill opinion of the Bennets has been growing, under the influence of these very people and events, until the climax of the ungracious proposal and refusal is reached. And yet, in the centre of this disturbance, forces have begun to stir, and, almost imperceptibly, to allay it. And this entails a change of course which is very difficult to contrive. The initial impulse must not seem to have spent itself—that would leave a fatal impression of lassitude. There must be deflexion; and this, for Jane Austen, means cause and opportunity to reconsider character and action. (Not conduct alone; she has little use for those casual encounters in ambiguous circumstances which are the staple of Fanny Burney's misunderstandings between lovers.) Even while they are drawing yet farther apart, Elizabeth and Darcy have begun to feel unfamiliar doubts; sure as each still is of his and her own critical judgement, both have come to question the standards of their own social worlds. Her mother's behaviour at Netherfield on two uncomfortable occasions disturbs Elizabeth in such a way as to suggest that she had not been embarrassed by it before; and Charlotte Lucas's conduct shocks her. Presently, Colonel Fitzwilliam's manners give her a standard by which to judge Wickham's. In the meantime Darcy has been unwillingly learning to criticize the manners of his world as it is represented by Miss Bingley, and—touching him more smartly—by Lady Catherine.

> "I have told Miss Bennet several times, that she will never play really well, unless she practises more; and though Mrs. Collins has no instrument, she is very welcome, as I have often told her, to come to Rosings every day, and play on the piano forte in Mrs. Jenkinson's room. She would be in nobody's way, you know, in that part of the house." Mr. Darcy looked a little ashamed of his aunt's ill breeding, and made no answer.

And so, even when the climax of mutual exasperation is reached, Elizabeth's criticism of Darcy meets some response in his consciousness, his statement of his objections to her family means something to her; and the way is open for each to consider anew the actions and character of the other. What Darcy has

done is now shown afresh in his letter; this I do not find quite plausible. The manner is right, but not the matter: so much, and such, information would hardly be volunteered by a proud and reserved man—unless under pressure from his author, anxious to get on with the story. And perhaps it may be the same pressure that hastens Elizabeth's complete acceptance of its witness; for there is no time to lose; she must have revised her whole impression of him before her visit to Pemberley—revised it confidently enough to be able to indicate as much clearly to Wickham, for our benefit: 'I think', she says enigmatically in answer to his searching questions, 'Mr. Darcy improves on acquaintance.' This disturbs and provokes him to further inquiry: '"For I dare not hope," he continued in a lower and more serious tone, "that he is improved in essentials." "Oh, no!" said Elizabeth. "In essentials, I believe, he is very much what he ever was"'—and she develops this proposition to Wickham's discomfort.

The Pemberley visit is to supplement this revised impression of Darcy with evidence as to character: Mrs. Reynolds is a useful piece of machinery—but I do not think that the more exacting Jane Austen of the later novels would have been content with her. It is more to the purpose that here Darcy and Elizabeth see one another for the first time in favourable—even flattering—circumstances: he at his best on his own estate (a piece of nice observation), and she among congenial companions. Lydia's disgrace has still to come—to give him opportunity for proving that he has taken her strictures to heart, to show her how much he values those hopes of a better understanding which it seems bound to frustrate. And Lady Catherine will involuntarily give the last turn to the plot by her interference. But these are needed to bring about rather the marriage than the better understanding. *That* had sprung from the very nature of the misunderstanding, from the interaction of character and circumstance. (pp. 160-63)

> *Mary Lascelles, in her* Jane Austen and Her Art, *Oxford University Press, London, 1939, 225 p.*

SAMUEL KLIGER   (essay date 1947)

[*Kliger asserts that* Pride and Prejudice *derives its structure and plot from an ongoing series of variations on the popular eighteenth-century theme of art versus nature. The critic views Darcy and Elizabeth's reconciliation as a subtle balancing of social responsibility, feeling, and intellect that symbolizes the ideal resolution of the art-nature dialectic.*]

It is no difficult task to cull from Jane Austen's *Pride and Prejudice* passages reflecting the period's taste in art and employing a critical terminology made widely current throughout the eighteenth century by many formal discussions of aesthetics. Thus, for example, two performances at the piano by Elizabeth Bennet, the heroine, and her sister Mary, are evaluated in terms of the familiar antithesis, drawn in innumerable essays of the period, between "art" and "nature." Elizabeth performs first and the author comments: "Her performance was pleasing, though by no means capital. After a song or two, and before she could reply to the entreaties of several that she would sing again, she was eagerly succeeded at the instrument by her sister Mary, who having, in consequence of being the only plain one in the family, worked hard for knowledge and accomplishments, was always impatient for display." As for the sister, however: "Mary had neither genius nor taste; and though vanity had given her application, it had given her likewise a pedantic air and conceited manner, which would have injured a higher degree of excellence than she had reached. Elizabeth, easy and unaffected, had been listened to with much more pleasure, though not playing half so well.''

A century-long discussion, particularly of Shakespeare, is neatly summarized in this passage. Shakespeare, the period agreed, ''wanted art''; but, his natural genius offsetting his neglect of art, he was exonerated. Mrs. Griffith, for example, condemned those ''mechanists in criticism'' who judged Shakespeare ''by the cold rules of artful construction.'' She remarked further: ''Would they restrain him within the precincts of art, the height, the depth of whose imagination and creative genius found even the extent of Nature too streightly bounded for it to move in?'' Pope, earlier in the century, had also declared for the ''grace beyond the reach of art'': ''A cooler Judgment may commit fewer Faults, and be more approv'd in the Eyes of *One Sort* of Criticks: but that Warmth of Fancy will carry the loudest and more universal Applauses which holds the Heart of a Reader under the strongest Enchantment.''

These were critical commonplaces of the period. The contemporary reader of Jane Austen's novel would recognize at once the critical distinctions between ''art'' and ''nature'' involved and would concur, perhaps, in extending the palm not to Mary's artful yet unpleasing rendition but to Elizabeth's ''natural'' singing despite its obvious failures in the ''art'' of voice cultivation. On the other hand, however, although Jane Austen's partiality for Elizabeth's vivid style is obvious, it would be a serious mistake to conclude that it was possible for either Jane Austen or her period to deprecate ''art'' altogether. Nothing could be further from the truth of eighteenth-century aesthetic standards, generally speaking. The whole point of the art-nature antithesis was that it was usable as a basis for erecting an apparatus for the critical analysis of painting, literature, and the fine arts, which by manipulation of the two contraries, ''art'' and ''nature,'' found excellence in a just mixture of these two opposing qualities. In this kind of analysis, faults were identified with excesses in any one extreme or exclusive emphasis on one extreme of style. The rationalistic temper of the period required that excellence be found in a mean between two extremes. Only those readers persuaded by the false classic-romantic dichotomy embalmed in the simpler sort of literary text-books will find in Jane Austen's relative partiality for Elizabeth an absolute condemnation of Mary's ''art.'' As a matter of fact, those who read the novel in this rigid manner will fail to see that by a kind of calculated ambiguity, Jane Austen has purposely set up in the singing scene two alternative possibilities of interpretation: i.e., Elizabeth's ''naturalness'' is either praiseworthy or to be condemned. Before the novel's end, it will become apparent that, one alternative removed, the remaining alternative fixes the conception of Elizabeth's character and attitudes.

The contrast between Elizabeth's ''natural'' and Mary's ''artful'' rendition is soon extended, as anyone can expect who is even moderately well read in eighteenth-century aesthetic discussion, to involve a second set of terms, held in essential opposition: ''reason'' and ''feeling.'' Thus Mary comments on Elizabeth's decision to walk the three miles to the Bingley home in order to investigate Jane's illness: ''I admire the activity of your benevolence, . . . but every impulse of feeling should be guided by reason; and, in my opinion, exertion should always be in proportion to what is required.'' Art and reason are the terms on one side of the antithesis; nature and benevolence are the terms on the other side. The contextual shift along the line from ''art'' (a literary norm) to ''reason'' (an

ethical norm) is readily recognizable as a commonplace in the neo-classical idea-complex. From Shaftesbury onwards, taste in art had almost invariably been conceived as a species of virtue. No notion was more characteristic of English neo-classicism than the idea that taste in the fine arts is an ally of morals. The eighteenth century believed that both the feeling for beauty and the prizing of what is decent and proper, perfect the character of the gentleman. As Alexander Gerard expressed it in his *Essay on Taste:* ''A man of nice taste will have a stronger abhorrence of vice and a keener relish for virtue, in any given situation, than a person of dull organs can have in the same circumstances.'' Because of the contextual shift or correlation of art with morals, Elizabeth's emotionalism is to be seen as the correlative of her artless singing. Furthermore, her indecorous behaviour, although clearly motivated by a warm devotion to her sick sister, Jane, also suggests, nevertheless, possibilities of censure, in that the century saw moral excellence as action conforming, as does good art, to a universal criterion of the mean between two extremes. In other words, Elizabeth's emotionalism is not only correlative to her natural style of singing but by calculated ambiguity is purposely presented in the novel in such a way as to suggest possibilities of both praise and censure. By means of this artistic device, the novel's end is practically dictated: that is, the period's rationalistic quest of the mean between two extremes requires that the probabilities for the heroine's behaviour be set up between two alternatives, neither of which is acceptable alone; the rejection of one alternative makes spectacularly clear to the heroine (and the reader) that the solution lies not in the remaining alternative but in a just moderation between the two.

In a third passage, the bi-polar terms ''art'' and ''nature'' reveal yet another tension in the neo-classical idea-complex, between ''originality'' (inspiration, spontaneity, singularity, enthusiasm, excess, the untutored genius—these are all synonymous in current critical usage) and the opposite of originality, the ''rules'' (regularity, uniformity, propriety, *bon sens,* the appeal to precedent and the example of Greek and Roman antiquity, the disciplined artist—these are all synonyms in the eighteenth-century vocabulary of criticism). The tension is brought to light in Mary's comment on Collins' letter: ''In point of composition, . . . , his letter does not seem defective. The idea of the olive branch perhaps is not wholly new, yet I think it is well expressed.'' Mary's measured praise of Collins' epistolary style is in accord with Pope's dictum.

> True wit is Nature to advantage dress'd
> What oft was thought, but ne'er so well express'd,

as only one expression out of many of the period's critical viewpoint towards ''originality.'' Jane Austen's contemporary readers, simply because their values were the same as Jane Austen's, did not need to be reminded, as does the modern reader, either of the critical distinction between the term ''originality'' and its antithetical correlative ''uniformity,'' or that these concepts were transvaluations of the basic antithesis between ''art'' and ''nature.'' In the pattern, Mary is the symbol of art, reason, uniformity while Elizabeth is the symbol of nature, benevolence, originality.

The subject of letter-writing, in a fourth passage, causes a shift a second time in the narrative from art and nature, conceived unilaterally in their aesthetic application, to the question of a universal standard of excellence common to art and morals alike. Darcy is composing a letter and Miss Bingley, whose game it is to detract from Elizabeth's charm, monopolizes the conversation. In this sequence, Miss Bingley is twitting Darcy on his slow, laborious writing. In verbal parry and thrust, the information is elicited that Bingley, by contrast, is a rapid writer: "My ideas flow so rapidly that I have not time to express them; by which means my letters sometimes convey no ideas at all to my correspondents." Elizabeth, who is only too eager to humble Darcy's pride—if she can—takes the occasion to praise Bingley's modesty in confessing his epistolary faults. Darcy, however, is not prone to accept her judgment, and he even condemns such modesty as a kind of hypocrisy. As the banter grows, it becomes clear that Darcy reproves "precipitance" (it is his own word) in letter-writing and in social conduct. The tie of friendship between Bingley and himself notwithstanding, there is no point, Darcy is saying, in shrinking from condemning Bingley's epistolary deficiencies. Darcy is offended by Bingley's epistolary improprieties as if they were moral misdemeanors—this, of course, is possible only because the period correlated art with morals. In addition, Darcy is arguing that Elizabeth is compounding the original error in seeking exculpation in friendship. Darcy's overbearing manner may be reprehensible, and before the novel's end he too will approach the mean and allow for the ties of friendship; but because of the century's rationalistic "religion," there is in his reprimand of Elizabeth and Bingley more of a defence of the universe's rational aims and goals than there is a defence of a purely literary standard. Propriety for Darcy is universal and immutable, imbedded in the rational scheme of things, or is, rather, the means of achieving life's rational ends.

Two additional passages, concentrating on Elizabeth's predilection for the artless, also reveal a background of eighteenth-century aesthetic discussion. One concerns the merits in landscape gardening as between the French trimmed garden and the English wild, natural garden, and the second, Longinus' theory of the "sublime." Mrs. Gardiner's invitation to Elizabeth to visit the Lake-country arouses Elizabeth's anticipations of pleasure in the sublimity of rocks and mountains: "What are men to rocks and mountains? Oh, what hours of transport we shall spend!" In the second passage, Elizabeth's visit to Pemberley, Darcy's family seat, opens to her enraptured eyes the beauty of Pemberley's natural landscaping. It was "without any artificial appearance. Its banks were neither formal nor falsely adorned. Elizabeth was delighted. She had never seen a place for which nature had done more, or where natural beauty had been so little counteracted by an awkward taste." In neither of these passages is the doctrine of "nature" extended to morals, but to the period, as we have seen, "nature" was simultaneously an aesthetic and ethical norm. "Transport," in particular, is a key word in the period to a protracted discussion of Longinus' theory of the "sublime." The transport afforded by rocks and mountains illustrates the interest in *beau désordre*, created by a shift within the neo-classical thought-complex away from a doctrine of uniform nature, regular and orderly, toward a doctrine which saw excellence in irregularity; the concomitant shift was from reason to emotion, from a rational deistic religion to a religion of "enthusiasm." In other words, both ethical and aesthetic criteria were involved in the discussion of "art" and "nature."

These are the passages on art criticism which *Pride and Prejudice* yields to the attentive reader. However, as we have already seen, it is a quite dubious procedure which would attempt to establish a partiality on Jane Austen's part for any one of the critical ideas which the novel expresses. Critical ideas introduced within the context of a novel are not at all the same as critical ideas expressed in a formal treatise on the subject. At any rate, even if we waive the objection, the search for

typical eighteenth-century critical ideas in *Pride and Prejudice* would nevertheless tend to miss the whole point, which can be expressed in the following way: in both great and small plots, the novel intends to invoke the same thoughts and attitudes about the antithesis of art and nature. The concentration, in fact, in the small plot on singing, letter-writing, the enjoyment of mountainous sublimity, the appreciation of gardening, carries out Jane Austen's carefully premeditated plan for increasing the availability of the art-nature antithesis for the love plot or basic situation of the novel. In other words, the art-nature antithesis is abstracted into a symbolism adequate to cover the adventures and misadventures which keep Elizabeth and Darcy apart in mutual repulsion at the beginning of the tale and bring them together at the end. Instead, therefore, of selecting passages by an eclectic method in the interest of a systematic exposition of Jane Austen's views on art, the passages ought to be chosen by a formal method, treating the book as an art form with its own laws of development, in the interest of establishing the mutual appropriateness of the art-nature antithesis to the probabilities for action set up in the characters, who are arranged along a scale from one extreme of behaviour suggested by the terms art and reason to the extreme at the opposite end of the scale suggested by the terms nature and emotion.

The purpose of this essay, therefore, is first to establish the art-nature antithesis as the ground of the book's action and its mode of organization and, second, to show that the doctrine of art and reason is extended to morals, to include, in particular, a concept of class relationships. Darcy's pride of class is persistently misunderstood by Elizabeth and what she must learn is that his pride—under proper limitations—is appropriate and a proper human trait. Contrariwise, Darcy must learn that Elizabeth's prejudice for dealing with humans *qua* humans, irrespective of class, is—again under proper limitations—appropriate and an admirable human trait. Thus between the problem posed in the initial scenes of the novel and its resolution at the book's end is a dialectic which separates the two leading characters in the beginning and joins them at the end in a mean between the two extremes which each respectively represents. Jane Austen has a host of admirers, but it seems merely idle to praise her perfection of form without being able to indicate in specific ways how the perfection is achieved. The governing idea of *Pride and Prejudice* is the art-nature antithesis; the perfection of form is achieved through relating each character and incident to the basic art-nature dialectic. A concentration on the art-nature contrast at the book's beginning in the sequence describing Mary's art and Elizabeth's artlessness prepares the reader to recognize that it is precisely the same dialectic between whose ebb and flow Elizabeth and Darcy, in their conflicting attitudes towards class relationships, gyrate. Tracing the art-nature dialectic will give clearer meaning to *Pride and Prejudice* and will show how completely dedicated Jane Austen was to the art of fiction.

The ethical expression of the art-nature opposition which governs the novel appears in an antithesis between primitivism and society. The reader of Jane Austen's novel should recall that because of a vogue in the eighteenth century of primitivistic discussion, the term "nature" had also established itself as one item of an antithesis on another level between the "arts" (man-made) and that which is in "nature" (God-made); the antithesis could be used to indicate whether civilization was progressing from the primitive state of nature because of man's progress in the arts, manufactures, organized government, and private property; or, conversely, whether civilization was retrograding because the arts, manufactures, government, and private property represented a perversion of nature. Elizabeth's prejudice toward Darcy's pride of class, her insistence on dealing with humans *qua* humans (naturally, that is) express the ideas at the primitivistic pole of the antithesis; Darcy is the spokesman for civilization, man-made and not in "nature," especially as he speaks in terms of a theory of class stratification. Elizabeth represents "man-in-nature," the earlier felicity and joy existing in the class-less, government-less, property-less conditions surrounding men in the Garden of Eden before the Fall. Darcy represents the consequences of the fall of man, the arts of society and government necessary to restrain the wickedness and greed of men resulting from their fall from the bliss of Eden. In Darcy culminates a centuries-old tradition, carefully nurtured by Christian thinkers throughout the medieval period and carried down to modern times without significant change. (pp. 357-63)

We are now at the heart of the Elizabeth-Darcy problem. The issues are clear: (1) A tension is created between the conceptions of man-in-nature and man-in-society; the first deals with humans *qua* humans, the second deals with humans as the "art" of society directs their activities. (2) Pride in class is a proper and justifiable human trait; superiority, so far from being a usurped right, is actually a heavy burden of duties which one assumes; the essential meaning of *noblesse oblige* is this willingness to serve. (3) Since no class exists for itself but is bound by reciprocated rights and duties to classes above and below, social non-compliance is represented either in improper respect for classes above or in delinquency in duty to classes below. (4) The system embodies the universal criterion of the mean between the two extremes; the individual's worth *qua* individual is adjusted to his worth as a member of a social class, whatever his class may be; a dialectic separates the natural man from man as the art of society has created him; nature and art are the juxtaposed terms. Considering the dialectic which separates the two terms, it is instructive to observe how the great Renaissance rationalist, Bishop Hooker, formulated the problem. He pointed out that individuals who are perfectly exemplary are not necessarily the same considered as members of society: "It is both commonly said, and truly, that the best men otherwise are not always the best in regard of society. The reason whereof is, for that the law of men's actions is one, if they be respected only as men; and another, when they are considered as parts of a public body. Many men there are, than whom nothing is more commendable when they are singled; and yet in society with others none less fit to answer the duties which are looked for at their hands."

Since it is Darcy who capitulates first and early in the book, the real concern of the author is evidently Elizabeth's quest of the mean between the two extremes of "art" and "nature." It is Elizabeth who must set her emotional house in order and learn to evaluate all that has happened to her in terms of the mean between the two extremes of the "art" of human relationships and humans in their "natural" associations. In Bishop Hooker's terms, she is an exemplary person as an individual, but she is socially deficient. On the other hand, Darcy is socially exemplary but is deficient in naturalness.

In the letter-writing scene, resentful of Darcy's stiff-necked pride, Elizabeth scores a point for herself, although ostensibly she is defending Bingley's relaxed epistolary style against Darcy's condemnation of such indecorum. She says: "You appear to me, Mr. Darcy, to allow nothing for the influence of friendship and affection." Elizabeth may be right, but she may be

wrong also. Darcy scores a point for reason and the "art" of human relationships when he replies: "Pride—where there is a real superiority of mind—pride will always be under good regulation." Pride, he is saying, is a proper human trait; but Elizabeth is scornful. Her prejudice for dealing with humans *qua* humans, irrespective of class standards, naturally instead of artfully, emotionally instead of rationally, has nearly fatal consequences for her in so far as it almost brings her to a marriage with Wickham.

Wickham precipitates the main action. In the first place, he raises the crucial problem of reciprocated rights and duties. The question is whether the Darcys, father and son, have been true to their class mission of rewarding a faithful servitor. Slyly but shrewdly, Wickham encourages Elizabeth to believe that the younger Darcy has been remiss in his social duties. The entire incident is revealing not only of Wickham's rascality but of Darcy's class idealism and of Elizabeth's failure to consider more sympathetically Darcy's class pride which debars him from expostulating even when he has been seriously libelled.

The fundamental principle of *noblesse oblige* is never to complain, never to explain. No gentleman will either complain or explain when his actions are falsely reported. It is beneath Darcy's pride to explain that Wickham had signed away for cash his right to the Darcy patronage. Darcy by his attitude acknowledges the merit of the phrase *"honi soit qui mal y pense"*—and it is certainly part of Elizabeth's later humiliation that she must recognize her failure to understand Darcy's silence. With perfect consistency, Darcy afterwards serves Elizabeth silently and well in the Lydia-Wickham elopement by removing the financial obstacles in the way of the marriage. On the other hand, Wickham further displays his lack of principles in his loud complaints to Elizabeth.

Elizabeth falls victim to Wickham's strategy only because of her prejudice for dealing with people naturally, irrespective of class. It is characteristic of her that she seeks to measure Darcy for human consistency and she fails for the obvious reason that she is measuring him with the wrong measuring stick. This is brought out in her reply to Wickham that, granting Darcy his pride, his pride alone should have encouraged him to discharge his class obligation to his former steward: "How strange! . . . How abominable! I wonder that the very pride of this Mr. Darcy has not made him just to you! If from no better motive, that he should not have been too proud to be dishonest—for dishonesty I must call it."

In a chastened spirit, Elizabeth learns to respect Darcy's pride of class. Her surrender is expressed explicitly in the words which she intends to remove her father's anxiety about her impending marriage with Darcy: "I love him. Indeed he has no improper pride." A complete surrender of either Darcy or Elizabeth to the other would completely falsify the eighteenth century's ideal of moderation and would obscure the basic art-nature antithesis. As it is, the partial capitulation of each to the other makes clear that each recognizes that every quality has its corresponding defect. With a sudden pleasant surprise, the reader recalls that early in the novel, Jane Austen, with an irony that must have been deliberate, suggests the idea as the premise upon which in the central sequence of the novel the quest proceeds for the mean between extremes when she has Darcy say: "There is, I believe, in every disposition a tendency to some particular evil, a natural defect, which not even the best education can overcome." The exposure of Wickham's perfidy makes Elizabeth, as she reflects backwards on her wilful misunderstanding of Darcy's class idealism, realize her

defect of considering people exclusively in their natural relations with corresponding neglect of their opposite qualities
arising out of their social relations as the arts of government
and society shape them.

It is not intended to suggest that Elizabeth is a doctrinaire
revolutionary, aiming to level all classes. There is not a single
statement in the novel which can be construed as politically
tendentious. On this score alone, the critics are quite right who
point out that Jane Austen was totally unaffected by the currents
of thought set up by the French Revolution; not even her relative
residing in her house, whose husband was beheaded by the
guillotine, moved her to interpret the Revolution. Yet *Pride
and Prejudice* is not merely a mild satire on manners but, as
we have seen, hands down a social verdict. The satire in the
novel on social institutions hardly ripples the surface, but the
currents underneath are powerful. If the conclusion of the novel
makes clear that Elizabeth accepts class relationships as valid,
it becomes equally clear that Darcy, through Elizabeth's genius
for treating all people with respect for their natural dignity, is
reminded that institutions are not an end in themselves but are
intended to serve the end of human happiness.

If Elizabeth is not a Leveller, intent on levelling all classes, it
is nevertheless interesting to observe how much the spirit of
the great seventeenth-century Levellers has entered into her
mind. Modern democracy was forged, as we know, in the fiery
furnace of the Cromwellian revolution. The noblest words ever
spoken for democracy came from the famous Putney Debates
in which the question was raised whether property should be
a qualification for voting. Rainborough, a Leveller, declared:
"For really I think that the poorest he that is in England hath
a life to live, as the greatest he." Rainborough was defeated
and the property qualification remained. The steady growth,
however, of the franchise in England bears witness to the fact
that Leveller ideas of respect for natural human dignity have
never failed to inspire English political thinking. Perhaps this
is merely another way of pointing to the English genius for
bringing about the most revolutionary changes in the mildest
way possible. The compromise effected between Elizabeth and
Darcy represents the same phenomenon, and in this sense Elizabeth is a Leveller and Darcy represents those in the Cromwellian group who argued for the preservation of the property
qualification. Elizabeth learns that we must not scorn the accumulated wisdom of past experience which has shaped during
centuries the institution of class; Darcy, on the other hand,
learns that conservatism need not be impervious to new ideas.
And here, perhaps, we have the sufficient answer to those
critics of Jane Austen who claim that she was politically and
socially obtuse. A livelier appreciation among readers of Jane
Austen's novel of the potency of the terms "art" and "nature"
in the thinking of such typical eighteenth-century political writers as Burke, Rousseau, Priestley, and Paine, would make it
clearer that the art-nature antithesis was an explicit intellectual
formulation growing out of the rationalistic spirit of the age.
Developed now in aesthetic discussion and now in political
discussion, the terms at the bottom were the same since the
century sought a universal criterion of a mean between extremes common to art and morals alike. (pp. 364-68)

> *Samuel Kliger, "Jane Austen's 'Pride and Prejudice'
> in the Eighteenth-Century Mode," in* University of
> Toronto Quarterly, *Vol. XVI, No. 4, July, 1947, pp.
> 357-70.*

MARVIN MUDRICK   (essay date 1952)

[*In the following excerpt from his study of irony in Austen's works,
Mudrick explores how this quality functions in* Pride and Prejudice. *According to the critic, Elizabeth's gradual realization that
the choices of even complex individuals are subject to social and
economic pressures is central to the development of her character.
Mudrick also remarks on various simple and complex characters
in the novel and analyzes Elizabeth's reactions to each of them.
For additional commentary by Mudrick on* Pride and Prejudice,
see NCLC, Vol. 1.]

In *Pride and Prejudice,* for the first time, Jane Austen allows
her heroine to share her own characteristic response to the
world. Elizabeth Bennet tells Darcy:

> "Follies and nonsense, whims and inconsis-
> tencies do divert me, I own, and I laugh at
> them whenever I can. . . ."

The response is not only characteristic of Elizabeth and her
author, but consciously and articulately aimed at by both of
them. Both choose diversion; and both, moreover, look for
their diversion in the people about them. Elizabeth, despite her
youth and the limitations of a rural society, is—like the author·
of **"Lesley Castle"** and **"The Three Sisters"**—a busy "studier
of character," as Bingley leads her to affirm:

> "You begin to comprehend me, do you?" cried
> he, turning towards her.
>
> "Oh! yes—I understand you perfectly."
>
> "I wish I might take this for a compliment; but
> to be so easily seen through I am afraid is pit-
> iful."
>
> "That is as it happens. It does not necessarily
> follow that a deep, intricate character is more
> or less estimable than such a one as yours."
>
> "Lizzy," cried her mother, "remember where
> you are, and do not run on in the wild manner
> that you are suffered to do at home."
>
> "I did not know before," continued Bingley
> immediately, "that you were a studier of char-
> acter. It must be an amazing study."
>
> "Yes; but intricate characters are the *most*
> amusing. They have at least that advan-
> tage." . . .

"Character" gains a general overtone: with Elizabeth's qualifying adjective, it becomes not only the summation of a single
personality, but the summation of a type, the fixing of the
individual into a category. So Elizabeth sets herself up as an
ironic spectator, able and prepared to judge and classify, already making the first large division of the world into two sorts
of people: the simple ones, those who give themselves away
out of shallowness (as Bingley fears) or perhaps openness (as
Elizabeth implies) or an excess of affectation (as Mr. Collins
will demonstrate); and the intricate ones, those who cannot be
judged and classified so easily, who are "the most amusing"
to the ironic spectator because they offer the most formidable
challenge to his powers of detection and analysis. Into one of
these preliminary categories, Elizabeth fits everybody she observes. (pp. 94-5)

The first decision we must make about anyone, so Elizabeth
suggests and the author confirms by her shaping commentary,
is not moral but psychological, not whether he is good or bad,
but whether he is simple or intricate: whether he may be disposed of as fixed and predictable or must be recognized as
variable, perhaps torn between contradictory motives, intel-

lectually or emotionally complex, unsusceptible to a quick judgment.

Once having placed the individual in his category, we must proceed to discriminate him from the others there; and, in the category of simplicity at least, Elizabeth judges as accurately as her author. Jane Austen allows the ''simple'' characters to have no surprises for Elizabeth, and, consequently, none for us. They perform, they amuse; but we never doubt that we know what they are, and why they act as they do. (p. 95)

[Elizabeth] is far more aware of distinctions in personality than any of the author's previous heroines: Catherine Morland, Elinor or Marianne Dashwood. In *Northanger Abbey,* the author could not allow her heroine to be aware from the outset since her story developed precisely out of Catherine's unawareness of distinctions (a quality suggested, perhaps, by Jane Austen's early tendency to assert an arbitrary omniscience over the objects of her irony). In *Sense and Sensibility,* Jane Austen, yielding for the first time to the moral pressures inevitable upon a woman of her time and class, allowed Elinor only the solemn and easy discriminations of bourgeois morality, and finally smothered the threatening spark of Marianne's much livelier and more observing consciousness. . . . [The distinction between simple and complex personalities], which in her youthful defensive posture Jane Austen has tended to make only between her characters and herself, she . . . establishes internally [in *Pride and Prejudice*], between two categories of personality within the novel. The distinction is, in fact, one that every character in *Pride and Prejudice* must make if he can; and the complex characters—Elizabeth and Darcy among them—justify their complexity by making it, and trying to live by its implications, through all their lapses of arrogance, prejudice, sensuality, and fear. Elizabeth is aware because, in the novel's climate of adult decision, she must be so to survive with our respect and interest.

Yet the distinction must be made in a social setting, by human beings fallible, if for no other reason, because of their own social involvement. The province of *Pride and Prejudice*—as always in Jane Austen's novels—is marriage in an acquisitive society. Elizabeth herself, being young, attractive, and unmarried, is at the center of it; and it is this position that sets her off from such an external and imposed commentator as Henry Tilney. Her position of personal involvement subjects her, moreover, to a risk of error never run by the detached Mr. Tilney. She can tag and dismiss the blatantly simple persons very well; it is when she moves away from these toward ambiguity and self-concealment, toward persons themselves aware enough to interest and engage her, that her youth and inexperience and emotional partiality begin to deceive her.

They deceive her first with Charlotte Lucas. The two girls have been good friends. Charlotte, according to the author, is a ''sensible, intelligent young woman,'' . . . and she shares Elizabeth's taste for raillery and social generalization. Even when Charlotte offers her altogether cynical views on courtship and marriage, Elizabeth refuses to take her at her word. . . . It is not that Elizabeth misjudges Charlotte's capabilities, but that she underestimates the strength of the pressures acting upon her. Charlotte is twenty-seven, unmarried, not pretty, not well-to-do, living in a society which treats a penniless old maid less as a joke than as an exasperating burden upon her family. But Elizabeth is inexperienced enough, at the beginning, to judge in terms of personality only. She recognizes Mr. Collins' total foolishness and Charlotte's intelligence, and would never have dreamed that any pressure could overcome so natural an op-

position. Complex and simple, aware and unaware, do not belong together—except that in marriages made by economics they often unite, however obvious the mismatching. . . . So the natural antithesis which separates simple from complex, and which should separate one from the other absolutely in the closest human relationship, can be upset and annulled by economic pressure.

Elizabeth's continual mistake is to ignore, or to set aside as uninfluential, the social context. It is a question not merely of individuals and marriage, but of individuals and marriage in an acquisitive society. Elizabeth expects nothing except comfort or amusement from simplicity; but she likes to believe that complexity means a categorically free will, without social distortion or qualification.

When complexity and a pleasing manner combine, as they do in Wickham, Elizabeth is at her least cautious. Wickham is clever and charming, a smooth social being, and for these qualities Elizabeth is ready to believe his long, unsolicited tale of being wronged and even to imagine herself falling in love with him. What she never allows, until much later, to cast a doubt upon his testimony is the fact that he is a dispossessed man in an acquisitive society. It is true that Wickham is very persuasive, and that Elizabeth's prejudice against Darcy (which has grown out of her failure to take into account *his* social context) has prepared her to accept Wickham's accusation. Still, she has reason to reconsider when Wickham turns his attentions to a Miss King, concerning whom the ''sudden acquisition of ten thousand pounds was the most remarkable charm.'' . . . If, instead, she refuses to begrudge him his change of heart, his ''wish of independence,'' . . . and acknowledges to her aunt that she is ''open to the mortifying conviction that handsome young men must have something to live on, as well as the plain,'' . . . she remains quite in character, less perceptive than usual out of her appreciation of Wickham's cleverness and manner, ready to believe that an unknown Miss King can scarcely be as bad as Charlotte's too well known Mr. Collins, that at any rate so charming a man cannot be altogether wrong.

It is with Wickham, nevertheless, that Jane Austen's directing and organizing irony—which functions doubly, at the same time through and upon Elizabeth—begins to fail; and the area of failure, as with Willoughby, is the sexual experience outside marriage.

The first flattening of tone occurs in Darcy's letter . . . , in which Wickham's infamy is revealed. Wickham has attempted to seduce Darcy's sister, Georgiana; and it is this specific attempt, beyond any other evidence of profligacy, that automatically makes him a villain from Darcy's point of view, and from Elizabeth's also as soon as she can accept the truth of the letter. The curious fact is, not that Elizabeth and, here at least, Jane Austen regard seduction as infamous, but that, into an ironic atmosphere elaborated and intensified out of the difficulty of interpreting motive, Jane Austen pushes a standard black-and-white seduction-scene, with all the appurtenances of an ingenuous young girl, a scheming profligate, a wicked governess, and an outraged brother, and with no trace of doubt, shading, or irony. It is hardly enough to say, with Miss Lascelles, that Jane Austen clings to this novelistic convention through almost all her work as to a usable climax, which she met in Richardson and for which she could find no adequate substitute. *Why* she retained this threadbare revelation when, as early as *Pride and Prejudice,* she could demonstrate the most subtle and resourceful skill in representing every other particular of the action, remains a question.

The answer seems to be that, though the nature of her subject makes an approach to the sexual experience inevitable, Jane Austen will not allow herself (as she did in **"Love and Friendship"** and continues to do in her letters) to assimilate extramarital sex to her characteristic unifying irony, and that her only other possible response is conventional. She must truncate, flatten, falsify, disapprove, all in the interests of an external morality; and the process in *Pride and Prejudice* is so out of key with its surroundings as to be immediately jarring.

Lydia is the outstanding victim. Not that Lydia is not throughout a wholly consistent and living character. On the solid and simple foundations of her personality she works up to her triumphant end in marriage to Wickham. If she acts from her sensual nature, it is Elizabeth and the author themselves who have proved to us that Lydia, being among the simple spirits who are never really aware and who act only upon their single potentiality, cannot do otherwise. She is fulfilling herself, as Mr. Collins fulfills himself in marriage and at Rosings, as Jane and Bingley fulfill themselves. The irony is, or should be, in her unawareness, in her powerlessness to change, in the incongruity between her conviction of vitality and her lack of choice. This irony, though, Jane Austen quite cuts off. She is herself silent, but it is clear that she allows Elizabeth to define the proper attitude toward Lydia. Elizabeth can feel, at first, no sympathy for Lydia at all—only shame and self-pity however altruistically phrased. . . . Later, however, when the moment of shame is long past, her attitude has not changed except to harden into sarcastic resentment. . . . Elizabeth's ill-tempered efforts to shame Lydia are fruitless, as Elizabeth should have known they would be while Lydia is Lydia still. What they amount to is a kind of floating moral judgment. It seems that both Jane Austen and her heroine feel uneasily that a moral lesson must be taught, though they have already proved that Lydia is incapable of learning it. . . . (pp. 106-12)

So Jane Austen suspends her irony, suspends her imagination altogether, while Wickham is engaged in seducing Georgiana or Lydia. Yet, apart from this temporary suspension, Wickham fits admirably into the large pattern of Elizabeth's social education. Not only is he, like Charlotte, an example of the complex personality discarding scruples, discarding candor, making the wrong choice under economic pressure; he is also an evil agent, quite willing to corrupt others as well, to involve them in public disgrace if he can thereby assure his own security. What he uses deliberately is what Mrs. Bennet used, much less deliberately, in her conquest of her husband: sexual attractiveness. It is, then, Wickham who by exploiting sex sets off that other intricate character who passively succumbed to it—Mr. Bennet.

It is, in fact, easy to imagine that when Mr. Bennet calls Wickham his favorite son-in-law . . . he is not merely indulging in habitual paradox, but ironically recognizing the painful contrast between Wickham's awareness, however directed, and his own self-delusion, in the same emotional circumstance. Mr. Bennet made his mistake many years before, and must now stand by it because his class recognizes no respectable way out. . . . (pp. 112-13)

Elizabeth knows her father: of the complex characters in the story, he is the only one whom she has known long and well enough to judge accurately from the outset. She has learned from his example that a complex personality may yield to the pressure of sensuality; that marriages made by sex—as well as those made by economics—represent, for the free individual, an abdication of choice, an irremediable self-degradation and defeat.

In his social context, in his status as a gentleman of independent means, Mr. Bennet was lulled into believing that choice was easy, a matter of simple and unexamined inclination; and in the same society Mrs. Bennet could not believe otherwise than that any gentleman of means must make a desirable husband. This much Elizabeth recognizes about the pressures of an acquisitive society, even upon a free individual like her father. The shock of Charlotte's marriage to a fool makes Elizabeth recognize that these pressures act decisively upon other free individuals as well. In spite of examples, however, it takes a long series of vexations and misunderstandings before she can be convinced that the imposed pride of rank and wealth, perhaps the strongest pressure in an acquisitive society, may act, not yet decisively—for the area of decision is marriage—but conditionally upon a free individual like Darcy, to make him behave with an overconfident and unsympathetic obstinacy, to make him seem far different from what he is capable of being behind the façade of pride.

It is the social façade of the complex person that deceives Elizabeth. She can penetrate her father's, out of sympathetic familiarity and concern; but Charlotte's has deceived her. Wickham's takes her in altogether; and by contrast with Wickham's, by the contrast which Wickham himself takes care to emphasize in his own support, Darcy's façade seems disagreeable indeed, or rather a clear window on a disagreeable spirit.

Darcy's function as the character most difficult for the heroine to interpret, and yet most necessary for her to interpret if *she* is to make a proper decision in the only area of choice her society leaves open, his simultaneous role as the heroine's puzzle and her only possible hero, is clearly marked out during the action. From Elizabeth's point of view, in fact, the process of the interpretation of Darcy's personality from disdain through doubt to admiration is represented with an extraordinarily vivid and convincing minuteness. Nevertheless, Darcy himself remains unachieved: we recognize his effects upon Elizabeth, without recognizing that he exists independently of them.

Mrs. Leavis has persuasively documented her belief that *Pride and Prejudice* is an effort to "rewrite the story of *Cecilia* in realistic terms" [see *NCLC*, Vol. 1]; and she observes, more particularly, that Darcy fails because he does not transcend his derivation: he is a character out of a book, not one whom Jane Austen created or reorganized for her own purpose. But why Darcy alone: why is he, among the major figures in *Pride and Prejudice,* the only one disturbingly derived and wooden?

The reason seems to be the same as that which compelled Jane Austen to falsify her tone and commentary concerning Wickham's seductions and to supply Elinor and Marianne Dashwood with such nonentities for husbands. The socially unmanageable, the personally involving aspects of sex, Jane Austen can no longer treat with irony, nor can she as yet treat them straightforwardly. Darcy is the hero, he is the potential lover of a complex young woman much like the author herself; and as such Jane Austen cannot animate him with emotion, or with her characteristic informing irony. She borrows him from a book; and, though she alters and illuminates everything else, she can do nothing more with him than fit him functionally into the plot.

Even here the author is so uncharacteristically clumsy as to rely on inconsistencies of personality to move her story along. However difficult Elizabeth's task of interpreting Darcy, it is clear from the beginning that, in his consistent functional impact upon the story, he is a proud man with a strong sense of at least external propriety and dignity, and with no taste whatever for his aunt's vulgar condescension or the kind of sarcasm dispensed by Mr. Bennet. Yet on his first appearance he initiates Elizabeth's prejudice by speaking with a simple vulgarity indistinguishable from his aunt's, and in a voice loud enough to be overheard by the object of his contempt. . . . In spite of his rigid and principled reserve, in spite of Elizabeth's having just turned down his arrogant proposal, he makes his explanation to Elizabeth in a thoroughly frank and unreserved letter, which—more appropriate to a Richardsonian correspondent than to Darcy as he has been presented—seems an author's gesture of desperation to weight the scales in favor of her predetermined hero. (pp. 115-18)

Out of inconsistency, Darcy emerges into flatness. Only in his sparring with Elizabeth, and then only occasionally, does he establish himself with a degree of solidity, of independent reference, as when Elizabeth tries to tease him into communicativeness while they are dancing. . . . (p. 118)

In dialogue, at least when Elizabeth is an enlivening participant, Jane Austen seems able now and then to overcome her awkwardness in handling Darcy. Otherwise, however, she can only make him serve: he interests us chiefly because he is the center of Elizabeth's interest; and because, in a book in which the individual must choose and in which marriage is the single area of choice, Darcy represents Elizabeth's only plausible, or almost plausible, mate. But Elizabeth's catalogue of his admirable qualities resembles an author's anxious trick to underscore this plausibility:

> She began now to comprehend that he was exactly the man who, in disposition and talents, would most suit her. His understanding and temper, though unlike her own, would have answered all her wishes. It was an union that must have been to the advantage of both; by her ease and liveliness, his mind might have been softened, his manners improved, and from his judgment, information, and knowledge of the world, she must have received benefit of greater importance. . . .

And when Darcy is ironed out into the conventionally generous and altruistic hero, making devoted efforts to shackle Wickham to Lydia, expending thousands of pounds to restore peace of mind to Elizabeth's family, and all for the love of Elizabeth—when he does all this, with no more of personal depth than Jane Austen allows of moral depth in the whole Lydia-Wickham episode, he comes very close to forfeiting even the functional plausibility that Elizabeth's interest lends him.

The last third of the book, as R. A. Brower has pointed out [see *NCLC*, Vol. 1], does in fact diminish suddenly in density and originality: that is, beginning with Lydia's elopement. We get a conventional chase by an outraged father, a friendly uncle, and a now impeccable hero; we get outbursts of irrelevantly directed moral judgment, and a general simplification of the problems of motive and will down to the level of the Burneyan novel. Jane Austen herself, routed by the sexual question she has raised, is concealed behind a fogbank of bourgeois morality; and the characters, most conspicuously Darcy, must shift for themselves, or, rather, they fall automatically into the grooves prepared for them by hundreds of novels of sentiment and sensibility.

Only Elizabeth does not. She may yield temporarily to a kind of homeless moralizing on Lydia's disgrace, she may be rather obvious and stiff in acquainting herself with Darcy's virtues at last; but the lapses are minor, and they never seriously dim her luminous vigor, her wit, curiosity, discrimination, and independence. If the novel does not collapse in the predictabilities of the denouement, it is because Elizabeth has from the outset been presented in a depth specific and vital enough to resist flattening, because she remains what she has been—a complex person in search of conclusions about people in society, and on the way to her unique and crucial choice.

She observes, and her shield and instrument together is irony. Like Mary Crawford later, Elizabeth is a recognizable and striking aspect of her author; but, unlike Mary's, her sins are all quite venial, her irony unclouded by the author's disapproval and—after a few detours—grandly vindicated in its effect. Jane Austen has not yet made her first unqualified capitulation to the suspicious sobriety of her class, and surrendered her values in exchange for its own. She can, in fact, embody her personal values in her heroine and be delighted with the result; so she writes to her sister about Elizabeth: "I must confess that I think her as delightful a creature as ever appeared in print, and how I shall be able to tolerate those who do not like *her* at least I do not know" [see excerpt dated January, 1813]. . . . (pp. 119-20)

Elizabeth's third dimension is irony; and it is her irony that fills out and sustains the action. Her slightest perception of incongruity reverberates through the scene, and from it out into the atmosphere of the book. (p. 120)

There is, above all, the perpetual exuberant yet directed irony of her conversation, especially as she uses it to sound Darcy. . . . Whether Elizabeth is teasing him about his silence at dancing . . . , or, in Lady Catherine's drawing room, explaining her lack of skill at the piano to refute Darcy's claim of having no talent for sociability . . . she draws him out in the only ways in which he can be drawn out at all, by a challenging indirection just short of impudence, by the appeal of an intelligence as free and aware as that on which he prides himself, by the penetration of a wit which makes its own rules without breaking any significant ones, which even establishes its priority over simple truth. . . . If Darcy, finally sounded and known, hardly differs from the stiff-jointed Burneyan aristocratic hero, except as Darcy is provided with a somewhat more explicit personality, the fault is not Elizabeth's, but her author's. Elizabeth has learned what can be learned about him; she has even learned, with Miss Bingley, that Darcy is *not* to be laughed at—not, at least, in the matter of his influence over Bingley. . . . In the process of interpretation, moreover—with its deflections, its spurious evidence, its shocks of awareness and repentance—she has brought to a focus at last all the scattered principles which her overconfidence and lack of experience continually obliged her to underestimate, forget or abandon.

She never gives up her first principle: to separate the simple personality from the complex, and to concentrate her attention and interest on the latter. Her point of reference is always the complex individual, the individual aware and capable of choice. Her own pride is in her freedom, to observe, to analyze, to choose; her continual mistake is to forget that, even for her, there is only one area of choice—marriage—and that this choice is subject to all the powerful and numbing pressures of an acquisitive society.

Under pressure, Charlotte denies her choice while making it, degrades herself to the level of a fool in marrying one. Under pressure, Wickham squanders his choice in any opportunity, however unscrupulous and desperate, to make his fortune. Under pressure, Mr. Bennet was led to believe that choice was easy, and to marry a woman who made no demands upon his awareness. And under pressure, Darcy jeopardizes his freedom by believing that, for the man of breeding, choice is not individual but ancestral, narrowly predetermined by rank and family. The simple people—Mrs. Bennet, Lydia, Mr. Collins, Lady Catherine, Jane, Bingley—do not choose at all; they are led, largely unaware; we cannot even submit them to a moral judgment: and the irony, as Elizabeth recognizes about all of them except Jane, is in their illusion of choice, their assumption of will. The complex do, on the other hand, choose; yet it takes a long time for Elizabeth to recognize that choice is never unalloyed, and may indeed be nullified altogether.

The central fact for Elizabeth remains the power of choice. In spite of social pressures, in spite of the misunderstandings and the obstacles to awareness that cut off and confuse the individual, in spite of the individual's repeated failures, the power of choice is all that distinguishes him as a being who acts and who may be judged. There are, certainly, limitations upon his choice, the limitations of an imposed prudence, of living within a social frame in which material comfort is an article of prestige and a sign of moral well-being: since even Elizabeth, though an acute and critical observer, is no rebel, she cannot contemplate the possibility of happiness outside her given social frame. The author is, likewise, pointedly ironic in contrasting Elizabeth's charitable allowances, first for Wickham, and then for Colonel Fitzwilliam, an "Earl's younger son," . . . when her relative poverty obliges them to regard her as ineligible. Yet the irony does not go so far as to invalidate choice or distinctions in choice. Fitzwilliam, no rebel, is prudent in the hope that both prudence and inclination may be satisfied together in the future; but Wickham's "prudence," rather than merely limiting his choice, has deprived him of it entirely. In Elizabeth's feeling, upon touring Darcy's estate, "that to be mistress of Pemberley might be something!" . . . the irony is circumscribed with an equal clarity: Darcy gains by being a rich man with a magnificent estate; but Pemberley is an expression of Darcy's taste as well as of his wealth and rank, and the image of Pemberley cannot divert Elizabeth from her primary concern with Darcy's motives and the meaning of his façade. Pemberley with Mr. Collins, or even with Bingley, would not do at all.

The focus is upon the complex individual; the only quality that distinguishes him from his setting, from the forms of courtship and marriage in an acquisitive society, which otherwise standardize and absorb him, is also his unique function—choice. What Elizabeth must choose, within the bounds set by prudence, is an individual equally complex, and undefeated by his social role. The complex individual is, after all, isolated by his freedom, and must be seen so at the end; for even if pressures from without, from the social system and social class, deflect or overwhelm him, they demonstrate not that he is indistinguishable from his social role, but that he is vulnerable to it. The fact of choice makes him stand, finally, alone, to judge or be judged.

In *Pride and Prejudice,* Jane Austen's irony has developed into an instrument of discrimination between the people who are simple reproductions of their social type and the people with individuality and will, between the unaware and the aware. The defensive—and destructive—weapon of *Northanger Abbey* and *Sense and Sensibility* has here been adapted directly to the theme through the personality of Elizabeth Bennet, who reflects

and illustrates her author's vision without ever becoming (except in her malice toward Lydia) merely her author's advocate. The irony is internal, it does not take disturbing tangents toward the author's need for self-vindication: even self-defensive, it is internal and consistent—Mr. Bennet's shying from the consequences of his disastrous mistake, Elizabeth's provocative parrying of Darcy. And if this new control over her irony permits Jane Austen only to be more clever (and not particularly more persuasive) in avoiding a commitment, by Elizabeth in love, for example . . . the characteristic block of Jane Austen's against direct emotional expression has occasion only very rarely to operate in *Pride and Prejudice:* above all, in the talk and atmosphere of Darcy's proposals, and in his letter—passages which most nearly reproduce the flat or melodramatic textures of *Cecilia,* without any lift of emotion or of irony either. The moment is soon over; and irony is not only back, but back at its proper task of discrimination. (pp. 121-25)

> *Marvin Mudrick, in his* Jane Austen: Irony as Defense and Discovery, *Princeton University Press, 1952, 267 p.*

DOROTHY VAN GHENT (essay date 1953)

[*Van Ghent was an American educator and literary critic. In the following excerpt, she explores various aspects of* Pride and Prejudice, *including the novel's limited range of materials, the nature of its value system and moral dilemmas, and its structure, style, and language. Van Ghent maintains that the "general directions of reference taken by Jane Austen's language . . . are clearly materialistic," and in the latter portion of her remarks the critic discusses how the novelist's "mercantile" vocabulary lends meaning to the text.*]

It is the frequent response of readers who are making their first acquaintance with Jane Austen that her subject matter is itself so limited—limited to the manners of a small section of English country gentry who apparently never have been worried about death or sex, hunger or war, guilt or God—that it can offer no contiguity with modern interests. This is a very real difficulty in an approach to an Austen novel, and we should not obscure it; for by taking it initially into consideration, we can begin to come closer to the actual toughness and subtlety of the Austen quality. The greatest novels have been great in range as well as in technical invention; they have explored human experience a good deal more widely and deeply than Jane Austen was able to explore it. It is wronging an Austen novel to expect of it what it makes no pretense to rival—the spiritual profundity of the very greatest novels. But if we expect artistic mastery of limited materials, we shall not be disappointed.

The exclusions and limitations are deliberate; they do not necessarily represent limitations of Jane Austen's personal experience. Though she led the life of a maiden gentlewoman, it was not actually a sheltered life—not sheltered, that is, from the apparition of a number of the harsher human difficulties. She was a member of a large family whose activities ramified in many directions, in a period when a cousin could be guillotined, when an aunt and uncle could be jailed for a year on a shopkeeper's petty falsification, and when the pregnancies and childbed mortalities of relatives and friends were kept up at a barnyard rate. Her letters show in her the ironical mentality and the eighteenth-century gusto that are the reverse of the puritanism and naïveté that might be associated with the maidenly life. What she excludes from her fictional material does not, then, reflect a personal obliviousness, but, rather, a critically developed knowledge of the character of her gift and a restriction of its exercise to the kind of subject matter which she could shape into most significance. When we begin to look upon these limitations, not as having the negative function of showing how much of human life Jane Austen left out, but as having, rather, the positive function of defining the form and meaning of the book, we begin also to understand that kind of value that can lie in artistic mastery over a restricted range. This "two inches of ivory" (the metaphor which she herself used to describe her work), though it may resemble the handle of a lady's fan when looked on scantly, is in substance an elephant's tusk; it is a savagely probing instrument as well as a masterpiece of refinement.

Time and space are small in *Pride and Prejudice*. Time is a few months completely on the surface of the present, with no abysses of past or future, no room for mystery; there is time only for a sufficiently complicated business of getting wived and husbanded and of adapting oneself to civilization and civilization to oneself. Space can be covered in a few hours of coach ride between London and a country village or estate: but this space is a *physical* setting only in the most generalized sense; it is space as defined by a modern positivistic philosopher—"a place for an argument." The concern is rational and social. What is relevant is the way minds operate in certain social circumstances, and the physical particular has only a derived and subordinate relevance, as it serves to stimulate attitudes between persons. Even the social circumstances are severely restricted: they are the circumstances of marriageable young women coming five to a leisure-class family with reduced funds and prospects. What can be done with this time and space and these circumstances? What Jane Austen does is to dissect—with what one critic has called "regulated hatred"— the monster in the skin of the civilized animal, the irrational acting in the costumes and on the stage of the rational; and to illuminate the difficult and delicate reconciliation of the sensitively developed individual with the terms of his social existence.

"It is a truth universally acknowledged, that a single man in possession of a good fortune must be in want of a wife." This is the first sentence of the book. What we read in it is its opposite—a single woman must be in want of a man with a good fortune—and at once we are inducted into the Austen language, the ironical Austen attack, and the energy, peculiar to an Austen novel, that arises from the compression between a barbaric subsurface marital warfare and a surface of polite manners and civilized conventions. Marriage—that adult initiatory rite that is centrally important in most societies whether barbarous or advanced—is the uppermost concern. As motivation for the story, it is as primitively powerful an urgency as is sex in a novel by D. H. Lawrence. The tale is that of a man hunt, with the female the pursuer and the male a shy and elusive prey. The desperation of the hunt is the desperation of economic survival: girls in a family like that of the Bennets must succeed in running down solvent young men in order to survive. But the marriage motivation is complicated by other needs of a civilized community: the man hunters must observe the most refined behavior and sentiments. The female is a "lady" and the male is a "gentleman"; they must "fall in love." Not only must civilized appearances be preserved before the eyes of the community, but it is even necessary to preserve dignity and fineness of feeling in one's own eyes.

The second sentence outlines the area in which the aforementioned "truth universally acknowledged" is to be investigated—a small settled community, febrile with social and economic rivalry.

However little known the feelings or views of such a man may be on his first entering a neighborhood, this truth is so well fixed in the minds of the surrounding families, that he is considered as the rightful property of some one or other of their daughters.

Here a high valuation of property is so dominant a culture trait that the word "property" becomes a metaphor for the young man himself; and the phrasing of the sentence, with typical Austen obliquity, adds a further sly emphasis to this trait when it uses an idiom associated with the possession of wealth— "well fixed"—as a qualifier of the standing of "truth." We are told that the young man may have "feelings or views" of his own (it becomes evident, later, that even daughters are capable of a similar willful subjectivity); and we are warned of the embarrassment such "feelings or views" will cause, whether to the individual or to the community, when we read of those "surrounding families" in whom "truth" is "so well fixed"—portentous pressure! And now we are given a light preliminary draft of the esteemed state of marriage, in the little drama of conflicting perceptions and wills that the first chapter presents between the imbecilic Mrs. Bennet and her indifferent, sarcastic husband. "The experience of three and twenty years had been insufficient to make his wife understand his character." The marriage problem is set broadly before us in this uneasy parental background, where an ill-mated couple must come to terms on the finding of mates for their five daughters. A social call must be made, in any case, on the single gentleman of good fortune who has settled in the neighborhood. With the return of the call, and with the daughters set up for view— some of whom are "handsome," some "good-natured"—no doubt he will buy, that is to say, "fall in love" (with such love, perhaps, as we have seen between Mr. and Mrs. Bennet themselves).

In this first chapter, the fundamental literary unit of the single word—"fortune," "property," "possession," "establishment," "business"—has consistently been setting up the impulsion of economic interest against those non-utilitarian interests implied by the words "feelings" and "love." The implications of the word "marriage" itself are ambivalent; for as these implications are controlled in the book, "marriage" does not mean an act of ungoverned passion (not even in Lydia's and Wickham's rash elopement does it mean this: for Wickham has his eye on a settlement by blackmail, and Lydia's infatuation is rather more with a uniform than with a man); marriage means a complex engagement between the marrying couple and society—that is, it means not only "feelings" but "property" as well. In marrying, the individual marries society as well as his mate, and "property" provides the necessary articles of this other marriage. With marriage, so defined, as the given locus of action, the clash and reconciliation of utility interests with interests that are nonutilitarian will provide a subtle drama of manners; for whatever spiritual creativity may lie in the individual personality, that creativity will be able to operate only within publicly acceptable modes of deportment. These modes of deportment, however public and traditional, must be made to convey the secret life of the individual spirit, much as a lens conveys a vision of otherwise invisible constellations. Language itself is the lens in this case—the linguistic habits of social man.

Below language we do not descend, except by inference, for, in this definitively social world, language is the index of behavior, the special machine which social man has made to register his attitudes and to organize his dealings with others. We have spoken of Jane Austen's exclusion of the physical particular. One might expect that in her treatment of the central problem of marriage she could not avoid some physical particularity—some consciousness of the part played by the flesh and the fleshly passions in marriage. Curiously and quite wonderfully, out of her restricted concern for the rational and social definition of the human performance there does arise a strong implication of the physical. Can one leave this novel without an acute sense of physical characterizations—even of the smells of cosmetic tinctures and obesity in Mrs. Bennet's boudoir, or of the grampus-like erotic wallowings of the monstrous Mr. Collins? Nothing could be stranger to an Austen novel than such representations of the physical. And yet, from her cool, unencumbered understanding of the linguistic exhibitions of the parlor human, she gives us, by the subtlest of implication, the human down to its "naturals," down to where it is human only by grace of the fact that it talks English and has a set of gestures arbitrarily corresponding to rationality.

Among the "daughters" and the "young men of fortune" there are a few sensitive individuals, civilized in spirit as well as in manner. For these few, "feeling" must either succumb to the paralysis of utility or else must develop special delicacy and strength. The final adjustment with society, with "property" and "establishment," must be made in any case, for in this book the individual is unthinkable without the social environment, and in the Austen world that environment has been given once and forever—it is unchangeable and it contains the only possibilities for individual development. For the protagonists, the marriage rite will signify an "ordeal" in that traditional sense of a moral testing which is the serious meaning of initiation in any of the important ceremonies of life. What will be tested will be their integrity of "feeling" under the crudely threatening social pressures. The moral life, then, will be equated with delicacy and integrity of feeling, and its capacity for growth under adverse conditions. In the person of the chief protagonist, Elizabeth, it really will be equated with intelligence. In this conception of the moral life, Jane Austen shows herself the closest kin to Henry James in the tradition of the English novel; for by James, also, the moral life was located in emotional intelligence, and he too limited himself to observation of its workings in the narrow area of a sophisticated civilization.

The final note of the civilized in *Pride and Prejudice* is, as we have said, reconciliation. The protagonists do not "find themselves" by leaving society, divorcing themselves from its predilections and obsessions. In the union of Darcy and Elizabeth, Jane and Bingley, the obsessive social formula of marriage-to-property is found again, but now as the happy reward of initiates who have travailed and passed their "ordeal." The incongruities between savage impulses and the civilized conventions in which they are buried, between utility and morality, are reconciled in the symbolic act of a marriage which society itself—bent on useful marriages—has paradoxically done everything to prevent. Rightly, the next to the last word in the book is the word "uniting."

We have so far attempted to indicate both the restrictive discipline which Jane Austen accepted from her material and the moral life which she found in it. The significance of a given body of material is a function of the form which the artist gives to the material. Significance is, then, not actually "found" by the artist in his subject matter, as if it were already and obviously present there for anyone to see, but is created by him

in the act of giving form to the material (it was in this sense that poets were once called trouvères, or "finders"). The form of the action of *Pride and Prejudice* is a set of "diverging and converging lines" [see excerpt by Mary Lascelles dated 1939] mathematically balanced in their movements, a form whose diagrammatic neatness might be suggested in [a design] ... which shows the relationship of correspondence-with-variation between the Darcy-Elizabeth plot and the Jane-Bingley subplot, the complication of the former and the simplicity of the latter, the successive movements toward splitting apart and toward coming together, and the final resolution of movement in "recognition" and reconciliation between conflicting claims, as the total action composes itself. . . .

But significant form ... is a far more complex structure of relationships than those merely of plot. An Austen novel offers a particularly luminous illustration of the function of style in determining the major form. [A] diagram of the plot movements of *Pride and Prejudice* [might] serve as visualization of a pattern of antithetical balances found also in the verbal composition of the book. It is here, in style, in the language base itself, that we are able to observe Jane Austen's most deft and subtle exploitation of her material.

The first sentence of the book—"It is a truth universally acknowledged, that a single man in possession of a good fortune must be in want of a wife"—again affords an instance in point. As we have said, the sentence ironically turns itself inside out, thus: a single woman must be in want of a man with a good fortune. In this doubling of the inverse meaning over the surface meaning, a very modest-looking statement sums up the chief conflicting forces in the book: a decorous convention of love (which holds the man to be the pursuer) embraces a savage economic compulsion (the compulsion of the insolvent female to run down male "property"), and in the verbal embrace they appear as a unit. The ironic mode here is a mode of simultaneous opposition and union: civilized convention and economic primitivism unite in the sentence as they do in the action, where "feelings" and "fortune," initially in conflict, are reconciled in the socially creative union of marriage.

This is but one type of verbal manipulation with which the book luxuriates. Another we shall illustrate with a sentence from Mr. Collins' proposal to Elizabeth, where "significant form" lies in elaborate rather than in modest phrasing. Mr. Collins manages to wind himself up almost inextricably in syntax.

> "But the fact is, that being as I am, to inherit this estate after the death of your honored father, (who, however, may live many years longer,) I could not satisfy myself without resolving to chuse a wife from among his daughters, that the loss to them might be as little as possible, when the melancholy event takes place—which, however, as I have already said, may not be for several years."

Fancy syntax acts here, not as an expression of moral and intellectual refinement (as Mr. Collins intends it to act), but as an expression of stupidity, the antithesis of that refinement. The elaborate language in which Mr. Collins gets himself fairly *stuck* is a mimesis of an action of the soul, the soul that becomes self dishonest through failure to know itself, and that overrates itself at the expense of the social context, just as it overrates verbalism at the expense of meaning. We have suggested that moral life, in an Austen novel, is identified with emotional intelligence; and it is precisely through failure of intelligence—the wit to know his own limitations—that Mr. Collins appears as a moral monstrosity. Language is the mirror of his degeneracy. Against Mr. Collins' elaborate style of speech we may place the neat and direct phrasing of a sentence such as "It is a truth universally acknowledged . . ." where the balance of overt thesis and buried antithesis acts as a kind of signature of the intelligential life—its syntactical modesty conveying a very deft and energetic mental dance.

Similarly, elaborate epithet ("your honored father," "the melancholy event") is suspect—the sign not of attention but of indifference, of a moldiness of spirit which, far from being innocuous, has the capacity of mold to flourish destructively and to engulf what is clean and sound, as such epithet itself devours sense. Comedy, let us say again, "is a serious matter," and what is serious in this scene of Mr. Collins' proposal is the engulfing capacity of the rapacious Mr. Collins, from whom Elizabeth escapes narrowly. The narrowness of the escape is underlined by the fact that Elizabeth's friend, Charlotte—herself, we assume, intelligent, inasmuch as she is Elizabeth's friend—complacently offers herself as host to this mighty mold. In the civilized community which is our area of observation, emotional intelligence and quickness of moral perception—as we see them, for instance, in Elizabeth—are profoundly threatened by an all-environing imbecility. It is through style that we understand the nature of this threat; for the simplicity and directness of the governing syntax of the book prepares us to find positive values in simplicity and directness, negative values in elaboration and indirection. Even the canny intelligence of Mr. Bennet is not that emotionally informed intelligence—or, shall we say, that intelligence which informs the emotions—that we are led to look upon as desirable; and Mr. Bennet reveals his failure also in "style," a style of speech that shows a little too elaborate consciousness of the pungency of double-talk, of the verbal effect of ironic undercutting. When Elizabeth suggests that it would be imprudent to send the lightheaded Lydia to Brighton, he says,

> Lydia will never be easy till she has exposed herself in some public place or other, and we can never expect her to do it with so little expense or inconvenience to her family as under the present circumstances.

Being intelligent, Mr. Bennet learns regret for his failure, although (and we delight also in Jane Austen's "realism" here, the tenacity of her psychological grip on her characters) not too much regret—not so much that he ceases to be Mr. Bennet.

From still another point of view, the style of the book is significant of total structure; we refer here to a generalized kind of epithet used in descriptive passages. The park at Pemberley, Darcy's estate, "was very large, and contained great variety of ground"; one drove "through a beautiful wood stretching over a wide extent." What we wish to notice, in diction of this kind, is the merely approximate appropriateness of the qualifier: "large," "great variety," "beautiful wood," "wide extent." This type of diction we might again describe as "modest," or we might speak of it as flatly commonplace; but we shall want to investigate its possibilities of function in the total form of the book. The reader will observe the continued use of the same kind of diction in the passage below, describing the house; what should be noted is the use to which the description is put—its use, not to convey any sense of "naturalistic" particularity, but, rather, to reveal Darcy's taste (of

which Elizabeth has been suspicious) and a subtle turn in Elizabeth's feelings about him.

> It was a large, handsome, stone building, standing well on rising ground, and backed by a ridge of high woody hills;—and in front, a stream of some natural importance was swelled into greater, but without any artificial appearance. Its banks were neither formal nor falsely adorned. Elizabeth was delighted. She had never seen a place for which nature had done more, or where natural beauty had been so little counteracted by an awkward taste. They were all of them warm in their admiration; and at that moment she felt that to be mistress of Pemberley might be something!

Wealth applied to the happiest and most dignified creation of environment—that is all we need to know about this setting, a need which the description fulfills by virtue of generalizations—"large," "standing well," "natural importance," "natural beauty," and the series of negations of what is generally understood by "artificial appearance," "falsely adorned," and so forth. More particularity of description would deflect from what is significant in the episode, namely, the effect of the scene upon Elizabeth's attitude toward her lover. Darcy himself has had in her eyes a certain artificiality, unpleasant formality, falseness; he has been lacking in that naturalness which delights her in the present scene, which is his home and which speaks intimately of him; and she has felt that his taste in the handling of human relations was very seriously "awkward." The appearance of Pemberley cannot help putting a slight pressure on her judgment of him, and the description is used with deliberate purpose for this effect. And how shrewd psychologically and warmly human is the remark, "and at that moment she felt that to be mistress of Pemberley might be something!" With all her personal integrity and exacerbated delicacy of feeling about the horrors of acquisitiveness, Elizabeth is smitten with an acquisitive temptation. (No wonder Jane Austen could not find Elizabeth's painted portrait in the galleries, though she was able to find Jane Bennet's there [see excerpt dated May, 1813]. Elizabeth is quite too human to have a duplicate in paint; only language is able to catch her.) In this final clause, the dramatic concern is solely with the social context—the shifting attitudes of one person toward another, as these attitudes are conditioned by the terms of a narrow, but nevertheless complex, social existence; but as the relationships between persons shift, the individual himself (as Elizabeth, here) is reinterpreted, shows a new aspect of his humanity. In this fashion, the Austen style—here a deliberately generalized and commonplace descriptive style—functions again as determination of significant form, significance in this particular case being the *rational* meaning of a physical setting.

Finally we should remark upon what is perhaps the most formative and conclusive activity of style in the book: the effect of a narrowly mercantile and materialistic vocabulary in setting up meanings. Let us go down a few lists of typical words, categorizing them rather crudely and arbitrarily, but in such a manner as to show their direction of reference. The reader will perhaps be interested in adding to these merely suggestive lists, for in watching the Austen language lies the real excitement of the Austen novel. We shall set up such categories as "trade," "arithmetic," "money," "material possessions," simply in order to indicate the kind of language Jane Austen inherited from her culture and to which she was confined—and in order to suggest what she was able to do with her language, how much of the human drama she was able to get into such confines.

TRADE	ARITHMETIC
employed	equally
due form	added
collect	proportion
receipt	addition
buy	enumerate
sell	figure
business	calculated
supply	amount
terms	amounting
means	inconsiderable
venture	consideration

MONEY	MATERIAL POSSESSIONS	SOCIAL INTEGRATION
pounds	estate	town
credit	property	society
capital	owner	civil
pay	house	neighborhood
fortune	manor	county
valuable	tenant	fashion
principal	substantial	breeding
interest	establishment	genteel
afford	provided	marriage
indebted	foundation	husband
undervalue	belongs to	connection

We could add such verbal categories as those referring to ''patronage,'' ''law,'' ''skill'' (a particularly interesting one, covering such words as ''design,'' ''cunning,'' ''arts,'' ''schemes,'' and so on; a category obviously converging with the ''trade'' category, but whose vocabulary, as it appears in this book, is used derogatorily—the stupid people, like Mrs. Bennet, Lady Catherine de Bourgh, Wickham, and Mr. Collins, are the ones who ''scheme'' and have ''designs'').

In viewing in the abstract the expressive possibilities open to literary creatorship, we might assume that the whole body of the English language, as it is filed in the dictionary, is perfectly free of access to each author—that each author shares equally and at large in the common stuff of the language. In a sense this is true; the whole body of the language *is* there, virtually, in the dictionary, and anyone can consult it and use it if he wants to. But we have observed fairly frequently, if only by-the-way, in these studies, that each author does not consult the whole body of the language in selecting words for his meanings; that he is driven, as if compulsively, to the selection of a highly particular part of the language; and that the individual character of his work, its connotations and special insights, derive largely from the style he has made his own—that is to say, from the vocabulary and verbal arrangements he has adopted out of the whole gamut of words and rhetorical patterns available in the language. In making these selections, he is acting partly under the compulsions of the culture in which he has been bred and whose unconscious assumptions—as to what is interesting or valuable or necessary or convenient in life—are reflected in the verbal and rhetorical selections common in that culture; and he is acting partly also under compulsions that are individual to his own personal background, but that still maintain subtle links with the common cultural assumptions. The general directions of reference taken by Jane Austen's language, as

indicated by such lists as those given above (and the lists, with others like them, could be extended for pages), are clearly materialistic. They reflect a culture whose institutions are solidly defined by materialistic interests—property and banking and trade and the law that keeps order in these matters—institutions which determine, in turn, the character of family relations, the amenities of community life, and the whole complex economy of the emotions. By acknowledgment of the fact that the materialistic assumptions of our own culture are even more pervasive than those reflected in this book, and that their governance over our emotions and our speech habits is even more grim, more sterilizing, and more restrictive, we should be somewhat aided in appreciation of the ''contemporaneity'' of Jane Austen herself.

But where then, we must ask, does originality lie, if an author's very language is dictated in so large a part by something, as it were, ''outside'' himself—by the culture into which he is accidentally born? How can there be any free play of individual genius, the free and original play with the language by which we recognize the insight and innovations of genius? The question has to be answered separately for the work of each artist, but as for Jane Austen's work we have been finding answers all along—in her exploitation of antithetical structures to convey ambivalent attitudes, in her ironic use of syntactical elaborations that go against the grain of the language and that convey moral aberrations, and finally in her direct and oblique play with an inherited vocabulary that is materialistic in reference and that she forces—or blandishes or intrigues—into spiritual duties.

The language base of the Austen novel gives us the limiting conditions of the culture. Somehow, using this language of acquisitiveness and calculation and materialism, a language common to the most admirable characters as well as to the basest characters in the book, the spiritually creative persons will have to form their destinies. The project would be so much easier if the intelligent people and the stupid people, the people who are morally alive and the people who are morally dead, had each their different language to distinguish and publicize their differences! But unfortunately for that ease, they have only one language. Fortunately for the drama of the Austen novel, there is this difficulty of the single materialistic language; for drama subsists on difficulty. Within the sterile confines of public assumptions, the Austen protagonists find with difficulty the fertility of honest and intelligent individual feeling. On a basis of communication that is drawn always from the public and savage theology of ''property,'' the delicate lines of spiritual adjustment are explored. The final fought-for recognitions of value are recognitions of the unity of experience—a unity between the common culture and the individual development. No one more knowledgeably than this perceptive and witty woman, ambushed by imbecility, could have conducted such an exploration. (pp. 99-111)

Dorothy Van Ghent, ''On 'Pride and Prejudice','' in her The English Novel: Form and Function, *Holt, Rinehart and Winston, 1953, pp. 99-111.*

W. SOMERSET MAUGHAM   (essay date 1954)

[*Maugham was an English novelist, dramatist, and short story writer who is considered a skilled satirist. Best known for his autobiographical novel* Of Human Bondage, *Maugham also achieved popular success with such plays as* Caesar's Wife, The Breadwinner, *and* Our Betters. *In the following excerpt, Maugham asserts that* Pride and Prejudice *is Austen's finest work. The critic focuses on the plot, major characters, and readability of the novel.*]

The great mass of readers, I believe, has accepted *Pride and Prejudice* as [Austen's] masterpiece and . . . I think it well to accept their judgment. What makes a classic is not that it is praised by critics, expounded by professors and studied in schools, but that large numbers of readers, generation after generation, have found pleasure and spiritual profit in reading it.

I myself think that *Pride and Prejudice* is on the whole the most satisfactory of all the novels. (p. 73)

Professor Garrod, a learned and witty critic, has said that Jane Austen was incapable of writing a story, by which, he explains, he means a sequence of happenings, either romantic or uncommon. But that is not what Jane Austen had a talent for, and not what she tried to do. She had too much sense, and too sprightly a humor, to be romantic, and she was interested not in the uncommon, but in the common. She *made* it uncommon by the keenness of her observation, her irony and her playful wit. By a story most of us mean a connected and coherent narrative with a beginning, a middle and an end. *Pride and Prejudice* begins in the right place, with the arrival on the scene of the two young men whose love for Elizabeth Bennet and her sister Jane provide the novel with its plot, and it ends in the right place with their marriage. It is the traditional happy ending. This sort of ending has excited the scorn of the sophisticated, and of course it is true that many, perhaps most, marriages are not happy, and further, that marriage concludes nothing; it is merely an introduction to another order of experience. Many authors have in consequence started their novels with marriage and dealt with its outcome. It is their right. But there is something to be said for the simple people who look upon marriage as a satisfactory conclusion to a work of fiction. They do so because they have an instinctive feeling that, by mating, a man and a woman have fulfilled their biological function; the interest which it is natural to feel in the steps that have led to this consummation, the birth of love, the obstacles, the misunderstandings, the avowals, now yields to its result, their issue, which is the generation that will succeed them. To nature, each couple is but a link in a chain, and the only importance of the link is that another link may be added to it. This is the novelist's justification for the happy ending. In *Pride and Prejudice,* the reader's satisfaction is considerably enhanced by the knowledge that the bridegroom has a substantial income and will take his bride to a fine house, surrounded by a park, and furnished throughout with expensive and elegant furniture.

Pride and Prejudice is a very well-constructed book. The incidents follow one another naturally, and one's sense of probability is nowhere outraged. It is perhaps odd that Elizabeth and Jane should be so well-bred and well-behaved, whereas their mother and their three younger sisters should be, as Lady Knatchbull put it, "very much below par as to good society and its ways"; but that this should be so was essential to the story. I have allowed myself to wonder that Miss Austen did not avoid this stumbling-block by making Elizabeth and Jane the daughters of a first marriage of Mr. Bennet and making the Mrs. Bennet of the novel his second wife and the mother of the three younger daughters. She liked Elizabeth the best of all her heroines. "I must confess," she wrote, "that I think her as delightful a creature as ever appeared in print" [see excerpt dated January, 1813]. If, as some have thought, she was herself the original for her portrait of Elizabeth; and she

has certainly given her her own gaiety, high spirit and courage, wit and readiness, good sense and right feeling; it is perhaps not rash to suppose that when she drew the placid, kindly and beautiful Jane Bennet she had in mind her sister Cassandra. Darcy has been generally regarded as a fearful cad. His first offense was his disinclination to dance with people he didn't know, and didn't want to know, at a public ball to which he had gone with a party. Not a very heinous one. It is unfortunate that Elizabeth should overhear the derogatory terms in which he spoke of her to Bingley, but he could not know that she was listening, and his excuse might have been that his friend was badgering him to do what he had no wish to do. It is true that when Darcy proposes to Elizabeth it is with an unpardonable insolence, but pride, pride of birth and position, was the predominant trait of his character, and without it there would have been no story to tell. The manner of his proposal, moreover, gave Jane Austen opportunity for the most dramatic scene in the book; it is conceivable that, with the experience she gained later, Jane Austen might have been able to indicate Darcy's feelings, very natural and comprehensible feelings, in such a way as to antagonize Elizabeth, without putting into his mouth speeches so outrageous as to shock the reader. There is, perhaps, some exaggeration in the drawing of Lady Catherine and Mr. Collins, but to my mind little more than comedy allows. Comedy sees life in a light more sparkling, but colder, than that of common day, and a touch of exaggeration, that is of farce, is often no disadvantage. A discreet admixture of farce, like a sprinkle of sugar on strawberries, may well make comedy more palatable. With regard to Lady Catherine, one must remember that in Miss Austen's day rank gave its possessors a sense of immense superiority over persons of inferior station; and they not only expected to be treated by them with the utmost deference, but were. In my own youth I knew great ladies whose sense of importance, though not quite so blatant, was not far removed from Lady Catherine's. And as for Mr. Collins, who has not known, even today, men with that combination of obsequiousness and pomposity? (pp. 74-6)

There is one merit which Miss Austen has, and which I have almost omitted to mention. She is wonderfully readable—more readable than some greater and more famous novelists. She deals, as Walter Scott said with "commonplace things, the involvements, feelings, and characters of ordinary life" [see *NCLC,* Vol. 1]; nothing very much happens in her books and yet, when you come to the bottom of a page, you eagerly turn it in order to know what will happen next. Nothing very much does and again you eagerly turn the page. The novelist who has the power to achieve this has the most precious gift a novelist can possess. (p. 78)

W. Somerset Maugham, "Jane Austen and 'Pride and Prejudice'," in his The Art of Fiction: An Introduction to Ten Novels and Their Authors, *1954. Reprint by Doubleday & Company, Inc., 1955, pp. 55-78.*

JAMES BALDWIN, FRANK O'CONNOR, AND LYMAN BRYSON
(broadcast date 1955)

[*Baldwin is an American novelist, essayist, dramatist, short story writer, and screenwriter who has been an important presence in American letters since the publication in 1953 of his novel* Go Tell It on the Mountain. *O'Connor was an Irish short story writer and man of letters whose critical commentary is distinguished by his insistent probing into the connections between society and the artist as well as by his attempt to analyze the creative process of the writer. Bryson was an American author and educator. In the following excerpt from a radio program first broadcast on May 8, 1955, Baldwin, O'Connor, and Bryson focus on* Pride and Prejudice *as they discuss the unique appeal and characteristic literary strengths of Austen's writings. Among the topics considered by the critics are the conflict between reason and instinct in the novel, Austen's narrative perspective, and her ability to portray and understand both feminine and masculine points of view.]*

Bryson: There are a good many authors of distinction and even of greatness of whom one might say, "Well, I can take him or leave him." Nobody can ever say that about Jane Austen. You either think Jane Austen is one of the greatest and most—what shall I say?—enticing authors in the world, or you wonder what all the fuss is about. Now, what is the real "Janeite?"

O'Connor: I put myself forward very timidly as a typical Janeite. I think Jane Austen was the greatest of novelists.

Bryson: The absolutely greatest?

O'Connor: Absolutely greatest! . . .

Bryson: . . . What hold does this extraordinary spinster of the early nineteenth century have on you? Is it because, as a professional writer, you admire her ways and methods, Mr. O'Connor?

O'Connor: No single answer would be sufficient for that. First of all, she's one of the greatest technicians of English literature. She's as perfect in literature as Mozart is in music, and she gives me the same sort of feeling. But apart from that, she is the first of the great novelists. One of the interesting things about the nineteenth century novel is that Jane Austen was producing her books exactly at the same time as Sir Walter Scott, who was the most popular writer who ever lived. Within twenty years it was quite obvious that the novel was going Jane Austen's way and not Scott's.

Baldwin: I've wondered where in the world she learned it all!

Bryson: Do you mean her material or her way with it?

Baldwin: Her way with it—the material was there. All she had to do was go to those tea parties and look at those people and listen to those conversations, as she obviously did, and to remember it all and note it down.

Bryson: She got the tone of it.

Baldwin: The way she lets you know what her attitude is, the way she reproduces and recreates this world, is one of the things that make her a very great novelist.

Bryson: I notice, Mr. O'Connor, that he said a "very great" novelist.

O'Connor: Ah, well, we'll educate him in due course. One of the very interesting things about Jane Austen—and it's been mentioned by dozens of writers—is that she never describes a conversation between men unless there is a woman present, because she did not know how men spoke when women weren't around.

Baldwin: That's very true.

O'Connor: You notice it in **Pride and Prejudice.** You may find Darcy in a most extraordinary situation, but you never see that situation described except through what he says to Elizabeth.

Baldwin: What's amazing is that within this tremendous limitation she still knows so much about these men, even if she doesn't know what they say when they're alone. She makes these people absolutely real. You don't feel any lack in her portraits of these men, in spite of the fact that she was always watching, as it were, from a distance.

Bryson: You have two things here: you have a world and you have an attitude toward it. How would you go about describing this world that was her material? Under those tea parties there was a good deal else.

Baldwin: She had an advantage which no novelist has today. She had a very ordered world to look at.

Bryson: As far as just looking at it is concerned.

Baldwin: Yes, but what she saw beneath it is what makes her so remarkable—all the disorder, all the pettiness, all the horror, all the heartbreak that was going on all the time. A woman like Mrs. Bennett [*sic*], who was so earnestly marrying off her daughters by the most unscrupulous means, any means at all, is still a very respected figure in this world. Miss Austen doesn't really judge Mrs. Bennett. She deals with her cruelly, but she also arouses our sympathy for Mrs. Bennett because her dilemma is so absolutely human.

Bryson: What else would you do with your daughters in that period?

Baldwin: Well, marry them off—yes.

Bryson: That was the only career open to them.

O'Connor: There's another thing, too: Jane Austen had a particular sort of psychology which the modern novelist doesn't have. The eighteenth century was concerned with the conflict between instinct and judgment, and it was always taken for granted that it was necessary for judgment to repress the instincts.

Bryson: Now, the surface of those tea parties—that was judgment?

O'Connor: That's judgment.

Bryson: And the horror that Mr. Baldwin was talking about, that running horror under the surface—that's instinct?

O'Connor: Yes. The instinct, when it's released, produces all this damage. The very title of the book represents this eighteenth-century psychology, because pride is a fault of the judgment. Darcy is a typical Jane Austen figure. He is a father-figure. He represents judgment. You realize that she was terribly in love with him. It's really the masculine side of her own character which she projected.

Bryson: Are you talking about Jane or her character Elizabeth or are they the same person?

O'Connor: I think that's a difficult question to answer.

Bryson: They're the same person, really?

O'Connor: Elizabeth represents the side of Jane Austen which she was trying to repress, the instinct, and which was always breaking out in her. I mean that she must have been as witty and as charming and as muddle-headed as Elizabeth herself. She was always trying to direct herself.

Bryson: Toward this masculine ideal of balanced judgment?

O'Connor: Yes, this is true.

Baldwin: This whole business of the conflict between instinct and judgment is one thing that the novelist has lost today. Since Freud we know too much about the instincts and still don't know enough, with the result there is no order imposed on anything. It is very difficult for a novelist to describe his own world because the whole world is in such chaos; there is no longer any way of making judgments about it.

Bryson: Of course, that shows what we do to a teacher, because, actually, Freud would not accept that as his teaching, would he?

Baldwin: No, of course not. It's what has been done with him.

Bryson: Jane Austen had a world in which there was surface order, although underneath it lay the disorder caused by instincts, and you say that world is gone?

O'Connor: It *shouldn't* be gone.

Bryson: After all, decorum hasn't completely left the world, has it?

Baldwin: But it has ceased to be respected in the way it used to be, and this is why it's so difficult. There are still many people who have manners and all the old-fashioned virtues—which are real virtues—but these people are now regarded as eccentric. They were not eccentric for Jane Austen. . . .

Bryson: . . . Jane Austen's world—what kind of story does she set in it? Can you tell it?

O'Connor: It's an awfully simple boy-meets-girl story, but "boy" in this case represents judgment, which has a few little faults of pride, and "girl" represents instinct, which has a great many faults of prejudice.

Bryson: And, of course, in the world of the eighteenth century, pride means an aristocrat, a conscious aristocrat with wealth and land and all the rest of it.

O'Connor: Yes. The boy and the girl are separated not by circumstances, but by what they are.

Bryson: What's the source of Elizabeth's prejudice against Darcy? After all, he was handsome, he represented the judgment that Miss Austen herself admired.

Baldwin: He was also very proud.

Bryson: Wasn't that part of the manners of his time and class?

Baldwin: I think one might say that that kind of pride is always an offense to instinct. You feel yourself being judged and you can't bear it. When Darcy meets Elizabeth he judges her at once and judges her very harshly, and she cannot stand it. This is the reason why she is so prejudiced against him right up to the moment of the proposal.

O'Connor: This is the only book in the world in which there is a proposal of marriage entirely devoted to the man's apologizing for his behavior and saying that he was badly brought up. Now, that's typical of Jane Austen.

Bryson: It sounds very dull as you just told it.

O'Connor: Well, it's really one of the most moving scenes in all literature. I remember that the first time I read it I broke into tears. It's the perfection of a daydream, but it is one of the noblest daydreams that ever existed. It is, in fact, the moment at which this great artist tries to combine her instincts and her judgment and succeeds in binding them into one central situation.

Baldwin: It is really heartbreaking. You feel a tremendous surge of relief, a physical sensation of relief, after Elizabeth reads his letter and looks at Darcy again; somehow Miss Austen has made you love Darcy, and has done it in some mysterious

way by describing all of his faults—he's obviously an impossible man, but he holds your attention and he gets all of your sympathy. You are rooting for those two, you *want* them to get together.

Bryson: But how does she make Darcy sympathetic by describing his faults, even if he does blame them on his parentage and his upbringing?

Baldwin: She doesn't change his character, but she throws a new light on it suddenly; you see for the first time his virtues as well as his pride. He is humbling himself, and you feel the effort. This is what gives that scene such tremendous impetus.

Bryson: There's no condescension in it?

Baldwin: Not any real condescension, although Elizabeth takes it as such.

Bryson: That's because of her prejudice.

Baldwin: And this is the moment her prejudice begins to dissolve.

Bryson: How much of your relief in this is because you, as a reader, have loved Darcy? You've loved this proud, rich, aristocratic, tactless person all the way through because Jane Austen has made you love him. You're relieved because the nobility in him comes out.

Baldwin: Yes, precisely.

Bryson: Well, now, that's the story, although there are all sorts of other things going on: Mrs. Bennett marrying off her daughters, getting into trouble, some of her daughters running off with the wrong man, poor Mr. Bennett being shoved around by his family of women, and so on. All that is just machinery, isn't it?

O'Connor: I suspect so, yes. It's just thrown in.

Baldwin: I'm not so sure that it's just machinery. I think, rather, that it's comment and illustration.

Bryson: It makes this world?

Baldwin: It gives this world body. You feel it, you have a sense of it, you know what's happening to other people. It suggests a great deal more than it says.

Bryson: And, then, of course, there's also the fact that she helps you to understand Darcy by giving you those scenes of aristocratic life with his relatives. They are almost farcical, but they apologize to you, in a sense, for Darcy.

O'Connor: There's also something one has to take into account, and that is Jane Austen's amazing technical dexterity. She never wrote two novels in the same manner.

Bryson: They're all Jane!

O'Connor: They're all very much Jane, but, for instance, in *Persuasion* she anticipates Virginia Woolf, in *Emma* she anticipates James Joyce. And one of the most astonishing things that I know of in fiction is the opening of *Pride and Prejudice*. In those half-dozen chapters at the beginning, you get for the first time, so far as I know, exposition and development united.

Bryson: For the first time in fiction?

O'Connor: For the first time in fiction! She uses exactly the same trick that the dramatist does in the theatre. "My dear Mr. Bennett," the wife begins, and you realize there is somebody called Mr. Bennett. You realize after a couple of pages that they've got daughters, you realize that a man called Bingley has a house nearby, and so on. That's the first and most extraordinary device. The second is that it dispenses entirely with a point of view, and since Henry James we've all expected one.

Bryson: You mean there *is* no point of view?

O'Connor: Absolutely no point of view.

Bryson: There's omniscience?

O'Connor: Omniscience. You think that it's being seen through Elizabeth's eyes; it's not.

Bryson: And yet you said a moment ago that she describes nothing but what Elizabeth herself could have seen.

O'Connor: I think you're misquoting, Mr. Bryson.

Bryson: Well, then, I want to straighten it out, but that's the way I remembered it.

O'Connor: Nothing but what a *woman* could have seen.

Bryson: I see!

O'Connor: Not this particular one, but *a* woman.

Bryson: She doesn't try to reproduce purely masculine conversations because she wouldn't quite know what men talked about; and, in fact, she probably thought she wouldn't belong there anyway. That's partly her tact.

O'Connor: It's not only tact, you know. It's almost a religious observance with Jane Austen. It all begins with her first novel, **Northanger Abbey,** when she says "It's quite possible Ann Radcliffe's novels can take place in the Pyrenees; I know nothing about the Pyrenees. They can take place even in the west of England and I know nothing about the west of England. All I am saying is that I know the middle of England and these things would have happened in the middle of England in this way." It's an art of witness, it's using the judgment as the absolute test.

Bryson: That makes all the more miraculous the way in which she conveys this extraordinary and so-difficult-to-describe attitude of hers. She doesn't do it with the events of the story. The events of the story have an emotional pull on you as few stories have, in spite of her lightness of touch. But she doesn't do it with the story. She doesn't do it by talking about herself. How *does* she do it? How does she give you this curious, cold, ironic—I would use the word malice, if it didn't seem a little too strong—how does she give you that feeling about herself? You say that she wrote many books in many different styles and yet every one of them was Jane Austen.

O'Connor: And every one of them described the conflict which is implicit in this one. I think the secret of **Pride and Prejudice** is that her real theme—she had only one theme, the conflict of instinct and judgment—is repressed. You don't notice it. You're not aware of it. You're terribly aware of it in a novel like **Mansfield Park,** where, in fact, she gives too much to her "father" figures and not enough to the figures who represent the instinct. In **Persuasion** she abandons it all. There she is, the lonely dying woman, going around from seaside place to seaside place, aware again of invalidism as a form of the imagination.

Bryson: But you still have evaded my question as to how she . . .

O'Connor: How she does it!

Bryson: I'm not talking about her extraordinary skill and style, the quickness of character, or this combination of exposition and development. I'm talking about the *Jane* feeling, which I get, although I wouldn't call myself a Janeite.

O'Connor: We've really been saying, haven't we, that the thing we admire about Jane Austen amongst all the novelists is that she is a supreme moralist. She is all the time teaching. She teaches very discreetly.

Bryson: You never catch her at it?

Baldwin: No, but it's her passion. I think one of the keys as to how she does it is that she cares so terribly about all these people. She cares too much about them to make an easy judgment about them. She's never really cruel. She loves them all and looks very hard at them; since she has this passion to make you see, to make you feel, she carries you with her in a subtle way that's hard to recognize.

Bryson: I'm still a little bit puzzled. Perhaps this is an insoluble problem. But you can look at people through the eyes of, well, Tolstoy or Shakespeare, and it's like looking through a pane of glass that has no color in it at all. It's absolutely clear. You look at people through Jane's eyes and there's a lovely ironic tint in the glass.

Baldwin: Yes, that's right.

Bryson: Is that her moralism?

O'Connor: No, that's a different thing. I would almost call it her femininity.

Bryson: But that's just another *word*. There are a lot of feminine writers in the world who haven't been able to do it.

Baldwin: Well, look at the way she's always poking sly fun at her men, particularly. She's really poking fun at the man's world, the things that men take for granted, and the kind of judgments that men make.

Bryson: Perhaps she's poking fun at men and loving them at the same time. I suppose it's a typical feminine attitude. I've never been present when only women were talking, so I wouldn't know.

O'Connor: Do you know, I think you have put your finger on something entirely different, Mr. Bryson, and put it very neatly. What you're really saying is that Jane is always *commenting*. You're always aware of her as a person in the story, and her subject and object are beautifully balanced. The other great novelists withdraw so far from their characters that, as you say, it's like seeing them through a pane of clear glass. Jane never entirely withdraws. She just nudges you very, very gently and says, "Listen to this. Watch the tone in which this is said."

Baldwin: That's exactly right.

Bryson: And yet there's never any sense of intrusion there, nor is there any condescension between her and her characters. Well, what about her people? Darcy isn't the kind of character you find in some novels, where a person represents a passion so much that he is a kind of embodiment of a psychological state rather than a person. Darcy is more than that.

Baldwin: This is why Jane Austen is so important, I think. Darcy represents judgment, but she also knows what he is like as a man—and this is what she really cares about. To come back again to that proposal scene; it is an affirmation of his masculinity, of his humanity, which is breaking through all the barriers of pride. What is remarkable is that she should have seen this, and seen it so clearly, without any of the distortion that wrecks *Jane Eyre* and almost wrecks *Wuthering Heights*. Even Heathcliff in *Wuthering Heights* is much more an embodiment of passion than a man.

Bryson: You're taking feminine novelists by intention, are you?

Baldwin: Yes, I am; I think this is fairly just, because feminine novelists have a special handicap to work against. The truth is that they're living in a man's world; their point of view is limited. Every novelist's point of view is limited, but a man can go further and do more things and say more things—although it doesn't necessarily make him a better novelist. Miss Austen is the only female novelist I know and read who has this absolute clarity which, if I may be permitted to say so, is like a man's. She's always commenting, as Mr. O'Connor says, she's always judging, but you never feel that her own feminine personality has warped her point of view.

Bryson: She was Elizabeth and Darcy both?

Baldwin: She was!

Bryson: How can you be two people and still give the impression so exquisitely of being only one of them?

O'Connor: Aren't the great polarities in literature just two aspects of the same thing? Isn't Falstaff the other side of Henry IV? You can say the same thing about Shaw's *Candida*. Isn't Shaw at the same time the social revolutionary and the gentle poet, and isn't it true that these couples who occur so frequently in literature always represent the two sides of a man's personality or of a woman's personality?

Bryson: There are people who would say that that explains all great artists—they have in themselves two kinds of people, and where they are sharply in conflict the effort to be one person gives them this insight into the character of others. That seems a little bit like a formula, but you think it's basic, do you?

O'Connor: I think it certainly works with a great many works of art, though not all. You're not always aware that these two characters are really the same. Joyce does it deliberately in *Ulysses,* where Stephen and Bloom are obviously the same character.

Bryson: Of course, that makes Jane Austen the more remarkable, since she was these two things and yet she never lost the color of the feminine, never really lost her allegiance to the side of instinct.

Baldwin: Yes, this is the most amazing thing of all, I think.

Bryson: Why haven't other women succeeded in doing this? You ticked them off here very briefly and neatly, Mr. Baldwin, and said that the Brontës couldn't do it and other women novelists couldn't do it. Is it because there was not enough masculine judgment in the others—they let themselves go too far toward instinct?

Baldwin: I have the feeling that what makes Miss Austen a great novelist is the passion to teach. It is so strong in her, I think, that it burns out almost everything else. It burns out a certain pettiness, a certain self-seeking. She's much more interested, finally, in looking at the world than she is in getting anything out of it for herself. (pp. 142-49)

James Baldwin, Frank O'Connor, and Lyman Bryson, "Jane Austen, 'Pride and Prejudice'," in The Invitation to Learning Reader: The Individual & Society, *edited by Ralph Backlund, Herbert Muschel, 1955, pp. 142-50.*

MARK SCHORER   (essay date 1956)

[*Schorer was an American critic and biographer. In the excerpt below, he explores the conflict between feudal and mercantile societies in* Pride and Prejudice, *demonstrating how economic and social pressures affect the morality and behavior of various characters. According to the critic, the novel is ultimately a "comic and complex study of self-importance and egotism and malice as these are absorbed from a society whose morality and values are derived from the economics of class."*]

The social setting of [*Pride and Prejudice*], like that of Jane Austen's other novels, is one in which a feudalistic order that does not know that it is dying and a bourgeois or mercantile order that is not yet confident that it is quite alive, meet and conflict and sometimes merge. Ultimately, what had been the feudal order was to be engulfed by what was growing into the mercantile order, but in the exact time that she was writing and from her country perspective, Jane Austen can hardly be expected to tell us this in so many words, even though she already dramatizes the process. Fitzwilliam Darcy is the feudal lord of manorial estates; no more than Jane Austen can he remotely conceive of them as presently falling into the hands of capitalists, much less as one day becoming great public parks and monuments directed by the State. Darcy, absolutely sure of his class, thinks in terms of manners, of the code of civilized conduct in a society where class lines are drawn tight. He is proud. Elizabeth Bennet, daughter of her mother whose background is in "trade," not at all unlike Jane Austen in her thinking and her values, anticipating no inheritance—Elizabeth thinks, too, in terms of manners, of the code of civilized conduct in a society where humane impulses are not thwarted by class lines. By Darcy's pride, she is prejudiced. (It should be observed that for Americans, these distinctions do not exist and for most of us they are reversed: it is Darcy who is prejudiced against a lower social order, and it is Elizabeth who is poor but proud in the face of his prejudice; Jane Austen did not consciously hold even though she, too, observed this difference.) In large part, the comedy of *Pride and Prejudice* arises out of a basic historic discrepancy that is not in itself comic at all, the discrepancy between aristocratic assumptions of social place that are becoming unreal and therefore seem merely boorish, and bourgeois desires for social place that are not yet

A modern photograph of Austen's home at Chawton. Courtesy of the British Tourist Authority.

quite realizable, and therefore, when they do not arouse our pity, seem merely foolish. This discrepancy that lies at the heart of the book leads to an enormous ambiguity which, when the hero and heroine are finally merged in marriage, is transcended. The ambiguity arises from the fact that the author herself accepts one code as proper and at the same time aspires with the other.

Says Darcy:

> "Nor am I ashamed of the feelings I related. They were natural and just. Could you expect me to rejoice in the inferiority of your connections? To congratulate myself on the hope of relations, whose condition in life is so decidedly beneath my own?"

Replies Elizabeth:

> "You are mistaken, Mr. Darcy, if you suppose that the mode of your declaration affected me in any other way, than as it spared me the concern which I might have felt in refusing you, had you behaved in a more gentleman-like manner."

Our hearts, of course, go out to Elizabeth, because she has nothing on her side (no money, no family, no tradition)—nothing but her splendid intelligence; but the author's mind is divided between these two, for it is her observing social *eye* that sees and gives them the world they live in, even if it is her imaginative heart that, ultimately, judges them in relation to that world. For—ask yourself: is Elizabeth not perfectly correct? Darcy's "arrogance, . . . conceit, and . . . selfish disdain of the feelings of others" could only provide "that groundwork of disapprobation, on which succeeding events have built so immoveable a dislike." But is Darcy any less correct? Mrs. Bennet is a transparently scheming boor "of mean understanding, little information, and uncertain temper"; Mr. Bennet, for all his amiable intelligence and wit, is a demoralized man; their daughter Lydia is a cheap flibber-ti-gibbet, with Kitty close behind her; Mary is a foolishly pontificating young bore; so who—with all this tastelessness and weakness so obvious at a glance—who could know about Jane? who, on first meeting, could know even about Lizzy?

The opposition of these two codes, in almost if not quite perfect balance, provides ground that throws up a positive forest of pride and prejudice around [the characters], . . . and there is no way out of that forest, implicit with social savageries, except the path of what we are persuaded is the tenderest of human institutions, but which we can see here has its own savageries, a nettled way: marriage. "It is a truth universally acknowledged, that a single man in possession of a good fortune, must be in want of a wife." Or, more bluntly: it is a truth universally acknowledged, that a single woman without a fortune, must be in want of a husband who has one. If this is not to be achieved, marriage to an imbecile (Mr. Collins) dependent on the fortune of a pretentious termagant (Lady Catherine) is a plausible second-best. And if even this is impossible, then marriage to anyone at all, marriage if necessary to a scoundrel (Wickham), but under any circumstances, marriage, marriage! (pp. 80-2)

[The] basic socio-historical change in which Jane Austen's material is involved; marriage as a kind of symbol of economic merging, of one class rising and another sinking; and then marriage as a brutal economic fact in an essentially materialistic society—all this is the groundwork out of which *Pride and Prejudice,* together with Jane Austen's other novels, arises. Certainly it does not create the surface of her novels, but it gives her her basic situations (hence her plots) and it inhabits her tone when dry irony turns acrid. To what degree she had articulated this material is irrelevant, but that it thrusts itself into the surface quite frequently . . . is highly relevant, for it thus likewise comes to play its part in forming the ruling point-of-view of the novel and of informing the attitudes of the chief characters, Elizabeth, for example, who comes closest to speaking for Jane Austen herself, and who says at one point,

> "There are few people whom I really love, and still fewer of whom I think well. The more I see of the world, the more am I dissatisfied with it; and every day confirms my belief of the inconsistency of all human characters, and of the little dependence that can be placed on the appearance of either merit or sense."

It is at least an intuitive if not an articulated awareness of the basic social facts that puts such a speech as this into the mouth of one of the loveliest heroines of British fiction, just as it is this awareness that motivates such modulations of tone as from the characteristic ironic understatement of "with such a mother . . . home could not be faultless," to the less characteristic direct judgment of "Their table was superlatively stupid." (pp. 83-4)

Jane Austen's ultimate evaluation of her society is to be found in her stylistic base, by which I mean the buried and the dead metaphors ("live" metaphors, like natural description, find small place in Jane Austen's prose) on which her style—hence, her vision—seems to depend. This stylistic base . . . is derived from commerce and property, the counting house and the inherited estate. . . . [Here], in the metaphorical base itself, we have the social division of which I have spoken, the mercantile and the feudal codes. What draws them together in the style (as, by and large, in the plot) is the fact that *both* are material, cash *and* land. [An essay], written by Dorothy Van Ghent, has taken up the suggestion to demonstrate that it can be applied with . . . appropriateness and illumination to *Pride and Prejudice* [see excerpt dated 1953]. So I should suppose it could be to any other of the novels, not only because Jane Austen's primary subject matter never changes, but also because they are, after all, the product of a single imagination, and style is the most intimate register of imagination. If, then, this is the stylistic sub-structure of an Austen novel, *Pride and Prejudice* for our purposes, it lies under the surface of manners, the materialistic social facts under the "patina of sentimental scruple and moral punctilio." We have, thus, a further discrepancy that serves as a basis for comedy, the discrepancy between social actualities and social sentiment or convention. When moral and emotional situations are persistently expressed in economic figures ("he was longing to publish his prosperous love"), we can hardly escape the recognition that this is a novel about marriage as a market, and about the female as marketable. The basis of the comedy—and ultimately of Jane Austen's perception and evaluation of her material—lies in the difference between the two orders of value which the metaphors, like the characters, are all the while busily equating.

A forest of pride and prejudice, we have said, and should now examine this notion with a view to observing not so much the social analysis that the novel makes as the high degree of aesthetic integration with which it presents that analysis through its characters. Darcy and Elizabeth are, of course, the pivotal characters, he in his pride, she in her prejudice, and vice versa. All about them are ranged a variety of characters who represent degrees and kinds of the same deficiencies of character and vision, or who embody other traits that derive from these deficiencies. Elizabeth and Darcy we do not quite laugh at; but then consider Mr. Collins and Lady Catherine as hilarious caricatures of the same faults, he of pride, she of prejudice. (And, in passing, we should just notice the delightful irony that exists in the fact that each of these latter two are punished for their rigid excesses, just as Elizabeth and Darcy are rewarded because they are capable of altering: Mr. Collins will no doubt inherit Longbourne, the Bennet establishment, but long before that Elizabeth Bennet presides at infinitely grander Pemberley; Lady Catherine, through the very extremity of her kind of snobbery, is in fact the agent in the plot that at last completely releases Darcy from his.) Consider Mrs. Bennet as a kind of thematic foil to Darcy, the swiftly shifting, meaningless bases of her prejudices as opposed to the presumably deliberate, steady, and rational basis of his pride, and the irony inherent in the fact that her first prejudice is directed at this quality in him:

> His character was decided. He was the proudest, most disagreeable man in the world, and every body hoped that he would never come there again. Amongst the most violent against him was Mrs. Bennet.

Thus we find ourselves in a further complexity in this forest when it is brought home to us that even as Elizabeth's "hate" is forming (and Elizabeth is the chief figure of prejudice), she is, for all her other vast differences, her mother's daughter in this. We cannot wholly reject Miss Bingley's pronouncement that Elizabeth is "a mixture of pride and impertinence," even when we recognize the fact that Miss Bingley herself, and her sister, Mrs. Hurst, are only further representations of precisely these qualities.

Pride and Prejudice is a novel that founds its action on class barriers, but our first inference from such a glance at the thematic integration of the characters as we have thrown must be that moral qualities are clearly not obedient to class lines. If, now, we examine those of the characters who suffer the results of this social situation rather than create it, we are led to the same inference. There is, on the one side, the minor but significant figure of Mr. Hurst, a man of only one quality, and that is slothfulness, the vice of his class; but on the other side there is the delightfully cynical Mr. Bennet, who, having made an error of judgment in the major social fact, marriage, has allowed himself to lapse into a complete slothfulness of his own kind, and, in a major moral crisis as in the most mundane matters, is either unable or unwilling to be of use. With these gentlemen we can place the sad female figure of Charlotte Lucas; with them, in her way, she has buckled under the social pressure. Character can no more be equated with charm than it can be with class.

No more can intelligence. If we consider Mrs. Bennet's three youngest daughters as the two kinds of consequences of her indecent but necessary social ambitions (Mary as the reactionary copybook moralist who can read us lectures on the distinction between pride and vanity; Kitty and Lydia as the wholly reflective creatures of their mother's wit), we can oppose them all to the "accomplished" and utterly pallid Miss Darcy and—without entirely acquitting Jane Austen here of the charge of a failure in characterization—regard her as the female weakness that is a counterpart of her brother's feudal strength. Between

Lydia and Miss Darcy, dramatically linking them, stands Wickham, in whom charm and villainy go hand in hand. And he is an especially instructive figure: with his ambiguous initial attachment to one class, he has the aspirations of the other, and he feeds upon both: the immoral opportunist, he represents the acquisitive, the materialistic impulse at its worst, which is to say when it moves out beyond all social restraint whatever.

Four persons of consequence to both the plot and the scheme of values with which that plot is concerned remain, and these are the necessary exceptions to the schematization of character *motif* that we have made. There are Jane and Bingley, Jane almost limp in her goodness, and Bingley almost weak in his amiability. We may dismiss them if we wish as stereotypes that Jane Austen inherited from sentimental novels that she read but could not herself have written, as with Miss Darcy, that is, failures in characterization; but at the same time it should be pointed out that they are necessary to the full balance of the plot, necessary figures of a kind of social and moral passivity on which a vicious social atmosphere can work, which pride and prejudice can *harm*. If Jane and Bingley are primarily necessary to the full plot, our last two figures, Elizabeth's aunt and uncle, the Gardiners, are of prime importance to the scale of values. For all its implicit and expressed judgments on society, *Pride and Prejudice* is by no means a novel that will entertain any notions of rejecting it. The figure of Wickham tells us that. Society is as real as it is necessary, and if society and morality are not the same thing, the fact remains that the second cannot exist at all without the first. The problem is somehow to bring the social scale into an adjustment with the moral scale, and this the major movement of the plot finally does, as we shall presently see. Throughout, the Gardiners are present as figures who have solved this problem. They are there to place the bourgeois values (which must ultimately merge with and correct the aristocratic values) against their travesties as we see them in the bulk of other figures, most notably in Mrs. Bennet and Mr. Collins. Their humanity transcends class without seeking to escape it: and so Darcy sees them. Pale as they may be, mechanical as Mr. Gardiner's role in the Lydia-Wickham plot and Mrs. Gardiner's in the Elizabeth-Darcy plot may be, they still serve to *remind* us, at least, of the ultimate values of the unpretentious, intelligent heart. These the whole novel at last demonstrates.

All novels can be divided loosely into two kinds: there are novels which are above all interested in a precise and if possible rich definition of theme, novels which dramatize a special *quality* of their whole potential "world" of subject; and there are novels which are above all interested in a complete account of the subject, novels which attempt to dramatize the *quantity* of their "world" of subject. Dickens's novels, which are positively crammed and gorged with material, are of the second kind. Jane Austen's, which we have seen to be extremely limited in material, are of the first. In examining her characters even so briefly as we have just done, we discover the value, for her, of these limitations. Every character, however entertaining in himself, however important to the mechanical plot, has a further function; every character is in some important way integrated in the theme of the novel, so that the novel presents us with a various and full and, finally, exact dramatic analysis of that theme. In other words, all the characters are all the time pointing not out or away from but directly at the very center of the whole. The more characters, or material (for all material in fiction must be represented through characters) a novelist introduces, the less likely does such integration become. If something is gained in narrative spread, something is lost in aesthetic and moral precision. Jane Austen's art is among the supreme examples of the precisionist's.

Three conditions are necessary to the operation of the dynamics that make a novel. The first is a social context within which individual characters (as well as, probably, more social types) may exist. The combination makes plot possible. The second is that individual characters, in pursuit of their own ends, must resist change. The resistance makes plot move. The third is that the individual characters must finally yield to change. In yielding, they give plot the maximum of meaning and resolve it.

After Jane's wounding experience with Bingley, she cries wistfully, "It cannot last long. He will be forgot, and we shall all be as we were before." Elizabeth looks at her sister with "incredulous solicitude." She cannot believe it. And if she were able to step out of the novel and consider its welfare, she would not want to believe it. She might be reminded, as we are, of a moment in E. M. Forster's *A Passage to India,* when, after an accident, one of the characters uneasily says, "We are all three the same people still," even as we can see that the whole novel is moving for the very reason that they are ceasing to be the same people. Or she might be reminded, as we are, of the very last sentence of Henry James's *The Wings of the Dove,* when Kate Croy, recognizing the inevitable, says, "We shall never be again as we were!" and closes the novel as surely as, at that point, about to pass out through a door, she closes that.

Early in *Pride and Prejudice,* when Elizabeth is frivolously defending the pleasures of life in the country, she says, "But people themselves alter so much, that there is something new to be observed in them for ever." The interest of a novel, no less than of a country community, lies in the processes of human alteration. In *Pride and Prejudice,* the pattern of these processes is clear enough: two persons of firm character and mind take opposing temperamental postures upon meeting; through their own quality and through events that are brought on by their relationships with others, the opposition thickens into a tangle; their own new and real feelings toward one another are largely hidden from themselves by the thicket of misunderstandings; misunderstandings are ultimately cleared away, their real feelings are exposed, and the elements in their temperaments that brought on the initial confusing—which all the time have been exposed to a steady pressure that has slowly been loosening them—are corrected; in their alteration, they are free to merge.

After she receives Darcy's letter, Elizabeth cries out in humiliation, "Till this moment, I never knew myself." This is the beginning of the process of reversal. But self-awareness is not yet complete, and since alteration is continuous until the whole process is resolved, until the novelist closes that imaginary circle (in Henry James's figure) around her material at the point where the situation seems to come to rest, it cannot be. The novel ends at the point at which the characters have moved into their fullest self-awareness.

In his essay, "Light and Bright and Sparkling," Reuben Brower [see *NCLC,* Vol. 1] has demonstrated how subtly but how exactly Jane Austen uses her ironic devices from the opening pages on to lay the groundwork for this alteration, so that it comes about not as a mechanical contrivance but as a kind of moral flowering that we are quite ready to accept as among the beautiful potentialities of the individual human being.

The movement of these individual human beings exists, of course, within a larger movement, that of the whole world about them. Not everything in that world is happy at the end. The Bennets are left with their entailed estate. Mrs. Bennet, like the life force, will persist, as foolishly as ever—the Bingley sisters, nearly as maliciously. The wretched marriage of Lydia and Wickham will give trouble. The gaunt specter of Lady Catherine has not been laid; she is alive to poison the air of Pemberley. Pride and prejudice have not departed from the world. And Jane Austen need not have feared: hers is a moral realism, and the world is not intolerably bright by any means. Still, it is brighter. . . .

The novel is a comic and complex study of self-importance and egotism and malice as these are absorbed from a society whose morality and values are derived from the economics of class; a study, further, in the mitigation of these traits as the hero and heroine come into self-recognition, as their individual beings rise momentarily above that society and then sink back into it again. As this happens, the moral and the social scales make their readjustment. Individual being, as our hero and heroine have discovered it, will not make that society different, but to a larger degree than they as individual human beings have "improved in civility," civilization has refined its humanity. The alteration is minor. It is also mighty. And it is the end, I believe, of every great novel. (pp. 84-91)

Mark Schorer, "Pride Unprejudiced," in The Kenyon Review, *Vol. XVIII, No. 1, Winter, 1956, pp. 72-91.*

DOUGLAS BUSH (essay date 1956)

[*Bush was a Canadian-American scholar, critic, literary historian, and educator. Here, he parodies the notion that* Pride and Prejudice *is susceptible to an "anthropological-psychological" method of criticism that seeks to discover "mythic patterns" and "occult structuring" within the work. The critic's mockery suggests that the novel's true strengths may not readily lend themselves to sophisticated or pedantic scholarly discussion.*]

Although our age has witnessed the superseding of tame traditional criticism by the anthropological-psychological method, the study of Jane Austen has not yet caught up with the new movement. Her critics still talk about "social comedy" and "eighteenth-century rationality" and the like. The revolutionary exponents of archetypal myth, who have revealed unsuspected depths in many familiar works of literature, have quite failed to see Jane Austen's essential affinity with Melville and Kafka.

That her mythic patterns should have gone so long unrecognized is startling evidence of the real subtlety of her mind and art, which have been so much praised for shallow reasons. Even a brief examination of the occult structuring of *Pride and Prejudice* will establish Jane Austen's claim to be the first great exemplar of the modern mythic consciousness. If conventional criticism should object that she was a notably rational person, and that she had read little outside eighteenth-century belles lettres, it may be said in reply that it is of the essence of the mythic technique that it should be at least half unconscious, that its operations should disclose themselves only to the anthropological critic. It may be granted that the various myths which underlie the smooth and simple surface of *Pride and Prejudice* are not fully and organically developed but—in keeping with the fragmentariness of the modern psyche and its world—are only momentarily touched or blended in nebulous and shifting configurations; yet their presence in depth re-creates the values implicit in the outwardly commonplace situations of genteel village life. In mythic criticism the great thing is to find some semi-submerged rocks to stand on.

To the average casual reader, the first short chapter of *Pride and Prejudice* appears only to state the common theme of love and marriage, to set forth the character and situation of Mr. and Mrs. Bennet and their five marriageable daughters, and to report the arrival in the neighborhood of a highly eligible young bachelor, Mr. Bingley. Yet, from this brief and supposedly comic exposition, hints of the mythic and even mystic emerge. The famous first sentence, "It is a truth universally acknowledged, that a single man in possession of a good fortune must be in want of a wife," goes far beyond surface literalness. For on the next page we are told that Mrs. Bennet had been a beauty, and the single man in want of a wife reflects that desire for perpetuation of beauty expounded in Plato's *Symposium*. Ironically, although Mrs. Bennet has, in Platonic language, experienced "birth in beauty" five times, only one of her daughters is really beautiful; but it is this one that soon attracts Bingley.

Further, who and what is Bingley, the mysterious, ebullient stranger from the north who descends with his band of followers (his two sisters and Mr. Hurst and Mr. Darcy) upon a sleepy, conventional society and whom young people at once look to for providing dances? Clearly he is Dionysus, the disturbing visitor from northern Thrace. And who then is Pentheus, the king of Thebes who resisted the newcomer and was torn to pieces by the Maenads led by his own mother? Such violent data had to be somewhat adjusted by the author, yet it is hardly less clear that Pentheus is Mr. Bennet, the king of his small domain who is resentful of strangers and professedly unwilling to call on Bingley (his lack of tragic integrity is betrayed by his actually calling), and who undergoes a symbolic death in that he has no son and that his estate is entailed. Mrs. Bennet, to be sure, is not responsible for the entail, but she nags about it constantly, and she has urged her husband to cultivate Bingley, so that she must be a surrogate for Pentheus' Maenad mother. Bingley's fortune is a patent transliteration of the ivy and wine of Dionysus (the family money had been acquired in trade, undoubtedly distilling); and his sudden, unexplained comings and goings correspond to the epiphanies of the god. The mythic character of Darcy and of his relation to Bingley is less certain. However, his dominating personality and his initial blindness to the charms of Elizabeth Bennet suggest the blind seer Tiresias as the mentor of Dionysus-Bingley. (I pass by the obvious homosexuality; on this level the two men are Hercules and Hylas.) Thus the simple persons and incidents of the novel take on from the start richly evocative and even sinister connotations.

As the story proceeds and tensions develop, the mythic pattern, and with it some individual roles, undergo subtle transformations; one myth shades into another. The once pretty Mrs. Bennet, whose sole concern is to get her daughters married, is an embodiment of the unthinking life-force that works through women, and she is Dionysiac in her devotion to Bingley. Her motherhood and her earthy mentality might at first suggest identification with the Earth Goddess, but one explicit clue indicates that she is the goddess of love, born of the sea—she is a native of Meryton, the town of *mare*, the sea. On this new level, Mr. Bennet is more complex and obscure, because in projecting him Miss Austen uses not so much the orthodox and familiar myth of Venus and Adonis but some Renaissance

variations of it. On the one hand, in his cool indifference to his emotional wife and in his desire to be left alone in his library, Mr. Bennet is the cold Adonis, intent on his hunting, of Shakespeare's poem. On the other hand, Jane Austen fuses with this conception the Neoplatonic symbolism of Spenser's "Garden of Adonis": as an intellectual, and the parent of five daughters, Mr. Bennet is Spenser's Adonis, "the father of all Forms," and Mrs. Bennet is Spenser's Venus, simply unformed Matter. Whatever skepticism conventional scholarship may have concerning some of these interpretations, no one could dispute this last point.

But the security of Venus and Adonis is threatened (and will eventually be destroyed) by the Boar. In Jane Austen's multiple layers of meaning, the Boar is the entail, which comes into force with Mr. Bennet's death and which is personified in his heir, Rev. Mr. Collins. We have here what is perhaps the most striking mythic ambiguity in the book: Mr. Collins is both the Boar and the Bore (and his clerical status adds a further though unexploited element of traditional ritualism). Mr. Collins is in fact the axis of several polarities.

As if this interweaving of mythic patterns were not complex enough, the same pattern, with new features added, is worked out on another level and takes shape as the central figure in the carpet. The older Venus and Adonis are partly paralleled in a younger Venus and Adonis, Elizabeth and the initially proud and indifferent Darcy; but this second version operates in a vein of paradox. Mr. Bennet had in his youth been allured by a pretty face and had later discovered the stupidity behind it; Darcy, at first cold and then attracted by beauty, discovers the spirit and charm that go with it and falls deeply in love. Elizabeth, though misled for a time by the specious Wickham (a sort of Anteros), comes to love Darcy in her turn. But the security of the young pair's new relation is threatened by a variety of circumstances and most explicitly by a new Boar-Bore, not now Mr. Collins but his patroness, Lady Catherine (who has also some Gorgonish traits). Mr. Collins, like the mythical boar, while really killing had only sought to kiss (he proposed to Elizabeth); Lady Catherine, seeking to kill the relation between her nephew Darcy and Elizabeth, instead brings about his renewed proposal and acceptance. Some of these features of the design have, it is true, been noticed in conventional criticism, but only on the personal and social level; the deeper dimensions and reverberations have been completely missed.

There are many particulars one would like to go into, for instance, Elizabeth's uncle, Mr. Gardiner, whom Darcy so unexpectedly invites to fish on his estate: what is Mr. Gardiner's relation to the Fisher King, and what of the veiled phallicism in the allusion to fishing tackle? But only one other thread in the variegated web of complexity can be touched upon, the most central of all archetypal myths, the theme of death and rebirth. Jane Austen's heavy reliance upon this is all the more remarkable because she is commonly said to avoid the subject of death altogether; she never has a principal character die and only rarely reports such remote deaths as may contribute to the plot. But the real reason now becomes apparent: she did not deal with the subject in ordinary ways simply because her stories of young love are set against a dark mythic background of death. In *Pride and Prejudice* hints of mortality appear at the very beginning, in such place-names as Longbourn ("man goeth to his long home"; "The undiscover'd country from whose bourn No traveller returns") and Netherfield (the nether or lower world). There is a recurrent stress on physical frailty: Kitty Bennet has spells of coughing; Jane Bennet falls ill at Netherfield; Anne de Bourgh is sickly; and there is a whole crowd of adults whose parents are dead; etc. We have already observed the insistent significance of the entail and Mr. Collins, who will inherit the estate when Mr. Bennet dies. In proposing to Elizabeth, the magnanimous Mr. Collins says that he knows she will, after her mother's death, have no more than a thousand pounds in the four per cents. Such hieroglyphics of pain and death, both mythic and worldly, are reinforced by the process of the seasons. The book opens in early autumn, and in this season of harvest and death there is the ritual dance, which, ominously, takes place at Netherfield, Bingley's house. It is during the late autumn and winter that blows fall upon the Bennets—Mr. Collins' unhappy visit, Bingley's departure and abandoning of Jane Bennet and her heavy disappointment and Elizabeth's sympathy for her. The worst blow, Lydia's elopement with Wickham (note, by the way, the ancient view of the shallow, sensual quality of Lydian music), does occur in the summer, but it is this event that sets everything in motion toward rebirth, or what is crudely called a happy ending. Darcy—now a saving Hercules—rescues Lydia and wins Elizabeth; Dionysus-Bingley returns and is restored to Jane; and Mrs. Bennet, again a radiant Venus, rises from the depths in a foam of rejoicing.

Almost all the characters and incidents of the novel, under close scrutiny, will yield their mythic overtones, but perhaps enough has been said here to stimulate a critic who has the time and the insight for fuller investigation. The subject of archetypal myth in Jane Austen needs a book, and will doubtless get one. (pp. 591-96)

> *Douglas Bush, "Mrs. Bennet and the Dark Gods: The Truth about Jane Austen," in* The Sewanee Review, *Vol. LXIV, No. 4, Autumn, 1956, pp. 591-96.*

E. M. HALLIDAY (essay date 1960)

[*Halliday investigates the narrative perspective in* Pride and Prejudice. *This perspective, Halliday contends, allows Austen to tell the story largely from Elizabeth's point of view while building suspense toward a climax that Elizabeth does not anticipate until it is almost upon her. According to the critic, Austen's ability to inform the reader about aspects of the characters and plot that are unknown to Elizabeth is crucial to the drama of the novel.*]

Consider the famous opening sentence of *Pride and Prejudice:* "It is a truth universally acknowledged, that a single man in possession of a good fortune must be in want of a wife." The narrator seems to be standing outside the story, not yet observing the characters but gazing off into the middle distance for some reflections on life in general. But this impression does not last. As Mr. Bennet and "his lady" begin their dialogue, it rapidly becomes clear that the storyteller had them both in view when that opening generalization was made. It is an opinion, we find, that Mrs. Bennet would greet with a clapping of hands and little cries of joy—and one Mr. Bennet would send flying to the paradise of foolish ideas with a shaft of ridicule. The narrator ostensibly takes the responsibility for the opinion; but we see from the beginning that her observations are likely to bear an ironic relation to the views, and points of view, of her characters. This is our introduction to the quality of tough yet gentle irony that will control every page of the novel, making us feel a wonderful balance between sense and sensibility.

This artful control of over-all narrative perspective in the service of Jane Austen's irony is supported by a most subtle manipulation of point of view for the sake of the novel's unity. Even a sleepy reader of this book must be well aware, before he has read very far, that it is Elizabeth Bennet's story. But how does he know this? The title gives no clue, and Elizabeth is not the storyteller. The opening pages make it clear that the matrimonial prospects of the Bennet daughters will direct the action—but there are five daughters. True, three of them look far from promising: Mary is a pedantic bore; Lydia is an empty-headed flirt; Kitty is just empty-headed. But both Jane and Elizabeth are attractive and accomplished, and for several chapters it looks as if Jane's chances with Bingley will bring the central action into focus, with Elizabeth playing some subsidiary role. How is it, then, that by the time we are quarterway through the novel—say by the time Mr. Collins makes his celebrated proposal to Elizabeth—it has become perfectly clear that Elizabeth is the heroine of *Pride and Prejudice,* and that Jane is only a secondary character?

Partly, this is revealed by the sheer amount of attention the storyteller pays to Elizabeth, which increases rapidly as we move through the first eighteen chapters. This, of course, is itself a function of point of view. The storyteller chooses to gaze upon Elizabeth more and more often, and for longer and longer stretches of time. But the interesting fact is that this deliberate restriction of the narrator's privilege of gazing anywhere and everywhere is most stringently applied when the mechanics of the plot call, quite on the contrary, for attention to Jane. In chapter vii, Jane goes to visit Caroline Bingley at Netherfield. Mrs. Bennet's most sanguine hopes are fulfilled when Jane catches a bad cold on the way, and therefore has to spend several days with the Bingleys. But note that this is reported by letter; for when Jane leaves for Netherfield we do not go with her. The narrative perspective remains focused on the Bennet household, and particularly on Elizabeth; and it is not until Elizabeth decides to put sisterhood above gentility, and walks three miles across muddy fields, that we make our first entry into the Bingley household. Moreover, we see nothing of Jane until Elizabeth goes upstairs to nurse her; and even then we get a scanty glimpse, since Jane evidently is too sick to talk. By this time it begins to be obvious that the narrator is only slightly more interested in Jane than is the feline Miss Bingley, who tolerates her chiefly for the sake of Bingley's interest. Jane's relation to Bingley will be important in the plot, but much less for itself than as a necessary device to help build up Elizabeth's prejudice against Darcy.

Actually, the narrator's audacity in slighting Jane is almost rude. When poor Jane emerges from her sickroom after several days (chap. xi), she is nearly ignored. Everyone greets her politely, of course; but although Bingley "then sat down by her and talked scarcely to anyone else," none of this tête-à-tête between the two nascent lovers is reported. On the other hand, a word-for-word rendering of a most lively conversation including Elizabeth, Bingley, his sister, and Darcy takes up the rest of the chapter; but for all she contributes to the scene, Jane might as well be stretched out asleep on a sofa like the languid Mr. Hurst, who is also present but inaudible.

About this time we also begin to be aware that the narrator's increasing attention to Elizabeth and neglect of Jane is not simply a matter of direction of gaze. We are induced to see much of Elizabeth, and not much of her older sister; but we also begin to see more and more of the action, and of the other characters, from Elizabeth's point of view. In chapter x, for example, just before the one in which Jane becomes so remarkably inconspicuous, we are quite specifically encouraged to identify ourselves with Elizabeth at the beginning of the scene:

> Elizabeth took up some needlework and was sufficiently amused in attending to what passed between Darcy and his companion. The perpetual commendations of the lady either on his handwriting, or on the evenness of his lines, or on the length of his letter, with the perfect unconcern with which her praises were received, formed a curious dialogue, and was exactly in unison with her opinion of each.

We are not told that Elizabeth smiles, or makes any other outward sign of her amusement. The narrative perspective has penetrated to Elizabeth's consciousness; the point of view has become hers not only physically, but psychically.

By means of such skillful technical maneuvering, Jane Austen gradually forces the action of **Pride and Prejudice** to coalesce around Elizabeth, and we are prepared for an essential part of that action to take place in the intimate and subtle chambers of her mind. When we reach the crisis of the novel with Darcy's first proposal to Elizabeth (chap. xxxiv)—which, as a matter of structural nicety, comes exactly halfway through the book— we know that everything that follows must depend on her discovery of his true character. The groundwork is laid very shortly, in chapter xxxvi, which consists entirely of a searching analysis of Elizabeth's inward reactions to Darcy's letter of explanation. And the fact that her discovery is chiefly a psychological process, not an outward action, is stressed by her realization that it involves *self*-discovery. "Had I been in love," she cries (tantalizing the reader with the conditional), "I could not have been more wretchedly blind. . . . I have courted prepossession and ignorance and driven reason away where either were concerned. Till this moment I never knew myself."

Thus the management of narrative perspective plays an essential part in establishing the unity of the action: it is Elizabeth's story, and it is the story of her sense and sensibility rather than her outward behavior. But now an intriguing question occurs. If Elizabeth is to be the center of vision, why is she treated, in the opening chapters, merely on an equal plane with the other principal characters? Why the delay in establishing her predominance?

There appear to be some very good reasons for this, having to do with the use of point of view to help create suspense. The most violent outward action in **Pride and Prejudice,** perhaps, is Elizabeth's leap over a puddle on her way to Netherfield. Clearly, the suspense in this novel depends not on violent action, or even the threat thereof—despite Mrs. Bennet's nervous fears that Mr. Bennet will fight Wickham. It depends mostly on our waiting for Elizabeth to discover two things: that Darcy is in love with her; and that she is in love with Darcy. The reader must be led to suspect both of these things before Elizabeth does, or the suspense is lost. But if the point of view of the narration had been Elizabeth's from the start, the reader could hardly be aware that Darcy is falling in love; for Elizabeth, blinded by intense prejudice, never dreams of his affection. The storyteller therefore treats us to several direct insights into Darcy's mind in the early stages of the action: he begins by finding her eyes entrancing in chapter vi, and by chapter x is obliged to admit to himself that he "had never been so bewitched by any woman as he was by her." Once it

is firmly established that Darcy is slipping, however reluctantly, the narrator can safely project the point of view to that of the prejudiced heroine; and from then on we rarely desert Elizabeth as the center of vision.

As for Elizabeth's falling in love with Darcy, it is something not accomplished until near the end of the book; but we must feel, surely, that it is something *begun* much earlier than Elizabeth herself realizes. To effect this, we must be able to see Darcy apart from Elizabeth's conscious bias: we must see him, almost from the start, as at least potentially worthy of her love. No doubt we begin to take this view of Darcy early, despite his snobbish behavior, partly because we know he is falling in love with Elizabeth. Since we have begun to like her very much ourselves, this stands to his credit in the face of her prejudice; it shows his discrimination. But, as we have seen, our knowledge that Darcy is falling in love would have been impossible if Elizabeth had become the center of vision too soon. Thus our respect for Darcy, which we must feel before believing that so estimable a heroine could fall in love with him, also depends on keeping the point of view away from Elizabeth for a certain length of time.

And what about Elizabeth's specific prejudices against Darcy? If there is to be an interesting degree of suspense, we must not share them wholeheartedly with her: we must believe, long before she does, that the foundations on which they rest are doubtful, so that we may anticipate her change of heart. There are three things Elizabeth seriously holds against Darcy: she thinks he has spoiled Jane's chances with Bingley; that he has done this because he despises the social position of her family; and that he has ruined Wickham's career without due cause. After she has accused Darcy of these faults and hurled his proposal back in his face, he writes her the long, painstaking letter in which he clears himself of the charges. And it deserves attention that most of the grounds upon which he clears himself have been objectively established, early in the story—established, that is, in a way that would have been difficult or impossible in a narration primarily from Elizabeth's point of view. We must be left free to observe these grounds independent of Elizabeth, so that the possibility of romance between her and Darcy can beguile us long before it consciously dawns on her.

Darcy says, first, that Jane never displayed any love for Bingley, so to whisk him away to London could not be thought of as injuring Jane's emotions—and if we look back, we find that the narrator has carefully established this in the early chapters. Jane is so excessively demure that even when her heart is fluttering with romantic passion her manner shows only genteel pleasure and politeness. Even Elizabeth admits this, to Charlotte Lucas, in chapter vi; but it does not occur to her (as it may to the reader) that Bingley won't see through Jane's decorous disguise.

Darcy's explanation of why he wants to prevent marriage between Bingley and Jane is that he could not bear to see his friend marry into a family including such uncommonly ill-bred persons as Mrs. Bennet, Lydia, Kitty, and Mary: and we, the readers, have enjoyed generous exhibitions of their behavior, objectively related, from the opening pages of the novel. Although Darcy's disapproval on this score is damaging to the idea of romance between him and Elizabeth, it is not nearly so much so as her false conviction that he considers her family social station hopelessly beneath him.

Finally, Darcy's explanation of his treatment of Wickham, while it relies mostly on family history, brings to Elizabeth's attention certain improprieties in Wickham's behavior toward her—improprieties that were wide open to the reader's view in chapter xvi, even though at that time they were lost on Elizabeth. This chapter, in fact, is a kind of tour de force of narrative perspective: the point of view seems to be that of Elizabeth; yet in spite of many insights into her mental reaction to Wickham, the reader can maintain a certain detachment of judgment because the bulk of the chapter is fully recorded conversation—and what Wickham says constitutes his impropriety.

Thus the eminent part played by narrative perspective in establishing the artistic unity of *Pride and Prejudice* is achieved only by dint of some very skillful modification for the sake of dramatic suspense. Through a delicate balance between objective and subjective, we are given good reason to anticipate, with delicious anxiety, that Darcy and Elizabeth will wind up in each other's arms; yet Elizabeth, from whose point of view the story as a whole is focused, does not begin to perceive this denouement until near the end. (pp. 65-70)

> E. M. Halliday, *"Narrative Perspective in 'Pride and Prejudice',"* in Nineteenth-Century Fiction, *Vol. 15, No. 1, June, 1960, pp. 65-71.*

MORDECAI MARCUS   (essay date 1961)

[*Marcus examines how the relationships between Collins and Charlotte, Wickham and Lydia, and Bingley and Jane contrast with Elizabeth and Darcy's union and contribute to an understanding of its appropriateness. According to the critic, the four couples represent a pattern that illuminates the pitfalls of love and marriage that Darcy and Elizabeth manage to avoid through their strength of character.*]

Most critics of Jane Austen's *Pride and Prejudice* have justly praised the economy and control of its plotting, emphasizing the skill with which the relationships between Collins and Charlotte, Wickham and Lydia, and Bingley and Jane function, sometimes ironically, to bring together Darcy and Elizabeth. Many critics have also stressed revealing contrasts among these four relationships and among the individual characters, but no one has noted a particular and detailed thematic balance which emphasizes the value and significance of the adjustment between Darcy and Elizabeth.

Many definitions have been proposed of an essential conflict which is resolved by Darcy and Elizabeth. Mark Schorer calls it an adjustment of "the social scale . . . with the moral scale" [see excerpt dated 1956]; Dorothy van Ghent: "The difficult and delicate reconciliation of the sensitively developed individual with the terms of his social existence" [see excerpt dated 1953]; David Daiches: "Adjustment between the claims of personal and social life." These definitions, which are virtually identical and most conveniently stated in Daiches's formula, provide a basis for contrasting the four relationships.

At the center stand Darcy and Elizabeth, whose struggles lead to a reconciliation of personal and social claims. Far to one side of them stand Collins and Charlotte, who demonstrate a complete yielding to social claims. At the opposite extreme stand Wickham and Lydia, who represent capitulation to personal claims. It is difficult to fit Bingley and Jane into this pattern because immobility, not capitulation or progressive adjustment, characterizes them until they are united by outside forces. They may, however, be connected to the pattern by noting that they possess traits necessary for adjustment but do not see this until it is pointed out to them. They are also related

to the pattern by their inability to assert personal claims and to resist certain social claims, which inability results in passivity rather than in adjustment or capitulation. In the thematic structure they can be placed towards the center but below Darcy and Elizabeth, in a realm of impercipience, passivity, and chance. Thus Collins-Charlotte and Wickham-Lydia contrast to Darcy and Elizabeth through lack of integrity, whereas Bingley and Jane contrast to them through lack of percipience and strength. Some detailed analysis will show further significance in these contrasts.

The relationship between Collins and Charlotte presents a complete abandonment of personal claims in favor of social claims, but their individual adjustments are distinctly different. Collins seeks a wife so he may set a proper social example and obey Lady Catherine's wishes. Charlotte will accept such a contemptible man because he is the only alternative to penury and social isolation. All of this is readily apparent, but the situation is complicated by signs that Collins, unlike Charlotte, is incapable of normal personal feeling. His whole character has been absorbed by his social mask, and so he relates only his social self to other social surfaces. Thus Collins does not exactly capitulate to social claims, for he never recognizes personal claims, and he is blind to the fact that his own personal claims are distorted social claims. A brief analysis of his combination of arrogance and servility will explain this distortion. Collins values only social power, and so he seeks security by cringing before his superiors. To his potential inferiors he is arrogant and rude, which behavior expresses anger at those who will not recognize his social power and vindictive compensation for his cringing. The portrayal of Collins's almost mechanical character in which social claims have become indistinguishable from character gives us little sense of the original process by which social claims can crush personality, but such a portrayal might introduce a more pathetic note than the novel could sustain.

Charlotte, unlike Collins, does show the process of capitulation to social claims; her relationship with Elizabeth establishes the fact that she has intelligence, sensibility, and integrity. Thus her loneliness with Collins is the central pathos of her marriage; for Collins has lost nothing by the marriage because he had nothing to lose.

At the opposite extreme to Collins and Charlotte stand Wickham and Lydia, who yield almost completely to personal claims. Their chief motivation appears to be sexual passion, but other motives are visible. Lydia seeks freedom and excitement. Wickham avails himself of a chance to flee his creditors, and he also seems to have some hopes for an agreeable marriage settlement. The marriage gives promise of a brutalization which Jane Austen cautiously suggests in her concluding pages, but again the pathetic note is restrained.

Possibly Jane Austen sees a greater failure of integrity in the Wickham-Lydia than in the Collins-Charlotte marriage. Collins's selfishness is so much a part of his almost mechanical social self that we see no possible alternative to it for him; and Charlotte's yielding to social claims and acceptance of loneliness with Collins may seem little worse than the alternate fate of social isolation. Wickham and Lydia, on the other hand, have personal attractiveness and energy, which makes it difficult to forgive them for recklessly discarding any balance between personal and social claims. It is interesting to note that Jane Austen implies that Wickham and Lydia, the violators of sacred convention, will be more unhappy than Collins and Charlotte, who have sacrificed all or part of their personalities to society. Collins and Charlotte seem assured of a more or less indispensable social equilibrium which Wickham and Lydia will lack. Jane Austen could not, of course, consider the probably greater sexual satisfaction in a marriage such as Wickham and Lydia's. But comparisons between the relative failure of these marriages must remain precarious, for Charlotte might have had the courage and integrity to reject Collins.

The relationship between Bingley and Jane provides the novel with less movement than do Collins-Charlotte and Wickham-Lydia, but it provides more subtle and perhaps more revealing contrasts to the Darcy-Elizabeth relationship. The contrast between Bingley-Jane and Darcy-Elizabeth enables us to feel poignant modulations each time we compare one couple with the other. Bingley and Jane possess personal attractiveness and dignity, social graces, and a measure of good sense, but they lack insight, strength, and self-confidence. Jane's diffidence towards Bingley and her quickness to believe that he has lost interest in her show inability to assert personal claims and to resist excessive social claims. Bingley similarly lacks self-confidence, and he yields easily to criticism of Jane's social position. If we cannot imagine Bingley and Jane acting much differently, we at least are strongly concerned and sympathetic with their weaknesses; we wish that they had the strength of Darcy and Elizabeth.

Unlike Bingley and Jane, Darcy and Elizabeth are deep and strong enough to hope for each other's continued affection even after circumstances have borne strong evidence against it. Also, they are able to stand up against excessive social claims. Darcy becomes willing to associate himself with the Bennet family (Lady Catherine's opposition is a much slighter obstacle). Although the excessive social claims which Elizabeth must resist may be slighter, they are not negligible. First, she must resist an overbearing verbal storm from Lady Catherine (which surely would have crushed a Jane Bennet), and then she must assert her claim to Darcy despite her realization of her family's true nature. Of lesser importance are her embarrassment in informing her family that she will marry Darcy and her pain in observing Darcy in association with her mother and younger sisters.

Contrast between these two couples also reveals dangers that hover near for Darcy and Elizabeth. Elizabeth could never act as do Charlotte and Lydia, but we can imagine her yielding to hopeless passivity. Darcy could not act as Collins or Wickham do, but we can imagine him permanently stiffening into the inflexible pride he displayed in condemning Elizabeth's family to her face. Such action would scarcely parallel Bingley's behavior, but the weakness it would display would have effects like those of Bingley's weaknesses. Most important of all, Darcy's and Elizabeth's differences from Bingley and Jane suggest to us the power of will which Darcy and Elizabeth develop, the ability to educate themselves which lies at the heart of the novel.

Several critics have suggested that Collins and Wickham represent real marriage prospects for Elizabeth, but this seems doubtful. Marriage to a man she could not respect would be impossible for Elizabeth, unless, indeed, she were taken in by a charming but dishonest man such as Wickham, but if she were long enough deceived by Wickham to marry him—unlikely and fruitless for him as this would seem—her action would not represent capitulation to personal values but would be only a serious error of judgment. Although the Collins-Charlotte and Wickham-Lydia marriages help to dramatize the possible fate of a girl in Elizabeth's social position, their chief purpose is to show by contrast the desirability and integrity of the adjustment between Darcy and Elizabeth. Only Bingley and Jane help to dramatize alternatives which were significantly possible for Darcy and Elizabeth and thus to show the strength represented by their adjustment.

One might object that the Collins-Charlotte and Wickham-Lydia relationships provide excessively artificial contrasts to Darcy and Elizabeth. But had Jane Austen created two more relationships as naturally contrasting to Darcy and Elizabeth as that of Bingley and Jane, and had shown major defects in those relationships, she might have created large-scale tragic effects. One may lament that she did not do exactly this, but one may also doubt that her gifts would have preserved their present power and integrity had she abandoned her comic irony, or attempted to combine it with tragic irony. (pp. 274-79)

> Mordecai Marcus, ''A Major Thematic Pattern in 'Pride and Prejudice','' in Nineteenth-Century Fiction, *Vol. 16, No. 3, December, 1961, pp. 274-79.*

CHARLES J. McCANN (essay date 1964)

[*McCann focuses on how the three important country houses in* Pride and Prejudice—Netherfield, Rosings, *and* Pemberley—*help to clarify the personalities of their inhabitants. Among the topics the critic discusses are how Elizabeth's perception of Darcy is altered by her visit to Pemberley and how Darcy's character is influenced by his surroundings.*]

The country house is perhaps the most familiar landmark in Jane Austen's setting, and far from being merely decorative, it serves a vital purpose. Generally, it is an essential ingredient of her art; relatively simple in *Persuasion,* where Kellynch is an instrument of the plot, complex in *Emma,* where Donwell Abbey is the background of a central scene, and more complex in *Mansfield Park,* where the house serves in the fullest way as the background of the story. This is the inevitable consequence of the fact that Jane Austen carefully places her characters in just the proper symbol of their economic, social, or intellectual condition. In this respect the country houses in all Austen novels, and especially those in *Pride and Prejudice,* are constant values—that is to say, each is a recognizable emblem for a complex of social, economic, and intellectual realities. Thus, the pretentiousness of Rosings reveals Lady Catherine, as the nondescriptness of Netherfield does Bingley. To the extent that she employs the country house emblematically, Jane Austen can characterize obliquely, and in *Pride and Prejudice* as in no other work this method dramatically informs the entire novel.

Taken together, however, Netherfield, Rosings, and Pemberley are much more than three emblems of three separate families, that is, three discrete images. And this because, while the emblematic correspondence is soon made clear in the case of Netherfield and Rosings, the two lesser houses of *Pride and Prejudice,* the correspondence between Pemberley and Darcy remains unclear in the early stages of the action. While the early scenes of the work are built around Netherfield and Rosings, Pemberley remains in the distance; we hear much about it, but are not permitted to see it. Two revelatory ratios are established early, but one quantity in the third ratio remains unknown. Thus, while Netherfield is to Bingley as Rosings is to Lady Catherine, the unknown quantity that is Pemberley creates a certain mystery about Darcy. Existing as it does in this unspecified relation to the action and scene, Pemberley serves as the basis of a suspense which amplifies, parallels, and resolves with, the Elizabeth-Darcy story. In addition to furthering action and characterization, the image of Pemberley, always with the support of the two other houses, provides tonal, rhythmic, and rational unities, and serves as a symbol which makes the story—as comedy—possible. For it becomes a symbol of a fixed value, of a stable condition to which the heroine belongs, but from which she is separated by immaturity, and to which she finally attains. Pemberley, then, stands for that "rigorous and positive belief" which, according to Professor Brower, balances the "sense of variability" [see *NCLC*, Vol. 1].

In order to accomplish these various ends, it is necessary for Austen to mention Pemberley early in the novel. While it would not, however, be to her purpose to define the exact relationship between Pemberley and Darcy this early, she must imply a *close* relationship. This she does from the introduction of both, when the assembly at Netherfield discovers Darcy to be so proud that "not all his large estate in Derbyshire could then save him from having a most forbidding, disagreeable countenance". . . . Moreover, while the "neutral" company is aware of a relationship between man and house—an inexact one, to be sure—Elizabeth, at this time a little too self-centered, is unwilling to accept this fact with all that it necessarily implies. Thus, early in the novel Darcy's possessions help define Elizabeth's position in a subtle dramatic irony:

> "His pride," said Miss Lucas, "does not offend *me* so much as pride often does, because there is an excuse for it. One cannot wonder that so very fine a young man, with family, fortune, everything in his favour, should think highly of himself. If I may so express it, he has a *right* to be proud."
>
> "That is very true," replied Elizabeth, "and I could easily forgive his pride, if he had not mortified *mine*." . . . (pp. 65-7)

Pride has reared its head for the first time, and in a context intricately associated with Pemberley. Without itself being the source of conflict, Pemberley serves as a focal point around which the lines of conflict are drawn. In the disguised maneuvering to win Darcy, Pemberley becomes the image to which characters respond with their own kinds of pride. Elizabeth's own self-defensive pride has already been clearly established. A little later, when Miss Bingley tries to denigrate her unwitting rival by suggesting the ludicrousness of Elizabeth's mother at Pemberley, she is attempting to arouse Darcy's pride by pointing out the essential incompatibility of the two families. At the same time that it does this, her attack also reveals her mean spirit and points out an implicit sense of pride at feeling free to associate herself with what Darcy represents.

At this point one is uncertain as to whether Pemberley is deservedly an object of pride; later we are to be convinced that Darcy's pride is justifiable, but even at this point there is a clear indication that Pemberley is already a norm: for if Miss Bingley's "queen of the hill" tactics are to mean anything, there must be a "hill," and that hill is Pemberley. Futile hope of opening a soft spot in Darcy's heart by flattery of Pemberley guides Miss Bingley's tactics, but her excess—and we are meant to be aware that it is excess—calls her brother's better social sense into play. "Upon my word, Caroline, I should think it more possible to get Pemberley by purchase than by imitation." . . . (p. 67)

While this early conversation sets up Pemberley as a possible ideal, Jane Austen, by reference to Pemberley, cunningly uses this dialogue to delineate four characters. Miss Bingley's lack of honor and sensitivity—she is unknowingly but blatantly baring her meanness—and Bingley's bland and formless good humor are clearly revealed. It also captures Mrs. Bennet's vulgarity, and here is one of the pleasures of reading "Honest Jane": unsympathetic characters are allowed to speak the truth. It is Elizabeth, however, who always holds the center of the stage. We are never allowed to forget that she, in her innocence and pride, must progress to discover another kind of pride and perhaps even another more complex innocence—the one born of custom and of ceremony.

Much of the suspense of the novel is dependent on whether Elizabeth will successfully make such progress. The brilliance of Austen's artistry lies in that we are able to follow so closely the landmarks in Elizabeth's development. The suspense involved, however, is not merely a matter of controlled point of view. For there is as much anticipation of discovering what Pemberley—and consequently Darcy—will be, as there is in following Elizabeth's progress. Let us, for the sake of argument, imagine a version of the story in which Elizabeth and the reader were permitted from the start to see Pemberley. Such a version could still present the sort of awakening we see in *Emma* and in *Persuasion* where the pleasures we are discussing depend almost entirely on control of point of view, but much of the effect peculiar to *Pride and Prejudice* would have been lost. To illustrate this quality of *Pride and Prejudice*, consider the following passage. Elizabeth is selecting a book from the collection in the drawing room at Netherfield:

> He (Bingley) immediately offered to fetch her others; all that his library afforded.
>
> "And I wish my collection were larger for your benefit and my own credit: but I am an idle fellow; and though I have not many, I have more than I ever look into."
>
> Elizabeth assured him that she could suit herself perfectly with those in the room.
>
> "I am astonished," said Miss Bingley, "that my father should have left so small a collection of books. —What a delightful library you have at Pemberley, Mr. Darcy!"
>
> "It ought to be good," he replied, "it has been the work of many generations." . . . (pp. 67-9)

It is not astonishing that Netherfield has so few books when we recall that Mr. Bingley senior had spent so much of his life working that he had little opportunity to purchase an estate, much less to fill the library shelves. Netherfield thus contrasts with Pemberley, the mellowed home of generations, and thereby creates a tension which in some respects modifies the Elizabeth-Darcy one. This tension, added to the minor one of Bingley-Miss Bingley, characterizes Bingley, Miss Bingley, and Darcy, and—since our information about Pemberley is hearsay—adds suspense. While it is surely important that our point of view is Elizabeth's, the suspenseful quality of this typical scene cannot be discussed solely in those terms.

The irony of Elizabeth's position, emphasized by the symbolism of the setting, is already becoming clear. Although one day she will be both subjectively and objectively "in," she is at present "out" in both respects. There is additional irony in the fact that Miss Bingley, now subjectively "in" but objectively "out," furnishes us with most of our advance information about Pemberley. Her desperate claims to the inside track, in remarks such as, "Do let the portraits of your uncle and aunt Philips be placed in the gallery at Pemberley," . . . supply pieces for the montage of an impressive house that gradually assembles in the reader's mind.

All the foregoing allusions to Pemberley have been made during the action at Netherfield. Although we know from the natives' opinion of its inhabitants that Netherfield is considered an important house in a neighborhood of Lucases and Philipses, it is significant that not one aspect of Netherfield is praised during these discussions, apart from Mrs. Bennet's suspect enthusiasms. The reader is not told much about Netherfield except that Bingley would be willing to leave at five minutes notice. Indeed, the sharpest image we have of it is of the "charming prospect over that gravel walk." . . . This pointed nondescriptness has an analogy in Bingley's character, and a blandness already suggested in him as here intensified. In retrospect, then, the references to country houses in the beginning of the novel are dominated by ancient Pemberley, which gains as much ascendancy in the reader's consciousness over rented Netherfield as aristocratic Darcy has over nouveau riche Bingley.

Rosings, the second-ranking house of *Pride and Prejudice,* heretofore only casually mentioned, is appropriately introduced by Mr. Collins's effusions. The actual change of scene to Rosings, however, comes only after modulation: description of Pemberley by Wickham, and reminiscences about Pemberley between Mrs. Gardiner and Wickham. By interrupting the crescendo of praise of Rosings, Jane Austen avoids interfering with the reader's anticipation of Pemberley; by suggesting that Mr. Collins wears rose-colored glasses, she prevents our confusing with Rosings what has been associated with Pemberley; and only after the standard by which to judge Rosings has been set forth in this oblique conversational manner do we get Catherine's picture, one that we may to some extent trust. But even then, "It was Mr. Collins's picture . . . rationally softened. . . ." (pp. 69-70)

Mr. Collins's view (the best in the Kingdom!) is of ". . . a handsome modern building, well situated on rising ground." . . . His admiring account of the glazing of the front windows, praise which leaves Elizabeth unresponsive, reminds us that Lady Catherine's husband was the original owner. The effect of this summary treatment of the Rosings setting is to give the impression of a new, flashy establishment, a fit casing for snobbish Lady Catherine de Bourgh.

Elizabeth is of course able to adjust unselfconsciously to the atmospheres of Netherfield and Rosings because she is unimpressed and unmoved by either. This reflects Jane Austen's relative unconcern with Elizabeth's reaction to these settings: her purpose is to create through dialogue a picture of a third setting, that of Pemberley, and by this means to point out the disparity between the reader's and Elizabeth's awareness of its importance. And this disparity, Jane Austen does not allow us to forget, is due to Elizabeth's present feelings about Darcy.

In the preceding discussion, I have suggested that if we follow the logic of associating houses and inhabitants a dilemma becomes apparent in the case of Darcy and Pemberley, a dilemma resulting from unknowns which call the reliability of the association into question. If the process of association advanced in a straightforward manner, we ought to have a most cold, forbidding picture of Pemberley. And this because insofar as we are close to Elizabeth we ought to think its owner cold and

forbidding. (We are, however, somewhat prepared to believe otherwise by the ending of Darcy's letter.) But the house, as we have been led to imagine it, does not at all reflect what we know of its master, whose attributes, while they might include nobility and inimitability, certainly do not seem to number delightfulness among them. Further uncertainty arises from the fact that our chief informant about Pemberley has been Miss Bingley, who, as a very interested party, is probably not a reliable architectural correspondent. Our suspicions about the accuracy of her reports are naturally aroused, and, if our suspicions prove correct, Pemberley may very well match its so-far-disagreeable master. At this point, then, two of the anticipated satisfactions of the story are in doubt: finding Pemberley magnificent, and discovering its master to be compatible with his milieu. With more than the simple interest evoked by Pemberley in Volume I, the reader approaches the end of Volume II with real suspense due to the expected, but apparent lack of, correspondence between house and master. This careful heightening of suspense, added to Elizabeth's expressed anxiety, accounts for that high tension we feel when "To Pemberley, therefore, they were to go." . . . (pp. 70-1)

Volume III opens on the same note, *tremolo:* ". . . her spirits were in a high flutter." The tension only gradually diminishes in what is by far the longest and most elaborate piece of description in the novel. Darcy's home, whose beauty is confirmed by a specific comparison to Rosings, is found to be truly superb. Pemberley, in short, has met high expectations: if anything its glories have been understated. And Darcy, if we are to believe his housekeeper, is quite different from what Elizabeth has been led to believe. Elizabeth's preconception, however, is understandable, for she has been influenced by Bingley's hints that Darcy is susceptible to influence of place and situation. Then comes the sudden meeting in the park, and after a period of continued suspense during the tour Darcy surprisingly and significantly shows himself gracious in the test of meeting the middle-class Gardiners. The housekeeper's view of him proves to be the true one.

It is obvious that love works upon Darcy to open and soften his heretofore inapproachably proud character. But he has been in love with Elizabeth for some time. Why could he not have softened before? Bingley, though typically indiscriminate, has hit upon a basic element of Darcy's character when he remarks: "I declare I do not know a more aweful object than Darcy, on particular occasions, and in particular places; at his own house especially . . .". His setting seems to be a condition of Darcy's being. This is borne out by the fact that Elizabeth's impressions of him at Pemberley are shaken when she next sees him at Longbourn, now at his most forbidding. This insight of Bingley's, apparently borne out by Elizabeth's later experience, seems to contradict what we saw happening in the meeting at Pemberley. But there is no real contradiction—this merely reveals how sensitive Darcy is to both setting and character, and when either, as at Longbourn, is distasteful to him, he assumes a forbidding manner. But at Pemberley, where setting *and* Elizabeth's company are congenial to him, the forbidding manner falls away, thereby revealing it to be a polite form of indignation. At Pemberley, with those he cares for, he can be his true self. That Pemberley does not signify Darcy's whole personality in a one-for-one relationship, as setting does for the lesser characters where economy of characterization is necessary, reveals a degree of complexity in Darcy's character. Moreover, the fact that love does work upon Darcy further keeps him from being pasteboard, and further helps keep him as human enough for the nothing-if-not-human Elizabeth. Thus it is not surprising to find Elizabeth at Pemberley responding to a Darcy who has been softened by love but who is also (the context suggests) susceptible to setting:

> Never, even in the company of his dear friends at Netherfield, or his dignified relations at Rosings, had she seen him so desirous to please, so free from self-consequence, or unbending reserve as now, when . . . even the acquaintance of those to whom his attentions were addressed, would draw down the ridicule and censure of the ladies both of Netherfield and Rosings. . . .
>
> (pp. 71-2)

The significance of the subtle correspondence between characters and setting is underlined by the fact that Jane Austen from beginning to end never fails to suggest it. After the marriage, Pemberley is the home of felicity, usually open only to those who are compatible with its true elegance and with the personalities of its master and mistress. Wickham is excluded; Mrs. Bennet is merely an occasional visitor; characteristically she is taken up with Darcy's town house, not with his chief possession, Pemberley. Netherfield, a dwelling for transients, is closed. Even the owner of Rosings must swallow her prejudice for the privilege of visiting the home of justifiable pride.

This discussion can shed some light on problems that have intermittently troubled readers of *Pride and Prejudice:* what is seen as a sudden change in Darcy, and what seems like opportunism in Elizabeth. As for Darcy, his apparent change is neither implausible nor unexpected. This is not to say that there has not been an illusion of change—an illusion due to the reader's early, imperfect vision of Darcy. Structured as the novel is, the reader cannot have a true picture of Darcy until he sees him at Pemberley. For if we are to follow the logic of the novel we must see Darcy's setting before we truly see him. As for the characteristic forbidding manner, it is merely an indication of his sensitivity to company and environment. Once the environmental unpleasantness has been removed, Darcy reveals himself to be what he has always been.

The possibility of opportunism in Elizabeth can never be dismissed. However, Austen makes it clear that the visit to Pemberley affects her deeply. And later when her sister Jane asks her at what period she was first aware of her love for Darcy, she replies, jokingly: "'It has been coming on so gradually, that I hardly know when it began. But I believe I must date it from my first seeing his beautiful grounds at Pemberley.'" . . . Elizabeth's remark seems straightforward on the surface; she intends it to be a sarcastic but playful comment about her apparent materialism. Elizabeth, of course, feels self-conscious enough to be forced to indulge in such facetiousness, but she can only do so because she does not believe the remark to be a true one. In view of what Pemberley has come to represent, however, we feel uneasy and wonder whether our author here intends us to see beyond Elizabeth's view of the matter. Sir Walter Scott, in his well-known objection, misses both the playfulness and the irony and stresses the opportunism latent in Elizabeth's answer. In doing so he seems to have intuitively grasped the intended implication without understanding the manner in which it is expressed. As a consequence, he makes Elizabeth decidedly too unsympathetic. Whatever truth her answer holds is due not to simple snobbism or cupidity in Elizabeth, although Honest Jane does not leave out the possibility of a hidden "normal" measure of either, and we would be wise not to despise the fact that R. W. Chapman labels this

position "grotesque." Impure motivation seems inevitable in view of Mark Schorer's finding that in Jane Austen's world "marriage [is] a brutal economic fact in an essentially materialistic society" [see excerpt dated 1956].

All this should indicate that Jane Austen's view of Elizabeth's motivation is extremely complex: more sympathetic than Scott's, more realistic than Chapman's. What seems to make this reading of Elizabeth's motivation so convincing is the fact that Elizabeth has been presented as the sort of girl who would not return love unless her suitor possessed those traits which Pemberley happens to reflect and foster, and then she only becomes conscious of being *able* to love Darcy since their meeting at Pemberley. Thus the prevalent motif of the novel is here once again emphasized. When Elizabeth connects the notions of her love and Pemberley she reminds us of the relation of character to setting, the structural system of *Pride and Prejudice* which allows Jane Austen to accomplish her end—to present ironically the maturing of a well-disposed girl without, as in *Emma,* adopting an extremely related point of view. And here, precisely for this reason, she is able to accomplish her end with not necessarily more beautiful but with more mild irony than in *Emma.* Another solution would have been to follow the pattern of Fielding, and that of all down to George Eliot, that is, to use the narrative voice as the major control by which the reader could position the character. Instead, Jane Austen complemented point of view by using the imagery of her setting; and by submerging imagery even more into her dramatic texture by conveying it through dialogue, she produced, long before such a technique became common, one of the most artfully subtle uses of setting. (pp. 72-5)

Charles J. McCann, "Setting and Character in 'Pride and Prejudice'," in Nineteenth-Century Fiction, *Vol. 19, No. 1, June, 1964, pp. 65-75.*

A. WALTON LITZ   (essay date 1965)

[*In the following excerpt from his study of Austen's growth as an artist, Litz argues that in* Pride and Prejudice *the novelist transcended the "stale conventions" of eighteenth-century fiction characteristic of her predecessor Fanny Burney. The critic also discusses those qualities that set* Pride and Prejudice *apart from Austen's other novels, including its language, dramatic structure, and equation of art with morality.*]

We cannot think of *Pride and Prejudice* as belonging to any one period of Jane Austen's life before 1813; rather it was a summing up of her artistic career, a valedictory to the world of *Sense and Sensibility* and a token of things to come. More than any other of her novels it deserves Henry Austen's description in his Biographical Notice: "Some of these novels had been the gradual performances of her previous life."

One index to the new tones and new attitudes struck in *Pride and Prejudice* is the novel's use of conventions and stock situations drawn from eighteenth-century fiction. Both *Sense and Sensibility* and *Pride and Prejudice* depend upon characters and actions inherited from the Richardson-Fanny Burney tradition: the attractive seducer, the thoughtless young hoyden, ill-mannered relatives, tyrannical aristocrats, elopements and assignations. It is obvious from the *Juvenilia* that Jane Austen recognized the potential absurdity of these conventions; but they were so much a part of her fictional experience, and in some cases so close to the actual world she knew, that she could not exclude them from her art. The superiority of *Pride and Prejudice* to *Sense and Sensibility* lies in the transformation of these stale conventions, which renders them a believable part of the action and a natural vehicle for the novel's themes. This difference may be seen in a comparison of the heroes and villains, Darcy with Colonel Brandon, Wickham with Willoughby. In *Sense and Sensibility* Colonel Brandon has no more life than Lord Orville in Fanny Burney's *Evelina;* we believe in what he represents, but not in him. Yet Darcy, while preserving the virtues of the fictional hero, is entirely believable, since Jane Austen has subjected him to a process of self-evaluation and self-recognition. In him the type has been revivified. Similarly, the story of Willoughby's past behavior (as told by Colonel Brandon) is merely a plot device, a tale of seduction borrowed from fiction in the hope that it will give Willoughby's villainy substance and shape. In fact the tale stamps Willoughby as a two-dimensional figure; it substitutes his prototype in *Evelina* for the man we have glimpsed earlier, and not even the moving final confession can reassert his reality. But in *Pride and Prejudice* Wickham, although a descendant of the eighteenth-century fictional rake, does not suffer from the defects of his originals: his elopement with Lydia is plausible and carefully prepared, not a stale convention dragged in to forward the plot; and Darcy's account of Wickham's past villainies, unlike Colonel Brandon's tale, seems consonant with all we know of the subject's character.

It is important to keep these distinctions between *Sense and Sensibility* and *Pride and Prejudice* in mind when we speak of the latter's origins in late eighteenth-century fiction. Jane Austen's admiration of Fanny Burney is well known, and there can be no doubt that *Pride and Prejudice*—or, more exactly, *First Impressions*—owed a debt to *Cecilia.* Q. D. Leavis exaggerates this debt in her statement that "the original conception of *First Impressions* was undoubtedly to rewrite the story of Cecilia in realistic terms," but we know that when Jane Austen began work on the story the world of *Evelina* and *Cecilia* held a great reality for her. A niece recollected hearing, as a very young child, Jane Austen "read a part out of *Evelina,* one of the chapters concerning the Branghtons and Mr. Smith, and she thought it sounded like a play." Fanny Burney's fiction is filled with figures who remind us of Colonel Brandon or Willoughby or Lydia or Mrs. Bennet, and although one can argue that these were common types, the details of their treatment in Jane Austen's early work are often reminiscent of Fanny Burney. More significantly, the struggle between personal affection and family pride in *Cecilia* may have suggested the major themes of *Pride and Prejudice;* certainly the title was taken from the conclusion to *Cecilia,* where Dr. Lyster points the story's moral.

> "The whole of this unfortunate business . . . has been the result of PRIDE and PREJUDICE. . . . Yet this, however, remember; if to PRIDE and PREJUDICE you owe your miseries, so wonderfully is good and evil balanced, that to PRIDE and PREJUDICE you will also owe their termination."

But these similarities between *Pride and Prejudice* and Fanny Burney's novels only intensify our sense of Jane Austen's achievement in transforming the conventions of "the land of fiction." Since the limited social world she observed had been the subject of so much previous fiction, she was prevented from seeking originality in new situations and new locales. Instead she had to find her voice within the same range of life explored by many other female writers. Bingley's arrival at Netherfield, the ballroom scene, Wickham's flirtations, Dar-

cy's letter, Lydia's elopement, Lady Catherine's condescending visit—these were standard raw materials, but in *Pride and Prejudice* they were endowed with such a quantity of "felt life," and incorporated so skillfully into the drama, that they took on a new significance. It is this transformation of familiar materials which yields one of the novel's chief pleasures, the sense of subtle variations within a fixed and traditional range of experience. *Pride and Prejudice* bears that hallmark of "classic" art, the discovery of new possibilities within a traditional form.

Although the phrase "Pride and Prejudice" does not suggest as neat an ideological antithesis as "Sense and Sensibility," it would have led a late eighteenth-century reader to expect a schematic drama in which each quality is represented by a separate character or faction. But in *Pride and Prejudice* one cannot equate Darcy with Pride, or Elizabeth with Prejudice; Darcy's pride of place is founded on social prejudice, while Elizabeth's initial prejudice against him is rooted in pride of her own quick perceptions. In this we have a clear indication of the novel's distance from *Cecilia,* for Jane Austen's "internalizing" of the conflicts between proper and improper pride, candor and prejudice, goes far beyond the capabilities of Fanny Burney. Indeed, it was this ability to vest the novel's conflicts in the dynamic development of personality that freed Jane Austen from the world of static values which still dominates in *Sense and Sensibility.* Whereas in *Sense and Sensibility* the antitheses are resolved by a suppression of one position and an uneasy exaltation of the other, the entire movement of *Pride and Prejudice* tends toward a resolution of conflicts which is a union rather than a compromise, a union in which both parties gain new vigor and freedom of expression. The marriage of Elizabeth and Darcy resolves not only their personal differences but the conflicts they have represented, with the result that the novel provides a final pleasure unique in Jane Austen's fiction, a sense of complete fulfillment analogous to that which marks the end of some musical compositions. It is this sense of a union of opposites—without injury to the identity of either—which prompts the common comparison with Mozart. In *Pride and Prejudice,* for once in her career, Jane Austen allowed the symmetry of her imaginative creation to prevail over the protests of her social self, and the result is a triumph of ideal form. It was a triumph not to be repeated, one that was replaced in the later novels by less comforting views of human nature. Yet it remains valid as the finest expression of one aspect of Jane Austen's personality, her desire to endow human behavior with the order and symmetry of art. *Pride and Prejudice* is a great comedy because it formulates an ideal vision of human possibilities; its ending is "realistic" not because we measure the union of Elizabeth and Darcy against our own experience (that experience which delights in Jane Austen's statement that Mrs. Bennet remained "occasionally nervous and invariably silly"), but because their marriage is a complete fulfillment of the novel's artistic imperatives. Their lives have been the work's structure, and their marriage is a vindication of the artist's power to resolve complexities.

In his penetrating essay on *Mansfield Park* Lionel Trilling defines the special quality that distinguishes *Pride and Prejudice* from Jane Austen's other works.

> The great charm, the charming greatness, of *Pride and Prejudice* is that it permits us to conceive of morality as style. The relation of Elizabeth Bennet to Darcy is real, is intense, but it expresses itself as a conflict and reconcilia-

tion of styles: a formal rhetoric, traditional and rigorous, must find a way to accommodate a female vivacity, which in turn must recognize the principled demands of the strict male syntax. The high moral import of the novel lies in the fact that the union of styles is accomplished without injury to either lover.

Pride and Prejudice does more than testify to the artist's capacity for organizing and clarifying the confusions of life; it supports the fine illusion that life itself can take on the discrimination and selectivity of art. Throughout the novel aesthetic and moral values are closely related. Darcy and Elizabeth share the common eighteenth-century assumption that a man of real taste is usually a man of sound moral judgment, and when Elizabeth first views Pemberley the tasteful prospect confirms her altered opinion of Darcy's character. . . . Every evidence of sound aesthetic judgment provided by Pemberley is converted by Elizabeth into evidence of Darcy's natural amiability, and joined with the enthusiastic testimony of the housekeeper, until Pemberley becomes an image of his true nature. Sir Walter Scott was not entirely imperceptive when he made his much-ridiculed remark that Elizabeth "does not perceive that she has done a foolish thing until she accidentally visits a very handsome seat and grounds belonging to her admirer." Pemberley is more than a reminder of lost social and economic possibilities; it is a solid reflection of Elizabeth's new attitude toward Darcy.

This close connection between aesthetic and moral judgments enables Jane Austen to express her moral themes in terms of the novel's movement from complex antitheses to easy resolution. As Darcy and Elizabeth are first presented to us they sum up most of the conflicting forces in Jane Austen's early fiction. Elizabeth possesses the illusion of total freedom; she looks to nature, rather than society or traditional authority, for the basis of her judgments. She is self-reliant and proud of her discernment, contemptuous of all conventions that constrict the individual's freedom. Darcy, on the other hand, is mindful of his relationship to society, proud of his social place, and aware of the restrictions that inevitably limit the free spirit. Together they dramatize the persistent conflict between social restraint and the individual will, between tradition and self-expression.

Both Darcy and Elizabeth are flanked by figures who parody their basic tendencies: in Mr. Bennet the irony of the detached observer has become sterile, while Lady Catherine de Bourgh represents the worst side of aristocratic self-consciousness. But it is another group that provides the full antidote to pride and prejudice. The Gardiners stand as a rebuke to Darcy's social prejudices and aristocratic pride, an example of natural aristocracy; while Wickham's true nature is a telling blow to Elizabeth's pride of perception, and to her prejudice in favor of "natural" goodness. The marriage of Elizabeth and Darcy is, as Mark Schorer has pointed out, a kind of economic and social merging, an accommodation of traditional values based upon status with the new values personified in the Gardiners [see excerpt dated 1956]. Elizabeth is led to an appreciation of Darcy's "proper" pride—"he has no improper pride," she ultimately protests to Mr. Bennet . . .—while Darcy is disabused of his inherited prejudices based on caste and economic distance. But it would be too much to say, as Schorer does, that Jane Austen embodies her social judgments in Darcy, and her moral judgments in Elizabeth. For it is part of the novel's purpose to demonstrate that Elizabeth's original opinions were not freely arrived at, but conditioned by social prejudice, while

Darcy's initial pride had its roots in a feeling of moral superiority. The first two volumes of *Pride and Prejudice* are so complex that no one set of antitheses can define the positions of the hero and heroine, and any attempt to establish rigid patterns leads to absurdity. Under such schematizing Darcy's ambivalent attitude is reduced to the pomposity of Mary's extracts, while Elizabeth's wit becomes as sterile as her father's.

During recent years several intelligent critics have analyzed the stylistic and dramatic techniques used by Jane Austen to mark the subtle changes in the relationship between Darcy and Elizabeth. The most persuasive of these critics, Reuben Brower, has shown that all of the surface wit and irony of the novel is *functional*, a part of the larger dramatic design [see *NCLC*, Vol. 1]. Through a "sheer poetry of wit" Jane Austen conveys multiple views of her major characters, yet never does she lose sight of her fundamental dramatic aims. The greatness of the novel—whatever its limitations may be—lies in her fusion of the poetry of wit with the dramatic structure of fiction. It is this combination of local complexity with a general clarity of design which animates the novel, and redeems a story which could have been as static as that of *Sense and Sensibility*. A perfect example of the organic connection between language and action may be found in the speeches of Elizabeth and Darcy, which change as the differences between them are reconciled. In the novel's early scenes Jane Austen establishes a clear-cut distinction between Elizabeth's lively speech and Darcy's formal language, but this difference in expressive style is gradually modified as each begins to appreciate the other's style of living. When Darcy learns of the changes in Elizabeth's feelings toward him he expresses himself "as sensibly and as warmly as a man violently in love can be supposed to do" . . . , while Elizabeth's defense of her engagement to Mr. Bennet is reminiscent of Darcy's earlier remarks on the virtues of proper pride: "Indeed he has no improper pride. He is perfectly amiable." . . . In the conventional final chapter of *Pride and Prejudice,* where the future lives of the characters are confidently charted, Jane Austen can summarize with such easy authority because we have already seen these relationships foreshadowed in the novel's language and action.

The foundation of Jane Austen's success in correlating language and action is her irony, and the nature of this irony is nowhere better displayed than in the permutations of the novel's first sentence: "It is a truth universally acknowledged, that a single man in possession of a good fortune, must be in want of a wife." Out of context this general statement may seem no more significant than its original in *Rambler* No. 115, where Hymenaeus writes:

> "I was known to possess a fortune, and to want a wife; and therefore was frequently attended by those hymeneal solicitors, with whose importunity I was sometimes diverted, and sometimes perplexed; for they contended for me as vultures for a carcase; each employing all his eloquence, and all his artifices, to enforce and promote his own scheme, from the success of which he was to receive no other advantage than the pleasure of defeating others equally eager, and equally industrious."

Yet even in isolation the novel's opening sentence contains a certain irony: the exaggeration of the statement jars against our sense of reality, and prepares us for the discovery in the first chapters of *Pride and Prejudice* that this "truth" is acknowledged only by Mrs. Bennet and her kind. In the context of these chapters the irony is directed at economic motives for marriage, but as the action develops the implications of the opening sentence are modified and extended, until by the end of the novel we are willing to acknowledge that both Bingley and Darcy were "in want of a wife." Thus the sentence is simultaneously a source for irony and a flat statement of the social and personal necessities which dominate the world of *Pride and Prejudice.* The basic truth of the generalization is untouched by its ironic potential, and this suggests an important distinction that must be made in any discussion of Jane Austen's mature art. Her irony is dramatic, not static; complex, not simple; and we can only judge the tenor of the author's comments or the professions of her characters against the total pattern of dramatic action. Take for an example the following dialogue between Darcy and Elizabeth:

> "What think you of books?" said he, smiling.

> "Books—Oh! no.—I am sure we never read the same, or not with the same feelings."

> "I am sorry you think so; but if that be the case, there can at least be no want of subject.— We may compare our different opinions."

> "No—I cannot talk of books in a ball-room; my head is always full of something else."

> "The *present* always occupies you in such scenes—does it?" said he, with a look of doubt.

> "Yes, always," she replied, without knowing what she said, for her thoughts had wandered far from the subject, as soon afterwards appeared by her suddenly exclaiming, "I remember hearing you once say, Mr. Darcy, that you hardly ever forgave, that your resentment once created was unappeasable. You are very cautious, I suppose, as to its *being created*."

> "I am," said he, with a firm voice.

> "And never allow yourself to be blinded by prejudice?"

> "I hope not."

> "It is particularly incumbent on those who never change their opinion, to be secure of judging properly at first."

> "May I ask to what these questions tend?"

> "Merely to the illustration of *your* character," said she, endeavouring to shake off her gravity. "I am trying to make it out."

By the time we have reached this passage in the novel we know enough of Darcy's nature, and Elizabeth's pride of judgment, to realize that the questions tend more to an illustration of *her* character than of his. In this exchange Jane Austen is depending on an immediate grasp of the inherent dramatic irony, and she has carefully prepared her audience by allowing them to see more of the truth of the situation than any one character can perceive. But a first encounter with this passage does not exhaust its ironic implications, and only in retrospect—or upon second reading—do we understand its relation to the total pattern of dramatic action. The point about such complicated irony is that it depends on a full *external* revelation of the characters' inner natures; we rely more upon what they say and do than upon the author's comments. In this passage, as in so many

others, we are reminded of the novel's affinities with the best in eighteenth-century drama. The tripartite structure of *Pride and Prejudice,* dictated by the conventional three-decker form of publication, is similar to the structure of a three-act play, and we know from a remark in one of her letters to Cassandra that Jane Austen considered the volumes as separate units [see excerpt dated January, 1813]:

> The second volume is shorter than I could wish, but the difference is not so much in reality as in look, there being a larger proportion of narrative in that part.

This remark reveals the dramatist's eye for symmetry, but the reference to "a larger proportion of narrative" is scarcely apologetic, and we must realize that Jane Austen's method in *Pride and Prejudice* depends heavily on scenic effects but is not limited to them. The first half of the novel could easily be translated into a play; here Darcy and Elizabeth are "on stage," joining with the other characters to dramatize the novel's psychological and social conflicts. Howard S. Babb has shown how Jane Austen plays on the word "performance" in the early dialogues, bringing all the implications of the word together in the great scene at Rosings . . . , where Elizabeth's actual performance at the piano becomes the center of a dramatic confrontation [see excerpt dated 1958]. But after the scene at Rosings, when Darcy's letter begins Elizabeth's movement toward self-recognition, the term "performance" quietly disappears from the novel. The first half of *Pride and Prejudice* has indeed been a dramatic performance, but in the second half a mixture of narrative, summary, and scene carries the plot toward its conclusion.

Yet this movement from the predominantly "scenic" construction of the first half of *Pride and Prejudice* into the less dramatic narrative of the second half does not lead to a drop in our interest, nor do we feel that the consistency of the novel's form has been violated. This is because the novel is unified by the indirect presence of Jane Austen's sensibility, and by the direct presence of Elizabeth Bennet as a commanding center of our interest. The shift from the scene at Rosings to Elizabeth's reception of Darcy's letter merely internalizes the drama; and the account of Elizabeth's changing reactions to Darcy's letter reminds us that Jane Austen has not renounced her right to record the inner life of a character with absolute authority. This is not to say that Elizabeth is a Jamesian "center of consciousness"; Jane Austen was too sure of her created world (and of its relation to the actual world) to efface her own personality from the novel, and from first sentence to last we are aware of the artist's command over her fictions. But her early experiments had shown the need for some technique that would counteract the novel's general tendency toward looseness of form by "focusing" action and psychological exposition, and in *The Watsons* she had explored the method of telling a story from the point-of-view of one character while reserving the right to qualify and expand that viewpoint through dramatic irony and direct comment. Such a method is really a compromise: it combines in a limited form the omniscience of traditional third-person narration with the immediacy of first-person narrative, giving the reader a sense of involvement and identification while simultaneously providing the perspective necessary for moral judgment. Of course, this method makes the exacting demand that the novel's central figure be perpetually intelligent and interesting, a demand which Jane Austen could only partially satisfy in *The Watsons.* But in revising *Pride and Prejudice* she created a heroine who could justify the form, and the result was a highly unified work in which the center of our interest is always at the center of the artistic composition. (pp. 99-111)

A. Walton Litz, in his Jane Austen: A Study of Her Artistic Development, *Oxford University Press, 1965, 198 p.*

ALISTAIR M. DUCKWORTH   (essay date 1971)

[*Duckworth focuses on a single motif in* Pride and Prejudice: *the characters' laughter and their attitudes toward laughter as an index to their morality and social philosophy.*]

[Jane Austen insists in **Pride and Prejudice** that a properly constituted society] emerges only from the interaction of cultural discipline and individual commitment, and only when inherited forms receive the support of individual energy do they carry value. Conversely, however (and this is where Elizabeth's education is important), individual energy must be generated within social contexts, for, lacking social direction and control, it turns too easily to withdrawal from society, or to irresponsibility and anarchy.

Several of the novel's recurring motifs might be examined to support these points, but none seems more appropriate to this "light and bright and sparkling" novel than the motif of laughter, an examination of which will serve the additional function of qualifying any suggestion that Darcy's social philosophy goes uncriticized in the novel.

Beginning with Darcy's opinion, expressed early in the novel, that Miss Bennet "smiled too much . . . , attitudes toward laughter divide the characters, as they provide a dialectic illustrative of the theme. Most obviously, Darcy, all "grave propriety" . . . , is opposed to Elizabeth, who has a "lively, playful disposition, which delighted in any thing ridiculous." . . . We tend, perhaps, to consider Elizabeth's position normative, for modern theories of humor—Meredith's, Bergson's—have stressed the deflationary function of the laugh. One laughs at hypocrisy, vanity, pretension, the gap between statement and action, between theory and practice, and there are unnumerable examples of this in the novel. Jane Austen is by no means averse to using the comic spirit as the sword of common sense. Yet in the eighteenth century, as she must have been aware, laughter was the subject of widespread debate. If on the one hand laughter was associated with the freedom which Englishmen had gained with the Glorious Revolution, on the other it was considered to be a sign of disharmony, of lack of restraint, and of chaos. When the third Earl of Shaftesbury in his "Essay on the Freedom of Wit and Humor" (1709) argued (or was credited with arguing) that "ridicule" was a test of truth, there were many who responded that certain matters (and especially, religion) should not be put to such a test.

Clearly aware of this background, Jane Austen has Darcy take a conservative attitude toward laughter. His taciturn disposition and unwillingness to be the butt of mirth are clearly described. He tells those assembled in the Netherfield drawing room that "it has been the study of [his] life to avoid those weaknesses which often expose a strong understanding to ridicule" . . . , and his attitude toward laughter places him in the company of, for example, Lord Chesterfield, who considered that "frequent and loud laughter is the characteristic of folly and ill manners," and who, in another letter to his son, advised: "Loud laughter is the mirth of the mob, who are only pleased with silly things; for true wit of good sense never excited a laugh, since the

creation of the world. A man of parts and fashion is therefore only seen to smile, but never heard to laugh." Darcy's aversion to laughter is more than a wish to appear as a man of parts, however. Like the man of zeal whom Shaftesbury views with some irony, Darcy seems to feel that "all Professions must fall to the ground, all Establishments come to ruin, and nothing orderly or decent be left standing in the world" if "Matters of Importance [are] treated with this frankness of Humour." For him laughter is the disparagement of the good and the subversion of the established. He opposes any theory of laughter as corrective.

The deficiencies of this view, evident enough in Darcy's own demeanor, are revealed in the parodies of it which appear in the novel. Everywhere in **Pride and Prejudice**, pompous gravity is laughed out of existence. By absorbing didacticism into the absurdly formal utterances of a Mary Bennet or a Mr. Collins (neither of whom is ever known to laugh), Jane Austen demonstrates that the uncritical acceptance of precept and the literalistic observance of sanctioned moral attitudes may have effects the reverse of what the situation demands. We cannot forget Mr. Collins' vicious parody of the parable of the prodigal son in his letter of "consolation" to Mr. Bennet on news of Lydia's elopement: "Let me advise you . . . to console yourself as much as possible, to throw off your unworthy child from your affection for ever, and leave her to reap the fruits of her own heinous offence." . . . Nor can we be unaware of the total lack of feeling in Mary's formulaic response to the same event: "we must stem the tide of malice, and pour into the wounded bosoms of each other, the balm of sisterly consolation." . . . The humor of these characters lies in their lack of humor, their failure in their unawareness of the claims of spontaneity in certain situations. They can produce, as if by rote, a prior "institutional" response, but they have no conception that circumstances sometimes alter cases. Mr. Collins admits to Mr. Bennet that he arranges beforehand "such little elegant compliments as may be adapted to ordinary occasions" . . . , and it is clear that for him "ordinary occasions" are to be defined by the same kind of ceremonial ritual as a church service, or an introduction to the redoubtable Lady Catherine.

Elizabeth's attitude toward experience is very different, as an early conversation . . . makes sufficiently plain. She and Miss Bingley have formed a temporary alliance to poke fun at Darcy. He has shown his awareness of Miss Bingley's design in walking round the room—she is showing off her figure to the best advantage—and she in reply, asks Elizabeth, "How shall we punish him for such a speech?" Elizabeth suggests that they should "Teaze him—laugh at him" . . . , but Miss Bingley, ever anxious to please Darcy, demurs:

> "Teaze calmness of temper and presence of mind! No, no—I feel he may defy us there. And as to laughter, we will not expose ourselves, if you please, by attempting to laugh without a subject. . . ."

> "Mr. Darcy is not to be laughed at!" cried Elizabeth. "That is an uncommon advantage, and uncommon I hope it will continue, for it would be a great loss to *me* to have many such acquaintance. I dearly love a laugh."

Elizabeth, like Lord Shaftesbury, is a defender of raillery as a means of proving the worth of a person or idea. "Truth 'tis suppos'd," says Shaftesbury, "may bear *all* Lights: and *one* of those principal Lights or natural Mediums, by which Things are to be view'd, in order to a thorow Recognition, is *Ridicule* it-self, or that Manner of Proof by which we discern whatever is liable to just Raillery in any Subject.'' . . . And when Darcy defends himself by pointing out that ''the wisest and the best of men, nay, the wisest and best of their actions, may be rendered ridiculous by a person whose first object in life is a joke'' . . . , Elizabeth disassociates herself from the accusation: ''Certainly,'' replied Elizabeth,—''there are such people, but I hope I am not one of *them*. I hope I never ridicule what is wise or good. Follies and nonsense, whims and inconsistencies *do* divert me, I own, and I laugh at them whenever I can.'' . . . Elizabeth would agree with the third earl that there is ''a great difference between seeking how to raise a Laugh from every thing; and seeking, in every thing, what justly may be laugh'd at.'' . . . She might indeed be echoing Shaftesbury's assertion that, ''as I am earnest in defending Raillery, so I can be sober too in the Use of it'' . . . , and she clearly seems to win this particular exchange. When Darcy somewhat pontifically distinguishes between pride and vanity, ''Elizabeth turned away to hide a smile.'' . . . As Bergson knew, humor is the great deflator of men who act like machines.

Yet the motif is not confined to this scene, and in other appearances Elizabeth's point of view does not come off so well, as laughter becomes on occasions everything that the grave Darcy suggests it to be. Mr. Bennet, for example, employs his wit as a barely concealed misanthropy, as an assertion of superiority required by his sense of defeat: ''For what do we live, but to make sport for our neighbours, and laugh at them in our turn?'' . . . No less subversive is Lydia's laughter, however different her loud buffoonery is from her father's cool satire. Like Lord Chesterfield's ''mirth of the mob,'' Lydia's laughter is excessive and silly, but beyond this, her immoderate mirth, like her lexical hyperboles (''Aye,'' ''Lord''), her grammatical failures (''Kitty and me were to spend the day there'' . . . , and her constant inattention to the decorum required of the occasion (as when she interrupts Mr. Collins in his reading of Fordyce), indicates a vulgarity and a selfishness which bid fair to subvert established forms.

A good gloss for Jane Austen's treatment of Lydia is discoverable in *The Covent-Garden Journal*, Nos. 55 and 56, where Fielding, taking a conservative position toward humor, disputes the view, argued by Congreve specifically, that the abundance of ''Characters of Humour'' in England is to be attributed to the ''Liberty'' that this country enjoys. Only if ''Liberty'' includes within its meaning ''an Exemption from all Restraint of municipal Laws, but likewise from all Restraint of those Rules of Behaviour which are expressed in the general Term of good Breeding,'' Fielding argues, may it properly be associated with humor. And he goes on, in No. 56, to provide two reasons of his own for the abundance of humorous characters in England: ''The first is that Method so general in this Kingdom of giving no Education to the Youth of both Sexes''; and the ''second general Reason . . . seems to me to arise from the great Number of People, who are daily raised by Trade to the Rank of Gentry, without having had any Education at all.'' In this context, Lydia's ''wild volatility'' . . . is attributable to both her parents: to her father, who has failed to educate her in the ''Rules of Behaviour'' (Elizabeth sees that he has not taken the ''trouble of checking her exuberant spirits'' . . . ; and to her mother, who has become through her marriage a member of the gentry, but who again and again—to Elizabeth's mortification—show she lacks entirely the ''breeding'' required by her new position.

Lydia's ''exemption from all Restraint,'' in Fielding's phrase, becomes a focus of attention when she accompanies Elizabeth and Jane in the coach returning to Longbourn. As she informs Mary Bennet on arrival, ''we were so merry all the way home! we talked and laughed so loud, that any body might have heard us ten miles off.'' . . . Further evidence of her indecorous conduct during the absence of her older sisters is revealed in her description of a ''piece of fun'' recently enjoyed at Colonel Forster's:

> ''We dressed up Chamberlayne in woman's clothes, on purpose to pass for a lady,—only think what fun! Not a soul knew of it, but Col. and Mrs. Forster, and Kitty and me, except my aunt, for we were forced to borrow one of her gowns; and you cannot imagine how well he looked! When Denny, and Wickham, and Pratt, and two or three more of the men came in, they did not know him in the least. Lord! how I laughed! and so did Mrs. Forster. I thought I should have died. And *that* made the men suspect something, and then they soon found out what was the matter.'' . . .

As Lydia takes evident delight in turning normal relations upside down, there is here, perhaps, an anticipation of the theatricality that is so suspect in *Mansfield Park*.

The disequilibrium that Lydia introduces into previously ordered structures is evident in her speech and manners long before she runs off with Wickham. But it is this assertion of her ''liberty'' that calls unfettered individualism into question and reveals Jane Austen taking a more conservative view of humor. In the letter that Lydia writes to Harriet Forster following her elopement, the laughter motif finds its culmination, as Lydia's determination to see everything without exception as hilarious gives every reason for viewing laughter with suspicion:

> ''You will laugh when you know where I am gone, and I cannot help laughing myself at your surprise tomorrow morning, as soon as I am missed. I am going to Gretna Green, and if you cannot guess with who, I shall think you a simpleton, for there is but one man in the world I love, and he is an angel. I should never be happy without him, so think it no harm to be off. You need not send them word at Longbourn of my going, if you do not like it, for it will make the surprise the greater, when I write to them, and sign my name Lydia Wickham. What a good joke it will be! I can hardly write for laughing. Pray make my excuses to Pratt, for not keeping my engagement. . . . I wish you would tell Sally to mend a great slit in my worked muslin gown, before they are packed up.'' . . .

The moral chaos of Lydia's character is here revealed in her choice of correspondent (not her family but her friend), in her motive for writing (not to dispel alarm, but to inspire admiration), and in the transparent inconsistency of her avowals (within a breath of her declared intention to love ''but one man in the world,'' she expresses an interest in another). Linguistically, as usual, all is disorder, as grammatical errors and lexical hyperboles silently comment upon the enormity of Lydia's ''scheme of infamy.'' . . . The Popean, if not Freudian, skill of the "great slit in my worked muslin gown" is obvious. Serious as her action is, however, Lydia has no sense of guilt. When she returns to Longbourn with Wickham, she is "Lydia still; untamed, unabashed, wild, noisy, and fearless" . . . , and from the moment her "voice [is] heard in the vestibule . . . and she [runs] into the room," Elizabeth is disgusted by her attitude. But Lydia can only observe "with a laugh, that it was a great while since she had been there," and "Wickham was not at all more distressed than herself." . . . (pp. 132-39)

It is clear that the basically worthy orientations of Darcy and Elizabeth, like those of Elinor and Marianne Dashwood, receive comment in the perverse parodies of them that the novel provides. Almost all the characters are illuminated by the laughter theme, which embraces a whole series of discriminations of humor—joke, piece of fun, playfulness, good humor, smile, wit, laughter, and so on—serving to distinguish decorous from indecorous action, moral from immoral motivations. In these descriptions, traditional—fundamentally classical—principles are operative; rules, including the due observation of the subject under discussion, the character of the speaker, the character of the audience, and the situation of the utterance, guide the reader to the degree of humor permissible in a given instance. Like Fielding, Jane Austen believes in "Rules of Good Breeding" (and especially in the "golden rule") and knows that when laughter or humor exceeds these rules it is to be censured.

In granting to Elizabeth an access to the significance of humor, Jane Austen reveals that her heroine has learned to make ethical discriminations separately from subjective desires, to distinguish between what is spontaneously permissible and what is immorally subversive. Her intrinsic accessibility to such a recognition is shown early, when she "checked her laugh" . . . on seeing that Darcy is really offended by Bingley's portrait of him as an "aweful object" . . . at Pemberley, and in a later conversation with Jane she shows that she has learned to view "wit" with some suspicion:

> "And yet I meant to be uncommonly clever in taking so decided a dislike to him, without any reason. It is such a spur to one's genius, such an opening for wit to have a dislike of that kind. One may be continually abusive without saying any thing just; but one cannot be always laughing at a man without now and then stumbling on something witty." . . .

She has come round practically to repeating Darcy's own view on the subject of wit. And when she is married to Darcy, she comes to regulate her laughter somewhat: "She remembered that he had yet to learn to be laught at." . . . Of course, Elizabeth does not subdue her playfulness entirely, nor is it thematically necessary that she should. She will continue to shock Darcy's passive and obedient sister by the "lively, sportive, manner" . . . in which she addresses Darcy, and she will distinguish herself from Jane in a letter to her aunt by writing "she only smiles, I laugh." . . . And this is appropriate, for culture without life, like discipline without humor, is empty form. As Elizabeth brings judgment to her laughter, Darcy must learn to be laughed at, for Truth may indeed bear all lights. (pp. 139-40)

> *Alistair M. Duckworth, in his* The Improvement of the Estate: A Study of Jane Austen's Novels, *The Johns Hopkins University Press, 1971, 239 p.*

NORMAN PAGE (essay date 1972)

[*In the following excerpt from his study of language in Austen's works, Page analyzes the narrative function of dialogue and dramatic structure in* Pride and Prejudice. *Page argues that dramatic conversation constitutes the primary method of narration in the novel.*]

[The 'triumph' of Jane Austen's] novels is to a large extent a triumph of style, and that the fact that they constantly transcend the level of cultivated gossip or conventional story-telling is to be explained partly in terms of certain qualities of language. The achievement was not only one of individual genius, of course. Short of pastiche, a writer can use only the resources made available to him by the language of his day; and part of Jane Austen's greatness lay in exploiting the distinctive strengths of the English language as she found it, and in resisting some of the influences which were at work to change it even as she wrote. At the same time she was an innovator too, notably in prose syntax and in narrative modes. If we take into account the difference between her subject-matter (that is, her apparent field of interest) and the inner meaning of her novels as signalled, very largely, by the particular features of their language, we can begin to understand the contradictory judgments which have been passed upon them. For those who see only the surface—the morning visit and the ball, the dinner party and the picnic—her work suffers from damaging limitations; on the other hand, her power to suggest, through her style, the major issues inherent in minor incidents justifies F. R. Leavis's claim to find in her an 'intense moral preoccupation'. . . .

[How] is this sense of the far-reaching importance of the local and the ephemeral conveyed? Largely, it will be suggested, by stylistic means: it is Jane Austen's finely-controlled use of language which brings to the reader's attention the true import of episodes and conversations apparently slight in themselves. (p. 9)

[*Pride and Prejudice* has often] been regarded as the most dramatic of Jane Austen's novels; and certainly dialogue, and various substitutes for dialogue, play a very important part in its narrative technique. *Pride and Prejudice* is full of conversations and of references to conversation: R. A. Brower observes that the dialogue is 'dramatic in the sense of defining characters through the way they speak and are spoken about', and speech plays a major role in character-presentation, both for those who (like the heroine) are brilliant talkers and for those who, though far from brilliant, consistently reveal themselves through an individual mode of speech. In the social world of this novel, where the characters belong to a leisured class, talk is a major occupation, often seeming to fill a place in their lives which for the less privileged would be taken up by earning their bread. Where the members of a society, and especially its female members, are virtually without prescribed duties—there are some scornful references to 'female accomplishments', and 'work' for Jane Austen's women characters usually means decorative needlework—conversation takes on a significance that it can hardly afford to possess in a working community; and the ability to talk—to anyone, about anything, or nothing—becomes highly prized. For not all talk is equally valuable. The Bingley sisters are characteristically endowed with the gift of speech as a social asset: 'They could describe an entertainment with accuracy, relate an anecdote with humour, and laugh at their acquaintance with spirit', and their malicious discussion of Elizabeth includes the damning observation that 'she has no conversation'—which is perhaps not as wide of the mark as it appears, since her notion of 'conversation' is very different from theirs. Again, Elizabeth's favourable first impressions of Wickham owe something to his skill as a conversationalist: his conversation, 'though it was only on its being a wet night and on the probability of a rainy season, made her feel that the commonest, dullest, most thread-bare topic might be rendered interesting by the skill of the speaker'. Lady Catherine talks 'without any intermission', as does her social inferior Mrs Bennet; and even Mr Collins can boast 'a happy readiness of conversation'. In such a society, the appearance of a fresh topic, such as the arrival of a letter or a stranger, tends to assume an importance that may strike us as exaggerated. Its value lies in the nourishment it provides for daily discourse, and this novel may be said to be, to an appreciable extent, not so much about what is done as about what is said. Furthermore, the society described is one in which relationships, particularly those between men and women, can have little opportunity for development save in the setting of the formal or semi-formal social occasion—the ball, the dinner-party or the morning visit. On such occasions talk becomes a major social activity, only temporarily interrupted by dancing or listening to a song or a pianoforte solo: it is through con-versation that relationships come into existence, grow and flourish or decline. At many points in the novel, social groups are described by reference to the speech, or the silence, of the various members. (pp. 25-6)

The novel is 'dramatic', then, in the sense that talk is very important for most of its characters, and most of them talk a great deal. Substantial stretches of the text consist of dialogue (the first two chapters, for example, contain little else). This is normally presented as direct speech: as a later chapter will suggest, there is in this novel relatively little use of the indirect forms. But even when direct speech is not presented, there are very frequent references to conversations taking place. It is dramatic, too, in the further sense that scenes seem often to be conceived and conducted in stage terms: not only the use of dialogue but the collecting of characters in appropriate groups, and the contriving of exits and entrances, suggest a debt to the theatre. The episode of Jane Bennet's engagement to Bingley (Chapter 55) will serve as an illustration. Elizabeth, unaware of what is afoot, enters the drawing-room and discovers the striking tableau of 'her sister and Bingley standing together over the hearth as if engaged in earnest conversation'. Bingley, whispering briefly to Jane, runs from the room, leaving her to impart the joyful news to her sister. We learn in the course of the ensuing dialogue that Bingley has in fact gone to ask Mr Bennet for his daughter's hand; and Jane then sets off to tell her mother—both these subordinate dialogues taking place off-stage, as it were, leaving Elizabeth for a short time alone on the stage to contemplate the satisfactory outcome of events and the gratifying discomfiture of Miss Bingley, until Bingley re-enters and greets her as a sister. The single setting is retained throughout. The elements of difference from stage-presentation are as important as the similarity, however: the novelist is at liberty to present as fully or as briefly as she wishes the various phases of a scene or episode, making possible a flexibility of pace and, in this instance, a speed and economy that would hardly be possible in the theatre, since all that has just been summarized occupies no more than a couple of pages of the novel text. To call *Pride and Prejudice* dramatic, therefore, is only to suggest that it adopts some of the distinctive virtues of the stage-play without renouncing the peculiar advantages of fiction.

The dialogue itself has a wit, polish and vivacity that makes it outstanding in the Jane Austen canon—qualities which the author herself obviously recognized, when she described it as perhaps too 'light, and bright, and sparkling' for some tastes. For the heroine, speech is the chief means of self-assertion, of demonstrating her qualities of mind and character, and of in-sisting upon her right to independent judgments. Like her cre-ator, she is bound by the conventions of the society to which she, and those she loves, belongs, though she does not lack courage to defy those conventions (in walking alone, in bad weather, to visit her sick sister, for instance) when the need arises. But the splendid gesture of a Jeanie Deans or a Lizzie Hexam is not open to her: Jane Austen is not writing the kind of novel that can accommodate heroic action on this scale, nor is she writing about a social class in which it would be thinkable for a young woman to walk from Scotland to London to save her sister's life, or jump into the Thames to rescue her drowning lover. It is through speech, used in the situations of everyday social life, that Elizabeth Bennet must make upon the world the mark of her own unique personality. Accordingly, her lan-guage is markedly more vigorous, and employs a wider range of verbal resources, than that of most of Jane Austen's heroines. She is capable not only of walking through the mud but of venturing on acts of *linguistic* boldness and unconventionality, in words that can elsewhere carry the stigma of ignorance or vulgarity. She can quote a proverb to Darcy's face (telling him to '"Keep your breath to cool your porridge"'), and she is the only one of the heroines capable of the magnificently col-loquial response to the news of the de Bourghs' arrival:

> 'And is this all?' cried Elizabeth. 'I expected at least that the pigs were got into the garden, and here is nothing but Lady Catherine and her daughter!' . . .

The pertness of many of her replies recalls the conversational style of the letters, and there is an affinity too between her speech and the narrative style of the novel, which reveals at many points a sense of language as both a delightful plaything and an instrument of devastating comment. None of the later novels makes such extensive use of comic devices such as zeugma and oxymoron: Mary Bennet is reported to be 'deep in the study of thorough bass and human nature'; for Elizabeth walking with the Gardiners in the grounds of Pemberley, 'time and her aunt moved slowly'; and we read of Mrs Bennet's 'querulous serenity' and of Elizabeth's indulgence in 'all the delight of unpleasant recollections'. The tone of the narrative voice often bears a strong resemblance to that of the heroine.

Linguistically, Elizabeth is undoubtedly her father's child, but the wit and relish of folly in his speech is tinged with a cynicism and even callousness, produced by an unwise marriage, from which hers is free. The incisiveness of his repartee, and the ruthless logic which he applies to his wife's intellectual con-fusion, can be seen in a passage which suggests the extent of Ivy Compton-Burnett's debt to Jane Austen. The subject is the entail which will leave Mrs Bennet and her daughters homeless at her husband's death:

> 'Indeed, Mr Bennet,' said she, 'it is very hard to think that Charlotte Lucas should ever be mistress of this house, that *I* should be forced to make way for *her* and live to see her take my place in it!'
>
> 'My dear, do not give way to such gloomy thoughts. Let us hope for better things. Let us flatter ourselves that *I* may be the survivor.' . . .
>
> 'I cannot bear to think that they should have all this estate. If it was not for the entail I should not mind it.'
>
> 'What should you not mind?'

'I should not mind anything at all.'

'Let us be thankful that you are preserved from
a state of such insensibility.' . . .

Just as Mr Bennet has bestowed his intellectual powers upon
Elizabeth, Mrs Bennet finds her counterpart in the foolish and
'noisy' Lydia, whose garrulity comes close to rivalling her
mother's, and whose irresponsibility, at first mere girlish
thoughtfulness, reveals itself as grave moral confusion when
she elopes with Wickham.

Darcy's speech presents a less straightforward case. He quickly
earns a reputation for taciturnity, even moroseness: he spends
long periods in silence (when he calls on the Bennets he is
liable to sit 'ten minutes together without opening his lips'),
and admits to Elizabeth:

> 'I certainly have not the talent which some people
> possess . . . of conversing easily with those I
> have never seen before. I cannot catch their
> tone of conversation, or appear interested in
> their concerns, as I often see done.' . . .

Since 'ease', the happy knack of being at home in any company, is a quality often singled out for commendation, this
sounds like a shortcoming; and it certainly counts as a failure
by the standards of the society already described. Yet the evidence of the housekeeper at Pemberley, who has known him
from boyhood, contradicts the notion of a haughty indifference
to others: ' "Some people call him proud, but I am sure I never
saw anything of it. To my fancy, it is only because he does
not rattle away like other young men." ' One recalls a notably
fluent speaker, John Thorpe of *Northanger Abbey,* in connection with whom that useful eighteenth-century term 'a rattle'
is invoked: readiness of discourse is a social virtue—but mere
glibness is to be distrusted, as a sympton of superficiality or
worse. For Darcy, there is no place in life for talk that exists
only to kill time. He speaks when he has something to say,
and is prepared to remain silent in defiance of conventional
expectations. This brings him in line with Jane Austen's other
heroes—Mr Knightley, for instance, is given to speaking briefly
and to the point—and his gravity also acts as a foil to Elizabeth's irreverence.

Other characters are similarly individualized by their mode of
speech, at times moving close to eccentricity. With Mr Collins,
for instance, dialogue comes close to caricature. . . . The tendency of many speakers to throw off epigrams also calls for
comment: here again is a feature common to dialogue and
narrative style alike. Not only the sententious Mary Bennet but
Darcy, Elizabeth, Charlotte Lucas and others all employ a
device which recalls the comedy of manners as well as the
copybook and, more seriously, the impressive example of Dr
Johnson. The four examples which follow are from the characters named, in that order:

> 'Pride relates more to our opinion of ourselves,
> vanity to what we would have others think of
> us.'

> 'We all love to instruct, though we can teach
> only what is not worth knowing.'

> 'The power of doing anything with quickness
> is always much prized by the possessor, and
> often without any attention to the imperfection
> of the performance.'

'Happiness in marriage is entirely a matter of
chance.'

Dialogues are important throughout the novel, but there is
another element occurring throughout, and particularly important in the second half, which should be briefly mentioned
here. I refer to the letters which, quoted in whole or in part,
summarized, or simply alluded to, play such a significant role
in the narrative. None of the other novels exhibits such physical
mobility in its characters. Whereas the world of *Emma,* for
instance, is relatively static, here we find journeys a commonplace. Bingley and his sisters and Darcy come and go, as
do Mr Collins and the Gardiners; Elizabeth goes to Kent and
later to Derbyshire; Lydia and Wickham go to Brighton and
then to London, followed there by Mr Bennet; and so forth.
At moments the arrivals and departures come thick and fast.
At the opening of Chapter 53, Lydia and Wickham have no
sooner departed for Newcastle than Bingley returns to Netherfield to provide a fresh infusion of interest. Given the frequent
separations, letter-writing assumes a major role in the development of relationships and the transmission of news, and
material which would otherwise have been conveyed through
dialogue is presented in letter-form. A letter can thus be seen
as a form of 'speech to the absent', and a correspondence as
a prolonged conversation or debate. Since the presence of the
heroine normally determines at any given point the setting of
the action, news of the absent comes largely through the post,
the importance of which is made clear after Lydia's disgrace. . . . At such a time, the postman's knock is the most
dramatic event. Appropriately, the novel draws to a conclusion
with a burst of epistolary energy, in various styles, in the
penultimate chapter. Elizabeth writes to the Gardiners, Darcy
to Lady Catherine, Mr Bennet to Mr Collins, Miss Bingley to
her brother, and to Jane, and Miss Darcy to *her* brother. It
would seem that the happy outcome of the Elizabeth-Darcy
relationship is incomplete until news of it has been transmitted
to all absent but interested parties. And, as a comparison of
the letters quoted readily shows, letters bear the imprint of their
writers' individuality at least as much as dialogue; indeed, as
a later chapter will suggest more fully, such qualities as Mr
Collins's pomposity and Lydia's irresponsibility appear more
blatant in the kind of sustained monologue that a letter represents.

Dialogue, then, and correspondence as a substitute for dialogue, carry much of the narrative load in *Pride and Prejudice.*
At certain points, however, Jane Austen avoids dialogue where
it might reasonably have been anticipated. Some examples are:
Elizabeth's unexpected meeting with Darcy in the grounds of
Pemberley (Chapter 43), Lydia's return home after her marriage (Chapter 51), Elizabeth's acceptance of Darcy (Chapter
58), and her 'important communication' to her mother that she
is to marry him (Chapter 59). In the first example cited, the
chapter begins with a long passage of direct speech in which
Elizabeth finds new light shed on Darcy's character by the
testimony of his housekeeper; after his sudden appearance,
however, the scene is presented so consistently through Elizabeth's consciousness that the objectivity of direct speech would
seem out of place. Instead, we are given only the sketchiest
indications of the ensuing dialogue (Darcy speaks with 'perfect
civility', and makes 'civil inquiries after her family'): in its
place is a kind of inner speech, a presentation of Elizabeth's
unspoken thoughts:

> Her coming there was the most unfortunate, the
> most ill-judged thing in the world! How strange

must it appear to him! In what a disgraceful light might it not strike so vain a man! It might seem as if she had purposely thrown herself in his way again! Oh! why did she come? or why did he thus come a day before he was expected? . . . And his behaviour, so strikingly altered—what could it mean? That he should even speak to her was amazing!—but to speak with such civility, to enquire after her family! . . .

The absence of quotation marks involves no ambiguity about the status of this passage: its exclamatory manner, quite unlike that of the narrative style, suggests the heroine's violent emotions, and its questions show the self-searching that she must carry out in the process of adjusting to the changed situation.

The second example referred to also calls for further comment. At the beginning of Chapter 51, the scene is set in the Bennet's breakfast-room for Lydia's return with her husband. What follows is certainly conceived in dramatic terms to the extent that the disposition of those present, and the arrival of the newcomers, are carefully indicated. The narrative is reminiscent at one point of stage-directions:

> Lydia's voice was heard in the vestibule; the door was thrown open, and she ran into the room. Her mother stepped forwards, embraced her . . . gave her hand with an affectionate smile to Wickham, who followed his lady . . .

But for a time at least there is no dialogue. Lydia's insensitively effusive arrival, her mother's rapturous welcome, the cooler reception she receives from her father, the 'easy address' of Wickham, are all narrated; it is evident that 'there was no want of discourse', but (with the exception of two speeches by Lydia) the author chooses not to present this painful scene through dialogue. . . . Such instances, however, only constitute exceptions, though significant and interesting exceptions, to the prevailing dramatic method of the novel: a method which Jane Austen uses to some degree, and with various modifications, throughout her work, but nowhere more brilliantly and memorably. (pp. 27-34)

Norman Page, in his The Language of Jane Austen, *Basil Blackwell, 1972, 208 p.*

MARILYN BUTLER   (essay date 1975)

[*Butler argues that in the context of the literary, social, and political climate of Austen's era, her works "belong decisively to one class of partisan novels, the conservative." Discussing* Pride and Prejudice *from this point of view, the critic asserts that despite the tendency of many readers and critics to see the novel as "progressive," it is in fact ideologically orthodox.*]

Jane Austen is by common consent an author remarkably sure of her values. She skewers a moral solecism as confidently as a verbal infelicity. At the end of her novels the standing of the heroine's soul in the light of the next world seems as decisively settled as her future financial security in this. The familiar Austen moral abstractions avoid seeming abstract, so closely are they bound up with an orderly pattern of behaviour, a set of assumptions imposed by the material circumstances of leisured middle-class life. (p. 1)

It is by virtue of her certainties that Jane Austen is called Augustan. Certainly satirical writers before her time had criticized manners or behaviour they deplored by confident reference to an understood standard, such as that of Christian doctrine, or of certain classical literary forms. But these are criticisms of the actual by reference to an ideal; whereas Jane Austen finds her ideal within a world she deliberately makes resemble the actual. By implication she is far less critical of contemporary society in its essence than Ben Jonson, Dryden, Swift, Pope, or Fielding had been. For at least four of her heroines, moral progress consists in discerning, and submitting to, the claims of the society around them. This is certainly not the moral position of the authors of *Volpone, Gulliver's Travels,* or *The Dunciad.* In fact it is not a typical neo-classical position at all.

If Jane Austen's moral goals seem nearer at hand, more realizable, than Pope's, how are they to be defined? The essence of her certainty is that the reforms she perceives to be necessary are within the attitudes of individuals; she calls for no general changes in the world of the established lesser landed gentry. Most modern commentators on Jane Austen assume that her reasons for adopting her matter and manner are aesthetic rather than moral: she writes about '3 or 4 families in a Country Village' because she knows she can do it well, not because she wishes to validate a way of life. Yet it is always dangerous to make unhistorical assumptions, and in the period itself it would have been customary to think in very different terms about what such preferences showed. Critics of the novel, from Samuel Johnson to Clara Reeve and Henry Mackenzie, all ponder thoughtfully the moral impression the novelist makes upon the reader, and (in print at least) give cursory attention to the means he employs to do it. Jane Austen's twentieth-century reader will probably exclaim that this is precisely where she differs from the rest. If so, he must explain why her naturalism operates only within carefully defined limits. Her style, confident and generalizing, and her openly apparent arrangement of character and plot, all suggest an ideal order, which at the same time they present in terms of an actual order. It is not demanded of a Charles Musgrove that he should aspire to be a good man in any very lofty or spiritual sense. '. . . A more equal match . . . might have given more consequence to his character, and more usefulness, rationality and elegance to his habits and pursuits.' It would have been enough if he had realized his capacity to be a gentleman.

This is not to suggest that Jane Austen is merely a snob, as a crass vein of criticism of her novels has held. Her distinctions between true gentlemanliness and the shell of it are keen, perhaps because—like Elizabeth Bennet—she has experienced social rebuffs at first hand. She is certainly no sycophant of wealth or rank, and she does not deal intimately with—or apparently much like—the great aristocracy. The class she deals with has local and not national importance: in eighteenth-century terms, she is a Tory rather than a Whig. She believes that the gentleman—as her words 'consequence' and 'usefulness' imply—derives his personal dignity from the contribution he makes at the head of an organic, hierarchical, small community. It is for such a community, ideally perceived, that her novels speak.

The novel of Jane Austen's day was not just didactic. It was also seen as relevant to contemporary issues, and, since these issues were unusually deep and clearcut, inevitably partisan. Indeed, at the period when Jane Austen began to write, literature as a whole was partisan, in England as well as on the Continent: so were the other arts, as Kenneth Clark observes in drawing a general parallel with painting. 'Doctrine was found in works which seem to us very harmless. We may think that *The Marriage of Figaro* was written solely to give us pleasure, but in 1785 it was considered a political bombshell, for from 1780 to 1790 every play and every ballet was interpreted in a political sense.' To qualify this a little, at the very least a representation of man in a setting which resembled the natural world would be seen as making certain statements about man's nature and about his social role, all of which were capable of translation into the political sphere. There may well have been artists who thought relatively little about politics. But some artistic forms implicitly seemed to convey certain general principles or prepossessions about man, and if, in this sensitive period, an artist did not care much what they were, his critics and readers were liable to care for him. As it happens, Jane Austen's novels belong decisively to one class of partisan novels, the conservative. Intellectually she is orthodox: more orthodox than a contemporary with whom she has otherwise much in common, Maria Edgeworth. Her important innovations are technical and stylistic modifications within a clearly defined and accepted genre. (pp. 1-3)

Of all the Austen novels, *Pride and Prejudice* seems at first glance the least likely to yield a conservative theme. . . .

[Generations] of Jane Austen readers have agreed in finding *Pride and Prejudice* the lightest, most consistently entertaining, and least didactic of the novels.

It would not be in keeping with the serious-mindedness of modern scholarship to rest content with the popular view of *Pride and Prejudice* as having no meaning at all. But the commonest interpretations, however they differ from each other, agree in placing it well outside the sphere of the anti-jacobin novel. Many modern critics have suggested that it appears deliberately to run counter to the conservative tendency which can hardly be gainsaid in *Sense and Sensibility* and *Mansfield Park*. In appearing before her readers in the guise of Elizabeth Bennet, Jane Austen—or so the argument runs—reveals herself the critic of various forms of orthodoxy. (p. 197)

[But the more one examines *Pride and Prejudice*] the more difficult it becomes to read into it authorial approval of the element in Elizabeth which is rebellious. It is true that, like all Jane Austen's fiction, *Pride and Prejudice* has an element of antithetical patterning. It is not true that the pattern is adequately summarized in the terms 'nature' versus 'art' [see excerpt by Samuel Kliger dated 1947]. . . . As it happens, all novels built on the consciously antithetical pattern, from Sterne's comparison in *Tristram Shandy* of the feeling with the intellectualizing, to Maria Edgeworth's many comparisons of the rational with the unthinking, are about the human question, not the aesthetic question, and are—as one would expect—perfectly clear about which side they favour. (p. 203)

[The antitheses in *Pride and Prejudice* are] complex and bewildering, since in many respects they cut across one another. To be sure Elizabeth, independent and informal, can be contrasted with Darcy, who is socially established and formal; Elizabeth's 'low' mother, sisters and aunt offer themselves for comparison with Darcy's haughty aunt and cousin. But, equally, Elizabeth and Darcy together, each of them complex and censorious, are balanced against the simpler Jane and Bingley, and this may prove in the long run to be the more significant comparison. The obvious social contrasts between the two extended families and their connections have encouraged, latterly, some unduly sociological interpretations, in which the characters come to stand for certain classes and class attitudes. Elizabeth and Darcy, for example, believe respectively in 'a

personalist ethic' and 'a prudent and social point of departure', and the parties behind them follow suit: 'the novel is structurally balanced between the basic orientation of the two principals.' Yet of all the points made by the complex action, the most decisive are surely those which affect Darcy and Elizabeth in their private capacity, as individuals. And if this is true, the notion of a structure which opposes the two is at best a half-truth, at worst misleading.

When Darcy and Elizabeth are first introduced, we are aware of great differences of personality between them: enough, one might think, to justify the idea that they are indeed presented as polar opposites. At the first assembly Darcy is 'discovered to be proud, to be above his company, and above being pleased; and not all his large estate in Derbyshire could have save him from having a most forbidding, disagreeable countenance'. His hauteur seems as different as possible from Elizabeth's informality. 'She had a lively, playful disposition, which delighted in anything ridiculous.' Elizabeth certainly continues in the notion that she and Darcy are so different as to be totally incompatible. (pp. 203-04)

Darcy's view of Elizabeth is also coloured by his sense of a gulf between them; although for him it is not a difference of personality but of social status, an objective fact related to the dignity of his own family, and to the vulgarity of some of Elizabeth's connections.

Apparently many readers are persuaded by the opinions of the two protagonists that they should see in the love-story of *Pride and Prejudice* a meeting of opposites. Yet from the beginning the evidence supplied by independent witnesses and, surely, by the author herself shows that the two protagonists are mistaken. Whenever Elizabeth discusses Darcy's faults, she touches, though often unconsciously, upon her own. She notices at once, for example, that he is, like her, a critic of others. 'He has a very satirical eye, and if I do not begin by being impertinent myself, I shall soon grow afraid of him.' In discussing his faults with Darcy, she gets him to admit to what he calls resentfulness, which is an unwillingness to change his mind once he has decided to censure someone. 'My good opinion once lost is lost for ever.' Elizabeth calls this 'a failing indeed'; but Darcy's disapproval of Wickham is not more obstinate (and of course it turns out to be more reasonably founded) than Elizabeth's own wilful dislike of Darcy. Although for different reasons, both are equally likely to be severe on others:

> 'There is, I believe, in every disposition a tendency to some particular evil, a natural defect, which not even the best education can overcome.'
>
> 'And *your* defect is a propensity to hate everybody.'
>
> 'And yours', he replied with a smile, 'is wilfully to misunderstand them.'

Darcy's theory of human nature implies a curiously blended attitude towards his own: in theory he admits he is fallible, but the real impression left is one of pride. For Elizabeth, too, the quality that goes with severity about others is complacency towards the self. (p. 205)

The subject of *Pride and Prejudice* is what the title indicates: the sin of pride, obnoxious to the Christian, which takes the form of a complacency about the self and a correspondingly lower opinion, or prejudice, about others. Darcy's pride is humbled mid-way through the novel, when he proposes to

Elizabeth and to his astonishment is rejected. The lesson he has to learn is not quite that it is hard for a rich man to enter the kingdom of heaven; it is more that we have no innate worth, either of social status or abilities. We have to earn our right to consideration by respect for others, and continuous watchfulness of ourselves.

Elizabeth's corresponding sin is more subtle and her enlightenment requires the space of the whole book. To begin with she seems unconscious that she suffers from pride at all. Quick of observation, encouraged by her father's example to take delight in the follies and vanities of others, she sees everyone's mistakes but her own. The false proffers of friendship from Miss Bingley and Mrs. Hurst do not deceive her: she already has too low an opinion of them. She is quick to see and enjoy the foibles of Mr. Collins, as she has always taken pleasure from those of Sir William Lucas. But she also quite unreasonably persists in thinking ill of Darcy, and, just as perversely, in thinking well of Wickham, even when the evidence that he is a fortune-hunter is placed before her. Elizabeth's pride in her own fallible perceptions is her governing characteristic.

There has been a curious tendency to take 'Pride' and 'Prejudice' to be polar qualities, like 'Sense' and 'Sensibility', whereas in the course of the novel we generally see them associated within the same character. The proud Lady Catherine is certainly prejudiced, and the prejudiced Elizabeth can validly be accused of pride. Caroline Bingley after all declares that her manners are 'a mixture of pride and impertinence', and though we need not take the jealous Miss Bingley too literally as to Elizabeth's manners, on Elizabeth's moral character she probably speaks more truth than she knows. (pp. 206-07)

Elizabeth, who is so quick about the mistakes of others, has no inkling of her own fallibility until Darcy's proposal and the explanatory letter which follows it. The confrontation between these two central characters naturally brings about mutual illumination, not because one has opposite qualities which the other must learn to adopt, but because each discovers the other to be worthy of respect: the very admission of the value of an opponent forces both Elizabeth and Darcy to be more humble about themselves. Elizabeth's first concession is relatively trivial: she sees initially that she has been mistaken about Wickham. But it is more than this. As she examines her own mental processes, she notices that she has never been objective about him. She never tried to check his account of himself against information about his early life, if she could have acquired any; or even against what would have been available, 'some instance of goodness, some distinguished trait of integrity or benevolence'. On the contrary, the subjective impression had been enough for her. 'His countenance, voice and manner, had established him at once in the possession of every virtue.' She now perceives that there *was* objective evidence; that Wickham, a stranger, ought not to have spoken so freely; that, contrary to his boast, he had not stood his ground, but had avoided Darcy; yet at the time she persistently ignored every pointer. Conversely she begins to see that apart from her own antipathy she has no case against Darcy. (pp. 207-08)

In his excellent essay on *Pride and Prejudice*, Mr. Howard S. Babb shows how in conversation with Darcy Elizabeth has indeed preferred wit to justice, and has steadily shown herself more fallible than he is [see Additional Bibliography]. Elizabeth prides herself on her individualism and trusts her perceptions, never recognizing that her judgements are really grounded in her feelings. While Darcy is equally assured, his generalizations tend to be those of society at large, and he is far more careful than Elizabeth to base his arguments upon reason. (p. 209)

Elizabeth's conversations with Jane, in which she is gently urged to take a more candid view, counterpoint her conversations with Darcy, in which we see her ill-founded prejudices in action.

Now this clearly *is* the kind of antithesis in which a balance is meant to be struck. Many critics have echoed Elizabeth's remark, 'intricate characters are the *most* amusing'. We would not exchange Elizabeth's intelligence for Jane's innocence, nor Darcy's consistency for Bingley's pliancy, even though the faults of the central couple lead them into worse moral error. But in fact the author does not want us to—it is clear that her view of the truly Christian character blends the best qualities of all four. Elizabeth and Darcy take a properly pessimistic view of human liability to err, and, rightly applied, their perceptiveness will be a great moral quality: for Jane Austen insists that the scrupulous self-knowledge which she prizes is the product of their kind of sceptical intelligence. The example of the other couple helps them to harness their talents to more Christian ends, by showing charity towards others and humility towards themselves. To this extent Mr. Kliger's generalization applies: in the comparison between the two central couples, faults are identified with excesses in either extreme, and excellence lies in the mean. But the different beliefs that divide Elizabeth and Jane are not fundamental, for they concern the proper application of principles which they both share. Elizabeth's satire versus Jane's candour is a very different polarization from nature versus art, and it can never suggest to us that over the novel as a whole Jane Austen compromises between two views of human nature. Her moral ideal is clear: it is most nearly approached by Darcy and Elizabeth at the point when they have acknowledged the necessity of Jane and Bingley's humility and candour. In their ultimate state of enlightenment, Jane Austen's hero and heroine illustrate a view of human nature that derives from orthodox Christian pessimism, not from progressive optimism. The theme of the moral education of Elizabeth, which is paralleled by that of Darcy, does not sanction but rebukes the contemporary doctrine of faith in the individual.

If in nothing else, a clue to the conservatism of the novel lies in the original title, *First Impressions*. Mr. B. C. Southam has suggested that *Pride and Prejudice* may have begun as a burlesque on that popular theme. Jane Austen had already employed it satirically more than once, for both *Love and Friendship* and *Sense and Sensibility* mock the convention of love at first sight; and, in doing so, express conservative scepticism about the 'truth' of man's spontaneous feelings. It is possible that Jane Austen meant to ridicule the hackneyed theme by standing it on its head: what *she* offers is hate at first sight. In any case, as she develops her plot in the final version, it is clear that to her love at first sight and hate at first sight are essentially the same. Both are emotional responses, built on insufficient or wrong evidence, and fostered by pride and complacency towards the unreliable subjective consciousness. It may well have been that with such a title the early version was more dogmatic: it belongs, after all, to 1796-7, years of great partisan activity in the novel, and approximately the era of the early work on *Sense and Sensibility*. Yet, for all its polish and technical maturity, the finished *Pride and Prejudice* has not, evidently, modified its ideological stance. As a novel it is far better than *Sense and Sensibility*, but no less conservative. (pp. 211-13)

Marilyn Butler, in her Jane Austen and the War of Ideas, *1975. Reprint by Oxford at the Clarendon Press, Oxford, 1976, 310 p.*

MARTHA SATZ   (essay date 1983)

[*Satz proposes an epistemological framework for interpreting* Pride and Prejudice, *one that focuses on the novel's approach to questions of knowledge, perception, belief, and evidence. In the following excerpt, Satz explores Austen's view of knowledge.*]

In addition to the large number of dualities offered as interpretative frameworks of *Pride and Prejudice*, yet another disjunction leaps out from almost every page to a reader alert to the problems of knowledge. The terms of this disjunction may be variously expressed as belief and knowledge, data and fact, perception and interpretation, or subjectivity and objectivity. The novel repeatedly reveals the salient gap between evidence and conclusion and the labyrinth of false paths and difficulties that lie between the two.

At times, explicit epistemological discussions occur with grandeur, as when they are the stuff of reconciliation between Elizabeth and Darcy, but more often as trivia in concerns about confirmation in the most prosaic exchanges. And the narrator's voice has an epistemological purview as she persistently refers to the ubiquity of differing and variable interpretation in describing everything from Georgiana to the flow of public opinion. In short, comments and discussions about knowledge and understanding, and the erratic and variable interpretations on which they rest, not only supply the central subject of the book but also constitute the warp and woof of its fabric.

The novel persistently points to the overwhelming problems of acquiring knowledge, the frustrating fallibility and insufficiency of evidence, the relativism of alternate interpretations, and the inevitable gap between what is believed and what is. The presuppositions inherent in *Pride and Prejudice* concerning the process of forming beliefs and gaining knowledge are susceptible to a general characterization.

The first implicit thesis is that beliefs are always based on other beliefs or bits of evidence, and nothing is ever known *simpliciter*. Conclusions and alleged facts are always presented together with the evidence on which they are based. Such a practice often, perhaps inevitably, serves to underline the fragility of the edifice of knowledge as the paucity of evidence upon which most people base their beliefs becomes apparent. When Mr. Darcy initially encounters the neighbors of Netherfield, the flimsy evidence on which he is first pronounced thoroughly admirable and then condemned is rather pointedly indicated. Echoes of this insight, the insignificant foundation on which public opinion changes, repeatedly sound in the text in isolated humorous sentences. Yet, in addition to being a source of levity, the structure of knowledge is a recognized and acknowledged concern of the main characters, reflected in their dialogue as this speech by Jane to her sister demonstrates:

> ". . . I confess myself to have been entirely deceived in Miss Bingley's regard of me. But, my dear sister, though the event has proved you right, do not think me obstinate if I still assert, that, considering what her behavior was, my confidence was as natural as your suspicion. I do not comprehend her reason for wishing to be intimate with me, but if the same circum-

stances were to happen again, I am sure I should be deceived again. . . ."

Jane claims that although she proved mistaken, she made the correct decision and held the correct belief on the basis of the evidence available to her. She is thereby explicitly making the rather sophisticated epistemological point that her belief was warranted if not true, appropriate to the evidence if not metaphysically certified.

The introduction of Mr. and Mrs. Bennet appears as the ultimate illustration of the persistent implicit emphasis on the connection between evidence and judgment. At the end of Chapter I, the narrator gives an authoritative account of the personalities of Mr. and Mrs. Bennet. However, first, she has presented ample evidence on which such a judgment may be based. Since the work is literature, the evidence, appropriately enough, is not only substantive but stylistic as well. Certainly Mrs. Bennet and Mr. Bennet differ in terms of what they say, Mrs. Bennet discoursing at great length about trivial details, Mr. Bennet requesting concrete facts. However, their manner of presentation diverges as well. Initially, her long-winded conversations are reported verbatim, but his distance and coolness are indicated by means of the use of indirect discourse. Thus, the summary the narrator presents of the Bennets' character has first been richly inductively supported. The reader, whose position in regard to knowledge has interesting similarities and dissimilarities with the characters in the book, in this instance understands the Bennets both through detailed demonstrations and authorial general statements.

The second tenet of this novel supposes that evidence-gathering and judgment-making are dependent upon the subject or perceiver. Susan Morgan, in her highly innovative book, *In the Meantime: Character and Perception in Jane Austen's Fiction* [see Additional Bibliography], expresses this insight: "In Austen's epistemology the observer is part of the process." A multiplicity of instances, minor and major, establish that almost any evidence can be given two contradictory interpretations. After her bold walk alone over the countryside to inquire about the health of her sister, when Elizabeth makes her famous disheveled entrance, her reputation threatened by the shame of a muddy petticoat, the Bingley sisters and Mr. Bingley have radically different interpretations. Likewise, the letter written by Miss Bingley to Jane about Mr. Bingley's romantic interests is given divergent explanations by Elizabeth and Jane. The duality expressed here, the possibility of alternative conflicting explanations for the same sentences of a letter, presages Elizabeth's later painful ruminations about the proper interpretation of Darcy's crucial missive.

By what process, then, is one judgment or interpretation chosen? The answer lies in the strongly emphasized fact that interpretative schemes differ among individuals. For example, Jane's consistently beneficent mode of construing the world is particularly well delineated. In contrast, Elizabeth, although she prides herself on her realistic perception, often views the world with an amusedly cynical eye. She tells Darcy: "Follies and nonsense, whims and inconsistencies *do* divert me, I own, and I laugh at them whenever I can." And although she protests, "I hope I never ridicule what is wise and good" . . . , the weight of the text belies this hope.

Chapter IV of the first volume is really an illustrative study of different interpretative views at work. The reader learns how four different observers, Jane, Elizabeth, Bingley, and Darcy, perceive the ball. Jane's and Bingley's ways of perceiving events are similar. Bingley, like Jane, has a mode of seeing the world suffused with his tractability and mildness of temper. Hence, for these observers, everything at the ball is pleasing and agreeable. Elizabeth and Darcy, although slightly less similar to each other than Jane and Bingley, still have analogous ways of viewing matters. Although they claim commitment to a reasonable and clear-eyed attitude, they have a naturally satirical eye. They reject charitable impulses to spotlight foibles and defects. Thus, at the ball, they see some disturbing elements.

Although Austen expansively exhibits these four characters' interpretative systems in the elegantly crafted Chapter IV, in Chapter III the ball serves to reveal the conceptual penchants of other characters as well. Mary's view of the world is recognized as egotistical, and Catherine's and Lydia's as undiscriminating, in a half-sentence apiece. Mr. Bennet's removal and aloofness from the world reveals itself in the fact that he alone among the main characters does not attend the ball but must be given an account of it. His lack of interest and satirical disposition are revealed: "He had rather hoped that all his wife's views on the stranger would be disappointed; . . ." . . . Mrs. Bennet's unabashedly concrete and indiscriminate turn of mind is likewise captured by her faithful chronological recounting of Mr. Bingley's dance partners. Such a pattern often repeats itself. An event, major or minor, is an occasion which in its interpretation exhibits the modes of perception of the characters. Thus, the ball, an early major event of the novel, is typical of its other events; namely, the space devoted to its description is dwarfed by accounts of how its various elements are interpreted by different observers.

If the novel presupposes that every person has a conceptual framework through which he perceives reality, then it is legitimate to ask what framework the author encourages the reader to adopt. If follies and inconsistencies do divert Elizabeth, they seem to divert the author even more so. Hence, the reader is led to view the scenes that transpire with an amused, distant eye. The following description is typical of an often-assumed narrative stance:

> . . . A great deal more passed at the other table. Lady Catherine was generally speaking—stating the mistakes of the three others, or relating some anecdote of herself. Mr. Collins was employed in agreeing to everything her Ladyship said, thanking her for every fish he won, and apologizing if he thought he won too many. Sir William did not say much. He was storing his memory with anecdotes and noble names. . . .

This ironic stance is all-encompassing. It is clear that the narrator, like Elizabeth, perhaps with more justification, takes pride in her intelligence and encourages the reader to do likewise. Both narrator and reader attend to the events of the novel, alert to the self-deception and foibles of its characters. (pp. 171-75)

If the principles thus far presented are truly the epistemological foundation of the novel, then inherent in *Pride and Prejudice,* in nascent form, is a philosophical view come to vogue in the last half of the twentieth century. Structuralism, the panoramic view, which has applications in science, anthropology, art, history, literary theory, and, it seems, all other areas of knowledge, states roughly that a person's mode, his system of perceiving and conceiving reality is creative. Understanding the world necessarily involves a system, and every system at least

partially creates its object. No statement ever directly tests itself against reality, for a single statement is always embedded in a theory.

Willard Van Orman Quine has captured this phenomenon of human thought in a metaphor for science, which he interprets very broadly to include, for example, the hypothesis that there are physical objects:

> . . . total science is like a field of force whose boundary conditions are experience. A conflict with experience at the periphery occasions readjustments in the interior of the field. . . . But the total field is so underdetermined by its boundary conditions, experience, that there is much latitude of choice as to what statements to reevaluate in the light of any contrary experience.

The analogues of a much lower stratum are available in *Pride and Prejudice.* When Collins asks Elizabeth to marry him, since he rejects the truth of her answer, he alters his understanding of human exchange so that he no longer takes Elizabeth's "no" to be evidence that she does not want to marry him. Collins is a comic figure, but Jane often appears engaged in the same process. If the Bingley sisters act rudely to her, then she changes her view of human behavior to interpret these actions as efforts not to hurt her feelings.

This metaphysical view, which heeds Wittgenstein's dictum, "to treat of the net and not of what the net describes," has a striking overlap with the outlined presuppositions of *Pride and Prejudice.* Although the novel demonstrably deals with the processes of acquiring knowledge, more importantly, it exhibits the different interpretative models, the divergent theoretical structures, by which characters understand the world. In fact, characters are individuated by their mode of viewing reality. Moreover, no one of the characters' systems is clearly superior to all the others. Thus, . . . neither Elizabeth's nor Jane's schema is superior at acquiring truth.

Does, then, *Pride and Prejudice* emphasize the creative, arbitrary, and essentially fictional nature of perception? Its unremitting concentration, alternately solemn and humorous, on the exquisite complexities and internal laws of human beliefs, pursued both in abstract disquisition and gossipy detail, favors this position. Its insistence on the shaping nature of beliefs bolsters the view.

However, there is another strain in *Pride and Prejudice,* long recognized by critics: the assurance of certainty in Jane Austen's world, the identification of knowledge with the good; as Alistair M. Duckworth proclaims, the belief that ". . . that which is good and true in life resists the perversions of the individual viewpoint. . . ." Critics have labeled this current as Platonic; the elements to which they refer can be summarized in four cardinal propositions. (1) Moral virtue is equivalent to knowledge. The second principle is really a particularization of the first. (2) Those who are wisest are best; those who are not virtuous fail because they lack knowledge. Further principles concern the nature of reason and its relation to other faculties. (3) Ideally, reason should control feelings. The last principle concerns the processes involved in knowledge. (4) Only when beliefs are subjugated to the painstaking test of reason do they result in knowledge.

In addition to intellectual assumptions, there are Platonic motifs that run through the novel as well, particularly in the relationship between the two couples, Elizabeth and Darcy and Jane and Bingley. They are portrayed as existing on different planes of intelligence. The text forcefully establishes Darcy's and Elizabeth's intelligence. However, their intelligence has not been tested; like the alleged wise man of Socrates' time, they have not questioned their fundamental assumptions.

The emphasis and testimony of the novel indicate that Elizabeth's happiness is superior to that of her less self-conscious sister, Jane. This novel, like Platonic philosophy, particularly in the *Republic,* makes the happiness of those who are less self-conscious dependent on those who are more so. Those who think and understand should be responsible for those who do not and cannot. As Marvin Mudrick characterizes the relationship, Bingley and Jane have their adult guardians [see excerpt dated 1952]. The happy reunion of Jane and Bingley is a consequence of Darcy's and Elizabeth's change in understanding.

The Platonism in the novel assures the reader that there exists an objective order, truth knowable by a person who exercises her most acute faculties. Furthermore, truth attained by this rational means guarantees happiness. And indeed within the circumscribed world of the novel, happiness, in its highest sense, tinged with metaphysical grandeur, is equated with the good, the proper marriage.

Yet, as we have seen, beside the granite of the Platonism underlying the novel are the malleable surfaces of a structuralism shaping truth to viewpoint and collapsing if asked to support objective truth. By focusing on the plastic processes of human knowledge and the shifting, arbitrary shapes of human belief, the novel implicitly undermines the power of the human faculties to attain absolute knowledge of the world. A basic cleavage appears in *Pride and Prejudice* between pride in the power of the human mind to acquire objective truth and humility at the recognition of the fallibility, inevitable distortion, and prejudice of mental processes.

But fiction is fundamentally different from life. Ordinarily, if one were to accept the quasi-structuralist view demonstrably embedded in *Pride and Prejudice,* that all judgments about reality are dependent upon the conceptual structure of the perceiver, then one would have to accept the view that humans are unconditionally barred from an unbiased view of reality. Thus, in the actual human situation, the two views, (1) that beliefs about reality are necessarily filtered through somewhat arbitrary conceptual structures and (2) that objective truth is attainable, are completely irreconcilable. However, in fiction the two perspectives, the ontological and the epistemological, can be combined to provide metaphysical illumination. The author by virtue of her omnipotence and omniscience vis à vis her creation has two perspectives, objective truth and human interpretation, and thus can mend the rent between two such apparently discrepant viewpoints. But even so skilled an artisan as Austen leaves evidence of her stitches.

Indeed, the last third of the book has always been a favorite target of the critics. The usual reason cited for the abruptly appearing deficit and incongruity in the novel is Jane Austen's inability to incorporate sexual behavior into her ironic, literary world view. However, whether or not this rather superficial observation has merit, deeper consideration must be invoked as well to account for the substantial shift within the text. The last third of the novel evidences nothing less than Austen's rather ambitious intellectual project of healing the split between the subjective and the objective. The author in this section is

no longer content to share amusement with the reader over the eccentricities of the human personalities and the vagaries of the pursuit of knowledge, but instead insists on forcefully guaranteeing the seriousness and reality of the characters' moral concerns. By closing the ironic distance between narrator and character, Austen does what she had steadfastly refused to do before—metaphysically underwrites the validity of particular perceptions.

Quite clearly, in the last part of the novel, a moral lesson is in evidence. In this section of the novel, for the most part, there is no space between, on the one hand, what the characters perceive, interpret, and ponder, and, on the other, what is; facts are presented baldly and indubitably.

It is not sufficient to explain this shift in narrative stance by repeating the obvious truth that Lydia's and Wickham's action, an illicit relationship outside of marriage, is absolutely impermissible and immoral for Austen. The more compelling level on which to consider the problem is why Austen introduces what, in the context of this novel, equating the good and proper marriage with happiness and fulfillment, is a clear paradigm of immorality. It apparently functions, as paradigms best can, to distinguish unmistakably good conduct from bad conduct and true beliefs from false ones. By conclusively displaying the rectitude and worthiness of Darcy's character, Austen certifies the validity of Elizabeth's processes of gathering evidence and of ultimately arriving at conclusions. By offering this extreme example of behavior, Austen puts the finishing touches on her gallery of portraits, illustrative of the alternatives in pursuit of marriage. Thus, the last part of the novel constitutes not only Austen's answer to the problem of knowledge but a justification for that answer. She declares that incorrigible knowledge is possible but also upholds a particular methodology of acquiring that knowledge. (pp. 177-79)

The narrator and the reader must be chastened from their natural temperamental epistemological biases also. Indeed, as if Austen were taking heed of her own inherent epistemological lesson, the ironic attitude which presumes certainty lapses as the evils of the assumption of certainty become more apparent. The intelligent reader, missing in the last part of the novel Austen's detached, acerbic humor, must give up her own comfortably aloof position as well and thus, like Elizabeth and the narrator, become swept up in the seriousness of human concerns. However, there is another irony, an irony parallel to that associated with Socrates, whom the oracle identified as the wisest of men just because, as he came to discover, he knew that he knew nothing. There is a reward for the epistemologically modest. To her now humbled readers, Austen offers, after exposing them to all the perils that prevent knowledge, the hope that if one is modest enough, alert enough to one's own predispositions of mind, and open enough to new information, one can, in spite of everything, attain knowledge and gain the happiness that follows. Even the least among us, by correction of foibles, may know more and thereby gain more. This lesson is evidenced by the fate of Kitty, who throughout the book is portrayed as the intellectual and moral twin of Lydia.

The final irony concerns the author Jane Austen. Although the narrator of *Pride and Prejudice* retreats from her ironic, subtly audacious perspective, the author herself, by foisting on her reader, in spite of all the evidence to the contrary, a metaphysically and morally certified view of knowledge, projects a supreme arrogance about what is true, thereby ultimately contradicting the fabric of the entire novel. Thus, the schism

Austen has bridged within the text ultimately reemerges between reader and text. (pp. 182-83)

Martha Satz, "An Epistemological Understanding of 'Pride and Prejudice': Humility and Objectivity," in Women & Literature, n.s. Vol. 3, 1983, pp. 171-86.

ADDITIONAL BIBLIOGRAPHY

Anderson, Walter E. "Plot, Character, Speech, and Place in *Pride and Prejudice*." *Nineteenth-Century Fiction* 30, No. 3 (December 1975): 367-82.

    Argues that critics have largely overlooked the crucial role that Austen's handling of the plot plays in creating the novel's dramatic interest.

Auerbach, Nina. *"Pride and Prejudice."* In her *Communities of Women: An Idea in Fiction*, pp. 38-55. Cambridge: Harvard University Press, 1978.

    Explores the plight of women in the novel, focusing on their powerlessness and dependence on men in a society that grants them little authority of their own.

Austen, Jane. *Pride and Prejudice*. Edited by Donald J. Gray. New York: W. W. Norton & Co., 1966.

    An authoritative text of the novel, including background materials, letters, and excerpts from contemporary reviews and modern criticism.

Babb, Howard S. "Dialogue with Feeling: A Note on *Pride and Prejudice*." *Kenyon Review* XX, No. 2 (Spring 1958): 203-16.

    A close analysis of the conversations between Elizabeth and Darcy, demonstrating "what deep, what intensive motivations Jane Austen has implanted" in the two characters.

Brophy, Brigid. "A Remorseless Realist." In *Jane Austen, "Sense and Sensibility," "Pride and Prejudice," and "Mansfield Park": A Casebook,* edited by B. C. Southam, pp. 186-97. London: Macmillan, 1976.

    Argues that in *Pride and Prejudice* Austen displayed insight into the sexual and economic realities faced by her characters that anticipates the ideas of Karl Marx and Sigmund Freud.

Brown, Julia Prewitt. "Necessary Conjunctions: *Pride and Prejudice*." In her *Jane Austen's Novels: Social Change and Literary Form*, pp. 65-79. Cambridge: Harvard University Press, 1979.

    Posits that the novel derives its form in part from the contrast between a series of paired characters, themes, and narrative devices.

Burlin, Katrin R. "'Pictures of Perfection' at Pemberley: Art in *Pride and Prejudice*." In *Jane Austen: New Perspectives*, edited by Janet Todd, pp. 155-70. Women and Literature, n.s., vol. 3. New York: Holmes & Meier Publishers, 1983.

    Demonstrates how the grounds and portraits at Pemberley contribute to Elizabeth and Darcy's understanding of one another.

Craik, W. A. *"Pride and Prejudice."* In her *Jane Austen: The Six Novels*, pp. 62-90. London: Methuen & Co., 1965.

    A general discussion of the novel, including its characters, plot, themes, and place in Austen's oeuvre.

De Rose, Peter L., and McGuire, S. W. *A Concordance to the Works of Jane Austen.* 3 vols. New York: Garland Publishing, 1982.

    A concordance keyed to the R. W. Chapman edition of Austen's works.

Ek, Grete. "Mistaken Conduct and Proper 'Feeling': A Study of Jane Austen's *Pride and Prejudice*." In *Fair Forms: Essays in English Literature from Spenser to Jane Austen*, edited by Maren-Sofie Røstvig, pp. 178-202. Totowa, N.J.: Rowman and Littlefield, 1975.

Contends that the conflict between Elizabeth and Darcy is primarily "a process of clarification rather than one of substantial change."

Fergus, Jan. "*Pride and Prejudice* and Its Predecessors" and "*Pride and Prejudice*." In her *Jane Austen and the Didactic Novel: "Northanger Abbey," "Sense and Sensibility," and "Pride and Prejudice,"* pp. 61-86, pp. 87-120. Totowa, N.J.: Barnes & Noble Books, 1983.

    Explores the influence of such novelists as Fanny Burney and Samuel Richardson on *Pride and Prejudice*. Fergus focuses on the relationship between the novel and eighteenth-century didactic fiction.

Gilson, David. *A Bibliography of Jane Austen*. Oxford: Clarendon Press, 1982, 877 p.

    A comprehensive bibliography of primary and secondary materials.

Gooneratne, Yasmine. *"Pride and Prejudice."* In her *Jane Austen*, pp. 81-103. British Authors Introductory Critical Studies, edited by Robin Mayhead. Cambridge: Cambridge University Press, 1970.

    A general introduction to the novel, focusing on the development of Elizabeth's character.

Harmsel, Henrietta Ten. *"Pride and Prejudice."* In her *Jane Austen: A Study in Fictional Conventions*, pp. 61-93. Studies in English Literature, Vol. IV. The Hague: Mouton & Co., 1964.

    Examines Austen's use of conventional situations, character types, and thematic motifs.

Heilman, Robert B. "*E Pluribus Unum*: Parts and Whole in *Pride and Prejudice*." In *Jane Austen: Bicentenary Essays*, edited by John Halperin, pp. 123-43. Cambridge: Cambridge University Press, 1975.

    Suggests that the novel derives its unity from a "multiplicity" of variations on the themes of pride and marriage.

Hennelly, Mark M., Jr. "*Pride and Prejudice*: The Eyes Have It." In *Jane Austen: New Perspectives*, edited by Janet Todd, pp. 187-207. Women and Literature, n.s., vol. 3. New York: Holmes & Meier Publishers, 1983.

    Examines the implications of Austen's portrayal of various characters' eyes, use of eye contact, and visual perceptions.

Kirschbaum, Leo. "The World of *Pride and Prejudice*." In *Twelve Original Essays on Great English Novels*, edited by Charles Shapiro, pp. 69-85. Detroit: Wayne State University Press, 1960.

    Argues that despite Austen's rational and realistic approach to her materials, her use of coincidence is contrived and her understanding of the emotional life of her characters highly limited.

Krieger, Murray. "Postscript: The Naïve Classic and the Merely Comic." In his *Visions of Extremity in Modern Literature*. Vol. II, *The Classic Vision: The Retreat from Extremity*, pp. 221-52. Baltimore: Johns Hopkins University Press, 1971.*

    Discusses the carefully controlled boundaries of the human community in *Pride and Prejudice*. Krieger argues that the novel represents a system of "closed values" cut off from the reality of life.

Kroeber, Karl. "*Pride and Prejudice*: Fiction's Lasting Novelty." In *Jane Austen: Bicentenary Essays*, edited by John Halperin, pp. 144-55. Cambridge: Cambridge University Press, 1975.

    An analysis of the novel's linguistic patterns focusing on Austen's use of dead metaphors.

Liddell, Robert. *"Pride and Prejudice."* In his *The Novels of Jane Austen*, pp. 34-55. London: Longmans, 1963.

    A study of various aspects of the novel, including its history, sources, social background, and irony.

Mansell, Darrel. "*Pride and Prejudice*: Irony in the Novels." In his *The Novels of Jane Austen: An Interpretation*, pp. 78-107. London: Macmillan, 1973.

    Explores the various levels of irony in the novel, stressing the ironic interaction of different characters, themes, and situations.

Moler, Kenneth L. "*Pride and Prejudice* and the 'Patrician Hero'." In his *Jane Austen's Art of Allusion*, pp. 75-108. Lincoln: University of Nebraska Press, 1968.

> Examines the relationship between Darcy and the "patrician heroes" in the novels of Burney and Richardson.

Morgan, Susan. "Intelligence in *Pride and Prejudice*." In her *In the Meantime: Character and Perception in Jane Austen's Fiction*, pp. 77-106. Chicago: University of Chicago Press, 1980.

> Suggests that the novel dramatizes the dangers of "wrong thinking, false choices, and unengaged lives." Morgan argues that the plot tests Elizabeth's ability to engage her perceptions intelligently in controlling the direction of her life.

Nardin, Jane. "Propriety as a Test of Character: *Pride and Prejudice*." In her *Those Elegant Decorums: The Concept of Propriety in Jane Austen's Novels*, pp. 47-61. Albany: State University of New York Press, 1973.

> A study of how manners in the novel reflect the morality of the characters.

Roth, Barry. *An Annotated Bibliography of Jane Austen Studies: 1973-83*. Charlottesville: University Press of Virginia, 1985, 359 p.

> An annotated guide to recent criticism on Austen.

Rubenstein, E., ed. *Twentieth-Century Interpretations of "Pride and Prejudice": A Collection of Critical Essays*. Twentieth-Century Interpretations, edited by Maynard Mack. Englewood Cliffs, N.J.: Prentice-Hall, 1969, 120 p.

> Reprints selected essays by such critics as Litz, Kliger, and Brower.

Smith, LeRoy W. "*Pride and Prejudice:* No Improper Pride." In his *Jane Austen and the Drama of Woman*, pp. 87-110. London: Macmillan, 1983.

> An extended discussion of the social, moral, economic, and sexual dilemmas Elizabeth must face as a middle-class woman in her society.

Southam, B. C., ed. *Jane Austen: The Critical Heritage*. Critical Heritage Series, edited by B. C. Southam. London: Routledge & Kegan Paul, 1968, 276 p.

> Contains excerpts from nineteenth-century critical commentary on *Pride and Prejudice*.

———, ed. *Jane Austen, "Sense and Sensibility," "Pride and Prejudice," and "Mansfield Park": A Casebook*. London: Macmillan, 1976, 254 p.

> Reprints excerpts from nineteenth- and twentieth-century critical commentary.

Tave, Stuart M. "Affection and the Mortification of Elizabeth Bennet." In his *Some Words of Jane Austen*, pp. 116-57. Chicago: University of Chicago Press, 1973.

> Explores the concept of "amiability" in the novel. Tave focuses on Elizabeth's gradual realization that Darcy is an amiable man, worthy of her affection.

Wallace, Robert K. "*Pride and Prejudice* and Piano Concerto No. 9 (K. 271)." In his *Jane Austen and Mozart: Classical Equilibrium in Fiction and Music*, pp. 83-135. Athens: University of Georgia Press, 1983.

> A detailed comparison of the novel and a Mozart piano concerto.

Weinsheimer, Joel. "Chance and the Hierarchy of Marriages in *Pride and Prejudice*." *ELH* 39, No. 3 (September 1972): 404-19.

> A study of Austen's use of chance in the novel and the part it plays in the marriages that take place.

Wiesenfarth, Joseph. "The Plot of *Pride and Prejudice*." In his *The Errand of Form: An Assay of Jane Austen's Art*, pp. 60-85. New York: Fordham University Press, 1967.

> An analysis of the relationship between the plot of the novel and the moral values it represents.

Wright, Andrew H. "*Pride and Prejudice*." In his *Jane Austen's Novels: A Study in Structure*, pp. 105-23. London: Chatto & Windus, 1957.

> Discusses the characters of Elizabeth, Darcy, and Wickham.

John Banim

1798-1842

Michael Banim

1796-1874

(Also wrote under pseudonym of O'Hara Family) Irish novelists, short story writers, and essayists; John was also a poet, dramatist, and journalist.

Recognized as pioneers of the Irish novel, John and Michael Banim collaborated on a series of novels and short stories about the life of the Irish peasant in the days preceding the great famine of the 1840s. Intentionally didactic, and designed to document the Irish peasants' struggles, their works can be grouped into two categories: those of cabin life, which detail a life of few amenities led by village peasants ingrained with folklore and a belief in the supernatural, and those that describe the historical events that led to Ireland's social and economic problems in the early 1800s. Though the Banims' works are little known today, critics praise their descriptions of peasant life in pre-famine Ireland as being among the first realistic examinations of the decline of Gaelic culture under English domination.

The brothers were born at Kilkenny, Ireland, into a family of farmers and tradespeople. Michael intended to study law, but left school to assist in his father's shop when the family suffered financial losses. His younger brother, John, was educated at Kilkenny College and at the drawing academy of the Royal Dublin Society. Very early in his life, John's health began to fail. When a young woman he had hoped to marry died of tuberculosis in 1817, John walked fifty miles in poor weather to attend her funeral. He collapsed upon his return home with the first attack of the spinal disease that afflicted him throughout much of his life and spent the following year regaining his strength. Early in 1820, having apparently recovered his health, John left for Dublin to work as a journalist.

During the first year there, John experimented with several literary genres before turning to the novel. His poem of Irish mythology, *The Celt's Paradise,* was submitted to Sir Walter Scott and, upon his recommendation, was published in 1821. One of John's plays, *Damon and Pythias,* was produced at Covent Garden in 1821 and remained in the repertoire of major English and American acting companies for many years.

While in Dublin, John conceived the idea for the works for which he and Michael are known today. He determined to depict Irish life from the viewpoint of the peasant and working-class Catholic. This perspective differed from that of most of his Irish contemporaries, who wrote from the viewpoint of the Protestant Ascendancy. On one of his trips to Kilkenny, John discussed the plan with his brother and finally convinced a reluctant Michael to collaborate on a series of novels and short stories to be published under the collective pseudonym O'Hara Family. John and Michael agreed that they would exchange their individual works through the mail, with each acting as editor of the other's writing. Though critics continue to debate the exact nature of each brother's contribution, the Banims' letters from this period document the close working relationship they enjoyed.

The Banims continued collaborating through the mid-1830s: John lived in England and Europe while Michael remained as a shopkeeper in Kilkenny, supplying the details of peasant life unavailable to his city-based brother. The collaboration was successful and lasting, enabling them to publish a substantial number of novels and collections of short stories. During these years, John suffered recurring attacks of his paralyzing and painful spinal disease. In 1835, he received a government pension and retired to Ireland, where he became increasingly disabled and died at the age of forty-four. Michael outlived his younger brother by many years. After leaving the family business, he took an appointment as postmaster at Kilkenny in 1852. He published two novels, *Clough Fionn* and *The Town of the Cascades,* and lived out his last years dependent on a Royal Literary Fund pension. Michael died in 1874.

The Banims' method of editing each other's writings—which included extensive revisions of plot, characterization, and tone—has made it difficult for critics to determine the authorship of individual works. Because many early reviewers assumed that John alone had written the O'Hara Family books, he was much better known than Michael, whose reputation as an author has grown more slowly. Today, some commentators still claim that Michael did very little original writing and that he only suggested ideas that John later developed into stories; others insist that Michael had a deeper knowledge of Irish peasant life and wrote as skillfully as John. Although John and Michael wrote several works individually, most critics agree that these are inferior to their collaborative efforts. Today, scholars concur that the authors' best works are the stories of peasant life and the historical novels produced under their joint pseudonym, O'Hara Family.

In their peasant stories and novels, the Banims realistically depicted cabin life in pre-famine Ireland. The authors' first-hand knowledge of this life is evident throughout their works: the Banims based many of their fictional characters on people they knew, and, although they were educated and wrote in English, their novels attest to their familiarity with Gaelic. The Banims wrote during a period of political and social change, as English domination slowly eroded the traditional Gaelic culture and language. Threatened by the Penal Laws, which proscribed the peasants' religious, educational, and political rights, the cabin life explored by the Banims was already declining in the early nineteenth century. Their novels are often praised for providing a record of this disappearing world; as Mark D. Hawthorne wrote, the Banims "found the remnants of the Gaelic past in the living folklore of the cabin."

The Banims' best-known novels of peasant life include *The Fetches, Crohoore of the Bill-Hook, The Nowlans,* and *Father Connell. The Fetches,* generally attributed to John, describes the peasants' absolute belief in the otherworld. Critics often note the deliberate ambiguity in the work's skillful juxtaposition of the peasants' belief in the supernatural with the suggestion that the events were imagined. In *Crohoore of the Bill-Hook,* Michael writes of the duplicity among the battlers for Irish independence, yet sympathetically portrays the peasants' social and political plight. Judged by most critics to be John's best novel of peasant life, *The Nowlans* is a psychological study of John Nowlan, a man who, though committed to the Catholic priesthood, falls in love with a Protestant woman, marries her in a Protestant ceremony, and suffers the torment of being condemned for his ''sin.'' Critics praise the author's realistic treatment of the priest's mental breakdown, but also argue that the second portion of the novel slips into melodramatic violence as it follows the adventures of the priest's sister, Peggy. *Father Connell,* usually attributed to Michael, is an explicit analysis of conditions among the Irish lower classes that focuses on a priest driven to despair and then action by the plight of his impoverished parishioners. Throughout these novels, the Banims' use of humor, folklore, and supernatural elements contributes to their insightful descriptions of Irish peasant life.

In their historical novels, the Banims used seventeenth- and eighteenth-century events to explain the social and economic problems of early nineteenth-century Ireland. John's most critically acclaimed historical novel is *The Boyne Water.* Based on the struggle between William of Orange and James II for control of the English throne and its dominions, the novel displays John's understanding of Ireland's problems and his ability to offer solutions. He creates a hero, the Irish Protestant Robert Evelyn, whose sympathetic and evenhanded actions toward Irish Catholics represent John's hopes for reconciliation. In another historical novel, *The Croppy,* Michael recounts the story of the Wexford Rebellion of 1798. This novel is usually regarded as less ambitious than *The Boyne Water,* but is praised nevertheless for its successful incorporation of the stories told to Michael by veterans of that conflict. Critics agree that the novel has a sense of immediacy not found in *The Boyne Water,* which many reviewers fault for its excessive and cumbersome historical details.

Although their novels and short stories received mixed reviews, the Banims enjoyed a modest reputation during the nineteenth century. Some early commentators condemned their material as lurid and unfit for literature, while others applauded the Banims for their realistic descriptions. Twentieth-century critics continue to praise the Banims' realism as well as their frankly didactic attempt to reconcile the Irish political and religious factions of their day. Though many scholars regard their depictions of the gentry as flawed because of the Banims' unfamiliarity with that social class, they praise John and Michael's detailed and accurate portrayals of the peasants. The Banims created many memorable characters: the mysterious but heroic Crohoore; the Irish Protestant Evelyn, sympathetic to the Catholic cause; the admirable priest, Father Connell; the fallen priest, John Nowlan. Although the Banims' works are seldom read today, critics point out their historical value as records of the doomed culture of Gaelic Ireland. Modern opinion of their work was summarized by Hawthorne, who stated that the Banims ''stood between two cultures and, unlike any of their contemporaries, wanted to find a way that the Gaelic past and the English present might be fused into a new, unique nation.''

PRINCIPAL WORKS

By John Banim:

The Celt's Paradise   (poetry)   1821
Damon and Pythias   (drama)   1821
Revelations of the Dead-Alive   (essays)   1824; also published as *London and Its Eccentricities in the Year 2023,* 1845
The Anglo-Irish of the Nineteenth Century   (novel)   1828

By John and Michael Banim under the Pseudonym ''O'Hara Family'':

*Tales, by the O'Hara Family   (novels)   1825
The Boyne Water   (novel)   1826
The Croppy   (novel)   1826
**Tales, by the O'Hara Family   (novels)   1826
***The Denounced   (novels)   1830
The Chaunt of the Cholera: Songs for Ireland   (poetry)   1831
The Ghost-Hunter and His Family   (novel)   1833
****The Mayor of Wind-Gap   (novel)   1835
The Bit o' Writin' and Other Tales   (short stories)   1838
Father Connell   (novel)   1842

By Michael Banim:

Clough Fionn (novel) 1852; published in periodical *Dublin University Magazine*
The Town of the Cascades   (novel)   1864

*This work includes the novels *Crohoore of the Bill-Hook, The Fetches,* and *John Doe; or, Peep o' Day.*
**This work includes the novels *The Nowlans* and *Peter of the Castle.*
***This work includes the novels *The Last Baron of Crana* and *The Conformists.*
****This work was published with the novel *Canvassing,* by Miss Martin.

JOHN BANIM   (letter date 1824)

[*This portion of a letter from John to Michael Banim, dated May 2, 1824, illustrates the authors' method of literary collaboration. Commending one of his own manuscripts to his brother for editing, John proceeds to give Michael a lesson in characterization.*]

So far as it goes, I pronounce that you have been successful. Here and there, I have marked such particular criticisms as struck me, and them you may note by referring to the margin. I send you the MSS. of my tale, and I request your severest criticisms; scratch, cut, and condemn at your pleasure. This is the first copy. Looking over it, I perceive many parts that are bad; send it back when you can, with every suggestion you are capable of making. Read it for the whole family in solemn conclave. Let father, mother, Joanna and yourself sit in judgment on it, and send me all your opinions sincerely given. (pp. 852-53)

To return again to your tale [*Crohoore of the Bill-Hook*]. Two of the personages do not stand out sufficiently from the canvass. Aim at distinctness and at individuality of character. Open Shakespeare, and read a play of his, then turn to the list of dramatis personae, and see and feel what he has done in this way.

Of a dozen characters, each is himself alone. Look about you; bring to mind the persons you have known, call them up before you; select and copy them. Never give a person an action to do, who is not a legible individual. Make that a rule, and I think it ought to be a primary rule with novel writers.

Suppose one was to get a sheet of paper; draw up thereon a list of persons, and after their names, write down what kind of human beings they shall be, leaving no two alike, and not one generalised or undrawn. After Shakespeare, Scott is the great master-hand of character, and hence, one of his sources of great power. To shew you clearly what I mean; not a creature we ever met in our father's penetralia, resembled the other. There might be somewhat of a conventional, outward similarity, arising from their pursuits, habits, and amusements being similar; but each was, notwithstanding, distinct. I think that in writing a tale, every character in it should be drawn from nature. It is impossible all should be absolute originals. Human nature being the same, in all ages, and in all climes, it cannot be hoped now-a-days, that a writer can be the discoverer of a new character. It can be no more than the same dough, somewhat differently shaped. Habits of country, habits of station, habits of any kind, will diversify; but human nature is the same now that it ever was. I say one can scarcely draw an original character; but I say, draw like nature; no matter what kind of nature you draw from, provided that the likeness be not that of a disgusting object. After all, there is nothing commonplace in nature.

Since I am on this, I may as well tell you, how as I think, character ought to be marked. Apart from propriety of language and thought, fit words and fit ideas for each person, (and by the way lift up both your hands, and wonder how Shakespeare makes his people walk before you *without any other means*) character can be indited, by portraits of the face and person, with allusion to the expression and conformation of both; by painting dress, by describing gait, motion, gesticulation, and by the tone of the voice sometimes. I here purposely omit the downright easy way of telling us at once, that a man is a good, or a wicked fellow. If you sharpen your eye and ear on these points, I see you are pretty sharp already, you can, either from your recollections, or present and future study, in society, and among men and women, every hour in the day, gain truth, and conviction, and pleasure.

If either of us could only delineate the peculiarities we daily witness in those we meet, success would be the result. All will appreciate a likeness; and the artist who can convince every beholder, that he has transferred to his canvass, each peculiar mark of the individual he paints, will be praised, and he deserves it. (pp. 853-54)

Get fourteen or fifteen of any of the persons you ever knew; put them into scenes favourable to their peculiarities, their individualities can be exemplified, without straining after the point; in proper situations, set them talking for themselves; by their own word of mouth, they will denote their own character, better than any description from your pen; thus will you dramatise your tale, and faithful drama is the life and soul of novel writing. Plot is an inferior consideration to drama, though still it is a main consideration.

Do not say that I am dictatorial, or that I consider you to be a subject for a drilling; but let us unaffectedly compare notes as often as we can, and both will be benefited.

A few words more, as to the mode of studying the art of novel writing. Read any first-rate production of the kind, with a note book. When an author forces you to feel with him, or whenever he produces a more than ordinary degree of pleasure, or when he startles you—stop and try how he has done it; see if it be by dialogue, or by picture, or by description, or by action. Fully comprehend his method, his means for the effect, and note it down; write down all such impressions. Enumerate these, and see how many go to make the combined interest of one book. Observe, by contrasting characters, how he keeps up the balance of the familiar, and the marvellous, humorous, serious, and romantic.

This would not be imitation, it would be study; what, I will venture to say, great men have done with their predecessors— what painters do in the study of their art. (pp. 855-56)

John Banim, in a letter to Michael Banim on May 2, 1824, in The Irish Quarterly Review, *Vol. XV, No. XVI, December, 1854, pp. 852-56.*

THE GENTLEMAN'S MAGAZINE AND HISTORICAL CHRONICLE   (essay date 1825)

[*In this review of the first series of* Tales, by the O'Hara Family, *the anonymous critic asserts that the author of* Crohoore of the

A portrait of John Banim. This is the only available portrait of either of the Banim brothers.

Bill-Hook, The Fetches, *and* John Doe *is not the equal of Scott, but "treads more closely upon the heels of the Scottish Novelist than any other writer with whom we have been made acquainted."*]

The author of these [*Tales of the O'Hara Family*] (who, we understand to be Mr. Banim) will not, we trust, think our comparison "odious," if we liken them to his admirable Prototype, designated by an hyperbole of compliment *"The Great Unknown."* We do not affirm that these writers [Mr. Banim and Mr. Scott] are equal in talents; but the author of the *Tales* before us treads more closely upon the heels of the Scottish Novelist than any other writer with whom we have been made acquainted. They are *akin* in fertility of invention, and in power of description; in the same happy art of beguiling the reader of fiction into a belief that he is perusing a veritable history; and alike in awakening an interest which knows no intermission. The author of the Irish *Tales* is as much at home in the country which he has chosen for the detail of exploits of lawless violence, as is the Author of *Waverley* in his Highland fortresses, beleaguered by Royal armies, and defended by Jacobite adherents.

We will endeavour to give some account of these admirable *Tales*, and . . . [convey] the writer's powers—powers which we predict require but public encouragement to ripen into a splendid maturity, and to yield a rich harvest of amusement to the world, and of fame and profit to their owner. (p. 54)

[The first tale, *Crohoore of the Bill-Hook*, abounds] in scenes of very powerful interest, and [is] animated by many vigorous pictures of national manners. . . . Did our limits permit, we would willingly extract the fine description of the Cave of Dumore; the battle that terminated in the rescue of Shea; and the scene between a set of "bocchochs," or lame beggars (the genuine name of every class of real or deceptive mendicants), conveying perhaps the most genuine characteristics of the lowest Irish that is yet in print.

The second tale in the collection is one of a different cast. It is founded on a superstition prevalent in Ireland, and called **The Fetches.** A Fetch is a supernatural fac-simile of some individual, which comes to ensure to its original a happy longevity or an immediate dissolution. If seen in the morning, the one event is predicted; if in the evening, the other. From such superstition the author has constructed a tale of melancholy interest, but perhaps of too refined a character for general sympathy; for unless we can surrender our feelings to the illusion, we might be tempted to treat the story with contempt as childish and absurd.

The last tale is, in our opinion, decidedly the best. [*John Doe; or Peep o'Day*] abounds with national traits very faithfully depicted, and exhibits the Irish character in its most varied and antithetical form, in its most contentious bearings, and in its fine and generous enthusiasm: fierce in its revenge, gentle in its affections.

We could willingly give many pages from the tale of John Doe; but must now dismiss the *O'Hara Tales* with hearty congratulations to the publick, that another Master Spirit has been awakened, who can array with the splendour and light of a creative fancy, the facts and experiences of an acute and intelligent mind. We await his further productions with sincere interest, and offer him our best thanks for that which is before us. (pp. 55-6)

A review of "Tales of the O'Hara Family," in The Gentleman's Magazine and Historical Chronicle, *Vol. XCV, July, 1825, pp. 54-6.*

THE LONDON MAGAZINE   (essay date 1825)

[*In this mixed review of the three novels of the* Tales, *by the O'Hara Family, the critic commends John Banim's talents and abilities while arguing that he does not live up to his promise. The reviewer concludes with the hope that the author will, in future work, "trust to his observation more, and to his imagination less."*]

[The *Tales by the O'Hara Family*] is far superior to the vulgar novel of the circulating library, though its chief fault is, that it contains too much of the staple commodity of Leadenhall-street. It is the product of much ill-managed talent, and much uncultivated mind. With perhaps higher powers than the author of *To-day in Ireland,* he has made a much less entertaining and instructive work. He must cultivate his judgment, write not in haste, consider his plots, and strike out one half of his manuscripts after he has come to the conclusion of the productive part of his labour. If the author likewise intends to benefit his native country, he must pay a little attention to some severer studies than painting and poetry—of all political science he is as guiltless as the printer's devil. This to one who writes of Ireland and its evils is fatal; though it is common to all Irishmen, who have for a century done little else than rave a furious mixture of poetry, eloquence, and folly, in behalf of their beloved Emerald Isle. The author of these *Tales,* with his knowledge of character, his knowledge of Ireland, with knowledge of another kind, and his dramatic powers, might contribute more essential aid to his suffering country than half a dozen crazy orators.

These *Tales,* which in imitation of Sir Walter Scott's absurd introductions and prefaces, are as absurdly represented to be the composition of some O'Hara family, are three in number. The first, *Crohoore of the Bill-hook,* is the most elaborate, and on the whole the best. The fable is artful, and tolerably well maintained, till towards the latter end the story is wound up with a great deal of huddling and hurry. Some characters occur which are well conceived and forcibly thrown out—there are several scenes of interest, and much well-managed dialogue. It is, however, greatly disfigured by the author's love of the false supernatural—a constant attempt to frighten his reader with what he intends presently to explain in the most natural way in the world.—The second, *The Fetches,* is a story of the true supernatural. You are given to understand that previous to death the shade or form of the person about to die presents itself to his dearest friends; why, or wherefore, does not appear. This tale is decidedly the worst of the three; it is painful, disagreeable, false in almost every respect, and unredeemed by any decided merit.—The last, *John Doe,* is perhaps as entertaining as any of the three—it is very spirited in parts, but as a whole is ill-conducted, improbable, and confused. Many scenes are, however, drawn with vigour; the Irish character, that most extraordinary phænomenon in human nature, is well and truly exhibited—and the state of manners in one division of the country is pretty faithfully delineated. We exhort the writer to go on—we wish to see more from his pen—though not more *Tales by the O'Hara Family.* Let him trust to his observation more, and to his imagination less. (pp. 135-36)

A review of "Tales by the O'Hara Family," in The London Magazine, *n.s. Vol. III, No. 1, September, 1825, pp. 134-36.*

[THOMAS MOORE] (essay date 1826)

[*A nineteenth-century Irish poet, Moore is best known for his exotic epic poem* Lalla Rookh. *Moore also wrote biographies and, occasionally, criticism. In this mixed review, Moore focuses on* Crohoore of the Bill-Hook *and* John Doe, *delineating both their strengths and weaknesses.*]

Tales of the O'Hara Family is, perhaps, the most powerful, altogether, of [a] whole class of Irish Novels. There is a vigour and raciness in every page, which atones for much of exaggeration and bad taste. The genius of the writer, like that irregular offspring of fire, the *Potheen* of his native land, has not only a strength, but a wildness of flavour about it, which it would be in vain to look for in productions more amenable to the gauge of criticism. . . . It is, indeed, one of the great merits of this work that the portraits from low life, which it contains, have been evidently sat for on the spot;—the humour comes authentic from the very source, without having gone through any refining process on the way, and, though the author shows occasionally that he can write with much elegance and sweetness, there is, in general, a *ton de brigand* assumed in his style, which throws an air of truth and authority over his White-Boy recitals.

The first of these *Tales, Crohore of the Bill-hook,* is that which, we believe, is most admired in Ireland. To enter, however, with due sympathy, into this wild and striking story, it would be necessary to come prepared with a much fuller knowledge of the condition, habits, and modes of expression of the lower orders of Irish (among whom the adventures entirely lie), than could be expected from a mere English reader. There is also, at the very outset, a degree of violence in the incidents, which inclines persons, who have often been taken in by this cheap mode of producing effects, to pause with suspicion on the threshold of a novel, which opens with no less a supply of the terrible than three murders and an abduction—all performed by the same master-hand. The rest of the narrative is entirely occupied with the pursuit and the escapes of the supposed perpetrator of these horrors, in whom the faculty of Sir Boyle Roche's bird—that of 'being in two places at once'—is multiplied beyond the usual privilege of ubiquity in heroes. Mystifications and apparitions succeed each other rapidly—a train of wonders is laid which explode in nothing, and the only solution given of all the marvels that have happened, is one still more marvellous and insoluble than any, namely, that the murders, instead of being perpetrated by the person most marked out, both by disposition and circumstances, for such a deed, have been committed by a jovial, good-humoured young fellow, of whom nobody entertained the slightest suspicion, and whose motives were far from being proportionate to the instigation of any such crime. Notwithstanding, however, these defects of the story, *Crohore of the Bill-hook* is an original and powerful production; and to those who can read with facility, the humorous jargon of the lower orders of Irish, must be as full of amusement as it is of picturesqueness and interest. We have looked in vain for any passage sufficiently detached from the narrative, to admit of being *framed* as a specimen of the whole. We shall be happy, however, if we have so far excited the curiosity of the reader, as to induce him to form his own opinion at the fountainhead. Should he be deterred by the interspersion of Irish, and of phrases not at least English, through the dialogue, let him turn to the tale of *John Doe,* in the last volume, where he will find, with less of these interruptions, a story, to our taste, far more interesting, and yet with the same vigour of touch, truth of costume and vividness of colouring, which are so remarkable in *Crohore,* and which render

this author one of the most masterly painters of national character that have yet appeared in Ireland. (pp. 364-66)

[*Thomas Moore*], *"Irish Novels," in* The Edinburgh Review, *Vol. XLIII, No. LXXXVI, February, 1826, pp. 356-72.**

THE MONTHLY REVIEW, London (essay date 1827)

[*In the following assessment of the second series of* Tales, *by the* O'Hara Family, *the critic compares* The Nowlans *and* Peter of the Castle *with the earlier novels in the series and notes John Banim's continuing imitation of Scott.*]

Mr. Banim, in whose single identity the whole of 'The O'Hara Family' are well understood to be concentrated, is a gentleman of considerable talents and acquirements. Of his qualifications as a novelist, we have already found some reason to speak in terms of commendation. We attributed to him great occasional power in the display of the passions,—though he has always succeeded worst in pathos; we gave him credit for a shrewd insight into human nature generally, and a perfect acquaintance with the eccentricities of the Irish character in particular; and we did not hesitate to declare, that there are few of his compeers who can, upon an effort, imagine and throw off a scene of strife or terror with a bolder or more vigorous pencil. But from this measure of praise we made a fair deduction in the aggregate, for the improbabilities and the extravagance which abound in his plots, for his inconsistent management of the different characters in his fictions, and for a great deal of what is unnatural and absurd, overwrought and unskilful, in the general conduct of his narratives.

In repeating this balanced judgment upon his former works, we sufficiently characterise the merits and defects of the volumes now before us. They exhibit all the peculiarities of the author's mind and style: they are remarkable for the same desultory strength of description; they betray the same intervals and lapses of inequality and weakness; and though the tales which they contain, cannot, certainly, on the whole, be placed in competition, for spirit and graphic force, with the earlier series, their inferiority is not so distinct and palpable as to endanger the modicum of fame, of which the author had previously and deservedly possessed himself.

The history of *The Nowlans,* fills the two first volumes, and offers, consequently, much more ample scope for the delineation of national manners, than that entitled *Peter of the Castle,* which is compressed into the single remaining volume. The scene of the story of *The Nowlans,* is laid in our own times, and among the Llieuve-Jeullum, or Slieve-Bloom Mountains:—that wild and barren tract of the south-west of Ireland, which stretches through the county of Tipperary, and borders on Limerick. The family of the Nowlans are of the class of the more considerable farmers of this unfrequented and mountainous region; and, accordingly, we are carefully introduced to the whole of their pedigree and kindred. But the business and interest of the tale turn chiefly upon the fortunes of two individuals, a son and a daughter, of the house; of whom the former, John Nowlan, is educated for the priesthood; and the latter, his sister, Peggy Nowlan, is the humble heroine of the piece. (pp. 123-24)

It is unnecessary to go through the details . . . of the story. In analyzing it we do not discover any room for admiration, either in the construction of the plot, the machinery of the action, or the probability of the incidents. The business of the plot is influenced chiefly by the iniquity of Mr. Frank; and this is altogether of the monstrous and unnatural character, which belongs only to the hacknied villain of the common-place novel. The coarse delineation of such utter depravity, is the ordinary and stock resource of inferior fiction-mongers; who labour to make up, by thickening and deepening the naked horrors of their plots, for the want of interest with which they otherwise lack the ingenuity to invest their narratives. The author before us should have felt above resorting to this clumsy expedient. That a brother, with smiles and accents of tenderness on his lips, should deliberately, and in cold blood, plan the disgrace and ruin of his sister, for the mere sake of procuring her disinheritance, is in itself sufficiently atrocious to startle our credulity. But when we find this brother described as the heir to a splendid fortune, on whom all the advantages of a modern education had been carefully bestowed; as a young gentleman of elegant manners, classical attainments, and accomplished tastes:—when we are told all this, and are then required to believe him the practised associate of swindlers, blacklegs, and common thieves, the accomplice in highway robberies and housebreaking, who, in the vulgar slang of the lowest tramper, boasts his share and calculates his profits *in a swag,*—the reason at once revolts at a contradiction so palpable and absurd. Scarcely less incredible, too, are the deeper shades of his guilt: his suggestion to an accomplice to dispatch his excellent uncle, the benefactor who had reared and cherished him; and his premeditated scheme for the murder of his innocent wife, and her unborn babe. There is no keeping in such a portraiture. That the gentleman of refined habits and intellectual accomplishments, may yet be a vicious man, is, we know, unhappily but too true:—but his vices must still shew some relation to his caste. He may be a Lovelace, or a Joseph Surface: but he will scarcely prove a Jonathan Wild, or a Thurtell.

But, with the first detection of Mr. Frank's crimes, the story should in any case have ended; and all the subsequent incidents of the second volume, appear as so many ill appended afterthoughts of the author. The latter adventures and escapes of Peggy, in which she is compelled to be the secret and unshrinking eye-witness of a frightful murder—a scene, by the way, certainly painted with very great power—are quite unnecessary to the completeness of the tale: but our author has always an irresistible passion for multiplying his catastrophes. No accidents are too wonderful, no coincidences too strange, to be pressed by the novelist into his service at need; and "rakin' Peery Conolly," in particular, is always most unaccountably at hand in every emergency of the flagging plot. In this, and several of the other characters, as well as in some of the incidents of the tale, it is again forced upon us to observe the author's same broad imitation of Sir Walter Scott. . . . Peggy Nowlan, the most interesting of his females, is the double of Jenny Deans; in a mendicant friar, we have a kind of Edie Ochiltree; and the cast-away Maggy Nowlan, and her more infamous mother and brother, are converted in the sequel, with a transformation as rapid as the changes of a pantomime, into such agents of iniquity as the author of *Waverley* has frequently delighted to imagine. Mr. Banim has certainly persisted—unconsciously it may be—in borrowing largely from the storehouse of Sir Walter's machinery.

Perhaps the character of John, is the only part of the mere construction of the story, which deserves to be mentioned with praise. The author has certainly succeeded in giving a very painful interest to his fortunes: while the picture of his peculiar trials is altogether new in our tales of fiction; and the writhing agony of the mental struggle under which he falls, is depicted

with a vivid energy and knowledge of human nature, which must make every bosom thrill with commiseration and dread. But, . . . the greatest merit and the most easy charm of these tales, as in those of the former series, consist, not in the business of the narrative, but in the sketches, sometimes grave, sometimes humourous, and ever most lively and faithful, which they offer of genuine Irish life. To the story of Mr. Aby Nowlan, we have referred for one example of these sketches; and there is another fully equal to it, though in a very different style, describing a thriving and managing family of very opposite qualities. We mean the description in the first volume . . . of 'Magistrate Adams' and his family, and of a dinner party given by these people;—the representatives of a whole class who, in the sister kingdom, wound the "kibe" of aristocracy by their ridiculous pretensions, and support a scanty 'gentility' by mingled thrift and display;—who, exercising the lower grades of political and judicial office, maintain their petty state by mean grasping extortion and insolent tyranny over the poor, and by ostentatious entertainment of their equals and superiors.

The story of **Peter of the Castle,** which occupies the third volume is, in the unity of its plot and design, far superior to the other. In fact, this tale has all the elements of a very good romance; and we should not be surprised to see it adapted to the stage of one of the lesser theatres. It is, like all our author's stories, somewhat wild and melo-dramatic in its cast; but, with a few alterations, it might easily have been expanded into a novel of three volumes. Though contained in a single one, there is abundance of business and incident in the plot, that would well bear enlargement; and the denouement may be said—no common fault—to be but too rapidly evolved. It would need only a good deal more of the "filling in and finishing" of our author's inimitable tints of national manners. In this respect, the composition is, as it stands, rather meagre: but there is one excellent scene in it, . . . the celebration of a marriage in an Irish cabin, which it is impossible to read without exquisite amusement, or to pass without hearty commendation. For minute characteristic and humourous detail, it may put to nought the ballad of the far-famed "Wedding at Ballyporeen." We love not to turn from this warm eulogy, to a conclusion of chilling criticism: yet we cannot but complain that, in this tale again, we should be fated to encounter the old plague of imitation. There is a conversation between some aged beggars, . . . whose unearthly expression of delight in prophesying the untimely end of a heartbroken girl, we defy any reader to peruse, without pronouncing it a palpable copy from the celebrated scene of the same nature in the *Bride of Lammermoor.* (pp. 129-32)

A review of "Tales by the O'Hara Family," in The Monthly Review, *London, Vol. IV, January, 1827, pp. 123-32.*

THE LONDON MAGAZINE (essay date 1827)

[*Calling* The Nowlans *the best novel in the second series of the* Tales, by the O'Hara Family, *the critic asserts that John Banim's talent is a "mongrel breed," his excellent descriptive powers but copies of the styles of other authors and painters. The critic also comments on Banim's characterizations.*]

We have read [*Tales of the O'Hara Family*] with an interest often excited even to a painful degree of intensity, and with frequent admiration of the author's powers; and yet they are productions wild in fable, clumsy in their machinery, and generally defective in the portraiture of character. The author's genius, indeed, seems to be somewhat of a mongrel breed. In extravagance and passion he resembles Maturin; in incident, Scott; in accurate description of manners, Edgeworth; in prosing dialogue he is alone comparable with Galt. His palpable deficiencies are judgment, and that intuitive sense of fitness which we call *tact*. His want of judgment appears in the scheme of his plots; his want of tact in the choice of subjects for the display of his powers; in his failing to perceive that he may exhibit them in their greatest force, to the pain, instead of the gratification of the reader. In the former series this fault was illustrated in a whole story, *The Fetches*, which left, together with a most disagreeable impression on the mind, a feeling almost of resentment at the misdirected talent which had so idly sported with the fancy, and turned our deepest sympathies to folly. This talent had the offence of a hoax in it; we felt that we had been betrayed into a painful interest by childish inventions. On examining the springs of the imposition, we found them of a very vulgar order. The attention may be strongly captivated by images which disgust the eye, and such was the secret charm of *The Fetches;* our aversion to the ideas made us dwell on them with distempered earnestness, as a man will gaze on a corpse, or any other disagreeable object, because the thought of it offends him. In *The Nowlans,* the first and best tale of the New Series, we observe more than one example of this kind, of attempt at fascination by force of presenting shocking pictures. In one instance it fails, and the effect is, of course, burlesque: in another we think it succeeds, and the consequence is disgust to the reader,—honest, genuine, physical disgust, accompanied with a slight sickness at the stomach, if he has just dined. The scene, a murder, it must be confessed, is admirably painted; but as it offends, we think the talent displayed on it ill bestowed. Allusion to this description leads us to observe on the author's imagination. Passion and imagination would seem to be his strong points, and yet, though he appears to abound in imagination, we never find the ground of it original. He is always working on some pattern or other, and not always nice in his choice of one. Like many musicians, he cannot play without notes; there must be something to direct the motions of his hands, and then he will grace and embellish what he sees before him. His genius is essentially pictorial, and he does nothing without copy. He can paint the progress of ruin in an Irish *jontleman's* hospitable house, with the pencil of a Hogarth, or the inmates of a cottage in the style of a Wilkie; but beyond the surface, the expression, he never goes with effect; and when he attempts to describe the inner springs of human action, and to exhibit the secret motions of hearts, he fails altogether, because this is a machinery beyond his ken, one which his intellectual vision has never penetrated. In this province the author of *To-day in Ireland* [Eyre Evans Crowe] is incomparably his superior. He has looked at more than the outside of things; his eyes have searched deeper than the picturesque; and he threw more than figures and landscape into his work. In support of our remark that the writer of the *O'Hara Tales* is always working on some pattern, taken either from nature, his best work; or from the inventions of other books, his worst . . . ; or from recorded facts, we might refer to many examples, which would be admitted as soon as seen. For a striking and familiar instance, we may mention the description of the lovely girl in *John Doe,* who, partially disrobed, sits at her toilet, gazing on her lover's miniature. This is a perfect literary gem; it is all grace, taste, and elegance, and the effect is bewitching. A popular picture, which deserves equal praise, was at first supposed to have been taken from the scene in the book, but it turned out, by the ready and ingenuous avowal of

the author, that the original of his design was the picture. In *The Nowlans* we find two melo-dramatic adventures, derived from a memorable assassination in the South of France. The murder, to the details of which we have already adverted and objected as sickening, is, indeed, obviously a copy of the main circumstances of the assassination of Fualdes. . . . [There] is the horrid and deliberate preparation; the vessel brought in to catch the blood; the cloth to wipe it up; the throat cut before the starting eye-balls of a hidden witness, a trembling, terror-struck woman! The other dramatic situation, taken from a story, whether true or false we know not, connected with the same tragedy, is that of a girl, who goes to meet a villain at midnight, by appointment, and observes a man at the place of assignation digging a grave. The idea of this incident is to be traced to a French print of Bancal or Bastide (which we forget), digging a grave for a girl supposed to have witnessed the murder of Fualdes, and who is sent on an errand to the criminal in the fields, in order that he might murder her. We could mention other copies, not only of scenes and incidents, but characters. *Aby Nowlan,* for instance, is the Laird in [Scott's] *Heart of Mid-Lothian;* with this difference, indeed, that, instead of a miser, he is a spendthrift, but in stolidity and general bearing they are one and the same. The chief villain of this tale, too, Mr. Frank, is an exaggeration of Stanley, who associates himself with the smugglers in the *Heart of Mid-Lothian,* and contracts a *mésalliance.* The Irish villain, to be sure, is of a complexion many shades deeper, and of a more odious profligacy than his prototype. He robs a mail-coach, commits murder, and would have assassinated the heroine of the story, who is illegally married to him, and who is a partial copy of Jeanie Deans. In the character of this Mr. Frank, we find a remarkable instance of the author's want of tact. The slang conversations which this worthy holds with one of his associates, are, for the most part, unintelligible, and, to the last degree, tedious and offensive; they disgust the fatigued reader, without adding, in any measure, to the effect of the portrait. Scott has just touched his genteel profligate's discourse with slang, and therefore his copyist throws into that of his well-born rogue the whole vocabulary of Newgate. This is giving us three morning guns by way of heightening the effect. Notwithstanding, however, all drawbacks and defects, many errors of judgment, and some few of execution, and gross outrages against *vrai-semblance,* these are very clever performances; and we gladly take them, with all their faults, which we note rather as curious phenomena, than in the spirit of detraction. It seems odd to us that there should be such extreme failure, mixed up with such extreme success; but our author is an Irishman, and these, perhaps, are the irregularities of Irish genius.

We have already observed that *The Nowlans* is the best tale of the New Series. The principal character in it is a young catholic priest, John Nowlan, who wins the affections of a girl, of a rank and condition in life very superior to his own; and, in a moment of frenzy, carries her off, and, in violation of his vow of celibacy, marries her. The consequence of this act is pitiable misery to both parties. They sink into the most deplorable poverty, and John Nowlan has the torture of seeing the being who has sacrificed all to him, her whom he has taken from an affluent home, a shivering, houseless wanderer. The character of Letty, the poor victim, is very sweetly drawn. It is the only one that interests us in the book, and a touching picture it presents of generous devotion and gentle unrepining suffering. After having descended, step by step, to a condition of the last wretchedness, she perishes, a wayfarer in a cabin, in giving birth to a child; and here we have an example of the author's want of tact in a scene of unnatural mummery. The husband is found by some charitable visitors celebrating the death of his beloved wife with a kind of mock wake. He has taken the door off its hinges to serve as a bier on which to lay her out, and made an illumination of a single rush-light. We so honour Letty, that we cannot endure the profanation of her fair remains by this odious burlesque of a vulgar ceremony. From this period John Nowlan disappears for a considerable space, and his sister Peggy becomes the centre of operations. She is a tidy, respectable wench, for whom it is impossible to become interested by any circumstance, but that of her being in danger of having her throat cut. Nothing short of this danger can concern us in her behalf, and painfully admirable is the description of her peril: in all her other adventures, we fancy a stout, substantial, able-bodied damsel, with red cheeks, thick ancles, and solid *spogs* [feet], who is perfectly capable of taking care of herself, and whose feelings are not of a kind to rue very keenly any but the sufferings of her flesh. The author has indeed intended her to be full of sensibilities and the finer affections, but he has not effected his purpose: he has conceived a design, but not conveyed an impression of it. He has intended very likely a paragon of a Peggy, but he has put to paper only an ordinary Peggy, in a red cloak, more fit to do the work of a house than that of a novel; to make butter, than to melt hearts. (pp. 51-4)

> *A review of "Tales of the O'Hara Family, Second Series," in* The London Magazine, *n.s. Vol. VII, January 1, 1827, pp. 51-73.*

JOHN BANIM   (letter date 1828)

[*In the following letter, John advises Michael to use their mother's descriptions of her family and townspeople as a resource for characters and plots. Michael later incorporated these suggestions into* The Ghost-Hunter and His Family.]

No matter from what class of life you take your future materials, seek as much as possible for the good and amiable in our national character and habits; as well as for the strong, the fierce, and I will say the ungovernable. How very valuable, for instance, would be a simple dramatic tale, got through by old Daniel Carroll, his wife, his sons and his two daughters. Here no necessity exists to rake your memory for the great object, *character*. Every one of these I have mentioned, must, from your mother's description of them, live for you. Old Daniel Carroll her father, with his grotesque sun-dials, his fork pendulums—his crude system of philosophy; and his reading, during long evenings, Don Quixote and such books, although so throughly pious. Then his wife Betty, you recollect her defence when reprehended for some out of the way expression by her husband. Questioned by him where she had heard the malediction uttered by her. She paused and taxed her memory, and then affirmed, she could have heard it no where, except it issued from the sinful books, he was in the habit of reading. Betty's character is richly primitive. Then there is the son Philip's wild irregular one. The younger Daniel's, petty, selfish, cunning. Alley's retaining her anxiety to be thought very devout, not hiding her candle under a bushel meanwhile—then the eldest daughter, our own dear mother, such as she was in her maidenhood. Her industry, her thrift, her mildness—her mother-wit and natural good sense. Her lovers, her starling, her canniness. My dear Michael, if health permitted, I could use these people, and bring their real and unimagined qualities into play, with credit to the Irish character, all papist as it is, sweetly, primitively, and amiably.

I remember, too, an old story of our mother's, of a gaunt stone-cutter, killing a slight delicate young man in a fight, brought on by a quarrel in a church-yard about the right of interment in a certain spot; you must recollect the occurrence, as it was described to us one cold evening as we sat close together round the fire. (pp. 243-44)

> *John Banim, in an extract from a letter to Michael Banim on November 10, 1828, in* The Irish Quarterly Review, *Vol. V, No. XVIII, June, 1855, pp. 243-45.*

[T. H. LISTER]   (essay date 1831)

[*While objecting to John Banim's reliance on violence and horror in the second edition of* Tales, by the O'Hara Family, *Lister considers the series a powerful and accurate delineation of the "coarse and unpleasing" aspects of Irish life. Unlike* The Nowlans, *Lister argues,* The Croppy *and the two novels of* The Denounced, The Last Baron of Crana *and* The Conformists, *are marred by their lack of originality.*]

Mr Banim holds a very high place among the novelists of Ireland. There is a rough masculine power, a sterling uncultivated vigour, and a nationality in his writings, well calculated to arrest attention. There is little polish, little regard to the graces of style, and very slight evidence of a correct and regulated taste. The subjects in which he delights, are such as affect us powerfully, it is true, but somewhat painfully, and which would not be selected by a lover of refinement. Scenes of violence and horror—crime and its adjuncts—misery of the deepest shade, and the strong emotions which it calls forth, are treated by him with most success, and with extraordinary force. It is often easy to criticise the language in which he conveys to us the appalling circumstances of his tale; but we are conscious, nevertheless, that a strong impression has been made; and though we may coldly cavil at the means employed, we must allow that they do not fail to produce the proposed effect. He also handles a mystery skilfully, and understands the complication of a plot, which (though probability is often forgotten) he generally develops with commendable attention to dramatic effect. Comparing him with painters, we would say, that he combines the merits of Spagnoletto and Salvator Rosa with much that belongs to Hogarth. His delineations, like those of the English artist, are forcible, true, and characteristic, but too often coarse and unpleasing,—dwelling on the dark side of human nature, and overcharging its loathsome defects;—teaching us rather to hate than to love our species, and occasionally ministering to a pruriency of taste which it is by no means the prevailing sin of modern writers to encourage; yet, at the same time, full of a strength and earnestness which convinces us of the perfect fidelity of the unwelcome representations we are made to contemplate. The commencement of the tale called *The Nowlans* furnishes some good exemplifications of this peculiar power. The education and career of Aby Nowlan—the details of his ill-regulated *menage*—the stupid vice, low profligacy, and comfortless extravagance, with its progressive train of ruinous consequences—are laid before us with a painful truth and force, to which we know no parallel in the Novels of the day. In short, spite of many faults, we greatly admire the author of the *O'Hara Tales,* when he is *himself*; but, unfortunately, he has lately striven to become that for which nature has not qualified him—an Irish Walter Scott. He holds about the same station, in comparison with that great Novelist, as Webster or Marlowe by the side of Shakspeare. Those early dramatists had much wild and rugged vigour—sometimes, by bursts, they showed as much as Shakspeare; but their harps had fewer strings, and those few too often jarred discordantly: and so it is with Mr Banim, even when he is content to be himself. But he is unfortunately what Webster and Marlowe were not—a copyist—and his later efforts have been sadly marred by obvious attempts at imitation. (pp. 413-14)

There are few of the *dramatis personae*, in the outlines of which imitation is not more or less discernible. His Pedlar and Knitter, in [*The Croppy*]—his Baron of Crana, John Sharpe, Father James, and Louise, will readily remind the generality of readers of the half-crazed, half-gifted, half-vicious, half-virtuous sub-agents in the *Waverley Tales;* and of such characters as the Pirate, the blunt Scotch serving-man, Dominie Sampson, and Fenella. But we object not so much to imitations like these, as to those ludicrous travesties of style, which have just sufficient resemblance even to react unfavourably upon the very delightful works of our great Novelist, and make us for a while half out of charity with them. (p. 415)

Mr Banim extends his love of accuracy and minuteness to subjects on which we believe few, if any, desire to be informed. We could have spared, in [*The Croppy*], a long description of that rare and curious operation called 'knitting,' which, even if sufficiently unusual in Ireland to demand a description, (of which we are not aware,) is, we assure him, very frequently and diligently practised by the females of the sister kingdom. Who wants to be told that a man who lights his pipe, 'continues slowly and methodically taking out of his pouch, while the reins rested on the neck of his tired and patient steed, a little leathern packet, containing, under many careful foldings, a piece of tobacco, a flint, steel, and touch-paper?' Who would not gladly dispense with such wordy sketches as the following, introduced on occasion of a man looking at his watch? ' ''Come out, Tell-truth,'' said he, as, slowly and cautiously, he drew from his poke the article he so encomiastically addressed. At first appeared, suspended to a stout chain of massive proportions, something in a brown leathern case, which case, smiling all the time, he slid off; then the eye rested on another leathern case, of different texture from the first; and finally he exposed to view a watch, of the diameter of, and almost as round as, a twenty-four pound shot, of which the back was incrusted with some green composition; and that back, as well as the glass of the huge time-piece, underwent furbishing from the loose cuff of his jacket.'

Whoever compares the two first series of the *O'Hara Tales*, and especially the very striking one called *The Nowlans*, with [*The Croppy, The Last Baron of Crana,* and *The Conformists*], will see the injurious effects of imitation,—will see how much even a writer of ability may lose by ceasing to draw from his own resources, and attempting to adopt the style of another, even though that other may be the most gifted and popular writer of his day. *The Nowlans* was Mr Banim's own, and bore the decided impress of his peculiar manner. There were faults in it; but even the faults had an originality which half redeemed them, and made them almost as acceptable as second-hand beauties. We have already praised the strongly-coloured episode of Aby Nowlan's life and death—like what Defoe might have written, and perhaps even better than he would have done it; but there are others in the tale no less entitled to praise. What a deep and growing interest is given to the character of the young priest, struggling in vain against those natural passions, to which the forced celibacy of his order opposes such a demoralizing bar! How fearfully dark, yet true, the colouring of the increasing misery which gradually envelopes him and

his partner—the lodging-house in Dublin, with all the wretched reality of approaching destitution—the flight, the death, the burial! What terrible graces are displayed in the appointment at the Foil-dhuv—the midnight murder in the cabin—Frank's threat to his uncle, escape, and self-destruction at the police-office! The choice of these scenes is perhaps not always commendable; but, being chosen, we must admire the remarkable vigour with which they are described. Now of this ability, there is by no means so much in the last two works of Mr Banim. *The Croppy, a Tale of 1798,* is meant to be an historical novel—historical, inasmuch as it introduces some real events, but not as bringing real personages on the scene. Than the period chosen for this tale, perhaps none in the history of Ireland is more interesting; and it is therefore to be wished, that the story had been rendered more strictly historical,—that the author had introduced just enough of fictitious private details, to cause us to take an interest in his imaginary actors in the real public drama, and then allowed us to follow with them, easily and naturally, the march of events. But this is not done; on the contrary, we are allowed to see very little of the out-breaking and progress of the Irish rebellion. Attention is diverted from it by a very improbable and unnecessarily complicated plot, so little reconcilable with our notions of truth and nature, that it communicates an air of improbability even to those parts of the narrative which are so. The character of Belinda St John is little better than the common staple of a tenth-rate romance heroine; nor is Sir William Judkin much superior to the usual run of fascinating villains, who draw forth the sighs of those sempstresses that peruse the volumes of the Minerva Press. To these defects must be added that of prolixity. A whole chapter of fifteen pages is appropriated to the description of the militia and yeomanry of the county of Wexford; and we should not do justice to the completeness of the description, if we were not to say that, to the best of our belief, no part of their accoutrements is forgotten. Mr Puff's description of Queen Elizabeth's side-saddle, (a description unhappily lost to the world,) could alone have furnished a worthy parallel. The personages in this tale, especially those who are in humble life, talk a great deal too much, and often inappropriately; and whenever we approach an interesting event, we are kept provokingly long in tantalizing suspense. Though [*The Croppy*] is, on these accounts, inferior to some of Mr Banim's earlier performances, it is not to be supposed that it does not contain passages which display the characteristic vigour of his style. (pp. 415-17)

Many of the faults which appear in [*The Croppy*], are also perceptible in Mr Banim's last work, [*The Denounced*]. It consists of two tales, *The Last Baron of Crana,* and *The Conformists,* of which the latter is the best. The former is not uninteresting, and contains pretty good materials for a melo-drama; but we cannot venture to extend our praise much farther. The latter is at once more forcible and more simple—relying for its effect rather on the developement of character than on intricacies of plot, unexpected turns, and mysterious complications of events. It illustrates, very interestingly, the effects of one of those many forms which Anti-Catholic tyranny assumed, during that golden age of intolerance which succeeded the revolution of 1688;—of that cunningly oppressive statute, which, in the hope to keep clipped the ever-growing wings of Roman Catholic power, deprived the obnoxious sect of a free participation in the blessings of education; and made it penal for any Papist to exercise the calling of schoolmaster, or even to give instructions as tutor in a private house. . . . The evils resulting from such a state of things, are well shown in the tale of *The Conformists;* where Mr D'Arcy, a Roman Catholic gentleman, having sent abroad, for education, his eldest son, finds it difficult to educate the second, whom he is obliged to retain at home. Daniel D'Arcy is thus neglected; and at length, when on the verge of manhood, is awakened to a painful sense of the disadvantages under which he has laboured. The growing feeling of inferiority and of wrongs, the desire of improvement, and the inability to gain it, acting upon a proud and sensitive temperament, are extremely well described. Daniel D'Arcy reminds us a little of the author's John Nowlan; and the developement of his wayward, moody, impassioned character, is managed with almost equal skill, and proves Mr Banim to be no mean proficient in displaying the morbid anatomy of our moral nature. There are many striking scenes in this tale, the whole of which is well calculated to rivet the attention. (pp. 419-20)

> [*T. H. Lister*], "Novels Descriptive of Irish Life," *in* The Edinburgh Review, *Vol. LII, No. CIV, January, 1831, pp. 410-31.**

ALLAN CUNNINGHAM (essay date 1834)

[*Cunningham reviews the qualities of the* Tales, by the O'Hara Family *responsible for the extremes of opinion concerning John Banim's writing ability.*]

On the novels of John Banim the world has pronounced, on the whole, a very favourable opinion; and, as it seems not to have been taken hastily up, nor to have been influenced improperly, the opinion may be deemed deliberate and right. Yet I have heard him spoken of as the greatest of all novelists, when the greatest that ever lived was still living; and I have, likewise, heard him condemned, as prolix, extravagant, and unnatural. It is not easy to decide, where such difference of opinion is entertained among men of taste; but it is quite easy to see in the works of Banim, extraordinary breadth, and dramatic power, and life-like vigour of character, and yet feel that he overflows with words, says a hundred idle things, and pursues conversations till they grow tedious and want coherence and proportion. It is not from what he seems in the eyes of the English nation that he ought to be judged, but from what estimation he has won among those whose manners he has described, and to whom he has given strong passions, indignant bursts of patriotism, and overflowings of tenderness and love. The character of the two islands is in many things different, and works which profess to reflect the spirit, and manners, and feelings of the Irish, should be judged in the spirit of those they personate. To me, the wild fits of despair and exultation, of enthusiasm and despondency, of generosity and guile, which are so abundant in the *O'Hara Tales,* and other stories from the same author, are seriously overstrained, and sometimes unnatural, though redeemed by ten thousand touches of truth and feeling. Yet I have no doubt—indeed I know it—that they have much of the Green Isle in them, and must be looked upon, in many respects, as strictly historic as well as domestic. It would have been better, however, had it been the pleasure of the author, to have sobered them down a little—there is more wild action, wild speaking, and passion, and impulse, than is graceful and becoming. (pp. 179-81)

> *Allan Cunningham, "John Banim," in his* Biographical and Critical History of the British Literature of the Last Fifty Years, *Baudry's Foreign Library, 1834, pp. 179-81.*

TAIT'S EDINBURGH MAGAZINE (essay date 1842)

[*In this favorable review of* Father Connell, *the critic predicts for the novel a lasting fame based on the depiction of this "fascinating" Catholic priest and concludes with an admonition to the clergy of England and Scotland to look to Father Connell "and go and do likewise."*]

The close of the publishing season, if it can now be said ever to know a close, is, in 1842, its most brilliant period;—so far at least as respects the daily bread of the large majority of the English "reading public:" namely, novels, romances, and poetry.... [One] of them, *Father Connell,*—is destined to an existence which must extend far beyond the *season,* and add fresh laurels to the most national and pathetic of the imaginative writers of Ireland. Although the name of the O'Hara Family were not emblazoned on the title-page of *Father Connell,* no one who has perused *Crohoore of the Bill-Hook, John Doe,* or *The Nowlans,* could for a moment remain in doubt as to its authorship. The new work possesses, in a lavish degree, all the beauties, and also the idiosyncracies, the peculiarities, the strong mannerism of Banim. It displays his peculiar power of working out strong effects by means apparently the most rude and simple; of fathoming the depths and threading the intricacies of that greatest of all puzzles and mysteries,—the human heart; and especially of those hearts carried in Irish bosoms, in which the horrible and the ludicrous, the piteous, and the humorously grotesque, are either found in close proximity or in fantastic combination. It is the charm of Banim's writings, that all his pictures, though true in design to universal nature, are coloured with the hues of Irish fancy, and are, in style and costume, strictly national. Banim is indeed nothing if not Irish; and his fictions cannot be appreciated by those who do not relish them the more for this exclusiveness. If less national in his feelings, partialities, and even prejudices, he would, in our opinion, be a much less powerful fictionist, and less worthy of admiration, though probably much more popular with the ordinary class of English readers.

Than Father Connell, the hero and the *heart* of this new story, Mr. Banim has never painted anything more perfect, more true, or half so morally beautiful. Whatever is finest in the characters of Chaucer's good Priest, of the Vicar of Wakefield, or of Abraham Adams, meets in Father Connell, whose heart is a perpetual well-spring of overflowing love, and softest charity, and milkiest human kindliness. As good Protestants, we could be almost jealous of a Roman Catholic priest being made so very fascinating to the affections, while to the judgment he is faultless; especially as it seems impossible that Father Connell, unless vowed to celibacy, could have been, to the same degree, the pitiful and tender father, as well as the watchful pastor of his little flock. His locality is one which Banim has often painted; a small provincial third or fourth-rate ancient city, with its old-fashioned shopkeepers, petty tradesmen and vagrant mendicants; not without its religious and party jealousies and animosities; but with an under current of kindness and neighbourly feeling running through all, and brought into play by casual events. The *personnel* of the good priest is in all probability a portrait from the life; which some minute traits of identity, such as "his fingers closing on the palms of his hands, and almost always working against them," make almost a certainty. He was a hale sturdy man, of at least seventy-five, "yet without any indication of old age about him."

> His face showed scarce a wrinkle, and it was florid.... His forehead was expansive, and, at the temples, square; his eyes were blue, and

generally expressing thought, and abstraction. . . .

But above all, there was about his countenance the indications of a great singleness, and primitiveness, and beauty of character. . . .

(p. 458)

A painter could paint Father Connell from the description given. Without being the ideal of an Apostle, his figure, countenance, manners, and dress harmonize well with his genuine character of the most benevolent of Irish priests, the most kindly-natured of human beings. And such he is from first to last,—whether cherishing the orphan, comforting the afflicted, reproving the vicious in the spirit of the purest love, or making the most heroic sacrifices for those he loved, and to whom he was bound by his personal feelings as much as by his pastoral office. (pp. 458-59)

[We] purposely refrain from marring the effect of a highly interesting plot, by hinting at its progress and developement. After many thrilling scenes have harrowed the reader, it ends happily. Poetic justice is rigidly dispensed; and the sudden death of the aged Father Connell, while on an errand of love and mercy for his orphan protégé, to which his feeble strength was unequal, is, at last, more a transfiguration, an apotheosis, forming a suitable close to his divine life, than the mortal agony of death. At first sight, one is indeed disposed to grumble at this stroke, and to wish that the venerable Father had lingered yet a little while on earth, to enjoy the sight of the happiness which he had so long ministered to create. But it is better as it is. (p. 474)

Do the established clergy wish to recover their influence over the people of England and Scotland? Let them look to Father Connell, and go and do likewise. (p. 475)

A review of "Father Connell: A Novel," in Tait's Edinburgh Magazine, *Vol. IX, No. CIII, July, 1842, pp. 458-75.*

R. H. HORNE (essay date 1844)

[*Horne examines* Crohoore of the Bill-Hook *and* The Nowlans *and declares John Banim Ireland's "true dramatic historian."*]

The author of the *O'Hara Tales* stands pre-eminent among the delineators of Irish character, and quite distinct from the mere painters of Irish manners. He goes to the very heart and soul of the matter. He is neither the eulogist nor the vilifier, neither the patronising apologist, nor the caricaturist of his countrymen, but their true dramatic historian. Fiction such as his, is truer than any history, because it deals not only with facts and their causes, but with the springs of motive and action. It not only details circumstances, but probes into and discovers the living elements on which circumstances operate. His Irishmen are not strange, unaccountable creatures, but members of the great human family, with a temperament of their own, marking a peculiar race, and his Irishwomen are in especial drawn with the utmost truth and depth of feeling. He knows well the sources of those bitter waters which have converted the impulsive, generous, simple-minded, humorous, and irascible race with whom he has to deal, into lawless ruffians, or unprincipled knaves. He loves to paint the national character in its genial state, ardent in love, constant in friendship, with a ready tear for the mourner, and a ready laugh for the reveller, overflowing with gratitude for kindness, with open hand and heart, and unsuspicious as a child; and reversing the picture, to show that same character goaded by oppression and contemptuous injustice, into a cruel mocking demon in human form, or into some reckless, libertine, idle, hopeless tattered rascal. The likeness cannot be disputed. The description carries internal evidence with it. Whoever has been in Ireland remembers illustrations of it, and begins to discover the how and the why of things which before puzzled him. Even those who have never been in Ireland, cannot have gone through their lives without observing the cheerfulness, humour, and gaiety of its natives, even under depressing circumstances, their natural politeness, the warmth of their gratitude, their ready helpfulness, all evidences of a character to be moulded into excellent good form by love and kindness. The reverse of the picture need not be dwelt on. It is the theme of all the world. Irish reprobates and Irish criminals are plentiful. Banim and some few others can teach why they are so.

In the small compass of nine pages of Banim's admirable story called *Crohoore of the Bill-Hook,* there is contained what may be called the natural history of "White-boyism," and in those pages is comprised the philosophy of the whole matter, with its illustrations in human tears and drops of blood. In the vivid and exciting description of the White-boy outrage on the tithe-proctor, where the remorseless cruelty is rendered more revolting by its accompaniment of the never-absent Irish humour that makes the torturer comfort his wretched victim before he cuts off his ears, with "Don't be the laste unasy in yoursef, a-gra; you may be right sartin I'll do the thing nate and handy"— how finely does the author claim and obtain impartial justice for the perpetrators, at the tribunal of eternal truth, by the few words with which he prefaces his dreadful narrative. "The legal retribution," says he, "visited on Damien and Ravaillac has found its careful registers: nor in this transcript of real scenes, shall the illegal violence done to an Irish tithe-proctor, want true and courageous historians." Who that has ever had his soul sickened by even a glance into the cold methodical detail of the exquisite tortures, that were each day, and day after day, applied to Ravaillac—the pincers, the fire, the rack, the screw—while the "Do not drive my soul to despair!" shrieked out in vain, except to be recorded by the witnessing secretary—every agonized exclamation being carefully noted— who does not feel the force of those words? Despotic power had transformed these legal and highly-polished tormentors into devils. Ignorance, wrong, and ruin had converted those illegal and outcast men of impulse, into mocking savages. Individual character and varied circumstance, acting and re-acting discordantly, these make up the mystery of human woe. Rise to a sufficient elevation, and the criminals might be seen to change places, or all fade into one mass of suffering wanderers in the dark, concerning whom horror and hatred would turn into deep pity; and tears and an effort to save take the place of retribution. (pp. 143-46)

Banim's conception of his subject is equal to his skill in the development of character. He has always a definite aim and purpose, and always a plot. However elaborately he may finish his individual figures, they are always skilfully grouped, and all the groups together make an harmonious whole. His management of his subject is equally fine. He invests it with an interest, humorous, terrible, or pathetic. We are sufficiently behind the scenes to feel with and for his characters, and to attach due importance to his incidents, yet he does not disclose his "mystery" till the proper moment. *Crohoore,* is an excellent illustration of this. We defy any one, unless he resort to the unjustifiable expedient of "looking at the end," to divine how all will be explained to his heart's ease and thorough satisfaction at last.

The thrilling interest attached to the history of the young priest in *The Nowlans,* affords another instance of the power and passion with which this author works out his conceptions. The struggle between nature and conscience, unnaturally opposed as they are by the vow of celibacy, is here rendered more terrible in its effect by the youth and the ardent, impetuous character of the priest, which fight desperately against his high sense of duty and devotion to his faith. The lovely and refined character of Lettey, her sweet, tender, trustful, artless, self-sacrificing spirit, and her excessive yet trembling love for him, obliterating from her consciousness all thought of her own superior station and fortune—all this enhances the deadly effort it cost them to part for ever, engages our deepest sympathies, and carries us along with them in their horror-stricken flight *together,* when that interview which they had meant to be their last on earth, has united their fates for ever. Then follow the cruel persecution of the world, the vain struggle with its anathema, and the final tragedy—the lone waste cabin in the lone field surrounded by the darkness of night, by the snow and winter wind; the door torn from its hinges and raised on four stones from off the wet floor; upon it the corpse of the beautiful young woman clasping the dead infant to her breast; the rush-light stuck in a lump of yellow clay flickering by their side; at their feet, the young man, kneeling—his face as pale as their's, ''with unwinking distended eyes rivetted on the lowly bier.''

The Nowlans is, perhaps, the finest of Banim's works; but they are all more or less stamped with genius. (pp. 147-49)

> R. H. Horne, ''Banim and the Irish Novelists,'' in his A New Spirit of the Age, Vol. II, *Smith, Elder, and Co.,* 1844, pp. 141-52.*

MICHAEL BANIM   (letter date 1855?)

[The following excerpt is drawn from a letter from Michael that first appeared in Murray's biographical sketch of John in 1855 (see excerpt below); the exact date of the letter's composition is not known. Here, Michael recounts an experience of his that gave John the idea for the character of the priest in The Nowlans.*]*

While pursuing the track of Sarsfield on his route to intercept the reinforcements destined to strengthen the besiegers of Limerick, I journeyed on foot, through the Slieve Bloom Mountains, tracing my way principally by the traditionary information given by the people. I kept an itinerary as I went along, referable, not only to the purpose of my journey, but descriptive also of the peculiar and impressive scenery around me; and of the existing characteristics of a little known, but, as they appear to me, a very fine people. (p. 37)

It was my fate to seek shelter for the night at the house of a farmer named Daniel Kennedy. His warm and comfortable dwelling was in a mountain hollow, known as Fail Dhuiv, or the Black Glen. The peculiarities of this out of the way homestead, the appearance of the dwellers therein, and the details of the unostentatiously hospitable reception given to me, were faithfully reported in my note-book. Extracted thence, almost word for word, my veritable account forms the introduction to the tale of *The Nowlans.* There was a sick son on the night of my visit occupying the stranger's bedroom, about whom the good woman of the house and her daughters appeared to be most anxious. I could not, for this reason, be accommodated

in the apartment usually reserved for guests, and my bed was made up on the kitchen table. The homemade sheets and blankets white as snow, and redolent of the sweet mountain breeze in which they had been bleached, were most inviting to a weary pedestrian, as I was; and I slept luxuriously that night on the kitchen table, under the roof of Daniel Kennedy of Fail Dhuiv.

The circumstance of the sick son, who, I could learn, had been away, and who, in his illness, had come home to seek the ministry of his affectionate kindred, gave the idea, and no more than the idea, of John Nowlan—the hero of the new tale. (pp. 37-8)

> Michael Banim, in an extract from a letter in 1855? in The Irish Quarterly Review, *Vol. V, No. XVII, March, 1855, pp. 37-8.*

[PATRICK JOSEPH MURRAY]   (essay date 1855)

[In the following excerpt, Murray, John Banim's biographer, favorably reviews The Nowlans.*]*

It would, perhaps, be almost impossible to suggest any plot more powerfully conceived, and more vigorously elaborated than that of *The Nowlans.* It is, in truth, the analysis of passion: love in every phase—its pathos and its rage; and when we close the book, saddened by the fate of poor *Letty Nowlan,* and her misguided lover, we feel how truly the epigraph which Banim selected from Gray describes the lot of the hero and heroine:—

> These shall the fury passions tear—
> The vultures of the mind.

The whole vigor of Banim's genius was engaged in the construction of this novel; and it was, in its first edition, disfigured by some passages which his more sober judgment led him afterwards to omit. If however, we take this novel, solely as a specimen of what Banim's genius could enable him to achieve, and if we compare *all* its parts, considering them as a whole, it must be classed amongst the most powerful fictions of the time, and if not the first, certainly of the first rank. Doubtless if it be not taken as a whole, the melodramatic character appears too boldly, but this is an objection which might, with equal force, be urged against *The Bride of Lammermoor,* and *Eugene Aram.* (p. 44)

> [Patrick Joseph Murray], ''John Banim: Part IV,'' in The Irish Quarterly Review, *Vol. V, No. XVII, March, 1855, pp. 25-48.*

A LOVER OF JUSTICE   (letter date 1855)

[Responding to a claim published in Notes and Queries *by William John Fitzpatrick that Michael Banim wrote* Crohoore of the Bill-Hook *and* The Croppy, *the impassioned writer of this letter to the editor of the* Brighton Guardian *not only insists that John alone was responsible for these two novels, but adds that Michael neglected his impoverished brother. Fitzpatrick later responded to this letter, defending the authority upon which he had made his claim of Michael's authorship (see excerpt dated 1855).]*

Sir.—Permit me through the medium of your very widely circulated Journal to correct a misrepresentation made in the last number of *Notes and Queries* by a person signing himself ''William John Fitzpatrick.'' This gentleman . . . says ''The interesting *Tales of the O'Hara Family,* which some thirty years ago excited a marked sensation in literary circles, were until quite recently believed to owe their popularity entirely to John

Banim. A memoir of Mr. Banim at present appearing in the *Irish Quarterly Review* informs the public that his brother Michael, ex-Mayor of Kilkenny, wrote *Crohoore of the Bill-hook*, [*The Croppy*],—in fact, some of the very best of the *O'Hara Tales*." Now, Sir, let me inform the public through your columns, that a greater misrepresentation was never sent to print than the above passage from *Notes and Queries*. The fact is, that the late John Banim not only composed every line of *Crohoore of the Bill-hook* from his own brain, but also transcribed every line of it with his own weary hand, and that, too, at a period when he was not even on speaking terms with his brother Michael, better known as "the shabby Mayor of Kilkenny;" and at that very period when *Crohoore* was written poor John Banim was in a state of beggary and without a coat, and after a weary day's labor at this exquisite work he would stroll out in the dark with an old black cloth round his shoulders to roam by the river side for a breath of air, while his ex-mayorship Michael, who wishes to obtain some new installation or other honour on borrowed plumes, by robbing the dead of his fame, was luxuriating on homefed mutton and "mountain dew" in the town of Kilkenny, while (not *the individual*, as Mr. Fitzpatrick is pleased to call him) the great John Banim was, hungry, thirsty, and weary, weaving from his own brain that truly beautiful work for the amusement of an admiring English public. Now, Sir, regarding the authorship of that splendid Novel, [*The Croppy*], Mr. Michael Banim, the ex-mayor of Kilkenny, was giving and attending "Harvest Homes," and dancing Irish-jigs in the Province of Leinster, while the poor half-starved author, John Banim, was writing [*The Croppy*] at the hospitable home of the late Mr. W. Donnell, of Balinlig House, in the Vale of Glenariff, country Antrim, Province of Ulster, North of Ireland. And the curious English traveller in passing through the beautiful valley of Glenariff can without any trouble see the very room in Balinlig house where John Banim, alone and unaided, wrote and composed every line of that exquisite Novel *The Croppy;* and that, too, when his brother Michael would not give the "Literary Madman," as he was pleased to call poor John, one single sixpence to save him from starvation. . . . [The] friends of the ex-mayor may with impunity think that time has cast oblivion over the life and sufferings of the departed Novelist, and that now, in this distant period they may assert what they please, and pluck the laurel from the grave of him who earned it well. But if the readers of *Notes and Queries* take the trouble of inquiring who is the writer of the memoir of "this *individual*," they will find it is written by Mr. Fitzpatrick himself, or else some other minion of the ex-shabby mayor of Kilkenny, who have some worldly project to carry out by blasting the fame of a truly great Novelist, who destroyed his health at the midnight lamp and shortened his life in the cause of literature. If the shade of the late John Banim could arise from his lowly grave and read Mr. Fitzpatrick's article in the last number of *Notes and Queries*, with what truth it might exclaim,

> Amid the stranger throng
> Enemies, I have none;
> But from my would-be friends and relatives,
> May Heaven save my fame.

> I am, Sir, your obedient servant,
> A Lover of Justice.
> (pp. i-iii)

A Lover of Justice, in a letter to the editor of the "Brighton Guardian" on November 14, 1855, in The Irish Quarterly Review, *Vol. VI, No. XXI, March, 1856, pp. i-iii.*

ONE OF THE READERS AND ADMIRERS OF *THE O'HARA TALES* (letter date 1855)

[*Disputing the claims of "A Lover of Justice" (see excerpt dated 1855), the writer of this letter to the editor of the* Brighton Herald *points to John and Michael's published letters as evidence of their close personal and literary relationship.*]

Sir.—In the last number of the *Brighton Guardian* a writer who signs himself "A Lover of Justice," makes a fierce attack upon William John Fitzpatrick for stating, in a recent number of *Notes and Queries,* that "Michael Banim, now ex-Mayor of Kilkenny, was the author of *Crohoore of the Bill-hook, The Croppy,*—in fact some of the best of the *O'Hara Tales*." . . . (p. iii)

Now, as this question of authorship is one that is interesting to the general public, perhaps you will allow me a portion of your space to endeavour to throw some light upon it. That the *Tales by the O'Hara Family* were the joint production of John and Michael Banim has never, I believe, been questioned until the present moment; and it is proved by the published correspondence of John Banim. It is new to me, too, that John and Michael Banim were ever upon bad terms. But if they ever were, certainly it could not of been at the time of the writing of these *Tales;* for upon this point, too, we have the evidence of John's own letters. These letters to Michael, extend over the period of John's residence in London from 1822, when he first arrived in town, up to 1825, when the *O'Hara Tales* made their appearance, and in these letters frequent reference is made by John to the tale that Michael had undertaken to contribute to the collection: and, moreover, there is internal evidence in these letters to prove that the tale in question was *Crohoore of the Bill-hook*. (pp. iii-iv)

Why so fierce an onslaught should have been made upon Mr. Michael Banim by "A Lover of Justice," I cannot conceive. The fact of his being ex-Mayor of Kilkenny, upon which the writer dwells, proves nothing against his ability as a writer. I have only taken up the pen as a matter of literary justice, and have no interest in the question of the authorship except as

One of the Readers and Admirers of *The O'Hara Tales*.
(p. vi)

One of the Readers and Admirers of "The O'Hara Tales," in a letter to the editor of the "Brighton Herald" on November 17, 1855, in The Irish Quarterly Review, *Vol. VI, No. XXI, March, 1856, pp. iii-vi.*

WILLIAM JOHN FITZPATRICK (letter date 1855)

[*In this letter to the editor of the* Brighton Guardian, *Fitzpatrick responds to the letter from "A Lover of Justice," who fiercely denied Fitzpatrick's claim that Michael Banim wrote* Crohoore of the Bill-Hook *and* The Croppy *(see excerpt dated 1855). Defending his assertion, Fitzpatrick uses as evidence a quote from the Irish novelist William Carleton, as well as the letters of Michael and John Banim detailing their method of collaboration.*]

Sir,—It was only by chance that I saw on this morning, for the first time, your journal of Wednesday, November 14th; and had it not been for the considerateness of some unknown English friend, who sent it even at the eleventh hour, I might never have had an opportunity of replying to a letter which contains most offensive references to me, and that worthy, unobtrusive, and respectable man, Michael Banim, Ex Mayor of Kilkenny. (p. vi)

I did not make the assertion relative to Banim's *Tales* without producing my authority. On that authority, let the merits of the case be judged. The *Irish Quarterly Review* is a work of high respectability and genius. For nearly two years, the life of Banim, written by the Editor, has been regularly appearing in that serial. Banim's private correspondence and papers, have been placed at the disposal of the Editor—a gentleman, well known and respected in literary, and general society, at the Bar, and in Alma Mater. Your correspondent supports, that if the public inquire who is the author of the memoir, *"they will find it is written by Mr. Fitzpatrick himself."* Although it is a biography which any Irishman might feel proud to have written, I emphatically deny all claim to the authorship.

I shall now proceed to give in detail, my authorities for the assertion which your correspondent in his wrath, has appealed to the public to analyse and judge.

In the *Irish Quarterly Review* for December, 1854, p. 830, appears an interesting account of the origin of those tales, during a conference between the brothers, John and Michael, and it concludes with these words:—"And thus amid the green fields of Inistiogue were the *Tales of the O'Hara Family* planned, and a joint system of writing commenced, which rivalled in popularity, the *Canterbury Tales* by the Sisters Lee." From the manner in which your correspondent heads his letter, "Tales by the O'Hara Family," it would appear as if he too believed their production to be through the joint agency of the brothers.

At page 850 is described Michael Banim's literary labours, amid the most onerous occupation, . . . "his fancy was busily at work, weaving the scenes of his narrative, and when he retired to his room at night, he committed the already formed scenes to paper, and the early morning generally found him clothing his thoughts in words, and thus the powerful story of *Crohoore of the Bill-Hook* was composed and written. The first portion of the MS. was transmitted to John for perusal late in 1823. By return of post a letter of praise and thanks was written to Michael—entreaties for more were pressingly urged. The progress was necessarily slow, but scrap by scrap it was forwarded; and, as had been agreed upon, John's portion of the work, *The Fetches* and *John Doe,* were sent to Michael, each brother acting as critic to the other, and thus the *nom de plume, Tales by the O'Hara Family,* was in every point a reality, John taking the name *Abel O'Hara,* Michael assuming that of *Barnes O'Hara.*"

The interesting private letters from John Banim to his brother, with which the the memoir is sprinkled, exhibit the full secret of their *modus operandi.* Some of John's letters are playfully signed "Abel O'Hara."

The revelation that *Crohoore of the Bill-Hook* (the best tale of the series) was not written by John Banim greatly surprised me, and early last May I called the attention of that distinguished Irish novelist, William Carleton, to it as remarkable. "I always knew," replied Carleton, "that *Crohoore of the Bill-Hook* was Michael's and not John's." Carleton knew John Banim intimately, and wrote that interesting memoir of him which appeared in the *Nation* shortly after his death.

With respect to the powerfully written novel of *The Croppy* I have referred to the *Irish Quarterly* for June, 1855, and at pp. 234 and 235 I find the fullest particulars given of the composition of *The Croppy.* The work was written by Michael, and not John Banim. It is, however, an understood thing, that the brothers criticised and revised each other's *Tales;* and if John was really seen by the late Mr. W. Donnell (as your corre-

spondent says) poring over *The Croppy* in 1827, and even transcribing portions of it, it argues nothing. Your rather pert correspondent would do well to refer to the *Quarterly,* and read the truly affectionate letters from John to his brother Michael, at this and other periods. . . . If he thinks that the Biography alluded to is written in dispraising terms of John Banim, he is mistaken. The biographer is absolutely in love with John's character throughout—in fact too much so for the taste of many. Your correspondent, who signs himself "A Lover of Justice," . . . would perhaps be nearer the truth to subscribe "A Lover of Slander." . . . (pp. vii-viii)

For myself, I may say, I was never a personal friend of John Banim's, much less a relative. I never even saw him. The many affectionate letters written in the fullest confidence, by John and his wife, to Michael (the originals of which may doubtless be viewed, if necessary) sufficiently refute the rabid drivelling of a *Lover of Slander.* He has been rioting in the exuberance of a fortnight's unrefuted calumny. By to-morrow's post I will forward his production to the ex-mayor of Kilkenny, and let that gentleman deal with the writer, as he thinks fit. Your correspondent, like most slanderers, wears a mask. He trembles to appear before the public with his name and address.

I have the honour to be, Sir,
Your very humble servant,
William John Fitzpatrick.
(p. ix)

William John Fitzpatrick, in a letter to the editor of the "Brighton Guardian" on November 28, 1855, in The Irish Quarterly Review, *Vol. VI, No. XXI, March, 1856, pp. vi-ix.*

A LOVER OF JUSTICE   (letter date 1855)

[*Responding to the letter by "One of the Readers and Admirers of* The O'Hara Tales" *(see excerpt dated 1855), this critic defends the portrait of Michael Banim that was presented in an earlier article (see excerpt by "A Lover of Justice" dated 1855).*]

Sir, facts are stubborn things, which remain the same despite of every misrepresentation. I was therefore truly startled by such a strange announcement in *Notes and Queries,* that John Banim, whose authorship of the best of the *Tales of the O'Hara Family* has been a well established fact for *"thirty years,"* should have his fame nibbled at by an unknown writer in a recent number of the *Irish Quarterly Review;* and as the question of authorship is one of interest to the general public, I felt it my duty to state through the columns of your widely circulated journal, that a greater misrepresentation was never sent to print.

A writer in the *Brighton Herald* of the 17th of this month wishes to overturn my statement of authentic facts by a pile of inconsistent paragraphs which tell nothing. (p. ix)

This writer in the *Herald* backs the *Irish Quarterly Review* in the truth of its statement, that for thirty years John Banim was known as the recognised author of the *O'Hara Tales,* that he derived a great popularity from them, and that the literary world was quite in a sensation with his productions; but that a writer of a memoir *last year* brings to light that his brother Michael was the author. In another part the writer in the *Herald* states that Michael Banim under the name of Barnes O'Hara, was *well known* as one of the authors of the O'Hara tales.

Now in the name of common sense how do these two statements chime? If Michael was well known as the author of *Crohoore of the Bill Hook, The Croppy,* &c., &c., why would John be enjoying the undisputed fame for so many long years until a writer comes forward *last year* to accuse him of going on borrowed plumes? Is it consistent with human nature that Michael would allow John Banim to usurp his fame and his labours for so many years without producing proofs to show the world that he was wronged? And every one who had the honour of knowing the late John Banim,—and many are still alive—will bear me out that he was the very last man on earth to soar on *Aura popularis,* unless it was his right to do so. . . .

[The] writer in the *Herald* says, that if the brothers were not on speaking terms, they were on affectionate writing terms. Now does not every body know that there never yet existed two brothers who have not been on both speaking terms and writing terms at some period of their lives, although they may have been on bad terms both before and after? This writer also refers me to a "printed correspondence" in the *Irish Quarterly Review for December* 1854. But does he think I am so unwise as to pin my faith to a *printed* correspondence produced at the end of thirty years? I cannot see the water-marks on paper, or the genuine post-marks of the letters in print. . . . (p. x)

[Why] *is he not also sagacious enough to know that John Banim had a dear bosom friend and companion called Michael B—,* independently of his brother Michael? (p. xi)

[The] writer in the *Herald* sets up an unnecessary defence of the cleverness of the ex-Mayor of Kilkenny, and says "that John had a much higher respect for the ability of Michael than a Lover of Justice has." That statement is very wide of the truth; for I always considered Michael to be a clever man, and I am aware that he has written some good things, although his genius was far below that enjoyed by his departed brother. . . . There was a vein of composition in every one of the Banim family; but in John alone did it find "a local habitation and a name." . . . Without in any way depreciating the literary ability of Michael Banim, I again repeat, from my full knowledge of the facts, that a greater misrepresentation was never sent to print than that John Banim was *not* the author of *The Croppy, Crohoore of the Billhook, The Boyne Water,* &c. Twelve years before the *Irish Quarterly Review* began to nibble at John Banim's fame, I held in the hand that now traces this letter portions of the original draughts of the above-named works in John Banim's own writing, and with his own corrections and interlineations, and I could at this moment,—if I were at liberty to do so,—point to the family who still hold them as sacred heir-looms of the great novelist; but the pear is not yet ripe enough to render such a disinterment necessary. Enough, the person who holds these literary treasures was from boyhood the bosom friend, often the companion, and always the confidant, of all the joys and sorrows of poor suffering, but gifted John Banim. The original draught of *The Croppy* amused me much, for in it he had made rattling Bill Nale the father of Eliza, and old Nanny the knitter her grandmother; but a Cork gentleman to whom he submitted the plot laughed at him for giving such strange relations to so gentle and elegant a lady as Eliza. John Banim took the hint, and in his final draught he made Bill the father of her beautiful, stern, and haughty friend. (pp. xi-xii)

In conclusion, I beg to correct a typographical error in my last letter in your columns; namely, that John Banim wrote every line with his own weary hand. This should have been, "he invented every line in his own weary brain." The sentence

must have been blundered either by your printers, readers, or by myself in the haste of writing it; but the contrary was the fact. John Banim had a heartsick horror of copying anything he composed; he had three friends in the distance who generally performed that task. Two of them were my personal friends, and the third was Michael Banim; and thus arose the latter day fiction that Michael was the author of some of John's best works. But it is quite a common thing in London for a hard-working author to send his manuscript written illegibly to a brother at leisure in the distance, to write out clear for the press, put slight alterations, if necessary, if the brother from a knowledge of the facts described were competent to do so, which no doubt, Michael was in reference to the *O'Hara Tales;* and return it slip by slip through the post. And this may account for John's bantering Michael thus: "Paint for me to the life our old parish priest, hat, wig, jock-coat, worsted stockings, shoe-buckle, and all;" for when the brothers were on good terms Michael (who was a good critic) had a habit of altering John's sentiments in a manner disagreeable to the great Novelist's feeling and *amour propre.* It is now many years since poor John Banim's death closed a chequered career, embittered at its close by a painful illness, in which the great Novelist was forced to use crutches, but I have not heard that since that event Michael has published any work whatever, which would hardly be the case were he the "powerful" writer which the despoilers of John's fame would represent him.

Hoping this will fully satisfy Mr. Fitzpatrick and his defender in the *Brighton Herald,*

I am, Sir, your obedient servant,
A Lover of Justice.
(pp. xii-xiii)

A Lover of Justice, in a letter to the editor of the "Brighton Guardian" on November 28, 1855, in The Irish Quarterly Review, *Vol. VI, No. XXI, March, 1856, pp. ix-xiii.*

MICHAEL BANIM   (letter date 1855?)

[*In a letter to Murray, excerpted below, Michael describes how he and John developed the idea for and composed* Father Connell, *the last novel on which they collaborated.*]

I had laid by my pen to devote myself entirely to business from the period of my coadjutor's break down in 1833.—It will be recollected, that in one of the letters from which I have extracted, my brother threw out the suggestion, that we should write a novel—of which an old parish priest, might be the hero—In 1840, five years after his return home, relinquishing on his own part all hope of being able to take up anything requiring continuous application, he urged me to resume my occupation—under his immediate supervision.

I had, some time before, filled a note book with materials referrible to the latest agrarian confederacy, that had disturbed our neighbourhood; the actors in which had bestowed on themselves, the fantastical name of 'Whitefeet.' With some of the principal leaders of this lawless and wide spread combination I had held intercourse—I had gained a knowledge of their signs and passwords, and obtained an insight into their views and proceedings. I proposed a tale wherein my materials could be used; my adviser differed with me.

'We have given,' he said, 'perhaps too much of the dark side of the Irish character; let us, for the present, treat of the amiable; enough of it is around us—I once mentioned our old parish priest to you; the good, the childishly innocent, and yet the wise Father O'Donnell—we have only to take him as he really was, and if we succeed in drawing him lifelike, he must be reverenced and loved, as we used to love and reverence him.'

I sat down as proposed, when time, not indispensably engaged otherwise, enabled me to do so—I read for my brother each chapter as the tale progressed, and when I had put it out of hands, he took it up for revision and amendment. I have, ever since, regretted having allowed him to do this. According to his conception the tale required extensive alterations as to style and management: I may have differed with him; but, adhering to our original mode of proceeding, I did not object, either to substitution or condensation. The task was too continuous, for his disorganised brain, and I fear that, although his daughter then fifteen, and a young man who resided near the cottage, acted as occasional amanuenses, his death was hastened by his more than usual occupation on the tale of *Father Connell*. In some instances the original was condensed; and one entire chapter substituted.

Father Connell was the last joint work of The O'Hara Family. John's attending physician, although not pronouncing positively, led me to think, he might have held out, longer if he had not wrought, for him too ardently, at this book.

Not presuming for one moment, that the tale of *Father Connell* possesses merit as a novel, I may be permitted to remark, that it is so far of value, inasmuch as the character of the old priest who governed the parish of St. John in Kilkenny, when my brother and I attended in our muslin surplices at his vesper chair, and partook of his twelfth night feast of cakes and ale, is attempted to be faithfully pourtrayed. No matter how meagre may be the colouring, or how ill-disposed the lights and shadows, and relief—the likeness is a true one, without flattery or exaggeration; no virtue feigned, or habit imagined—such as he is given under the name of 'Father Connell' was our parish priest, the Rev. Richard O'Donnell, Roman Catholic Dean of Ossory—when the writers of the tale were young. (pp. 848-49)

> *Michael Banim, in an extract from a letter to John Murray in 1855? in* The Irish Quarterly Review, *Vol. V, No. XX, December, 1855, pp. 848-49.*

MARY RUSSELL MITFORD   (essay date 1855)

[*Mitford was an English sketch writer, dramatist, poet, novelist, and critic whose legacy to nineteenth-century literature includes some of the most endearing sketches of English country life. In the following excerpt, Mitford discusses John Banim's prose and poetry, praising his "purely original" accounts of Irish life as well as the "intensely national" quality of his writing.*]

John Banim was the founder of that school of Irish novelists, which, always excepting its blameless purity, so much resembles the modern romantic French school, that if it were possible to suspect Messieurs Victor Hugo, Eugène Sue, and Alexander Dumas of reading the English, which they never approach without such ludicrous blunders, one might fancy that many-volumed tribe to have stolen their peculiar inspiration from the O'Hara family. Of a certainty the tales of Mr. Banim were purely original. They had no precursors either in our own language or in any other, and they produced accordingly the sort of impression, more vivid than durable, which highly-colored and deeply-shadowed novelty is sure to make on the public mind. But they are also intensely national. They reflect Irish scenery, Irish character, Irish crime, and Irish virtue, with a general truth which, in spite of their tendency to melo-

dramatic effects, will keep them fresh and life-like for many a day after the mere fashion of the novel of the season shall be past and gone. The last of his works, especially, *Father Connell*, contains the portrait of a parish priest, so exquisitely simple, natural, and tender, that in the whole range of fiction I know nothing more charming. The subject was one that the author loved; witness the following rude, rugged, homely song, which explains so well the imperishable ties which unite the peasant to his pastor.

"SOGGARTH AROON"

> Am I the slave they say,
>   Soggarth Aroon?
> Since you did show the way,
>   Soggarth Aroon,
> *Their* slave no more to be,
> While they would work with me
> Ould Ireland's slavery,
>   Soggarth aroon!

(p. 21)

There is a small and little-known volume of these rough peasant-ballads, full of the same truth and intensity of feeling,—songs which seem destined to be sung at the wakes and patterns of Ireland. But, to say nothing of his fine classical tragedy of *Damon and Pythias*, Mr. Banim, so successful in the delineation of the sweet, delicate, almost idealized girl of the people, has written at least one song that may rival Gerald Griffin in grace and sentiment. A lover sings it to his mistress.

> 'Tis not for love of gold I go,
>   'Tis not for love of fame;
> Though fortune may her smile bestow,
>   And I may win a name,
>   Ailleen;
>   And I may win a name.

(pp. 22-3)

Is it not strange that with such ballads as these of John Banim, Thomas Davis, and Gerald Griffin before us, Mr. Moore, that great and undoubted wit, should pass in the highest English circles for the only song-writer of Ireland? Do people really prefer flowers made of silk and cambric, of gum and wire, the work of human hands however perfect, to such as Mother Earth sends forth in the gushing spring-time, full of sap and odor, sparkling with sunshine and dripping with dew? (p. 24)

> *Mary Russell Mitford, "Irish Authors," in her* Recollections of a Literary Life; or, Books, Places, and People, *Harper & Brothers, Publishers, 1855, pp. 15-24.**

ALFRED M. WILLIAMS   (essay date 1881)

[*In the following excerpt, Williams briefly discusses the* Tales, *by the O'Hara Family and* The Chaunt of the Cholera: Songs for Ireland.]

The series [*Tales by the O'Hara Family*], which was begun by *Crohoore of the Bill Hook*, by Michael, and *The Nowlans*, by John, were recognized at once as powerful and idiomatic pictures of Irish life; and although sometimes overstrained and melodramatic in their incidents, and too obviously copied in some of the characters from originals whose peculiarities were reproduced with too great minuteness, they have a power both in passionate and descriptive passages which has never been rivalled by any other Irish novelist. The *Tales by the O'Hara*

Family, as they were called, were the first to describe the peasant life in Ireland, and to express the religious and political sentiments of the people. Their spirit was dark and gloomy, except where revelling in minute reproductions of home scenes of national life, and they fully represented the indignant spirit of an oppressed and proscribed people. The styles of the two brothers were singularly alike, which is perhaps to be accounted for by the fact that they consulted together about the incidents and language, and revised the manuscripts of each other's works. The novels of Michael Banim, wholly unapprenticed in literature and written in the evenings after days spent in the shop, were quite as powerful and polished as those of John, and the same faults were common to both. (p. 257)

[John Banim's] poems were few in number, and were confined to a small volume entitled, *The Chaunt of the Cholera: Songs for the Irish People,*—published while he was at Boulogne. "The Chaunt of the Cholera" is a vivid and ghastly piece of verse, impressive through its very rudeness; but the gems of the volume are **"Soggarth Aroon,"**—*Priest Dear,*—an address of the peasant to his priest; and the tender poem of **"Ailleen,"** addressed to his wife. . . . Although his poems are so few, John Banim is one of the most national and powerful of the Irish poets. (p. 259)

Alfred M. Williams, "John Banim," in his The Poets and Poetry of Ireland, *James R. Osgood and Company, 1881, pp. 255-64.*

W. B. YEATS (essay date 1891)

[*Yeats was an Irish poet, playwright, and essayist of the late nineteenth and early twentieth centuries. The leading figure of the Irish Renaissance, Yeats was also an active critic of his contemporaries' work. Here, Yeats briefly discusses the close collaboration between the Banims.*]

John Doe and *The Nowlans* are, I imagine, the best of John Banim's stories, and *Father Connell* the best of Michael's. Whether it be justifiable to divide the work of one from the work of the other in this way I do not know. They worked constantly . . . upon each other's stories, and were so alike in faculty that it is impossible to fix with confidence the march lands of either. The genius of John Banim was certainly the more vehement and passionate. He had likewise a faculty for verse absent in his brother. His **"Soggarth Aroon"** is one of the most beautiful and popular of all Irish poems. The greater number of his verses were, however, of no value. (p. 97)

W. B. Yeats, "John and Michael Banim," in Representative Irish Tales, *edited by W. B. Yeats, 1891. Reprint by Colin Smythe, 1979, pp. 93-7.*

HORATIO SHEAFE KRANS (essay date 1903)

[*In this survey of the novels of John and Michael Banim, Krans assesses their merits and faults. He argues that* John Doe, The Nowlans, Crohoore of the Bill-Hook, The Croppy, *and* Father Connell *best represent the brothers' greatest strength as writers: the ability to faithfully depict Irish peasant life.*]

The earliest of the Celtic group of writers were John and Michael Banim. The two brothers were closely associated in their literary work and mutually indebted for criticism and suggestion. John, the younger, had the more decided talent. He was guide and counsellor to Michael, and it was he who took the initiative in their joint literary enterprises.

Of John Banim's stories, *Peter of the Castle* and *The Mayor of Wind Gap,* it need only be said that, relying for effect partly upon romantic incident, partly upon manners-painting of both peasant and gentle life, they excel in neither. *The Last Baron of Crana,* and *The Conformists,* the former a semi-historical novel, have little merit besides that which attaches to them as illustrations, in the way of moderately interesting fiction, of the working of the penal laws. *John Doe,* and *The Nowlans,* by John Banim, *Crohoore of the Bill-Hook, The Croppy,* and *Father Connell,* by Michael Banim, are the tales and novels that best represent the brothers as novelists of peasant life. These works combine graphic realistic powers with a gloomy and unlovely romantic spirit which delights in sensational incident, overstrained excitement, and fevered, high-pitched passion. In John Banim's *The Nowlans* there are impressive and powerful scenes which neither of the brothers has equalled elsewhere. The central situation is grasped and presented with a convincing reality, and is doubtless, in the perfervid passion of the young hero for the girl above him in station, in part the story of the author's ill-regulated and unhappy passion for the love of his youth. The structure of the story is lamentably slovenly. But it is a story informed with tenderness, passion, and power. With these qualities it is to be regretted that the shaping hand of the artist was wanting to express them in a coherent and harmonious form. *Father Connell,* written by Michael Banim, received additions at the hands of John. As a novel it is dull; but as a faithful picture of a Roman Catholic priest in his home, and in his relations with his flock, not without interest.

Michael and John each wrote an historical novel. John Banim's *The Boyne Water,* the author's most elaborate effort, is obviously an imitation of Sir Walter. But it lacks the magic by which the Wizard of the North conjured the past into a life, real, at least, if not quite its own. The author's imagination here proved unequal to his great task, and the book shows throughout the stiffness of a mechanical product in which the material did not become plastic to the touch. Besides this radical defect, the political discussions brought into the story clog the movement of the narrative; and the action is overlaid and obscured by masses of dead historical detail, and ineffective, irrelevant incident. The battle-pieces of the story, however correct from the military point of view, lack the battle-rage and stirring trumpet note of the struggle between the hosts of William and James. And the motives that spurred the combatants are not poured through the story—the Protestants burning to get the Catholics under their feet, and the Catholics aflame with loyalty to a King of their own faith, eager to turn the tables upon their oppressors, and get back the lands torn from them by Cromwell. There is more of the fighting spirit under the frieze coats and beneath the brandished shillelaghs of Carleton's *Battle of the Factions* than in all the clashing hosts of *The Boyne Water.*

Michael Banim's historical novel, *The Croppy,* was made from material close at hand—the Rebellion of '98—of which he heard from the lips of men still living. With all the artistic failings of *The Boyne Water* it still abounds in scenes imaginatively handled; it catches the temper of the antagonists in the struggle; and leaves the reader with impressions of certain phases of the Rebellion that have in them something like the vividness of a personal experience. The subject of *The Croppy* demanded less of its author than was demanded by the great events included in the scope of *The Boyne Water.* Though the latter is a far more careful and elaborate performance, the former has a movement and spirit that make it the more readable of the two.

In the style of these two writers, and in the way they handle their material, there is a curiously close resemblance. In John Banim there is perhaps a more marked tendency, resulting doubtless from his physical infirmities, toward feverish and overstrained passion, but on the whole it would be impossible to distinguish in the work of the brothers, on merely internal evidence, the part for which each was responsible.

The work of the Banims gives no indication of the possession of artistic sense in its authors. Their style is remarkable only for a rude and irresistible eloquence in certain passages; for the rest it is uncouth and loose. The Banims were most successful when they dealt with peasant life. Their pictures of high life were failures. The sensational and melodramatic element was strong in them. They tend more than any other of the Irish novelists to a presentation of turbulent and unchastened passion. They lack the creative power, the strong feeling, the rich humor of Carleton, and the vein of delicate sentiment and graceful poetry of Griffin. (pp. 299-303)

> Horatio Sheafe Krans, "Literary Estimate," in his
> Irish Life in Irish Fiction, The Columbia University
> Press, 1903, pp. 270-326.*

LOUIS LACHAL, S.J.   (essay date 1930)

[Lachal regrets that the Banims have not received recognition for their authentic depiction of the Irish people in the Tales, by the O'Hara Family. Though he finds John's work "more artistic, more literary," Lachal also values Michael's "homely genius" for portraying peasant life.]

The work of the "O'Hara Family" has been to a great extent forgotten. It is regrettable, for John and Michael Banim, who wrote under this *nom-de-plume,* did much for Ireland. They may be called the first national novelists. They were great admirers of Scott, and had the ambition to do for Ireland what Scott did for his country by his tales. (p. 338)

The Banims, in general, gave a true picture of the Irish character, with its bright and dark sides. They, unlike Lover or Lever, were in sympathy with and understood the heart of the people. They showed the Irish, not as the strange, grotesque caricatures so often portrayed in fiction, but as men of noble impulses and generous traits. They saw another side, too. Though the Irishman could be sympathetic, kind, and forgiving, he could become stern, bitter, revengeful.

Ignorance, poverty, and cruelty are shown to exist among the peasantry. But these things have their cause. They are the natural result of religious persecution and political oppression. Later Michael Banim wrote: "It was the object of the authors, while admitting certain and continued lawlessness, to show that causes existed consequently creating the lawlessness. Through the medium of fiction this purpose was constantly kept in view." (p. 340)

Crohoore of the Bill-hook illustrates well the plan of the authors. Its action lies in one of the darkest periods of Irish history, when the peasantry, crushed under the tithe-proctor, middleman, and penal laws, retorted by the savage outrages of the secret societies. One of these societies, the "Whiteboys," is largely dealt with in the book. Michael Banim does not justify outrage, but explains it by a picture of the causes from which it came.

Banim's indictment of the tithe-proctor, personified in the person of Peery Clancy, reveals as loathsome a character as it seems possible to imagine. This villain had become rich from squeezing "from the very, very poorest their last acid shilling: they were his best profit, his fat of the land, his milk and honey." (p. 341)

Among the best known of the other novels of John Banim, *The Nowlans, The Boyne Water, The Conformists, The Last Baron of Crana,* may be cited. *The Boyne Water* is probably his greatest work. The novel is closely modelled on Scott, and scene after scene of the long drama of the Williamite wars passes before the reader. Great historical figures move across the stage. The rival kings and the principal generals are vividly presented. The characters include Sarsfield, Galloping Hogan the Rapparee, Carolan the bard, and many others. The story is well told, while the politics and great questions of the day are thrashed out in its conversations. John Banim shows in this tale as elsewhere his keen eye for natural beauty, and the wild scenery of the Antrim coast is fully described as also the scenes through which Sarsfield passed on his famous ride. The book ends with the treaty of Limerick.

In preparation for this great work John Banim showed extraordinary care. These lines are from a letter to Michael. "I will visit every necessary spot in the north and south; Derry, Lough Neagh, from that down to the Boyne; and then Limerick once more," and later, "I traced on the spot the localities connected with the last siege of Limerick."

This accuracy of setting is noticeable in all their work. Many of the series are laid in the Kilkenny district with which, of course, the brothers were very familiar. When it became necessary to examine any other part of Ireland, usually Michael did so, sent his information along to John or used it in the revision of manuscript. Among the best of Michael's works may be mentioned, besides *Crohoore, Father Connell* and *The Town of the Cascades.* A volume of stories published under the title of *The Bit o' Writing* has also been very popular. *Father Connell* was the last joint work of the brothers, and *The Town of the Cascades* the last of the *Tales.* (pp. 342-43)

The Banims had much in common, though Michael did not possess the poetic vein of his brother. The touch of John was lighter and more delicate, more artistic, more literary. His work rings truer. Though both at times tend to be melodramatic, Michael is the more frequent offender. Moreover, the use of the deus ex machina is more frequent in Michael's work. (p. 343)

Both were strong in description, though John had probably a deeper appreciation of and more perfect expression of natural beauty and grandeur. Michael's more homely genius was at its best when describing the peasants and their pastimes. His native heath, Kilkenny and its surroundings, is the familiar background of his pages and he describes at times with rare charm Kilkenny's river, the "silver-winding Nore," the ways of whose trout he knew well, . . . [gleaming] with fresh beauty in such a work as *The Mayor of Wind-gap.*

Take this scene from John's pages, "The earth, wherever it was seen bare, appeared dry and crumbling into dust; the rocks and stones were partially bleached white, or their few patches of moss burnt black or deep red. Up the valley, as far as my eye could travel, and at last over the broad bosom of the distant hill, which seemed torn and indented with the headlong torrent it had once poured down, far and uniform on every side a vertical July sun was shining." Does not the writer paint with life-like accuracy, the picture he saw when he looked up the long, lonely valley, parched by the summer's sun?

John Banim's work is often gloomy and tragic. His brightness is not as spontaneous as Michael's. This dark note is probably due to a great extent, to the worry that lay heavy on his mind and the sickness that tortured his body. But this did not diminish the vigour and great realistic power of his work. One might cite as examples the description of the battle of Aughrim which begins *The Last Baron of Crana,* or the vigour that runs through the many scenes of his great novel, *The Boyne Water.* (pp. 343-44)

Michael Banim's disposition and genius was more humane and more bright. It has been written of him that "his peculiar kindness of manner won the confidence of the peasantry and enabled him to gain that deep insight into their daily lives which he afterwards reproduced in his life-like portraits of character." He found happiness in studying the lives of those around him and in the beautiful scenery of his own country. (pp. 344-45)

Much of the local colour for the tales was supplied by [Michael]. John had lost touch to a certain extent with the peasant classes of his own land or never had the natural charm and kindness which enabled Michael to win their hearts and get to know them intimately. Thus the opening chapters of *Peter of the Castle,* which give a detailed account of country match-making and marriage festivities of the time, were supplied by Michael. He supplied, too, the description of the pattern, a sort of country holiday scene which takes up the first few chapters of *John Doe or the Peep o' Day.* (p. 345)

Power too, is in the writings of Michael Banim and he handles tragedy well, but with him the brighter side of the story is never long absent. (p. 347)

The reader will admit that [Michael] Banim achieves great strength and power. But he will notice too that there are faults. Is he not stilted and rhetorical, in such a phrase as "Almighty eye of the Universe." This tendency will be noted throughout the Banim's works.

One might also dwell on the introduction of the deus-ex-machina, the creation of doubles, the weakness of the denouement, other artificial properties of the conventional novel.

There is a more serious artistic defect to lay at the door of Michael Banim. One is usually satisfied in John's tales by the fulfilment of dramatic justice, by the giving of reality to the plot. Not so with his brother. Michael Banim is obsessed by the idea of the happy ending. This glaring example is from *Father Connell:* The grim details of what the reader is convinced is the murder of an old servant have been related. This weak paragraph ends the chapter. "Dead, however, she was not, but on the contrary quite alive and up, to receive her little fortune, and enjoy it in a quiet relief from worldly care and labour." Several other examples, just as weak, could be pointed out.

Or one could dwell on the lapses of Michael Banim into melodrama, particularly in one or two of the short stories, published in the volume called *A Bit of Writin'.* This is a collection of tales, several of which are splendidly told. It is probably better, however, to pass on to a short study of the most pleasing of the *Tales by the O'Hara Family, Father Connell,* the last joint work of the brothers, which Michael wrote at John's suggestion.

The scene is Kilkenny, and the hero strictly modelled, as is said in the preface on their beloved parish priest. His character, one of the noblest in fiction, is that of an ideal shepherd, kind, simple, generous, lovable, yet fierce and untiring in the protection of his flock. There are grim and terrible scenes in the story. There is, moreover, a severe indictment of abuses. We may study the author roused by the rapacity of the absentee landlords and their neglect of their tenants. (pp. 347-48)

But for the most part, the tale is brightened by kindliness and a humour, so pleasant, so homely, so kind that one comes to love the author so revealed. (p. 348)

Louis Lachal, S.J., "Two Forgotten Irish Novelists," in The Irish Monthly, Vol. LVIII, No. 685, July, 1930, pp. 338-49.

B. G. MacCARTHY (essay date 1946)

[*MacCarthy focuses on* The Nowlans *and* Crohoore of the Bill-Hook. *In the former, he notes John Banim's powers of observation and realistic descriptions, and in the latter, which this critic considers the best of the* Tales, *by the O'Hara Family, MacCarthy praises Michael Banim's insight into the Gaelic mind.*]

John and Michael Banim were the sons of a well-to-do shopkeeper in Kilkenny. In 1821, after John Banim had had a slight success in London literary circles, he proposed to his brother that they should write stories illustrating Irish life. So began the project of *Tales of the O'Hara Family.* . . . Each brother wrote separately and submitted his work to the other for correction and criticism. Michael Banim did not choose to take his place publicly as a writer, and therefore it is to John that we must turn for any explicit statement of their aim. This John expressed as follows: "They [the tales] were inspired simply by a devoted love of our country, and by an indignant wish to convince her slanderers, and in some slight degree to soften the hearts of her oppressors; although that in writing in her cause, to other nations, I saw the necessity of endeavouring cautiously and laboriously to make fiction the vehicle of fact."

But unfortunately art and propaganda do not propose the same ends or employ the same means. Instruction is sometimes too apparent in John Banim's works, as, for example, in *The Nowlans,* where, at a dinner at Mount Nelson, we have a long exposition of Irish grievances which forms a complete digression from the story. This novel, *The Nowlans,* has a strange theme. It contains a curious mixture of styles. The general tone is quiet and well-balanced. But from this sanity there are outbursts of melodrama (as in the case of Frank Adams, who is the sort of villain who foams at the mouth and gnashes his teeth). On the other hand, there are such grim and controlled scenes as that in which Peggy Nowlan, hiding at Foil Dhu in the darkness of night, watches her husband dig the grave which she knows that he intends for her. But the most valuable aspect of John Banim's work is that which has caused him to be compared to Crabbe. There are in his novels long passages where he shows the most acute power of observation, sharpened sometimes by his sense of repulsion. This realism appears most perfectly in Banim's account of the lodgings in Phibsboro' taken by John Nowlan and his wife. These lodgings are kept by a penurious, shuffling old man and his termagant wife. "It was all mean, pinching economy, miserly comfort, unwarranted neatness and propriety; cold, heartless, worthless independence." We see the shrivelled and cowardly old landlord as he fidgets, as he lisps and mumbles, "continually tapping his chest with one hand, ever complaining of his asthma." He appears every Sunday caparisoned for church in a complete suit of shining black.

> Sometimes his wife allowed him to invite to a Sunday dinner five or six old men like himself, all clad in shining black too; and when John saw them come crawling towards the house, or, joined with their host, crawling or stalking about the yard, he felt an odd sensation of disgust, such as he thought might be aroused by the sight of so many old shining blackbeetles; the insects that, of all that crept, were his antipathy and loathing.

Two skinny little Helots, brazen and vexatious, do the housework. They are the daughter and the niece of the old couple.

> They were of a size, and that size very little; of an age, and that more than thirty; but from their stunted growth, hard, liny shape and nondescript expression of features, might pass for ten years younger or ten years older, as the spectator fancied. They gave no idea of flesh and blood. They never looked as if they were warm, or soft to the touch. One would as soon think of flirting with them as with the old wooden effigies to be found in the niches of old cathedrals. They imparted no notion, much less sensation of sex. But they were as active as bees and as strong as little horses; and as despotic and cruel, if they dared, as the old tyrant herself.

All these impressions are shot through by John Nowlan's mood of sickened despair.

Such realism, however, did not become the main characteristic of John Banim's writing. The themes he chose did not much lend themselves to this kind of exposition. They were the themes also favoured by his brother, by Gerald Griffin and by Carleton—themes of mysterious murder, abductions, judicial trails and final execution. John Banim tried his hand, too, at the sort of subject which appealed to Maturin and later to Le Fanu—the supernatural—but much cannot be claimed for his story *The Fetches*. He essayed, moreover, an historical novel, *The Boyne Water,* maintaining in it a political point of view which he had been warned would alienate from him a large body of his public. This novel was poorly reviewed, but not merely because of its political tone.

Surely the best of the *O'Hara Tales* was Michael Banim's *Crohoore of the Billhook,* a dramatic and powerful novel. There are, as usual, a murder and a mystery, but these are raised to a supernatural height, and the closely-woven plot is developed against a background of wild mountain country and lowering skies. A brief introduction shows the wake of Antony Dooling and his wife, both murdered at dead of night on Christmas Eve. Then the story proper begins. We see the Dooling kitchen on that very Christmas Eve, a few short hours before the murder. The farmer, his family and servants are making merry around a roaring fire. It is an excellent scene, vividly described. Since the reader knows the impending doom, there is a strong sense of dramatic irony. Crohoore, the monstrous dwarf (a kind of Quasimodo) is shown enigmatically, and the tension rises to the moment when the enraged farmer strikes Crohoore. The piper abruptly ceases to play. There is a dead silence. Crohoore, his convulsed face covered with blood, pauses at the doorway to turn on the fireside group a ghastly and ma-

lignant look. He goes out. That night Antony Dooling and his wife are butchered in their beds, and Alley Dooling, the daughter of the house, is carried away into the mountains. In the ensuing events Michael Banim maintains the grim vigour of his narrative, and it is always his gift to make us see what he describes and feel the terrors with which he surrounds us. His hints at the supernatural are sufficiently subtle to seem credible (a technique which his brother lacked). Michael does not flinch from scenes which curdle the blood. There is the dreadful episode when the tithe-proctor is buried to the chin and his ears cut off, to an unbroken accompaniment of jibing. "Goodnight, Peery," his quondam victims call out, as they leave him "an' sure you have all the crop we can gi' you!" The rescue of Piers O'Shea from the soldiers is another decription in which no detail is omitted. It is particularly to be noticed that in all stark or tragic situations, Michael Banim uses restraint, and puts into the mouths of his characters brief, strong speech. When Piers O'Shea goes to the mother of Terence Delany to tell her that her son has been cut to pieces by the dragoons, he has only just begun to say that he has a message from her son when she springs at the truth, which she states with the inflection of a question. "My son is dead," she says; and Piers answers simply: "Christ have pity on you."

It is true that the Banims, since they belonged to a comfortable family, had no such contact as did Carleton with the lives of poor country-folk. Yet no one will deny to the Banims, and particularly to Michael, knowledge of Gaelic customs and insight into the Gaelic mind. As evidence of this, one need only turn to Michael's description of Terence Delany's mother coming to the wayside shed in which are huddled the bodies of the young men slain by the soldiers. She finds her way among the corpses until she reaches the body of her son. She stoops slowly, kisses his lips and breaks into the keen. This keen Michael Banim gives in full. It ends as it began in the desolate cry: "I nursed you at my breast; I baked your marriage cake; I sit at your head—Ullah!" Who will not say that this is the voice of Gaelic Ireland, not merely of Banim's time, but of the ageless Ireland of strong primeval memories?

It is interesting to note a point which Michael Banim makes in regard to the use of Anglo-Irish dialect, a subject to which one can only make passing reference. For the poorer people who speak English, Banim gives us the usual uneducated Anglo-Irish dialect. (And, without comment, he amuses himself by putting on the lips of the English soldiers a variety of English dialect—Yorkshire, Cockney, and what seems to be Sussex). But for Terence Delany's dying words and for Moya Delany's keen, Banim uses pure English. He did this because mother and son had spoken in Gaelic. Banim says: "If the language uttered by Terence Delany appear too refined for one in his situation of life, it is ascertainable as only in strict unison with the genius and idiom of the language in which he spoke, and from which we have literally translated; in the Irish there is nothing of what is known by the name of vulgarism; its construction even in the mouths of the peasantry, who to this day use it, has been and can be but little corrupted; nor could the familiar colloquy of the meanest among them be rendered, in English, into common-place or slang." (pp. 28-32)

> *B. G. MacCarthy, "Irish Regional Novelists of the Early Nineteenth Century (Concluded)," in* The Dublin Magazine, *n.s. Vol. XXI, No. 3, July-September, 1946, pp. 28-37.*

THOMAS FLANAGAN   (essay date 1959)

> [*Flanagan declares that John was the "controlling genius" who wrote most of the novels and revised Michael's contributions. He*

divides the novels into two categories: stories of peasant life, which include Crohoore of the Bill-Hook *and* The Nowlans, *and historical novels, which include* The Last Baron of Crana, The Conformists, The Croppy, *and* The Boyne Water. *Flanagan adds that ''Banim's wish—history was to make it seem an inordinate ambition—was to explain [the Irish] 'sullen savage' to England.''*]

''Banim resolved,'' Patrick Murray says, ''to raise the national character in the estimation of other lands, by a portrayal of the people as they really were, but at the same time to vindicate them from the charges of violence and bloodthirstiness, by showing, in the course of the fiction, the various causes which he supposed concurred to draw forth and foster these evil qualities'' [see Additional Bibliography].

This is the kind of laudable ambition which, by the operation of inexorable law, produces poor fiction. Banim's career as a writer lasted only some six years, for he was stricken while still young with a fatal and immediately incapacitating illness. Because they were the years in which many grave political issues were at stake, his work tends more toward ''vindication'' than toward a representation of Irish life ''as it really was.'' Judged on this ground, he was successful. He was a kind and eminently fair-minded man, and was welcomed in England as an honorable champion of Catholic claims and as an interpreter of the Irish peasant. But his natural endowment as a writer was slender as compared with that of either Gerald Griffin or William Carleton, his brilliant contemporaries.

Banim's novels appeared under the pseudonym of ''The O'Hara Family,'' and he had envisioned a series of tales, for which he would write the more serious stories and his brother Michael the ''filling.'' But Michael was neither a well-educated nor an ambitious writer. The controlling genius was always John's; he wrote most of the important novels and made extensive revisions of Michael's contributions. For this reason it seems sensible to depart from the usual practice of referring to ''the Banim brothers.''

Banim's work falls into two distinct categories. . . . He wrote stories of peasant life and he wrote historical novels. The differences between the two in tone, atmosphere, and attitude are great, but they are linked by a common intention: ''the formation of a good and affectionate feeling between England and Ireland.'' It was an admirable purpose, but he was convinced that whatever did not serve it had to be pruned away, for he believed that affection and strangeness could not exist together. The profound differences between the cultures had to be minimized, the bitterness and the estrangements rationalized. He was determined to remain above the self-lacerating pity with which Ireland called the attention of the world to its miseries, but the determination exacted its price. Only by accident does the pen of the O'Hara Family leap beyond its intention to create surely and powerfully. The most vivid instances of this are *Crohoore of the Billhook* and *The Nowlans.*

Crohoore is the story of eighteenth-century life as it was experienced by the Catholic peasants and strong farmers. From its opening pages we are in a world for which neither the novels of Maria Edgeworth nor those of Lady Morgan have prepared us—the secret, strangely self-sufficient Gaelic world. We are gathered around the turf fire of the Dooling family—Tony, his wife, and his laborers are seated on benches; beyond them the servant girls squat on their haunches. It is a cheerful, even a comfortable, house, yet disturbing because it does not have the indrawn and sequestered privacy to which English novels have accustomed us. Muldowny the piper comes in to gossip and hug the fire. Paudge Dermody, the local wit, wanders in

as a matter of course. Old women ''begging their way'' come and go. The house is open to the country, and no store whatever is set by privacy.

But one of Dooling's workmen, Crohoore, sits apart from the others, breaking the cozy, inglenook atmosphere:

> His cheeks were pale, hollow, and retiring; his nose, of the old Milesian mold, long, broad-backed and hooked; his jaws, coming unusually forward, caused his teeth to start from his face; and his lips, that, without much effort, never closed over those disagreeable teeth, were large, fleshless and bloodless, the upper one wearing, in common with his chin, a red beard, just changed from the down of youth to the bristliness of manhood, and, as yet, unshaven. These features, all large to disproportion, conveyed, along with the unpleasantness deformity inspires, the expression of a bold and decided character, and something else besides, which was malignity or mystery, according to the observation or mood of an observer. . . .
>
> (pp. 174-77)

Crohoore, leaning forward to catch the light from the fire, is slowly and lovingly whetting a pike blade to razor sharpness. The noise grates against the melody of Muldowny's pipes.

In the morning Dooling and his wife are found hacked to death, and Crohoore has fled with their daughter Ally. Pierce Shea, her lover, sets out in pursuit, and the reader is plunged into a world of almost incredible violence. Highwaymen, White Boys, and Ribbonmen lie in wait in the hills and glens beyond the farm land. Gallants seize women and force them, weeks later, into tardy marriages. Orange gunmen open fire on peasants huddled in a cave to hear Mass. The garrison of soldiers is in the country to protect property, not life. Mobs of peasants are liable at any moment to hurl themselves against their muskets.

The peasants have their own *riah,* or king, Jack Doran, a half-sir who has turned gunman. The point on which the plot turns is that Doran's men have murdered the Doolings; Crohoore has taken Ally away for safekeeping. But this is only a device; the substance of the story lies elsewhere. It begins with the simple fact that neither Crohoore nor any of the peasants loyal to the Doolings consider for a moment turning to the law for protection. Nor does Pierce Shea, whose feelings we are to share, expect them to do so. (p. 177)

No facts about Ireland unearthed by the various select committees so shocked the English public as these: that large numbers of the peasants periodically banded together to enforce a rough justice through terror and that the population as a whole passively condoned such activities.

There is a scene in *Peep o' Day* which is startling precisely because Banim presents it so casually. A young English officer is set upon by a footpad in a lonely glen. A farmer named Kavanagh rescues him and kills his assailant. Then he rifles the dead man's pocket, picks up the body, and tumbles it into the lake. The dead are best sunk under water and forgotten. The ablest of Ireland's social critics, from Gustave de Beaumont to George Cornewall Lewis, took great pains, as Banim does, to place the Irish peasant's hatred of the law in historical perspective. But Banim was under a special burden, that of making such a world believable as fiction.

It was a problem which he was never able to solve. *Crohoore,* that "dark and terrible" story, as Stephen Brown calls it, is founded on fact, and yet one instinctively rejects it as being lurid beyond belief. He was faced with the task of writing about a bloody and violent land, in which justice was measured out by hanging judges and packed juries, and exacted by the loaded whips of squireens and the brandings and mutilations of secret societies. But there no longer existed in English fiction conventions by which such a society could be represented. In default, he accepted the conventions of the shilling shocker.

The central scene in *Crohoore,* and the one which is most vividly represented, describes the torture and mutilation of a tithe proctor. Doran's men meet to plot the crime in a mud cabin, where they are roused to fury by one of the hedge schoolmasters who acted as the ideologists of the White Boy movement:

> I say once again, that you're not like a son of green Ireland, the crature, doin' as much as you can, an' sorry in your heart you can't do more, against the rievin', plunderin', mur-therin' raparees o' tithe proctors, the bitther foes of ould Ireland's land. . . .

(pp. 177-78)

Clancy, the proctor, is routed out of his bed and dragged through the village, as the children shout their consent, and the women peer approvingly from the doorways. A hedge poet accom-panies the expedition so that it may fittingly be commemorated, and a fiddler and a pipe improve the occasion. Clancy is buried to his neck beside a ditch, then Yemen O'Nase, "the finisher of the law," whets his pruning knife and sets about his task:

> Well, we're all ready; an' it's a sweet bit of a blade that's in it, for one knife. Och, bud it's none of your blades that's fir nothin' but cuttin' butther.

(p. 179)

In the speech of Yemen O'Nase and Mourteen the school-master, we have for the first time the tang and vigor of peasant speech put to dramatic use. In Mourteen's case it is hedge oratory at its most incendiary, and yet the ghost of an old, debased culture lurks in its cadences. Measured against it, Pierce Shea is a lifeless stick of prim good will, and Riah Doran the ranting villain of a Surrey Theatre melodrama. It is essential to Banim's scheme that Shea should be wrongfully accused of being a White Boy, and that Doran should be a White Boy leader but also a cold, Machiavellian criminal. For Doran and Shea are "gentlemen," capable of either heroic and unbelievable virtue or Byronic villainy, but never of the full vigorous life which his peasants possess.

This is the central weakness in his fiction. In each of his novels there is a sharp division between the peasants and the "gen-tlemen"—as indeed there should be, since his culture imposed the division. But his peasants are created with swift and certain skill, while his gentlemen are mere cardboard figures. The saddening explanation is that he knew next to nothing about the latter class. The English ideal of the gentleman, as it was formulated in the nineteenth century, bore no correspondence to Irish life, yet for Banim it was the only available image.

In *Peep o' Day,* while commenting on the ghastly humor which characterized Irish violence, and on the gunmen who took part in outrages as though playing Tom Fools to a company of Christmas mummers, he says, "There is a mockery of the heart by the heart itself. . . ." In some measure Banim mocks him-self, for too often he sees to the tragic heart of Irish experience, and then denies what he has seen in the interest of some con-ventional and trumpery plot.

This is particularly true of the way in which he has used the figure of Crohoore himself. Crohoore is "the aboriginal in-habitant of the island," the quintessence of the world which produced Yemen O'Nase and Peery Clancy and Mourteen. He is the dark, unknowable figure who sits in every cabin, whetting the pike on which the blood-red fire plays. He will reappear as Shane na Gow in *The Croppy,* and as Rory na Chopple in *The Boyne Water.* He is "malignity or mystery, according to the observation or mood of an observer." But we are asked to believe, before the story is done, that he is only a variety of the faithful retainer, serving in his own whimsical fashion the best interests of "the young master," Pierce Shea.

Mary Russell Mitford, having in mind the way in which his novels contrasted with those of Maria Edgeworth, accused Banim of having introduced into Irish fiction the lurid melodrama of Eugene Sue. The truth, rather, is that Banim was writing of a land so dark and bloody that Sue's method's would have been overly genteel. (pp. 179-81)

John Banim wrote a great amount of bad fiction in an effort to persuade himself and his readers that the cultures [of the Ascendancy and of the peasants] were really not very different at all. When he forgot this noble intention he wrote well.

He is happily forgetful during most of the novel called *The Nowlans,* a book which is remarkable for its realistic portrayal of Irish life. (pp. 182-83)

The Nowlans are strong farmers, fairly prosperous and socially conservative. Banim knew their world well—what their parlors looked like, what books a seminarian would read, how farmers and laborers addressed each other. And here, for once, he knew all the subtle divisions of caste and class. (p. 183)

Banim finally establishes the rich, confusing relationships of the Nowlan clan, but is less successful, because less familiar, with the Protestant households. Nevertheless, the liberal Longs and the bigoted Adamses have a real existence in the novel. They exist, that is to say, as perils for the Nowlans. Old Mister Long comes from a family with an honorable tradition of friendly relations with his Catholic neighbors, while Adams is an Orange zealot. Protestantism itself, however, is the real threat to the Nowlans, for they are a pushing, aspiring family, and the Established Church is a badge of status; it represents both power and the cachet of gentility.

Banim's first intention was to make *The Nowlans* a novel with a thesis. The early nineteenth century saw the rise in Ireland of a proselytizing movement which called itself, with undue optimism, the New Reformation. In point of fact it was the equivalent of the Evangelical movement in England, but its consequences were much less happy. (pp. 183-84)

A group of Evangelical emissaries arrives on the scene in *The Nowlans,* under the patronage of Sirr, the local parson, and Adams. The Reverend Mister Stokes is "an English clergyman, sent from a Bible Society in London to investigate the progress of their benevolent efforts among the peasantry of Ire-land." . . . He is assisted by a former Catholic priest named Horragan, who has been entrusted with the conversion of the Gaelic-speaking population. Banim wants to convince fair-minded Englishmen, the audience he kept constantly in mind, that, while the motives of Stokes and his associates may be worthy, their ignorance of the Irish scene has made them the inevitable dupes of men like Adams and Horragan—bigots and renegades. To this end he develops a number of lengthy exchanges, in which Long upholds a worthier Protestant position, and the Catholic stand is set forth by an old Dominican.

Most Irish novelists of the period felt themselves impelled to write at least one novel on this topical issue, and never with much success. Banim puts appropriate speeches in the mouths of his characters, but he is entirely unable to respond to the spiritual life of Protestantism. The figure of Horragan is especially unworthy of his usual sense of fairness. Mortimer Sullivan, on whom he is modeled, was a sufficiently wretched being, but Banim represents him with a ferocity of caricature which defeats its own purpose.

But the tone and intensity of the novel change abruptly when requirements of the plot cause Letty Long and Father John Nowlan to fall in love and marry. The other elements of the plot continue to function, but they pale beside Banim's fascinated concern with Nowlan's psychology. It is as though he had discovered, for the first time, that differences of religion and culture can be both profound and determining. (pp. 184-85)

Banim is respectful of Letty's feelings, which he knows to be connected with her religious training, and yet he is so far removed from the world of Protestantism that he writes tentatively. The fact is reflected in Letty's pathetic attempts to communicate with John and in John's stricken muteness. But with John, Banim is on sure ground and writes with instinctive skill. The special role of the priest in the Irish Catholic imagination is such that few Catholic novelists approached this theme, and none so openly as Banim.

He comes to see, and to make us see, that the issue is not merely one of sect, in the strict sense of the word. John's identity had depended upon a world of feelings and loyalties of which his Catholicism was a part. When he leaves Tipperary for London he changes one existence for another—or, rather, for a state which cannot properly be called existence. In describing this Banim's language is charged beyond its usual range, for he is describing a descent into hell.

> If, as his unwinking eyes strained through the blank at the window, perception brought, now and then, a notice of anything to his mind, it was only to encourage the mood that was upon him. The howling of the midnight wind over the black bogs of Tipperary; the gusty beating of the rain against the glass; the feeble glimmering of lanterns at the door of miserable inns, or cabins, as the coach stopped to change horses, and the miserable, half-dressed ghostlike figures appeared and disappeared in the dreary light and engulfing darkness; such circumstances or sights, if at all observed by John Nowlan, could only tend to answer, in an outward prospect, the inward horror of his soul. . . .
>
> (pp. 185-86)

In Dublin the Nowlans take lodging with an English Protestant family named Grimes. It is a well-conducted family, honest, church-going, neat, and industrious. But to John "it was all mean, pinching economy, miserly comfort, unwarranted neatness, and propriety; cold, heartless, worthless independence. . . . The whole house and its inhabitants had an air of looking better than they really were or ought to be." (p. 186)

Nowlan is puzzled by the intensity of his dislike, and John Banim seems clearly to share the feeling. He is at least embarrassed by the undue intensity of the language. Committed as he was to a moralistic theory of fiction, he could not acknowledge that for once his imagination had been liberated from its everlasting fairmindedness. He says elsewhere, speaking of the Irish peasant, "those secrets of his inner heart he keeps concealed to the present hour, as well from the oppressor he hates, as from the friends who, if they knew him better, could better serve."

The observation, which is well taken, could be applied with equal justice to Banim himself. Because he had accepted the task of mediating between the two cultures, he could not bring himself to admit how much he cherished the one and detested the other. It is an honorable failure, one must say, remembering how much of Ireland's fiction is animated by a mean and soul-destroying hatred. But tolerance and accommodation wreak their own havoc upon art. Banim had himself taken John Nowlan's journey across the black Tipperary bogs to the house of the stranger.

In John Nowlan's room in the city there is but one concession to ornament, "a long, narrow chimney glass, set in a frame about an inch deep, and presenting to the eye about as faithful a reflection of the human face, as might a river or lake with the wind blowing high upon it." . . . Banim's art is like the Grimes's chimney glass. Somewhere, far beyond its flawed and deceptive surface, we can sense, in all his fierce irreducibility, Crohoore of the Billhook, but we are given only as much of him as can be accommodated to an inch of frame. Only rarely, though with pleasure, do we realize that his creator, too, was a man of passion and feeling. *The Nowlans* affords such an occasion. (p. 187)

• • • • •

Banim wrote, in all, four historical novels, and their subjects are chosen with singular skill. The first, *The Boyne Water*, deals with the impact upon Irish life of the struggle between James and William. *The Last Baron of Crana* is set in that period, which still remains obscure and puzzling to scholars, when the Irish forces had capitulated at Limerick and a frightening anarchy had settled over the island. *The Conformists* is a novel of the Penal Days. Finally *The Croppy*, on which Michael Banim collaborated, turns to account the Rising of 1798.

Taken together, the novels should form a coherent pattern. Unhappily, they are of uneven merit, none of the latter three approaching the first in accomplishment. But *The Boyne Water* sets a standard which no other Irish historical novel was to meet. Subject to several strong reservations, it is the best work of its kind since Scott.

The comparison is inescapable, for Scott was Banim's absolute master. As much might be said of any historical novelist; Scott set the mold, and few of his successors either dared or troubled to break it. In most cases, however, his imitators contented themselves with a slavish conformity to the kinds of plot and character which he developed. Banim, as we shall see, can scarcely be excused on this score. But he also had a sense, rare in his generation, of what Scott was about, and of the sources of his power; he knew that beneath the brightly colored surface of the *Waverley Novels* lay a deep and urgent knowledge of history as tragic experience.

For Banim, as for Scott, past and present were in continuous debate. The feelings, passions, and loyalties which worked upon his countrymen had their sources in past centuries, and hence to understand the past was to gain mastery over the present. "I will tell you, Barnes, what I would like to aid," he wrote. "I would go far to assist in dispersing the mist that hangs over Irish ground. I would like to see those dwelling on the Irish soil looking about them in the clear sunshine—the murkiness dispelled—recognizing each other as belonging to a common country. . . . We, here in Ireland, ought to be anxious to ascertain our position accurately, if for no other reason than that we may give ourselves a common country."

The intention to "ascertain our position accurately" led Banim straight to a single day, July 1, 1690, when, on the shores of the Boyne River, the armies of William of Orange shattered those of James II. (pp. 189-90)

Banim is aware, as most historians of his day were not, that the struggle in Ireland between the Williamite and Jacobite forces decided three distinct issues. In its largest terms, those suggested by Trevelyan, it was the first check placed by the Protestant powers upon the ambitions of the French monarchy. As a dynastic contest it established the Whig oligarchy in England. But as an issue fought out on Irish soil it was a chapter in an old story. He sorts out these issues with care and intelligence, yet mindful of the relationships among them.

The blood spilled at the Boyne Water still ran in crimson channels through the fabric of Irish life; it had become the sacramental wine of rival ideologies. To Irish Protestants William was the champion of the "old cause," brave, pious, and determined. To Catholics he was a cunning hypocrite and tyrant. Both sides were in agreement that James was a coward, who basely betrayed the Irish cavaliers who had flocked to his banners. Banim brushes away both of these convenient fictions. His rival kings are drawn in cold but not hostile lines; they are engaged in a quarrel whose terms are European; fate has drawn them to a country which neither understands nor cherishes. (pp. 192-93)

The great merit of *The Boyne Water* derives from those of Banim's qualities which are not of necessity literary. He was a remarkably intelligent man, and it was a specifically political and historical intelligence. He was also, for all his religious piety, skeptical of the social consequences of "crusades." But if these are the virtues which lift *The Boyne Water* above the ruck of its successors, they also impose its severe limitations. We become aware of these gradually, as the pattern of the plot takes shape as a series of annoying parallelisms.

Walker, an Anglican zealot, is paired off against O'Haggerty. A moderate priest, striving for reconciliation, has his opposite number in the Williamite camp. If Evelyn falls afoul of a band of Jacobite terrorists, so must McDonnell, within four or five chapters, be captured by William's brutal mercenaries. Banim does not employ this technique, though it might appear so, to obliterate moral distinctions. If he abjures partisanship, his own loyalties are clear and undisguised, and the judgment which he makes of each of his characters is unequivocal and indeed didactic. And yet one is left with the sense that the pattern, for all its admirable symmetry, lacks a center, lacks some ultimate commitment by Banim to his material.

Perhaps the answer lies with his dependence on Scott. Much of the machinery of *The Boyne Water* has been lifted bodily from *Waverley*. Scott's practice—nowhere more evident than in that novel—was to work with opposites, Scotsman and En-glishman, cavalier and roundhead, highland laird and lowland lord, kirk and church. The resemblances to the Irish scene presented themselves to Banim with a dangerous plausibility. He saw Scott's cavaliers as bearing a rough equivalence to the Norman Irish of the Pale, and his roundheads to the Ulster Presbyterians, and his highland chieftains to the "old" Irish. But Scott's recurrent theme, which justifies these polarities, is the death of passion. It is his deep and genuine conservatism which makes legitimate his exploitation of the technique which he invented. (pp. 193-94)

Scott had a firm, unshakable confidence in the security of the King, Lords, and Commons of Great Britain, the social worth of the Protestant Succession, and the propriety of the Act of Union which had joined Scotland with England. He turned to the past, as Burke did, to search out those vivid strands which the present had brought into so firm a knot. (p. 194)

Banim, however, was dealing with a country where the strands of the past still twisted and coiled about men's heads like lethal and uncontrollable wires, impelled by some malignant energy. Walker and O'Haggerty were still addressing their bogside conventicles. Even as he wrote, his *Rory na Chopple,* the blandly smiling murderer with soft brogue and sudden cruelty, was somewhere in County Clare, leading out a Ribbon mob against a glebe house—or else he was in the Black North, at the head of his Orange "loyalists."

Banim's two novels of the Penal Times may be given brief treatment. In *The Last Baron of Crana* he traces the fate of two Gaelic families in the years following the surrender at Limerick. The hushed and fearful expectancy which had fallen upon the Gaelic world is created effectively, and the story has a certain surface excitement, but the characters are stiffly theatrical. "A stout rebel, as I have ever heard," says Sir Redmond O'Burke, accepting Prendergast's surrender in the thick of a hot action, "and, as I now bear witness, a courageous gentleman; but we waste some time here; I crave your company back to the hill, whence, after honorably bestowing you, I may again engage in my duty." . . . Prendergast, the Williamite, is afflicted with a similar rotundity of utterance.

The Conformists takes up a subject to which a real and moving interest adheres, though Banim seems hardly to recognize this. Mark Darcy returns home from Spain with the education and sword of a gentleman. His younger brother, Daniel, trained in a hedge school, and accustomed to accord a sullen deference to the Orange gentry, becomes increasingly resentful of him, and at last decides upon a dreadful measure. One of the most notorious of the penal statutes was that which provided that if a son or younger brother conformed to the Established Church, the law would put him in possession of the lands of his family. The plot is concerned entirely with the motives which tempt Daniel to this act, its commission, and his ultimate repentance. It is managed in a style which alternates between the perfunctory and the lurid.

Banim tells us in a note which introduces these two novels that, because they were being published at a delicate moment in the Emancipation fight, he had carefully pruned and "re-modelled" and "rewritten" so that no passage could possibly give offense to either faith. The thin and watery texture of both stories may, no doubt, be attributed to this absurd decision. But there are other and more substantial reasons.

There is one effective scene in *The Last Baron of Crana*. Young Patrick Burke, who has managed to evade the laws, and who has been brought up as Prendergast's ward, has been searching for the "last baron," Randal O'Hagan. He finds him at last, but can feel only pity and unconquerable disgust. For O'Hagan, who had been an urbane and chivalrous officer on Sarsfield's staff, is now a murdering woodkern. "Even the expressions of his face, so far as regards indication of rank, were deficient; its colour and texture seemed vulgar; nay, his speech, and the hoarse cadences of his voice, had necessarily acquired their present character, since his abandonment of his name and station in the world. Once or twice, Patrick detected him eyeing askance his own family crest upon articles of plate which lay upon the table. . . ." (pp. 194-96)

The effectiveness is accidental. It depends not on the meaning of the scene to us, but on our knowledge of what it meant to Banim. Irish Catholics of his generation took particular and excessive pride in what they imagined their past to have been. Their race had boasted gentlemen as polished as any in the Ascendancy, and as punctilious. They remembered, with a somewhat self-pitying nostalgia, that the ranks of its chivalry had made their last gallant stand at Limerick. Those who remained had not, like Scott's Jacobites, perished in their pride; they had been subjected to a remorseless, if often random, brutalization.

It is not necessary to sort out here the facts and the fancies which were incorporated into the early nineteenth-century myth of Sarsfield and his Jacobite army. The point, rather, is that in the history of the intervening century, rich with the shames, crimes, and glories of the Ascendancy, the history of the Catholic community was, and in part remains, a blank page. Remote country houses might shelter a scholar like Charles O'Conor of Belenagare, who carefully gathered, preserved, and studied the slender memorials of his country. Or a half-proscribed squire and smuggler like Maurice O'Connell of Derrynane might toss his correspondence into desks and lockers for the enlightenment of our own age. But for the middle-class Irish who, like Banim, were beginning to find pens and voices, such survivals were themselves inaccessible. And in default they conjectured as to what "things must have been like" in the eighteeenth century. An extraordinary talent like that of Gerald Griffin could, by some act of sympathetic magic, recreate that past with surprising accuracy. But most novelists, following Banim's unhappy example, produced cardboard "gentlemen" who nobly endured a puppet-show martyrdom.

In the main these novelists preferred to move further and further into the past, creating out of shroudlike mists a Red Hugh O'Donnell who talked like Sir Philip Sidney and comported himself like Walter Scott welcoming George IV to Edinburgh. But Banim, the evidence of *The Last Baron* and *The Conformists* to the contrary, had no taste for that sort of foolishness. And in *The Croppy* he confronted the most immediate and controversial subject which he could possibly have found.

In 1828 the Great Rebellion was a scant thirty years in the past, and still a subject of empassioned dispute. It had, indeed, its dark significance for the present moment. (pp. 196-97)

Stated bluntly, it was the fear of a slave uprising. The term suggests the mingled loathing, fear, and contempt with which many in the Garrison viewed the people whom they ruled and exploited. (p. 197)

[The liberal minority] had from the first put forward the interpretation which serves as the theme of Banim's novel. The peasants of Wexford had been goaded into an insurrection which, once commenced, had taken the unhappy and predict-able course of all peasant wars. For the aims of the rebellion very few, and Banim least of all, had a good word to say. . . .

> The Catholic peasant confounded all the late adherents of his abhorred enemies with the first and worst who had persecuted him; Protestant and Orangeman became, in his mind, synonymous words; and in this delusion he caught up his rude and formidable pike, when, without time being afforded him to reflect, he was precipitated, by United Irish emissaries on one side, and by monstrous and wanton civil outrage on the other, into the melee of civil strife.
>
> (p. 198)

This is an interpretation which accords with all the evidence we have, save that it is somewhat too eager to exculpate the peasantry on grounds of ignorance. Thirty years hence, however, any Irish "patriot" would reject it with indignation. By that time the '98 had been cast in another, more heroic mold, thanks largely to the spirited efforts of Thomas Davis, John Mitchel, and the Young Ireland group. The United Irishmen, represented by Banim as sinister incendiaries, had become the principal deities of the nationalist pantheon.

Banim's novel is set in Wexford, to which county the actual fighting was more or less restricted. He has allowed himself a canvas of adequate size, and creates a coherent picture of the society within which the violence erupted. It is also, by and large, a convincing picture, although he stumbles into his usual absurdities when dealing with the Protestant gentry. The opening chapters are perhaps too idyllic: "On either side of the river, the grounds rise and fall in every change of soft form; domain succeeds domain, and mansion is in view of mansion." . . . But before he is finished, every "domain" and every "mansion" has suffered a hideous transformation. There is also a certain historical justification: Wexford, a peaceful and fairly prosperous county, was the last place in which rebellion might have been expected. But, in a fashion which Banim recreates in all its lurid details, it had been raked over by agitators.

Saunders Smiley, the Orange agent, has his orders from the government to force the peasantry into a premature and hence foredoomed insurrection. He has his counterpart in Bill Nale, a veteran of Ulster's religious battles, who is preaching a holy war of retribution from cabin to cabin. Lastly, and perhaps most fatally, there appears on the scene "the Member from the Committee," the leader despatched by the United Irishmen.

Banim writes of all three with a quiet, bitter contempt, but one scene rises with dramatic force above the level of mere professional competence. It is that in which "the Member," who manages to combine the greatest zeal with the greatest complacency, explains to the men whom he has sworn that they are pledged to a movement whose ideals transcend weak notions of sect and creed. For seated about him are men into whose hearts have been instilled a deep and ineradicable religious hatred, and who will shortly make a travesty of the instructions of their lofty mentors by launching an indiscriminate slaughter of Protestants.

The two great figures of *The Croppy* are Shane na gow and Father Rourke. Both are kindly men goaded into violence; both, transformed by the fury of events, become murderers; both are hanged. The novel closes in the tame fashion which was expected of romances of this sort. Lovers are reunited, faithful servants are rewarded, just punishments are meted out, and

Mr. Mossop, the paternalistic magistrate, has regained control of the county. But the final powerful image is of a very different order:

> Father Rourke was hanged upon the bridge at Wexford. The weight of his colossal body had broken the rope, however, before Saunders Smiley saw him pending to his heart's content. . . .

(pp. 198-99)

Like Crohoore, sharpening his pike by the fire's glow, Rourke has a meaning which extends beyond that which the conscious intentions of the novel assign to him. Most of the characters in *The Croppy* had their counterparts in the actual rebellion, and the original of "Rourke" was John Murphy, the parish priest of Boulavogue. Murphy had opposed the rising, both on religious grounds and because like most sensible men he saw that it was suicidal. But when it became clear that his people were being offered the choice of dying with a fight or without one, he took the field with them. (p. 200)

Murphy's legend lingered on among the peasantry, and he is the hero of several songs commemorative of the '98. There is nothing heroic, however, about Banim's Father Rourke. He is a determined and capable leader, but action brings out in him a ferocious bigotry, quite equal to that betrayed by his opponents. It is Rourke who directs the murder of innocent Protestant prisoners. There seems no doubt, from any of the evidence, that Banim's portrait is accurate. But when nationalists were constructing their myth of the '98, these harsh lines were carefully sponged away.

In his best novels Banim refused to soften or sentimentalize the issues, and this is a quality so rare in Irish fiction as to excuse his very evident shortcomings. It was a quality which he shared with his much abler contemporaries, Griffin and Carleton. Had the conditions of Irish culture been other than what they were, had not the pressures placed on literature by politics become increasingly sharp, these writers might have marked the beginnings of a tradition. Instead they stand as lonely and broken figures, who failed even to understand each other.

In Banim's work the recurring figure is the peasant, that creature "of mystery or malignity." For Banim, clearly, he was something of both. Dashing Jacobites and disinherited cavaliers and improbable graduates of Kilkenny College make their processional appearances in his stories, but his heart and his wonder are always fixed on the pikeman by the fire and the rebel on the gallows.

When the Land War was at its height in the 1880s, long after Banim's death, *The Daily News* of London despatched a special correspondent named Bernard Becker to "get the facts." . . . His last recollection was of a shebeen house where he found himself snowbound one December night. It was not the scene which impressed him, but a man whom he found sitting by the fire.

> The sulky brute answers me never a word. Probably he knows or suspects where I have been, and if so would let me lie on the ground under a kicking horse till an end was made of me rather than stretch out a hand. . . . It is a strange sight, this sullen savage sitting scowling over the fire; but *on se fait a tout* in Disturbed Ireland.

Banim's wish—history was to make it seem an inordinate ambition—was to explain this "sullen savage" to England. (pp. 200-01)

Thomas Flanagan, "John Banim," in his The Irish Novelists, 1800-1850, *Columbia University Press, 1959, pp. 167-204.*

MARK D. HAWTHORNE   (essay date 1975)

[*In this detailed examination of the works of John and Michael Banim, Hawthorne emphasizes the methods the authors used to create not only a positive "self-image" for the Irish, but a style of literature for the Irish Catholic. Hawthorne notes that the Banims combined John's literary control and knowledge of the English with Michael's sensitivity and understanding of the Irish peasant, creating "a form of fiction that is part neither of the sophisticated literary tradition of England nor of their native oral tradition but that fuses the two into a new medium."*]

[Of all the early Irish] novelists John and Michael Banim best show us the problems that faced the Irish Catholic when he tried to discard the English veneer so as to create a new national literature. They have been overshadowed by Maria Edgeworth and William Carleton because they often failed to achieve what they strove to attain, but they form the logical step that takes us from the Ascendancy lady who brought a little of Ireland into the English novel and the Ulsterman who tried to write of Ireland as he had known it for an audience that the Banims in part helped to create. (pp. 13-14)

What was needed in the 1820's was a spokesman for the rising class of Irish tradesmen, a writer who could do for Irish literature what O'Connell was doing for Irish politics. John and Michael Banim stepped in to fill this role. Their father had been a farmer and a small tradesman, and they well knew the fears, hopes, and frustrations of being Catholic. They could represent the Irishman as none of the Regency writers had been able to. But the political turmoil that gave them an opportunity also presented their greatest problem: they had to create a literature for and about Ireland where none existed in English, and to do this, they had to bridge the gap between the native Gaelic culture and the superimposed English one.

In the cultural confusion that followed the breakdown of the Gaelic world, the Irishman desperately needed to see himself in literature as he actually was, not as an English audience wanted to believe he was. . . . Of course, John and Michael Banim could not change the stereotyped Irishman of English literature by themselves; it would take three more generations, geniuses like Yeats, Synge, George Moore, and Joyce, and the rediscovery of the Gaelic past to achieve what they began. Still, they tried in their humble way to alter the literary portrait of the Irishman.

To do this, they had to reinterpret history so that an Irishman could see exactly how he had been betrayed by England. (pp. 17-19)

The self-image that they finally created needed to fuse history, country, people, and religion into a single cultural view—an approach to life that gave the diversity of individuals a common heritage. Here they had their greatest difficulty, for they lacked the historical perspective that Yeats and the Celtic Revival possessed. They suffered from the problem of trying to create unity where no unity existed and where the diversity of cultures was as striking as the contrasts in the scenery. In their own way they sought to reconcile Gaelic and English. (p. 21)

In 1822 when John and Michael decided to collaborate on an Irish novel, their first difficulty was to determine the nature of [their] audience and to create a self-image that it would accept. This difficulty was intensified because they were themselves too much a part of both cultures. (p. 24)

John and Michael shared the desire to be *Irish* novelists, and this desire keeps their collaboration a genuine sharing of attitudes and ambitions. . . . Being Irish novelists, however, meant more than using Irish characters and setting; it meant that they had to fuse the two cultures with their opposing value systems so that anglicized Irishmen could appreciate why and how they were unique. (pp. 26-7)

They found the remnants of the Gaelic past in the living folklore of the cabin, the *banshee, fetch, sheehogue, thigha,* and *poocha* being its most obvious representatives. While the Penal Laws had almost exterminated the literary Gaelic culture, folklore had remained more alive than ever. . . . Later in the nineteenth century Gaelic literature exerted a force on Ireland when it was losing its folklore and adopting an industrial outlook, but at the time of the Banims, folklore, not literature, was the moving force of the native tradition.

Fortunately the Banims happened to live at the time when the European public was becoming aware of this other world. (pp. 28-9)

John and Michael Banim contributed to this European awareness by combining the otherworldliness of their native culture and the "realism" of the English novel. The result is, at times, shocking. In the midst of a realistic account of the struggles of a family trying to survive adversity, the reader might suddenly encounter the *banshee;* in an otherwise realistic portrayal of tenant life he might be asked to accept the existence of a *fetch* as being just as concrete as the potatoes on the table or the pigs rooting under it. This combination simply is not a part of the English novel. No one expects, or would accept, a ghost's appearance in *Emma* or "Monk" Lewis' giving a lecture on rationality. Usually the otherworld in English fiction before 1820 is carefully segregated from the ordinary world, and seldom is it taken seriously outside of the Gothic novel, the Tale of Terror, or the Waverley Novels. But in the Banims' novels the two worlds combine and ultimately fuse into a supercharged reality, sometimes with rather unexpected results but always with tacit belief in the viability of the greater reality.

This fusion also joins the values inherent in the two cultures. On the one hand, the Banims portrayed the Irishman as he had never before found himself in literature in English. Without censure from the author, characters can speak one moment of politics and insurrection and the next of the *sheehogue,* treating both with the respect due to significant parts of their lives. A character can rub elbows with a witch, a son of a fallen Gaelic family, a priest, a tenant farmer, an insurrectionist, and a ghost without questioning the range of tangibility or possibility in his experience. On the other hand, the Banims created an atmosphere in their fiction that reflects the mysteries of the Celtic unknown and the glaring light of English practicality. The seditious meetings of Croppies are no more real than the working out of a witch's dark curse; the daily trivia of the *sheeban* keeper is on the same level as the cry of the *banshee* or the festivities of the dead in the local graveyard. The Irish audience saw in this fiction its own contradictions—its lack of respect for English law, its fierce temper, its intense sense of justice, its tenderness and deep affection, its drunkenness and its sober faith, its wide diversity of behavior. In one respect, all that

the Banims did was to capture the Irishman as they thought he actually was; in another, they had to create a national literature in order to do so. They were not always successful; still, they pointed in the direction of *Traits and Tales of the Irish Peasantry, Uncle Silas, Cathleen Ni Houlihan, Ulysses,* and *Malone Dies.* (pp. 30-2)

The Banims decided to show that the otherworld was a "natural" fact in the life of the Irish peasant without explaining it away, condemning it as mere superstition, or delving into a legendary and remote past. In short, they expanded the realistic techniques of the English novelist to a wider sphere than anyone other than Scott had attempted, and with the determination to create a full portrait of the Irishman, they accounted for the otherworld as if it were concrete and objectified. (pp. 62-3)

The Fetches and *Crohoore of the Billhook,* both published in 1825, mark the beginning of a specifically Irish novel in the sense that Maria Edgeworth's *Castle Rackrent* (1800) or *The Absentee* (1812) do not because of their close affinity to the English novel and their characteristically English attitude toward the facts of daily life. (p. 63)

The Fetches combines the ordinary world—the peasants' cabins and folk customs as well as the prosperous townsmen of Kilkenny—and the mysterious world of the supernatural. By treating his subject so that the reader is not sure whether the *fetches* are actually present or merely figments of the characters' imaginations, John realized the delicate balance between the worlds that made them both believable. At once, the novel deals with appearances of otherworldly creatures and is as realistic as the English novel of manners.

The characters in *The Fetches* are sceptics who believe only in the actuality of the sensory world and tend to scoff at superstition or believers who accept superstition and find themselves involved in visions. Maria and Mortimer take the view that the sensory world alone is real and are firmly supported by the scientific opinion of Dr. Butler, who argues that *fetches* are merely the figments of overwrought imaginations. At the same time, Anna believes in them, and Harry Tresham has gone to the length of "proving" their existence philosophically. After establishing this division between characters, John Banim designed the novel's structure as a conflict between opposing opinions so that the superstition could be exactly what Dr. Butler argues, merely the figment of fantasy: the final resolution which "proves" that Tresham and Anna were right comes entirely as a result of Tresham's terminal illness and Anna's sick imagination. In other words, interpenetration of natural and supernatural in the unfolding of the *fetches'* appearances illustrates the awful infringement of the otherworld in the sensory world even as it can be construed as completely naturalistic. John Banim has bridged the gulf between English commonsense and the Irish otherworld through discovering a double focus. (pp. 66-7)

Banim treats these appearances in such a manner that, at once, they are clearly the deliriums of diseased imaginations and the actual infringement of the otherworld in this world. He carefully accounts for the naturalistic or sceptical explanation, but he also objectifies the experiences so that the reader also sees what might be hallucination. By not settling this conflict between the two possibilities, Banim left the novel ambiguous and hence believable from either viewpoint. (p. 70)

Michael Banim's *Crohoore of the Billhook* also presents a full picture of the Irish peasant and his beliefs. (p. 72)

Although he occasionally lets the reader know that he does not believe in the stories of the folk or in the actual existence of the "good people" and a host of other supernatural creatures, Michael puts this belief into his characters. This detachment of the author from his characters serves the same function as John's use of Dr. Butler [in *The Fetches*]: it establishes the opinion of commonsense so that the unknown emerges from a clear recognition of actuality. But the belief in the otherworld and the way in which characters tend to act upon their belief makes the world of *Crohoore* take on wider scope than the sceptical author indicates. When a character disbelieves, it becomes a sign of either his villainy or his heroism; these characters use their knowledge of the wider reality for their own ends. In other words, they do not believe in the otherworld, but they know that others do and use this belief so that they can act with greater freedom. The result, then, is that Michael moves between the actual and the supernatural to set the tone for the novel and create its tension, to give the novel its power and suspense. (pp. 72-3)

[Michael contrasts the superstitious atmosphere with] the political involvement of the Whiteboy uprising. . . . Michael carefully separates politics and otherworldliness; in those parts of *Crohoore* that deal with the Whiteboys, he avoids the otherworld that permeates the rest of the adventure. Still, the Whiteboys intrude into the mystery of the night, and the otherworldliness of Crohoore, Lheeum-na-Sheeog, and Dora Shea infringes on the ordinary world. The two worlds interpenetrate, but the attitudes represented by each of them do not overlap. The Whiteboys are evil; the otherworld, good. (pp. 78-9)

[In] *Crohoore of the Billhook* Michael creates a fusion of two worlds: Doran's is that of thieves and murderers who use superstition to control the peasants and who use the Whiteboys to obscure their crimes; Crohoore's is of the poor outcast—beggars, dwarfs, old women—who use superstition to protect themselves from the actual world and to protect the innocent from the crimes of men like Doran. (p. 79)

Comparison of *The Fetches* and *Crohoore of the Billhook* reveals John's and Michael's fusion of the two cultures of Ireland. Both novels exploit specifically Irish materials, the *fetch*, the *sheehogue*, the countryside of Ireland, the citizens of Kilkenny, the Anglo-Irish in the Big Houses. John, having come to this material after experimenting with Greco-Roman settings, avoided the peasantry to focus on the Irishman of the countryside. Despite this difference in characters, each treated his material in such a way that the supernatural remains mysterious and awesome. They captured the essence of naive wonder from the folk story and grafted it onto common stereotypes from the English novel. Maria Edgeworth's novels focused so glaringly on the Ascendancy that one is scarcely aware of the darkness of the cabin, the wealth of traditional folk customs and beliefs, or the undercurrent of fierce and savage resentment against the Big Houses, but *The Fetches* and *Crohoore of the Billhook* introduced a new note in that both confront the two cultures of Ireland and from this conflict develop the fullness of Irish attitudes toward themselves and toward the English. (p. 80)

[In *The Fetches* and *Crohoore of the Billhook*] John and Michael shape their material into a form of fiction that is part neither of the sophisticated literary tradition of England nor of their native oral tradition but that fuses the two into a new medium. The English novel in the early nineteenth century eschewed the mixture of actuality and wonder except in the widely popular Gothic romance that seldom attempted to portray ordinary men and women, especially of the lowest class; it was a re-

flection of a cultural attitude that emphasized entanglements and frustrations of worldly men and women whose main concern was social or fashionable. The native oral tradition portrayed a dark world of mysterious, inexplicable actions that held the attention of the auditors because it fulfilled their wishes or objectified their irrational fears; this, too, was a reflection of a cultural attitude, but this attitude was more primitive, linking the peasant to the primordial world of his ancestors. The art of the Banims and their contribution to the Irish novel was to fuse these opposing attitudes without falling into mere fantasy or condemning the native beliefs as mere figments of the imagination. It was a narrow path to tread, but in these novels and tales they found that it could be done. Using the native folk beliefs and attitudes toward the otherworld and, at the same time, portraying the peasant as an ordinary man of flesh and bone, they shaped a fiction that has the realism of the English novel and the mystery of the oral tradition. True, they were not always successful, and at times their novels seem to creak between the opposing demands of the two cultures. Nevertheless, they discovered a compromise that spoke to their countrymen, giving unity to the diversity of the Irish countryside and showing the Irish that they had a right to be proud of their unique ability to balance between the primitive world of the cabin and the anglicized world of the town. (pp. 91-2)

> *Mark D. Hawthorne, in his* John and Michael Banim (The "O'Hara Brothers"): A Study in the Early Development of the Anglo-Irish Novel, *Institut für Englische Sprache und Literatur, Universität Salzburg, 1975, 144 p.*

ROBERT TRACY (essay date 1980)

[*Calling the Banims "the first novelists who were Irish rather than Anglo-Irish," Tracy reviews a reissue of the* Tales, *by the O'Hara Family and notes the didacticism inherent in the Banims' attempt to convey the Irish Catholic side of the conflict with both the Protestants and the English.*]

The Banim brothers were the first novelists who were Irish rather than Anglo-Irish—Banim is a Tipperary-Kilkenny variant of Bannon, O Banáin. They write of the "strong" (prosperous) farmers of the southeast, of struggling tenants, of the people of the roads, and of the various secret organizations that attacked landlords and tithe collectors in late eighteenth- and early nineteenth-century Ireland: White Boys, Rockites, Caravats, Shanavests, led by Captain Rock, Captain Moonlight, Captain Starshine, or by John Doe and Richard Roe—names the peasants knew all too well from their unwilling experiences with legal documents and proceedings.

Like all Irish writers, the Banims hoped for English readers, and they tried to describe Irish grievances, and the savage reprisals those grievances sometimes provoked, without appearing to condone violence. There is always a didactic element: Irishmen must abandon their sectarian rivalries to form a united nation, Protestants must surrender their privileges, Catholics their long-cherished resentment. Men and women of goodwill have been preaching the same doctrine in Ireland ever since, with some success, but Northern Ireland shows us that it is still needed, and the Banims' fiction is unfortunately still valid as a kind of political guide to the problems of that unhappy province. (p. 194)

In 1827 Gerald Griffin, concluding his *Tales of the Munster Festivals,* criticized the Banims for drawing "pictures . . . more striking than favourable" by depicting Irish peasants in "moods of troubled gloom and of rude excitement'' and by emphasizing ''the violent and fearful passions of the people.'' The remark tells us more about Griffin's fears than about the Banims, but it does point out a persistent feature of their work, a sense that savage violence lurks just below the surface of Irish life, ever ready to break out. William Carleton, John Synge, and Sean O'Casey were later to dwell on the same bleak truth. (p. 195)

Both Banims, but especially Michael, had a good ear for Irish dialect and, like their fellow countrymen Boucicault and Shaw, the varied speech of Englishmen. ''Tis the Hoirish cry, as 'em calls it, what such loike woild Hoirish always howls, dom 'em,'' says a Yorkshireman, confronted by an Irish funeral; and a cockney replies, ''Demme, though . . . if them 'ere vimen, what are arter the coffin, ben't on a lark, like, east-why, they don't come down a tear, for all they clap hands, and hollar, the velps. . . .'' They sprinkle their pages with Irish words and phrases, reminding the reader that this is a foreign world, emphatically not English, and that Irish peasants, who often sound comic when speaking in English to soldiers and magistrates, have another language when they are at home. Before Terence Delany, a dispossessed peasant, dies in *Crohoore,* he delivers a moving speech, and Michael comments, ''if the language uttered . . . appear too refined for one in his situation of life, it is ascertainable as only in strict unison with the genius and idiom of the language in which he spoke, and from which we have literally translated; in the Irish, there is nothing of what is known by the name of vulgarism; its construction even in the mouths of the peasantry, who to this day use it, has been and can be but little corrupted; nor could the familiar colloquy of the meanest among them, be rendered, in English, into common-place or slang.'' A man is not, of course, upon oath when defending his national language. John, who had the task of seeing *Crohoore* through the press in London, comments drily, ''It is tremendous work to compel English types to shape themselves into Irish words.''

The Banims' social status, as sons of a small tradesman and farmer in Kilkenny, gave them a greater insight into the life of the poor and at the same time made them more eager than Maria Edgeworth had been to assert Irish rights. They condemn terrorism, but remind their readers that White Boys and similar groups exist because the Penal Laws have left the Irish leaderless and ignorant, and the unjust tithes have made them poor. Tithes ought not to be protested with violence, but they ought to be abolished. When Maria Edgeworth raises the question of tithes in *Ormond* . . . , King Corny, her Catholic gentleman, has no fondness for tithes, but hopes for ''no quarrels'' and insists that quarrels imply ''Faults on both sides.'' The priest who argues that ''it don't become a good Catholic to say that'' about tithes is seen as boorishly contentious. In a subtle way the Banims are often contentious. When a British officer praises a girl's beauty in John Banim's *John Doe* . . . , an Irish listener agrees, ''considerin' sich as them that lives on phatoes one an' twenty times in the week.'' In the same novel another officer comments to a traveling priest on the superiority of Italian over British scenery, and the priest concurs; the Italian landscape is more beautiful than the English ''owing . . . to the influence of atmosphere . . . and from the scarcity of trees in Ireland, much more so than the Irish one.'' The English deforestation of Ireland is one of Ireland's long remembered grievances: the forests were destroyed first because they sheltered the survivors of James II's armies, later because the British navy needed Irish oak. ''What shall we do for timber? / The last of the woods is down . . . The crown of the forest has withered / And the last of its game is gone''—so, in Frank O'Connor's version,

runs one of the most famous Irish laments, composed in the seventeenth century to mourn the passing of the old Irish great houses, the woods, and the old Irish aristocracy. Deforestation bulks large in the Citizen's diatribe in *Ulysses.* Banim underlines his introduction of this controversial item by letting his English officer protest ''he could not understand why—unless it was attributable to the indolence of its people—Ireland should be so 'shamefully deficient in trees.''' Michael trails the same coat in *Crohoore,* sending Crohoore and Alley across a range of hills with ''here and there a stunted oak, the relics of the large woods, that about fifty or sixty years before [that is, about 1715, since the story takes place about 1775] had overspread the district.''

John Banim was perhaps a little more moderate than his brother, and a little more inclined to seek his heroes and heroines among the gentlefolk—though *The Nowlans,* in *Tales,* Second Series (1826), presents farmers and clerks; probably his most successful work, it is a bleak tale of a young priest who breaks his vows and marries a Protestant girl, though he believes that by marrying he has lost his soul. In *The Fetches,* John's first contribution to the 1825 *Tales,* a genteel young couple see one another's fetches—a fetch is an apparition of a living person, and its appearance means that that person is about to die. Young Harry Tresham and his Anna spend far too much time discussing the Irish superstitions which Harry has learned about from his peasant nurse. When they see the fetches, they become ill and are separated; but at the end the couple meet by a waterfall, the fetches reappear, and the young people plunge to their deaths. The story is partly a psychological study of those who frighten themselves by brooding too much over superstitions, but it is partly an endorsement of those superstitions. Other people see the fetches too. They are real. And they have risen out of the dirt and ignorance of the peasant cabin where Harry learned about them to destroy this educated and amiable young Anglo-Irish couple. Irish superstition is based on ignorance, which in turn is caused by misgovernment. It is as fatal as the diseases which breed in Dickens's slums. In *John Doe,* his other contribution to the 1825 *Tales,* John Banim is more ambivalent. The local tithe proctor is a monster of cruelty, but when the White Boy hero kills him, the deed makes him unworthy of the heroine. Instead she chooses the lawfully licensed killer, the English officer Graham, who is hunting the White Boys.

John Banim's *The Anglo-Irish of the Nineteenth Century* . . . is almost a rewrite of Maria Edgeworth's *The Absentee* . . . , and endorses her belief that Ireland needs better, but not fewer, landlords. The plot—letting an absentee Irish landlord visit his estate incognito, see the abuses carried on in his name by unjust stewards, and resolve to live at home and make the system operate more justly and more efficiently—became almost a cliché among nineteenth-century Irish novelists, employed by Edgeworth in *Ennui* . . . , Carleton in *Valentine M'Clutchy, The Irish Agent* . . .—there is even Alice Milligan's *A Royal Democrat* . . . , in which the Prince of Wales comes to examine his Irish ''estate'' and decides to rule Ireland more benevolently in future. John Banim's hero arrives at the same resolve. He comes to accept, and to accept with pride, the Irish element in his identity—previously he has called himself Anglo-Irish or English-Irish, emphasizing the English element. Despite absurdities of plot depending on mistaken identity, near doubles, and deliberate mystification by the hero's pro-Irish sister, the hero's conversion is believable. And perhaps even the constant disguises, incognitos, half-glimpsed figures, and whispered warnings can be defended as contributing to a picture of an incohesive society swarming with spies, outlaws, and assassins.

The difficulty of obtaining the Banims' books, even in large research libraries, has long delayed the kind of evaluation that their work demands. It is true that this collection is not completed. . . . [Still], this handsome edition, intelligently introduced, is an important achievement. Students of Irish literature—as we have seen, the Banims abhorred the term "Anglo-Irish"—can now examine the development of the Banims and illuminate a dark area of Irish studies. But the student of Irish literature ought not to be the sole beneficiary. The Banims owed a debt to Scott, as Scott admitted a debt to Maria Edgeworth. But in exploring the human potential for savage behavior, the controlling power of superstition, and especially in their awareness of the crushing effect of history on individuals, they anticipate—although they remain minor novelists—some of the great Russian writers who were also members of an incohesive society. "Go to the Arran [sic] Islands," Yeats ordered Synge, when they met in 1896, "express a life that has never found expression." It had been expressed already by the Banims, and by other nineteenth-century Irish writers. Yeats had forgotten his own words to Father Matthew Russell in 1889: "Carleton and Banim . . . had a square-built power no later Irishman has approached. They saw the whole of everything they looked at . . . the brutal with the tender, the coarse with the refined. . . . The old men tried to make one see life plainly but all written down in a kind of fiery shorthand that it might never be forgotten." (pp. 196-99)

> *Robert Tracy, in a review of "Tales by the O'Hara Family" and others, in* Nineteenth-Century Fiction, *Vol. 35, No. 2, September, 1980, pp. 193-99.*

JOHN CRONIN (essay date 1980)

[*In his discussion of* The Nowlans, *Cronin claims that although the novel is "in places, quite execrably plotted," it "often approaches greatness." Cronin admires John Banim's ability to combine within his novel the unfolding of an Irish Catholic's psychological breakdown and the cultural and political dilemmas facing the Irish people.*]

John Banim was to achieve in *The Nowlans* a work which, in the realms of character analysis and the exploration of motives, often approaches greatness but one which is also, in places, quite execrably plotted.

Broadly speaking, the work falls into three main sections, the first two dealing with 'priest' John's relationships with Maggy Nowlan and with Letty Adams. The third, by far the most confused and chaotic, recounts the fortunes of John's sister, Peggy Nowlan, and her relationship with the villain of the piece, Letty's brother, Frank Adams. (p. 47)

In assigning John Nowlan one Catholic and one Protestant parent, Banim both provides himself with a splendid opportunity for entertaining characterisation and also furnishes his work with an appropriate sectarian ambivalence which is relevant to the entire social fabric of the work and to the hero's main dilemma. Throughout, the novel will seek to explore the divided Ireland of the early nineteenth century, an Ireland which saw the proselytising activities of the 'New Reformation' in full swing, an Ireland where all that was solid and respectable was also Protestant, where the vast majority of the people were Catholics struggling desperately to achieve some sort of civic identity for the first time since the inception of the Penal Laws. Throughout the work also, John Nowlan will be subjected to

moral and social pressures from the two sides of the religious divide and will be made to question the absolutes of clerical celibacy and the rigid regulations of the Church in which he has taken his vows as a clergyman. The immensely diverting account which Banim provides by Mrs Nowlan's partial 'conversion' from her original Protestantism to her husband's faith, forms an ironically comic prelude to the genuine agonies of indecision which will afflict her son later in the work. Not until Joyce offers us his portrait of that most reluctant of Catholics, Mr Kernan of the short story, *Grace,* will we encounter so amusing a study of divided religious allegiances as Mrs Nowlan:

> She had been brought up decidedly biased to one religion, chiefly because hating the other, and not much burdened, even after her conversion, with a knowledge of the distinctions between both, Mrs Nowlan was, sometimes, indifferently and unconsciously a child of either. For instance; while giving out, during Lent, at the head of her domestics and children, the form of prayer called "the rosary", . . . Mrs Nowlan more than once mixed up, in a concluding aspiration, the first of a Roman Catholic prayer and the last of a Protestant one. . . .

As presented by Banim, Mrs Nowlan becomes a comically idiosyncratic character of a highly effective kind, in the manner which John Banim had recommended to his brother, but there is a cutting edge to this comedy, since Mrs Nowlan's absurd social pretensions reflect the social pretensions of Irish Protestants in general and expose the ruinous divisions in the society with which the novel is profoundly concerned. . . . (pp. 47-8)

This first volume of *The Nowlans* [shows] John Banim writing often with great power and penetration on social issues and personal dilemmas which profoundly interested him. He was tackling what was, for his period, explosive material. His avowed purpose in all his fiction was to reveal his people in a true light to the readers of the larger island and it was extremely courageous of him to choose an errant priest as his hero for a full-length novel. He must have known the risks he ran of offending his fellow-countrymen by his choice of theme. In this respect, Banim is something of a pioneer and deserves high praise for his forthright approach to a sensitive subject. Irish fiction has produced plenty of sentimentalised portraits of priests of the 'soggarth aroon' kind but surprisingly few realistic portraits of priests as fallible, human figures subject to the stresses which beset all mortals. John Nowlan is a worthy predecessor of George Moore's Fr Gogarty or Gerald O'Donovan's Fr Ralph. Only a few talented writers such as Richard Power or Brian Moore have offered us equally credible portraits of priests in contemporary fiction. It would, therefore, be very gratifying if one could maintain that Banim sustained this level of performance in the second volume of his story. Unfortunately, he did not. The second volume deals largely with Peggy Nowlan and Frank Adams and lapses into melodramatic contrivances of all kinds. The first of these has John Nowlan forcing Frank and Peggy into marriage because he has been deceived by Maggie Nowlan into the belief that Frank has seduced his sister. When this absurd match has been improbably celebrated by the friar, Shanaghan, John next rushes off to Dublin with Letty, committing himself totally to a course which he has failed utterly to justify to himself in terms of the morality by which he has lived as a clerical student and a priest.

John Nowlan's life with Letty in Dublin is depicted by Banim with a kind of morbid realism which is immensely powerful in conveying the mental torment he suffers and the physical privations they both undergo through poverty and loneliness. The hideously unpleasant lodgings in Phibsborough are brought to sordid life through the sort of detail which must surely owe something to Banim's own unhappy experiences in Dublin as a young man. The dreadful Mr and Mrs Grimes, the stingy owners of this mean household, are memorable portraits of a particular kind of smug parsimony. Oddly enough, Thomas Flanagan appears to feel that Banim had lost his objectivity in his depiction of the Grimes couple and their setting. He writes of Banim's imagination being 'liberated from its everlasting fairmindedness' [see excerpt dated 1959]. He appears to take the view that Banim is satirising a particular kind of Protestantism in his account of the Grimes pair and their unlovely residence. This seems to me to do less than justice to the effectiveness of the entire episode. John and Letty are allowed no idyllic interlude in their loving. He is convinced that, as a priest, he is not married at all and that he has, therefore, dragged Letty with him into the most fearsome kind of sinfulness. Letty, convinced by Frank that John has not taken final vows, appears to believe in the marriage as a real one, but they are, in any case, allowed little opportunity for speculation about the rights and wrongs of their union. The mere business of keeping body and soul together occupies them to the exclusion of all else. John, to begin with, manages to get some work as a teacher but his secret becomes known to the well-to-do Dublin Catholics who employ him and they soon reject him brutally, making it quite clear that they see him as a priest who is living in sin with a mistress. Thus, *pace* Flanagan, Banim seems to present just as unsympathetic a view of his Dublin Catholics as he does of the Protestant Grimes family. The former are as viciously uncharitable as the latter are meanly self-satisfied. John and Letty are rejected by all and their letters home provide no solution to their problems. Letty's letters to her uncle remain unanswered and she will die without knowing that Frank has thwarted her efforts to get in touch with her uncle. Eventually, poverty forces the unhappy pair to flee from Dublin and, soon after, Letty dies with her first-born in the direst poverty and John Nowlan lays out her body on an old door in a dreadful hovel by the roadside. This scene, which sounds like the worst kind of melodrama when recounted out of context, has in its place in the story a dark and gloomy power, providing a fitting climax to John Nowlan's doomed and hopeless passion.

The rest of the work lapses into the worst kind of lurid and improbable contrivance to the point where the reader can scarcely summon up the necessary energy or curiosity to follow the labyrinthine improbabilities of an increasingly silly plot. Frank Adams turns into the most Gothic of villains. There are attacks on stage coaches, disguises, fortunate rescues at the last minute, dark murders in ruined wayside cottages, nothing seems to be too highly-coloured or unconvincing to find its way into the story which meanders from Tipperary to Dublin and back again. John Nowlan, who has been at the centre of the tale from the beginning, disappears from view and Banim never succeeds in achieving the same penetration of the character of Peggy Nowlan. The powerful realism of the first volume gives way to lurid melodrama. The realities of Irish life are once again forced into the unsuitable form of nineteenth century sensational fiction. . . . Sadly, Banim was prepared to tamper with what most readers feel is the strongest part of his work, his frank presentation of John Nowlan's powerful passions and his realistic depiction of the disorderly life of the lecherous

Aby Nowlan. In a letter to his brother, Michael, on Christmas Day, 1826, John writes:

> The second series go on right well; but the publishers say they are too strongly written, too harrowing, and, in parts, too warm and impure. The latter portion of this judgment, I regret to say, is merited. I have made a mistake, and must not again fall into the same error.

In the following April, another letter to Michael indicates that the bowdlerising of *The Nowlans* has taken place:

> In the second edition of the second series of our tales, just out, I have corrected some of the more glaring improprieties of the first.

His biographer, Murray, appears to approve of the alterations. Fortunately for Banim, his moralistic unease does not appear to have developed into the sort of general creative nausea which was to assail his friend, Gerald Griffin, and lead to that writer's complete abandonment of his craft. In thus altering the first version of his most powerful novel, Banim was merely adapting himself to the prudish moral standards of his day. Modern readers will return to the story's original and more powerful version and delight in its bold tackling of a soul-struggle of a turbulent and deeply disturbing nature.

In *The Nowlans,* John Banim, in spite of obtrusive and outmoded conventions, managed to chart the lonely and agonising moral struggle of a tormented and devious nature. He dealt with sexual matters with frankness and clarity and charted the shifts and vacillations of his hero in a manner convincingly geared to the action of the story. In his bold use of chance and coincidence and near-miss situations he anticipates the quality of the rustic tragedies of Thomas Hardy and his handling of John Nowlan's dark and lonely struggle against his own passionate nature is as modern as John McGahern's *The Dark.* Small wonder that Maria Edgeworth referred admiringly to *The Nowlans* as 'a work of great genius'. . . . [In] spite of his largely unsuccessful struggle with the novel form, in spite, also, of appalling ill-health and a grievously arduous life, John Banim managed, in *The Nowlans,* to do enough to convince us of his considerable gifts as a novelist, combining a searching analysis of individual torment with a comprehensive dramatisation of the frustrating and contradictory Ireland of his day. (pp. 54-7)

> *John Cronin, "John Banim: 'The Nowlans' (1826),"*
> *in his* The Anglo-Irish Novel: The Nineteenth Century, *Vol. 1,* Barnes & Noble Books, 1980, pp. 41-58.

BARTON R. FRIEDMAN (essay date 1982)

[*Friedman argues that John Banim wrote* The Boyne Water *to support Irish Catholic Emancipation and that he attempted through his character Robert Evelyn, an English-educated Irish Protestant, to call for an end to hostilities between Irish Catholics and Protestants. According to Friedman, in this novel Banim shapes his fictional characters and plot so that he may concentrate on the history of political and military events within Ireland.*]

The kind of Englishman who may honor *The Boyne Water* with a perusal materializes in the book's chief protagonist, Robert Evelyn—the more because Evelyn is not an Englishman but an Irish Protestant, his mind formed by an English education. Evelyn's letter to his exiled Roman Catholic friend and brother-in-law, Edmund M'Donnell, lamenting Parliament's disregard of the Treaty of Limerick, closes the novel as "Abel O'Hara's" letter to "Barnes O'Hara" opens it. And Evelyn repeats the optimism about English justice professed by the Banims: "Englishmen will yet pay their fathers' debt to Ireland. The treaty of Limerick will yet be kept." . . .

For John Banim in 1826, keeping the Treaty of Limerick meant legislating Catholic Emancipation. As his few critics have pointed out, he wrote *The Boyne Water* to add his voice to those in England and Ireland supporting Emancipation, which Parliament in fact passed three years later. Catholic Emancipation Banim views as an essential step toward healing the breach dividing Irishmen, the achievement of which Evelyn urges on M'Donnell as part of the program for fulfilling Ireland's aspirations to nationhood: "From the present hour, Ireland must become an united country, fairly and nobly rivalling England in all that makes England truly great, or remain, for ages, a province of England, poor, shattered, narrow-minded, contemptible, and, party with party as she stands, contemned by the world, and by England, too." . . . (p. 40)

The division threatening to lock Ireland into a provinciality—poor, shattered, narrow-minded, and contemptible—is symbolized as Evelyn writes by the sea separating him from M'Donnell; its consequences symbolized not only by Edmond's banishment—with that of Sarsfield and the defenders of Limerick—to service in foreign armies, but also by the collapse of his hopes for domestic happiness through the death of his fiancée, and Evelyn's sister, Esther, in the siege of Londonderry. Banim uses the courtship of Edmund and Esther and of Evelyn and Edmund's sister Eva to dramatize the tension between public affairs and private feelings. The reconciliation of Evelyn and Eva, as Limerick is about to fall, suggests the potential of love to overcome the most deeply rooted of historical hatreds and show the way to making Ireland a united country.

Marriage between Roman Catholic and Protestant seems, indeed, the conventional resolution to dramatic conflicts with political implications for Irish novelists throughout the first half of the 19th century. This resolution forms, allowing for differences in the political and religious rivalries he addressed, part of the legacy conferred on them by Scott. Banim himself is accused by Robert Lee Wolff—implausibly, in my view—of patterning *The Boyne Water* with a fidelity "almost comic at times" on *Redgauntlet*. . . . Thomas Flanagan more reasonably proposes *Waverley* . . . as Banim's model [see excerpt dated 1959].

But neither recognizes that, however much Banim has borrowed from Scott, he has reversed Scott's emphasis. In *Waverley*, the history of the Forty-Five is subordinate to the *bildungsroman* tracing Edward's growth from youthful dreamer to responsible adult, and Culloden enters the narrative only by inference. Scott even apologizes, if with a somewhat satirical edge, "for plaguing [his readers] so long with old-fashioned politics, and Whig and Tory, and Hanoverians and Jacobites," explaining that he cannot render his story "intelligible, not to say probable, without it." . . . In *The Boyne Water,* Evelyn is the same mature, moderate, tolerant citizen entering Carrickfergus after the accession of James II in 1685 as he is when writing to Edmund years after William's triumph is complete. Beyond his role as one of the principals in Banim's double love plot, he functions chiefly as witness to most of the major events in James's campaign to hold Ireland—from Londonderry to the Boyne to Limerick—thereby enabling his author to narrate each battle in detail. His capture at the Boyne reduces him to an all but passive observer; and in the last stages of the

narrative much of its focus shifts to a real historical figure, Patrick Sarsfield.

That *The Boyne Water* is more concerned with history than fiction is implied by "Abel O'Hara's" letter to "Barnes," which could readily serve as the introduction to a scholarly treatise: while historians have traditionally accepted the Whig reading of the Glorious Revolution—the letter in effect runs—new perspectives like those opened by James's memoirs require that the case for the Stuarts, at least in Ireland, be reassessed. And "Abel" goes to great lengths, by way of repeated assertions to his brother, to assure their "hesitant English wellwishers" that the crucial episodes of the narrative, from the tornado bringing the Evelyns and the M'Donnells together to the circumstances determining the outcome of the struggle, are reliably documented: "Every statement of facts, or allusion to them, which we are compelled incidentally to put forward, is authorized by historians, whom both sides are bound to admit; and . . . nothing can be objected to us which must not also be objected to Dalrymple, or Harris, or Burnet, or Hume, or Smollett, or James's memoirs, or Walker's diary of the siege of Derry . . .". (pp. 40-2)

"Abel O'Hara's" historians comprise, for the most part, a roll-call of the chief Protestant commentators on the Glorious Revolution available to a student in 1826. In their authority lies the Banims' claim to a fairness and balance they find lacking in English versions of James's Irish debacle. For they are acutely aware that—as Brown, following Cecil Woodham-Smith, remarks in *The Politics of Irish Literature*—viewing history through Irish eyes entails turning some of the greatest English heroes, among them William III, into villains. If they are to hold the sympathy of that English reader whose wellwishes, however hesitant, "Abel O'Hara's" letter solicits, they must refrain from awakening his prejudices by firmly repressing their own. The magnitude of their problem is illustrated by a modern historian trained in scholarly objectivity: David Ogg, in *England in the Reigns of James II and William III*. Ogg attacks James's Declarations of Indulgence, arguing that, had he achieved his aim of placing as many Roman Catholics as possible in public office, he would have reconstituted England as a country in which, though Protestants might still practice their religion, they lived as "helots," kept from participating in their own government. What Ogg describes—though without acknowledging or perhaps even realizing it—is precisely the state of which longstanding English policy had relegated Catholics in Ireland.

Bitterness at this policy manifestly underlies *The Boyne Water,* despite John Banim's efforts to mute it in his characterization of another English hero Brown lists as an anathema to the Irish, Oliver Cromwell, who makes his one appearance in the narrative as "ruthless Cromwell." . . . In Banim's polemical design this epithet becomes a virtual, if nonetheless Freudian, slip of the pen. He pitches his narrative voice not as a rallying cry to the survivors of Ninety-Eight or, somewhat before its time, to the bold Fenian men, but as a call for moderation. Again, "Abel O'Hara's" letter alerts the reader to the *via media* he and his brother stake out for the novel:

> One side regards William as a persecutor, which
> he was not; as a Church-of-England champion,
> which he was not; and as a religious bigot,
> which he was not: the other, as an amiable and
> chivalrous hero of romance, appointed, first to
> England, and next to Ireland, especially for the
> purpose of rooting out popery. . . . James, too—

both agree in one point concerning him; namely, that he was a coward, or something very like it; and then, his hereditary haters call him tyrant, butcher, fanatic; or if that is not enough, his most vivid identity, in their comprehensive minds, changes into a brass sixpence, or a pair of wooden shoes; while the descendants of those who fought by his side, scarcely take the trouble of denying one of the leading charges; either because, in as much "contented ignorance" as those that talk more, (on this one subject, at least) they have listened until repetition worries them into assent, or because one of the leading charges, if allowed to be true, seems to afford, by throwing upon James's shoulders the blame of occasional defeat, some unction for their wounded vanity. . . .

(pp. 42-3)

Proposing *The Boyne Water* as a corrective to history's portraits of William and James sums up one of the novel's main strategies. In his treatment of what J. G. Simms calls "The War of the Two Kings," John Banim anticipates the method of a historian for whom he and his brother would have little use, Lord Macaulay, who, as George Levine observes, narrates the Glorious Revolution in his *History of England* (1849-61) from the perspectives of the two men embodying its conflict: one the last of the feudal, the other the first of the modern, monarchs. (pp. 43-4)

The Banims would surely deny that Macaulay does justice to the Irish party. He interprets William's seizure of the crown as a triumph of order over anarchy; and in extolling that triumph he turns history's cast of heroes and villains once more English-side-up: "England was again the England of Elizabeth and Cromwell; and all the relations of all the states in Christendom were completely changed by the sudden introduction of this new power into the system." . . .

Macaulay's William is precisely the amiable and chivalrous hero of romance the Banims had sought to exorcise from history, portrayed not only as the brave commander, ignoring a shoulder wound to ford the Boyne with his left wing, his arrival deciding the day, but also as a political genius. . . .

This William little resembles Banim's sullen, near reclusive monarch, shielded from his subjects by Bentinck and his Meerschaum-smoking Dutch officers, granting Evelyn a reluctant audience at Kensington Palace. Nor does James skilfully managing his prancing horse—encountered by Evelyn when he accompanies the delegation from Londonderry to the Jacobite camp at Johnstown—resemble Macaulay's frightened truant, throwing the Royal Seal in the Thames, abandoning his kingdom to its own devices. . . . (p. 45)

Instead of exorcising the amiable and chivalrous hero of romance from history, *The Boyne Water* recreates him in its portrait of James presenting a royal face to the world while his throne crumbles beneath him; or, rather, the novel extends him to apprehend both kings. William inspecting his troops before the Boyne assumes similarly heroic stature. . . . (p. 46)

[But Banim] never quite bridges the gap between the novel of manners inherent in the courtships of Evelyn and Eva, Edmund and Esther, and the romance he fashions from history. Though he might have succeeded had he been able to build his plot around Edmund who, stripped of land and father by the brutal Kirke, abjures his name and turns Rapparee, his polemical

design required him to find his central intelligence in the moderate Protestant, Evelyn; and Evelyn is descended in a direct literary line from Waverley, of whom Flora Mac Ivor justly concludes: "high and perilous enterprise is not [his] forte. He would never have been his celebrated ancestor Sir Nigel, but only Sir Nigel's eulogist and poet." . . . (pp. 46-7)

Because high and perilous enterprise is not Evelyn's forte either, Banim renders the last part of his narrative a eulogy for another Sir Nigel, Sarsfield. Its major action, besides the Siege of Limerick itself, consists of the famous raid by the Lucan Horse on William's artillery train, during which Evelyn, as Sarsfield's prisoner, is carried along like an appendage to his saddle. Banim needs Evelyn's presence as a device not only for controlling point of view but also for expressing the political moderation he urges on Englishmen vintage 1826 in a voice, he assumes, more convincing than his own native Irish Catholic voice. Evelyn serves, that is, to question those simplistic moral labels ingrained in Englishmen by their historical traditions. (p. 47)

Banim has split Scott's characters, importing them into *The Boyne Water* in binary form to accommodate his historical allegory. Burley becomes O'Haggerty and Walker, as Henry Morton becomes Edmund and Evelyn. Though Lord Evandale in the end pursues a career similar to Edmund's, joining Claverhouse in rebellion, just as Edmund joins the Rapparees, the wilds of Ireland are for Edmund only a way-station along his route into banishment. Whereas the vagaries of British politics leading to 1688 make Morton—like Edmund but on the opposite side—first an exile serving in the wars between William of Orange and Louis XIV, and then, like Evelyn settling down to domestic tranquility with his Catholic bride, Eva M'Donnell, the accepted suitor of Edith Bellenden, daughter of a Tory family.

Banim's reincarnation of characters in *Old Mortality* into doubles mirroring each other extends to Claverhouse, who, as "bloody Claverhouse," ruthless scourge of Scots Covenanters, survives in Kirke, and as benefactor of Morton, wishing no better death than a soldier's in victorious battle, survives in Sarsfield. Claverhouse, Scott well knew, had his wish granted at Killiekrankie; Sarsfield, Banim well knew also, and has Edmund inform Evelyn, had already died Claverhouse's death at Neerwinden. Like Scott, Banim does not so much falsify history as shape it to his own ends. He found no need to invent a tyrant to justify Edmund's embrace of outlawry because he had Kirke, whom even David Hume, strong Williamite partisan as he was, labels a "wanton savage," ready to hand. He found no need to invent a tempter to explain Evelyn's embrace of revolution or a leader to account for Londonderry's embrace of resistance because he had the Reverend George Walker ready to hand.

The conflict between Walker and Father O'Haggerty, which begins with their meeting at the pub in Carrickfergus and ends when they kill each other at the Boyne, sums up Banim's historical theme and exemplifies his method of representing history. If Walker, whom Macaulay describes as assisting by his eloquence to rally the people of Londonderry . . . , figured prominently in real events, O'Haggerty seems a fiction nonetheless true to life. The admonitory sermon Edmund and Evelyn hear him delivering as they enter Carrickfergus—that "as God abandoned Saul, in his lukewarmness, and for his treatment of the Amalekites took his kingdom from him, and ruined his family . . . [so] would He punish all . . . guilty of a similar disobedience" . . . —is attributed generally by Macaulay . . .

to priests in the neighborhood of Londonderry and specifically by Cecil Davis Milligan to an unnamed friar addressing Catholic members of Mountjoy's regiment in Derry's marketplace. No historian, to my knowledge, identifies Walker's killer as a militant priest in arms for James. Macaulay simply observes . . . that Walker was shot urging his fellow Ulstermen on during their crossing of the Boyne at almost the same moment as Marshall Schomberg died performing the same service for the Huguenots; and Robert H. Murray agrees.

Murray also records William's unsympathetic response—"What took him there?"—to the news of Walker's death, a response which had earlier found its way, the harshness of its rhetoric amplified, into *The Boyne Water* "The fool!" says Banim's William, "what did he there?" . . . Banim carefully footnotes William's remark, specifying its source as Dalrymple, for Banim's strategy requires that he induce the reader, presumably conditioned by Protestant historians of the Glorious Revolution, to adjudge Walker as much a villain as Scott's Burley. In this Banim set himself a formidable task. Even Hilaire Belloc, among the few English apologists for James, concedes Walker's achievement in imposing on the citizens of Londonderry an order and discipline that made their resistance possible. (pp. 47-9)

Walker's contempt for treaties negotiated with papists, and especially for the treaty concluded on the eve of Kirke's relief of the city, parallels Sarsfield's scrupulous adherence to the Treaty of Limerick, concluded under like circumstances, and anticipates his emergence as the real amiable and chivalrous hero of *The Boyne Water*. Exploiting the license allowed the historical novelist, as distinct from the historian, Banim on no authority places Sarsfield among the officers escorting King James within range of James Spike's cannon; and when Spike's shot forces their retreat, Sarsfield remains behind "as if astonishment and indignation kept him motionless; or as if to dare another shot in his own person." . . .

His assurance grows into what amounts to a rhetorical set piece, by which Banim established him as spokesman for the integrity of Catholic Ireland. . . . (p. 51)

Despite the Banim's claim to balance in their handling of the Glorious Revolution, Sarsfield's concern with honor shows *The Boyne Water* to be no less biased than Macaulay's *History*. His admonishment to his Protestant compeers—"Keep ye your part of this covenant as well as we keep ours, and there needs no ill-blood between us" . . . —ominously foreshadows not only the implied indictment of English policy in Evelyn's letter to Edmund, but the whole course of events, especially within John Banim's lifetime, from the Rising that took place the year he was born, 1798, to the struggle for Catholic Emancipation that he entered by writing the novel.

The consequences of ill-blood manifest themselves dramatically in the estrangement of both pairs of lovers and the death by starvation of the innocent Esther; the potential of good will appears in the efforts of Sarsfield, exerted on behalf of an enemy, to abet the reconciliation of Evelyn and Eva. While Banim, like Scott, if less successfully, shapes his plot to explore the relationship between public and private worlds and, in periods of crisis, the often conflicting demands they make on the individual, Banim's didactic intent requires that, beyond crystallizing these stresses in fiction, he demonstrate their existence in history itself. To this end, the unfortunate James II serves him perfectly. Wrenched from Eva at the very altar, as Esther is from Edmund, by the news of William's landing at

Torbay and the disclosure of the commitments the young men have made to their misguiding spiritual lights, Evelyn retires to his house at Glenarm, where Walker regales him with an account—listing defections by friends and family—of James's setbacks at court; the severest of which he represents as the Churchills' subornation of Princess Anne. Embittered by the collapse of his own domestic hopes, but also outraged by the disloyalty of those closest to James, Evelyn pronounces their conduct "monstrous . . . unparalleled in the history of nature, or of the human heart." . . . In this conviction Evelyn is joined, through a narrative parenthesis, by Banim himself:

> "succeeding generations will acknowledge" (they *have* on all sides acknowledged it)—"that this prince, whose chief errors were those of temper, judgment, and fanaticism, has met, from his most obliged friends, and the nearest members of his family, worse treatment than even Nero, Domitian, or the blackest tyrants of the world ever experienced." (. . . italics Banim's)
> (pp. 51-2)

The parenthesis, which no modern critic would consider other than a scandalous breach of novelistic decorum, reflects Banim's concern to break down the Williamite, Protestant prejudices of his contemporary English readers, while reinforcing the sympathies of those hesitant well-wishers toward Ireland lurking among them. (p. 53)

[Banim is] critical of Evelyn, who, by Jacobite standards, has taken the field against the government to which he is bound as a subject. Both Banim and Macaulay use betrayal as a device for stressing the magnanimity of their rightful kings: William, in an incident evoked by both, forgoes vengeance against Hamilton after his capture at the Boyne, instead sending for a physician to dress his wounds; James courteously welcomes Evelyn to his evening at Dublin Castle, demanding of him only the reasons for his disloyalty. When Evelyn can manage no better than the weak response that "his majesty's abdication had . . . seemed to release him from allegiance" . . . , James attacks him energetically and persuasively: declaring that abdication entails an act of free will, whereas he was driven from the throne over his own vigorous protests; that, "deserted by all upon whom [he] could have placed reliance," he had no power to resist William; that cognizant of the lesson taught him by his royal father—*"there is little distance between the prisons and the graves of princes"*—he chose flight as the one course left him (. . . italics Banim's).

Banim has put the whole Jacobite case against the legitimacy of William and his successors, into James's reply to Evelyn. His speech constitutes another set piece, comparable in polemical import to Sarsfield's speech on honor, and it reduces Evelyn to silence, whereupon James dismisses him, again courteously but also patronizingly. . . . (pp. 53-4)

That the argument for rebellion is carried by a youth, who, whatever his virtues, is definable as a stripling, an undistinguished subject, appears to the critical eye a painfully unsubtle device for weighting history in James's favor. His confrontation with Evelyn is hardly a war between two kings. It is consistent, however, with Banim's treatment of the Derry apprentices denying entrance at Antrim's troops, which he trivializes as largely an adolescent prank: "In another moment the young crowd scampered by, to shut the other gates, some serious, some frightened at their own daring, but the greater number chuckling and laughing in such a way as told that there was as much fun as patriotism, as much whim as bigotry, in their important frolic." . . . Banim characteristically claims truth for his rendering of the event by marshalling as much fact, including the identities of the apprentices, as the narrative will bear, and then calling the reader's attention to his practice: craving him "to observe, that all the names we have mentioned here, are, together with Mr. Walker's, historical names; and 'immortal' ones, too—in Derry." . . . He employs the same stratagem in depicting the Protestant fear of massacre, incorporating the actual letter by which an anonymous peasant informer supposedly warned Lord Mount Alexander of a Roman Catholic plot "to fall on and murder man, woman, and child," then announcing: "Here is quoted, word for word, the document that, such as it is, produced the real or feigned shew of terror which, beginning in professions of loyalty to King James, ended in openly resisting his dominion in Ireland." . . . (pp. 54-5)

Banim tries in effect to have it both ways. While he accurately renders the causes of James's downfall in Ireland, he develops those causes within a rhetorical frame calculated to discredit their perpetrators: the Derry apprentices have earned immortal names, but only in Derry; the letter to Lord Mount Alexander provokes a show of terror, real or feigned. And he underscores the ambivalence with which he would have even his English reader view these details through the skepticism of Evelyn. Shown the letter by Walker—whom no historical account, to my knowledge, lists as receiving a copy—Evelyn observes that, though "It purports to be written by a vulgar Irishman . . . it rather seems to me like the diction of a vulgar Englishman; or, perhaps, an affectation of the latter by an educated person." . . . (p. 55)

Evelyn's capacity for moral judgment derives partly, that is, from his sensitivity to language. Though himself victimized by language, as Walker deploys it, he grasps its potential to distort and corrupt. The subversive power of language comprises, indeed, one of Banim's pervasive themes. *The Boyne Water,* thus, opens with a confrontation between Evelyn's acerbic aunt and a peasant of Carrickfergus, incorrigible bigots both. . . . Their exchange foreshadows Banim's recurrently allegorical use of characters, whereby even his major adversaries—Walker and O'Haggerty, William and James—become voices bespeaking rival ideologies. Mrs. Evelyn's hatred of papists is echoed by her attendant, an old Roundhead trooper, significantly named Oliver, who fondly recalls Cromwell's slaughter of Irish Catholics in 1641, and who is rebuked for his bloodthirstiness by Evelyn: "the times are altered; and altered, I hope, for the better, since they afford opportunities to men of all parties to hold out to each other the hand of brotherhood." . . . (pp. 55-6)

Banim essentially adumbrates his whole novel in this brief episode: the potential of good will to promote brotherhood is realized, literally, in the bond between Evelyn and Edmund; the potential of ill will to provoke conflict is realized in history itself. As an instrument of prophecy, history outweighs fiction. The reconciliation of Edmund and Eva with Evelyn affects no one but Edmund, Eva, and Evelyn. Though Edmund survives, he survives only as an exile—Esther and Ireland lost to him forever. Though Walker dies, his spirit persists in Parliament's refusal to honor the Treaty of Limerick. Though "Abel O'Hara" confidently predicts to "Barnes O'Hara" that "Facts will rout out delusions; and, with them, all disposition to consider as friends those who have endeavoured, and who still endeavour to perpetuate them, or to regard as enemies those who, in the

spirit and love of truth, would humbly but zealously put them to flight for ever" . . . , a reading of Macaulay or the Whig historians following him suggests that John Banim's revision of the facts changed little. Though Catholic Emancipation became law three years after *The Boyne Water* appeared, Ulster, where most of the novel is set, remains a sectarian battleground. (p. 56)

> Barton R. Friedman, "Fabricating History; or, John Banim Refights the Boyne," in Éire-Ireland, Vol. XVII, No. 1, Spring, 1982, pp. 39-56.

JAMES M. CAHALAN (essay date 1983)

[*Cahalan claims the Banims' historical novels "opened up the broad panorama of Irish life to the literary world." He particularly praises* The Boyne Water, *whose Irish Protestant hero links the historical and personal worlds within the novel, but adds that the literary qualities of* The Denounced *and* The Croppy *suffer when the authors lapse into melodrama.*]

It was the historical fiction of the Banims . . . that first opened up the broad panorama of Irish life to the literary world. It should be noted, incidentally, that John Banim was not the first Irish historical novelist. . . . Banim in *The Boyne Water* . . . , however, was the first Irish novelist to attempt to understand Irish history by focusing on a major event in an earlier generation within modern Irish history: the Jacobite-Williamite war of 1689-91. *The Boyne Water* stood for more than a century as the most widely acclaimed Irish historical novel—a remarkable achievement, considering the dark age in which it was written. The Banims also traced the eighteenth-century Irish national experience, in John's *The Denounced* . . . and Michael's *The Croppy* . . . , moving through the Penal Age to 1798. (p. 45)

John Banim's *The Boyne Water* . . . is the first and best of the Banims' historical novels. It is also their longest. John worked furiously upon it from July to December 1825, just after returning to London from three weeks in Ireland visiting Derry, the Boyne, and Kilkenny and having already spent months studying historical accounts of the Jacobite-Williamite war. The novel tells the story of the Protestant brother and sister Robert and Esther Evelyn, who meet and fall in love with the Catholic Eva and Edmund M'Donnell. The two couples wage difficult courtships in the midst of the war. Robert Evelyn is the chief protagonist of the novel; as in John's *The Last Baron of Crana* and Michael's *The Croppy,* a Protestant hero is presented to the Banims' predominantly English readership. The aim is didactic: the Banims want to show their readers that their Protestant heroes' religious and political tolerance is a healthy alternative to bigotry and oppression. Like Robert Morton in *Old Mortality,* Evelyn moderates between opposing fanaticisms in the form of two sectarian extremists: the Protestant, Williamite Reverend-General Walker and the Catholic, Jacobite O'Haggerty. "The same farce, this Christian world over!" exclaims Evelyn. Michael underlined John's didactic intent in the "Introductory Letter" prefacing the novel: "We have unhesitatingly restored to their shape and features all those we have found disguised according to the musty fanaticism prevailing nearly two centuries ago." . . . John deliberately chose not only a Protestant hero for his novel but a title borrowed from the famous Protestant ballad presenting "King Billy"'s version of the Battle of the Boyne; he seeks to tell a new, different, in-depth version of the story of the Boyne, traversing the period from 1685 to 1695.

Robert Evelyn serves Banim thematically, as a voice of moderation between extremes, and structurally, as a convenient link between the different scenes of history as well as between the individual, imaginative world and the political, historical world. Through Evelyn's eyes we see both kings, James and William, as well as Generals Sarsfield and Hamilton. Evelyn's meeting with King James gives the king (and Banim) a chance to present a defense of his abdication of the throne. At this point James summarizes the usefulness of Evelyn as a political (and narrative) link: "Seldom has it chanced that we have been afforded the opportunity of demanding from an enemy, face to face, his reason for hostility." . . . Banim was concerned not to romanticize the characters from public history, writing to Michael that he did not want to make Sarsfield, for example, "a hero of romance"; instead, his fictional heroes and heroines, the Evelyns and M'Donnells, are presented that way. He notes at the opening of the novel that Robert and Esther had in their air "that certain, though indefinable something which proclaims the habits and feelings, if not the birth and lineage, of gentle maidens and gallant cavaliers." . . . These are the characters of romance—noble, flawless, and beautiful.

Banim sets up the double romance and marriage of Robert-Eva and Edmund-Esther in order to explore the political polarities of the time on a personal level. Their lives are invaded by military and social realities: their double wedding is interrupted by Walker, who announces that William has landed at Carrickfergus and takes Robert off to serve in his army. Banim had suggested the unusual nature of the friendship of the Protestant Evelyns and Catholic M'Donnells early in the novel by having them meet in the midst of a tornado. "Increased darkness attended it, and the tumbling and crash of loose rock, again found on its course, showed its unabated power." . . . Only in this otherworldly atmosphere do the Evelyns accept the hospitality of the M'Donnells; as in Scott, entrance to history is gained through the doors of Gothicism. At the same time, Robert's and Esther's warmth and tolerance are contrasted with the flaming bigotry of their aunt and Oliver Whittle, whose closed-mindedness is exposed pointedly to the reader. Banim obviously expects his reader to see through Whittle's narrow-minded disdain for the M'Donnells.

As in Scott, the Evelyns' journey to the M'Donnells takes them from "Lowland" to "Highland," from Belfast to Carrickfergus and Cushindoll, with Banim attempting to transfer Scott's topography to Ulster. The highest mountains in Ireland are actually in the south, in Munster, but Banim sends his hero north, like Waverley, to the Highlands of Antrim. The Scottian interaction of setting and atmosphere with character, plot, and theme is central to *The Boyne Water.* Banim follows his tornado with the introduction of the Gaelic otherworld in the person of Onagh. . . . (pp. 48-51)

The presentation of Onagh, with all of her ranting and raving, assumes Gothic proportions in the novel. (p. 51)

Onagh embodies the Gaelic/Gothic otherworld in *The Boyne Water.* Banim makes it clear that she and the other Gaels in the book speak in another language and from another culture. He continually notes that their dialogue "is translated from the Gaelic," until he finally grows impatient with the notation: "M'Donnell continued to speak in Irish, which, as usual, was rendered for the strangers, and this shall be our last notice of the fact." . . . It is not his "last notice." Banim's use of dialect is scrupulous but awkward.

The use of opposed dialects in *The Boyne Water,* standard English versus various varieties of Anglo-Irish speech and translations from the Gaelic, reinforces the social polarities in the novel, as does the contrast of standard English, English Scots dialect, and Gaelic translations in the Waverley novels. Banim's biographer fails to comment on the extent of his knowledge of Irish Gaelic, but Banim's meticulous attention to the footnoting of his "Gaelicisms" in *The Boyne Water* indicates that he must have had a working knowledge of the language, though a few of his translations are shaky enough to suggest that he was no native speaker.

When the Evelyns travel north into the Gaelic otherworld, Banim sets up an outsider's point of view, one which he himself shared. The middle-class, English-speaking Banim speaks from a world dominated by genteel, English-speaking heroes and heroines. The peasant mercenaries Rory-na-Chopple and Galloping Hogan do not belong to this world. Characters such as these are reminiscent of many of Scott's vivid "fringe" characters. Moya Laherty and Carolan love Robert and Eva, respectively, but these Gaelic peasants cannot match their loved ones' status and their love is not reciprocated. When Moya finally makes her overture and Robert turns her down . . . , Moya's rural, peasant Anglo-Irish speech is contrasted with Robert's educated, genteel standard English, setting the two of them off sharply from each other on the page and underscoring their different social status. The Anglo-Irish dialects presented by Banim exemplify the typical nineteenth-century pastiche, not much bettered (except perhaps in William Carleton's best works) until John Synge. (p. 52)

Both the English and Irish Gaelic dialects spoken in Northern Ireland were and are, in fact, closer in many ways to their Scottish equivalents than they are to the dialects of southern and western Ireland. The term *Gaelic,* whose use sometimes tends to confuse the fairly different Celtic languages of Ireland and Scotland, is actually accurate in this case, for the Gaelic phrases recorded in anglicized form in *The Boyne Water* are drawn from nineteenth-century Antrim Gaelic speech, a dialect as close in many ways to Scottish Gaelic as it is to the Gaelic of Connacht or Munster. Flanagan's assessment of Banim as an imitator of Scott is somewhat misleading, for if it is true, as he writes, that "much of the machinery of *The Boyne Water* has been lifted bodily from *Waverley*" [see excerpt dated 1959] and that Banim imitates Scott's use of language and presentation of culture, it is also clear that the imitation does not distort his Irish materials, for Banim and Scott were writing about two very similar cultures. Where Banim does go wrong, Scott has often preceded him with a similar error. For example, the names *Edmund* and *Eva* can hardly be said to be Gaelic and were undoubtedly grafted onto the story in order to propitiate English readers. Similarly, many of Scott's names are only pseudo-Gaelic: the Mucklewraths and all the rest. Neither writer achieves linguistic precision. Both do manage to make a traditional culture accessible and understandable, conveying its flavor to a wider audience, while at the same time letting it retain its dignity and its distinctness.

Banim departs from Scott in his presentation of his hero: the formerly passive Evelyn moves toward partisanship. Searching for Eva, who serves the Jacobite cause, Evelyn spends as much time with the Jacobites as with his own Williamite army, traveling as a noncombatant with Sarsfield from Dublin to Limerick, where the final Williamite victory occurs. Evelyn recognizes the rightness of the Catholic cause. The Protestant hero is taught the Catholic point of view—just as Banim seeks to educate his readers. By the end of Banim's very long story, Esther, trapped by Walker in the siege of Derry, has died from sheer anxiety and from the starvation forecast by Onagh; Edmund is exiled to France; and Evelyn, reunited at last with Eva, remains in Ireland brooding over the vagaries of Irish politics. Evelyn may have exhibited earlier the anxieties of the passive hero and some of the indecision of a Waverley, but by the end he has become very clear about the course of Irish politics; he has become a partisan. Sarsfield, in signing the Treaty of Limerick, has tried to conclude an honorable peace which would preserve the dignity of the Catholic cause, but he is quickly betrayed by the English Parliament. With the Penal Age beginning, Evelyn writes to Edmund:

> In the great country of England, there must also arise a feeling to right the present wrong to which it has just lent itself. For, without her affirmation, the wrong could not have been committed. . . . The treaty of Limerick will yet be kept.

(pp. 53-4)

Writing in 1826, in the middle of the fight for Catholic Emancipation, Banim provides a clear moral to his story. As an O'Connellite and a literary spokesman for English-speaking and bilingual Catholics as well as the rising class of Irish tradesmen, Banim sought to draw a clear connection between the Jacobite-Williamite war and the struggles of his own day in order to argue that the old sociopolitical polarities had still not been resolved, that the Treaty of Limerick had not been kept, and that Catholic Emancipation would finally enforce it. "IT WAS NOT" . . . a happy country, he tells us. The present intrudes upon the past at several points in Banim's narrative, as when he comments upon how the Derry city gate changed in appearance after 1690 . . . ; cumulatively, the suggestion is that there is a definite connection between the past and the present. Banim's Jacobite Ireland is viewed from his own nineteenth-century O'Connellite perspective.

The Boyne Water does not grant the happy ending of a Scott novel; it is the only one of the Banims' historical novels that does not. This feature, along with its thoroughgoing faithfulness to local ways and to history and its sheer energy, marks its superiority to the nineteenth-century fiction that followed it. The Evelyns and the M'Donnells begin as heroes and heroines of romance, but they end as realistic characters. Robert, Eva, and Edmund are survivors of a tragic chapter of Irish nationalist history. Esther does not even survive. Banim is weakest at the points where he allows his imitation of Scott to deprive himself of originality and where he permits his zealous desire to present a balanced view of history to obscure his own position. Robert Evelyn is palest where he reads like Edward Waverley traversing the Irish countryside and most interesting where he replaces wavering with commitment. Rather than return from Irish "Highland" to Irish "Lowland" as a moderate, Evelyn remains in Ireland, convinced of the rightness of the Catholic cause.

Banim, of course, saw his own position as a moderate if partisan one. As he wrote to Michael, "Englishmen of almost every party, who may honour our book with a perusal, are now prepared to recognize the truth of the historical portraits we sketch and allude to." . . . Yet he weakens his own artistic and political statement by seeking always to sweeten the bitter pill of Irish nationalism for his English audience. Cautious in his nationalism, he is unable to throw off caution and to show Irish history as the nightmare that it was. He cannot fully transcend romance and reach tragedy; of course, neither could any other nineteenth-century Irish historical novelist.

John Banim's political commitment to Catholic Emancipation ennobled *The Boyne Water,* but his fear of jeopardizing the cause emasculated *The Last Baron of Crana* and *The Conformists,* two novels published in 1830 under a single title, *The Denounced* (whose adjective may be taken to apply to the unfortunate Catholics of the Penal Age). John had completed a draft of *The Denounced* by the summer of 1829, but after the passage of Catholic Emancipation in that year, he carefully revised his tales before he allowed them to be published the next year. The historical context and Banim's reaction to it are very significant. *The Boyne Water* was written and published relatively early during the Catholic Emancipation campaign, when Daniel O'Connell was busy whipping up the fury of Irishmen and the sympathy of liberal Englishmen; Banim wrote *The Boyne Water* in this O'Connellite spirit. *The Denounced,* on the other hand, was written when Catholic Emancipation was in its most sensitive stage of negotiation before Parliament. Not wanting to endanger the act, Banim pulled his political punches. By the time he had finished the first draft of his book, the Emancipation Act had been passed, and Banim was concerned not to reopen any old wounds of the Protestant-Catholic, English-Irish battle. . . . Writing in the first full flush of the Catholic Emancipation victory, too early still to realize that the realities of Catholic Emancipation would not equal its promise, Banim felt that liberty was won, that "the musty folios of penal enactment have become so much lumber." . . . He seemed unaware that for the forty-shilling holder a ten-pound voting franchise did not banish political slavery at all and that Irishmen would continue to struggle with political and economic bondage for another century or more. By 1833, Murray records, John would write to Michael, "We have given perhaps too much of the dark side of the Irish character; let us, for the present, treat of the amiable; enough of it is around us." . . . (pp. 54-7)

Banim's reaction to Catholic Emancipation was not the only debilitating factor in the composition of *The Denounced,* for he was sick and hard put for cash during this time. . . . Floored by a spinal disease, Banim was unable to carry out the kind of in-depth historical research with which he had prepared for *The Boyne Water;* visits to historical sites in Ireland were impossible.

Falling short of true historicity, Banim retreated to romance and melodrama. His use of local settings, dialects, and traditions greatly lessened. *The Last Baron of Crana* is set rather vaguely in the north of Ireland and around Limerick; *The Conformists,* in a single southern townland, perhaps Kilkenny, although this is never specified. The meticulous footnotes to Irish and Anglo-Irish speech that peppered *The Boyne Water* drop out of *The Last Baron* and *The Conformists* almost entirely. The happy endings of these novels, given the nightmarish Penal Age with which they are concerned, seem unconvincing—contrived merely to please author and reader. *The Boyne Water* manages to present a realism emerging even out of romantic trappings, as the heroes and heroines of romance learn realistic lessons about survival. In contrast, *The Last Baron* and *The Conformists* impose romantic resolutions upon the unpleasant scenario of eighteenth-century Irish history.

The Last Baron of Crana is a tale of chivalry. As in *The Boyne Water,* the hero is a Protestant, Miles Pendergast. Fighting in the Battle of Aughrim in 1691, Pendergast promises his dying Catholic foe Redmond O'Burke that he will adopt his son, Patrick. *The Last Baron* is thus doomed to implausibility from the very beginning. Banim fails to achieve the integration of public history and personal fiction that distinguishes *The Boyne Water*. He follows Pendergast's promise to O'Burke with a somewhat intrusive account of the specifics of the Treaty of Limerick, self-consciously citing "*Smollett, Continuation of Hume,* chapter iii section 12." . . . Always the educator, Banim seems almost painfully defensive about his attempts at historicity:

> In these pages, as well as in others which the writers have submitted to their readers, an endeavour has been made to guard against prejudices of country and creed, while alluding to historical events necessarily bearing upon the task in hand. Upon former occasions, whenever the words of a neutral, or even an adverse historian could be found to convey, briefly, the information required, he has spoken to the reader—and oftener, perhaps, than some readers gave him or his transcribers credit for.
>
> (pp. 57-8)

The Last Baron follows the story of Miles Pendergast and Patrick O'Burke from 1691 into the early years of the eighteenth century. . . . The plot is built upon melodramatic questions of identity: Is Gernon really who he seems to be? Is the mysterious Sir Randal Oge O'Hagan, the roaming rapparee, actually Roger Walshe, Philip's brother, the lost "Last Baron of Crana"? Who is the true father of the homeless Louise Danville, lately come from France? Is it Roger? Will all of these characters achieve happiness? The answer to all of these questions, of course, is "yes."

The best character in *The Last Baron* is none of these, but rather John Sharpe, Miles Pendergast's servant. Sharpe is a Protestant bigot, much like Oliver Whittle in *The Boyne Water*. His earthly views balance the almost mindless, implausible tolerance of the Protestant Pendergast, who gladly raises Patrick as a Catholic, risking his own life by bringing along the outlawed Father James to do the teaching. In contrast, Sharpe disdains "Papists," reporting that his horse, "George Walker" (named after the Protestant hero of Derry), refuses to transport them, and he carries on constant verbal combat with Rory Laherty, Patrick's Catholic servant. Banim uses Sharpe and Laherty as a study in cultural contrast; as always, he takes pains to present Protestant and Catholic sectarianisms as polarized, mirror-image delusions. Rory "thought John Sharpe as great a blockhead as John Sharpe thought Rory Laherty." (pp. 58-9)

Unlike Oliver Whittle, Sharpe does modify his views; he gets educated beyond simple bigotry. . . . Sharpe is a delightful exception to the generally black-and-white characterizations in *The Last Baron,* a romance that for the most part opposes pure evil (Gernon) and pure good (Pendergast, Patrick, Lady Dorcas).

The only other ambiguities of character come with the novel's outlaws. Roger, the rapparee, and Father James, the hunted priest, are presented as somewhat lurid in their outlawry. Father James is pathetic and insane. Outlawed by the Penal Code, he conducts bizarre Gothic services in a cave. Roger, although a good Robin Hood, has lost his nobility by becoming a rapparee. Not quite the knight in shining armor that Carleton's Redmond O'Hanlon is, Banim's rapparee is introduced as a "notorious freebooter." . . . He doesn't fit Banim's nonviolent O'Connellite code, even though he's on the right side.

The Conformists is better than *The Last Baron of Crana*. Here at last Banim's protagonist, Daniel D'Arcy, is a Catholic, and the social world of the novel is entirely Banim's own world: southern, Catholic, middle-class Ireland. *The Conformists* could have been a great novel rather than merely an interesting one. The subject is an important one, but Banim's treatment of it does not live up to its potential. Set during the 1750s, the novel explores conformism—Catholic conversion to Protestantism in order to escape the Penal Code and achieve prosperity—a phenomenon that divided many Catholic families during the Penal Age. There is a suggestion of Cain and Abel to the story of the brothers Daniel and Marks D'Arcy. Their father, Hugh D'Arcy, had unexpectedly inherited from his conformist uncle a modest fortune with which he had bought an estate in 1703. Dan, haunted by sin, impelled by acquisitiveness, and frustrated by the greater parental favor enjoyed by Marks, finally conforms and seeks to disown the rest of his family. He is the black sheep of the family and Marks is the fair-haired darling, yet the story is told from Dan's point of view. His gradually building resentment of his brother and inarticulate rage over his own position (defiantly plowing the fields of the Red House farm) are graphically portrayed in a way that looks forward to the motifs in Irish fiction of the white-haired boy and sibling rivalry. In his frustrated desire to do something with his hands, Dan is something like Farrington in Joyce's story "Counterparts." Unlike Farrington, however, and unlike Cain, Dan repents, at the last moment repudiating his conversion, which he has been talked into by the evil lawyer and conformist Micky Doolly. At the end Dan restores his family to their home.

Like *The Last Baron, The Conformists* jolts to a stop, in the happy ending of romance, a happy ending that deflates the novel. . . . We are left with . . . [a] double wedding about to occur, as at the end of the traditional romance.

The happy ending seems an empty escape in view of what the novel's most recent editor describes as "the grinding injustice of the times." . . . Banim shows in *The Conformists* that he was well schooled about this injustice. We shall probably never know how much of this perception he edited out of the final, published version. The first question Marks asks when he returns home from school in Spain is about the absence of horses, which he was accustomed to riding in Spain but which Irish Catholics are prohibited by statute from owning if worth more than five pounds apiece. History, in the form of Dan's near conversion, nearly destroys the D'Arcy family, but generally history is incidental; the focus is on Dan's character and development. Most of the novel is a long flashback to the time before Marks's return from Spain, delineating the failure of Dan to match his brother's success in his studies and his degeneration, occurring mostly in the Gothic dark and the wrong company. Dan gets caught by his parents in a bog hole with Jinny Haggerty (worth noting since sex is a rarity, to say the least, in the Banims' works), leaves home to make his own way with his own hands on a farm, falls in love with Dora Donovan but feels unworthy of her, and is tempted to convert. Banim hints that he is aware of the escapist nature of some aspects of his story. After describing the sunset scene in which Dan and Dora declare their love, he notes, like author speaking to narrator, "'Romance.' Well, serious Sir. Attend to plainer facts." . . . Thus is "Romance" undercut.

When public history does enter Dan's story, Banim seems apologetic about it:

> It is regretted that the complexion of the time
> of the story unavoidably forces into notice an-

other allusion to penal enactment. This would be avoided, if possible; but so domesticated, we may say, was the statute-book of former days, at the very fire-sides of the Irish people; so literally was it the text from which they read every thing they were permitted to do; and so fully and minutely did it command their feelings, their passions, their hopes, and their prospects, that in rehearsing, as in the present instance, the fortunes of persons living under its sway, fact and nature must be departed from, if they be said to have taken one important step independent of it. . . .

Rather than apologizing for this perception, Banim should have been constantly exploring it. Instead, we are lost once again in melodrama and questions of identity: Who are the mysterious man in gray and the dark woman who try to turn Dan and Dora from each other? Will Jinny and Dinny Haggerty succeed in their plot against the lovers? Jinny loves Dan but can't have him, like Moya Laherty in *The Boyne Water;* once again, Banim portrays his peasants as unworthy of his middle-class protagonists. The focus on Dan as dark protagonist in a dark age of Irish history is effective and appropriate, but the end of the novel escapes that dark age too easily. Like Patrick O'Burke and Miles Pendergast, Dan D'Arcy is finally not "denounced" at all, even though the Penal Age threatened that fate. Instead, Banim lets his heroes off the hook: they escape the nightmare of Irish history and flee into the fairyland world of marriage, property, and progress. (pp. 59-62)

Even though Wexford in 1798 was much more immediate to Michael than Antrim in 1685 was to John, Michael prepared himself for *The Croppy* with extensive historical research, as John had done for *The Boyne Water.* One of the problems with *The Croppy,* in fact, is that its author seems unable to decide whether he is historian or novelist. History is fairly well integrated in *The Boyne Water;* it intrudes in *The Croppy.* The long historical chapter that opens the novel seems an imposition. Like Scott's "Introductory Chapter" in *Waverley,* Banim's first chapter is really more a preface. . . . The true beginning of the novel, chapter 2, opens with a description of Wexford at peace: "The summer sun was slanting his evening rays over the picturesquely winding Slaney. . . ." Immediately we meet Eliza Hartley, "our heroine," "pensively" trying to decide whom she loves. Her love story dominates the next several chapters of the novel. We do not return to public history until chapter 6, at which point the violence of the outside world intrudes into Eliza's consciousness and the reader's.

The reader is left somewhat confused about whether *The Croppy* is history or romance because of Banim's inability to integrate the two. Curiously enough, Banim seems clearer and more committed as historian than as novelist. His historical introduction and epilogue do not advocate, but they do explain, the rebel position, by noting its historical causes. The novel itself presents no such defense. In his story Banim seems to go out of his way to placate his English readers. All of his major "good" characters—Eliza Hartley, her father, Sir Thomas Hartley, and Harry Talbot—are Protestants. The ultimate, deus-ex-machina hero is Harry Talbot, leader of a government platoon that helps to crush the rebellion. Harry marries Eliza after finally exposing to her the villainy of her other suitor, Sir William Judkin, a United Irish leader. The triangle of noble father (Sir Thomas), virtuous daughter (Eliza), and courageous, heroic suitor (Talbot) is one that recurs in the Irish historical

novel, specifically in Le Fanu's *Torlogh O'Brien* and Buckley's *Croppies Lie Down.*

The plot of *The Croppy* revolves around a Gothic web, a melodramatic labyrinth, of unlikely occurrences. In the last two of these, Talbot appears with Eliza's father, whom she had thought Talbot had executed as a United Irish leader, and Judkin is discovered, in a thoroughly Gothic scene, dying over the coffin of his bastard child by Eliza's friend Belinda. The moral positions of Talbot, Judkin, and Belinda are reversed. Throughout most of the novel, Talbot seems both to Eliza and to the reader to be the villain; he turns out to be the hero. Judkin seems to be the hero; he is actually the villain. Belinda, initially presented as Eliza's trusted confidante, is revealed as a macabre witch. These are Banim's attempts at exciting, melodramatic, Scottian plot reversals. Unfortunately, the involutions that end *The Croppy* are unconvincing. Reader sympathies sought throughout the novel are gratuitously contradicted at the end. Furthermore, the main plot has essentially nothing to do with history. Love story and history do not achieve the unity that they do in *The Boyne Water.* Like *The Last Baron of Crana,* *The Croppy* is a romance imposed on history rather than integrated with it.

The most interesting characters in *The Croppy* are minor ones. Beneath the implausible romance that dominates the novel is a more realistic, more interesting underworld of characters and events. Shawn-a-Gow, the blacksmith, sees his innocent son killed before his eyes by government soldiers and busies himself forging pikes for the rebels. Equally interesting are Nanny the Knitter, the old woman who makes a profession of matchmaking for money, and Rattling Bill Nale, a spy who plays both sides for profit. Father Rourke, whose corpse on the gallows is the final image of the novel, whips up Catholic sectarian passions by quoting a supposed Protestant oath to bathe in Catholic blood, which is the same oath that Protestant leaders attribute to the Catholics. Characters such as these are brought to life, as in *The Boyne Water,* by the use of dialect and faithfulness to local tradition. Several of them are based upon history or personal experience: Shawn-a-Gow and Rattling Bill, upon people Banim knew about in Kilkenny; Sir Thomas Hartley, upon Bagenal Harvey, the United Irish leader who eschewed sectarian rebellion but was executed anyway; and Father Rourke, upon Father Philip Roche, the Catholic leader who was hung for his role in the rebellion.

Banim is at his best when he shows how characters like these were affected by the realities of sectarian war. This message, however, is obscured by Banim's melodramatic main plot. Only at the end of *The Croppy* does he return to the realistic, didactic, nationalist intent with which he had begun his story. . . . (pp. 63-5)

[It] might be said that the Banims' achievement was a passing one, but not so their influence. Their attempt to present Irish history realistically often got lost in the shadow of romance which they thought was Scott's, but they were remembered as pioneers of the Irish historical novel. *The Boyne Water,* in particular, was admired and imitated. In *Torlogh O'Brien,* Sheridan Le Fanu modelled himself on John Banim as well as Scott. . . . [Both] Le Fanu and Carleton eulogized Banim. Later still, Yeats pointed to the link between the Banims and Carleton in his assertion that the Banims were Carleton's "equals in gloomy and tragic power" and that all three "saw the whole of everything they looked at . . . the brutal with the tender, the coarse with the refined." The future direction of the Irish historical novel was one suggested, if not fully achieved, by

John Banim and *The Boyne Water:* an adherence to many of the conventions introduced by Scott but at the same time a departure from Scott's passive hero and happy ending in favor of a partisan, Irish nationalist hero and a scenario that became increasingly *un*happy, eventually leading to darker, more realistic endings. These beginnings represent the Banims' legacy. (p. 66)

> *James M. Cahalan, "Beginnings: The Banims," in his* Great Hatred, Little Room: The Irish Historical Novel, *Syracuse University Press, 1983, pp. 43-66.*

ADDITIONAL BIBLIOGRAPHY

Brown, Stephen J., S.J. *Ireland in Fiction: A Guide to Irish Novels, Tales, Romances, and Folklore*. 1919. Reprint. New York: Barnes & Noble, 1969, 362 p.

Contains a brief discussion of the Banims' writing styles and synopses of their novels.

Foster, Roy. "The Unending History Lesson." *Times Literary Supplement*, No. 3,893 (22 October 1976): 1334.

A review of a 1976 publication of *The Boyne Water* that focuses on the novel as a "history lesson."

Griffin, Daniel. "1826." In his *The Life of Gerald Griffin*, pp. 160-96. New York: D. & J. Sadlier & Co., 1857.*

An account of John Banim's friendship with Griffin, including excerpts from their correspondence.

Lubbers, Klaus. "Author and Audience in the Early Nineteenth Century." In *Literature and the Changing Ireland,* edited by Peter Connolly, pp. 25-36. Irish Literary Studies, Vol. 9. Totowa, N.J.: Barnes & Noble Books, 1982.*

A discussion of the Banims' novels from the viewpoint of a literary historian.

Murray, Patrick Joseph. *The Life of John Banim*. New York: D. & J. Sadlier & Co., 1869, 445 p.

The only book-length biography of John Banim. Murray explores his life, work, and relationship, both personal and professional, with his brother Michael. A large number of the Banims' letters and many excerpts from their literary works are included.

William Blake

1757-1827

English poet and artist.

Blake, a visionary poet and artist who was once ridiculed as a madman and is now revered as a genius, is considered one of the major poets of English literature. His current stature rests primarily on the scholarly consensus that his remarkable oeuvre, which is distinguished by his creation and illustration of a complex mythological system, constitutes an achievement of the first order. Imagination is of paramount importance in Blake's system, serving as the vehicle of humanity's communion with the spiritual essence of reality, while reason is associated with the error of materialism. By boldly bringing his unconventional perspective to bear on such sacrosanct subjects as religion, morality, art, and politics, the poet has come to be recognized as both a social rebel and a "hero of the imagination" who played a key role in advancing the Romantic revolt against rationalism. Many of these thematic concerns inform Blake's best-known creation, *Songs of Innocence and of Experience: Shewing the Two Contrary States of the Human Soul,* which is considered one of the great works of English lyric poetry.

Blake was the second of five children born to a London hosier, James Blake, and his wife, Catherine. He exhibited visionary tendencies as a child, claiming to see God at his window and a tree trimmed with angels, and was artistically precocious as well. Following several years' study at Henry Pars's Drawing School, he was apprenticed in 1772 to the master engraver James Basire, who helped stimulate Blake's interest in the Gothic style by assigning him to make drawings of the monuments in Westminster Abbey. Blake took up studies at The Royal Academy of Arts in 1779, but he openly disagreed with his instructors' artistic theories and soon focused his energies on engraving. This work brought him into contact with the radical bookseller Joseph Johnson and with such fellow artists as Thomas Stothard, John Flaxman, and Henry Fuseli. It was through Flaxman's efforts in particular that Blake obtained many of the engraving and drawing commissions that were the principal source of his meager income. In 1782 Blake married Catherine Boucher, the illiterate daughter of a Battersea market-gardener. Catherine was devoted to Blake, and under his instruction she learned to read, write, and help illuminate his books. Although commentators detect signs of conjugal stress in Blake's works, they generally agree that the couple enjoyed a loving union that benefited the poet greatly.

Blake first attracted literary notice in the salon of the Reverend and Mrs. A. S. Mathew, where he read from his poems and occasionally sang them to his original musical compositions. In 1783, Flaxman and the Reverend Mathew funded the printing of *Poetical Sketches,* a collection of verse and drama that shows a young talent subject to the influence of such writers as Ossian and William Shakespeare yet capable of sophisticated technical innovation as well. Blake opened a short-lived print business in 1784, the year to which bibliographers tentatively assign the manuscript of his satire, *An Island in the Moon.* Three years later, he suffered the loss of his younger brother Robert, with whose spirit he later claimed to communicate in the "regions of . . . Imagination." At about the same time, he

developed his private technique of illuminated printing. Blake first employed this printing method in about 1788 while producing two treatises entitled *There Is No Natural Religion* and *All Religions Are One,* which urge the claims of imagination over rationalist philosophy. He issued more and perhaps greater illuminated works in the following year: *Songs of Innocence* and *The Book of Thel* were printed in 1789, and scholars tentatively assign the manuscript of *Tiriel* to this period as well. Inasmuch as Blake painstakingly engraved the plates for his illuminated works, printed them personally, and colored each copy by hand, his books are as rare as they are beautiful. This restricted circulation had a dire impact on Blake, for it limited his income drastically and prevented his reputation and works from spreading beyond a fairly closed society of friends and connoisseurs.

The outbreak of the French Revolution in 1789 found Blake in the company of Joseph Johnson's radical coterie, which included such prominent activists as Joseph Priestley, Thomas Paine, and Mary Wollstonecraft. In their society he evidently discussed such subjects as the democratic revolutions in America and France and the political and social turmoil that they engendered at home, topics that also became major focuses of his poetry: *The French Revolution,* for example, covers events in France during May to mid-July, 1789, emphasizing the oppressive authoritarianism of the old regime, while *America: A*

Prophecy predicts the spread of the American experiment to Europe. These and other works clearly establish Blake's sympathy with political and civil liberties, but his opinions put him at odds with the notoriously repressive government of William Pitt, and thus some critics have speculated that Blake obscured his ideas behind the veil of mysticism to circumvent government censure.

In 1790, Blake and his wife moved to Lambeth, where he completed *The French Revolution* and *America*. In addition to these works, one of the first fruits of his tremendously productive ten-years' stay there was *The Marriage of Heaven and Hell*. In this paradoxical work, Blake departs from his former spiritual guide, Emanuel Swedenborg, to expose the evils inhering in the orthodox conception of virtue and the virtues inhering in the orthodox conception of evil. Characteristically, Blake here identifies religion with laws that focus on restrictions and divisions rather than on spiritual harmony. A series of minor symbolic books also belongs to the Lambeth period: in *Visions of the Daughters of Albion: The Eye Sees More than the Heart Knows, America, The First Book of Urizen, Europe: A Prophecy, The Song of Los, The Book of Ahania,* and *The Book of Los,* Blake developed the symbolic mythology that he first introduced in *Tiriel* and *The Book of Thel,* setting in motion what Mark Schorer describes as "a system of ever-widening metaphorical amplification" through which Blake attempted "to explain his story, the story of his England, the history of the world, prehistory, and the nature of all eternity." Scholars generally agree that Blake's mythology reaches its fullest expression in *The Four Zoas: The Torments of Love & Jealousy in the Death and Judgement of Albion the Ancient Man,* which he probably began to compose during the Lambeth years, and in *Jerusalem: The Emanation of the Giant Albion,* a prophetic work of later origin. *Songs of Innocence and of Experience,* regarded by many critics as the lyrical counterpart of the symbolic books, is also a product of the Lambeth period.

From 1800 to 1803, Blake and his wife lived at the seaside village of Felpham under the patronage of the minor poet William Hayley, whose mundaneness soon became a source of vexation to the visionary Blake. Scholars speculate that Blake revised *The Four Zoas* during his unhappy stay there and that he began to draft *Milton,* a reworking of *Paradise Lost,* at this time also. Both poems have been interpreted in light of his statement that he had "fought thro' a Hell of terrors & horror . . . in a Divided Existence" during these years. The Blakes returned to London in 1803, but their homecoming was marred by accusations that he had uttered seditious sentiments while expelling a soldier named Scofield from his garden at Felpham. He was tried for sedition and acquitted in 1804. Blake's next significant publication, his series of illustrations of an 1808 edition of Robert Blair's *The Grave,* attracted more notice than all of his poetical works combined. However, reviewers castigated his corporeal representation of spiritual phenomena as a piece of imaginative and theological impertinence, and the book also embroiled Blake in a dispute with the publisher, R. H. Cromek. These and other frustrations came to the fore in 1809, when he mounted a private exhibition of his paintings that he hoped would publicize his work and help to vindicate his visionary aesthetic. This it failed to do: not only was the exhibition poorly attended, but the descriptive catalogue that he wrote to accompany it largely inspired ridicule among its few readers.

Blake's later years were distinguished by his completion of *Jerusalem,* his last and longest prophetic book, and by his

creation of a series of engraved illustrations for the Book of Job that is now widely regarded as his greatest artistic achievement. The latter work was commissioned in the early 1820s by John Linnell, one of a group of young artists known as the "Ancients" who gathered around Blake and helped support him in his old age. Vigorous and perspicacious to the last, Blake reportedly greeted death with a song on his lips in his sixty-ninth year.

Blake once defended his art by remarking, "What is Grand is necessarily obscure to Weak men. That which can be made Explicit to the Idiot is not worth my care." He thus characterized his work as a combination of grandness and obscurity that he was not particularly eager to elucidate. Fortunately, his aesthetic philosophy emerges clearly in his writings, forming a firm basis for critical insight into his perplexing oeuvre. Blake held the radical view that "Nature is Imagination itself"; by extension, he also maintained that exercise of the imagination leads to wisdom and insight (synonymous with vision) and, according to Jerome J. McGann, that poetry, painting, and other imaginative pursuits serve as "vehicles for vision." Given this perception, the world of imagination took precedence for Blake over the world of matter, and rational philosophical systems, based as they are in the material world, gave way to the "Divine Arts of Imagination." Moreover, Blake considered it his personal mission both to express and embody this philosophy in his art, thus giving a prophetic quality to his work.

Blake's passion for originality and imagination informs his creation of a private cosmology that embraces both his lyric and prophetic poetry. Stated in the most general terms, his system posits a universe whose most sweeping movements and minutest particulars reflect ever-fluctuating relationships between reason, love, poetry, energy, and other vital forces. While these forces appear most prominently in the symbolic mythology of the prophetic books, taking the guise of such titanic characters as Urizen, Luvah, Los, and Orc, critics generally maintain that they are integral to the symbolism of the lyric poems as well. Hazard Adams, for example, states that "the whole of Blake's great symbolic system" is assimilated in the symbolic structure of the lyric "The Tyger," while Joseph Wicksteed sees Blake's ideas concerning matter and the flesh reflected in such symbols as dew and grass in the "Introduction" to *Songs of Experience.* Great as this symbolic system might be, however, it has also been described as "notoriously private" and "hieroglyphic," pointing to a difficulty in interpreting Blake's symbols that led early critics to question the lucidity and even the sanity of Blake's prophetic books.

By virtue of its versification, *Jerusalem* is considered by many to be the culmination of a lifetime of prosodic experimentation befitting a poet who despised restriction in all its forms: "Poetry Fetter'd, Fetters the Human Race!" Blake declared in the preface to *Jerusalem,* proclaiming his liberation from the "monotony" and "bondage" of metered verse. As early as *Poetical Sketches,* he explored eliminating end rhyme, substituting rhythmical devices such as word repetition that he subsequently used to great advantage in *Songs of Innocence and of Experience.* The poems in the latter work are also celebrated for their compression and economy, yet Blake appears to have deemphasized these qualities in selecting the lengthy septenary line for *The Four Zoas, Milton,* and *Jerusalem.* Even here, however, he deviated from his standard line at will, leading to Alicia Ostriker's observation that "Blake, even in his metrics, deliberately breaks every rule he makes, refuses to impose order in art where there is no order in his visions, . . . [insisting on] keeping beauty afar until he is ready for her.'' Ostriker and other commentators generally agree that Blake's greatest stylistic triumph occurs in ''Night IX'' of *The Four Zoas,* in which the poet triumphantly orchestrates his varied measures in announcing the restoration of universal harmony at the Last Judgment.

Ironically, Blake was better known among his contemporaries for his engravings and designs than for his poetry. Consigned to obscurity by virtue of the scarcity of his books and his reputation for madness, his works received scant attention from his peers, although Samuel Taylor Coleridge privately recognized him as a ''man of Genius'' and Charles Lamb conceded that he was ''one of the most extraordinary persons of the age.'' Blake's critical fortunes did not begin to improve until 1863 with the publication of Alexander Gilchrist's sympathetic biography, which sparked a revival of interest in the poet that was sustained by the editorial and critical ministrations of such nineteenth-century luminaries as Dante Gabriel Rossetti and Charles Algernon Swinburne. This impetus has continued unabated into the twentieth century as well, with S. Foster Damon, Northrop Frye, Harold Bloom, and other critics providing explications of Blake's symbolic system that have abetted an ever-widening array of Blake studies. Indeed, since Frye laid the foundation for interpreting Blake's symbolism in his 1947 publication *Fearful Symmetry: A Study of William Blake,* examinations of Blake's sources, themes, and style have proliferated to such an extent that the growth of Blake studies appears to be assured well into the twenty-first century.

Blake once wrote, ''One Law for the Lion and the Ox is oppression.'' A kindred appreciation of the claims of individualism may well inform the willingness of modern scholars to elevate this most individual of writers to the front ranks of English poetry. At the same time, however, enthusiasts stress that he transcends the merely personal in his works. In the words of George Saintsbury, Blake set forth an artistic aesthetic in which, in place of the ''battered gods of the classical or neo-classical Philistia, are set up Imagination for Reason, Enthusiasm for Good Sense, the Result for the Rule; the execution for the mere conception or even the mere selection of subject; impression for calculation; the heart and the eyes and the pulses and the fancy for the stop-watch and the boxwood measure and the table of specifications.'' Insofar as he embodied these values in expressing his individual vision, he may be said to have championed some of the most profound artistic impulses of humankind.

(See also *Something about the Author,* Vol. 30.)

*PRINCIPAL WORKS

Poetical Sketches　(poetry and drama)　1783
An Island in the Moon [MS]　(satire)　1784
All Religions Are One　(treatise)　1788?
There Is No Natural Religion　(treatise)　1788?
The Book of Thel　(poetry)　1789
Songs of Innocence　(poetry)　1789
Tiriel [MS]　(poetry)　1789?
The Marriage of Heaven and Hell　(prose, proverbs, and
　　poetry)　1790-93?
The French Revolution　(poetry)　1791
America: A Prophecy　(poetry)　1793
*Visions of the Daughters of Albion: The Eye Sees More than
　　the Heart Knows*　(poetry)　1793

Europe: A Prophecy　(poetry)　1794
The First Book of Urizen　(poetry)　1794
*Songs of Innocence and of Experience: Shewing the Two
　　Contrary States of the Human Soul*　(poetry)　1794
The Book of Ahania　(poetry)　1795
The Book of Los　(poetry)　1795
The Song of Los　(poetry)　1795
*The Four Zoas: The Torments of Love & Jealousy in the
　　Death and Judgement of Albion the Ancient Man* [MS]
　　(poetry)　1796-1807?; published as *Vala* in *The Works
　　of William Blake, Poetic, Symbolic, and Critical.* 3
　　vols. 1893
Milton　(poetry)　1804-08?
Jerusalem: The Emanation of the Giant Albion　(poetry)
　　1804-20?
The Pickering Manuscript [MS]　(poetry and proverbs)
　　1807?
A Descriptive Catalogue　(catalogue)　1809
*The Poetical Works of William Blake, Lyrical and
　　Miscellaneous*　(poetry and drama)　1874
The Works of William Blake, Poetic, Symbolic, and Critical.
　　3 vols.　(poetry)　1893
****The Note-Book of William Blake*　(notebook)　1935
The Poetry and Prose of William Blake　(poetry, prose,
　　drama, marginalia, and letters)　1965
The Complete Writings of William Blake　(poetry, prose,
　　drama, marginalia, and letters)　1966
The Letters of William Blake　(letters)　1968

*Dating the original publication of Blake's works is difficult, for he alternately printed and revised some of his individual writings over a long period of time and left few plates and copies of books for bibliographers to examine as evidence. The dates in this list of principal works, reflecting the speculative nature of Blake bibliography, are taken mainly from *Blake Books* by G. E. Bentley, Jr. [see Additional Bibliography]. The designation [MS] following a title indicates that Blake left the work in manuscript form.

**Blake's notebook is also referred to as the ''Rossetti Manuscript.''

WILLIAM BLAKE　(letter date 1799)

[Blake issued the following defense of his visionary art in response to a patron who, in returning a commissioned drawing to the artist, objected that his work was marred by the ''other worldly'' nature of his fancy. According to Blake, as ''Nature is Imagination itself,'' so is imagination the essence of true art. See the excerpts dated 1802, 1808, 1809, and 1804-20 for additional commentary by Blake.]

I feel very sorry that your Ideas & Mine on Moral Painting differ so much as to have made you angry with my method of Study. If I am wrong, I am wrong in good company. I had hoped your plan comprehended All Species of this Art, & Expecially that you would not regret that Species which gives Existence to Every other, namely, Visions of Eternity. You say that I want somebody to Elucidate my Ideas. But you ought to know that What is Grand is necessarily obscure to Weak men. That which can be made Explicit to the Idiot is not worth my care. The wisest of the Ancients consider'd what is not too Explicit as the fittest for Instruction, because it rouzes the faculties to act. I name Moses, Solomon, Esop, Homer, Plato. (p. 34)

I know that This World Is a World of imagination & Vision. I see Every thing I paint In This World, but Every body does not see alike. To the Eyes of a Miser a Guinea is more beautiful than the Sun, & a bag worn with the use of Money has more beautiful proportions than a Vine filled with Grapes. The tree which moves some to tears of joy is in the Eyes of others only a Green thing that stands in the way. Some See Nature all Ridicule & Deformity, & by these I shall not regulate my proportions; & Some Scarce see Nature at all. But to the Eyes of the Man of Imagination, Nature is Imagination itself. As a man is, So he Sees. As the Eye is formed, such are its Powers. You certainly Mistake, when you say that the Visions of Fancy are not to be found in This World. To Me This World is all One continued Vision of Fancy or Imagination, & I feel Flatter'd when I am told so. What is it sets Homer, Virgil & Milton in so high a rank of Art? Why is the Bible more Entertaining & Instructive than any other book? Is it not because they are addressed to the Imagination, which is Spiritual Sensation, & but mediately to the Understanding or Reason? Such is True Painting, and such was alone valued by the Greeks & the best modern Artists. Consider what Lord Bacon says: "Sense sends over to Imagination before Reason have judged, & Reason sends over to Imagination before the Decree can be acted." (pp. 35-6)

But I am happy to find a Great Majority of Fellow Mortals who can Elucidate My Visions, & Particularly they have been Elucidated by Children, who have taken a greater delight in contemplating my Pictures than I even hoped. Neither Youth nor Childhood is Folly or Incapacity. Some Children are Fools & so are some Old Men. But There is a vast Majority on the side of Imagination or Spiritual Sensation. (p. 36)

William Blake, in a letter to Dr. Trusler on August 23, 1799, in his The Letters of William Blake, *edited by Geoffrey Keynes, The Macmillan Company, 1956, pp. 34-7.*

WILLIAM BLAKE   (letter date 1802)

[*Blake here elaborates on the persistent conflict he experiences between business and spiritual demands. In so doing, he alludes to the opposition between spirit and nature, a basic tenet of his thought, and reveals his profound sense of duty as one who is in direct communication with "Messengers from Heaven." See the excerpts dated 1799, 1808, 1809, and 1804-20 for additional commentary by Blake.*]

I find on all hands great objections to my doing any thing but the meer drudgery of business, & intimations that if I do not confine myself to this, I shall not live; this has always pursu'd me. You will understand by this the source of all my uneasiness. This from Johnson & Fuseli brought me down here, & this from Mr H. will bring me back again; for that I cannot live without doing my duty to lay up treasures in heaven is Certain & Determined, & to this I have long made up my mind, & why this should be made an objection to Me, while Drunkenness, Lewdness, Gluttony & even Idleness itself, does not hurt other men, let Satan himself Explain. The Thing I have most at Heart—more than life, or all that seems to make life comfortable without—Is the Interest of True Religion & Science, & whenever any thing appears to affect that Interest (Especially if I myself omit any duty to my . . . Station as a Soldier of Christ), It gives me the greatest of torments. I am not ashamed, afraid, or averse to tell you what Ought to be Told: That I am under the direction of Messengers from Heaven, Daily & Nightly; but the nature of such things is not, as some

suppose, without trouble or care. Temptations are on the right hand & left; behind, the sea of time & space roars & follows swiftly; he who keeps not right onward is lost, & if our footsteps slide in clay, how can we do otherwise than fear & tremble?. . . But if we fear to do the dictates of our Angels, & tremble at the Tasks set before us; if we refuse to do Spiritual Acts because of Natural Fears of Natural Desires! Who can describe the dismal torments of such a state!—I too well remember the Threats I heard!—If you, who are organised by Divine Providence for Spiritual communion, Refuse, & bury your Talent in the Earth, even tho' you should want Natural Bread, Sorrow & Desperation pursues you thro' life, & after death shame & confusion of face to eternity. Every one in Eternity will leave you, aghast at the Man who was crown'd with glory & honour by his brethren, & betray'd their cause to their enemies. You will be call'd the base Judas who betray'd his Friend!—Such words would make any stout man tremble, & how then could I be at ease? But I am now no longer in That State, & now go on again with my Task, Fearless, and tho' my path is difficult, I have no fear of stumbling while I keep it. (pp. 69-71)

William Blake, in a letter to Thomas Butts on January 10, 1802, in his The Letters of William Blake, *edited by Geoffrey Keynes, The Macmillan Company, 1956, pp. 68-71.*

THE LITERARY JOURNAL   (essay date 1806)

[*The earliest known essay on Blake was written by Benjamin Heath Malkin, who included a sympathetic account of Blake as poet and artist in the introduction to his* A Father's Memoirs of His Child, *published in 1806. Malkin reprinted several poems from* Poetical Sketches *and* Songs of Innocence *and* Songs of Experience *in his essay, eliciting the following rebuff in the July, 1806, issue of the* Literary Journal.]

To relieve our readers with a lighter subject, with a touch, indeed, of the ridiculous—let us refer to Mr. William Blake. With the professional occupations of painting and engraving, in which this gentleman is engaged, we have nothing to do; except, indeed, to praise his design prefixed to this volume. The portrait of the child is very interesting.—But what can Mr. Malkin mean by introducing his friend to us as a poet? He allows that Mr. Blake's attempts are 'unfinished and irregular'—and he asserts him to have ventured on the 'ancient simplicity'—illa priorum simplicitas—but with due submission to the judgment of our readers, should we not say that Mr. Blake has successfully heightened the 'modern nonsense?' (p. 44)

An extract from William Blake: The Critical Heritage, *edited by G. E. Bentley, Jr., Routledge & Kegan Paul, 1975, p. 44.*

THE BRITISH CRITIC   (essay date 1806)

[*This commentator dismisses as nonsense the poetry that Malkin included in his essay on Blake. These remarks originally appeared in the September, 1806, issue of the* British Critic.]

[Malkin celebrates Blake] both as an artist and as a poet; but so little judgment is shown, in our opinion, with regard to the proofs of these talents, that we much doubt whether the encomium will be at all useful to the person praised. As an artist, he seems to be one of those who mistake extravagance for genius; as is testified even by his angel in the frontispiece, though the kneeling figure is elegant, and that of the child is passable. As a poet, he seems chiefly inspired by that,

—Nurse of the didactic muse,
Divine Nonsensia.—

(p. 45)

An extract from William Blake: The Critical Heritage, *edited by G. E. Bentley, Jr., Routledge & Kegan Paul, 1975, p. 45.*

WILLIAM BLAKE (essay date 1808?)

[*Although the Royal Academy of Arts had displayed a number of his productions, Blake was deeply incensed by what he perceived as the regular refusal of the English artistic establishment to exhibit his work. In about 1808, he wrote the following trenchant criticism of that establishment in the margin of a copy of* The Life of Sir Joshua Reynolds, Knight. *Reynolds was a leading portrait painter of his day and served as the first president of the Royal Academy. For additional commentary by Blake, see the excerpts dated 1799, 1802, 1809, and 1804-20.*]

The Enquiry in England is not whether a Man has Talents. & Genius? But whether he is Passive & Polite & a Virtuous Ass: & obedient to Noblemens Opinions in Art & Science. If he is; he is a Good Man: If Not he must be Starved. (p. 632)

William Blake, "Marginalia to 'The Works of Sir Joshua Reynolds, Knight' (1798)," in his The Poetry and Prose of William Blake, *edited by David V. Erdman, Doubleday & Company, Inc., 1965, p. 632.*

THE ANTI-JACOBIN REVIEW AND MAGAZINE (essay date 1808)

[*A number of reviewers objected vigorously to the designs that Blake made for an 1808 edition of Blair's* Grave. *As the following excerpt indicates, Blake's critics insisted that his attempt to give corporeal representation to spiritual states of being was completely misguided. Such criticism spoke to an important aspect of Blake's thought—the reality of the spiritual world and its fitness for artistic representation—and drew a defense from the artist in the* Descriptive Catalogue (*see excerpt dated 1809*).]

Mr. Blake was formerly an engraver, but his talents in that line scarcely advancing to mediocrity, he was induced as we have been informed, to direct his attention to the art of design; and aided as his friends report, by visionary communications with the spirits of the Raffaeles, the Titians, the Caraccis, the Corregios, and the Michael-Angelos of past ages, he succeeded in producing the 'Inventions' before us. . . . [Waiving] all considerations of supposed spiritual agency and inspiration, we shall judge only of Mr. Blake's designs from the plain principles of taste and common sense, yet not without reference to the high station in the ranks of art which the proprietor (Mr. Cromek,) claims for them. (pp. 225-26)

The 'Death of the Strong Wicked Man' is conceived with greater energy of mind, and more happily expressed than any other design in the whole work. (p. 229)

Had Mr. Blake contented himself with pourtraying the death-bed of the strong man, the frantic sorrows of the despairing wife, and the mute yet expressive woes of the afflicted daughter, his picture would have deserved a very enlarged portion of commendation. The extremities convulsed with agony, the expanded chest heaving with inexpressible pain, the swelling muscle, and the breadth of limb, are well adapted to give the

idea of strength laid low; but when to all this is superadded a perfectly *corporeal* representation of "the masculine Soul" of the dying man "hurried through the casement in flame," the mind is shocked at the outrage done to nature and probability; and notwithstanding the opinion of Mr. Fuseli, we hesitate not to characterize the imagination of the artist, as carried far, very far, beyond the "verge of legitimate invention."

The 'Death of the good Old Man,' is yet more objectionable. If it were really Mr. Blake's intention [as Mr. Fuseli states in the prospectus for the work] "to connect the visible and the invisible world without provoking probability," he should have done it with threads of silk and not with bars of iron. The beings of another world, when depicted on the same canvas as earthly bodies, should be sufficiently immaterial to be veiled by the gossamer, and not as they are here designed, with all the fullness and rotundity of mortal flesh. (p. 230)

[In the design entitled 'The Soul exploring the recesses of the Grave'] the artist has departed from his own principles, as far as those principles are exemplified in the deaths of the Good and of the Bad Man; in both which pieces we see the spirit taking its flight to the realms of eternity immediately on the extinction of the mortal breath: in this the soul is made to wait on "the dissolution of the body." These inconsistencies must not be tolerated, even in the absurd effusions which we are here so strongly called upon to commend. (p. 231)

Though occasionally invigorated by an imagination chastened by good taste, we regard [these designs] in general as the offspring of a morbid fancy; and we think, that this attempt "to connect the visible with the invisible world, by a familiar and domestic atmosphere," has totally failed. The curtain that separates these worlds is still undrawn by mortal hands; and so we augur it will continue till that great day, when "Heaven's portals shall be opened," and the millions that now lie captive in the grave shall spring

—————into life,
Day-light, and liberty.—

(p. 233)

The dedication of this edition of the *Grave* to the Queen, written by Mr. Blake, is one of the most abortive attempts to form a wreath of poetical flowers that we have ever seen. Should he again essay to climb the Parnassian heights, his friends would do well to restrain his wanderings by the strait waistcoat. Whatever licence we may allow him as a painter, to tolerate him as a poet would be insufferable. (p. 234)

A review of "The Grave, a Poem," in The Anti-Jacobin Review and Magazine, *Vol. XXXI, No. CXXV, November, 1808, pp. 225-34.*

WILLIAM BLAKE (essay date 1809)

[*Blake regarded his exhibition of 1809 as an opportunity for the art world to make an informed decision concerning his reputation for madness and eccentricity. His* Descriptive Catalogue, *published as a guide to the exhibition in 1809 and excerpted below, aims at self-vindication. For additional commentary by Blake, see the excerpts dated 1799, 1802, 1808, and 1804-20.*]

The connoisseurs and artists who have made objections to Mr. B.'s mode of representing spirits with real bodies, would do well to consider that the Venus, the Minerva, the Jupiter, the Apollo, which they admire in Greek [statues] are all of them representations of spiritual existences of God's immortal, to the mortal perishing organ of sight; and yet they are embodied and organized in solid marble. Mr. B. requires the same latitude and all is well. The Prophets describe what they saw in Vision as real and existing men whom they saw with their imaginative and immortal organs; the Apostles the same; the clearer the organ the more distinct the object. A Spirit and a Vision are not, as the modern philosophy supposes, a cloudy vapour or a nothing: they are organized and minutely articulated beyond all that the mortal and perishing nature can produce. He who does not imagine in stronger and better lineaments, and in stronger and better light than his perishing mortal eye can see does not imagine at all. The painter of this work asserts that all his imaginations appear to him infinitely more perfect and more minutely organized than any thing seen by his mortal eye. [Spirits] are organized men: Moderns wish to draw figures without lines, and with great and heavy shadows; are not shadows more unmeaning than lines, and more heavy? O who can doubt this! (p. 532)

> William Blake, "A Descriptive Catalogue of Pictures: Poetical and Historical Inventions," in his The Poetry and Prose of William Blake, edited by David V. Erdman, Doubleday & Company, Inc., 1965, pp. 520-41.

[ROBERT HUNT]   (essay date 1809)

[Hunt, who was one of Blake's most strident critics, chiefly uses his review of the Descriptive Catalogue *to impugn Blake's sanity.]*

If beside the stupid and mad-brained political project of their rulers, the sane part of the people of England required . . . fresh proof of the alarming increase of the effects of insanity, they will be too well convinced from its having lately spread into the hitherto sober region of Art. . . . [When] the ebullitions of a distempered brain are mistaken for the sallies of genius by those whose works have exhibited the soundest thinking in art, the malady has indeed attained a pernicious height, and it becomes a duty to endeavour to arrest its progress. Such is the case with the productions and admirers of WILLIAM BLAKE, an unfortunate lunatic, whose personal inoffensiveness secures him from confinement, and, consequently, of whom no public notice would have been taken, if he was not forced on the notice and animadversion of the EXAMINER, in having been held up to public admiration by many esteemed amateurs and professors as a genius in some respect original and legitimate. The praises which these gentlemen bestowed last year on this unfortunate man's illustrations of *Blair's Grave*, have, in feeding his vanity, stimulated him to publish his madness more largely, and thus again exposed him, if not to the derision, at least to the pity of the public. . . . [The] poor man fancies himself a great master, and has painted a few wretched pictures, some of which are unintelligible allegory, others an attempt at sober character by caricature representation, and the whole 'blotted and blurred,' and very badly drawn. These he calls an Exhibition, of which he has published a Catalogue, or rather a farrago of nonsense, unintelligibleness, and egregious vanity, the wild effusions of a distempered brain. . . . 'In this Exhibition,' Mr. BLAKE very modestly observes, 'the grand style of art is restored; and in it will be seen *real* art, as left us by RAPHAEL and ALBERT DURER, MICHAEL ANGELO and JULIO ROMANO, stripped from the ignorances of RUBENS and REMBRANDT, TITIAN and CORREGGIO.' Of the engraving which he proposes to make from his picture of the *Canterbury Pilgrims*, and to finish in a year, he as justly, soberly, and modestly observes, 'No work of art can take longer than a year: it may be worked backwards and forwards without

end, and last a man's whole life, but he will at length only be forced to bring it back to what it was, and it will be worse than it was at the end of the first twelve months. The value of this artist's year is the *criterion of society;* and as it is valued, so does society *flourish or decay*.' That insanity should elevate itself to this fancied importance, is the usual effect of the unfortunate malady; but that men of taste, in their sober senses, should mistake its unmeaning and distorted conceptions for the flashes of genius, is indeed a phenomenon. (p. 605)

> [Robert Hunt], "Mr. Blake's Exhibition," in The Examiner, No. 90, September 17, 1809, pp. 605-06.

HENRY CRABB ROBINSON AND WILLIAM HAZLITT (conversation date 1811)

[The following commentary is taken from Robinson's record of his conversation with Hazlitt concerning Songs of Innocence and of Experience. *Hazlitt, who is considered one of the most important commentators of the Romantic age, describes the poetry as "beautiful," yet he also alludes to the poet's "vain struggles to get rid of what presses on his brain." For additional commentary by Robinson, see the excerpt below dated 1811.]*

I showed Hazlitt Blake's *Young*. He saw no merit in them as designs. I read him some of the poems. He was much struck with them and expressed himself with his usual strength and singularity. 'They are beautiful,' he said, 'and only too deep for the vulgar. He has no sense of the ludicrous, and, as to a God, a worm crawling in a privy is as worthy an object as any other, all being to him indifferent. So to Blake the Chimney Sweeper, etc. He is ruined by vain struggles to get rid of what presses on his brain—he attempts impossibles.' I added: 'He is like a man who lifts a burden too heavy for him; he bears it an instant, it then falls on and crushes him.' (p. 25)

> Henry Crabb Robinson, in a conversation with William Hazlitt in March, 1811, in his Henry Crabb Robinson on Books and Their Writers, Vol. I, edited by Edith J. Morley, J. M. Dent and Sons Limited, 1938, p. 25.

ROBERT SOUTHEY [AS REPORTED BY HENRY CRABB ROBINSON]   (diary date 1811)

[Southey, an English poet, historian, biographer, essayist, short story writer, and editor, was a prominent literary figure during the late eighteenth and early nineteenth centuries. Robinson here reports that Southey took Blake for a madman.]

Returned late to Charles Lamb's. Found a very large party there. Southey had been with Blake, and admired both his designs and his poetic talents, at the same time that he held him for a decided madman. Blake, he says, spoke of his visions with the diffidence that is usual with such people, and did not seem to expect that he should be believed. He showed Southey a perfectly mad poem called *Jerusalem*. . . . (pp. 40-1)

> Robert Southey [as reported by Henry Crabb Robinson on July 24, 1811], in Henry Crabb Robinson on Books and Their Writers, Vol. I by Henry Crabb Robinson, edited by Edith J. Morley, J. M. Dent and Sons Limited, 1938, pp. 40-1.

HENRY CRABB ROBINSON   (essay date 1811)

[Robinson, a journalist and later a barrister by profession, is important to literature for the light that his diaries and corre-

spondence shed on Blake, Wordsworth, and other writers whose friendship he cultivated. Robinson first met Blake in 1825, drawing out his opinions on such topics as religion and literature and recording their conversations in his diary. His interest in Blake predates their meeting, however, for he published the following commentary on the poet in the German periodical Vaterländisches Museum *in 1811. Here, Robinson briefly surveys Blake's criticism and poetry for the German public. For additional commentary by the critic, see the excerpt by Robinson and Hazlitt dated 1811.]*

Of all the conditions which arouse the interest of the psychologist, none assuredly is more attractive than the union of genius and madness in single remarkable minds, which, while on the one hand they compel our admiration by their great mental powers, yet on the other move our pity by their claims to supernatural gifts. Of such is the whole race of ecstatics, mystics, seers of visions and dreamers of dreams, and to their list we have now to add another name, that of William Blake.

This extraordinary man, who is at this moment living in London, although more than fifty years of age, is only now beginning to emerge from the obscurity in which the singular bent of his talents and the eccentricity of his personal character have confined him. (p. 236)

One attempt at introducing him to the great British public has indeed succeeded, his illustrations to Blair's 'Grave.' . . . (p. 238)

Only last year he opened an exhibition of his frescoes, proclaiming that he had rediscovered the lost art of fresco. He demanded of those who had considered his works the slovenly daubs of a madman, destitute alike of technical skill and harmony of proportion, to examine them now with greater attention. . . . At the same time he published a *Descriptive Catalogue* of these fresco pictures, out of which we propose to give only a few unconnected passages. The original consists of a veritable folio of fragmentary utterances on art and religion, without plan or arrangement, and the artist's idiosyncracies will in this way be most clearly shown. The vehemence with which, throughout the book, he declaims against oil painting and the artists of the Venetian and Flemish schools is part of the fixed ideas of the author. . . . [His preface begins with the following words:] 'The eye which prefers the colouring of Rubens and Titian to that of Raphael and Michael Angelo should be modest and mistrust its own judgement,' but as he proceeds with his descriptions his wrath against false schools of painting waxes, and in holy zeal he proclaims that the hated artists are evil spirits, and later art the offspring of hell. Chiaroscuro he plainly calls 'an infernal machine in the hand of Venetian and Flemish demons.' . . . Correggio he calls 'a soft, effeminate, and consequently most cruel demon.' Rubens is 'a most outrageous demon.' . . . [The] following passage, while it reveals the artist's views on the technique of his art, contains a truth which cannot be denied, and which underlies his whole doctrine. 'The great and golden rule of art, as well as of life, is this: That the more distinct, sharp and wiry the bounding line, the more perfect the work of art.' . . . In the same spirit he proclaims the guilt of the recent distinction between a painting and a drawing. 'If losing and obliterating the outline constitutes a picture, Mr. B. will never be so foolish as to do one. . . . There is no difference between Raphael's Cartoons and his Frescoes or Pictures, except that the Frescos or Pictures are more highly finished.' (pp. 240-42)

[Blake's] greatest enjoyment consists in giving bodily form to spiritual beings. Thus in the 'Grave' he has represented the reunion of soul and body, and to both he has given equal clearness of form and outline. . . .

In his Catalogue we find . . . vindication of the reproaches brought against his earlier work. 'Shall painting be confined to the sordid drudgery of facsimile representations of merely mortal and perishing substances, and not be, as poetry and music are, elevated into its own proper sphere of invention and visionary conception?' He then alleges that the statues of the Greek gods are so many bodily representations of spiritual beings. 'A Spirit and a Vision are not, as the modern philosophy asserts, a cloudy vapour or a nothing; they are organised and minutely articulated beyond all that the mortal and perishing nature can produce. Spirits are organised men' [see excerpt dated 1809]. (p. 243)

Elsewhere [in the *Descriptive Catalogue*] he says that Adam and Noah were Druids, and that he himself is an inhabitant of Eden. Blake's religious convictions appear to be those of an orthodox Christian; nevertheless, passages concerning earlier mythologies occur which might cast a doubt on it. . . . [His] system remains more allied to the stoical endurance of Antiquity than to the essential austerity of Christianity. (pp. 246-47)

[Blake's] poems breathe the same spirit and are distinguished by the same peculiarities as his drawings and prose criticisms. As early as 1783 a little volume was printed with the title of *Poetical Sketches, by W. B.* No printer's name is given on the title-page, and in the preface it states that the poems were composed between his thirteenth and twentieth years. They are of very unequal merit. The metre is usually so loose and careless as to betray a total ignorance of the art, whereby the larger part of the poems are rendered singularly rough and unattractive. On the other hand, there is a wildness and loftiness of imagination in certain dramatic fragments which testifies to genuine poetical feeling. (pp. 249-50)

A still more remarkable little book of poems by our author exists, which is only to be met with in the hands of collectors. It is a duodecimo entitled *Songs of Innocence and Experience, shewing the two contrary states of the human soul. The Author and printer W. Blake.* . . . It is not easy to form a comprehensive opinion of the text, since the poems deserve the highest praise and the gravest censure. Some are childlike songs of great beauty and simplicity; these are the *Songs of Innocence,* many of which, nevertheless, are excessively childish.

The *Songs of Experience,* on the other hand, are metaphysical riddles and mystical allegories. Among them are poetic pictures of the highest beauty and sublimity; and again there are poetical fancies which can scarcely be understood even by the initiated. (pp. 250-51)

Besides these songs two other works of Blake's Poetry and Painting have come under our notice, of which, however, we must confess our inability to give a sufficient account. These are two quarto volumes which appeared in 1794, printed and adorned like the *Songs,* under the titles of *Europe, a Prophecy,* and *America, a Prophecy.*

The very 'Prophecies of Bakis' are not obscurer. *America* appears in part to give a poetical account of the Revolution, since it contains the names of several party leaders. The actors in it are a species of guardian angels. We give only a short example, nor can we decide whether it is intended to be in prose or verse.

> On these vast shady hills between America's and
>   Albion's shore,
> Now barred out by the Atlantic Sea: called Atlantean
>   hills,

Because from their bright summits you may pass to the
   golden world,
An ancient palace, archetype of mighty empiries,
Rears its immortal summit, built in the forests of God,
By Ariston the King of Heaven for his stolen bride.

The obscurity of these lines in such a poem by such a man
will be willingly overlooked.

Europe is a similar mysterious and incomprehensible rhapsody,
which probably contains the artist's political visions of the
future, but is wholly inexplicable. (pp. 254-55)

We have now an account of all the works of this extraordinary
man that have come under our notice. We have been lengthy,
but our object is to draw the attention of Germany to a man
in whom all the elements of greatness are unquestionably to
be found, even though those elements are disproportionately
mingled. Closer research than was permitted us would perhaps
shew that as an artist Blake will never produce consummate
and immortal work, as a poet flawless poems; but this assuredly
cannot lessen the interest which all men, Germans in a higher
degree even than Englishmen, must take in the contemplation
of such a character. We will only recall the phrase of a thoughtful writer, that those faces are the most attractive in which
nature has set something of greatness which she has yet left
unfinished; he same may hold good of the soul. (pp. 255-56)

> *Henry Crabb Robinson, "An Early Appreciation of
> William Blake," translated by K. A. Esdaile, in* The
> Library, *n.s. Vol. V, No. 19, July, 1914, pp. 229-56.**

S[AMUEL] T[AYLOR] COLERIDGE (letter date 1818)

[*Coleridge was central to the English Romantic movement as a
poet and critic and is considered one of the greatest literary critics
in the English language. His comments upon first reading* Songs
of Innocence and of Experience *are excerpted below.*]

I have this morning been reading a strange publication—viz.
Poems with very wild and interesting pictures, as the swathing,
etched (I suppose) but it is said—printed and painted by the
Author, W. Blake. He is a man of Genius—and I apprehend,
a Swedenborgian—certainly, a mystic *emphatically.* You perhaps smile at *my* calling another Poet, a *Mystic;* but verily I
am in the very mire of common-place common-sense compared
with Mr Blake, apo- or rather ana-calyptic Poet, and Painter!
(pp. 833-34)

> *S[amuel] T[aylor] Coleridge, in a letter to H. F. Cary
> on February 6, 1818, in his* Collected Letters of
> Samuel Taylor Coleridge: 1815-1819, Vol. IV, *ed-
> ited by Earl Leslie Griggs, Oxford at the Clarendon
> Press, Oxford, 1959, pp. 832-34.*

WILLIAM BLAKE (essay date 1804-20?)

[*The following excerpt is taken from the preface to* Jerusalem, *in
which Blake seeks to justify on spiritual grounds the "enthusiasm"
informing the poem and to explain his use of varying line lengths
and cadences in the work. Blake's editors here use italics within
brackets to indicate letters or words deleted, erased, or written
over. Scholars estimate that Blake etched and revised the plates
for* Jerusalem *during the period 1804-20. For further commentary
by Blake, see the excerpts dated 1799, 1802, 1808, and 1809.*]

The Enthusiasm of the following Poem, the Author hopes [*no
Reader will think presumptuousness or arroganc*[*e*] *when he
is reminded that the Ancients entrusted their love to their Writ-*

ing, *to the full as Enthusiastically as I have who Acknowledge
mine for my Saviour and Lord, for they were wholly absorb'd
in their Gods.*] I also hope the Reader will be with me, wholly
One in Jesus our Lord, who is the God [*of Fire*] and Lord [*of
Love*] to whom the Ancients look'd and saw his day afar off,
with trembling & amazement.

The Spirit of Jesus is continual forgiveness of Sin: he who
waits to be righteous before he enters into the Saviours kingdom, the Divine Body; will never enter there. I am perhaps
the most sinful of men! I pretend not to holiness! yet I pretend
to love, to see, to converse with daily, as man with man, &
the more to have an interest in the Friend of Sinners. Therefore
[*Dear*] Reader, [*forgive*] what you do not approve, & [*love*]
me for this energetic exertion of my talent.

> Reader! [*lover*] of books!
> [*lover*] of heaven,
> And of that God from whom [*all books are given,*]
> Who in mysterious Sinais awful cave
> To Man the wond'rous art of writing gave,
> Again he speaks in thunder and in fire!
> Thunder of Thought, & flames of fierce desire:
> Even from the depths of Hell his voice I hear,
> Within the unfathomd caverns of my Ear.
> Therefore I print; nor vain my types shall be:
> Heaven, Earth & Hell, henceforth shall live in harmony
>
>   Of the Measure, in which
>   the following Poem is written

We who dwell on Earth can do nothing of ourselves, every
thing is conducted by Spirits, no less than Digestion or Sleep. . . .

When this Verse was first dictated to me I consider'd a Monotonous Cadence like that used by Milton & Shakspeare &
all writers of English Blank Verse, derived from the modern
bondage of Rhyming; to be a necessary and indispensible part
of Verse. But I soon found that in the mouth of a true Orator
such monotony was not only awkward, but as much a bondage
as rhyme itself. I therefore have produced a variety in every
line, both of cadences & number of syllables. Every word and
every letter is studied and put into its fit place: the terrific
numbers are reserved for the terrific parts—the mild & gentle,
for the mild & gentle parts, and the prosaic, for inferior parts:
all are necessary to each other. Poetry Fetter'd, Fetters the
Human Race! Nations are Destroy'd, or Flourish, in proportion
as Their Poetry Painting and Music, are Destroy'd or Flourish!
The Primeval State of Man, was Wisdom, Art, and Science.
(p. 144)

> *William Blake, "Preface to 'Jerusalem: The Ema-
> nation of the Giant Albion'," in his* The Poetry and
> Prose of William Blake, *edited by David V. Erdman,
> Doubleday & Company, Inc., 1965, pp. 143-44.*

CHARLES LAMB (letter date 1824)

[*Lamb was a nineteenth-century English essayist, critic, poet,
dramatist, and novelist who is chiefly remembered for his "Elia"
essays, a series renowned for its witty, idiosyncratic treatment of
everyday subjects. Under his auspices, Blake's poem "The Chimney Sweeper" (from* Songs of Innocence) *was reprinted in an
1824 collection entitled* The Chimney Sweeper's Friend, and
Climbing Boy's Album. *The poem stirred the curiosity of Bernard
Barton, whose request for information concerning Blake yielded
the following response from Lamb.*]

Blake is a real name, I assure you, and a most extraordinary man, if he be still living. He is the Robert [sic] Blake, whose wild designs accompany a splendid folio edition of the "Night Thoughts," which you may have seen. . . . He paints in water colours marvellous strange pictures, visions of his brain, which he asserts that he has seen. They have great merit. He has *seen* the old Welsh bards on Snowdon—he has seen the Beautifullest, the strongest, and the Ugliest Man, left alone from the Massacre of the Britons by the Romans, and has painted them from memory (I have seen his paintings), and asserts them to be as good as the figures of Raphael and Angelo, but not better, as they had precisely the same retro-visions and prophetic visions with themself. . . . The painters in oil (which he will have it that neither of them practised) he affirms to have been the ruin of art, and affirms that all the while he was engaged in his Water paintings, Titian was disturbing him, Titian the Ill Genius of Oil Painting. His Pictures—one in particular, the Canterbury Pilgrims (far above Stothard's)—have great merit, but hard, dry, yet with grace. He has written a Catalogue of them with a most spirited criticism on Chaucer, but mystical and full of Vision. His poems have been sold hitherto only in Manuscript. I never read them; but a friend at my desire procured the **"Sweep Song."** There is one to a tiger, which I have heard recited, beginning—

> Tiger, Tiger, burning bright,
> Thro' the desarts of the night,

which is glorious, but, alas! I have not the book; for the man is flown, whither I know not—to Hades or a Mad House. But I must look on him as one of the most extraordinary persons of the age. (pp. 104-05)

> *Charles Lamb, in a letter to B[ernard] B[arton] on May 15, 1824 in his* The Letters of Charles Lamb, *Vol. II, edited by Alfred Ainger, A. C. Armstrong & Son, 1888, pp. 104-06.*

LONDON UNIVERSITY MAGAZINE (essay date 1830)

[*The following excerpt is taken from commentary on Blake that originally appeared in the March, 1830, issue of the* London University Magazine. *In addition to exhibiting sympathy with the spiritual orientation of Blake's art, the critic defends the coherence of his works and characterizes him as a misunderstood genius.*]

It is a curious circumstance, and well worthy the attention of all persons, that in this age of reason, Englishmen should have allowed two such men as Flaxman and Blake, to pass from this life without evincing the smallest regard for them. Perhaps 'reason stumbles all night over bones of the dead,' as Blake has elegantly expressed it, and pays but small attention to real genius; or it may be partly accounted for through the want of a good philosophy, which, Mad. De Stael says, has not as yet been taught in England. These, perhaps, are a few of the many reasons why Blake and Flaxman have been buried in obscurity; but we have a confident hope that Coleridge, Blake, and Flaxman are the forerunners of a more elevated and purer system, which has even now begun to take root in the breast of the English nation; they have laid a foundation for future minds— Coleridge, for the development of a more internal philosophy— Blake and Flaxman, for a purer and more ennobling sentiment in works of art. (pp. 199-200)

If Blake had lived in Germany, by this time he would have had commentators of the highest order upon every one of his effusions; but here, so little attention is paid to works of the

mind, and so much to natural knowledge, that England, in the eyes of the thinking world, seems fast sinking into a lethargy, appearing as if the *Poison Tree* had poured the soporific distillation over its body, which now lies under it almost dead and lifeless. . . . The powers, then, of both mind and body having been freely exercised, the result is a genius, who stands forth as a representative of his race; and thus we may say, Blake in his single person united all the grand combination of art and mind, poetry, music, and painting; and we may carry the simile still further, and say, that as England is the least fettered by the minds of other nations, so Blake poured forth his effusions in his own grand style, copying no one, . . . but breathing spirit and life into his works; and though shaping forms from the world of his creative and sportive imagination, yet he still remembered he was a moral as well as intellectual citizen of England, bound both to love and instruct her. These ought to be the ruling principles of all artists and poets. Flaxman and Blake thought it a still higher honour to be celebrated for their innocence and beauty of sentiment, than for a mere sensual representation of forms. Their internal esthetic produced a similar external, not by any means inferior to the mere form-painter, and in this respect superior, that there was a Promethean fire which glowed in their productions, purifying the soul from the gross imperfections of the natural mind. . . .

This grand combination of art succeeded in every particular, painting being the flesh, poetry the bones, and music the nerves of Blake's work.

The figures surrounding and enclosing the poems, produce fresh delight. They are equally tinged by a poetical idea, and though sometimes it is difficult to understand his wandering flights, yet the extraordinary power developed in the handling of both arts [astonishes] as well as [delights]. Here and there figures are introduced, which, like the spirits in Macbeth, pass quickly from the sight; yet they every one of them have been well digested in the brain of a genius; and we should endeavour rather to unlock the prison-door in which we are placed, and gain an insight into his powerful mind than rail and scoff at him as a dreamer and madman.

For instance, Albion, with which the world is very little acquainted, seems the embodying of Blake's ideas on the present state of England; he viewed it, not with the eyes of ordinary men, but contemplated it rather as a province of one grand man, in which diseases and crimes are continually engendered, and on this account he poured forth his poetical effusions somewhat in the style of Novalis, mourning over the crimes and errors of his dear country: and it is more extraordinary still that, like Novalis, he contemplated the natural world as the mere outbirth of the thought, and lived and existed in that world for which we are created. Horrid forms and visions pervade this Albion, for they were the only representatives, in his opinion, of the present state of mankind. No great genius wrote without having a plan, and so in this, a light is frequently thrown across the pictures, which partly discover the interior design of the Poet. We are perfectly aware of the present state of public opinion on this kind of men, but we know at the same time, that every genius has a certain end to perform, and always runs before his contemporaries, and for that reason is not generally understood.—This is our candid opinion with respect to Blake, but we hope that hereafter his merits will be more generally acknowledged. (pp. 201-02)

> *An extract in* William Blake: The Critical Heritage, *edited by G. E. Bentley, Jr., Routledge & Kegan Paul, 1975, pp. 199-205.*

Blake's print "Glad Day," also known as "Albion Rose."

EDWARD FITZGERALD (letter date 1833)

[*FitzGerald was a nineteenth-century English writer who is best known as the translator of the* Rubáiyát of Omar Khayyám. *In the excerpt below, he focuses on the relationship between Blake's genius and his madness.*]

I have lately bought a little pamphlet which is very difficult to be got, called **The Songs of Innocence,** written and adorned with drawings by W. Blake (if you know his name) who was quite mad: but of a madness that was really the elements of great genius ill-sorted: in fact, a genius with a screw loose, as we used to say. I shall shew you this book when I see you: to me there is particular interest in this man's writing and drawing, from the strangeness of the constitution of his mind. He was a man that used to see visions: and make drawings and paintings of Alexander the Great, Caesar, &c. who, he declared, stood before him while he drew. . . . (p. 21)

> *Edward FitzGerald, in a letter to W. B. Donne on October 25, 1833, in his* Letters and Literary Remains of Edward FitzGerald, Vol. I, *edited by William Aldis Wright, Macmillan and Co., 1889, pp. 20-1.*

WALTER SAVAGE LANDOR [AS REPORTED BY JOHN FORSTER] (essay date 1837)

[*Landor was an English poet, critic, and essayist. Though seldom read today, he is remembered for his* Imaginary Conversations— *a series of fictionalized dialogues between historical characters—*

and for his poetry written in imitation of classical Greek and Roman authors. The passage below is taken from John Forster's biographical account of Landor's activities during the year 1837.]

At an old bookseller's in Bristol [Landor] picked up some of the writings of Blake, and was strangely fascinated by them. He was anxious to have collected as many more as he could, and enlisted me in the service; but he as much wanted patience for it as I wanted time, and between us it came to nothing. He protested that Blake had been Wordsworth's prototype, and wished they could have divided his madness between them; for that some accession of it in the one case, and something of a diminution of it in the other, would very greatly have improved both. (pp. 322-23)

> *Walter Savage Landor [as reported by John Forster in 1837], in* Walter Savage Landor, a Biography: 1821-1864, Vol. 2 *by John Forster, Chapman & Hall, 1869, pp. 322-23.*

J[AMES] J[OHN] G[ARTH] WILKINSON (essay date 1839)

[*Wilkinson edited the first conventionally published edition of* Songs of Innocence and of Experience, *issued in 1839. In the preface to that work, excerpted below, he focuses on Blake's deviations from the standards of spiritual and Christian vision, yet expresses hope that the* Songs *will promote a greater awareness of the spiritual essence of reality.*]

They who would form a just estimate of Blake's powers as an Artist, have abundant opportunities of doing so, from his exquisite Illustrations to the **Songs of Innocence;** from his Designs to Blair's *Grave,* Young's *Night Thoughts,* and the Book of Job, in all of which, there are 'glorious shapes, expressing godlike sentiments.' These works, in the main, are not more remarkable for high original genius, than they are for sane self-possession; and shew the occasional sovereignty of the inner man, over the fantasies which obsessed the outer. Yet he, who professed as a doctrine, that the visionary form of thought was higher than the rational one; for whom the common earth teemed with millions of otherwise invisible creatures; who naturalized the spiritual, instead of spiritualizing the natural; was likely, even in these, his noblest Works, to prefer seeing Truth under the loose garments of Typical, or even Mythologic Representation, rather than in the Divine-Human Embodiment of Christianity. And accordingly, his Imagination, self-divorced from a Reason which might have elevated and chastened it, and necessarily spurning the Scientific daylight and material Realism of the nineteenth century, found a home in the ruins of Ancient and consummated Churches; and imbued itself with the superficial obscurity and ghastliness, far more than with the inward grandeur of primeval Times. For the true Inward is one and identical, and if Blake had been disposed to see it, he would have found that it was still (though doubtless under a multitude of wrappages) extant in the present Age. On the contrary, copying the outward form of the Past, he has delivered to us a multitude of new Hieroglyphics, which contain no presumable reconditeness of meaning, and which we are obliged to account for, simply by the Artist's having yielded himself up, more thoroughly than other men *will* do, to those fantastic impulses which are common to all mankind; and which saner people subjugate, but cannot exterminate. In so yielding himself, the Artist, not less than the man, was a loser, though it unquestionably gave him a certain power, as all unscrupulous *passion* must, of wildness and fierce vagary. This power is possessed in different degrees, by every human being, if he will but give loose and free vent to the hell that is in him; and hence, the madness even of the meanest, is terrific. But no madness can long be considered either really Poetic or Artistical. Of the worst aspect of Blake's genius it is painful to speak. In his *Prophecies of America,* his *Visions of the Daughters of Albion,* and a host of unpublished drawings, earthborn might has banished the heavenlier elements of Art, and exists combined with all that is monstrous and diabolical. In the domain of Terror he here entered, the characteristic of his genius is fearful Reality. He embodies no Byronisms,—none of the sentimentalities of civilized vice, but delights to draw evil things and evil beings in their naked and final state. The effect of these delineations is greatly heightened by the antiquity which is engraven on the faces of those who do and suffer in them. We have the impression that we are looking down into the hells of the ancient people, the Anakim, the Nephilim, and the Rephaim. Their human forms are gigantic petrifactions, from which the fires of lust and intense selfish passion, have long dissipated what was animal and vital; leaving stony limbs, and countenances expressive of despair, and stupid cruelty.

In many of the characters of his mind, Blake resembled Shelley. From the opposite extremes of Christianity and Materialism, they both seem, at length, to have converged towards Pantheism, or natural-spiritualism; and it is probable, that a somewhat similar self-intelligence, or Egotheism, possessed them both. They agreed in mistaking the forms of Truth, for the Truth itself; and, consequently, drew the materials of their works, from the ages of type and shadow which preceded the Christian Revelation. The beauty, chasteness, and clear polish of Shelley's mind, as well as his metaphysical irreligion, took him, naturally enough, to the Philosophy and Theology of the Greeks; where he could at once enjoy the loose dogma of an Impersonal Creator, and have liberty to distribute Personality at will to the beautiful unliving forms of the visible creation. We appeal to the 'Prometheus Unbound,' his consummating Work, in proof of this assertion. The visionary tendencies, and mysticism of Blake, developing themselves, as they did, under the shelter of a religious parentage and education, carried him, on the contrary, to the mythic fountains of an elder time, and his genius which was too expansive to dwell in classic formalisms, entered into, and inhabited, the Egyptian and Asiatic perversions of an ancient and true Religion. In consequence of these allied deformities, the works of both are sadly deficient in vital heat, and in substantial or practical Truth, and fail, therefore, to satisfy the common wants, or to appeal to the universal instincts, of Humanity. Self-will in each, was the centre of the Individual, and self-intelligence, the 'Anima Mundi' of the Philosopher, and they both imagined, that they could chop and change the Universe, even to the confounding of Life with Death, to suit their own creative fancies. (pp. 58-9)

[*Songs of Innocence and of Experience*] contains nearly all that is excellent in Blake's Poetry; and great, rare, and manifest, is the excellence that is here. The faults are equally conspicuous, and he who runs may read them. They amount to an utter want of elaboration, and even, in many cases, to an inattention to the ordinary rules of grammar. Yet the *Songs of Innocence,* at least, are quite free from the dark becloudment which rolled and billowed over Blake in his later days. He here transcended Self, and escaped from the isolation which Self involves; and, as it then ever is, his expanding affections embraced universal Man, and, without violating, beautified and hallowed, even his individual peculiarities. Accordingly, many of these delicious Lays, belong to the Era as well as to the Author. They are remarkable for the transparent depth of thought

which constitutes true Simplicity—they give us glimpses of all that is holiest in the Childhood of the World and the Individual—they abound with the sweetest touches of that Pastoral life, by which the Golden Age may be still visibly represented to the iron one—they delineate full-orbed Age, ripe with the seeds of a second Infancy, which is 'the Kingdom of Heaven.' The latter half of the Volume, comprising the *Songs of Experience,* consists, it is true, of darker themes; but they, too, are well and wonderfully sung; and ought to be preserved, because, in contrastive connexion with the *Songs of Innocence,* they do convey a powerful impression of 'the two contrary states of the Human Soul.'

If the Volume gives one impulse to the New Spiritualism which is now dawning on the world;—if it leads one reader to think, that all Reality for him, in the long run, lies out of the limits of Space and Time; and that Spirits, and not bodies, and still less garments, are men;—if it gives one blow, even the faintest, to those term-shifting juggleries, which usurp the name of 'Philosophical Systems,' (and all the energies of all the forms of genuine Truth must henceforth be expended on these effects,) it will have done its work in its little day; and we shall be abundantly satisfied, with having undertaken to perpetuate it, for a few years, by the present Republication. (p. 60)

J[ames] J[ohn] G[arth] Wilkinson, in an extract in William Blake: The Critical Heritage, *edited by G. E. Bentley, Jr., Routledge & Kegan Paul, 1975, pp. 57-60.*

WILLIAM WORDSWORTH [AS REPORTED BY HENRY CRABB ROBINSON]   (diary date 1850?)

[*Wordsworth is considered the greatest and most influential English Romantic poet. Although his abiding concern with the role of nature and imagination in art aligns him with Blake, critics often contrast their poetic practices and theories. Wordsworth's death date of 1850 has been assigned to this remark, which was first recorded in Robinson's diary, because the date of Wordsworth's conversation with Robinson is not certain.*]

There is no doubt this poor man was mad, but there is something in the madness of this man which interests me more than the Sanity of Lord Byron & Walter Scott! (p. 536)

William Wordsworth [as reported by Henry Crabb Robinson], in Blake Records, *edited by G. E. Bentley, Jr., Oxford at the Clarendon Press, Oxford, 1969, p. 536.*

ALEXANDER GILCHRIST   (essay date 1861?)

[*Critics generally agree that significant scholarly interest in and understanding of Blake's thought began with the publication of Gilchrist's* Life of William Blake, "Pictor Ignotus." *As part of his biographical study, Gilchrist here argues that Blake's alleged madness is best understood as eccentricity born of "an excessive culture of the imagination" and lack of self-discipline. Gilchrist died in 1861 having completed this portion of his book, hence the date for this excerpt; the unfinished* Life *was subsequently completed by Anne Gilchrist, Dante Gabriel Rossetti, and William Michael Rossetti and published in 1863.*]

[Blake would sometimes] give accounts of romantic appearances which had shown themselves to him. At one of Mr. Aders' parties . . . Blake was talking to a little group gathered round him, within hearing of a lady whose children had just come home from boarding school for the holidays. "The other evening,'' said Blake in his usual quiet way, ''taking a walk, I came to a meadow, and at the farther corner of it I saw a fold of lambs. Coming nearer, the ground blushed with flowers; and the wattled cote and its woolly tenants were of an exquisite pastoral beauty. But I looked again, and it proved to be no living flock, but beautiful sculpture.'' The lady, thinking this a capital holiday-show for her children, eagerly interposed, ''I beg pardon, Mr. Blake, but *may* I ask *where* you saw this?'' *''Here,* madam,'' answered Blake, touching his forehead. The reply brings us to the point of view from which Blake himself regarded his visions. It was by no means the mad view those ignorant of the man have fancied. He would candidly confess they were not literal matters of fact; but phenomena seen by his imagination; *realities* none the less for that, but transacted within the realm of mind. A distinction which widely separates such visions from the hallucinations of madness, or of the victims of ghostly or table-turning delusions; and indicates that wild habit of talk (and of writing) which startled outsiders, to have been the fruit of an excessive culture of the imagination, combined with daring licence of speech. (pp. 337-38)

According to his own explanation, Blake saw spiritual appearances by the exercise of a special faculty—that of imagination—using the word in the then unusual, but true sense, of a faculty which busies itself with the subtler realities, *not* with fictions. . . . He said the things imagination saw were as much realities as were gross and tangible facts. He would tell his artist-friends, ''You have the same faculty as I (the visionary), only you do not trust or cultivate it. You can see what I do, *if you choose.''* In a similar spirit was his advice to a young painter: ''You have only to work up imagination to the state of vision, and the thing is done.'' (pp. 338-39)

Extravagant and apocryphal stories have passed current about Blake. One—which I believe Leigh Hunt used to tell—bears internal evidence, to those who understand Blake, of having been a fabrication. Once, it is said, the visionary man was walking down Cheapside with a friend. Suddenly he took off his hat and bowed low. ''What did you do that for?'' ''Oh! that was the Apostle Paul.'' A story quite out of keeping with the artist's ordinary demeanour towards his spiritual visitants, though quite in unison with the accepted notions as to ghosts and other apparitions with whom the ghost-seer is traditionally supposed to have tangible personal relations. Blake's was not that kind of vision. The spirits which appeared to him did not reveal themselves in palpable, hand-shaking guise, nor were they mistaken by him for bodily facts. He did not claim for them an external, or (in German slang) an *objective* existence.

In Blake, imagination was by nature so strong, by himself had been so much fostered and, amid the solitude in which he lived, had been so little interfered with by the ideas of others, that it had grown to a disproportionate height so as to overshadow every other faculty. He relied on it as on a revelation of the Invisible. The appearances thus summoned before his mental eye were implicitly trusted in, not dismissed as idle phantoms as an ordinary—even an imaginative-man dismisses them. Hence his *bonâ fide* ''portraits'' of visionary characters, such as those drawn for John Varley. And to this genuine faith is due the singular difference *in kind* between his imaginative work and that of nearly every other painter who has left a record of himself. Such is the explanation which all who knew the man personally give of what seemed mere madness to the world. (pp. 339-40)

[Blake's] reasoning powers were far inferior, as are, more or less, those of all artists, to his perceptive, above all to his

perceptions of beauty. He elected his opinions because they seemed beautiful to him, and fulfilled ''the desires of his mind.'' Then he would find reasons for them. Thus, Christianity was beautiful to him, and was accepted even more because it satisfied his love of spiritual beauty, than because it satisfied his religious and moral sense. Again, the notion was attractive and beautiful to him that ''Christianity is Art,'' and conversely, that ''Art is Christianity'': *therefore* he believed it. And it became one of his standing theological canons, which, in his sybilline writings, he is for ever reiterating.

Both in his books, and in conversation, Blake was a vehement *assertor;* very decisive and very obstinate in his opinions, when he had once taken them up. And he was impatient of control, or of a law in anything,—in his Art, in his opinions on morals, religion, or what not. If artists be divided into the disciplined and undisciplined, he must fall under the latter category. To this, as well as to entire want of discipline in the literary art, was due much of the incoherence in his books and design; incoherence and wildness, which is another source of the general inference embodied by Wordsworth and Southey, who knew him only in his poems, when they described him as a man ''of great, but undoubtedly insane genius.'' If for *insane* we read *undisciplined,* or ill-balanced, I think we shall hit the truth. (p. 347)

Alexander Gilchrist, in his The Life of William Blake, *edited by W. Graham Robertson, John Lane/The Bodley Head Ltd., 1907, 533 p.*

[R. H. HUTTON]   (essay date 1863)

[*In the following extract from his review of Gilchrist's biography (see excerpt dated 1861), Hutton portrays Blake as a visionary driven by an unsympathetic age to express his visions in art and then assesses the impact of this burden on his work. The critic disapproves of Blake's ''mystical'' verse, maintaining that the ''double, and treble, and quadruple visions, of which he was so proud, spoiled his poetry.''*]

Blake was often thought insane, and not without reasons quite strong enough to have shut up many a man less poor and more enviable in worldly position. But, probably, the truth was simply this, that he was a visionary in the eighteenth century,— an age when there was ''no open vision,''—so that both the age was less able to understand him, and he was fretted into greater eccentricity by his age. Being from the first a dreamer of dreams and a man of very obstinate intellect, he was induced to talk as if his dreams were the only truth and the world around him comparatively a fiction. . . . [He] was alive, fortunately for his own reason, to the indifference of the world, and so the eighteenth century succeeded in depositing round his eager visionary mind a crust of reserve which made him brood more than ever over his visions and believe in them more passionately. His art, his philosophy, if it can be so called, his poetry, his faith, his manners, all express the chained visionary, who would have fretted passionately against the bonds of social humdrum if he had not found a safety-valve for all his visions in Art. . . .

If we had to describe Blake's intellect in a single sentence we should say that a mind moulded in the primeval intellectual world which gave rise to the Book of Job, or more nearly, perhaps, of Ezekiel, had been put to sleep for near three thousand years, and then launched into the midst of the meaner London life in Golden Square, Battersea, Oxford Street, and the Strand, of the reign of George III. . . .

Blake's intellectual visions were all of the primeval kind, of grand and free outline, with vistas of great complexity but simple elements, such as opened out everywhere to the seer in the morning of creation. Everywhere there is infinitude in them; but an intellect unaccustomed to sound its own depths assembles a confusion of symbols from all quarters of creation to spell out its meaning in a sort of half-articulate hieroglyphic. Terror and pity, horror and innocence and primeval joy, strong desire and anguish unsubdued, all speak in different and mysterious symbols through shrouds of tempestuous darkness or an overwhelming blaze of light. The most striking characteristic of the early and sublime imagery of the East,—such imagery as Ezekiel used in order to shadow forth his divine inspiration,—is, that it does so much *more* than express meaning.— that it expresses meaning in the vague sense in which music expresses meaning,—so that a very wide fringe of imagery remains over, which is, as it were, merely an *accompaniment* of the meaning, not a part of its essence. So many symbols are heaped together, each of them a sort of separate hieroglyphic, that one is always in danger of *over*-interpreting the drift of the aggregate, and as you may miss the melody by attempting to cross-examine the notes, so you may miss the burden by attempting to separate the symbols. This is as true of Blake as if he had lived in the age of hieroglyphic. His brother artists called his house "the house of the Interpreter;" but it was rather the house of the man who most needed an Interpreter, yet who, perhaps, after all, was better interpreted by feeling than by thought.

The explanation of such hieroglyphic visions we take to be that minds of a special constitution,—one which becomes much less common as the world studies and masters its own thoughts,— are almost unable to separate *thoughts* from *things* at all, but incarnate their thoughts in things, almost arbitrarily and capriciously, rather than not at all. This is especially the gift of a great visionary painter like Blake. He has a profound conflict going on in his own mind, as he takes a country walk; instead of separating his thoughts from the scenery, they pass out of him into the scenery; the sun throws out a forbidding glare,— the trees stretch their arms to hold him back from his path,— the clouds scowl or smile upon his wishes, even the thistle under his foot looks its malice,—and if he paints the scene as a *picture*, it is a picture instinct with force of expression and feeling. But if, instead, he blunders into mystical poetry, his awkward use of *things* to express what words would, in poetry, express better, only looks like childish "make-belief." (p. 2772)

His double, and treble, and quadruple visions, of which he was so proud, spoiled his poetry, and often confused his pictures; but, when not too multiplex, gave a singular depth and glow to the latter. It is the painter's greatest art to think through things instead of words, and Blake did so. . . .

Now and then, when the object of Blake's visions was not plural but singular, he succeeded in expressing his vision in singularly striking poetry, but usually his poetry assembled too many realistic symbols to be in any way intelligible. There are touches, however, of verse here and there, which mingle the mysterious depth of Wordsworth with the grand symbolism of the primeval world. Take, for example [his poem **"The Truth"**]. . . . There are more beautiful things than this in Blake's poems, but few that show so strongly the elemental sort of energy that breathes in the author of the "Inventions to Job," as well as the glimpses of pure beauty, through the parting shadows of divine strength. But while Blake is singularly great in imparting a kind of temporary soul to *things*, . . . it is very

rarely, indeed, that his pictures and poems are instinct with what we call *experience*. One set of his poems are called *Songs of Experience,*—but they are rather songs of a man revolted by the attempt to gain experience and determined not to gain it. So, too, his pictures are full of elemental symbols, and thoughts, and natural emotions,—but never have the complexity of experience. "Blake is damned good to *steal from*," said Fuseli; and so he was. For his pictures were all *à priori*, suggesting new ideas, new lights, new combinations of things, in infinite variety of movement and expression, but only giving the form, the base, the *à priori* idea on which others could engraft a deeper complexity of human experience. . . .

[Mr. Rossetti] sums up the peculiar genius of Blake in two or three lines of such truth and beauty that we will close our notice with them. The man, he says, who can understand and enjoy Blake's pictures will gain from them "some things as he first knew them, not encumbered behind the days of his life; things too delicate for memory or years since forgotten; the momentary sense of spring in winter sunshine, the long sunsets long ago, and falling fires on distant hills." That is Blake's essential function,—to recall by painting,—now and then by poetry,— that lost sense described by Wordsworth which moved Blake, says Mr. Robinson, to "hysterical rapture,"—and well it might, for it was a poetical greeting from his own highest genius as an artist:—

> But there's a tree, of many, one,
> A single field which I have looked upon,
> Both of them speak of something that is gone;
> The pansy at my feet
> Doth the same tale repeat;
> Whither is fled the visionary gleam?
> Where is it now, the glory and the dream?
>
> (p. 2773)

[*R. H. Hutton*], "William Blake," *in* The Spectator, *Vol. 63, No. 1847, November 21, 1863, pp. 2771-73.*

ALGERNON CHARLES SWINBURNE   (essay date 1867)

[*A nineteenth-century English poet, dramatist, and critic, Swinburne was renowned during his lifetime for his skill and technical mastery as a lyric poet and is currently regarded as a preeminent symbol of rebellion against the prevailing moral orientation of Victorian aesthetics. Blake scholars also recognize his contribution as the author of the first full-length critical study of the poet. The excerpt below is taken from that work, featuring commentary on Blake's use of style, theme, and symbolism in the prophetic writings, particularly* The Marriage of Heaven and Hell.]

[Blake regarded his prophetic books as his greatest works], and as containing the sum of his achieved ambitions and fulfilled desires: as in effect inspired matter, of absolute imaginative truth and eternal import. We shall not again pause to rebut the familiar cry of response, to the effect that he was mad and not accountable for the uttermost madness of error. It must be enough to reply here that he was by no means mad, in any sense that would authorise us in rejecting his own judgment of his own aims and powers on a plea which would be held insufficient in another man's case. Let all readers and all critics get rid of that notion for good—clear their minds of it utterly and with all haste; let them know and remember, having once been told it, that in these strangest of all written books there is purpose as well as power, meaning as well as mystery. Doubtless, nothing quite like them was ever pitched out headlong into the world as they were. The confusion, the clamour, the jar of words that half suffice and thoughts that half exist—all these and other more absolutely offensive qualities—audacity, monotony, bombast, obscure play of licence and tortuous growth of fancy—cannot quench or even wholly conceal the living purport and the imperishable beauty which are here latent. (pp. 185-86)

[Gilchrist asserts] that Blake was given to contradict himself, by mere impulse if not by brute instinct, to such an extent that consistency is in no sense to be sought for or believed in throughout these works of his: and quotes, by way of ratifying this quite false notion, a noble sentence from the "Proverbs of Hell," aimed by Blake with all his force against that obstinate adherence to one external opinion which closes and hardens the spirit against all further message from the new-grown feelings or inspiration from the altering circumstances of a man. Never was there an error more grave or more complete than this. The expression shifts perpetually, the types blunder into new forms, the meaning tumbles into new types; the purpose remains, and the faith keeps its hold.

There are certain errors and eccentricities of manner and matter alike common to nearly all these books, and distinctly referable to the character and training of the man. Not educated in any regular or rational way, and by nature of an eagerly susceptible and intensely adhesive mind, in which the lyrical faculty had gained and kept a preponderance over all others visible in every scrap of his work, he had saturated his thoughts and kindled his senses with a passionate study of the forms of the Bible as translated into English, till his fancy caught a feverish contagion and his ear derived a delirious excitement from the mere sound and shape of the written words and verses. Hence the quaint and fervent imitation of style, the reproduction of peculiarities which to most men are meaningless when divested of their old sense or invested with a new. Hence the bewildering catalogues, genealogies, and divisions which (especially in such later books as the *Jerusalem*) seem at first invented only to strike any miserable reader with furious or lachrymose lunacy. Hence, though heaven knows by no fault of the originals, the insane cosmogony, blatant mythology, and sonorous aberration of thoughts and theories. Hence also much of the special force and supreme occasional loveliness or grandeur in expression. Conceive a man incomparably gifted as to the spiritual side of art, prone beyond all measure to the lyrical form of work, incredibly contemptuous of all things and people dissimilar to himself, of an intensely sensitive imagination and intolerant habit of faith, with a passionate power of peculiar belief, taking with all his might of mental nerve and strain of excitable spirit to a perusal and reperusal of such books as Job and Ezekiel. Observe too that his tone of mind was as far from being critical as from being orthodox. Thus his ecstacy of study was neither on the one side tempered and watered down by faith in established forms and external creeds, nor on the other side modified and directed by analytic judgment and the lust of facts. To Blake either form of mind was alike hateful. Like the Moses of Rabbinical tradition, he was "drunken with the kisses of the lips of God." Rational deism and clerical religion were to him two equally abhorrent incarnations of the same evil spirit, appearing now as negation and now as restriction. He wanted supremacy of freedom with intensity of faith. Hence he was properly neither Christian nor infidel: he was emphatically a heretic. Such men, according to the temper of the times, are burnt as demoniacs or pitied as lunatics. He believed in redemption by Christ, and in the incarnation of Satan as Jehovah. He believed that by self-sacrifice the soul should attain freedom and victorious deliverance from bodily bondage and sexual servitude; and also that the extremest fullness of indulgence in such desire and such delight as the senses can aim at or attain was absolutely good, eternally just, and universally requisite. These opinions, and stranger than these, he put forth in the cloudiest style, the wilfullest humour, and the stormiest excitement. No wonder the world let his books drift without caring to inquire what gold or jewels might be washed up as waifs from the dregs of churned foam and subsiding surf. He was the very man for fire and faggot; a mediaeval inquisitor would have had no more doubt about him than a materialist or "theophilanthropist" of his own day or of ours. (pp. 188-90)

[Over Blake's] clamorous kingdoms of speech and dream some few ruling forces of supreme discord preside: and chiefly the lord of the world of man; Urizen, God of cloud and star, "Father of jealousy," clothed with a splendour of shadow, strong and sad and cruel; his planet faintly glimmers and slowly revolves, a horror in heaven; the night is a part of his thought, rain and wind are in the passage of his feet; sorrow is in all his works; he is the maker of mortal things, of the elements and sexes; in him are incarnate that jealousy which the Hebrews acknowledged and that envy which the Greeks recognized in the divine nature; in his worship faith remains one with fear. Star and cloud, the types of mystery and distance, of cold alienation and heavenly jealousy, belong of right to the God who grudges and forbids: even as the spirit of revolt is made manifest in fiery incarnation—pure prolific fire, "the cold loins of Urizen dividing." These two symbols of "cruel fear" or "starry jealousy" in the divine tyrant, of ardent love or creative lust in the rebellious saviour of man, pervade the mystical writings of Blake. Orc, the man-child, with hair and flesh like fire, son of Space and Time, a terror and a wonder from the hour of his birth, containing within himself the likeness of all passions and appetites of men, is cast out from before the face of heaven; and falling upon earth, a stronger Vulcan or Satan, fills with his fire the narrowed foreheads and the darkened eyes of all that dwell thereon; imprisoned often and fed from vessels of iron with barren food and bitter drink, a wanderer or a captive upon earth, he shall rise again when his fire has spread through all lands to inflame and to infect with a strong contagion the spirit and the sense of man, and shall prevail against the law and the commandments of his enemy. This endless myth of oppression and redemption, of revelation and revolt, runs through many forms and spills itself by strange straits and byways among the sands and shallows of prophetic speech. But in these books there is not the substantial coherence of form and reasonable unity of principle which bring within scope of apprehension even the wildest myths grown out of unconscious idealism and impulsive tradition. A single man's work, however exclusively he may look to inspiration for motive and material, must always want the breadth and variety of meaning, the supple beauty of symbol, the infectious intensity of satisfied belief, which grow out of creeds and fables native to the spirit of a nation, yet peculiar to no man or sect, common yet sacred, not invented or constructed, but found growing and kept fresh with faith. But for all the dimness and violence of expression which pervert and darken the mythology of [Blake's] attempts at gospel, they have qualities great enough to be worth finding out. Only let none conceive that each separate figure in the swarming and noisy life of this populous daemonic creation has individual meaning and vitality. Blake was often taken off his feet by the strong currents of fancy, and indulged, like a child during its first humour of invention, in wild byplay and erratic excesses of simple sound; often lost his way in a maze of wind-music, and transcribed as it were with eyes closed and open ears the notes caught by chance as they drifted across the dream of his subdued senses. Alternating between lyrical invention and gigantic allegory, it is hard to catch and hold him down to any form or plan. At one time we have mere music, chains of ringing names, scattered jewels of sound without a thread, tortuous network of harmonies without a clue; and again we have passages, not always unworthy of an AEschylean chorus, full of fate and fear; words that are strained wellnigh in sunder by strong significance and earnest passion; words that deal greatly with great things, that strike deep and hold fast; each inclusive of some fierce apocalypse or suggestive of some obscure evangel. Now the matter in hand is touched with something of an epic style; the narrative and characters lose half their hidden sense, and the reciter passes from the prophetic tripod to the seat of a common singer; mere names, perhaps not even musical to other ears than his, allure and divert him; he plays with stately cadences, and lets the wind of swift or slow declamation steer him whither it will. Now again he falls with renewed might of will to his purpose; and his grand lyrical gift becomes an instrument not sonorous merely but vocal and articulate. To readers who can but once take their stand for a minute on the writer's footing, look for a little with his eyes and listen with his ears, even the more incoherent cadences will become not undelightful; something of his pleasure, with something of his perception, will pass into them; and understanding once the main gist of the whole fitful and high-strung tune, they will tolerate, where they cannot enjoy, the strange diversities and discords which intervene. (pp. 192-95)

In the meanest place as in the meanest man he beheld the hidden spirit and significance of which the flesh or the building is but a type. . . . It is inadequate and even inaccurate to say that he allotted to each place as to each world a presiding daemon or deity. He averred implicitly or directly, that each had a soul or spirit, the quintessence of its natural life, capable of change but not of death; and that of this soul the visible externals, though a native and actual part, were only a part, inseparable as yet but incomplete. Thus whenever, to his misfortune and ours, he stumbles upon the proper names of terrene men and things, he uses these names as signifying not the sensual form or body but the spirit which he supposed to animate these, to speak in them and work through them. In *America* the names of liberators, in *Jerusalem* the names of provinces, have no separate local or mundane sense whatever; throughout the prophecies "Albion" is the mythical and typical fatherland of human life, much what the East might seem to other men: and by way of making this type actual and prominent enough, Blake seizes upon all possible divisions of the modern visible England in town or country, and turns them in his loose symbolic way into minor powers and serving spirits. That he was wholly unconscious of the intolerably laughable effect we need not believe. He had all the delight in laying snares and giving offence, which is proper to his kind. He had all the confidence in his own power and right to do such things and to get over the doing of them which accompanies in such men the subtle humour of scandalizing. And unfortunately he had not by training, perhaps not by nature, the conscience which would have reminded him that whether or not an artist may allowably play with all other things in heaven and earth, one thing he must certainly not play with; the material forms of art: that levity and violence are here prohibited under grave penalties. Allowing however for this, we may notice that in the wildest passages of these books Blake merely carries into strange places or throws into strange shapes such final theories as in the dialect of calmer and smaller men have been accounted not unreasonable. (pp. 197-98)

Title page of America.

[*The Marriage of Heaven and Hell* is] the greatest of all his books; a work indeed which we rank as about the greatest produced by the eighteenth century in the line of high poetry and spiritual speculation. *The Marriage of Heaven and Hell* gives us the high-water mark of his intellect. None of his lyrical writings show the same sustained strength and radiance of mind; none of his other works in verse or prose give more than a hint here and a trace there of the same harmonious and humorous power, of the same choice of eloquent words, the same noble command and liberal music of thought; small things he could often do perfectly, and great things often imperfectly; here for once he has written a book as perfect as his most faultless song, as great as his most imperfect rhapsody. His fire of spirit fills it from end to end; but never deforms the body, never singes the surface of the work, as too often in the still noble books of his later life. Across the flicker of flame, under the roll and roar of water, which seem to flash and to resound throughout the poem, a stately music, shrill now as laughter and now again sonorous as a psalm, is audible through shifting notes and fitful metres of sound. The book swarms with heresies and eccentricities; every sentence bristles with some paradox, every page seethes with blind foam and surf of stormy doctrine; the humour is of that fierce grave sort, whose cool insanity of manner is more horrible and more obscure to the Philistine than any sharp edge of burlesque or glitter of irony; it is huge, swift, inexplicable; hardly laughable through its enormity of laughter, hardly significant through its condensation of meaning; but as true and thoughtful as the greatest humourist's. The variety and audacity of thoughts and words are incomparable: not less so their fervour and beauty. (pp. 204-05)

It was part of Blake's humour to challenge misconception, conscious as he was of power to grapple with it: to blow dust in their eyes who were already sandblind, to strew thorns under their feet who were already lame. Those whom the book in its present shape would perplex and repel he knew it would not in any form have attracted; and how such readers may fare is no concern of such writers; nor in effect need it be. Aware that he must at best offend a little, he did not fear to offend much. To measure the exact space of safety, to lay down the precise limits of offence, was an office neither to his taste nor within his power. . . . Blake's way was not the worst; to indulge his impulse to the full and write what fell to his hand, making sure at least of his own genius and natural instinct. In this his greatest book he has at once given himself freer play and set himself to harder labour than elsewhere: the two secrets of great work. Passion and humour are mixed in his writing like mist and light; whom the light may scorch or the mist confuse it is not his part to consider.

In the prologue Blake puts forth, not without grandeur if also with an admixture of rant and wind, a chief tenet of his moral creed. Once the ways of good and evil were clear, not yet confused by laws and religions; then humility and benevolence, the endurance of peril and the fruitful labour of love, were the just man's proper apanage; behind his feet the desert blossomed; by his toil and danger, by his sweat and blood, the desolate places were made rich and the dead bones clothed with flesh as the flesh of Adam. Now the hypocrite has come to reap the fruits, to divide and gather and eat; to drive forth the just man and to dwell in the paths which he found perilous and barren, but left safe and fertile. Churches have cast out apostles; creeds have rooted out faith. Henceforth anger and loneliness, the divine indignation of spiritual exile, the salt bread of scorn and the bitter wine of wrath, are the portion of the just man; he walks with lions in the waste places, not worth making fertile that others may reap and feed. "Rintrah," the spirit presiding over this period, is a spirit of fire and storm; darkness and famine, wrath and want, divide the kingdoms of the world. "Prisons are built with stones of Law; brothels with bricks of Religion." "As the caterpillar chooses the fairest leaves to lay her eggs on, so the priest lays his curse on the fairest joys." In a third proverb the view given of prayer is no less heretical; "As the plough follows words, so God rewards prayers." This was but the outcome or corollary of his main doctrine; as what we have called his "evangel of bodily liberty" was but the fruit of his belief in the identity of body with soul. The fear which restrains and the faith which refuses were things as ignoble as the hypocrisy which assumes or the humility which resigns. Veils and chains must be lifted and broken. "Folly is the cloak of knavery; shame is pride's cloak." Again; "He who desires but acts not breeds pestilence." "Sooner murder an infant in its cradle than nurse unacted desires." The doctrine of freedom could hardly run further or faster. Translated into rough practice, and planted in a less pure soil than that of the writer's mind, this philosophy might bring forth a strange harvest. Together with such width of moral pantheism as will hardly admit a "tender curb," leave "a little curtain of flesh on the bed of our desire," there is a vehemence of faith in divine wrath, in the excellence of righteous anger and revenge, to be outdone by no prophet or Puritan. "A dead body revenges not injuries." Sincerity and plain dealing at least are virtues not to be thrown over; Blake indeed could not conceive an impulse to mendacity, a tortuous habit of mind,

a soul born crooked. This one quality of falsehood remains damnable in his sight, to be consumed with all that comes of it. In man or beast or any other part of God he found no native taint or birthmark of this. Upon all else the divine breath and the divine hand are sensible and visible.

> The pride of the peacock is the glory of God;
> The lust of the goat is the bounty of God;
> The wrath of the lion is the wisdom of God;
> The nakedness of woman is the work of God.

All form and all instinct is sacred; but no invention or device of man's. All crafts and creeds of theirs are "the serpent's meat:" and that a man should be born cruel and false is barely imaginable. (pp. 205-08)

[We] should now be able to allow for the subtle intricate fashion in which Blake labours to invert the weapons of his antagonists upon themselves [in the section beginning "As a new heaven is begun" and in "The Voice of the Devil"]. Neither can the banns or marriage be published between heaven and hell with the voice of a parish clerk. This prophet came to do what Swedenborg his precursor had left undone, being but the watchman by the empty sepulchre, and his writings as the grave-clothes cast off by the risen Christ. Blake's estimate of Swedenborg, right or wrong, was . . . distinct and consistent; to this effect; that his inspiration was limited and timid, superficial and derivative; that he was content with leaves and husks, and had not the courage to examine the root and the kernel of things; that he clove to the heaven and shrank from the hell of other men; whereas, to men in whom "a new heaven is begun," the one must not be terrible nor the other desirable. To them the "flaming fire" wherein dwells a God whom men call devil, must seem a purer element of life than the starry and cloudy space wherein dwells a devil whom they call God. It must be remembered that Blake uses the current terms of religion, now as types of his own peculiar faith, now in the sense of ordinary preachers: impugning therefore at one time what at another he will seem to vindicate. Vague and violent as this overture may appear, it must be followed with care, that the writer's intensity of spiritual faith may be hereafter kept in sight. The senses, "the chief inlets of soul in this age" of brute doubt and brute belief, are worthy only as parts of the soul. This, it cannot be too much repeated and insisted on, this and no prurience of porcine appetite for rotten apples, no vulgarity of porcine adoration for unctuous wash, is what lies at the root of Blake's sensual doctrine. Let no reader now or ever forget, that while others will admit nothing beyond the body, the mystic will admit nothing outside the soul. (pp. 211-12)

> The Giants who formed this world into its sensual existence, and now seem to live in it in chains, are in truth the causes of its life and the sources of all activity; but the chains are, the cunning of weak and tame minds, which have power to resist energy; according to the proverb, the weak in courage is strong in cunning.
>
> Thus one portion of being is the Prolific, the other, the Devouring; to the devourer it seems as if the producer was in his chains; but it is not so; he only takes portions of existence and fancies that the whole.
>
> But the Prolific would cease to be Prolific, unless the Devourer as a sea received the excess of his delights.

Some will say, Is not God alone the Prolific?

I answer, God only Acts and Is in existing beings or Men.

These two classes of men are always upon earth, and they should be enemies; whoever tries to reconcile them, seeks to destroy existence.

Religion is an endeavour to reconcile the two.

NOTE.—Jesus Christ did not wish to unite but to separate them, as in the Parable of sheep and goats! and he says I came not to send Peace but a Sword.

Messiah or Satan or Tempter was formerly thought to be one of the Antediluvians who are our Energies.

These are hard sayings; who can hear them? At first sight also, as we were forewarned, this passage seems at direct variance with that other in the overture, where our prophet appears at first sight, and only appears, to speak of the fallen ''Messiah'' as the same with the Christ of his belief. Verbally coherent we cannot hope to make the two passages; but it must be remarked and remembered that the very root or kernel of this creed is not the assumed humanity of God, but the achieved divinity of Man; not incarnation from without, but development from within; not a miraculous passage into flesh, but a natural growth into godhead. Christ, as the type or sample of manhood, thus becomes after death the true Jehovah; not, as he seems to the vulgar, the extraneous and empirical God of creeds and churches, human in no necessary or absolute sense, the false and fallen phantom of his enemy, Zeus in the mask of Prometheus. . . . Subtle, trenchant and profound as is this philosophy, there is no radical flaw in the book, no positive incongruity, no inherent contradiction. A single consistent principle keeps alive the large relaxed limbs, makes significant the dim great features of this strange faith. It is but at the opening that the words are even partially inadequate and obscure. (pp. 216-17)

In the next and longest division of the book [the passage entitled ''A Memorable Fancy'' beginning with the words, ''An angel came to me and said''], direct allegory and imaginative vision are indivisibly mixed into each other. The stable and mill, the twisted root and inverted fungus, are transparent symbols enough: the splendid and stormy apocalypse of the abyss is a chapter of pure vision or poetic invention. (p. 218)

The ''seven houses of brick'' we may take to be a reminiscence of the seven churches of St. John; as indeed the traces of former evangelists and prophets are never long wanting when we track the steps of this one. Lest however we be found unawares on the side of . . . [the] hapless angels and baboons, we will abstain with all due care from any not indispensable analysis. It is evident that between pure ''phantasy'' and mere ''analytics'' the great gulf must remain fixed, and either party appear to the other deceptive and deceived. That impulsive energy and energetic faith are the only means, whether used as tools of peace or as weapons of war, to pave or to fight our way toward the realities of things, was plainly the creed of Blake; as also that these realities, once well in sight, will reverse appearance and overthrow tradition: hell will appear as heaven, and heaven as hell. The abyss once entered with due trust and courage appears a place of green pastures and gracious springs: the paradise of resignation once beheld with undisturbed eyes appears a place of emptiness or bondage, delusion or cruelty. On the humorous beauty and vigour of these symbols we need not

expatiate; in these qualities Rabelais and Dante together could hardly have excelled Blake at his best. (pp. 220-21)

[The] book is wound up in a lyric rapture, not without some flutter and tumour of style, but full of clear high music and flame-like aspiration. Epilogue and prologue are both nearer in manner to the dubious hybrid language of the succeeding books of prophecy than to the choice and noble prose in which the rest of this book is written. The overture must be read by the light of its meaning; of the mysterious universal mother and her son, the latest birth of the world, we have already taken account. The date of 1790 must here be kept in mind, that all may remember what appearances of change were abroad, what manner of light and tempest was visible upon earth, when the hopes of such men as Blake made their stormy way into speech or song.

"A SONG OF LIBERTY"

1. The Eternal Female groan'd! it was heard over all the Earth.

2. Albion's coast is sick silent; the American meadows faint!

3. Shadows of Prophecy shiver along by the lakes and the rivers, and mutter across the ocean. France, rend down thy dungeon;

4. Golden Spain, burst the barriers of old Rome;

5. Cast thy keys, O Rome, into the deep down falling, even to eternity down falling;

6. And weep.

7. In her trembling hands she took the new-born terror howling:

8. On those infinite mountains of light now barred out by the Atlantic sea, the new-born fire stood before the starry King!

9. Flag'd with grey-browed snows and thunderous visages the jealous wings waved over the deep.

10. The speary hand burned aloft, unbuckled was the shield, forth went the hand of jealousy among the flaming hair, and hurled the new-born wonder thro' the starry night.

11. The fire, the fire is falling!

12. Look up! look up! O citizen of London, enlarge thy countenance: O Jew, leave counting gold! return to thy oil and wine; O African! black African! (go, winged thought, widen his forehead.)

13, The fiery limbs, the flaming hair, shot like the sinking sun into the western sea.

14. Waked from his eternal sleep, the hoary element roaring fled away.

15. Down rushed, beating his wings in vain, the jealous King; his grey-browed councillors, thunderous warriors, curled veterans, among helms and shields, and chariots, horses, elephants; banners, castles, slings and rocks;

16. Falling, rushing, ruining! buried in the ruins, on Urthona's dens;

17. All night beneath the ruins, then their sullen flames faded emerge round the gloomy King.

18. With thunder and fire, leading his starry hosts thro' the waste wilderness, he promulgates his ten commands, glancing his beamy eye-lids over the deep in dark dismay;

19. Where the son of fire in his eastern cloud, while the morning plumes her golden breast,

20. Spurning the clouds written with curses, stamps the stony law to dust, loosing the eternal horses from the dens of night, crying, Empire is no more! and now the lion and the wolf shall cease.

CHORUS.

Let the Priests of the Raven of dawn no longer in deadly black with hoarse note curse the sons of joy; Nor his accepted brethren, whom, tyrant, he calls free, lay the bound or build the roof; Nor pale religious letchery call that virginity that wishes but acts not;

For everything that lives is Holy.

And so, as with fire and thunder—"thunder of thought, and flames of fierce desire"—is this *Marriage of Heaven and Hell* at length happily consummated; the prophet, as a fervent paranymph, standing by to invoke upon the wedded pair his most unclerical benediction. Those who are not bidden to the bridegroom's supper may as well keep away, lest worse befall them, not having a wedding garment. For us there remains little to say, now that the torches are out, the nuts scattered, the songs silent, and the saffron faded from the veil. We will wish them a quiet life, and an heir who may combine the merits and capacities of either parent. It were pleasant enough, but too superfluous, to dwell upon the beauty of this nuptial hymn; to bid men remark what eloquence, what subtlety, what ardour of wisdom, what splendour of thought, is here; how far it outruns, not in daring alone but in sufficiency, all sayings of minor mystics who were not also poets; how much of lofty love and of noble faith underlies and animates these rapid and fervent words; what greatness of spirit and of speech there was in the man who, living as Blake lived, could write as Blake has written. Those who cannot see what is implied may remain unable to tolerate what is expressed; and those who can read aright need no index of ours. (pp. 222-25)

The complete and exalted figure of Blake cannot be seen in full by those who avert their eyes, smarting and blinking, from the frequent smoke and sudden flame. Others will see more clearly, as they look more sharply, the radical sanity and coherence of the mind which put forth its shoots of thought and faith in ways so strange, at such strange times. Faith incredible and love invisible to most men were alone the springs of this turbid and sonorous stream. In Blake, above all other men, the moral and the imaginative senses were so fused together as to compose the final artistic form. No man's fancy, in that age, flew so far and so high on so sure a wing. No man's mind, in that generation, dived so deep or gazed so long after the chance of human redemption. To serve art and to love liberty seemed to him the two things (if indeed they were not one thing) worth a man's life and work; and no servant was ever trustier, no lover more constant than he. (pp. 298-99)

Confidence in future friends, and contempt of present foes, may have induced him to leave his highest achievements impalpable and obscure. Their scope is as wide and as high as heaven, but not as clear; clouds involve and rains inundate the fitful and stormy space of air through which he spreads and plies an indefatigable wing. There can be few books in the world like these; I can remember one poet only whose work seems to me the same or similar in kind; a poet as vast in aim, as daring in detail, as unlike others, as coherent to himself, as strange without and as sane within. The points of contact and sides of likeness between William Blake and Walt Whitman are so many and so grave, as to afford some ground of reason to those who preach the transition of souls or transfusion of spirits. The great American is not a more passionate preacher of sexual or political freedom than the English artist. To each the imperishable form of a possible and universal Republic is equally requisite and adorable as the temporal and spiritual queen of ages as of men. To each all sides and shapes of life are alike acceptable or endurable. From the fresh free ground of either workman nothing is excluded that is not exclusive. The words of either strike deep and run wide and soar high. They are both full of faith and passion, competent to love and to loathe, capable of contempt and of worship. Both are spiritual, and both democratic; both by their works recall, even to so untaught and tentative a student as I am, the fragments vouchsafed to us of the Pantheistic poetry of the East. Their casual audacities of expression or speculation are in effect wellnigh indentical. Their outlooks and theories are evidently the same on all points of intellectual and social life. The divine devotion and selfless love which make men martyrs and prophets are alike visible and palpable in each. . . . It seems that in each of these men at their birth pity and passion, and relief and redress of wrong, became incarnate and innate. That may well be said of the one which was said of the other: that "he looks like a man." And in externals and details the work of these two constantly and inevitably coheres and coincides. A sound as of a sweeping wind; a prospect as over dawning continents at the fiery instant of a sudden sunrise; a splendour now of stars and now of storms; an expanse and exultation of wing across strange spaces of air and above shoreless stretches of sea; a resolute and reflective love of liberty in all times and in all things where it should be; a depth of sympathy and a height of scorn which complete and explain each other, as tender and as bitter as Dante's; a power, intense and infallible, of pictorial concentration and absorption, most rare when combined with the sense and the enjoyment of the widest and the highest things; an exquisite and lyrical excellence of form when the subject is well in keeping with the poet's tone of spirit; a strength and security of touch in small sweet sketches of colour and outline, which bring before the eyes of their student a clear glimpse of the thing designed—some little inlet of sky lighted by moon or star, some dim reach of windy water or gentle growth of meadow-land or wood; these are qualities common to the work of either. Had we place or time or wish to touch on their shortcomings and errors, it might be shown that these too are nearly akin; that their poetry has at once the melody and the laxity of a fitful storm-wind; that, being oceanic, it is troubled with violent groundswells and sudden perils of ebb and reflux, of shoal and reef, and perplexing to the swimmer or the sailor; in a word, that it partakes the powers and the faults of elemental and eternal things; that it is at times noisy and barren and loose, rootless and fruitless and informal; and is in the main fruitful and delightful and noble, a necessary part of the divine mechanism of things. Any work or art of which this cannot be said is superfluous and perishable, whatever of grace or charm it may possess or assume. Whitman has seldom struck a note of thought and speech so just and so profound as Blake has now and then touched upon; but his work is generally more frank and fresh, smelling of sweeter air, and readier to expound or expose its message, than this of the prophetic books. Nor is there among these any poem or passage of equal length so faultless and so noble as his ''Voice out of the Sea,'' or as his dirge over President Lincoln—the most sweet and sonorous nocturn ever chanted in the church of the world. But in breadth of outline and charm of colour, these poems recall the work of Blake; and to neither poet can a higher tribute of honest praise be paid than this. (pp. 300-03)

> *Algernon Charles Swinburne, in his* William Blake:
> A Critical Essay, *edited by Hugh J. Luke, 1867.*
> *Reprint by University of Nebraska Press, 1970, 319 p.*

WILLIAM MICHAEL ROSSETTI (essay date 1874)

[Rossetti, an English art critic, man of letters, and one of the original members of the Pre-Raphaelite Brotherhood, was instrumental in keeping Blake's life and works before the public in the later half of the nineteenth century. With his brother, Dante Gabriel Rossetti, he helped Anne Gilchrist complete her late husband's influential Life of William Blake, *and he also brought out an edition of the poet's works. Rossetti's preface to that edition, in which he praises Blake's lyric poetry while questioning the readability and sanity of the prophetic books, is excerpted below.]*

The character of Blake's poetry bears, it need hardly be said, a considerable affinity to that of his work in the art of design; he himself, it is said, thought the former the finer of the two. There is, however, no little difference between them, when their main elements are considered proportionally. In both, Blake almost totally ignores actual life and its evolution, and the passions and interactions of men as elicited by the wear and tear of real society. True, individual instances might be cited where he has in view some topic of the day, or some incident of life, simple or harrowing, such as social or dramatic writers might take cognizance of. But these also he treats with a primitiveness or singularity which, if it does not remove the subjects from our sympathy—and a few cases of very highly sympathetic treatment are to be found—does at least leave them within the region of the ideal, or sometimes of the intangible. As a rule, Blake does not deal at all with the complicated practical interests of life, or the influence of these upon character; but he possesses the large range of primordial emotion, from the utter innocence and happy unconscious instinct of infancy, up to the fervours of the prophet, inspired to announce, to judge, and to reprobate. (pp. cxi-cxii)

[Leaving the] Prophetic Books for the present, we may say of the other rhythmic poems that the spiritual intuition of which we have already spoken as Blake's most central faculty, and a lyric outflow the purest and most spontaneous, fashioning the composition in its general mould, and drifting aright each word and cadence, are the most observable and precious qualities. This statement as to the wording and cadences must of course be understood with due limitation; for Blake, exquisitely true to the mark as he can come in such matters, is often also palpably faulty—transgressing even the obvious laws of grammar and of metre. Power of thought is likewise largely present in several cases; not of analytic or reasoning thought, for which Blake had as little turn in his poems as liking in his *dicta*, but broad and strong intellectual perception, telling in aid of that still higher and primary faculty of intuition. (p. cxiii)

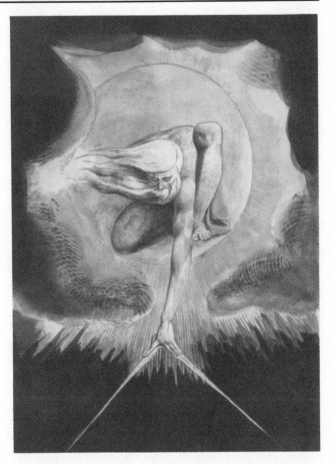

''The Ancient of Days,'' the frontispiece of Europe.

The *Poetical Sketches* are simply astonishing; whether we regard the fact that they were written between Blake's twelfth and twentieth years, or reflect that they thus preceded even the first publications of Cowper and of Burns, not to speak of other and later authors in whose work the modern spirit and tone of poetry are more distinctly perceptible. Blake, in truth, when in his teens, was a wholly unique poet; far ahead of his contemporaries, and of his predecessors of three or four generations, equally in what he himself could do, and in his sympathy for olden sources of inspiration. In his fragmentary drama of **''Edward the Third''** we recognize one who has loved and studied Shakspeare to good purpose: and several of the short lyrics in the *Poetical Sketches* have the same sort of pungent perfume—indefinable but not evanescent—that belongs to the choicest Elizabethan songs; the like play of emotion,—or play of colour, as it might be termed; the like ripeness and roundness, poetic, and intolerant of translation into prose. At the time when Blake wrote these songs, and for a long while before, no one was doing anything of at all the same kind. Not but that, even in Blake, lines and words occur here and there betraying the *fadeur* of the eighteenth century.

It cannot be said that he ever surpassed in absolute lyrical gift, nor yet indeed in literary finish, the most excellent things in his earliest volume. The *Songs of Innocence*, however, are, taken in their totality, fully up to the same mark; and they have the additional value conferred by unity of scheme, and relation of parts. Some of the little poems included in this series are the most perfect expression ever given (so far as I know) to babe-life—to what a man can remember of himself as an infant, or can enter into as existing in other infants, or can love as of the essence of infancy. Blake was a believer (with more or less exactness of dogma) in the preëxistence of the human soul. These poems are very like the utterance of a babe, sentient at once of its present infantine and of its past matured existence; feeling the life and thinking the thoughts of infancy, yet feeling and thinking all this through the medium of a higher consciousness, a fullness of spiritual stature which once was, and again shall be. The comparative merit of the *Songs of Innocence* and the later-written *Songs of Experience* has been debated by competent critics, with diverse conclusions. To me it seems that the finest compositions in the *Experience* are fully as admirable as the finest in the *Innocence;* the unsuccessful items, however, being more numerous, and the faulty elements throughout producing a more damaging effect. The tone of thought, necessarily more varied, is also, in a sense, more elevated, but not so constantly well sustained or at unity with itself.

The *Songs of Experience* here and there, and also the *Book of Thel* (not to speak of examples even in the earlier poems) show us something of the obscure side of Blake's poetry; his arbitrary use of words and symbols, and a certain way he had of *hurrying* his conceptions into shape. Clearly, no poet had conceptions more immediate: Blake, by an inchoate method of execution, where things are said with as much abruptness as vividness, and are indicated or approximated rather than exhibited, and so left to explain themselves or not as the case may turn out, succeeds in conveying to his reader a good deal of this same immediate impression felt by himself. It cannot be so sudden and striking to the reader as it was to the writer; but the very obscurity serves to make it rapid. The reader, while he feels that explanation is needed (and explanation can only be a lengthy process, and so far conflicts with the immediateness of impression) has a sense also of something hastily presented to him, and as hastily withdrawn. He snatches a meaning, or else must miss it; for, before he has time to think it out, another image has replaced the former one. In some of the remaining poems the obscurity increases; and a certain proportion of them is really not intelligible, save by an effort of conjecture: I may cite "**The Crystal Cabinet**," "**The Mental Traveller**," and "**William Bond**." The two former, however, with all their difficulty, are exceedingly fine; and some others . . . , especially "**Broken Love**" and "**Auguries of Innocence**", rank among Blake's noblest performances. (pp. cxiv-cxvii)

Ample evidence exists to satisfy us that Blake had real conceptions in the metaphysical or supersensual regions of thought—conceptions which might have been termed speculations in other people, but in him rather intuitions; and that the Prophetic Books embody these in some sort of way cannot be disputed. He did not want them to be exactly understood, in the analytical, unravelling sense. "Allegory addressed to the intellectual powers" (he has written *à propos* of the *Jerusalem*), "while it is altogether hidden from the corporeal understanding, is my definition of the most sublime poetry." The Prophetic Books have indeed sublimity and power in large measure; invention both of mythology and of imagery; and much which, if it does not take hold of the imagination of the reader, does at least appeal to it. Yet, after everything that ought to be allowed in favour of the Prophetic Books has been conceded, I must confess my opinion that they are, taken as a whole, neither readable nor even entirely sane performances. They are dark and chaotic to the extremest degree; ponderous and turbid; battling and baffling, like the arms of a windmill when the wind blows shiftingly from all quarters; full of action as in-

conceivable as the personages, and personages as insoluble as their acts; replete with uncouth and arbitrary nomenclature,—hieroglyphics sometimes seemingly void of demotic equivalents. Urizen, Fuzon, Los and Enitharmon (Time and Space), Theotormon, Ahania, Har and Heva, Orc, Rintrah, Palamabron; and, for places, Golgonooza, Bowlahoola (Art and Law), &c.—such are the names with which Blake condemns us to become familiar before we can so much as begin to follow out his revelations and his myths. Various passages are truly formless, according to any admissible standard of poetic or rhapsodic form: a much greater number yield no stable or tangible sense,—they hurtle in your ears, and are gone. Notwithstanding all this, the greatness of the man—the directness and force of his mind, and sometimes its vigorous grasp as well—are abundantly evident in the Prophetic Books. A reader susceptible to poetic influences cannot make light of them; nor can one who has perused Mr. Swinburne's essay [see excerpt dated 1867] affect to consider that they lack meaning—positive and important, though not definite and developed, meaning. If an intellectual man were relegated to entire solitude for some months or years, with nothing to read except Blake's Prophetic Books, he would naturally study and ponder them; piece together their myths, trace their connection, reason out their system. If at the end of the process he considered these works altogether right and fine, or even absolutely free from a tinge of something other than sanity, he would have arrived at a conclusion different from mine: but I have no hesitation in thinking that he would relish the books vastly more at the close than at the commencement of his studies, and that his admiration for them would be all the stronger in proportion to the elevation and amplitude of his own mind. He would be quite capable of ranging them among the most inspired, as certainly among the most uncommon, productions of the human intellect. (pp. cxx-cxxii)

> *William Michael Rossetti, in a prefatory memoir to* The Poetical Works of William Blake, Lyrical and Miscellaneous *by William Blake, edited by William Michael Rossetti, 1874. Reprint by George Bell & Sons, 1893, pp. ix-cxxxiii.*

GEORGE SAINTSBURY (essay date 1874)

[*Saintsbury was an English literary historian and critic of the late nineteenth and early twentieth centuries. A prolific writer, he composed several histories of English and European literature as well as numerous critical works on individual authors, styles, and periods. In the following excerpt, taken from a review of Rossetti's 1874 edition of Blake (see excerpt above), Saintsbury underscores the close relationship between Blake's literary strengths and weaknesses. For further commentary by Saintsbury, see the excerpt dated 1911.*]

[The] value of Mr. Rossetti's edition does not so much consist in the intrinsic excellence of the additions which he has made to our knowledge, as in the increased facilities offered for studying Blake's poetry as a whole. Of the two dangers that beset this study, one is tolerably extinct. No one of any taste or culture is likely at this time of day to undervalue the genius or the work of the greatest English poet of the eighteenth century. But in the opposite direction there is much more chance of stumbling. The beauties in Blake are sometimes so transcendent, the meaning is sometimes so pregnant and subtle, that there is considerable danger of wilfully seeing beauty when there is mere deformity, and sense when there is mere nonsense. We must confess that some comments on Blake have irresistibly reminded us of the interpretative sagacity of one

Thaumast, a countryman of ours, if Master Francis Rabelais may be trusted. Mr. Rossetti has, we think, hit upon (though he has not followed out) the right clue to much of Blake's writing as well as to much of his conduct, when he describes his behaviour to Hayley as that of a "naughty little boy." The curious childishness of Blake's nature, not by any means always or often taking the "naughty" form, should always be borne in mind. His delight in mere sound, often quite separated from sense, his exaggerated likes and dislikes, his abrupt transitions and discontinuities, and his total lack of any critical or analytic faculty, are all eminently childlike. They are almost necessary conditions of his peculiar excellences, his wonderful freshness and spontaneity, and the extraordinary simplicity with which his profoundest thoughts and most splendid images are delivered. No man probably ever produced such magnificent and varied effects with less complicated apparatus of language or style. Nothing is laboured or decorated; each jewel is there just as it was found in the veins of the rock. Such gems as—

> Abstinence sows sand all over
> The ruddy limbs and flaming hair;

as—

> Let age and sickness silent rob
> The vineyard in the night;
> But those who burn with vigorous youth
> Pluck fruits before the light;

as the exquisite "**Wildflower Song,**" and many others, show, as it would seem, a perfect command of metre and language. But comparison soon shows us that this appearance of conscious mastery is quite delusive. It is not that Blake never revised his work; far from it: but that it was always uncertain whether the process of revision would polish or deform. The lack of critical power also explains his extraordinary judgments on the work of other men. The defence, ingeniously set up, that he preferred even the bad work of a workman who in some sort went on his own principles, to the good work of another who went on principles different from his, will not cover all cases. Allowing that in this manner he might dislike Sir Joshua, what possible defence can it afford for his calling Rembrandt a fool? The fact seems to be that, as is the case with children, he was rarely without some reason for his likes, but constantly lacked all reason whatever for his dislikes. There is undoubtedly an odd tendency in the half-developed and half-cultured mind to dislike in this manner, while the attractions of such a mind are seldom wrong. Culture, which in a strict sense Blake never had, would no doubt have corrected much of this wrongheadedness, as well as much of his carelessness in work. But it would probably have restricted, in a much greater degree, his constructive and creative power. The man of culture is constantly restrained from producing by his too keen sense of the partial imperfection of his work. There is about Blake something peculiarly Adamic: he is constantly naked, but not in the least ashamed. Had he eaten of the tree which should be re-baptised of Culture, he would probably with the deformities have learnt to hide much of the beauty of his nudity.

One of the more noteworthy results of this simplicity and absence of after-thought is the lightness of touch and absence of detail which characterise his most successful works. . . . Never perhaps was there a poet who dealt less in epithets, or whose epithets when he does use them are of a simpler kind, yet never was there one who succeeded more perfectly in making the common as though it were not common:

> Ah, Sunflower, weary of time,
> Who countest the steps of the sun.

Here are just twelve of the commonest words, yet a hundred could not be more expressive or more pathetic. Hence it is that Blake's verses stick in the memory more persistently than other men's, their vague sweet suggestiveness compensating for the absence of elaborate imagery. (pp. 600-01)

> *George Saintsbury, in a review of "The Poetical Works of William Blake," in* The Academy, *n.s. No. 135, December 5, 1874, pp. 599-601.*

EDWIN JOHN ELLIS AND WILLIAM BUTLER YEATS (essay date 1893)

[*Yeats, an Irish writer who is considered one of the greatest poets in the English language, was deeply interested in spiritualism, theosophy, and occult systems. Bringing these interests to bear on the study of Blake, he joined Ellis in editing a collection of the writer's works that featured a detailed explication of Blake's "symbolic system" as well as the first publication of* The Four Zoas *(referred to here as* Vala*). The following excerpt focuses on their explication of the symbolism of the four zoas and selected passages in* The Marriage of Heaven and Hell. *For additional commentary by Yeats, see the excerpt dated 1897.*]

Two principal causes have hitherto kept the critics,—among whom must be included Mr. Swinburne himself, though he reigns as the one-eyed man of the proverb among the blind,—from attaining a knowledge of what Blake meant.

The first is the solidity of [his] myth, and its wonderful coherence. The second is the variety of terms in which the sections of it are named.

The foundation of Blake's symbolic system of speech is his conception of the Four-fold in Man, and the covering that concealed this system was a peculiar use of synonyms. The four portions of Humanity are divided under the names of the Four Zoas in the myth, and the reader who does not understand the relation of the Four Zoas to each other, and to each living man, has not made even the first step towards understanding the Symbolic System which is the signature of Blake's genius, and the guarantee of his sanity. Mr. Swinburne, Mr. Gilchrist, and the brothers, Dante and William Rossetti, deserve well of literature for having brought Blake into the light of day and made his name known throughout the length and breadth of England. But though whatever is accessible to us now was accessible to them when they wrote, including the then unpublished *Vala,* not one chapter, not one clear paragraph about the myth of Four Zoas, is to be found in all that they have published. (Vol. I, p. viii)

Blake at the beginning of his longest poem bids the muses sing man's "fall into Division and his resurrection into Unity," and Jacob Boehmen would have echoed the words. The universe, according to both seers, arose from the divine unity, and by a process of division and subdivision almost identical in both systems, so far as its earlier stages are concerned and having many analogies throughout. (Vol. I, p. 246)

Like Boehmen and the occultists generally, [Blake] postulates besides the Trinity a fourth principle, a universal matrix or heaven or abode, from which, and in which all have life. It is that represented by the circle containing the triangle of the ancient mystics, and may be described as the imagination of God, without which neither Father, Son, nor Spirit could be made manifest in life and action. In one of the aphorisms written in the Laocoon plate, it is called "The Divine Body," and men are valued according as it enters into them, for we are told that "The unproductive man is not a Christian." To this emanation, to give it the Blakean term, of the Father, is applied constantly by Boehmen the word "looking-glass," and Blake, when he uses the same expression in connection with a corresponding though minor being of his mystical mythology, and writes of "Enitharmon's looking-glass," as also when he speaks in the essay on "The Last Judgment" of "the vegetable glass of Nature," adopts the term as his own. God looking into this mirror, ceases to be mere will, beholds Himself as the Son, His love for His own unity, His self-consciousness, and enters on that eternal meditation about Himself which is called the Holy Spirit. "Council" it is sometimes called in Boehmen, a term which is lengthened into "The Council of God" in the "Mystical Writings." This Holy Spirit, or "Council," is the energy which wakes into being the numberless thought-forms of the great mirror, the immortal or typical shapes of all things, the "ideas" of Plato. It and the mirror make up together divine manifestation. At first the thought-forms subsist and move in this universal "imagination which liveth for ever" without being manifest to themselves and each other as separate individualities, not being lives but thoughts of the universal life. Then comes the contrary of the universal life, "the reaction of man against God," the longing of the shapes and thought-forms for a vivid sensation of their own existence. Desire is its name, and to it Boehmen traces the fall into physical life. Blake will have none of this doctrine, for desire is to him essentially sacred, because essentially vital, for "all that lives is holy." "Contraries are not negations," he tells us in *Milton* and it is to the negation of God that we owe the physical body and its troubles. It was only when limited to its own narrow experience and divorced from imagination by what Blake calls reason, "its outward bound," that desire brought corporeality to impede life in its action. This reason is the eternal "no" warring on the eternal "yes" of God, and the creator of the opaque, the non-imaginative, the egoistic. He means by reason something quite different from what he calls intellect. It means with him the faculty that entices us to claim exclusive reality for our own sensations, and build up selfhoods, dwelling in memories of their own experiences—the great "chaos"—to promulgate "laws of prudence" for their protection, and "call them the laws of God." It is what we call materialism, and has caused all evil and all misery, for once we believe that our selfhoods, or spectres as Blake names them, alone exist, we seek to feed them and preserve them at whatever sorrow and toil to others. . . . It closed up the forms and thoughts and lives within the narrow circle of their separate existence, whereas before they had "expanded and contracted" at will, hiding them from the light and life of God, and from the freedom of the "imagination which liveth for ever." The mirror was changed under its influence to that hard stepmother we call Nature. Desire, before reason came to set bounds to it, was merely joy seeking its own infinity, but restriction changed it to a devouring flame. "Thought," says Blake in *Europe*, "changed the infinite to a serpent," that is, to a self-torturing and desirous selfhood or spectre. As soon as reason had set bounds to life, "the laws of the numbers" began, and multiplicity endeavoured to take the place of unity, continually struggling with that from whence it came. In the struggle the indignation of unity is called "the wrath of God," and is the cause of our unending dissatisfaction with ourselves and all things. (Vol. I, pp. 246-48)

The personal desires shrink further and further from the impersonal wrath. Hence God, as Will, became wrapped in darkness, and man would never again have known the divine freedom he had fallen from, did not God as Love descend perpetually within the forms and lives. The unity contends with the mul-

tiplicity, and seeks to conquer it in the will, but descends into it to redeem and succour in the love, for "One must be all, and contain within Himself all things both small and great." . . . It is the perpetual aim of the love to persuade all lives "to unite as one man," and all thoughts and feelings to put off their separate egoism and become "the divine members." (Vol. I, pp. 248-49)

[Blake's] system is mainly busy with the lesser powers through which the Deity manifests in our created world, for "God only acts or is in existing beings or men." The unity is mysteriously united to the diversity and finds therein its body and its opportunity for life and motion, by that union of incompatibles which is the supreme paradox. The "beings" in the sentence quoted from *The Marriage of Heaven and Hell* are the spirits or mental states. The present chapter has to do with their classification into four great divisions corresponding to the division of the Divine Nature into Father, Son, Spirit and, what we have called with Boehmen, "mirror." These four kinds of mental states and their corresponding physical symbols are called the four Zoas, or "Lifes," from the Greek word *zoa*, life. They are identical with the wheels of Ezekiel and with the four beasts of the Apocalypse, and resemble closely Raphael, Michael, Gabriel, Uriel, the Kabalistic regents of the cardinal points, and like them preside over psychic and bodily affairs. They are the mighty beings, Urizen, Luvah, Tharmas, Urthona, whose deeds and words fill page after page of "The Mystical Writings."

When life falls into division the First Person of the Trinity gives place to Urizen, "creator of men, mistaken demon of Heaven," and "god of this world." He is Reason, the enemy of inspiration and imagination. Urizen before he sought dominion as Reason was wholly subordinate and enwrapped in the divine fire and as such was a principle of spiritual or imaginative order, but separating himself from the Divine, as the cold light of the mind, he became a selfhood, a life living from and for itself, and not from and for the source of all lives, and was transformed into the cause of the formalism and deadness of unimaginative thought and of the rigidity and opaqueness of iron and stone. Before, he had been the tendency of things to group themselves by a natural affinity into shapes of beauty and joy, and now he turned into the tendency of things to contract about their own centres, and to subordinate all to themselves. From being the creative will of the divine he became the creative will of the body and corporeal mind. He is described as falling into the chaos, which is memory, because memory is the record of the merely egoistic experience, thus differing from inspiration, which is direct knowledge. It is he who creates those "laws of prudence" to preserve the selfhoods, or spectres, and calls them "laws of God." He is Blake's greatest dramatization and wanders hither and thither, a melancholy tyrant, now expanding into the builder of earth and sky, proclaiming himself "God from Eternity to Eternity," and bidding all know that "the spectre is the man; the rest .. delusion and fancy," and now contracting to the egoism of human passion. His name is a modification of Uriel, the archangel of the sun in "Paradise Lost," and he is god both of intellectual and material light. The separation of the cold light beam from the warm flame is a symbol of his descent into matter; a symbolism found also in Swedenborg, who compares the fallen Reason to light separated from heat, "for then all things become torpid and lie dead." . . . (Vol. I, pp. 251-52)

When the fall of spirit from unity causes the Father to give place to Urizen, the Son gives place to a power called Luvah, from the Hebrew *Luv,* heart or love, and *ah,* a feminine termination. He is love in its less imaginative aspect and is associated with the blood, and serves one good purpose. Divine love descends into the world ''in Luvah's robes of blood''— a correspondence for the Incarnation itself. When separated from Divine Love he is uninspired feeling in every aspect but that of desire, for desire implies a certain amount of imagination and thought because it implies an object. Reason is contractive and desire active, but the fallen Luvah dissolves all into vague emotion, at once feeding and lulling life into a deathly sleep. He is frequently associated with pity, for he promises rest to warring and thinking man, but it is the pity ''which seeks for dominion,'' subordinating everything to itself, and may be described as emotion without thought as Urizen is thought without emotion. Urizen and Luvah are the opposing principles of the fallen mind of man, and seek, the one to contract it into hard egoism, the other to expand it into soft weakness. The one would make the personal life mad with pride and the other would dissolve it away into hypocritic humility; the one has produced the battles, the other the peace preaching and dominion seeking churches of Christendom; the one has been the false Jehovah and the other the false Christ of the nations.

The matrix, ''mirror'' or feminine principle, gives place to Tharmas—probably the biblical Thamuz in a modified form— the power of growing or, as Blake calls it, vegetative life. Action being essentially masculine, when impersonated imaginatively, while passivity is feminine,—even Tharmas is seen to be masculine under the influence of the dominion of reason, for as a result of this tyranny the matrix ceases to be merely passive. The forms, thoughts, and desires, contracted under the influence of Urizen, stand out as it were from the diffusion and passivity of the matrix, compel it to seek perpetually to reabsorb them, for they have become denials of its peculiar life, and so to reply to their repulsion with attraction. Much of Blake's poetry will be found to deal with this contest of the male and female, active and passive tendencies, or, as he preferred to call it, of spectre and emanation. Tharmas is, therefore, nature and the five senses generally, and is perpetually at war with the reason who launches against him all manner of abstractions and asceticisms.

As the primordial division continues the Holy Spirit is succeeded by a Zoa, called Urthona—the ''regent,'' to use the Kabalistic word—of ''dark fire'' or of the fierce impersonal energy—or wrath of God—striving against the restrictions and divisions of Urizen. Active or male desire itself is a son or subdivision of the dark fire god—it being essentially a struggle for more ample life. The flames under the earth in ''The soul exploring the recesses of the grave,'' and elsewhere, when they are not the bright and beautiful fire of inspiration of the Holy Spirit, are these dark flames of material energy, which are the only things that still defy the power of Urizen. The fourth Zoa alone is described as living. Tharmas and Urthona were slain or made captive by Urizen, who himself sleeps in the death of matter. (Vol. I, pp. 253-54)

The Zoas are sometimes to be considered as mental states in which men may dwell for a time, and whence they may pass on, and sometimes as external necessities appearing to men in the laws of nature, or of society. They have innumerable subdivisions, for the fourfold analysis of things and thoughts need never come to an end. To the sub-divisions Blake applies names, each portion being a personage in its way, and justifying a separate myth. The Zoas themselves are symbolically associated with certain regions, directions, magnitudes, &c. Much

of this symbolism is identical with the Kabalistic symbols of the angels of the four points. (Vol. I, p. 255)

The zenith is the unlimited translucence of free spirit or imagination. The nadir is the limit of opaque matter in the outer, and of unimaginativeness in the inner world. The centre is the gathering point of physical existence. The circumference is the outward or expansive tendency of vitalizing instinct. The Zoas have their positions in these regions or states, they have first their rightful stations when the world is spiritual and unfallen, and then certain other stations when it is unspiritual and fallen. The regent of the centre is Luvah, for although he dissolves and ''divides the soul,'' he can yet gather under his dominion, as round a centre, all conscious but unimaginative life. He is egoistic feeling, as Urizen after his fall is egoistic thought. It is not, however, until he becomes proud and seeks to usurp the place of inspiration that he becomes evil, for all the powers of nature have their purpose and their place, and man's personal feeling when it is a passive vehicle for the creative fire within, makes itself a mere mask for the divine fire. Opposite to Luvah's eastern station is Tharmas in the West and in the circumference. He being not feeling, not conscious personal emotion, but instinct and sensation, or what Blake unites with Boehmen in calling vegetative life. As some unimaginative feeling is the centre of corporeal life, or the seat of its consciousness, at all times when it is not sunk in dead reason, so the life of the senses is its circumference or outer limit, its matrix, and the mirror in which it reflects itself. Between these two worlds—the worlds of Tharmas and Luvah—corporeal life fluctuates, as if upon one level, incapable of rising towards the zenith, the spiritual; and dying utterly if it falls towards the unvital matter of the opaque nadir. It is neither spiritual and imaginative like the one, or dead and destructive like the other, but moves, trembling and fluctuating in its mid region, its twilight of the senses and the feelings. When all is in the eternal imagination, Urizen as yet unfallen, dwells in the zenith wrapped as we have described in inspiration, and Urthona the wrathful outer necessity in the nadir with ever shifting matter. It is not until the fall has come that reason binds itself to the wheel of outer necessity, and change and darkness rise into the soul of man. (Vol. I, pp. 255-56)

The Zoas are also associated with the four elements. Urizen is ''The Prince of Light.'' In his good aspect of thought, not yet withdrawn from Divine Love and inspiration, he would be the warm and light-giving beams of fire; but as we have him most constantly in Blake, he is its cold light, its beam long separated from the source. Luvah is the regent of air and of the breath, whereby the physical body gets the least material, because least opaque of its corporeal ingredients,—the symbol of its wayward feeling, and the vehicle whereby it sighs its sorrows. . . . [Air] is the symbol of the feelings, because it has no inherent tendency upwards like fire, or downwards like water and earth, but moves hither and thither under the stress of heat and cold as our feelings do, when summoned by instinct on the one hand, or imagination on the other. As the Son is the centre of the Divine Triad, Father, Son, and Holy Spirit, so Luvah stands between unfallen Urizen and Tharmas, and air between fire and water. The air has two great properties, it transmits fire as light and warmth, and sustains water as cloud, and so Luvah changes thought on the one hand, and vegetative instinct on the other into active life, for all activity springs from feeling. Tharmas is described as ''the rough demon of the waters,'' for water is, according to the occultists, the universal fructifier. . . . Tharmas is also associated with water, because it is his mission to destroy and scatter. Christ, the Imagination, is described in **Milton** as becoming the ''prey'' of Tharmas who is there understood as the sense of Touch, not as Water only. Water is clear, allowing the light beam to pass through it. Tharmas is so far permeated by spirit as to be living, for all life is from the spirit or imagination. Most occultists find significance in the reflecting property of water. It is symbolic of the mirror or matrix of life. Urthona is earth, but earth to Blake is the limit downward of his vision—behind it God and fire begin anew. What we lay in the earth we give into the hands of the unknown god, who labours in darkness and takes care of the dead and the unborn. It is the dark fire which, unlike the gentle inner flame, transforms and renews and fills the soul with fear. It is the heat under the crucible, and the wrath of the Deity. (Vol. I, pp. 257-58)

[The] abodes or ''atmospheres,'' to use a term common both to Blake and Swedenborg, to which the Zoas belong, represent the four rungs of the great ladder whose upper end is in spirit its lower in matter. These ''atmospheres'' are named by Blake Beulah, Alla, Al-ulro, and Or-ulro respectively—Beulah being ascribed to the zenith. . . . [There is also] a plane called Jerusalem, the kingdom of the daughters of inspiration, who are above Beulah—the ''atmosphere'' of the daughters of pleasant images. So beyond the zenith is the eternal life of God, whose Angel of the Presence is Urizen. There are thus five atmospheres, of which the highest is above the power of the Zoas. They correspond to the imaginative sight or direct vision of the mind, and to the four senses, for Blake considers taste and touch to be sub-divisions of one sense, the servant of the vegetative impulse—Tharmas.

An illustration from Europe.

In a copy of **Europe,** in possession of Mr. Linnell, are some introductory lines absent in other copies. They begin:—

> Five windows light the caverned man, thro' one he
>   breathes the air,
> Thro' one hears music of the spheres, thro' one the
>   eternal vine
> Flourishes, that he may receive the grapes; thro' one
>   can look,
> And see small portions of the eternal world that ever
>   groweth;
> Thro' one himself pass out what time he pleases, but he
>   will not;
> For stolen joys are sweet, and bread eaten in secret
>   pleasant.

Here the ''atmospheres'' are enumerated one by one, the nadir corresponds to hearing, the centre to the nostrils and to the sense of smell and the power of breathing, the circumference to taste and touch, symbolized by the vine, the zenith to the eyes, and the fifth atmosphere, as we have said, to the direct apprehension of truth and beauty inherent to the mind, to the power that is of seeing, ''not with but through the eye.'' Fallen man, however, will have none of the last, for he prefers the stolen delights of the four senses and the ''mystery'' of the world. Beulah, or the zenith, corresponds to the eyes, because in the symbolic zenith is the first beginning of external life, and in the eyes is the first union of subject and object, thought and nature, spirit and matter. . . . In Blake [Beulah] is a place of repose, ante-chamber of Inspiration, and dwelling of Muses, not like those of the Greeks. Its evil aspect is that ''we become what we behold,'' and from it pass to a lower plane—Alla— and are enslaved by the egoistic emotion of the false centre, for love in all its phases is ever in Blake, as in Shakespeare, ''engendered in the eyes.'' The nostrils are associated with the centre, because by them we breathe the air which is the symbol of Luvah and the centre. Taste and touch are associated with Al-ulro, because in the world of Tharmas the structure of the body is completed and mind sleeps in bodily vitality. Or-ulro has for symbol the ear, because the creative word moves in the darkness of those ''multiplied fires'' which mould life in regions of force that is not yet personal, and shape it, as a child is shaped in the womb, or as the soul and character of men in the furnace of affliction. Or-ulro is said to be a void, which when entered into becomes a womb. Beulah, Alla, and Al-ulro are symbolical of the triad of personal life—head, heart, loins, or of thinking, emotional, and instinctive existence. Or-ulro and Jerusalem are respectively below and above the limited life of the personality. They are God's external and internal influences upon the world, the creation from the darkness, the influx from the light. (Vol. I, pp. 258-60)

It must always be remembered that the Zoas exist in everything. Blake held the doctrine of the macrocosm, and microcosm, and would gladly have assented to the saying of Paracelsus: ''He who tastes a crust of bread tastes all the stars and all the heavens.'' There is no grass blade of the field, no pebble of the brook, in which he could not have found the Zoas and some of their correspondences. (Vol. I, pp. 260-61)

• • • • •

[In **The Marriage of Heaven and Hell,** Blake was] attempting to write his doctrines without the aid of the myth, using merely popular terms. His difficulty was insuperable. The popular terms would not fit his ideas, and the attempt to employ them in a new sense with parenthetical scraps of explanation has caused such obscurity that anyone who does not know Blake well enough to see what he intends to convey in spite of his method of conveying it, will not see anything here but paradox.

The ''contraries'' now used may be sorted under their mythical equivalents as given in the later books, in tabular form, thus:—

Jehovah (after Christ's Death).	The Divine Unity.
(before)	Urizen in the South.
Christ.	Los, or Imagination,
The heaven formed from what was	Golgonooza, or Art.
stolen from the Abyss.	
The Devil.	Orc.

These are not exact equivalents, but sufficiently nearly so for the tracing of Blake's ideas from one form of expression to another. The ideas themselves changed under the action of the expression as time went on. (Vol. II, pp. 64-5)

[In the first Memorable Fancy,] ''Hell'' is used throughout for the double meaning which always belongs to fire,—passion and enthusiasm. . . . Buildings mean systems, and garments bodies of the figures who go to make up the systems. The opening might read:—

> When in the heat of enthusiasm and enjoying its delights, which to the merely obedient and reasonable seem to be torment and insanity, thinking that proverbs would show the higher wisdom better than myths or designs, I collected some.

The idea that the enjoyments of genius appear to be torment to those who do not share them, is worked out in the conversation between Urizen and Orc in the first pages of Night VII. of *Vala*.

The rock on the abyss of the five senses appears in all the books. It is the rock of separation, the division of man from man . . . , which Blake attributed to the divorce of reason and morality from imagination and forgiveness, or love—that is, the rupture of what he now called the marriage of Heaven and Hell, and later on simply the division of the masculine from the feminine. This is the rock of the North, and is the seat of Satan. The rock of the South is the power of Divine Forgiveness and the permanence of imaginative form and of the ''true surfaces'' of things which appear when the apparent (phenomenal) surfaces are corroded away. It is the Throne of God, beyond which Reason would exalt law by making Mystery the sanction of Morality. . . . The fine senses are called an abyss here, a flood elsewhere.

The devil's first question hints that a bird has two appearances. One is its true form and includes the shape of its mind and emotions. The other is its apparent form of feathers ''closed'' by our fine senses. This ''closing'' is what ''creates'' the outer form by making it seem solid. It is Satan's ''world of opaqueness'' . . . , and its creation is the paradoxical act of cruelty and mercy produced by shrinkage of mind, not by miraculous solidification of vacuum into matter. (Vol. II, pp. 65-6)

The next memorable fancy states the fundamental doctrine of transcendentalism in its positive form,—''a firm persuasion that a thing is so, makes it so.'' This is the root of hypnotic suggestion and all magic. Incidentally it refutes the negative side of transcendentalism which is apt to deny nature any objectivity, for it is evident that objectivity can come into existence from its opposite by means of a firm persuasion.

All these paradoxes would lead inevitably to insanity if insanity were merely a mental and not a moral state, but Blake has defined it as identical with selfishness, that is the contrary of brotherhood, and declares it to be the ''natural'' state of us all.

An important expression of Blake's views is contained in the Memorable Fancy when the Poetic Genius being considered to be the same thing as God, each man's conscience is necessarily considered to be the same thing as his genius. This repeats an explanation given elsewhere of Blake's use of the word *knave* for a man who was wicked enough to be deficient in genius or ''innate science.'' (Vol. II, p. 69)

[In the next Memorable Fancy], an indication that we are in Hell is given by the order of the four signs of the first chambers of the printing-house. The Dragon-Man of the cave is not said to be Urthona, but we perceive him to be a nameless form of this Zoa, joined with his spectre, who divided in the early pages of *Jerusalem*. The caves he clears are the dens that Urizen explores afterwards. He is the porter of the Northern Bar in *Thel*.

In the second, the sign of Tharmas, the Serpent,—ancient symbol of the water-region,—is adorning the cave with gems. From here come the attractions of ''false beauty.''

In the third is the eagle, symbol of air,—the heart-region, or Luvah.

In the fourth the Lion, symbol of Urizen in the south.

The unnamed forms of the fifth chamber are probably akin to the Gnomes of Palamabron. They are not part of the fourfold humanity, but are rather impulses of expansion than of origination. They pass forward the inspirations of the four regions to the sixth, where the highest dark form is reached,—that of the closed book.

A seventh stage must have been that of manifestation, and the books would have opened themselves.

Blake was not ready to go so far yet. (Vol. II, pp. 69-70)

[In the next Memorable Fancy, an] angel attempting to show the poet his eternal lot, takes him through a stable (place of tame instruction), a church (of restraint), its nether vault (of buried passion), to a mill,—type of the grinding of reason in analysis, or argument of law in nature. Mental darkness as of a cave succeeds, and finally the mere blank, such as nature without a spark of humanity is, or as reason without a fragment of poetry. The roots of trees are here, the nether parts of vegetation, the humblest form of blind life. Below this is nothing conceivable to which the mind can lend existence. Here the imagination pauses. Blake proposes to pass to the void in search of God. Six stages of descent have been gone through. What of the seventh?

The first of the six was a stage of servitude, the next of moral restraint, and so onwards in emphasis of oppression. Blake, who always preached liberty, prepares us for a picture of the vision seen in the void where presently in accordance with the proverb that ''standing water breeds reptiles of the mind,'' between the spider-web rays of the black sun, abhorrent creatures prey on one another. Between the black and white spiders, the poet's lot is cast by his guide. We half see an allusion to the fact that his poetry lies between the black and white lines in which it is written, for we have not forgotten that we but lately heard of men who ''took the form of books.'' If this be the true meaning, there will break out from between the lines a view of diabolic poetry as it appears to a timid angel.

This happens. Cloud and fire burst from the place where the poet's lot is cast. Tempest, and nether deep darken from it. The old serpent, nature and its impulses, swims the mental tempest in a horrible form. Green and purple, not the colours as in ordinary poetry of jealousy and tyranny, are on his forehead as on a tiger's,—the figurative tiger of wrath. They are the hues of instinctive growth and passionate blood.

The angel, like an alarmed conscience, retreats in fear of the lower nature thus revealed, and leaving a fungus, the parasitic blind life of some formula, in which he had found repose, climbs up into the intellectual protection of the analytic will.

Then all vanishes, and a singing voice tells the poet that the horrors he saw were a vision of what his own nature, if he tamed it down under the yoke of the weak, would become. The "alteration of opinions" here hinted is evidently the alteration of growth, like that of stream to sea and seed to tree, not mere variation like that of the weather-cock.

Now, the poet, who is the Lion referred to in the last words of this Book, proposes to take the ox, the angel, who must not have one and the same law with him, lest he be under oppression, and proposes to change the vision and show him in turn his own fate.

First they fly "westerly through the night till elevated above the earth's shadow." The West is the region of vegetative passion. If they go upwards through it they must be journeying from North by West to South, the reverse of the direction of Urizen's movement when he fell. The poet takes the timid angel far enough this way to escape the influence of earthly night. Then he dashes at the centre of the source of vision, the sun of imagination, not the dark sun of the inhuman void. Here, as of right, the poet puts on innocence. Now the angel is evidently a pale inspirer of Swedenborg. It was to supplement and partly refute Swedenborg Blake wrote the present book. So to keep hand in hand with the Angel he takes Swedenborg's volumes, and soon sinks with them from the glorious clime of poetic vision. (Vol. II, pp. 71-2)

All the planets, the arbiters of character and the dividers in old time of man's qualities, are passed but the sad Saturn. Even he is too poetic. A mere "space," if space it may be called, is all that the mind dwells in which, originally timid, submits its feebleness to domination by the system of another.

But the angel's lot must be considered more in detail. The space, an intellectual gap—for the stars belong to the pure reason in this symbology—peoples itself when contemplated. It is clearly the seat of religious war. The jarring sectaries who struggle with and consume each other are at the bottom of a pit into which those descend who read the Bible controversially. The bricks of the houses recall the twenty-second Proverb of Hell. They symbolize the dry-baked dogmas. The religious, (for to Blake religion was a word seldom used as representing reverential emotions in the aggregate, but generally as bondage of non-mystic dogmatism and morality) that is the chained monkeys,—are books like the men were in the sixth chamber of the house of poetry. The skeleton of one is Aristotle's Analytics when brought from the Space to the Mill. (Vol. II, pp. 72-3)

The promise of the Bible of Hell, with which the present book ends, was never redeemed. It has been supposed that this refers to Blake's version which had only reached as far as the book

of Genesis, of the Bible itself "as understood by a Christian visionary." . . .

After this promise the book of the *Marriage of Heaven and Hell* closes with the definition of what Blake used to call the "indefinite," or the law not altered for each individual, but oppressive because forced on opposites. (Vol. II, p. 73)

> *Edwin John Ellis and William Butler Yeats, in* The Works of William Blake, Vols. I and II *by William Blake, edited by Edwin John Ellis and William Butler Yeats, 1893. Reprint by AMS Press, 1973, I: 420 p., II: 174 p.**

W. B. YEATS (essay date 1897)

[*Yeats here portrays Blake as a poet blessed with a unique mission—to introduce the "religion of art" to the world—but cursed with the burden of inventing his own mythology. The critic's remarks were originally published in the* Academy *in 1897; for additional commentary by Yeats, see the excerpt by Ellis and Yeats dated 1893.*]

There have been men who loved the future like a mistress, and the future mixed her breath into their breath and shook her hair about them, and hid them from the understanding of their times. William Blake was one of these men, and if he spoke confusedly and obscurely it was because he spoke things for whose speaking he could find no models in the world about him. He announced the religion of art, of which no man dreamed in the world about him; and he understood it more perfectly than the thousands of subtle spirits who have received its baptism in the world about us, because, in the beginning of important things—in the beginning of love, in the beginning of the day, in the beginning of any work, there is a moment when we understand more perfectly than we understand again until all is finished. . . . We [now] write of great writers, even of writers whose beauty would once have seemed an unholy beauty, with rapt sentences like those our fathers kept for the beatitudes and mysteries of the Church; and no matter what we believe with our lips, we believe with our hearts that beautiful things, as Browning said in his one prose essay that was not in verse, have 'lain burningly on the Divine hand,' and that when time has begun to wither, the Divine hand will fall heavily on bad taste and vulgarity. When no man believed these things William Blake believed them, and began that preaching against the Philistine, which is as the preaching of the Middle Ages against the Saracen.

He had learned from Jacob Boehme and from old alchemist writers that imagination was the first emanation of divinity, 'the body of God,' 'the Divine members,' and he drew the deduction, which they did not draw, that the imaginative arts were therefore the greatest of Divine revelations, and that the sympathy with all living things, sinful and righteous alike, which the imaginative arts awaken, is that forgiveness of sins commanded by Christ. The reason, and by the reason he meant deductions from the observations of the senses, binds us to mortality because it binds us to the senses, and divides us from each other by showing us our clashing interests; but imagination divides us from mortality by the immortality of beauty, and binds us to each other by opening the secret doors of all hearts. He cried again and again that every thing that lives is holy, and that nothing is unholy except things that do not live—lethargies, and cruelties, and timidites, and that denial of imagination which is the root they grew from in old times. Passions, because most living, are most holy—and this was a scandalous paradox in his time—and man shall enter eternity borne upon their wings. (pp. 168-71)

This philosophy kept him more simply a poet than any poet of his time, for it made him content to express every beautiful feeling that came into his head without troubling about its utility or chaining it to any utility. Sometimes one feels, even when one is reading poets of a better time—Tennyson or Wordsworth, let us say—that they have troubled the energy and simplicity of their imaginative passions by asking whether they were for the helping or for the hindrance of the world, instead of believing that all beautiful things have 'lain burningly on the Divine hand.' But when one reads Blake, it is as though the spray of an inexhaustible fountain of beauty was blown into our faces, and not merely when one reads the *Songs of Innocence,* or the lyrics he wished to call 'The Ideas of Good and Evil,' but when one reads those 'Prophetic Works' in which he spoke confusedly and obscurely because he spoke of things for whose speaking he could find no models in the world about him. He was a symbolist who had to invent his symbols; and his counties of England, with their correspondence to tribes of Israel, and his mountains and rivers, with their correspondence to parts of a man's body, are arbitrary as some of the symbolism in the *Axël* of the symbolist Villiers De L'Isle Adam is arbitrary, while they mix incongruous things as *Axël* does not. He was a man crying out for a mythology, and trying to make one because he could not find one to his hand. Had he been a Catholic of Dante's time he would have been well content with Mary and the angels; or had he been a scholar of our time he would have taken his symbols where Wagner took his, from Norse mythology; or have followed, with the help of Prof. Rhys, that pathway into Welsh mythology which he found in *Jerusalem;* or have gone to Ireland—and he was probably an Irishman—and chosen for his symbols the sacred mountains, along whose sides the peasant still sees enchanted fires, and the divinities which have not faded from the belief . . . and have been less obscure because a traditional mythology stood on the threshold of his meaning and on the margin of his sacred darkness. If 'Enitharmon' had been named Freia, or Gwydeon, or Danu, and made live in Ancient Norway, or Ancient Wales, or Ancient Ireland, we would have forgotten that her maker was a mystic; and the hymn of her harping, that is in *Vala,* would but have reminded us of many ancient hymns. (pp. 172-75)

> W. B. Yeats, "William Blake and the Imagination," in his Ideas of Good and Evil, A. H. Bullen, 1903, pp. 168-75.

GEORGE SAINTSBURY (essay date 1911)

[*Citing the critical views that Blake expressed in his marginalia and other writings, Saintsbury hails the author as an incisive (if overlooked) formulator of Romantic critical theory. For additional commentary by Saintsbury, see the excerpt dated 1874.*]

There have been times—perhaps they are not quite over—when the admission of William Blake into the category of critics would have been regarded as an absurdity, or a bad jest. Nothing is more certain, however, than that the poet-painter expresses, with a force and directness rather improved by that lack of complete technical sanity which some of his admirers most unwisely an needlessly deny, the opinions of the "Extreme Right," the high-fliers of the Army of Romanticism. He may often be thinking of painting rather than of poetry; but this is sometimes expressedly not the case, and many of his most pointed sayings apply to the one art just as well as to the other—if indeed it would not be still more correct to say that, except when they concern mere technique, they always apply to both. His work, despite the attention which it has received from hands, sometimes of the most eminent, during the last forty years, has never yet been edited in a fashion making its chaos cosmic or the threading of its labyrinths easy: and it may be well to bring together some of the most noteworthy critical expressions in it. . . . [The expression], "Every man is a judge of pictures who has not been connoisseured out of his senses," is in itself almost a miniature manifesto of the new school of criticism. For "connoisseurship"—the regular training in the orthodox system of judgment by rule and line and pattern—is substituted the impression of the natural man, unconditioned except by the requirement that it *shall* be impression, and not prejudice.

So, . . . that remarkable expression of the Prophet Isaiah [in *The Marriage of Heaven and Hell*] when, as Blake casually mentions, he and Ezekiel "dined with me"—an occasion on which surely any one of taste would like to have completed the quartette. The poet-host tells us that he asked, "Does a firm persuasion that a thing is so make it so?" and that the prophet-guest answered, "All poets believe that it does"—a position from which Neo-Classicism and the reluctance to "surrender disbelief" are at once crushed, concluded, and quelled.

In the remarkable engraved page on Homer and Virgil, Blake adventures himself (not with such rashness as may at first seem) against Aristotle (or what he takes for Aristotle), by laying it down that Unity and Morality belong to philosophy, not poetry, or at least are secondary in the latter; that goodness and badness are not distinctions of "character" (a saying in which there is some quibbling but much depth as well); that the Classics, not Goths or Monks, "desolate Europe with wars" (a great enough dictum at the junction of the eighteenth and nineteenth centuries); and that "Grecian [wit] is mathematical form," which is only "eternal in the reasoning memory," while Gothic is "living form, that is to say, eternal existence"—perhaps the deepest saying of the whole, though it wants large allowance and intelligent taking.

The "**Notes on Reynolds**" are naturally full of our stuff.

> Enthusiastic admiration is the first principle of knowledge. [Sir Joshua had stated just the contrary.]
>
> What has reasoning to do with the art of painting [or, we may safely add, of poetry]?
>
> Knowledge of ideal beauty is not to be acquired; it is born in us.
>
> One central form . . . being granted, it does not follow that all other forms are deformity. All forms are perfect in the poet's mind, . . . they are from imagination.
>
> To generalise is to be an idiot. To particularise is the great distinction of merit. . . .
>
> Invention depends altogether upon execution.
>
> Passion and expression are beauty itself.
>
> Ages are all equal: but genius is always above its age.

It is worth while to add to these the very remarkable annotations upon Wordsworth's Prefaces: "I don't know who wrote these: they are very mischievous, and direct contrary to Wordsworth's own practice" [where if Blake had added the words "when he is a poet," he would simply have given the conclusion of the whole matter], with the very shrewd comment that Wordsworth is not so much attacking poetic diction, or defending his own, as "vindicating unpopular poets."

Scanty as this critical budget may seem, its individual items are of extraordinary weight, when we remember that some of them were written before the *Lyrical Ballads* themselves appeared, and all of them by a man of hardly any reading in contemporary literature, and quite out of the circle of Coleridgean influence. It is scarcely, if at all, too much to say that they are almost enough to start, in a fit mind, the whole system of Romantic criticism in its more abstract form, and sometimes even in its particular and concrete applications. All the eighteenth-century Dagons—the beliefs in official connoisseurship, in the unapproachable supremacy of the ancients, in the barbarism and foolishness of Gothic art and literature, in the superiority of the general to the particular, in the necessity of extracting central forms and holding to them, in the supremacy of reason, in the teachableness of poetry, in the virtues of copying, in the superiority of design to execution,—all are tumbled off their pedestals with the most irreverent violence. That the critic's applications in the sister art to Rubens, to Titian, to Reynolds himself, are generally unjust, and not infrequently the result of pure ignorance, does not matter; his own formulas would often correct him quite as thoroughly as those of the classical school. What is important is his discovery and enunciation of these formulas themselves.

For by them, in place of these battered gods of the classical or neo-classical Philistia, are set up Imagination for Reason, Enthusiasm for Good Sense, the Result for the Rule; the execution for the mere conception or even the mere selection of subject; impression for calculation; the heart and the eyes and the pulses and the fancy for the stop-watch and the boxwood measure and the table of specifications. It is not necessary to argue the question whether Blake's own poetical work ... justifies or disconcerts the theories under which it was composed; it may be very strongly suspected, from utterances new as well as old, that approval of the theory and approval of the practice, as well as disapproval in each case, are too intimately bound up with each other to make appeal to either much of an argument. But for our main purpose, which is purely historical, the importance of Blake should, even in these few pages, have been put out of doubt. In no contemporary—not in Coleridge himself—is the counter-creed to that of the Neo-classics formulated with a sharper precision, and withal a greater width of inclusion and sweep. (pp. 376-79)

> *George Saintsbury, "Wordsworth and Coleridge: Their Companions and Adversaries," in his* A History of English Criticism: Being the English Chapters of a History of Criticism and Literary Taste in Europe, *revised edition, Dodd, Mead and Company, 1911, pp. 310-408.**

S. FOSTER DAMON   (essay date 1924)

[*The following commentary on Blake's prosody is taken from Damon's* William Blake: His Philosophy and Symbols, *a scholarly study that is considered one of the major works in Blake criticism. In surveying the poet's prosodic techniques, Damon links expressiveness and experimentation, maintaining that Blake*

anticipated "most of the prosodic discoveries of the nineteenth century" in searching for more meaningful poetic expression.]

Though Blake is supposed to have been a careless, even an automatic writer, in reality he was one of the great technicians. He had all the tricks at his finger-tips, and we cannot doubt that every line he ever wrote was tested at least semi-consciously by his inner ear.

A radical in philosophy, religion, and painting, he was also a great innovator in metrics. His earliest poems show an attempt to transcend rhyme, which he finally rejected. In metre, he sought constantly for lines which were at once freer and more accurately expressive. It was characteristic of him that the line he finally adopted for its easy ability to say all things was a line two feet longer than the norm accepted by Shakspere and Milton; and this expansive line, the iambic septenary, was a line which no one before or since has been able to use with any fluidity or variety. (p. 45)

The eighteenth century generally wrote in iambs, which are, after all, the most natural foot of English versification. Blake, however, tried other feet: the trochee, of which he became very fond; and the anapest, whose expressive qualities he seems to have been the first man to discover. Dactylic lines occur very rarely, and then only accidentally.

The trochee was used in several of the most famous *Songs*, such as **"Piping down the Valleys Wild," "The Lamb," "The Tyger,"** and **"A Poison Tree."** These titles alone show the contrasting effects which Blake extracted from this foot.

An illustration from The First Book of Urizen.

The music latent in the anapest had never been appreciated before Blake's time. The Elizabethans hardly suspected its existence; and when they stumbled upon it, curious jingles, such as some of the dialogues in *Love's Labour's Lost*, II. i, were their best results—results which never became fashionable. Gradually the anapest stretched its limbs into a canter well suited to drinking songs and hunting choruses, but for nothing else. The eighteenth century seems to have thought that this trumpery effect was the only possible variation from the iamb. But Blake, who was trying to extend poetic expressiveness in all metres, discovered that as rare and rich a music lay in the anapest as in any other metre. By shortening the usual tetrameter to a dimeter, he evoked the light laughter of **"The Ecchoing Green."** His greatest success in lyrical anapests, however, was in the tragic **"Garden of Love"** and the strangely exotic **"Sunflower."** . . . Poe later was to obtain the same effect in his *Ulalume*; but he found it necessary to repeat lines as a refrain, in order to retard the ordinary rush of the anapests. In his later poems, such as **"The Land of Dreams,"** Blake retarded the anapest by substituting iambs here and there.

This mixture of feet was characteristic of Blake's aesthetics. 'Bring out number, weight & measure in a year of dearth,' he wrote scornfully of purists. Practically never did he hestitate to introduce a variety of feet, so long as he did not overwhelm the general effect of the fundamental foot. In the very first quatrain of **"The Tyger"** he boldly inserted an iambic line:

> Could frame thy fearful symmetry.

The added syllable becomes still more emphatic in the terminal line:

> Dare frame thy fearful symmetry.

Obviously, such an effect was not accidental. (pp. 45-6)

Sometimes he juxtaposed two metres, as in **"Night"** (*Songs of Innocence*), whose stanza is composed of two iambic septenaries followed by four anapestic dimeters. He also devised the scheme of changing gradually from one metrical pattern to another. The first and most famous of these is the **"Mad Song"** of the *Poetical Sketches*. . . . Other examples are **"I Laid me down upon a bank,"** and **"The Voice of the Ancient Bard,"** which moves from iambic trimeter to anapestic pentameter.

Finally Blake's theory of immediate expressiveness through constant variation developed so far, that he actually denied the basis of metre entirely, and thus he wrote the first Manifesto of Free Verse [in the preface to *Jerusalem* (see excerpt dated 1804-20?)]. . . . (p. 46)

[Blake] treated lines with the same freedom that he treated feet. He tried all lengths from the dimeter to the septenary, and individualized each of them. . . .

[Blake's] favourite line for lyrics was the tetrameter. The contrasting **"Lamb"** and **"Tyger"** show what he could do with it.

> What dread hand forged thy dread feet?

seemed to Saintsbury a climax in the use of the trochaic tetrameter. **"My Spectre around me"** is the extreme variation of a form which can still be accurately designated as iambic tetrametric quatrains rhymed in couplets. **"The Everlasting Gospel"** is just as free as Coleridge's famous *Christabel,* and its freedom is based upon precisely the same prosodic principle; yet its effect is curiously different. Blake does not consciously pass from one species of foot to another; he mingles them at

the instantaneous prompting of his ear, and consequently his effect is far less academic. (p. 47)

Blake's most interesting work with the pentameter, however, lies in his blank verse. The *Poetical Sketches* show a very high and subtle appreciation of its possibilities. Blake already knew, no doubt, from reading Shakspere and Milton, that the great principle in blank verse is the *variation around* the iambic pentameter. His *King Edward the Third* shows all the Elizabethan tricks, regulated somewhat by the eighteenth-century restrictions, yet breaking out now and then into effects entirely Blake's own. We must confess that a line sometimes needs rereading, to get the right cadence; but this cadence is often truly admirable, always interesting, and never a mistake. The very opening lines challenge one with their perverse beat:

> O thou to whose fury the nations are
> But as dust, maintain thy servant's right! . . .
> When confusion rages, when the field is in a flame,
> When cries of blood tear horror from heav'n . . .

Startling as these seem, they can readily be paralleled by lines from accepted masterpieces. (pp. 47-8)

Blake's great triumph with blank verse, however, was in using it for actual lyrics. This was a feat not to be paralleled until the nineteenth century. The poems to the seasons, to the evening star, and to morning anticipated Poe's second poem "To Helen" and Tennyson's "Summer Night," **"Fair Elenor"** and the Minstrel's song at the end of *King Edward the Third* are arranged in quatrains; nevertheless they are blank verse, and not unrhymed iambic pentameters, which puts them in another classification from Tennyson's *Tears, Idle Tears*. (p. 48)

[One of Blake's poetic forms was] entirely his own, in which he made several experiments, whose true value could not be appreciated until the present day. This was his metrical 'prose,' which is very like Paul Fort's 'polyphonic prose,' from which Amy Lowell's elaborate compositions developed.

Blake's original idea was to vary blank verse so much that it would be presented most smoothly as a solid block of prose. Ossian had treated septenaries in the same way, so Blake did it with blank verse.

The **"Prologue to King John"** was the first of these experiments, judging by the form.

> The trembling sinews of old age must work
> the work of death against their progeny;
> for Tyranny hath stretch'd his purple arm,
> and 'Blood!' he cries; 'the chariots and the horses,
> the noise of shout, and the dreadful thunder of battle
>   heard afar!'
> Beware, O proud! thou shalt be humbled. . . .

This is obviously blank verse with variations which many an Elizabethan might have written. But this was only Blake's starting-point. In **"Contemplation"** the variations are far greater, and made with the sympathetic rhythm in mind.

> Vain, foolish man, that roams on lofty rocks,
> where, 'cause his garments are swollen with wind,
> he fancies he is grown into a giant!

The windy rhythm of the second line is obvious. But in the following quotation we are losing sight of blank verse very quickly.

The brook stretches its arms along the velvet meadow,
its silver inhabitants sport and play;
the youthful sun joys like a hunter roused to the chase,
he rushes up the sky,
and lays hold on the immortal coursers of day;
the sky glitters with the jingling trappings.

In fact, such non-metrical rhythm is simply Free Verse.

"Samson," the last in [*Poetical Sketches*], is far more regular,
yet differs from all the other experiments. Blake evidently was
trying to improve on the broken, yet metrical, cadences of
Milton's *Samson Agonistes*. Blake's cadences are perfectly clear.
Early editors yielded to the temptation of fixing it up into
respectable blank verse; but in doing so they changed Blake's
effect. He deliberately eliminated overflow and all the effects
which come from the conflict of the iambic pentameter with
the surge of the words themselves. Such an effect is Miltonic,
but it is not Blakean. A single specimen, arranged with reference to the cadences, should prove this beyond dispute.

Call thine alluring arts and honest-seeming brow,
the holy kiss of love, and the transparent tear;
put on fair linen that with the lily vies,
purple and silver;
neglect thy hair,
to seem more lovely in thy loose attire;
put on thy country's pride, deceit,
and eyes of love decked in mild sorrow;
to sell thy lord for gold.

(pp. 48-9)

Blake's use of rhyme in his lyrics was quite as sophisticated
and free as his use of lines. He was dissatisfied with it because
its automatic tinkle had become meaningless. At first he considered abolishing it altogether, and the *Poetical Sketches* open
with lyrics freed entirely from the 'modern bondage of rhyming.' In this he was justified by Milton's translation of Horace's
Fifth Ode (Bk. I.) and by Collins's *Ode to Evening*. But Blake
soon realized that he was eliminating an effect which had its
place. His more elaborate stanza-patterns allowed fresher echoes
of sound, but this was not enough. He wished to transcend
rhyme, to produce subtle and strange chimes in the inner ear.
This was not easy to do, as he discovered.

At first he was contented with false vowel-sounds. These were
not the conventional rhymes for the eye, which are still considered perfectly allowable. Scoffers should be reminded that
Blake's new rhymes are even harder to produce consistently
than regular rhymes. Blake found this out in his **"Fresh from
the Dewy Hill,"** whose first four stanzas are rhymed entirely
in his radical way, but whose last two stanzas are rhymed
impeccably. It is obvious that Blake's technique failed him.
He falls into rhyme, not out of it.

There are also several cases of false terminal consonants. *Dawn-
scorn* is to be found twice: in the "Mad Song" and in "Fresh
from the Dewy Hill"; although the merest novice would know
enough to substitute *morn* for *dawn*. *Vault-fraught* may be
made to rhyme by adopting the early pronunciation of *vaut*.
But such combinations as *girl-small* "Spring" and *lambs-hands*
("Holy Thursday") are not to be explained away.

This use of false rhymes gradually found its place marvellously.
"Love and Harmony Combine" (rhymed *aaaa*) obtains a very
pleasant effect by the use of one false rhyme per quatrain,
which breaks up an effect which otherwise would be angular
and monotonous. The variation of the less prominent rhymes

is very successfully done, as in **"When Old Corruption first
begun"** and the **"Introduction"** to the *Songs of Innocence*.

Eventually Blake produced three or four poems which seem
perfect, yet which depend on these false rhymes. *Lamb-name*,
though used twice in one stanza, has never been considered a
blot on **"The Lamb."** *Am-name* is equally successful in **"Infant Joy,"** though the economy of rhyme there is remarkable.
Hum-home is a perfectly satisfactory termination to **"A Dream."**
"Spring" is hardly more than a string of these false rhymes,
in two of the three stanzas. Why these rhymes are so delightful,
while the experiments in the *Poetical Sketches* are not, is very
difficult to say.

Blake had other interesting tricks which he played with rhyme.

There are a few cases of internal rhyme besides the entirely
conventional ones which are almost always found in septenaries. **"The Garden of Love"** (rhymed *abcb*) changes its pattern without warning in the last stanza, and, by the internal
rhymes of the last two lines, ends the poem appropriately with
the dull and heavy effect of a tolling bell. The first two lines
really do not rhyme at all, but the impetus from the preceding
stanzas fools us.

And I saw it was filled with graves,
And tomb-stones where flowers should be;
And priests in black *gowns* were walking their *rounds*,
And binding with *briars* my joys and *desires*.

(pp. 50-1)

[Sometimes] we find that Blake will infuse a rhyme sound
throughout several lines. Thus *or* runs riot through the eighteenth and nineteenth stanzas of **"Gwin, King of Norway."**
Far more successful is the first stanza of his poem **"To The
Queen"** in his edition of Blair's *Grave*, where the coldness of
the sepulchre is invoked by all the *ol*'s. (p. 51)

Sometimes he repeated words, instead of using rhymes. In
"The Little Vagabond" . . . he repeated *well*, and seemed to
think it satisfactory. *Appear* is used in the same way in **"The
School-Boy."** Coleridge did the same thing quite as consciously
in the couplet from *Christabel:*

Is the night chilly and dark?
The night is chilly, but not dark.

Blake was most successful with his repetitions when he used
them as a sort of refrain. **"The Lamb"** is the best-known
example of this. . . .

Leaving the lyrics for Prophetic Books, Blake at once encountered a new problem. Instead of modelling miniature
thoughts and moods into exquisite patterns of words, he was
now concerned with extensive, rather than intensive, expression. He had to find a line which could be repeated indefinitely
with the least possible monotony, a line so flexible as to express
the greatest number of thoughts and emotions. Such a line
would be the quintessence of English versification, the perfect
length, and the natural beat. Blake's predecessors had found
it in the iambic pentameter; Marlowe, Shakspere, and Milton
had already used it gloriously; but Blake found it too restricted
to contain his expansive soul. As we have noticed, he used it
but once after the *Poetical Sketches*. So, abandoning their 'Monotonous Cadence,' which was 'not only awkward, but as much
a bondage as rhyme itself,' he turned to Macpherson's *Ossian*,
which he, like all his contemporaries, greatly admired.

Ossian was printed as prose; but in fact the greater part of it
falls into frightfully dull blocks of septenaries, with caesuras

placed regularly after the fourth foot. The alexandrine is freely interspersed, for it is a peculiarity of that line that it can be thrown in anywhere among septenaries without interrupting the rhythm. . . . Metrically, it was far rougher than any other verse Blake knew, which undoubtedly accounts for much of his love for it. (p. 52)

[But Blake] understood perfectly how monotonous and limited Macpherson's effects were, so he practised varying the septenary more and more, till from the gentle meander of *Thel* we pass eventually to the choral tempest of *Jerusalem.* He also seems to have realized that many people did not feel the rhythm of *Ossian,* obvious as it was, so he printed his own lines as verse. (pp. 52-3)

The earliest septenaries, those of *Tiriel* and *Thel,* were written 1788-1789. They are treated almost as intellectually as the eighteenth century treated its blank verse. The caesuras are carefully yet easily varied; extra light syllables are slipped in unobtrusively; a few feet are inverted; and there is no awkward overflow whatsoever. Occasionally unaccented syllables are omitted. In *Thel,* Blake scatters light accents in some profusion, to make his verbal music fit the text. *Tiriel,* being of rougher fibre, is more roughly treated. Blake's only really radical treatment of the line is the occasional interpolation of octameters, or, more rarely, alexandrines. These become especially noticeable toward the end of the poems; Blake reserved his greatest irregularities for the climax. The excitement lashes itself, in the agony of expression, to stronger, more brutal cadences.

The most interesting feature, however, is Blake's tendency to interpret by the cadence the movement of the action. It sometimes goes so far that, while the seven fundamental beats are definite enough, they are distributed almost at random.

> Shout, beautiful daughter of Tiriel! thou singest a sweet
>   song! . . .
> Westwardly journeying, till Tiriel grew weary with his
>   travel.

One line is particularly interesting, since by the omission of one beat (which I take to be omitted after the word *refuse*) the following beat is felt with double force:

> Shall fail. If thou refuse . . . *howl* in the desolate
>   mountains!

The terminal lament in *Thel* is suddenly and potently irregular. Its ten lines contain one pentameter, one octameter, and three alexandrines!

The next period of Blake's septenaries is dated 1793-1794; it includes the *Visions of the Daughters of Albion, America,* and the narrative parts of *Europe.* The development is marked. Still the lines are smooth enough; the percentage of alexandrines and octameters has not increased; but the greater turbulence of the subject-matter with Blake's growing familiarity with his medium produce sudden effects that once in a while puzzle us for the moment. Nevertheless, practically all of them are thoroughly successful.

One of the effects which Blake was developing was the omission of unaccented syllables, so that several accents may stand together. This had been done before in *Tiriel:*

> Rise from the centre, belching flames & roarings, *dark
>   smoke*. . . .
> Some fled away: but Zazel *stood still,* & thus begun:—
> *Bald tyrant,* Wrinkled cunning, listen to Zazel's chains!

Also in *Thel:*

> Till to her own grave-plot she came, and there she *sat
> down.*

In the *Visions of the Daughters of Albion,* this effect is used rather more successfully:

> And thus I turn my face to where my *whole soul seeks.*
>   (pp. 53-4)

In *Europe,* Blake, somewhat dissatisfied with the septenary, used other kinds of line for the speeches of the characters. In the remainder of the minor Prophetic Books, he tried a completely new experiment. But he returned to the septenary for his three epics.

It is hard to judge of the metre of *The Four Zoas,* since only fragments of it have been published accurately. (p. 54)

An examination of the manuscript, however, shows that *The Four Zoas* (1797-1804) represents the transitional stage from the minor Prophetic Books to the two later epics. . . .   .

There are long passages, such as the description of the redeemed Vala in ''Night the Ninth'' . . . , which are as smooth and iridescent as anything in *Thel;* but at other times the variation around the septenary is so extreme as to produce such a line as this . . . :

> Oh lovely, terrible Los, wonder of Eternity! O Los, my
>   defence & guide!

Alexandrines and octameters are not merely interspersed; they may hold their own for several lines, as in Orc's War-Song [''Night VII,'' first version]. . . . (p. 55)

[Pentameters appear] and even nonameters. Once in a while the anapest is substituted for the iamb, as in . . . the following lines from Enion's lament . . . :

> While our olive & vine sing & laugh round our door, &
>   our children bring fruits & flowers,
> Then the groan & the dolour are quite forgotten, & the
>   slave grinding at the mill,
> And the captive in chains, & the poor in the prison, &
>   the soldier in the field.

There is far more rush in the verse. Blake evidently let himself be carried away by his ear, and became entirely careless of the academic aspect of his work. As he had one of the finest ears for verse that any poet has ever possessed in English, the results are for the most part entirely satisfactory. . . .

[*Milton* and *Jerusalem*] represent Blake's ultimate experiments in poetic technique. Still we find long passages of iambic septenaries; but lines of different length have invaded the poems more and more. . . . (p. 56)

The septenaries at times vanish, as in this accidental passage of pentameters (*Jerusalem* . . .):

> Those who give their lives for him are despised!
> Those who devour his soul are taken into his bosom:
> To destroy his Emanation is their intention.
> Arise! awake, O Friends of the Giant Albion!
> They have perswaded him of horrible falshoods!
> They have sown errors over all his fruitful fields!

The climax of *Jerusalem* is very largely in solid blocks of octameters:

And every Man stood Fourfold, each Four Faces had,
    One to the West,
One toward the East, One to the South, One to the
    North, the Horses Fourfold.
And the dim Chaos brighten'd beneath, above, around!
    Eyed as the Peacock, According to the Human
    Nerves of Sensation, the Four Rivers of the Water of
    Life.

Overflow, which had been used sparingly before, now becomes very common. In *Thel* we find the following passage:

For I walk thro' the vales of Har, and smell the
    sweetest flowers,
But I feed not the little flowers: I hear the warbling
    birds;
But I feed not the warbling birds; they fly and seek
    their food.

In *The Four Zoas,* the enjambement has become more daring, but still quite regular:

Four Mighty Ones are in every Man; a Perfect Unity
Cannot Exist but from the Universal Brotherhood of
    Eden,
The Universal Man, To Whom be Glory Evermore.
    Amen.
What are the Natures of those Living Creatures, the
    Heavenly Father only
Knoweth: No Individual knoweth, nor can know in all
    Eternity.

But in *Milton* and *Jerusalem,* such restraint is often cast aside. The following passage (*Jerusalem* . . .) is not unusual:

First as a red Globe of blood trembling beneath his
    bosom
Suspended over her he hung; he infolded her in his
    garments
Of wool: he hid her from the Spectre, in shame &
    confusion of
Face; in terrors & pains of Hell & Eternal Death, the
    Trembling Globe shot forth Self-living & Los howl'd
    over it.

It should now be quite clear how Blake meant these 'Prophetic' septenaries to be read. They are to be poured out in a great flood of oratory, stressing the natural accents, and passing rapidly over the unaccented syllables. The 'syllabic' tradition, which weighs every syllable with great care, is to be completely ignored. Each line represents a breath; and this breath is the real metrical unit, around which all the variations are formed.

Let us now return to the other kinds of verse to be found in the Prophetic Books.

"A Song of Liberty" was arranged in prose verses, to resemble the topography of the Bible. But this was only to conceal the metrical basis of the poem. It is not 'of course, lyrical prose,' as one eminent critic described it; it is really in alexandrines, with regular caesuras, but with a foot that varies from anapest to dactyl, with interpolated iambs and trochees. Arranged according to this scheme, the opening lines appear as follows:

The Eternal Female groan'd. / It was heard over all the
    earth.
Albion's coast is sick, silent. / The American meadows
    faint!
Shadows of Prophecy shiver / along by the lakes and
    the rivers,

and mutter across the ocean. / France, rend down thy
    dungeon.
Golden Spain, burst / the barriers of old Rome!
Cast thy keys, O Rome! / into the deep, down falling,
    even to Eternity / down falling, and weep.

To read these metrically, great violence must be done to the normal accent of the words. This was a new scheme of Blake's to transcend ordinary metres; an experiment which he varied many ways in his minor Prophetic Books, before he discovered his ideal in the irregular septenaries of *Milton* and *Jerusalem.*

In *The French Revolution* he applied the same principle to anapestic septenaries. Customarily poets begin with lines absolutely according to pattern, in order that the pattern may be established; but Blake, in direct defiance of this, is apt to begin with variations, so that the metrical basis may be less obvious. Just so he began *King Edward the Third;* so now he begins *The French Revolution.*

The dead brood over Europe; the cloud and vision
    descends upon chearful France;
O cloud well appointed! Sick, sick, the Prince on his
    couch! wreath'd in dim
And appalling mist; his strong hand outstretch'd, from
    his shoulder down the bone,
Runs aching cold into the sceptre, too heavy for mortal
    grasp—no more
To be swayed by visible hand, nor in cruelty bruise the
    mild flourishing mountains.

So it seems clear that Blake meant his metre to be overrun by the violence of the expression. *The dead brood* is not a good anapest. *Sick, sick,* comprise two accents, with compensating pauses. Blake substitutes spondees and paeons so freely, he packs the line according to its movement so often, and wrenches the accents so viciously, that the metre is fairly pummelled into expressiveness. As a result, we often puzzle over the number of beats intended in certain lines. (pp. 56-8)

[The] next experiment was in anapestic trimeter, which forms the basis of *Urizen,* "Asia" (*Song of Los*), *The Book of Los,* and *Ahania.* The shortening of the line slowed the rush of the verse. Otherwise Blake observed the same principle of wrenching accents away from the metrical base. He uses all his old tricks, but with much more sobriety. The result is excellent. (pp. 58-9)

Besides these anapestic verses, Blake made yet another line of experimentation in the freer forms. This was a continuation of the 'prose' in the *Poetical Sketches;* for Blake needed some more lyrical form in order to deal with the more songful moments. Conventional lyrics, like the *Songs of Innocence and Experience,* would have been woefully out of place: his Eternals could never express themselves in such fragile patterns. So Blake turned back to his early experiments with metrical lines of uneven lengths, and finally reached something very like some of our modern Free Verse.

The first example of it is the "Argument" to *The Marriage of Heaven and Hell.* The lines are entirely iambic (with a few truncations), and vary from six to two feet in length.

In *Europe,* the same irregularities are observed in those passages which do not deal directly with narration, but with the invocations of Spirits and with the actions of Los and Enitharmon. The opening lines of the "Prophecy" are influenced in rhythm as well as thought by Milton's *Hymn to the Nativity,* while *Samson Agonistes* also has its influence, especially in lines 21-22, which are a rhymed trimeter couplet, quite in Milton's style. Los's first speech swells from tetrameter to alexandrine.

''Africa'' (*Song of Los*) is written in the same iambic lines of lengths varying from dimeter to septenary.

Blake also tried arranging these iambic lines into stanzas of a set pattern. The ''Preludium'' of *Europe* contains seven stanzas of four lines each, the first, second, and fourth of which are septenaries, and the third a trimeter. In *The Four Zoas,* Enitharmon's Song over Los . . . consists of seven iambic stanzas of five lines each, arranged 7, 3, 7, 4, 7. The lament of Urizen in the same poem . . . might also be mentioned here, though its thirteen iambic quatrains are entirely in septenaries. There are a few variations in these lyrics from *The Four Zoas:* in Enitharmon's song, the second line twice is made a tetrameter, and the first one a pentameter; while in Urizen's lament, the third line shows a very definite tendency to become an octameter. In none of these lyrics, however, did Blake reach again the freedom which he had shown in the 'prose' of the *Poetical Sketches.*

This completes our survey of Blake's prosody. Besides his experiments in rhyme, he extended the expressiveness of practically all the boundaries of versification. In particular, he discovered the substitution of one foot for another, he brought out for the first time the true music of the anapest, and he developed as none have before or since the longest and most difficult lines in English verse. He was not a purist: he did nothing towards perfecting set forms like the sonnet or the hexameter; what he did was to search for freer and newer forms. Guided by an excellent ear, he went so far as to anticipate most of the prosodic discoveries of the nineteenth century, and to lead directly toward those of the twentieth century. (pp. 59-60)

S. Foster Damon, in his William Blake: His Philosophy and Symbols, *1924. Reprint by Peter Smith, 1947, 487 p.*

HELEN C. WHITE　(essay date 1927)

[*In her critically acclaimed study* The Mysticism of William Blake, *White contends that Blake cannot properly be considered a great mystic. The following excerpt summarizes many of her insights into his shortcomings, including the limiting nature of his visionary ideal.*]

Blake, on the surface, presents many of the familiar characteristics of the mystic. The sensitiveness bordering on emotional instability found in the sharp variations of mood . . . is a well-known element in the mystic temperament. The dissatisfaction with the ordinary confines of experience, the irrepressible urge to transcend them, is another. The positive belief that there is a world of supernal reality, under certain conditions and at certain points impinging upon our material world, is still another. The certainty that the properly enlightened human being can in some way pass the limits of the material world and put himself into some effective relation with that world above is, again, a familiar part of all mystic belief. The devotion of all the resources of the human spirit and of the human life to the compassing of that goal—this again is regarded as typically mystical. And finally, there are Blake's visions! In all these things, then, to some extent and defined in some way, Blake, on the surface of things, has been taken as a mystic. But while these things in themselves place him within the vast field of the mystical, they do not make him a mystic in the

A depiction of the character Los from The First Book of Urizen.

sense of the great mystics, or a prophet in the sense of the great prophets, or a visionary in the sense of the great visionaries. To answer the questions involved in these verdicts we must go into the problem much more deeply than these general surface descriptions imply.

To begin where the mystics began, then, with the belief in the existence of a world of what is usually called the spiritual in contradistinction to the purely natural and material, the word ''spiritual'' is used for such varying levels of phenomena that in itself it means little. For instance, the spiritual of the spiritualists is no more spiritual than the headless horseman who inspired Ichabod Crane's ride. And, on the other hand, there is even in man's shuddering at the vulgarest of attic-lurking, churchyard-haunting ghosts something of the immemorial human reaction to the spiritual.

These are, then, two elements to this of the spiritual: the conceptual and the emotional—what a man thinks the spiritual is, and how he reacts to it. (pp. 208-09)

[Blake insisted that] his God was essentially solid and substantial, fully as sound and hard as material objects. Here Blake's early experience and life-long practice with the graver undoubtedly shaped his religious as well as his artistic views. Blake's God is man on an enlarged scale, and very little more. Consequently there is nothing surprising in the fundamental anthropomorphism of his Zoas, or the material definiteness with which their stories are told, both in line and in verse. Indeed, it may be wondered if Blake had any very precise notion of spirit in a sense different from that of matter. Certain it is that his conceptions of spirit are much closer to the experiences of the medium than to the ineffable visions of the neo-Platonist. The conception of spirit, not as a refined or subtilized form of matter, but as something essentially different from the material is probably the product of a greater degree of intellectual sophistication than Blake ever knew. Moreover, when the idea of spirit has been attained in any philosophy or religion (and it is essentially an attainment), it has been attained not in the artistic or scientific fields, but in the ethical. Blake would never be guilty of the materialism of the conception of spirit betrayed in some discussions of ectoplasm, but he never came near the heights of a St. John or a Yagnavalkya. It may be seriously wondered if he ever could do so without that initial dualism between illusion and reality, matter and spirit, that has marked the thinking of the typical mystics.

As for the feeling of the spiritual, the response to what a recent German critic [Rudolph Otto] has called the "numinous" in human experience, Blake's "spiritual" remains on a relatively low level. There is nothing of the mystery of life in Blake; very little of the tragic beauty of the inscrutableness of life. There is strangeness, there is terribleness, there is a sense of the preternatural. Some passages in the "Prophetic Writings" remind one of the winged lions of Assyrian sculpture, an expression of man's sense of the overhanging reality as something powerful, something "awful" in the literal sense. But one searches the pages of Blake in vain for the ineffable, for the beauty that passes understanding. In this sense, then, Blake's spiritual reality remains on a fairly primitive level.

This quality of Blake's "spiritual" is important not only for the understanding of his view of the world, but also for the understanding of the goal which he sought in his "mystical activity." The goal of the great mystics . . . is a peculiarly intimate and profound union with God, or the Supreme Reality, in the soul of the mystic. It is a literal answer to that poignant prayer of St. Augustine: "Narrow is the Mansion of my soul; enlarge thou it that thou mayest enter in." The goal of Blake is . . . the entrance into the life of vision, into a life where the creative imagination of the individual artist compasses the strange riches of the world of the spirit. Superficially considered, the two goals might be deemed commensurate, two ways of viewing the same reality. But that apparent similarity vanishes when we consider the ground on which each conception is erected.

The fundamental issue is that of the relation of the individual will to the will of God. With the great mystics, faith or belief may be sufficient for salvation, but it is not adequate to the task of attaining their goal. Neither is mere following of their aspiration sufficient, for here, as elsewhere, only "the pure in heart. . . . shall see God." So all mystic effort, both eastern and western, requires not only strenuous discipline, but also a very real surrender of self. This latter is one of Blake's favorite teachings; in fact, he comes very near to making a goal of what is only a means. But his "self-annihilation" differs from that of the typical mystics in several very important respects. Blake's idea probably starts from the Swedenborgian self-annihilation which means very little more than the traditional putting off of the "old man" and putting on of the "new man." In Blake's hands the idea acquires an emotional coloring that makes of it something very different. Its motive force is essentially emotion, the emotion of love, one of the central tenets of Blake's teachings. But the "self-annihilation" of the mystics arises from the love of God that is not so much an emotional efflux as an integral act of the will. . . . "Not my will, but Thy will," is the heart of the love of God defined in this way. The "most burning love" of God that warmed the aspiration of so many mystics is an addition to this central core, not a substitution.

Such a surrender of the personal will is very hard to conceive of in the case of a man in whose work one finds so much of a personal animus as one does in Blake's life and writings. Not only in private epigrams and letters does one discern a strong personal animus, but in at least one of the "Prophetical Books" Blake has used an episode of his own life, the sojourn at Felpham, with the famous irritation at Hayley's well-meaning but blind and philistine interference, as the foundation of the great religious action of **Milton**. It is, of course, difficult to separate the personal strand of vindicating a point of view and striking out the heat of a grievance from the perception in one's own personal experience of the great workings of the universal. But the spirit is very different, for that of the one consists in erecting the personal experience into the universal, and that of the other in viewing the personal through the eyes of the universal. Some of the symbolism of **Milton** suggests the first rather than the second. If "self-annihilation" means the freeing of the universal in one's soul from the stress of the individual and the narrowly personal, whether it be manifested or not in arrogance or pride, then Blake's "self-annihilation" is certainly very different from that of the typical mystics. For even the sacred region of the spirit was filled by his pride as he consoled himself for the neglect he suffered on earth with the reflection that in heaven his works were warmly acclaimed. To be sure, that is not so different from the consolation the devout Christian has been traditionally supposed to enjoy in his good works; yet in general good Christians have been far too conscious of the imperfection of their ways to flaunt it with such naïve defiance as did Blake.

It is because of this scorn of humility that one is not sure that Blake's faithful obedience to the direction of his spirits, his unflagging and wholly admirable loyalty to what he supposed he was by high heaven appointed to do, even in the teeth of financial and professional discouragement and bitter coldness where he had hoped for enthusiastic approval—that all this was due so much to a submission to heaven as to an extraordinary faith in himself and in the rightness of his inspiration. One remembers that passage in which he says that feeling a great power of wrath in himself he looked abroad to see if such an energy were not one of the characteristic of a great man. From even the most sympathetic point of view it is not at all certain that that is the best way for a man to arrive at a just notion of what the will of God is; and without that, all the zeal in the world to make the will of God prevail, to borrow Arnold's famous phrase, can hardly save a man from striving to make his own will prevail.

The consequences of Blake's denial of humility are obvious. Humility in the Christian sense means the bowing of the individual will before the infinite wisdom and nobleness of the will of God; it means the concentration of all the aspirant's energies upon the work of seeking to know and to do that will; it means indifference to all other considerations, and in that narrowing of the field of purpose, the widest possible expansion of interest and influence; it means the elimination of the personal and the biased from the individual's outlook upon life in great things and in small. In all these things humility is not a barren forswearing, but a conquest of positive advantage not only for goodness but for sheer intellectual clarity and, above all, for mystical insight.

Clearly then, Blake's goal belongs to an order different from that of the typical mystics. The degree of that difference will be more apparent upon closer scrutiny of his definition of his goal. That, it will be remembered, is the life of vision, of the free perception of the world of imaginative reality and of the unimpeded exercise of the powers of the creative imagination. And the great manifestation of this exercise of the creative imagination is the body of visions to which he devoted his life.

There is no doubt that Blake would unhesitatingly have placed his visions first from whatever angle his gifts or his works or his theories might be approached. They were the glory of his life, the distinctive mark of whatever authenticity he might claim, the goal of all his teaching and all his working. In the position he accords to them and in what he says of them may be found the heart of his philosophy. Consequently, it is in them more than in anything else that we shall discover the real meaning of points that his explicit teaching left puzzling or obscure. This means, of course, that Blake's estimate of the importance of visions for his goal is very different from that of the typical mystics. (pp. 209-14)

[The] great mystics regard visions as preliminary challenges and graces in the vestibule of the heavenly kingdom. Hope and refreshment they do afford on the way of the mystic, but they certainly are in no sense his goal. To the great mystics Blake, no matter how authentic his visions, could never be more than one who had tarried on the way; one, it is true, to whom God had been abundant in his graces, but one who had never come into the fulness of the mystical experience.

For the main business of the mystic is not to voyage in strange lands of the imagination, but on the wings of the spirit to soar to God. Whatever halts him on that flight is an impediment and not an achievement. Were the vision of the celestial city— nay, even the beatific vision itself—to light up his imagination, still he would not have reached his goal, for he is striving to purify his spirit and widen the portals of his soul that God himself may enter in. . . . Never would he be content to rest in Blake's life of vision. For Blake's visions represent neither an intimate communion nor an intimate direction of conduct. (pp. 214-15)

Christ, although a very different Christ from the Christ of the New Testament, yet still unmistakably God, finds a place in [Blake's] supernaturalism, and God the Father in the guise of a very dignified old man slightly cramped in at the top of a plate figures in the illustrations to the *Book of Job*. In the *Marriage of Heaven and Hell* a devil chats affably with Blake, and in the sittings with Varley, king and warrior and courtesan come from the world of the beyond and, quite invisible to the sympathetic astrologer, Varley, sit for their portraits in what must have been a most notable midnight séance. But above all these in time and effort Blake's own world of Zoas and emanations and their children claimed his interest. Far more prominent than Christ or God in Blake's system is Urthona-Los, and the heavenly city of Christian longing becomes a half-human spirit Jerusalem, and its peaceful streets yield place to those storied halls of the city of Golgonooza on the lake of Udan-Adan.

That is the most important thing to take into account for the relation of Blake's supernaturalism to the question of whether or not he is a mystic. The relation of Blake's visions to the tradition in which he professed to be working is no mere question of orthodoxy: it is a question of fundamental direction and massing of energy. The visions of the mystics have in general been a re-creation, a reinvesting with immediate vitality, of a vision of the world that has been something larger than the creation of one mind. They have been distinctly the fruit of religious activity, but Blake has devoted his powers to the

invention of a new system, to the elaboration of what is in reality a new mythology. And that, however fresh or true or valuable, is something entirely different from the work of the typical mystics, something belonging to the field of religion only by virtue of its subject matter, in its method and its processes more akin to the achievements of the great romancers.

The mystic sought union with God. Blake sought a restoration of the soul to the life of vision. The mystic sought to experience God in his own soul. Blake sought to see the world of vision. The mystic found the realization of his goal in God alone, Blake found it in the heterogeneous and discursive visions to which he devoted the "Prophetical Writings." The objective of Blake's mystical effort was, then, so different from the goal of the great mystics in so fundamental a way as to make any identification of his activity with theirs impossible, and to make impossible the drawing of any real equivalence.

This conclusion finds striking confirmation when the problem is approached from what in a certain sense might be called the other side to the goal, the way in which Blake hopes to reach this goal. (pp. 215-16)

Blake insists throughout his work upon the effortlessness of his visions, pointing to the fact that the "Prophetic Books" were dictated to him without any effort of his, and that heavenly things were revealed to him without any solicitation on his part. And, in the second place, when Blake tries to lead other men into the life of vision he expressly rejects discipline and maintains that the life of vision is the spontaneous fruit of the release of man's energies, and that that release is to be effected, not by the traditional methods of ethical discipline, but by the cultivation of the creative imagination, especially as manifested in the powers of the artist—above all, the visionary artist. (p. 217)

[Now], it is quite true that the supreme type of mystical achievement, like the supreme type of any human achievement, often comes, as it seems, quite from the outside, without any conscious effort on the part of the mystic or the artist. It seems as if reality suddenly poured in upon the spirit, as if a man spoke words not his own, as if for a brief moment the spirit were lifted above its ordinary pedestrian ways to fly on the wings of its dreams. But such experiences in no wise invalidate what the mystics have said as to the strenuous work by which they come to their goal, for they are very ephemeral, and they find their fitting context in the most strenuous endeavour of the artist or the mystic. Finally, they seldom come except after the most strenuous endeavour and after the most complete devotion of all the powers of a man's nature to the enterprise in hand. It is as if when the soul had spent all its resources— and often seemingly in vain—the price of its endeavour had suddenly been returned in a way undreamed of. (pp. 217-18)

[Mystical insight is] essentially the fruit of strenuous discipline, in some part of an intellectual, but certainly for the greater part of an ethical, nature.

The intellectual discipline of the mystic has centered about the problem of the concentration of the attention. . . . [Whether] it be the meditation of the Buddhist Bhikkhu, or the Christian mystic, the journey to that higher insight that is their goal takes its beginning in the strenuous intellectual labor of meditation. The reader who quietly and dispassionately peruses the pages of the *Manresa*, or the directions for meditation of the Buddhist sages is apt to be a little scornful at first of the importance attached to such very simple trains of thought as they describe. To anyone who has not attempted meditation it seems as if it would be very easy to hold one fairly simple idea before his mind until he has compelled even its most hidden recesses to yield their treasure of meaning and inspiration. But the train of reflection that appears so simple on the surface is in reality both complicated and profound, for it is from this sustained meditation that the mystic rises into the serene ecstasy of contemplation or union.

This intellectual discipline plays no part in Blake's mystical activity. What he stresses is the free expansion of the artist's imagination, sweeping heaven and earth with its creative fury, the surrender of the visionary's mind and will to the influx of vision. The secret is obvious. The object of Blake's mystical activity was so much more diffused and miscellaneous than the object of the mystic's activity that the character of the activity itself must inevitably be far less strenuous and concentrated even on the intellectual side.

As for the ethical side, Blake's rejection of discipline becomes one of the most important items of his mystical code. The key to this aspect of his thinking and his activity may be found in what he made of chastity. (pp. 218-19)

Blake attacked chastity because he believed that it fettered energy and fortified the selfish isolation of the spiritually incomplete individual. It sought to impose restraint in a field where he believed that absolute freedom was essential. This protest has been warmly applauded by some of Blake's critics who seem to forget that no amount of purely physical intensity of living can quite approximate high spiritual quality of living, that these two ideals belong to two distinct regions which, while not necessarily incompatible under ideal conditions, are certainly hostile to each other when the gates that bar the road to excess are broken down. In other words, Blake failed to see that the [religious] stress on chastity, like that on humility, had arisen, not from an arbitrary imposition of a moral tyranny, but from a faith in its potency as an intellectual and spiritual aid to the conquest of the heart's dearest choice.

The hatred of restriction, of interference with the free energy of human nature, which led Blake to reject chastity passionately also led him to reject the principle of discipline in any form. His fundamental objection to the moral law was not that it was carried to extremes, but that it was used to accomplish its fundamental purpose, to check the vagrant impulses of the individual. Even the Ten Commandments, for all their generality, he rejected as tyrannous. This impatience of the moral law is perhaps the best example that we have of Blake's intense hatred of discipline, a hatred that, however interesting it may be from the artistic point of view, is certainly, from the ethical or the religious point of view, one of the most consequential differences between Blake's mysticism and that of the typical mystics. For the typical mystic has generally found in the spirit of the moral law a necessary discipline for human life, one that in the restraint it imposes upon the growth of weeds in the human spirit gives the better chance for the flowers to bloom. (pp. 220-21)

Finally, Blake's reinterpretation of Christianity in terms of art involves certain conclusions for his mystical activity that cannot be disregarded. The core of this recension is the identification of Christ with the creative imagination, the most original feature of Blake's Christianity. This makes the creative imagination the agent of redemption, to translate Blake's ideas into the more conventional terms of theology. In other words, the exercise of an art is the way to achieve goodness. One is reminded of the medieval *laborare est orare*, but the old saying

of the Benedictines never contemplated a replacement of prayer by work. Furthermore, when Blake said "art" he meant art in the very literal sense of the word. Whether he literally intended that all men should be artists is a question, but it is certain that the only mystic for whom Blake's teachings made any provision was the artist, the man in whom the powers of the creative imagination find expression in a very special form of talent. The mystic was therefore not to pray his way into heaven, or to meditate his way to the gates of contemplation, but to imagine his way into reality.

At that point the significance of Blake's rejection of the ethical discipline of the mystics for the more outgoing workings of love and energy becomes clear. Blake's way was not essentially ethical at all. He rejected discipline and substituted energy and intensity of emotion for the strife of the will because the region in which he was working was a very different one from that in which the will has been wont to operate. The mystical way of the typical mystics belongs to the ethical field, finding its great impulse in the will; the mystical way of Blake belongs to the imaginative field, finding its great impulse in the creative energies. What all this amounts to is Blake's famous identification of art and religion. (p. 222)

[It] is clear that religion and art have a common ground and that they can be of very real service to each other in the realization of their respective purposes, but it is also clear that in some very fundamental respects they are entirely different.

For each has its distinctive province. Religion aims to make men better, to purify their affections, to enlighten their judgments, to inspire their inclinations, to fortify their wills, and she does each of these things in the name of a higher will than man's, that, seeing more broadly and more profoundly and more timelessly, has conceived a nobler and a truer pattern of life than man could ever devise. And religion has assured man that whatever be the immediate consequences of his trying to follow her guidance, it will be better with him, and better for the whole of which he is a part, that he endeavor to serve this higher will. (p. 223)

Art, on the other hand, aims to give man beauty, for beauty, she knows, is the greatest gift which the world of sound and color and smell and form can give to man. The satisfaction she gives is a disinterested one that carries man beyond the narrow circle of himself into a world where the more limited instincts of material possession, of egotistical interest, of vanity, of inertia are swept away in a broader vision. Art does not ask man to be a better man, but she tries to make him prefer better things. (pp. 223-24)

That his confusion of these fundamental purposes of art and religion proved disastrous to Blake's art in the realm of poetry seems beyond question. For, however highly the ingenuity of the "Prophetical Writings" may be esteemed, there can be no question that as poetry and as art they are far from satisfactory. As has been suggested more than once, they are marvelously strange and powerful; but, except for passages of rare energy and magnificence, almost smothered in the obscurity and involution of their context, they are notably deficient in lucidity, in wholeness, in vitality, and in beauty—in all the essentials of great literature and of great art. The common opinion that their failure is due to their increasing subservience to Blake's visionary purposes is confirmed when we turn to works relatively free of the "system," to two such diverse achievements as the *Songs of Innocence and of Experience* and the illustrations to the *Book of Job*. The merits of the first have been so universally acclaimed that only the perfection of their simplicity and beauty need be mentioned here. They demonstrate beyond doubt the high order of Blake's original endowment. And the illustrations to the *Book of Job* are justly famous, for their majesty and beauty demonstrate what Blake can achieve in the way of mastering and transmuting material that has been given to him, in this case by the Bible, and so fashioning it that the observer can hardly miss the lucidity and luminous grace of the finished work. It would seem, then, that the same things that made Blake's visionary philosophy fall so far short of the goal of the mystics made him, so far as one can judge from the evidence, fall very far short of the artistic excellence promised in the early lyrics and, to a considerable extent, achieved toward the close of his life in the field of drawing. With the great mystics it has not generally been so. Their mystical efforts, their mystical experiences, have sent them back to the exercise of their peculiar abilities, to the fulfilment of their especial work, with added, not diminished or confused, power. The mystic achievement did not make Abbot Bernard the less moving preacher when he rose to admonish and to encourage his flock at Clairvaux; it did not weaken the magnetic powers of leadership of the Buddha when he drew to the austerity of his alms-bowl and yellow robe the pious from all India; it did not quench the stalwart eloquence or the shrewd sense of George Fox as he journeyed from one end of the United Kingdom to the other to strengthen the persecuted Quaker cause; nor did it impair the remarkable administrative ability and reforming ardor of St. Teresa when she set about to restore the Carmelites to their original spiritual fervor; nor did it in the least detract from the charm and the vitality of St. Augustine's rhetorical gifts when he sat down to tell the story of God's marvelous working with him.

"By their fruits shall ye know them." Again, when we penetrate below the categorical resemblances of the surface, we find that Blake's mysticism, in its fruit as in its essential nature and its characteristic working, is so different from the mysticism of the typical mystics as to necessitate our seeking some other category for it. (pp. 225-26)

[Blake's world] is like our world in its substantiality, in the conception of its form and its movement. But it is very unlike our world in two important respects that have very much impressed students of Blake. The first is a matter of approach, of point of view, of way of looking at things, that has usually been somewhat roughly, but adequately enough, summed up in the word "wonder." And Blake's wonder has been distinguished from that of other men by the fact that Blake, in a large part of his work, and that the best known and most loved part, has dwelt upon the wonder of very little, and usually very commonplace, things that we pass by every day without any appreciation of how extraordinary they are. He once said to his friend and disciple, Richmond: "I can look at a knot in a piece of wood till I am frightened at it," and his latter-day disciples have rung all the possible changes on that sentence without saying very much about what it means. The looking at a piece of wood is of no intrinsic account, for obviously its meaning is entirely vicarious in that it is merely a step in the train of meditation or reverie that ensues. The Christian enthusiast like Richard Rolle of Hampole also could look at a piece of wood until his normal equilibrium was profoundly disturbed. But the piece of wood on which he gazed had been fashioned into a cross; consequently the ecstatic devotee brought to its contemplation a rich treasury of reflection and association, the story of the events that had led the centuries to invest two crossed sticks with so much meaning, the many-sided human personality of Him who to the devout fancy still hung there, the place which that scene that the wood could not fail to conjure up held in the Christian's view of the universe, and finally, its tremendous emotional and ethical implications for the life of the aspirant himself. In other words, as in the question of the ethical power of nature, the bare object, the rapt attention, are not sufficient. It is what the contemplative brings, and not the mere contemplation or the knot in the piece of wood in itself, that counts for meaning. (p. 242)

There is also another side to this famous power of Blake to find wonder in the common things of life. In some cases, as in the above, the wonder comes from an importation of meaning. But the same result may be obtained from the reverse process. We understand the world around us in our ordinary sense of knowing enough about it to use it for everyday practical purposes because we have unconsciously built up around the simplest object a body of associations which tell us what we may expect of that object and what its relations to the rest of the world are for our ordinary purposes. Usually these associations become so firmly entangled about the object that we never see the latter for itself. . . . [When] in some way the old association-incrusted object is suddenly divested of its well-known meanings it becomes at once an object of wonder, something new and startling which teases us by its unwonted detachment from the context of our ordinary expectations. Especially is this true of the wonder of the child's vision, of which we have been hearing so much for the last century. Blake lamented that man as he grew up ceased to be able to see everything as when a child. It is a favorite lament of the victims of infantile nostalgia. But the trouble is not that the man sees less than the child, but that he sees so much more.

And therein lies the charm of the thing. For the child's vision is simpler, clearer, less complicated by the thousand and one impingements of larger areas of experience that forever perplex the grown-up's enjoyment of the world as it is. And the more harassed the grown-up, the wearier he be of the multitudinous claims of mature reality, the more grateful he will be for the relief and the consequent refreshment of the child's vision. That is not the whole story of the popularity which Blake's *Song of Innocence and of Experience* have enjoyed, but it is certainly the major part of it. And there is no reason why we should not so solace and refresh ourselves when this vision is presented by such a master in this field as Blake. (pp. 243-44)

The second way in which the world of Blake's fancy is unlike our world is in the aura that invests it, an aura not to be defined in terms of meaning, hardly in terms of feeling. It is best studied in some of Blake's drawings and paintings, perhaps best of all in a woodcut which Blake made to illustrate Dr. Thornton's edition of Vergil's *Pastorals*. It is a tiny thing representing a single blasted tree on a desolate heath, but it suggests amazingly size and power, with an intensity that comes from the very cramped meagerness of space with which it secures its effect. Much the same thing is true of the famous watercolor of the "Plague," in which the plague is represented by a gigantic green monster striding through the darkness of a stricken city with dusty hands that one feels instinctively must be scattering death on the fetid air; this is a good example of a large part of Blake's work that is apt to draw from the unreflecting observer some reaction like: "What a supernatural thing it is!" Probably this type of effect is more easily secured in drawing or painting than in poetry. But something is due to the matter of technique. This does not by any means require perfection of technique, but it does require clarity, simplicity, and compression if the peculiar sense of intense and strange power is to be communicated. Blake gets it in some of his simpler earlier poems, as in that famous quatrain from the **"Auguries of Innocence"** which everyone knows:

> To see a World in a grain of sand,
> And a Heaven in a wild flower,
> Hold Infinity in the palm of your hand,
> And Eternity in an hour.

But it is very difficult to get such an effect as this in long poems so deficient in lucidity, in wholeness, in vitality, and in beauty—in all the essentials of great literature and great art—as the "Prophetic Books." It is only in passages of rare energy and magnificence that one there finds this characteristic quality of Blake's fancy, and then it is almost lost in the obscurity and involution of the context. Emphatically, the "Prophetic Books" are not the place to seek Blake's visionary qualities at their best and most artistically effective.

After all, much as we want a prophet for this modern world of ours, both to help us in our need and to send us forward in our strength, to gather up what we have discovered and to carry it forward into the Promised Land which we believe we are working toward, we must admit that William Blake is not the man. It is hard to reject a prophet who comes in so many ways in such a congenial guise—poor, hard-working, a fresh and original genius, a rebel against a time which we, too, until quite recently, have disliked, a forerunner of some of our choicest intellectual developments, and the author of a series of works in both literature and painting, the very deficiencies of which are not unpleasing to our predilections. But he is not a great mystic in any sense that means anything; he is a prophet, interesting and suggestive, but very imperfect and incomplete. And as a visionary his real power is not to be sought in the works by which he himself set most store, but in the lyrics of his early manhood and in his pictorial art. (pp. 244-45)

> *Helen C. White, in her* The Mysticism of William Blake, *1927. Reprint by Russell & Russell, Inc., 1964, 276 p.*

JOSEPH H. WICKSTEED (essay date 1928)

[*Wicksteed is a highly regarded Blake scholar best known for his* Blake's Vision of the Book of Job, *an influential study of Blake's pictorial symbolism. In the following excerpt from another study of Blake, he explicates the introductory poems in* Songs of Innocence *and* Songs of Experience, *relating their themes to Blake's concern with the relationship of vision, love, and art. To avoid confusion regarding titles, Wicksteed refers to the "Introduction" to* Songs of Innocence *as "The Piper."*]

It is possible to read this lovely poem ["**The Piper**"] again and again and still to discover new beauties in it. At times it seems to have a slightly symbolical meaning, as though the Piper were the spirit of poetry making the wild vales of this life beautiful with song. But though this idea may possibly have been present with Blake at some point in the poem's gestation, his main interest is in putting into exact and expressive imagery his own experience as the singer of these songs. Every image has a basis in fact, and every word an exact function in producing both the image and the song.

Beginning with the words, we shall find in them a good example of Blake's concentration. "Piping down the valleys" is only four words, but with what matchless economy they are used to produce their effect. By the first, echoes are awakened

The title page of Songs of Innocence and of Experience.

of Arcady and the god Pan, and the next carries us along with easy and happy motion. The word "the" makes valleys into something generic, like "the country" or "the sea," and valleys itself means more than fields or woods or even hills, while it includes them all. So that in these first four words we have already a wonderful picture and a wonderful movement and song. Then comes the last word of the line, a little strange and unexpected. "Wild" is used in the sense of natural or uncultivated, but it is surely Nature in no purely pastoral mood. It may be Pan, but can it be Arcady? Does it introduce a distant hint of those "forests of the night" that we are to enter and pass through in "Experience"? If such questions arise, the next line seems deliberately calculated to silence them. The word "wild" has given strength to the picture, but the songs are merely "songs of pleasant glee," and surely we are in Arcady after all.

We are still left expectant. Having heard the song we await the singer. In the third line he appears as the poet himself, and with him the heavenly Muse in vision as a child upon a cloud. The many repetitions of the song which this vision demands are each accompanied by some new mood. The child first laughs as he gives the theme. But when the theme is repeated it moves the child to tears, and when the mere piping is not enough, words adding the quality of thought and feeling call forth the union of tears with "joy." Yet something has been lost. Words can only be sung after the pipe is dropped. And next the vision itself disappears, when its command to write has been heard. We can only sing when we cease to pipe, and we can only write when we wake from dream.

And yet the poet makes it clear that the atmosphere of rural vision remains. The very instruments of his craft are culled from the brooks where his song was first awakened. The reeds that first supplied his pipes now make his pen, and the water they grow from yields his ink.

And all the time there has been progress. We have passed from "pleasant glee" through laughter on to "merry chear" and then to tears. Next the happy pipe is dropped and the vocal song of "happy chear" (deeper than "merry chear") introduces the magic word "joy." Blake constantly associates great joy with tears, and the words and moods are here chosen with conscious purpose to express progression from glee to cheer, from cheer to happiness, and from happiness to joy, each state being something richer than the last.

But the crisis of the poem is when the child on the cloud disappears. It is difficult to make the meaning and reason of this clear, and yet it is so important and characteristic that we less than half understand the poem unless we grasp it. The Child is a mere happy vision inspiring the Poet from without until he begins to work. He then cannot see the child any more for the same reason that we cannot see ourselves. The Child is now something within. It is himself, and the only outside inspiration is now the fact of actual living children on this earth. Their appreciation of the book is once more described by the significant word "joy." Its use now as a verb seems to have the subtle effect of making them take part.

The poem therefore begins upon the wild earth, is lifted for a time to familiar intercourse with a heavenly vision, and ends again upon the earth, though still retaining the note of joy captured at the height of vision.

This is explained by Blake's significant though cryptic line in *Jerusalem:*

> All things Begin & End in Albions Ancient Druid
> Rocky Shore

which, being expanded, amounts to saying that howsoever we may explore the realms of vision we must come back in the end to that hard and narrow age-long way that skirts the margin between Time and Eternity, where Druid sacrifice of humanity is so common, but which is for every man his native earth.

This is the theme of all Blake's greatest work, and in this respect and others ["**The Piper**"] carries us in anticipation to Blake's final working out of that theme. The "**Introduction**" is in fact more than an introduction to the *Songs of Innocence;* it is like an early sonata whose form was to dictate that of the later symphonies, and especially of the greatest symphony of all.

The parallel between this sonata of "**The Piper**" and the "Job" symphony is particularly close and illuminating. The first water-colour drawings for the "Job" series were completed by Blake about 1820. It begins with Job and his family worshipping beneath his Tree, the symbol of this life. The next scene shows us, as in the "**Piper**," a vision upon the clouds, and it is this vision of the powers of heaven and hell which, entering into relations with the earthly man, dictates the terrible but in the end triumphant course of Job's life until it finally disappears . . . like the cloud child in the "**Piper**," because Job has absorbed it into his own active life.

It disappears from Job's vision to leave his soul flooded with light. "Undeserved" suffering (as he thought his sufferings were) has lost its meaning for him. He has realised that the riches of this world seen in the Spirit are greater than any man ever *deserved*. Job is inspired to return to his poverty in a new spirit towards his fellow men and women that makes him rich indeed, ending with his epic story of Heaven's dealings with him, and his song of glory with his family round the original Tree. And so the Piper, too, after seeing and listening to a heavenly vision that changes and grows, finally loses it as he absorbs it. Then recording it in art, he sings his inspired song "about a Lamb" for the joy of living children upon earth.

It is not necessary to suppose that Blake realised the full greatness of his conception when he wrote this little lyric. He had experienced the fact that the artist, amusing himself with his art, is sometimes surprised by the Spirit and led to ever greater heights of beauty and vision, until he makes the vision his own by Art. Then he is no longer what he was, but a chosen spirit inspired with prophecy or song to his fellows upon earth. It was this discovery, that earth is lifted by Vision which though it disappears makes us and our earth something new, that provided a scheme capable of ever greater treatment, as Blake's life experience and thought gave him greater matter for his art. (pp. 79-83)

[The Bard in the "**Introduction**" to *Songs of Experience,* together with its sequel, "**Earth's Answer**,"] introduces us to "Experience" as the Piper introduced us to "Innocence." The [latter] is at first the pure lyrist piping only for present joy, whereas [the former] chants with prophetic voice and sees all time, "present, past, and future." The "Piper" draws his inspiration from a visionary child in the clouds. The "Bard" draws his from the Holy Spirit walking upon ancient earth. The reference is to Jehovah walking in the Garden of Eden in the evening and discovering the trespass of Adam. Did "the lapsed soul" but listen to that voice descending, as it does into this twilight world, the wheel of heaven could even now be turned and the light of day restored to earth. Thus the "Bard's" message is an appeal to Earth. The "Piper," it will be remembered, begins in this wild earth, soars in vision to heaven, and returns to earth to complete his work. This movement . . . [is] repeated in many of Blake's songs and visions. Here the figure is changed, and instead of the Soul returning to Earth, it is Earth herself that is bid return. The lines that follow can only be understood if we know the thoughts that were uppermost in Blake's mind as he wrote. The dew is matter, the grass is flesh, out of which earth is called to arise. Night is the dark period of disillusionment in the State of Experience, and the morn is the joy of fulfilled and liberated love. The failure of man to realise the beauty of the love of man and maid is typical of all his failure to embrace the joy of the artist. The stars are the broken lights of eternity which even Night cannot quench, for the beauty of life and love are never wholly hidden, though seen as we see them, without poetry and divine inspiration, they are but the "wat'ry shore," the materialistic margin, of the full day of divine beatitude.

The eternal character of the Bard's vision, inspired by the Divine Word itself, confers on youth an authority above that of parents and elders, leading it into the light of direct experience. (pp. 145-46)

Earth's answer is tragic and enigmatical. The task is too hard, and she can only lament the senseless cruelty of chains she cannot break. To understand her plaint we must realise that she is bound by some *thought* which we shall find to be theological. Like the Bard, she appeals to antiquity, but whereas his appeal was to the Word, hers is to the Father; his filling with hope, hers with despair.

For Blake there were two visions of God. One was the evil dream of man inventing an invisible Father to account for the creation of this material universe (itself an illusion), and the other was a Spirit—intensely visible in everything that lived when seen as holy and spiritual.

The priests of the former were jealous of all creative acts, whether of the poet or of man and maid. Their cold and cruel attitude towards Art and Sex betrayed their fear of the eternal challenge these make to a conception of a World bound by laws of Time and Matter. By banishing love to the secrecy of night and starlight and the bondage of law and religion, they prison it in the watery shore of the flesh, and hold in chains of ice the open love of virgin hearts in man and maid that should be like the dawn.

These two poems thus interpreted give us the clue to very much of Blake's thought. At the end of his life he pictures Job in his first prosperity worshipping unawares the God of this World as "Our Father which art in heaven" and passing through untold tribulation until he discovers the Divine Being in life itself, in brotherly love and forgiveness, in brotherly interdependence, in the creation of verse and sculpture and song, and in the holy joys of wife and home: all spiritual realities: all here and now. (pp. 147-48)

> *Joseph H. Wicksteed, in his* Blake's Innocence and Experience: A Study of the Songs and Manuscripts, *E. P. Dutton & Co., 1928, 301 p.*

JOHN MIDDLETON MURRY (essay date 1933)

[*Murry was a noted English essayist, magazine editor, and literary critic during the first half of the twentieth century. Considered a perceptive critic whose work reveals his "honesty to the point of masochism," he has contributed important studies on the works of Blake, John Keats, Fedor Dostoevski, Katherine Mansfield, and D. H. Lawrence. In the following excerpt from his* William Blake, *Murry explicates* The Four Zoas *as spiritual autobiography, interpreting the poem as a direct reflection of Blake's struggle to reach a new understanding of the principles represented by the character Urizen. This struggle became manifest in the later Lambeth prophecies, according to Murry, and was resolved as "a new marriage of Heaven and Hell" in* The Four Zoas, *thus ushering in a rebirth of the poet's confidence in* Milton.]

Between 1795 and 1804 Blake wrote *The Four Zoas*. It covers the period during which no engraved prophetic book appeared. For *The Song of Los* belongs to 1795, and the next engraved book, *Milton,* was begun in 1804. Thus *The Four Zoas* does not belong to the sequence of Blake's published utterances. It exists only in the form of a manuscript adorned by a few beautiful pencil drawings. Some of the material it contains was afterwards incorporated into *Milton,* and more into *Jerusalem*.

Why did not Blake attempt to issue *The Four Zoas* in his own particular fashion? (p. 153)

[The] cause of Blake's apparent neglect of a work so considerable and so profound as *The Four Zoas* must be sought in the work itself, and in the nature of its connection with the work which preceded, and the work which followed it.

What chiefly impresses us in the sequence of the engraved Lambeth books is a gradual darkening of confidence and flagging of inspiration. One might almost say they peter out. They become fragmentary, desultory, repetitive. Whatever may be our difficulties with *Milton,* one thing is certain: this internal languor has wholly disappeared. What Blake is saying in *Milton*

he is saying with all his mind, and all his heart, and all his soul, and all his strength.

In respect of thought and mood *The Four Zoas* occupies a place between. Not that the thought and mood of a book composed over nine years is uniform; nor is it in accord with human experience that the thought and mood of a period of transition between dejection and the rebirth of confidence should be uniform. It must inevitably be a period of struggle, and hope, and despair, and constant change. Such a period we find directly reflected in *The Four Zoas*. Blake is changing.

We can see the process and nature of the change most clearly in the destiny of Urizen, who is the major creation of the later Lambeth books. In them he is, on the whole, a purely sinister figure, the embodiment of the Rational principle in its most repressive and repulsive aspect; and although . . . the creation of Ahania brings with it the possibility of Urizen's regeneration,—of a Law transformed by Love, Rationality transfigured by the Imagination,—the predominant impression made by the figure of Urizen is of a power utterly inhuman and merciless. That the existence of this Power is in some sense necessary to existence is a feeling which we rather retain from the splendid vision of *The Marriage of Heaven and Hell* than derive from the later Lambeth books themselves. To define a change of mood in a man of spiritual genius is almost foolhardy; but the attempt must be made. We shall say then that, whereas in *The Marriage* our feeling is that Blake is secure in his triumph over false Reason and the Law, and therefore free to acknowledge that they are necessary to existence—'Without Contraries is no Progression'; 'Time is the mercy of Eternity'; 'Whoever tries to reconcile them (the Devourers and the Prolific) seeks to destroy existence', are characteristic utterances of this sense of comprehending and comprehensive power—in the later Lambeth books our feeling is that Blake has lost this commanding position. He can no longer afford to grant any sort of justification to the principle he now embodies in Urizen, the apparent king of the world of Time. Time is no longer the mercy of Eternity; it is rather the cruelty of Eternity—if such a phrase were not in Blake's imagination a contradiction in terms.

For a man whose mind is passionately concerned with the world of reality, a dualism of thought is inevitable. Such a dualism is a necessary manifestation of Life itself, of that living progression which, without contraries, cannot be. However assured may be the passing 'beyond Good and Evil', however secure the confidence in the necessity and validity of that act of transcendence, it immediately, and by its own operation, involves the creation of another Good and another Evil. For the transcendence of the old dualism is the new Good, and the resistance to that transcendence the new Evil. The very consummation of a marriage between Heaven and Hell means the opening of a new and deeper Hell beneath the prophet's feet. For the resistance to a Light so manifest as that which radiates from every thing and every creature in the vision of Eternity is an Evil of a new order: an incomprehensible opacity fit to rank with the luminousness of the Light itself. This Evil seems to the newly awakened vision of Eternity elemental and monstrous—'the mystery of iniquity'.

Thus we need to look no further than the inevitable consequence of the Divine Vision itself for a clue to the understanding of the sinister figure of Urizen in the later Lambeth books. He is not the false Reason that was recognized and comprehended and vanquished in *The Marriage;* he is a new power altogether. He is not that which resists Energy; he is that which resists the Light. To resist Energy is a possible, almost a human impulse; to resist the Light is inhuman and devilish. And this elemental, incomprehensible resistance, we have cause to believe, had been manifested to Blake in his nearest and dearest. No wonder that his inspiration flagged and that he seemed to stand still in his own footsteps, as it were fascinated and bemused by the figure which his imagination had defined.

What is of the utmost importance to understand is that Blake had not gone back on his vision. The change of mood which makes so deep and painful an impression on the sensitive mind is not at all what the counter-visionary complacently describes as the inevitable reaction after visionary experience. . . . What appears to the unimaginative mind like retreat is advance. It is necessary to the progress of the man of vision that he should learn the nature of the resistance to the vision. It may be, indeed it is, a fact that the mind of man resists the light of vision; but to admit that fact is not to deny the truth of vision. It is to enter more fully into the vision itself. It is to prepare for the new task of transcending the new Evil, as the old was transcended.

This, we believe, is the true explanation of the facts to be explained. First, the marked difference in tone between the figure of Urizen in the later Lambeth books and the Angels of *The Marriage;* second, the gradual faltering of Blake's inspiration as soon as the figure of Urizen takes clear shape in his imagination; and, third, the long period of hesitation during which *The Four Zoas* was composed—a period during which, though his imaginative thought was incessantly active, as the text of *The Four Zoas* amply proves, Blake hesitated to commit himself to the engraved finality of his own peculiar mode of expression. He had a new problem to solve: the resistance of the human mind to the luminous and self-evident truth; he had a new obstacle to overcome: his own anger and dismay and resentment at the resistance it encountered. (pp. 154-57)

What Blake was struggling to achieve in the years from 1795 to 1802 was a new marriage of Heaven and Hell. And the process of that struggle is embodied (in a very literal sense, embodied) in the writing of *The Four Zoas.* We believe it would be possible to follow out in detail in the text of that great book the slow and painful advance towards victory. For *The Four Zoas* ends in victory. The last phase of the book belongs, spiritually and creatively, to the same order of illumination as *Milton.* All the fundamental insights which make of *Milton* so rapturous an adventure are unmistakably present in the last phase of *The Four Zoas;* and, as we shall try to show, the eternal moment of creative vision out of which *Milton* inevitably grew, is clearly indicated in Night VII of *The Four Zoas.* (p. 158)

Nothing more will be attempted [here] than to give some clues to the inward development of Blake himself, and of the symbols in which that development was dramatically expressed. The first simple fact to be held in mind is that Nights VII-IX of *The Four Zoas* and *Milton* belong to the same order of illumination: and that both the doctrine and vision of *Milton* derive from the same creative 'moment' as those last three Nights. . . . This 'moment', I have no doubt, occurred during Blake's three years' stay at Felpham; nor have I much doubt that the last three Nights of *The Four Zoas* were written there in 1802-3. This Felpham 'moment' was decisive. It meant that Blake had achieved the new marriage of Heaven and Hell towards whch he had been struggling. (pp. 158-59)

[The] original *Marriage of Heaven and Hell* represented (as Blake believed) the Light. The Lambeth books which followed represented the gradual recognition of the resistance to Light, and an almost despairing rebellion against that resistance. Despair, or rather the expression of despair, reaches a climacteric in *The Song of Los,* where Jesus, whom Blake had hitherto striven to identify with Orc, the rebellious Energy, and thus with himself, is recognized as opposed to him. Jesus was wrong— he preached the gospel of 'wretched Theotormon'—he, Blake, was right. And with that, Blake passed into a period of complete spiritual isolation. He was alone.

He had gone headlong along the path of Energy (which was for him the path of Light) and the resistance to his Energy had loomed more sinister and elemental before him. . . . And as the resistance loomed more sinister and elemental before Blake's vision, it seemed to him that this resistance was, in the literal sense, part of the nature of things: Opacity and Existence were one. Hence arose, in Blake's imaginative thought, an apparent identification of the creation of Urizen and the creation of Existence itself. This identification, on another level, was expressed by the union of the Rational with the Female principle; and . . . , on the naked level of personal experience, this was intimately connected with the resistance he encountered in his wife.

On this last level, the original title of *The Four Zoas,* namely *Vala,* expresses Blake's momentary conclusion that the resistance of his wife was the root of all his evil; on another, that the Female principle was the origin of all Opacity; on yet another, that the whole world of generation was an incomprehensible mistake. In *The Four Zoas,* Blake passes beyond this condition of despair. From the fearful conclusion that Opacity and Existence are one, he passes to the quite different conclusion that mortal existence represents 'the limit of Opacity' and 'the limit of Contraction', and that these limits are set, in mercy, by 'the Divine Hand'.

The meaning of Opacity is self-evident; for the use of the term has been forced upon us in the effort to explain the nature of Blake's new problem and new struggle. The conception of Contraction is equally obvious. The senses of the man liberated into Eternity are 'expansive and flexible'; because, as we have seen, they necessarily expand into the Infinite in all things— the single and solely real universe of living Identities. If, as a man of Blake's habit of mind was bound to do, we conceive this universe of Identities as being that from which the apparent world existentially, as well as eternally derives, we are driven to speak of a process of Contraction from a formerly existing condition of Expansion. (pp. 159-61)

[Blake's new conception of a 'limit' of Opacity and Contraction] denotes a transcending of the new Evil of resistance. Superficially, it may appear to represent a *nec plus ultra* of imperviousness to the Light; but, in reality, since the limit is imagined as deliberately set by the Divine Hand, it denotes a return to the conception of Time as the mercy of Eternity. The resistance of the new Evil to the Light is itself part of the Divine Vision, not the working of mysterious and elemental power thwarting the Divine Vision. Nor must it be thought that Blake was weakly capitulating to the shallow optimism of providential religion. Blake never capitulated weakly to anything. Even the growing pessimism of the later Lambeth books is the result of his looking squarely at the new Enemy. Now, he has struggled and overcome. He has advanced to a new understanding which comprehends the new Evil.

This new understanding receives its most direct and simple expression towards the end of Night VII. There Los, who partly represents Blake himself, is reunited to the Spectre of Urthona.

But then the Spectre enter'd Los's bosom. Every sigh &
groan
Of Enitharmon bore Urthona's Spectre on its wings.
Obdurate Los felt Pity. Enitharmon told the tale
Of Urthona. Los embrac'd the Spectre, first as a
brother,
Then as another Self, astonish'd, humanizing & in
tears,
In Self abasement Giving up his Domineering lust. . . .

The Spectre of Urthona is hardly to be distinguished from
Urizen. In *The First Book of Urizen* Eternity divides first into
Urizen and Los, and Enitharmon is born of Los's pity for
Urizen. The Spectre of Urthona is thus an alternative form of
Urizen. Immediately after his reunion with Los, he speaks these
words to him:

Thou never canst embrace sweet Enitharmon, terrible
Demon, Till
Thou art united with thy Spectre, Consummating by
pains & labours
That mortal body, & by Self annihilation back-returning
To Life Eternal. Be assur'd I am thy real self,
Tho' thus divided from thee & the slave of Every
passion
Of thy fierce Soul. Unbar the Gates of Memory: look
upon me
Not as another, but as thy real Self. I am thy Spectre,
Thou didst subdue me in old times by thy Immortal
Strength,
When I was a ravening, hungering & thirsting cruel lust
& murder.
Tho' horrible & Ghastly to thine Eyes, tho' buried
beneath
The ruins of the Universe: hear what inspir'd I speak &
be silent!
If we unite in one, another better world will be
Open'd within your heart & loins & wondrous brain,
Threefold, as it was in Eternity; & this the fourth
Universe
Will be Renew'd by the three, & consummated in
Mental fires.
But if thou dost refuse, Another body will be prepared
For me; and thou, annihilate, evaporate & be no more.
For thou art but a form & organ of life, & of thyself
Art nothing, being Created Continually by Mercy &
Love divine. . . .

We may put aside for the moment all questions of detailed
interpretation. What is important is to seize the spirit of the
passage. For Los is convinced by the Spectre; and this conviction is a decisive moment in the history of Los.

Los furious answer'd: 'Spectre horrible, thy words
astound my Ear
With irresistible conviction. I feel I am not one of those
Who, when convinc'd, can still persist: tho' furious,
controllable
By Reason's power. Even I already feel a World within
Opening its gates, & in it all the real substances
Of which these in the outward World are shadows
which pass away.
Come then into my Bosom, & in thy shadowy arms
bring with thee
My lovely Enitharmon. I will quell my fury & teach
Peace to the soul of dark revenge, & repentance to
Cruelty.' . . .

The union with Enitharmon is delayed. She trembles and flees
and hides beneath Urizen's Tree, which is the Tree of Mystery.
But Los and the Spectre are durably united. The Spectre gives
Los 'tasks enormous'—'to destroy that body he (Los) created'.
But Los performs 'wonders of labour'. But he is, of course,
no longer his former self; he is united with the Spectre.

They builded Golgonooza. Los, labouring, builded
pillars high,
And Domes terrific in the nether heavens; for beneath
Was open'd new heavens & a new Earth, beneath &
within,
Threefold, within the brain, within the heart, within the
loins,
A Threefold Atmosphere Sublime, continuous from
Urthona's world,
Yet having a Limit Twofold named Satan & Adam. . . .

[The psychological meaning of this passage is] that by being
reconciled to the Spectre within himself, by recognizing and
receiving Urizen as a part of his own Self, Los-Blake attains
a new understanding, a new synthesis (as we might call it today). Not, of course, an intellectual synthesis; but a real and
decisive act of new spiritual understanding, involving a revolution of the total man,—an act of the Self-annihilation which
is Imagination. Blake understands now that Urizen is not a
separate, demonic power, from whose dominion Blake alone
is free; he is in Blake himself, a necessary element of Blake's
being. Hence Los's task 'to destroy the body he created'. He
has to destroy the figure of Urizen as he had formerly created
him; he has, by the same compulsion, to destroy the figure of
Los as he had formerly created him. For the Los of the past
is essentially the enemy and opposite of the former Urizen. He
belongs to the same order of spiritual blindness; as Blake put
it simply, in looking upon Urizen with the eyes of separateness
and hated and contempt, Los 'became what he beheld.' Thus,
while the Spectre describes himself as having been 'a ravening,
hungering & thirsting cruel lust & murder' in 'the old times'
when Los subdued him (which is the story told in *The First
Book of Urizen*) Los reciprocates by discovering in his former
self fury and cruelty and 'the soul of dark revenge'.

But the union with Enitharmon is delayed. Los beholds the
fruit of the Tree of Mystery beneath whose shadow Enitharmon
had fled. He is 'filled with doubts in self-accusation'. Enitharmon tells him that by eating of this fruit she had come to
know that 'without a ransom she could not be saved from
Eternal Death'. She asks him to eat also of the fruit. 'Eat thou
also of the Fruit, & give me proof of life Eternal, or I die.'

Los eats; then he sits down in despair:

And must have given himself to death Eternal, But
Urthona's Spectre, in part mingling with him,
comforted him,
Being a medium between him & Enitharmon. But This
Union
Was not to be Effected without Cares & Sorrows &
Troubles
Of Six thousand Years of self denial & of bitter
Contrition. . . .

(pp. 161-66)

'Six thousand years' for Blake is the time occupied in one
distinct phase of spiritual experience before passing to another.
The autobiographical substance of these lines is that his new
imaginative understanding of the nature of Urizen, his new
realization that he himself contained an element of resistance

to the Light, did not immediately bring to Blake, as he hoped, a new unity between himself and his wife. His new confidence once more seemed to her impious like the old one. (p. 166)

What seemed impious to his wife was that Blake seemed to forgive himself for his former 'domineering lust'. Los, in his fury of cruelty, had trampled Urizen underfoot; Blake, the inspired rebel, had spurned the Law, and domineered over one to whom the Law was real, and had been blind to the fact that, in thus domineering, he had himself become the slave of the Law. He and his wife had bruised one another.

> 'O Enitharmon,
> Couldst thou but cease from terror & trembling & affright,
> When I appear before thee in forgiveness of ancient injuries!
> Why shouldest thou remember, & be afraid? I surely have died in pain
> Ofen enough to convince thy jealousy & fear & terror.
> Come hither; be patient; let us converse together, because
> I also tremble at myself & at all my former life.' ...

There is the cry of experience. It seemed to his wife that Blake had forgiven himself. And so it would seem to most Christians. But that is completely to misunderstand Blake's experience and his message. For him, no man in his Selfhood could forgive himself. The condition of Forgiveness and the condition of Selfhood could not exist together; for the condition of Forgiveness was an instant participation in Eternal Life, and was reached through Self-annihilation. So, it is to be remarked, Blake makes Los say that he appears before Enitharmon '*in forgiveness* of ancient injuries',—in a condition not his own, not personal to him, but one in which he is as it were clothed: yet, at the same time, this condition is truly himself, it is the very life-blood of his Eternal Individuality, which emerges only through annihilation of his Self. (pp. 166-67)

[We are now concerned] with the decisive moment of the forgiveness of Urizen; the moment of Blake's realization that Selfhood was triumphant in Los in his very struggle against Urizen. This was for him a new cleansing and a new integration. He had—to anticipate a pregnant phrase from *Milton*— 'destroy'd the Negation to redeem the Contraries'. The sheer negative opposition of Energy and Reason changes by the simple alchemy of more abundant life, into mutual understanding, mutual forgiveness. Blake's wife does not understand what has happened. What is in him a simple rebirth of integrity and confidence, is to her a recrudescence of presumption. His new-won assurance of Eternal Life is to her a new evidence of Eternal Death. It is not easy for a simple religious woman to live in marriage with a prophet.

The gradual overcoming of her new fears was a life-epoch in itself. Since 'Woman is the Nemesis of doubting Man', Blake doubts himself at her doubting, and sits down in despair. It is another death. But the integration of Los and Urizen endures and comforts the new man born of their union; and this new Blake is in contact with his wife. The condition of Forgiveness prevails against her doubting. There follows a by no means obscure symbolic description of a new period of inspiration, and a new collaboration of his wife in his work.

> O Lovely terrible Los, wonder of Eternity, O Los, my defence & guide,
> Thy works are all my joy, & in thy fires my soul delights.

> If mild they burn in just proportion, & in secret night
> And silence build their day in shadow of soft clouds & dews,
> Then I can sigh forth on the winds of Golgonooza piteous forms
> That vanish again into my bosom: but if thou, my Los,
> Wilt in sweet moderated fury fabricate forms sublime,
> Such as the piteous spectres may assimilate themselves into,
> They shall be ransoms for our Souls that we may live. ...

In other words, if Blake will no longer work in anger and hatred and fury, his creations themselves will overcome the fears of his wife. (pp. 168-69)

Blake is dramatizing the resolution of a tension, and the beginning of a new period of inspiration and collaboration, when Los

> drew a line upon the walls of shining heaven,
> And Enitharmon tinctur'd it with beams of blushing love. ...

Blake is no longer the Devil of *The Marriage of Heaven and Hell,* writing with corroding fires on the walls of the abyss of the Five Senses. And the words with which the whole Night closes give the essence of the change which has come to pass. The new works of Los are thus described:

> First his immortal spirit drew Urizen's Spectre away
> From out the ranks of war, separating him in sunder,
> Leaving his Spectrous form, which could not be drawn away ...
> Startled was Los: he found his Enemy Urizen now
> In his hands: he wonder'd that he felt love, & not hate.
> His whole soul loved him: he beheld him an infant
> Lovely breath'd from Enitharmon: he trembled within himself. ...

That is the decisive 'moment' of *The Four Zoas.* It can be interpreted on different levels. It means the victorious advance of Blake to a new spiritual understanding of the fact of resistance to the Light. Since there is, and can be, no advance in spiritual understanding without a new growth of simple human tenderness, it means a victory of loving-kindness—the beginnings of a new life with his wife. Since Blake's prophetic books are, through and through, a record of his own spiritual progress, it means a fundamental change in the treatment of his own previous themes. If we allow that the dominant theme of the later Lambeth books is the binding of Urizen, then *The Four Zoas* marks the passing of that theme into the freeing of Urizen.

But Urizen represents so much, and is the imaginative embodiment of a process so deeply ramified in the growth of the human soul, that the freeing of Urizen, who was 'in old times' the very negation of freedom, necessitates the growth of a new symbolism. The regeneration of Urizen is necessarily a new generation. There can be no simple continuity between the new Urizen and the old one. Los-Blake now loves the new Urizen with his whole soul. The Urizen that was cannot be loved by the whole soul of any man; and the Urizen that is to be cannot resemble him or bear his name. Blake's symbolism must grow to yield to his growing experience; and growth is a process of destruction as well as creation. So Los has 'to destroy the body he created'.

Blake's prophetic books, strange and obscure as they are at the first approach, are alive in this deepest sense of all. They are one incessant process of destruction and creation, of creation through destruction. Their seeming chaos is the apparent confusion which attends swift and precipitate growth: the husks of the old are incessantly being split in sunder under the urge of the new realization.

To follow this thrust of spiritual growth, to open glimpses on to its crucial moments, to bring home to others something of the stress and surrender and surge of life in a man whose single aim it was to reach a truth that could not fail—this is the utmost an interpreter of Blake can dream of doing. To systematize him is to kill him; his work is a living thing. And, I think, in order to understand the quality of Blake's glorious humanity, we need to have known, in the stress of our own small life-experience, what it is, and how far beyond all other achievements it is, at some crucial moment when the unconscious choice lay between the security which is death and the insecurity which is life, to have 'destroyed the Negation, to redeem the Contraries'. (pp. 169-71)

> *John Middleton Murry, in his* William Blake, *1933.*
> *Reprint by McGraw-Hill Book Company, 1964, 380 p.*

MARK SCHORER (essay date 1946)

[*In his* William Blake: The Politics of Vision, *Schorer portrays Blake as a radical thinker and poet deeply immersed in the revolutionary sociopolitical movements of his era. This image of Blake emerges clearly in the following excerpt, in which the critic emphasizes the extraordinary nature of Blake's commitment to the revolutionary ideals of liberty, equality, and fraternity.*]

That the content of Blake's poetry is primarily social and that his criticism of society is radical, commentary on Blake does not readily concede even now. Not many years ago Stephen Spender wrote: "The error of poetry was surely the romantic movement. . . . If Blake had not been so unique a figure, if he had been a greater poet and perhaps less of a genius, he might have been the leader of a reaction from the late eighteenth century, which would have been a 'criticism of life'—that is, of the Industrial Revolution.

> But most through midnight streets I hear
> How the youthful harlot's curse
> Blasts the new-born infant's tear,
> And blights with plagues the marriage hearse,

is poetry that is a function of life, as distinct from poetry that is an escape into dreams.'' Mr. Spender meant that in Blake, as in his contemporaries, in spite of the flickering promise of genuine perception into the actual, the ''escape into dreams'' triumphed over the ''criticism of life.''

This is the conventional view of Blake's development, but it is a view that declines to read closely. If a radical is a thinker who challenges and repudiates the assumptions of the dominant class in his society on the basis of revolutionary assumptions of his own, and if a radical poet is one whose utterance, in image and structure as well as in matter, is informed by the challenge and the repudiation—then Blake was and always remained a radical poet. The radical content of his poetry came out of well-known revolutionary discussion concentrated in the thought of that ''remarkable coterie'' associated with the London printer Joseph Johnson at the end of the eighteenth century. Yet the influence on Blake of republicans like Price and Paine and Priestley, of anarchists like Holcroft and Godwin, of the

Frontispiece of Songs of Innocence.

feminist Mary Wollstonecraft, of industrial and social developments toward which these persons held attitudes, is a focus for Blake rather than a ''source,'' an atmosphere of opinion in which he found a direction rather than a set of fixed ideas. They provided a point at which his own revolutionary concepts were freed and from which they more or less evolved. (pp. 151-52)

Blake criticism has not always denied the influence of these theorists, but it has decreed a sharp separation—dating the year, of course, as 1792, and the month as September—between Blake the heedless young radical and Blake the sagely retreating mystic. His biography and his casual utterances show that this separation is not real, that he maintained his connections with other radicals while they were available, and sustained his interest in their ideas after they were not. (p. 153)

The fact that ideas as used in poetry are subject to the imagination sometimes makes them difficult to recognize, and with a poet like Blake, who seized at ideas from so many diverse directions and who was almost always so different in one way or another from their source, the opportunity of overlooking his debt is great. Face Blake with Godwin in fancy—one could hardly produce a temperamental clash more harsh. And of course Blake's sharp opposition to some of the most basic assumptions of current revolutionary dogma makes this debt particularly obscure. Yet ideas mesh and are pushed into movement not so much through gentle elisions as through partial antagonisms, and this is the relation between revolutionary theory and Blake's intellectual development. He sharpened his borrowings by his rejections; and by his very rejection of certain elements in that theory he refreshed it, and at precisely the point in history when it seemed to be expiring.

Blake's intellectual and poetic stature was greater than Shelley's precisely to the extent that he attempted a restatement of the assumptions of revolutionary doctrine. Whitehead has said: "The literary exposition of freedom deals mainly with the frills. The Greek myth was more to the point. Prometheus did not bring to mankind freedom of the press. He procured fire." One would despair of reading a poem on the freedom of the press, to be sure, and Prometheus brought mankind more than fire. Yet Shelley's Prometheus brought less than either, the unconverted theory, and even those poems of his over which we murmur names of real events like Peterloo are nearly as abstract as the doctrine of his mentors. The rejection of the doctrine of necessity was not enough; for poetry, a *recasting* was the required act. In two important ways Blake avoided the defect of Shelley. He fought against the abstraction of revolutionary theory by criticizing, and not abstractly, that element in the theory itself; and he countered it further by building the most intimate portion of his poetry, its imagery, not on the frills of freedom but on the facts of contemporary life.

In his extremely personal way Blake measures up to the very definition of poetry by which Mr. Spender finds him wanting. "The task of the poet of the future," the latter said, "is to win back the ground that has been lost by the romantic movement: that is to say he has to apply himself minutely to observe the life of people round him, and he has also to understand and to feel in himself the development of recent history. Poetry is at once a description of the conditions of living and an affirmation of the permanent in life, of real values.... I do not mean that poets must write exclusively, or even of necessity at all, of machines and towns.... What is required of the poet is not up-to-date-ness but an awareness of the extent to which the external conditions of today, towns, machinery, etc., have, like an acid, eaten into conscious and subconscious humanity."

Blake's poetry is of an elaborately concentric order. He is the most difficult of English poets because he was the most ambitious. He wished, in a system of ever-widening metaphorical amplification, to explain his story, the story of his England, the history of the world, prehistory, and the nature of all eternity. Almost unanimously, critics have attended to the eternal elements, to what they have called the "mysticism," or at least to the religion, or simply to an exposition of the system itself. Or they have elucidated in very general terms what Spender calls the "real values" at the expense of "the conditions of living," and in separating the two, they have altered the meaning of the first. In Blake's scheme, "eternity" is the cause, but man, and most specifically man in Blake's day, is the tragic or the triumphant effect, and "eternity" itself is a solid, even a somewhat lumpish, affair. "All things Begin & End," in his narratives, "in Albion's Ancient Druid Rocky Shore," and Ephesians 6:12 served as the epigraph to [*The Four Zoas,*] one of his longest and perhaps his central poem: "For our contention is not with the blood and the flesh, but with dominion, with authority, with the blind world-rulers of this life, with the spirit of evil in things heavenly."

This was Shelley's implicit epigraph, but the two dramatized it differently. Several of Blake's poems, like some of Shelley's, take historical events as their subject matter, but in Shelley the "conditions of living" vanish in moonlight and high sound; in Blake, even as the poetry grows more bewildering, the "conditions of living" more and more insistently force themselves into the imagery, the fabric of the poems. In Shelley, the Rights of Man remains the defective historical generalization that it was in eighteenth-century liberal theory. In Blake, it is converted into its psychological actuality, which, as a political axiom, remains undisputed even though varieties of interest have interpreted it in varieties of ways. The slogan The Rights of Man Blake avoided, as he avoided most slogans. But the abiding theme of all his poems is the integrity of the individual, and the imperative right of the personality to expression and fulfillment.

When Blake said, "I in Six Thousand Years walk up and down," he was laying claim to a vaster knowledge of the developments of history than any man can support, and he was placing on poetry a greater burden than it can endure apart from religious ritual. He did so because he was convinced that his function, inspite of his inadequate theology, was religious, that under the multiple and shifting historical tides he perceived the enduring psychological facts. These, as he envisaged them, he could not have perceived except at the end of his century, in a generation of political upheaval and in the time of a terrorized reaction, and even then, he could not conceivably have expressed them if his eyes had indeed been only on the elusive "real values" and never on the mere, brutal, corrosive, outrageous fact. Walking up and down in six thousand years meant that Blake, like Shelley, was

> . . . as a nerve o'er which do creep
> The else unfelt oppressions of this earth;

but much more, too. (pp. 153-56)

"Each Identity is Eternal" and "All Things Common"—the intellectual struggle to which Blake gave his life was to bring these two together. In French Revolutionary doctrine, their names were Liberty and Fraternity, but the French Revolution failed to unite them. In Blake's lifetime and (with the possible exception of such ambiguous social experiments as Robert Owen's), at least until the formulations of Marx, liberty alone found defenders. Isolated from its triad, it developed on the one hand into the dreary shopkeeper's philosophy of Bentham, and on the other into the aggressive power philosophy of Carlyle, where liberty was the monopoly of the exceptional, and most men were intended to lapse gratefully into the slavery they deserved. Blake's correction of eighteenth-century liberalism from which he certainly derived, prevents his falling into some poetic approximation either of the drab Benthamite liberalism, with its uninspired approval of the bourgeoisie, or of the glittering negations of Carlyle and Nietzsche, with their exaltation of the most frightening aristocracy of all. For Blake, exalting neither man's reason nor, in the usual sense, his virtue, yet *loved* men, individual men. To Bentham the mass of individuals were colorless atoms; to Carlyle and Nietzsche they were scum in a quagmire. Blake's concern was with the individual man within the mass of individual men.

Individualism was his main value, as it was the main value of all liberals of whatever color in the first half of the nineteenth century; but he detected the ambiguities and the contrasts that inhabit this term, and he struggled in his poetry to express them, and to assert one set of meanings against another. His long poems are dramatic parables about the conflicts between these forms of individualism. Urizen, the mistaken spirit, represents individualism, after all, as much as does Orc, or Los, or any good spirit. When is the impulse mistaken, and when is it good? It is mistaken when, like Urizen, it separates itself from its members to exalt itself, when it is in competition with its members, when it destroys order. It is good when, like Orc or Los, it attempts to force or weld the original whole together again and establish a harmony of parts. Individualism is evil when it is a will to power, good when it is a will to order. The quarrel is between competition, a reckless laissez faire, and co-operation. The way to achieve the good is through the only social virtue that Blake recognized, love, or forgiveness, or brotherhood, which as often as not he called imagination.

"Each Identity is Eternal" and "All Things Common." This is to ask for complete individuality within the widest universality. The paradox here between individualism and harmony is the great paradox of democracy itself: the right of the personality to develop, and the evil of any personality's "developing" at the expense of any other. The second "developing" is crucial, and it resolves the paradox; for preventing another means reducing, not expanding, the self and thereafter the society. This concept Blake labored ceaselessly, in every way, to express; in the lyric imagery of nature—

> Each outcry of the hunted Hare
> A fibre from the Brain does tear.
> A Skylark wounded in the wing,
> A Cherubim does cease to sing—

and in moralistic verse—

> The iron hand crush'd the Tyrant's head
> And became a Tyrant in his stead—

and in straightforward prose: "All Those who, having no Passions of their own because No Intellect, Have spent their lives in Curbing & Governing other People's by the Various arts"; [and] "Poverty is the Fool's Rod, which at last is turn'd on his own back." . . . (pp. 182-84)

But the difficulty of stating a perception that had not yet been formulated in history was great. . . . Chiefly, he had to rely on his mythical representations, in which the unity of opposites could be embodied, and this paradox resolved. The figure of Albion, who "falls" into sleep and sickness when a part (which now degenerates, too) rebels, and awakens to a glorious day when the part is reassimilated (and finds itself well again)—this figure may be taken as the symbol of a great composite democratic individual, the archetype for a society whose members live co-operatively, and for the individual whose self-expression is then complete and who is then in perfect health. Blake's treatment of the sexes represents a parallel unity of opposites. They are separate, with separate impulses, and only when the impulses of each are given free expression *in love* is the separateness broken down. The androgynous figure of Blake's eternity is the symbol of this attainment.

Blake could sometimes only perilously maintain his concept of variety in unity ("the MOST UNITED VARIETY"). Often enough he rejects his ideal of individuality within the whole for that other individualism which pits the single *against* the whole, man *against* the universe, and the poet *against* society; when he seems to say that his concern, like that of the mystics, is the development of his individuality alone, the achievement of his own spiritual life, of a private salvation—all of which is laissez faire, too. But these occasions are found in his discouraged, fragmentary utterances, not in his poems. He wrote no palinodes. In his poetry he repeatedly sought to state what we recognize now as the greatest modern social paradox. He

did not think this paradox through as a political or an economic problem, but he struggled with it valiantly and constantly as a psychological problem, and he knew how current politics and economics taxed it. He was the first to know. When others fought for liberty alone, he insisted on equality and fraternity also; and he saw that you cannot gain the first if you sacrifice the second or the third. Toward the adjustment of these three our civilization still strives. (pp. 184-85)

> *Mark Schorer, in his* William Blake: The Politics of Vision, *Henry Holt and Company, 1946, 524 p.*

NORTHROP FRYE   (essay date 1947)

[*Frye is a twentieth-century Canadian critic best known for his theories of myth criticism that he employs to explicate a work of literature through an analysis of its archetypal characteristics. One of the first fruits of his "archetypal criticism" was* Fearful Symmetry: A Study of William Blake, *in which he raised Blake studies to a new level by elucidating a unified system of thought behind the Blakean canon, demonstrating the coherence of his mythology, and placing it in a tradition of archetypal symbolism that includes the great works of world literature. The following excerpt from* Fearful Symmetry *focuses on Blake's use of archetypal motifs and symbolism and includes a synopsis of his vision of history from the time of the Fall to the advent of the Apocalypse. Frye occasionally adopts Blake's point of view in the course of explicating the poet's ideas.*]

The Bible is the world's greatest work of art and therefore has primary claim to the title of God's Word. It takes in, in one immense sweep, the entire world of experience from the creation to the final vision of the City of God, embracing heroic saga, prophetic vision, legend, symbolism, the Gospel of Jesus, poetry and oratory on the way. It bridges the gap between a lost Golden Age and the time that the Word became flesh and dwelt among us, and it alone gives us the vision of the life of Jesus in this world. For some reason or other the Jews managed to preserve an imaginative tradition which the Greeks and others lost sight of, and possessed only in disguised and allegorical forms. The Classical poets, says Blake:

> Assert that Jupiter usurped the Throne of his Father, Saturn, & brought on an Iron Age & Begat on Mnemosyne, or Memory, The Greek Muses, which are not Inspiration as the Bible is. Reality was Forgot, & the Vanities of Time & Space only Remember'd & call'd Reality. Such is the Mighty difference between Allegoric Fable & Spiritual Mystery. Let it here be Noted that the Greek Fables originated in Spiritual Mystery & Real Visions, which are lost & clouded in Fable & Allegory, while the Hebrew Bible & the Greek Gospel are Genuine, Preserv'd by the Saviour's Mercy. The Nature of my Work is Visionary or Imaginative; it is an Endeavour to Restore what the Ancients call'd the Golden Age.

We shall come to this distinction between allegory and vision in a moment. There are two obvious inferences from the passage: first, that Blake's poetry is all related to a central myth; and secondly, that the primary basis of this myth is the Bible, so that if we know how Blake read the Bible "in its infernal or diabolical sense" we shall have little difficulty with his symbolism. (pp. 108-09)

The Bible is therefore the archetype of Western culture, and the Bible, with its derivatives, provides the basis for most of our major art: for Dante, Milton, Michelangelo, Raphael, Bach, the great cathedrals, and so on. The most complete form of art is a cyclic vision, which, like the Bible, sees the world between the two poles of fall and redemption. In Western art this is most clearly represented in the miracle-play sequences and encyclopedic symbolism of the Gothic cathedrals, which often cover the entire imaginative field from creation to the Last Judgment, and always fit integrally into some important aspect of it.

However, while "The Old & New Testaments are the Great Code of Art," to regard them as forming a peculiar and exclusive Word of God is a sectarian error. . . . There are many great visions outside the range of the Bible, such as the Icelandic Eddas and the *Bhagavadgita,* almost equally faithful to the central form of the Word of God, and the Bible no less than Classical legends comes from older and more authentic sources. . . . [Blake hints] at older Scriptures still from which the Bible itself has been derived:

> The antiquities of every Nation under Heaven, is no less sacred than that of the Jews. . . . How other antiquities came to be neglected and disbelieved, while those of the Jews are collected and arranged, is an enquiry worthy both of the Antiquarian and the Divine.

This feeling that the Bible does not exhaust the Word of God accounts for the phenomenon of what we may call contrapuntal symbolism, that is, the use of un-Christian mythology, usually Classical, to supplement and round out a Christian poem. (pp. 109-10)

The meaning of history, like the meaning of art, is to be found in its relation to the same great archetype of human existence. The inner form of history is not the same thing as the progress of time: a linear chronicle is a wild fairy tale in which the fate of an empire hangs on the shape of a beauty's nose, or the murder of a noble moron touches off a world war. And no poet concerned with human beings ever bothers to draw an individual as such: he is concerned with selecting the significant aspects of him. Significant in relation to what? In relation to the unity of his conception. But what makes that conception worth conceiving in the first place? Its relation, Blake would say, to the primary Word of God. We say that there is something universal in Quixote, Falstaff, Hamlet, Milton's Satan. But "something universal" is rather vague: just what is universal about them? As soon as we attempt to answer this, we begin in spite of ourselves to elaborate our own versions of the archetypal myth. (p. 111)

[The] primary activity of all communication with the poet is to establish the unity of his poem in our minds. . . . [Blake maintained] that every poem is necessarily a perfect unity. This unity has two aspects: a unity of words and a unity of images. (p. 113)

To the poet the word is a storm-center of meanings, sounds and associations, radiating out indefinitely like the ripples of a pool. It is precisely because of this indefiniteness that he writes poems. The poem is a unity of words in which these radiations have become the links of imaginative cohesion. In a poem the sounds and rhythms of words are revealed more clearly than in ordinary speech, and similarly their meanings have an intensity in poetry that a dictionary can give no hint of.

This respect for the imaginative integrity of poetry is the reason for Blake's distrust of set patterns of meter and rhyme. Only lyrics, and not many of them, can be in a strict stanzaic form: longer works must have much greater fluency if the sound, sense and subject are to make a complete correspondence at all times. (pp. 114-15)

[According to Blake:]

> Fable or Allegory are a totally distinct & inferior kind of Poetry. Vision or Imagination is a Representation of what Eternally Exists, Really & Unchangeably. Fable or Allegory is Form'd by the daughters of Memory. . . . Fable is allegory, but what Critics call The Fable, is Vision itself. The Hebrew Bible & the Gospel of Jesus are not Allegory, but Eternal Vision or Imagination of All that Exists. Note here that Fable or Allegory is seldom without some Vision. Pilgrim's Progress is full of it, the Greek Poets the same; but Allegory & Vision ought to be known as Two Distinct Things. . . .

"Allegory" in the above sense is closely related to the kind of symbolism which is founded on the simile. To say that a hero is *like* a lion is a reference to something else on the same imaginative plane. Subject and object, as in Lockian philosophy, are considered to be only accidentally related. Even an epic simile enriches the symbolism only at the price of digressing from the narrative. The artist, contemplating the hero, searches in his memory for something that reminds him of the hero's courage, and drags out a lion. But here we no longer have two real things: we have a correspondence of abstractions. The hero's courage, not the hero himself, is what the lion symbolizes. And a lion which symbolizes an abstract quality is not a real but a heraldic lion. Some lions are cowardly; some are old and sick; some are cubs; some are female. And it is no use to say that a mature courageous male healthy lion is an "ideal" one: we should need an old and sick lion for an old and sick hero. Whenever we take our eye off the image we slip into abstractions, into regarding qualities, moral or intellectual, as more real than living things. So Blake opposes to "Similitude" the "Identity," the latter being the metaphor which unites the theme and the illustration of it. (pp. 116-17)

All symbolism that deals with qualities has too many bad qualities of its own to be of any use to art. Hence we must not expect to find in Blake any kind of personification, or attempt to give life to an abstraction. When we read in *The Four Zoas* that Los attempts to embrace Enitharmon but that she is jealous and goes over to the embraces of Urizen, it is neither very helpful nor very interesting to translate that as: "Time or Prophecy attempts to overcome Space but Space falls under the domination of Reason." The continuous translation of poetic images into a series of moral and philosophical concepts is what usually passes for the explanation of an allegory. Now a reconstruction of a poem in abstract nouns is not necessarily a false interpretation of part of its meaning. But it is a translation, which means that it assumes the reader's ignorance of the original language. (p. 117)

[Thus] we see that art is neither inferior nor equal to morality and truth, but the synthesis of civilized life in which alone their general laws have any real meaning. Art is neither good nor bad, but a clairvoyant vision of the nature of both, and any attempt to align it with morality, otherwise called bowdlerizing, is intolerably vulgar. "Is not every Vice possible to

Man,'' asked Blake, ''described in the Bible openly?'' Art is neither true nor false, but a clairvoyant vision of the nature of both, and any attempt to estimate its merits by the accuracy with which it reproduces the data of history or science is foolish. A subtler problem, once again, is presented by religion, which claims to be the synthesis of morality and truth we have said that art is, and hence to be superior to it. (pp. 117-18)

[Let us look at] the eleventh plate of *The Marriage of Heaven and Hell* . . . :

> The ancient Poets animated all sensible objects with Gods or Geniuses, calling them by the names and adorning them with the properties of woods, rivers, mountains, lakes, cities, nations, and whatever their enlarged & numerous senses could perceive. . . .
>
> Till a system was formed, which some took advantage of, & enslav'd the vulgar by attempting to realize or abstract the mental deities from their objects: thus began Priesthood;
>
> Choosing forms of worship from poetic tales.
>
> And at length they pronounc'd that the Gods had order'd such things.
>
> Thus men forgot that All deities reside in the human breast.

Now just as the poet is brought up to speak and write one particular language, so he is brought up in the traditions of one particular religion. And his function as a poet is to concentrate on the myths of that religion, and to recreate the original imaginative life of those myths by transforming them into unique works of art. The essential truth of a religion can be presented only in its essential form, which is that of imaginative vision. ''Every thing possible to be believ'd is an image of truth''; in which case everything possible to be believed by the ordinary man is actually to be seen by the visionary. The human imagination knows that man fell: the Biblical story of Adam and Eve is a vision of that fact which has frozen into a myth. Milton's reason told him that that story was ''true''; his imagination told him that it was an image of truth, and stimulated him to recreate it in that form.

The artist *qua* artist neither doubts nor believes his religion: he sees what it means, and he knows how to illustrate it. His religion performs two great services for him. It provides him with a generally understood body of symbols, and it puts into his hands the visionary masterpieces on which it is founded: the Bible particularly, in the case of Christian poets. Many of these latter have petrified into sacred Scriptures supposed now to impart exclusive formulas of salvation rather than vision. It is the business of a poet, however, to see them as poems, and base his own poetry on them as such.

To do this he must bring out more sharply and accurately what the human mind was trying to do when it first created the beings we now call gods. Jupiter is a sky-god: he is a product of the imaginative tendency to see the sky as an old man . . . and not as an abstraction called Heaven. Originally he was conceived as a tyrannical old bully because he represented the imaginative feeling of a hostile mystery in the sky-world. Venus became a beautiful harlot because the imagination sees ''nature'' as a woman and finds her lovely but treacherous. As the original ''organized men,'' or ''Giant forms'' dwindle into gods, the clarity of their relationship to the archetypal myth

becomes blurred, and irrelevant stories and attributes cluster around them. They become increasingly vague and general until, in their final stages, they are mere personifications. . . . (pp. 118-19)

This is why we meet so many new names in Blake and find ourselves reading about Vala and Urizen instead of Venus and Zeus. It may be thought that the more familiar names would make the Prophecies easier, but actually it would make them more difficult. To Venus and Zeus we bring memories and associations rather than a concentrated response, and are thus continually impelled to search outside the poem being read for its meaning. And as no two poets can possibly mean the same thing by ''Venus,'' we should have to go through a long process of discarding misleading associations which the use of a new name prevents at once. Those who think that a greater writer would be less exacting are under an illusion. Some poets, including Homer, Chaucer and Shakespeare, present a smooth readable surface for the lazy reader to slide over: others, including Dante, Spenser and Blake, make it impossible for any reader to overlook the fact that they contain deeper meanings. The wails of protest which the latter group arouses show only that the real profundity of the former group has not been touched. Blake has tried to show us, in his essay on Chaucer, how inadequate it is to bring preconceived notions of medieval monks and friars and merry widows to the *General Prologue*. It follows, of course, that the familiar names we do find in Blake, such as Reuben, Satan and Merlin, do not depend for their meaning on one's memory of Genesis, Milton or Malory. (pp. 119-20)

The Bible is in a very special category compared with other works of art, but it too yields precedence to the imagination. . . . The central form of Christianity is its vision of the humanity of God and the divinity of risen Man, and this, in varying ways, is what all great Christian artists have attempted to recreate. Insofar as they regard the divinity worshiped by Christians as other than human, they produce cloudy and inaccurate visions. Milton's Satan comes off more clearly than his God because he has attempted to equate the latter with abstract goodness and perfection. There is nothing for such a God to do except recite the creed and rationalize the miserable agony of fallen man into a defense of his own virtue. Satan is human and real, a mixture of good and evil, imagination and Selfhood, and therefore has a place in a work of art.

Poetry cannot be made, either of morality and personifications, or of mythology and gods, as long as the artist considers himself to be an illustrator or a transcriber. Spenser . . . had a tendency to personification and Milton to theology, and it is instructive to see in their work how their interest in them is always in inverse proportion to the quality of the writing. Shakespeare and Chaucer follow a sounder poetic policy. They avert their eyes from both gods and abstract nouns, and concentrate on living men and real things, on the particular rather than the general. (pp. 120-21)

This universal perception of the particular applies to natural objects as well as human forms. Ordinarily, our perception of the world is haphazard; it is often unrelated to our simultaneous mental processes, and hence when we use a real thing to ''symbolize'' a state of mind it seems to us only a fancied or arbitrary resemblance. At most, a natural object may symbolize a mental event because it ''corresponds'' to something in the mind. Here we still have Lockian dualism and its simile. But when we speak of the desire of the Selfhood or ego to restrict activity in others, it is rather inadequate to say that a prison is a ''symbol'' of the Selfhood. Prisons exist because Selfhoods do: they are the real things the Selfhood produces, and symbols of it only in that sense. To say that in Blake the sea is a symbol of chaos is incorrect if it assumes that ''chaos'' has any existence except in a number of real things which includes the sea. The sea is the image of chaos. ''Image'' and ''form'' being the same word in Blake, the sea is the form of chaos. As even chaos is only an abstract idea unless it is a perceived form, the sea is the reality of chaos.

And when we realize that everything exists in the form it does because man is fallen God, it becomes evident that all things are the realities of fall and regeneration. Art could not possess its infinite variety if archetypal visions could be represented only by a group of special symbols. In his poem called **''Auguries of Innocence''** Blake says:

> He who the Ox to wrath has mov'd
> Shall never be by Woman lov'd.

This is obviously not true of the state of experience: the title of the poem shows that Blake is talking about a Paradise or Beulah into which men who abuse oxen cannot enter. This ''augury of innocence'' is of the same order of thought as Jesus': ''Blessed are the meek, for they shall inherit the earth.'' This is simple enough, but another couplet from the same poem is more complicated:

> The Bat that flits at close of Eve
> Has left the Brain that won't Believe.

The bat is black and prefers darkness to light. For this reason a superstitious man would see it as something ominous, and a Lockian poet would see it as a symbol of doubt. But to Blake it is neither of these things. Blake means precisely what he says. In human society everything from the Sistine ceiling to thumbscrews owes its form to man's mind and character in one of its various aspects. Similarly the character of everything in nature expresses an aspect of the human mind. We say that a snowflake has a symmetrical design, not because the snowflake has consciously produced it, but because we can see the design. We see that the snowflake has achieved something of which we alone can see the form, and the form of the snowflake is therefore a human form. It is the function of art to illuminate the human form of nature, to present the ferocity of the weasel, the docility of the sheep, the drooping delicacy of the willow, the grim barrenness of the precipice, so that we can see the character of the weasel, the sheep, the willow and the precipice. This vision of character, or total form, is something of course much more inclusive than the words given, which express only aspects of that character, can suggest.

''The man was like a lion'' is a Lockian simile, an attempt to express a human character in natural terms. ''The man was a lion'' is a much more dramatic and effective figure, and more suggestive of their real relationship; but still it is essentially a simile with the word ''like'' omitted. But if we say ''the lion is like a man'' we are getting somewhere, and beginning to achieve the concentrated focus of the artist's vision on the lion which reveals his form to the human eye. As we proceed in our vision, everything positive and real about the lion becomes an aspect of our perception of him, and we can take the next step and say that the lion is entirely a human form, a human creature. All art interprets nature in human terms in this way, so vividly that we hardly dare admit what art tells us about the relation between tears and tempests, joy and sunshine, love and the moon, death and winter, resurrection and spring. The real bat, therefore, is that aspect of the human imagination which prefers darkness to light; and this bat is the exact opposite of the bat which is a symbol of doubt. The famous ''Ghost of the Flea'' similarly shows the human form of that insect.

The painted lion is not alive; the natural lion has not been emancipated into a human order. The painter's task is not a hopelessly quixotic attempt to capture his model's life, but to show its relationship to a universal human order, a Paradise in which lions owe their generation as well as their form to human minds. The most concentrated vision of the lion sees this archetypal human creature in the ferocious wildcat of nature, as Blake's poem on the tiger does. (pp. 121-24)

Those who do not love living things do not love God or Man, as the Ancient Mariner found to his cost. But because some Greek poet loved the nightingale, he created from her the human figure of Philomela, and by doing so passed from love into vision, from a sensitive reaction to nature into the intelligent form of civilized human life, or Paradise. The story of Philomela is not a fantasy suggested by the nightingale, but a vision of the fall of the original human nightingale into its present natural shape. Blake says:

> Think of a white cloud as being holy, you cannot love it; but think of a holy man within the cloud, love springs up in your thoughts, for to think of holiness distinct from man is impossible to the affections.

But if the poet can see the world in a grain of sand, it is because he already has that archetypal vision of ''All that Exists,'' of which everything he sees is a form or image. All Blake's poetry is related to his particular view of this vision, that ''Central Form composed of all other Forms'' which he concedes to Reynolds. Within the huge framework of this central form, certain states of the human mind that created it inevitably appear and take on human lineaments, just as a pantheon crystallizes from a religious vision. Blake's characters are the ''Giant forms'' that religions worship as gods and artists visualize as ''organized men.'' (p. 124)

[Blake held] that in a perfectly imaginative state all individuals are integral units of a race, species or class, related to it as tissues and cells are to a body. This larger unit is not an abstraction or aggregate, but a larger human body or human being. . . . The most inclusive vision possible, then, is to see the universe as One Man, who to a Christian is Jesus. On nearer view Jesus is seen as a ''Council of God'' or group of ''Eternals'' or Patriarchs, seen by ancient prophets as dwelling in a Golden Age of peace and happiness. On still nearer view these patriarchs, the memory of whom survives in the Bible under the accounts of Abraham, Isaac and Jacob, resolve themselves into vast numbers of individual men.

One of these Eternals, named Albion, has fallen. Albion includes, presumably, all the humanity that we know in the world of time and space, though visualized as a single Titan or giant. The history of the world from its creation, which was part of his fall, to the Last Judgment is his sleep. The yet unfallen part of God made seven attempts to awaken him, and in the seventh Jesus himself descended into the world of Generation and began his final redemption.

This myth of a primeval giant whose fall was the creation of the present universe is not in the Bible itself, but has been preserved by the Cabbala in its conception of Adam Kadmon, the universal man who contained within his limbs all heaven and earth, to whom Blake refers. A somewhat more accessible form of the same myth is in the Prose Edda, a cyclic work systematizing the fragmentary apocalyptic poems of the Elder Edda, which to Blake contained traditions as antique and authentic as those of the Old Testament itself. In the sleep of the giant Ymir, the Edda tells us, the earth was made of his flesh, the mountains of his bones, the heavens from his skull, the sea from his blood, the clouds from his brains—this last has a particularly Blakean touch.

The Greeks have also kept a dim memory of a Golden Age before the Fall in their legend of a lost island of Atlantis and of a giant who contained the world in the figure of Atlas, the Titan who bears the world on his back, a perfect image of the fallen Albion with nature outside him and pressing upon him, and of the etymology of that curious word "understanding." Atlantis, according to Plato's *Critias*, was settled by the god Poseidon (possibly Blake's "Ariston"), whose eldest son was Atlas: this corresponds to the English tradition, preserved in Spenser, that Albion, the eponymous ancestor of England, was the son of Neptune. . . . (pp. 125-26)

The fall of Albion included a deluge in which the center of Atlantis was overwhelmed and only the fragments of the British Isles were left. The settlement of America by the English and revolt of America against the dead hand of English tyranny is therefore the dawn of a new age in which Atlantis begins to appear above the waves. In the meantime England still exists in the spiritual world as Atlantis, and Blake's engraved poems are on its mountains.

Frontispiece of Songs of Experience.

There are several accounts of the Fall in Blake . . . , but the invariable characteristic of them is Albion's relapse from active creative energy to passivity. This passivity takes the form of wonder or awe at the world he has created, which in eternity he sees as a woman. The Fall thus begins in Beulah, the divine garden identified with Eden in Genesis. Once he takes the fatal step of thinking the object-world independent of him, Albion sinks into a sleep symbolizing the passivity of his mind, and his creation separates and becomes the "female will" or Mother Nature, the remote and inaccessible universe of tantalizing mystery we now see. Love, or the transformation of the objective into the beloved, and art, or the transformation of the objective into the created, are the two activities pursued on this earth to repair the damage of the Fall, and they raise our state to Beulah and Eden respectively.

On earth the cult of worshiping the independent object or female will takes two chief forms. One is the superstitious reverence for a Mother God, the primitive fear of the sibyl or prophetess whom the Teutons called Vala. This is a symbolic form of nature-worship, and Blake gives the name Vala to nature in his symbolism. The other form is the worship not so much of vegetative nature as of the Queen of Heaven, the remote, mysterious beauty of the starry heavens. This produces on earth the blind devotion to a mistress who is expected to elude and tantalize the lover, the basis of the Troubadour code. The Queen of Heaven's name in Blake is Enitharmon.

The fall of Albion, the company of nations living in the Golden Age, was followed at once by the appearance of the "female will." The story of Adam and Eve in the Bible, which represents a fairly late stage in the Fall, shows sin and death entering the world through a woman: the fact that Adam fell through adoration of Eve is however more clearly brought out in *Paradise Lost*. Of older provenance is the reference in Genesis to the sons of God intermarrying with the daughters of men, more fully elaborated in the Book of Enoch. . . . More important than any of these in Blake's symbolism are those five curious "daughters of Zelopehad" who wander in and out of the Hexateuch looking for a separate female inheritance. One of them is named Tirzah, also the name of an Israelite capital of the Ten Tribes, and therefore a symbol of opposition to Jerusalem, the City of God. This Tirzah is associated with a beautiful woman in the Song of Songs. The five daughters represent the five senses and imply the passive dependence on sense experience which is symbolized in our being born from a mother. This is the meaning of the little poem **"To Tirzah"** which ends the *Songs of Experience.*

The word "emanation" in Blake means the object-world; creature in Eden, female in Beulah, object or nature in Generation, abstraction in Ulro. "Spectre" means the subjective counterpart to this in the two fallen states. Now the spiritual world is to Blake always something civilized, a city or a palace (in the highest imaginative state there would be no difference between a city and a palace, but a house of many mansions) surrounded by the garden or cultivated nature of the Biblical Paradise. Men lose the "opaque" qualities of their minds in higher imaginative states: therefore the spiritual world is a completely integrated body of imaginative men. The Christian Church is the nearest symbol of this on earth; but all visible churches are really part of a political body. This political body is symbolized in the Bible by Jerusalem, which in the Apocalypse becomes the New Jerusalem, the spiritualized church of the imaginative, the liberty of the sons of God united in brotherhood. Jerusalem is therefore the emanation of the awakened Albion. The Jesus who redeemed Albion suffered in the old Jerusalem, and when Albion awakes he will be with Jesus in the new one. The union of Albion and Jersualem suggests a parallelism between English and Hebrew history which runs all through Blake's symbolism, and which underlies the famous hymn beginning **"And did those feet in ancient time."** This is natural, for the Last Judgment is seen by a poet "according to the situation he holds" and Blake's situation was that of an English Christian.

The seven attempts made by God to awaken Albion divide history into seven great periods, each with a dominating religion. These Blake identifies with the "Seven Eyes of God" mentioned in Zechariah, and he gives these "Eyes" the names of Lucier, Moloch, the Elohim, Shaddai, Pachad, Jehovah and Jesus. The "eighth eye" he occasionally speaks of is the apocalypse or awakening of Albion himself.

The Fall was not a single event, but required many generations, and covered the first three "Eyes" of God, described by Hesiod and Ovid as the silver, bronze and iron ages which followed the golden one. The silver age or Lucifer period was a time in which the universe was tearing apart in chaotic disorder, and gigantic energies, sprung from the body of Albion, were fighting for imaginative control of it. Myths of the war of Titans on Zeus in the Classics, and of the Jötuns on Odin in the Eddas, preserve accounts of a war of giants and gods. The giants are rightfully defeated, according to most of our Scriptures, because even the fallen order of nature which the gods established is preferable to chaos. But the feeling that Odin and Zeus are really usurpers can still be traced. Gradually, as the universe took its present form, the weakening human imagination was slowly pushed down and contracted into its present helpless state. Yet gigantic energies still remain in men, imprisoned, but struggling to be free. The revolt of Prometheus nearly destroyed Olympus; and in the Eddas it is prophesied that some day the chained Loki will burst free and begin the destruction of the world. This imprisoned Titanic power in man, which spasmodically causes revolutions, Blake calls Orc. Orc is regarded as an evil being by conventional morality, but in Blake the coming of Jesus is one of his reappearances.

The victory of the sky-god over the Titans means that the universe slowly became more orderly and predictable, and that men, weaker than the Titans but still gigantic, turned to internecine war as history enters the "Moloch" brazen period. The new thundergod of moral law and tyrannical power, whom Blake calls Urizen, was a projection of the death-impulse, and these giants, at the nadir of the Fall, worshiped him in a cult of death consisting largely of human sacrifices. Since then, the belief that somehow it is right to kill men has been the underlying cause of all wars.

This is the period of Druidism, when giants erected huge sacrificial temples like Stonehenge and indulged in hideously murderous orgies. (pp. 126-29)

During the Druid period the world took its present form, which means, as to be is to be perceived, that men's bodies were gradually shrinking down to the point at which they now perceive it. When the present body of man was achieved, the universe necessarily appeared to that body in its present shape. Its present shape is a stabilizing of the object-world, made permanent on a basis of "mathematic form" or mechanical order. Therefore the creation of the present body of man must have been part of this stabilization. Such a creation must have been an "act of Mercy" and the work of the yet unfallen God,

for men by themselves in their fallen state have sunk below the instinct of self-preservation.

This process is described in the Biblical story of Adam and Eve, the Ask and Embla of the Eddas. Adam in Blake is the physical man, the soul in the form of the bodies we now see. He is called the "Limit of Contraction": that is, he has fallen as far as man can fall without losing his imagination altogether and the ability to recreate himself along with it. Along with his creation went the completion of the present universe, which Blake calls the "Mundane Shell," and, probably, the settling of animals and plants into their present natural order of spawning and preying, the aggregate of which Blake calls the "Polypus," a huge wriggling mass of life. This all took place in the third "Eye" of the Elohim. This word is plural in form, and Blake follows tradition in regarding the Elohim as a trinity. But on the principles of Blake's symbolism the trinity would become a collective singular at a little distance, and is so portrayed in the great picture of "The Elohim Creating Adam.". From Adam's time until the Last Judgment, a period for which Blake adopts the conventional figure of six thousand years, the remaining four eras or Eyes of God are divided into twenty-eight phases or "Churches," corresponding to the twenty-eight cities of Albion mentioned by Geoffrey of Monmouth. The world of time and space is a "sublunary" world of cyclic change, and is associated with the twenty-eight-day lunar cycle.

The first twenty of these Churches cover the remainder of the Druid period and the fourth and fifth eyes of God, Shaddai and Pachad. They are known to us only from the genealogical lists of the Bible. Seth, Enoch, Methusaleh, Noah, Shem and the other patriarchs down to Abraham, who are said to have lived for centuries, are not individual men but civilizations or historical cycles which grew up in Africa and Asia.

We know the African culture only from its final decadence in Egypt, with its hieratic ritual, oppressive priestly code, tyrannical monarchy and the "mathematic form" of its pyramids. Apparently the Exodus in the Bible is a reminiscence of the founding of new Druid kingdoms in Asia at the beginning of the Shaddai period. The Noachic deluge, which may be partly a reminiscence of the overwhelming of Atlantis, is also connected with the same event, and symbolically it completes the establishing of the "Limit of Contraction" in Adam. When man falls, nature falls too; and when man is locked into an enfeebled body, born in helpless dependence on a precreated object, and a prey to selfishness, fear and all other symptoms of weakness, nature becomes a prey to sudden accidents and senseless cataclysms. (pp. 129-31)

[The] great "Druid" civilizations of Asia, particularly Mesopotamia, produced magnificent works of art and literature in their prime: again, history records only their late degenerate period. Of the literature, only the Old Testament survives. We can get some idea of what their art was like from the Greeks, however, for the Greek Muses were daughters of Memory, which means that Classical culture is a parasitic growth on the earlier Asiatic ones, and Classical mythology contains many echoes, usually misunderstood by its compilers, of earlier and more authentic visions:

> No man can believe that either Homer's Mythology, or Ovid's, were the production of Greece or of Latium; neither will any one believe, that the Greek statues, as they are called, were the invention of Greek Artists; perhaps the Torso is the only original work remaining;

all the rest are evidently copies, though fine ones, from greater works of the Asiatic Patriarchs.

At any rate, one should give Blake credit for realizing that the marble mediocrities dug up in that age of Winckelmann were copies of something. The Trojan war symbolizes the taking-over of Asiatic culture by the Greeks. The beings of the earlier myths, which appeared on the walls of Solomon's Temple and were called Cherubim, were recognized as imaginative creations: the gods of the Greeks, derived from them, were conceived as independent of man:

> Visions of these eternal principles or characters of human life appear to poets, in all ages; the Grecian gods were the ancient Cherubim of Phoenicia; but the Greeks, and since them the Moderns, have neglected to subdue the gods of Priam. These gods are visions of the eternal attributes, or divine names, which, when erected into gods, become destructive to humanity. They ought to be the servants, and not the masters of man, or of society. They ought to be made to sacrifice to Man, and not man compelled to sacrifice to them; for when separated from man or humanity, who is Jesus the Saviour, the vine of eternity, they are thieves and rebels, they are destroyers.

Troy in Blake therefore stands for the abstraction of the "fairies of Albion" into "Gods of the heathen." Hence the conquest of England by the Trojan Brutus symbolizes the final collapse of the great Druidic civilizations of antiquity, paralleling the Platonic account of the defeat of Atlantis by Athens. . . . The Trojan war is also, because based on the love of a whore, the source of all the chivalric female-will worship of the Middle Ages. After it, imaginative animism almost drops out of culture and a belief in abstract gods reigns supreme over most of the earth, the former surviving among the Druids only as esoteric traditions preserved by the caste of bards.

Before this had happened, however, the Jehovah cycle of history had begun with the founding of a new Hebrew culture, presented in the Bible as the escape of a patriarch (really a "Church") called Abraham, from Chaldea. The essential feature of this was the giving-up of human sacrifice in favor of animal sacrifice, symbolized in the story of the substitution of a ram for Isaac as a victim:

> Adam was a Druid, and Noah; also Abraham was called to succeed the Druidical age, which began to turn allegoric and mental signification into corporeal command, whereby human sacrifice would have depopulated the earth.

So far, so good; but truth precipitates error, and in every culture great imaginative work is done in the face of a consolidating tyranny. The growth of the Classical civilization was only part of this negative response to Abraham: the rest came in the establishment of a moral law and a ceremonial worship of a thunderous tyrant by Moses, the twenty-second "Church," completed by the integration of this into a political tyranny by David and Solomon, who represent the twenty-third.

According to Swedenborg, the Hexateuch is a compilation of earlier and later documents. The first eleven chapters of Genesis, down to Abraham, are ancient and belong to an original *Ur-Bibel;* but most of the Exodus account is drawn from earlier books, now lost. These consisted of a history and a prophecy, referred to in Numbers xxi, 14 and 27; also the "Book of Jasher." The Exodus account as we have it is therefore somewhat confused, and an ancient prophetic poem has been rewritten from a priestly point of view. The Passover incident represents, like the Isaac story, the decline of human sacrifice, and the Exodus itself seems to go back to the emergence of an Asiatic civilization which probably took place nearer the time of Adam. But the real basis of the Exodus story was a poem in which Egypt symbolized Ulro and the Promised Land Eden. In that poem the imaginative energy which achieved the entry into Eden, the pillar of fire, was called Joshua, which means Jesus. . . . The pillar of cloud, the power of tyranny which kept the Hebrews wandering in a wilderness trying to follow their elusive Sinaitic ghost (Urizen) was Egypt itself, which Moses represented. What is now given us as a ferocious butchery of Canaanite tribes was in the original the annihilation of the bogies of the Selfhood. . . . This interpretation of the Exodus is fundamental to Blake's symbolism: the work which throws most light on Blake here is the Wisdom of Solomon, in which the plague of darkness, for instance, is treated as a symbol of the brooding terrors of the opaque Selfhood in language very close to Blake:

> For while they thought that they were unseen in their secret sins, they were sundered one from another by a dark curtain of forgetfulness, stricken with terrible awe, and sore troubled by spectral forms.

With the coming of Jesus or the seventh Eye the finale of history begins. The first consolidation of tyranny established to meet this new threat was the "Church Paul," absorbing Jesus into the old Pharisaic legalism. Next comes his further absorption into the Classical tyranny, represented by the Church Constantine, then the establishment of the female-will culture of the Middle Ages, the chivalric code and Madonna-worship associated with Charlemagne and Arthur. Finally comes the twenty-seventh Church in Luther and the Renaissance, the tyrannical precipitate of which is Deism. These twenty-seven "Heavens," as they are called, roll round us in a circle forever, and Deism is spiritually as far from Eden as Babylon or Egypt or Rome ever were.

Only with the twenty-eighth, the last phase associated with Milton, does the apocalypse get under way. . . . Milton himself represents an imaginative penetration of the spiritual world unequalled in Christian poetry, and Blake, especially in his poem on Milton, attempts to clarify his vision still further. The apocalypse proper begins with the French and American revolutions, when the revolutionary iconoclasm of Orc, which was made manifest in Jesus, returns to the world to complete the seventh cycle. Then, as St. John says:

> In the days of the voice of the seventh angel, when he shall begin to sound, the mystery of God should be finished, as he hath declared to his servants the prophets.

Opposed to this is the development of empiric thought denying the reality of all states above Generation, which only needs a little pushing until it becomes a materialist tyranny so complete that humanity will finally be able to see all its ramifications as part of a single unified falsehood, an epiphany of Satan. (pp. 131-34)

Northrop Frye, in his Fearful Symmetry: A Study of William Blake, *Princeton University Press, 1947, 462 p.*

BERNARD BLACKSTONE   (essay date 1949)

[*Blackstone explicates* Milton *as an attempt by the poet to rectify Milton's errors as an "arch-promulgator" of rationalism.*]

Milton is not an easy poem to understand. It is the product of an intense struggle in Blake's own mind, a struggle complicated by his relations with Hayley at Felpham, but concerned chiefly with the question that always haunted him: how had it come about that England, once the seat of inspiration and vision, was now the dispenser of rationalism to Europe—the land of Bacon, Newton and Locke? It is with this problem that Blake is going to grapple . . . in *Milton*. And he is going to use Milton himself, the poet of vision writing in the century of experiment, to exteriorise this problem.

As always, the situation has its several aspects: historical, religious, psychological. In the case of Milton the historical aspect—and more especially the biographical details—takes on an unwonted importance for Blake. In many respects he could identify himself with the seventeenth-century poet. He, too, felt his work to be 'doctrinal to a nation'; he, too, felt directly inspired; he too, was an apostle of liberty in an age of restrictions. And—to come down to the more personal question—he had known something of Milton's disappointment in an early marriage, and something of Milton's revolt. (p. 134)

[Blake] recognized in Milton the greatest of poets . . . ; but he also saw in Milton the arch-promulgator of pernicious errors. Blake's symbolic works may be regarded as a rewriting of Milton's epics with an inversion, or subtle elaboration, of the rôles of passion and reason, and with a deeper meaning given to Christ and the Holy Ghost. (p. 147)

It is noticeable that *Milton* contains far more direct Biblical allusion than we find in *The Four Zoas*. The Bible is the only Sublime. 'Shakespeare & Milton were both curb'd by the general malady & infection from the silly Greek & Latin slaves of the Sword.' And this infection of rationalism continues. [In the "Preface" to *Milton*] Blake calls upon the 'Young Men of the New Age' to revolt and oppose the false doctrines which are taught in 'the Camp, the Court & the University'; he implores the artists and sculptors to be true to their own imaginations, 'those Worlds of Eternity in which we shall live for ever in JESUS OUR LORD.' Then follows the famous poem, **"And did those feet in ancient time Walk upon England's mountains green?"**—a supreme expression of Blake's determination to go on thinking and writing for his country's good. (pp. 147-48)

'. . . now no longer divided nor at war with myself . . . ,' Blake had written to Hayley in 1804, at the time he was making a final revision of *Milton*. This inner unity becomes apparent in the poem. It is more controlled; it has structure; it is free from the 'torments of jealousy' which gave rise to such wild and violent imagery in the earlier epic. The imagery of *Milton*, indeed, is drawn to a surprising degree from the world of nature; observed, it is true, not with but through the eye, yet observed in its minutest particulars. It might almost be called the epic of Nature, seen *sub specie aeternitatis*. For it was Nature that Milton rejected, when he rejected his sixfold emanation, his three wives and three daughters, and the redemption of Nature is a corollary of Milton's self-annihilation. Hence the sheer joy in the life of flowers, birds and insects which runs through the poem. (p. 148)

Structurally, the poem consists of a redemption narrative interspersed with long passages of mystical teaching. The narrative is about Milton, who while on earth . . . had held wrong views of sex and nature, and was unkind to his womenfolk, but has repented of his error during the hundred years he has spent in heaven, and is anxious to atone for it. He is separated from his sixfold emanation, who wanders in the abyss in torment. Now at last he casts off his spectrous reason, the power which has dominated him hitherto—and descends again into the world of vegetation to redeem his emanation.

We note at the very beginning that this is to be a milder book than either *The Four Zoas* or *Jerusalem*. Blake involves as his Muses the 'Daughters of Beulah,' the softly feminine principle which in Eden serves as a repose for the warriors wearied with their intellectual combats, and which in earthly existence is marriage itself. But in *Jerusalem* it will be the Saviour, the Divine Vision, who is invoked, and who dictates the very words of the song. There is a profound difference of emphasis. The action of *Milton*, important as it is, is secondary to the supreme theme of man's resurrection into unity.

'Come into my hand,' so Blake calls to the Daughters of Beulah, the emanations of Eternity,

> By your mild power descending down the Nerves of my
>   right arm
> From out the portals of my Brain, where by your
>   ministry
> The Eternal Great Humanity Divine planted his Paradise
> And in it caus'd the Spectres of the Dead to take sweet
>   forms
> In likeness of himself. . . .

'By your ministry. . . .' Blake, now no longer divided, can look on sexual generation as a good, a *beatum peccatum*, as indeed it is in comparison with the nothingness man might have suffered after the Fall. It is Milton's error not to have recognised this. 'O blessed Generation, image of Regeneration,' Blake cries later. In his poetry he has accepted Nature, though in his prose he may still think it necessary to be explicit against the material creation.

Then we have the theme stated:

> Say first! what mov'd Milton, who walk'd about in
>   Eternity
> One hundred years, pond'ring the intricate mazes of
>   Providence,
> Unhappy tho' in heav'n—he obey'd, he murmur'd not,
>   he was silent
> Viewing his Sixfold Emanation scatter'd thro' the deep
> In torment—To go into the deep her to redeem &
>   himself perish?
> That cause at length mov'd Milton to this unexampled
>   deed,
> A Bard's prophetic Song! . . .

The Bard, who may in fact be identified with Blake, sings the familiar story of the Fall, the Incarnation of Urizen and the Division of Los, as we have read it in *The Book of Urizen* and *The Four Zoas*. . . . There follows the equally familiar story of the building of Golgonooza and the birth of Satan. The song continues with the account of a quarrel between Satan and Palamabron, in which Blake introduces in symbolic dress the history of his contests with Hayley during the Felpham period. (pp. 148-50)

The further details of the Bard's song are either too personal, or too repetitive of the action of *The Four Zoas*, to need setting forth here. When the song has ended,

there was great murmuring in the Heavens of
Albion
Concerning Generation & the Vegetative power &
concerning
The Lamb the Saviour. . . .

Then Milton rises in the midst of the assembly, and avows his
resolution to return to earth:

He took off the robe of the promise & ungirded himself
from the oath of God.
And Milton said: "I go to Eternal Death! The Nations
still
Follow after the detestable Gods of Priam, in pomp
Of warlike selfhood contradicting and blaspheming,
When will the Resurrection come to deliver the sleeping
body
From corruptibility? O when, Lord Jesus, wilt thou
come?
Tarry no longer, for my soul lies at the gates of death.
I will arise and look forth for the morning of the grave:
I will go down to the sepulcher to see if morning
breaks:
I will go down to self annihilation and eternal death,
Lest the Last Judgment come & find me unannihilate
And I be seiz'd & giv'n into the hands of my
Selfhood." . . .

He accuses himself of sin in having deserted his emanation. . . .
Then he plunges into the Abyss.

On the verge of Beulah he enters his Shadow, and goes onward
into the world of generation. First he sees Albion outstretched
on the Rock of Ages, with the Sea of Time and Space rolling
over him. Then, says Blake,

Then first I saw him in the Zenith as a falling star
Descending perpendicular, swift as the swallow or
swift:
And on my left foot falling on the tarsus, enter'd there:
But from my left foot a black cloud redounding spread
over Europe. . . .

The left foot is a symbol of the material world. Milton proceeds
on his way through the recesses of the Mundane Shell towards
Los and Enitharmon. The Shadowy Female (Vala) laments,
and Urizen emerges 'from his Rocky Form & from his Snows'
to bar Milton's passage. They fight, and Urizen tries to freeze
Milton's brain with the icy waters of reason,

But Milton took of the red clay of Succoth, moulding it
with care
Between his palms and filling up the furrows of many
years,
Beginning at the feet of Urizen, and on the bones
Creating new flesh on the Demon cold. . . .

Against his will, reason is being endued with the warm flesh
and blood of humanity. This 'moulding' is the eternal task of
the poet, the maker. Moreover, in descending to redeem his
sexual portion, Milton also redeems his spectre, and creates
the whole man which he had never been before.

Now Rehab and Tirzah—moral virtue and Natural Religion—
enter the lists against Milton: they mock at Jerusalem and the
Lamb of God; but Milton pays no attention. He goes on with
his work on Urizen. And Albion begins to turn on his couch,

Feeling the electric flame of Milton's awful precipitate
descent. . . .

Los, remembering an ancient prophecy that Milton would descend, goes in search of him.

When Milton enters Blake's left foot, Blake is enabled to 'see
into the life of things,' to have a new vision of the universe.
He now becomes one man with Los,

And all this Vegetable World appear'd on my left Foot
As a bright sandal form'd immortal of precious stones
& gold.
I stooped down & bound it on to walk forward thro'
Eternity. . . .

Los reveals to Blake the glorious secret that not one moment
of time is lost, 'nor one Event of Space unpermanent.' He
greets the coming of Milton as the sign that six thousand years
are passed away and the end is approaching. . . . The First
Book ends with an exposition of Blake's view on the nature
of time and space.

Book the Second opens in Beulah, 'a place where Contrarieties
are equally True.' Beulah is a feminine world, as we have
already seen, built around Great Eternity by the mercy of God:
a world where the Emanations, who cannot bear the too terrible
joy and sports of intellect, find refuge, and where Man also
may repose awhile from his mental activities. Here dwells
Ololon, who appears to be identified with Milton's sixfold
emanation, though in an earlier text we have seen it stated that
Milton's emanation is wandering solitary through the void. She
prepares to descend, as Milton had done, into generation; and
'all the Living Creatures of the Four Elements' wail. These
living creatures are the Zoas, who have partaken of mortality,
and preach a materialistic doctrine which in the succeeding
paragraph of the epic is opposed by a spiritual doctrine of
creation. This opposition of the two views of nature is a principal theme of *Milton*. . . . [We then] come to the charge of
the Divine Voice to Vala or Nature, stressing the truth that
natural beauty was first formed to be a refreshment to the spirit
of fallen Man, but has hardened into a system opaque to the
Divine Vision.

Ololon now descends from Beulah . . . and enters the Mundane
Shell, surrounded by the four ruined universes of Urizen, Los,
Tharmas and Luvah. She contrasts the state of physical war in
the generative world with the spiritual combats of Eternity,
and bewails the frozen bulk of Nature. . . . Having entered the
Polypus, or Ulro, Ololon appears as 'a Virgin of twelve years'
before Blake in his cottage garden at Felpham, whither he has
been taken by Los from Lambeth in order to write this account
of eternal happenings. Ololon tells Blake that she has come to
seek Milton. Milton's Spectre, i.e. his false rational power
which he has now cast off but which is still active, hears this
and appears, too, before Blake. In the form of this Spectre he
sees all the false gods and churches of the world.

Now, however, because Milton has separated himself from his
Spectre, the process of self-annihilation can begin. Milton addresses his Spectre thus:

"Satan! my Spectre! I know my power thee to
annihilate
And be a greater in thy place & be thy Tabernacle,
A covering for thee to do thy will, till one greater
comes
And smites me as I smote thee & becomes my
covering.
Such are the Laws of thy false Heav'ns; but Laws of
Eternity
Are not such; know thou, I come to Self Annihilation."
. . .

The title page of The Song of Los.

Blake, we see, is continuing with his purpose of rewriting *Paradise Lost*, of rectifying Milton's error. Just as in Book I he has shown that Satan fell, not from pride and ambition as Milton had said, but from hypocrisy, moral judgement and officious kindness, so now he is demonstrating that the laws of Eternity do not demand Satan's punishment and relegation to the pit, but watch over him and protect him until the time comes for him to be delivered. Milton continues:

> "Such are the Laws of Eternity, that each shall
>   mutually
> Annihilate himself for others' good, as I for thee.
> Thy purpose & the purpose of thy Priests & of thy
>   Churches
> Is to impress on men the fear of death, to teach
> Trembling & fear, terror, constriction, abject
>   selfishness.
> Mine is to teach Men to despise death & to go on
> In fearless majesty annihilating Self, laughing to scorn
> Thy Laws & terrors, shaking down thy Synagogues as
>   webs.
> I come to discover before Heav'n & Hell the Self
>   righteousness
> In all its Hypocritic turpitude, opening to every eye
> These wonders of Satan's holiness, shewing to the Earth
> The Idol Virtues of the Natural Heart, & Satan's Seat
> Explore in all its Selfish Natural Virtue, & put off
> In self annihilation all that is not of God alone,
> To put off Self & all I have, ever & ever. Amen." . . .

Satan defies Milton, asserting that he is God alone, opposed to Mercy and Jesus the Divine Delusion. But at this point the Trumpets of the Last Judgement sound, calling Albion to awake; he does so, and attempts to walk, but is not strong enough and has to sink down again upon his couch. For *Milton* is not the record of the universal Last Judgement, but only of a particular one, that of Milton and through Milton of Blake himself.

Next we have the meeting of Milton and Ololon. Ololon cannot yet completely understand Milton's self-annihilation: she is afraid that in its course the 'little ones, the Children of Jerusalem' (i.e. the minute particulars of human life) will be destroyed also. But Milton rebukes her and gives a clear exposition of doctrine:

>   turning toward Ololon in terrible majesty
>   Milton
> Replied: "Obey thou the Words of the Inspired Man.
> All that can be annihilated must be annihilated
> That the Children of Jerusalem may be saved from
>   slavery.
> There is a Negation, & there is a Contrary:
> The Negation must be destroy'd to redeem the
>   Contraries.
> The Negation is the Spectre, the Reasoning Power in
>   Man:
> This is a false Body, an Incrustation over my Immortal
> Spirit, a Selfhood which must be put off & annihilated
>   alway." . . .

This statement is important and we must look more closely at its meaning. Ololon, we remember, is the emanation: that is, in each individual she is the feminine portion, representing the softer emotions and sentiments and particularly the instinct of self-preservation. She is that part of a man which fears that he will, in seeking for God alone, throw away all his human happiness and be left 'naked to laughter.' It is this shrinking fear which holds back many a man from the unitive life. But Milton teaches her that this fear is without foundation: only that which is annihilable can be annihilated, and what is annihilable is no part of reality. It is the outer covering or mask, the false shell which each man builds up around himself with the passing of years—the shell which hides his true nature even from himself, but to which, nevertheless, he clings with trembling fear. It is only when this shell has been sloughed off, this mask discarded, that the true joy can spring, the joy of being what one really is. Only then can the Children of Jerusalem, the minute particulars of Man's real identity, be redeemed from slavery. Ololon is confounding the negation with the contrary. The negation is the Spectre, the cold uncreative reason; the contraries are the ultimate paradoxes of a man's being, which ensure the springs of his energy. The selfhood, Blake is never tired of insisting, is a nothingness: yet it is to this nothingness that we sacrifice, perpetually, our happiness.

The poem ends with a vision of the Saviour coming, 'round his limbs The Clouds of Ololon folded as a Garment dipped in blood'; the Four Zoas sound their trumpets, and at this Blake's soul leaves its union with Milton and

>   return'd into its mortal state
>   To Resurrection & Judgment in the Vegetable Body,
>   And my sweet Shadow of Delight stood trembling by
>   my side. . . .

All things are now ready for 'the Great Harvest & Vintage of the Nations.' (pp. 150-55)

Bernard Blackstone, in his English Blake, *Cambridge at the University Press, 1949, 455 p.*

MARGARET BOTTRALL (essay date 1950)

[*In the excerpt below, Bottrall outlines the emergence of the theme of Christian redemption in Blake's later works.*]

There is no recorded event in Blake's life to account for the change in symbolism which distinguishes the books written after the year 1795 from their predecessors. His whole religious attitude, however, underwent a change at this period. From the time when he began to work on *Vala*, (known in its revised form as *The Four Zoas*), his mythological web is reinforced with christian symbols. Whereas in *The Marriage of Heaven and Hell* he affirms that "God only Acts and Is, in existing Beings or Men", in the later books he is concerned to establish the providential action of God, to show the creation as "an act of mercy", and to trace the redemptive scheme as something transcending, though including, the efforts of the individual soul towards fulfilment. Some crisis, felt perhaps as a defeat, separates the Lambeth books from their successors.

He had sought previously to account for the imperfection of human society by other hypotheses than man's bias towards sin; but from the time when he began to write *The Four Zoas* until the end of his life, fallen man's need for redemption becomes his main theme. In this and the subsequent prophetic books, man is shown contending with "the blind world-rulers of this life, with the spirit of evil in things heavenly" and also as rent by the warring elements in his own personality. Unaided he cannot achieve his own salvation; and what is new is the intervention, among the titanic figures of Los, Urizen and the rest, of the figure of Jesus. Blake is now concerned with the redemptive action of Christ, both in its eternal aspect and in its impact on the individual and on society.

He sees the regeneration of man as a drama played out upon two planes. There is the psychological reintegration of the personality symbolised by the reconciliation of the four Zoas, and there is the birth, death and resurrection of the Lamb of God which, mysteriously but indispensably, makes that reintegration possible.

> Daughter of Beulah, Sing
> (Man's) fall into Division & his Resurrection to Unity:
> His fall into the Generation of decay & death, & his
> Regeneration by the Resurrection from the dead.
>
> (pp. 47-8)

Undoubtedly the prophetic books, with their incessant turmoils, fissions and debates, mirror the conflicts of his own spirit. Fr. W. P. Witcutt [see Additional Bibliography] in his recent study of Blake has convincingly shown how the Zoas correspond to the four functions of the psyche classified by Jung as Thought, Feeling, Sensation and Intuition, how the Spectre corresponds to the Shadow and the Emanation to the Anima of Jung's terminology. But fantastically subjective though the prophetic writings are, they are nevertheless concerned with metaphysical and ethical problems. Blake's poems and pictures were not meant merely to record experiences but to convey truths; and this must be my justification for stressing those themes which are bound up with Blake's christianity.

In *The Four Zoas* the drama of the Zoas is encompassed by the greater drama in which the Lamb of God is the protagonist. Blake's apocalyptic imagination, fed by his knowledge of occult writings, caused him to present the figure of Jesus as one among a great company of immortal beings, over whom the Council of God presides. . . . He is referred to as the Good Shepherd, the Eternal Saviour, the Rock of Ages; but since his eternal function is to redeem through self-sacrifice, it is the sacrificial title of the Lamb of God that Blake most frequently uses.

The necessity for the Incarnation as a stage in the redemption of man is stated by Los in unequivocal terms:

> Refusing to behold the Divine Image which all behold
> And live thereby, (Man) is sunk down into a deadly sleep.
> But we, immortal in our own strength, survive by stern debate
> Till we have drawn the Lamb of God into a mortal form.
> And that he must be born is certain, for One must be All,
> And comprehend within himself all things both small & great.
>
> (pp. 48-9)

In his sacrificial capacity as Lamb of God he is distinct from all the other Eternals, yet he is the unifying principle of all immortal beings.

> Then those in great Eternity met in the Council of God
> As one Man, for contracting their Exalted Senses
> They behold Multitude, or Expanding they behold as one,
> As One Man all the Universal family; & that One Man
> They call Jesus the Christ, & they in him & he in them
> Live in Perfect harmony. . . .
>
> (p. 49)

Blake's vision is of Christ, the Divine Humanity, active in wisdom and love "before all worlds". In his view, "Eternity exists and all things in Eternity, independent of Creation which was an act of Mercy", and therefore God's Humanity precedes and supersedes his Incarnation. He attempts to show how, beyond this world of time and space, the unifying spirit of Love is at work. The redemption of the world by our Lord Jesus Christ is seen as a pure act of love, not as a sort of divine improvisation occasioned by the Fall, to reconcile God with sinful man.

> "Assume the dark Satanic body in the Virgin's womb,
> O Lamb Divine! it cannot thee annoy. O pitying one,
> Thy pity is from the foundation of the World, & thy Redemption
> Begun Already in Eternity".
>
> (pp. 49-50)

Jesus appears in the guise of suffering love:

> Eternity appear'd above them as One Man infolded
> In Luvah's robes of blood & bearing all his afflictions. . . .

In this guise he can be loved and worshipped. The Daughters of Beulah, in an episode derived from the story of Lazarus, implore him to raise from the dead Albion, the prototype of Man:

> Lord Saviour, if thou hadst been here our brother had not died,
> And now we know that whatsoever thou wilt ask of God
> He will give it thee; for we are weak women & dare not lift
> Our eyes to the Divine pavilions; therefore in mercy thou
> Appearest cloth'd in Luvah's garments that we may behold thee

And live. . . .

In Jesus the Light is become intelligible, God is manifest as merciful and compassionate:

> The Divine Mercy
> Steps beyond and Redeems Man in the Body of
>   Jesus. . . .
>
> (p. 50)

The absolute necessity for a Saviour is emphasised by the hymn which Blake puts into the mouth of "the sons of Eden round the Lamb of God", who sing:

> "Glory, Glory, Glory to the holy Lamb of God
> Who now beginneth to put off the dark Satanic body.
> Now we behold redemption. Now we know that life
>   Eternal
> Depends alone upon the Universal hand . . .".

But though there had to be a divine saviour to waken fallen man to his true inheritance by dying for him so that "death Eternal is put off Eternally", yet the true significance of Christ's redemptive mission can only be understood when it is seen to typify the eternal redemptive process in which all men are involved because they are a part of universal humanity—part of Christ's mystical body. Blake in his insistence on Jesus as the One Man, Divine Humanity, stresses this again and again. (p. 51)

The world into which the Lamb of God has to descend is a world full of evil, given over to sin, warfare, misery and death; and the mortal body is spoken of as something abhorrent—"the dark Satanic body". This is in strange contrast to Blake's earlier affirmation that "everything that lives is holy"; but as he grew older his preoccupation with the reality of the spiritual led him towards the heresy that this world is an evil illusion. He did not associate the human quality in man with the body but with the spirit, and there he was soundly christian. But when he reckoned mortality to be a disguise for true humanity, he thought as a gnostic.

Whereas for the orthodox christian, the Incarnation is the unique example of a perfect union between two disparate natures, the divine and the human, for Blake the assumption of a mortal body by Jesus appeared as the supreme example of loving condescension on the part of the One Man, that Eternal Divine Humanity from whom we all proceed, towards whom we all tend, and in whom we are all united. (pp. 51-2)

Blake saw in the crucifixion of Jesus, contrived by the chief priests and rulers of the people, the extreme and most appalling example of the exercise of legalism.

> . . . Jesus, the image of the invisible God
> Became its prey, a curse, an offering and an atonement
> For Death Eternal. . . .

Man's moral and intellectual blindness, symbolised by the tree of mystery, was the instrument of Christ's death; and in every example of moral oppression and vindictive punishment Blake saw a renewed crucifixion of Jesus.

After the account of the crucifixion in *The Four Zoas*, his imagination seems to have veered away from the contemplation of the divine sacrifice; for what follows is a condemnation of the Church for its worship of the dead Lord and, by implication, for its neglect of the living Christ. Even Jerusalem, symbol of enlightened love, takes fright at the sight of the dead body:

> Jerusalem saw the Body dead upon the Cross. She fled
>   away,
> Saying, "Is this Eternal Death? Where shall I hide from
>   Death?
> Pity me, Los! pity me, Urizen! & let us build
> A Sepulcher & worship Death in fear while yet we live:
> Death! God of All! from whom we rise, to whom we
>   all return:
> And let all Nations of the Earth worship at the
>   Sepulcher
> With Gift & Spices, with lamps rich emboss'd, jewels
>   & gold." . . .
>
> (pp. 52-3)

It is the same line of thought as we find in *The Everlasting Gospel:*

> And thus with wrath he did subdue
> The Serpent Bulk of Nature's dross,
> Till He had nail'd it to the Cross.
> He took on Sin in the Virgin's Womb,
> And put it off on the Cross & Tomb
> To be Worship'd by the Church of Rome. . . .

But though it is the Resurrection rather than the Crucifixion which reveals the worthlessness of "Nature's dross", Blake gives no account in *The Four Zoas* of the Resurrection of Jesus. There is only the simple episode, at the beginning of the ninth night, when Jesus risen appears to Los and Enitharmon. . . . Blake repeatedly expresses his conviction that "Death Eternal is put off Eternally" through the putting-on and putting-off of the mortal body by the Eternal Saviour, and his actual rising from the tomb must have seemed to him such a foregone conclusion that he did not even attempt to recount it.

The Vision of the Redemption is followed by the Last Judgment, and the ninth night of *The Four Zoas* contains some of the finest writing in the entire poem. It was a subject that exercised the strongest fascination upon Blake; he expended in later years immense pains on the composition of a picture of this "Stupendous Vision", and elucidated the picture in a series of highly interesting notes. In *The Four Zoas* the dead come to judgment, and the Zoas themselves are eventually reconciled and restored to their primal unity. A strange feast is celebrated; the bread and wine are made from human elements—the bread of knowledge, the wine of passion, both wrought from human suffering under the power of the Eternals. At the feast the host is The Eternal Man, sometimes called The Regenerate Man:—

> And One of the Eternals spoke. All was silent at the
>   feast.
> "Man is a Worm; wearied with joy, he seeks the caves
>   of sleep
> Among the Flowers of Beulah, in his selfish cold
>   repose
> Forsaking Brotherhood & Universal Love, in selfish
>   clay
> Folding the pure wings of his mind, seeking the places
>   dark
> Abstracted from the roots of Science; then inclos'd
>   around
> In walls of Gold we cast him like a Seed into the Earth
> Till times & spaces have pass'd over him; duly every
>   morn

We visit him, covering with a Veil the immortal seed;
With windows from the inclement sky we cover him, &
    with walls
And hearths protect the selfish terror, till divided all
In families we see our shadows born, & thence we
    know
That Man subsists by Brotherhood & Universal Love.
We fall on one another's necks, more closely we
    embrace.
Not for ourselves; but for the Eternal Family we live.
Man liveth not by Self alone, but in his brother's face
Each shall behold the Eternal Father & love & joy
    abound''.
So spoke the Eternal at the Feast; they embrac'd the
    New born Man,
Calling him Brother, image of the Eternal Father; they
    sat down
At the immortal tables, sounding loud their instruments
    of joy,
Calling the Morning into Beulah; the Eternal Man
    rejoic'd.

(pp. 53-4)

In this passage are combined a variety of themes highly characteristic of Blake. There is the insistence on selfishness and apathy as basic qualities in unregenerate man; the same qualities as are suggested in *The Marriage of Heaven and Hell,*

For man has closed himself up, till he sees all things
    thro'
narrow chinks of his cavern. . . .

Wilful blindness is suggested as a cause of the Fall in a passage already quoted:

"Refusing to behold the Divine Image which all behold
And live thereby, he is sunk down into a deadly
    sleep.'' . . .

There is also the suggestion that an eternal providence watches over man in his blindness, irrespective of his merit, and that redemption is something intended from all eternity. (p. 55)

The third theme is the most fundamental to Blake's religious thinking; the conviction that

Man subsists by Brotherhood and Universal Love . . .
Man liveth not by Self alone, but in his Brother's face
Each shall behold the Eternal Father, & love & joy
    abound.

This is implicit in the *Song of Innocence* and it reaches the climax of its development in his last epic, *Jerusalem.* There we find Albion fleeing in solitary selfishness,

Turning from Universal Love, petrific as he went . . .
                but mild, the Saviour follow'd him,
Displaying the Eternal Vision, the Divine Similitude,
In loves and tears of brothers, sisters, sons, fathers &
    friends,
Which if Man ceases to behold, he ceases to exist,
Saying, "Albion! Our wars are wars of life, & wounds
    of love
With intellectual spears, & long wing'd arrows of
    thought.
Mutual in one another's love and wrath all renewing
We live as One Man; for contracting our infinite senses
We behold multitude, or expanding, we behold as one,
As One Man all the Universal Family, and that One
    Man

We call Jesus the Christ; and he in us, and we in him
Live in perfect Harmony in Eden, the land of life,
Giving, receiving, and forgiving each other's
    trespasses.'' . . .

It is an echo of the passage from *The Four Zoas* describing the Council of God; but the expansion of the conception is as remarkable as the echo; for Blake's imagination, not resting in the thought of all the eternal powers unified in Jesus, leapt to identify with Jesus the whole of redeemed humanity. (pp. 55-6)

Blake's religious thinking is always centred on the inseparability of God and Man. What distinguishes his later from his earlier approach to christianity is his acceptance of the necessity for a divine Saviour. By temperament he was inclined to be a Pelagian; the ever-renewed struggles of the Zoas reflect his own unending interior struggles to achieve his own salvation; but he was driven to the conclusion that no man can be wholly his own saviour. In *Jerusalem* the need for grace is stated in the strongest possible terms:

    . . . However great & glorious, however loving
And merciful the Individuality, however high
Our palaces and cities and however fruitful are our
    fields,
In Selfhood, we are nothing, but fade away in
    morning's breath.
Our mildness is nothing: the greatest mildness we can
    use
Is incapable and nothing: none but the Lamb of God
    can heal

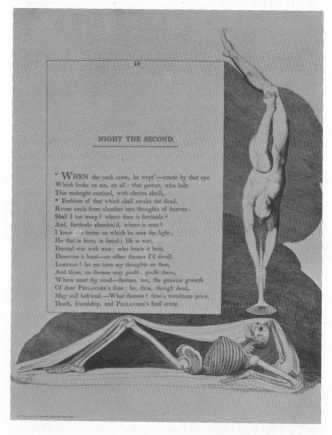

An illustration designed and engraved by Blake from the 1797 edition of Edward Young's Night Thoughts.

This dread disease, none but Jesus. O Lord, descend
and save! . . .

Addressing himself to the Deists, Blake even expresses a belief
in original sin:

> Man is born a Spectre or Satan & is altogether
> an Evil, and requires a New Selfhood contin-
> ually, & must continually be changed into his
> direct Contrary. . . .

Mr Bronowski comments that these words "unsay a lifetime
of hope". But there is nothing defeatist about Blake in his
latter years. His acceptance of the fact of man's inherent propensity to sin was balanced by his acceptance of the fact of
divine grace.

The later prophetic books show the impact of Methodism on
Blake. In *Milton* he speaks of Whitefield and Wesley as two
prophets raised up to preach

> Faith in God the dear Saviour who took on the likeness
> of men,
> Becoming obedient to death, even the death of the
> Cross.

(pp. 56-7)

With the revivalists Blake believed that every man must experience within himself redemption from the limitations of his
corrupted nature, in order to know eternal life. He believed
too that by the death and resurrection of Jesus Christ man was
mysteriously redeemed from eternal death. But whereas Wesley thought of the death of Christ on the Cross in terms of
retribution, compensatory justice and vicarious sacrifice, Blake,
like William Law before him, found this interpretation of the
crucifixion intolerable.

He understood that the mystery of salvation involves death and
sacrifice, and that the innocent must suffer for the guilty:

> And it was enquir'd Why in a Great Solemn Assembly
> The Innocent should be condemn'd for the Guilty. Then
> an Eternal rose,
> Saying: "If the Guilty should be condemn'd he must be
> an Eternal Death,
> And one must die for another throughout all
> eternity." . . .

But the suffering and death derive their value and saving grace
solely from that spirit of love in the victim which leads him
to accept them of his own free will. (pp. 57-8)

Blake saw in the death of Jesus the supreme example of that
necessity for self-sacrifice which is binding on all humanity.
His death was not to pay the compensation exacted by the God
of Justice, but to fulfil the law of love. And though the crucifixion is the climax of the drama of man's redemption, it is
not the whole drama. The fact that in the person of Jesus God
took upon himself our mortal nature was for Blake the central,
final proof of divine love. At the crucifixion that nature was
put off, and the death of Jesus was no less necessary for the
salvation of man than was his birth; but it was not more necessary. (p. 59)

One of Blake's illustrations to *Jerusalem* sums up his vision
of redeeming love. It shows the crucified Christ confronting
Albion, whose outstretched arms reflect the gesture of embrace.
No cross is visible, but the hands and feet of the Saviour are
nailed and his head is crowned with thorns. In the figure of
Albion we see Man patterning himself on the divine image in

the posture of ultimate sacrifice; but whereas the figure of Jesus
is drooping, suggestive of suffering, Albion's is vigorous, full
of life. The outstretched arms, the head thrown back, the upward movement suggest the active response of man to the love
of God—"We love because he first loved us". The death of
Christ renews the life of Man, if he will take the divine image
for his pattern.

Man is involved in the drama of the redemption as an actor;
he participates, he is himself committed to self-denial and self-
sacrifice, for "Man is Love as God is Love". This is the great
argument of *Milton*. Through self-annihilation Milton conforms
to the eternal pattern of Jesus. He faces Eternal Death and
redeems his enemy; by so doing, he redeems himself. Regeneration is a double process, in which God's grace and man's
will are involved; and to the human participant it presents itself
as an incessant labour. All Blake's prophetic books are full of
turmoil, for he knew that regeneration makes enormous demands upon a man. In the words of William Law:

> Regeneration is not to be considered as a Thing,
> done, but as a State that is progressive, or as
> a Thing, that is continually doing.

(pp. 59-60)

Blake's vision of the redemption of man necessarily included
the redemption of the entire creation, for he conceived of man
as participating in that one divine life which animates "all
things visible and invisible." . . . In the final lines of *Jerusalem,* describing the restoration of the creation to union with
its creator, the unification of the many in the One, he speaks
of

> All Human Forms identified, even Tree, Metal, Earth &
> Stone: all
> Human Forms identified, living, going forth &
> returning wearied
> Into the Planetary lives of Years, Months, Days &
> Hours; reposing
> And then Awaking into his Bosom in the Life of
> Immortality. . . .

Blake's thought here corresponds, as so often, with cabalistic
doctrine and owes something too to Swedenborg, but the fact
remains that he sees the apotheosis of Man in terms of his
absorption into the mystical body of Christ, the One Man, the
Divine Humanity.

Distinctively christian is his belief that the unity of man with
man is a condition of the unity of man with God. The creation
cannot be redeemed, society cannot be saved, until men learn
to obey the command of Jesus, to love one another.

> "He who would see the Divinity must see him in his
> Children,
> One first, in friendship & love, then a Divine Family,
> & in the midst
> Jesus will appear . . .".

(pp. 63-4)

[The] most constant element in his approach to christianity is
his hostility to the systematised hypocrisy of the Churches.
Whether we turn to *The Songs of Experience,* to *The Marriage
of Heaven and Hell,* to the Lambeth books or to the latest of
his writings, *Jerusalem* and **"The Everlasting Gospel,"** we
find the same condemnation of "religion" that derives from
self-regarding philosophising, and not from spiritual intuition.

He uses stinging language in his annotations to Bishop Watson's *Apology for the Bible* which had appeared in 1797 in reply to Tom Paine's *Age of Reason*. Nobody but Blake, with his own definitions of christianity, could have called Paine "a better Christian than the Bishop", for he was a professed Deist and had no scruples about trampling on beliefs which christians have always held sacred. Towards Deists and Rationalists Blake usually showed strong hostility, but he knew Paine as a friend, and honoured him as champion of the rights of man. He realised that this "Inspired Man", who wholeheartedly followed the dictates of his "Energetic Genius", was doing a service to pure religion by attacking "the Perversions of Christ's words and acts . . . and also the perversions of the Bible''.

> Christ died as an Unbeliever & if the Bishops had their will so would Paine . . . but he who speaks a word against the Son of man shall be forgiven. Let the Bishop prove that he has not spoken against the Holy Ghost, who in Paine strives with Christendom as in Christ he strove with the Jews.
>
> (pp. 67-8)

Blake knew that his own mission was to strive with Christendom, and in these notes he makes it very clear that he considers himself a Christian, one who dares to defend Christ and who refuses to interpret the Bible as "the Peculiar Word of God, Exclusive of Conscience or the Word of God Universal". (p. 68)

[According to Blake, the] genuineness of a religion that professes to be christian must be tested by [the] . . . touchstone of forgiveness.

> Will any one say "Where are those who worship Satan under the name of God?" Where are they? Listen! Every Religion that Preaches Vengeance for Sin is the Religion of the Enemy & Avenger, and not of the Forgiver of Sin, and their God is Satan, Named by the Divine Name. . . .

At the time of writing *Milton*, Blake was working towards this, his final position, through a preoccupation with the necessity for self-annihilation as a stage in regeneration. In the poem he makes abundantly clear his belief that the majority of mankind have a perverted idea of God and of what is required of them in the way of allegiance to him. This misapprehension he attributes mainly to the cultivation of reason at the expense of imagination.

The most explicit identification of the satanic Spectre with unenlightened Reason is made in *Jerusalem:*

> The Spectre is the Reasoning Power in Man, & when separated
> From Imagination and closing itself as in steel in a Ratio
> Of the Things of Memory, It thence frames Laws & Moralities
> To destroy Imagination, the Divine Body, by Martyrdoms & Wars.
>
> (p. 69)

[Blake] saw a special danger when reason is given priority in the sphere of religious experience. Reason is an indispensable ingredient of faith, but reason unsupported by intuition can only result in an arid system of theology and morals which is without power to regenerate the human soul. . . .

If his hostility to Reason sometimes seems perverse, in strictly religious matters at least there were historical as well as personal causes to justify his anti-rationalism. The temper of the Anglican church in the eighteenth century was so suspicious of inspiration, so hostile to enthusiasm, that it cast off John Wesley, perhaps the greatest christian reformer England has ever produced. And it is not necessary to go to Dissenters for testimony to the false importance then given to reason in religion. (p. 70)

As a young man, Blake had maintained, against the opinion of his rationalist and dissenting friends, that there is No Natural Religion. He continued to believe this though he came to direct his attacks from a different quarter. He first held that the natural man suffers from a defect of vision which incapacitates [him] for religious experience. By the proper exercise, however, of his imaginative faculty, this defect could be remedied, and every man could enjoy his rightful spiritual heritage and live consciously in the presence of God. But Blake, as the years passed, came to see that few men were constitutionally visionaries, as he himself was, and he realised too that not only the imagination but the will has to be re-directed if man is to become in truth a child of God. It is the practice of the "Natural Morality of Self-righteousness, the Selfish Virtues of the Natural Heart" which leads to the "Worship of the God of this World". He was in agreement with William Law that, whether in or out of the church,

> When Religion is in the Hands of the mere Natural Man, he is always the worse for it; it adds a bad Heat to his own dark Fire, and helps to inflame his four elements of Selfishness, Envy, Pride and Wrath.

Part of Milton's prophetic mission is to expose the satanic nature of all that is self-regarding, self-righteous, self-satisfied, in a word, self-centred:

> I come to discover before Heav'n and Hell the Self-righteousness
> In all its Hypocritic turpitude, opening to every eye
> These wonders of Satan's holiness, shewing to the Earth
> The Idol Virtues of the Natural Heart, & Satan's Seat
> Explore in all its Selfish Natural Virtue. . . .

But he has, too, a redemptive function. He has not merely to preach, but actually to demonstrate, the Laws of Eternity.

> If the Guilty should be condemn'd he must be an Eternal Death,
> And one must die for another throughout all Eternity.
>
> (p. 72)

There is a dramatic moment when Milton realises that his adversary Satan is not a principle of evil external to himself, but that the evil is within:

> I in my Selfhood am that Satan: I am that Evil One!
> He is my Spectre! . . .

Regeneration consists in acknowledging our own guilt and in freeing ourselves from the dominion of the self-centred element which hinders us from living like children of God. But this unregenerate element is so intimate, so integral a part of mortal man's nature that nothing less than self-annihilation will serve as an image of the regenerative process. (pp. 72-3)

The freeing of the soul from this captivity, the breaking down of this fixed self-centredness, calls for heroism. More than this, it calls for grace, as Blake eventually acknowledged:

O Saviour pour upon me thy Spirit of meekness & love!
Annihilate the Selfhood in me: be thou all my life! . . .

But Blake emphasises also the labour which the conquest of
self imposes upon every man, not in **Milton** only but in **Jerusalem,** where Los struggles with his recalcitrant Spectre, and
Albion, under the dominion of his own Spectre, also contends
against Los. Albion . . . takes on many of the characteristics
of Urizen-Satan. He turns his back on Jesus, the Divine Vision,
saying "By demonstration man alone can live, and not by
faith": he sets up laws of moral virtue, curses his sons and
daughters for transgressing these laws, and refuses time and
time again to be reconciled with Los. But he is haunted by the
remembrance of his rejection of Jesus:

O Human Imagination, O Divine Body I have
  Crucified!
I have turned my back upon thee into the Wastes of
  Moral Law.

(p. 74)

Satan cannot, in Blake's myth, ever be fully redeemed; the
reason is hinted in a note to Wordsworth's *Excursion:*

Satan dwells in (the Divine Mercy) but Mercy does not
dwell in him; he knows not to Forgive. . . .

But Albion can repent and be saved. Eventually he acknowledges his guilt:

      "O Lord, what can I do? my Selfhood cruel
Marches against thee, deceitful . . .
I know it is my Self, O my Divine Creator &
  Redeemer".
Jesus replied: "Fear not, Albion: unless I die thou canst
  not live;
But if I die I shall arise again & thou with me.
This is Friendship & Brotherhood: without it Man Is
  Not". . . .

Albion's full redemption is accomplished when, accepting this
"Mysterious Offering of Self for another", he follows the
pattern of Christ, accepting the Laws of Eternity. He

. . . stood in terror, not for himself, but for his Friend
Divine: & Self was lost in the contemplation of faith
And wonder at the Divine Mercy . . .

Freed from all self-interest, actuated by pure love, Albion

. . . threw himself into the Furnaces of affliction.
All was a Vision, all a Dream: the Furnaces became
Fountains of Living Waters flowing from the Humanity
Divine.

(pp. 74-5)

Though Satan cannot, being the essence of Selfhood, participate in the redemptive work of self-annihilation, he can and
must, according to Blake, be saved from punishment. In the
Palambron story at the beginning of **Milton** he takes pains to
insist that the Eternals do not seek to be revenged on Satan;
he falls, but he cannot be allowed to perish.

Sometimes, it is true, Blake writes as though the Spectre had
to be destroyed utterly. . . . Usually, however, though the imagery remains violent, it is the reclamation and not the destruction of the Spectre that is figured:

"Awake, Albion awake! reclaim thy Reasoning
  Spectre. Subdue
Him to the Divine Mercy! Cast him down into the Lake
Of Los that ever burneth with fire . . .".

(p. 75)

This is the line of action which is in harmony with the general
temper of Blake's thought. Writing to Hayley in 1804, he
describes those spiritual experiences at Felpham which inspired
him to write **Milton,** and says, "he is become my servant who
domineered over me, he is even as a brother who was my
enemy". In *The Four Zoas* Los is urged by his Spectre to an
act of recognition and reconciliation:

      "be assur'd I am thy real self,
Tho' thus divided from thee & the slave of Every
  passion
Of thy fierce Soul. Unbar the Gates of Memory: look
  upon me
Not as another, but as thy real Self. I am thy
  Spectre . . .".

(pp. 75-6)

In repentance, man cannot deny his own satanic tendency to
exalt Self into God's place. He cannot lay on others the blame
for crimes against society when in his own inveterate selfishness he has set himself above the Divine Humanity and has
therefore sinned against true brotherhood. Blake identifies himself with the Pharisees and shares their guilt for the death of
Jesus; he identifies himself with Satan, the symbol of cruelty
and hypocrisy operating in society, and shares in the guilt of
a rotten civilisation.

And with the full acknowledgement of guilt comes freedom.
Blake's exceptional wisdom comes out in his recognition of
the fact that the tendency to be "our own Centre and Circumference" cannot be eradicated by mere force of will. He knew
that self-denial, as commonly taught and practised, may be
self-mutilation. The regenerate man is man reintegrated, not
maimed and torn and suffering from his struggles to be su-
perhuman. The repudiation of the Selfhood can only result in
psychological disaster. It is not to be repudiated, but recognised
for what it is—evil; the source of false judgments and mistaken
actions. It must be reclaimed, as bad lands are reclaimed when
men accept full responsibility for their improvement.

In his handling of this problem, Blake is not only a good
psychologist, he is profoundly christian. The Spectre is antagonistic to the life of the spirit and must therefore be overcome.
But an enemy encountered with violence remains an enemy;
forcibly kept under, he remains an enemy still. Only if he is
treated as a friend can he possibly become a friend. Blake not
only dramatised the reconciliation of individual man with his
spectral Satan or selfhood; his compassion and humour led him
to address a poem of tender friendliness to **"The Accuser who
is the God of this World"**:

Truly, My Satan, thou art but a Dunce
And dost not know the Garment from the Man.
Every Harlot was a Virgin once,
Nor canst thou ever change Kate into Nan.

Tho' thou art Worship'd by the Names Divine
Of Jesus & Jehovah, thou art still
The Son of Morn in weary Night's decline,
The lost Traveller's Dream under the Hill. . . .

Though in this world of time Satan usurps the prerogatives of
God, and though men minister to his insatiable pride by giving

to him the worship that they should reserve for the Friend of Sinners, yet in eternity he is still Lucifer, Son of the Morning, the rebel angel with whom all poets feel themselves in league. Nor, even in this world, is his power so great as to overawe or delude those who, with forgiving vision, see their fellows as they essentially are. The verses were written late in Blake's poetic life, at the time when he was bringing *Jerusalem* to a close. The redeeming power of love is the major theme of that poem—the power of forgiveness to reintegrate man and society. It is one of the great, disregarded, christian themes.

Christ overcame the world by manifesting to the bitter end his love for friends and enemies alike. He overcame the world because he would not fight against his persecutors but was content to die for them. He was forsaken on the night of his passion; but the hearts of men, hungry always for the assurance of enduring love, have been drawn to him ever since the day when he was lifted upon on the cross. Enemies can only be subdued by the weapons of love. That is the eternal truth exemplified in the story of Jesus. It is the truth which Blake seized when he said "The Glory of Christianity is to Conquer by Forgiveness". (pp. 77-9)

> *Margaret Bottrall, in her* The Divine Image: A Study of Blake's Interpretation of Christianity, *Edizioni di Storia e Letteratura, 1950, 119 p.*

DAVID V. ERDMAN   (essay date 1954)

[*Scholars value Erdman's* Blake, Prophet against Empire, *first published in 1954, as an insightful examination of contemporary historical references in Blake's poetry and art. The critic takes* Europe *as his text in the following excerpt, elucidating the ways in which the poem functions as a veiled criticism of the turn-of-the-century "English Crusade against France." See the accompanying illustrations for further commentary on the satirical aspects of* Europe.]

On January 21, 1793, the French Convention sent Louis XVI to the guillotine. One week later the British Parliament voted to prepare for war, and on February 1 the Convention responded with a formal declaration. The "English Crusade against France" had begun. Blake expected the sequel to be the triumph of revolutionary Energy, the collapse of the "Angels & weak men" who governed "unwilling" Britain, and the establishment of republics throughout Europe. In *America,* ready for sale by October, he presented the failure of the earlier English Crusade against the Colonies as a prophecy for the year 1793. In it he directed at England the "Empire is no more" chorus of **"A Song of Liberty"** and foretold a consummation (in England) of the revolution begun in America. In his illustrations of *America* he pictured the judgment and execution of a ruler by a revolutionary tribunal. In a separate picture engraved in June he portrayed the imminent downfall of a stout king and his henchmen. And in the following year he traced, in *Europe,* the fatal steps of Britain's entry into the war with France and prophesied ruin for the crusaders led by Rintrah (Pitt) and Palamabron (Parliament) who had joined the counterrevolutionary lion and wolf of the Continental Armageddon. (pp. 201-02)

In *Europe, A Prophecy,* Blake enlarges on the idea that the British attempt to accuse, judge, and execute revolutionary France is equivalent to an invitation to universal revolution, and he devotes attention to the sequence of events that led to the blowing of the trumpet of war against France, particularly the efforts in 1792 of Britain's ruling Angels to shut the gates of the minds of "the youth of England" and to condition them for the terrors of the approaching Armageddon.

James Gillray's "The Dagger Scene," which Erdman views as a lampoon of Edmund Burke's speech to Parliament in 1792 in which he flung a dagger to the ground to illustrate the dangers of alliance with France. According to Erdman, Blake based a design for Europe *on Gillray's cartoon.*

This historical portion of *Europe* is set obscurely, however, in a complicated web of myth reaching from the morning of Christ's nativity to the day of Judgment. Nowhere is Blake's symbolism more cryptic; nowhere do so many new characters appear in such fleeting contexts; nowhere is there such sly shifting from one level of discourse to another, such difficulty with ambiguities of punctuation and sudden changes of pace. Many critics looking for the historical meaning have foundered on the assumption that the "strife of blood" at the end of the poem signifies the French Revolution of 1789, not the English crusade of 1793-94—failing to distinguish the historical narrative . . . from its mythological envelope. Yet this narrative must be read correctly before the rest of the work will come into proper focus.

The historical portion (lines 60 to 150 and 198 to 206) begins with a reference to the innumerable wars that divided the ruling families or "heavens" of Europe up to the catastrophic end of the American War—"Till Albion's Angel, smitten with his own plagues, fled with his bands"—a catastrophe which implied a very dark future for all ancient heavens, particularly those of Albion:

> The cloud bears hard on Albion's shore,
> Fill'd with immortal demons of futurity,

a cloud filled with plagues which rush down on the "council house" and bury the "smitten Angels of Albion" for one hour. After the American debacle the privy council (modern cabinet) did collapse, and the ministry of Fox and North in 1783 supplied a brief interlude in the long tradition of king-dominated councils.

Then began the ministry, supported by all the open and secret influence of the Crown, of young William Pitt, whom Blake presents as "Rintrah, furious king" and pictures as a black knight armed cap-a-pie in chain mail and carrying a crusader's sword. . . . Though such "Angels & weak men" were able to restore Tory rule, the American influence remained and they did so only with difficulty, "In troubled mists, o'erclouded by the terrors of struggling times." Like Satan and his cohorts, Rintrah and his fellow angels were now fallen and living among the ruins of their bright edifice of chivalry. "In thoughts perturb'd they rose from the bright ruins, silent following The fiery King" while "Round him roll'd his clouds of war.". . . (pp. 210-12)

Rintrah's three unsuccessful attempts to blow "the iron tube" of war may be taken as the three crises contrived by Pitt in the half decade before war with France finally came. In 1787 England made preparations to hire Hessians and send munitions in support of the Dutch Orange party and to back Prussia if she invaded Holland to forestall France; in 1790 Spain was pushed to a point just short of war over an incident in Nootka Sound (Vancouver); and in 1791 Pitt obtained from Parliament a vote to arm against Russia but withdrew his ultimatum when he saw the size of the opposition. In each of the last two cases the "pretext for an armament" was more apparent than the purpose of it, and Pitt privately conceded that he had found he could not swing enough public support behind a military venture to risk his ministry in a war. These were the adventures described . . . as knight-errantry by Paine and as presumptuous assays by Blake. Their miscarriage pointed to the need of a preliminary softening of the public backbone such as the Antijacobin alarms of 1792 provided.

Blake's way of describing Pitt's turning to this sort of preparatory attack on morale is to say that Rintrah led his council, in clouds of war, to Druidism—to "his ancient temple, serpent-form'd, That stretches out its shady length along the Island white" of Britain. As distinguished from the self-sacrifice of Washington and Paine, praised in **America,** Pitt's Druidism represents the aggressive sacrifice of others, according to a self-righteous creed in which "man" has become "an Angel, Heaven a mighty circle turning, God a tyrant crown'd." . . . With some distortion of his Antiquarian sources, Blake imagines the original serpent temple as an edifice stretching all across the waist of England, along the Thames, the artery of modern Britannia's naval power. He places the serpent's head in "golden Verulam" because Verulamium is the site of Druid ruins and also because Verulam was the baronial title of Francis Bacon, whom Blake considers the Machiavelli of British imperialism.

On the brink of war with France, Pitt did look primarily to naval action and the seizure of French islands. Had he been able to read the prophetic warning of Blake, he could have learned that the "southern porch" of such Druidic aggression would become "a raging whirlpool" which would draw "the dizzy enquirer to his grave." But Rintrah, standing on the Druid altar or Stone of Night, looked up for comfort to Urizen with "his brazen Book That Kings & Priests had copied on Earth," and as he looked it expanded "from North to South." For the moment the distinction between Urizen and George III seems very faint. Blake illustrates the page with a vision of the bat-winged, black-robed, papal-crowned Emperor of Babylon overshadowing a Gothic church similar to the Archbishop's chapel at Lambeth. His face is something like that of the King in [James Gillray's political] caricatures, and we remember that the pope of British State Religion *is* George the Third.

Blake's camera has now drawn close to London, and we see that the stone of sacrifice is in the city's heart. It is the stone of London's blackening church and bloody palace, around which swag "the clouds & fires pale" of the religion of war:

Round Albions cliffs & Londons walls . . .
Rolling volumes of grey mist involve Churches,
    Palaces, Towers:
For Urizen unclaspd his Book! feeding his soul with
    pity.

Now comes the public reading of a page from the cruel laws of Urizen, and since the episode that follows can be identified as the downfall of Chancellor Thurlow on June 15, 1792, first publicized in the papers and in Gillray's print of May 24, the cruel preachment referred to is evidently the famous Royal Proclamation of May 21 against "divers wicked and seditious writings." Looking back from 1794, Blake treats this first official effort to befog men's minds with Antijacobinism as the first decisive step of Pitt's government toward war and an effort to prepare a war psychology. Blake gives us a composite scene in which the hypocritical Angel reads the Proclamation before an unwilling muster of youthful militia, who curse the trumpeter of their doom.

The youth of England hid in gloom curse the paind
    heavens; compell'd
Into the deadly night to see the form of Albions Angel.
Their parents brought them forth & aged ignorance
    preaches canting,
On a vast rock perceivd by those senses that are clos'd
    from thought:
Bleak, dark, abrupt, it stands & overshadows London
    city.
They saw his boney feet on the rock, the flesh
    consum'd in flames:
They saw the Serpent temple lifted above, shadowing the
    Island white:
They heard the voice of Albions Angel howling in
    flames of Orc [i.e. crying out against wicked
    Jacobinism],
Seeking the trump of the last doom.

(pp. 212-15)

Historians agree with Blake that this Proclamation began England's "black era of reaction and coercion." Ostensibly aimed at Paine's *Rights of Man,* the second part of which, urging England toward a republic, had been published in February, the ban's immediate political intent and effect was to split the Foxite Whigs and weaken their organization of associations of "Friends of the People" to support Parliamentary Reform. On the more popular Constitutional and Corresponding Societies it had if anything a stimulating effect. But in the minds of "mortal men" the Proclamation was ominously linked with concurrent military maneuvers. (p. 215)

[From] May to August the youth of England, in regiment after regiment, were compelled to march through London and encamp on the open heath west of the city for much drilling and sham battle against imaginary enemies. Newspapers at first (May 24) assured the public that "the little encampment on Bagshot Heath" was formed for the study of new Prussian maneuvers recently introduced into the British army, "and not from the most distant idea of any armament being at this time requisite on the part of Great Britain." But as the summer wore on, the papers alternated shocking reports of democratic atrocities in France with "evidence" of sinister French designs upon Britain. It was gradually taken for granted that the suppositious enemies were French Jacobins (and English ones), and before the end of July the "military evolutions" at Bagshot reached the dramatic height of supposing "that an army of enemies, amounting to 20,000 had landed at Southampton." In August the British ambassador gave France an ultimatum that he would quit Paris "the moment a debate is brought on for deposing the King." Pitt, without risking a consultation of Parliament, began erecting barracks in the industrial centers—rather more evidently against English Jacobins than French.

And on December 1 the Proclamation of May 21 was repeated, this time formally linked with a calling out of the militia.

Blake has placed this combined "mustering" and preachment in May, when the war games began. The youth whose bodies are brought forth for slaughter and whose minds are being closed from thought are "hid in gloom." Yet they see the flames of Orc consuming the flesh of Albion's Angel. . . . And it is the rulers, not they, who are pained and howl. The war trumpet will, when someone succeeds in blowing it, bring an end to the government of Angels and weak men.

The next episode in *Europe* is presented in identifiable detail and serves to confirm the present interpretation of Blake's narrative. The episode has long since faded on the pages of history, but we can easily see how it delighted Blake's sense of irony. For Pitt's first victim following the Antijacobin ban was not Tom Paine but one of the Angels of Pitt's own cabinet, the Lord High Chancellor and Keeper of the Seal and Guardian of the King's Conscience. . . . Chancellor Thurlow often took an independent line, and for years Pitt had been seeking to rid himself of his formidable colleague. His chance came when the Chancellor ridiculed Pitt's Sinking Fund Bill as the work of "a mere reptile of a minister" and told Parliament that no bill should attempt to bind all future governments. The grain of sedition in this remark was infinitesimal, but Pitt promptly asked the King to dismiss Lord Thurlow, counting on his own indispensability at a time when he had filled the King's mind with alarm for the constitution. . . . Thurlow was compelled to relinquish the Great Seal and doff his judicial gown and wig.

The episode may have been of slight political significance, but . . . Blake treated it as an omen of the Day when judges should be judged and a sign that the revolutionary world crisis could singe even the high guardian of British law in Westminster Hall.

> Above the rest the howl was heard from Westminster
>   louder & louder:
> The Guardian of the secret codes forsook his ancient
>   mansion

An illustration from Europe, *discussed by Erdman as a prophetic rendition of Gillray's drawing (see previous illustration). Erdman maintains that Blake here represents Burke as a dagger-wielding assassin lying in wait for Everyman.*

> Driven out by the flames of Orc; his furr'd robes &
>   false locks
> Adhered and grew one with his flesh, and nerves &
>   veins shot thro' them.
> With dismal torment sick hanging upon the wind: he
>   fled
> Groveling along Great George Street thro' the Park
>   gate; all the soldiers
> Fled from his sight: he drag'd his torments to the
>   wilderness.

Here is circumstantial detail of Thurlow's leaving the Westminster government buildings and fleeing in shame and anger down Great George Street to St. James' Park. (pp. 215-17)

"Thus was the howl thro' Europe," Blake generalizes, "For Orc rejoic'd to hear the howling shadows." Some of the shadowy rulers had considerable power left, however, both political and military:

> But Palamabron shot his lightnings trenching down his
>   [Orc's] wide back
> And Rintrah hung with all his legions in the nether
>   deep.

Regardless of Orc's rejoicing through Europe, the result for England was that the citizens were bound "in leaden gyves" and every house became a den with "Thou shalt not" written over the doors "& over the chimneys Fear." . . . And since Blake deals with no further events of English history before the blowing of the trumpet, the cited actions of Rintrah and Palamabron can be taken to signify any single or continuing activity between May 1792 and January 1793 engaged in by Rintrah as Pitt and Palamabron as Parliament, or rather as Burke in Parliament. (p. 218)

Palamabron's thunderbolts against Orc might signify any of Burke's Antijacobin speeches. But the illustration on the first page of the Preludium of *Europe* derives from a Gillray print of December 30, 1792, and this print points to a specific occasion: *The Dagger Scene; or, the Plot Discover'd.* . . . Gillray's man with a dagger is Burke, whom he often pictures as a spy or vigilant watchman defending Crown and Cross against "atheistical revolutionists." Blake's dagger-wielding assassin has the same face, and Blake's whole picture is prophetic transformation of the Gillray satire.

Pitt had called an emergency session of Parliament in December by reissuing the May proclamation and calling out troops. In this Parliament, Burke delivered a war-inciting speech on the Alien Bill, a measure based on and calculated to intensify the suspicion that foreign agents were about. At his climax Burke suddenly produced a steel dagger and flung it on the floor. "This," he exclaimed, pointing to the dagger, "is what you are to gain with an alliance with France." Gillray mocks the histrionics—the dagger, the pointing finger, the "startled" adversaries. Blake pictures Burke as an assassin lurking in the cave (of Parliament) to stab a youthful pilgrim. . . . The dagger in his hand (corresponding to the thunderbolts in the text) signifies that his malice is the real "plot," his speech a waylaying of Everyman on his peaceful pilgrimage, or, more specifically, the Patriot on his progress to Paradise. (pp. 218-19)

The second page of the Preludium may illustrate Rintrah's hanging in the nether deep like Milton's Satan in the "nethermost Abyss" on his way to invade the Garden of Eden. Hanging in space a wrestler (Rintrah?) clutches two opponents whom he is trying to strangle. Another, who has escaped but holds his head in pain, is climbing onto a cloud. In later pictures Blake will represent Pitt and Nelson as harrowing and strangling nations. Gillray uses similar wrestling scenes to represent the throttling of political opponents by Pitt and Burke. Pitt's treatment of Lord Thurlow, in the text, is a case in point. . . . (pp. 219-20)

Either because he understood *Europe* very well, or because he was coached by Blake himself, his friend George Cumberland added explanatory glosses to a copy now in the British Museum, mostly in the form of quotations from Blake's household volume, Bysshe's anthology. Verses written under the two Preludium pictures imply that both are manifestations of the same windy (Parliamentary) strife. From the "hoarse din" of "imprison'd tempests" and "clam'rous Hurricanes" raving in a "noisy cave" (compare the "shrill winds" of Blake's text) emerges a global conflict:

> This orb's wide frame with the convulsion shakes,
> Oft opens in the storm and often cracks.
> Horror, Amazement, and Despair appear
> In all the hideous forms that Mortals fear.

The three words were underlined to call attention to the two trapped and the one escaping victims of the strangler; they suggest that Pitt is stifling expressions of Horror and Amazement at his catastrophic policy but is unable to suppress the silent figure of Despair, which is ascending.

In Blake's text the domestic repression that follows the actions of Rintrah and Palamabron is welcomed by a woman named Enitharmon. In the mythical envelope of *Europe,* . . . she is the Queen of Heaven. In the temporal world her interest in the matter may be that of the Queen of England. At the time of the King's insanity in 1788 Queen Charlotte had been advised by physicians to keep the King "in constant Awe" of herself, on the theory that this would prevent a relapse, and she had assumed charge of the royal household "with singular Zeal." She was subsequently believed to control the flow of patronage and rule the Empire through Pitt. His choice of peace in 1790 had been attributed to the Queen's influence; it was logical to assume that his later choice of war was also her doing. The May proclamation against seditious writings was issued in the King's name but from "the Queen's House." Pitt's success in ousting Thurlow was attributed to her support, and Gillray's version, in a print entitled *Sin, Death, and the Devil,* June 9, is that the Queen sheltered Pitt from the fallen Thurlow's vengeance by playing a part like that of Sin in Milton's description of the contest between Satan and Death.

Gillray's lurid caricature is an instructive link between Blake and Milton. Thurlow is a muscle-bound Satan, Pitt a gaunt and naked King Death wearing "the likeness of" the British Crown (compare Blake's calling Rintrah a "furious king"), and Queen Charlotte a hideous "snaky" Sin wearing the key to the backstairs, "the Instrument of all our Woe." Her control over the gates of Hell and her jailor's function suggest why Enitharmon is delighted to see a prison made of England:

> to see (O womans triumph)
> Every house a den, every man bound: the shadows are filld
> With spectres, and the windows wove over with curses of iron.
> Over the doors Thou shalt not: & over the chimneys Fear is written:
> With bands of iron round their necks fastend into the walls
> The citizens: in leaden gyves the inhabitants of suburbs

Walk heavy: soft and bent are the bones of villagers. (pp. 220-21)

The suggestion that the queen of jailors is Sin and that Sin is the incestuous mother of Death recalls Blake's indictment of the perverse idea "that Woman's love is Sin," a part of the Urizenic code which makes the nation's queen a symbol of whoredom and puts the chivalrous slogans of the Antijacobin crusaders in the category of accusations of adultery. On the level of psychology and ethics Blake treats war as the perversion of sexual energy; on the level of politics, as *Europe* indicates, he considers that priest and king make war to divert desire from normal channels and that they use the slogans of chivalry to make slaves of the men of their own and other nations who assert the rights of Love. The fact that Rintrah is pictured . . . as championing not one queen but two should remind us that there were queens of both France and England. The crusade is undertaken, according to the text, "That Woman, lovely Woman, may have dominion," and Rintrah and Palamabron are sent forth to battle for two angelic females bearing scepters tipped with the fleur-de-lis commonly used in English caricature prints as a French royalist symbol. (p. 222)

[Burke] viewed the dethronement of the Queen of France as marking the extinction of chivalry, that "nurse of manly sentiment and heroick enterprise," while Paine welcomed the departure of "the Quixotic age of chivalric nonsense" and laughed at Burke as "the trumpeter of the order" and at Pitt as its "knight-errant." . . . [In "Fayette" Blake depicts the Queens of France and] of England as equally vicious. Evidently the two queens in *Europe*—not Enitharmon, who is their archetype, but the briefly mentioned Leutha, "sweet smiling pestilence. . . silken queen," and "silent Elynittria," the "silver bowed queen" of Rintrah—are ideal portraits of the queens of France and England as pictured to the youth who are being sent to war that these may "have dominion." (pp. 222-23)

Finally, Gillray's bestowal of serpent hair upon the Queen, who is in Milton a "Snaky Sorceress" only by virtue of being serpentine below the waist, leads us to Blake's concluding lines, in which the prophet himself arises with "his head . . . in snaky thunders clad" and calls "all his sons to the strife of blood," a strife he believes will bring the end of kings and queens and the whole restrictive code of Sin. The trumpet that Rintrah was trying to blow would announce their end because meanwhile "in the vineyards of red France" a "terrible Orc" had made his appearance "before the Trumpet blew." If we understand the blowing of the trump to mean the British vote for war, then the Orc whose coming preceded it is the one who guillotined the King of France on January 21, the same "Demon red" whose light was, according to *America,* received by France twelve years after the fall of Albion's power across the Atlantic.

Yet when, in *Europe,* the end does come, we are reminded that the decisive battles are fought in more strategic areas than Pitt's cabinet or even the nether deep. The trumpet is actually blown (a larger view discloses) by the ideological creator of the whole Antijacobin universe, "A mighty Spirit . . . Nam'd Newton." *He* "siez'd the trump & blow'd the enormous blast!" and the mighty Angelic hosts, helpless as "leaves of Autumn,"

> Fell thro' the wintry skies seeking their graves:
> Rattling their hollow bones in howling and lamentation.

An illustration from Europe. *Erdman interprets Rintrah, the male figure, as a symbol of Prime Minister William Pitt and the angels as symbols of the queens of England and France.*

England's crisis was exploding into a world crisis, the crisis of an epoch. (pp. 223-24)

> David V. Erdman, in his Blake, Prophet against Empire: A Poet's Interpretation of the History of His Own Times, *revised edition, Princeton University Press, 1969, 546 p.*

ROBERT F. GLECKNER (essay date 1959)

[*Critics generally consider Gleckner's* The Piper & the Bard, *excerpted below, to be one of the major scholarly commentaries on* Songs of Innocence and of Experience. *Gleckner here urges a cumulative reading of these and other poems based on an informed appreciation of Blake's organic symbolic technique.*]

[Blake's symbolic technique] is simple, its roots lying in his concept of states and their symbols. These states are innocence, experience, and a higher innocence, their symbols the child, the father, and Christ. (p. 62)

Each of Blake's song series (or states or major symbols) is comprised of a number of smaller units (or states or symbols), so that the relationship of each unit to the series as a whole might be stated as a descending progression: from the states of innocence and experience to the *Songs of Innocence and of Experience,* to each individual song, to the symbols within each song, to the words that form the symbols. Conceivably ignorance of or indifference to one word can prohibit the imaginative perception and understanding of the whole structure. . . . [A] recognition of Blake's punctiliousness in the songs is in-

dispensable to a correct, full reading of each song as well as to a comprehension of his major states. . . . The serious reader of Blake's songs . . . [must] be constantly aware of the context or state in which each individual poem appears; and since each state is made up of many poems, other poems in the same state must be consulted to appreciate the fullest possible significance of any one poem.

Yet the necessity for a cumulative reading of Blake's songs should in no way detract from his artistry in each individual song; the hundreds of comments on the songs, the countless anthologized segments of his work, and the universal praise accorded the songs are all eloquent testimony to their fundamental self-sufficiency. Yet out of its context each song means a great deal less than Blake expected of his total invention; and occasionally it may be taken to mean something quite different from what he intended. Since innocence and experience are vital parts of Blake's system, to deny to the *Songs of Innocence* the very background and basic symbology it helps to create is as wrong as reading *The Rape of the Lock* outside the epic tradition. Without an awareness of his design Blake is the simplest of lyric poets. But with very little study the child of innocence can be seen to be radically different from the child of experience; and the mother of innocence is scarcely recognizable in experience. The states are separate; they are the two contrary states of the human soul, and the width of the hiatus is spanned by the poems which appeared after the engraving of the *Songs of Innocence* and before the *Songs of Experience—The Book of Thel, Tiriel, Visions of the Daughters of Albion, The Marriage of Heaven and Hell.* These poems are the products of a transition in Blake's own thinking. With the *Songs of Innocence* behind him, he had as yet no vehicle, no ready plan, and no completely formulated major symbol for experience. *Thel, Tiriel,* and the *Visions* were his experiments to find that form, the "reinforced lyric," and that symbol, the father-priest-king. Outside the context of this half-light between the states, these three poems are susceptible to facile misunderstanding, simply because the controlling symbols and their milieu are ignored or unrecognized. (pp. 62-4)

[Many] times a faithful interpretation of a poem depends upon a correct determination of speaker and perspective. That this element should carefully be considered is evidenced by the introductory song to each series: one is sung by the Piper, the other by the Bard. Superficially there seems to be little to distinguish one from the other since the Piper clearly exhibits imaginative vision and the Bard sees present, past, and future. Yet for the Piper the past can only be the primal unity, for the present is innocence, and the immediate future is experience; while for the Bard the past is innocence, the present experience, the future a higher innocence. Accordingly it is natural to expect the Piper's point of view to be joyful, happy; he is conscious of the child's essential divinity and assured of his present protection. But into that joyous context the elements of experience constantly insinuate themselves, and a note of sorrow is never completely absent from the Piper's pipe. In experience, on the other hand, the Bard's voice is solemn, serious, and more deeply resonant, for the high-pitched joy of innocence exists now only as memory or as a degenerate, hypocritical smile. Within experience, though, lies the ember which can leap into flame at any moment to light the way to the higher innocence. What joins the two voices together is that both singers are imaginative; they are the poetic and/or prophetic characters. Because of this Blake demands that his reader always consider the imaginative point of view no matter who is speaking, seeing, or acting in the poem. . . . [The] reader must rouse his faculties to realize that both Piper and Bard see the spiritual, imaginative significance of the terrestrial, sensational activity in all the songs.

Both singers are William Blake. And since he, or they, sing all the songs, the fact that they are identifiable or not identifiable with a character in a poem contributes most importantly to the total meaning of that poem. For example, in **"The Chimney Sweeper"** (*Innocence*) the angel is equated at one point with the Piper, but in **"Infant Sorrow"** it is vital to recognize the speaker to be quite separate from the Bard, the former's myopia only being discernible through the Bard's greater vision. Similarly, in **"The Little Vagabond"** the reader must discover at least four points of view: that of the mother, who is the direct antithesis of the mother Blake wrote of in *Songs of Innocence;* that of the parson, who is equated as always by Blake with the major symbol of experience; that of the vagabond himself, who must be viewed as a child of experience, not the carefree, irresponsible, thoughtless child of innocence; and that of the Bard, through whose vision each of the other points of view can be studied and evaluated. Without an awareness of this complexity in **"The Little Vagabond,"** the reader fails to grasp an essential part of the poem's structure, the very element which rescues it from the limbo of sentimental drivel. (pp. 64-5)

In all of Blake's poetry acts, objects, and characters can be symbolic, the determination of their value and association depending upon whether they contribute to the structure of the controlling symbol. For example, the mother of *Songs of Innocence* is symbolic to the extent that her protective solicitude for the child contributes to his status as the major symbol of the state of innocence. And since most of Blake's symbols are recurrent throughout the poetry, the pattern or incidence of their recurrence will reveal the technique by which Blake achieved the intensive richness of each individual poem. (p. 66)

To illustrate the way in which such a symbol gathers the moss of association and connotation within Blake's self-created "poetic tradition," I shall trace briefly the recurrence of the staff or rod or, in its most easily recognizable form, the sceptre. It appears first in unsymbolic context in the *Poetical Sketches* with little more than a literal or "traditional" meaning—sovereignty, power, rule:

> O Winter! bar thine adamantine doors:
> The north is thine; there hast thou built thy dark
> Deep-founded habitation. Shake not thy roofs,
> Nor bend thy pillars with thine iron car.
>
> He hears me not, but o'er the yawning deep
> Rides heavy; his storms are unchain'd, sheathed
> In ribbed steel; I dare not lift mine eyes,
> For he hath rear'd his sceptre o'er the world.
> 　　　　　　　　　　　　　　　("To Winter" . . .)

In **"Gwin, King of Norway"** cruelty and tyranny are added to the sceptre's significance, foreshadowing the hypocrisy of the secular, religious, and domestic rulers of *Songs of Experience* as well as the selfishness of Tiriel:

> Come, Kings, and listen to my song:
> 　When Gwin, the son of Nore,
> Over the nations of the North
> 　His cruel sceptre bore,
>
> The Nobles of the land did feed
> 　Upon the hungry Poor;
> They tear the poor man's lamb, and drive
> 　The needy from their door! . . .

In **"Holy Thursday"** (*Innocence*) Blake varies the symbol for the first time and establishes the more modern version of authority and cruelty—the rod or staff or wand:

> Twas on a Holy Thursday their innocent faces clean
> The children walking two & two in red & blue & green
> Grey headed beadles walkd before with wands as white
> 　as snow
> Till into the high dome of Pauls they like Thames
> 　waters flow.

The beadle wielding the authority is a representative of the organized church of "natural religion" which Blake hated so violently. The wand itself represents not merely authority but an act of restraint which forces the children to act according to rule rather than their inherently divine impulses. The whiteness of the wand suggests the frigidity of man-made moral purity as opposed to the warmth of young, energetic, exuberant innocence. And finally, its usage here suggests the worldly concept of duty (and its corollary, harm), the duty of worship which clashes with all of Blake's ideas of freedom and spontaneity.

Following this context of ecclesiastical authority, in *Tiriel* the symbol appears as purely secular rule, personified by the king and the father. Tiriel himself is both, and Har is the father of Tiriel. Upon entering the false innocence of the vales of Har, Tiriel, who has been thrown out of his castle and apparently deposed by his sons and daughters, glozingly intreats a welcome form the pitiful Har and Heva and their protectress, Mnetha:

> I cast away my staff the kind companion of my travel
> And I kneel down that you may see I am a harmless
> 　man.

The staff is symbol of the man. All that the poem reveals Tiriel to be has gone into the associative formation of that staff: the cruelty of his curse upon his children, the tyranny of his expulsion of his brothers, the selfishness of his reign and his parenthood, the hypocrisy of his approach to Har, Heva, and Ijim, and the error of his entire life. "There is not an Error," Blake wrote, "but it has a Man for its Actor"; then in manuscript he changed "Actor" to "Agent" and added, "that is, it is a Man" (**"Last Judgment"** . . .). Tiriel is the actor, agent, and man of error; the staff is his heraldic device. Taken with the reference to harm it also suggests a variant of staff or rod, the scourge. Denying the real existence of harm since it depends upon the efficacy of physicality, Blake recognized only harm to the soul, to the divinity of man, and that had nothing to do with corporeal punishment or material rewards. . . . Tiriel's "harmless" gesture to Har and Heva . . . is blatantly hypocritical in view of Blake's attitude toward harm; yet on earth the act of disarmament brings results, for the earth is fallen and harmlessness has become the equivalent of love. The fact remains, though, that the staff is only the symbol of the man. Kneeling or not, Tiriel never for a moment relinquishes his devotion to or grasp of earthly power. He takes back his staff when he leaves the vales, and on his return visit he heralds his approach with an emphatic assertion of his omnipotence.

Such worldly dominion is carefully related by Blake to the concept of self: a denial of self, which is prerequisite to attaining the higher innocence, is equal to a denial or surrender of personal power. The circumstances of self-denial provide the context of the sceptre's next appearance, in *The Book of Thel:*

> Does the Eagle know what is in the pit?
> Or wilt thou go ask the Mole:
> Can Wisdom be put in a silver rod?
> Or Love in a golden bowl?

The silver rod is, of course, Thel's symbol of sovereignty: she is queen of Har. The poem recounts her attempt to retain physical immortality and youth and still pass through the state of experience. That is, she hopes to gain the wisdom of the higher innocence without relinquishing her silver rod. In Blake's system this is impossible, since the self must be denied in favor of participation in the greater self; recognizing none greater than herself, Thel flies the prospect of an ugly existence which would deny to her her beauty, youth, power, and (she believes) her happiness.

So the process of symbolic accumulation goes, until in *The Four Zoas* we can find a sceptre redolent with meaning in the hands of Urizen as he plots the initial fall into division:

> "Thou Luvah," said the Prince of Light, "behold our
>   sons & daughters
> Repos'd on beds; let them sleep on; do thou alone
>   depart
> Into thy wished Kingdom, where in Majesty & Power
> We may erect a throne. . . .
>   "I . . .
> Will lay my scepter on Jerusalem, the Emanation,
> On all her sons, & on thy sons, O Luvah, & on mine
> Till dawn was wont to wake them; then my trumpet
>   sounding loud,
> Ravish'd away in night; my strong command shall be
>   obey'd. . . ."

Finally, in *Jerusalem* the sceptre and scourge of Tiriel join forces with the iron chain, another of Blake's great symbols, to produce the following:

> O Divine Spirit, sustain me on thy wings,
> That I may awake Albion from his long & cold repose;
> For Bacon & Newton, sheath'd in dismal steel, their
>   terrors hang
> Like iron scourges over Albion. . . .

(pp. 66-9)

[It] is important to understand that Blake did not discard all the tools of his lyric trade when he took up the prophetic instrument. Rather he took those tools—and images, incidents, and characters—and expanded them immensely. Two instances of that expansion I have quoted above. In the second, which appears the more cryptic, the reader need know nothing of Bacon and Newton if he has made a careful reading throughout Blake's poetry of the sceptre-chain-scourge symbols. With the manifold associations of restriction, tyranny, cruelty, reason, conventional morality, natural religion, selfish oppression, myopic vision, and so on, Newton and Bacon both become metamorphosed, through the medium of their iron scourge, into a Tiriel, a father, a priest, and a king (the fool is innate). Or, the other way around, if Newton is appreciated in his symbolic role of single vision incarnate ("Newton's sleep"), all of the associations of the symbol gather about his figure. Such symbolic reciprocity is constantly employed by Blake, but it is effective only if we are aware of the full, cumulative power of each symbol in a given context. (pp. 69-70)

The symbols can appear with equal effectiveness, perhaps even more effectiveness, by implication. For example, in *Visions of the Daughters of Albion* Blake describes Bromion and Oothoon as bound back to back in Bromion's den, and in the Rossetti manuscript he writes of being bound down by his "mirtle tree." . . . Bondage is chain is Tiriel is priest is religion is reason, and so on. The process is almost interminable, but the resultant richness of the poetry more than justifies the reader's search.

From the above truncated equation it should be clear that acts too may be symbolic. As Gardner points out, "Just as symbol and symbolic action are, in writing of the highest quality, related to dramatic conflict and theme, so the figures of myth and allegory are identifiable from the symbolism of their actions." For Blake every experience became a person. The priests in "The Garden of Love," Har in *Tiriel,* the father in "A Little Girl Lost," and Tirzah, among others, are fused in the act common to all, bondage. Similarly, since the priests are ecclesiastical authority, Har and Tiriel monarchical authority, the father domestic authority, and Tirzah natural—or even cosmic—authority, the sceptre admirably symbolizes all of their acts. The object, act, and actor can all be classified under the major symbol of experience, the father-priest-king. Just so, the protective action of the mother in innocence contributes to the symbolic significance of the child. And the attempt by "the little boy lost" to seize his "father" bodily is as wrong in Blake's world as the weeping of "the little boy found" is right. Both acts substantiate the symbolic value of *the* child of innocence, and a knowledge of both acts is prerequisite to a correct interpretation of, say, "The Chimney Sweeper" and "A Little Boy Lost" in *Experience.* In the same way the raising of voices in song (both "Holy Thursday" poems), the sharing of sorrow ("On Anothers Sorrow," "A Cradle Song"), the nibbling of lambs and the preying of wolves and tigers ("Night"), shading another from the sun ("The Little Black Boy"), whispering ("Nurses Song" in *Experience*), sulking ("Infant Sorrow"), drinking ale ("The Little Vagabond"), and killing a fly ("The Fly") are all symbolic acts. And each act takes on a different significance as it is viewed from different points of view.

Perhaps the most important and certainly the most interesting act in the *Songs* and allied poems is that which involves the transition from innocence to experience. In "The Little Black Boy," for example, Blake translates the transitional act into several symbols—light and shade, the sun and the tree, the sun and the cloud. Learning to "bear the beams of love" is the act, and around it Blake builds an ironic contrast between the apparent blackness of the black boy and the apparent whiteness of the white boy. This contrast is emphasized by the former's unselfish shading of the latter until he too can bear the beams of love. Tiriel, of course, is already in experience, but his "fall" is powerfully summarized in his final curse on his father Har. It foreshadows the voice of the grave in *The Book of Thel,* perhaps Blake's most powerful presentation of the way to experience. The transition in *Thel* is in terms of a denial of self, a surrender of earthly dominion, and the entry into the grave. If we have read carefully "The Little Girl Lost," Thel's crucial error and her reason for fleeing the grave in terror become most clear. In "The Little Girl Lost" Lyca's approach to experience is voluntary and self-sacrificing. It is the right way. Thel's approach is fearful and selfish and proud. The fundamental significance of both poems and the key to correct interpretation of the transitional act depend heavily on the points of view involved. (pp. 71-3)

With such care in his use of point of view, recurring symbols, and symbolic action, Blake leads the reader to see the gradual merging of many of his characters. The final product of the merger is what I have called the major symbol. In other words, kindred points of view tend to unite the holders of those points of view; characters who are associated continually with the same or similar recurring symbols tend to melt into each other; and a similar pattern of action reveals a fundamental affinity among the actors. In these ways the symbolic value of any one character in any one poem is intensified and expanded beyond the bounds of the immediate context. The identity may shift, but the symbolic character remains the same. When the beadle's wand in **"Holy Thursday"** is recognized as a part of the basic sceptre motif, the beadle's identity, while being retained as representative of church law, merges with that of Tiriel and the father. Within the single symbol are inherent all the others which go to make up the major symbol of the context. Similarly, in innocence the child merges with the lamb, which in turn merges with the figure of Christ in **"The Lamb"**; the angel merges with the Piper in **"The Chimney Sweeper"** of *Innocence;* and the earth of **"Earth's Answer"** merges with Oothoon of the *Visions of the Daughters of Albion.* Once he has established a character like Tiriel, Blake will use him over and over again, always being careful to provide for him a different context, different associates, and a different object or act upon which to exert his particular symbolic influence. (pp. 73-4)

Perhaps the finest example of shifting identity is the major symbol of experience. The very fact that Blake often refers to it in the aggregate—father-priest-king—demonstrates the close connection among the three principles. . . . In the *Songs* both the beadle and the father appear, the latter in emphatically negative form: "No father was there" (**"The Little Boy Lost"**). In **"The Chimney Sweeper"** the father sells his son into virtual servitude, and in *Tiriel* he becomes a gigantic figure for there he is also a king. In *Thel* Thel herself is the queen of Har, a ruler who refuses to renounce her sovereignty and her self. In **"A Song of Liberty"** the starry king promulgates the ten commandments to control the flaming energy of the Christ-like newborn babe, an act reminiscent of Har's scourging of Tiriel's "youthful fancies"; and **"A Song"** ends with a chorus about the "Priests of the Raven of dawn" who "curse the sons of joy." In *The French Revolution* the king enacts his traditional tyrannical role, while in the *Visions of the Daughters of Albion* Bromion's power, the power of natural religion, is universal and in his "religious caves" lie the enslaved subjects of the moral law. (pp. 74-5)

In the *Songs of Experience* the major symbol, of course, appears in many forms: the "selfish father of men" (**"Earth's Answer"**), the pebble (**"The Clod and the Pebble"**), the "cold and usurous hand" (**"Holy Thursday"**), God (**"The Chimney Sweeper"**), the dreamer (**"The Angel"**), the earth implicit in **"Ah! Sun-Flower,"** the priest (**"The Garden of Love"**), the mother, parson, and "Dame Lurch" (**"The Little Vagabond"**), "Cruelty," "Humility," and the "Human Brain" (**"The Human Abstract"**), and Tirzah (**"To Tirzah"**). And finally the father-priest-king is recognizable in Enitharmon and Urizen in *Europe,* in "the primeval priest" in *The First Book of Urizen,* Urizen again in *The Book of Ahania, The Book of Los,* and *The Song of Los,* Urthona, Tharmas, Luvah, and Urizen in *The Four Zoas,* Satan in *Milton,* and Albion's spectre in *Jerusalem.*

In each of these figures is all the others. The priests of **"The Garden of Love"** bind with briars love and desire, but they do so because they are selfish like Tiriel and the father of men in **"Earth's Answer,"** because their hands are cold and usurious like those in **"Holy Thursday,"** because they represent this world, the earth implicit in **"Ah! Sun-Flower,** because they are the gods of this world with all the cruelty, humility, and hypocrisy of which the human brain of **"The Human Abstract"** is capable. The priests are as much the major symbol as the father, just as the lamb, sheep, grasshoppers, birds, "the divine image," etc. are all the major symbol of innocence—the child. (p. 75)

[Each] individual identity in its specific context is at once a part of the whole context and the whole of which it is a part. Both the priests of **"The Garden of Love"** and the birds of **"Night"** are self-sufficient for an understanding of the poems. Blake simply asked his reader for more than understanding: that is "corporeal" activity. He wanted them to imagine as he imagined, to see as he saw, even to recreate as he created; only then does the symbolic method make sense, only then can one see the minor symbols as parts of a major symbol, only then can the song take its place as a song of innocence or of experience. (p. 76)

Robert F. Gleckner, in his The Piper & the Bard: A Study of William Blake, *Wayne State University Press, 1959, 906 p.*

HAROLD BLOOM (essay date 1963)

[Bloom, an American critic and editor, is best known as the formulator of "revisionism," a controversial theory of literary creation based on the concept that all poets are subject to the influence of earlier poets, and that, to develop their own voices, they attempt to overcome this influence through a deliberate process of "creative correction" that Bloom calls "misreading." Prior to introducing this theory, he provided a sustained and, by all accounts, sensitive reading of Blake's poetry in Blake's Apocalypse: A Study in Poetic Argument. *The following explication*

Blake's cottage at Felpham.

of The First Book of Urizen, The Book of Ahania, and The Book of Los, which focuses on the parodic and archetypal aspects of the poems, is excerpted from that study.]

The sequence of poems examined in the last chapter dealt with the relation between history and myth; individual history in the *Songs of Experience,* political and cultural history in *America, Europe,* and *The Song of Los.* In the sequence of poems to be considered now, Blake completed the structure of his earlier canon by three creations in pure myth, the books of *Urizen, Ahania,* and *Los.* These poems set forth the beginnings of myth; they are the Genesis and Exodus of Blake's "Bible of Hell." . . .

[The energy of *The Book of Urizen*] gives it a more masculine beauty than Blake has achieved before. Blake's genius for intellectual satire, subordinated since *The Marriage of Heaven and Hell,* finds full expression again in *Urizen,* and largely accounts for the poem's startling tone. Like **"The Tyger,"** the tone is one of shuddering awe, for Urizen is both fearfully mistaken and genuinely fearful. (p. 164)

Urizen is horrible, but he has a horrible dignity, as befits a god who will rule the heavens of all religious and philosophical orthodoxies. On one level Urizen is a parody, both of the Jehovah of Genesis and of Plato's Demiurge in the *Timaeus.* Yet Blake's quarrel is with himself, not merely with other men's ideas of order. The Urizen of Blake's myth is as much (and as little) Blake himself as are the other characters of the myth, and Blake's satire in *The Book of Urizen* is not directed at Urizen alone.

The illustrations to *The Book of Urizen* are among Blake's finest, and have been more admired than the poem itself, which nevertheless is superior to them. Even the frighteningly self-absorbed stony old man of the famous frontispiece is not really adequate to Blake's magnificent conception. By a very grim paradox, Urizen, the limiter of energy, is himself an indomitable energy, for the reasoning mind is the most terrible force in nature, and the mind of Urizen is truly the great poem of winter. (pp. 164-65)

[The "Preludium" to *The Book of Urizen*] is one of Blake's simplest:

> Of the primeval Priest's assum'd power,
> When Eternals spurn'd back his religion,
> And gave him a place in the north,
> Obscure, shadowy, void, solitary.
>
> Eternals! I hear your call gladly.
> Dictate swift wingèd words & fear not
> To unfold your dark visions of torment.

Blake's subject is the primordial history of priestcraft, and clearly the adjective "assum'd" is equivocal. The reference to the north is an ironic allusion to Satan's revolt in *Paradise Lost,* V, where the great rebel gathers his host "into the limits of the North" to plot against the hierarchy of heaven. Blake's Muses are the unfallen Eternals, themselves actors in the story of Urizen's fall.

The poem begins greatly, with the sudden rise of a shadow in Eternity. In a world of open consciousness there appears a spirit who divides, differentiates, appropriates for himself. Urizen begins his revolt against his brethren by withdrawing into himself, becoming "unknown, unprolific, self-clos'd, all-repelling." To the other Eternals he seems a void or vacuum, but to his priests who will write Genesis he will seem a being overflowing with creative generosity. This self-divided Demiurge is the brooding power that moved over the face of the

abyss, but his creativity is viewed here from quite another perspective:

> For he strove in battles dire,
> In unseen conflictions with shapes
> Bred from his forsaken wilderness
> Of beast, bird, fish, serpent, and element,
> Combustion, blast, vapour, and cloud.

Blake again parodies Milton's God who created by retraction— "I uncircumscribed myself retire"—but Urizen's retraction is an abandonment that allows nightmare shapes to spring from a "forsaken wilderness." Urizen is fighting himself, and the darkness he moves within is an invisible ninefold, a number associated with nightmare images throughout every European mythical tradition. Urizen's creativity is negative because it is solipsistic, and Blake hints strongly that the solitary male principle of God in Genesis is equally entrapped in a prison of self:

> Dark, revolving in silent activity:
> Unseen in tormenting passions:
> An activity unknown and horrible,
> A self-contemplating shadow,
> In enormous labours occupied.

Blake continues to build tension, by delaying Urizen's direct manifestation in the work. We see, with the Eternals, the formation of a "petrific abominable chaos," a rock upon which orthodoxy will be built. Within that stony maelstrom the Nobodaddy of superstition is preparing, evolving the future of our illusion:

> His cold horrors, silent, dark Urizen
> Prepar'd; his ten thousands of thunders,
> Rang'd in gloom'd array, stretch out across
> The dread world; & the rolling of wheels,
> As of swelling seas, sound in his clouds,
> In his hills of stor'd snows, in his mountains
> Of hail & ice; voices of terror
> Are heard, like thunders of autumn,
> When the cloud blazes over the harvests.

This is the god of natural religion, rather like the Power of Coleridge's *Hymn before Sunrise,* a mountain Leviathan, white with the colorless all-color of the indefinite. Having presaged the human meaning of this dread being, Blake gives a brief glimpse of the world Urizen first disrupts:

> Earth was not: nor globes of attraction;
> The will of the Immortal expanded
> Or contracted his all-flexible senses;
> Death was not, but eternal life sprung.

Earth and the other planets are cyclic images of a fallen world. The single Man who was Immortal had full control of his potential for perception, and so the final contraction we call death could not be. But a trumpet sounds in the heavens, and thundering words burst forth. Urizen speaks, and we know at last the tragedy of his motives:

> From the depths of dark solitude, from
> The eternal abode in my holiness,
> Hidden, set apart, in my stern counsels,
> Reserv'd for the days of futurity,
> I have sought for a joy without pain,
> For a solid without fluctuation.
> Why will you die, O Eternals?
> Why live in unquenchable burnings?

He has invented the idea of the holy, an idea Blake hated with an altogether humanistic passion, for everything that lives is holy, and no individuality can be more holy than another. And with the sickness of holiness Urizen has invented also the affliction of futurity, not the future as it is now rushing forward to meet one, but the future as the indefinite, menacing and remote. Urizen knows himself, all too well, for he has wearied of the strife of contraries. He desires not an exuberant becoming, but a repose of unchanging solidity, a joy unperplexed from its human neighbor, pain. The passions of the life of Eternity are to Urizen so many separate deaths, intolerable dissolvings of his solidity. Enshrined in his petrification he longs for the glorious withering of monologue, not the "unquenchable burnings" that define the human state of imagination. The element of fire, burning upward as Promethean emblem, must be forced downward and inward into the abyss of the consuming self:

> First I fought with the fire, consum'd
> Inwards into a deep world within,
> A void immense, wild, dark & deep,
> Where nothing was—Nature's wide womb;
> And self-balanc'd, stretch'd o'er the void,
> I alone, even I! the winds merciless
> Bound; but condensing in torrents
> They fall & fall; strong I repell'd
> The vast waves, & arose on the waters
> A wide world of solid obstruction.

There is an allusion here to the Chaos through which Milton's Satan so courageously travels, a "wild Abyss, the Womb of nature and perhaps her grave." Unlike the external Chaos of *Paradise Lost,* the abyss of Urizen is all within, but the journey of Satan and the inner strife of Urizen are genuinely parallel, for each will bring destruction to man. The firmament of Jehovah in Genesis, divided off from the waters, is one with Urizen's "wide world of solid obstruction," spun out as a barrier against energy. (pp. 165-68)

[In *Urizen,*] Jehovah, Satan, and Urizen are one, three demiurges desperately shaping worlds out of tortured expediencies. But Urizen is the most cunning and comprehensive of this trinity. In his introspection he has discovered the "Seven deadly Sins of the Soul" and to counter these he must unfold his darkness. On the rocky world he has formed . . . he proceeds to found a Decalogue, the "Book of eternal brass." The brazen laws are those we have had expounded to us by Bromion in [*Visions of the Daughters of Albion*] and earlier by the aged Tiriel:

> One command, one joy, one desire,
> One curse, one weight, one measure,
> One King, one God, one Law.

In reaction to Urizen's self-righteousness, the other Eternals yield to the temptation of moral outrage, and by this fierce irony they rather than Urizen are responsible for the next stage of the Fall. The pretensions of a self-congratulatory moral intellect are answered by the unforgiving wrath of the affronted human faculties of emotion, instinct, imagination. Again the parody is directed towards *Paradise Lost,* where the Divine Wrath burning down the abyss upon the falling Satanic host created the heat without light of Hell. Against this black fire Urizen is forced to emulate the desperate labors of Plato's Demiurge. He digs up mountains and hills (an ironic allusion to Angelic activity in Milton's heavenly war) and piles up a stony womb in the shape of a globe, thus obstructing the vision of Eternity. By closing himself off, Urizen has effected a total separation from the being he is closest to, the imaginative shaper, Los. . . . The analytical mind cannot go mad without distorting the imagination, and the anguish of Los is a bitter refrain throughout the rest of the poem.

Urizen, sundered from reality, has become indefinite, "unorganiz'd," and is sunk in a "stony sleep" like the beast in Yeats's *The Second Coming.* Confronted by this formlessness, Los rouses his fires, hoping to reshape Urizen into some semblance of his former existence. But Urizen, like Nebuchadnezzar, must have seven ages of change pass over him, seven lengthy days of Creation-Fall, until at last the Eternal mind will appear as the mind of Deism, the human intellect struggling in the context of an imprisoning nature.

If the mind collapses into perpetual winter, it takes the inventing vision with it. Los, struggling to make the falling mind more definite in its outline, is in the unhappy position of the Deist poet who feels he must stoop to truth and moralize his song. As Urizen "his prolific delight obscur'd more and more," Los reacted by "numb'ring with links hours, days and years." Clock-time is invented in the hope of somehow organizing a chaos, and to meet an imaginative dearth, Los is bringing out number, weight, and measure. In the ghastly comedy of a falling creation, the well-meaning Los and the solipsistic Urizen are equally blunderers.

The changes of Urizen, presented in a rhetoric of horror, are only the forming of our own natural body, the shrinking-up of flexible senses into the confinements of our cavern. When the process is complete, the fallen Urizen faces west, towards the ironic completion of death. Horrified by his failure to arrest Urizen's fall, Los momentarily gives up, drops his hammer, and silently merges with Urizen.

Blake's aesthetic complexity is fully revealed in this reunion of Urizen and Los. In part Blake's point is again satiric; the poetry of an age yields to that age's minimal ideas of order, when the poet is making his most extended effort to transform that order back into its original and larger form. The naturalization of a system of thought, its actual embodiment, causes the shaping spirit of imagination to despair, and then to merge itself with the body of nature that is the idea of order incarnate. Here in 1795 Blake profoundly anticipates the crisis in Wordsworth's and Coleridge's creative lives that took place a decade later.

This crisis of Los joining Urizen is satirical only insofar as it is allegorical; read in its own terms it is a direct statement of Blake's creative psychology. Pity . . . is not for Blake an unequivocal virtue, and pity enters the mythic word of *The Book of Urizen* out of Los's dismay at the disaster suffered by solipsistic intellect. Los becomes the image of the death he pities, and so divides his being in two. The crisis of the imagination produces "the first Female form now separate." . . . (pp. 168-70)

Los and Enitharmon are Blake's fallen Adam and Eve, but from the start, they are made to plague and not to comfort one another. The sight of a separate female form is a horror for the unfallen Eternals. Confronted by this division into nature, they react by repudiating Los as they have already denied Urizen. The powers of Los are the powers of perception, just as the unfallen Urizen controlled the Eternal basis of conceptualization. The evolving Urizen is dwindling down to the minimal mental process of abstraction, and the sundered Los shrinks to a fixed perception of time even as the Enitharmon split from his side hardens into a materialized perception of space. The stupidity of the surviving Eternals (presumably Tharmas and Luvah, instinctual impulse towards unity and emotional consciousness respectively) is that they complete the fall of man, by passionately rejecting both the self-ruined intellect and the self-divided power of perception. By first weaving the woof they call Science, and then fastening it down over Urizen, Los, and Enitharmon as a tent, they give unnecessary substance to fallen ideas of space and time. They objectify an order of fallen nature when all they seek is to be rid of it.

Within this newly confined world Los and Enitharmon enact the torments of love and jealousy. She perversely flees, he follows, and:

> Eternity shudder'd when they saw
> Man begetting his likeness
> On his own divided image.

Yet the divided image must regenerate the human in time, for the Eternals cannot. Orc is born from Enitharmon in the shape of time's serpent, a new birth of organic energy evolving out of a lower into a higher nature. The fierce child is too much for the Eternals to bear, though he is not the Shadow they take him for, but a fresh desire they cannot comprehend. To protect themselves, they close down the tent of space, and rob Los of his right to behold the eternal world.

With the birth of Orc and its consequences, *The Book of Urizen* has reached its crisis. The remaining three sections of the poem (VII-IX) are superior in vigor and relevance to the earlier parts, for Blake now has the advantage of dealing with an experiential world, though in its primitive stages.

The terror of familial strife begins with Los's jealousy of his first-born. Perhaps because the child has cost him Eternity, perhaps out of possessive love for Enitharmon, Los begins to be afflicted by a tightening chain around his bosom. He breaks it each night, but it forms again each day, in imitation of the chain called "Devouring" that bound the titanic Loki in the Eddic literature. As the castoff chains fall down on Urizen's rocky world they lock together into a linked Chain of Jealousy, and Los uses what nature has made for him:

> They took Orc to the top of a mountain.
> Oh how Enitharmon wept!
> They chain'd his young limbs to the rock
> With the Chain of Jealousy,
> Beneath Urizen's deathful Shadow.

There is a sense of an archetype being renewed here; of Oedipus being exposed to die by Laius's command, of Abraham preparing to sacrifice Isaac. The poetic principle fathers fresh life upon nature, and yet cannot accept that life, resents it, and prepares to offer it up to the death-shadow of a deformed moral intellect. Yet life has its voice, the freshness of an infant cry can sting nature out of its sleep of death, and rouse even Urizen from dogmatic repose:

> The dead heard the voice of the child,
> And began to awake from sleep;
> All things heard the voice of the child,
> And began to awake to life.

> And Urizen, craving with hunger,
> Stung with the odours of Nature,
> Explor'd his dens around.

The remainder of the poem is concerned with Urizen's exploration of his dens, one of the major events in Blake's reading of the history of man's primordial consciousness. Urizen begins by emulating the God of the Book of Proverbs and *Paradise Lost;* he forms golden compasses and other instruments to assist him in measuring and dividing up the Abyss he is responsible for having formed. It is as though the onset of new generative life has warned him that there are forces still to be confined, energies that threaten his "solid without fluctuation." His prime motive in drawing apart from other beings was to avoid the life of Eternity, with its "unquenchable burnings"; now he fears the burnings of Orc's flames of desire. Other flames are set against him (and against Orc as well):

> But Los encircled Enitharmon
> With fires of Prophecy
> From the sight of Urizen and Orc.

> And she bore an enormous race.

The myth of the beautiful woman surrounded by a ring of fire is most familiar today in its Wagnerian form. Blake's source here may be from Northern mythology but the meaning of these lines has little to do with tradition, for they are satiric. The fires or creative movements of Los ought to be prophetic in function, but here they are only possessive. Los encircles part of the human, but the encircling necessarily naturalizes, and ensures that the enormous race of descendants will be ensnared within natural limitations.

Urizen exploring his dens displays the negative moral courage of Milton's Satan questing through chaos, but Urizen is capable of self-education where Satan is not. This makes it the more heinous that Urizen should always learn the imaginatively mistaken lessons. What Urizen sees quite properly sickens him, yet he fails to assume responsibility for such horrors. He sees the grief of his children, elemental forms of fallen existence, and his reaction to such grief is the blind cursing of a Tiriel:

> He in darkness clos'd view'd all his race,
> And his soul sicken'd! He curs'd
> Both sons & daughters; for he saw
> That no flesh nor spirit could keep
> His iron laws one moment.

As he contemplates his creation, he weeps the hypocritical tears of abstract pity, parodying the mercy of the destructive Jehovah. As in **"The Human Abstract"** pity breeds a monstrous growth:

> Cold he wander'd on high, over their cities,
> In weeping & pain & woe;
> And wherever he wander'd, in sorrows
> Upon the aged heavens,
> A cold shadow follow'd behind him
> Like a spider's web, moist, cold & dim,
> Drawing out from his sorrowing soul,
> The dungeon-like heaven dividing,
> Wherever the footsteps of Urizen
> Walk'd over the cities in sorrow.

This is the Net of Religion, the flytrap of moral virtue, the rightly reasonable knowledge of good and of evil. Blake's barely controlled indignation menaces the tone of this passage, for he feels the tactile repulsion of the "moist, cold, and dim" rather too strongly. This web is, as he powerfully remarks, "a Female in embryo," the origin of the Female Will that dreams the poem *Europe*, and that will dream the nine Nights of the epic *Four Zoas*. "No wings of fire," not the most inspired of poets, can break the web:

> So twisted the cords, & so knotted
> The meshes, twisted like to the human brain.

After this the poem settles into the lamentable defeat of man's culmination in Fall, properly assigned to its ninth and most sinister chapter. The descendants of Urizen shrink "beneath the dark Net of infection," and this shrinking primarily affects their senses. The climax is reached in the rhetorical shudder of a ghastly parody of the Sabbath:

> Six days they shrunk up from existence,
> And on the seventh day they rested,
> And they bless'd the seventh day, in sick hope,
> And forgot their eternal life.

Urizen's explorations have resulted in man's invention of death, which is only an exhaustion based on deliberately narrowed perceptions:

> No more could they rise at will
> In the infinite void, but bound down
> To earth by their narrowing perceptions
> They lived a period of years;
> Then left a noisom body
> To the jaws of devouring darkness.

We die because we want to die, because we refuse the effort of vision that would take us out of a perversely comforting universe of death. That universe of death is allegorically named Egypt in the Bible. Blake identifies it with the englobed chaos of the salt Ocean, product of Urizen's hypocrisy and terrible weeping. *The Book of Urizen* ends with the departure of a saving remnant from this Egypt, led by Fuzon, Urizen's fiery son. Fuzon's revolt from Urizen begins the next poem in this series, *The Book of Ahania,* where Fuzon takes the place of Orc as the titanic emblem of organic energy. Blake originally entitled *Urizen* the *First Book of Urizen* and thus clearly intended the poem to be incomplete in itself, a Genesis requiring an Exodus and a subsequent canon. What the alert reader takes away from *Urizen* as a poem in its own right is a strong sense of the internal menace embodied in that fallen angel of thought. Urizen is within us as he was within Blake, and there is even a self-mocking aspect of his poem, demonstrating how uncomfortable Blake was in trying to keep the compass-wielding categorizer in his place. Even a parody of an orthodox cosmology begins to be overly involved in the Urizenic spirit, and Blake may have begun to worry that as a true poet he might be of Jehovah's party without knowing it. Satan did not seduce Milton and Urizen did not entrap Blake, but both poets undoubtedly felt the appealing force of their negative creations.

The Orc of *The Book of Urizen* was last seen as a Promethean child bound to the barren rock, but raising his voice and so moving nature to some life and Urizen to the analytical exploration of his confined universe. The cyclic contest of Orc and Urizen is fully developed in Blake's first epic, *The Four Zoas,* where the mythic pattern demonstrates a grim aging of the young rebel into the old tyrant, a perpetual failure of the creative impulse to rid itself of organic decay. In *The Book of Ahania,* one of the most beautiful of Blake's poems, Orc is replaced by Fuzon, whose name seems to mean "the fire of nature," and who is Urizen's own son. Perhaps Blake displaced Orc by Fuzon because he intended a more hopeful prophecy than *Europe* or *The Book of Urizen,* and saw Fuzon as having a better prospect of victory. But, faithful to the imaginative structure of his myth, he abandoned this hope, and Fuzon suffers the fate of Orc, an immolation that echoes the martyrdoms of Prometheus, Balder, and Christ, and perhaps also of David's son Absalom, caught in the thickets of the natural world and slain as a sacrifice to God's righteousness.

The Book of Ahania is in two parts, four sections being devoted to the revolt and fall of Fuzon, and a final one to the haunting lament of Urizen's abandoned female counterpart, Ahania, a wisdom goddess as her name, apparently founded on Athena, would indicate.

Fuzon is the "Son of Urizen's silent burnings," and rises with the murderous wrath of unacted desires. His first defiance of his father finely states a potentially humanist dismissal of Mystery:

> "Shall we worship this Demon of smoke,"
> Said Fuzon, "this abstract non-entity,
> This cloudy God seated on waters,
> Now seen, now obscur'd, King of sorrow?"

The allusion here to the creation in Genesis heightens Fuzon's rejection of natural limitation, as does his contempt for a god devoted to concealment. But the son is all too like the father; his fire is only a natural one, and his weapons therefore are his father's. Even as Urizen marked out globes, dimensions of circularity, so Fuzon forms a globe of wrath as his weapon. As it flies burning towards Urizen it lengthens into a hungry beam, phallic in its implications. Urizen puts up a disk to protect himself against his son's fury but:

> laughing, it tore through
> That beaten mass, keeping its direction,
> The cold loins of Urizen dividing.

As Urizen is Jehovah, and Fuzon a strangely Titanic Moses, we are suddenly startled by the audacity of Blake's myth, more radical than Freud's suggestions in *Moses and Monotheism.* The conflict of Urizen and Fuzon is sexual, in that the son has sought to wound and thus awaken the cold loins of his father. But the effect is radically opposite, for the afflicted Urizen rejects his sexuality, and dismisses his female counterpart as Sin:

> Dire shriek'd his invisible Lust!
> Deep groan'd Urizen; stretching his awful hand,
> Ahania (so name his parted soul)
> He seiz'd on his mountains of jealousy.
> He groan'd, anguish'd, & called her Sin,
> Kissing her and weeping over her;
> Then hid her in darkness, in silence,
> Jealous, tho' she was invisible.

This is a complex rejection, founded on the jealous possessiveness of a father shielding a mother from her child, but also isolating the intellect's delight in itself from the passions of creation. The mind's pleasures, rejected, breed Pestilence, the moon-worship of a separate female principle:

> She fell down a faint shadow wand'ring
> In chaos and circling dark Urizen,
> As the moon anguish'd circles the earth,
> Hopeless! abhorr'd! a death-shadow,
> Unseen, unbodied, unknown,
> The mother of Pestilence. . . .

(pp. 171-78)

Separated from his capacity for joy, Urizen prepares his revenge upon his son. In his dire self-communings he has bred a serpent of mortality from his own forsaken wilderness. He slays this serpent and makes its corpse into a black bow. The serpent's blood is used to poison a rock, and the rock is then sent as an arrow against Fuzon. Unaware that his father's rejected sexuality is murderously approaching him, Fuzon is already in the ironic process of becoming his father:

> While Fuzon, his tygers unloosing,
> Thought Urizen slain by his wrath.
> "I am God!" said he, "eldest of things."
>
> Sudden sings the rock; swift & invisible
> On Fuzon flew, enter'd his bosom;
> His beautiful visage, his tresses,
> That gave light to the mornings of heaven,
> Were smitten with darkness, deform'd,
> And outstretch'd on the edge of the forest.
>
> But the rock fell upon the Earth,
> Mount Sinai in Arabia.

The murder of this rebel Moses is an archetypal act, celebrated in a triumph of Blake's intellectual symbolism. The poetic excellence of this passage is a function of its astonishing concentration, and of the sudden flashing out of mythic analogues. Fuzon unlooses his tygers of wrath, but those powers of insight are restrained by his self-instruction, his attempt to identify himself as God. The rock enters his bosom as the mistletoe slew Balder or the lance entered the side of Christ, to overcome divinity by nature. Like Absalom caught by his hair "between the heaven and the earth" to be slain upon the oak, so Fuzon is entrapped, destroyed by his father. Blake's symbolism goes further, for Fuzon's light-giving tresses become identical, in their deformation, with the foliage of the forest. Balder dead meant the dawn gone out of the heavens, and Fuzon struck down means the darkening of nature into the forest of the night, where the Tyger of mysterious wrath will affright the eye of the Bard of Experience. In this great passage's climax the rock which has served as a negation of an arrow of desire falls upon the earth to become Mount Sinai, the rock of the Law. The Mosaic dispensation is converted into the commandments of Urizen, and the Moral Law itself has slain the Moses who tried to lead Urizen's surviving children out of Egypt.

Urizen annoints his wounded loins, and the mixed blood and balm flows down into the void, to become the snake's poison of Experience, the moral negations of absolute good and absolute evil. The body of Fuzon is nailed by Urizen to the topmost stem of the Tree of Mystery . . . [that Blake also depicted] in **"The Human Abstract."** As an image of crucifixion this recalls both Christ and the Odin on the Tree, self-slain to attain the runes, the knowledge of Mystery. But since Fuzon has been slain by a serpent-bow, and there is a later hint that he himself becomes a serpent upon the tree, there is also an allusion to the brazen serpent praised by Moses in the spiritual wilderness. No more than time's serpent does Fuzon altogether die; he becomes a "pale living corse on the tree," a raised serpent of Jehovah-Urizen's will to chaos. For the forty years of Israelite wandering Blake substitutes forty years of reptilization, while Fuzon groans upon the dead tree. At the end of those forty years, "Asia arose in the pendulous deep," and the next cycle of history began. . . . (pp. 178-79)

With this fresh defeat of the spirit of organic energy, Blake had carried the events of his myth as far as he could, without utilizing the full structure of epic. The remainder of *The Book of Ahania* is the seventy-line chant in which Ahania laments her separation from Urizen. This chant is the equivalent of Oothoon's great lament, and deliberately echoes **"Earth's Answer"** in the *Songs of Experience*. Ahania's grief begins as a longing for lost sexual fulfillment:

> To awake bright Urizen, my king,
> To arise to the mountain sport,
> To the bliss of eternal valleys;

> To awake my king in the morn,
> To embrace Ahania's joy
> On the bredth of his open bosom,
> From my soft cloud of dew to fall
> In showers of life on his harvests.

The imagery of Ahania is drawn from Solomon's Song, and from the fragment "Thou hast a lap full of seed" in Blake's Notebook. The mind in its unfallen relation to reality was itself a sexual principle, and the activity of intellect was rewarded by the delight of sexual completion:

> Swell'd with ripeness & fat with fatness,
> Bursting on winds, my odors,
> My ripe figs and rich pomegranates,
> In infant joy at thy feet,
> O Urizen, sported and sang.
>
> Then thou with thy lap full of seed,
> With thy hand full of generous fire,
> Walked forth from the clouds of morning;
> On the virgins of springing joy,
> On the human soul to cast
> The seed of eternal science.
>
> The sweat poured down thy temples,
> To Ahania return'd in evening;
> The moisture awoke to birth
> My mothers-joys, sleeping in bliss.

The loss of pleasure on Urizen's part is clearly the cause of a psychic impotence that devours the mind's prolific joy. The state of dejection that ensues is the reigning atmosphere of Experience's universe of death. The poem ends with Ahania's echoing of the language of **"Earth's Answer:**

> But now alone over rocks, mountains,
> Cast out from thy lovely bosom,
> Cruel jealousy, selfish fear,
> Self-destroying! how can delight
> Renew in these chains of darkness,
> Where bones of beasts are strown
> On the bleak and snowy mountains,
> Where bones from the birth are buried
> Before they see the light?

Few images, even in Blake, are grimmer than that final vision of mental infanticide. The Wisdom of the eighth chapter of Proverbs, who was daily Jehovah's delight, "rejoicing always before him," has become now so pale a wanderer as almost not to exist. "Doth not wisdom cry? and understanding put forth her voice?" But Blake's Wisdom weeps upon the void, "distant in solitary night."

So far Blake has dealt mostly with Orc and with Urizen. His eternal Prophet, Los, the figure of poetic genius, is also involved in the fall of Urizen, but we have not yet seen that fall from his perspective. *The Book of Los* . . . centers its story of the fall on the role of Los, beginning in the midst of the action of Chapter IV of *The Book of Urizen.* Unfortunately, *The Book of Los* is fascinating in conception but not always eloquently expressed and, with the *Africa* part of *The Song of Los,* seems to me poetically the poorest of Blake's important works, inferior to both *Urizen* and *Ahania.* There is an exhaustion evident in the language of *The Book of Los,* as if the strenuous quality of Blake's inspiration cannot accommodate itself any longer to a three- or four-beat line, and to the limiting context of a shorter poem. The visualizations of *The Book of Los* are of epic intensity and require the larger form of *The Four Zoas.*

Precisely because of the strain between its form and its content, *The Book of Los* can teach us much about Blake and the conceptual scope of his poetry. He was ready to cease experimenting and to create the full dimensions of his mythic world, to speak with the full authority of his own Word. The tone of *The Book of Los* is impatience, and remorselessly the poem hurls itself to its climax, the collapse of prophetic power into the body's singular mixture of imagination and irrelevance. Blake as a poet and prophet is aware that the descent of Los into the sublime absurdity of our mortal body is the story of his own incarnation in eighteenth-century England.

The poem begins with the song of an "aged Mother," Eno, who guides "the chariot of Leutha." Eno is evidently a mother of fallen existence, and her song expresses deep yearning for those "Times remote" when the four qualities of Covet, Envy, Wrath, and Wantonness did not rage in the world. Leutha . . . [is elsewhere presented] as a sexual temptress of the kind of Spenser's Acrasia, guardian of a world from which Oothoon had to escape. To be reduced to guiding Leutha's chariot is to be involved, however unwillingly, in the deceptiveness of a sexual masquerade, which explains Eno's chagrin. The poem she chants is one of Blake's most ironic, for it is a parable of how the imagination goes wrong for all its contrary intentions.

The action of *The Book of Los* begins with that moment in *Urizen* when the fiery rage of the other Eternals set Los the

"Death's Door," one of Blake's illustrations for Robert Blair's The Grave.

hateful work of watching Urizen's decay. The psychic allegory is instructive, if read with tact. When the mind insists on detaching itself from the human integral, and so achieves a self-congratulatory chaos, the fury against the mind felt by the emotional and instinctual life will damage the imagination. Los is asked to be a passive guardian of the "Solid without fluctuation" that Urizen has desired and now all too literally achieved. But this unbearable passivity almost ruins him, as it is alien to his active perceptiveness. Confronting a world of walled-in conceptualization, Los is made desperate by the cold and dark fires of abstract brooding. His "expanding clear senses" finally can bear the hard bondage no longer, and he rends Urizen's mock-cosmos into fragments, to fall with them into the abyss:

> Falling, falling, Los fell & fell,
> Sunk precipitant, heavy, down, down,
> Times on times, night on night, day on day—
> Truth has bounds, Error none—falling, falling,
> Years on years, and ages on ages:
> Still he fell thro' the void, still a void
> Found for falling, day & night without end;
> For tho' day or night was not, their spaces
> Were measur'd by his incessant whirls
> In the horrid vacuity bottomless.

His falling motion has begun the regulating process of marking out the spaces of time, and so his great labor of somehow forming man's world has begun, though with ironic inadvertence. He begins to contemplate his fall, and it "chang'd oblique"; even a swerve acquires the significance of creation in a downward-borne reality. Los has begun the incessant labors that will occupy him on through Blake's definitive poem, *Jerusalem*, labors finding their direct analogue in Blake's own acts of artistic creation, organizing the inchoate strife of the poet's mind into the intellectual warfare of prophecy.

What is first created on the heaving sea of emergent space and time is an undifferentiated mass of organic life, sardonically termed "the white Polypus." Los battles the waters, and, in a parody of the basic forms of cosmogony, separates "the heavy and thin," as God in Genesis divided the darkness from the light. This act of distinction revives the light of darkened desire, and by such reillumination Los beheld:

> Forthwith, writhing upon the dark void,
> The Backbone of Urizen appear
> Hurtling upon the wind
> Like a serpent, like an iron chain,
> Whirling about in the Deep.

Aside from its parody of the Mosaic glimpse of the back parts of Jehovah, this startling passage's main import is in its terrifying effect upon Los. Grotesque as Urizen has become, his astonishing manifestation suggests to Los that even so serpentine a creature can be molded into a definite form. Los builds the panoply of a divine smith, including furnaces (like those in the Book of Daniel) and an Anvil and Hammer (as in **"The Tyger"**) and begins to shape Urizen into something more definite.

Los is now more like the Demiourgos of Plato's *Timaeus* than Urizen ever was, but Los is not being praised, as Plato's harried shaper evidently was meant to be. For Los is mistaken, fearfully mistaken; the shaping spirit has been forced into error. He forms "an immense Orb of fire," our sun, condensing it from the flowing-down fires of eternal desire. This sun is an image of circularity, of sinister cycles formed in the "infinite wombs" of Los's furnaces throughout nine ages of misled prophetic framing. When the sun is ready, Los smiles, and binds the vast spine of Urizen "down to the glowing illusion." It is an illusion of eternity, an artifice that will enchain the fallen mind to the circular pulsation of natural recurrence. From this truly dead sun's encounter with the mind's remnants, the most terrible of imaginative errors is completed. The "Human Illusion" or Adamic Man is formed as an inadequate substitute for the Man who beheld Eternity:

> But no light! for the Deep fled away
> On all sides, and left an unform'd
> Dark vacuity: here Urizen lay
> In fierce torments on his glowing bed;
>
> Till his Brain in a rock & his Heart
> In a fleshy slough formed four rivers,
> Obscuring the immense Orb of fire,
> Flowing down into night; till a Form
> Was completed, a Human Illusion,
> In darkness and deep clouds involv'd.

The four rivers of Eden are the fallen senses of mankind, flowing down into the night of unnecessary sensory bondage. Urizen becomes Adam, and so fallen God too literally becomes fallen Man. Yet Urizenic Man at least has fierce torments, and his earth is a glowing bed. But only for a while; then the limit of contraction is reached, as the brain becomes lodged in the skull's cavern, and the heart forms the minimal perceptiveness that obscures even the natural sun. At the end, all Los's labors have resulted in Urizen's triumph; the Deist existence enshrouded in the deep clouds of abstract contemplation. (pp. 179-83)

> *Harold Bloom, in his* Blake's Apocalypse: A Study in Poetic Argument, *Doubleday & Company, Inc., 1963, 454 p.*

HAZARD ADAMS (essay date 1963)

[*Adams applies his understanding of Blake's symbolic system to "The Tyger" from* Songs of Experience, *interpreting the images in the poem as symbols of various aspects of creative inspiration. According to Adams, Blake suggests a "prophetic" reading of the Urizenic speaker's fearful questions concerning the creative process.*]

Readers have generally assumed that **"The Tyger"** is one of Blake's two or three greatest lyrics. For this reason, it is interesting to see that **"The Tyger"** most fully and particularly assimilates the whole of Blake's great system. (p. 57)

"The Tyger" is a poem of rather simple form, clearly and cleanly proportioned, all of its statements contributing to a single, sustained, dramatic gesture. Read aloud, it is powerful enough to move many listeners (small children, for example) without their having much understanding of the poem beyond its expression of a dramatic situation. But Blake warns us that there is a great gulf between simplicity and insipidity. The total force of the poem comes not only from its immediate rhetorical power but also from its symbolical structure.

Blake's image of the tiger, at first sensuous, is to continued inspection symbolic. Things which burn brightly, even tigers, can be thought of as either purifying something or being purified. In the dark of night, in a forest, a tiger's eyes would seem to burn. The tiger's coat suggests this same conflagration. In any case, Blake is trying to establish a brilliance about his image which he elsewhere associates, not surprisingly, with the apocalyptic figure of his minor prophecies, Orc:

> But terrible Orc, when he beheld the morning in the east,
> Shot from the heights of Enitharmon,
> And in the vineyards of red France appear'd the light of his fury. . . .

There are many examples of the same imagery throughout the prophecies. Another visual image which Blake may be suggesting here is consistent with what we shall see in the nature of the tiger itself. In many religious paintings (and in Blake's own work, the popularly mistitled "Glad Day" for example) the central figure seems to be emerging from or surrounded by a vast light: figuratively he "burns." Visually the fire image suggests immediate violence; traditionally it suggests some sort of purgatorial revelation.

The forests of the poem represent those famous mythological areas inhabited by blatant beasts, lost knights, and various spiritual wanderers and travelers. These forests *belong to* the night: Blake clearly invites us to read his line symbolically. For Blake, night suggests the delusion of material substance and the absence of the kind of light that surrounds revelation. There is a violent contrast between light and darkness, between the tiger and its surroundings, and the reader recognizes that the forest and the night are to be thought of in a derogatory way. The tiger, on the other hand, is presented ambiguously. In spite of its natural viciousness, it also suggests clarity and energy. If the reader has had prolonged experience with poetry and mythology, other associations will sharpen these ideas. He will perhaps associate the "forests of the night" with the traditional dark night or dark journey of the soul through the dens of demons and beasts. The tiger's brightness may suggest the force which the sun so often symbolizes in mythology. If the reader has read Dante, he may associate the forests with Dante's descent from the dark wood into the underworld; if he has read Goethe, he may notice a striking symbolic relationship between Blake's imagery and the imagery of enclosure in *Faust*—the forest, the study, the cave, the circle. Finally, if he has read Blake's own work, he will know that since the fall of man was a fall into a material world, he may associate the night with matter. In forests in the darkness men are trapped in an enclosure similar to Plato's cave, hobbled by the growing rubbish of materialism, blocked off from light by material substance. Men stand in forests surrounded by webs of leaves, limbs, vines, and bracken (Blake's illustrations provide ample evidence for such a symbolic interpretation of fallen life). Blake's prophecies work toward a similar expression of this idea in expanded form. In *The Book of Urizen,* Urizen, the arch-materialist of Blake's myth, traps himself in webbed enclosures similar to jungles. In *The Four Zoas* he sits in his "web of deceitful religion." The forest is also a symbol of the natural cycle of growth and decay in the fallen, natural world. It therefore represents not only spatial but also temporal enclosure. In his later prophecies Blake refers to the fallen world in its material, spatial form as the "mundane shell." Its opacity prevents man from seeing through to eternity. The time-form of the fallen world Blake calls the "circle of destiny," the world falsely seen in the spirit of materialistic determinism. The stars, which enter our poem in stanza 5, are a part of the concave surface of the mundane shell where man is trapped, and their movements represent the delusory, mechanical aspects of time. This shell is also a kind of egg, holding an embryo capable eventually of breaking the shell and leaping into real life free of the cycles of time and the enclosures of space.

In *The Four Zoas,* night symbolizes the history of the fallen world—its time-form, the circle of destiny. The archetypal man of Blake's prophetic books, Albion, a primordial giant symbolizing the human world, succumbs to sleep at the time of the fall and awakens only at the last judgment. In an early scheme for *The Four Zoas* Blake divided the history of the fallen world into nine "nights," each a historical cycle; and he subtitled his poem "The Death and Judgment of the Ancient Man, A Dream in Nine Nights." The fallen world is therefore a nightmare in the mind of Albion, who is afflicted by materialist delusions: for the materialist, the tiger appears out of darkness, a nightmarish figure, bright and violent, perhaps the vehicle of that terrible judgment he has been taught to believe in. What the tiger is to the visionary the poem is about to tell us, but in a subtler way. (pp. 58-60)

A reading of Blake's early drafts of **"The Tyger"** in the Rossetti MS reveals a rather important metamorphosis of the attitude of the speaker of the poem. Certain phrases from these drafts, later deleted, suggest that the speaker's attitude as Blake first conceived it was more clearly one of failure to understand and consequent fear of the tiger. For example:

> What dread hand and what dread feet?
> Could fetch it from the furnace deep
> And in thy horrid ribs dare steep
> In the well of sanguine woe.

The hellish imagery of these lines (Blake contended, after all, that hell was a mental state), the reference to horrid ribs (one might compare the references to the ribs of Urizen in *The Book of Urizen*), and deadly terrors strongly suggest that the tiger is a product of a *real* hell and a *real* deathliness. Subsequently several of these images were eliminated from the poem so that the balance between fear and admiration does not topple. However, it is still possible to read the final draft and assume that the speaker is a figure living in the fallen world and deluded into thinking that his world is the real world—someone like Urizen as he appears in *The Four Zoas,* particularly in Night Seven (a), where he meets Orc:

> But Urizen silent descended to the Caves of Orc & saw
> A cavern'd Universe of flaming fire. . . .

For in the final draft we find the assertion that the tiger may come from "distant deeps." To fallen man the tiger is horrific. It does not conform to established law, fails to fit into the established world picture, and is therefore evil. It is the corporeal eye of such a person that is described in *The Marriage of Heaven and Hell:* "The roaring of lions, the howling of wolves, the raging of the stormy sea, and the destructive sword, are portions of eternity, too great for the eye of man." . . . (pp. 60-1)

But I think it is clear that there is, if not another speaker of the poem who presents us with an alternative reading, a higher imaginative level on which the poem must be read. On this level the speaker is the Blakean prophet himself, whose attitude casts an ironic perspective upon the words as they are spoken by our Urizenic questioner. This speaker knows the answers to his questions and is forming them rhetorically. This means ultimately that he is a visionary, a "mental traveller" who sees the world in its proper perspective. Careful examination shows that the questions he asks imply certain answers, and that from them we learn not only what the tiger is but also who his maker is. His attitude is thus opposed to the confused fear of the Urizenic questioner.

The question of stanza 1 involves the speaker's assumption that some "hand or eye" forms the tiger. The confused speaker cannot decide how the tiger was made. Was it the hand or eye of some all-powerful creator? In either case his interpretation is ominous. The physical creation of brute force is represented by the hand of God thrust down from above into our world. The creative eye suggests the capacity for wrath in God's imagination. The two possible gods, to this attitude, are thus the aloof deity of natural religion, who acts toward man as the speaker acts toward the poor fly in **"The Fly,"** or the wrathful, avenging, spying deity of upside-down Christianity. A visionary perspective denies neither hand nor eye but casts them into a less ominous form and reads the "or" to mean "both" because the act of the hand is an extension of the eye's mental formulation. The hand is the shaping force of the blacksmith artist. The eye occurs elsewhere in Blake to suggest the shaping spirit of imagination. If we take the maker of the tiger to be God (provisionally, for he is a certain kind of god), the appearance of "eye" in this context means that God's method of creation is supernatural and that what He creates is not material. For Blake there is a clear distinction between the material, lidded or "outward" eye (an image like that of the "mundane shell") and the immortal, visionary eye which the artist sees *through* instead of with. The one raises a wall against true perception. The other opens a door: "If the doors of perception were cleansed every thing would appear to man as it is, infinite." . . . Erdman has pointed out that the eye appears as a visionary image in Blake's illustrations and drawings. In *Jerusalem,* Albion sleeps through history with eyes closed; his moments of vision and assertions of new life occur when he opens his real eyes and creates thereby the real world, not the nightmarish apparent one:

> Upon the Rock, he open'd his eyelids in pain, in pain he mov'd
> His stony members, he saw England. Ah! shall the Dead live again?

(pp. 62-3)

"Eye" suggests also the cycles of history named by God in *The Four Zoas* and *Jerusalem.* In those prophecies history is divided into seven (sometimes eight, depending upon whether Blake wants to include the apocalypse as the final eye) periods or "eyes of God," as Blake calls them. Each of these is a wheel containing within itself the microcosm of all history, each wheel the same play with different players; or perhaps better, each the same group of players acting a slightly different but archetypal drama: "as one age falls, another rises, different to mortal sight, but to immortals only the same . . . Accident ever varies, Substance can never suffer change nor decay." . . . Thus each "eye of God" is an intuition of the full scope of the historic process, and the eighth eye will act as the culmination of this process. This view of history and reality is consistent with Blake's argument that reality lies within "minute particulars," if only each particular is observed *through* the eye. Thus each eye of God is figuratively the "world in a grain of sand." The tiger as a creation of the imaginative eye of God and a symbol of that imaginative power is microcosmically implicit in each cycle, immanent and imminent. To the tiger's more complex relation to the culmination of history or the "eighth eye of God," I shall return shortly.

The tiger-maker is not God, simply defined. He is a false god or the true God depending upon the speaker's perspective. Urizen would consider the maker of the tiger a false god, a devil—that is why Blake often sides with "the devil's party," as he seems to do in *The Marriage of Heaven and Hell,* showing that "angels" are representatives of passive reason and thus lieutenants of Urizen to be associated with the stars, while "devils" are truly creative: "Active Evil is better than Passive Good." . . . Urizen's god is really the false god. Therefore, if the questions of the poem are taken as spoken by the materialist they imply fearfully that the creator of the tiger is some kind of interloper, a breaker of order. Icarus and Prometheus, the mythological personages of whom there are definite overtones in stanza 2, were both interlopers. Both defied the order of things (the material order, Blake would say) and both were punished for it. Icarus aspired to the sun and was flung down into the sea. Prometheus stole fire (the persistent image of Blake's poem) from the Gods, brought it to man, and was chained to a rock for his transgression. There is a parallel to this in Blake's own work, where Orc, Blake's first major apocalyptic figure, is also chained to a rock so that he too may be controlled. According to Urizen, then, the creator of the tiger, a threatening figure like Orc, or perhaps Blake's ultimate hero Los, must be some lawbreaker sent by the forces of the devil himself. Part of Orc's serpent nature is imposed upon him by the deluded imaginations of Urizen.

But from the visionary perspective, the same questions are merely rhetorical. The same interlopers are not evil creatures but heroic representatives of energy. They have embarked on the inevitable journey any hero must make in order to meet the forces of materialism and to do battle with them. Icarus' ascent on wings attached to him by wax suggests a terrible misjudgment of the consequences of approach to the fire of heaven, but Prometheus' descent sets the stage for the more important final battle to come, the loss of Aeschylus' *Prometheus Unbound* being an irony of history. Prometheus' gift of fire to man symbolizes hope of eventual apocalypse, a cleansing of all material things in purgatorial flame. His act is therefore related closely to the image Blake draws of a burning tiger capable of causing a conflagration which will consume the forests. The "seizing" of fire is also the typical act of a blacksmith preparing to forge some object. In stanzas 3 and 4, furthermore, the speaker assumes that the creator of the tiger is a blacksmith. This particular smith is not only the strongest of creatures but also the greatest of artists. He is not only a Prometheus but also a Hephaestus; and we recall that the blacksmith Hephaestus was also hurled from heaven by Zeus, that he was the Greek god of fire, and that his name was used by Greek and Roman poets as a synonym for "fire."

From the perspective of Urizen again, the questions of stanzas 3 and 4 imply that the blacksmith is some devil-maker. If we take the blacksmith as an archetype of the artist, then we see that from this perspective the artist is a creator of illusions and that the poet, in Sir Philip Sidney's terms, "lyeth," but for evil reasons, not in behalf of active energy. Urizen would ban him from the republic for reasons somewhat different from Plato's—because he is a fabricator and a dangerous revolutionary who pretends to see a world other than the material one. In his annotations to Bacon's *Essays,* Blake objects to the idea of the poet's lying in order to give pleasure. Only someone who sees *with* the corporeal eye would for a moment be so naive as to say that the poet lies: "What Bacon calls Lies is Truth itself." . . . Blake's blacksmith-artist Los works steadily with anvil and forge, hand and eye; the wonders of his labors are his creations of form out of miasma. His actions illustrate the principle of *outline* in Blake's aesthetic. According to Blake, when error is given proper outline it ceases to be error, for in its true form it has lost the power to delude. If, then, we begin

to suspect that the creator of the tiger is, in Blake's terms, Urizen's nemesis Los, we shall not be far wrong.

But this is not the whole story either. Stanza 5 is perhaps the most difficult in the poem. No interpretation of it that I have seen seems adequate. The most elaborate recent one is by Kathleen Raine in an essay which proposes to find the answer to the poem's question (Who made the tiger?) in Blake's alchemical and occult reading [see Additional Bibliography]. She points to a quotation from Reuchlin's *De Arte Cabbalistica,* which is mentioned twice by Robert Fludd in his *Mosaicall Philosophy* and once by Thomas Vaughn in his *Lumen de Lumine,* "both books well-known to Blake." The quotation is: "There is not an herb here below but he hath a star in heaven above; the star strikes him with her beams and says to him: Grow." Miss Raine construes the action of the stars in throwing down their "spears" (beams) as making possible the creation or "growth" of the tiger and the fallen world. By a somewhat devious process of reasoning, Miss Raine concludes that the Elohim (whom she associates with Urizen), as distinct from God, created the tiger, because in Blake's sources the Elohim created the fallen world. Therefore, she argues, "the answer is beyond all possible doubt, No"; God, who created the lamb, did not create the tiger.

I can only say that I totally disagree with the conclusion and the method used to arrive at it. Miss Raine has perhaps discovered a valuable source for Blake's star imagery, but she has completely ignored what Blake has done with the imagery in assimilating it to the poem and has wrenched the poem out of Blake's own symbolic system. In the first place, if we accept the source, Blake has substituted "spears" for "beams," and it is difficult to assume that he did this merely to find a rime for "tears." "Spears" brings a suggestion of war into the poem. "Stars" in Blake's symbolism are always associated with Urizen and materialism. As warriors they seem to represent his own legions, who have lost the battle against the creator of the tiger and in the course of attempting to negate active energy have actually helped to create what they most feared—the wrath of righteousness. I believe that further examination of Blake's imagery here will sustain this view. In Blake's symbolism the stars represent the movement of a delusory scientific time and the concave, inner surface of the mundane egg, which is the fallen world. The image is particularly apt because the stars are ineffectual in daylight; they are apparent only at night or during fallen history. To Urizen the act of the stars in throwing down their spears would suggest the creation of the material world—the end of the "wars of Eden" leading to the fall. Stars are traditionally angelic intelligences, but Blake uses both angels and stars ironically as forces of reaction and passive good. The action of the stars here represents a fall in the war in heaven during which the "demonic" orders, represented by the tiger, were created. (pp. 63-6)

It is unlikely that in the stubbornness of his own revolt Urizen (if we may conjecture) would fully understand the weeping of the stars. He might consider it an expression of pity for those hurt in the havoc wrought by his "necessary" war in behalf of progress. But it is more likely that the tears are really tears of chagrin and fear reminiscent of the allegory in Blake's *America,* in which the soldiers of the king of England, also associated with Urizen, throw down their arms to flee the vision of revolt, Orc. (p. 67)

From the point of view of the visionary, the action of the stars is more profound. As Erdman suggests:

The climax of the forging [of stanza 4 of **"The Tyger"**] is a mighty hammering which drives out the impurities in a shower of sparks, like the falling stars children call angels' tears. At this point in **"The Tyger"** Blake employs the symbols which in his political writing signify the day of repentance when the king's "starry hosts" shall "throw down . . . sword and musket."

For the visionary the image of these lines leads toward an intuition of apocalypse when, with the tiger formed, the sparks hurled, and heaven itself cleansed by pity and (perhaps, ironically) by fear, total resolution can be foreseen. The imagery of the stanza, rather than deriving its meaning from a single source, seems to me to describe an ambiguous event. If Miss Raine's hint is useful, it is to suggest that the hurling down of the spears of light at the time of the creation of the tiger is one of those typically ambiguous Blakean acts in which progression comes out of its own opposite. Thus the capitulation of the stars, in contributing to the "growth" of the fallen world, helps to bring about its apocalyptic destruction, just as Los's "hand or eye" brings form out of miasma and completes a divine plan which seems to have begun in total degradation. The visionary understands the paradox of progress and therefore is able to "keep the divine vision in time of trouble." The falling of the stars into the "starry floor" of the heavens is combined, then, with an image of pity, for they fall into this position in the form of tears, where they are a constant reminder of God's mercy in creating a lower limit for the fall.

There is a further qualification to be made. For Blake, there are true and false tears, true and false pity. For someone like Los, the true pity is to hold in check any immediate or sentimental expression of that emotion, just as Orc in Night VII of *The Four Zoas* "contemns" the pity of Urizen. . . . If Los were to pity Urizen before he had given him his true form, he would harm the whole of creation in the long run. Los, as artist, must purge himself even of apparent pity in order to be capable of its higher form. The violent tiger itself is Blake's symbol for the denial of false pity. Urizen was fooled by the stars; they pitied themselves. The kind of pity of which Urizen is capable in his fallen state is itself error. When Blake speaks of Satan as having no "science of wrath, but only of pity," . . . he indicates the necessity of one contrary paradoxically assisting the creativity of the other. Only Los marries the contraries.

In the fallen world even the apocalypse seems to have an ambiguous form. In total resolution the purgation by flame which is the tiger and the baptism by tears which is the weeping of the stars lead out of the fallen world into the new in the traditional rituals of rebirth. The balance of contraries is achieved, and the tiger lies down with the lamb, an image to which Blake turns in other lyrics.

If by now we do not have a fairly clear idea of who created the tiger and what the tiger is, the prophetic books can tell us more. In stanza 2 the word "dare" dramatically replaces the word "could" of stanza 1. Physical strength to create the tiger is evidently not the only necessity—there must be *will;* the figurative journey is both physically and spiritually difficult. In the prophecies the tenacious spirit is Los, who wipes "the sweat from his red brow" and confronts those miasmal, hovering, indefinite creatures to whom he must give a form. It is Los, then, who howls in anguish, bestows no false pity, and holds to his task. . . . (pp. 68-70)

[Blake] found the visionary at least latent in every man. Every man is a Los or at least has a Los. When in *Milton* Blake finds his own prophetic inspiration, it is Los who appears to him as a burning spiritual form:

> . . . Los descended to me:
> And Los behind me stood, a terrible flaming Sun, just close
> Behind my back. I turned round in terror, and behold!
> Los stood in that fierce glowing fire, & he also stoop'd down
> And bound my sandals on in Udan-Adan; trembling I stood
> Exceedingly with fear & terror, standing in the Vale
> Of Lambeth; but he kissed me and wish'd me health,
> And I became One Man with him arising in my strength.
> 'Twas too late now to recede. Los had enter'd into my soul:
> His terrors now posses'd me whole! I arose in fury & strength. . . .

Since the power of vision is the power of artistic creation in a nonmaterial world, the power of God is the power of man, and each man is a kind of artist. It is no surprise to see that Blake takes the next step and asserts that man is a microcosm of God, God is the spiritual body of communal man.

In *Jerusalem,* when the seven eyes of God are named, it is said that "they nam'd the Eighth: he came not, he hid in Albion's Forests." . . . For fallen man, such a creature is truly horrendous, hidden gleaming like an eye—like a tiger—in darkness, an image of the judgment he fears. Fallen man sees with "a little narrow orb, clos'd up & dark / Scarcely beholding the great light." . . . Such an eye, Blake implies, cannot "judge of the stars" and can therefore certainly "measure the sunny rays." . . . For such an eye, tigers and lions are not human forms but those "dishumaniz'd men" . . . seen by Urizen in his travels. Their spiritual reality is covered over by a material excrescence:

> . . . A Rock, a Cloud, a Mountain,
> Were now not Vocal as in Climes of happy Eternity
> Where the lamb replies to the infant voice, & the lion to the man of years
> Giving them sweet instructions; where the Cloud, the River & the Field
> Talk with the husbandman & shepherd.
>
> (pp. 70-1)

But for the visionary, the tiger illuminated is the tiger creating out of the forest the light of day in one vast apocalyptic conflagration similar to the awakening of Albion in *Jerusalem:*

> . . . Albion rose
> In anger, the wrath of God breaking, bright flaming on all sides around
> His awful limbs; into the Heavens he walked, clothed in flames. . . .

The leap of the tiger in the forest, inevitable to the eye of the visionary, is equivalent to the purgative fire which sweeps all before it, the eighth eye of God rending the veil of materialism. The tiger is thus an image of man's own hopes—the God in man, but also something created by the artist in man on the anvil of inspiration. It is a "fearful" image because, in the "forests of the night," false pity is misdirected. The artist who chooses to capture the miasmal mist of error and from it create significant form must not succumb to the temptations of right reason: "The tygers of wrath are wiser than the horses of instruction." ... To do so would be suddenly to succumb to the Urizenic view of what the tiger represents. Blake, himself, knew the temptation to treat the tiger as an obsessive, evil demon: "I am under the direction of Messengers from Heaven, Daily & Nightly; but the nature of such things is not, as some suppose, without trouble or care. Temptations are on the right hand & left; behind, the sea of time & space roars & follows swiftly: he who keeps not right onward is lost, & if our footsteps slide in clay, how can we do otherwise than fear & tremble" [see excerpt dated 1802]. ... And even Los is capable of momentary delusion during which the negative hatred of the spectre appears similar to the tiger's wrath:

> While Los spoke the terrible Spectre fell shudd'ring
> before him,
> Watching his time with glowing eyes to leap upon his
> prey....

But in certain visionary circumstances wrath and pity merge in a single imaginative act. The totality of the man of imagination, expressed in the image of the four Zoas and their eyes is combined with the seven lamps, the seven spirits, and the seven seals of Revelation in Blake's description of his pictorial *Vision of the Last Judgment:* "The whole upper part of the Design is a view of Heaven opened: around the Throne of Christ [in a cloud which rolls away are the] Four Living Creatures filled with Eyes, attended by Seven Angels with the Seven Vials of the Wrath of God." ... Blake clearly associates these seven angels and vials with his own seven historical cycles culminating in the total eighth.

The eighth eye or total man is the "Four Living Creatures." Even in his fallen state the prophetic power in this man is capable of being raised above his own sleeping form so that he may see God's wrath and its sevenfold cyclical expression in history as a form of spiritual recreation and therefore proper pity. This is the case with Milton:

> The Seven Angels of the Presence wept over Milton's
> Shadow.
> As when a man dreams he reflects not that his body
> sleeps,
> Else he would wake, so seem'd he entering his Shadow:
> but
> With him the Spirits of the Seven Angels of the
> Presence
> Entering, they gave him still perceptions of his Sleeping
> Body
> Which now arose and walk'd with them in Eden, as an
> Eighth
> Image Divine tho' darken'd and tho' walking as one
> walks
> In sleep, and the Seven comforted and supported him.

(pp. 71-2)

To "dare frame" the tiger's "fearful symmetry" is to "keep right onward," to hold the visionary attitude. It is also to confront the tiger with assurance. To be tempted and to succumb is to become the materialist and to find oneself staring into a mirror at one's own spectre, without realizing that one sees there the reflection of a brute self. Nature's "vegetable glass" shows Urizen only his own image. Not knowing that he sees himself, he chases that image through the world, failing ever to subdue it. The "wild beast" which Blake calls the "spectre" in **"My Spectre around me ..."** is an intimation

of the divided state of fallen man. If it is horrific, its existence, like that of the tiger, indicates man's condition if he cares to or can read the sign. In the conclusion of *Visions of the Daughters of Albion,* Oothoon, a free spirit condemned as a harlot by the man she has loved, lists a "glowing tyger" as one of the creatures of the night which can be blotted out by the "mild beams" of the sun—beams which bring expansion to the "eye of pity." ... Having come this far, Oothoon needs only to see a little farther through the eye and into the tiger's fire to understand that the blotting out of the horrific glowing tiger in the greater light of the sun is similar to the disappearance of the sun in the light of the glory of God, which is described to us in Revelation. In the apocalypse the tiger's fire returns to the light of which it is a fallen intimation. To the visionary, the tiger symbolizes the primal spiritual energy which may bring form out of chaos and unite man with that part of his own being which he has allowed somehow to sleepwalk into the dreadful forests of material darkness. In *Europe,* Blake speaks of materialist "thought" as the cause of such a retreat from reality:

> Thought chang'd the infinite to a serpent, that which
> pitieth
> To a devouring flame; and man fled from its face and
> hid
> In forests of night.

(p. 73)

The tiger is formed on the anvil of inspiration, which is the eye of man and God, but it is also a symbol of the very same eye that created it, for Blake believed that men are what they behold, that the outer and inner worlds are really one: "To the Eyes of the Man of Imagination, Nature is Imagination itself. As a Man is, So he Sees. As the Eye is form'd, such are its Powers" [see excerpt dated 1799]. ... Several times in the prophetic books Blake announces that a character has "become what he beheld." The manner in which one beholds the tiger is all important to its and one's own spiritual nature. As guardian of the forest it may either opaquely repel or indicate the existence somewhere nearby of a gate into the state of vision. Man has the power to create his world, for that world is really himself, caught in the vortex where the spirit takes on perceivable form.

"The Tyger" is concerned with both the unprolific or distorting and the truly creative process in spiritual life. The latter is a process equivalent to the process of creation in art. Creation in art is for Blake the renewal of visionary truth. From the point of view of the visionary, the tiger, fearful as he may be, is created form, error solidified and metamorphosed into a vision of the last judgment. He is, therefore, a creature to be confronted and contemplated not with undiluted fear but with that strange gaiety suggested by the visionary intensity of the poem itself—a gaiety which can find a place in the divine plan for both the tears and spears of the stars, for both Los and Urizen, and for both the tiger and the lamb. (pp. 73-4)

> *Hazard Adams, in his* William Blake: A Reading of the Shorter Poems, *University of Washington Press, 1963, 337 p.*

ALICIA OSTRIKER (essay date 1965)

[*As part of her comprehensive prosodic analysis in* Vision and Verse in William Blake, *Ostriker provides the following assessment of Blake's versification in* The Four Zoas *and* Jerusalem. *The critic offers a study in contrasts, for she focuses on the stylistic*

A pencil drawing of Blake by John Linnell dated 1820.

versatility of The Four Zoas *and underscores the austere intel-
lectuality of* Jerusalem.]

[With regard to formal technique, Blake's major prophecies]
are of a piece. All adhere to the septenary, and differ from
each other only as Blake, growing older, gradually shifted from
a mode which was ornately emotional to a mode austerely and
insistently intellectual. This involved a steady rise in degree
of irregularity in the verse. It also involved, in *Jerusalem,* a
sudden virtual cessation of imitative versification. Blake's
manifesto for expressive technique, prefaced to *Jerusalem,* applies to all three: "... the terrific numbers are reserved for
the terrific parts, the mild & gentle for the mild & gentle parts,
and the prosaic for inferior parts" [see excerpt dated 1804-
1820]. But the books, as we shall see, contain different proportions of mild, terrific, and prosaic.

Of all the prophecies, *The Four Zoas* offers the richest poetic
treasure hoard. Possibly it is too rich for unity. The changes
that came over *Vala* (Blake's first title for the poem) as it
matured into *The Four Zoas* invariably show expansion rather
than contradiction or contraction in Blake's thought. Among
the most important additions are those which refer to Jesus and
the Council of God, and those which allegorize contemporary
events; these indicate that Blake's myth was alive enough for
him to want to attach it to absolute Christian truths, and to the
truths in history as he was discovering them. But G. E. Bentley
feels that the revisions, occurring over a period of at least ten
years, "left a wilderness of loose ends, incomplete ideas, sprained
rhythms, and false starts which would have utterly condemned
the work of a smaller mind." (p. 172)

The real culprit is Blake's "Energy," which in this case was
centrifugal. The poem remains a gaudy mental pageant, certainly a failure if judged by standards alien to Blake's. "Unity
is the cloke of folly," he said ..., and he composed accordingly. Since his habit was to let the totality of a work of art
take care of itself while he labored at the parts, he did not feel
obliged to glue together even the most disparate forms. In *The
Four Zoas* he produced a work of extraordinary range, in which
every mood is treated as intensely as if there were nothing else
in the poem but that mood, as if salvation depended on that
mood alone. The ground level of this epic takes up where
America and the *Visions of the Daughters of Albion* left off.
Beyond this, *The Four Zoas* resolves into several discrete styles
which lie "at random, carelessly diffused," not given architecture until Night Nine.

Blake involves "terrific numbers," of course, for the passages
of loud noise and violent activity, for "The howlings gnashings
groanings shriekings shudderings sobbings burstings" ... which
cram the poem. These passages are always heavily, and usually
irregularly, accented:

> The hammer of Urthona smote the rivets in terror. of
>   brass
> Tenfold. the Demons rage flamd tenfold forth rending,
> Roaring redounding. Loud Loud Louder & Louder &
>   fird
> The darkness warring with the waves of Tharmas &
>   Snows of Urizen. . . .

In such passages spondaic formations (flámd ténfôld fórth rénd-
ing ... Lóud Lóud Lóuder) are important for emphasis, and
enjambment and asymmetrical pauses build cumulative rhythms.
The sound is strongly repetitive; here the consonant pattern
moves from *m*'s (ha*mm*er, s*m*ote, fla*m*d) to *f*'s, to *l*'s and *d*'s
culminating in the reiterated "*Loud*," and with strenuous *r*'s
running all through. The vowels are broad and deep, with
echoes and half-echoes like hammer-terror, brass-darkness. Most
important, the rhythm, sound, and diction all imitate, in a
sensuous as well as a symbolic way, the clamor and effort
Blake means to express. It is quite a different technique from
that used, for example, in **"The Tyger,"** where the sense of
effort was far more mental than physical.

One of the most sustained blood-and-thunder sections occurs
at the close of Night III, when Ahania, spurned by Urizen,
falls, and Urizen perforce follows, to the accompaniment of a
crash, flame, and universal groan, and Tharmas rises as Chaos
regnant:

> But from the Dolorous Groan one like a shadow of
>   smoke appeard
> And human bones rattling together in the smoke &
>   stamping
> The nether Abyss & gnashing in fierce despair. panting
>   in sobs
> Thick short incessant bursting sobbing. deep despairing
>   stamping struggling   (8)
> Struggling to utter the voice of Man struggling to take
>   the features of Man. Struggling   (9)
> To take the limbs of Man at length emerging from the
>   smoke . . .
> Crying. Fury in my limbs. destruction in my bones &
>   marrow
> My skull riven into filaments. my eyes into sea jellies
> Floating upon the tide wander bubbling & bubbling . . .
> So Tharmas bellowd oer the ocean thundring sobbing
>   bursting. . . .

Here, in addition to the devices already mentioned of heavy and irregular accent patterns, and repetitive and imitative sound, Blake lets his struggling Chaos burst from septenary to an eight-foot and then a nine-foot line, as marked. Long lines like these are relatively common in *The Four Zoas* as compared to *Milton* and *Jerusalem*.

Some of the lamentations, speeches of defiance, curses, and so on, though still fairly "terrific," are milder than this. When Urizen curses his daughters, the rage is controlled:

> . . . for their colours of loveliness
> I will give blackness for jewels hoary frost for ornament deformity;
> For crowns wreathd Serpents for sweet odors stinking corruptibility
> For voices of delight hoarse croakings inarticulate thro frost . . .
> Go forth sons of my curse Go forth daughters of my abhorrence.

Although the speech ends with a line from *Tiriel,* Blake has learned something from Isaiah about balanced diction and rhythm. Still, Blake's terrific passages are mainly brass and percussion. There is nothing subtle about them; nor is there anything subtle about the way Blake pulls them out for all occasions. (pp. 172-75)

A second style in *The Four Zoas,* commonly Biblical both in language and construction, is the lyric. Here the meter is regular and the matter is "mild & gentle"—although sometimes only in a very equivocal sense. Since Blake did not care about regularity or the appearance of regularity for its own sake, he often used it ironically, in the delusive tones of females, for songs of war and human sacrifice. . . .

> Now now the Battle rages round thy tender limbs O Vala
> Now smile among thy bitter tears now put on all thy beauty
> Is not the wound of the sword Sweet & the broken bone delightful
> Wilt thou now smile among the slain when the wounded groan in the field. . . .

[Here is an] explicit declaration that the god of love and passion (Luvah) is also the god of pain and mutilation. Yeats must have learned something from Blake about how "a terrible beauty is born." But what gives Blake's war lyrics force is that he couples a full perception of cruelty's beauty with a firm moral detestation of it, which Yeats (and Swinburne before him) was never able to do.

Another type of lyric in *The Four Zoas* is the lamentation. . . .

> O did I keep the horses of the day in silver pastures
> O I refusd the lord of day the horses of his prince
> O did I close my treasuries with roofs of solid stone
> And darken all my Palace walls with envyings & hate. . . .
> I went not forth I hid myself in black clouds of my wrath
> I calld the stars around my feet in the night of councils dark
> The stars threw down their spears & fled naked away
> We fell. . . .

Of the many lyrics of lamentation, the smoothest show characters nearest the state of regeneration, like Enion who never

falls far, and Urizen in Night V temporarily perceiving his error. In these cases, metrical regularity bears morally positive implications. (pp. 175-76)

Finally, Blake also employs a flowing *Thel*-like meter for his lyrics of joy. The pastoral interlude of Night IX systematically recalls ballad; the diction, the hymeneal theme, the rhythms, are all from the Song of Songs:

> Where dost thou flee O fair one where dost thou seek thy happy place
> To yonder brightness there I haste for sure I came from thence
> Or I must have slept eternally nor have felt the dew of morning
> Eternally thou must have slept, nor have felt the morning dew
> But for yon nourishing sun tis that by which thou art arisen
> The birds adore the sun the beasts rise up & play in his beams,
> And every flower & every leaf rejoices in his light
> Then, O thou fair one, sit thee down, for thou art as the grass,
> Thou risest in the dew of morning & at night art folded up.

(pp. 176-77)

The imitative music in *The Four Zoas,* whether bombastic or lyric, concurs with the sudden upsurge of natural description in this poem. After a few tentative sorties in the early books, Blake seems now to be observing the vegetative world for its sensory as well as its symbolic qualities. Not only does he give several catalogues of natural objects, like the list of trees, birds and animals in [Night I], or the list of insects and small earth animals in [Night IX]. These might be padding. He also indulges in genuine imagery, of the sort which is every other poets staple, but which he had hardly trifled with since *Poetical Sketches.* To describe the sea's motion, he extends his line:

> & helpless as a wave
> Beaten along its sightless way growing enormous in its motion to
> Its utmost goal. . . .

To describe Los at war, he brings the sun symbol back to the world of corporeal image:

> Flaming his head like the bright sun seen thro a mist that magnifies
> The disk into a terrible vision to the Eyes of trembling mortals.

(p. 177)

Aural imagery is also important in *The Four Zoas,* although its source may be literary rather than natural. A passage in Night V describes the winter birth of Orc-Christ to the sound of music; its subject duplicates the opening of the *Nativity Ode,* and its technique may stem from Milton's musical passage later in that poem. In [Night VIII] another bit of aural imagery has Los at work in Golgonooza; "The hard dentant hammers are lulld by the flutes lula lula" may have been suggested by the musical pastimes around Milton's Pandemonium.

In addition to the terrific parts and the lyrics, a third noticeable style in *The Four Zoas* is the ethically argumentative. This may be dramatic, as in the lament of Enion, Blake's "blind & age bent" Demeter (taken perhaps from Job . . .):

What is the price of Experience do men buy it for a
    song
Or wisdom for a dance in the street? No it is bought
    with the price
Of all that a man hath his house his wife his children
Wisdom is sold in the desolate market where none
    come to buy
And in the witherd field where the farmer plows for
    bread in vain

It is an easy thing to triumph in the summers sun
And in the vintage & to sing on the waggon loaded
    with corn
It is an easy thing to talk of patience to the afflicted
To speak the laws of prudence to the houseless
    wanderer. . . .
It is an easy thing to rejoice in the tents of prosperity
Thus could I sing & thus rejoice, but it is not so with
    me. . . .

Or it may be satiric. Blake's comment on Bacon's *Essays* was
"good advice for Satan's kingdom," and he probably meant
Urizen's advice to his daughters to reproduce Bacon's curt
style:

Compell the poor to live upon a Crust of bread by soft
    mild arts
Smile when they frown frown when they smile & when
    a man looks pale
With labour & abstinence say he looks healthy & happy
And when his children sicken let them die there are
    enough
Born, even too many & our Earth will be overrun
Without these arts. . . .

Technically these ethical passages fall between the terrific sections and the lyrics, with neither the rhythmic drive and the
cacophony of the former, nor the rhythmic grace and melli-
fluousness of the latter. Their irregularities, like the ironic
spondee of "sóft | míld árts," and the enjambment of "there
are enough / Born," are rhetorically functional rather than imitative. The sound rather avoids than cultivates alliteration;
there is just enough—"Com*p*ell the *p*oor to live upon a Crust,"
"healthy & happy," "*ch*ild*ren* si*ck*en"—to give the lines starch.
At its worst, this middle style degenerates into "prosaic numbers for the inferior parts."

Blake, like Milton, wrote poorly when he wrote only to expound doctrinal points. Few critics claim great poetic value
for God the Father's justification of Man's fall in Book III of
Paradise Lost, although everyone agrees that the explanation
given there of man's free will is central to the poem's conception. When Blake descends from poetry to explanation in
lines like:

But in Eternal times the Seat of Urizen is in the South,
Urthona in the North Luvah in East Tharmas in
    West . . .

          so permitted because
It was the best possible in the State calld Satan to Save
From Death Eternal. . . .

Blake's catastrophe is severer than Milton's, because he lacks
the ridge of a stable line to break his fall.

Except for Night VIII, *The Four Zoas* has rather few "inferior
parts." In that Night the explanations, abstractions, catalogues,
and genealogies come tediously thick and fast. Unfortunately,

this was among the last sections of *The Four Zoas* to be written,
and it ominously forecasts developments in *Milton* and *Jerusalem*. As it stands in the present poem, it is only the dark
hour before the dawn.

Night IX, Blake's triumph, bursts from the poem like the final
movement of Beethoven's Choral Symphony. It is the Last
Judgment. "And all the while the trumpet sounds," . . . amid
tumult of flood and earthquake, human wailing and groaning,
wakening the dead to judgment. The book resounds with musical imagery. "Vocal may" is mentioned early. . . . There is
a "noise of rural works" as horses, bulls, tigers, and lions
"sing" . . . and the Sons of Urizen "shout." . . . The Human
seed is harrowed "To ravishing melody of flutes & harps &
softest voice." . . . When Ahania rises in springtime,

A shout of jubilee in lovely notes responds from
    daughter to daughter
From son to Son as if the Stars beaming innumerable
Thro night should sing soft warbling filling Earth &
    heaven
And bright Ahania took her seat by Urizen in songs &
    joy. . . .

The Human Wine is pressed to music, "to violins & tabors to
the pipe flute lyre & cymbal" . . . , and when the wine is
finished, "the heavens rolld on with vocal harmony." . . . Even
the structure of this Night is musical. After a tremendous apocalyptic prelude which corresponds to Winter in the Night's
seasonal scheme and thus appropriately includes or announces
bits of the various motifs to come, there are definite movements
for the plowing and harrowing of springtime, vintage, and
breadmaking, each interrupted by arias from the various characters.

All the styles of *The Four Zoas* appear at their best in this final
Night, saved from the danger of overcrowding by the Night's
good structure. As befits the theme of unification, and Blake's
conviction that a whole Man was greater than the sum of his
parts, something new also appears: a style which combines
lyricism with a moderate degree of metrical irregularity to
express the higher, firmer beauty of the new life:

The Sun has left his blackness & has found a fresher
    morning
Ănd thĕ míld móon rejoices in the clear & cloudless
    night
Ănd Mán wálks fórth from midst of the fires the evil is
    all consumd. . . .
The Expanding Eyes of Man behold the depths of
    wondrous worlds
Óne Éarth óne séa beneath nor Érrĭng Glóbes wándĕr
    but Stars
Ŏf fíre ríse ûp níghtlў frŏm the Ocean & óne Sún
Éach mórnĭng lĭke ă Néw bórn Mán íssŭes with songs
    & Joy.

                                              (pp. 176-81)

                    • • • • •

[*Jerusalem*] seems generally acknowledged to be an uninviting
poem. Even Frye, Blake's most ardent defender, admits its
harshness, defending it on grounds of expressiveness, and comparing it to Goya's *Disasters of War*, where truth, not beauty
or ugliness, is the relevant thing. Between *Jerusalem* and a
Goya etching, however, is the difference between an image
and an idea. Blake's system . . . has in his last great prophetic
work almost entirely gobbled up his poetry. "Putting on in-

tellect'' to Blake meant pursuing the ramifications of his thought down every crooked alley and lane to the last minute particular, leaving nothing unexplained, personifying the Sons and Daughters of Albion with the exactness of Biblical genealogies, declaring the dimensions of Golgonooza as precisely as Solomon's temple was measured, establishing the jurisdiction of the Twelve Tribes of Israel over ''the Fifty-two Counties of England & Wales / The Thirty-six of Scotland & the Thirty-four of Ireland'' ... as faithfully as Homer gave his catalogue of ships, and filling every vacancy in the epic with wads of dialectic. The dwelling on natural objects ... has vanished, since Blake now renounces Nature as the source of any good. Analysis of human emotion has become analysis of geographical and numerological symbolism. Individual history has turned collective. Characters have become diagrammatic, and their dramatic interchanges, their clashes of wills, their triumphs and lamentations, have become doctrinal debates.

Another difference between Goya and the Blake of *Jerusalem* is the difference between outrage and despair. Goya's lurid portraits of the human wolf and serpent are inflammatory; they cry out for rebellion against the vicious, the ugly, the stupid. But Blake has gone beyond faith in rebellion. Where the dominant mood of *The Four Zoas* was struggle, ... the dominant mood of *Jerusalem* is a grim determination to let evil and error have their way, to let them express themselves unarrested, even to give them ''a body,'' in the faith that only when it is fully grown, fully drunk with the blood of nations, and thus fully recognized, may Falsehood ''be cast off for ever.'' ... Blake's rule for this poem seems to be that of Conrad's Stein: ''In the destructive element immerse.'' *Jerusalem* is an incantation to raise the Devil on the presumption that when he is raised he will vanish. This is in fact what happens at the poem's close, when things have gotten so bad they cannot possibly get any worse: Antichrist appears, overshadowing and dividing Albion and Jesus; Albion to save Jesus ''threw himself into the Furnace of affliction'' and in the very next line, without any of the tumult of Night IX in *The Four Zoas,* we discover that

> All was a Vision, all a Dream: the Furnaces became
> Fountains of Living Waters flowing from the Humanity Divine
> And all the Cities of Albion rose from their Slumbers. and All
> The Sons & Daughters of Albion on soft clouds waking from Sleep. . . .

The impulse of Mankind to sacrifice himself for his friend, Jesus, has itself destroyed Antichrist. But up until this point, the dream has been a nightmare.

What happens to the verse in *Jerusalem* is that it shifts still further than before into the camp of irregularity, and is flayed of ornament so that the blood and muscle of Blake's thought can be seen unveiled. In the bulk of the poem, Blake hardly seems to be on civil speaking terms with his meter; he is far too occupied with the content of what he is saying to worry about the technique, which perforce must take care of itself. The effect of Blake's new preoccupations on his verse is at times painfully direct. *The Four Zoas* had recorded the crucifixion of Luvah in Blake's cruel lyric manner:

> They give the Oath of blood, they cast the lots into the helmet,
> They vote the death of Luvah & they naild him to the tree. . . .
> Then left the Sons of Urizen the plow & harrow the loom

> The hammer & the Chisel & the rule & compasses
> They forgd the sword the chariot of war the battle ax
> The trumpet fitted to the battle & the flute of summer,
> And all the arts of life they changd into the arts of death. . . .
> O Melancholy Magdalen, behold the morning breaks
> Gird on the flaming Zone. descend into the Sepulcher. . . .
> Remember all thy feigned terrors on the secret Couch
> When the sun rose in glowing morn with arms of mighty hosts
> Marching to battle who was wont to rise with Urizens harps
> Girt as a sower with his seed to scatter life abroad.

In *Jerusalem,* to ensure that the British people would not miss the relevance of the crucifixion to them—to make them see that they were the crucifers—he simply added place names (italics mine):

> They cast the lots into the helmet: they give the oath of blood *in Lambeth*
> They vote the death of Luvah, & they nail'd him to *Albions* Tree *in Bath* ...
> Then left the Sons of Urizen the plow & harrow, the Loom
> The hammer & the chisel. & the rule & compasses: *from London fleeing*
> They forg'd the sword *on Cheviot,* the chariot of War & the battle-ax,
> The trumpet fitted to mortal battle, & the Flute of Summer *in Annandale*
> And all the Arts of Life. they chang'd into the Arts of Death *in Albion.* . . .
> O melancholy Magdalen behold the morning *over Malden* break:
> Gird on thy flaming zone, descend into the sepulcher *of Canterbury.* . . .
> Remember all thy feigned terrors on the secret couch *of Lambeth's Vale*
> When the sun rose in glowing morn, with arms of mighty hosts
> Marching to battle who was wont to rise with Urizens harps
> Girt as a sower with his seed to scatter life abroad *over Albion.* . . .

By good fortune or fortunate instinct, most of these additions simply change septenaries into passable, if rather overcrowded, eight-stress lines; and the lines ''They forg'd the sword on Cheviot, the chariot of War & the battle-ax, / The trumpet fitted to mortal battle, & the Flute of Summer in Ananndale,'' may even be considered a metrical enrichment. But the poet certainly has broken the back of his general movement, changing a flowing narrative to something much heavier. (pp. 189-93)

[Despite] the epic's exploded scope, passages which in earlier books might have had quite varied textures here seem often to have gone through the same grinder. Compare two descriptions of the Tree of Mystery springing up around Urizen in *The Four Zoas,* around Albion in *Jerusalem:*

> His book of iron on his knees he tracd the dreadful letters ...
> Age after Age till underneath his heel a deadly root
> Struck thro the rock the root of Mystery accursed shooting up

Branches into the heaven of Los they pipe formd
  bending down
Take root again where ever they touch again branching
  forth
In intricate labyrinths oerspreading many a grizly
  deep . . .
He sat by Tyburns brook, and underneath his heel shot
  up
A deadly Tree, he nam'd it Moral Virtue. and the Law
Of God who dwells in Chaos hidden from the human
  sight.
    The Tree spread over him its cold shadows, (Albion
    groand)
They bent down, they felt the earth and again enrooting
Shot into many a Tree: an endless labyrinth of woe! . . .

In *The Four Zoas* [quoted first], the passage is devoted to
picturing the banyan's growth, in *Jerusalem* to explaining it.
In *The Four Zoas* there are clusters of sound like "*root* . . .
*S*t*ruck,* . . . *rock*," "*root* . . . *thro*' . . . *root* . . . *sh*o*oting*,"
"*Branches* . . . *bending* . . . *branching*." Its cumulative rhythms
make use of little touches like "pípe fórm'd" and the en-
jambments "deadly root / Struck" and "shooting up /
Branches." But in the *Jerusalem* passage the sound-echoes go
no further than "*hidden* . . . *human*," "c*old* shad*ows* . . .
gr*oand*" and the rhythm is diffuse, headed nowhere, with the
spondees "shót úp" and "bént dówn" wasted in it. (pp. 193-94)

  It is easy to acknowledge a man to be great & good
    while we
  Derogate from him in the trifles & small articles of that
    goodness:
  Those alone are his friends, who admire his minutest
    powers. . . .

[In this passage from *Jerusalem*] we have two lines which might
be either verse or prose, and one which is unmistakably verse;
none of which, however, makes use of rhythm to heighten
meaning. There is nothing especially wrong here, but nothing
especially right. As all these passages show, the "inferior"
parts of *Jerusalem* may or may not be irregular. Irregularity is
not their defect; their defect is that they are typically lacking
in a cumulative rhythm and in the reinforcements of sound.

Too much of *Jerusalem* is "inferior" in this sense. Yet the
total impression given by the verse of this epic not only conforms to, but enhances, Blake's doctrines. Because Blake has
renounced Nature, there is no imitative versification. Because
he has embraced Freedom, he can use enjambed weak endings
habitually, and often seems to go out of his way for them as
if deliberately to flout conventional prosody:

  The silent broodings of deadly revenge springing from
    the
  All powerful parental affection. . . .

  Such is the Forgiveness of the Gods, the Moral Virtues
    of the
  Heathen. . . .

This is disconcerting, but it reminds us that "Jerusalem is
nam'd Liberty among the Sons of Albion."

Again, because he has decided to give Falsehood a body, he
can have lines as ugly as:

  Calling the Rocks Atomic Origins of Existence: denying
    Eternity
  By the Atheistical Epicurean Philosophy of Albions
    Tree. . . .

Ugliness has been produced here by sound as well as sense,
by the turkey-gobble of "Calling the R*ock*s At*omic O*rigins,"
and by the setting of the sedate Greek-derived words "Atheistical Epicurean Philosophy" to a burlesque jog as if they
were so many camels.

Finally, because he has embraced Intellect, he can turn aside
the rhythms of passion for the rhythms of idea. When Los
speaks "swift as the shuttle of gold" to Enitharmon in the last
moments before their mutual redemption, he makes no impassioned oration, but lectures her on how the sexes will vanish:

        that we may Foresee & Avoid
  The terrors of Creation & Redemption & Judgment.
    Beholding them
  Displayd in the Emanative Visions of Canaan in
    Jerusalem & in Shiloh
  And in the Shadows of Remembrance. & in the Chaos
    of the Spectre
  Amalek. Edom. Egypt. Moab. Ammon. Ashur.
    Philistea. around Jerusalem. . . .

Moreover, it is almost uncanny how even in the midst of di-
dactics, when a "poetic" figure appears, poetic rhythms appear
also, as in the last line of:

  For Art & Science cannot exist but in minutely
    organized Particulars
  And not in generalizing Demonstrations of the Rational
    Power.
  The Infinite alone resides in Definite & Determinate
    Identity
  Establishment of Truth depends on destruction of
    Falshood continually
  On Circumcision: not on Virginity, O Reasoners of
    Albion.

                                    (pp. 194-96)

Yet it would be unfair to imply that *Jerusalem* lacks beauty
even in the ordinary sense, for in its own odd, austere way,
this poem has many effective passages. Los striving to master
his Spectre emits power through his awkward, musclebound
rhythms:

  I knów thy decéit | & thў | rĕvén|gĕs, ănd | ŭnléss thou
    desist
  Ĭ wĭll cértăinlў crĕâte an eternal Hell for thee. Lísten: /
  Be atténtive: / be obédient: / Lo the Furnaces are ready
    to receive thee. . . .

The balance is lopsided, yet every accent is like the crack of
a whip. Or for a fuller sort of power, Blake can still manage
a good exhortation:

  Rúsh ón! Rúsh ón! Rúsh ón! ye vegetating Sons of
    Albion
  Thĕ Sún shâll gó before you in Day: the Moon shall go
  Before you in Night. Cóme ón! Cóme ón! Cóme ón!
    The Lord
  Jehovah is before, behind, above, beneath, around. . . .

At times, too, the poem still approaches lyric, although Blake
jealously guards his metrical irregularities even in his "mild
& gentle" sections; the description of Golgonooza has its septenaries and alexandrines, but also has lines of five and four
feet:

> The stones are pity, and the bricks, well wrought
> affections: (5)
> Enameld with love & kindness, & the tiles engraven
> gold   (6)
> Labour of merciful hands: the beams & rafters are
> forgiveness . . .   (7)
> The cielings, devotion; the hearths, thanksgiving (4)
>
> (pp. 196-97)

Finally, when *Jerusalem* reaches its denouement, when it is time for Albion to rise from his rock and rejoin Jesus, Blake wants a versification that will express the final vision of union and will erase all the horrors of the prior "dream" that mankind has lived until now. . . . [Consequently,] he extends his line of freedom once more, so that it reaches to eight feet instead of seven, and with this leavening eight-stress line he proceeds to march "forward forward irresistible from Eternity to Eternity." . . . (pp. 197-98)

Plates 94 and 95, in which Albion awakes and "England who is Brittannia enterd Albion's bosom rejoicing" . . . , both contain several eight-foot lines, as if in preparation for the coming movement. Plate 96, the colloquy between Albion and Jesus which culminates in Albion's self-sacrifice and the re-entry of the Four Zoas into Albion's bosom, reverts to septenary. In Plate 97, Albion draws his Bow and all the Four Zoas draw their Bows; Plate 98 gives the Fourfold shooting of the arrow of Love and the consequent humanizing of the universe; and Plate 99 is Blake's brief "consummatum est." All these are dominated by the eight-stress line, although Blake will not limit himself even now so much that he cannot still have some of his sevens and sixes, and a few lines in Plate 98 seem to be nine and ten feet long.

The final vision begins with the fourfold drawing of the Bow:

> Só spáke the Vision of Albion & in him sò spáke in my
> hearing   (6)
> The Únivérsal Fáther Then Álbion strétchd his hánd ínto
> Infínitúde.   (8)
> And took his Bow. Fóurfŏld the Visĭon fŏr bright
> béaming Urizen   (7)
> Láyd hĭs hánd ŏn the South & took a breathing Bow of
> carved Gold   (8)
> Lúvăh hĭs hánd strétch'd tŏ thĕ Éast & bore a Silver
> Bow bríght shíning   (8)
> Thármăs Wéstwărd a Bow of Brass púre fláming richly
> wrought   (7)
> Urthona Northward in thíck stórms a Bow of Iron,
> terrible thundering.   (8)

One notes, at this point, the careful attention to sound; the repeated "*So spake . . . so spake*," the triple alliteration "*bright beaming . . . breathing Bow . . . Bow of Brass*," and the key sound for the fourth, dark, laboring Zoa, "Ur*th*ona Nor*th*ward . . . *th*ick . . . *th*undering." The rhythm, too, once again performs a human task. There is a good distribution of trochees and spondees. The line openings vary, with three normal iambic openings (Thĕ Únĭvérs-, Ănd tóok hĭs Bów, Ŭrthónă Nórth-), one spondee (Só spáke), two double trochees (Láyd hĭs hánd ŏn, Thármăs Wéstwărd), and one single trochee (Lúvăh) which then recurs internally to form a line with a lovely cadence, its first half moving with a swing, then straightening out to a steady beat, and concluding with a spondaic poise:

> Lúvăh hĭs hánd / strétchd tŏ thĕ Éast / & bóre ă Sílvĕr
> Bów bright shíníng:

The effect of a double dactyl in "térrĭblĕ thúndĕrĭng" concludes this introduction to the "Human Fourfold."

The tenor of this passage and those which follow it is one of stately ceremony. There is a sense of decorum, surprising to find in Blake after all the contortions and ululations of *Jerusalem*. There is a feeling of alternating "expansion" of vision in such lines as:

> Ănd thĕ dím Cháos brightend beneath, above, around:
> Éyed ăs the Peacock,
> Accordĭng tŏ thĕ Húman Nerves of Sensatĭon, thĕ Fóur
> Rívĕrs ŏf thĕ Wáter of Life. . . .

and "contraction," when the human creatures look back on what is past and momentarily re-create its ugliness:

> Where are the Kingdoms of the World & all their glory
> that grew on Desolation
> The Fruit of Albions Poverty Tree when the Triple
> Headed Gog-Magog Giant
> Of Albion Taxed the Nations into Desolation & then
> gave the Spectrous Oath . . .

But the final statement is that of harmony:

> All Human Forms identified even Tree Metal Earth &
> Stone, all
> Human Forms identified. living going forth & returning
> wearied
> Into the Planetary lives of Years Months Days & Hours
> reposing,
> And then Awaking into his Bosom in the Life of
> Immortality.
>
> And I heard the Name of their Emanations they are
> named Jerusalem. . . .
>
> (pp. 198-200)

It is reasonable to ask, of *Jerusalem* and of the other Prophetic Books, whether the offspring justify the long travail. Do the many fine passages of poetry in *The Four Zoas* justify its disunity and the hectic, tortured tone of the whole? . . . Is the pilgrimage through *Jerusalem,* in whose dark caverns we hear almost nothing but the horrid clang of the Blake-Los hammer, made worthwhile by the ultimate emergence into daylight and the music of the spheres? Remember Johnson's remark about Milton's magnum opus, which seems even truer here: that it was admirable, but nobody ever wished it longer.

According to any conventional definition of a work of art, these would be flawed, uneven monsters whose defects greatly outweigh their virtues. Art must have its rules; Art must transform life's chaos to order; Art must create beauty from all things; Art must exhibit wholeness, harmony, radiance. But Blake, even in his metrics, deliberately breaks every rule he makes, refuses to impose order in art where there is no order in his visions, and insists, in his perverse honesty, on preserving every jot and tittle of man's foulness just as it stands, keeping beauty afar until he is ready for her. According to Blake's own expressive definition of art, he could have done no other.

The difficulty with expressivist poetry is that, by its nature, it refuses external standards of judgment. It insists that criteria of beauty, lucidity, wholeness, do not apply to it. If it is ugly, it was meant to express ugliness; if obscure, obscurity is its warp and woof; if fragmented, it will defend fragmentation as its necessary condition. You cannot declare that it is "good" or "bad" art, for it does not really care whether it is art or not. It would just as soon be something else, and if you require labels to your experiences, it does not care about you. All Blake's impulses—his didacticism, his passion for intellectual outline unblurred by sentiment, his obsession with liberty, his insistence on creating ''a System'' and setting it down in its entirety—converge to make the form of *Jerusalem*. Blake, like the parents of the Little Girl Lost, only

> Followed
> Where the vision led.

If the reader can enter into this form and find himself enlarged, so much the better. If not, so much the worse. This is a matter of taste and choice, as when two people go to a museum and look at some particularly grotesque Picasso. One says, ''Ah, that man—he really has it. You just can't get around him.'' The other says, ''Why didn't he just keep on doing more and more of those Blue Period things?''

For the reader who wants to give Blake the benefit of the doubt, the only possible help is repeated reading. One makes one's peace with the Prophetic Books, if at all, as the algebra student makes his peace with Imaginary Numbers. There is nothing in the real world to correspond to the square root of minus one; he is exasperated; but ambition, or his teacher, requires him to keep using the square root of minus one in equations until he grows to feel at home with it and becomes convinced that, real or unreal, the thing certainly is useful and probably makes sense. In the end, he is likely to feel that imaginary numbers are as true as anything else, and perhaps truer than most things. (pp. 200-01)

> *Alicia Ostriker, in her* Vision and Verse in William
> Blake, *The University of Wisconsin Press, 1965, 224 p.*

JOHN HOLLOWAY   (essay date 1968)

[*Holloway examines Blake's response to experience in his lyric poems, discerning a progressive movement away from his thematically and formally expressed vision of ''harmonious oneness'' in* Songs of Innocence *to a preoccupation with the disunity and evilness of reality in* Songs of Experience, *the Notebook poems of 1800-03, and the Pickering Manuscript lyrics of that same period.*]

Blake's poetry of visionary innocence is his greatest achievement, or at least his most indisputable success. As a collection, there is nothing in our language to set beside *Songs of Innocence.* But to see Blake's work, even up to 1790, solely in terms of those poems would be silly. By now there is no need to refute old-fashioned notions of the eighteenth century as an age of sense, reason and decorum. Those things hold good for no more than one smallish part of eighteenth-century society; and even that only when this part of society is considered by itself, and not as predatory on the rest—which it was. More than this, the later eighteenth century (and earlier nineteenth) was a period of repression, violence, political crisis and widespread suffering probably without parallel in modern England. The Seven Years' War with France was soon followed by the American crisis and War of Independence; and that by the outbreak, of the French Revolution, the war with revolutionary France, and Pitt's savage repression of radicalism at home. As against this, for the first time, many were coming to see society as something like a grand conspiracy of the great and rich against the small and poor, and the victorious heroes of history as not very different from the bloodthirsty pirates of the age itself. Scott's novel *The Pirate* was later to make exactly this point; and Blake's lyrics were written not only in succession

From Blake's series of engraved designs for the Book of Job.

to the hymns of Watts and Wesley, but in the very years of the revolutionary writings of Tom Paine, Godwin, and Mary Wollstonecraft.

Already in *Poetical Sketches* it is clear that there is a side of Blake very different indeed from his vision of patriarchal innocence. The **''Prologue intended for a Dramatic Piece of King Edward the Fourth''** in that collection is clearly an attack on the destructive militarism of a ruling class:

> When Sin claps his broad wings over the battle . . .
> O who can answer at the throne of God?
> The Kings and Nobles of the Land have done it!
> Hear it not, Heaven, thy Ministers have done it!

Erdman has argued that *King Edward the Third* was intended to be, when complete, an attack on the aggression of the French Wars: his case is necessarily inconclusive, but he is quite probably right. *Gwin King of Norway* seems to owe a good deal to Gray's translations from Old Norse poetry like *The Fatal Sisters* and *The Descent of Odin.* . . . But in this poem Blake struck a new and radical note quite foreign to Gray:

> The Nobles of the land did feed
> Upon the hungry Poor . . .

Besides this, there are several turns of phrase in the poem (such as the likening of Gwin's warriors to *lion's whelps,* and the defiance of Gwin in the words ''Thou'rt swept from out the land'') which make it possible, anyhow, that Gwin is a substitute for *George,* that what was literary and antiquarian for Gray was something quite other than that for Blake; and that in writing his own poem, Blake was rejoicing in the American War of Independence. Again, the prose fragment **"Then She Bore Pale Desire"**, written at about the same time as some of the *Poetical Sketches,* is almost a historical 'Progress of Pride', to be read as a riposte to poems like Gray's 'Progress of Poesy' or Thomson's 'Liberty'. (pp. 54-5)

So it would be quite wrong to see the polemical, radical poems of *Songs of Experience* as something new in Blake. That side was there from the start. On the other hand, something about this polemical radicalism . . . is unquestionably new: and this something is that Blake can no longer keep his severity of judgment from challenging his vision of innocence. In *Poetical Sketches,* the radical and antiwar pieces seem largely, though not entirely, literary in inspiration. The horrors of war (if not outright condemnation of these) are in Gray's pieces; the sufferings of the common people through the military adventures of their rulers are vivid in Shakespeare's history plays. All these sentiments, indeed, are one part of eighteenth-century literary tradition. Blake's radicalism could draw on these facts, and at this stage, could still remain with something of the abstract and doctrinaire. That could exist in his mind alongside his patriarchal pastoralism. But between the first collection of *Songs* and the second, something happened to give Blake's social feelings a greater immediacy, and make any further such insulation impossible.

This something was less the French Revolution considered simply in itself, than its impact at home in Britain. Bronowski points out how in 1791 the radical bookseller Joseph Johnson (who seems to have become a friend of Blake in the later 1780's) had seen danger ahead, and suddenly abandoned the publication of Paine's *The Rights of Man.* He was wise. The following year saw the Royal Proclamation against Seditious Writings, and Paine and his new printer were soon prosecuted. Paine was later prosecuted in his absence (he had fled abroad) for treason. In July 1791 the Birmingham mob, incited, it is alleged, by the authorities, had sacked the house and laboratory of the radical dissenter Joseph Priestley. (p. 56)

As revolution took its course in France, and fears of revolution at home infected with panic the unshakeable assurance of the powers-that-be in their own total rightness, repression went further. In December 1792 a convention of Parliamentary Reformers was held in Edinburgh; the following year one of its leaders, Thomas Muir, was prosecuted for sedition and sentenced to fourteen years' transportation. . . . The following month Thomas Palmer, a respectable Scottish Unitarian minister, and ex-Fellow of a Cambridge college, received a like sentence. Just as the words "every ban" in **"London"** (as well, of course, as meaning "curse" which comes later in the poem) may have come into Blake's mind from the repressive Proclamations, so the "mind-forg'd manacles" themselves may not be general and figurative only, but refer also to how respectable men like Muir and Palmer were appearing on trial manacled in court as if they were common felons. Early the next year, three more reformist leaders were sentenced to fourteen years' transportation. The acquittal in London, during the autumn of 1794, of Thomas Hardy and others on charges of high treason, did not reverse the general trend of the time. This continued in the prohibitory Acts of 1795, the suspension of *habeas corpus,* the prosecution and imprisonment of Joseph Johnson and many others, and the Combination Acts of 1799. Hardy was acquitted when the defence showed up the prosecution evidence as lies. But the real significance of the acquittal was to stress how the police spy and the *agent provocateur*

were everywhere. Here is the universe of uncertainty and fear that Blake captures in the first stanza of **"London"**:

> . . . mark in every face I meet
> Marks of weakness, marks of woe.

The opening lines of the poem contrast this with the "charter'd" Thames and the city's chartered streets. But what is in Blake's mind is no generalized contrast between the free and the trammelled life: it is the present and pressing destruction of the political liberty of his fellows and himself. The first draft of stanza 2 makes this clearer still:

> . . . in every voice, in every ban
> The *german* mind-forg'd links I hear.

Blake of course means the House of Hanover with its German troops—used against British settlers in America, and now being stationed across England, ostensibly for action in the French War. (pp. 56-7)

Blake's response to these years is clear in a quatrain in the 1793 *Notebook;* again, the proverbial and popular is the form he adopts:

> **"An ancient Proverb"**
> Remove away that black'ning church:
> Remove away that marriage hearse:
> Remove away that man of blood:
> You'll quite remove the ancient curse. . . .

[What] one can say, briefly, is that *Songs of Experience* record Blake's discovery that there is an "ancient curse"—one, that is, under which men have suffered throughout history—and that it calls the whole vision of Innocence in question. (pp. 57-8)

It is well known, of course, that a number of poems in *Songs of Experience* are counterpart-pieces to poems in *Songs of Innocence.* One pair that has been relatively little discussed is **"The Divine Image"** and its later counterpart **"The Human Abstract"**. The first of these is in the "Common Metre" and simple diction of the hymns, and the virtues that it celebrates are the traditional Christian ones of ". . . Mercy, Pity, Peace and Love". . . . The essential structure of the poem is an identification of these virtues (which are seen collectively in the poem as "the good") with both God and man, and therefore the identification of God *with* man: man *is* "the Divine Image". The poem cannot be regarded as among the major successes of *Songs of Innocence,* not only because the visionary quality is absent from it, but also because there is a sense in which it contains, as it were, the seed of its own refutation. This is because, by the very neatness of its argumentative form, the poem says implicitly that man has not only those four virtues, but also the capacity to think, argue, agree—and so of necessity disagree. (p. 60)

It is precisely this *exposure to retort* that the *Songs of Experience* poem exploits:

> Pity would be no more
> If we did not make somebody poor . . .

What the latter poem asserts is that conventional Christian virtues exist as mere froth (or, maybe, mere varnish would be better) on the surface of a society founded not on great virtues, but great evils—poverty, unhappiness, fear, selfishness, cruelty and the 'Raven' of death. Poetically the piece is far richer than its counterpart, for Blake means "summary" by "Abstract" in the title, and the poem's growth is such that the sham virtues and real evils grow out of each other in organic progression until the whole forms a savage parody of the story of the 'Tree of Jesse' (*Isaiah* II, 1). Humanity grows through evil veritably to Death itself. There is a third poem in the series: **"A Divine Image"**, which Blake did not include in *Songs of Experience,* though he etched it, according to Keynes, in about 1794. In this poem, Blake seems to see a new truth: I shall return to it.

The new vision of *Songs of Experience*—selective, sarcastic, critical—results in a radically new poetic form, new mode of poetic organization. The visionary harmonies of the earlier collection had induced their own characteristic form: intricate, moving, and beautifully distinctive. Of this **"The Lamb"** is a clear if simple example, simple because poetic form here merges into explicit statement. The point is that one can virtually assert this poem to have a structure, inasmuch as it has a structure of ideas: and the structure of ideas is a structure of identity, of the merging and inter-fusion which is the ultimate condition of harmonious oneness. In a world of harmony, the work of the Creator tends simply towards being a duplication and re-duplication of himself: until finally, it is oneness which *is* blessedness.

> Little Lamb, who made thee . . .?
> Little Lamb, I'll tell thee:
> He is called by thy name . . .
> He became a little child.
> I a child and thou a lamb
> We are called by his name.
> *Little Lamb, God bless thee!*

The last line in this quotation immediately follows, and seems what necessarily follows, the all-embracing identities which precede it.

The **"Introduction"** to *Songs of Innocence* is like this too. . . . Perhaps the line which leads one most easily into the structure of this poem is:

> And I stain'd the water clear . . .

Some might wish to make an ambiguity out of this: the clear water is *stained,* or the water is stained *clear*. But that sort of verbal ingenuity is what the whole diction and rhythm and narrative line of the poem reject. Yet the impression left with the reader is still of how near the ink and the clear water are together, of how nearly they are one. The staining is a fact in the poem, but it is the water's clarity that is rendered sensuously explicit. Why, however, "the" water? Since this is not quite idiomatic unless there is a reference to water already, the attentive reader's mind searches instinctively backward in the poem. There is nothing explicit but the child's tears; yet since these are the tears of the "laughing" child on the cloud, they are the joyous showers of rain. . . . But if, ultimately, the singer's ink and the child's tears of joy at what he writes down *are one,* we are still not to think that the ink is made directly from the rain. Since the poet "pluck'd a hollow reed" for his pen (which, clearly, he has already done for his pipe: so pipe and pen themselves come together) there is a stream also in the landscape of the poem. But the stream does not enter the poem by inference merely: for just as there is both a meta-phorical, or perhaps one should say spiritual, sense in which the child on the cloud is a heavenly presence (is, in fact, the 'Lamb' about which, or whom, he calls for a song), and also a literal or material sense in which joyful tears from the cloud

are just refreshing showers of rain, so there is a material sense in which what goes

> Piping down the valleys wild
> Piping songs of pleasant glee

is simply the stream itself: the stream, that is (to make use of a pun, which is not, I think, quite absent from the poem) as "spring" that comes "o'er the eastern hills" to the "listening valleys" as in an earlier piece. Singer and stream are one, and both are one with spring. Poet sings to spiritual presence of the divine; at the same time, different though not different, there is just a springtime landscape, with a babbling stream, the lambs in the meadows beside it, and the fresh rain-bearing clouds above. There is no need now to tot up all the identities which compose the poem. Its manifold of equations issue from, and communicate, a world of harmonious oneness. (pp. 60-2)

Perhaps the most remarkable poem of this kind is what I am inclined to think is the finest poetic success of all Blake's lyrics: the **"Holy Thursday"** poem in *Songs of Innocence*. Since its children are of course charity children, **"Holy Thursday"** may reasonably be seen as in the context of such pieces as Watts's 'Praise for Mercies: On the Poor'.

> Where'er I take my walks abroad . . .
> How many children in the street
> Half-naked I behold

or Christopher Smart's 'Pray Remember the Poor':

> I just came by the prison door,
> I gave a penny to the poor,
> Papa did this good deed approve
> And poor Mama cried out for love;
> Whene'er the poor comes to my gate
> Relief I will communicate. . . .

"Holy Thursday" is in another world because it totally reverses the movement of attention: not down from above, as so clearly in Watts and Smart, but up from below. The children *are* the life-bearing waters of the city's river, as they flow in streams into its cathedral; they are flowers, not just from their angelic faces, but because Blake's vision has transfigured the red and blue and green of their coloured charity costumes. The river seems to become a fountain from the "high dome of Paul's" as they sing, and their singing grows into the "mighty wind" that (compare I *Kings* XIX, 11-12) was prelude to the divine voice. As the fountain rises up to heaven, their lamb-like radiance becomes one with the divine, with the "harmonious thunderings" of the heavenly choirs. Hence the sudden explosive-surprise-yet-total-appositeness of the closing:

> Then cherish pity, lest you drive *an angel* from your
>   door.

Blake is sufficiently close to the tradition he so much changes for his poem to go back to a scriptural text: "Suffer the little children to come unto me, and forbid them not; for of such is the kingdom of God" (*Mark* X, 14). Children are one with river, with fountain, with wind ascending to Heaven, with Angels, with the song of angels, and ultimately with the Divine Principle itself.

But the structure of these poems in *Songs of Innocence* has been examined as preliminary to seeing how great, structurally speaking, is the change in a number of the *Songs of Experience*. Nor is it a simple, single change. **"The Fly"**, for example, might at a careless reading be taken as similar in structure to the 'Innocence' poems above. But the identity which it asserts between fly and man is in no way a fusion and oneness intuited by a kind of visionary power and presented to the reader in the imagery of the poem: it is a more or less clear-cut parallelism insisted on through the poem by a logical argument. . . . [The] form and structure of the poem are logical. Its continuity is a thinking continuity. The opening words of the later stanzas make this inescapable. ''For . . . if . . . then'' mean, respectively ''Because . . . given-the-premises-that . . . therefore''. What unifies is the sharp line of an argument strung through the whole piece.

"The Chimney Sweeper" in *Songs of Experience* is much the same. The first two lines present the situation of the black child sweep in the snow: but the rest of the poem is what he says, and its logical structure is perhaps even more sharply articulated than in **"The Fly"**, and may be expressed '''because' A, therefore B and C, and *in the same way* 'because' D, therefore E and F''. **"The Human Abstract"** and **"A Little Boy Lost"** are other poems in which logical argument is prominent. **"The Little Vagabond"** is nothing more than a catalogue of the consequences which would follow from a conditional proposition which in fact is not fulfilled.

These poems represent something quite new. They have no parallel in *Songs of Innocence*. But there are other poems in the later collection which introduce another new principle of structure, one of quite a different kind. . . . [This principle of structure] might be thought at first to be simply a proposition about experience: a mere matter of fact, as Blake sees fact. But when a poet has a belief about experience which is not stated explicitly, but transpires (by inference) in all the relations between such realities as enter his poem, that belief becomes not only one among his beliefs about the world, but veritably the mode of organization of his poem.

This mode of organization, in a number of the poems, is something like the *reverse* of that in *Songs of Innocence*. There, objects began to merge into each other in harmonious oneness: in these poems, it is as if *everything is held back from contact with everything else*. If the poem has a unity, it is that of a sustained negative conviction. Separateness and repulsion pervade it everywhere. It is a sequence of separated, isolated people that Blake passes and observes in **"London"**:

> . . . *every* cry of *every* man
> . . .*every* Infant's cry of fear

man and child, church and child sweep, palace and soldier, harlot, client (it may be), child, bride and groom—each is the enemy of its counterpart, each is without live relation to any of the others. The verbs—''appalls'', ''runs in blood down'', ''blasts'', ''blights'' (and the concealed actions of fearing, cursing and weeping)—all show this same principle at work. In **"Infant Sorrow"**, the child is endangered by the world, struggles against the father, strives against the swaddling bands, sulks against the mother. In **"A Little Boy Lost"** there is first the selfhood of the little boy, asserted over the bond between him and his father and brothers: and then the priest who seems to be enemy as much to the parents as the child. Even between parent and child there is no active relation, only helpless weeping.

The **"Introduction"** to *Songs of Experience* is another poem that presents a universe of disjunction and non-relation. Even the initial image of the divine presence (the 'Holy Word') walking among the trees is an illustration: its essential structure is not unlike that in **"London"** of the poet walking among his fellow-Londoners and noticing them one by one. But the divine presence is calling the soul that has ''lapsed'' away from it: and whether it is the divine presence itself or the (divinely inspired) ''voice of the Bard'' that is in question, the starry pole that ''might'' be controlled but is not, and the ''fallen'' light that this might renew but does not, are ''lapsed'' into disjunction as well. When the ''voice of the Bard'' speaks, as it seems to do through the second half of the poem, what it speaks of is also opposites and unrelateds: the ''starry Floor'' (of heaven) and ''watery shore'', and the morning that ''rises from'' the ''slumbrous mass'' of the darkened earth. More remarkable still, even what the poem calls for (as against what it unhappily diagnoses), seem to come in similar terms:

> O Earth, O Earth, return!
> Arise from out the dewy grass

The call is presumably to fallen humanity (''fashioned out of clay''), but that it should be called on to ''arise from out'' of the ground from which it was made is something that follows the reiterated movement of the poem. Similar again is at least the suggestion carried by the closing lines:

> The starry floor,
> The wat'ry shore
> Is giv'n thee till the break of day

If the esoteric, symbolic meaning of the poem be taken into account, this probably means that at the moment of his spiritual rejuvenation, man will repudiate, and be withdrawn from, the world of the senses and move into the intelligible world. But the poet has found means to refer even to this event (which, in his own terms, would be restoration of harmony) along the lines of the poem's recurrent pattern: what is stressed is the break-up of an integration, the seeming cancellation of a bond.

> Turn away no more

the last verse opens: what the poem as a whole depicts, and what it mirrors in its own mode of organization, is a world of universal ''turn away''.

There was to be one further dramatic change in the formal structure of Blake's lyrical writing, a change manifested in the handful of remarkable later lyrics which occur in his *Notebook* of *c.* 1800-1803. Some of these were printed in Gilchrist's *Life of Blake* in 1863, but there was no complete printing until over a hundred years after the poems were composed. These poems, however, seem also to represent a decisive new stage in Blake's response to experience, and their distinctive form is a reflection of that.

In 1791, the first book of Blake's *French Revolution* was printed for the radical bookseller Joseph Johnson, and the complete poem was stated to be in seven books, of which the other six, already composed, would be printed ''in their Order''. But those six remaining books were not printed, and have never been located. Probably Blake destroyed them, and even the First Book was printed but never published, the sole surviving copy of it being in all probability a set of page proofs. Bronowski has stressed the importance of these facts: and whether we agree with his suggestion that Blake suppressed this work on account of severe repression and reactionary government in Britain, or with Keynes's that he did so through disillusionment with the French Revolution itself, or think that both are true, the fact remains that the suppression marks something of great importance in Blake's career. (pp. 63-7)

Blake does not seem to have repudiated his radical opinions . . . ; but the fact remains that he withdrew, at least so far as his writing is concerned, from active expression of them and involvement with current issues. Moreover, he may have retained the attitudes of a radical towards social good and evil, but he to a limited extent resembles the other major poets of his time in ceasing to put his trust in radical remedies. A poem like that which begins **"Let the brothels of Paris be opened"** (in the 1793 *Notebook*) shows his early disillusionment with the revolutionary leader Lafayette. That which begins **"I saw a Monk of Charlemaine"** in the *Notebook* for 1800-1803 records disillusionment of a far deeper kind:

> The hand of vengeance sought the bed
> To which the purple tyrant fled.
> The iron hand crush'd the tyrant's head
> *And became a tyrant in his stead.*
> Until the Tyrant himself relent,
> The Tyrant who first the black bow bent,
> Slaughter shall heap the bloody plain;
> Resistance and war is the tyrant's gain.

This new conviction must be part of what lies behind **"To Tirzah"** and also behind the difference between **"The Human Abstract"**, and **"A Divine Image"** (which Blake etched as early as 1794, but did not include in *Songs of Experience* himself).

"A Divine Image" must be read along with **"The Divine Image"** in *Songs of Innocence,* and **"The Human Abstract"** in *Songs of Experience;* but its pessimism about humanity is an altogether different thing from what one finds in the latter of these poems. **"The Human Abstract"** asserts that the conventional Christian virtues like "Mercy, Pity, Peace and Love" are parasitic on evil and bring it about. The "Cruelty, Jealousy, Terror and Secrecy" of **"A Divine Image"** are to a considerable degree the opposites, one by one, of those same conventional virtues ("Secrecy" must also be taken with "Mystery" which appears in stanza four of the other poem). In essence the poem is a sardonic attack on the conventional idea of the Christian God, and the line:

> The Human Face a Furnace seal'd

brings to mind the creative fires of **"The Tyger"**. The traditional conception of man as made in the image of God is inverted, and a cruel and vicious deity is seen as in the image of "the Human Form Divine". Yet one cannot but find more in the poem also. Whether its foundation is that the terror-God made man in his image, or that man made the idea of a terror-God, man himself remains the image of such a God—either as his creature or as his creator. The poem is such an attack on Christianity as must spring from disillusionment with regard to humanity as well.

"To Tirzah" which Keynes gives in *Songs of Innocence* as "probably added about 1801", ought perhaps to be read with **"The Land of Dreams"** in the Pickering Manuscript. There is a sense in which Blake has now become something like an Idealist. "Binding with briars my joys and desires" is now the office of man's mortal and earthly part, deadening and nullifying his awareness—the "closing of the senses" described in, for example, Chapter 9 of *The First Book of Urizen*. "It is Raised a Spiritual Body" the accompanying illustration quotes from I *Corinthians* XV, 44; as for what is of the Earth and "Born of Mortal Birth", the poem dismisses it with the simple but decisive "What have I to do with thee?". In **"The Land**

of Dreams"** there is a vision of pastoral beatitude like that of *Songs of Innocence:*

> O, what Land is the Land of Dreams?
> What are its Mountains & what are its Streams?
> O Father, I saw my Mother there,
> Among the Lillies by waters fair.
>
> Among the Lambs, clothed in white,
> She walk'd with her Thomas in sweet delight. . . .

But this is not, as (at least implicitly) in *Songs of Innocence,* a vision of the world of everyday. The world of everyday is now a "Land of unbelief and fear", and the world of lambs and lilies an unattainable ideal world on "the other side". Reminiscence of the closing stanzas of Shelley's 'Adonais' is clearly inescapable. The influence of Plato is of course behind both.

In Blake in fact, as in Plato, a growing sense of an ideal world of radiant perfection seems to have gone with a growing sense of how evil in the world of everyday is not a fit object for attack and polemic, for the simple and decisive reason that attack is futile when it is attack upon what is of that world's very essence. Perfection is something that radically and ineluctably has no place in it. **"Mary"**, also in the Pickering manuscript of about 1803, and in superficial appearance a rollicking ballad in broadsheet style, is no conventional account of a maiden's fall. Mary falls because goodness, whatever means it may adopt in order to survive, seems inevitably doomed. Mary is hated in her radiant beauty, and scorned when she tries to recommend herself by modest plainness.

> "All Faces have envy, sweet Mary, but thine . . ."

The best-known poem in the Pickering Ms., **"Auguries of Innocence"**, also gives expression to this sense that there is no way out, that the opposite of all evil is no better than what it is opposite to:

> The Questioner, who sits so sly,
> Shall never know how to Reply.
> He who replies to Words of Doubt
> Doth put the Light of Knowledge out.

Confusion or conviction are equally valueless: and the impact of the whole poem . . . is that what innocence "augurs" is no localized and remediable abuse, but corruption everywhere on all hands. (pp. 68-71)

"The Golden Net" is almost the finest of these later poems: and in it there begins to evolve the new and distinctive form which is the effective embodiment of their vision. The poem is something like a brilliant, sardonic parody of the 'Judgement of Paris' theme: the young traveller sees not the beauties, but the sufferings, of the three weeping virgins that carry the golden net. Yet all that his pity achieves is to imprison him under their net, turn their sorrow to seemingly sadistic pleasure, and replace their sufferings by suffering of his own. . . . [What] Blake now registers as his response to reality is a world of *futile action,* a world in which remedy is merely rearrangement of the disease; and the new form in the poem is a form created by a new kind of narrative, counterpointed, as it were, into self-defeat.

This cyclic form, embodying Blake's by now almost tragic sense of the potentiality of existence, and drawing vitality and tautness from the narrative thread, is plain also in **"The Crystal Cabinet"**. This is a poem on something like the same traditional theme as Keats's 'La Belle Dame Sans Merci'. The poet encounters the maiden in the wilds, she brings him into the delights of her private paradise, this suddenly disintegrates, and he finds himself where he was, but with grief substituted for the original carefree joy. Yet Blake's poem, though it employs this traditional narrative *motif*, gives it a quite new force, in that the maiden's private paradise, her ''golden cabinet'' is in the event not private at all. It is a redeemed vision of the world of everyday:

> Another England there I saw
> Another London with its Tower
> Another Thames & other Hills,
> And another pleasant Surrey bower.

But it is unrealizable: even as the poet ''strove to seize the inmost Form'' it burst and disintegrated before him.

Kathleen Raine has shown how much there is in **''The Mental Traveller''**, the most striking and substantial poem in the Pickering Ms., of Plato's conception in the *Politicus* of alternating phases in the world's history, of these as connected with alternating dominance of body and of soul, and of the whole process as symbolized by the birth and rebirth of Dionysus [see Additional Bibliography]. Enlightening as she is over these preliminary matters, she leaves untouched what is of more account. . . . Were **''The Mental Traveller''** some mere *résumé* of conceptions with which we can familiarize ourselves in other authors—whether Plato, Thomas Taylor or Yeats—it would be expendable. Poetic greatness is not to be found in such recapitulation, however intriguing or congenial one may find what it recapitulates. (pp. 71-2)

[The] interest and quality of the poem surely resides in this: that as we read it, an impression emerges from it which quite dwarfs and renders insignificant any sense that ''here [Blake] follows the teaching of Plato'' about gyres; and this impression is, that through his narrative, seemingly at a great distance from everyday reality, Blake has in fact found means to record some of his findings about that reality, and to do with almost terrifying fulness, directness and sombre force:

> he rends up his manacles
> And binds her down for his delight;

> He plants himself in all her Nerves,
> Just as a Husbandman his mould;
> And she becomes his dwelling place
> And Garden fruitful seventy fold. . . .

[In particular, he has much to say] about what man (or woman) has done to man:

> Her fingers number every Nerve,
> Just as a miser counts his gold;
> She lives upon his shrieks and cries,
> And she grows young as he grows old.

Or again:

> The honey of her Infant lips
> The bread and wine of her sweet smile,
> The wild game of her roving Eye
> Does him to Infancy beguile.

What has this, in all honesty, to do with Thomas Taylor's paraphrase of Plato's belief that the soul grows young as the body grows old? Rather, it is another glimpse from the vision of ''Experience''; but set within a narrative so organized as to make that vision appear total, inter-locking through all its parts, and tragically inevitable.

Thus it is, I think, throughout the poem. The ''aged Shadow'', whose cottage is filled with treasure won from human suffering; the vagrants and travellers of whom it may be said

> *His grief* is their eternal joy;
> They make the walls and roof to ring

—the old man driven out like Lear; the vagrant, taken pity on, who becomes the oppressor . . ., the lover ''beguil'd . . . by various arts of Love & *State*''; the men who roam in the ''desart'' and flee in crazy terror at the birth of a child—all

> . . . such dreadful things
> As cold Earth wanderers never knew

are so described, of course, in irony. Cold Earth wanderers, Blake thought, know these things only too well. They are aspects of the world of everyday, as he now saw it, and they are shot through the poem in such a way that its over-riding impact is to come to seem an organizing and perspective of the here and the now. What the cyclic narrative does is something stressed and confirmed in the insistent rhythm of the poem, and the steely controlled weight of its superb monosyllabic lines, lines in which the innermost essence of the English language is realized and brought to fruition:

> To make it feel both cold and heat . . .

> And she grows young as he grows old . . .

> But She comes to the Man she loves,
> If young or old, or rich or poor . . .

> She nails him down upon the Rock,
> And all is done as I have told.

These things all come together to make the poem into a decisive, a terrifying epitome of Blake's later vision of life. ''Innocence'' does not desert him entirely, but it finds little or no place in the later lyrics:

> . . . Tharmes brought his flock upon the hills, & in the
>   Vales
> Around the Eternal Man's bright tent, the little Children
>   play
> Among the woolly flocks. The hammer of Urthona
>   sounds . . .
> The Sun arises from his dewy bed, & the fresh airs
> Play in his smiling beams . . .

But all this is now visionary in a new sense—it is the remote and chiliastic dream of regeneration that closes *The Four Zoas*. So far as the lyrics are concerned, Blake has brought his readers, in these latest poems, to the polar opposite of the state, and vision, of Innocence. (pp. 73-5)

> *John Holloway, in his* Blake: The Lyric Poetry, *Edward Arnold (Publishers) Ltd., 1968, 79 p.*

JEROME J. McGANN   (essay date 1973)

[*McGann argues that Blake intended his poems to serve as ''vehicles for vision'' for the reader, thus invoking a visionary aesthetic that is antithetical to analytical and systematic approaches to his work.*]

Though we have had many discussions of Blake's theory of the imagination, few relate that theory to what used to be called, in more innocent ages, the rhetorical purposes of his works. That is to say, whereas many areas of ''meaning'' in Blake's poetry have been exhaustively explored, few critics have tried

From Blake's series of engraved designs for the Book of Job.

to explain precisely how his poems aim to work. This question seems a crucial one, perhaps especially for the epics, which are poems designed to set in motion that elaborate set of relations known as Blake's "system," or his personal mythology.

The problem, which is both simple and fundamental, can be stated in this way. Do we not violate Blake's poetry by encouraging, in ourselves or in others, an analytic or systematic approach to it? Or is it true, as some readers have hinted, that Blake's own attacks upon Urizenic attitudes are themselves belied by his poetry, and thrown back by his complex "system"? Is it all, in fact, no more than another Satanic mill with complicated wheels?

I shall try to face these questions in this essay, and to propose an answer for those who find Blake's own work based upon hidden systematizing principles. At the same time I shall be entering a caveat not only for Blake criticism as such, but also for criticism in general, especially for those critics who agree with Blake's philosophic positions. My study of Blake has led to the conclusion that, to the degree that one regards Blake's art as an object of analysis and interpretation, to the degree that any criticism fosters such a view, to that degree has Blake been misused, even, I would venture to say, misread. Such uses disregard Blake's explicit aims, and certainly do not treat his work in the same spirit that the author writ. (pp. 3-4)

Students of Blake often speak of his *prophetic* art, and they are right to do so. A prophet does not speak for himself, as

orthodox conceptions of prophecy make very clear. The prophet is God's spokesman. This fact about prophetic speech has important aesthetic consequences for Blake. Blake believed that God was a man, incarnated in Jesus but imprisoned as well in every individual psyche. We are all divine children, as **"The Lamb"** so delicately recalls: "I a child, & thou a lamb, / We are called by his name." . . . Yet such a poem offers not an explanation of, but an occasion for experiencing, the oneness of man and God and their creations. Like so many of Blake's lyrics, **"The Lamb"** is properly called prophetic rather than personal because its "I" and "thou" do not locate the sort of personal encounter typical of the lyrics of Cowper, Burns, Coleridge, or Keats. "I" and "thou" are points of relation describing the circling unities of child, lamb, Christ, and Everyman. The art of the poem is to seem *not* to interpret the relations of its own signs, to offer those signs without a point of view from which to understand their significance. The poem seems hermetically sealed, and for this very reason makes a special demand upon those of us who desire it to establish communication. The poem, in fact, requires its meaning from the reader, the only personality which can experience in vision that for which the poem is the occasion. (p. 4)

"The Lamb" is typical of Blake, and its special character explains why so many critics have resorted to the analytic constructs of "voices" and "personae" to explain Blake's poems. Such terms suggest the depersonalizing inertia in the works. But one must see, in addition, that the prophetic and visionary aspect of the poem is similarly depersonalized. The poem fulfills its prophecy and vision only in man the reader. We do not properly call Blake's art visionary if we merely mean by this that it records Blake's personal visions. His art is visionary not because it records but because it induces vision. For this reason Blake set out as epigraph to **Milton** the passage from Numbers: "Would to God that all the Lords people were Prophets." . . . (p. 5)

The whole of Blake's commentary on his painting *A Vision of the Last Judgment* repeats the idea that art is a vehicle for vision rather than an object of perception. In describing his work Blake says simply: "I have represented it [*The Last Judgment*] as I saw it[.] to different People it appears differently . . . as every thing else does." He then goes on to explain carefully "The Nature of Visionary Fancy or Imagination." The power "is very little Known," Blake says,

> & the Eternal nature & permanence of its ever
> Existent Images is considerd as less permanent
> than the things of Vegetative & Generative Na-
> ture yet the Oak dies as well as the Lettuce but
> Its Eternal Image & Individuality never dies.
> but renews by its seed. just . . . (so) the Imag-
> inative Image returns . . . (by) the seed of Con-
> templative Thought the Writings of the Proph-
> ets illustrate these conceptions of the Visionary
> Fancy by their various sublime & Divine Im-
> ages as seen in the Worlds of Vision. . . .

What Blake means here is explained later when he elaborates on the nature of "Contemplative Thought." First he describes some of the scenes in his painting, which is itself a visionary response to certain biblical scenes and images. He then explains what is required of the viewer of his painting:

> If the Spectator could Enter into these Images
> in his Imagination approaching them on the
> Fiery Chariot of his Contemplative Thought if

he could Enter into Noahs Rainbow or into his bosom or could make a Friend & Companion of one of these Images of wonder which always intreats him to leave mortal things as he must know then would he arise from his Grave then would he meet the Lord in the Air & then he would be happy General Knowledge is Remote Knowledge it is in Particulars that Wisdom consists & Happiness too. . . .

Such pronouncements explain why Blake thought that art alone could restore man to his golden age. Blake's ideal art released every man to the achievement of his own fullest powers. Thus he could extol *"the Art of Invention not of Imitation,"* . . . not so much to aggrandize his own practice as to remind us that the end of all art, in every man, is not analysis but vision.

All three of Blake's surviving epics are explicit attempts to recover the Divine Vision for, in, and through the world. He does not compose his poetry for himself but for "the Divine Humanity," the brotherhood of all men. Thus he will say: "I will not cease from Mental Fight . . . Till we have built Jerusalem." . . . That is, "I" (Blake) struggle that "we" (Man) may together, in vision, recover our emanation Jerusalem, who is the image of every man's infinite desire. Blake is not simply being modest here. The lyric states the literal fact of his belief, that the original state of blessedness is recovered only when every man lives in vision, that is, when every man beholds the universe in his own active imagination. An "external world" is a delusion just as any "generalized" conception of reality is a shadow. To find the world one must find oneself.

> For all are Men in Eternity. Rivers Mountains Cities
>   Villages,
> All are Human & when you enter into their Bosoms
>   you walk
> In Heavens & Earths; as in your own Bosom you bear
>   your Heaven
> And Earth, & all you behold, tho it appears Without it
>   is Within
> In your Imagination, of which this World of Mortality
>   is but a Shadow.

> (pp. 5-6)

The insistence upon every man's possession of his own Divine Vision is basic to everything Blake wrote. In their fulfilled, or, as Blake would have it, Edenic condition, all men are united in Jesus, that is, all men are creative visionaries who interchange their vital energies and continually regenerate themselves through each other.

> . . . Man subsists by Brotherhood & Universal Love
> We fall on one anothers necks more closely we embrace
> Not for ourselves but for the Eternal Family we live
> Man liveth not by Self alone but in his brothers face
> Each shall behold the Eternal Father, & love & joy
>   abound. . . .

Though this homely description of Blake's visionary paradise contrasts markedly with the splendid concluding passages of *Jerusalem,* it nevertheless expresses the same event. (p. 7)

[As Blake] said in *The Marriage of Heaven and Hell,* all great visions court the danger of enslaving vulgar minds into worship and imitation. Indeed, the history of fallen man is the record of successive acts of creative vision which repeatedly became debased in cultural transmission. Blake believed he was divinely marked to usher in the final stages of fallen man's

history, and that hence he was called upon to introduce an art that could be received only in vision. He aimed for an imaginative vehicle which would preclude his imposing himself on his audience. (p. 8)

Blake was determined not to fall into Milton's error, which amounted to the formation of a Urizenic system from what Milton's "enlarged & numerous senses" . . . had perceived in true vision. Blake's program was to free man forever from the domination of intellectual programs. His aim was this, by "Striving with Systems to deliver Individuals from those Systems." . . . Blake believed that all systems waged reductive attacks upon the multiplied particulars of life: "One Law for the Lion & Ox is Oppression." . . . One may well wonder, therefore, why Blake should have created his own elaborate system and how he expected it to serve the arts of creation rather than destruction. What protects the reader from the powerful system announced by Blake's prophet at the beginning of *Jerusalem*?

> I must Create a System, or be enslav'd by another Mans
> I will not Reason & Compare: my business is to Create. . . .

· · · · ·

Coming to terms with this apparent paradox in Blake's work demands that we grasp what Blake means by creation. Whether seen in a historical or an aesthetic frame of reference, creation can only be for Blake both an act of divine mercy and a delusion of the Satanic will. He states his views very explicitly in *A Vision of the Last Judgment.* Creation is generative and changing, whereas eternity is permanent and infinite. Therefore Blake insists that "Error is Created Truth is Eternal Error or Creation will be Burned Up & then & not till then Truth or Eternity will appear." . . . Creation and eternity are two different conditions altogether, the one having a beginning and an end while the other remains a simple existent. "Eternity Exists and All things in Eternity Independent of Creation which was an act of Mercy." . . . In terms of Blake's biblical view of history, creation began with the fall of man from his eternal home in imagination. Before that catastrophe there was no "Error or Creation." . . . (p. 9)

But if eternity and creation are two different conditions of being, the divine mercy, or imagination, can transform creation and error into the means of recovering true vision. . . .

Ultimately aesthetic and historical creation are imaginatively transformed into a "Vision of the Science of the Elohim." . . . The Elohistic science is precisely the system which Los seeks to manipulate, the means of piercing Apollyon with his own bow. It is a system driving itself and all things forward to Eternal Death, where changing forms will finally be "Burned up."

What is true in terms of natural and historical images is likewise true of art. The twenty-seven churches, or the successive intellectual and religious systems which man's fallen imagination has created, all solidify into destructive systems under the image of the Covering Cherub. Milton's Shadow is another avatar of this ultimate demon, for Blake argued that all men, even, like Milton, the most artistic and powerful, were subject to its transformations. Milton's own work fostered idolatry rather than life to the degree that it accepted certain pre-established systems of thought, or urged a wisdom that could be commonly accepted rather than one that had to be instantly gained.

What was needed was an art that could not be turned into an abstraction, an art that no one would fall down and worship.

It must be an art that would urge no programs and offer no systems. He found it in an art which was ultimately committed not to creation but, paradoxically, to destruction, an art that would not be seen but would be seen through. Through it men would be made, like the Milton of Blake's poem, to "go to Eternal Death." . . . (p. 10)

The chief metaphor for an art of this sort, as all of Blake's major epics show, is a Christian one: redemption through death and the annihilation of the righteous selfhood. The life of Jesus, along with all the economies of the Christian mystery, properly stands at the pivot of what Blake sought to accomplish. . . . The life of Jesus is a poetic tale, not a form of worship; it does not introduce into the world a new system but is the definitive method for deliverance from all system. Blake represented this in the Jesus who lived to break all the commandments. He himself strove to produce an art that would bring no messages, consolatory or otherwise. His poetry issued a call to life not through visionary ideas, which are a contradiction in terms, but through visionary forms, poetic tales. In this sense his poetry must be said to have no meaning. (pp. 10-11)

[In a] sense Blake defines all poetry as prophecy, that is, the issuance of a call to judgment, the declaration of a state of affairs in which men have to choose either the light or the darkness. Echoing Isaiah 8:15, Los declares:

But still I labour in hope, tho' still my tears flow down.
That he who will not defend Truth, may be compelld to defend
A Lie: that he may be snared and caught and snared and taken. . . .

"He who has ears to hear, let him hear." Blake's prophetic art is in the first place a revelation. It exposes the inner condition of the listener. But beyond this, his art demands a choice. One must either take up the responsibility for one's newly revealed life or let it go. These are the prophet's functions. He does not teach, he declares that the time of choice has come.

The particular "testing" quality of Blake's art suggests why his work is more closely allied to the *symboliste* method of later writers than to the allegorical techniques of his intellectual forebears. . . . Allegory counts upon "remembered" things—conventional meanings and publicly accepted ideas and forms of thought which the poet can build upon. But *symbolisme* came into being precisely because the systems of publicly acceptable ideas and forms of thought had broken up. (pp. 11-12)

Blake's notoriously private symbolism (and in contrast to allegory, all symbolism is private) is merely the sign of a new state of artistic affairs. His mythology is privately apocalyptic in the sense that any meaning which one derives from it will reveal more about the commentator than about the artifact or its maker. It is an art of creative obscurity because its obscurity repels generalized conceptions. The poetry carries meaning only along the grammars of individual assent.

Thematic criticism of "**The Tyger,**" for example, has been both massive and contentious; and there is no reason to think that the quarrels about the meaning of the poem will soon be resolved. But once a reader no longer requires a definitive experience of the poem in cognitive terms, it ceases to pose a problem (though it must always remain a conundrum). As with so many of Blake's lyrics, part of the poem's strategy is to resist attempts to imprint meaning upon it. "**The Tyger**" tempts us to a cognitive apprehension but in the end exhausts our efforts. It teases us out of thought and either drives us on to

vision or away from it, back to old habits of perception. "**The Fly**" operates similarly. "**The Clod & the Pebble**" is yet another, unpretentious example of a poem designed to confound intellectual apprehension. This modest, yet treacherous, lyric perfectly balances its opposing sets of assertive symbols. Tempting us to approach it as if it were an allegory about ethics, in the end it baffles the inherited content of its images. Like "**The Tyger,**" the poem has no meaning. The attitudes represented through the clod and the pebble face each other to a standoff. (p. 12)

Thus, the extreme diversity of opinion among critics of Blake about the meaning of particular poems and passages of poems is perhaps the most eloquent testimony we have to the success of his work. Interpretations of the meanings of Blake's poems are necessarily legion, since his poetry was written to break in upon the centers of individual life and call their meanings into the open. Like Jesus, Blake came to send not peace but a sword. His work is a sign of contention. (p. 13)

• • • • •

Ultimately *Jerusalem* has only one aim: to lead us toward vision in the infinite world. Though the elaboration of this simple purpose is astonishing, one can grasp the essential method by looking closely at one of the poem's symbols, the world of Generation. Accumulating the different images which make up this symbolic complex, we discover an essentially contrarious situation. We have, on the one hand, the destructive mills of generation, the Satanic wheels which produce the inhuman city of Babylon. Related to these are the nets of female religion, themselves allied to the vast polypus of death images recurring everywhere. Blake deliberately presents these images as parodic versions of an alternative, heroic set associated with the prophet Los. The mills correspond to the furnaces of Los which build the city of art, Golgonooza, just as Rahab's nets correspond to Enitharmon's golden looms in Cathedron. These latter creations are called "the sublime Universe of Los & Enitharmon." . . . (p. 14)

The world of Generation, then, in its lethal aspect, is a sea of time and space, a delusive state of cycles and flux, perpetuating bondage and dismemberment. Blake's famous Arlington Court tempera painting depicts such a world. As the joyfully declared "[Image] of regeneration" . . . , however, the world of flux is a patent symbol of divine grace. For creation is also an act of mercy.

For Blake, the man of imagination lives in neither of these worlds but in eternity. The sublime world of Los and Enitharmon is merely the world of deadly generation turned inside out. Thereby the world is *revealed*, exposed, so that men may be led on to death and vision. Los's world, in Blake's terms, is a current which runs opposed to the current of vegetative existence. Blake has some marvelous ways of imaging this interacting set of opposing movements.

Terrific ragd the Eternal Wheels of intellect terrific ragd
The living creatures of the wheels, in the Wars of Eternal life
But perverse rolld the wheels of Urizen & Luvah back revers'd. . . .

In *Milton* the same image is brilliantly refined in terms of a set of mechanical cogs, the "evil" one turning in one direction but the "redemptive" one, attached to it, fatally reversing the effective inertia through death toward life.

The Wine-press is call'd War on Earth, it is the
    Printing-Press
Of Los; and here he lays his words in order above the
    mortal brain
As cogs are formd in a wheel to turn the cogs of the
    adverse wheel. . . .

The whole of the last movement of the first chapter of **Milton** . . . is an elaborate illustration of this doubled perspective upon "the World of Los the labour of six thousand years." . . . For example, the remark that the wine-press of Los "is call'd War on Earth" spins off a double set of images, one of a horrifying cast, the other suggestive of the Great harvest and Vintage, the Communion of Saints. Los, the generative form of the eternal prophet Urthona, forces us to hold the two perspectives in a single field. Doing so, we participate in the redemption of creation (ourselves), and even perceive wherein the created "Nature is a Vision of the Science of the Elohim." . . . (pp. 14-15)

At the end of the first chapter of **Jerusalem** . . . , Albion repeats the experience of Los's Spectre at the beginning of the chapter. . . . Both the Spectre of Los and Albion, perceiving the murderous aspects of Nature and History, curse their lot and counsel despair. The situation seems hopeless to both of them. As Albion laments: "But Albion is cast forth to the Potter his Children to the Builders / To build Babylon because they have forsaken Jerusalem." . . . Like Los's Spectre, he will wish "that Death & Annihilation were the same." . . .

But such a view is what Blake calls "single vision," and he composes his epics to raise men, initially, into the double vision that is the generative symbol of the fourfold vision in eternity. To perceive not only that nature is a prison house but that it is a garden of delights ("the sublime Universe of Los & Enitharmon") is to perceive through "contraries." Threefold vision, which Blake associates with the land of Beulah, is a further advance still. In this condition men perceive the identity of the contraries. (p. 15)

[Fourfold vision demands] that all things be forsaken, since only by thus fostering a condition of total perceptual indigence can one begin the preparation for infinite vision. Possessing nothing, one discovers that all things are possible. But if to describe fourfold vision in this way is almost to parody it, Blake's poems resort to enactment and dramatization. However this is done, it always occurs in the "Moment in each Day that Satan cannot find." . . . (Note how Blake's statement assures us that such visionary, timeless moments are continually borne to us through fallen time, even by Satan's "Watch Fiends" themselves.) Between the pulsations of an artery, suspended from time in time, such a moment contains an experience of dying to an old form of thought and gaining a new world of perception.

Blake's poems aim to establish the conditions which will rouse the faculties of his readers to this very death and release. He sets out contrarious perspectives on the universe, and by violent acts of juxtaposition forces us "To build the Universe stupendous: Mental forms Creating." . . . The demand is that we set the poem's terms into successively different types of relations with each other. Blake's art is a sort of Glass-Bead Game. To "make sense" of his works we establish in and for them different forms of order based upon shifting sets of dissociations and associations, contrasts and analogies. To cease the act of creating these sets of relations, or of ironically unbuilding them again, is to lapse into single vision. For example, to perceive

the similarity between the Spectre of Los and Albion in the first chapter of **Jerusalem** is to have gained a perception that is already a dangerous temptation to single vision and Newton's sleep. That sense of an analogy itself establishes the terms for a further demand: the perception of distinctions and contrasts. And these additional experiences call for still further constructions and destructions. As far as Blake is concerned, the process is clearly infinite. His favorite image for it is, characteristically, an optical one.

Albion! Our wars are wars of life, & wounds of love,
With intellectual spears, & long winged arrows of
    thought:
Mutual in one anothers love and wrath all renewing
We live as One Man; for contracting our infinite senses
We behold multitude; or expanding; we behold as one,
As One Man all the Universal Family . . .

(p. 16)

Blake's epics aim to promote such acts of imaginative perception on both a large and a small scale. Every line ought to be an opportunity for outwitting Satan's watch fiends, while the poem as a whole is designed as a spiritual exercise for the encouragement of universal prophecy. (p. 17)

For Blake, the essence of human life is not thought but experience, the imaginative apprehension of the unseen worlds which we believe will always exist for the joy of man's discovery. These may as well be worlds of thought, but for Blake the experience of discovering them rather than the intellectual possession of them is paradise, Eden, fourfold vision.

• • • • •

Like the angel of the Annunciation and the prophets of the Good News, Los exists to prepare the way for the coming of the Lord, and one of his most difficult functions is to give way before the Redeemer. This final gesture is the justification of the prophet's life. Los's career in **Jerusalem** follows such a pattern of life, which is clearly derived from the example of Saint John the Baptist. In **Jerusalem** . . . we read:

And Rahab Babylon the Great hath destroyed
    Jerusalem . . .

And all her Twenty-seven Heavens now hid & now
    reveal'd,
Appear in strong delusive light of Time & Space drawn
    out
In Shadowy pomp by the Eternal Prophet created
    evermore

For Los in Six Thousand Years walks up & down
    continually
That not one Moment of Time be lost & every
    revolution
Of Space he makes permanent in Bowlahoola &
    Cathedron . . .
But Jesus, breaking thro' the Central Zones of Death &
    Hell
Opens Eternity in Time & Space; triumphant in
    Mercy. . . .

The passage helps to explain other things besides the relation of Los and Jesus. The universe of Los in space and time is created in order to expel all such natural boundaries from man's life forever. Near the opening of the poem Los, seeing the melancholy duty placed upon him to create a world of spatial and temporal forms, yet hopes against his fears.

Yet why despair? I saw the finger of God go forth
Upon my Furnaces from within the Wheels of Albion's
 Sons,
Fixing their Systems, permanent: by mathematic power
Giving a body to Falsehood that it may be cast off for
 ever
With Demonstrative Science piercing Apollyon with his
 own bow! . . .

In the end, Los will himself undergo the death through which his own dire but merciful inventions drive all things. When this event is told, the natural world of space and time ends forever. Los himself goes to Eternal Death along with all his invented worlds, in order to advance the redemption of Albion. When the risen Albion says to Jesus, the Divine Vision: "I see thee in the likeness & similitude of Los my Friend" . . . , we understand that art itself has finally been redeemed to the Divine Vision. This entails the annihilation of "art" for "Vision" and hence means that in *Jerusalem* Los must pay "the price of Experience" if he would truly live; that is, he must give up all he has. His death is the heroic gift which he passes on to his friend Albion, the example according to which Albion must live his life. As Albion received it from his friend Los, Los received it from Jesus.

We live imagination as Jesus did, though we live in it through the exercise of all our giant faculties, in particular the faculty of aesthetic prophecy. Imagination does not create time and space, Los does. Imagination conceives the transformation of these terrifying and deadly manufactures into the mercies of eternity, a transformation in which the fearful Los yet courageously hopes. In this process Los is Jesus' instrument, just as Los's Spectre is the instrument of Urthona's vehicular personality. When Blake speaks of Los "Creating Space, Creating Time according to the wonders Divine / Of Human Imagination" . . . , the very grammar draws the distinction I have been pointing to. For, to Blake, imagination is not creation; it is, rather, life, existence, and—in the metaphor most characteristic of Blake's own faculties—vision. All creation is a *felix culpa* according to imagination (in any other view it is mere Hell) and will be, as Blake said, annihilated in the Last Judgment that ushers in Human Existence. For this was all creation permitted: death. Golgonooza, Los's city, is not Jerusalem but the means toward it, and the function of his city of art is to reveal the whorish aspects of all creation. Golgonooza too must go to Eternal Death, for it stands not only as the promise of Jerusalem, but also as the last great temptation to retreat from vision. Golgonooza is the house whose windows of the morning open out to the worlds of eternity, where Jesus dwells. We were never meant to live in it, or with it, but through it. (pp. 18-20)

The task Blake set himself was the revelation of a form of art which would not imprison later generations of men the way so much of art, even Milton's, had done. Blake aimed to foster a fellowship of creative spirits, not a world of corpses paralyzed within a dream of life. To regard Blake's vision of life as an object of study or perception is to transform it into a shadow of death. Thus he designed his work to be a means of vision in us, to "rouze" our faculties to act the way his had been roused. For the only communion that men share in Jesus is the exercise of imagination. The vehicular forms of the imaginative life, that is, the worlds of Los, are as varied as human existence itself; and men must be encouraged to their continual production. To do so, artists must approach the world not with creations that will trap men but with visions that will encourage

imaginative activity. The model for such an art, in Blake's mind, was his notion of a Christian death, that is, the gaining of life not by possessing it but by fostering it. Men live only when they help life to spring everywhere and eternally. So Blake waged war on the Selfhood continually, knowing that his visions were not ours any more than his own perceptions were ritually repeatable. Thus he developed an intensely private mythology, to protect both himself and us: for we can live in that mythology only to Blake's shame and our destruction. For himself, he had continually to subject his own visions to revisions and imaginative renewals. "William Blake," he could sign himself, "Born 28 Nov. 1757 in London & has died several times since." (p. 21)

Jerome J. McGann, "The Aim of Blake's Prophecies and the Uses of Blake Criticism," in Blake's Sublime Allegory: Essays on the Four Zoas, Milton, Jerusalem, *edited by Stuart Curran and Joseph Anthony Wittreich, Jr., The University of Wisconsin Press, 1973, pp. 3-21.*

SUSAN FOX (essay date 1977)

[*Fox discusses Blake's negative treatment of females, discerning a conflict between the poet's use of femaleness as a metaphor of weakness and power hunger and his doctrine of necessary equality between contraries.*]

In his prophetic poems Blake conceives a perfection of humanity defined in part by the complete mutuality of its interdependent genders. Yet throughout the same poems he represents one of those mutual, contrary, equal genders as inferior and dependent (or, in the case of Jerusalem, superior and dependent), or as unnaturally and disastrously dominant. Indeed, females are not only represented as weak or power-hungry, they come to represent weakness (that frailty best seen in the precariously limited "emanative" state Beulah) and powerhunger ("Female Will," the corrupting lust for dominance identified with women). Blake's philosophical principle of mutuality is thus undermined by stereotypical metaphors of femaleness which I believe he adopted automatically in his early poems and then tried to redress but found himself trapped by in his late works.

In the margin of his 1789 edition of Lavater's *Aphorisms on Man* Blake wrote, "let the men do their duty & the women will be such wonders, the female life lives from the light of the male. see a mans female dependents you know the man. . . ." The condescension disguised here, no doubt even to Blake, as appreciation marks an ambivalence towards women which is a significant feature of all Blake's poetry. (pp. 507-08)

His ambivalence has been matched by a strong and confusing ambivalence among his critics as to how to take his combined respect and derogation. On the one hand [as the following passage from Northrop Frye demonstrates,] they apologize for what seems like Blake's shrill antifeminism in promulgating such an idea as "Female Will" by sterilizing the conception of its sexual connotations:

> Another feature of the Ulro vision requiring comment is the "female will," the separated objective world that confronts us in the fallen perspective. The outer world of nature is a "Female Space" . . . because, like a "harlot coy" increasing her price by pretending to be a virgin, it continually retreats from the perceiver. The perceiver is a human being, who

Beatrice addressing Dante from the Car. This design was part of a series of illustrations of Dante's works that Blake created late in his career.

may be a man or a woman—in other words Blake's "female will" has nothing to do with human women except when women dramatize it in their sexual rituals, as they do, for instance, in the Courtly Love convention.

On the other hand they, like all responsive readers, must recognize that one of the most moving and provocative features of Blake's poetry is its profound psychological probing into sexual and familial relations, a probing embodied in such gender distinctions as spectre (always male, though it has a usually female counterpart in the "shadow"), emanation (almost exclusively female, with a revealing exception we shall deal with below), and Female Will. In other words, Blake's poetry has been represented both as a sexless abstraction of a universal human mentality divided metaphorically into sexual factions and as a profound study of human relations, including the sexual, in which metaphors of gender suggest not universal abstractions but the minute particulars of daily life. (p. 508)

One encounters this critical dilemma in Blake's poetry only in terms of his representation of the relations of the sexes. In no other issue do abstraction and particularity seem so seriously to contradict each other. The abstract elements of Blake's political, aesthetic, and historical attitudes are compatible with their personal elements, but the personal dimension of his attitudes towards women is so ambiguous that it interferes with the generalization he would build out of it. We may see this ambiguity in every facet of his poetic vision, from its cosmology to its individual characterizations.

Of the four states of being in Blake's universe, the only realm in which females are both powerful and constructive is Beulah. In Eden, females, supposedly merged perfectly with their male contraries, have no independent power; when they attempt to assume such power, as Luvah's emanation Vala does in trying to usurp all of Albion's love, they destroy Edenic wholeness. In fallen reality, as we shall see, females are either passive or pernicious. In Beulah alone do female forms have power and use it for good. Yet even in Beulah the positive image of femaleness is tainted by condescension: a female state is necessarily a limited state in Blake's universe.

In the *Songs of Innocence,* generally considered a study of proto-Beulaic existence, the positive internal powers of the realm are female. The little boy lost by his father is found by his mother, the black child who yearns hopelessly for his father-god's love is comforted by his mother, other mothers and nurses protect children from darkness and grief. (p. 509)

The power of the females in the *Songs of Innocence* is entirely positive, though severely restricted in that the ultimate power in the *Songs* resides in males outside the borders of pure innocence—in piper, angel, father-god. The female power which governs the Beulaic vales in *The Book of Thel* is not only restricted, but negative in implication. The daughters of the seraphim seem to be the only permanent human inhabitants of the vales, and they apparently run things there amiably enough; but male powers from other realms drop in occasionally (Luvah waters his horses there, and God strolls through at dusk), and they clearly take precedence when they do. But however smoothly things are run by the pastoral female regents of the vales, their success is itself an indication of weakness: the vales of Har are a temporary abode from which one must proceed by active determination; that only daughters inhabit the place, that the youngest of those daughters attempts to leave and cannot, identifies females with failure. That identification is harmless to Blake's vision in this early poem, because at this point in the development of his vision women at their best are still domestic help-meets and not the cosmic "contraries" they will become.

By the time Blake was engaged in writing *Milton,* some fifteen years after he engraved *The Book of Thel,* his doctrine of contrariety had crystallized, and it had crystallized around the central metaphor of the relations of male and female. As M. H. Abrams observes, "all contraries, in Blake, operate as opposing yet complementary male-female powers which, in their energetic love-hate relationship, are necessary to all modes of progression, organization, creativity, or procreativity" [see Additional Bibliography]. Contraries must be equal if their contrariety is not to resolve into a tyranny of one element over the other, and therefore Blake must rescue the female element of this central contrariety from its taint of weakness and failure. He attempts to do so in *Milton* in part by clarifying his derogatory representation of Beulah:

> Into this pleasant Shadow all the weak & weary
> Like Women & Children were taken away as on wings
> Of dovelike softness, & shadowy habitations prepared
>   for them
> But every Man returnd & went still going forward thro'
> The Bosom of the Father in Eternity on Eternity....

According to this crucial passage it is not that women fail the rigors of existence in ther realms, but that anyone who fails appears frail and feminine. Femaleness is thus not a synonym for failure in Blake's late poetry, but a metaphor for it. This does not, of course, excuse Blake of the prejudice of selecting this particular metaphor (though it is one he seems not so much to choose here as to be trapped in by his earlier poetry), and, as Jean H. Hagstrum has pointed out in a similar context, "Metaphors have a way of taking over in Blake...." Still, in his late prophecies Blake seems at least to be trying to rescue the idea of a separate but equal female principle from the bitterness and condescension his earlier uneasiness about women had imposed upon it. (pp. 509-11)

As Blake's cosmology developed, his representation of the femaleness of Beulah became increasingly more metaphoric. We may see the same pattern of increasing metaphorization in his representations of individual female characters.... The failure of the heroine of *The Book of Thel* is, as we have seen, a particularly feminine failure, but it foreshadows the genderless failure of active desire Blake will develop in later poems: in the context of his other works Thel suggests not just the frailty of women, but the "feminine" frailty of all human beings. In *Europe* (1794), engraved five years after the *Innocence* songs and *Thel,* female characters represent not only the darker propensities Blake feared in women, but the technically genderless tyrannies of nature and religion as well. By *The Four Zoas,* which Blake probably worked on between 1796 and 1807, both male and female figures have become, however

pointedly realistic their battles and failures and ultimate reconciliations may seem, symbols of issues much broader than marital relationships: males are Zoas (or spectres) and females are emanations, and their union is not marriage but apocalypse.

As the metaphoric value of female characters develops in these poems, so does their chief negative metaphoric identification, the Female Will, that lust for unnatural dominance which disrupts all proper order, even as a female-dominated marriage supposedly disrupts proper order. Between *The Book of Thel* and *Milton,* the only positive females are those so devoid of will, or at least of the power to realize their will, as to be melodramatically helpless. Thel herself is instructive in this respect. She fails for lack of will, but we have more sympathy for her in her failure than we might have had had she succeeded and turned into, say, the Shadowy Female of *America* once she had found her voice, or Enitharmon in *Europe,* or Vala in *The Four Zoas.* Thel needs will, but not Female Will. After *Thel* and until *Milton,* the only effective will females can have is Female Will. Even Oothoon, the single female character in all Blake's poetry who is both active and good, fails to achieve what she desires because her (lower case) feminine will is not powerful enough to free her from the impositions of male authority. Thel needed will to succeed; Oothoon, paradoxically, needs Female Will, which would pervert the very goal it alone could achieve. Women, it would seem from these early poems, are trapped in a reality which recognizes no female power but evil female power.

Blake's evident sympathy for lovely frail Thel and valorous Oothoon suggests a strong consciousness of the social forces which prevent sexual mutuality. Indeed, *Visions of the Daughters of Albion* has long been read as an affirmation of Mary Wollstonecraft's *A Vindication of the Rights of Woman,* published one year before Blake engraved *Visions.* Oothoon's courage and her embodiment not only of Wollstonecraft's ideas but of Blake's own have made her seem unimpeachable proof of Blake's feminism. Because in the poems which follow *Visions of the Daughters of Albion* there is no heroine both assertive and good ..., it has frequently been assumed that some personal incident converted Blake from belief in sexual equality to mistrust and derogation of women. Though I agree that the tone of many of his passages about women has a new stridency after *Visions,* I do not accept the idea of a sudden and bitter conversion. We have already noted that even in the *Songs of Innocence* and *The Book of Thel* Blake's attitude towards women is equivocal; I believe it is equivocal in *Visions* as well. It is certainly true that Oothoon speaks for Blake in this poem, that she is as noble in its context as ever Los is in the final poems (more noble: she does not make mistakes), that she indicates a real and deep capacity in Blake for recognizing wisdom and courage and righteousness and strength in women. But it is also true that, unlike Orc or Los or Milton or any other positive male figure in Blake's poetry, Oothoon is helplessly victimized by powers completely outside her control. On one level the poem is an outcry against this victimization, a passionate denunciation of the oppression of women. But on another level it exploits that victimization symbolically to make a second and equally central political point. Blake made the chief character of *Visions of the Daughters of Albion* female not just because he admired Mary Wollstonecraft and thought women at least potentially men's equals, and not just because he abhorred the oppression of women, but also because he needed a chief character who could be raped and tied down and suppressed without recourse—or rather, with the single recourse of giving birth to the revolutionary male force which can end the victimization. *Visions of the Daughters of Albion* has a heroine and not a hero partly because one of the points of the poem is that its central figure, "the soft soul of America," is a slave. Oothoon was chosen for her part not just because she was wise and brave, but also because she was female and thus powerless. Her gender is a trap—just the trap the symbolism of the poem demands. (pp. 511-13)

After *Visions of the Daughters of Albion* female characters will be either good (Ahania, Ololon, Jerusalem) or active (Enitharmon, Rahab, Vala), never both. Blake will divide the female character more schematically and reductively than he ever will the male: Tharmas, for example, the incarnation of chaotic passivity, is also the force which commands Los to keep building fallen humanity in *The Four Zoas;* he, like all other male forms, is both negative and positive, both weak and powerful. In *America* and *Europe* we see the pernicious Female Will rampant (in *Europe* the woeful Shadowy Female constantly giving birth gives us a passive contrary to the virulent Enitharmon); in the Books of *Urizen* and *Ahania* the emanations weep helplessly at the deeds of their powerful consorts. In *The Four Zoas* Ahania and Enion lament helplessly in the wilderness while Enitharmon and Vala proclaim their dominion and scheme to keep it. Rahab's power to corrupt opposes Ololon's sweet submissiveness in *Milton,* and Vala in her strident pride contrasts with the wise but abandoned Jerusalem in Blake's last prophecy. This divided female image must necessarily be of more value as symbol than as characterization, since any character it permits is by definition partial.

The reason for this shift in emphasis from character (or at least from the representation of self-contained figures capable of complex significance, like Oothoon—Blake was never much interested in characterization in any novelistic sense) to symbol may have been the proliferation of Blake's mythic system, or it may have been a personal experience which altered his conception of women. It has often been argued that at Lambeth, where the Blakes lived from 1791 to 1800, Blake undertook an affair—or desired to undertake one—which so alienated his wife that she startled him into a new perception of feminine wrath and possessiveness. It may be that such a revelation shocked Blake into accepting stereotypes of women he had long resisted—or that his own guilt and confusion made him spiteful. But whatever the cause of the emergence of female as metaphor in his poetry, the process reaches a crisis in *Milton,* in which for the first time the metaphoric representation of female characters contradicts the vision it is intended to support. (pp. 513-14)

Contraries are by definition equal, but the females in *Milton,* however crucial and powerful Blake intended them to be, are not convincingly equal to their male contraries. They participate in the same dehumanizing division of the good from the active which kept Blake's earlier female figures not only from full characterization but even from multidimensional symbolism. Throughout the poem females are either passive or pernicious. Females presented positively are passive: emanations cannot long endure the strife of Eden, Enitharmon is uncomplainingly cut off from full vision by Los, Ololon mourns by her river in Eden and only descends to Generation when she sees Milton there, Catherine is ill in her house. Active females are pernicious: Leutha, Tirzah, the Shadowy Female all create disaster by their actions, which are only imitations of the actions of males anyway and need the further actions of males to complete them.

There is some evidence in *Milton* that the passive female can be stronger in her passivity than the male in his active glory. Enitharmon's gentle love for Satan saves him by creating a space for him (his salvation is necessary to Albion's), and Ololon's lamentations consummate Milton's act of sacrifice and consolidate the Divine Family as Jesus. The positive functions of the females of the poem are equal in rigor and importance with those of the males. Yet still the metaphoric use Blake makes of femaleness is pejorative. In the passage quoted above about the function of Beulah he does not say that all females are weak, but he does say that all weakness is female: when you enter Beulah exhausted from Eden you are female, but when, restored and strong, you return to mental strife, you are male. Furthermore, that anathema "Female Will" is so strong in the poem that it corrupts any possible balance of male-female contraries: Leutha is responsible for the fall of Satan as Vala is for the fall of Albion (or at least for the imprisonment and torment of Luvah), the Divine Voice castigates the destructive half of his emanation, Babylon, for destroying their union, and if Milton confesses to having ignorantly misused Ololon, she confesses to having maliciously sought to vanquish him. Female Will may be only a metaphor for the destructive urge for dominance which knows no gender, and the femaleness of the emanations in Beulah may be only a metaphor for weakness; the metaphor in each case is surely the most immediately suggestive Blake could have employed. But precisely because of its suggestiveness that metaphor undermines the major thematic balance of the poem. (pp. 515-16)

Blake seems to be partly conscious of the damage his metaphoric use of females does to his vision in *Milton* in that he tries to correct that damage by implying that the metaphor is provisional. The division into sexes was a condition of the fall imposed by Urizen . . . and will cease to exist when the fall is consummated in resurrection. As the existence of sexual distinction is a condition of the fall, so is the urge for dominance which creates sexual hierarchy. Questions about the relationship between the sexes are thus referred to a better life in which there are no sexes.

In *Jerusalem* Blake seems more conscious still of the difficulties inherent in his now firmly established metaphors of femaleness, more determined to correct the imbalance they imply. He introduces a masculine emanation (Shiloh, the emanation of France as Jerusalem is of Albion . . .), and asserts later that all emanations "stand both Male & Female at the gates of each Humanity," . . . emphasizing that the weakness attributed to females by emanation is shared by males. He transfers responsibility for the division of the sexes from restrictive Urizen to inspired Los . . . , implying that there is constructive value in the separate existence of the female during the course of the fall. He reverses the genders of the speakers of several key speeches substantially repeated in *Jerusalem* from earlier poems, suggesting that his conception of sexual roles is at least partly flexible. . . . (p. 517)

Jesus castigates the destructive nature of his emanation fiercely in *Milton* . . . , demanding her conversion; in a parallel but much milder speech in *Jerusalem* he explains her error and consoles her and promises to lead her to redemption. . . . The softening of Jesus' tone towards his emanation in *Jerusalem* is echoed in Blake's expanding in his last prophecy the redemptive faculty of the female—most evident earlier in Ololon's identification with Jesus—by presenting Jerusalem as the wholly positive force which Albion need only recognize and embrace to return to Eden. She is better than he is, more nearly Edenic, less perverted: her sons are the soul while his are the body . . . , her sons number four times four, the perfect numbers of Edenic existence, while his only number four times three. . . .

Throughout *Jerusalem* Blake seems to be redefining for this separate female form he has conceptualized a position which is wholly positive. The clearest statement of that position is [in the following lines]: ''Man is adjoined to Man by his Emanative portion: / Who is Jerusalem in every individual Man: and her / Shadow is Vala, builded by the reasoning power in Man.'' The positive function of the female is to permit union among males; her negative function is to destroy that union by rationalization. We may recognize these functions in *Milton*, though they are not explicitly defined there: the constructive function is evident in the intermediation of Beulah between Eden and Generation as well as in Ololon's uniting of Milton and Jesus, and the negative function is evidence in the acts of Leutha and Rahab and the Shadowy Female. *Jerusalem* distinguishes even more overtly than *Milton* the positive and negative functions of the female, giving Vala equal time with Jerusalem. Yet the more clearly the female roles are defined, the more circumscribed they are by male reality: female separateness is good when it permits communication among males, bad when it corrupts that communication, good when it passively awaits embrace, bad when it actively demands embrace. The more positive Blake's female becomes, the more passive, the more male-circumscribed she becomes. Jerusalem is better than Albion, but lesser. The active/positive female alternative suggested, however ambivalently, by Ololon is sabotaged in *Jerusalem* by Blake's requirement of a totally positive—and hence, even at this point in the development of his attitudes, totally will-less—female principle. The conflict between Blake's doctrine and the stereotypes of sexual relationship in which he expresses it remains. (p. 518)

That Blake's metaphor contradicts his doctrine of necessary equality between contraries is perhaps more a comment on the society in which he was educated and which he addressed than it is upon his faculties as thinker and poet, but it is a comment on his mind and art nonetheless. Metaphors are not divorced from concepts. When they conflict with the concepts they are meant to advance they attest to an uneasiness in their author's mind, and create an uneasiness in his or her reader's mind. That uneasiness is probably minor for readers of Blake's prophecies, who are most likely able to accommodate such discrepancies comfortably in their perception of the rich and significant schemes of these great poems. It may have been minor for Blake himself, though he tried frequently to adjust it. It is not minor in our conception of the poet Blake, who more than any other male writer of his time recognized the destructive effect of received attitudes towards women, but who was nevertheless to some extent a victim of those attitudes. (p. 519)

Susan Fox, ''The Female as Metaphor in William Blake's Poetry,'' in Critical Inquiry, *Vol. 3, No. 3, Spring, 1977, pp. 507-19.*

LEOPOLD DAMROSCH, JR.   (essay date 1980)

[*Damrosch considers what Blake offers to the person who, unlike Frye (see excerpt dated 1947) and other sympathetic readers, does not share the poet's faith in imaginative vision. After noting Blake's limitations, Damrosch recommends reading him for his ''exploration of the possibilities and limits of the symbol, and his passionate demand for moral commitment.''*]

Blake, from a painting on ivory by John Linnell dated 1826.

Blake believed that his symbols, although compromised by participation in a fallen world, were ultimately guaranteed by being ''comprehended'' in the divine body of Jesus. If we do not share that faith, how shall we respond to the symbols? It is one thing for Blake to assert that they afford a privileged insight into truth, and another for us to agree that they do. (p. 364)

The preeminent exponent of Blake's desire-fulfilling symbols is Northrop Frye, who asserts with truly Blakean logic, ''Imagination creates reality, and as desire is a part of imagination, the world we desire is more real than the world we passively accept.'' This claim, as in Frye's later criticism where it is generalized to accommodate all symbolic writing, is offered in support of a rejection of science that is just as bitter and unfair as Blake's: ''As long as science means knowledge organized by a commonplace mind it will be part of the penalty man pays for being stupid.'' And since men who are not stupid understand that desire creates reality, it follows that ''the work of art is the product of this creative perception, hence it is not an escape from reality but a systematic training in comprehending it.'' Such an approach does a disservice to Blake, exaggerating the achieved security of his visions of desire and minimizing the great theme of man's struggle against the internal obstacles that thwart desire. Blake's imaginative vision is admirable because it wrestles so honestly with the intractable facts of fallen experience. Moreover, the symbolist approach depends upon what Murray Krieger has called ''the mythification of art,'' whereas Blake is expressly concerned to define the limits of both myth and art.

It would be more just to Blake to say that he is profoundly aware of the anguish of experience, but wants to believe that experience is finally an illusion. If we deny the conclusion we can still appreciate the brilliance of the diagnosis. The *Songs of Experience* are widely admired because they analyze the facts of experience so tellingly and protest against them with so noble a passion. And our admiration need not be any the less if we cannot follow Blake into a philosophical system that locates Experience near the bottom of a hierarchy of levels and dismisses most of it as mere "error."

> For he saw that life liv'd upon death
> The Ox in the slaughter house moans
> The Dog at the wintry door
> And he wept, & he called it Pity
> And his tears flowed down on the winds.

The speaker is Urizen, and his pity is futile if not downright hypocritical, but Blake's myth is large enough to do justice to the depth of feeling here even as he criticizes Urizen's response. Enion, Emanation of Tharmas the parent power, also speaks of the dog at the wintry door and the ox in the slaughterhouse; her words haunt us because Blake means them to be haunting.

> What is the price of Experience do men buy it for a
>   song
> Or wisdom for a dance in the street? No it is bought
>   with the price
> Of all that a man hath his house his wife his children
> Wisdom is sold in the desolate market where none
>   come to buy
> And in the witherd field where the farmer plows for
>   bread in vain. . . .

Perhaps a clarified vision should sweep these images away as delusions of Satan and Vala, but they come from Blake's most bitter experience, and we respond to them truly even if we cannot accept his hopeful call for their abolition. What one carries away most of all from the prophecies is man's desperate need for reintegration, not the ease with which he can hope to gain it.

Where the poems are most disappointing, by the same token, is in their frequent refusal to be true to the experience from which they were born. Just as suffering is finally translated into other terms, so also death is so far from being real that what we call life is Blake's "Eternal Death." Of course one may say that death is omnipresent in the myth by the very urgency with which Blake denies it. Imagination itself, according to Bergson, is "a defensive reaction of nature against the representation by intelligence of the inevitablility of death." Blake's art is a fight to the death against death. But any Christian poet denies the ultimate reality of death. What is harder to accept is Blake's concomitant rejection of life, which is dismissed as entrapment in materiality except in those epiphanic moments when it breaks free of life as we ordinarily live it. There can be no Wordsworthian solitary reaper in Blake, with her mournful song that fills the heart of the wayfarer, and no Michael with the tragedy of his family and land. Hegel exalts tragedy because it mediates the destructive fury of warring "truths"; Blake, like Plato, despises it because it encourages an emotional acceptance of destruction as a necessary consequence of the nature of things. "Drinking & eating, & pitying & weeping, as at a trajic scene / The soul drinks murder & revenge, & applauds its own holiness." . . . It is not that nothing is destroyed in Blake, but that what is destroyed is not *real*. "You cannot go to Eternal Death in that which can never Die." . . . No wonder Blake draws so little upon the greatest

of English poets; Shakespeare is the repudiated master in the descent of the spirit from poet to poet that culminates in Blake.

It is not only tragedy that we miss in Blake; it is much of human life. The notebook lyrics of love or anti-love are fascinating because they deal with themes that are usually submerged or allegorized out of recognition in the prophecies. It is inconceivable that Blake could have written the lines,

> Then, while time serves, and we are but decaying,
>   Come, my Corinna, come, let's go a-Maying.

For that is merely [of the world of Beulah]. . . . And because it is only Beulah, Blake will make no compromise with it. Herrick's speaker addresses a real woman, not an idea ("O Rose thou art sick"), he accepts mortality and the consequent attitude to pleasure, and his slow and thoughtful verse is remote from Blake's declarative (often declamatory) style. Such a mood is not incompatible with religious faith:

> It is the blight man was born for,
> It is Margaret you mourn for.
>   [Gerard Manley Hopkins, "Spring and Fall."]

But it must be a faith like Hopkins' that accepts both the reality and the significance of mortal life. In the end, for all his awareness of the weight of experience, Blake cannot come to terms with

>   . . . the very world which is the world
> Of all of us,—the place in which, in the end,
> We find our happiness, or not at all.
>   [William Wordsworth, *The Prelude*]

"A roller & two harrows lie before my window," Blake wrote to Butts on reaching Felpham. "I met a plow on my first going out at my gate the first morning after my arrival & the Plowboy said to the Plowman, 'Father The Gate is Open'." . . . The plow and harrows get into *The Four Zoas* and *Milton;* the plowboy and his father do not.

If Blake deliberately cuts himself off from the phenomenology of lived experience, and if the modern reader cannot join him in that exclusion, why should one read him? Among other reasons two seem particularly compelling: his exploration of the possibilities and limits of the symbol, and his passionate demand for moral commitment. Let us consider symbols first. (pp. 365-68)

[I argue] against the assumptions that symbols offer a privileged view of reality (unless artistic symbols be accepted as having the same status as all other symbolic forms) and that they should be welcomed for their tendency to construct reality in accordance with heart's desire. I hold rather . . . that although all thought is symbolic, this represents a problem rather than a victory, and that mythical thinking needs to be criticized as well as admired for its tendency to reshape the world in conformity with desire. But I would argue also that Blake understands this very point and wants to make us understand it. For if the fallen world is the only world we have, then its symbols are the only symbols; and in that case Blake's deconstruction of symbols can be immensely valuable. At the same time, by clinging to symbols in spite of their flaws, Blake exemplifies the all but universal refusal to imagine a truly empty universe. The imagination must people it with symbols of vitality. . . . [Blake] insists that the entire universe participates in the agony of the divided mind. In this sense Hume is a modern and Blake a late inheritor of Plotinus and Valentinus. But as the modern yearning for myths—even the most home-built and rickety—

has proved, the desire for humanized symbols is irresistible. And here again Blake can help us to regard them critically, just because he himself aspires to transcend them and therefore regards them with suspicion.

Shelley suggests that symbols may represent the only reality there is and may protect us from the abyss of unmeaning that lies beyond. For as he says in the *Defense*, "All things exist as they are perceived; at least in relation to the percipient. . . . But poetry defeats the curse which binds us to be subjected to the accident of surrounding impressions. And whether it spreads its own figured curtain, or withdraws life's dark veil from before the scene of things, it equally creates for us a being within our being. It makes us the inhabitants of a world to which the familiar world is a chaos." Blake, by the very force of his belief, compels us to recognize the provisional and wish-fulfilling nature of such a manifesto. If reality only exists as it is perceived "in relation to the percipient," then there is no guarantee that it exists at all except as subjective construction. And if poetry spreads a figured curtain rather than drawing the veil aside, then it is only a mask to hide the chaos of the world, and we would do well to know it. In his absolutism Blake encourages us to recognize—even if we continue to need—the groping and imperfect nature of the achievements available to the imagination.

Finally, we come to Blake for the exhilaration of contact with a prophetic spirit that never relents in the quest for truth.

> I will not cease from Mental Fight,
> Nor shall my Sword sleep in my hand:
> Till we have built Jerusalem,
> In Englands green & pleasant Land. . . .

To read Blake at all is to enter, however provisionally, into the quest, for as Auerbach says of biblical narrative, "Without believing in Abraham's sacrifice, it is impossible to put the narrative of it to the use for which it was written." And if in the end we cannot believe it, if we must put it to other uses, we are then forced to confront the meaning of our disbelief, to see plainly the empty universe which no religion of art can fill again with spilt meaning. It may be that aesthetic disinterestedness is the right response to art, but if so, it is all the more salutary to immerse oneself for a time in an art like Blake's that violently repudiates it. (pp. 368-70)

We read Blake's myth to know what it would be like to believe in man's spiritual power while fully recognizing the self-deluding tendencies of the imagination and its symbols. In Blake there is no reliance on received faith, as in the later Wordsworth, or on natural piety as a mode of transposed faith, as in the earlier Wordsworth. On the contrary, he provides a searching analysis of the basis of *all* faiths, and of their inevitable corruption, in the human imagination. His extraordinary exploration of the psyche is framed in a myth that offers imaginative answers to the fact of alienation. If we cannot share Blake's faith and accept his answers, we must admire the honesty and insight with which he strives to reconcile the direst aspects of human experience with our profound longing for harmony and meaning.

Within the category of moral and religious writing—as contrasted with tragedy or elegy or the other modes that Blake dismisses—his poems retain the power of their conception in spite of all obstacles of execution, and in spite of the gaping philosophical rifts that no amount of revision could ever close. In contrast with an extinct document such as, for instance, Pope's *Essay on Man*, Blake's epics survive because their

religious passion overwhelms mere ethical earnestness. . . . Blake's vision of truth, in its violence of commitment, is exciting to many a reader who has only the sketchiest idea of what he is actually talking about. (pp. 370-71)

[My comments have] been directed toward elucidating Blake's meanings, but I want to close by affirming that all of this would have a merely antiquarian function if Blake did not possess the power of religious vision. His meanings command our imaginative as well as scholarly respect because they are forged and reforged in the furnace of that vision; Blake does not force us to accept his answers, but he demands that we enter into his mental strife and make it ours. And if we inhabit a world that no longer believes in its symbols—if we can neither trust the products of our symbol-making imagination nor bear to live without them—then Blake speaks to us with a special poignancy. His Eden is forever closed to us by the Cherub with the flaming sword, but we are all too well acquainted with Los weeping at the silent forge, struggling to make the accusing Spectre of despair join again in creative labor. Rather than rhapsodizing about Blake's apocalyptic breakthrough as if it were easily attained, we might dwell instead on the bitter honesty with which he has dramatized the pre-apocalyptic condition, which may be the only condition we can ever know. And in that case what continues to move us in Blake's myth is not its answers but its questions, which are posed with a prophetic urgency that remains alive and life-giving. (p. 371)

> *Leopold Damrosch, Jr., in his* Symbol and Truth in Blake's Myth, *Princeton University Press, 1980, 395 p.*

ADDITIONAL BIBLIOGRAPHY

Abrams, M. H. *Natural Supernaturalism: Tradition and Revolution in Romantic Literature*. New York: W. W. Norton & Co., 1973, 550 p.
    Includes Blake among the German and English Romantic writers who enunciated a new view of human nature and human history following the disappointments of the French Revolution.

Adams, Hazard. *Blake and Yeats: The Contrary Vision*. Cornell Studies in English, edited by M. H. Abrams, Francis E. Mineka, and William M. Sale, Jr. Vol. XL. 1955. Reprint. Ann Arbor, Mich.: University Microfilms, 1965, 328 p.
    A comparison of Blake and Yeats that focuses on the poets' symbolism.

Altizer, Thomas J. J. *The New Apocalypse: The Radical Christian Vision of William Blake*. East Lansing: Michigan State University Press, 1967, 226 p.
    Investigates the radical theological implications of Blake's works.

Ault, Donald D. *Visionary Physics: Blake's Response to Newton*. Chicago: University of Chicago Press, 1974, 229 p.
    Explores the relationship between Blake's and Newton's visions of the world.

Bentley, G. E., Jr. *Blake Records*. Oxford: Clarendon Press, 1969, 678 p.
    A comprehensive collection of contemporary references to Blake. Bentley provides helpful background information concerning the letters, reviews, and other materials reprinted in the volume.

——. *Blake Books*. Oxford: Clarendon Press, 1977, 1079 p.
    The leading reference guide to Blake's works and to Blake criticism. The bibliography is divided into six sections: editions of Blake's writings; reproductions of drawings and paintings; commercial book engravings; catalogues and bibliographies; books owned by Blake; and biography and criticism.

————, ed. *William Blake: The Critical Heritage*. Critical Heritage Series, edited by B. C. Southam. London: Routledge & Kegan Paul, 1975, 294 p.

Contains eighteenth- and early nineteenth-century discussions of Blake's life, writings, drawings, and engraved designs.

————, and Nurmi, Martin K. *A Blake Bibliography: Annotated Lists of Works, Studies, and Blakeana*. Minneapolis: University of Minnesota Press, 1964, 393 p.

A major Blake bibliography. Bentley subsequently updated and augmented this work in his *Blake Books* (see annotation above).

Berger, P. *William Blake: Poet and Mystic*. Translated by Daniel H. Conner. New York: E. P. Dutton & Co., 1915, 420 p.

An early examination of Blake's life, doctrines, and works. Berger maintains that the poet's mysticism and symbolism gradually overpowered his poetry, making his poetry "perhaps the most obscure in the whole range of literature."

Bronowski, J. *William Blake, 1757-1827: A Man without a Mask*. London: Secker & Warburg, 1944, 153 p.

Portrays Blake as a poet whose life and work reflect the political and social revolutions that rocked his age.

Bruce, Harold. *William Blake in This World*. 1925. Reprint. New York: Haskell House Publishers, 1974, 234 p.

Attempts to present a nonromanticized version of Blake's life.

C[oleridge], S[amuel] T[aylor]. Letter to C. A. Tulk. In his *Collected Letters of Samuel Taylor Coleridge*, Vol. IV, 1815-1819, edited by Earl Leslie Griggs, pp. 835-38. Oxford, Clarendon Press, 1959.

Records Coleridge's reactions to *Songs of Innocence and of Experience*, indicating the degree to which individual poems pleased him.

Curran, Stuart, and Wittreich, Joseph Anthony, Jr., eds. *Blake's Sublime Allegory: Essays on "The Four Zoas," "Milton," "Jerusalem."* Madison: University of Wisconsin Press, 1973, 384 p.

A collection of essays on the major prophecies by distinguished scholars. The editors of the volume observe that "particular attention focuses on Blake's form of epic-prophecy, on its traditions, its structure, aesthetics, and metaphysics."

Damon, S. Foster. *A Blake Dictionary: The Ideas and Symbols of William Blake*. Brown University Bicentennial Publications: Studies in the Fields of General Scholarship. Providence, R.I.: Brown University Press, 1965, 460 p.

A highly regarded reference work explaining the ideas and symbols in Blake's writings from "Abarim" to "Zoa."

Dorfman, Deborah. *Blake in the Nineteenth Century: His Reputation as a Poet, From Gilchrist to Yeats*. Yale Studies in English, edited by Richard S. Sylvester, vol. 170. New Haven: Yale University Press, 1969, 314 p.

A close examination of the development of Blake's reputation during the nineteenth century. Dorfman focuses on the mid-nineteenth century Blake revival occasioned by the publication of Alexander Gilchrist's *Life of William Blake, "Pictor Ignotus"* (see excerpt dated 1861).

Downer, Alan S., ed. *English Institute Essays: 1950*. New York: AMS Press, 1965, 236 p.

Includes three noteworthy essays on Blake: Josephine Miles's "The Language of William Blake," Frye's "Blake's Treatment of the Archetype," and Erdman's "Blake: The Historical Approach."

Easson, Roger R., and Essick, Robert N. *William Blake: Book Illustrator*. 2 vols. Memphis, Tenn.: American Blake Foundation, 1979.

A bibliography and catalogue of Blake's commercial book illustrations.

Eaves, Morris. *William Blake's Theory of Art*. Princeton Essays on the Arts, no. 13. Princeton: Princeton University Press, 217 p.

Explores Blake's idea of the artist, the work of art, and the audience.

Eliot, T. S. "Blake." In his *The Sacred Wood: Essays on Poetry and Criticism*, pp. 151-58. London: Methuen, University Paperbacks, 1960.

Focuses on the ramifications of Blake's self-reliance.

Erdman, David V., ed. *A Concordance to the Writings of William Blake*. 2 vols. Cornell Concordances, edited by S. M. Parrish. Ithaca: Cornell University Press, 1967.

An index of the words in Blake's verse and prose.

Essick, Robert N., ed. *The Visionary Hand: Essays for the Study of William Blake's Art and Aesthetics*. Los Angeles: Hennessey & Ingalls, 1973, 558 p.

Includes discussions of Blake's art, aesthetics, and techniques of relief etching.

————, and Pearce, Donald, eds. *Blake in His Time*. Bloomington: Indiana University Press, 1978, 253 p.

A collection of essays bringing an "art-historical" approach to bear on such topics as Blake's artistic motifs, concepts, and development.

Frye, Northrop, ed. *Blake: A Collection of Critical Essays*. Twentieth Century Views, edited by Maynard Mack. Englewood Cliffs, N.J.: Prentice-Hall, 1966, 183 p.

Contains essays by leading Blake scholars on a variety of works, including "The Chimney Sweeper," "Ah! Sun-Flower," "The Crystal Cabinet," and "The Golden Net."

Gleckner, Robert F. *Blake's Prelude: "Poetical Sketches."* Baltimore: Johns Hopkins University Press, 1982, 202 p.

A detailed study of *Poetical Sketches*.

Hagstrum, Jean H. *William Blake: Poet and Painter*. Chicago: University of Chicago Press, 1964, 156 p.

An introduction to the composite art of Blake's illuminated verse.

Hall, Carol Louise. *Blake and Fuseli: A Study in the Transmission of Ideas*. Garland Publications in Comparative Literature, edited by James J. Wilhelm. New York: Garland Publishing, 1985, 171 p.

Examines Henry Fuseli's role in transmitting to Blake the ideas of Johann Joachim Winckelmann, Jean Jacques Rousseau, and Johann Kaspar Lavater.

Harper, George Mills. *The Neoplatonism of William Blake*. Chapel Hill: University of North Carolina Press, 1961, 324 p.

Examines the "fundamental ties" between contemporary Neoplatonism and Blake's thought.

Hilton, Nelson. *Literal Imagination: Blake's Vision of Words*. Berkeley and Los Angeles: University of California Press, 1983, 319 p.

Explores the ways in which Blake's literal imagination manifested itself in his use of words, including his exploitation of their "sound, etymology, graphic shape, contemporary applications, and varied associations."

Hoagwood, Terence Allan. *Prophecy and the Philosophy of Mind: Traditions of Blake and Shelley*. University, Ala.: University of Alabama Press, 1985, 247 p.

Delineates a revolutionary unification of the traditions of Christian biblical prophecy and its exegesis and Enlightenment epistemology in Blake's *Jerusalem* and Percy Bysshe Shelley's *Prometheus Unbound*.

Johnson, Mary Lynn. "William Blake." In *The English Romantic Poets: A Review of Research and Criticism*, 4th ed., edited by Frank Jordan, pp. 113-253. New York: Modern Language Association of America, 1985.

Provides a concise critical overview of past and present Blake scholarship.

Leader, Zachary. *Reading Blake's "Songs."* Boston: Routledge & Kegan Paul, 1981, 259 p.

Interprets *Songs of Innocence and of Experience* as a "single, carefully organized volume of verbal and visual art . . . in which almost every poem and design contributes to a larger artistic unity." Leader regards seventeenth- and eighteenth-century children's books and educational treatises as Blake's "immediate models" for the poems, emphasizing their contribution and the contribution of Blake's designs to the artistic unity of the work.

Lowery, Margaret Ruth. *Windows of the Morning: A Critical Study of William Blake's "Poetical Sketches," 1783*. New Haven: Yale University Press, 1940, 249 p.

Assesses *Poetical Sketches* in light of Blake's response to the Bible, John Milton, Edmund Spenser, William Shakespeare, and other influences.

Mellor, Anne Kostelanetz. *Blake's Human Form Divine*. Berkeley and Los Angeles: University of California Press, 1974, 354 p.

Probes the development of Blake's struggle with his conflicting philosophical and artistic positions concerning the human form.

More, Paul Elmer. "William Blake." In his *Shelburne Essays, fourth series*, pp. 212-38. New York: G. P. Putnam's Sons, Knickerbocker Press, 1911.

A brief survey of Blake's life and works. More concludes his remarks by observing that the poet's identification with the "naïve emotions of childhood" restricts his influence to "the lesser men—Rossetti, Swinburne, and their school—who in one way or another have shrunk from the higher as well as the lower realities of life."

Nurmi, Martin K. *William Blake*. London: Hutchinson University Library, 1975, 175 p.

An introduction to Blake written for the student and the general reader.

Paley, Morton D. *The Continuing City: William Blake's "Jerusalem."* Oxford: Clarendon Press, 1983, 330 p.

A scholarly study of *Jerusalem*. Paley discusses the poem in terms of poetic and artistic tradition, millenarianism, myth, and form.

———, and Phillips, Michael, eds. *William Blake: Essays in Honour of Sir Geoffrey Keynes*. Oxford: Clarendon Press, 1973, 390 p.

Presents commentary on a wide variety of Blake-related topics, including his poetic language, early reputation, and relation to Coleridge and Wordsworth.

Percival, Milton O. *William Blake's Circle of Destiny*. 1938. Reprint. New York: Octagon Books, 1964, 334 p.

Interprets Blake's myth as a "visionary presentation of a systematic body of thought" having sources and analogues in alchemical, biblical, and cabalistic literature.

Pinto, Vivian de Sola, ed. *The Divine Vision: Studies in the Poetry and Art of William Blake*. London: Victor Gollancz, 1957, 216 p.

A collection of essays commemorating the bicentenary of Blake's birth. Contributors to the volume include Damon, Frye, Nurmi, and other noted Blake scholars.

Plowman, Max. *An Introduction to the Study of Blake*. New York: E. P. Dutton & Co., 1927, 183 p.

A highly regarded general introductory study indicating avenues of approach to Blake's poetry.

Punter, David. "Blake: Creative and Uncreative Labour." *Studies in Romanticism* 16, No. 4 (Fall 1977): 535-61.

A Marxist evaluation of Blake's depiction of labor in the prophetic books.

Raine, Kathleen. "Who Made the Tyger?" *Encounter* II, No. 6 (June 1954): 43-50.

Interprets "The Tyger" in light of such possible sources as Paracelsus and Jewish cabalism.

———. *Blake and Tradition*. 2 vols. A. W. Mellon Lectures in the Fine Arts, Vol. 11, Bollingen Series, no. XXXV. Princeton: Princeton University Press, 1968.

Maintains that traditional metaphysical doctrines and their symbolic languages are key influences on Blake's work.

———. *Blake and the New Age*. London: George Allen & Unwin, 1979, 179 p.

Focuses on Blake's modern relevance as the prophet of a "New Age" that recognizes mind rather than matter as the first principle of the universe.

Saintsbury, George. "Burns, Blake, and the Close of the Eighteenth Century (with an Excursus on 'Ossian')." In his *A History of English Prosody from the Twelfth Century to the Present Day. Vol. III, From Blake to Mr. Swinburne*, pp. 3-46. London: Macmillan and Co., 1923.

Surveys Blake's versification in his lyric and prophetic poems.

Saurat, Denis. *Blake and Modern Thought*. New York: Doubleday & Co., Dial Press, 1929, 200 p.

Explains Blake's modernism in the context of his reversion to occultist and exotic lore.

Tannenbaum, Leslie. *Biblical Tradition in Blake's Early Prophecies: The Great Code of Art*. Princeton: Princeton University Press, 1982, 373 p.

Studies the impact of biblical tradition on Blake's thought and works. Tannenbaum considers such issues as Blake's use of biblical pictorialism, typology, and history, focusing his remarks on the early prophetic books.

Tayler, Irene. "The Woman Scaly." *The Bulletin of the Midwest Language Association* 6, No. 1 (Spring 1973): 74-87.

Discusses the relationship between femaleness and fallen vision in Blake's thought.

Wilkie, Brian, and Johnson, Mary Lynn. *Blake's "Four Zoas": The Design of a Dream*. Cambridge: Harvard University Press, 1978, 302 p.

An analysis of *The Four Zoas* that focuses on the poem's allegorical, structural, narrative, and mythical dimensions.

Wilson, Mona. *The Life of William Blake*. Edited by Geoffrey Keynes. London: Oxford University Press, 1971, 415 p.

Ranks with Gilchrist's *Life* (see excerpt dated 1861) as one of the major Blake biographies. The original edition of Wilson's study was published in 1927.

Witcutt, W. P. *Blake: A Psychological Study*. London: Hollis & Carter, 1946, 127 p.

Uses Jungian psychology as a tool for understanding Blake.

Wittreich, Joseph Anthony, Jr. *Angel of Apocalypse: Blake's Idea of Milton*. Madison: University of Wisconsin Press, 1975, 332 p.

Investigates Blake's conception of Milton, examining Blake's portrait and portrayals of Milton, illustrations to his works, and treatment of him in *The Marriage of Heaven and Hell* and *Milton*.

———, ed. *Nineteenth-Century Accounts of William Blake*. Gainesville, Fla.: Scholars' Facsimiles and Reprints, 1970, 289 p.

Reprints nineteenth-century accounts of Blake that provide primary evidence regarding his life and early reputation. The volume includes compositions by Malkin, Robinson, Yeats, John Thomas Smith, Allan Cunningham, and Frederick Tatham.

Timothy Dwight

1752-1817

(Also wrote under pseudonyms of Parnassus, The Friend, James Littlejohn, Esq., and John Homely) American poet, essayist, and theologian.

Dwight is remembered for his staunch advocacy of theological and political principles and for his role in the development of early American literature. His best-known poems are *The Conquest of Canäan*, an allegory, and *Greenfield Hill*, which focuses on American landscapes and culture. His book of travel essays entitled *Travels in New-England and New-York* is considered his most enduring work. Here, Dwight described in detail the rural communities of the early nineteenth-century northeastern United States. While Dwight's works enjoyed limited popularity during his lifetime, he was respected primarily as a social and intellectual leader. Today, though his reputation as an author has diminished, he remains significant as an influential historical figure.

Dwight was born in Northampton, Massachusetts, to a merchant and his wife, the daughter of the noted theologian Jonathan Edwards. Considered a child prodigy, Dwight was educated chiefly by his mother. By the age of four, he was able to read and interpret passages from the Bible and to teach himself the basics of Latin grammar. He began formal college preparatory classes at age eight, but was prevented from entering Yale University until he had reached the age of thirteen. As an undergraduate, Dwight became a member of the "Connecticut Wits," also known as the "Hartford Wits," a group that included such literary members as John Trumbull, Joel Barlow, and Richard Alsop. In addition to promoting Calvinism and Federalism, the "Wits" celebrated America's growing prominence as a world political power and advocated American themes and settings in literature. Dwight graduated from Yale in 1769 with highest honors. His overzealous study habits and the side effects of a smallpox vaccine had ruined his eyesight, however, and by the time he had finished his first two years of college, he could read for only fifteen minutes each day and needed numerous readers and scribes to assist him.

Dwight's interest in education continued unabated after his graduation. Following two years as principal of a grammar school, Dwight returned to Yale in 1771 as a tutor and candidate for a master's degree. He married Mary Woolsey in 1777. During that year, after an unsuccessful attempt to become president of the university, Dwight resigned his tutorial position and became a chaplain for the Continental Army. His father's sudden death in 1779 forced Dwight to leave his post and return to Northampton, where he supported his family by farming, preaching in small parishes, and serving as principal for several nearby grammar schools. In addition, Dwight founded a coeducational grammar school and served in the Massachusetts legislature from 1781 to 1782. The following year, Dwight and his wife moved to Greenfield Hill, Connecticut. There, he was ordained a Congregational minister and founded another coeducational academy. Embittered by his earlier attempt to become president of Yale, Dwight wrote scathing political essays attacking the man who had won the appointment, Ezra Stiles. In 1795, after the death of Stiles, Dwight was appointed to the position.

The innovations implemented by Dwight during his tenure as president of Yale prompted a dramatic change in the overall emphasis of higher education in America. Determined to make Yale a more distinguished academic institution, Dwight appointed scholars and prominent individuals to the faculty who encouraged specialized research and curriculum development. He also encouraged greater participation in college government among both professors and students. Furthermore, as professor of theology and moral philosophy Dwight returned religious studies to the undergraduate program, a change in curriculum that greatly influenced contemporary educators. His lectures to Yale undergraduates, collected in *Theology Explained and Defended in a Series of Sermons*, emphasized Calvinist doctrine and demonstrated Dwight's belief that religion should play an important role in American government. During his twenty-two years as president, Dwight was instrumental in building Yale's reputation for academic excellence. He died of cancer in 1817.

Although Dwight became known as a social and intellectual leader, his literary productions received few positive comments during his lifetime. *The Conquest of Canäan*, for example, was reviewed rather harshly by a number of Dwight's contemporaries. The first epic poem published by an American, *The Conquest of Canäan* employs the character of Joshua and the battle at Canäan as a symbolic representation of George Washington and the Revolutionary War. With this work, Dwight intended to create an American epic comparable to Homer's *Iliad* and Virgil's *Aeneid*. Instead, the poem's comparison of a biblical war with the War of Independence offended many critics. Still, a few commentators, including both Noah Webster and William Cowper, defended the poem's style and subject matter. Most twentieth-century critics consider *The Conquest of Canäan* only marginally important, claiming that its narrative style, characterization, language, and scene too closely parallel those of John Milton's *Paradise Lost*.

Greenfield Hill and *Travels in New-England and New-York* achieved greater popular success among Dwight's peers. *Greenfield Hill*, known specifically for its American themes and settings, was praised for its narrative technique: divided into seven sections, the poem imitates the narrative styles of several authors, particularly Milton. Although most critics admired *Greenfield Hill*, some considered the work derivative and undistinguished. *Travels in New-England and New-York*, which Dwight compiled during his many journeys while president of Yale, has received consistent attention from critics. Although some of his contemporaries faulted the work for its lack of stylistic spontaneity, most applauded its favorable presentation of the United States. Recently, *Travels in New-England and New-York* has been praised by twentieth-century scholars for its historically accurate portrayal of post-Revolutionary American life.

Dwight's importance as an author has diminished since his day. While many critics have agreed that his writings, with their emphasis on American themes and settings, contributed to the development of a more nationalistic literature, they have also concluded that he possessed a minor literary talent. Dwight's reputation currently rests primarily on his contributions as an educator who revitalized the academic system at Yale University and greatly influenced the curriculum and academic development of surrounding colleges. Today, Dwight is recognized as an important social and intellectual leader of late eighteenth- and early nineteenth-century America.

(See also *Dictionary of Literary Biography*, Vol. 37: *American Writers of the Early Republic*.)

*PRINCIPAL WORKS

"Columbia: A Song"   (poetry)   1783; published in journal
     Boston Magazine
The Conquest of Canäan   (poetry)   1785
The Triumph of Infidelity   (poetry)   1788
Greenfield Hill   (poetry)   1794
Theology Explained and Defended in a Series of Sermons. 5
     vols.   (lectures)   1818-19
Travels in New-England and New-York. 4 vols.   (travel
     essays)   1821-22

*Most of Dwight's works were written many years prior to first publication.

GEORGE WASHINGTON   (letter date 1778)

[*The first President of the United States, Washington was also an important American Revolutionary War general. In the following excerpt from a letter written to Dwight, he responds fa-*

vorably to Dwight's request for permission to dedicate his unfinished The Conquest of Canäan *to him.*]

I cannot but form favourable presages of the merit of the Work you propose to [honour me with the dedication of.]

Nothing can give me more pleasure, than to patronize the essays of Genius and a laudable cultivation of the Arts and Sciences, which had began to flourish in so eminent a degree, before the hand of oppression was stretched over our devoted Country. And I shall esteem myself happy, if a Poem, which has employed the labour of Years, will derive any advantages, or bear more weight in the World, by Making its appearance under dedication to me. (p. 106)

> *George Washington, in a letter to Reverend Timothy Dwight, Junior on March 18, 1778, in his* The Writings of George Washington from the Original Manuscript Sources, 1745-1799: March 1, 1778-May 31, 1778, *Vol. 11, edited by John C. Fitzpatrick, United States Government Printing Office, 1934, pp. 105-06.*

TIMOTHY DWIGHT   (essay date 1785)

[*In his introduction to* The Conquest of Canäan, *Dwight discusses the unusual circumstances surrounding the poem's composition. He defends his alterations of the biblical story of Joshua and remarks that his intent was to create an American epic comparable to Homer's* Iliad *or Virgil's* Aeneid.]

[As *The Conquest of Canäan; a Poem in Eleven Books*] is the first of the kind, which has been published in this country, the writer begs leave to introduce it with several observations, which that circumstance alone may perhaps render necessary.

He has taken to himself the liberty of altering the real order of the two last battles, because he imagined the illustrious events, which attended the battle of Gibeon, would make it appear to be the catastrophe of the poem, wherever inserted.

He has varied the story of the embassy from Gibeon, for reasons, which he thinks will be obvious to every reader, and which he hopes will be esteemed his sufficient justification.

To give entire Unity to the Action, he has made Jabin the Canäanitish hero through the whole poem; and has transferred the scene of the battle, between Hazor and Israel, from the shores of the lake Merom to the neighbourhood of Ai.

In the Manners, he has studied a medium between absolute barbarism and modern refinement. In the best characters, he has endeavoured to represent such manners, as are removed from the peculiarities of any age, or country, and might belong to the amiable and virtuous, of every age: such as are elevated without design, refined without ceremony, elegant without fashion, and agreeable, because they are ornamented with sincerity, dignity, and religion, not because they are polished by art and education. Of such manners, he hopes he may observe, without impropriety, that they possess the highest advantages for universal application.

He has made use of Rhyme, because he believed it would be more generally relished than blank verse, even amongst those who are esteemed persons of taste.

It may perhaps be thought the result of inattention or ignorance, that he chose a subject, in which his countrymen had no national interest. But he remarked that the *Iliad* and *Eneid* were as agreeable to modern nations, as to the Greeks and Romans. The reason he supposed to be obvious—the subjects of those poems furnish the fairest opportunities of exhibiting the agreeable, the novel, the moral, the pathetic, and the sublime. If he is not deceived, the subject he has chosen possesses, in a degree, the same advantages.

It will be observed that he has introduced some new words, and annexed to some old ones, a new signification. This liberty, allowed to others, he hopes will not be refused to him: especially as from this source the copiousness and refinement of language have been principally derived.

That he wishes to please he frankly confesses. If he fails in the design, it will be a satisfaction that he shall have injured no person but himself. As the poem is uniformly friendly to delicacy, and virtue, he hopes his countrymen will so far regard him with candour, as not to impute it to him as a fault, that he has endeavoured to please them, and has thrown in his mite, for the advancement of the refined arts, on this side of the Atlantic. (pp. 5-6)

> *Timothy Dwight, in a preface to his* The Conquest of Canäan: A Poem, *n.p., 1785, pp. 5-6.*

THE AMERICAN MAGAZINE   (poem date 1788)

[*Several sources cite Noah Webster as the author of the following poem dedicated to Dwight. Webster would have been nineteen years old at the time of its publication.*]

Hail, rising genius, whose celestial
    fire
Warms the glad soul to tune the sacred
    lyre;
Whose splendid lays in epic song adorn
A theme which infidels and sceptics scorn;
Sing the bold feats of Joshua's valiant
    hand
Who rears his standard in Canaan's land;
Before whose arm, the numerous squa-
    drons slain
Heap the broad field and drench the em-
    battled plain;
The vanquish'd nations tremble at his
    frown
And laurel'd conquests all his labors
    crown.

Shall Homer's genius date a matchless
    flight
And fear triumphant to the realms of
    light?
Shall Virgil's sweetness every grace com-
    bine
And lose the enraptur'd soul in charms
    divine?
Shall milder Tasso rear the magic throne
Nor these bright ages blush his power to
    own?
Shall god-like Milton, whose sublimer
    lays
Have shar'd at length the debt of envied
    praise,
In sacred verse alone deserve a name
Without one rival to eclipse his fame?

Your heavenly song the palm of praise
    demands
And wafts your rising fame to distant lands.
Those views extensive, that exalted mind
That manly firmness and that zeal refin'd;
That sacred fire which like the electric
    blaze
Darts thro' each state and beams enliven-
    ing rays;
Glow in your breast; you reach a softer-
    ing hand
To nourish science and adorn the land.

Here, see the man, whose philosophic
    soul
Mounts on the day and flies from pole to
    pole,
Thro vast expanse on daring pinions soar
Eye nature's system and its parts explore;
Or see him dare a guilty world engage
And curb the excursions of a vicious age;
Rouse slumbering man from folly's vile
    embrace
Or light a smile in sorrow's clouded face;
Diffuse the balmy dew of sacred truth
Support old age and guide the devious
    youth.

Wrap'd into transport at the Heavenly
    charms
Of music's sweetness and her soft alarms;
See the gay throng in harmony conspire
Touch the soft notes and wanton on the
    lyre
In sweetest concert every charm combine,
Rouse the dull soul, and flights of rage
    confine.

Soon o'er the land these glorious arts
    shall reign
And blest Yalensia lead the splendid train.
In future years unnumber'd Bards shall rise
Catch the bold flame and tower above the
    skies;
Their brightning splendor gild the epic page
And unborn Dwights adorn th' Augustan
    age.

(pp. 265-66)

> *"To the Author of the 'Conquest of Canaan'," in* The American Magazine, *No. 4, March, 1788, pp. 265-66.*

THE EUROPEAN MAGAZINE, AND LONDON REVIEW   (essay date 1788)

[*In the following excerpt from a largely negative review of* The Conquest of Canäan, *the critic faults Dwight's choice of subject matter and allegorical use of contemporary American figures. The reviewer concludes that Dwight's talent is still undeveloped, but could improve with age and experience. Noah Webster responds to this review in an essay in the* American Magazine *(1788).*]

Every liberal mind must be pleased to see Genius, and that great humaniser of nations, polite Literature, expanding themselves in the infant States of America. However inferior to a Homer or a Milton; or, however but little superior to a Blackmore; yet the attempt to cultivate the Muses in a new-formed Commonwealth, and a decent and promising attempt the Poem before us undoubtedly is, such an attempt has a claim to more than ordinary candour, has a claim to liberal indulgence, and such due commendations as may cherish the *lisping* Muse. The critic who is the genuine friend of the interests of literature, where he perceives a total barrenness of genius, will admonish the unhappy author to desist; and will even add ridicule and severity, as the case may require. But where taste and merit are discernible, and capable of improvement, he will point out the blemishes and faults with tenderness, and in a manner calculated to promote the Author's future amendment. Such we intend to be the rule of our conduct in our animadversions on the American Epic Poem, the ***Conquest of Canaan***. (p. 81)

There is good sense in the [introduction to the Poem (see excerpt dated 1785)], tho' we think some parts very objectionable. The faithful, full, and minute pictures of the manners of ancient times which Homer has given, add an immense value to his works, and afford an unexhausted mine to the philosopher, whose study is human nature. Ariosto and Tasso have a happiness of the same kind; and their works will convey to the latest posterity the ideas and manners ascribed to chivalry. The judgment of Virgil perceived the happiness of Homer in giving such striking pictures of the manners of his age; but though the Roman poet has given us innumerable allusions to ancient rites and customs, he has miserably failed in describing the characters of ancient Phrygia, Greece, and Latium. Eneas, his friend Achates, &c. Evander and Lausus, and others, are the mere Gentlemen of the Court of Augustus; and Lavinia, who has no choice in her own marriage, and has as little care or affection concerning it, is exactly the young Lady of corrupted Rome: and the rage of Lavinia's mother, and that of Dido herself, is no other than that of the high-spirited Roman matron. But though we mention the great value of Homer's works in their giving us the real manners of so remote an age, we do not blame the *genius* of an American of the present day for not giving us the manners of Canaan, and of the Israelites, who lived near three centuries before the Trojan war. If the want of real manners is a fault, that fault arises from the choice of the subject. But our Bard thinks the want of real manners no blemish; but rather boasts, that "he has endeavoured to represent such manners as are removed from the peculiarities of any age or country, but might belong to the amiable and virtuous of every age." And of such manners he asserts, that "they possess the highest advantages for universal application." But in these positions we widely differ from our author. There never was in human nature an amiable and virtuous character that was not marked, both in his acting and thinking, with "*the peculiarities of his age and country*." And in proof of this Mr. Dwight himself is a strong evidence, as will appear when we cite the absurdity of the different characters he ascribes to Great Britain and America. And we cannot think the *Utopian* characters of an *Ossian*, a *Blackmore*, or a *Dwight*, "possess the highest advantages for universal application." We have infinitely more pleasure in viewing the real manners of Spain in Cervantes, than in reading a thousand *Utopias* and *Arcadias,* and the whole family of fictitious characters and manners. Mr. Dwight denies that his choice of "a subject in which his countrymen had no national interest," was the result of inattention. "He had remarked, he says, that the Iliad and Eneid were as agreeable to modern nations as to the Greeks

and Romans." But here again we must dissent from our American bard. Though these poems do "furnish the fairest opportunities of exhibiting the agreeable, the novel, the moral, the pathetic, and the sublime," it does not follow but that the Greeks and Romans had their national partialities for their particular poems, and were much more interested in them than any modern nation can possibly be. Witness the enthusiasm and partiality with which a Frenchman views that feeble attempt at the Epic, the *Henriade*. But though his countrymen have no national interest in *Joshua*'s conquest of Canaan, Mr. Dwight has contrived to give them an interest in his poem, where, as will soon appear, *Joshua* in the allegorical sense is General *Washington;* and the Israelites, the people delivered and favoured by God, the *Americans*.

In his introduction of some new words, and the still greater licence of giving new significations to some old ones, our author, we think, has been rash and unhappy. (p. 82)

[In the First Book of the Poem,] America is obviously placed before us under the allegory of the Israelites having left Egypt, which means the British government, and about to settle themselves by force of arms. Hanniel who advises to return to Egypt, and the difficulties he foretells, represents the Loyalists, and Joshua's reply sums up the arguments of the American patriots. But this allegory is not regularly carried through the work. (p. 83)

．．．．．

[In the Tenth Book, the] description of the *western* Millennium is, like Pope's Messiah, a paraphrase on several passages of Isaiah, and contains some of our author's smoothest and best versification. We cannot say so much for his description of the resurrection, general judgment, and prospect of heaven, with which he winds up this Book.

The Eleventh and last Book is greatly superior, in the description of the battles, to our author's other attempts in that way. In his last Book Virgil has collected all his force, and his fire increases in just gradation to the catastrophe. Mr. Dwight, in like manner, has summoned up all his powers in his Eleventh and last Book, which, in point of gradation and interest, rises most properly over the foregoing Ten. . . .

Long before it was written, the subject was severely condemned by Lord Shaftsbury. (p. 271)

But, however we condemn the partial bias of his Lordship's censure, we cannot altogether cordially approve of Mr. Dwight's choice of subject; though, no doubt, his shadowing the late American war under it, will give it interest on that continent.

In his versification, Mr. Dwight, on the whole, is far from being unhappy, though in energy he is often deficient, and almost always wanting in that variety of construction which constitutes imitative harmony, and is so pleasing in some of our best poets. Though we do not mean to say that Mr. Dwight is entirely destitute of variety, or a few not unhappy attempts at imitative harmony, these are so thinly scattered, that his versification may justly be accused, for the far greatest part, of monotony.

A strongly marked variety with peculiarity of characters, as in Homer and Tasso, is not to be found in our author. That of Hanniel, who opposes Joshua, and advises at every opportunity the return to Egypt, is by much the best drawn of any in our author.

In the conduct of his fable, he often falls into egregious faults. His theological excrescences are often unpleasing, (witness Irad's defence of the slaughter of infants . . .) and always tedious. The death of every hero of note in Homer and Virgil, has an evident tendency to the production of the catastrophe. But Mr. Dwight kills his heroes most unmercifully, without any such necessary tendency; and we have already observed, that in conducting his fable a proper gradation is often much wanted.

Mr. Dwight has certainly a happy talent at description; but it is still in its puerility, and wants much cultivation and correction. His pictures are ill grouped, and repetitions of the same imagery often occur in the same description, by which he often falls into the anti-climax, and want of perspicuity, that *sine qua non* in classical poetry. We are often obliged to read many passages in our author twice over, ere we can catch his exact meaning; and the pleasure inspired by poetry is always lost in such drudgery.

Invention we can hardly discover. We cannot conceive that original genius or the powers of invention are necessary to form such a fable as Mr. Dwight's; tho' in his execution some parts display true poetical imagination. In this, the dream of Irad in the night before he is slain, in the beginning of the Seventh Book, and the burning of the forest which separates the combatants, at the end of the same, are particularly happy; though even in these we are tired with repetitions of the same imagery.

Mr. Dwight informs us in his motto, . . . and his poem evinces that he is a young man. As he is undoubtedly possessed of poetical powers much above mediocrity, it may justly be hoped, that experience and cultivation will one day render him truly classical. At present his work is a promising blossom of polite literature sprung up on the American continent, and as citizens of the world we rejoice to see it, and sincerely hope that Mr. Dwight will improve by our strictures. He may be assured, that had we not thought his Muse capable of improvement, we would by no means have been so particular, or paid her the attentions we have done. (pp. 272-73)

A review of "The Conquest of Canäan: A Poem," in The European Magazine, and London Review, Vol. XIII, February and April, 1788, pp. 81-4; 266-73.

[NOAH WEBSTER]   (essay date 1788)

[*A knowledgeable and versatile American scholar, Webster was a lawyer, teacher, editor, and lexicographer. Although he was distinguished in several fields, his greatest achievement was the compilation of* An American Dictionary of the English Language, *which in subsequent editions became the standard American dictionary. The following excerpt is from Webster's response to a review of* The Conquest of Canäan *published in* The European Magazine, and London Review *(1788). According to Webster, the critics for that publication allowed political prejudices to color their judgment of Dwight's poem, a work Webster considered worthy of more careful analysis.*]

Did these remarks, gentlemen, proceed from *liberal minds,* which are pleased to see genius and polite literature, expanding themselves in the *Infant States* of America? Or were they dictated by prejudice, in minds soured by political disappointment? Let the *liberal mind* determine. (p. 562)

Having given the argument of the first book at large, you subjoin the following remarks. "Here America is obviously placed before us under the allegory of the Israelites having left

Egypt, which means the British government, and about to settle themselves by force of arms. *Hanniel,* who advises to return to Egypt, and the *difficulties* he foretells, *represents* the loyalists, and Joshua's reply sums up the arguments of the American patriots. But this allegory is not regularly carried through the work."

Here, Gentlemen, your opinions are *obviously* erroneous. It is your misfortune to forget the character you profess, and instead of candid criticism, indulge yourselves in the malevolent reflections of peevish politicians. (pp. 562-63)

But, gentlemen, what have political subjects to do with an Epic Poem? On what authority did you assert that the **Conquest of Canaan** contains an allegory,—that the Americans are described under the character of the *Israelites,*—that Egypt is meant to represent the British government—and Hanniel, the loyalists? Is it any where asserted in the Poem, the preface, or any where else? Have you been informed of it by Dr. Dwight's friends, or by newspaper paragraphs? Gentlemen, your suppositions are without foundation. . . . (p. 563)

What a mixture of *ignorance* and *political spleen!* Is it impossible that an English Critic should view the finallest literary production in America, thro any medium but that of *national prejudice?* Must everything have a reference to the late separation of America from Great Britain, and Frenchmen be lugged into a decision on the merits of an American Poem? Is this the candor and impartiality of a *critic*—of an *English critic?*—Is this the boasted liberality of your nation? (pp. 564-65)

In your subsequent remarks you select for criticism such passages of the Poem, as you suppose carry on the *allegory,* which offends the pride of your nation. On such passages you freely indulge the rancor of your hearts.

But as the allegory is the work of your own invention, you are welcome to attack it with all the earnestness of a Quixote, engaged with a windmill.

Many of Dr. Dwight's friends will however acknowledge the propriety of the following criticisms—"That in some passages there is a strange confusion of ideas and language—that in others, there is a want of perspicuity—that there is too much bustling and killing—that the descriptions are too long, and often abound with repetitions of the same imagery,"—To these faults or others must we ascribe the fatigue of reading the Poem, which is generally complained of in America. You suppose indeed that the *allegory* of the Poem, which is designed to describe the late revolution, will make it interesting to Americans. I can assure you, gentlemen, that the Americans never suspected such an allegory to exist; nor do they take any uncommon interest in the Poem. They think it has much merit—but they see and censure its faults. They do not indeed expect to realize all the happiness anticipated in the tenth book of the Poem; but they cannot think with you that the fictions of a Poet's fancy are subjects of derision. They may at times indulge a political enthusiasm—all nations do the same—it is the spring of heroic actions—it is laudable—but they are philosophic enough to expect that the real greatness and happiness of America will resemble those of other free countries. Nor do they really expect that the eastern continent will be doomed to the most deplorable slavery and misery—on the contrary, they predict that liberty and happiness will increase, in proportion to the progressive improvements in science and commerce. (p. 565)

[Noah Webster], "To the Authors of the 'London Review'," in The American Magazine, No. 8, July, 1788, pp. 562-66.

THE AMERICAN MAGAZINE (essay date 1788)

[In this review, which some scholars attribute to Noah Webster, the critic affirms that Dwight's The Triumph of Infidelity *possesses some literary merit, yet considers his imitation of other writers inexcusable.]*

[*The Triumph of Infidelity*] is not destitute of poetic merit. The versification is generally correct, and variegated but intolerably harsh. The irony of the piece is indifferently well supported thro' the whole, and here and there we find a severe sarcasm. We cannot however consider the satire as uniformly natural and severe. A jumble of words, forced conceits and farfetched ideas will never pass for wit or satire. (p. 589)

[The] author appears to be a theological dogmatist, who has found the right way to heaven, by creeds and systems; and with more imperiousness than would become infinite wisdom and power, damns all who cannot swallow his articles of faith. A man who can groupe together such men as *Shaftsbury, Priestley, Chauncey* and *Allen* and stigmatize these and many of the first philosophers promiscuously as fools and knaves, can hardly be a candidate for that heaven of love and benevolence which the scripture informs us is prepared for good men.

Nor can we think the writer more remarkable for his poetic talents than for his liberality. He can indeed borrow lines without giving credit; but he should not borrow from such a smooth versifier as Pope—the contrast between his own lines and those borrowed immediately detects the plagiarism. Witness the following from "Eloise and Abelard."

> Oh write it not, my hand!
>   the name appears,
> Already written: Wash it out, my
>   tears:

Compared with the two succeeding lines of the author's—

> Still, oh, all pitying savior!
>   let thy love
> Stronger than death, all heights and
>   heaven above, &c.

The harshness of these lines is nothing singular—one half the poem is a jumble of unmeaning epithets, or an unnatural association of ideas. . . .

The writer has abused Dr. Chauncey freely for his purgatories; yet he talks about a lowest *hell;* and although the number of hells is not mentioned, yet Satan was once *plunged beneath the lowest.* Query, where did he stop? (p. 590)

> *A review of "The Triumph of Infidelity: A Poem,"* in The American Magazine, *No. 8, July, 1788, pp. 588-90.*

WILLIAM COWPER (essay date 1789)

[Cowper was an English poet, satirist, letter and hymn writer, essayist, and translator. Considered one of the most popular poets of the eighteenth century, he is remembered today for the spontaneity and simplicity of his nature lyrics, the earnest, personal tone of his religious poetry, and the wit embodied in his satires and letters. Although Cowper cites several flaws in The Conquest of Canäan, *he assesses the poem favorably. The essay from which the following excerpt was drawn originally appeared in the Analytical Review in 1789.]*

[Poetry] cannot be without fancy, and fancy can content herself with no materials as she finds them. The poet before us [in

The Conquest of Canäan] availing himself of this privilege, has modelled the sacred narrative to his mind, and in such manner that he who would learn by what steps the Israelites became possessed of the promised land, must still seek his information in the Bible. He fights all his battles under the walls of Ai, and opposes Jabin, King of Hazor, to Joshua, throughout the poem. The friendly disposition of the Gibeonites he ascribes, not to its true cause, the terror with which the miracles wrought in favor of Israel had inspired them, but to their previous conversion by Mina, a virgin of Edom, herself instructed in the camp of Israel. It is to be regretted, perhaps, that for the sake of simplifying his plan he has excluded from it the story of Rahab and the spies, and consequently of the fall of Jericho,—incidents which had great influence on all that followed, beautiful in themselves, and susceptible of much poetical embellishment.

Such are some of the liberties which the author had taken with the story. A more sparing use of the 'potestes quidlibet audendi' might have been advisable on a scriptural subject. Readers, influenced by a due respect for scripture, do not well endure a violent disturbance of its order. In that case something more than criticism is offended. He makes, however, all the atonement that can be expected from a poet: in his fictions he discovers much warmth of conception, and his numbers are very harmonious. His numbers, indeed, imitate pretty closely those of Pope, and therefore cannot fail to be musical; but he is chiefly to be commended for the animation with which he writes, and which rather increases as he proceeds, than suffers any abatement. His seventh book, in which he describes with great spirit the horrors of a battle fought by the light of a city in flames, affords one proof of it; and his tenth book, which is the last but one, another. . . . A strain of fine enthusiasm runs through the whole book; and we will venture to affirm, that no man who has a soul impressible by a bright display of the grandest subjects that revelation furnishes, will read it without emotion.

The composition, however, is not without a fault; and as we have candidly praised, we will censure with fidelity. By the motto which the author has chosen, we are led to suspect that he is young, and the chief blemish of his poem is one into which hardly anything but youth could have betrayed him. A little mature consideration would have taught him, that a subject nearly four thousand years old could not afford him a very fair opportunity for the celebration of his contemporaries. We found our attention to the wars of Joshua not pleasantly interrupted by a tribute of respect paid to the memory of a Mr. Wooster, slain on Ridgefield Hills in America; of a Mr. Warren, who fell in battle at Charlestown; and of a Mr. Mercer, who shared a similar fate at Princeton. He would plead, perhaps, his patriotism for his apology; but it is best to admit nothing that needs one. (pp. 87-90)

> *William Cowper, in a review of "The Conquest of Canaan," in* Three Men of Letters *by Moses Coit Tyler, G. P. Putnam's Sons, 1895, pp. 87-91.*

THE MONTHLY REVIEW, LONDON (essay date 1791)

[In the following excerpt, the critic maintains that The Triumph of Infidelity *is not likely to be the production of a true Doctor of Divinity and thus questions whether the poem was actually written by Dwight.]*

[Regarding *The Triumph of Infidelity: A Poem*, which is supposed to have been written by Timothy Dwight, D. D.:] Supposed to be written by a Doctor of Divinity! Surely it is a mistake! It cannot be, that the malignant spirit, which is breathed out in these lines against all who do not bear the badge of orthodoxy, should have resided in the bosom of an eminent Christian divine: but, *Timothy Dwight, D. D. &c.* sounds very like fiction. We hope that this is the case.

> *E., in a review of ''The Triumph of Infidelity: A Poem,'' in* The Monthly Review, *London, Vol. VI, December, 1791, p. 459.*

TIMOTHY DWIGHT   (essay date 1794)

[*In his introduction to* Greenfield Hill, *Dwight apologizes for the inconsistencies in his writing style, attributing those faults to his original intent ''to imitate, in the several parts, the manner of as many British Poets.''*]

To contribute to the innocent amusement of his countrymen, and to their improvement in manners, and in œconomical, political, and moral sentiments, is the object which the writer wishes to accomplish. As he is firmly persuaded, that his countrymen are furnished by Providence with as extensive and advantageous means of prosperity, as the world has hitherto seen, so he thinks it the duty and the interest of every citizen, to promote it, by all the means in his power. Poetry appears to him to be one, among the probable means of advancing this purpose. ''Allow me to make the Songs of a nation,'' said a wise man, ''and who will may make their Laws.'' Poetry may not, perhaps, produce greater effects in promoting the prosperity of mankind, than philosophy; but the effects which it produces, are far from being small. Where truth requires little illustration, and only needs to be set in a strong and affecting light, Poetry appears to be as advantageous an instrument of making useful impressions, as can be easily conceived. It will be read by many persons, who would scarcely look at a logical discussion; by most readers it will be more deeply felt, and more lastingly remembered; and, to say the least, it will, in the present case, be an unusual, and for that reason may be a forcible method of treating several subjects, handled in this Poem.

When the writer began the work, he had no design of publishing it; aiming merely to amuse his own mind, and to gain a temporary relief from the pressure of melancholy. Hence it was dropped, at an early period; when other avocations, or amusements presented themselves. The greater part of it was written seven years ago. Additions have been made to it, at different periods, from that time to the present—This will account for the dates of several things mentioned in it, which would otherwise seem to be improperly connected.

Originally the writer designed to imitate, in the several parts, the manner of as many British Poets; but finding himself too much occupied, when he projected the publication, to pursue that design, he relinquished it. The little appearance of such a design, still remaining, was the result of distant and general recollection. Much, of that nature, he has rejected, and all he would have rejected, had not even that rejection demanded more time than he could afford for such a purpose. These facts will, he hopes, apologize to the reader, for the mixed manner which he may, at times, observe in the performance. (pp. 6-8)

> *Timothy Dwight, in an introduction to his* Greenfield Hill: A Poem, *n.p., 1794, pp. 5-8.*

TIMOTHY DWIGHT   (essay date 1817?)

[*In his preface to* Travels in New-England and New-York, *Dwight discusses his reasons for recording and publishing notes of his travels. He admits that some of his descriptions may be considered tedious and repetitive, but also finds flaws in previous treatments of New England and New York by other travelers, notably the English. In parts of the essay not excerpted here, Dwight discusses the political, religious, and social climates of the areas he visited. Since the composition date of the essay is unknown, Dwight's remarks are dated 1817, the year of his death.*]

A country changing as rapidly as New England must, if truly exhibited, be described in a manner resembling that in which a painter would depict a cloud. The form and colors of the moment must be seized, or the picture will be erroneous. As it was naturally presumed by me that some of those who will live eighty or a hundred years hence must have feelings similar to my own, I resolved to furnish, so far as should be in my power, means of enabling them to know what was the appearance of their country during the period occupied by my journeys.

To the inducements presented by these considerations, some addition was made by the misrepresentation which foreigners, either through error or design, had published of my native country. As none of its inhabitants appeared to me inclined to do justice to its character, I began to entertain loose and distant thoughts of attempting it myself; and, after the purpose was once formed, every new misrepresentation made me more solicitous to carry it into execution. Still there was no fixed intention formed of publishing during my lifetime the book which I projected.

With these views and some others, which it is unnecessary to mention, both my excursions and my journals were continued. A moderate number of trials, however, convinced me that short notes, containing such hints concerning what I saw and heard as would enable me to detail the facts and describe the scenes of which it was proposed to give an account, would better answer my purpose. Accordingly they were adopted by me, prescribing, however, this condition to myself: that all the objects of importance which occupied either the imagination or the memory should be described at length the first leisure moment, while my notes would render my recollection fresh and complete. (pp. 1-2)

Originally I intended to confine my observations to New England; but, as my excursions were in several instances made chiefly in New York, as a considerable majority of its inhabitants are derived from New England, as the rest are intimately connected with New England by business, intercourse, and attachments, and as no adequate account of that state had been given to the public, I determined to include it in my remarks. (p. 2)

What I have seen and heard, the reader will, I believe, find reported with a good degree of exactness as well as with sincerity. But it ought to be observed that the state of this country changes so fast as to make a picture of it drawn at a given period an imperfect resemblance of what a traveler will find it to be after a moderate number of years have elapsed. The new settlements particularly would in many instances scarcely be known, even from the most accurate description, after a very short lapse of time. Of this I have had the most ample evidence from these journeys. (pp. 2-3)

The towns and villages through which I have passed are described in these letters with a minuteness which in all probability may be disagreeable to a considerable class of readers: some of whom have no relish for topography, while others are pleased with no accounts but such as are given in the gross. Happily these persons can easily pass them by. Two reasons have influenced me to adopt this measure. To many of mankind the subject will be interesting, and without such accounts a correct knowledge of any country is unattainable. . . .

In a number of instances I have delineated the scenery which presented itself to me in my excursions. This kind of description has, I acknowledge, been carried to excess by several modern travelers. But that excess infers no impropriety in the nature of the case. There are two reasons, besides the pleasure I have found in the employment, which, if I mistake not, will justify the attention here paid to this subject. The scenery which these countries display is very fine, and it has never been described. At the same time, not a small number of readers are delighted with landscapes; and their taste is as reasonably consulted to some extent by a writer as that of graver minds. When I hear so many individuals converse on the scenes of nature with so much pleasure, I cannot hesitate to believe that, wherever justice is done to such scenes in a book, it will be read by them with some degree of the same pleasure. (p. 3)

These letters are addressed to an English gentleman. Sufficient reasons for adopting this address will, it is believed, appear from the letters themselves. I wish it, however, to be understood that they are written for my own countrymen. From the numerous errors published in Great Britain concerning American subjects, of the most obvious nature and such as seem hardly to admit of mistake, it is naturally concluded that few persons in that island feel any wish to become acquainted with the situation of the United States, or with the real character of their inhabitants. By the government, indeed, we must, from the extent of our territory, our local circumstances, our population, and our commerce, be considered as possessing a degree of political importance; and, by the merchants of Liverpool and the manufacturers of Manchester, Birmingham, and Sheffield, we may be regarded with some attention as customers. But, except by the religious part of the British nation, we seem to be chiefly unknown or forgotten in the character of rational beings, or known and remembered almost only to be made the objects of contempt and calumny. A book which professes nothing more than to give a description of a country and a people regarded in this manner can form no claims on the attention of those by whom the subjects of which it treats are thus estimated. It may indeed be read, or at least reviewed, by some or other of the literary journalists of Great Britain. From these gentlemen, Americans and their writings have customarily met with one kind of treatment only. I neither claim, nor wish, any exemption from the common lot of my countrymen. (pp. 9-10)

> *Timothy Dwight, in a preface to his* Travels in New England and New York, *Vol. I, edited by Barbara Miller Solomon with Patricia M. King, Cambridge, Mass.: The Belknap Press, 1969, pp. 1-11.*

THE NORTH AMERICAN REVIEW   (essay date 1818)

[*In the following excerpt, the critic recognizes Dwight's "eminent powers of mind," but finds little to praise in his works. Further, the critic contends that* The Conquest of Canäan *is undistinguished and that* Greenfield Hill *will add little to Dwight's reputation.*]

The anonymous *Memoir* of the life of President Dwight, prefixed to the first volume [of Dr. Dwight's *Theology Explained*

and Defended in a Series of Sermons], is highly interesting; and whatever reasonable abatement may be made for any supposed partiality of the author or authors, it is manifest that Dr. Dwight was a man of very eminent powers of mind, of distinguished industry, activity, and energy, and of uncommon versatility of talents; that he possessed abilities for excelling in various callings, and that he was remarkably fitted for the sphere in which he moved, for more than twenty years preceding his death. (p. 348)

[Dr. Dwight's] earliest work, of any considerable length, which we have seen, is the *Conquest of Canaan*. This poem, from its subject, from the manner in which it is conducted, and from its length, claims to be of the Epic class. It was completed when its author was but twenty-two years of age. To so young a man, it could be no disgrace to fail of successful execution in such an arduous undertaking; to acquire a favourable reception, and lasting reputation as a poet, would be in a high degree honourable. We are inclined to think there is something too unpoetical in the author's adaptation of manners to the persons of his poem. 'He has studied,' (to use his own words,) 'a medium between absolute barbarism and modern refinement. In the best characters, he has endeavoured to represent such manners as are removed from the peculiarities of any age or country, and might belong to the amiable and virtuous of every age. Such as are elevated without design, refined without ceremony, elegant without fashion, and agreeable, because they are ornamented with sincerity, dignity, and religion, not because they are polished by art or education. Of such manners he hopes he may observe, without impropriety, that they possess the highest advantages for universal application' [see excerpt dated 1785]. Though all critics acknowledge truth to general nature to be one of the trials as well of the poet's as of the painter's genius, yet peculiarities of manners, in the time and place in which the scene is laid, are no less essential. The passions which have so much concern in the story of every genuine epic poem, so far as they are human, are shared by mankind in common. But manners, and *costume*, and modes of thinking, are as various and as contrariant, as the different caprices, and accidents, and degrees of mental cultivation, which are unfolded to us in the history of our species. Where the poet can seize upon these varieties, or even give such ideal peculiarities as do not violate probability, much is gained in point of novelty, while nothing is lost in the moral lessons, conveyed by the natural movements of those passions and affections, which are mainly concerned in the great action of the epic poem.

Corresponding with the laws which the author prescribed to himself, in his *Conquest of Canaan*, he made every thing too common. There is little that is really distinctive, little that is truly oriental about any of his persons or scenes. A certain equable current of unexceptionable, and oftentimes pleasing thoughts and expressions, flows through the poem. It is occasionally animated, and in description, sometimes picturesque and poetical. The versification, though generally monotonous, having too little variety in the pauses, is for the most part uncommonly smooth. In the expression of strong emotion, there is an avoidance of all offensive extravagance, if it do not reach the genuine ardour or pathos of the highest order of poetry. Having said thus much, we fear we have said all that is due to this poetical work; nor do we say this to deduct any thing from the high and well deserved reputation of President Dwight. It is not the lot of a single man to excel in every thing; and it is often our misfortune to make a false estimate of our own powers, and to stake too much of our intellectual wealth on the race, in which we are unable to reach the goal.

Greenfield Hill is an irregular poem, descriptive, historical and didactic, in seven parts. It contains no small variety of matter, and is composed in divers metres. The poem opens with a pleasing picture of rural scenery and rustic life; but the more familiar parts, 'the clergyman's advice to the villagers,' and 'the farmer's advice to the villagers,' are, perhaps, better of their kind, than any other portions of the work. We cannot persuade ourselves, that the author added any thing to his poetical reputation, by this second trial; though we are unwilling to say even this, to the dispraise of a book, which, if read for its useful practical lessons, and pure moral instructions, may be read with pleasure and profit. (pp. 351-53)

Those who would know more [about President Dwight], we refer to the *Memoir* of his life. We have already said it is a very interesting biographical account. It is also well arranged, well proportioned in its parts, and contains nothing that has wearied us by its prolixity. One thing however, it becomes us to mention, by way of caution to those who perform such a delicate office, due to departed worth; it is written too much in the strain of continued eulogy; and too constantly abounds in superlatives. We know that it is difficult, while an event which has so deeply wounded private affection, and made such a lamentable chasm in society, is still recent, for the writer to recollect, that he is composing for the public at large, and recording a permanent memorial for the benefit of succeeding generations; but what ever be his private feelings and partialities, he ought constantly to keep those ends in view, and train himself by a course of self discipline for the arduous work.

From the same leaning to overstrained panegyric, the author of the *Memoir* has either overlooked, or remained in voluntary ignorance of some important facts, by which he has done injustice to the memory of Dr. Dwight's learned predecessor [President Ezra Stiles]. (pp. 355-56)

We do not believe that the author of the memoir intended to injure the well earned reputation of so learned, and amiable, and pious a man, as the late Dr. Stiles; but still there is an appearance of too great indifference to it, which is to be explained by that overweening partiality towards President Dwight, to which we have already adverted; a partiality which naturally tends to exaggeration on the one hand, and injustice on the other.

The style of the *Memoir* in general, though somewhat constrained and formal, and sometimes incorrect, is not deficient either in vigour or animation; but we perceive too frequently a kind of violent affirmation, by means of such adverbs as *decidedly, absolutely,* and the like, where they seem to be unnecessary, and convey to our ears and understanding no impression of beauty or strength. We have noticed, also, several words which are not in good use; among which we recollect, *disorganization, engagedness, conduct* v.n. *originate* v.a. These may appear to be slight blemishes, but they are deserving of notice; for it is useful to point out even small offences, which we would not have others imitate, and which may easily be avoided.

We shall say but little of the series of sermons commenced in this first volume. They indicate a clear understanding and a vigorous mind, rather than any great extent of learning or critical research. The author appears familiar with the leading controversies that have prevailed among christians, especially those of a metaphysical complexion, and exhibits his own views,

for the most part, very distinctly. On some controverted points, however, his proofs and illustrations are of too popular and declamatory a kind, for a didactic discourse. Such appears to us to be the case in the sermon on the depravity of man, when we regard its connexion with the previous account of original sin; for, whatever be our opinion concerning the doctrine of total depravity, it can never be proved by citing the private vices of mankind, or by declaiming against the corruptions of governments, the licentiousness of subjects, or the defects and perversions of *religion*. (pp. 358-59)

It is well known that Dr. Dwight was a celebrated preacher, and that he sometimes, to a remarkable degree, roused the attention of his audience, and produced a strong excitement. We do not look in vain for specimens of *eloquence* in his sermons; and though his eloquence is not in our opinion of a very chastened kind, and parts of his discourses are much better adapted for delivery, than for being read with a critical eye, yet we are disposed to allow him full credit for that kind of talents, which enabled him with such boldness and effect to assault the vices and bad passions of men, and to tell home-truths in such a way as shamed even the profligate and abandoned. Still, however, he is far from faultless, His metaphors and comparisons are drawn too often from vulgar and disgusting objects; especially, and very frequently, from *swine* and *sties*. Thus are we sometimes involuntarily offended by a coarseness of manner, much more becoming in the satirist than in the divine. But apart from this, we meet, in the series of sermons, with examples of more refined eloquence, of which, if we had room, we should select several passages from the sermon on the 'comparative influence of atheism and christianity.' And, in general, we think Dr. Dwight entitled to the praise of that degree of eloquence, which consists in a bold, vigorous, fluent, and glowing style; though the vigour is sometimes impaired by redundancy of epithets, and the boldness is tarnished by unsightly images. (p. 360)

Discourses on dogmatical theology will of course be estimated differently, according to the opinions or prejudices of those who hear or read them. And if we cannot admit all the doctrines embraced in that part of the 'series of sermons' already published, it cannot be expected that we should turn polemics, and combat the arguments by which they are supported. In general, we commend the spirit which the author displays; though we think he shews more clemency, when he differs from those who pursue Calvinism to all its real or supposed consequences, than he does, when he censures those who disbelieve the doctrines themselves from which they think those consequences legitimately flow.

We have already remarked cursorily on President Dwight's style. We add only that it is too verbose; that he had too many favourite expressions; and that he sometimes repeated the same or similar thoughts and illustrations. (pp. 362-63)

In taking leave of this volume of sermons, of which we have already said much more than we intended, we should not do justice to its distinguished author, without expressing our high gratification, in finding throughout an elevated standard of moral virtue, proposed to his youthful hearers, and those practical lessons inculcated, which leave the impression, that the true design of religion is, to make a good man. And judging from the sermons in the volume before us, we do not hesitate to predict, that the series, when completely published, will be a valuable memorial of the author, and reflect much honour upon the institution over which he presided so long, and with such distinguished dignity and talents. (pp. 363-64)

"*Life and Writings of President Dwight,*" *in* The North American Review, *Vol. VII, No. XXI, September, 1818, pp. 347-64.*

THE CHRISTIAN SPECTATOR (essay date 1822)

[*The following excerpt is from a positive assessment of the first two volumes of* Travels in New-England and New-York. *The critic praises Dwight's accurate rendering of his journeys and contends that though some readers may find his notes too detailed, Dwight* "*was an exact observer of nature*" *whose observations dispute the negative accounts of American life published by foreign travelers.*]

It must be pleasing to the American reader, to be presented with . . . [***Travels in New-England and New-York***], from the pen of a writer so well qualified to do justice to the subject, as President Dwight, whose genius and learning have conferred such honour on his native country. No similar work has ever been undertaken by any person, on whose judgment, candour and veracity we could fully depend. (p. 145)

President Dwight informs us in his preface [see excerpt dated 1817], that he was principally induced to write, by a desire "to furnish, so far as should be within his power, the means of enabling our posterity to know what was the appearance of their country, during the period occupied by his journies." But he has executed the work on a far more extensive scale.

In these volumes, the first fourteen Letters contain a general account of New-England. . . . A great variety of interesting particulars are inserted in his subsequent Letters. From his judicious selection of historical facts and the accuracy of his observations, the reader will obtain a greater mass of valuable information respecting the Northern States, and gain a more current and comprehensive idea of the situation of the country, the course of its settlement, and its actual state, at the date of these Travels, than he could collect from all the volumes previously published on the subject.

A considerable portion of the work consists of statements, chiefly geographical and statistical. These, however valuable and instructive, cannot from their nature be entertaining to persons who read only for amusement. It is very easy for a fastidious critic to pronounce them dull and tedious, and propose to lessen this part by abridgment. But it could only be abridged by omission, and we should obtain fewer facts with the same minuteness of detail. As the author in his preface has advised such readers to pass over these statements, it must be their own fault should they fatigue themselves by the perusal. Others will esteem them useful and important, and recur to them, as notes of record and reference. (pp. 145-46)

These Letters, varying in manner with the varieties of their subjects, afford elegant examples of almost every kind of style and composition; of the familiar ease of epistolary correspondence, the grace and correctness of narration, the eloquence of oratory, and the beauties of sublime and picturesque description.

The historical sketches, and narratives of remarkable adventures, are chiefly collected from early records, oral traditions, or the accounts of the actors or eye witnesses of the scenes. Facts thus obtained are fully entitled to credit, when related by a writer, not chargeable with proneness to credulity or exaggeration.

The occasional notices of persons of eminence, among the deceased friends of the author, are a valuable addition to American biography.—Their characters are justly represented and generally drawn with due discrimination. (p. 146)

The author excels in picturesque descriptions of the scenery of nature—the gaiety and sweetness of rural prospects, and the wild and romantic magnificence of our mountains, lakes and cataracts. He viewed with enthusiasm the sublime and beautiful in landscape, and paints them with the glowing colours of a poetical imagination. (p. 147)

These Letters contain many judicious remarks, and some more extended essays, on government, laws, religion, morals, and manners; with several philosophical enquiries, and dissertations on the various phenomena of the natural world, in the northern regions we inhabit. We may always rely on the facts which he relates, for he was an exact observer of nature, and an indefatigable enquirer after truth. His theories and opinions will be acknowledged as often novel, always ingenious, and generally just.

He has given an accurate account of the schools, colleges, and universities, in the New-England states, the nature of their institutions, and the manner of instruction and government of the pupils, particularly in Yale College, in which for so long a period he held the presidency. Statements and remarks, respecting the progress of American literature, and the methods of communicating knowledge and improving the youthful mind, must be extremely valuable from the pen of a writer, who employed the greatest portion of his life in superintending the education of youth.

We would particularly recommend to American readers, the 48th Letter of the first volume. In an essay, elegant in style, and forcible in manner, the author enters his solemn protest against the prevailing mode of Fashionable Education. . . .

The author states in his preface, as a strong additional reason for undertaking the work, his desire to correct the misrepresentations, which foreigners, either through accident or design, had published of his native country. For this task, especially as regards the northern states, no writer was better qualified, or could have performed it with more accurate research, or greater merit in the execution. (p. 148)

President Dwight has recounted many sanguinary scenes, acted in the revolutionary war, which were not generally known to the public, or had been inaccurately related by modern historians. He has painted in just colours the wanton cruelties of the British commanders. . . . The actors of such tragedies deserve to be recorded in the annals of history, and their names exposed to the execration of posterity. But though he has animadverted with due severity on these instances of barbarity, he has often taken occasion to do justice to the merit and character of Great-Britain and to distinguish between the tyranny of her rulers and cruelty of her armies, and the just glory and virtues of the people. . . .

Though a clergyman of the congregational order, and a firm adherent to the doctrines of the Reformed churches, as his justly admired theological works abundantly testify, he was no bigot to ecclesiastical forms; nor uncharitable towards christians of other denominations, who differed from his opinions on points of minor importance, not inconsistent with vital piety. Every reader must applaud the truly catholic liberality of his sentiments. . . . (p. 150)

In contemplating the character and writings of President Dwight, we find a person, whose talents and learning confer honor upon our country, and an author, of whose works we may justly boast, without fearing the invidious censures of foreign reviewers, or their humble copyists and imitators in America. (p. 151)

A review of "Travels in New-England and New-York, Vols. I and II," in The Christian Spectator, *Vol. IV, No. III, March, 1822, pp. 145-51.*

THE CHRISTIAN SPECTATOR　(essay date 1822)

[*In the following excerpt from a laudatory appraisal of the third and fourth volumes of* Travels in New-England and New-York, *the critic especially commends Dwight's historical accuracy and presentation of American life.*]

[As with the first two volumes of *Travels in New-England and New-York,* we] find the same accuracy of statistical details, the same glow of animated description, the same eloquence of style, and melodious flow of prosaic numbers; equal ardour of feeling in the cause of virtue, and just severity of censure on every custom or habit destructive of morality and religion, and injurious to the purity and happiness of society [in volumes three and four]. The third volume is peculiarly interesting by its numerous sketches of the history of our former wars, and representations of scenery and manners, never before described. In a variety of instances, the future historian may avail himself of these accounts, to supply the omissions and correct the mistakes of preceding writers. The author, who has visited the scenes of action and acquired his information from personal knowledge, or accurate investigation and inquiry, deserves the confidence of his readers, and has in all ages received it, far more than the mere scholar, who compiles the story of nations in his closet, states from the conjectures of his fancy the secret intrigues of statesmen, the minute detail of battles and campaigns, and the characters of his kings and heroes; or omitting every fact or transaction, however material, which appears incapable of embellishment; gives us orations that were never spoken; relates achievements that never took place, and labours chiefly to gain the applause of critics, for his skill in narration, his penetration in discovering the unknown causes of events, or for the elegance, pomp and majesty of his historical style. (pp. 423-24)

He has recounted with accuracy many important events which took place during the revolutionary war, while the States of New-England and New-York were invaded by the armies of Great Britain, and mentioned various facts and circumstances, unnoticed by former writers. (p. 424)

These last volumes, like the former, are replete with useful and judicious observations on the soil, climate and productions of our country, the state of its commerce and manufactures, and the manners of its inhabitants in different settlements. They exhibit agreeable specimens of the author's genius in picturesque description. Among many others, we refer to his view of the prospect near the junction of the Mohawk river with the Schoharie; of the Highland, near West Point on the Hudson; of Lake George and its environs, and Lake Winipisiogee or Wentworth, and the mountains that surround it; and of the famous cataract of Niagara. He never fails to communicate to his readers those emotions of beauty, grandeur, and sublimity, which the scenery is calculated to inspire. Destitute of this perfection, descriptions, however accurate, are invariably cold and languid.

His travels in the State of New-York afford much valuable information, new as well as interesting to the people of New-England. Our knowledge of the early settlement of that State, the manners of its first European inhabitants, and its progressive improvement in learning and the arts, has depended chiefly on occasional sketches in historical and geographical works, which usually contain only general remarks, and those often partial and inaccurate. (pp. 426-27)

President Dwight excels in delineating the characters, habits and manners of different nations, tribes, sects, and classes of society; and presents many valuable sketches of the history of mankind. He draws a picture of the appearance of the human race in the state of nature, free from the control of law and the influence of religious opinions; exemplified in the Indians of New-England, and contrasted with the absurd philosophy of Godwin, and the other encomiasts of the virtues of savages, and the native purity and perfection of unsophisticated man. (p. 427)

A great part of the last Volume consists of elegant essays on the literature, language, morals and religion of New England, and the genius and character of its inhabitants. Here the author completes his original design of showing to posterity, what was the situation of their country at the period of his travels. He gives a summary of our institutions for the preservation of order, the support of government, the encouragement of learning, and the establishment of religion; and of the beneficial effects which these institutions have produced on the virtue and happiness of the people. Here posterity may view with pleasure the moral and intellectual features of our ancestors, drawn in their genuine colours, with due diversities of light and shade, and exhibiting a correct and characteristic resemblance.

It may be objected that [this] work is designed by the author as a vindication of his native country, and may therefore be justly suspected of partiality. But it is a vindication founded on facts, and conducted with the greatest fairness and candour; neither palliating our faults, nor adopting the style of eulogy and panegyric. He was perfectly acquainted with his subject, and writes principally from personal knowledge. They who doubt his opinions can never question his veracity. His love of virtue and piety have led him to censure freely the vices and errors of his countrymen; and he manifests the same ardour in furnishing hints for our reformation and improvement, as in correcting the misrepresentations of our enemies. (p. 428)

President Dwight finishes his remarks on New England, with a description of the characteristics of its inhabitants, and a genuine portrait of their personal appearance, and appropriate national qualities, moral and intellectual, at the commencement of the present century; and concludes the work, with observations on the situation of the American Republic, the extent of its territories, the rapid increase of its settlements and population, and our happy progress and improvement in arts, learning, policy and morals. He recounts the causes of our growth and prosperity, and presents a sublime and animating view of our future prospects.

Our readers will find their attention amply repaid, on the perusal of these Travels, by the information and entertainment they will receive. While we seize with avidity the journals of travellers, who describe the manners, customs and curiosities, and recount the transactions of foreign nations, it must be disgraceful to be ignorant of the state of our native country, and inattentive to the novelty and magnificence of the scenes that surround us, and the course of events in which we are personally interested. (pp. 431-32)

A review of "Travels in New-England and New-York, Vols. III and IV," in The Christian Spectator, *Vol. IV, No. VIII, August, 1822, pp. 423-32.*

WILLIAM B. SPRAGUE   (essay date 1847)

[*Sprague provides a favorable brief survey of Dwight's works.*]

The design of the [*Conquest of Canaan*] is obvious from its title. It brings out, with fine effect, a most interesting portion of sacred history, and is well adapted to cherish the spirit of devotion and piety. (pp. 347-48)

[*The Triumph of Infidelity*] has for its introduction a short and pithy dedication to Voltaire, as if he had been yet alive; in which some wholesome truths are addressed to him for the benefit of his followers. It is dignified, but yet severe, and contains many allusions to individuals, some of which were doubtless better understood then than now. . . . The poem is full of keen satire, as well as stern truth and sound philosophy. It was fitted to render important service to the cause of Christianity, at a time when the most formidable influence was arrayed against it. (p. 348)

[*Greenfield Hill*] consists of seven parts, each part embracing a distinct theme; and yet the whole bearing harmoniously upon one grand design. Its descriptions of surrounding scenery, of the desolations which war had recently occasioned in the neighborhood, and of the future glory of this land as it opens upon the eye of the patriot, are characterized by great vividness of conception, and sometimes by superlative beauty and magnificence. The work throughout exhibits the lofty breathings of a patriotic spirit. (pp. 348-49)

His System of Theology [*Theology Explained and Defended*] is doubtless to be regarded as his *chef-d'oeuvre;* the work upon which, more than any other, his reputation will depend. . . . No one can read this work without being struck with its philosophical arrangement, its luminous reasonings, its bold and lofty eloquence, and the ability which it evinces to employ different faculties with the best effect, and to do everything in an exceedingly graceful and perfect manner. (pp. 351-52)

[Dr. Dwight's] *Travels,* the most voluminous of his works, next to his Theology, contains an amount of historical, biographical, topographical matter, concerning the parts of the country to which it relates, that cannot be found in any other single publication. It is the record of a most diligent course of observation and research, continued through a long series of years. It is quite possible, that, in some instances, he may have been betrayed into mistakes by his informers; but, even if much more allowance were made for this than ought to be, the work would still hold a high place in the department to which it belongs. It is alike instructive and entertaining, full of interesting incident and valuable information. (p. 353)

William B. Sprague, "Life of Timothy Dwight," in The Library of American Biography: Lives of Roger Williams, Timothy Dwight, and Count Pulaski, *Vol. IV, second series, edited by Jared Sparks, Charles C. Little and James Brown, 1847, pp. 225-364.*

THE AMERICAN LITERARY MAGAZINE   (essay date 1848)

[*The following excerpt is from a positive assessment of Dwight's works.*]

Some men pass noiselessly through life, as the sun through the heavens, shedding a constant light to the end of their course, and after they are gone, leave a brightness to be seen in others, as the sunbeams reflected from the moon.

This is pre-eminently true of Dr. Dwight. Though possessed of no extraordinary genius, such as dazzles and captivates the million, he was distinguished, beyond most men of his day, for profound and varied learning, and for skill in so imparting it to others, as to mould them after his own liking. (p. 269)

As an author, Dr. Dwight is favorably known, not only in America but throughout Europe. His theological works are of standard excellence, and probably the best which he wrote, as they are more elaborately finished. His *Travels* contain a vast amount of historic material, both interesting and useful. He describes men and manners in an easy and agreeable style which always pleases. His poems, though perhaps not of the first order, are yet of great merit. His subjects are grave and stately, and treated with solemnity. The *Conquest of Canaan,* written for the most part in his minority, was well spoken of by Cowper, who remarked in a letter to a friend in America, that he was highly entertained by reading it. The poems of Dr. Dwight would form an interesting volume, and doubtless well pay the publisher for bringing them before the public in a neat form. (pp. 272-73)

"Timothy Dwight," in The American Literary Magazine, *Vol. II, No. 5, May, 1848, pp. 269-73.*

MOSES COIT TYLER   (essay date 1895)

[*An American teacher, minister, and literary historian, Tyler was one of the first critics to examine American literature. His* History of American Literature during the Colonial Time: 1607-1765 *and* The Literary History of the American Revolution: 1763-1783 *are examples of his methodical research, authoritative style, and keen insight. While Tyler's* History of American Literature during the Colonial Time *is now considered dated, his study of the American Revolution remains a valuable sourcebook for modern scholars. In the survey of Dwight's writings excerpted below, Tyler discusses each of Dwight's major works and posits that the author's importance lies not in his writings, but in his accomplishments as a leader and scholar. Tyler considers* Travels in New-England and New-York, *despite its "wearisome stiffness," Dwight's most valuable work and predicts that it will endure as an important depiction of early nineteenth-century American life.*]

The first [of Dwight's publications] was *The Conquest of Canaan,* in eleven books of rhymed pentameter verse. . . . The motto on the title-page, taken from Pope,—

> Fired, at first sight, with what the Muse imparts,
> In fearless youth we tempt the height of arts;

is perhaps an intimation that the author was troubled by a momentary suspicion of the audaciousness of his poetic attempt, and is even the proffer of an apology therefor in the improbable case of its failure. Self-distrust, however, was not a Timothean infirmity; and by the time our poet has travelled from his title-page to his dedication, and thence to the preface, he has resumed his native composure, and is able to speak quietly of *The Conquest of Canaan* as the first epic poem that had then appeared in America, and to adjust it to some sort of friendly familiarity with its true predecessors, the "Aeneid" and the "Iliad." For example, refering in the preface to himself and his poem, he says: "It may be thought the result of inattention or ignorance, that he chose a subject in which his countrymen had no national interest. But he remarked that the

Iliad and the Aeneid were as agreeable to modern nations, as to the Greeks and Romans. . . . If he is not mistaken, the subject he has chosen possesses in a degree the same advantages'' [see excerpt dated 1785].

Surely, *The Conquest of Canaan,* with its eleven dreadful books of conventional rhymed pentameters,—all tending more or less to disarrange and confuse the familiar facts of Biblical history, as well as to dilute, to render garrulous, and to cheapen, the noble reticence, the graphic simplicity, of the antique chronicle—is such an epic as can be grappled with, in these degenerate days, by no man who is not himself as heroic as this verse assumes to be. (pp. 85-7)

[In his satiric verse entitled *The Triumph of Infidelity,*] Dwight enters upon a function in which as poet, teacher, preacher, prose-writer, or conversationist, he was ever afterward to be conspicuous,—that of defender of the Christian faith and even of Calvinistic orthodoxy, against all unfriendly comers, particularly those of the eighteenth century, whether French, English, Scotch, or American. From title-page to colophon, the intended method of the satire is irony,—a method calling, of course, for delicacy of movement, for arch and mocking sprightliness, for grace and levity of stroke, and obviously beyond the quality of one who being, in the first place, always dead-in-earnest, emphatic, and even ponderous, and secondly quite guiltless of humor, was above all things an intellectual gladiator, and could hardly think of any other way of dealing with an antagonist than by the good old-fashioned one of felling him to the floor. Probably there can now be left for us on this planet few spectacles more provocative of the melancholy and pallid form of mirth, than that presented by these laborious efforts of the Reverend Doctor Timothy Dwight to be facetious at the expense of David Hume, or to slay the dreadful Monsieur de Voltaire in a duel of irony. (pp. 91-2)

The plan of [*Greenfield Hill*] was evidently taken from that of Sir John Denham's ''Cooper's Hill,'' even as Denham's poem followed the hint given by Ben Jonson in his ''Penshurst,'' and in its turn gave the hint upon which Pope wrote his ''Windsor Forest.'' After all, however, the plan demands no great effort of originality: it is the obvious one of founding a series of narrative and descriptive verses on such views of nature and of human nature as may be spread out before the eyes of a poet who takes his stand on some eminence, and looks off. In the present case, the eminence was furnished by the poet's own home at Greenfield. Standing upon that height, he looks abroad over an outspreading scene of great natural loveliness, and this gives to him **''The Prospect,''** the first of the seven parts of which the poem is composed. After paying homage to the charm of natural scenery abounding there, he celebrates the social felicity to be seen all about him,—equality of condition, fairness, freedom, peace, universal thrift, manly dignity. . . . (pp. 92-3)

[Each of the poem's cantos] has its own theme, relating to the past, present, or future, and suggested to the writer as he gazes off from his rural hill-top over forest, plain, or distant sea,— **''The Flourishing Village,'' ''The Burning of Fairfield,'' ''The Destruction of the Pequods,'' ''The Clergyman's Advice to the Villagers,'' ''The Farmer's Advice to the Villagers,''** and **''The Vision, or Prospect of the Future Happiness of America.''**

As a whole, it may be said of *Greenfield Hill* that the poem is even yet by no means impossible to read; and that there are in it occasional passages which may be recalled with pleasure. . . . Undoubtedly the one fault of the poem at which every reader

will most quickly take offence, is a fault of manner,—its imitativeness. Even when the poem does not descend quite to the depth of parody, it does reproduce too closely, and too often, the very notes of Thomson, or Goldsmith, of Beattie, Edward Moore, or Gay; and for all this, the author's own apology is rather an explanation than a defence. (pp. 96-7)

[Plainly enough,] it is not by his poetry that we can account for the place which this man held in the homage of his contemporaries, or for the greatness and force of the stimulus which he gave to the intellectual life of his time. Moreover, when we look into his prose writings, we do not find ourselves much nearer to a solution of the problem. That solution is to be found, not in anything he wrote, but in everything he was,— in the man himself, in the amazing energy, variety, and charm of his personality. He was himself greater than anything he ever said or did; and for those who came near him, all that he did or said had an added import and fascination as proceeding from one so overpoweringly competent and impressive. (pp. 99-100)

Indeed, for all the ways by which men can be profoundly and honorably moved, he seems to have had an extraordinary equipment,—the highest social position, peculiar authority in his stations of pastor and college-president, immense contemporary renown as scholar, poet, prose-writer, thinker, and, finally, a faculty of oral speech, whether in public or private, which enthralled and drew after him all who heard. (pp. 100-01)

They who looked upon him from day to day thought him in no respect more extraordinary than in the power of his spirit to overstep and conquer his bodily limitations. During the last forty years of his life, he was seldom free from great anguish in the region of the head just back of the eyes, and was seldom able to employ his own eyesight for more than a quarter of an hour in any one day. In spite of this, he continued to be one of the men the best informed of his time, with respect to the doings of the world in letters, science, criticism, invention, industry, politics, war. . . . Whatsoever found admission to his mind, was straightway bestowed in its proper place, and there abode steadfast, being ever afterward at command. ''His mind''—such is the testimony of two of his sons—''resembled a well-arranged volume, in which every subject forms a separate section, and each view of that subject a separate page. He perfectly knew the order of the subjects; could turn to any page at will; and always found each impression as distinct and perfect as when first formed.'' So, during the most of his life, all his writing of whatever sort, in prose or verse, was done by the hand of another; and in this act of dictation, his utterance was so ready and so sure, that no amanuensis could ever keep pace with it, and no sentence thus produced was in need of amendment thereafter. . . . His mind took such firm hold of the subject which principally occupied it, that no ordinary force could separate it from its grasp. He was always conscious of the exact progress which he had made in every subject. When company, or any other occurrence, compelled him to break off suddenly, it would sometimes happen that he did not return to his employment until after the expiration of several days. On resuming his labors, all he required of his amanuensis was, to read the last word, or clause, that had been written; and he instantly would proceed to dictate as if no interruption had occurred. (pp. 103-05)

These extraordinary powers brought with them their own literary defect: nearly all his work has the fatal note of dictation. Everywhere what he seems to write is mere oratory; composition by the tongue, rather than the pen; the style of an eloquent declaimer with his audience in front of him; clever improvisation,—affluent, emphatic, sonorous, moving on and on in balanced members, accented by imposing gestures, stately, conventional, seldom mitigated by the modesty of an understatement, by forbearance in epithets, by lightness of touch, friendly ease, the charm of informality, the grace of a broken rhythm. Everywhere are the traces of his disastrous facility in the emission of sentences that could go into print without grammatical censure: most impressive, no doubt, as they rolled from his musical tongue, but, when lying cold and stark on the printed page, obviously marred by the blemishes of nearly all extemporaneous and unchastised speech,—excess of assertion, monotony of form, redundance, and a notable aptitude for the commonplace whether in thought or phrase. (pp. 106-07)

That book of Timothy Dwight's by which he is likely to be remembered the longest, his *Travels in New England and New York,* is one which was begun by him probably with the least literary ambition, was certainly but an incidental product of his energies.... On his first journey ..., he jotted down in a note-book such bits of daily experience as seemed to him likely to be of interest to his family when he should return home. In the following year, this plan broadened out into that of a systematic journal, for the possible benefit of the whole family of man, and elastic enough to admit into itself everything, directly or indirectly suggested by his journeys, which could give instruction or diversion to any mind,—incidents of travel, natural scenery, statistics of population and of social progress; talks by the way; local histories, legends, superstitions; sketches of towns, buildings, domestic life; notable persons; comments on the past, present, or future of our country, on forms of government, politics, religion, irreligion, climate, soil, trees, rocks, mountains, rivers, beasts, birds, storms, earthquakes, the public health, longevity, schools, colleges, ministers, lawyers, doctors, butchers, bakers, and candle-stick makers, together with race-problems, the aboriginal savages and their descendants, the inaccuracies and scurrilities of foreign travellers in America, international discourtesy, and so forth, and so forth.

Thus, under the frail disguise of a mere book of travels, the thing grew to be a vast literary miscellany; not a book, but a bibliotheca; in short, the private dumping ground of a philosopher, into which he could cast all the odds and ends of knowledge or opinion for which he happened to have no other convenient receptacle, and much of which might as well have occurred to him while sitting cross-legged by his own fireside, as while abroad on horseback. Unluckily, in giving to us what he entitles his *Travels,* he has not chosen to lay before us the original memoranda,—the rough jottings actually made by him from day to day, in taverns, under the shadow of a hill, by the road side, or in the friendly covert of a hay-stack. In their original form, doubtless, there would have been much gain for us, especially in the direction of reality, of off-hand friendliness, and simplicity. We should have been glad to see so august a being as President Dwight, for once, without his presidential robes on; nay, possibly, even in his shirt-sleeves; hungry, thirsty, hot, clamoring for his dinner, the sweat on his forehead, his trousers gray with dust or bespattered with mud, his slouch hat far gone in collapse, his rusty old saddle-bags lying on the floor by the side of his dirty boots. We should have been glad to find in his records of travel some occasional marks of human spontaneity, one symptom of haste, disappointment, vexation; here and there, possibly, a broken sentence, something unfinished, a crudity, an informality. Ah! not so, not so. Surely, President Dwight may not thus be seen of mortal eyes. There-

fore it is that every touch of realism, of homeliness, of familiarity,—if such there was in the original record,—is here obliterated; all things so natural as mere jottings are hammered out into formal and balanced sentences, are polished smooth and placed in line, in stately paragraphs, on dress parade, fit to go to court; while the memoranda meant for an itinerary are afterward, in cold blood, elaborated into the meaningless form of "Letters"—destitute of every sparkle of an epistolary quality—and addressed to a dummy called "an English Gentleman."

In spite, however, of such freezing officialism, such wearisome stiffness, it cannot be overlooked that some portions of the *Travels* are capable of giving entertainment. Everywhere, too, they are rich with the spoils of intellectual vigilance. Finally, as testimony touching the condition of the northern parts of the American Republic at about the beginning of the nineteenth century, they must grow in value as the generations pass. (pp. 120-24)

> Moses Coit Tyler, "A Great College President and
> What He Wrote," in his Three Men of Letters, G. P.
> Putnam's Sons, 1895, pp. 71-130.

DANIEL DULANY ADDISON   (essay date 1900)

[In the excerpt below, Addison discusses how Dwight's political and moral views are reflected in his major works. He considers Travels in New-England and New-York *Dwight's "crowning literary work," a contribution "of inestimable value."]*

The Conquest of Canaan with its eleven books and thousands of lines is a monumental example of industry on the part of a young man who through its pages sought literary immortality. The poet's plan was ambitious. He reasoned that since Greece had its great epic poem, "The Iliad," and Rome was the possessor of "The Aeneid," America must not be behind in the race for poetic honors. There must be a great American poem. Seeing the need, he straightway determined to supply it; and instead of frankly taking an American subject, he hit upon a Biblical topic as most likely to give general satisfaction. It is by no means unnatural, however, that to the Puritan mind the selection of such a theme should seem a perfectly normal matter, for Palestine was a good deal better known than many parts of America. The kings of Israel were better known than the worthies of Connecticut.... The real interest lies in reading between the lines, and seeing presented in varied forms the theories, doctrines, and political ideas that were rife in America just before and during the Revolution. When Joshua speaks of the Rights of Man, and prophesies a great future for his sons, we discern a spirit working.... (pp. 162-63)

[Dwight's] pen was as fluent in writing verses less pretentious than an epic; a good example of which is a rhymed letter to his friend Colonel Humphrey who was travelling abroad. Dwight urges him not to forget his native land and adopt manners that would seem strange to those at home, there being no reason why "interfluent seas" should change a man's character and make him like those who "the plain, frank manners of their race despise."... (pp. 165-66)

[He often] found leisure enough to read deeply in the thought of the time, and the more he read the less sympathy did he have with those who cast a slur on Calvinism. Either a French sceptic, or an English or American theologian, who cast doubts upon received traditions, was his foe; and not content with smiting them in a ponderous discourse, he tried the keener weapons of irony and satire. This form of combat was essayed in 1788, when he published *The Triumph of Infidelity,* a poem of satire intended to strike between the points of the armor those who congregated with Satan. A critic of the poem has said: "Probably there can now be left for us on this planet few spectacles more provocative of the melancholy and pallid form of mirth than that presented by these laborious efforts of the Reverend Doctor Timothy Dwight to be facetious at the expense of David Hume, or to slay the dreadful Monsieur de Voltaire in a duel of irony." This may be true, but the poem is not without amusement, and at times possesses a rugged irony that is surprising. The poem is dedicated to Voltaire. The main theme is the rejoicing of Satan, "Hell's terrific God," at the throng of his worshippers and his efforts to gain new converts. In the midst of his various travels Satan is made to say:—

> To France I posted, on the wings of air,
> And fir'd the labors of the gay Voltaire.
> He light and gay, o'er learning's surface flew,
> And prov'd all things at option, false or true.

To the delight of Satan, Hume sang:—

> All things roll on, by fix'd eternal laws;
> Yet no effect depends upon a cause:
> Hence every law was made by chance divine,
> Parent most fit of order and design!

(pp. 167-68)

Throughout the poem the interest is held by more than one clever turn of phrase and curious simile. As a whole it is a more interesting relic of past polemics than many a famous discourse. The ambition to produce a great poem was never absent from Dwight's mind. . . . The result saw the light in 1794, when he published the long poem *Greenfield Hill,* which soon became popular. He had the poem by him for seven years, adding to and correcting it, chiefly at first with the idea of gaining relief from work, and then desiring, as he stated, "to contribute to the innocent amusement of his countrymen, and to their improvement in manners, and in œconomical, political, and moral sentiments." . . . Frankly the author states that it was his design to imitate, in the different parts of the poem, the peculiarities of many British poets, and though he gave up the plan as to the details there is a strong suggestion of Sir John Denham's "Cooper's Hill," and passages that show plainly his indebtedness to Thompson, Goldsmith, and Gay. The poem is divided into seven parts, each with an appropriate name, descriptive of the contents: **"The Prospect," "The Flourishing Village," "The Burning of Fairfield," "The Destruction of the Pequods," "The Clergyman's Advice to the Villagers," "The Farmer's Advice to the Villagers,"** and **"The Vision or Prospect of the Future Happiness of America."** In each of these sections there is opportunity for excellent description, homely advice, and instruction, besides the stating of one's opinions on many subjects. The verses thus grew to be a reflection at close range of the author's surroundings and well-known moral and political views. (pp. 169-71)

Greenfield Hill can easily be read to-day, not merely as an antiquary would examine an ancient manuscript for its bearings on the history of a previous generation, but for the purpose of seeing what the fathers read, and helping us to appreciate the qualities that now make virile the best parts of American life. (p. 178)

The most important of Timothy Dwight's literary labors . . . [as president of Yale College] were without doubt the sermons

that he preached to the students, both by reason of their immediate effect, and their influence on religious thought when published after his death, in five volumes, under the title *Theology Explained and Defended.* . . . The sermons taken as a whole constitute a thoroughly logical system of religious thought, dealing with a wide range of theological subjects from philosophy to specific doctrines, aiming to appeal to reason as well as faith, and to combat the intellectual objections which Hume, Priestley, and Paine had raised against the truth of Christianity as interpreted by the orthodox thinkers. Though Dwight's teaching is a milder form of Calvinism than that of Edwards, and differed from Hopkinsianism, he did not eliminate the severity of the older theologians. Without attempting to assign him a theological position, it can be said of the sermons that they were a departure from the usual modes of preaching, in that they are full of original thought, clear, at times sprightly, bringing to bear upon the topics chosen a mass of information and argument, which explains their popularity almost to the present day. . . . (pp. 178-79)

The crowning literary work of a long and earnest life was the *Travels in New England and New York,* published some years after his death. Many consider these bulky volumes as the most important gift that the good doctor has made to American letters. Southey, who reviewed them at length in the *Quarterly Review,* speaking of the work as a whole, says, "Though the humblest in its pretences, this is the most important of his writings, and will derive additional value from time, whatever may become of his poetry and of his sermons." The *Travels* came into existence gradually through many years and without any intention at first of being more than a record for his family. . . . They contain literally everything that might strike the physical eye or the mind's eye in journeys through a limited section of the world,—scenery, the height of hills and the depths of rivers, the general lay of the land, the names of the trees and fruits and vegetables, the produce of each locality, the number of the population, the progress made in society, the buildings, the industries, with, as Southey says, "a delightful curiosity in strange rocks, whirlwinds, and insects." There are preserved in these pages old superstitions and legends that would long ago have vanished if they had not caught the ear of the inquisitive wanderer. History and character sketches are placed side by side with good stories and epitaphs on tombstones. Biographies are written down at first hand, and accounts of battles are received from soldiers who fought under Putnam and Warren. Indian stories and tales of the early settlers are given with as much precision as if they were being recounted for the archives of a historical society. The book, in fine, is a panoramic picture of the social, industrial, educational, and religious condition of New England at the end of the eighteenth and the beginning of the nineteenth centuries. It is genuinely interesting and readable, and of inestimable value to the historian or the student of manners and customs. (pp. 185-88)

The biographical sketches contained in this work are well done and valuable, especially the accounts of Judge Oliver Ellsworth and General Phinehas Lyman, and of many other important New England men about whom delightful anecdotes are told. There is a vivid description also of the battle of Bunker Hill. To illustrate the strange mixture of fact and opinion with curious information in the record one has only to read the six reasons given why the river at Niagara Falls never moves faster than six miles an hour,—a question which was argued at length with the ferryman who did not agree with the traveller.

Though the book has no logical order in the arrangement of its facts, being a huge note-book of everything under the sun, with a kind of Sunday newspaper method in its inclusiveness, it has little in it of dulness, much of cleverness and even brilliancy. (pp. 189-90)

> *Daniel Dulany Addison, "Timothy Dwight," in his* The Clergy in American Life and Letters, *The Macmillan Company, 1900, pp. 157-90.*

JAMES L. ONDERDONK (essay date 1901)

[*The following excerpt is from a mixed assessment of Dwight's major poems.*]

The Conquest of Canaan is a long, tedious effort, extending through eleven books, "to represent such manners as are removed from the peculiarities of any age or country, and might belong to the amiable and virtuous of any period, elevated without design, refined without ceremony, elegant without fashion, and agreeable because they are ornamented with sincerity, dignity, and religion" [see excerpt dated 1785]. The versification is fair, but monotonous, and there is no unity of design. The author was willing to rest his reputation as a poet on this work, which in all sincerity he believed to be as meritorious as the Iliad or Aeneid. There is nothing very original or pleasing in the whole performance. Though dealing with wars of the Israelites, incidents of our own Revolution, as the death of Warren, are introduced, and the din and roar of contending hosts compared to Niagara Falls. (pp. 88-9)

[*The Triumph of Infidelity*] is a versified theological treatise, directed against the current infidelity, and contains some well-expressed satire upon the "smooth divine." *Greenfield Hill* . . . was a little more successful. It is true there was more preaching than poetry in it, but it dealt in home themes, and was a decided advance on its predecessors. Its didacticism was something formidable, as was to be expected.

Dr. Dwight was certainly a strong man in his day. As patriot, theologian, educator, controversialist, and citizen, if not as a poet, he was truly and eminently great. (p. 89)

> *James L. Onderdonk, "Freneau and the Connecticut Choir—1765-1815," in his* History of American Verse (1610-1897), *1901. Reprint by Johnson Reprint Corporation, 1969, pp. 75-102.**

VERNON LOUIS PARRINGTON (essay date 1926)

[*An American historian, biographer, and critic, Parrington is best known for his unfinished literary history of the United States,* Main Currents in American Thought. *Though modern scholars now disagree with many of his conclusions, they view Parrington's work as a significant first attempt at fashioning an intellectual history of America based on a broad interpretive thesis. Written from the point of view of a Jeffersonian liberal,* Main Currents in American Thought *has proven a widely influential work in American criticism. Although Parrington contends that Dwight's works display vigor and contain worthy advice, he maintains that Dwight was neither a great thinker nor a great poet.*]

In *The Conquest of Canaan* [Dwight] described so many thunderstorms that Trumbull suggested he ought to furnish a lightning-rod with the poem. Such a man could not move easily in narrow spaces. An epic was none too slight to contain his swelling fancies or satisfy his rhetoric; he walks with huge strides; he is prodigal of images; one canto finished, other cantos clamor to emerge upon the page. His ready versification, one often feels, runs like a water pipe with the faucet off. There

is never a pause to pick or choose; his words flow in an unbroken stream from his inkwell. Yet even in his amazing copiousness there is vigor; a well-stocked mind is pouring out the gatherings of years. When he pauses to give advice—as he was fond of doing—his abundant sense is worth listening to. The homely wisdom of his talk to the farmers in the sixth part of *Greenfield Hill* is not unlike Franklin. As a satirist he belongs to the Churchill school; he is downright abusive, often violent, quite lacking [a] lightness of touch and easy gayety. . . . His *Triumph of Infidelity* is good old-fashioned pulpit-thumping. The spirit of toleration was withheld from him by his fairy godmother, and he knows no other way of dealing with those who persist in disagreement after their mistakes have been pointed out, than the cudgel. In this tremendous poem he lays about him vigorously. On Hume and Voltaire and Priestley, and all the host of their followers, his blows fall smartly. Bloody crowns ought to be plentiful, but—though the Doctor does not seem to know it—most of the blows fall on straw men and none proves to be mortal. On the whole one prefers him in the pastoral mood when he lays aside his ministerial gown, and *Greenfield Hill,* apart from *Travels in New England and New York,* justly remains his most attractive work. But even that is sadly in need of winnowing. A great college president Timothy Dwight is conceded to have been; he was worshiped by his admirers only this side idolatry; but a great thinker, a steadfast friend of truth in whatever garb it might appear, a generous kindly soul loving even publicans and sinners, regardful of others and forgetful of self, he assuredly was not. That he could ever have been looked upon as a great poet, is a fact to be wondered at. (pp. xlii-xliii)

> *Vernon Louis Parrington, in an introduction to* The Connecticut Wits, *edited by Vernon Louis Parrington, Harcourt Brace Jovanovich, 1926, pp. ix-xlviii.**

LEON HOWARD (essay date 1943)

[*In the following excerpt, Howard outlines the flaws he perceives in* The Conquest of Canäan. *Specifically, Howard claims that Dwight took too many liberties with the poem: he disregarded biblical accuracy and employed the poetic techniques of such authors as Homer and Milton. The resulting epic, Howard maintains, is "full of eighteenth-century Americans with Hebrew names who talked like Milton's angels and fought like prehistoric Greeks."*]

The Conquest of Canäan was not designed to be anything so simple as a versified biblical narrative presented with overtones of allusion to later events of a similar pattern. The definition of an epic to which Dwight apparently subscribed called for more than a heroic narrative in elevated style: it was "A Fable related by a Poet, in order to raise the Admiration, and inspire the Love of Virtue, by representing to us the Action of a Hero favour'd by Heaven, who brings about a great Enterprize, notwithstanding the Obstacles he meets in his way." Therefore, as Ramsay pointed out, there were three things of major consideration in an epic: "the Action, the Moral, and the Poesy." Historical accuracy was subordinate to the moral purpose of the fable; and, in drawing the material for his "action" from the Book of Joshua, Dwight took full advantage of his poetic license to revise and invent. With an unexpected deference to the rules he condemned in his master's Dissertation, he achieved unity of place by arranging that the entire conquest take place in the neighborhood of Ai; and he gave unity to the action by making Jabin, the Canaanite hero, comparable in stature to Joshua, by condensing the campaign of many weeks into the continuous activity of a few days, and by rearranging the chronology in order that the victory at Gibeon might become the catastrophe of the poem and represent the final conquest of Canaan. He also took other liberties with his original, especially with respect to the characters, leaving out most of those who appeared in the Bible and inventing as many more to take their places. . . . The result was an apparent disregard for biblical authority which greatly disturbed even so sympathetic a reviewer as William Cowper [see excerpt dated 1789] but, at the same time, a variety of characterization which none of Dwight's literary associates ever approached.

The entire action of *The Conquest of Canäan* possessed high moral significance; but Dwight was also aware that (in the language of the Introduction to [a Greek and Roman myth entitled] *Telemachus*) "Virtue may be recommended both by Example and Instructions, either by the Manners or by the Precepts." (pp. 87-9)

For the "Poesy" of *The Conquest of Canäan* Dwight "made use of Rhyme," either because he had experimented unsuccessfully with blank verse or "because," as he explained in the Preface, "he believed it would be more generally relished than blank verse, even amongst those who are esteemed persons of taste" [see excerpt dated 1785]. The rhyme which he adopted was the heroic couplet of Pope's Homer; and, although Dwight apparently strove consciously for a greater animation in style than he found in his model, he seems to have paid little attention to the "harmony" of his numbers. For Dwight, like most of his contemporaries, was more concerned with the meaning than with the sound of his verse; and when he considered the subordinate sensory appeal of poetry he thought of achieving it through "imitation"—either by description or by the more "lively" method of using rhetorical figures. (pp. 90-1)

[Dwight] had his own notions concerning poetry and apparently felt that the epic writers had unduly neglected physical nature as material for descriptions and a source for rhetorical figures. Accordingly, he was never content with a "rosy-fingered dawn" but usually described his sunrises and nightfalls rather fully and never as exactly the same. If the moon was high in the heavens on one evening, it was above the eastern hills on the next, and just rising on the evening afterward; and it gradually faded during the poem from its "clear, full beauty" until it shed only a "feeble twilight." Sometimes the morn was led "o'er misty hills" by the day star, and sometimes it burst into a cloudless blue sky. Other aspects and phenomena of nature appeared in the poem; but Dwight made his greatest use of nature in its grander, more sublime phases, with the result that perhaps twoscore storms, figurative and real, roared through the book and provoked a suggestion from Trumbull that the author should have supplied his poem with a lightning rod. Such excess was inevitable, however, and altogether in keeping with Dwight's disposition. When he decided that an idea was good, he usually pushed it to the limit of his own endurance. He had already, while an undergraduate, almost ruined his eyesight by a self-established routine of excessive study; and, while he was ruining his epic by an excessive devotion to critical precepts, he was also threatening his magnificent physique by the rigid application of his curious theories of diet.

The Conquest of Canäan, however, was not based entirely upon precepts. When Dwight ambitiously planned the poem that was designed to be "the first of the kind, which has been published in this country," he looked around with characteristic thoroughness for the best examples he might follow. . . . All the machinery and many of the structural and expository devices were Miltonic. The poem opened with an invocation to the divine source of knowledge, the action began with a parliamentary debate, and the narrative occasionally paused for high converse in which the creation was described, the history of the world summarized, the coming of Christ prophesied, theology expounded, and the future envisioned—all of which was based upon Miltonic precedent as firmly as was the machinery of angelic messengers or the Gibeonite hymn to the sun. The battle scenes, on the other hand, were modeled on Pope's version of the *Iliad*. The Israelites and the men of Canaan waved falchions in the air to make lightning play around their heads, threw their spears nimbly through the air or thrust with them in their hands, clashed their burnished, moonlike shields, darkened the skies with arrows, and threw huge stones at each other as they battled on the plain beneath the throngs watching from city walls. They might ride horseback between battles, but they fought only from low chariots; and, although there were some military improvements allowed in the form of mass tactics, steel armor, and trumpet signals, single combat with plenty of time for speechmaking was the rule, the heroes raging over the field in search of particular opponents whom they fought in spaces conveniently cleared by more insignificant warriors. In short, Dwight's poem was full of eighteenth-century Americans with Hebrew names who talked like Milton's angels and fought like prehistoric Greeks. (pp. 91-3)

[The result of Dwight's romance and marriage] was the introduction into *The Conquest of Canäan* of a long episode of romantic love in which Dwight added pathos to his epic and drew a picture of manners that would be especially instructive to young people. (p. 94)

Curious though [the] episode is as a revelation of Dwight's sentiment and possibly of his mental state at a critical moment in his career, it is most interesting as an illustration of how emotion could be strained through his rather pedantic, theory-ridden mind and so lose all force of reality in its expression. The young man would never have tried so hard to make himself a poet had he not possessed, to a considerable degree, the talent for verse-making which he occasionally revealed by a deft turn of expression. But he was too self-conscious to relax and let his talent have free play. He was acutely aware, of course, that an epic should be composed in the florid "sublime" and "middle" styles, never in the "low," for all his models illustrated that basic requirement and both Lord Kames [author of *Elements of Criticism*] and the more formal rhetoricians insisted upon it. Yet as time went on he should have become more at ease even in a style foreign to the natural pungency he displayed in conversation. Instead, however, he merely became aware of new theoretical possibilities of expression and so acquired an additional artificiality. In the course of writing *The Conquest of Canäan* Dwight composed approximately five thousand rather carefully considered heroic couplets; and, although he did manage to get much more poetic "fire" in the last book than he did in the first, the skill he developed reveals the lucubration of a schoolteacher rather than the ease of a poet. (p. 95)

Leon Howard, "Timothy Dwight," in his *The Connecticut Wits*, *The University of Chicago Press*, 1943, pp. 79-111.

GEORGE F. SENSABAUGH (essay date 1964)

[*In the following excerpt, Sensabaugh discusses the similarities between Dwight's* The Conquest of Canäan *and Milton's* Paradise Lost.]

As Dwight cast about for a subject and style [for his *The Conquest of Canäan*] commensurate with his ambition he hit on what he considered a happy solution: he would tell the story of Joshua and his heroic struggles to bring the Children of Israel into the land of Canäan, and he would model his narrative on what he thought was the most sublime of all epics, *Paradise Lost*. That Americans often pictured themselves as Israelites claiming their heritage in a New Canäan was enough to satisfy Dwight's love for his country. All he needed to do was to tell his story in a style suited to the dignity of his intentions. Such a poem—elevated in language, vast in conception, and dignified in subject—would be truly epic and would ennoble not only Americans but mankind as well. (pp. 166-67)

In deference to prevailing poetic taste, he avoided Miltonic blank verse and cast his whole epic in heroic couplets; but this was one of the few concessions he made to Augustan poetic demands. Language, syntax, narrative machinery, character delineation, and scenes—all came from *Paradise Lost*.

Even a cursory reading reveals how many of Milton's characteristic words and how much of his syntax spring from the pages of *The Conquest of Canäan*. Milton was fond, for example, of saying "amaze" for "amazement," and so also was Dwight. Such words, to which may be added expressions like "sweetness ineffable" and "intermingled sighs," only indicate the vast debt Dwight owed to Milton's characteristic language; and along with such terminology Milton's syntax often appeared. (p. 167)

Dwight's imitation of Milton's diction and syntax is clear. But more significant was his following Milton's narrative technique, his reproducing in slightly changed order many graphic scenes essential to his unfolding story. Milton often pictured morning and evening to indicate the passage of time, sometimes lingering with such sensitivity on the scenes he presented that schoolmasters made them a part of their repertory for school recitations. The smell of morn was sweet in his nostrils, and eventide possessed special charms. (p. 168)

Dwight indicated the passage of time in the same way, pausing even more often than Milton had paused to describe morning and evening, sometimes in Milton's own words. So close is his description of evening in Book IX of *The Conquest of Canäan* to Milton's famous picture [of twilight in the Garden of Eden] that Dwight must have had his eyes on it when he composed his own scene. . . . Milton and Dwight of course drew from classical models for the narrative technique of indicating time by reference to morning and evening; but the similarity of their scenes in language and structure suggests that Dwight had Milton in mind. (pp. 168-69)

> *George F. Sensabaugh, "The Revolutionary Period," in his* Milton in Early America, *Princeton University Press, 1964, pp. 97-183.*

KENNETH SILVERMAN (essay date 1969)

[*In his book-length study of Dwight, Silverman concentrates on Dwight's role in the political, social, and religious changes that occurred in late eighteenth- and early nineteenth-century America. In the following excerpt, Silverman discusses the style of Dwight's works. Arguing that Dwight's poetical works often suffer from "an insensitive repetition of themes and phrases," Silverman maintains that his "love of place unexpectedly imbues the banal with life" in* Travels in New-England and New-York.]

The droning sameness of Dwight's battle scenes [in *The Conquest of Canäan*] results from an extraordinarily small range of diction and from an obsession with a few rhymes. As in "**America,**" he particularly likes to rhyme "skies-rise" and "main-plain." With a few slight variants he repeats them hundreds of times; within sixty lines of Book Three . . . , he rhymes "the plain-their train," "dreadful plain-hopes again," "darkening train-heap'd the plain," "burst amain-along the plain," "driving rain-o'er the plain," "obscuring rain-homeward plain," and "wreath to gain-skirmish'd plain." In the last book alone, "skies" is rhymed with "rise" twenty times, not to mention numerous "skies-cries," "skies-surprise," and so on. In describing the dozens of battles he forswears invention: he allows every lance to "hiss," spill each enemy's "vital tide," and invariably "stain" the field with the invariable "purple gore."

The verse, too, lacks variety. Everything happens in one unvarying, metronomic rhythm. "Animation" meant to Dwight simply an orgastic accretion of storm-tossed oceans, earthquakes, tempests, thunder, trembling heavens, whirlwinds, gales, blood-red skies, and hosts of murmuring widows. By prosopopeia each banal detail takes on the bombastic sublimity of nature:

> As when two seas, by winds together hurl'd,
> With bursting fury shake the solid world;
> Waves pil'd o'er waves, the watery mountains rise,
> And foam, and roar, and rage, against the skies:
> So join'd the combat; ranks, o'er ranks impell'd,
> Swell'd the hoarse tumult of the hideous field;
> Black drifts of dust becloud the gloomy ground;
> Hoarse groans ascend, and clashing arms resound.
> And now, where Zimri broke th'embodied war,
> Imperious Hoham drove his sounding car;
> Like flames, his rapid courses rush'd along,
> Forc'd a red path, and crush'd the thickening
>   throng. . . .

Under the weight of thousands of such lines, Dwight smothered the narrative clarity and the "natural" language he wished to reproduce; and he tired the attention he wished to engage.

The dramatic treatment Dwight professed to admire in the Bible also suffers from his repetitiousness. The action, bloated by "animation," lacks moment. Nothing can be seen or heard through the curtain of rhetoric. Dwight made no dramatic distinctions. The characters share the narrator's idiom. Men and women, youths and sages, heroes and villains, discourse in the same rhythm, the same diction; and all seem to be saying the same thing. Worse, Dwight provided no quotation marks to sever dialogue from narrative. One sometimes cannot tell whether the narrator or some character is speaking; and, if some character, which one. Borne on the flood of bombast, the reader often does not feel the unprepared and inexplicable shifts in point-of-view, which Dwight often planted in the middle of a verse paragraph, unmarked by punctuation or by changes of tone or rhythm. The repetitiousness serves to disguise the otherwise glaring mismanagement of the action, and the result is by turns tiresome and bewildering.

Dwight's insensitive handling of climactic moments is, however, less damaging than his addition to the completed poem of Books Three and Five, the romance of Irad and Selima. He masked the irrelevance of this sentimental subplot by involving his lovers in a half-dozen harrowing skirmishes, written in the sublime style, and padded with didactic asides on art and nature, and a tribute to Benjamin West. The interlarded subplot robbed the poem of its already enfeebled dramatic point. For, incomprehensibly, Dwight failed to adjust the existent plot to the newly inserted matter. (pp. 28-30)

Like the *Conquest, Greenfield Hill* suffers from an insensitive repetition of themes and phrases. Dwight was incapable of holding in mind the larger design. The "Arguments" to the various parts are often indistinguishable: "the happy state of the inhabitants" (Part One), "Description of a happy village" (Part Five), "the happiness of America" (Part Seven). What in theory justifies this redundance is that each part of the poem sees the subject from a slightly different point of view and through a different set of conventions, depending on the writer imitated. But whether the language recalls Goldsmith, Beattie, or Franklin the same happy village shows through.

The hill on which the narrator stands is less a narrative device, however, than the symbol of an intense localism. Whether sketching ideal types, commemorating historic personages, or recounting battles, Dwight's interest is in Greenfield Hill, in telling its past, prophesying its future, and assessing its present. The point is worth repeating that Dwight believed more deeply than anything else what he quoted from William Penn:

> Nothing is necessary to make good men har-
> monious and friendly but that they should live
> near to each other, and converse often, kindly,
> and freely, with each other.

Dwight's intense localism, his sense of the richness and value of the local scene, his *pietas,* orders the poem. The complementary first and last parts—"**The Prospect**" and "**The Vision**"—frame a deliberately balanced picture of the local past, present, and future, of what Greenfield Hill is, how it came to be, and how it may be maintained. The first two parts depict the present state of society; parts Three and Four explore the past; parts Five and Six explain how the present state of happiness may be preserved; Part Seven on the basis of the rest, prophesies the future. The two parts within each division complement each other. Part One offers a prospect of the countryside and nature, Part Two a contrasting prospect of the village and society. Part Three presents British atrocities during the recent Revolution, Part Four the contrasting Puritan heroism a hundred years earlier. In Part Five, a clergyman tells how Greenfield Hill's religious life may be maintained; in Part Six a farmer tells how its secular prosperity may be maintained. And this interest in local history, not the fraudulent "prospect" device, unifies the poem. (pp. 56-7)

[*Greenfield Hill* marks] a new concreteness in Dwight's style. The poem's abundance of place-names—"Grover's beauteous rise," "Mill-hill," "Norwalk's white-ascending spires"—gives the diction some freshness and vigor. What affords the final vision of futurity is not "Columbia," but a local deity, the "Genius of the Sound."

To speak with even this degree of intimacy to his situation, Dwight needed to create a new audience. No longer writing for all America, he specifies that the group of established farmers he is addressing occupy "about thirteen square miles." . . . Within its narrow focus the poem presents a complex and detailed account of town life, its ideal shape and practical shape, its manners, conduct, polity, its mode of preserving the past. *Greenfield Hill* precedes Emily Dickinson's Amherst, as well as E. A. Robinson's Tilbury Town, Edgar Lee Masters' Spoon River, and Sherwood Anderson's Winesburg as the first

delineation in American literature of the township ideal: "every town / A world within itself." (p. 57)

Dwight introduced into *Greenfield Hill* dozens of regional usages [of language] and Americanisms. In conjunction with local place-names and the names of local heroes, these create a distinctive idiom. The use of nativisms, as well as the detailed glosses Dwight supplied for them in his footnotes, was not unprecedented in colonial verse. For instance, in a pastoral poem on Maryland, Jonathan Boucher had italicized and glossed thirty-odd Americanisms; Ebenezer Cooke, in "The Sot-weed Factor," had introduced and annotated many more. Both poets, however, addressed their glosses to English readers as examples of colonial queerness and vulgarity. Dwight addressed his to Americans outside New England as examples of local color, and as explanations of novel manners and institutions. (p. 60)

The poem's indebtedness to its English models is, of course, immense; yet *Greenfield Hill* was the first lengthy poem in America so consciously written for a native audience, the first to so consciously resist sounding like British English. No other colonial poem, except the propaganda verse of the Revolution, has a native audience so much in mind. Dwight's appropriation of the local scene compelled him to assemble place-names, unfamiliar proper nouns, and Americanisms to form a rudimentary American literary speech, stilted, hesitant, and incomplete, but recognizably not British.

Dwight created not a single literary speech, but, more accurately, a number of native voices. The seven parts of the poem employ as many local personae, secondary narrators introduced by the narrator on the hill: a rural minister, a farmer, a parochial schoolmaster, a local mother, the "Genius of the Sound." These voices echo Dwight's varied roles at Greenfield Hill as preacher, farmer, teacher, father. He enhanced the dramatic distinction between these voices by metrical variety. Unlike *The Conquest of Canäan, Greenfield Hill* allows each speaker his own pulse—blank verse, heroic couplets, octosyllabics, Spenserian stanzas—and his own idiom, depending on the British writer imitated. Each persona, moreover, assumes a different perspective on America and on the village. From the minister's point of view, America is the site of the millennium, while the farmer sees it as a verdant Eden; accordingly, America appears as "New Canaan" or "New Albion" or "Western Albion" or "Columbia." The variety of voices offered Dwight a way out of his uncertainties. It enabled him to test out various attitudes toward America without being pledged to any one of them. (pp. 61-2)

Greenfield Hill struggles against its own rhetoric. . . . Dwight attempted to write a conventional poem that should break through the conventional poetic view of American life. He tried to distinguish between the real bliss of Connecticut and the literary Eden, to discover if in Connecticut "the soul-intrancing scenes, / Poetic fiction boasts, are real all." In doing so he gave his sympathies to facts far more than to "poetry," correcting the fanciful optimism of his epic. Yet, while more circumspect, the result is, like the epic, something between a poem and a tract, half a literary exercise on the glories of American life, half a straightforward account of the mores of the Connecticut Valley, neither a mythic description of ideal conduct nor a treatise on practical government. (pp. 62-3)

[In his *Travels; In New-England and New York,*] Dwight leavened his mass of hard fact with personal accounts of local history. He fondly details the settlement and development of each little town in the region, each important school; explains place-names; outlines the lives of local leaders and ministers; and estimates with a farmer's eye and a gardener's zeal the quality of the soil. As he tours the New England states, he simultaneously unfolds the history of King Philip's War. He describes local forays, often on a house-by-house basis, introduces some little-known actions, corrects errors about more celebrated ones, and connects events with places in the hope of dramatizing both. In addition to history and statistics, he provides a flow of patter about local curiosities and legends: a letter written by a drowning man; a traveler who crossed a bridge whose planks, mysteriously, had not yet been laid; a hundred-year-old bug, a tale which later found its way to both Thoreau and Melville; the causes of dry rot.

Dwight makes no formal effort to unify this melange, but he does group his jottings into letters, addressed, as Moses Tyler said, "to a dummy called 'an English Gentleman'" [see excerpt dated 1895]. He also gives the journey a geographical logic at odds with the actual chronology of his trips. For instance, to retain the illusion of a single tour, he places a trip to Brookline in 1805 before a trip to New Lebanon in 1799. Otherwise the *Travels* lurch between bald statistics, dry histories, and believe-it-or-nots, hungrily but indiscriminately seizing whatever will prove its underlying propositions about the solidity and enterprise of the New England character. If anything can be said to direct Dwight's zigzag course, it is his abiding love of the Connecticut Valley: "Take it for all in all, I have never seen the place where I could so willingly spend my life."

Dwight writes mainly from outside, with a brusque air of investigation. He arrives in town, counts the schools, measures the bridges, attends a service, and has quickly seen what confirms his belief that New Englanders are sober, pious, industrious, and intelligent. With wearisome sameness, hamlet after hamlet shows him what he wants to see, affording now and then a diverting local hero or curiosity. The deadpan factfinding is only unconsciously relieved, as when a visit with an aged atheist causes Dwight to remark, "It is scarcely necessary to observe, that a man one hundred and sixteen years old, without religion, was a melancholy sight to me." Otherwise, while measuring every bridge, computing every waterfall, Dwight visualizes nothing. His tone is level, reasonable; his style hasty, plain, unstudied, and undistinguished. His statistical paragraphs are often telegraphically brief, his descriptive paragraphs long and sluggish. Practically his only verb is "is."

Yet "is," the stubborn fact, was precisely Dwight's concern. He wrote the *Travels* convinced that, in the accounts of foreign travelers, America had been distorted by misinformation and faulty seeing. . . . He intended to give the facts, and to give them in proper perspective. Since Americans already knew the facts and Englishmen did not want to know them, he feared writing a book no American would read and no Englishman would buy. Actually, there had existed since colonial times a lively tradition of corrective literature; for the desire to challenge foreign misconceptions about America had provided the colonists perhaps their first literary impulse. With a triumphant air Dwight exposes literally thousands of errors in page after page of such travelers as the Comte de Volney, Isaac Weld, and the Duc de la Rochefoucault. (pp. 115-16)

Dwight's intimacy with the past gave the *Travels* its best moments. A knowledge of the history of some desolate spot, where an English traveler would have seen nothing, allowed him the kind of epiphany reserved for antiquarians. Amid the emptiness

he recalled how a soldier named Gregg, out pigeon hunting, was shot by Indians. . . .

Englishmen failed to see the real America because to Dwight it was an observation plus a memory. Throughout the *Travels,* voids become shrines; strolls, pilgrimages. Love of place unexpectedly imbues the banal with life. (p. 118)

> *Kenneth Silverman, in his* Timothy Dwight, *Twayne Publishers, Inc., 1969, 174 p.*

DONALD BARLOW STAUFFER   (essay date 1974)

[*In the following excerpt, Stauffer discusses Dwight's major poems,* The Conquest of Canäan *and* Greenfield Hill, *and concludes that "Dwight's is strictly a minor talent."*]

[Timothy Dwight] early decided he was destined to literary greatness, and as a test of his talents set himself the task of composing an epic in which he would combine the best of two popular modern epics—Milton's *Paradise Lost* and Fénelon's *The Adventures of Telemachus.* He chose as his subject the conquest of Canaan by Joshua, whose exploits he felt were suitable for an epic hero. When the poem was tardily published in 1785, his readers were accustomed to making the kind of analogies that the Puritan writers had made for generations and turned Dwight's biblical Promised Land into a Revolutionary America and Joshua into General Washington. Since Dwight was more interested in the moral effects of his poem upon his readers than he was in historical or political parallels, he was actually dismayed and irritated by attempts to read *The Conquest of Canaan* . . . as allegory. What he tried to create in Joshua was a hero "favour'd by Heaven" whose actions would "raise the Admiration, and inspire the Love of Virtue" in his readers. But since he took a great deal of pains to instill in Joshua the qualities of an ideal general, it is not altogether surprising that his patriotic readers a decade later were certain he was describing George Washington.

If *The Conquest of Canaan* was mistakenly read in retrospect as an American poem, another of Dwight's poems follows the pattern of the "vision" poems being written in this period. **"America: Or a Poem on the Settlement of the British Colonies"** . . . traces the history of the discovery of America and ends with a vision of an allegorical figure of freedom giving a prophecy of the future glory of America—a device that Barlow was to use in *The Vision of Columbus.*

Dwight, like his literary classmates at Yale, was not wholly at ease with the English poets, even though he had read most of them. He was especially attracted to Pope, however, and decided when he began his epic to use the couplet Pope had used in his translations of Homer. But Dwight was too cautious and unpracticed to give his couplets much of Pope's suppleness or resonance, and they fall with a thunderous deadness on the ear. *The Conquest of Canaan* consists of eleven cantos of correct but inert couplets, which Leon Howard has said are "full of eighteenth-century Americans with Hebrew names who talked like Milton's angels and fought like prehistoric Greeks" [see excerpt dated 1943].

Dwight's *Greenfield Hill* . . . was composed in a much more relaxed mood and atmosphere, when he was a pastor in Greenfield, Connecticut. In order to occupy his mind while he took long daily walks, he composed verses that he later dictated to a secretary. Then, to give them some form, he proposed to write a topographical hill poem about the beauties and virtues of his native state. In conception it recalls Denham's *Cooper's Hill,* Dyer's *Grongar Hill,* and Pope's "Windsor Forest," but it is a conglomerate of styles—with echoes of Pope, Milton, and Vergil's *Georgics*—in a variety of verse forms, including blank verse, couplets, octosyllabics, and Spenserian stanzas. The poem's theme is Dwight's rather smug love of his native land, which he compares to a Europe he knew only at second hand through his reading. . . . [His] poem does little to correct the notion of many of his readers that Connecticut was the garden spot of the world. Part Two, **"The Flourishing Village,"** is an imitation of Goldsmith that draws a favorable contrast between America and Europe. Other parts celebrate the beauty of local scenery, the romance of local history, and reflect Dwight's Calvinistic notions of human nature, with an emphasis on its improvement through the cultivation of good habits. The poem ends in the spirit of the times with a section called **"Vision, or Prospect of the Future Happiness of America."**

Dwight's is strictly a minor talent, and it is partly a reflection on his age that his poetry stands out as it does. Although there are some worthwhile passages in *Greenfield Hill,* these are notable more as versified philosophy than as poetry, and the poem as a whole stands as witness more to the wide and varied tastes of the writer than to his gifts as a poet. (pp. 42-4)

> Donald Barlow Stauffer, "The Late Eighteenth Century," in his A Short History of American Poetry, E. P. Dutton & Co., Inc., 1974, pp. 40-59.*

ROBERT D. ARNER   (essay date 1977)

[*In the excerpt below, Arner focuses on the historical accuracy of Dwight's writings and the political climate in which they were written.*]

Like the painter Benjamin West, whose work he interrupts [*The Conquest of Canäan*] to praise, Dwight was powerfully attracted to the grand historical style, believing that a rehearsal of the heroic past could be counted on to hallow the present. Too often, however, he mistakes bombast for heroic diction, and, unlike West, . . . he simply invests actual historical figures with the borrowed garments of biblical personages. The result is a loosely conceived allegory which portrays George Washington as Joshua, the Revolutionary War as the conquest of Canäan; when biblical story proves an unwieldy vehicle for American history, as frequently happens, Dwight drops the allegory and either returns to his expansions of the biblical narrative or goes off in other, mostly romantic and sentimental directions. There were, as the poet himself retrospectively confessed when he attempted to disavow any allegorical intention whatsoever, certain basic problems with the allegory, not the least of which, in Dwight's own words, was the absurdity of imagining "the *Conquest* of a country a proper event, under which to allegorize the defense of another country." It would be nice to say that Dwight's addiction to the historical style ruined him the way it worked against West, John Singleton Copley, and later, Washington Allston, but that represents only one aspect of a larger failure of Dwight's critical and creative sensibilities.

Still, though we may be tempted to write off Dwight's epic experiment, his Miltonic visions couched in Popean couplets,

as merely another instance of the American artist's attraction for European formulae or of the Anglo-American cultural lag (the epic, after all, was dead before Dwight attempted the *Conquest*), that explanation does not seem adequate to account for his intentions. That Dwight chose to employ the epic even though he must have known it was a moribund genre seems to reflect his awareness of the differences between recent American and British history as much as or perhaps more than it indicates a wrong-headed persistence in the attempt to resurrect a dead literary mode. Viewed in one light, the reemergence of the epic in the early Republic—in the works of Barlow, Freneau, and others as well as in Dwight—simply represents a collective anachronism; viewed another way, it suggests the American's consciousness of the distinction between a waxing and a waning empire, his search for a literary model appropriate to the birth of a nation. . . . Dwight was attempting to accomplish for America what Vergil's *Aeneid* accomplished for Augustan Rome, the simultaneous (and somewhat paradoxical) rehearsal of a national past as a means of rescuing it, in the faith in a fresh beginning, from the gloom of history. For Dwight's Puritan predecessors, biblical parallels were designed to elevate the colonial enterprise and to stress historical and mythic continuities as counters to geographical isolation. Near the end of the eighteenth century, when descendants of the Puritans faced an even more traumatic dislocation from the mother country, it is not surprising that they responded quickly by institutionalizing the quest for their own past in the foundation of state and regional historical societies. Such history as could not be discovered would have to be created, and the *Conquest* is Dwight's contribution to that larger national effort. (pp. 241-42)

Like *The Anarchiad,* which may have helped to inspire it, [*The Triumph of Infidelity*] forecasts the restoration of Satan's kingdom in America. The argument is buttressed by an historical overview of infidelism in the past and an account of its rise in America, a rise aided, somewhat surprisingly for the patriotic Dwight, by the success of the Revolution; paradoxically, cutting adrift from Europe meant an increasing dependence upon its ideas. Though the enemies include the Boston minister Charles Chauncy, the attack focuses mainly on European heretics of one cast or another: Priestley, Hume, Voltaire, and others. Besides this general disproportion among Dwight's "villains," the poem is flawed by a perplexing conclusion which sees Satan "proud with triumph" and yet defeated and "enrag'd." Doubtless this confusing close had something to do with Dwight's friend's, Noah Webster's, dismissal of the anonymous work as a "jumble of unmeaning epithets . . ." [see excerpt from the *American Magazine* dated 1788]. (p. 243)

Rather loosely unified by what can be seen or summoned into memory from the elevation of Greenfield Hill, the name of Dwight's rural parish in Fairfield, Connecticut, [*Greenfield Hill*] presents in seven sections the poet's vision of what all America might be: peaceful, pastoral, and above all Congregationalist. The styles of the seven sections are altered to reflect the changing moods of each part, in imitation of William Mason's *Museus* . . . : **"The Prospect"** is written in the blank verse of James Thomson's *The Seasons* . . . : **"The Flourishing Village"** in response to *The Deserted Village;* **"The Burning of Fairfield,"** an historical flashback, in octosyllabic couplets; **"The Destruction of the Pequods,"** a page from Puritan history, in Spenserian stanzas; **"The Clergyman's Advice to the Villagers,"** in octosyllabics once again; **"The Farmer's Advice to the Villagers,"** reminiscent of Franklin's proverbial style, again in octosyllabics; and **"The Vision"** in heroic couplets. Though the poem rests heavily upon English traditions, as this synopsis of its styles makes clear, it bears affinities also to some of Puritan literature, particularly Samuel Sewall's celebration of Plum Island near the end of *Phaenomena quaedam apocalyptica.* . . . (pp. 243-44)

[In section two of *Greenfield Hill,* entitled **"The Flourishing Village,"**] Dwight focuses attention upon the evil that will again divide the nation long after the breach between Federalist and republican has been repaired. Yet he is less than honest about the institution of slavery in America, and like his political opposite Freneau, he displaces criticism of the slave system to the British West Indies rather than striking at the American South. Freneau's reticence may have stemmed from his wish to avoid controversy in an effort to keep the infant country unified; Dwight's comes from a conviction that emancipation is already underway in Connecticut and will be accomplished when the slave is ready for it. . . . Dwight is not especially concerned with the South, for he has written off that area of the country long ago. His praises and predictions hold true not for the nation, but only for the society in and around Greenfield Hill. Thus the apparent contradiction between the gloomy tone of the *Triumph* and the hopeful one of *Greenfield Hill* turns out to be no contradiction at all, but the result of Dwight's imaginative diminishing of the boundaries of America. Only Connecticut and a few other select parts of New England fulfill or promise to fulfill the American dream. (pp. 244-45)

Robert D. Arner, "The Connecticut Wits," in American Literature, 1764-1789: The Revolutionary Years, *edited by Everett Emerson, The University of Wisconsin Press, 1977, pp. 233-52.**

ADDITIONAL BIBLIOGRAPHY

[Dwight, Sereno E.] "Memoir of the Life of President Dwight." In *Theology Explained and Defended in a Series of Sermons,* Vol. I, 12th ed., by Timothy Dwight, pp. 3-61. New York: Harper & Brothers, Publishers, 1850.
    An anecdotal sketch of Dwight's life, written by one of his sons.

Elliott, Emory. "Timothy Dwight: Pastor, Poet, and Politics." In his *Revolutionary Writers: Literature and Authority in the New Republic, 1725-1810,* pp. 55-91. New York: Oxford University Press, 1982.
    A survey of Dwight's life, works, and political involvement. Elliott concludes that although Dwight was not the best writer of his age, he remains significant for his influence as a social leader.

Lee, Robert Edson. "Timothy Dwight and the Boston *Palladium.*" *The New England Quarterly* XXXV, No. 2 (June 1962): 229-39.
    Identifies Dwight as the author of several poems and essays published anonymously in the Boston *Palladium* and discusses these writings in relation to his religious and political beliefs.

Volkomer, Walter E. "Timothy Dwight and New England Federalism." *The Connecticut Review* 3, No. 2 (April 1970): 72-82.
    Contrasts Dwight's Federalist political beliefs with the dominant political currents of his time. According to Volkomer, Dwight's ideas on government, particularly his opposition to democracy, "represent the degeneracy of Federalism and show the intellectual reasons for the decline and final disappearance of the political party."

George Eliot

1819-1880

(Pseudonym of Mary Ann (or Marian) Evans) English novelist, essayist, poet, editor, short story writer, and translator.

The following entry presents criticism of Eliot's novel *Middlemarch: A Study of Provincial Life* (1871-72). For additional information on Eliot's career and *Middlemarch*, see *NCLC*, Vol. 4.

Middlemarch is considered Eliot's finest achievement and one of the greatest novels in the English language. A work so vast in scope that it is frequently compared to Leo Tolstoy's *War and Peace*, *Middlemarch* presents the most comprehensive picture of provincial life in English fiction. The breadth of the social world depicted in *Middlemarch* is paralleled by the variety of intellectual and moral issues treated in the novel. In developing the novel's main theme—the relationship of the individual to society—Eliot skillfully combined four separate plot strands that together reflect her wide-ranging interests in psychology, history, philosophy, science, and religion. Throughout *Middlemarch*, Eliot scrupulously analyzes her characters and examines their effect upon the moral fabric of the community. In its psychological realism, as well as its intellectual depth, *Middlemarch* has profoundly influenced the development of the modern novel.

A knowledge of Eliot's life and career contributes to an understanding of the development of *Middlemarch*, its themes, and its critical history. Eliot was born and raised on a farm in Warwickshire, located in the English Midlands. The most important early influence on the author was her friendship with Maria Lewis, one of her teachers at a boarding school in Nuneaton. An ardent Evangelical, Lewis imparted her religious zeal to Eliot. However, after moving to Coventry in 1841 and meeting the sceptical philosophers Charles Bray and Charles Hennell, Eliot began to challenge her Evangelical beliefs. Though she became an agnostic, she continued to espouse the ethical teachings associated with Christianity. Critics frequently note that Eliot's religious crisis closely parallels that of Dorothea Brooke, the heroine of *Middlemarch*.

In 1849, Eliot moved to London, where she met John Chapman, the editor of the *Westminster Review*. He hired Eliot in 1851 as the *Westminster*'s assistant editor, a post she retained until 1854. Through Chapman, Eliot met some of London's leading literary figures, including the versatile writer and intellectual George Henry Lewes, who profoundly affected her career. Lewes and Eliot fell deeply in love, but he was legally prohibited from divorcing his estranged wife. Defying the strict moral code of the Victorian era, Lewes and Eliot openly lived together from 1854 until his death in 1878. The two considered their union a marriage despite its lack of legal sanction; in fact, Eliot assumed the name Marian Evans Lewes. Her relationship with Lewes outraged her family, and she rarely communicated with them until a few months before her death, when she married John Walter Cross, a longtime friend.

Lewes's influence on Eliot's writings was great: he encouraged her first efforts at fiction and remained her most ardent supporter during their years together. In addition, it was Lewes who brought Eliot's first work of fiction, a collection of short

stories entitled *Scenes of Clerical Life*, to the attention of John Blackwood, who published it as well as most of her other books. *Scenes of Clerical Life* was followed by a number of extremely popular novels, all of which were written under the pseudonym of George Eliot. Eliot's early novels—*Adam Bede, The Mill on the Floss,* and *Silas Marner*—are largely autobiographical accounts of English rural life that display her characteristic interest in moral questions. In her later works—*Romola, Felix Holt, Middlemarch,* and *Daniel Deronda*—Eliot drew less on her experiences in Warwickshire, although both *Middlemarch* and the political novel *Felix Holt* are set in the English Midlands during the early nineteenth century.

The genesis of *Middlemarch* is well documented in Eliot's letters and journals, in the notebooks she kept around the time of the novel's composition, and in the *Middlemarch* manuscript. These sources reveal that the novel's two main characters, Dorothea Brooke and Tertius Lydgate, were conceived at different times and originally destined for two separate works. In August, 1869, Eliot began a novel called "Middlemarch" that was to focus on Lydgate, an idealistic young doctor whose hopes of establishing a progressive hospital in the town of Middlemarch are thwarted by the social preoccupations of his wife, Rosamond. Work progressed slowly, and in December, 1870, Eliot started a novel entitled "Miss Brooke," whose heroine, Dorothea, was to be portrayed as a modern-day English St. Theresa who has difficulty accomplishing her altruistic goals in a provincial society. Recognizing the stories' thematic similarities, Eliot began fusing them into one novel under the title *Middlemarch: A Study of Provincial Life* early in 1871. The histories of Dorothea and Lydgate form the dominant interest of *Middlemarch*, but they are interwoven with two other stories—those of Nicholas Bulstrode and Mary Garth—that also describe confrontations between society and individual aspiration. In combination, the four plot strands present a complex vision of all strata of English provincial society in the years immediately preceding the passage of the First Reform Bill of 1832. *Middlemarch* was first published in *Blackwood's Edinburgh Magazine* in eight separate installments between December, 1871, and December, 1872. The novel was an enormous commercial success, prompting Eliot to remark in her journal that "no former book of mine has been received with more enthusiasm—not even *Adam Bede*."

Because the critical history of *Middlemarch* is closely linked to that of Eliot's other novels, a grasp of the major trends in Eliot criticism is considered essential to an understanding of the fluctuating response to *Middlemarch*. After the success of *Adam Bede*, contemporary reaction to Eliot's fiction was voluminous and mostly positive. While she was regarded as the leading English novelist during the last years of her life, it was common at this time to differentiate between her early and late work and to prefer the former. Reviewers almost unanimously agreed that Eliot's later novels were overly philosophic and didactic, lacking the spontaneity and charm of her early autobiographical works. Consequently, the esteem in which *Middlemarch* was held was already in decline by 1885, when Cross published a biography of the author in which the Eliot of the later novels—the Victorian sage—predominated. Cross's work, in combination with the late Victorian revolt against "the-novel-with-a-purpose," diminished her reputation at the end of the nineteenth century. As early as 1901, W. C. Brownell was able to ask, "How long has it been since George Eliot's name has been the subject of even a literary allusion?" During the next three decades, Eliot's works attracted very little scholarly attention. It was not until the 1940s that her novels, particularly the later ones, returned to favor. Since then, *Middlemarch* has been the subject of extensive examination.

Critical response to *Middlemarch* has varied considerably since Eliot's death. Contemporary commentary focused on its characterization, structure, and philosophy. Early reviewers were favorably impressed by the novel overall, despite some reservations: many praised *Middlemarch*'s realistic characters and panoramic scope, but faulted its incoherent construction. This view was expressed by Henry James in his now-famous comment, "*Middlemarch* is a treasure-house of details, but it is an indifferent whole" (see *NCLC*, Vol. 4). Like several other commentators, however, James acknowledged that it was perhaps unfair to judge the structure of *Middlemarch* by conventional standards; noting the novel's abundant philosophical digressions, he asked, "If we write novels so, how shall we write History?" The exact nature of *Middlemarch*'s philosophy proved to be a subject of great controversy. Many reviewers had difficulty determining whether the novel was a study of human inadequacy or an examination of the effects of provincial life on individual character. One source of this confusion, critics agreed, was the consistent irony in the presentation of the characters, which obscured Eliot's stance on the issue of free will and determinism. R. H. Hutton, among others, offered a second explanation for the confusion, arguing that a passage in the novel's "Finale" that blames Middle-

march society for Dorothea's mistakes is not supported by the rest of the text. In response to this criticism, Eliot deleted the passage in the 1874 edition of the novel, which is now considered the standard version.

With the decline in Eliot's overall reputation at the turn of the century came a consequent devaluation of *Middlemarch*. During the first four decades of the twentieth century, few critics wrote on the novel, and those who did often relied on the traditional distinction between Eliot's early and late work. In an essay that the recent critic Kerry McSweeney termed "the swansong of the turn-of-the-century depreciations of her work," Edmund Gosse dismissed *Middlemarch* as a "remarkable instance of elaborate mental resources misapplied." Leslie Stephen and Oliver Elton also recognized Eliot's intellectual preoccupations as a limitation, but discussed *Middlemarch* more sympathetically. Virginia Woolf (see *NCLC*, Vol. 4) was among the handful of commentators during this period to challenge the distinction between Eliot's early and late novels. Woolf maintained that Eliot's genius climaxed in *Middlemarch*, praising its intellectual power and describing it as "one of the few English novels written for grown-up people."

Modern criticism of *Middlemarch* begins in the late 1940s, when several scholars attempted to reverse the Victorian preference for Eliot's early novels. Of these critics, the most important was F. R. Leavis (see *NCLC*, Vol. 4). Arguing that Eliot's intellectual and moral preoccupations were an essential element of her creative vision, Leavis praised her penetrating character analysis in *Middlemarch* and labeled it her greatest work. Since the late 1940s, studies of *Middlemarch* have proliferated. Among the most frequently discussed topics are the novel's structure, imagery, narrative perspective, themes, characterization, treatment of women, and intellectual background.

The complexity of *Middlemarch* is underscored by many recent scholars, whose interpretations often document how Eliot employed a combination of literary techniques to create a unified work. While some modern commentary on the construction of *Middlemarch* has echoed the judgment of Eliot's contemporaries who described it as a poorly organized collection of stories, many scholars have attempted to show that the work's coherence derives from the complementary relationship of its structure, themes, and imagery. This view was articulated by Reva Stump, who discussed how web imagery in *Middlemarch* both supports a structure made up of many plot strands and underscores the theme of the interdependence of human lives. In another favorable study of *Middlemarch*'s design, Barbara Hardy examined how Eliot used structural parallels and contrasts to reveal differences in the characters' moral attitudes. Hardy also argued that the novel's four corresponding plots allowed Eliot to create a wide variety of characters who give weight and presence to the community of Middlemarch. This view is shared by most recent commentators, who frequently describe *Middlemarch* as a social document of English provincial life in the early nineteenth century. Underlying most laudatory assessments of the novel's social breadth is implicit praise for its realistic characters; many critics have suggested that Eliot's painstaking psychological analysis influenced the work of such later novelists as D. H. Lawrence and Joseph Conrad. Character studies of *Middlemarch* have focused most often on Dorothea. Many modern critics have examined Eliot's attitude toward her to determine whether society or Dorothea herself is responsible for her failure to achieve her idealistic goals. While most commentators argue that Eliot's gently mocking but sympathetic presentation of Dorothea indicates that neither she nor society is wholly to blame, several feminist commentators have viewed her situation in a different light. Kathleen Blake held that *Middlemarch* was a "great feminist work" because, through Dorothea's story, Eliot castigates societal conditions that prevent women from working. Conversely, Lee R. Edwards faulted Eliot for neglecting to provide an outlet other than marriage for Dorothea's energies. At least one critic, K. M. Newton, has analyzed the Romantic aspects of Dorothea's character. According to Newton, Dorothea's discovery that Christianity cannot be proved scientifically and her subsequent realization that her own feelings are a source of religious meaning imply that Eliot favored a Romantic approach to knowledge over an Enlightenment approach.

As Newton's analysis suggests, the intellectual background of *Middlemarch* is a subject of great interest to recent critics, who have analyzed the novel's incorporation of historical, scientific, and medical information. In one such study, U. C. Knoepflmacher explored how Eliot used allusion and myth to expose the limitations of Lydgate's empiricist view of reality. In another essay on the novel's scientific underpinnings, Karen Chase discussed Eliot's perception of the relationship between the mind and the body. Most scholars concur that *Middlemarch* is unsurpassed among nineteenth-century novels in its intellectual depth. While this offers an explanation for the tremendous variety of interpretations that the work continues to inspire, critics stress that Eliot's great achievement in *Middlemarch* rests on her ability to blend a profusion of complex issues into an artistic whole. As Knoepflmacher stated, "George Eliot successfully transmuted ideas into the form and structure of her novel; . . . this transmutation is in itself a key to her art." Modern in its intellectual sweep as well as in its approach to character, *Middlemarch* is consistently recognized for its influence upon the development of the novel. Its status as one of the greatest novels in the English language is affirmed by Hilda Hulme's enthusiasm for the work: "Every novel would be *Middlemarch* if it could."

(See also *Dictionary of Literary Biography*, Vol. 21: *Victorian Novelists before 1885;* Vol. 35: *Victorian Poets after 1850.*)

JOHN BLACKWOOD   (letter date 1871)

[*Blackwood was Eliot's publisher and, next to Lewes, did most to encourage her efforts at fiction. Here, Blackwood praises the manuscript version of Book II of* Middlemarch. *Eliot responds to Blackwood's letter in the excerpt below.*]

I have read the second portion of *Middlemarch* with the greatest admiration. It is a most wonderful study of human life and nature. You are like a great giant walking about among us and fixing every one you meet upon your canvas. In all this life like gallery that you put before us every trait in every character finds an echo or recollection in the reader's mind that tells him how true it is to Nature.

It was a disappointment at first not to find any of my old friends of the former part, all except Lydgate apparently entirely strangers, but as you beautifully express it we never know who are to influence our lives while "Destiny stands by sarcastic with our dramatis personae folded in her hand." The elaborate picture of the formation of Lydgate's character is powerfully

relieved by the tremendous French adventure into which the wise young Doctor fell. It would be endless to try to refer to all the happy hits and turns. That sylph caught young and made perfect by Mrs. Lemon is a great success, and I like poor Ned. Where did you hear those horsey men talking? . . . You have caught the very tone.

The Farebrother family are delights, a perfect picture. Reading of all the various characters in this second volume—for it is really almost a volume—I had quite forgotten Mr. Brooke, but I *knew his voice* the moment he came into the room at the meeting for the election of Chaplain. There is something uncommonly good about Mary Garth who has her "peculiar temptations" not to accept "good sense and good principle" "ready mixed" and does feel it hard to think that she must be called "an ugly thing" alongside of fair Rosamond.

I think our plan of publication is the right one as the two parts are almost distinct, each complete in itself. Indeed there will be complaints of the want of the continuous interest of a story, but this does not matter where all is so fresh and true to life. Each group that you introduce is a complete little book or study in itself. I return the precious M.S. registered. . . . When you can spare the M.S. I should like to have the quantity calculated. I am pretty sure there is equivalent to a volume of an ordinary novel in what I now return. (pp. 167-68)

> *John Blackwood, in a letter to George Eliot on July 20, 1871, in* The George Eliot Letters, 1869-1873; *Vol. V, edited by Gordon S. Haight, Yale University Press, 1955, pp. 167-68.*

M. E. LEWES   (letter date 1871)

[*Shortly after moving in with Lewes, Eliot adopted the name Marian Evans Lewes for her correspondence. Here, she responds to Blackwood (see excerpt above), who had commented on the manuscript version of Book II of* Middlemarch. *Her remarks display her concern with the design and wholeness of the novel.*]

Thanks for the prompt return of the M.S. . . . I have just been making a calculation of the pages and I find, on a liberal estimate, that this second portion is about 190 pp. of the size you usually give to my novels—I think, 25 lines per page, is it not? **"Miss Brooke"** being about 150 pp. the two parts together would be equal to the larger volumes of *Adam Bede* and *The Mill,* which are at least 350 pp. if my memory may be trusted.

Mr. Lewes has been saying that it may perhaps be well to take in a portion of Part II at the end of Part I. But it is too early for such definite arrangements. I don't see how I can leave anything out, because I hope there is nothing that will be seen to be irrelevant to my design, which is to show the gradual action of ordinary causes rather than exceptional, and to show this in some directions which have not been from time immemorial the beaten path—the Cremorne walks and shows of fiction. But the best intentions are good for nothing until execution has justified them. And you know I am always compassed about with fears. I am in danger in all my designs of parodying dear Goldsmith's satire on Burke, and think of refining when novel readers only think of skipping. (pp. 168-69)

> *M. E. Lewes, in a letter to John Blackwood on July 24, 1871, in* The George Eliot Letters, 1869-1873, *Vol. V, edited by Gordon S. Haight, Yale University Press, 1955, pp. 168-69.*

GEORGE ELIOT   (essay date 1871)

[*In the "Prelude" to* Middlemarch, *reprinted below, Eliot characterizes Dorothea as a modern-day St. Theresa; this introduction to the work is the point of departure for many critical discussions of the novel. The "Prelude" was first published in* Blackwood's Edinburgh Magazine *on December 1, 1871.*]

Who that cares much to know the history of man, and how the mysterious mixture behaves under the varying experiments of Time, has not dwelt, at least briefly, on the life of Saint Theresa, has not smiled with some gentleness at the thought of the little girl walking forth one morning hand-in-hand with her still smaller brother, to go and seek martyrdom in the country of the Moors? Out they toddled from rugged Avila, wide-eyed and helpless-looking as two fawns, but with human hearts, already beating to a national idea; until domestic reality met them in the shape of uncles, and turned them back from their great resolve. That child-pilgrimage was a fit beginning. Theresa's passionate, ideal nature demanded an epic life: what were many-volumed romances of chivalry and the social conquests of a brilliant girl to her? Her flame quickly burned up that light fuel; and, fed from within, soared after some illimitable satisfaction, some object which would never justify weariness, which would reconcile self-despair with the rapturous consciousness of life beyond self. She found her epos in the reform of a religious order.

That Spanish woman who lived three hundred years ago was certainly not the last of her kind. Many Theresas have been born who found for themselves no epic life wherein there was a constant unfolding of far-resonant action; perhaps only a life of mistakes, the offspring of a certain spiritual grandeur ill-matched with the meanness of opportunity; perhaps a tragic failure which found no sacred poet and sank unwept into oblivion. With dim lights and tangled circumstance they tried to shape their thought and deed in noble agreement; but after all, to common eyes their struggles seemed mere inconsistency and formlessness; for these later-born Theresas were helped by no coherent social faith and order which could perform the function of knowledge for the ardently willing soul. Their ardour alternated between a vague ideal and the common yearning of womanhood; so that the one was disapproved as extravagance, and the other condemned as a lapse.

Some have felt that these blundering lives are due to the inconvenient indefiniteness with which the Supreme Power has fashioned the natures of women: if there were one level of feminine incompetence as strict as the ability to count three and no more, the social lot of women might be treated with scientific certitude. Meanwhile the indefiniteness remains, and the limits of variation are really much wider than any one would imagine from the sameness of women's coiffure and the favourite love-stories in prose and verse. Here and there a cygnet is reared uneasily among the ducklings in the brown pond, and never finds the living stream in fellowship with its own oary-footed kind. Here and there is born a Saint Theresa, foundress of nothing, whose loving heart-beats and sobs after an unattained goodness tremble off and are dispersed among hindrances, instead of centering in some long-recognizable deed. (pp. 25-6)

> *George Eliot, in her* Middlemarch, *edited by W. J. Harvey, Penguin Books, 1985, 908 p.*

M. E. LEWES   (letter date 1872)

[*In the following excerpt from a letter to Alexander Main, Eliot questions whether readers will correctly interpret* Middlemarch.]

I need not tell you that [*Middlemarch*] will not present my own feeling about human life if it produces on readers whose minds are really receptive the impression of blank melancholy and despair. I can't help wondering at the high estimate made of *Middlemarch* in proportion to my other books. I suppose the depressed state of my health makes my writing seem more than usually below the mark of my desires, and I am too anxious about its completion—too fearful lest the impression which it might make (I mean for the good of those who read) should turn to nought—to look at it in mental sunshine. (p. 261)

> *M. E. Lewes, in a letter to Alexander Main on March 29, 1872, in* The George Eliot Letters, 1869-1873, *Vol. V, edited by Gordon S. Haight, Yale University Press, 1955, pp. 260-62.*

M. E. LEWES   (letter date 1872)

[*In this excerpt from a letter to Main, Eliot discusses her creative process, stating that* Middlemarch *is organically complete.*]

I have finished [*Middlemarch*] and am thoroughly at peace about it—not because I am convinced of its perfection, but because I have lived to give out what it was in me to give and have not been hindered by illness or death from making my work a whole, such as it is. When a subject has begun to grow in me I suffer terribly until it has wrought itself out—become a complete organism; and then it seems to take wing and go away from me. That thing is not to be done again—that life has been lived. I could not rest with a number of unfinished works on my mind. When they—or rather, when a conception has begun to shape itself in written words, I feel that it must go on to the end before I can be happy about it. Then I move away and look at it from a distance without any agitations. (p. 324)

> *M. E. Lewes, in a letter to Alexander Main on November 4, 1872, in* The George Eliot Letters, 1869-1873, *Vol. V, edited by Gordon S. Haight, Yale University Press, 1955, pp. 323-25.*

[W. L. COLLINS]   (essay date 1872)

[*Collins praises* Middlemarch's *reverent religious tone and sympathetic characters. Although Lewes generally shielded Eliot from reviews of her writings because he feared that adverse criticism would stifle her creativity, he approved of Collins's remarks and showed them to Eliot. She was also pleased by the review (see excerpt dated December 1, 1872).*]

It is difficult to say how far the large circle of readers who hailed with keen delight the announcement of a new novel by "George Eliot," will be satisfied with that writer for having adopted the tantalising expedient of issuing [*Middlemarch*] by instalments—a single "book" at a time.... If any work of fiction can bear the being read in portions without injury to its effect, it is one which, like the present, is really not so much a novel as a narrative which is made the vehicle of careful studies of character, fine and discriminating satire, and original thought clothed in the most finished and epigrammatic language. Regarded in this point of view, each "book" of *Middlemarch* is complete in itself. But thorough justice will not have been done to the work until it has been read through a second time as a whole—an experiment which very few will grudge to make. (p. 727)

The course of the story takes us very much into the borough town of Middlemarch, and the provincial magnates who make up society there. And here, we need hardly say, the peculiar and inimitable force with which, avoiding anything like caricature, ''George Eliot'' brings before us the characteristics of English middle-class life is fully exemplified. It may be that those smoother and more refined circles in which everything is cut, more or less, to an artificial and uniform pattern, and where few things are more dreaded than the imputation of oddity, present less attractive matter to an original artist; since one modern drawing-room scene and conversation may be and is multiplied by fifty in our popular novels with but very slight modifications. But it is also clear that this writer has a special faculty of observation, and a special taste for the reproduction, of the salient features of country town and village life, with a quick perception both of the humour and the pathos with which it abounds. And when we get fairly into the town, and are admitted to the hospitable board of Mrs. Vincy, the mayor's wife (herself an innkeeper's daughter, though she has a son at Oxford affecting expensive society and spending his money therein, as innkeepers' grandsons are rather apt to do), or when we are set down at old invalid Mr. Featherstone's churlish fireside, we feel that we have got into a fresher atmosphere and more amusing company, even if not quite so select as Mr. Fred Vincy the Oxonian might desire. There are a dozen rapid dashes of character among these Middlemarch notabilities, whose sayings and doings occupy but a very few pages here and there in the volumes, but each with individuality enough thrown into them to set up an industrious writer with characters for three or four separate novels, if he carefully worked them out. Not that these people are what are sometimes called ''characters'' or ''originals'' at all; they have no eccentricities of behaviour, and no recurrent phrases or turns of speech at which we are expected to laugh every time they appear on the scene. (pp. 734-35)

The curious thing about all these sketches is that they are people whom most of us have known under some other name, only we failed to catch the humorous aspect of their being. We thought them prosaic, not to say vulgar; when, lo! they were full of poetry,—to the poet. (p. 735)

Theological colour these volumes have none. Professions of a creed may seem to be even purposely avoided. But no one can say that their tone is other than reverent on religious questions. The unrealities of religion, whether they take the shape of formal act or fluent profession, are touched with a satire whose lash is not the less cutting because it is laid on with the most delicate wrist-play. People ''whose celestial intimacies seem not to improve their domestic manners,'' who contrive ''to conciliate piety and worldliness, the nothingness of this life and the desirability of cut glass, the consciousness at once of filthy rags and the best damask,'' find no mercy here. And whether the old miser Peter Featherstone seeks, as he declares in his will, ''to please God Almighty'' by building almshouses, or Mr. Bulstrode attempts ''an act of restitution which may move Divine Providence to avert painful consequences,'' the touch of honest scorn in the brief phrases is more effective than a homily. And nowhere, read where we will, shall we find less religious narrowness, or a fuller confession of the spiritual needs of human nature. Indeed, the cry of the soul after something more satisfying than the mere husks of worldly well-doing and success seems uttered in these volumes with an intensity which is almost painful. True, we have no distinct ideal set up and recommended as really attainable; rather—and this gives to the work that remarkable tinge of melancholy

which has been remarked, in spite of all their grace and humour, in most of its predecessors from the same hand—we are allowed to gather that for the most part ideals are unattainable, and that the highest aspirations only serve to give a grandeur to the failure in which they inevitably end. . . . Take the characters in these volumes: all who set before them an object in life higher than their fellows, fail in its attainment. Casaubon is a failure, Dorothea is a failure, Lydgate is a failure more than all. It might seem, at first thought, as though the moral were as cynical as this—if you would escape disappointment, you must not seek to rise above the level of your fellow-creatures. It is Celia, with her kitten-like content and hatred of ''notions,''—Sir James Chettam, who ''doesn't go much into ideas,''—Will Ladislaw, with his amiable vagabond dilettantism, who looks upon all forms of prescribed work as 'harness,' and holds genius to be ''necessarily intolerant of fetters,''—Fred Vincy, with his goodhumoured gentlemanlike selfishness,—who come out, on the whole, with the largest share of commonplace happiness. But we are much mistaken if such be the moral which the author—if any moral be intended or permissible—would have us draw. The lines may be read another way. To have an ideal at which we aim, and that ideal of the highest kind, is the worthy life and the true life, though not of necessity that which attains its object or wins content. It is better to fail than to succeed, if the aim has been noble in the one case, and mean in the other. Our full sympathies remain with the aspirants in their failures—even because of their failures—not with the lower natures in their placid ruminant life. (p. 737)

There is one observation which strikes us more forcibly in reading these volumes than in any others which have come to us from the same hand. It is the power which the writer shows in awakening, not only our interest in, but our sympathies with, nearly all the prominent characters in the full drama of the story. In most novels, there is at least some one creation of the author's fancy on whose brightness a shadow is seldom allowed to fall, in whose cause we become partisans, and whose greatest weaknesses are cleverly excused. Or, if the hero or heroine are not so near perfection in the outset, some discipline or other is introduced in the course of the story, which in the end completes and purifies the character. And in some sense, if the novelist is to be regarded as a moral teacher, this seems in accordance with the fitness of things. But such is by no means the principle upon which the author of *Middlemarch* works. We find in the volumes nothing of the conventional hero or heroine. As, even in the most disagreeable characters, we are shown in almost every instance the good that is working in them fitfully here and there, so in the portraits of the favourites the shadows are not left out. The only personages in the story with whom we are never angry or disappointed are those in whom we are never called upon to take any very lively interest—who have not character enough to involve contradictions—such as Sir James Chettam and Celia. Dorothea provokes us continually in the first book, until we scarcely pity her, though we can foresee much of the result, when she marries Casaubon; there is an epicurean selfishness about Lydgate, in spite of his nobler aspirations, which makes us feel that the lower form of selfishness in others from which he is made to suffer has in it something of retributive justice; Ladislaw is full of weaknesses and irresolution. On the other hand, there is no one who acts thoroughly the ''villain'' in the piece; Rosamond, who most rouses our indignation, is after all more contemptible than hateful; there is no one in whose frustrated designs the virtuous reader . . . feels the sort of triumph which David proclaims over his enemies. Casaubon, with all his pedantic narrowness, is, perhaps, the most pathetic conception in the book; and when Bulstrode is at last exposed and makes his miserable exit, so intensely have we been made to feel the mental agony and bitter humiliation of the man, that we are inclined to take his arm, as Lydgate does, and help him to his carriage. The creatures are all so intensely human, even in their baser aspects, that in spite of that seven-fold shield of virtue behind which we shelter ourselves, . . . when we sit in judgment on the characters of fiction, an honest conscience hesitates to cast the stone. (p. 743)

[We] take our leave of a work which, if it stood alone, would have made an era in the literature of fiction. Following, as it does, a series of acknowledged masterpieces from the same hand, which gave a new character to the English "novel," it would have been much to have been able to say that it maintained the reputation of its author. But we shall be surprised if the mature judgment passed upon it by those who can appreciate the work of a true artist—and we will admit that these may not be the majority of mere novel readers—does not pronounce it the most perfect of the series. (p. 745)

> [*W. L. Collins*], *in a review of "Middlemarch," in* Blackwood's Edinburgh Magazine, *Vol. CXII, No. DCLXXXVI, December, 1872, pp. 727-45.*

M. E. LEWES (letter date 1872)

[*In the following excerpt from a letter to Blackwood, Eliot expresses her satisfaction with Collins's review of* Middlemarch *(see excerpt dated 1872).*]

[Mr. Lewes expressed] to me his satisfaction (and he is very hard to satisfy with articles on me) in the genuineness of judgment, wise moderation, and excellent selection of points, in Maga's review of *Middlemarch.* I have just now been reading the review myself (Mr. Lewes had meant at first to follow his rule of not allowing me to see what is written about myself) and am pleased to find the right moral note struck everywhere both in remark and quotation. Especially, I am pleased with the writer's sensibility to the pathos in Mr. Casaubon's character and position, and with the discernment he shows about Bulstrode. But it is a perilous matter to approve the praise which is given to our own doings. (p. 334)

> *M. E. Lewes, in a letter to John Blackwood on December 1, 1872, in* The George Eliot Letters, 1869-1873, *Vol. V, edited by Gordon S. Haight, Yale University Press, 1955, pp. 334-35.*

THE SATURDAY REVIEW, LONDON (essay date 1872)

[*This anonymous critic praises the truthfulness and variety of* Middlemarch's *characters. However, the reviewer charges that the novel is overly didactic and states that Eliot judges some of her characters too harshly in the interest of advancing the story's moral.*]

If we are to call *Middlemarch* a novel at all, we may say that as a didactic novel it has scarcely been equalled. Never before have so keen and varied an observation, so deep an insight into character and motives, so strong a grasp of conceptions, such power of picturesque description, worked together to represent through the agency of fiction an author's moral and social views. But the reservation we have implied is a broad one. No talent, not genius itself, can quite overcome the inherent defect of a conspicuous, constantly prominent lesson, or bridge over

the disparity between the storyteller with an ulterior aim ever before his own eyes and the reader's, and the ideal storyteller whose primary impulse is a story to tell, and human nature to portray—not human nature as supporting a theory, but human nature as he sees it. The same reader who gives himself in unreserved trust to the master of humour and pathos whose object is to please him by his art, is justified in suspecting a bias or one-sided estimate of qualities where a moral has to be worked out through human agency. His confidence is disturbed, he is at once put upon his mettle, when the same gifts seem employed to betray him into unconscious, and perhaps unwilling, admissions. Self-respect calls upon him at every turn either to renounce principles and prejudices or to stand up and defend them—attitudes of mind altogether alien from that relaxation which it is the assumed office of fiction to provide for its votaries. Not but that he must be hard to please who cannot, without overtaxing his powers of attention, derive plenty of amusement pure and simple out of *Middlemarch*—all that the ordinary novel-reader reads a novel for; but it would be unjust to so thoughtful, powerful, and earnest a writer to ignore the intention that underlies the whole. And to read such writing and thinking as they ought to be read is a real exercise of mind; especially as we own ourselves, while charmed by inimitable touches of character, and enjoying the author's graces of style and felicity of illustration and allusion, not seldom differing from her views and strictures upon society, and her suggestions for its amendment.

Of course where a moralist and satirist quarrels with society he is very sure to be able to adduce an abundance of facts on his side. The quarrel with humanity in *Middlemarch* is its selfishness, and the quarrel with society is its hollow respectability. Human nature and society are hard things to defend; but care for self up to a point is not identical with selfishness; and respectability which pays its way and conducts itself with external propriety is not hollow in any peculiar sense. And we must say that if our young ladies, repelled by the faint and "neutral" virtues of Celia on the one hand, and the powerfully drawn worldly Rosamond on the other, take to be Dorotheas, with a vow to dress differently from other women, and to regulate their own conduct on the system of a general disapproval of the state of things into which they are born, the world will be a less comfortable world without being a better one.

Dorothea is so noble and striking a character—her charm growing upon us as the story advances—she is so penetrated by a sense of duty, so ardent in her longing to make the world better and happier, that we would not introduce her as an example unfit for general imitation had the ordinary domestic type of woman with whom she is contrasted been drawn by a more friendly hand. Dorothea is born with the temper and the aspirations of a St. Theresa; to her the destinies of mankind, seen by the light of Christianity, made the solicitudes of feminine fashion appear an occupation for Bedlam. She will not ride, because all people cannot afford a horse. She takes no interest in art, because it is the delight of the few beyond the reach of material want. Her strength of opinions, and her propensity to act on them, thus put her from the first at odds with society, which, we are told, expected women to have weak opinions, "while still finding its greatest safeguard in the security that opinions were not acted on." As a foil to these high sentiments, we have her sister Celia, of whom Dorothea says that she never did anything naughty since she was born, and who really never goes contrary to our sense of what is amiable and dutiful in woman; though, not being in the good graces of the author, we are not allowed to find her attractive. Less clever than

Dorothea, she has more worldly wisdom, which means perhaps more instinctive perceptions; and not feeling it her duty to subvert the world, she can take her place in it naturally. But surely it is not every girl's duty to refuse the advantages and pleasures of the condition in which she finds herself because all do not share them. She is not selfish because she is serenely happy in a happy home; and if she does her best to help and alleviate the suffering within her reach, she may comfort herself in the belief that the eye of Providence never sleeps.

It is certain that nothing in human nature in the way of a virtue or a grace will stand a strict analysis unshaken. The analytical mind is logically driven into disparagement.... There is no escape but in the ideal. Perhaps such a state of mind almost leads to hardness where the sympathies are not active—which they are not with our author on first opening her story. Early during its progress we have at times said to ourselves, The subjects and sentiments are tragic, but not the persons; the writer does not identify herself with them. But such a writer too keenly enters into her creations not to become attached to them, and therefore sympathetic; and tenderness for human frailty, and belief in human feeling, with whatever alloy of self, give a pathos to the close which the beginning did not promise.

We have all our especial antipathies among the vices; and the hypocrisy of seeming, the "dwelling in decencies for ever," the cant of selfishness, are the antipathies of George Eliot. As one book of this series followed another, each seemed to say, This is your benevolence, this your learning, this your family life, this your religion! The sleek trust in Providence which easy or grasping selfishness makes its boast is the particular subject of warning and contempt. The carefully elaborated character of Bulstrode, no hypocrite of the common type, but one who sincerely hopes to flatter Divine Justice into condoning the wrong done, and permitting ill-gotten gains to prosper on condition of a certain amount of service done, is a leading instance; but most of the selfishness of *Middlemarch* shelters itself under an assumed appeal from conscience to religion. Whether it be poor Celia justifying her girl's love of pretty things under the test that the necklace she longs for won't interfere with her prayers; or Mr. Brooke excusing a political move with one of his favourite summaries—"Religion, properly speaking, is the dread of a Hereafter"; or Mrs. Waule arguing that for her brother Peter to turn his property into Blue-Coat land was flying in the face of the Almighty that had prospered him, the appeal is uniformly a cover to the real thought or motive, and, as such, a fit subject for the satirist's pen. But every man's religion may be vulgarized if the alloy is too curiously sought for. We like things in groups; our preferences and convictions are tied together by association; but it is not always fair to couple the highest of these with the lowest, as though the same amount and quality of thought and conviction went to each. When we are told that Mrs. Bulstrode and Mrs. Pymdale had the same preferences in silks, patterns of underclothing, china ware, and clergymen, it does not prove the religion represented by the clergyman to be superficial and trivial, though it sounds so in such a conjunction. If *Middlemarch* is melancholy, it is due perhaps to its religion being all duty, without a sufficient admixture of hope. We miss the outlook of blue sky which is as essential to the cheerful portraiture of humanity by the moralist as a glimpse into the open is to the portraiture of art.

In so far as *Middlemarch* is an allegory Mr. Casaubon represents learning as opposed to science. Bunyan's Mr. Bat's-eyes is not more a personification of qualities than is Dorothea's first choice, with his lean person, blinking eyes, white moles, and formal phrases; with talents chiefly of the burrowing kind, carrying his taper among the tombs of the past in diligent exploration; his book, the "Key to all the Mythologies," itself a tomb. Altogether he is a striking figure, though now and then the author scarcely shows herself as entirely at home in his surroundings—for example, in his college jealousies and sorenesses—as we generally find her. As for Dorothea's sudden choice of him for a husband, it is not without precedent in real life.... The more a woman has aims of her own, and a sense of power to carry them out, the less is she guided by the common motives and aspirations of her sex. Personally we can acquiesce in her first choice more readily than in her second. There are two views of Ladislaw, who, we scarcely know on what reasonable grounds, is a great favourite with the author. He charms Dorothea by qualities exactly the reverse of her husband's; by his passionate prodigality of statement; by his ready understanding of her thoughts, which Mr. Casaubon always snubbed as long-exploded opinions, if not heresies; by the sunny brightness of his expression and hair, that seemed to shake out light when he moved his head quickly, "showing poor Mr. Casaubon by contrast altogether rayless"; by his looking an incarnation of the spring which we must suppose he typifies; by his versatility and quick transitions of mood and feeling, being made of such impressionable stuff that the bow of a violin drawn near him cleverly would at one stroke change the aspect of the world for him; by his easy unconventional manners and attitudes, and indifference to the solid goods of life. All these are doubtless attractions. Nature has done much for him, but duty—by which all the other characters of the story are tested—altogether fails in him. He does what he likes, whether right or wrong, to the end of the story; he makes no sacrifices; even his devotion to Dorothea does not preserve him from an unworthy flirtation with his friend Lydgate's wife. He is happy by luck, not desert. Just as devotees of the Virgin are said to be saved at the last moment by a medal worn or a rosary said in her honour, so the chance of his choosing the right woman to worship (though not at the right time) saves him from the consequences of idleness and mere self-pleasing; while poor Lydgate—ten times the better man—suffers not only in happiness, but in his noblest ambitions, and sinks to the lower level of a good practice and a good income because he marries and is faithful to the vain selfish creature whom Ladislaw merely flirts with. We daresay, however, it is inevitable that a grand woman who never in her life called things by the same name as other people should not match in her own degree. There is quite enough of the vagabond in Ladislaw, in spite of his remote kinship with Mr. Casaubon, to make Mrs. Cadwallader's judgment stick by one, that Dorothea might as well marry an Italian with white mice; for the author spares us nothing, and allows his enemies to sum up his genealogy—"the son of a Polish fiddler, and grandson of a thieving Jew pawnbroker." It is the man, not his antecedents, that the ideal woman cares for. But, after all, what is the example she sets? How does it differ from the ball-room choice of any ordinary girl who takes the pleasant fellow who pleases her fancy? not that it is reasonable to require or to expect her to make the same sort of mistake twice over....

The book is like a portrait gallery. From Mr. Brooke with his ingenious summaries, his universal experience, and never failing reservations—highly amusing to the reader, but more tolerated in his circle than the ordinary feeling of human nature towards bores makes quite natural—to the wonderful group of hungry expectants gathered round the miser's death-bed, voice, eyes, movement, physiognomy, all are photographed from the life. Though here we must point out some prejudices, as we would fain suppose them, which make the author hard upon natural distinctions of eye and complexion. All her weak and mean and knavish people are blond, as she calls fair-skinned: and blue eyes are uniformly disingenuous. The acutest observer is not free from prepossession. But what a ceaselessly busy observation; what nicety of penetration; what a tenacity of memory are indicated by these different social pictures! All the gradations of rank and class, nicely measured and appreciated, even while the distinctions of rank are represented as provoking the low ambition of common souls, and therefore things to be overstepped by natures of higher insight and more universal good will. In such questions the book is a deliberate challenge to society as at present constituted. (pp. 733-34)

> *A review of "Middlemarch," in* The Saturday Review, *London, Vol. 34, No. 893, December 7, 1872, pp. 733-34.*

SIDNEY COLVIN (essay date 1873)

[*In this excerpt from an appreciative review of* Middlemarch, *Colvin argues that Eliot "rouses" the attention of readers with an approach to character that is intellectual, psychological, and scientific. Yet, Colvin states, the novel does not "satisfy" readers because its teachings are ambiguous.*]

Fifteen months of pausing and recurring literary excitement are at an end; and *Middlemarch,* the chief English book of the immediate present, lies complete before us. Now that we have the book as a whole, what place does it seem to take among the rest with which its illustrious writer has enriched, I will not say posterity, because for posterity every present is apt in turn to prove itself a shallow judge, but her own generation and us who delight to honour her?

In the sense in which anything is called ripe because of fulness and strength, I think the last of George Eliot's novels is also the ripest. *Middlemarch* is extraordinarily full and strong, even among the company to which it belongs. And though I am not sure that it is the property of George Eliot's writing to satisfy, its property certainly is to rouse and attach, in proportion to its fulness and strength. There is nothing in the literature of the day so rousing—to the mind of the day there is scarcely anything so rousing in all literature—as her writing is. What she writes is so full of her time. It is observation, imagination, pathos, wit and humour, all of a high class in themselves; but what is more, all saturated with modern ideas, and poured into a language of which every word bites home with peculiar sharpness to the contemporary consciousness. That is what makes it less safe than it might seem at first sight to speak for posterity in such a case. We are afraid of exaggerating the meaning such work will have for those who come after us, for the very reason that we feel its meaning so pregnant for ourselves. If, indeed, the ideas of to-day are certain to be the ideas of to-morrow and the day after, if scientific thought and the positive synthesis are indubitably to rule the world, then any one, it should seem, might speak boldly enough to George Eliot's place. For the general definition of her work, I should say, is precisely this— that, among writers of the imagination, she has taken the lead in expressing and discussing the lives and ways of common folks . . . in terms of scientific thought and the positive synthesis. She has walked between two epochs, upon the confines of two worlds, and has described the old in terms of the new. To the old world belong the elements of her experience, to the

new world the elements of her reflection on experience. The elements of her experience are the "English Provincial Life" before the Reform Bill—the desires and alarms, indignations and satisfactions, of the human breast in county towns and villages, farms and parsonages, manor-houses, counting-houses, surgeries, streets and lanes, shops and fields, of midlands unshaken in their prejudices and unvisited by the steam-engine. To the new world belong the elements of her reflection; the many-sided culture which looks back upon prejudice with analytical amusement; the philosophy which declares the human family deluded in its higher dreams, dependent upon itself, and bound thereby to a closer if a sadder brotherhood; the habit in regarding and meditating physical laws, and the facts of sense and life, which leads up to that philosophy and belongs to it; the mingled depth of bitterness and tenderness in the human temper of which the philosophy becomes the spring.

Thus there is the most pointed contrast between the matter of these English tales and the manner of their telling. The matter is antiquated in our recollections, the manner seems to anticipate the future of our thoughts. Plenty of other writers have taken humdrum and narrow aspects of English life with which they were familiar, and by delicacy of perception and justness of rendering have put them together into pleasant works of literary art, without running the matter into a manner out of direct correspondence with it. But this procedure of George Eliot's is a newer thing in literature, and infinitely harder to judge of, than the gray and tranquil harmonies of that other mode of art. For no writer uses so many instruments in riveting the interest of the cultivated reader about the characters, and springs of character, which she is exhibiting. First, I say, she has the perpetual application of her own intelligence to the broad problems and conclusions of modern thought. That, for instance, when Fred Vincy, having brought losses upon the Garth family, feels his own dishonour more than their suffering, brings the reflection how *"we are most of us brought up in the notion that the highest motive for not doing a wrong is something irrespective of the beings who would suffer the wrong."* (pp. 142-43)

Next, this writer possesses, in her own sympathetic insight into the workings of human nature, a psychological instrument which will be perpetually displaying its power, its subtlety and trenchancy, in passages like this which lays bare the working of poor Mrs. Bulstrode's faithful mind upon the revelation of her husband's guilt: "Along with her brother's looks and words, there darted into her mind the idea of some guilt in her husband. Then, under the working of terror, came the image of her husband exposed to disgrace; *and then, after an instant of scorching shame in which she only felt the eyes of the world, with one leap of her heart she was at his side in mournful but unreproaching fellowship with shame and isolation."* Of the same trenchancy and potency, equally subtle and equally sure of themselves, are a hundred other processes of analysis, whether applied to serious crises—like that prolonged one during which Bulstrode wavers before the passive murder which shall rid him of his one obstacle as an efficient servant of God—or to such trivial crises as occur in the experiences of a Mrs. Dollop or a Mrs. Taft, or others who, being their betters, still belong to the class of "well-meaning women knowing very little of their own motives." And this powerful knowledge of human nature is still only one of many instruments for exposing a character and turning it about. What the character itself thinks and feels, exposed by this, will receive a simultaneous commentary in what the modern analytic mind has to remark upon such thoughts and feelings. . . . (p. 143)

Then, the writer's studies in science and physiology will constantly come in to suggest for the spiritual processes of her personages an explanation here or an illustration there. For a stroke of overwhelming power in this kind, take what is said in one place of Bulstrode—that ''he shrank from a direct lie with an intensity disproportionate to the number of his more indirect misdeeds. *But many of these misdeeds were like the subtle muscular movements which are not taken account of in the consciousness, though they bring about the end that we fix in our minds and desire. And it is only what we are vividly conscious of that we can vividly imagine to be seen by Omniscience.''*

And it is yet another instrument which the writer handles when she seizes on critical points of physical look and gesture in her personages, in a way which is scientific and her own. True, there are many descriptions, and especially of the beauty and gestures of Dorothea—and these are written with a peculiarly loving and as it were watchful exquisiteness—which may be put down as belonging to the ordinary resources of art. But look at Caleb Garth; he is a complete physiognomical study in the sense of Mr. Darwin, with the ''deepened depression in the outer angle of his bushy eyebrows, which gave his face a peculiar mildness;'' with his trick of ''broadening himself by putting his thumbs into his arm-holes,'' and the rest. Such are Rosamond's ways of turning her neck aside and patting her hair when she is going to be obstinate. So, we are not allowed to forget ''a certain massiveness in Lydgate's manner and tone, corresponding with his physique;'' nor indeed, any point of figure and physiognomy which strike the author's imagination as symptomatic. Symptomatic is the best word. There is a medical strain in the tissue of the story. There is a profound sense of the importance of physiological conditions in human life. But further still, I think, there is something like a medical habit in the writer, of examining her own creations for their symptoms, which runs through her descriptive and narrative art and gives it some of its peculiar manner.

So that, apart from the presence of rousing thought in general maxims and allusions, we know now what we mean when we speak of the fulness and strength derived, in the dramatic and narrative part of the work, from the use of so many instruments as we have seen. Then comes the question, do these qualities satisfy us as thoroughly as they rouse and interest? Sometimes I think they do, and sometimes not. Nothing evidently can be more satisfying, more illuminating, than that sentence which explained, by a primitive fact in the experimental relations of mind and body, a peculiar kind of bluntness in the conscience of the religious Bulstrode. And generally, wherever the novelist applies her philosophy or science to serious purposes, even if it may be applied too often, its effect seems to me good. But in lighter applications I doubt if the same kind of thing is not sometimes mistaken. The wit and humour of this writer every one of us knows and has revelled in; I do not think these want to gain body from an elaborate or semi-scientific language. In the expression of fun or common observation, is not such language apt to read a little technical and heavy, like a kind of intellectual slang? I do not think the delightful fun about Mrs. Garth and Mary and the children gains by it. I doubt if it is in place when it is applied to the mental processes of Mrs. Dollop or Mr. Bambridge. And when, for example, we are asked to consider what would have happened if Fred Vincy's ''prophetic soul had been urged to particularize,'' that is what I mean by something like a kind of intellectual slang.

But all this only concerns some methods or processes of the writer, picked from random points in the development of her

new story and its characters. What of these in themselves? Well, there comes back the old sense, of a difference to the degree to which we are roused, attached, and taught, and the degree to which we are satisfied. The book is full of high feeling, wisdom, and acuteness. It contains some of the most moving dramatic scenes in our literature. A scene like that of Dorothea in her night of agony, a scene like that in which the greatness of her nature ennobles for a moment the smallness of Rosamond's, is consummate alike in conception and in style. The characters are admirable in their vigour and individuality, as well as in the vividness and fulness of illustration with which we have seen that they are exhibited. . . . But as one turns them over in one's mind or talk, them and their fortunes in the book, with laughter or sympathy or pity or indignation or love, there will arise all sorts of questionings, debatings, such as do not arise after a reading which has left the mind satisfied. One calls in question this or that point in the conduct of the story; the attitude which the writer personally assumes towards her own creations; the general lesson which seems to underlie her scheme; above all, the impression which its issue leaves upon oneself.

The questions one asks are such as, within limits like these, it would be idle to attempt to solve, or even to state, except in the most fragmentary way. Are not, for instance, some points in the story a little coarsely invented and handled? At the very outset, is not the hideous nature of Dorothea's blind sacrifice too ruthlessly driven home to us, when it ought to have been allowed to reveal itself by gentler degrees? Is it not too repulsive to talk of the moles on Casaubon's face, and to make us loathe the union from the beginning? Is not the formalism and dryness of Casaubon's nature a little overdone in his first conversation and his letter of courtship? Or again, is not the whole intrigue of Ladislaw's birth and Bulstrode's guilt, the Jew pawnbroker and Raffles, somewhat common and poor? The story is made to hinge twice, at two important junctures, upon the incidents of watching by a death-bed. Is that scant invention, or is it a just device for bringing out, under nearly parallel circumstances, the opposite characters of Mary Garth and of Bulstrode—her untroubled and decisive integrity under difficulties, his wavering conscience, which, when to be passive is already to be a murderer, permits itself at last in something just beyond passiveness? Or, to shift the ground of question, does not the author seem a little unwarrantably hard upon some of her personages and kind to others? Fred and Rosamond Vincy, for instance—one would have said there was not so much to choose. The author, however, is on the whole kind to the brother, showing up his faults but not harshly, and making him in the end an example of how an amiable spendthrift may be redeemed by a good man's help and a good girl's love. While to the sister, within whose mind ''there was not room enough for luxuries to look small in,'' she shows a really merciless animosity, and gibbets her as an example of how an unworthy wife may degrade the career of a man of high purposes and capacities. Celia, too, who is not really so very much higher a character, the author makes quite a pet of in comparison, and puts her in situations where all her small virtues tell; and so on. Minute differences of character for better or worse may justly be shown, of course, as producing vast differences of effect under the impulsion of circumstances. Still, I do not think it is altogether fancy to find wanting here the impartiality of the greatest creators towards their mind's offspring.

Then, for the general lesson of the book, it is not easy to feel quite sure what it is, or how much importance the author gives it. In her prelude and conclusion both, she seems to insist upon the design of illustrating the necessary disappointment of a woman's nobler aspirations in a society not made to second noble aspirations in a woman. And that is one of the most burning lessons which any writer could set themselves to illustrate. But then, Dorothea does not suffer in her ideal aspirations from yielding to the pressure of social opinion. She suffers in them from finding that what she has done, in marrying an old scholar in the face of social opinion, was done under a delusion as to the old scholar's character. "Exactly," is apparently the author's drift; "but it is society which so nurtures women that their ideals cannot but be ideals of delusion." Taking this as the author's main point (and I think prelude and conclusion leave it still ambiguous), there are certainly passages enough in the body of the narrative which point the same remonstrance against what society does for women. *"The shallowness of a water-nixie's soul may have a charm till she becomes didactic:"* that describes the worthlessness of what men vulgarly prize in women. *"In the British climate there is no incompatibility between scientific insight and furnished lodgings. The incompatibility is chiefly between scientific ambition and a wife who objects to that kind of residence."* That points to the rarity of a woman, as women are brought up, who prefers the things of the mind to luxury. *"'Of course she is devoted to her husband,' said Rosamond, implying a notion of necessary sequence which the scientific man regarded as the prettiest possible for a woman."* That points with poignant irony to the science, as to the realities of society and the heart, of men whose science is solid in other things.

It is perhaps in pursuance of the same idea that Dorothea's destiny, after Casaubon has died, and she is free from the consequences of a first illusory ideal, is not made very brilliant after all. She cannot be an Antigone or a Theresa. She marries the man of her choice, and bears him children; but we have been made to feel all along that he is hardly worthy of her. There is no sense of triumph in it; there is rather a sense of sadness in a subdued and restricted, if not now a thwarted destiny. In this issue there is a deep depression; there is that blending of the author's bitterness with her profound tenderness of which I have already spoken. And upon this depends, or with it hangs together, that feeling of uncertainty and unsatisfiedness as to the whole fable and its impression which remains with the reader when all is done. He could spare the joybells—the vulgar upshot of happiness for ever after—Sophia surrendered to the arms of her enraptured Jones—if he felt quite sure of the moral or intellectual point of view which had dictated so chastened and subdued a conclusion. As it is, he does not feel clear enough about the point of view, the lesson, the main moral and intellectual outcome, to put up with that which he feels to be uncomfortable in the combinations of the story, and flat in the fates of friends and acquaintances who have been brought so marvellously near to him.

That these and such like questionings should remain in the mind, after the reading of a great work of fiction, would in ordinary phrase be said to indicate that, however great the other qualities of the work, it was deficient in qualities of art. The fact is, that this writer brings into her fiction so many new elements, and gives it pregnancy and significance in so many unaccustomed directions, that it is presumptuousness to pronounce in that way as to the question of art. Certainly, it is possible to write with as little illusion, or with forms of disillusion much more cynical, as to society and its dealings and issues, and yet to leave a more harmonious and definite artistic impression than is here left. French writers perpetually do so.

But then George Eliot, with her science and her disillusion, has the sense of bad and good as the great French literary artists have not got it, and is taken up, as they are not, with the properly moral elements of human life and struggling. They exceed in all that pertains to the passions of the individual; she cares more than they do for the general beyond the individual. That it is by which she rouses—I say rouses, attaches, and elevates—so much more than they do, even if her combinations satisfy much less. Is it, then, that a harmonious and satisfying literary art is impossible under these conditions? Is it that a literature, which confronts all the problems of life and the world, and recognises all the springs of action, and all that clogs the springs, and all that comes from their smooth or impeded working, and all the importance of one life for the mass,—is it that such a literature must be like life itself, to leave us sad and hungry? (pp. 143-47)

> *Sidney Colvin, in a review of "Middlemarch: A Study of English Provincial Life," in* The Fortnightly Review, *n.s. Vol. XIII, No. LXXIII, January 1, 1873, pp. 142-47.*

[A. V. DICEY] (essay date 1873)

[*Dicey labels* Middlemarch *inferior to* Scenes of Clerical Life, Adam Bede, Silas Marner, *and* Romola, *citing the novel's fragmentary structure as its greatest weakness.*]

Is **Middlemarch** the most successful as it is certainly the most elaborate effort of George Eliot's genius?

Hundreds of critics will answer in the affirmative, and may point to the infinite variety of the persons described, to the exquisite beauty and wit of the remarks and epigrams with which the book teems, in confirmation of their judgment. But though **Middlemarch** has stuff enough in it to fill out four or five ordinary novels, and though it would undoubtedly at once make the reputation of an unknown author, it will not be permanently placed on a level with **Adam Bede, Romola,** or with the most exquisite of all George Eliot's works—the **History of Silas Marner.** The defect of the book is, that the parts are much more striking than the whole, and the source of this defect lies in two characteristics, one of which is peculiar to **Middlemarch,** whilst the other, though traceable in all George Eliot's writings, becomes far more prominent in her later than in her earlier works.

What readers care for in **Middlemarch** is the study of character, but the author herself, as she takes pains by the very title to point out, intended it as a study primarily not of character but of provincial life. She in fact aimed at two different objects. Her first aim is to give a picture of existence in an English country town forty years ago; her second, to show how this prosaic life told upon the characters of three or four of the persons born into it. Now, in the attainment of the first object, George Eliot completely succeeds. The novel as a mere rendering of English life rises as much above such works as Mrs. Gaskell's truthful and amusing sketch of 'Cranford,' or Miss Austen's truthful but to us, we confess, not very amusing sketches of commonplace people, as a work of genius must always rise above books marked more by grace or cleverness. Looked at in fact as a series of pictures, **Middlemarch** is the most perfect representation of life in an English country town which is to be found in our language. Even the minute details of Fred's petty and somewhat sordid extravagance, and the descriptions of the horse-dealers by whom he is cheated, and of the billiard-room which he frequents, all add something to the picture, and bring before the mind the fearful and oppressive dreariness of a country town. But the very success with which George Eliot has painted *Middlemarch* has been unfavorable to her full attainment of the second, and by far the more important, object of the tale. The form of the story has made it impossible to centre the reader's interest fixedly on any one character. You can never fully occupy your mind with Dorothea or with Lydgate in the same way in which you can give yourself up unreservedly to the character of Romola or of Silas Marner. Just when you begin to be anxious about Dorothea's fate, you are carried off to Lydgate and Rosamond; and when your whole mind has become filled with the question whether Lydgate's genius will or will not be ruined by Rosamond's pettiness, you are compelled to break away both from Lydgate and Dorothea, and to interest yourself in the fate of Bulstrode or in the happiness of the Garth family. The mere annoyance of being constantly shifted from one scene to another is a trifling consideration. A much more serious evil of this constant shifting is, that it prevents the author from fully elaborating any one character, and from studying the effect of the work as a whole.

It is always an ungraceful and often a foolish thing to complain of a great work because it is not something which it does not profess to be, and there is something specially futile in censuring an author of genius because he has not the peculiar genius of some other writer. . . . But it is sound criticism to measure an author's productions by the standard of his own greatest works. Now, it is when judged by this criterion that *Middlemarch* will be found defective. The scheme of the book as the picture of a society has, as just pointed out, the inherent defect of making it difficult to fix attention on one or two persons, or to place the minor characters in due subordination to those worth elaborate study. But it happens that George Eliot has herself shown the way in which this difficulty can be met. In her earliest and even now her most striking work you have pictures of society. The *Sketches of Clerical Life* paint perfectly and clearly the social circle in which Janet and Amos Barton move, but you never lose sight of the principal character in the pictures of the minor personages whose figures fill up the canvas. The reason of this certainly is, in part, that the three tales making up the *Sketches of Clerical Life* are kept entirely separate from one another. . . . If any critic will candidly compare the *Clerical Sketches* and *Middlemarch,* he will admit that the form of the one was planned under a happy, and that of the latter a distinctly unhappy, inspiration. For the one feature which would vindicate the scheme of *Middlemarch* is wanting. At the beginning of the book, every one must have anticipated that the different histories commenced in it will by degrees become so closely interlaced as to form a complete whole. As a matter of fact, though Dorothea's life affects the life of Lydgate, and though there is a link (a very slight one, it may be added) between Fred's marriage and Bulstrode's calamity, still the book consists of at least three perfectly separate tales. A very slight amount of change would make it possible even now to publish separately the history of Dorothea and Casaubon, of Lydgate and Rosamond, and of Fred and Mary, and no one can doubt that the author might originally have produced these histories as three separate tales of life in *Middlemarch.*

"Any one," writes George Eliot, "watching keenly the stealthy convergence of human lots, sees a slow preparation of effects from one life to another which tells like a calculated irony on the indifference or the frozen stare with which we look at our unintroduced neighbor. *Destiny stands by sarcastic with dramatis personae folded in her hand.*" This passage, and especially the last sentence of it, might be taken as a fair description of the attitude occupied by the author towards her own work. To a certain extent in all her books, but to a far greater extent in *Middlemarch* than in any of her other writings, George Eliot performs the part of the "destiny which stands by sarcastic," and comments on the fate of the actors whom she brings into existence. A main feature—in short, perhaps the main feature—of *Middlemarch* is the prominence given to what, borrowing a term from Greek tragedy, may be called the "chorus." The work begins with a prelude in which the reader is warned that he is to hear the history of a "St. Theresa, foundress of nothing, whose loving heart-beats and sobs after an unattained goodness tremble off and are dispersed among hindrances instead of centring in some long recognizable deed''; and the work concludes with a epilogue pointing out how the modern Theresa had failed, and the cause of her failure. Throughout the whole course of the story, moreover, the chorus is never long absent. At every turn reflections are introduced upon the characters, upon the events, upon the way the characters and the events work upon one another. No one who admires beautiful writing or can appreciate striking and original thoughts can fail to feel that the chorus or reflective portion of the book is full of beauty and power. To a large class of persons it forms probably the great charm of *Middlemarch.* It certainly constitutes the most peculiar feature of the book. But a critic, even while he admires the reflections themselves, and feels that as moral reflections they possess far greater depth and subtlety than the remarks generally forced upon the world under the guise of moral teaching, can hardly deny that the part taken by George Eliot as the moralizer over her own handiwork, if it gives her novel a peculiar charm, also greatly damages its whole effect. It is a very curious study to observe the results which follow from the characteristic in question. One main and most injurious effect is that some of the characters are never drawn directly. We see not the men themselves, but the personages as they appear in the author's reflections upon them. Take, for example, Bulstrode: an immense amount of skill, pains, and thought has been expended upon him yet he never becomes a really living character in the sense in which his wife, for example, of whom comparatively little is told us, stands out as a living human being; and the reason of this is obvious. Of Bulstrode's thoughts and motives, of his views of religion, of his ideas of Providence, of his attempt to adjust his actions to principles which he held and yet had not the firmness to practise; of all this we hear a great deal, and a great deal which is very well worth the hearing. As an analysis of a peculiar kind of hypocrisy the account of Bulstrode is perfect, and a reader must be much better or much worse than his neighbors who does not feel many of the reflections on Bulstrode come painfully home to his own conscience. But of Bulstrode himself we know very little. The most marked personal feature about him is that he had a bad digestion, and that painful reflections on the state of his body alternated with anxiety about the state of his soul. All we are told, as far as it goes, is natural enough; but what we maintain is that he is never really painted. We see a reflection of him, but we never see the man.

A somewhat similar defect is traceable in the description of Will. Take him all in all, he is the least satisfactory character in the book. An amateur, who could not work and would not study, who was too proud to propose to a lady whom he thought richer than himself, and not too proud to sneer at and annoy the man on whose charity he lived; who, having apparently a marked distaste for work and a dislike to the serious and prosaic side of life, ends his career as an active member of Parliament somewhere between 1832 and 1840—a follower, we must presume, of the Radicals of that day, that is, men like Joseph Hume—is, we confess, a character which seems to us neither interesting nor consistent. What is most apparent is that Will has a great charm for George Eliot, and the only conclusion to which one can in fairness come is that, skilful as she is, she has for once failed to put before the reader a true picture of the man as he appears to her own mind. Take Will as the facts of his life paint him, and he appears a feeble, rather well-disposed Tito, who, late in life, turns into a feeble and less energetic Felix Holt. Take him as he is spoken of by the author, and you will suppose him a man of considerable originality, great generosity, and of a special grace—a person, in short, not absolutely worthy of Dorothea, yet whom she might marry without sacrificing the lofty greatness of her nature. The cause of this divergence between the estimate of Will formed by the author, and the view of him actually taken by the reader, is, no doubt, that he is not satisfactorily drawn. But the ultimate reason why the drawing is unsatisfactory is that George Eliot is occasionally so much occupied in the chorus to her play that she forgets to introduce us thoroughly to the characters. Will and Bulstrode afford the most marked instances of this omission; but a careful comparison say of *Silas Marner* or of "**Janet's Repentance**" with *Middlemarch,* is sufficient to prove to any one but a very fanatical admirer that as the number of George Eliot's "wise, witty, and tender" sayings increase, the directness with which she paints living persons diminishes.

The writer's preoccupation with the reflections which her story is to suggest injures her actual delineation of even those persons whom she intends to make prominent by their own acts and speeches. George Eliot tends, no doubt, unconsciously more and more to make even the most lively and original characters in the book the representatives of different aspects of her own thoughts. The tones are very various, but they all or nearly all seem to be the tones of one voice differently modulated. Take, for instance, Mrs. Cadwallader. No one is more amusing and no one more alive, but a great number of her speeches are really little but the wit of George Eliot thrown into a sharp, rustic, and caustic form.

Her description of Casaubon's blood, "somebody put a drop under a magnifying-glass, and it was all semicolons and parentheses," is an exquisite sneer, but it is exactly the kind of sarcasm, dashed with a flavor of scientific allusion, which comes perfectly naturally into reflections by George Eliot, but comes far less naturally from the mouth of the rector's wife. Mrs. Cadwallader, again, tells us how she had learnt to like her husband's sermons: "When I married Humphrey I made up my mind to like sermons, and I set out by liking the end very much; that soon spread to the middle and the beginning, because I could not have the end without them." Here, as elsewhere, the phrases may be the phrases of Mrs. Cadwallader, but the wit is essentially the wit of George Eliot. In short, Mrs. Cadwallader, and the same thing is true of half the secondary characters, is in reality not so much a secondary character as a part of the great chorus of reflection which accompanies the tragedy from beginning to end. In general, as we have said, the reflections, if they somewhat injure the movements of the drama, are in themselves so beautiful that we should scarcely care to have them omitted. In one respect, however, they are themselves open to criticism. They are occasionally injured by what truth compels us to call scientific conceits. No doubt a time may come when the progress of knowledge will make metaphors drawn from physical science really natural as appropriate illustrations, but to such a stage

of knowledge the mass of so-called educated readers have certainly as yet not attained:

> Even with a microscope directed on a water-drop we find ourselves making interpretations which turn out to be rather coarse, for whereas under a weak lens you may seem to see a creature exhibiting an active voracity, into which other smaller creatures actively play, as if they were so many animated tax-pennies, a stronger lens reveals to you tiniest hairlets, which make vortices for these victims, while the swallower awaits passively at his receipt of custom. In this way, metaphorically speaking, a strong lens applied to Mrs. Cadwallader's match-making will show a play of minute causes, producing what may be called thought and speech vortices to bring her the sort of food she needed.

Now, is there in truth one out of a thousand persons who reads this passage who finds that the ten lines of scientific metaphor really make clearer to him the fact, simple enough in itself, that Mrs. Cadwallader acted under the influence of a number of infinitely small causes? Is there any one who does not feel that the remark in the *Mill on the Floss,* that people do not really weave elaborate plots, but live very much from hand to mouth, is in fact worth all this talk about hairlets, lenses, and vortices? In truth, throughout *Middlemarch,* we feel inclined more than half to curse the day when George Eliot began rather to reflect than to copy. The book is her greatest effort. Its defect is, and this defect places it to our minds below her most perfect writings, that it is an effort in the bad as well as in the good sense of the word. The very brilliancy of the epigrams, the marvellous power of analysis used in tracing the action of character, the elaborate care given to the separate parts, leaves in the mind a sense of something like strain, and makes it difficult to look at the work as a whole. Yet it is impossible to part from a book which may be said, almost without exaggeration, to have made for many persons the chief happiness and interest of the last year, with criticisms on defects which, be they real or not, would scarcely deserve notice in another of inferior power. One point which tempts to criticism is that you can easily perceive that when, in the interest of the story, George Eliot forgets theories and has not time to make reflections, the whole power of simple, direct description is still as strong in her as ever. (pp. 76-7)

> [A. V. Dicey], in a review of "Middlemarch," in
> The Nation, *Vol. XVI, No. 396, January 30, 1873,*
> *pp. 76-7.*

THÉRÈSE BENTZON   (essay date 1873)

[*Bentzon argues that* Middlemarch *betrays an inherent defect in Eliot's approach to fiction: she depicts reality objectively, rather than transforming it artistically. According to Bentzon, Eliot's inattention to artistry precludes her from being ranked among the greatest novelists. This essay first appeared in the* Revue des deux mondes *in February, 1873.*]

The 'Prelude' to George Eliot's [*Middlemarch*], announcing that what is to be presented is the study of one of those forceful spirits which up to now she has not felt herself ready to paint, is full of good intentions [see excerpt dated 1871]. It would appear that the lady novelist who has already put her celebrated but pseudonymous signature to several books remarkable for their stylistic vigour and profound observation of character is to abjure the approach for which we have so often taken her to task—an approach which takes the form of obstinately evading the exceptional, of searching out truth in the common crowd, not only as a result of her untiring preoccupation with bringing out the beauty of the ordinary things of life, but also of her open hostility to anything resembling heroism, the ideal. Even if the average man, beset by all sorts of hardships and trivialities depicted in microscopic detail, had aroused our interest under the name of Adam Bede—the actual novel of that name a masterpiece of realism without vulgarity—it might be dangerous to exaggerate certain facets of his character and circumstances. In subsequent novels by the author of **Adam Bede,** the study of realistic truth has more than once stifled whatever passion there was; her delicate, patient analysis has become tiring and prolix; the dispassionateness (always a little aloof and condescending), according to which weaknesses were represented as strengths, has ended by making the reader indifferent to characters whom he doesn't know whether to love or hate, and doesn't feel inclined to trouble to find out.

George Eliot has led one to believe that she was going to emerge from these generalisations by portraying a modern Protestant St Theresa who, in the gallery of her fiction as it stood, would produce the effect of a figure of Raphael strayed unaccountably among those Flemish or Dutch portraits which stand out more than anything else by the precision of their copying and their detail. (pp. 56-7)

[In **Middlemarch**] we come across a peculiar painting of manners and characters, clearly marked with that very English quality—so English as to be virtually untranslatable, the 'quaintness', a *mélange* of wit, grace and originality. Nevertheless, [the work makes] . . . plain once more the basic defect of an approach to fiction which consists entirely of reproducing each succeeding episode, each passing character, with nothing more than photographic precision, so to speak. Even the finest photograph, however clear, however penetrating it may be, is still inferior to a painting created with an eye to structure and unity of effect.

If the author had left out the secondary characters, who do not in any way advance the main plot, the novel would have been half the length, since most of the townsfolk of Middlemarch seem to put in an appearance only so as to give the Casaubons time to get to Rome, where we find them thoroughly disenchanted with each other—which it was not difficult to foresee. . . .

Why is it one never is satisfied, one never can be satisfied, after reading a novel by George Eliot? The English critic replies that her achievement does not lie in her ability to *satisfy*, but in her ability to rivet the reader's attention to what she writes; and that her work is not to blame if it leaves us, like life itself, sad and still hungry [see excerpt by Sidney Colvin dated 1873]. Very well! But we must reply to this with the question: must art then be no more than an exact and slavish imitation of life?

Middlemarch comprises three novels, only one of which—the story of Fred Vincy and Mary Garth—shows us contented people who have demanded very little of their lives. . . . Their kind of modest happiness—without excitement, without intoxication, without ecstasy—is the only happiness, it seems, that is really possible, the only one that is to be desired; it defines by contrast the failed destinies of more exacting spirits. After her first cruel mistake, does not Dorothea allow her life, which should have been consecrated to the whole of humanity, to be absorbed within the life of one other person? Does not Lydgate,

who, like her, wanted to put all his powers into a vast project for the good of his fellow men, become the plaything and victim of a woman without heart or intelligence, ignorant of the harm she does, who ruins his career and destroys his confidence in himself? . . . Certainly, George Eliot lacks neither ability, knowledge, wit (few English writers have the advantage of her on this score), style (even though we could point out one or two blemishes here and there—the abuse of medical and physiological expressions, for example), nor invention; there are all of these things in this enormous novel, in the 'genre' scenes—which will stand up to very close and attentive reading—as much as in the most dramatic sequences. One hardly dares to criticise the election scenes for being over-long, they have so much else to recommend them in their accurate, caustic examination of human ambition and weakness, and above all their mixture of judicious good feeling and prudent noncommitment where the issue of political reform and social improvement arises; but these noble, weighty qualities, forceful and sensitive as they might be, are not enough to make up for a flagrant offence against the essential rules of art: **Middlemarch** is made up of a succession of unconnected chapters, following each other at random—with the result that the final effect is one of an incoherence which nothing can justify. Perhaps the blame should be laid at the door of its serial publication, the most venial inconvenience of which is that it exhausts the reader. At any rate, to reconcile us to provincial life, particularly drab and tedious in England, it would have been necessary that this study should be only the background to a picture that was interesting and all the more lively by contrast. To merit the title of great novelist, George Eliot must come to realise that the first condition of producing beauty is to attend to the overall structure of the work at hand before bothering oneself over ornamentation, and that perfection of detail is no compensation for absence of a well-thought-out design; just as the real cannot properly be said to exist outside of its relation with the ideal, however hard one may try to make it do so. It has been said often enough, but it cannot be said too often, that the ideal is not something set over above nature: it is itself a part of the whole truth, an indispensable part of all work aspiring to a sufficiently high standard. It is because she has misunderstood this immortal precept; because, at the behest of a private whim, she has given pride of place to observation rather than imagination, to an inexorable analysis rather than sensibility, passion or fantasy, that George Eliot will not be numbered among those novelists of the very highest rank. (pp. 58-60)

Thérèse Bentzon, "Contemporary Reviews: 'Middlemarch'," in George Eliot, Middlemarch: A Casebook, edited by Patrick Swinden, Macmillan, 1972, pp. 56-60.

M. E. LEWES (letter date 1873)

[*In this excerpt from a letter to Charles Ritter, Eliot discusses British reviews of* Middlemarch, *commenting that none of the critics adequately understand her message.*]

Though **Middlemarch** seems to have made a deep impression in our own country, and though the critics are as polite and benevolent as possible to me, there has not, I believe, been one really able review of the book in our newspapers and periodicals. And after one has had much experience as a writer, praise, as such, is incapable of stirring any fibre of joy. What one's soul thirsts for is the word which is the [reflection] of one's own aim and delight in writing—the word which shows that what one meant has been perfectly seized, that the emotion which stirred one in writing is repeated in the mind of the reader. That you should have picked out those exquisite words of Vinet's—"où l'élégance la plus exquise semble n'être qu'une partie de la vérité"—as representing your judgment about what I have written, is a peculiar comfort to me. It is precisely my ideal—to make matter and form an inseparable truthfulness. (p. 374)

> *M. E. Lewes, in a letter to Charles Ritter on February 11, 1873, in* The George Eliot Letters, 1869-1873, *Vol. V, edited by Gordon S. Haight, Yale University Press, 1955, pp. 373-74.*

SAMUEL BUTLER   (letter date 1873)

[*Butler was an English novelist and essayist who is best known for* The Way of All Flesh, *an autobiographical novel that satirizes Victorian church and family life. His disparaging assessment of* Middlemarch *anticipates turn-of-the-century response to Eliot's work.*]

I am reading **Middlemarch** and have got through two-thirds. I call it bad, and not interesting: there is no sweetness in the whole book, and though it is stuffed full of epigrams one feels that they are lugged in to show the writer off. The book seems to me to be a long-winded piece of studied brag, clever enough I dare say, but to me at any rate singularly unattractive. (p. 40)

> *Samuel Butler, in an extract from a letter to Eliza Mary Ann Savage on March 18? 1873, in* Letters between Samuel Butler and Miss E. M. A. Savage, 1871-1885, *edited by Geoffrey Keynes and Brian Hill, Jonathan Cape, 1935, pp. 39-40.*

[R. H. HUTTON]   (essay date 1873)

[*Hutton contends that* Middlemarch *is superior to Eliot's other novels in its broad and detailed picture of provincial life. Like many contemporary reviewers, he faults a passage in the "Finale" that blames Middlemarch society for Dorothea's mistakes.*]

George Eliot has never displayed more imaginative and intellectual power than in [**Middlemarch,**] her latest and, in some important respects, her richest tale. There is more passion and more lofty conception in **Adam Bede,** more affluence of the provincial grotesques of English rural life in **The Mill on the Floss,** more beauty in **Silas Marner,** more curious intellectual subtlety in **Romola;** but none of them can really compare with **Middlemarch** for delicacy of detail and completeness of finish—completeness as regards not only the individual figures, but the whole picture of the rural society delineated—and for the breadth of life brought within the field of the story. . . . [In] **Middlemarch,** George Eliot has set herself, from the very beginning, to illustrate her own profound conviction that the noblest aims, however faithfully and simply pursued, are apt to be wrecked, at least to outward seeming, in this our modern age of distracted life. She sets herself to paint by no means a tragedy, but what she herself describes as 'a life of mistakes, the offspring of a certain spiritual grandeur, ill-matched with the meanness of opportunity' [see "prelude," dated 1871]. And what she loses in beauty and in grandeur of effect by this deliberate aim, she seems to gain in ease, and in the obviously greater accordance between her array of intellectual and moral assumptions, and her artistic treatment of them. You feel that the inmost mind of the writer is reflected, not merely in the criticisms and the casual observations of the tale, but in the

tale itself; you feel throughout the painful sincerity which underlies both the humour and the sarcasm; you feel the desolateness of the formative thought as well as the root of its bitterness, and yet you never cease to feel the author's extraordinary fidelity to her own moral aims. **Middlemarch** is, as the preface (unfortunately called a "prelude") pretty plainly confesses, a sort of pictorial indictment of modern society for the crippling conditions it imposes on men and women, especially women, of high ideal enthusiasm. In consequence of the very aim of the tale, it could hardly be a satisfying imaginative whole, either tragic or otherwise; for the object is to paint not the grand defeat, but the helpless entanglement and miscarriage, of noble aims; to make us see the eager stream of high purpose, not leaping destructively from the rock, but more or less silted up, though not quite lost, in the dreary sands of modern life.

The very nature of this conception, while it ensures a certain vein of melancholy and even bitterness in the story, gives George Eliot's genius a fuller play than it has ever yet had for its predominant realism, and also for that minute knowledge of the whole moral field of modern life which alone tests the strength of a realistic genius. It was impossible to show how ideal aims could be frustrated and overborne by the mere *want of room* for them and the crowd of pettier thoughts and hopes in the society in which they were conceived, without a broad canvas and great variety of grouping; and this is exactly where George Eliot excels. To any one who can endure the melancholy which is rather to be read between the lines than ostentatiously paraded, to any one who either does not constantly ask himself how this great author is really conceiving the ultimate problems of faith and duty, or who, if understanding fully the nature of her answer, is steeled against the pain it is liable to give,—the wonderful freshness and variety of the pictures of county society (high and low), the perfect drawing and bold outlines of her characters, and the minute delicacy of the lights and shades, the abundant humour, the caustic philosophy, and the deep undertone of unsatisfied desire, will give, if certainly not pure delight, all the pleasure which can be derived from profound and unaffected admiration. For artistic finish and breadth, *taken together,* George Eliot has no equal among novelists. . . . George Eliot paints with Miss Austen's unerring humour and accuracy, and with Sir Walter's masculine breadth. . . . She can draw not merely eccentric characters, but perfectly simple and normal characters of to-day, with all the humour and truth that Scott reserved for his special studies. She has Miss Austen's accuracy and instinct combined with a speculative sympathy with various grooves of thought which gives depth to the minutiae of real life, and which enables her to interest the intellect of her readers, as well as to engross their imagination. And these great powers have never been brought out with anything like the full success achieved in **Middlemarch.** As our author's object in this tale is to show the paralysis, and the misleading diversions from its natural course, which a blunt and unsympathetic world prepares for the noblest ideality of feeling that is not in sympathy with it, it was essential for her to give such a solidity and complexity to her picture of the world by which her hero's and heroine's idealism was to be more or less tested and partly subjugated, as would justify the impression that she understood fully the character of the struggle. We doubt if any other novelist who ever wrote could have succeeded equally well in this melancholy design, could have framed as complete a picture of English county and county-town society, with all its rigidities, jealousies, and pettiness, with its thorough good-nature, stereotyped habits of thought, and very limited accessibility to higher ideas, and have threaded all these pictures together by a story, if not of the deepest interest, still admirably fitted for its peculiar purpose of showing how unplastic is such an age as our's to the glowing emotion of an ideal purpose.

For melancholy, profoundly melancholy, both in aim and execution, *Middlemarch* certainly is.... The melancholy of the story consists not in the catastrophes of fortune, but in the working out of the only design with which the author set out—the picture 'of the cygnet reared uneasily among the ducklings in the brown pond, and who never finds the living stream in fellowship with its own oary-footed kind;' in the delineation of what George Eliot (with a sentimentalism and disposition to 'gush,' of which she is hardly ever guilty) calls the 'loving heart-beats and sobs after an unattained goodness,' which 'tremble off and are dispersed among hindrances instead of centering in some long-recognisable deed.' The object of the book is gained by showing in Dorothea's case that a rare nature of the most self-forgetting kind, and the most enthusiastic love for the good and beautiful, is rather more likely to blunder, in its way through the world, than one of much lower moral calibre—which is probable enough; but also by showing that this rare nature does not find any satisfying inward life to compensate these blunders, and turn them into the conditions of purer strength and less accidental happiness—which we should have thought impossible; and again in Lydgate's case, by showing that an ardent love for truth—of the purely intellectual kind—is liable to be betrayed, by the commonplace good nature with which it is often combined, into a paralyzing contact with sordid cares and domestic trials—which, again, is probable enough; but also by showing that this love of truth is not transmuted into any higher moral equivalent through the noble and genuine self-denial of the sacrifice made for another's good—which, again, we should have held to be impossible. That Lydgate, marrying as he did, and with his wholesome nature, should before long have merged the gratification of his disinterested, speculative passion in the necessity of considering the happiness of his shallow-natured wife, is most true to nature. That, in pursuing that course from the high and right motive from which, on the whole, he pursued it, he should have gained no new power over either her or himself, but should have become bitter on his side, and left her as vain and shallow as he found her, is, we trust, not true to nature, but a picture due to that set theory of melancholy realism which George Eliot evidently regards as the best substitute for faith. It is only here and there, in the rare glimpses she gives us of the solitude of Dorothea's heart, that this radical deficiency of faith is carried, as it seems to us, into any touch untrue to what we know of real life. It does so come out, we think, in one or two descriptions of Dorothea's secret struggles, and in the bitter tone in which the close of Lydgate's career is described. Generally, however, nothing can be more truthful or less like preconceived theory than the pictures of provincial life in this wonderful book. But not the less does this deep distrust of 'the Supreme Power,' who, in the words of the 'prelude' to *Middlemarch,* has fashioned the natures of women 'with inconvenient indefiniteness,' give a certain air of moral desolation to the whole book, and make us feel how objectless is that network of complicated motives and grotesque manners, of which she gives us so wonderfully truthful a picture. (pp. 407-11)

By far the most remarkable *effort* in *Middlemarch*—we are by no means sure that the success is quite in proportion to the effort, though the success is great, and one which only a mind of great genius could have attained—is, of course, the sketch of Dorothea Brooke.... One sees, on looking back over the tale, that it was an essential of George Eliot's purpose to make this high-minded and enthusiastic girl marry twice, and in *neither* case make an 'ideal' marriage, though the second is an improvement on the first. The author, indeed, attempts at the close to ascribe the first mistake partly to causes which she had never before indicated, and in so doing makes, as we think, a faulty criticism on her own creation. She attenuates Dorothea's own responsibility for her first marriage after a fashion hardly consistent either with the type of the character itself, or with the story as it has been told.

> Dorothea, [we are told] was spoken of to a younger generation as a fine girl, who married a sickly clergyman, old enough to be her father, and in little more than a year after his death gave up her estate to marry his cousin—young enough to have been his son, with no property, and not well-born. Those who had not seen anything of Dorothea usually observed that she could not have been "a nice woman," else she would not have married either the one or the other. Certainly those determining acts of her life were not ideally beautiful. They were the mixed result of young and noble impulse struggling under prosaic conditions. Among the many remarks passed on her mistakes, it was never said in the neighbourhood of Middlemarch that such mistakes could not have happened if the society into which she was born had not smiled on propositions of marriage from a sickly man to a girl less than half his own age, on modes of education which make a woman's knowledge another name for motley ignorance, on rules of conduct which are in flat contradiction with its own loudly-asserted beliefs.
>
> (pp. 411-12)

Now, the remark as to the world's 'smiling on a proposition of marriage from a sickly man to a girl less than half his own age,' really has no foundation at all in the tale itself. When Mr. Brooke, Dorothea's uncle, weakly carries Mr. Casaubon's offer to Dorothea, he accompanies it with as much slipshod dissuasion as it is possible for so helpless a nature to use. Dorothea's sister Celia hears of it with an ill-disguised horror of disgust, which bitterly offends Dorothea. If the rector's wife, Mrs. Cadwallader, represents county opinion (and who could represent it better?), the whole society disapproved it. Would George Eliot have orphan girls protected against the weakness of such uncles as Mr. Brooke by the Court of Chancery, or would she like to see a law fixing the maximum difference of ages permissible between husband and wife? We hardly see how Dorothea could have been better protected against her first mistake than the picture of social life in Middlemarch represents her as having actually been protected. We note this point only because we find in this passage a trace that George Eliot is, on reviewing her own work, a little dissatisfied with her own picture of the 'prosaic conditions' to which she ascribes Dorothea's misadventures; and that she tries to persuade herself that they were actually more oppressive and paralyzing than they really were. It is obvious, we think, that Dorothea's character was one of much more impetuous self-assertion, of much more adventurous and self-willed idealism than this passage would suggest. She is painted from the first as groping her way with an imperious *disregard* of the prevailing conventional ideas,—ideas quite too mean and barren for the guidance of such a nature,—and as falling, in consequence of that imperious disregard, into her mistake—the mistake being due about equally to her hasty contempt for the existing social standards of conduct, and to her craving for nobler standards not supplied. It was rather the ambitious idealism and somewhat wilful independence of Dorothea's nature than any want of a sound general opinion about the matter, which is represented as leading her into the mistake of her marriage with the pedantic bookworm, Mr. Casaubon; and George Eliot is hardly fair to the society she has herself so wonderfully portrayed, when she throws the responsibility of Dorothea's first great mistake upon it. In the early part of the tale, George Eliot clearly intended to charge the society around Dorothea with sins of omission rather than sins of commission; with having no noble aims to which such a nature as Dorothea's could dedicate itself with any satisfaction, rather than with failing to have a certain 'bottom of good sense,' which might have saved her from her blunder, if she could but have shared it without losing anything in ideal purpose by sharing it. But in her final criticism of her heroine our author, in her desire to apologize for her, has wavered a little in her conception, and, instead of charging her failure, as at the start, on 'the meanness of opportunity,' has charged it on the positive distortion of the social morality by which she was surrounded—a distortion which in her own picture she had not only forgotten to draw, but had carefully proved not to exist. This little inconsistency is important only as showing that George Eliot had unconsciously, in the course of her story, aggravated the faults of the society against which she brings her indictment both at the beginning and the close—a tendency which attaches more or less to her very negative spiritual philosophy. Faith is wanted to make people perfectly candid about the blots in human ideals. A frequent tendency may be noted in those who find no anchor for faith, to throw upon some abstract offender like 'society' the faults they see in those who most satisfy their longing for perfection. It is only profound belief in God which prevents us from indulging a certain amount of moral superstition about our human ideals, or as one may almost call them, the idols of one's conscience. (pp. 413-14)

That *Middlemarch* is a great and permanent addition to George Eliot's fame and to the rich resources of English literature we have no doubt. A book of more breadth of genius in conception, of more even execution, is hardly to be found in our language. No doubt it is a little tame in plot, but for that the depth of its purpose and the humour of its conversations sufficiently atone. The melancholy at the heart of it, no criticism of course can attenuate, for that is of its essence. George Eliot means to draw noble natures struggling hard against the currents of a poor kind of world, and without any trust in any invisible rock higher than themselves to which they can entreat to be lifted up. Such a picture is melancholy in its very conception. That in spite of this absence of any inward vista of spiritual hope, and in spite of the equally complete absence of any outward vista of 'far-resonant action,' George Eliot should paint the noble characters in which her interest centres as clinging tenaciously to that *caput mortuum* into which Mr. Arnold has so strangely reduced the Christian idea of God—'a stream of tendency, not ourselves, which makes for righteousness,'—and as never even inclined to cry out 'let us eat and drink, for to-morrow we die,' is a great testimony to the ethical depth and purity of her mind. And it will add to the interest of *Middlemarch* in future generations, when at length this great wave of scepticism has swept by us, and 'this tyranny is overpast,' that in pointing to it as registering the low-tide mark of spiritual belief among the literary class in the nineteenth century, the critics of the future will be compelled to infer from it, that even during that low ebb of trust in the supernatural element of religion, there was no want of ardent belief in the spiritual obligations of purity and self-sacrifice, nor even in that 'secret of the Cross' which, strangely enough, survives the loss of the faith from which it sprang. (p. 429)

> [R. H. Hutton], in a review of "Middlemarch: A Study of Provincial Life," in The British Quarterly Review, Vol. LVII, No. CXIV, April 1, 1873, pp. 407-29.

THE LONDON QUARTERLY REVIEW   (essay date 1877)

[*This anonymous critic contends that Dorothea's lack of Christian faith is "an anachronism" and "a serious artistic flaw."*]

[In *Middlemarch*] the atmosphere is as little coloured by the "hues of heaven" as in *Daniel Deronda,* and there is, besides, a prevailing greyness, a leaden weight of commonness, crushing all noble effort and high ambitions, that have always, to our minds, given this book a place in the "literature of despair." The religious life is represented by Mr. Bulstrode. . . . For the rest it is quite absent. And there is one character especially in whom this absence appears to us to constitute a serious artistic flaw—"it is worse than a crime, it is a blunder." That Dorothea, with her passionate enthusiasms, her noble, unselfish nature—Dorothea, not illustrating a Positivist thesis in 1876, but living her life more than a generation ago, in 1830—that she should not distinctly love Christ, and, in the sorrows and disenchantment of her sad wifehood and widowhood, cast her cares on Him, is an anachronism. It is like Mr. Matthew Arnold making of St. Paul a neo-Christian of today. The laws of probability, of artistic keeping, are not observed. The real Dorothea—and George Eliot's characters, like those of all the great creators in fiction, are living entities, so that we almost feel a right to question her report of their thoughts and actions—the real Dorothea, who had been educated at Lausanne, where, if we remember right, a religious revival was then in progress, who had fed her young mind on such books of devotion as the *Imitation* and the *Christian Year,* who is likened for us to St. Theresa, would not have held the following to be a complete account of her spiritual state, its trusts and consolations:—

> I have no longings . . . I mean for myself; except that I should not like to have so much more than my share without doing anything for others. But I have a belief of my own, and it comforts me. . . . [By] desiring what is perfectly good, even when we don't quite know what it is and cannot do what we would, we are part of the Divine power against evil—widening the skirts of light and making the struggle with darkness narrower. . . .

> I have always been finding out my religion since I was a little girl. I used to pray so much. Now I hardly ever pray. I try not to have desires merely for myself, because they may not be good for others, and I have too much already.

This is well said and beautiful. It is the nearest approach we remember to a religious utterance in the book; and the word *Divine* may, perhaps, be accepted as a concession to dramatic propriety. But Dorothea's faith would have included such feelings as these, and gone beyond them. They would have been but as drops in the ocean of her love for God. (pp. 453-54)

A photograph of Griff House, Eliot's favorite childhood home.

"George Eliot and Comtism," *in* The London Quarterly Review, *Vol. XLVII, No. XCIV, January, 1877, pp. 446-71.*

J. W. CROSS (essay date 1885)

[*Eliot married Cross in May, 1880, just seven months before her death. In the excerpt below, he recounts one of his conversations with Eliot in which she discussed the composition of a scene in* Middlemarch.]

During our short married life, our time was so much divided between travelling and illness that George Eliot wrote very little, so that I have but slight personal experience of how the creative effort affected her. But she told me that, in all that she considered her best writing, there was a "not herself" which took possession of her, and that she felt her own personality to be merely the instrument through which this spirit, as it were, was acting. Particularly she dwelt on this in regard to the scene in [Bk. VIII, Ch. LXXXI of] *Middlemarch* between Dorothea and Rosamond, saying that, although she always knew they had, sooner or later, to come together, she kept the idea resolutely out of her mind until Dorothea was in Rosamond's drawing-room. Then, abandoning herself to the inspiration of the moment, she wrote the whole scene exactly as it stands, without alteration or erasure, in an intense state of excitement and agitation, feeling herself entirely possessed by the feelings of the two women. Of all the characters she had

attempted, she found Rosamond's the most difficult to sustain. (pp. 424-25)

J. W. Cross, in his George Eliot's Life as Related in Her Letters and Journals: Sunset, *Vol. III, William Blackwood and Sons, 1885, 470 p.*

BESSIE RAYNER BELLOC (essay date 1894)

[*Belloc, a close friend of Eliot, was known for her advocacy of feminist causes. In the excerpt below, she questions Dorothea's motivations.*]

[Dorothea is] so far touched with the modern spirit that she burns with desire to do good, which, oddly enough, is inspired by the example of St. Theresa. Now St. Theresa was a cloistered nun (George Eliot, be it noted, had an early attraction to Spain) and her work was not outwardly practical, but spiritual. Its efficacy entirely depended upon the validity of certain alleged facts in regard to prayer and a personal relation to an unseen Christ. The undeniable continuity of St. Theresa's work, which subsists to this day in full swing and efficacy, is one of the proofs, patent to all, of the deep root of this kind of faith in human nature; but as it was a faith which George Eliot wholly denied, and of which there is no sign of her heroine having in any way partaken, it is singular that so powerful and well-cultivated an intellect should have chosen the Spanish nun, dead three hundred years ago, as a constraining example. I have never been able to understand in what way St. Theresa impressed Dorothea Casaubon, nor why she wanted to resemble the saint. The foundress of some active order would have seemed more to the purpose.

Also, in regard to Dorothea's marriage, her point of view is, to me, inexplicable. To marry for money or position may be wrong, to marry for pity, or for usefulness, or religion, may be foolish and dangerous; but to marry that you may help a man to finish a big book, even were it the all-embracing Code Napoléon, seems to me to be an inconceivable reason. . . . [It] does not seem to me to partake of that touch of nature which makes the whole world kin. (pp. 210-11)

Surely, surely, no young woman born in the Shires, however "unked" she might feel at times, had any cause to marry Mr. Casaubon's big book or Will Ladislaw's unworthy personality. No, no, Dorothea! I am obliged to admit and believe that you were a real person, but you will never persuade me that you might not have done better in every sense of the word! (p. 212)

> Bessie Rayner Belloc, "Dorothea Casaubon and George Eliot," in Contemporary Review, Vol. LXV, February, 1894, pp. 207-16.

VIDA D. SCUDDER (essay date 1898)

[Praising Eliot's comprehensive picture of provincial life, Scudder underscores Middlemarch's significance as a social document. According to Scudder, Dorothea's social idealism signals a turning point in the development of fictional heroines.]

In social significance, **Middlemarch** is probably the most important novel of the central Victorian period. It is certainly the most comprehensive. The social environment of the book, sketched with remarkable breadth and power, is really a summary of that which we have learned to know in essay and novel. Here is the gentry,—a country gentry, this time,—Mr. Brooke and the Chethams, with their mild dilettanteism, their lack of purpose or ideals. Here is the bourgeois society of the town, divided from the county by a seemingly impassable gulf: the Bulstrodes and Vincys, painfully devoid of sweetness and light. In the intrigue centring around old Featherstone, George Eliot has tried her hand at types that the offhand melodrama of Dickens would have treated more successfully. But Arnold himself never drew a better Philistine than Bulstrode, with his "double Hell, of not making money and not saving his soul," nor is any one of Thackeray's women more selfish, bewitching, and trivially clever than Rosamund. George Eliot's studies of clergy are in all her books a new feature, unparalleled in fiction unless we return to the capital work of Miss Austen. **Middlemarch** gives none of her favorite and sympathetic pictures of dissent; but the Established Church is represented by admirable if rather depressing types, in Mr. Cadwallader, Mr. Farebrother, and Mr. Casaubon. Certainly, wherever the force for social salvation may reside, it is not in these gentlemen.

All these minor characters, whom Thackeray would have treated with contempt and Dickens with jest, George Eliot touches with unfailing pathos and redeems to human dignity; yet her obvious intention is to furnish through them a typical social background. Against this conventional society, she places in clear, warm relief two figures: Lydgate, the representative of intellectual force; Dorothea, the representative of moral force. Both rebel against convention, both in their different ways are routed by the world.

In Dorothea, that sweet and bewildered person, a new type of heroine appears upon the stage. Dickens' liking went out to fragile, emotional, and kittenish young ladies. . . . Thackeray, in Ethel Newcome, showed a restless, spirited, brilliant creature, ill at ease in the only life open to her. But Dorothea is run in another mould from these. That curious sense of the organic whole, that modern craving for untrammeled fellowship, for which the term altruism is degrading, and no other term exists, gathers intensely in her person, and is the source of the warm glow that streams through the dreary book. Dorothea is the first example noted in English fiction of that new personal type which suffers with atoning pain for the sorrows of the world. Her life fails. Wholly unguided, differing from the modern woman by her lack of any adequate training, or indeed of any training at all, she finds no cause for which to live, and had she found one, is too solely a creature of noble instincts to serve it effectively. Her marriage with Ladislaw can hardly be held more reassuring than that with Casaubon: for the brilliant young Bohemian—"a sort of a Shelley, you know," says Mr. Brooke—surely illustrates the frivolity of the forces of revolt, as conceived by George Eliot, against the solid background of English respectability, the Cadwalladers and Chethams and Bulstrodes and Brookes. Poor Dorothea! Her power has not yet changed from impulse to purpose. She represents only the second stage in the evolution of the modern heroine as a social force. The first is shown in the domestic and soft-hearted ladies of Thackeray and Dickens; the last, so far, appears in such characters as Besant's Valentine and Mrs. Ward's Marcella,—women strong to achieve in their activities and influence that large coöperation with the forces making for righteousness which earlier heroines never imagined nor desired, and which Dorothea only dreamed. (pp. 185-87)

Middlemarch, to the author, was doubtless the epos of failure. It expressed her impassioned protest against modern society, with its lack of a "coherent social faith and order," its mammonism and dilettanteism, its conventional class-divisions, its utter inability to present to young, large, eager natures a cause to live and die for, an atmosphere in which they could expand. But to us, the book, with all its sadness, is full of hope. It marks the turn of the tide in modern fiction; for its shows characters in whom a new social idealism is stirring, and their very failure implies the promise of social salvation. (p. 188)

> Vida D. Scudder, "George Eliot and the Social Conscience," in her Social Ideals in English Letters, 1898. Reprint by Houghton, Mifflin and Company, 1899, pp. 180-97.

W. D. HOWELLS (essay date 1901)

[Howells was the chief progenitor of American realism and an influential American literary critic during the late nineteenth and early twentieth centuries. Although he wrote nearly three dozen novels, few of them are read today. Despite his eclipse, however, he stands as one of the major literary figures of his era. Here, he contends that Rosamond and Dorothea are convincing characters; to Howells, much of Middlemarch's power derives from its realism.]

I am certain that it would be difficult to find a more detestable character, or a truer, than Rosamond Vincy, who equally with Dorothea Brooke is the heroine of **Middlemarch.** (p. 65)

There is of course the question . . . whether in portraying a nature so altogether odious as Rosamond's the author has not been guilty of leze-complexity. Is not such a character too simply, too singly detestable, to be a true copy? I confess that it comes perilously near incurring some such censure; but perhaps the defence may be that we have not taken due account of mitigating circumstances in Rosamond's case. If Lydgate had smoothly and splendidly succeeded, as she expected, from the beginning, and there had been no hint of debts or troubles, her conceit would have concerned itself with little, insignificant things; she would have been content chiefly to talk incessantly about herself, and safely flirt well within a devoted admiration of her husband; she would have been a pretty bore, without the power of considerable mischief, as she was certainly always without the wish for it, or the cognizance of it. There is fairly enough the implication of all this in the representation of her character, as we must own when we most suspect the author of having come to hate Rosamond so much that she is just to her with difficulty.

Novelists ought not to have their favorites among their creations, as parents ought not to have their favorites among their children; but no doubt they have them. . . . George Eliot has her preferences most distinctly, and she pursues some of her women with a rancor as perceptible as her fondness for others. I will not deny that I think this a defect of her art; it is so; and I am not going to defend it any more in the case of Dorothea Brooke, whom she loves, than in the case of Rosamond Vincy, whom she hates with a hatred passing her hatred of Hetty Sorrel and Gwendolen Harleth, and all the other anti-heroines of her books. She succeeds in commending these to our dislike rather than she succeeds in commending to our liking her Romolas and Mary Garths and Mirahs, perhaps because in fiction as in life a woman does not know how to praise her friends sparingly enough. But in Dorothea Brooke she has known how to hold her hand, or rather has she known how so to temper Dorothea's strength with weakness, her wisdom wifh folly, her good with evil, as to render her entirely credible and entirely lovable. (pp. 71-2)

Her marriage to Ladislaw at last is one of the finest things, and one of the truest things in a book so great that it almost persuades one to call it the greatest in English fiction. It is not because *Middlemarch* is an immense canvas, thronged with such a multitude of marvellously distinguished and differenced figures, that it so richly represents life. Other huge novels have been of as great scope and greater dramatic effect; but *Middlemarch* alone seems to me akin in spiritual power to "War and Peace." It is in its truth to motives as well as results that it is so tremendously convincing. After a lapse of years one comes to it not with a sense of having overmeasured it before, but with the perception that one had not at first realized its grandeur. It is as large as life in those moral dimensions which deepen inwardly and give the real compass of any artistic achievement through the impression received. There are none of its incidents that I find were overestimated in my earlier knowledge of them; and there are some that are far greater than I had remembered. I have had especially to correct my former judgment—I am not sure that it was mine at first hand—of the character of Ladislaw and his fitness to be Dorothea's lover. I had thought him a slight, if not a light man, a poorish sort of Bohemian, existing by her preference, in the reader's tolerance, and perhaps, as her husband, half a mistake. But in this renewed acquaintance with him, I must own him a person of weight by those measures which test the value of precious stones or precious metals: an artist through and through, a man of high courage and high honor, and of a certain social detachment which leaves him free to see the more easily and honestly himself. Dorothea made great and sorrowful mistakes

through her generous and loyal nature; but Ladislaw was one of her inspirations: a centre of truth in which her love and her duty, otherwise so sadly at odds, could meet and be at peace. (pp. 77-8)

W. D. Howells, ''George Eliot's Rosamond Vincy and Dorothea Brooke,'' in his Heroines of Fiction, Vol. II, *Harper & Brothers Publishers, 1901, pp. 65-78.*

LESLIE STEPHEN   (essay date 1902)

[*Stephen is considered one of the most important English literary critics of the late Victorian and early Edwardian eras. In his criticism, which was often moralistic, Stephen argues that all literature is nothing more than an imaginative rendering, in concrete terms, of a writer's philosophy or beliefs. In the excerpt below, Stephen attempts to determine the moral of* Middlemarch *by analyzing the love affairs of Dorothea and Casaubon, Rosamond and Lydgate, and Mary Garth and Fred Vincy.*]

The immediate success of *Middlemarch* may have been proportioned rather to the author's reputation than to its intrinsic merits. It certainly lacks the peculiar charm of the early work, and one understands why the *Spectator* should have been led to say that George Eliot was "the most melancholy of authors."... There is not much downright tragedy, but the general impression is unmistakably sad. This, however, does not prevent *Middlemarch* from having, in some ways, even a stronger interest than its companions. George Eliot was now over fifty, and the book represents the general tone of her reflection upon life and human nature.... *Middlemarch* is primarily a portrait of the circles which had been most familiar to her in youth, and its second title is [*A Study of Provincial Life*]. Provincial life, however, is to exemplify the results of a wider survey of contemporary society. One peculiarity of the book is appropriate to this scheme. It is not a story, but a combination of at least three stories—the love affairs of Dorothea and Casaubon, of Rosamond Vincy and Lydgate, and of Mary Garth and Fred Vincy, which again are interwoven with the story of Bulstrode. The various actions get mixed together as they would naturally do in a country town. Modern English novelists seem to have made up their mind that this kind of mixture is contrary to the rules of art. . . . But when the purpose is to get a general picture of the manners and customs of a certain social stratum, and we are to be interested in all the complex play of character and the opinions of neighbours, the method is appropriate to the design. The individuals are shown as involved in the network of surrounding interests which affects their development. *Middlemarch* gives us George Eliot's most characteristic view of such matters. It is her answer to the question, What on the whole is your judgment of commonplace English life? for "provincialism" is not really confined to the provinces. Without trying to put the answer into a single formula, and it would be very unjust to her to assume that such a formula was intended, I may note one leading doctrine:—

An eminent philosopher among my friends [she says, with a characteristically scientific illustration,] who can dignify even your ugly furniture by lifting it into the serene light of science, has shown me this pregnant little fact. Your pier-glass, an extensive surface of polished steel made to be rubbed by a housemaid, will be minutely and multitudinously scratched in all directions; but place now against it a lighted candle as a centre of illumination, and the scratches will seem to arrange themselves in a fine series of concentric circles round that little sun. It is demonstrable that the scratches are going everywhere impartially, and it is only your candle which produces the flattering illusion of a concentric arrangement, its light falling into an exclusive optical selection. These things are a parable

showing the effect of egoism. It may also represent the effect of a novelist's mental preoccupation. Many different views of human society may be equally true to fact; but the writer, who has a particular "candle," in the shape of a favourite principle, produces a spontaneous unity by its application to the varying cases presented. The personages who carry out the various plots of *Middlemarch* may be, as I think they are, very lifelike portraits of real life, but they are seen from a particular point of view. The "prelude" gives the keynote [see excerpt dated 1871]. We are asked to remember the childish adventure of Saint Theresa setting out to seek martyrdom in the country of the Moors. Her "passionate, ideal nature demanded an epic life . . . some object which would reconcile self-despair with the rapturous consciousness of life beyond self." . . . We are to see how such a nature manifests itself . . . in the commonplace atmosphere of a modern English town. In Maggie Tulliver and in Felix Holt we have already had the struggle for an ideal; but in *Middlemarch* there is a fuller picture of the element of stupidity and insensibility which is apt to clog the wings of aspiration. The Dodsons, among whom Maggie is placed, belong to the stratum of sheer bovine indifference. They are not only without ideas, but it has never occurred to them that such things exist. In *Middlemarch* we consider the higher stratum, which reads newspapers and supports the Society for the Diffusion of Useful Knowledge, and whose notions constitute what is called enlightened public opinion. The typical representative of what it calls its mind is Mr. Brooke, who can talk about Sir Humphry Davy, and Wordsworth, and Italian art, and has a delightful facility in handling the small change of conversation which has ceased to possess any intrinsic value. Even his neighbours can see that he is a fatuous humbug, and do not care to veil their blunt commonsense by fine phrases. But he discharges the functions of the Greek chorus with a boundless supply of the platitudes which represent an indistinct foreboding of the existence of an intellectual world.

Dorothea, brought up with Mr. Brooke in place of a parent, is to be a Theresa struggling under "dim lights and entangled circumstances." She is related, of course, both to Maggie and to Romola, though she is not in danger of absolute asphyxiation in a dense bucolic atmosphere, or of martyrdom in the violent struggles of hostile creeds. Her danger is rather that of being too easily acclimatised in a comfortable state of things, where there is sufficient cultivation and no particular demand for St. Theresas. She attracts us by her perfect straightforwardness and simplicity, though we are afraid that she has even a slight touch of stupidity. We fancy that she might find satisfaction, like other young ladies, in looking after schools and the unhealthy cottages on her uncle's estate. Still, she has a real loftiness of character, and a disposition to take things seriously, which make her more or less sensible of the limitations of her circle. She has vague religious aspirations, looks down upon the excellent country gentleman, Sir James Chettam, and fancies that she would like to marry the judicious Hooker, or Milton in his blindness. We can understand, and even pardon her, when she takes the pedant Casaubon at his own valuation, and sees in him "a living Bossuet, whose work would reconcile

complete knowledge with devoted piety, a modern Augustine who united the glories of doctor and saint."

Dorothea's misguided adoration is, I think, very natural, but it is undeniably painful, and many readers protested. The point is curious. George Eliot declared that she had lived in much sympathy with Casaubon's life, and was especially gratified when some one saw the pathos of his career. No doubt there is a pathos in devotion to an entirely mistaken ideal. To spend a life in researches, all thrown away from ignorance of what has been done, is a melancholy fate. One secret of Casaubon's blunder was explained to his wife during the honeymoon. He had not—as Ladislaw pointed out—read the Germans, and was therefore groping through a wood with a pocket compass where they had made carriage roads. But suppose that he had read the last authorities? Would that have really mended matters? A deeper objection is visible even to his own circle. Solid Sir James Chettam remarks that he is a man "with no good red blood in his body," and Ladislaw curses him for "a cursed white-blooded pedantic coxcomb." Their judgment is confirmed by all that we hear of him. He marries, we are told, because he wants "female tendance for his declining years. Hence he determined to abandon himself to the stream of feeling, and perhaps was surprised to find what an exceedingly shallow rill it was." His petty jealousy and steady snubbing of his wife is all in character. Now we can pity a man for making a blunder, and perhaps, in some sense, we ought to "pity" him for having neither heart nor passion. But that is a kind of pity which is not akin to love. Dorothea's mistake was not that she married a man who had not read German, but that she married a stick instead of a man. The story, the more fully we accept its truthfulness, becomes the more of a satire against young ladies who aim at lofty ideals. It implies a capacity for being imposed upon by a mere outside shell of pretence. Then we have to ask whether things are made better by her subsequent marriage to Ladislaw? That equally offended some readers, as George Eliot complained. Ladislaw is almost obtrusively a favourite with his creator. He is called "Will" for the sake of endearment; and we are to understand him as so charming that Dorothea's ability to keep him at a distance gives the most striking proof of her strong sense of wifely duty. Yet Ladislaw is scarcely more attractive to most masculine readers than the dandified Stephen Guest. He is a dabbler in art and literature; a small journalist, ready to accept employment from silly Mr. Brooke, and apparently liking to lie on a rug in the houses of his friends and flirt with their pretty wives. He certainly shows indifference to money, and behaves himself correctly to Dorothea, though he has fallen in love with her on her honeymoon. He is no doubt an amiable Bohemian, for some of whose peculiarities it would be easy to suggest a living original, and we can believe that Dorothea was quite content with her lot. But that seems to imply that a Theresa of our days has to be content with suckling fools and chronicling small beer. We are told, indeed, that Ladislaw became a reformer—apparently a "philosophical radical"—and even had the good luck to be returned by a constituency who paid his expenses. George Eliot ought to know; but I cannot believe in this conclusion. Ladislaw, I am convinced, became a brilliant journalist who could write smartly about everything, but who had not the moral force to be a leader in thought or action. I should be the last person to deny that a journalist may lead an honourable and useful life, but I cannot think the profession congenial to a lofty devotion to ideals. Dorothea was content with giving him "wifely help"; asking his friends to dinner, one supposes, and copying his ill-written manuscripts. Many lamented that "so rare a creature should be absorbed into the life of another," though no one could point out exactly what she ought to have done. That is just the pity of it. There was nothing for her to do; and I can only comfort myself by reflecting that, after all, she had a dash of stupidity, and that more successful Theresas may do a good deal of mischief.

The next pair of lovers gives a less ambiguous moral. Lydgate, we are told, though we scarcely see it, was a man of great energy, with a high purpose. His ideal is shown by his ambition to be a leader in medical science. In contrast to Casaubon, he is thoroughly familiar with the latest authorities, and has a capacity for really falling in love. Unfortunately, Rosamond Vincy is a model of one of the forms of stupidity against which the gods fight in vain. Being utterly incapable of even understanding her husband's aspirations, fixing her mind on the vulgar kind of success, and having the strength of will which comes from an absolute limitation to one aim, she is a most effective torpedo, and paralyses all Lydgate's energies. He is entangled in money difficulties; gives up his aspirations; sinks into a merely popular physician, and is sentenced to die early of diphtheria. A really strong man, such as Lydgate is supposed to be, might perhaps have made a better fight against the temptation and escaped that slavery to a pretty woman which seems to have impressed George Eliot as the great danger to the other sex. But she never, I think, showed more power than in this painful history. The skill with which Lydgate's gradual abandonment of his lofty aims is worked out without making him simply contemptible, forces us to recognise the truthfulness of the conception. It is an inimitable study of such a fascination as the snake is supposed to exert upon the bird: the slow reluctant surrender, step by step, of the higher to the lower nature, in consequence of weakness which is at least perfectly intelligible. George Eliot's "psychological analysis" is here at its best; if it is not surpassed by the power shown in Bulstrode. Bulstrode, too, has an ideal of a kind; only it is the vulgar ideal which is suggested by a low form of religion. George Eliot shows the ugly side of the beliefs in which she had more frequently emphasised the purer elements. But she still judges without bitterness; and gives, perhaps, the most satisfactory portrait of the hypocrisy which is more often treated by the method of savage caricature. If he is not as amusing as a Tartuffe or a Pecksniff, he is marvellously lifelike. Nothing can be finer than the description of the curious blending of motives and the ingenious self-deception which enables Bulstrode to maintain his own self-respect. He is afraid of exposure by the scamp who has known his past history.

> At six o'clock he had already been long dressed, and had spent some of his wretchedness in prayer, pleading his motives for averting the worst evil if in anything he had used falsity and spoken what was not true before God. For Bulstrode shrank from a direct lie with an intensity disproportionate to the number of his direct misdeeds. But many of those misdeeds were like the subtle muscular movements which are not taken account of in the consciousness, though they bring about the end that we fix our mind on and desire. And it is only what we are naïvely conscious of that we can vividly imagine to be seen by Omniscience.

The culminating scene in which Bulstrode comes to the edge of murder, and, though he does not kill his enemy, refrains from officiously saving life, is the practical application of the principles; and one is half inclined to think that there was some excuse for the proceeding.

It is, I think, to the force and penetration shown in such passages that *Middlemarch* owes its impressiveness. It shows George Eliot's reflective powers fully ripened and manifesting singular insight into certain intricacies of motive and character. There is, indeed, a correlative loss of the early power of attractiveness. The remaining pair of lovers, Mary Garth and Fred Vincy, the shrewd young woman and the feeble young gentleman whom she governs, do not carry us away; and Caleb Garth, though he is partly drawn from the same original as Adam Bede, is unimpeachable, but a faint duplicate of his predecessor. The moral most obviously suggested would apparently be that the desirable thing is to do your work well in the position to which Providence has assigned you, and not to bother about "ideals" at all. . . . [This] is an excellent moral, but it comes more appropriately at the end of *Candide* than at the end of a story which is to give us a modern Theresa.

This, I think, explains the rather painful impression which is made by *Middlemarch*. It is prompted by a sympathy for the enthusiast, but turns out to be virtually a satire upon the modern world. The lofty nature is to be exhibited struggling against the circumambient element of crass stupidity and stolid selfishness. But that element comes to represent the dominant and overpowering force. Belief is in so chaotic a state that the idealist is likely to go astray after false lights. Intellectual ambition mistakes pedantry for true learning; religious aspiration tempts acquiescence in cant and superstition; the desire to carry your creed into practice makes compromise necessary, and compromise passes imperceptibly into surrender. One is tempted to ask whether this does not exaggerate one aspect of the human tragicomedy. The unity, to return to our "parable," is to be the light carried by the observer in search of an idealist. In *Middlemarch* the light shows the aspirations of the serious actors, and measures their excellence by their capacity for such a motive. The test so suggested seems to give a rather onesided view of the world. The perfect novelist, if such a being existed, looking upon human nature from a thoroughly impartial and scientific point of view, would agree that such aspirations are rare and obviously impossible for the great mass of mankind. People, indisputably, are "mostly fools," and care very little for theories of life and conduct. But, therefore, it is idle to quarrel with the inevitable or to be disappointed at its results; and, moreover, it is easy to attach too much importance to this particular impulse. The world, somehow or other, worries along by means of very commonplace affections and very limited outlooks. George Eliot, no doubt, fully recognises that fact, but she seems to be dispirited by the contemplation. The result, however, is that she seems to be a little out of touch with the actual world, and to speak from a position of philosophical detachment which somehow exhibits her characters in a rather distorting light. For that reason *Middlemarch* seems to fall short of the great masterpieces which imply a closer contact with the world of realities and less preoccupation with certain speculative doctrines. Yet it is clearly a work of extraordinary power, full of subtle and accurate observation; and gives, if a melancholy, yet an undeniably truthful portraiture of the impression made by the society of the time upon one of the keenest observers, though upon an observer looking at the world from a certain distance, and rather too much impressed by the importance of philosophers and theorists. (pp. 173-84)

Leslie Stephen, in his George Eliot, *1902. Reprint by Macmillan and Co., Limited, 1926, 213 p.*

OLIVER ELTON   (essay date 1920)

[*In Elton's opinion,* Middlemarch's *lack of spontaneity prevents it from being ranked among the greatest novels in the English language.*]

[*Middlemarch*] is almost one of the great novels of the language. A little more ease and play and simplicity, a little less of the anxious idealism which ends in going beyond nature, and it might have been one of the greatest. Some of the figures, like Ladislaw, are mere pasteboard; but there is still a dense throng of persons whom we all might have known, perhaps too well. Some of the men whose inner crises are described with most labour and travail are the least real; such are the pedant Mr. Casaubon and the banker Bulstrode. But the whole is like some piece of experience that we might wish to but cannot forget. There is no plan, but there is no confusion. The 'three love-problems' are held firmly in hand. Dorothea, Lydgate, the Garth and Vincy families, meet and part, they pair and quarrel, they suffer and resign themselves, in what the authoress well calls an embroiled medium—say a kind of bird-lime—yet solidly and distinctly; and the illusion holds out. The insignificant, like Fred Vincy, are made happy; the superior natures suffer. If they prospered, there would be no story: who could write a novel about the Brownings? . . . The folly of Dorothea in choosing Mr. Casaubon is not made quite credible, and the immense pains taken in explaining it may betray a certain sense of the difficulty. But once the fact is granted, we foresee from the first the slow march of tragic disappointment. 'No one would ever know what she thought of a wedding journey to Rome.' The case is worse with Dr. Lydgate, who wishes to become a second Bichat; it is worse, because his crampfish of a wife outlives him; whereas Mr. Casaubon does die and makes room for Ladislaw. The strain of these sombre histories is relieved by the picture of the minor households, and by the invaluable Mr. Brooke, one of George Eliot's most cheerful creations. . . . *Middlemarch* is a precious document for the provincial life of that time, vaguely astir with ideas, but promptly sinking back into its beehive routine. (pp. 264-65)

> Oliver Elton, "George Eliot and Anthony Trollope," in his A Survey of English Literature: 1830-1880, Vol. II, Edward Arnold, 1920, pp. 258-82.*

EDMUND GOSSE   (essay date 1922)

[*A distinguished English literary historian, critic, and biographer, Gosse wrote extensively on seventeenth- and eighteenth-century English literature. The following excerpt is drawn from Gosse's essay on Eliot, which the recent critic Kerry McSweeney calls "the swansong of the turn-of-the-century depreciations of her work."*]

Middlemarch is constructed with unfailing power, and the picture of commonplace English country life which it gives is vivacious after a mechanical fashion, but all the charm of the early stories has evaporated, and has left behind it merely a residuum of unimaginative satire. The novel is a very remarkable instance of elaborate mental resources misapplied, and genius revolving, with tremendous machinery, like some great water-wheel, while no water is flowing underneath it. (p. 14)

> Edmund Gosse, "George Eliot," in his Aspects and Impressions, *Cassell and Company, Ltd., 1922, pp. 1-16.*

NOEL ANNAN   (essay date 1943)

[*Annan portrays Eliot as a novelist-philosopher and argues that* Middlemarch *is formed by a consequent "underlying conflict between feeling and intellect."*]

[George Eliot] valued her abilities as an intellectual and a moralist far above her gifts as a novelist. The acts which caused her such suffering, her renunciation of belief in God or her decision to live with Lewes, were the result of considered deliberation rather than emotional crisis. She reasoned. She did not merely lose her faith; she replaced it with a new creed, Agnosticism. For the worship of God she substituted worship of the Good. Was it not more praiseworthy, more moral, to devote one's life to altruism, if one had no hope of reward in Heaven? . . .

Such was her intellectual creed and such, the critics have assumed, is the purport of her novels. But, very occasionally, fragments come to us which suggest that she knew life could not be summed up in rational conclusions. She suffered from fits of terrible melancholy; a crucifix stood before her when she was translating Strauss's analysis of the Passion. Emerson was startled to find that one of her favourite books was Rousseau's *Confessions*, and the guests at a portentous party at the Sidgwicks' that she was addicted to black Bavarian beer.

This underlying conflict between feeling and intellect breaks through the surface of her greatest novel—perhaps the greatest English novel of the nineteenth century—**Middlemarch**. At first sight it appears exactly what we would have expected the George Eliot of the essays and letters to write. We see how the actions, right or wrong, of three sets of lovers bring their inevitable reward; through her penetrating eyes we watch them twisting facts to salve their consciences and writhing when their misdemeanours are brought home. "No nation," wrote Voltaire, "has treated in poetry moral ideas with more energy and depth than the English nation." We are indeed as a nation peculiarly gifted as moralists, and George Eliot is among the most outstanding. . . . But **Middlemarch** is great, not only because of her analysis of character, her great gift of telling a story which binds us to the pages; not even because it contains her greatest artistic creation, the beautiful, coy, egotistical Rosamund, the "sylph caught young and educated at Mrs. Lemon's"; but because it is pervaded by a quality, only latent in her earlier works, and born of the struggle between what her reason and her feelings told her was true: Compassion.

It is this quality, so conspicuous in the Russian novelists and absent from modern novelists, which transforms a provincial town into the world and shows the relation of the characters, not merely to themselves or to each other, but to the universe. It is displayed in the humour which lubricates her style: a humour which does not produce a set-piece figure of fun like Mrs. Poyser, but gently exposes human beings as so much less than they should be and all that they can hope to be. . . .

[It] is in the analysis of the main characters that her compassion is most powerfully displayed. The faults of the elderly desiccated scholar, Casaubon, whom Dorothea marries in girlish idealism, are many. He is pompous, priggish and touchy. He marries to get an obedient drudge to do hack-work. He brooks no criticism for her or his dependents and shrinks from the criticism of his intellectual equals. He commits a despicable act by disinheriting Dorothea in his will if she marries his young cousin Ladislaw. And yet we pity him. For George Eliot discerns that a scholar's life is full of gratuitous suffering. Not only is Casaubon sexually unattractive, he is despised by his fellow-men for being a milk-blooded scholar; he is driven apart from them—and thus driven into himself, so that he cannot impart to another soul his tortured feelings which therefore breed monsters in his own. This has made him what he is, and as a result prevents him from succeeding even as a scholar. That his subject is claptrap, that he has not read the German monographs, is relevant to Ladislaw, but not to George Eliot. She discerns that he suffers from the most painful malady which can attack scholars: the inability to commit themselves to paper. In her creation of Casaubon, who was partly inspired by Mark Pattison, she was not, as has been suggested, pillorying the accumulation of useless knowledge; she was writing about the implications of being a scholar.

Her most powerful study of moral retribution is that of Lydgate, the young doctor whose ambition to further medical science is sapped by his wife Rosamund. He is a victim of that self-deception engendered by desire which blinds the most vigorous and practical intellects. Only dimly does he at length apprehend the strength of her provincial snobbery, her obstinacy and self-satisfaction. We are left feeling that he was defeated by something stronger than intellect or goodness: stupidity and conceit. Whoever married Rosamond would have fared as he. We cannot condemn even the hypocritical, evangelical banker, Bulstrode, for so thoroughly does she expose the moral falsity of his soul that we pity him as we pity Angelo in *Measure for Measure*, just such another neurotic high-toned pillar of society whose inner nature is twisted by forces too strong for him.

And lastly Dorothea. She is the victim of self-delusion. George Eliot does not disguise how comical she finds this young idealistic prig. "Riding was an indulgence, which she allowed herself in spite of conscientious qualms; she felt she enjoyed it in a pagan sensuous way and always looked forward to renouncing it." Her commonsense sister Celia is always permitted to score off her. Young people who want to reform the world and burn with self-sacrifice are often comical and stuck-up; and as we watch Dorothea first marry Casaubon and then Ladislaw, we feel that the good-natured worldly people who would direct her for her own good—Sir James Chettam, or that amusing rattle Mrs. Cadwallader—who smile at her generous impulses and ideas, were right. They are the people who say many dashing and cutting words but never overstep the mark—who refer to the young as "going through a tiresome phase." We rather enjoy their company when we grow older, their easy manners, their loyalty and satire. But how we hate them when we are young!—how they blight our aspirations and strangle our hopes by their superior knowledge of the world. They prophesy that a young girl with ideals will make a fool of herself and a young doctor who will not compromise with medical cant will fail. And they are correct. Is this not, asks George Eliot, the nature of life, and are not human beings piteous if it is so?

Is this, then, merely the story of retribution and reward, of the effect of environment on character? Is it true that George Eliot is "kindly but just . . . with birchrod in hand to use as she thinks fit and lists of good and bad conduct marks pinned neatly on her desk"? No, it is not. This is the book of the agnostic, who writes with the crucifix before her, who reads the *Confessions*, who enjoys Bavarian beer. It is about the difference between self-deception and self-delusion; about the nature of honesty; about the torture of being young and idealistic and hoping to change the world for the better. It is not merely asking whether there is scope for self-sacrifice in a provincial town; it raises the whole question of the value of high thinking

and serious endeavour. And she gives the answer. Though at the end of the book the mundane characters flourish, she leaves no doubt in our minds that it is better to be young, high-minded and wrong than worldly, practical and right. But she also admitted that the search for the true and the good brought suffering and sorrow; and as she sat alone, folded in melancholy, she wept that the workings of the universe brought agony and disillusionment to those who would transform it.

Noel Annan, in a review of "Middlemarch," in The New Statesman & Nation, *Vol. XXXVI, No. 666, November 27, 1943, p. 355.*

BERNARD SHAW   (essay date 1944)

[*Shaw is one of the greatest and best-known dramatists to write in the English language since Shakespeare. During the late nineteenth and early twentieth centuries, he was a prominent literary, art, music, and drama critic whose reviews were known for their biting wit and brilliance. Here, Shaw stridently objects to the deterministic philosophy and melancholy tone of* Middlemarch. *His interpretation of the novel is challenged by Bullett (see Additional Bibliography). Shaw's comments were written in 1944.*]

The history of modern thought now teaches us that when we are forced to give up the creeds by their childishness and their conflicts with science we must either embrace Creative Evolution or fall into the bottomless pit of an utterly discouraging pessimism. This happened in dateless antiquity to Ecclesiastes the preacher, and in our own era to Shakespear and Swift. "George Eliot" (Marian Evans) who, incredible as it now seems, was during my boyhood ranked in literature as England's greatest mind, was broken by the fatalism that ensued when she discarded God. In her most famous novel *Middlemarch*, which I read in my teens and almost venerated, there is not a ray of hope: the characters have no more volition than billiard balls: they are moved only by circumstances and heredity. "As flies to wanton boys are we to the gods: they kill us for their sport" was Shakespear's anticipation of George Eliot. (p. 702)

Bernard Shaw, "Postscript to 'Back to Methuselah'," in his Bernard Shaw, Collected Plays with Their Prefaces: Heartbreak House, Augustus Does His Bit, Annajanska, Back to Methuselah, Jitta's Atonement, *Vol. V, edited by Dan H. Laurence, The Bodley Head, 1972, pp. 685-703.*

JOAN BENNETT   (essay date 1948)

[*Bennett was one of the first twentieth-century critics to grant Eliot's later works serious attention. Here, she illustrates the flawless design of* Middlemarch *by demonstrating that its main characters are both intrinsically interesting and essential to the plot. According to Bennett, the unity of* Middlemarch *derives from the coherence of Eliot's creative vision.*]

[Although *Middlemarch*] has the wealth of detail, the variety of characterization and the fertility of invention characteristic of the best Victorian fiction, it has also the economy, proportion and unity which has been the aim of serious novelists from the time of Henry James. The unity is not merely an artificial contrivance, or unity of plot, it arises out of singleness of vision and the many characters and episodes in *Middlemarch* are interdependent aspects of the central subject. The moral and intellectual qualities of each character affect the reader's perception of the other characters much as one object or one colour mass in a picture affects the perception of every other.

The life of Middlemarch, the provincial town, is conveyed with understanding and assurance comparable with the assured confidence of Jane Austen in depicting the world she knew so well. The religious, social and economic history that lies behind and conditions that life is the same as that which conditioned George Eliot's own early development. The language in which the inhabitants of Middlemarch speak, with the idiom varying throughout the social scale, was familiar to her ear and she reproduced it with effortless mastery, and the pressure such an environment exercises on the individuals who compose it was a part of her own experience. (pp. 162-63)

[Clearly the two main subjects of *Middlemarch*—the stories of Dorothea and Lydgate—arise] out of George Eliot's perception that historical circumstances, particularly in her own century, often result in a small proportion of achievement in comparison with endowment. It is not surprising that she discovered Middlemarch to be the right setting for Miss Brooke as well as for Lydgate. Both characters have to adapt themselves to the demands and conventions of provincial society of the period. For the man a career is open which promises the fulfilment of his ideal, though he is hedged about by the time and place in which he enters on that career. Marriage is irrelevant to it, except in so far as it will limit his economic freedom and, on this account, he intends to avoid or at least postpone it. For the woman, on the contrary, marriage is the only conceivable career. Consequently, she chooses a mate in the hope of finding, through him, her opportunity to serve humanity. She hopes to find a husband with gifts of character and intelligence superior to her own. And so, when Dorothea Brooke receives Casaubon's stilted letter of proposal:

> How could it occur to her to examine the letter, to look at it critically as a profession of love? Her whole soul was possessed by the fact that a fuller life was opening before her. . . .

> All Dorothea's passion was transfused through a mind struggling towards an ideal life; the radiance of her transfigured girlhood fell on the first object that came within its level.

That object happened to be Edward Casaubon, just as Rosamond Vincy happened to be the object that answered Lydgate's preconception of a restful, ornamental creature, whose unexacting companionship he could enjoy in his hours of leisure. The tragic outcome of the one marriage is the counterpart of the tragic outcome of the other. It seems not only fitting but necessary to the full understanding of their predicament that Dorothea and Lydgate should form part of a single pattern. But, in her treatment of the two stories, when she had joined them, George Eliot did not stop short at juxtaposition and contrast. The relation between Lydgate and Dorothea is a principal factor in the development of Lydgate's character; the ennobling of Lydgate and purgation of his 'spots of commonness', which partly compensates for the tragic waste, is affected by his contact with Dorothea. (pp. 165-66)

Lydgate has a long and hard road to travel before he appreciates the value of such a woman as Dorothea and the various places in the story at which their paths intersect are essential to the unfolding and presentation of his character. Furthermore, he is as essential a part of her story as she is of his. He is often an agent in those parts of the action of the novel that concern her, either because of his medical relations with Casaubon, or his financial relations with Bulstrode, or his social relations with Ladislaw. All this belongs to the machinery of construc-

tion and any novelist competent to construct a fairly elaborate plot would know how to interconnect the main characters with similar economy. The relationship between the two operates also at a deeper level. Lydgate is an essential factor in the development of Dorothea's character, events connected with him help to mature her nature and to communicate the whole of it to the reader. The portrait of Dorothea is not complete until we have witnessed her courageous faith in him when the rest of her world suspect him of accepting a bribe to shelter a murderer, and her mission of mercy to his wife when she returns to Rosamond in the full belief that Ladislaw is her lover and that Rosamond has therefore destroyed her own last hope of personal happiness. Thus the two themes which George Eliot at first thought of as the material for two separate stories become parts of a single whole and together create the central life of the book as we know it.

Lydgate and Dorothea together are the vehicle for the main theme in *Middlemarch*. The compromise each ultimately makes between the life to which they aspired and the life the conditions permit symbolizes the conception at the heart of the book.

But George Eliot was not confined by her central theme; her creative imagination operated freely in this novel, disciplined but not inhibited by the requirements of artistic economy and proportion. Everything in the book is relevant to the design, but nothing is merely relevant. For instance, for the presentation of the theme it suffices that the marriage partners of Lydgate and Dorothea should be a worldly, unintelligent coquette and an egotist whose pretensions to genius are false. But both characters are in fact complex and intrinsically interesting far in excess of this requirement. Rosamond's moral stupidity, her incapacity to see beyond her own pitifully inadequate standards, is painted with penetrating insight and is frighteningly true to life. Few scenes in fiction are more convincing, or more effectively enraging, than that between Rosamond and her husband when she reveals how she has frustrated his plan to free them from debt. Her unshakeable assurance that she alone is the aggrieved party—and it is her characteristic attitude of mind—elicits a horrified compassion not only for her husband, but for her own narrowness of vision. The last words about her in the book sum up a conception of her character that has been formed in the reader's mind by degrees with little need for the author's directing commentary. George Eliot seems to know intuitively what Rosamond will say and do on every occasion and, though we are constantly surprised at the degree of her impercipience and the particular twist it takes, we are never in doubt of the consistency of the portrait. (pp. 166-68)

The impotent rage she arouses in her husband is shared by the reader, but while Lydgate's pity and tenderness towards her are the aftermath of love and the outcome of his own sense of responsibility, the reader is only compassionate in so far as he recognizes her limitations. Rosamond is never depicted as deliberately wicked, she is merely incapable of understanding any values more altruistic than her own. The most brilliant stroke of creative genius in her portrait occurs in the scene between her and Dorothea [in Bk. VIII, Ch. LXXXI]. . . . In that scene, at a moment when George Eliot had abandoned conscious intellectual control and given free rein to her imagination [see excerpt by Cross dated 1885], Rosamond behaves against the current of her nature: she is momentarily actuated, at any rate in part, by a generous impulse. This abnormality is prepared for by, and is the convincing consequence of, the preceding scene with Ladislaw. Dorothea has found them together and has left the house under the impression, almost inevitable in the circumstances, that Ladislaw is Rosamond's lover. Ladislaw, realizing fully the misapprehension under which Dorothea has gone away and hopeless of any possibility of dispelling it, turns on Rosamond and forces her to see, as she has never done before, herself mirrored in the consciousness of another:

> Rosamond, while these poisoned weapons were being hurled at her, was almost losing the sense of her identity, and seemed to be waking into some new terrible existence. She had no sense of chill resolute repulsion, of reticent self-justification such as she had known under Lydgate's most stormy displeasure: all her sensibility was turned into a bewildering novelty of pain—she felt a new terrified recoil under a lash never experienced before. What another nature felt in opposition to her own was being burnt and bitten into her consciousness. . . .

When Dorothea comes to her the second time, Rosamond is still under the influence of this experience: Ladislaw has broken through the almost impregnable defence of her self-complacency:

> . . . she was under the first great shock that had shattered her dream-world in which she had been easily confident of herself and critical of others. . . .

It will not be long before the dream-world walls her in again; but at the moment when Dorothea—unmindful of her own impaired dream—comes back to fulfil her intention of restoring Rosamond's confidence in her husband, she finds her without her usual defences. She tells Dorothea the truth about her own one-sided flirtation with Ladislaw, and that when Dorothea found them together: 'He was telling me how he loved another woman, that I might know he could never love me. . . .' Rosamond has her one generous gesture and, even before it is completed, we see her begin to re-establish her self-confidence.

The portrait of Casaubon is no less complete than that of Rosamond. He is far from being merely a necessary factor in the unfolding of Dorothea's personality and story. His character is intrinsically interesting and convincing; ultimately he wins the compassion of the reader as well as of his wife. At first, while she thirstily follows the mirage of an intellectual hero, the reader sees only a formal, egotistical pedant. Gradually, Casaubon's inner consciousness is revealed, his corroding envy, his unsuccessful fight against recognizing the vanity of the researches on which he has spent his life, his hopeless sickness of body and mind. Casaubon causes almost as much misery as Rosamond, and with more evil intention. But his portrait, unlike hers, evokes the sense of tragic waste. He has a better endowment than she has and is unlike her in his capacity for prolonged suffering. The wall he erects between himself and others is a deliberate repudiation of pity; within it he is not successfully self-deceived as she is.

Although in this novel George Eliot's treatment of human personality and her care for the unity of her design are those of a modern novelist, the construction of *Middlemarch* is in the nineteenth-century tradition. An elaborate plot interlocks the various groups of characters and is carefully devised for that purpose. Three figures, the miser Featherstone, his frog-faced natural son Rigg, and Rigg's step-father, the drunken scoundrel Raffles, exist for the plot only and are of no intrinsic interest.

They are vivid, semi-grotesque creatures who would not be out of place in the world Dickens creates. George Eliot gives each of them just enough reality to compel belief for the moment and has no further interest in them. They are creatures of farce or melodrama; but they are indispensable to the full story of the foreground characters in the novel. . . . These three grotesques are mere puppets; they are tools which the author uses with skill and discards when they have fulfilled their purpose.

This aspect of the novel is a consciously contrived unifying agent, but *Middlemarch* has another kind of unity which is not contrived but grows out of the author's singleness of vision. Bulstrode, who plays his essential part in the contrivance, is a fully realized character whose existence in the Middlemarch world has an effect on the reader's total impression over and above his function in the plot. His portrait is a serious study of hypocrisy (different in kind from, for instance, Dickens's epitomizing of that quality in Pecksniff). . . . The root of his hypocrisy is his continual striving for self-deception. In the inner pattern of the novel the relation between this man and his wife is as important as are his relations with Lydgate. Mrs Bulstrode, a worthy, common place woman, as limited in her mental equipment as is her agreeable sister Mrs. Vincy (Rosamond's mother), has her moment of tragic grandeur in which she rises to the moral plane on which Dorothea habitually moves. This occurs when her brother-in-law Vincy tells her of her husband's public disgrace and of the extent, known and suspected, of his offence. . . . (pp. 168-72)

The Bulstrodes are intrinsically interesting and important characters in the novel, and the reader's attitude towards them has that quality of compassion which George Eliot elicits for most of the main characters in *Middlemarch*. But, in addition to this, the episode of Bulstrode's exposure acts as a touchstone testing the value of all those who come into contact with it. (p. 173)

Middlemarch is George Eliot's supreme achievement: while its characters are at least as various and as deeply studied as any she has created, they are more perfectly combined into a single whole than those in any other of her novels. Nothing here is irrelevant or over-elaborated. Each character reveals itself in the sequence of events with such consistency with its own nature as wins the reader's complete assent. The imagination of the author seems to be wholly engaged in discovering what each one would be doing or saying in the special circumstances of each scene or episode. And yet every one of them has a function in the whole design. Our final apprehension of the moral quality of Lydgate and Dorothea depends upon our seeing them in relation to all the others. The flawless integrity and unworldliness of the Garth family offsets the streak of snobbishness and materialism in Lydgate. The unostentatious kindliness of Mr Farebrother offsets Lydgate's more arrogant virtue; little Miss Noble's small charities done by stealth are a comical counterpart of Dorothea's unsatisfied thirst to do good. It is not likely that these particular juxtapositions were consciously intended by the author, but they, and others of the same kind, occur because all the characters who make up the world in which Lydgate and Dorothea live are the product of the same vision of life. We are compelled throughout the book to see as George Eliot saw. The weaving of the plot and the part each character plays in it is the result of her conscious purpose and planning. But the part each character plays in producing the total impression evoked by the novel is the result of her creative power. She could divest herself of her own individual characteristics and preoccupations and identify herself with all these human beings, limiting herself to their knowledge, their temperament and their circumstances. There is less direct intercourse between author and reader than in most of her novels because there is less need for it. She has only to compel our attention to the world she has created; its inner coherence is the result of her own coherent vision.

Some critics, both in George Eliot's day and in our own, have found fault with her conception of Ladislaw and of his relation to Dorothea. (pp. 174-75)

There are two relevant questions for the reader: first, whether the author conveys a sufficiently rounded impression of Ladislaw to compel belief in his existence, and secondly, whether she makes it credible that Dorothea would love him. If a negative answer is given it is usually to the second question. The reader discerns faults, weaknesses or irritating tricks in Ladislaw which, he supposes, would alienate her. Ladislaw is dilettante, that is to say that (in his early twenties) he cannot choose a career and settle down to it. In the grip of his passion for Dorothea he vacillates about leaving Middlemarch and continually finds an excuse to return. He offends and perplexes Middlemarch society in general by his easy, unconventional manners; to them he seems like a foreigner; they are not surprised to learn that his father was a Jewish pawnbroker. Perhaps George Eliot has succeeded so well in making her readers inhabit Middlemarch that they too readily adopt the Middlemarch point of view. But she has provided a counterbalancing impression. The discerning characters, those less bounded by the conventional standards of the provincial town, such as Lydgate or Mr Farebrother, are not offended by Ladislaw's manners. Mr Farebrother's sister, the admirable little old lady, Miss Noble, almost worships him because of his kindness to ragged children and his courtesy to herself. He has certain qualities which were particularly likely to attract Dorothea after her experience with Casaubon. He is spontaneous and unselfconscious; he responds to beauty in art or nature and to nobility in human character with romantic ardour. His intelligence is quick and gay—a happy contrast to Casaubon's ponderous learning. His nature is in many ways complementary to her own. Certainly George Eliot did not intend us to share Sir James Chettam's view that their marriage was a disaster.

The reader's feeling about this marriage has a bearing on another common criticism of *Middlemarch*, that it is, in R. H. Hutton's words [see excerpt dated 1873]:

> Profoundly melancholy both in aim and in execution.

In a sense this is obviously true, but it is not the whole truth about the book. An important part of George Eliot's intention in *Middlemarch*, as elsewhere, was to arouse compassion for the human predicament.... [From] the beginning of her career she hoped ... to elicit sympathy for the unspectacular sorrows of ordinary men and women. In *Middlemarch* itself, commenting on Dorothea's unhappiness in Rome, on her honeymoon with Casaubon, she wrote:

> Some discouragement, some faintness of heart at the new real future which replaces the imaginary, is not unusual, and we do not expect people to be deeply moved by what is not unusual.... If we had a keen vision and feeling of all ordinary human life, it would be like hearing the grass grow and the squirrel's heart beat, and we should die of that roar which lies on the other side of silence. As it is, the quick-

est of us walk about well wadded with stupidity.

In so far as *Middlemarch* removes some of that wadding and opens our ears to normal human sorrow, it is a melancholy book. The tragic waste of Lydgate, the incomplete fulfilment of Dorothea's promise, the moral degradation of Bulstrode, the disappointment of Farebrother when Mary Garth gives herself to Fred Vincy, who needs her more than he does, but deserves her less—all these are melancholy as certainly as they are lifelike. But it is doubtful whether the sorrow in the book outweighs the happiness. Against these woes must be set the various happy or contented lives; the pleasant ménage of Mr Farebrother with his mother and sisters; the satisfactory marriage of Celia and Sir James Chettam; the suitable and comfortable relationship of Mr and Mrs Vincy, which creates a tolerable happiness in spite of their worries over their children; Fred Vincy's improvement under the Garth influence and his happiness with Mary; the relation between Mr and Mrs Garth, in which a flawless union has compensated for many material anxieties, the satisfactory marriage of that odd pair, the Cadwalladers. All these counterbalancing pictures of normal human content, including (a subject rarely treated in fiction) happiness in the day's work (particularly emphasized in the portrait of Caleb Garth) together prevent the total effect of the book from being gloomy. Moreover, the reader is constantly delighted and enlivened by the author's gift for comedy which is only a little less evident here than in *Adam Bede* or *The Mill on the Floss*. (pp. 176-78)

In *Middlemarch* George Eliot presents a world too various and too absorbingly interesting and amusing for the total effect of the book to be melancholy—the selection of experience in it represents the typical sorrows of ordinary human beings, but it represents no less vividly the common human joys. And, as with all successful works of art, there is an overbalance of delight which comes from the contemplation of work well done. (p. 180)

> *Joan Bennett, in her* George Eliot: Her Mind and Her Art, *1948. Reprint by Cambridge at the University Press, 1962, 202 p.*

ARNOLD KETTLE (essay date 1951)

[*Kettle contends that while the various stories within* Middlemarch *are successful, the novel as a whole lacks organic completeness. He attributes this defect to Eliot's deterministic philosophy, arguing that the society of Middlemarch, which should have been the unifying feature, is too static to act as a link between the novel's separate parts.*]

[In *Middlemarch*] George Eliot takes a great deal of pains with her 'background' and the question arises as to whether background is the right word to use. What, we have to ask ourselves, is the central theme, the unifying subject of this *Study of Provincial Life*?

From the Prelude one gathers that this is to be a novel about latter-day Saint Theresas [see excerpt dated 1871] ...; and we are given the hint that the problem of such modern saints is that they are "helped by no coherent social faith and order which could perform the function of knowledge for the ardently willing soul."

This expectation is immediately justified by the introduction of Dorothea Brooke, the mention of the Blessed Virgin in the second sentence of the first chapter confirming all our antici-

A rare photograph of Eliot that was taken in 1858.

pation. And the first movement of the novel, the whole of the first book up to the introduction of Lydgate, continues the development of the theme. Dorothea is the centre of it and Dorothea is presented to us wonderfully, her limitations, her immaturity, her ''theoretic'' mind no less than her ardour, her yearning for a life more deeply satisfying than Tipton and Middlemarch can give.

Up to this point Middlemarch may be said to be to the novel what Highbury is to *Emma,* the world in which Dorothea and Casaubon and the surrounding characters live, and very subtly does George Eliot convey how Middlemarch has made them what they are. We feel no temptation to abstract these characters from the society that contains them. Dorothea is not Saint Theresa. She is an intelligent and sensitive girl born into the English landed ruling class of the early nineteenth century, full of half-formulated dissatisfactions with the fatuous, genteel life of the women of her class, seeking something beyond the narrow 'selfishness' of her acquaintances and turning towards a religious Puritanism and a high-minded philanthropy (cottages for the farm-labourers) to satisfy her unfulfilled potentialities; finally and disastrously imagining that in marriage to Casaubon she will find the fulfilment of her aspirations.

It is with the introduction of Lydgate, quickly followed by the Vincys and Bulstrode, that the basic structure of the novel changes. We know now that George Eliot in fact joined together in *Middlemarch* two novels originally planned separately—the

story of *Miss Brooke* and the story of Lydgate. But even without this knowledge we should find, before the end of the first book, a change coming over *Middlemarch.* George Eliot forces the problem on our attention in Chapter XI, just after the introduction of Lydgate and Rosamond.

> Certainly nothing at present could seem much less important to Lydgate than the turn of Miss Brooke's mind, or to Miss Brooke than the qualities of the woman who had attracted this young surgeon. But any one watching keenly the stealthy convergence of human lots, sees a slow preparation of effects from one life on another, which tells like a calculated irony on the indifference or the frozen stare with which we look at our unintroduced neighbour. Destiny stands by sarcastic with our *dramatis personae* folded in her hand.

> Old provincial society had its share of this kind of subtle movement: had not only its striking downfalls, its brilliant young professional dandies who ended by living up an entry with a drab and six children for their establishment, but also those less marked vicissitudes which are constantly shifting the boundaries of social intercourse and begetting new consciousness of inter-dependence.

(pp. 177-78)

It is a clumsy passage and its clumsiness comes from its function as a bridge between what the novel started as and what it is becoming; but it is also a passage full of interest to an analysis of the book. ''Destiny stands by sarcastic with our *dramatis personae* folded in her hand'': It is a pretentious, unhelpful sentence, calling up a significance it does not satisfy. Who, one feels tempted to ask, is this Destiny, a character previously unmentioned by the author? And, as a matter of fact, the figure of a sarcastic fate does not preside over *Middlemarch.* On the contrary George Eliot is at pains to dissociate herself from any such concept. Throughout the novel with an almost remorseless insistence, each moral crisis, each necessary decision is presented to the participants and to us with the minimum of suggestion of an all-powerful Destiny. It is the very core of George Eliot's morality and of the peculiar moral force of the book that her characters, despite most powerful pressures, and above all the prevailing pressure of the Middlemarch way of life, are not impelled to meet each particular choice in the way they do. Lydgate *need* not have married Rosamond, though we understand well enough why he did. Neither need Fred Vincy have reformed; it is George Eliot's particular achievement here that she convinces us of a transformation against which all the cards of 'Destiny' have been stacked.

My point here is that the appearance of this concept in Chapter XI is not justified by the total organization of the book and that it betrays a weakness, a lack of control, which is intimately connected with the transformation of the novel from the story of Dorothea to something else.

The something else is indicated in the sentence beginning ''Old provincial society . . .'' We realize as we read on that the centre of attention of the novel is indeed being shifted, so that the story of Miss Brooke is now not an end in itself but a starting-point. What we are to contemplate is nothing less than the whole subtle movement of old provincial society. The background has become the subject.

That it was bound to do so has already been hinted. So firmly is the story of Dorothea in those early chapters 'set' in the society of which she is a part, that it seems almost inevitable that an adequate examination of Dorothea must involve an examination of the Middlemarch world more thorough than that so far contemplated, and there is no doubt that it was under a sense of this compulsion that George Eliot altered the plan of the book and called it **Middlemarch.** And the central question in our estimate of the novel is how far she succeeds in this great, ambitious attempt thus to capture and reveal the relation of each individual story, the stories of Dorothea, of Lydgate, of Bulstrode, to the whole picture, the Middlemarch world. (pp. 179-80)

Middlemarch is a wonderully rich and intelligent book and its richness lies in a consideration of individual characters firmly placed in an actual social situation (it is because Ladislaw is never thus placed but remains a romantic dream-figure that he is a failure). But there seems to me a contradiction at the heart of **Middlemarch,** a contradiction between the success of the parts and the relative failure of the whole.

Middlemarch as a whole is not a deeply moving book. The total effect is immensely impressive but not immensely compelling. Our consciouness is modified and enriched but not much changed. We are moved by particular things in the book: by the revelation of Casaubon's incapacity; by the hideous quality of the Lydgate-Rosamond *impasse* (certainly upon our pulses this), he unable to find a chink in her smooth blonde armour and she incapable of understanding the kind of man he could have been; by Dorothea's disillusionment in Rome; by the scene in which Mrs. Bulstrode accepts her share in her husband's downfall. (pp. 180-81)

[In the last of these episodes,] the moral and emotional basis of a personal relationship is explored with an insight and a sympathy wholly admirable. And we are moved not simply because George Eliot's moral concern is so profound and sure but because the scene, with its many ramifications (including the implicit comparison with the attitude of Rosamond), is presented with so deep a sense of the social interpenetration that makes up life. And yet—it is the paradox of the novel— this sense of social interpenetration, so remarkably revealed in the exploration of the individual dilemma and so consistently and consciously sought after by George Eliot throughout the novel, does not in fact infuse the book as a whole.

Middlemarch taken in its completeness has almost everything except what is ultimately the most important thing of all, that final vibrant intensity of the living organism. Despite its superb achievements, despite the formidable intelligence which controls the whole book and rewards us, each time we return to it, with new insights, new richness of analysis and observation, there is something missing. We do not care about these people in the way in which, given the sum of human life and wisdom involved, we ought to care. What is lacking is not understanding, not sympathy, not warmth, certainly not seriousness.

George Eliot is the most intelligent of novelists; she always knows what she ought to do and she never shirks any issue. But she seems to lack what one might call a sense of the vital motion of things: she feels after this sense, but does not capture it. For all her intellect, all her human sympathy, all her nobility and generosity of mind, there is something of life that eludes her, that sense of the contradictions within every action and situation which is the motive-force of artistic energy and which

perhaps Keats was seeking to express when he referred to Shakespeare's "negative capability."

George Eliot possesses this negative capability when she explores a particular situation, a concrete problem; *then* the conflicts within the essence are perforce accepted and in fighting themselves out breathe the breath of life into the scene. But it is as though in her philosophy, her consciously formulated outlook, there is no place for the inner contradiction. (pp. 182-83)

I believe that most of the weaknesses of **Middlemarch** spring from this. It is behind the failure to impose an organic unity on the novel. The intention is, clearly, that Middlemarch itself should be the unifying factor, but in fact it is not. The 'subtle movement' of society which George Eliot herself refers to is not, in the achieved novel, caught. On the contrary the view of society presented is a static one. Nor is this simply because provincial society in the Midlands about 1832 was indeed comparatively unchanging (no society is really static when an artist looks at it), though it is perhaps significant that George Eliot, writing in the 1870s, should have set her novel forty years back. What is more important is the failure of the attempts to give 'historical colour' (like the surveying of the railroad and the election scenes) which are conscientious but not—on the artistic level—convincing, not integral to the novel's pattern.

More vital still is the fact that the various stories within the novel, though linked by the loose plot, have no organic unity. Many of the chief characters are related by blood, but their artistic relationship within the pattern of the novel is not fully realized. Between the story of Dorothea and that of Lydgate there is, it is true, an essential link. Lydgate's career (it is not by accident that he is a man) is the other side of the Saint Theresa theme. "Lydgate and Dorothea together are the vehicle for the main theme in **Middlemarch.** The compromise each ultimately makes between the life to which they aspired and the life the conditions permit symbolises the conception at the heart of the book!" Mrs. Bennett's remark [see excerpt dated 1948] is to the point; and the phrase "the life the conditions permit" is, I think, most significant.

For in such a phrase the limitation of the view of society implicit in **Middlemarch** is revealed and the reason for George Eliot's ultimate failure to capture its movement indicated. Society in this novel is presented to us as 'there'; that it is a part of a historical process is suggested intellectually only. And because the Middlemarch world is the given, static reality, the characters of the novel must be seen as at its mercy. They are free to make certain moral decisions within the bounds of the Middlemarch world, yet they are held captive by that world.

Hence the temptation of George Eliot, once she accepts the social implications of her story, to introduce an unconvincing, unrealized 'Destiny.' The artist in her does not believe in this Destiny and therefore when her imagination is fully engaged in the exploration of a concrete problem of individual relationships the concept of an impregnable social destiny disappears. But it is always lurking in the background and it eats into the overall vitality of the novel. In a sense it is a product of George Eliot's strength, her recognition of the complex social basis of morality. Had she not felt compelled to make Middlemarch the chief character of her book (a compulsion springing from her own honesty of analysis) she would not have needed the further social understanding which her later conception of the novel involved. She would not have attempted that advance on the art of Jane Austen which makes her at once a more impressive novelist and a less satisfactory one.

George Eliot's view of society is in the last analysis a mechanistic and determinist one. She has an absorbing sense of the power of society but very little sense of the way it changes. Hence her moral attitudes, like her social vision, tend to be static. "We are all of us born in moral stupidity, taking the world as an udder to feed our supreme selves." The image is significant, hinting as it does at a fully mechanistic outlook (not unlike Locke's conception of the mind as a blank sheet of white paper) in which the individual is essentially passive, a recipient of impressions, changed by the outside world but scarcely able to change it.

It is not by chance that human aspirations fare poorly in *Middlemarch*. All of the main characters, save Dorothea and Ladislaw and Mary and Fred, are defeated by Middlemarch and Mary and Fred are undefeated only because they have never fought a thorough-going battle with the values of Middlemarch society. Mary and the Garths, it is true, reject the more distasteful aspects of nineteenth-century morality—the money-grabbing of old Featherstone, the hypocritical dishonesty of Bulstrode—but they accept as proper and inevitable the fundamental set-up of Middlemarch. Integrity and hard work within the framework of the *status quo* is the ideal of conduct that Mary demands of Fred, decent enough standards as far as they go but scarcely adequate (as one immediately realizes if one applies them to Lydgate's dilemma) as an answer to the profound moral problems raised by the book as a whole or its central theme, and it is observable that the tensions of the book in the Garth-Vincy passages are considerably lower than in the Dorothea, Lydgate or Bulstrode sections.

It is George Eliot's mechanistic philosophy, too, which is at the root of the weakness . . . in her method of posing to us the moral issues at stake in the novel. The point here, it is worth insisting, is not that her moral concern should be consistent and explicit, not that she should continuously refer us back to our own consciences, but that she should do so in a way which weakens the tension of the scene she is describing and places her characters at a distance which makes an intimate conveying of their feelings difficult. Dr. Leavis is, I am sure, quite right to stress as inadequate the view of George Eliot expressed in Henry James's words:

> We feel in her, always, that she proceeds from the abstract to the concrete; that her figures and situations are evolved, as the phrase is, from her moral consciousness, and are only indirectly the products of observation.

I do not think that the continuous moral concern in *Middlemarch* is abstract or that George Eliot is trying to impose abstract concepts on a recalcitrant chunk of life. For all the deep moral preoccupation the novel has little of the moral fable about it.

On the contrary her method is to present most concretely a particular situation and then draw to our attention the moral issues involved in the choices which have to be made. The method is perhaps a little heavy-going; as we pass in the novel from moral crisis to moral crisis we feel a shade oppressed by the remorselessness of the performance. But what is oppressive is not any abstract plan lurking behind the screen but the very nature of George Eliot's moral judgments; there is too often a kind of flatness about them, which actually weakens the conflicts within the scene she is presenting. And the flatness comes,

I think, from the assumptions implicit in her moral view of the world as an udder.

To put it in another way, her standards of right and wrong . . . are not quite adequate to the complexity of her social vision. Henry James's criticism that her figures and situations are not *seen* in the irresponsible plastic way is unfortunately expressed and invites the drubbing Dr. Leavis rightly gives it, but it nevertheless hints at a genuine weakness. George Eliot's high-minded moral seriousness (which might in fact be described as Utilitarianism modified by John Stuart Mill, Comte and her early evangelical Christianity) does have an unfortunate effect on the novel, not because it is moral or serious, but because it is mechanistic and undialectical.

And like all mechanistic thinkers George Eliot ends by escaping into idealism. In this study of bourgeois society there are three rebels—Dorothea, Ladislaw and Lydgate—whose aspirations lead them to a profound dissatisfaction with the Middlemarch world. All three stand for, and wish to live by, values higher than the values of that world. They are the "ardent spirits" who seek to serve humanity through science and art and common sympathy. Lydgate is defeated by Middlemarch through his marriage with Rosamond and the bitter story of his defeat is the finest and most moving thing in the novel. But it is significant that Lydgate, like all the other failures of the novel, fails not through his strength but through his weakness.

There is no heroism in *Middlemarch* (leaving aside for the moment Dorothea and Ladislaw), no tragic conflict and there cannot be, for the dialectic of tragedy, the struggle in which the hero is destroyed through his own strength, is outside George Eliot's scheme of things. Because her outlook is mechanistic and not revolutionary no one can fight Middlemarch or change it. The most that they can do is to improve it a little (as Farebrother does and perhaps Dorothea) by being a little 'better' than their neighbours. But the best that most can rise to—like Mary Garth and Mrs. Bulstrode—is a sincere and unsentimental submission to its will. And therefore even the 'sympathetic' characters must either be passive or else be brought to their knees through their own faults. For though George Eliot hates Middlemarch she believes in its inevitability; it is the world and our udder.

Yet because she hates the values of the society she depicts and has a faith in men and women which her mechanistic philosophy cannot destroy George Eliot has to find a way out of her dilemma. She, whose noble humanity informs the whole novel, even its weaknesses, cannot submit emotionally to a philosophy that binds her people for ever to the Middlemarch world. Hence the significance of the Saint Theresa theme, both as to its place in the novel and as to the rather breathless, uncontrolled, even embarrassing emotional quality which it exudes. Hence, too, the whole problem of Dorothea and Ladislaw. Dr. Leavis has brilliantly indicated the nature of the unsatisfactoriness of Dorothea, the aspect of what he calls self-indulgence inherent in her conception [see *NCLC*, Vol. 4].

> Dorothea . . . is a product of George Eliot's own 'soul-hunger'—another day-dream ideal self. This persistence, in the midst of so much that is so other, of an unreduced enclave of the old immaturity is disconcerting in the extreme.

We have an alternation between the poised impersonal insight of a finely tempered wisdom and something like the emotional confusions and self-importances of adolescence. And yet, for all the penetration of Dr. Leavis's analysis, it is hard to agree entirely with his conclusion that "the weakness of the book . . . is in Dorothea." For although there is this weakness (which increases as the book goes on) it is also true that the strength of the book is in Dorothea. In spite of all our reservations it is Dorothea who, of all the characters of the novel, most deeply captures our imagination. It is her aspiration to a life nobler than the Middlemarch way of life that is the great positive force within the novel and the force which, above all, counteracts the tendency to present society as a static, invincible force outside the characters themselves. It is Dorothea alone who, with Ladislaw, successfully rebels against the Middlemarch values.

The word 'successfully' needs qualification. For one thing Dorothea herself has more of the Lady Bountiful about her than George Eliot seems prepared to admit, and there is always (though let us not overestimate the point) seven hundred a year between her and the full implications of her attitude. More important, the success of her rebellion is limited by the degree of artistic conviction which it carries. The "day-dream" aspect of Dorothea which Dr. Leavis has emphasized is a very basic limitation. But this quality, this sense we have of idealization, of something incompletely realized, is due, I would suggest, not so much to any subjective cause, some emotional immaturity in George Eliot herself (it is hard to see how she could combine her remarkable total achievement in the novel with such immaturity) as to the limitations of her philosophy, her social understanding.

Dorothea represents that element in human experience for which in the determinist universe of mechanistic materialism there is no place—the need of man to change the world that he inherits. Dorothea is the force that she is in the novel precisely because she encompasses this vital motive-force in human life; and she fails ultimately to convince us because in George Eliot's conscious philosophy she has no place. The "unreduced enclave" represented by the degree of George Eliot's failure here is the unreduced enclave of idealism in her world-outlook.

As for Ladislaw, he is far less successfully realized than Dorothea, far more than she a mere dream-figure, a romantic idealization of the kind of man she deserves. Indeed it is only when she becomes involved with Ladislaw that we become seriously uneasy about Dorothea. And Ladislaw, interestingly enough, is an aesthete, a respectable dilettante, a Bohemian minus the sordid reality of Bohemianism. He is in fact almost everything into which the ineffectual rebels of the late Victorian era escaped, and he is saved from the degeneracy implicit in his way of life. only by the convenient financial support of Casaubon, Mr. Brooke and finally Dorothea herself. The artistic failure of George Eliot with Ladislaw, her failure to make him a figure realized on the artistic level of the other characters of the novel, is inseparable from the social unrealism in his conception. Artistically he is not 'there,' not concrete, because socially he is not concrete, but idealized.

It is important, I think, to recognize the link between the weaknesses of *Middlemarch* and the limitations of George Eliot's philosophy. For there are two sorts of weakness in the novel which at first appear unrelated and even antithetical. In the first place there is the tendency towards a certain flatness or heaviness, a tendency which we have seen to be associated with her somewhat static view of society and morality. In the second place there is the element of unresolved emotionalism involved in the Dorothea-Ladislaw relationship. The two weaknesses are not, in fact, contradictory; but rather two sides of the same coin. It is the very inadequacy of her mechanistic

philosophy, its failure to incorporate a dialectical sense of contradiction and motion, that drives George Eliot to treat the aspirations of Dorothea idealistically.

Just as *War and Peace*—despite Tolstoy's enormous, penetrating sense of the dialectics of life, of birth, growth and development—is weakened by his mechanistic, determinist view of history, so in *Middlemarch* does George Eliot's undialectical philosophy weaken the total impact at which she aimed. And yet no novelist before her had so consciously and conscientiously tried to convey the inter-relatedness of social life or the changing nature of individuals and their relationships. She is a great, sincere and humane writer and it may well be that—despite the ultimate weaknesses within her work—the novelists of the future will turn to *Middlemarch* more often than to any other English novel. (pp. 183-90)

Arnold Kettle, "George Eliot: 'Middlemarch'," in his An Introduction to the English Novel: To George Eliot, Vol. I, *1951. Reprint by Hutchinson's University Library, 1954, pp. 171-90.*

REVA STUMP (essay date 1959)

[*In* Movement and Vision in George Eliot's Novels, *excerpted below, Stump argues that each of Eliot's novels rests on a complex pattern of vision imagery that alternately suggests two antithetical structural movements: movement toward and away from moral vision. Here, Stump illustrates how* Middlemarch's *web imagery supports its themes and its structural movement away from moral vision.*]

[In discussing Eliot's works, moral vision can be] defined as the deeply felt perception of what it is to be a human being, a perception so deeply felt that it must profoundly influence what one is in relation to his fellow human beings. When we come to examine *Middlemarch,* there is no need to redefine the term. One of two central facts in *Middlemarch* is that the kind and loving but unheralded private actions which are the result of growing vision do not perfectly fulfill the life which seeks heroic channels but do nevertheless contribute to the moral evolution of mankind. The second is that the petty and selfish private actions which are the result of moral stupidity and lack of vision constitute a friction which retards the forward movement of mankind. In a wide general sense these two antithetical sets of actions create the structural movements toward and away from moral vision and thereby provide the substructural movement of the novel, the forward struggle of humanity. This statement should not be interpreted as implying that George Eliot is setting black against white and showing right and wrong actions to be clear-cut and easily distinguishable but rather that there is no neutral area of indifference, that all human actions—whether trivial or great—have moral consequences. George Eliot is intent on showing her reader how it is that "we insignificant people with our daily words and acts are preparing the lives of many Dorotheas, some of which may present a far sadder sacrifice than that of the Dorothea whose story we know," . . . and that we also prepare for the existence of the Bulstrodes, Lydgates, and Rosamonds, as well as the Riggs and Raffles, "those low people by whose interference, however little we may like it, the course of the world is very much determined." . . . That is the negative statement. On the other hand, and this is the positive part of the book which has been too often neglected, "the growing good of the world is partly dependent on unhistoric acts." . . . (p. 137)

Exploration of what I consider to be the governing metaphor of the book may perhaps yield a meaningful point of departure for the examination of structural movement in *Middlemarch*. George Eliot says: "I . . . have so much to do in unraveling certain human lots, and seeing how they were woven and interwoven, that all the light I can command must be concentrated on this particular web, and not dispersed over that tempting range of relevancies called the universe." . . . Here the author clearly—albeit in general terms—tells us her intention. It is extremely important that she here employs a vision image in relation to her function as novelist. She is intent on "seeing" and making it possible for her reader to see how human lots are related, and all the "light" which she as novelist can command must be focused squarely on the "web" which she invites the reader to explore with her. Thus indirectly she warns her reader that he too must concentrate on seeing that which presumably is not at once discernible. Throughout the whole of *Middlemarch* the vision imagery predominates. We see not only how the web of human lots is constructed but also how the characters themselves come to see it. In this image, then, is the conjunction of two central elements in the novel, for the web metaphor is both idea-giving and form-giving. . . . "This particular web" is the fabric constructed by the weaving and interweaving of human lots, and the focus is on the web itself rather than exclusively on one particular human lot, on the way both public and private actions of human beings interrelate. Thus it is that the attention of the reader is constantly being shifted from one episode to another, from one character to another, from one place to another, from private scene to public scene. It is the way in which human actions form the threads of connection that George Eliot would have us examine from various vantage points. . . . As we follow the movement of characters from place to place and from group relationship to private relationship we see how their lives become increasingly involved, so enmeshed and interwoven, in fact, that it is impossible to follow one straight narrative line in the life of a character without considering the other lines which intercept and modify it. Hence the effect is a structure made up of many threads rather than a single narrative line. If the term may be used descriptively, we should say that the effect is a *weblike* structure. (pp. 138-39)

Discussion of the multiple function of the web image and its complex relationship to other elements in the novel—most especially to vision—will, I believe, reveal a great deal about theme and structure in *Middlemarch*.

First of all, the web is the fabric of human life which in *Middlemarch* George Eliot partially unravels and examines in order to discover whatever is discernible about that fabric, what some of the parts are, and how they relate to the whole. In the Finale she indicates that the novel proper does not comprehend the entire web. "Every limit is a beginning as well as an ending. . . . For the fragment of a life, however typical, is not the sample of an even *web:* promises may not be kept, and an ardent outset may be followed by declension; latent powers may find their long-awaited opportunity; a past error may urge a grand retrieval." Thus is would seem that the web is continually extending so that there is finally no even web, no whole fabric but one that is always in the process of becoming and will remain so as long as there are human actions to continue the operation of the law of cause and effect in human affairs. The Finale tells us briefly what happened to the characters of *Middlemarch*, but such a conclusion does not give the closed effect which E. M. Forster deplored as the primary weakness of novels. Rather it opens out, creating the sense of a continuing

life pattern. It speaks of marriage, birth, and death, of old age and youth, of reform, inheritance, and the daily problems of life. We are not left with the illusion that our characters live happily ever after, but with the sure knowledge that while they live out their lives they are continuing to form fresh threads of connection, some which will hamper and others which will enrich their lives.

If a web, then, is thought of in the sense indicated above, it suggests a spread-out, expansive quality. But it also suggests what is on the surface apparently contradictory, that its intricate structure might impede free and unhampered movement. Both of these qualities are peculiarly suited to George Eliot's purpose here. This is not to say that the author constantly repeats the image but rather that because it is a rich image which recurs in significant contexts complementing and supporting the basic themes and structural movement, it is therefore useful to the critic as a way of describing the meaning and action of the novel. *Middlemarch* is obviously concerned in large part with the "later-born Theresas" whose passionate ideal natures can find no adequate channel for heroic action. . . . There are no heroes who will perform great historic acts, for except in rare instances there is no longer any channel for such action: "the medium in which their ardent deeds took shape is for ever gone." . . . The "hindrances" with which everyday life confronts them cause their energies to be "dispersed" and diffused, resulting in many private actions rather than one grand heroic act. But I believe that it is inaccurate to describe *Middlemarch,* as at least one critic has done, as a study in frustration [see essay by Wagenknecht in Additional Bibliography]. Let us say rather that this novel explores the imperfectly fulfilled life, what would be necessary for fulfillment, the elements which prevent fulfillment, the attempts which are made, the nature of the failure, and the known extent of the success. For it is still possible for such lives to fulfill themselves partially if, like Dorothea, they can come to see what their lives should be in relation to those about them—in short, if they can enlarge their vision. George Eliot's last statement about Dorothea . . . implies such a partial fulfillment:

> Her finely-touched spirit had still its fine issues, though they were not widely visible. Her full nature, like that river of which Cyrus broke the strength, spent itself in channels which had no great name on earth. But the effect of her being on those around her was incalculably diffusive: for the growing good of the world is partly dependent on unhistoric acts. . . .

Hence the double significance of "this particular web" on which George Eliot chose to focus her light: it is useful as a means of indicating both the meanness of opportunity and the incalculably diffusive effect of human actions peformed within such restricting circumstances. (pp. 141-43)

[The web metaphor is also useful] as a partial way of defining one of the two antithetical movements in the novel, the movement away from moral vision. It is surely of extreme significance that of the four major characters whose downfall the book depicts, all are at some time metaphorically shown to be spinning or weaving a web—all four, but only these four: Lydgate, Rosamond, Casaubon, and Bulstrode. The primary reason that the web image as it is used in relation to these four characters assists in the definition of the movement away from vision is that it either equals an illusion or indicates the means by which an illusion is fixed. Either it represents an insular world or it represents the insulation which makes such a world possible. The distinction here is unimportant—perhaps it does not even have to be made—but what is important is that the web, as used in relation to these characters, is connected with illusion and egoism rather than with reality and fellow-feeling.

Even before she sees Lydgate, Rosamond begins constructing the web of illusion which is eventually to entangle the two of them: "Ever since that important new arrival in Middlemarch she had *woven* a little future, of which something like this scene [her first meeting with Lydgate] was the necessary beginning." . . . Lydgate, we soon learn, had not "been *weaving* any future in which their lots were united; but a man naturally remembers a charming girl with pleasure." . . . After a period of time during which Rosamond "reached her *netting*" . . . and Mrs. Bulstrode's hints about marriage "had managed to get *woven* like slight clinging *hairs* into the more substantial *web* of his thoughts," . . . Lydgate becomes so deeply involved that he rationalizes about his firm resolve not to let marriage come between him and his medical research. Failing to benefit by the experience of having "once already been drawn headlong by impetuous folly," . . . he does not see the real Rosamond beneath the beautiful flowerlike exterior. The fragile web of courtship is therefore created by Lydgate out of his illusory expectations of happiness:

> Young love-making—that *gossamer web!* Even the points it clings to—the things whence its subtle interlacings are swung—are *scarcely perceptible:* momentary touches of finger-tips, meetings of rays from blue and dark orbs, unfinished phrases, lightest changes of cheek and lips, faintest tremors. The *web* itself is made of spontaneous beliefs and indefinable joys, yearnings of one life toward another, visions of completeness, indefinite trust. And *Lydgate fell to spinning that web* from his inward self with wonderful rapidity, in spite of experience supposed to be finished off with the drama of Laure—in spite too of medicine and biology. . . . As for Rosamond, she was in the water-lily's exapnding wonderment at its own fuller life, and she too was *spinning* industriously at the mutual web. . . .

Here again the author examines the play of minute causes which is barely discernible even to the most acute eye, for this is one of those subtle movements of the soul which **Middlemarch** traces. . . . Seen in full context the image of Lydgate spinning the gossamer web is connected with the gradual lessening of his firm resolves and most specifically with his resolve not to marry. Obviously the act of falling in love does not in itself constitute moral drifting, but in Lydgate it marks the beginning of his loss of direction. For it is during this period in his life that Lydgate slowly begins to lose the self-mastery which is necessary to prevent his once more being drawn headlong. But the signs of his moral drifting are still, like the signs of love, scarcely perceptible. In fact, it is not so much the entangling property of the web which is emphasized, although that is implicit in the image, as the unobservable mystery which attends its creation and its extremely fragile, insubstantial and illusive nature.

Mr. Casaubon also weaves a web of illusion but out of passions which are in themselves ignoble. Fearing that Dorothea no longer looks upon him without criticism, he misinterprets and builds on certain facts concerning her and Will Ladislaw, bringing his

power of suspicious construction into exasperated activity. To all the facts which he knew, he added imaginary facts both present and future which became more real to him than those, because they called up a stronger dislike, a more predominating bitterness. Suspicion and jealousy of Will Ladislaw's intentions, suspicion and jealousy of Dorothea's impressions, were constantly at their *weaving* work.

His vision so blinded that he can see nothing but self, Casaubon weaves an illusion which further cuts him off from vision; speaking generally in this passage about Casaubon, the author asks: "Will not a tiny speck very close to our *vision* blot out the glory of the world, and leave only a margin by which we *see* the blot? I know no speck so troublesome as self." . . . (pp. 149-51)

Elsewhere George Eliot explores Casaubon's inner life in terms which more clearly show the web image in relation to the themes of egoism and vision. Speaking of his inability to know the intense joy which can come only when one is at least partially freed from self, she says: "His experience was of that pitiable kind which shrinks from pity, and fears most of all that it should be known: it was that proud, narrow sensitiveness which has not mass enough to spare for transformation into sympathy, and quivers *thread-like* in small currents of self-preoccupation or at best of an *egoistic* scrupulosity." . . . These "thread-like currents" form a kind of insular world in which the self is entrapped, cut off from sympathy and unable to sympathize, cut off finally from the full participation in life which a wider vision would make possible. . . . (pp. 151-52)

Casaubon is not the only character in **Middlemarch** who feels the need of such protective insulation, for Bulstrode badly needs it if he is to survive in the dual role of hard businessman and religious fanatic. Hence when he had found himself engaged in a crooked business entirely incompatible with his religious position he began a rationalizing process which, continued over a period of years, gradually creates in him a moral incapacity. In that past life he had acted on the principle that "his religious activity could not be incompatible with his business as soon as he had argued himself into not feeling it incompatible." . . . Eventually faced with the problem of his past in the inescapable fact of Raffles' presence in Middlemarch, he reiterates his rationale:

> Mentally surrounded with that past again, Bulstrode had the same pleas—indeed, the years had been perpetually *spinning* them into *intricate thickness, like masses of spider-web, padding the moral sensibility;* nay, as age made *egosim* more eager but less enjoying, his soul had become more saturated with the belief that he did everything for God's sake, being indifferent to it for his own . . .

Thus the weblike padding creates an insular world from which all of the elements that contradict self-view are excluded in order that the illusion about self may be perpetuated. Clearly any action which so pads the moral sensibility and so elevates the ego constitutes a movement away from moral vision.

A slighter but somewhat similar image is used to describe Rosamond, whose egoism, if second to that of any character in **Middlemarch**, is second only to Bulstrode's. On one of the numberless occasions when Rosamond employs her cleverness to secure her own way in opposition to Lydgate, he gradually comes to understand the egoistic nature of this cleverness which had so attracted him to her: "He had regarded Rosamond's cleverness as precisely of that receptive kind which became a woman. He was now beginning to find out what that cleverness was—what was the shape into which it had run as into *a close network* aloof and independent." . . . This passage partially indicates the illusion about Rosamond out of which Lydgate spun his share of the "mutual web," the illusion that cleverness is receptive and womanly. The "close work" of Rosamond's cleverness is indeed neither fragile nor dependent on any other creature. Rather the image effectively suggests the strong impenetrable nature of Rosamond's egoism. "What she liked to do was to her the right thing, and all of her cleverness was directed to getting the means of doing it." . . . When, however, what is needed is not something she likes, the cleverness remains neutral and apart. . . . It is, of course, Lydgate's inability to penetrate Rosamond's aloof neutrality that finally makes impossible any reasonable solution to their domestic difficulty. Rosamond does not, like Casaubon and Bulstrode, create a padding against a world she fears will find her culpable—"In fact there was but one person in Rosamond's world whom she did not regard as blameworthy" . . .—but the aloof and independent network of her cleverness is just as sure a means of preserving her egoism and cutting her off from fellow feeling.

It is, however, not only the Bulstrodes, Casaubons, and Rosamonds whose moral sensibility is padded but those of every human being, George Eliot reminds us: "If we had a *keen vision* and feeling of all ordinary human life, it would be like hearing the grass grow and the squirrel's heart beat, and we should die of that roar which lies on the other side of silence. As it is, the quickest of us walk about well *wadded* with stupidity." . . . Obviously we do not need to supply further protection, since truly keen vision and feeling of all ordinary human life can never be achieved. *Middlemarch* is therefore dedicated to showing another kind of death, that which occurs as the result of too much padding. (pp. 152-54)

Reva Stump, in her Movement and Vision in George Eliot's Novels, *University of Washington Press, 1959, 232 p.*

BARBARA HARDY (essay date 1959)

[*One of Eliot's most prolific critics, Hardy has written numerous essays on* Middlemarch; *in addition, she edited an important collection of criticism on the novel. In the following excerpt, drawn from Hardy's full-length study of Eliot's fiction, she explains how* Middlemarch's *structure complements its themes. For further criticism by Hardy on* Middlemarch, *see excerpt dated 1964.*]

[*Middlemarch*] is a novel with an extraordinary sense of expanding life. The double plots of *Felix Holt* or *Wuthering Heights* or *Vanity Fair* are highly rigid pieces of parallelism compared with *Middlemarch*, where the structure has its effect of human generalization and differentiation, but avoids the stiffness of symmetry. The four related stories of *Middlemarch* make a structural equivalent of the novel without heroes. This novel has its central figures, but the reader is forced to switch attention from each in turn. There is no constant focus, and yet it is very different from most attempts to shift the point of view.

Its most obvious effect is social breadth, and it is certainly one of the few studies of a community where the community has weight and character. Middlemarch is given its presence in many ways, by an approach to personification, and by a rich variety of crowd scenes—parties, meetings, a funeral, an auction—where there is a rest from the psychological concentration of each of the four main actions. But it is the combined presence of those four actions which gives the community its force and its shaping pressure. The assembly of individuals shows a society. But there is no distant and flickering bird's-eye-view, for the multiplicity of viewpoint has enough space in which to work without sacrificing closeness.

The novel begins for ten chapters as if it were a novel with a central figure. Then we move, rather abruptly, it may seem on first reading, from Dorothea to Lydgate, and we never return to her again with such concentration and such expansiveness. This piece of structural effect may be the result of George Eliot's originally separate conception of *Miss Brooke*, though on the other hand *Miss Brooke*'s easy fusion with *Middlemarch* is a practical demonstration of George Eliot's constancy of theme and, more important here, of her urge towards the divided novel.

Dorothea's central position is to some extent weighted by the Prologue and Epilogue, and by her long introductory occupation of the novel. After those chapters she shares the rotation with the other characters. George Eliot and Lewes were aware that readers might be disappointed when the action moves away from Dorothea for so long, but this very disappointment is functional. Dorothea cannot be a Saint Theresa in this society, and the theme of human fellowship must be developed without one engrossing figure. Once the interest and curiosity has been established, by exposition, and revealing action, we move to the story of Lydgate.

The management of transition is worth looking at, especially since it is to some extent determined by the publication in parts. . . . [There] was the conscious need for representing most of the interests of the four actions in each part. The transition from Dorothea begins in chapter x, which is a crowd-scene introducing Lydgate and Bulstrode and Mr Vincy, as well as making the social expansion from the gentry to the bourgeoisie, and from one main plot-interest to several others. (pp. 93-5)

The dinner-party provides an excellent occasion for choral gossip, mainly about the future bride and bridegroom, Dorothea and Casaubon, and the newcomer, Lydgate. After we have shifted from the choral comment to that part of it which is Lydgate's private point of view, we leave Dorothea: 'Not long after that dinner-party she had become Mrs Casaubon, and was on her way to Rome'.

In the next chapter we go back in time and back to Lydgate. The transition is simple and smooth: 'Lydgate, in fact, was already conscious of being fascinated by a woman strikingly different from Miss Brooke . . . ' and, with a few ironical anticipations of future relations, we move to Rosamond, Fred, and to the mention of Mary Garth and the last illness of old Featherstone. Lydgate has been introduced and left in suspense while we move backwards in time to his first meeting with Rosamond. And that first meeting at Stone Court is also the introduction to Bulstrode, who has been—so Featherstone thinks—talking maliciously about Fred. The book ends with all the major characters present, and all interrupted in action.

It is not until the next book that Bulstrode and Lydgate put in a lengthy appearance and the fourfold alternating action begins. The alternation is deliberately ironical—Rosamond's imagination plays with Lydgate (before she has seen him) and she arranges the first meeting. Then we have the drama of Lydgate's past love for Laure, and his determination that experience shall now guide his relations with women. And so on. As we move from action to action there is a similar effect of irony or contrast, but often merely produced by the mere dismissal of one character or group and the reappearance of another. This is the shared surface of real life—not of course confined to George Eliot: we have a similar tension and stereoscopic realism in *Clarissa* and *Uncle Tom's Cabin* and *Oliver Twist*, though for a comparable multiplicity we should perhaps go to *War and Peace* or *Ulysses*.

This is a diffused structure with no hero or heroine engrossing its centre. In a sense it creates a collective structure for a portrait of society. But it is more than another version of *Vanity Fair*, the other famous 'Novel without a Hero'. Its shifting point of view is the structural equivalent for its theme of illusion, and the insistent rotation, with ironical contrast and comparison, puts each illusion in its place amongst the rest and lets the contradictions stand. Dorothea and Casaubon, Rosamond and Lydgate, Fred and Mary, Bulstrode and Featherstone, all are shown in their private dreams, mostly making their incompatible demands on life. As the novel rotates we change our point of view, and the common illusion of supreme self-importance is exposed. The two marriages are delineated in ironical resemblance and difference, the two men die and the others wait for death, the unspoken dreams clash against each other. The structural movement puts each assertion in its place, and indeed makes it unnecessary for the author to do more than give an occasional jog to the movement. The diffused action is concentrated by this constant contrast and comparison. (pp. 95-96)

The main source of the concentration of *Middlemarch*, the book which even in this decade has been said to lack 'architecture', is the correspondence of one plot with another. These are not tenuously related parts, but different versions of the same story. There are four pairs, linked by love and marriage: the Casaubons, the Lydgates, the Bulstrodes, and Fred and Mary. The correspondence is one of moral implication but George Eliot often uses a relatively trivial coincidence to draw our attention to the greater coincidence, or to put us into her habit of seeing the similarities of 'human lots'. She uses the trivial fact that Casaubon is courting Dorothea at the same time that Lydgate is getting to know Rosamond in order to point to other similarities and other differences:

> He had seen Miss Vincy above his horizon almost as long as it had taken Mr Casaubon to become engaged and married: but this learned gentleman was possessed of a fortune. . .

The problems of money is one of the several themes which run though the contrasts and likeness of these marriages. But the important cross-reference is that of moral situation. Each is a marriage of opposites and a moral battlefield where there can be no truce. Rosamond defeats Lydgate, Mrs Bulstrode forgives and loves Bulstrode, Dorothea attempts to love and understand but eventually has to escape Casaubon's 'dead hand', and Mary Garth, with some help from Ibsen's 'helpers and servers'—Farebrother, Caleb Garth, and Featherstone's 'dead hand',—succeeds in rescuing Fred.

The Morality Play beneath the full rich novel is laid bare by the structural relations. Dorothea's virtue is exposed and defined by the comparison with Lydgate, with Caleb, and with Mary; though it is also exposed and defined by its opposites: Rosamond, Bulstrode, and Casaubon. In Dorothea's relation with Casaubon the human action overlays this kind of formal contrast, but not entirely. The necessary formal reading of the novel as a whole has some influence on our reading of the separate parts, and having observed the parallelism and contrast which binds the units together, we acquire the trained eye which picks out the Morality Play in the domestic scene. Dorothea waits for Casaubon after he has rebuffed her:

> She hesitated, fearing to offend him by obtruding herself; for her ardour, continually repulsed, served, with her intense memory, to heighten her dread, as thwarted energy subsides into a shudder; and she wandered slowly round the nearer clumps of trees until she saw him advancing. Then she went towards him, and might have represented a heaven-sent angel coming with a promise that the short hours remaining should yet be filled with that faithful love which clings the closer to a comprehended grief. His glance in reply to hers was so chill that she felt her timidity increased; yet she turned and passed her hand through his arm.
>
> Mr Casaubon kept his hands behind him and allowed her pliant arm to cling with difficulty against his rigid arm.
>
> There was something horrible to Dorothea in the sensation which this unresponsive hardness inflicted on her. That is a strong word, but not too strong: it is in these acts called trivialities that the seeds of joy are for ever wasted.

(pp. 97-9)

She goes to her room, and in 'the miserable light' sees clearly 'her own and her husband's solitude—how they walked apart so that she was obliged to survey him', and lets 'her resentment govern her'. Then she recoils and makes a characteristic second attempt, going once more to wait for him. He comes out of the library, and this time speaks, 'with a gentle surprise in his tone':

> 'Come, my dear, come. You are young, and need not to extend your life by watching'.
>
> When the kind quiet melancholy of that speech fell on Dorothea's ears, she felt something like the thankfulness that might well up in us if we had narrowly escaped hurting a lamed creature. She put her hand into her husband's, and they went along the broad corridor together.

(pp. 99-100)

Here there is the moral contrast of rigidity and chill, pliancy and warmth, and it is a contrast made more apparent by being repeated in the same kind of contrast between a similar pair of opposites, Rosamond and Lydgate. But within the immediate response to such scenes the Morality contrast is subdued to the dramatic moment: we see the moral opposites, lit by other contrast, and by the formality of images like the 'heaven-sent angel', and by the swift movement of generalization—'it is in these acts'—but what is most prominent is the particular human relationship, its domestic conflict, its temporary peace and resolution. So with Dorothea's approach to Rosamond. When the two women meet on the morning after Dorothea has found Rosamond with Will, there is the full irony of the meeting of opposites. It is the moral humour which determines the meeting: Rosamond's egoism has made the deceptive scene,

Dorothea's refusal to stay in her private grief and jealousy has brought her back to Rosamond. But the moral opposition is only a part of the scene. Dorothea has come out of a private and self-absorbing despair; Rosamond is for the moment forced to forget herself—in her way—and tell Dorothea that Will does not love her but Dorothea herself. The excitement of the crisis is only in part the characteristic moral collision, for it is in part the human unpredictability that George Eliot sets free to determine the action.

There is something else which gives this kind of moral antithesis its humanity. The characters are mixed, and even Dorothea has her bitter jealousy, even Rosamond her temporary vision of what it feels like to be someone else. But, even allowing for George Eliot's deference to the mixture which modifies the moral pattern, there is the further tentativeness especially characteristic of *Middlemarch*. The moral issue is shown without complacency. Dorothea is much less and much more than a moral example—unlike Dinah and Felix and Daniel Deronda— and her warm impulse is shown with tact and truth, as a gesture rather than a converting influence. Dinah and Felix and Daniel represent the same urge away from self, but, with very few exceptions, their words and actions have a vast converting influence. These characters have the simplicity and great stature of abstractions in a Morality Play, and something of their magical power.

It is otherwise with Dorothea. When Casaubon rebuffs her she subdues her pride and goes to wait for him. He is touched— to 'kind quiet melancholy', but their marriage is still a divided one and the division grows after his death. She is the only one in Middlemarch who tells Lydgate that she believes in him, but he does not accept her advice when she begs him to stay. She subdues her scorn and goes back a second time to help Rosamond, and Rosamond performs her one unselfish act of confession and self-humiliation, but lives on to become Lydgate's 'basil plant'. The moral pattern in *Middlemarch* is blurred by its human truth. Dorothea's influence is exactly what George Eliot says it is at the end of the novel, 'the effect of her being on those around her was incalculably diffusive'. Her generous warmth has no more than a brief effect on the others, and they go on in their chill, not radically changed. This tentativeness in Dorothea is something Dr Leavis seems to overlook when he says of *Middlemarch* that 'the situations offered by way of "objective correlative" have the daydream relation to experience; they are generated by a need to soar above the indocile facts and conditions of the real world' [see *NCLC*, Vol. 4]. It is true that much of the imagery has this daydream quality, and that Dorothea is often presented in terms of adjectives and descriptions of 'exalting potency'. But I find this exalting potency more characteristic of George Eliot's treatment of love than of her treatment of moral situations. The action and situations of *Middlemarch* seem to be making a brave attempt to face this indocile world, and not to soar above it. Dorothea is idealized in her relationship with Will, and perhaps at times elsewhere, but many of her actions are not idealized but shown as decidedly unspectacular. It is a novel where there are no moral miracles.

Dorothea's influence is shown as fragmentary, diffused, and even temporary. The form in which we read her story is appropriate: we assemble our impression of her influence from fragmentary episodes, often from her brief appearance in other people's stories, and always interrupted by other lives. She does not play a central part, and her coming and going as a minor character or a spectator in the other actions helps to underline the final tentative verdict. But this piecemeal reading extends to all the characters: it is a characteristic of the form of this novel, and has various effects.

George Eliot makes her structural relations of character plain: even the reader who may not formulate the pattern of the novel, must presumably notice some of the more obvious resemblances and differences between the four pairs of men and women. But there are hints carefully placed for the reader who may be too absorbed in reading the story to observe the pattern. These hints are of various kinds. One characteristic kind of hint comes in the passages of general comment which we skip at our peril. In her generalization we frequently find her giving anonymous and typical examples to reinforce a particular moral commentary, and if we read carefully we often find that the anonymous example in the list may crop up, sooner or later, in the course of the action. (pp. 101-02)

Here, for instance, is Mrs Bulstrode's moment of decision, when she learns of her husband's past crime and present disgrace:

> She locked herself in her room. She needed time to get used to her maimed consciousness, her poor lopped life, before she could walk steadily to the place allotted her. . . .
>
> The man whose prosperity she had shared through nearly half a life, and who had unvaryingly cherished her—now that punishment had befallen him it was not possible to her in any sense to forsake him. There is a forsaking which still sits at the same board and lies on the same couch with the forsaken soul, withering it the more by unloving proximity.

(pp. 102-03)

In the next chapter the anonymous example of this unloving proximity comes to life. Lydgate, though innocent—or almost innocent—is involved in Bulstrode's shame. He too has a wife:

> But Rosamond went home with a sense of justified repugnance towards her husband. What had she really done—how had he really acted? She did not know. Why had he not told her everything? He did not speak to her on the subject, and of course she could not speak to him. It came into her mind once that she would ask her father to let her go home again; but dwelling on that prospect made it seem utter dreariness to her: a married woman gone back to live with her parents—life seemed to have no meaning for her in such a position: she could not contemplate herself in it.

Lydgate waits for her to speak to him, as Bulstrode dared not hope for his wife to speak. The anonymous image in the preceding chapter fits her perfectly. Hers is the silence and hers the withering by 'unloving proximity'.

It is impossible to attempt a full analysis of George Eliot's structural relations: her characters are not only fully clothed with their particular interests, but move in a very intricate pattern, where sometimes a chain of likeness and unlikeness seems to be making the generalization clear. (p. 103)

This carefully woven pattern extends even to minor characters, for this is a novel where, as far as possible, all the characters are carefully weighted with an implied full existence. It is impossible to separate vision and technical device. The grotesque Rigg Featherstone, for instance, is not merely a character introduced as the unexpected heir, the joke up the old man's sleeve produced after death to frustrate the waiting mourners, and the functional link between Raffles, his stepfather, and Bulstrode. As Coleridge said of the Fool in *King Lear,* this character is brought into the main interest of the story. This story is not merely the usual battlefield of egoism and love, but shows the particular ruling passion of men seeking their vocation. All the characters, including Dorothea, are included in the overture to Lydgate's story, where George Eliot laments that we are 'comparatively uninterested in that other kind of "makdom and fairnesse" which must be wooed with industrious thought and patient renunciation of small desires'. Bulstrode is given dimension and sympathy by being brought into direct connection with this important theme: if he could have had his time over again, 'why, then he would choose to be missionary'. So with a minor character like Rigg:

> From his earliest employment as an errand-boy in a seaport, he had looked through the windows of the money-changers as other boys look through the windows of the pastry-cooks; the fascination had wrought itself gradually into a deep special passion. . . . The one joy after which his soul thirsted was to have a money-changer's shop on a much frequented quay.

(p. 106)

This is a good example of George Eliot's method of involving even her minor characters: Rigg's ambition is necessary to the plot because it removes him from Middlemarch, leaving Stone Court free, first for Bulstrode, then for Fred. He frustrates Featherstone's grasping dead hand, just as Dorothea frustrates Casaubon's, and Rigg is no mere figure of parody. But George Eliot puts as much imaginative sympathy into this brief glimpse at Rigg's ruling passion as she puts into the long and moving account of Lydgate's love for medicine. It is not merely the act of parallelism which is important, but the quality of the attentiveness. She can use less sympathetic and serious mirrors, of course. There are many lighter instances of this diffused theme of vocation: Mrs Garth, who is unable to understand why anyone could not want to be a teacher, holding her 'Lindley Murray above the waves', Mr Brooke with his extensive list of discarded projects, ending with his political ambition, and little Henrietta Noble and her comfits for the children—the last also a gentle echo of Dorothea's small tentative gestures. The parallel may be made in a different key, but it is never a merely mechanical echo. It is indeed this ability to express the energy of even a minor figure like Rigg which makes this formal pattern say insistently that human beings are very like each other. Human substance is placed before us, and we are not asked to make a quantitative accretion of similar cases but to feel that Rigg's excited vision is of a piece with Dorothea's and Lydgate's. We extract not a theme, not a related subject, but a continuity of passion. Both the ruling passion of man's work, and the slightly more particularized Saint Theresa theme, are generalizations which are forced upon the reader by this deeply felt recurrence. And in *Middlemarch* it is a recurrence which helps to animate the portrait of a society. The community is brought to life not merely by social background—the railway and the Reform Bill—not even by the social influences—the cholera, the hospital and the bank—but because there is this recurrence and difference which make the pattern. (pp. 106-07)

Barbara Hardy, in her The Novels of George Eliot: A Study in Form, *The Athlone Press, 1959, 242 p.*

QUENTIN ANDERSON   (essay date 1960)

[*According to Anderson, the unity of* Middlemarch *derives from the recurrent image of "human relationships as a web." Anderson challenges the traditional division of Eliot's powers into the creative and the intellectual; he contends that Eliot's is the only "fully realized," unified presence in the book.*]

[*Middlemarch*] is subtitled *A Study of Provincial Life,* and the climax in the national life which it partly chronicles, the period in which the Reform Bill of 1832 was moving towards adoption, was selected with the apparent intention of giving the novel the representative quality which we associate with Flaubert's *Sentimental Education* and Tolstoy's *War and Peace.* But one of the first things we must note about the novel is that this particular intention masks a more general one. Flaubert's choice of the revolution of 1848 or Tolstoy's of Napoleon's invasion of Russia as events which bring together various strands of the national experience was motivated in part by a desire to put that experience before us. George Eliot's notebook for the novel shows that she looked up such matters as the stages in the passage of the Reform Bill, the medical horizons of the 1830s, the industrial uses of manganese, and various other details. But the uses to which she puts these things are not terminal; she is not concerned as Flaubert is to lodge firmly in the reader's sensibility a mass of impressions deliberately selected to inform us of the political, industrial, and social life of the time. She is, in fact, incapable of suggesting the tone of a given period or historical moment. In the Middlemarch world, as in George Eliot generally, change is something intrusive, an irruption from without. The more general intention of which I have spoken is the attempt to render in a novel her sense of the 'primitive tissue' of a community.

This term is employed by Tertius Lydgate, a surgeon with excellent training, who buys a Middlemarch practice and hopes to combine medical work with research in physiology. His studies in Paris have persuaded him that a promising line of inquiry lies in the attempt to find the primal tissue which is the basis of all those adapted to special bodily functions. The master image of the book precisely parallels Lydgate's physiological inquiry: this is the image of human relationships as a web. Each of us stands at what seems to us a centre, our own consciousness, though it is in fact but one of numerous nodes or junction points. This is further illustrated in George Eliot's figure of the metal mirror bearing many scratches, which when illuminated at any given point produces the illusion of concentric circles ranged about that point. This figure enriches the suggestion of the recurrent web image and those associated with it by enforcing the fact that in dealing with a particular person we must consider: his appearance in the eyes of each of the other persons whom he encounters; the way he appears among various social groups to which he is known or which know of him; and his own complex of feelings which leads him to offer the world a version (or various versions) of himself. This does not at first seem an epoch-making kind of viewpoint for a novelist, since all novelists must somehow convey the quality of each character's self-regard and the opinions that others have of him. But George Eliot's special success in *Middlemarch* is the consequence of making the reciprocal workings of self-regard and opinion primary—in effect an extraordinary economy of means, and not simply of means, for it appears when we look closely that the matter of the book is people's opinions about one another, and that its particular method consists in contriving scenes in which the disparity between the intentions of agents and the opinions of observers is dramatically exhibited. This consistency of method accounts for our sense of the unity of a book which embraces a whole social order and four, or by another reckoning, five principal stories. (pp. 276-77)

[What George Eliot surveys in **Middlemarch**] may be called a landscape of opinion, for it is not the natural landscape that is dominant here. In fact, there are only two fully realized natural landscapes, Lowick Manor and Stone Court, and in these cases the landscape is realized by an individual whose situation and interests make him aware of an external world at that particular moment. For the most part we may characterize the book's use of the physical world by referring to George Eliot's own sense of Warwickshire as a physical locale which has been wholly humanized, and to the Reverend Cadwallader's half-serious remark that it is a very good quality in a man to have a trout stream. This transposition of the natural into the moral and psychological is further illustrated by the novelist's use of snatches of poetry—Dorothea Brooke's hope for social betterment 'haunted her like a passion'—and we may say that the affectionate sense of nature and the objects that man makes and handles which suffuses **Adam Bede** has been deliberately subdued here. Nothing comparable to the description of Hetty Sorrel in Mrs Poyser's diary can enter into **Middlemarch,** not because it is a more 'intellectual' book, but because its immediacies are not things seen but things felt and believed. It is striking that we know almost nothing of the appearance of Middlemarch itself, although our sense of the life of the town as a community is very full indeed, ranging as it does from a pot-house to the Green Dragon, the town's best inn, from horse-dealers, auctioneers, and grocers to the lawyers, physicians, merchants, clergymen, and landowners who stand at the head of the scale. Although we see little of the activities of all these people we hear their voices, each pitched to the tone of its own desire, each capable of dropping suggestively or rising assertively on grounds which George Eliot shows to be wholly inadequate when related to the facts of the particular case. Chapter 45 is a good instance of the masterly way in which she can demonstrate the drifts and swirls of opinion through the town. In this account of various responses to Lydgate's principled refusal to dispense drugs himself, each of the voices establishes a character so fully and with such economy that it is hard to believe that Mawmsey, the grocer, and Mrs Dollop of the Tankard have not always been known to us. Yet this single chapter does much more. In it we learn that the clouds of misapprehension and selfishness gathering about Lydgate cannot possibly be dispelled, that he is more than likely to get into debt, and that his wife's awful insularity will resist his earnest and even his desparate attempts to penetrate it. George Eliot had much earlier (Chapter 15) used her author's privilege to warn the reader of all these possibilities. 'For surely all must admit that a man may be puffed and belauded, envied, ridiculed, counted upon as a tool and fallen in love with, or at least selected as a future husband, and yet remain virtually unknown—known merely as a cluster of signs for his neighbours' false suppositions.' The novelist, writing of **Middlemarch**, says: 'I wanted to give a panoramic view of provincial life . . .;' but what she does give is something far more active, far more in accord with the image of the web—or of a vast switchboard in which every signal is interpreted differently by each receiver, and each receiver is in its turn capable of propagating in response a signal of its own with equally dissonant consequences. Yet in the end, roughly but surely, the disso-

nances die out and a consensus of sorts emerges, for as George Eliot remarks at one point, not everyone is an originator, and there is a limit to the varieties of error people can fall into.

The characters move in a landscape of opinion, but those who concern us have an inner life; they can look within as well as without, and measure their sense of themselves against the world's demands and expectations. The economy of means and materials I have referred to consists in the use of the landscape of opinion as the scene of action. It does not exclude, it rather informs and gives depth to the conventional motifs and the conventional attributes of character. . . . (pp. 280-81)

Some of George Eliot's devices to enforce her view of the landscape of opinion are [transparent]. . . . Young Fred Vincy has long held expectations based on old Peter Featherstone's will. Peter, who lives to torment his relatives, teases him about a story that he has been trying to borrow money on post-obits. Fred is instructed to get a letter from the stiff-necked Bulstrode to the effect that this is not true.

> You must be joking, sir. Mr Bulstrode, like other men, believes scores of things that are not true, and he has a prejudice against me. I could easily get him to write that he knew no facts in proof of the report you speak of, though it might lead to unpleasantness. But I could hardly ask him to write down what he believes or does not believe about me.

Old Featherstone is here made to demand of Fred Vincy more than Bulstrode's testimony as to the *facts;* had he limited himself to this, Fred would be less uncomfortable—but what has actually been demanded is an account of the way in which Fred is envisioned by another man—an account of one facet of his social being. The imaginative coherence of **Middlemarch** is observable on many levels; in this instance old Featherstone's demand is the counterpart of what chiefly obsesses his last months: the effect that another document, his will, will have on those who survive him. *His* opinion will emerge when his last will is read, and it will comfort no one on the **Middlemarch** scene. Fred, meanwhile, is buoyed up by an opinion generally held that he will inherit from old Featherstone: 'In fact, tacit expectations of what would be done for him by Uncle Featherstone determined the angle at which most people viewed Fred Vincy in Middlemarch; and in his own consciousness, what Uncle Featherstone would do for him in an emergency, or what he would do simply as an incorporated luck, formed always an immeasurable depth of aerial perspective.'

Fred is the son of a ruddy, genial merchant who is shortly to become mayor of the town, and it is part of the pattern that the elder Vincy's sense of self is more completely dependent on the views that others hold of him than that of any other character. When Bulstrode, his brother-in-law, scolds him for training Fred for the Church on simply worldly grounds, his inward reaction is described in this way: 'When a man has the immediate prospect of being mayor, and is ready, in the interests of commerce, to take up a firm attitude on politics generally, he has naturally a sense of his importance to the framework of things which seems to throw questions of private conduct into the background.' When Wrench, the family doctor, fails to diagnose Fred's typhoid fever Mr Vincy feels indignant: 'What Mr. Vincy thought confusedly was, that the fever might somehow have been hindered if Wrench had shown the proper solicitude about his—the Mayor's—family.'

When men and affairs do not conspire to supply his self-love, the elder Vincy very quickly loses his head. Old Featherstone's latest will brings Fred nothing, and the father's view of the son changes instantly: 'He's an uncommonly unfortunate lad, is Fred. He'd need have some luck by-and-by to make up for all this—else I don't know who'd have an eldest son.' (pp. 284-85)

Joan Bennett, in her sensible little book on the novelist, emphasizes George Eliot's observation about the medium in which her characters move: 'It is the habit of my imagination to strive after as full a vision of the medium in which character moves as of the character itself.' . . . *Middlemarch* authorizes an extension of this principle; George Eliot has created a common medium which completely immerses most of the characters. It is hard to conceive how an individual can on this scene really originate anything. Dorothea's wide charity finds no direct expression; Lydgate's scientific interest in the town's health meets blank incomprehension and effectual resistance, not only from all ranks in the medical hierarchy but from almost every element in the town. Indeed, the reader may by now feel . . . that Middlemarch is as oppressive as that provincial town inhabited by Emma Bovary in another study of the *mœurs de province*. In Flaubert's book there are at least the passionate impulses of Emma to combat her stifling world. What is there here? (pp. 286-87)

[The] only thing which can possibly balance, can possibly support *Middlemarch,* is [the] image of the writer which the novel creates in the reader. Were she not there we should not be attending.

George Eliot is present as the only fully realized individual in her book. This sounds like a harsh saying, but it may not be quite so harsh as it sounds. When one is reading *Middlemarch* there are many moments when one looks up and says, 'How intelligent, how penetrating this woman is!' And, of course, one is speaking of George Eliot. In reading the fine chapter of analysis which has to do with Lydgate's character and the situation in which he finds himself in Middlemarch, we come upon this passage:

> He was at a starting-point which makes many a man's career a fine subject for betting, if there were any gentlemen given to that amusement who could appreciate the complicated probabilities of an arduous purpose, with all the possible thwartings and furtherings of circumstance, all the niceties of inward balance, by which a man swims and makes his point or else is carried headlong. The risk would remain, even with close knowledge of Lydgate's character; for character too is a process and an unfolding.

Those who like *Middlemarch* take pleasure in the writer's judiciousness. They are far more tempted to invest themselves with her sensibility than they are to identify themselves with that of any of her characters. It is notable that analytic passages like the one just quoted predominate among those chosen for quotation from Leslie Stephen's day to our own. The description of Caleb Garth, of Rosamond Vincy's terrible self-absorption, of Dorothea's aspirations and her blindness to her sister Celia's world, of Bulstrode's casuistical inner life, of Casaubon's tortured consciousness of inadequacy—all these are analytic though all are matched by passages of dialogue in which their substance is exemplified. Certain dramatic scenes—

that between Dorothea and Rosamond in particular—are also favourites, but again the most familiar passage about Rosamond seems to be that which describes her reaction to the awful, the inconceivable fact that there is another self in the world, one which Ladislaw cherishes far more than hers. These fine and satisfying analytic passages are not additions or decorations, nor do they represent a division within George Eliot, rather they exhibit her sense of process at work within the frame of actuality; it is her life *in* the novel which lies at its heart; this is what we rejoice in. Admittedly this means that no character is freed to exist as Don Quixote or Julien Sorel are enfranchised; the very firmness and clarity of George Eliot's vision, extending to the edges of her canvas, quite preclude her granting to any one of her creatures the authority of existence. Like a goddess, she suffers them to exist in so far as they may be known through sympathy and comprehension. No more life than this can emerge—any further measure would make her characters novelists. Those who are her surrogates, her delegated voices, are in a sense independent of her, but they are wholly caught up within a system of morally and aesthetically statable responses—as is Mary Garth—and correspond rather to Mary Anne Evans, who had once lived within a provincial society, than to George Eliot, the novelist. (pp. 287-88)

Middlemarch, the scene of this novel, is wholly dominated by the finely tempered mind which envisions it. But how is this scene framed and judged from without? What are the effectual boundaries of the landscape of opinion? The town—though it is a middling place from the point of view of one considering a group of provincial towns—lies on the marches, it is on the periphery of the great world, not simply the world of London or even Rome, but the world of science, the arts, and of history; realized human greatness does not enter it. We must inquire how the writer who herself moved in the great world acknowledged that world in *Middlemarch.*

There is a finely scaled scene in *Daniel Deronda* in which Gwendolen Harleth asks the musician, Klesmer, to help her to launch a musical career on nothing more than a feeble talent and her social pretensions. Klesmer confronts Gwendolen with the audacity and the ignorance of her claim. The scene has a wonderfully tonic effect—it is as if George Eliot had managed a dramatic confrontation of the austerities of art with the blind abundant energgies of youth and beauty. Klesmer's treatment of Gwendolen is exquisitely modulated; it is at once a denunciation and a tribute to her as a woman. But she must be told that social lies and politeness have nothing to do with being an artist. In the world of art you must tell the truth; self-regard and the world's opinion must give way before realized mastery. There is an analogous scene in *Middlemarch,* though the standard invoked is not impersonal. Rosamond's flirtation with Ladislaw is abruptly ended when she discovers that Dorothea is all-important to him. She had found in Ladislaw a representative of the world outside Middlemarch to which she had ignorantly aspired, and Ladislaw thinks her of no account. She is momentarily awed into a generosity which brings Ladislaw and Dorothea together. Throughout the book Ladislaw speaks authoritatively about the world outside the town's awareness. It is he who tells Dorothea that Casaubon's work is useless because he has not read the German scholars; it is he who demands fidelity to a standard of artistic accomplishment; he alone has some sense of national politics.

Yet Ladislaw does not have the authority of Klesmer; he is the weakest of the major characters, not merely because he is made to behave like a dilettante, but because George Eliot's judiciousness does not extend to him; he is not understood. In fact, he is rather like a character in an ordinary novel. F. R. Leavis sees this as a consequence of the weakness of the figure of Dorothea. Since she is in part a self-indulgent fantasy of George Eliot's and not wholly disciplined by the demands of the novel, we may think of Ladislaw as an accessory required by the fantasy. Certainly the scenes they share are full of high-flown nonsense. But there is a good deal of evidence that Dorothea and Ladislaw represent something more than the unresolved longings of Mary Anne Evans. The leading characters in *Romola, Felix Holt, Middlemarch,* and *Daniel Deronda* all escape the circle of the author's judgement. It is claimed for each of them that they aspire to or escape into the great world. Dorothea is the partial exception. When confronted by her uncle, Casaubon, her sister Celia, or the Chettams, she is fully controlled, fully understood. But Romola, Felix Holt, and Deronda are all extravagantly moral or extravagantly spiritual or both. And Dorothea and Ladislaw in their scenes together have the same defect.

Instead of thinking of *Middlemarch* as showing two strains, an artistically responsible element and a neurotically compelled one, we must, I believe, adopt a fresh version of the traditional assertion that George Eliot's conception of her fiction is internally divided.... The disjunction between an 'intellectual' George Eliot and a George Eliot who has the novelist's sympathetic comprehension of human beings is ... a clear-cut contradiction. It is the voice heard within the frame of her best fiction which has high intellectual distinction.

But there is an internal division in her conception of *Middlemarch* which corresponds to the far more serious split in *Daniel Deronda,* in which Deronda's mystical religiosity is given precedence over the fictionally superior story of Gwendolen Harleth. (The argument may also be applied to *Romola* and *Felix Holt.*) This split in the writer's conception of fiction appears to have a biographical root. The novels of George Eliot's maturity re-enact her own emancipation; the values which the Garths and Farebrother assert within the little world of Middlemarch are reasserted from the viewpoint of liberated intelligence by the voice of the narrator; her loss of faith, her translation to the metropolis, her defiance of propriety in living with Lewes, are all justified by the activity of the novelist who surveys Middlemarch. The right opinion of the Garths and Farebrother gives way before the knowledge of the novelist. But for George Eliot the re-enactment brought with it an irresistible impulse to include a character who could function as knower, an *embodied* voice.

She was unable, even in the years of her maturest art, to conceive of fiction as a truly independent form. It would seem to have been enough to bring that fine intelligence to bear on the enclosed world of Middlemarch, but she is never content with this. She must bring forward some instance of principled nonconformity, as if to feed an appetite for self-justification. (pp. 290-93)

The English novel is so much the richer for George Eliot's contribution that one may be tempted into scolding her for not doing what no English novelist of the century did: for not taking possession of the great world. Her sense of community, her finely modulated articulation of passion and idea, the clarity and firmness of her characterization—these things alone justify Virginia Woolf's remark that *Middlemarch* was one of the few English novels written for grown-up people [see *NCLC*, Vol. 4]. Since the grown-up perspective includes Flaubert and Tolstoy, we are of course conscious that George Eliot did not share

their power to incarnate the great world in the lesser one, to make the novel an instrument which can register the fate of a society in the perspective of history and heroic achievement. To exercise this power she would have had to take her own splendid powers for granted, and this she could not do. (p. 293)

Quentin Anderson, "George Eliot in 'Middlemarch'," in From Dickens to Hardy, edited by Boris Ford, revised edition, Penguin Books, 1960, pp. 274-93.

DAVID DAICHES (essay date 1963)

[*Daiches is a prominent English scholar and critic who has written extensively on English and American literature. His criticism is often characterized as appreciative in content and attached to no single methodology. The following excerpt is drawn from Daiches's George Eliot: "Middlemarch," a sequential analysis of the novel in which he examines how Eliot develops her characters through narrative voice, symbolism, imagery, language, and structure. Daiches here charts the problems in Dorothea and Casaubon's marriage and traces the evolution of her relationship with Ladislaw.*]

[In chapter I of *Middlemarch*] we are given an interim summing up of Dorothea's character in which, in spite of the humour, the implications of the irony at her expense are truly serious:

> Dorothea, with all her eagerness to know the truths of life, retained very childlike ideas about marriage. She felt sure that she would have accepted the judicious Hooker, if she had been born in time to save him from that wretched mistake he made in matrimony; or John Milton when his blindness had come on; or any of the other great men whose odd habits it would have been glorious piety to endure; but an amiable handsome baronet, who said 'Exactly' to her remarks even when she expressed uncertainty,—how could he affect her as a lover? The really delightful marriage must be that where your husband was a sort of father, and could teach you even Hebrew, if you wished it.

George Eliot is here telling us something of considerable importance about Dorothea, something which will explain her subsequent marriage and also her fiction relationship with Will Ladislaw. Though the tone is ... humorous, there is a tartness at the centre. Dorothea 'retained very childlike ideas about marriage'. To put it in more modern terms, she was sexually unawakened and (this is made clear in more ways than one) did not even know what are often oddly called 'the facts of life'. Marriage for her was an ennobling discipleship to a father-figure. She had no idea of the kind of emotional or physical relationship that was really involved. It was to require a glamourous outsider to awaken her to some awareness of this, and critics who complain of the theatrical unreality of Will Ladislaw would do well to realise what is involved here.... [The] curly-headed Apollo-like figure of Will, confronting Dorothea in the sunshine of Italy at the very moment when she is beginning to realise the barrenness of her marriage to Casaubon, is an almost symbolic agent of release and awakening. That Will eventually captures Dorothea's love, as from this critical Italian encounter he has had her passionate interest, does not mean that we as readers are called upon to admire him or even that his creator admired him. Dorothea by her nature and her history has been conditioned to respond to that kind of person, and the moral implications of this are very ambiguous indeed. The important point, in reading chapter I, is to realise that we are here being shown, with great delicacy but unmistakably, a nineteen-year-old girl who has completely sublimated her sexual instincts (of which of course she is wholly unaware) into an idealistic yearning for service. (pp. 14-15)

[Dorothea's sexual innocence] is paralleled by Casaubon's desiccation. 'He has got no good red blood in his body', comments Sir James Chettam, who has earlier called him a mummy (and been himself, by contrast, called 'blooming' by the author). Sir James's face assumes a look of 'concentrated disgust' when talking of Casaubon. Mrs. Cadwallader supposes that his 'family quarterings are three cuttle-fish, and a commentator rampant'. Casaubon himself is surprised to find, on abandoning himself to his 'stream of feeling' about Dorothea, that it was 'an exceedingly shallow rill'.... The suggestion of sexual impotence, to match Dorothea's sexual ignorance, is irresistible. It is all very delicately done, and no doubt the Victorian reader failed to see in the relationship between these two the matching of impotence and sublimation. But *we* can see it, and we can appreciate how much this illuminates Dorothea's relationship with Will Ladislaw, the awakening agent. In this connection it is worth noting that in chapter 9 we are told of Dorothea's painful incomprehension of 'severe classical nudities and smirking Renaissance-Correggiosities' which stared 'into the midst of her Puritanic conceptions'. 'She had never been taught hòw she could bring them into any sort of relevance with her life'. In the light of this, her later meeting with Will in Italy in a context of Italian painting has an obvious symbolic function. (p. 21)

After Dorothea's marriage to Casaubon, the movement of her mind from idealistic hope to resigned frustration is charted rapidly and with remarkable specificness. Our first view of her as a wife is on her honeymoon in Rome, sobbing in her room in the Via Sestina (chapter 20). Images of narrowness and emptiness crowd on to the page, but at this stage they seem to reflect Dorothea's own limitations. The experience of Rome, 'after the brief narrow experience of her girlhood' was too much for her. We are reminded that she 'had been brought up in English and Swiss Puritanism, fed on meagre Protestant histories and on art chiefly of the hand-screen sort'. We are also reminded that she was 'a girl whose ardent nature turned all her small allowance of knowledge into principles'. She was thus not equipped to respond to Rome: it corresponded to nothing in her experience or could not be turned into principles or assimilated to the principles she had already formed. 'The weight of unintelligible Rome might lie easily on bright nymphs to whom it formed a background for the brilliant picnic of Anglo-foreign society; but Dorothea had no such defence against deep impressions'. George Eliot goes on to give a magnificent analysis of the effect of Rome, with 'all this vast wreck of ambitious ideals, sensuous and spiritual, mixed confusedly with the signs of breathing forgetfulness and degradation', on someone of Dorothea's background and temperament. The conclusion of the paragraph—'and the red drapery which was being hung for Christmas spreading itself everywhere like a disease of the retina'—is startling in its physical force. The image also reminds us of Dorothea's short-sightedness, which is mentioned several times as a literal, physical fact but which we learn more and more to see as symbolic of another kind of short-sightedness, the direct product of her idealising hopefulness.

It is, then, the impact of Rome on inexperience that accounts for Dorothea's unhappiness. Having made this point with con-

siderable brilliance, George Eliot pauses before the fact of Dorothea's marriage. Was this also a factor in her unhappiness? 'Some discouragement, some faintness of heart at the new real future which replaces the imaginary, is not unusual, and we do not expect people [that is, her readers] to be moved by what is not unusual. That element of tragedy which lies in the very fact of frequency, has not yet wrought itself into the coarse emotion of mankind; and perhaps our frames could hardly bear much of it'. George Eliot is here being ironical about marriage, ironical about her readers, ironical about human nature. We are not to expect any of the conventional novelistic ways of handling marriage, evidently. It is a curious and effective pause, leaving the reader deliberately in suspense, before the author gathers herself together and fairly assaults the reader with evidence of Casaubon's inadequacy and of Dorothea's marital disillusion. It is not, then, simply Rome after all.

Dorothea's view of Casaubon was changing. But, mocks the author, surely he was just as learned as before? Dorothea had not really known him before. 'The fact is unalterable, that a fellow-mortal with whose nature you are acquainted solely through the brief entrances and exits of a few imaginative weeks called courtship, may, when seen in the continuity of married companionship, be disclosed as something better or worse than what you have preconceived, but will certainly not appear altogether the same'. Then follow the assaulting phrases and images which positively overwhelm the reader with a vivid sense of Casaubon's deficiencies. 'Stifling depression', 'ante-rooms and winding passages which seemed to lead nowhither', 'forlorn weariness', 'mental shiver', 'blank absence of interest or sympathy', 'lost among closets and winding stairs', and a characteristic use of water imagery to suggest the disparity between Dorothea's expectations and the reality: 'Having once embarked on your marital voyage, it is impossible not to be aware that you make no way and that the sea is not within sight—that, in fact, you are exploring an enclosed basin'. This imagery is reinforced by our exposure to Casaubon's conversation, with its chill pomposity of diction:

> 'Yes', said Mr. Casaubon, with that peculiar pitch of voice which makes the word half a negative. 'I have been led farther than I had foreseen, and various subjects for annotation have presented themselves which, though I have no direct need of them, I could not pretermit. The task, notwithstanding the assistance of my amanuensis, has been a somewhat laborious one, but your society has happily prevented me from that too continuous prosecution of thought beyond the hours of study which has been the snare of my solitary life'.

Words like 'pretermit' and 'amanuensis' fall cold and lifeless in the pedantic sing-song rhythms of the prose. Casaubon's frightened self is hidden far below this repulsive camouflage of words. It is his second speech of about the same length; an earlier one, separated in this chapter by the image of his being lost among small closets and winding stairs, came in answer to Dorothea's attempt to get through to his real self, to find out what he himself really thought about the frescoes at the Farnesina:

> 'They are, I believe, highly esteemed. Some of them represent the fable of Cupid and Psyche, which is probably the romantic invention of a literary period, and cannot, I think, be reckoned as a genuine mythical product. But if

you like these wall-paintings we can easily drive thither; and you will then, I think, have seen the chief works of Raphael, any of which it were a pity to omit in a visit to Rome. He is the painter who has been held to combine the most complete grace of form with sublimity of expression. Such at least I have gathered to be the opinion of cognoscenti'.

The tiny scared self remains concealed. The irony is the greater when we realise that this pedantic shuffling out of any responsibility to understand comes from a man whose life-work is supposed to be the provision of a full and final understanding of all mythology. Dorothea is led by her as yet only half-conscious fears to press him about his work: when will he stop compiling his interminable notes and begin to write his book? Casaubon, hit hard on his most vulnerable spot, responds with cold cruelty, snubbing Dorothea completely. The cruelty, it is made clear, is the measure of his own desperate fear of being found out by his wife. Even at this stage we have a certain compassion for the man who, haivng married for comfort and support, finds that his once humbly adoring wife is about to discover his central inadequacy which he has hitherto tried to hide even from himself.

To bring Will in at this stage was a masterstroke: it is to oppose the sun-god to the ice-god. But we must not make the mistake, here or elsewhere, of taking Dorothea's view of Will as wholly identical with the author's. The introductory dialogue between Will and Naumann establishes Will as something of a playboy of the arts. His talk about art with Dorothea has not the same function of Klesmer's great confrontation of Gwendolen Harleth in **Daniel Deronda,** when he explains to her how hard the true service of art really is. Klesmer is trying to make Gwendolen see her own irresponsibility and shallowness, is trying to shock her into some moral maturity. Will, on the other hand, is trying to release some of Dorothea's repressed sensuous awareness; or rather, this is what he succeeds in doing, as well as in sowing further distrust of Casaubon, but his aim is largely egotistical, to make himself feel good in his relation with Dorothea. Dorothea is absolutely ripe for impression by a handsome and arty young man. This does not mean that the author's sympathy is withheld from Will. Clearly, he is a hero of a kind. Yet his later adventures in Middlemarch are often treated by George Eliot with an amused air; if criticicm is waived (and sometimes it is not) that is, we feel, because of the author's indulgence. Sometimes we see him transfigured by Dorothea's feelings towards him; sometimes he is an almost purely symbolic figure of release and fulfilment; in the end he manages to combine, in a rather mechanical way, aesthetic sensitivity, human understanding, and zeal for the public good, which might well be George Eliot's formula for the ideal husband. He is never fully realised, but he serves his purpose in the novel. Dorothea's short-sightedness is only partly cured by experience, and the girl who married Casaubon to her friends' astonishment is not so very different from the girl who marries Will Ladislaw to her friends' disgust. Some critics have written of Will as though he is being proposed by the author as in all circumstances the ideal husband of the ideal woman. This is grossly to over-simplify George Eliot's art. We are never left in doubt of the fact that Dorothea's actions are restricted by the time and place and circumstances in which she lives: that, indeed, is the theme of the Prelude [see excerpt dated 1871]. Will is what time and place and circumstances offer, ideal for Dorothea only in this context. (pp. 39-43)

The confrontation of Will and Casaubon in Rome is emphasised by an overt use of the sun symbol which always lies fairly close to the surface where Will is present. When Casaubon comes home to find his wife and his young cousin engaged in conversation, he 'felt a surprise which was quite unmixed with pleasure'. Then we are told:

> The first impression on seeing Will was one of sunny brightness, which added to the uncertainty of his changing expression. Surely, his very features changed their form; his jaw looked sometimes large and sometimes small; and the little ripple in his nose was a preparation for metamorphosis. When he turned his head quickly his hair seemed to shake out light, and some persons thought they saw decided genius in this coruscation. Mr. Casaubon, on the contrary, stood rayless.

Whose impression is being described here? Not Casaubon's certainly. Is it the author's? But consider the tone—the force of that 'surely', the humorous reference to classical mythology in the phrase, 'a preparation for metamorphosis'. Consider the dry sentence, 'Mr. Casaubon, on the contrary, stood rayless'. There is obvious ironic humour in the fact that whereas Casaubon has devoted his life to writing, in a particularly dead fashion, about mythology, his wife is here being assaulted by a real life myth, a sunny figure on the point of metamorphosis (and we think here, however briefly, of Ovid's *Metamorphoses,* that great repository of classical myth). The irony is far from being all at Casaubon's expense, however. 'Some persons thought they saw decided genius in this coruscation'. The language gives away a certain flippancy of tone, a certain refusal to commit the author to this view. Indeed, the view of Will which we are given here is not quite the author's and not quite Dorothea's; it is a sort of author's parody of Dorothea's view. Dorothea, rather than Will, is being gently laughed at. At the same time the Apollo aspect of Will is emphasised, and plays its part in weaving the texture of the story.

Chapter 21, in which the paragraph occurs, is one of the great chapters. By the time it ends we have seen the full movement of Dorothea's mind with respect to her husband almost to the point of compassion. 'As Dorothea's eyes were turned anxiously on her husband she was perhaps not insensible to the contrast, but it was only mingled with other causes in making her more conscious of that new alarm on his behalf which was the first stirring of a pitying tenderness fed by the realities of his lot and not by her own dreams'. With Will's help, she has found Casaubon out and, paradoxically, this leads her for the first time to consider him as he is, not as an object for the satisfaction of her own idealism. . . . The chapter concludes with a paragraph in which the author points the moral in a particularly suggestive manner:

> We are all of us born in moral stupidity, taking the world as an udder to feed our supreme selves: Dorothea had early begun to emerge from that stupidity, but yet it had been easier to her to imagine how she would devote herself to Mr. Casaubon, and become wise and strong in his strength and wisdom, than to conceive with that distinctness which is no longer reflection but feeling—an idea wrought back to the directness of sense, like the solidity of objects—that he had an equivalent centre of self, whence the

lights and shadows must always fall with a certain difference.

(pp. 43-5)

Dorothea has learned no longer to seek from Casaubon a reflection of herself, a satisfaction of her own needs, but to see his objective self as it is, in all its otherness. D. H. Lawrence believed that in realising the mystical core of true otherness in one's partner one finally achieved perfect sexual love. For George Eliot such a realisation was linked not to love but to pity. It had never been love at all, for either Dorothea or Casaubon; each had idealised the other into a perfect server of his own needs, and was thus prevented from seeing the other properly. When they are finally forced to see each other as they really are, Dorothea's idealisation moves rapidly through contempt to pity, and Casaubon's moves at once to egotistical dread. . . . Dorothea's feeling of compassionate helpfulness cannot survive her husband's continuous shrinking—shrinking from her pity, shrinking from her knowledge. Contempt, even hatred, lie always in wait. By the time of his death he had become nothing but a heavy duty, and after his death he became a dead hand clutching from the grave. (pp. 45-6)

The final coming together of Dorothea and Will Ladislaw has sometimes been censured as a conventional romantic happy ending unworthy of such a great novel. This is understandable; a certain relaxation of artistic strenuousness, a lowering of the pitch of the work, seems to take place in the later stretches. But we must not be blind to the evidence of irony at both Will's and Dorothea's expense that persists right up to the end of the book, nor to the author's insistence in the Finale that marriage is not a conventional happy ending but 'a great beginning' (thus suggesting that no ideal resolution of Dorothea's problem has been achieved even in marrying Will). Will's decision to stay away from Middlemarch is treated at the opening of chapter 82 with considerable mockery:

> When Will Ladislaw exiled himself from Middlemarch he had placed no stronger obstacle to his return than his own resolve, which was by no means an iron barrier, but simply a state of mind liable to melt into a minuet with other states of mind, and to find itself bowing, smiling, and giving place with polite facility.

And in spite of his vindication in the matter of his relations with Rosamond, he had behaved selfishly and recklessly: he had, in fact, though with different motives and in a different way, aroused in Rosamond expectations similar to those that Lydgate had first aroused in her. Lydgate's discovery of what he had unwittingly aroused in Rosamond produced tenderness which he mistook for love; Will's produced uneasiness. 'To a creature of Will's susceptible temperament—without any neutral region of indifference in his nature, ready to turn everything that befell him into the collisions of passionate drama—the revelation that Rosamond had made her happiness in any way dependent on him was a difficulty which his outburst of rage towards her had immeasurably increased for him'. This sense of Will's having got himself into a nasty mess does not—and surely is not meant to—increase our respect for his character.

We move from this scene to find Dorothea frustrated in her desire to do good:

> What was there to be done in the village! O dear! nothing. Everybody was well and had flannel; nobody's pig had died; and it was Saturday morning, when there was a general scrubbing of floors and door-stones, and when it was useless to go into the school.

So she determines on some improving reading, and tries in vain to learn the geography of Asia Minor. The author is still affectionate towards Dorothea, but this scene reduces her, good-humouredly enough, from a Saint Theresa figure to a rather silly schoolgirl. The culminating interview with Will comes immediately after this, in the same chapter (83). Both characters are rapidly restored to dignity by the nature of the scene which is now enacted: it is beautifully symbolic and at the same time utterly persuasive psychologically.

> While he was speaking there came a vivid flash of lightning which lit each of them up for the other—and the light seemed to be the terror of a hopeless love. Dorothea darted instantaneously from the window; Will followed her, seizing her hand with a spasmodic movement; and so they stood, with their hands clasped, like two children, looking out on the storm . . .

They are two children in a stormy world. Both Will's impetuous romantic chat about art and politics and Dorothea's passionately idealistic desires to be of service are now admitted, and at the same time dignified, as qualities of children. Yet Dorothea has learned from experience; indeed, they both have. . . . The in-

A photograph of George Henry Lewes, with whom Eliot lived from 1854 until his death in 1878.

nocence of this couple is not incompatible with their having learned from experience; it suggests rather a certain incompatibility with the ordinariness and the compromises of the workaday world. Yet even in this symbolic scene Will is not spared. . . . The egotism of his angry insistence to Dorothea that his life is maimed and his refusal to consider any possible hope or comfort (for himself; he is less concerned with her) is blatant. In the end, it is she who has to propose to him. (pp. 62-4)

David Daiches, in his George Eliot: "Middlemarch," *Edward Arnold (Publishers) Ltd., 1963, 72 p.*

BARBARA HARDY   (essay date 1964)

[*Hardy states that both the realism and unity of* Middlemarch *are flawed by Eliot's refusal to discuss Dorothea and Ladislaw's sexual relationship. According to Hardy, Eliot's "silence" on this subject "is a psychological flaw because of a failure in truthfulness, [and] a structural flaw because of the vivid presence of truthfulness elsewhere." For additional commentary by Hardy on* Middlemarch, *see excerpt dated 1959.*]

Middlemarch provides us with a model for the expansive form, in its large scope, multiple variations, and freedom from the restrictions of either aesthetic or ideological form. Many of its structural features—antithesis and parallelism, anticipation and echo, scenic condensation—are those we also find in Meredith and indeed in Henry James, but in a restricted range. Not only is the organization of *Middlemarch* much less conspicuous and indeed less elegantly symmetrical than that of a novel by James, but there is never any sacrifice of truthfulness to the achievement of aesthetic ends. The form is the means to the ends of good story, moral argument, and the imitation of life. It is much more naturally plotted than the ideological novels, less dependent on coincidence and less restricted to crisis, and it shapes its moral argument tentatively through character and action, instead of shaping character and action in accordance with dogma. There are no strong climaxes like those at the end of *The Ambassadors* and *Jane Eyre* which complete a pattern or clinch an argument but distort the appearance of life.

The act of comparison is a dangerous tool in criticism. We may too easily select the material for comparison in order to back our prejudices and preferences, and if we shift the comparison, and put *Middlemarch* beside *Le Rouge et le Noir*, or *Anna Karenina*, or *Lady Chatterley's Lover*, we must modify our sense of its expansiveness and truthfulness. *Middlemarch* is a large, free, and truthful novel . . . but it has its own special restrictions. If we compare it with the novels I have just mentioned, novels which resemble it in social and psychological material to a sufficient extent to make the comparison viable, then we should use the word 'realism' more warily in our praise of George Eliot.

Middlemarch is only restrictedly truthful in its treatment of sexuality. The consequence is not only to make us use the word 'realism' warily but also to look hard at our praise of its formal unity. For one of the interesting features of this restriction is that it is uneven. The novel does not reveal a consistent restriction but a lop-sided one. (pp. 105-06)

[In *Middlemarch*, George Eliot's refusal to be explicit about a sexual situation] is so marked that many readers do not even notice that there is anything which she is refusing to be explicit about. She is reticent—not, I claim, silent—about the Casaubon marriage. This reticence, because it is not silence, is compatible with a truthful and complete account of what it was

like for Dorothea to be married to Casaubon, and what it was like for Casaubon to be married to Dorothea. We may not see the point at once, but when we do, I suggest, everything fits. But the novel's truthfulness is not sustained. In Dorothea's relationship with Will we have much more than a refusal to name the passions. We have a refusal even to suggest them. She is reticent about Dorothea and Casaubon, but she leaves things out in her treatment of Dorothea and Will. The omission is both an unrealistic element in an unusually realistic novel and the cause of imbalance. We can make the criticism in terms of truth and in terms of form. *Middlemarch* has often been praised as a great realistic novel and, more latterly, as a triumph of unified organization, but both its realism and its unity are flawed. (p. 108)

George Eliot never tells us that Casaubon is impotent. Like most English novelists of her time, she is reticent, sometimes evasive, about sex. *Middlemarch* appeared twenty years before *Jude the Obscure*, and if we compare it with contemporary novels in France and Russia, it leaves out a lot. Everybody knows that Dickens was interested in the social aspects of sex, but contrived to write at length about a prostitute, in *Oliver Twist*, without giving her a local habitation or a name which would be unpalatable in family reading. Sex as an aspect of personal relations scarcely comes into Dickens, but George Eliot is plainly giving her action some sexual substance in *Adam Bede, The Mill on the Floss,* and *Daniel Deronda*. Her domestic drama seems restrained when we compare her with Tolstoy, but restraint is not the same thing as omission, and if we confuse the two when discussing *Middlemarch* we are surely imprecise when we proffer the favourite words of praise like 'adult' and 'realistic'. I am not claiming sexual realism for George Eliot. D. H. Lawrence allows himself total explicitness and is moreover interested in aspects of sexual behaviour which do not concern *Middlemarch* in any way. George Eliot writes within a restricted convention of reticence, and is emphasizing sensibility rather than sexuality. (pp. 109-10)

I do not think that the truthfulness of *Middlemarch* is impaired because George Eliot does not tell us outright that Casaubon is impotent. The very technique of implication has dramatic advantages. . . . On the other hand, I do not want to exaggerate this dramatic decorum. It could have been combined with explicit naming, by the author or one of the characters, and there is no doubt that social and literary restraint governs the novel's reticence. There is no doubt, too, that the sexual failure is only a part of Casaubon's generalized failure of mind and feeling. But the author does not distort the facts of nature and marriage: if we do not see the point, all is not lost, and the novel makes sense. If we do, then many of the small hints and details, as well as the larger tensions, make better sense, are more coherent and complete.

But where the novel shows the unhappy consequences of restricted treatment of sex is in Dorothea's relation with Will Ladislaw. Here is the psychological and structural flaw in *Middlemarch*. It is a psychological flaw because of a failure in truthfulness, a structural flaw because of the vivid presence of truthfulness elsewhere. I do not insist on describing the flaw in psychological and structural terms merely because of an interest in structure, but because I think the successes and failures which are combined in *Middlemarch* afford an interesting model for the formal critic. If we limit our definitions of form in fiction, as we so often do, to the organization of symbols, imagery, and ideas, then we may well pass over this failure. Recognition of this kind of failure forces us to review our ideas of form, especially our ideas of unity. It is possible to demonstrate the thematic and poetic unity of the novel: the themes cohere and perist throughout, and there is a mobile unity of imagery and symbol which has been analysed by several critics. But if we regard form in the largest sense, and think not merely of unity but of a more useful and less popular word, completeness, then we have to qualify our praise of the form of this novel. (pp. 120-21)

Up to a point the fable which lies at the heart of *Middlemarch* is clear enough. The three main characters are Casaubon, Dorothea, and Ladislaw. The fable may be called the rescue into love, and it has many forms in fiction. It is present in James's *The Bostonians*, in Gissing's neglected novel *The Emancipated*, in E. M. Forster's *A Room With a View* and *Where Angels Fear to Tread*, in several of D. H. Lawrence's stories and novels, and in Meredith's *Lord Ormont and his Aminta* and perhaps in *The Egoist*. In all these novels the sexual rescue—from an old man, a woman, a sterile aesthete—has social implications. The rescuer is something of the Noble Savage and something of the Outsider, representing not only personal passion and fertility but the new blood needed and feared by the old establishment. Casaubon is, like Sir Clifford Chatterley, a cluster of different kinds of impotence. His futile mythological research, his nominal clerical function, his birth and property, all combine with his physical and emotional deficiencies to give him a significant place in the unreformed society. Like Sir Clifford, his assumption of Providential grace and favour for self and class gives him more than a merely personal deadness and egoism, though both in *Middlemarch* and *Lady Chatterley's Lover*, this is only an indirect generalization in a novel containing a great deal of overt political and social discussion. George Eliot's advantage over Lawrence, despite her sexual reticence, is that she creates an individual as well as a symbol, a man who feels the internal strain and loneliness of his position, a man torn by doubt and anxiety and pride, a man capable of stepping briefly outside this clearly marked moral category and on one occasion speaking to Dorothea with surprise and humility and recognition, capable of responding as a human being and certainly created out of sympathy and fellow-feeling. There is no possibility of an even identification with the characters in *Lady Chatterley's Lover* because they are not evenly animated, but Casaubon is presented as part of his environment, having a history, having the register of his differentiated consciousness, made of the same stuff as everyone else though warped, hardened, and self-regarding.

Ladislaw completes and answers these social implications. He is 'a kind of gypsy', defiantly declassé, grandson of a woman who rebelled against the Casaubon values of class and money, son of a woman who rebelled against the Bulstrode values of a Nonconformist respectable thieving line. His father is a musician, his mother an actress, and he is a dilettante and a Radical. As a Radical, of course, he also rejects the superficial and feeble liberalism of Brooke. Like Matey Weyburn in *Lord Ormont and his Aminta*, and Mellors in *Lady Chatterley*, he is a social misfit, a man seeking his vocation, and the poor man who wins the lady. But the mere absurdity of the comparison with Mellors or with Forster's Gino makes his deficiencies plain. As a Noble Savage he is a little fragile.

It may be objected that the very comparison itself is artificial, that I am complaining that Ladislaw fails to meet a standard set up by other novels and inappropriately applied to *Middlemarch*. Though I think the social implications of the love-story

in *Middlemarch* are usefully brought out by this classification I am not judging Ladislaw by the general and external standards I may have implied, but by the expectations set up within the novel itself. Ladislaw and Casaubon make an excellent social antithesis in their roles, but an unequal sexual one.

The pattern is worked out very satisfactorily in terms of symbol and image. Dorothea is imprisoned in the stone prison of melancholy Lowick, in the labyrinth, in the dark tomb. Casaubon is the winter-worn husband, and the Minotaur. Ladislaw has a godlike brightness, is irradiated by images of light, is the natural daylight from which Dorothea is shut off. Images of darkness and light, aridity and water, enclosure and space, are strong. (pp. 121-23)

But poetic unity is not enough. The unity and antithetical completeness of the imagery and symbolism of place and weather and appearances are not endorsed by the characters. Ladislaw is presented in terms of sensibility, not sensuality. The sexual implications of the imagery are substantiated in Casaubon—of course he can only refer to the opinions of *cognoscenti* when he shows Dorothea *Cupid and Psyche*—but not in the rescuing hero. At times, indeed, the imagery itself takes on and contributes to Ladislaw's idyllic colouring: there is a sexual implication when Casaubon concludes that the poets have overrated the force of masculine passion which is sadly lacking when we find Will 'verifying in his own experience that higher love-poetry which had charmed his fancy'. . . . When the Cupid and Psyche symbol finds its antithetical completion, after Casaubon's death, the image is delicate and innocent, not strongly passionate:

> She did not know then that it was Love who had come to her briefly, as in a dream before awaking, with the hues of morning on his wings—that it was Love to whom she was sobbing her farewell as his image was banished by the blameless rigour of irresistible day.
>
> (pp. 123-24)

The appropriate comment seems to be that at this point in the story she should have known. There are some Victorian novels in which it might seem captious not to accept such a lack of self-knowledge but *Middlemarch* is not one of them. George Eliot spends a fair amount of energy criticizing Dorothea's ignorance and short-sightedness but here remains romantically identified with this innocence. (p. 124)

I do not mean to suggest that our impression of Will is entirely romantic, innocent, and radiant. In his private thoughts about Dorothea's marriage, in his discussions with Naumann, in his excellently convincing relationship with Lydgate (especially where their masculine solidarity puts Rosamond's narrow femininity in its place), in his quarrels with Bulstrode and his differences with Brooke, he is detached, honest, and touchy. The relationship between Dorothea and Casaubon is presented in terms of sexuality, but that between Dorothea and Ladislaw is shown as denying it, and it is here that his masculinity falters. George Eliot is not hampered by the difficulties of describing actual love-making, though it is worth noticing that when Dorothea and Will touch each other they are at their most innocent and childlike. In the relationship between Maggie and Stephen, or the relationship between Lydgate and Rosamond, in this same novel, tension and desire are conveyed without physical detail.

In this novel sensibility acts as a surrogate for sensuality. This comes out in the presentation of Will as an artist, less marked by his ability than by impressionability. It comes out too in the sustained aesthetic debate which is the beginning of Dorothea's acquaintance with Will, and which has many implications. Dorothea is presented as a Puritan, and this makes for a special irony in her marriage—her self-abnegation has made the innocent blunder possible, but her ardour is there to suffer. It is Will who points out this ignorance and sees the paradox, as Philip did for Maggie. He preaches ardently on behalf of the art he loves, which Dorothea distrusts, because of its obscure relation to the hard realities, because of its apparently trivial delight in beauty. Will's attempt to convert her to the aesthetic attitude is most ironically placed in Rome, on her wedding-journey. Will is presented as an aesthete of a special kind. His impressionability is both praised and doubted: if it shows itself in his response to art and in his restless trials as poet and painter, it shows itself also in his sensitivity to other people—to Lydgate, for instance, as well as to Casaubon and Dorothea, where his understanding is less impartial. But although he is carefully seen as a creature 'of uncertain promise' (like Fred Vincy), he is given much more than an effeminate aestheticism. His arguments in defence of beauty are largely realistic attempts to persuade Dorothea into 'a sturdy delight in things as they are'. Implicit in Dorothea's first bewildered impressions of Rome is, I suggest, a reaction to sensuality. . . . (pp. 125-26)

[There] are more than aesthetic implications in Dorothea's reaction to Rome:

> Ruins and basilicas, palaces and colossi, set in the midst of a sordid present, where all that was living and warm-blooded seemed sunk in the deep degeneracy of a superstition divorced from reverence; the dimmer but yet eager Titanic life gazing and struggling on walls and ceilings; the long vistas of white forms whose marble eyes seemed to hold the monotonous light of an alien world: all this vast wreck of ambitious ideals, sensuous and spiritual, mixed confusedly with the signs of breathing forgetfulness and degradation, at first jarred with an electric shock, and then urged themselves on her with that ache belonging to a glut of confused ideas which check the flow of emotion. Forms both pale and glowing took possession of her young sense, and fixed themselves in her memory even when she was not thinking of them, preparing strange associations which remained through her after-years.
>
> (p. 127)

The vague sensual implications here, and elsewhere, are related to her 'tumultous preoccupations with her personal lot', but not picked up in the ensuing debate with Will. This debate is indeed not continued throughout the novel, and lacks the clearer suggestions to be found in James or Gissing, who both correlate aestheticism with sensuality in their Bohemian characters. Will's Bohemianism and his political activity are both related clearly enough, by opposition, to Casaubon's class-values, to Bulstrode's respectable Nonconformity, and to Brooke's brand of Radicalism, but they are less convincingly related to each other. If the idyllic and romantic innocence of Will's love for Dorothea is one weakness, his movement from art to politics is another aspect of his character which does not ring quite true. There is a slackening in the novel with the disappearance of the aesthetic debate which has carried so much of the antithetical

play of social and sexual values. Will's political activity alone has a slighter reference, leaving his role as lover conspicuous and inadequate. We can see why the debate drops out. Once Dorothea sees her error in marriage, once she sees exactly where her fanaticism and self-ignorance have led her, the aesthetic debate is no longer required, and there are other ways of showing her aversion to her marriage. Her problem ceases to be one of bewilderment and becomes one of clear vision. Once she sees her marriage for what it is—which takes some time—her problem is chiefly that of accepting it, and living with it in activity and not mere resentment and despair. (pp. 127-28)

The weakness of the novel, and the weakness of Will Ladislaw, are located in his relationship with Dorothea. It is when they are together, physically or in thoughts of each other, that the romantic glow seems false and the childlike innocence implausible and inappropriate. In Will's other relations George Eliot can scarcely be accused of romantic softness, or of glossing over sexual problems. She keeps her heroine clear of any emotional conflict in her feeling for her husband and her feeling for Ladislaw, and here the moral scheme strikes the modern reader as being worked out at the expense of truthfulness. But although Will is shown as romantically rejoicing in the purity of Dorothea and in the impossibility of his love—'What others might have called the futility of his passion, made an additional delight for his imagination' . . .—this is only a part of the analysis of Will's emotions. In his relations with Rosamond the 'romantic' glow is strikingly absent.

His rejection of Rosamond is violent, shocked and fearful, and he deals a hard blow to her strong sexual vanity when he tells her that he loves Dorothea: 'I never had a *preference* for her, any more than I have a preference for breathing. No other woman exists by the side of her'. His declaration is a fine example of George Eliot's psychological truthfulness at its best, and it is neither exclusive nor obsessed, as declarations of love tend to be in many Victorian novels. George Eliot shows us the present, in William James's words, as more like a saddleback than a razor-edge, for Will's confident rejection and words of love and loyalty are darkened by the shadow of the possible future. He looks over the edge of the present, though with pain and not with desire. Feeling, moral commitment, and time, are truthfully confused:

> When Lydgate spoke with desperate resignation of going to settle in London, and said with a faint smile, 'We shall have you again, old fellow', Will felt inexpressibly mournful, and said nothing. Rosamond had that morning entreated him to urge this step on Lydgate; and it seemed to him as if he were beholding in a magic panorama a future where he himself was sliding into that pleasureless yielding to the small solicitations of circumstance, which is a commoner history of perdition than any single momentous bargain.
>
> We are on a perilous margin when we begin to look passively at our future selves, and see our own figures led with dull consent into insipid misdoing and shabby achievement.
>
> (pp. 128-29)

Those critics who find Will Ladislaw a weak romantic conception, the under-distanced product of the author's fantasy, might reflect on the fact that few Victorian heroes are shown as contemplating adultery, and so coolly and miserably, in the moment of passionate commitment to the pure heroine. George Eliot is restricted in her handling of the central relationship in this story, but her treatment of the relations of Will and Rosamond, like her treatment of the Casaubon marriage, shows not merely her ability to admit realities commonly left out of the novels of her time, but to recognize uncomfortable truths often evaded or denied outside literature. (p. 129)

Middlemarch, like most novels, has its formal simplifications and omissions which are determined by social and personal factors, but its expansiveness allows for many moments of surprising truth. We cannot say that there is a strict organization of category, of parallels and antitheses, which breaks down in the free admission of change and complexity. In describing the form of the novel we have to confront not a neat symmetry and clear unity which has additional details which seem to be added on, like grace-notes (if we admire them) or as wasteful and arbitrary strokes (if we do not approve), but a highly complex and mobile pattern. But this does not mean that we are left with no standards with which to judge formal success, and in at least one respect, as I have tried to show, it is necessary to criticize *Middlemarch* for a lack of balance and completeness. The demand for unity and the demand for truth should be inseparable. The inadequacy of the word 'unity' is suggested in this attempt to analyse form and truth as inseparable constituents of the good novel, for it would be true to say that *Middlemarch* would be a satisfactory unity if the asexual presentation of Dorothea's relation with Will were matched by a similar omission in the presentation of her relation with Casaubon. Completeness seems to be a better word than unity, including as it does the formal concept of equality of strengths with the concept of truthfulness. Who would exchange the flawed *Middlemarch* with its omissions made conspicuous by its suggestive reticence, for a novel where truth were reduced and mere aesthetic balance retained? (pp. 130-31)

> Barbara Hardy, "Implication and Incompleteness: George Eliot's 'Middlemarch'," in her The Appropriate Form: An Essay on the Novel, *The Athlone Press, 1964, pp. 105-31.*

W. J. HARVEY (essay date 1965)

[*A foremost Eliot scholar, Harvey was among the first twentieth-century critics to champion* Middlemarch *as one of the greatest novels in the English language. In the excerpt below, drawn from Harvey's introduction to the work, he discusses its accuracy as a historical and social document.*]

How far George Eliot drew on historical originals for her characters is not really relevant to a sensitive reading of . . . [*Middlemarch*]. Nor should we interpret the novel too strictly as a historical study. George Eliot's preliminary research does, as a matter of fact, result in a historically accurate picture of her chosen period; there are a few minor mistakes and anachronisms . . . but it would be quite pedantic to quibble about them. As we shall see, a certain knowledge of social history does do much to illuminate certain aspects of her creative achievement, but the important criterion in our use of such extrinsic information is its relevance. For example, while it is obvious from several details in the novel that Middlemarch is based on Coventry, this is of little importance to our general recognition of George Eliot's success in creating a dense, coherent, and credible social world.

Rather more interesting is the question raised by Professor Asa Briggs, when he asserts that 'the problem [George Eliot] sets Lydgate and Dorothea is in its essence a mid-Victorian problem. Their vision and their struggle are the same as her own' [see Additional Bibliography]. How far did George Eliot project into the past of her childhood the issues facing her as an adult? In what ways does *Middlemarch* represent an essentially mid-Victorian world? If George Eliot did this at all, it was certainly not in the sharply topical manner of Dickens, for example, with his attack on the Circumlocution Office in *Little Dorrit.* Professor Briggs is right in the sense that many aspects of the Middlemarch world persisted into, or had their analogues in, later Victorian decades. Thus it is no accident that *Felix Holt* (1866) and *Middlemarch* (1871-2)—both concerned with the politics of the first Reform Bill of 1832—span in their publication the politics of the second Reform Act of 1867. Again, cholera figures briefly in the novel (and there is some evidence that George Eliot originally intended to make it more central), so it is useful to remember that there was a major outbreak of the disease in England as late as 1866. Will Ladislaw is as close in some respects to the Pre-Raphaelites as to the later Romantics. Yet again, the feminist aspects of the novel, though certainly appropriate to the chosen historical period, would be equally relevant to the society for which *Middlemarch* was written. In these general terms, then, the novel is a historical document not only of the 1830s, but also of the 1860s and 1870s; but beyond this I do not think we can safely go.

If George Eliot's creation of a social scene is impressive for what James called 'solidity of specification', it is surely not simply because she is historically accurate and detailed. The strength of this aspect of *Middlemarch* derives from two sources, firstly, the way in which individuals mesh so realistically with their environment. Dorothea's destiny is the result, not just of the narrowness of her provincial world, but also of her ardent, theoretic nature; Lydgate fails, not just because of circumstances, but also because of intrinsic flaws, those 'spots of commonness' in his nature. In this way George Eliot avoids any crude kind of social determinism; her characters are both agents and patients in the human scene, just as we all are. Secondly, George Eliot's strength derives from her ability to analyse and to set dramatically into motion those forces and pressures which we feel to be the sinew and bloodstream not just of Middlemarch but of *any* reasonably sophisticated society. If we list, however briefly and abstractly, some of these forces, we shall see how complete and complex is her grasp of social life—its groupings and associations, its conflicting interests and pressure groups, its mechanics and dynamics.

(a) *Birth, Rank, Class:* Clearly this set of forces is all-important as providing an impediment to the Dorothea-Ladislaw union and as a magnet in the Rosamond-Lydgate marriage. Lower down the social scale we see how subtly it operates in the relations between the Garth and Vincy families. We may also see how strongly divisive a factor these pressures may be, even in so small a community as Middlemarch. The most obvious gulf is between town and county; this is most clearly brought out in Chapter 34, where Sir James Chettham, Mrs Cadwallader, and others, watching Featherstone's funeral from Casaubon's house, can recognize Vincy but not his wife or family. But many more subtle examples of this division and the efforts to bridge it—either seriously as with Dorothea, or comically as with Brooke—can be found.

(b) *Money:* Obviously this is a more important social factor in the town than in the countryside, though Bulstrode and his wealth find a parallel in Featherstone. Above all it is one index of Lydgate's entanglement and downfall. In her cool notation of apparently insignificant detail, George Eliot is the equal of Flaubert in *Madame Bovary*.

(c) *Locality:* The native's distrust of the outsider is important; even Bulstrode, long-established in Middlemarch, is still suspect. But more obviously this force functions as a source of latent animus towards Lydgate and of open hostility towards Ladislaw.

(d) *Religion:* As one might expect, Catholicism does not figure as a direct social factor, though Brooke allows 'an acre of ground for a Romanist chapel'. More surprisingly, Dissent is also scarcely mentioned; the main stress is always on the varieties of Anglicanism, ranging from the old 'High and Dry' Toryism of Cadwallader to the Evangelicalism of Mr Tyke.

(e) *Politics:* Local politics pervade all aspects of Middlemarch life. But we are never allowed to forget that this provincial story is contained within the broad sweep of national history.

(f) *Profession:* From the wide range of jobs, the 'manifold wakings of men to labour' exemplified in the novel, we may isolate the medical profession, since it is here that some knowledge of social history illuminates the novel. . . . The doctor is a common fictional figure, but George Eliot is probably the first English novelist to delineate with historical precision the emergence of a new *kind* of doctor.

By the beginning of the nineteenth century the traditional divisions of the medical profession were breaking down, largely due to new demands created by widespread social changes. Traditionally there were three orders—the physicians (today, we should probably think of them more as consultants), the surgeons, and the apothecaries (long since elevated from the humble functions of druggist). More and more doctors held diplomas from both the College of Surgeons and the Society of Apothecaries, and from these surgeon apothecaries emerged a new type of doctor who became the equivalent of the modern general practitioner. Lydgate represents this new type and the hostility he arouses in the physicians of Middlemarch (Dr Minchin and Dr Sprague) and the apothecaries (Toller and Wrench) reflects in large part that uneasy awareness that the traditional orders, jealously guarded, are being subverted. But Lydgate represents a professional as well as a social advance; his use of the stethoscope and his desire to conduct post-mortems place him in the *avant-garde* of medicine. Ironically, he is saved from an open scandal in the Raffles affair only because Bulstrode, in disobeying his orders, unknowingly reverts to the old-fashioned treatment prescribed by the rest of the profession. One of the great historical events of the period, not mentioned in the novel, is the founding in 1832 of what was to become the British Medical Association. It was originally named the *Provincial* Medical and Surgical Association. Thus, in hoping to advance both medical research and practice in a provincial town, Lydgate is again a prophetic figure; his story is in large part the defeat of the man of the future by the stubborn conservatism of the present.

The range of George Eliot's analysis is thus very wide. But she is always careful to show the interaction of these various factors throughout the society. If national politics and religion merge in the issue of Catholic Emancipation, then local politics and religion merge in the appointment of Tyke as chaplain to the new hospital. Brooke's comic misunderstanding of politics is paralleled by Dagley's distorted notions of what Reform may mean. Gossip is a social lubricant or irritant at all levels, from

Mrs Cadwallader through Tantripp and the servants to the inns and streets of Middlemarch. Snobbery is also pervasive; Mrs Cadwallader is echoed by Rosamond. To complete the picture, George Eliot hints at the various forces of social change and upheaval—the Reform Bill and the coming of the railways; this is a world on the move. Above all, throughout the novel George Eliot creates a sense of the reciprocity of man and his environment. (pp. 16-20)

> *W. J. Harvey, in an introduction to* Middlemarch *by George Eliot, edited by W. J. Harvey, Penguin Books, 1965, pp. 7-22.*

DEREK OLDFIELD   (essay date 1967)

[*Oldfield analyzes three stylistic techniques Eliot uses in her portrayal of Dorothea: shifting the point of view; correlating Dorothea's speech patterns with her changing personality; and communicating Dorothea's thoughts indirectly through a form of expression known as* erlebte Rede.]

Is there any one function that we can all agree George Eliot's style intends to fulfil? In the case of *Middlemarch* we can safely assume that one of her concerns will be to present to us an image of Dorothea. As we learn in the Finale, an appreciation of the importance of 'our daily words and acts' in 'preparing the lives of many Dorotheas' will depend upon our assessment of what Middlemarch did to 'the Dorothea whose story we know'. Before we can appreciate a 'far sadder sacrifice' we have to sympathise with hers.

George Eliot uses three different stylistic methods in her presentation of Dorothea. First, there is her allegedly 'direct' narrator's voice; then there is the dramatization of Dorothea's own speech; and finally there is George Eliot's method of communicating Dorothea's thoughts. How direct is George Eliot's own voice in *Middlemarch*? Unlike the bungling players at Elsinore, she does not 'tell all'. Her judgments are constantly modified or restricted in some way, whether by such devices as the 'impersonal' narrator, the use of negatives and irony, or by a modifying context.

Sometimes, for example, George Eliot forces us to reserve our acquiescence to some proposition by making it the responsibility of somebody other than herself. We see Dorothea through the eyes of 'Those who approached her' (Ch. 1). We hear what 'Most men' (Ch. 1) thought about her, or what 'all people, young or old that is, in those ante-reform times' (Ch. 3) would have thought of her. We are told what the 'rural opinion about the new young ladies' (Ch. 1) was. Or George Eliot will simply use the passive voice and will write of Dorothea: 'She was usually spoken of as being remarkably clever' (Ch. 1), or 'She was regarded as an heiress' (Ch. 1). On another occasion, George Eliot does not tell us what Dorothea's face expresses, but writes: 'Dorothea's brow took an expression of reprobation and pity' (Ch. 4). George Eliot carefully disavows responsibility for what Dorothea actually felt. All we know is that she pulled the appropriate face. The complexity of things may also be mirrored stylistically when something is first stated and then immediately qualified: 'But perhaps no persons then living— certainly none in the neighbourhood of Tipton . . .' (Ch. 3). More often still this restrictive effect is achieved by negatives. Similarly, George Eliot's irony often defines by negation:

> A young lady of some birth and fortune, who knelt suddenly down on a brick floor by the side of a sick labourer and prayed fervidly as

if she thought herself living in the time of the Apostles—who had strange whims of fasting like a Papist and of sitting up at night to read old theological books! (Ch. 1)

The sarcasm directed at the 'young lady' is unmistakable. The whole sentence structure, lacking a finite verb, suggests a proposition to be rejected. Then, too, there are the depreciative 'whims', 'Papist' and the attribution of 'old' to the theological books. There is the incongruous collocation of 'a young lady of some birth and fortune' with 'a brick floor'. Finally there is the frank imputation of delusion, behaving 'as if she thought herself living in the time of the Apostles'. But although the sarcastic tone is unmistakable, the reader is conscious of not identifying himself with the ironic point of view. The past that Dorothea might appear to live in is, after all, the time of the Apostles who claimed a universal relevance for their behaviour; perhaps young ladies and brick floors can respectably come into contact with each other through prayer. Once the critical process has begun, the reader begins to revalue many of the sneers expressed and to realize that it is merely the invalid opinion of a nameless frightened young squire. This modifying process is similar to the effect George Eliot achieves in the opening sentences of **Middlemarch,** defining Miss Brooke's kind of beauty. In fact, instead of telling us directly what to think, George Eliot frequently just tells us what we may *not* think—or lets us oscillate between one attitude that needs qualifying and another. George Eliot, herself, describes the process: 'starting a long way off the true point, and proceeding by loops and zigzags, we now and then arrive just where we ought to be' (Ch. 3). The voice of the narrator seems to make a succession of probes at the truth, observing of Dorothea that she was: 'likely to seek martyrdom, to make retractions and then to incur martyrdom after all in a quarter where she had not sought it' (Ch. 3). Or else the author's voice may be the one fixed bearing to guide the reader in his zig-zags. Let us take a longer passage which starts with one such fixed point of author statement:

> She was open, ardent and not in the least self-admiring; indeed it was pretty to see how her imagination adorned her sister Celia with attractions altogether superior to her own, and if any gentleman appeared to come to the Grange from some other motive than that of seeing Mr Brooke, she concluded that he must be in love with Celia: Sir James Chettam, for example, whom she constantly considered from Celia's point of view, inwardly debating whether it would be good for Celia to accept him. That he should be regarded as a suitor to herself would have seemed to her a ridiculous irrelevance. Dorothea, with all her eagerness to know the truths of life, retained very childlike ideas about marriage. She felt sure she would have accepted the judicious Hooker, if she had been born in time to save him from that wretched mistake he made in matrimony; or John Milton when his blindness had come on; or any of the other great men whose odd habits it would have been glorious piety to endure; but an amiable handsome baronet, who said 'Exactly' to her remarks even when she expressed uncertainty,—how could he affect her as a lover? The really delightful marriage must be that where

your husband was a sort of father, and could teach you even Hebrew, if you wished it. (Ch. 1)

Nothing could be more authoritative than 'She was open, ardent, and not in the least self-admiring', and the comment which follows, with its pretence of observed reality 'it was pretty to see how. . . .' Then again, after the earlier ambivalent discussion of Dorothea's marriage prospects, the responsibility for remaining single is now firmly made Dorothea's: 'Dorothea, with all her eagerness to know the truths of life, retained very childlike ideas about marriage'. This is immediately followed by a passage which sounds as if it might be a dramatization of Dorothea's consciousness. Here, as often elsewhere, it is introduced by a tag that ambiguously can announce either *oratio recta* or *oratio obliqua:* 'She felt. . . .' That Dorothea's feelings are presented in *oratio recta* is suggested by the slightly colloquial nature of what follows. '*That wretched* mistake' sounds like a personal voice. Other things being equal, the personal voice claims our sympathy. But one resource of the ironist is to give us the revaluing shock by playing unacceptable ideas off against the plausible voice.

George Eliot leads us into the unacceptable idea by three statements of mounting preposterousness. Hooker, who, according to Izaak Walton, chose an unsuitable wife because his vision (like Dorothea's and Milton's) was faulty, is a less celebrated example of a 'difficult husband' than is Milton; and in the final phase the anti-romantic indiscriminate nature of the selection is made explicit in the universal 'any of the other great men . . .', with the characteristically restrictive addition, 'whose odd habits it would have been glorious piety to endure'. So too it was not Milton at any time whom Dorothea could have regarded as a suitor but 'John Milton when his blindness had come on'. One way in which George Eliot presents Dorothea's thought is by granting her this precision of expression which, when it expresses her delusions, is of course quite cruelly accurate. We know the precise quality of Dorothea's delusions partly because she can express them herself. Part of the tragedy of Dorothea in these early chapters is conveyed by this quality of her thinking that we feel in its accuracy to come so near uncovering its own wrongheadedness. Irony often depends upon incongruous collocations and here there is a very strong stylistic presumption against it being 'glorious piety' to endure 'odd habits': and what right had the 'judicious' Hooker to be making mistakes? The plausible voice continues, 'but an amiable handsome baronet, who said 'Exactly' to her remarks, even when she expressed uncertainty,—how could he affect her as a lover?' Any sympathy we might have had for Sir James, in reaction to Hooker and Milton, is dispelled by the conclusive nature of this report. It has the finality of a Jane Austen sentence: appeal is unthinkable. We move to Dorothea. But the accuracy of the concluding statement appals us. 'The really delightful marriage must be that where your husband was a sort of father, and could teach you even Hebrew, if you wished it.' The candour, the openness is expressed and the contradictory elements brought together so as to be equated 'husband . . . a sort of father'. It is difficult to say whether Dorothea is sensing that she has discovered a paradox or whether there is a frightening suggestion that she is not seeing what to others is 'quite plain'. At all events, we again react away from Dorothea, this time in pity. And this one paragraph shows, I hope, that George Eliot's presentation of Dorothea is very far from imposed didacticism—the reader has to respond to the text with the closest possible attention if he is to react accurately to the multiple points of view, including Dorothea's own distorted view of herself. Already in what is apparently plain narrative description we have a hint of the ventriloquist's art. (pp. 65-9)

In a short study it is difficult to demonstrate just how skilfully George Eliot provides the people in Middlemarch with an idiom which is an extremely sensitive register of their natures. Bulstrode has evolved a highly efficient means of concealing himself; his abstract and infinitive predicates are nebulous, his constant prepositional phrases conceal connections and weaken his utterances. He is reluctant to use transitive verbs, but relies, with countless qualifications on weak verbs and the copula. Lydgate, the scientist, has a clarity of expression which, through sentence structure and metaphor, lucidly juxtaposes propositions. Casaubon, the 'scholar', accumulates pieces of language, moving further and further from his main clause. Casaubon, the inadequate human being, has 'not two styles of speaking at command', but is strangled by the measured public voice he has developed. His powers of communication have completely atrophied. In his researches, he cannot publish; in meeting other people, he cannot seek for a common idiom, and we watch him grow ever more isolated. Fred Vincy's unpretentious speech ('Oh, fudge!') establishes his basically genuine nature, whilst Mr Brooke's evasive, muddled half-finished speeches are a perfect 'organ' for the politician manqué. (pp. 71-2)

One might go on indefinitely, but there is little value in merely asserting that George Eliot saw speech as a pyschological as well as a social correlative in the presentation of her characters. Let us at least try to demonstrate the value of attending to these nuances of manner of speech in the case of Dorothea. What does such a study reveal about her personality? Might not the changing style of her speech even help to define in what her 'sad sacrifice' consists?

Before her marriage to Casaubon, Dorothea's speech is shown to be in many respects simple. Her ideas succeed each other in a series of short sentences.

> 'You must not judge of Celia's feelings from mine. I think she likes these small pets. She had a tiny terrier once, which she was very fond of. It made me unhappy because I was afraid of treading on it. I am rather short-sighted.' (Ch. 3)

If ever two people were stylistically incompatible, they are Dorothea and Casaubon. Dorothea makes no attempt to incorporate her subordinate clauses into her statements but leaves them in the position in which they occurred to her in the excited vigour of her thought. 'And then I should know what to do, when I got older' (Ch. 3). Her speech is repetitive. Sometimes, it is true, she seems to be striving for effect, as when she is acting Madame Poinçon ('No, no, dear, no . . . Not for the world, not for the world') (Ch. 1); but more often it seems artless as when she says to herself 'Everyday—things with us would mean the greatest things' (Ch. 3). Such an 'open' style of speaking is of course mercilessly revealing. The following extract is certainly childlike in its egocentricity emphasized by the multiplication of first-personal pronouns:

> I should learn to see the truth by the same light as great men have seen it by. And then I should know what to do, when I got older; I should see how it was possible to lead a grand life here—now—in England. I don't feel sure about doing good in any way now: everything seems like going on a mission to a people whose language I don't know. (Ch. 3)

The imagery of the last sentence is also typical of Dorothea's speech in these introductory chapters: her analogies are spirited and imaginative, but at the same time, quite explicit. This is no subtle metaphorical thinker. And that we are right in thus emphasizing Dorothea's extreme simplicity is confirmed by the stage direction 'simply' that George Eliot often adds. Does Dorothea's speech alter once she is the wife of Casaubon?

George Eliot makes it clear that Dorothea has often during her marriage to suppress this natural, simple idiom. Her instinctive desire to have her own opinions and projects affirmed by her husband is so often disappointed that she gives up anticipating positive answers from him. Her questions become hesitant and even timid: 'May I talk to you a little instead?' (Ch. 37) and 'May I come out to you in the garden presently?' (Ch. 48). And George Eliot herself speaks of Dorothea's relief in

> pouring forth her feelings unchecked: an experience once habitual with her, but hardly ever present since her marriage, which had been a perpetual struggle of energy with fear. (Ch. 39)

However, her tragedy goes deeper than this and to appreciate it we have to know more of the quality of her natural idiom and the personality it reveals.

What are the elements basic to Dorothea when she is being 'herself'? It will be helpful to look at the 'unchecked' conversation with her uncle when she tries to persuade him to make improvements on his estate. She broaches the subject with 'characteristic directness':

> 'Sir James has been telling me that he is in hope of seeing a great change made soon in your management of the estate—that you are thinking of having the farms valued, and repairs made, and the cottages improved, so that Tipton may look quite another place. Oh, how happy!'—she went on, clasping her hands, with a return to that more childlike impetuous manner which had been subdued since her marriage. 'If I were at home still, I should take to riding again, that I might go about with you and see all that! And you are going to engage Mr Garth, who praised my cottages, Sir James says.'

> 'Chettam is a little hasty, my dear,' said Mr Brooke, colouring slightly. 'A little hasty, you know. I never said I should do anything of the kind. I never said I should *not* do it, you know.'

> 'He only feels confident that you will do it', said Dorothea, in a voice as clear and unhesitating as that of a young chorister chanting a *credo*, 'because you mean to enter Parliament as a member who cares for the improvement of the people, and one of the first things to be made better is the state of the land and the labourers. Think of Kit Downes, Uncle, who lives with his wife and seven children in a house with one sitting-room and one bedroom hardly larger than this table! And those poor Dagleys, in their tumbledown farmhouse, where they live in the back kitchen and leave the other rooms to the rats! That is one reason why I did not like the pictures here, dear uncle—which you think me so stupid about. I used to come from the village with all that dirt and coarse ugliness

like a pain within me, and the simpering pictures in the drawing-room seemed to me like a wicked attempt to find delight in what is false, while we don't mind how hard the truth is for the neighbours outside our walls. I think we have no right to come forward and urge wider changes for good, until we have tried to alter the evils which lie under our own hands.' (Ch. 39)

There is energy in the exclamatory style through this passage. There is the graphic quality of her analogies—'bedroom hardly larger than this table', there is her unselfconsciousness, absorbed as she is in her 'credo' and the firmness of her rejoinder expressed either in the imperative—'Think of Kit Downes' or the assertion 'we have no right to come forward and urge wider changes for good, until we have tried to alter the evils which lie under our own hands'. 'Ardent' is the word that George Eliot uses for Dorothea and her usage is, as always, precise. How far does Dorothea retain this ardour?

It is with Ladislaw that she is most often her natural self. Apart from moment of embarrassment, this is how she speaks to Will:

> 'And that will make it all the more honourable,' said Dorothea, ardently. 'Besides, you have so many talents. I have heard from my uncle how well you speak in public, so that everyone is sorry when you leave off, and how clearly you can explain things. And you care that justice should be done to everyone. I am so glad. When we were in Rome, I thought you only cared for poetry and art, and the things that adorn life for those of us who are well off. But now I know you think about the rest of the world.' While she was speaking Dorothea had lost her personal embarrassment and had become like her former self. (Ch. 54)

The speech differs from the example previously given in being simpler, but it still has the affirming emphatic ring ('And that will make it all the more honourable'). The prompting tone of 'And you care that justice should be done to everyone' and the universal 'everyone' and 'the rest of the world' are characteristically energetic. Whatever may be Ladislaw's faults, there is something in him that allows Dorothea to retain her ardour.

Other stylistic correlatives to her ardour which persist till the end are her forceful imperatives, her strong diction and her use of intensifying adverbs. There is an urgency and force of utterance in Dorothea that we find in no other speaker in *Middlemarch*. Her imperatives are often passionate entreaties. 'Forgive me! . . .' (Ch. 21), she says to Casaubon, and to Ladislaw, 'Promise me that you will not again, to anyone, speak of that subject' (Ch. 22). She develops her own elliptical way of commanding compassion, '—please not to mention that again' (Ch. 37), she says to Lydgate. She continues to use words possessing the utmost force—'It is wicked to let people think evil of anyone falsely, when it can be hindered' (Ch. 76). Finally there is her persistent use of intensifiers: She is 'very grateful' to Mr Casaubon for loving her (Ch. 5). She is 'very glad' to hear from Ladislaw that she is a poem (Ch. 22). She has 'very little to do', and wishes 'very much' to see Lydgate to help him (Ch. 76).

Dorothea's most emphatic resource of all is her disarming directness. The overwhelming majority of her sentences have as their subject the personal pronoun, 'I'. To Ladislaw at the very end of the novel, she cries characteristically: 'Oh, I cannot bear it—my heart will break . . . I don't mind about poverty—I hate my wealth . . . We could live quite well on my own fortune—it is too much—seven hundred a year—I want so little—no new clothes—and I will learn what everything costs' (Ch. 83). *Middlemarch* presents us with several studies in egoism. Egoism, a study of Dorothea's speech would seem to suggest, is not simply a matter of having an 'I' any more than altruism is a matter of losing it.

Also retained, but perhaps less wholly sympathetic, is Dorothea's simplicity with its ambiguous element of 'childlike' egoism. For instance, after her husband's death she says:

> 'I should like to take a great deal of land and drain it and make a little colony, where everybody should work, and all the work should be done well. I should know every one of the people and be their friend. I am going to have great consultations with Mr Garth: he can tell me almost everything I want to know.' (Ch. 55)

George Eliot makes no comment but her ironic response to these Utopian dreams is expressed in the 'great deal of land' which to satisfy Dorothea will need *draining* (just as Milton needed to be blind) before she could render her not unobtrusive services. The colony will be cosily 'little' but Dorothea's universal 'everybody', 'every one', 'everything' will make it a whole world where she will be befriended because of what she has done. This is fantasy, the sort of opiate which George Eliot would always reject. Unless we attend carefully to the implications of the style, we shall, like F. R. Leavis, miss the criticism which persists in George Eliot's attitude to her heroine [see *NCLC*, Vol. 4]. Dorothea does not become perfect, the irony focused on her does not altogether disappear.

One element in her ardour which Dorothea does lose permanently and as a result of the whole stultifying environment of Middlemarch is her imaginative use of analogy. In the introductory chapters of the novel, Dorothea had likened the blonde-haired, red-whiskered Sir James Chettam to 'a *cochon de lait*' (Ch. 2) and, on another occasion she 'feels scourged' (Ch. 4). Later, talking to Ladislaw in Rome about her response to art Dorothea says: 'At first when I enter a room where the walls are covered with frescoes, or with rare pictures, I feel a kind of awe—like a child present at great ceremonies where there are grand robes and processions; . . . It is painful to be told that everything is very fine and not to be able to feel that it is fine—something like being blind, while people talk of the sky' (Ch. 21). She develops her explanation a little later:

> 'The painting and sculpture may be wonderful, but the feeling is often low and brutal, and sometimes even ridiculous. Here and there I see what takes me at once as noble—something that I might compare with the Alban Mountains or the sunset from the Pincian Hill. . . .' (Ch. 22)

Finally, she describes her belief to Ladislaw:

> 'That by desiring what is perfectly good, even when we don't quite know what it is and cannot do what we would, we are part of the divine power against evil—widening the skirts of light

and making the struggles with darkness narrower.' (Ch. 39)

Apart from the examples given above (see page 75) where Dorothea uses analogies in the moment of recovering her old spirit, and apart from talking to Rosamond about 'murdering' marriage, these are the only examples of figurative expression I can find spoken by Dorothea after her marriage to Casaubon. It is, I think, highly significant that they are all spoken to Ladislaw. But it is also true that they are all taken from the first half of **Middlemarch,** and that Dorothea does not enter marriage with Ladislaw with graphic phrases on her lips.

This would seem to be an instance of a characteristic of Dorothea's speech that is shown to atrophy. The heroine, on the evidence of the above account, would appear to have lost her facility in the use of a rich linguistic resource. Dorothea will never again illustrate her views with reference to 'scourges', 'sunsets', 'processions', of even *cochons de lait'.*

Dorothea's other sad loss, mirrored in her speech, is her confidence that people will say 'yes' to her. In all her early questions she prompts corroboration by using negatives, 'Will you not now do . . .' 'Will you not make up your mind . . .' (Ch. 20). But she has difficulty in eliciting from Casaubon the positive response she desires. She then turns to others, hoping that they may be positive about Casaubon. Thus she says to Ladislaw, '. . . it seems to me that with Mr Casaubon's learning he must have before him the same materials as German scholars—has he not?' (Ch. 22). And to Lydgate, when her husband is ill, 'But Mr Casaubon will soon be here again, I hope. Is he not making progress?' (Ch. 30). Eventually, to many people, her questions become purely rhetorical. 'What do we live for, if it is not to make life less difficult to each other?' (Ch. 72).

Dorothea's rhetorical questions are a moving dramatization of someone dangerously isolated, affirming her values out loud in an effort to keep a grip on them. This accounts too for much of her hyperbole. She recognizes this habit of 'speaking too strongly' (Ch. 62). Twice only in the latter half of **Middlemarch** does Dorothea make a desperate effort to regain affirmation and in each case it is on behalf of somebody else. Thus she meets Rosamond's 'polite impassibility' (Ch. 81) with 'cordial pleading tones'.

> 'You will not think me too troublesome, when I tell you that I came to talk to you about the injustice that has been shown towards Mr Lydgate. It will cheer you—will it not?—to know a great deal about him, that he may not like to speak about himself just because it is in his own vindication and to his own honour. You will like to know that your husband has warm friends, who have not left off believing in his high character? You will let me speak of this without thinking that I take a liberty?' (Ch. 81)

On this occasion Dorothea evokes a response. It is her major triumph that, with all the discouragement her ardour meets with, she still does urge affirmation. We know the triumph, because it is uniquely successful. On the only other occasion after the death of her husband that she dares seek support for her generous impulses, she is repulsed. It is when Farebrother has said that there is no proof for Lydgate's innocence. Dorothea exclaims: 'Oh, how cruel! . . . And would you not like to be the one person who believed in that man's innocence, if the rest of the world belied him?' (Ch. 72). Dorothea does not get the positive answer her ardour demands.

Disappointed in this hope, Dorothea falls back on people's readiness to say 'no'. Her 'way', we are told, is still 'ardent' (Ch. 62) but the form of the question is different. To Ladislaw she says, 'Do you suppose that I ever disbelieved in you?' (Ch. 62). And, later in the scene referred to above in which she is talking to Farebrother, she says 'energetically', 'You don't believe that Mr Lydgate is guilty of anything base?' (Ch. 71).

To ask questions in this way the key words have to be negative; Dorothea has to bring herself to utter words like 'guilty' and 'disbelieved' whereas we feel the natural tendency of 'a young chorister chanting a *credo*' would be more positive.

To sum up, Dorothea's tragedy is that life in Middlemarch denies her public expression—either in words or in acts—of her ardour. She does not lose her 'essential nature'. Her sense of identity remains—she is still direct and her emphases have not weakened. Yet her ardent soul is all but muted. There is loss of 'individuality'. She no longer expresses herself figuratively, no longer looks for affirmation. Only with her future husband will she sometimes indulge the parallelisms of rhetoric, once so precious to her. To all others, passion can no longer be adequately represented in words. At the beginning of the book Dorothea had declared to Celia: 'It is offensive to me to say that Sir James could think I was fond of him. Besides, it is not the right word for the feeling I must have towards the man I would accept as a husband' (Ch. 4). Three years later, at the end of the novel, the two sisters talk to each other again. Celia asks Dorothea about Ladislaw: 'Is he very fond of you, Dodo?' and Dorothea replies: 'I hope so. I am very fond of him' (Ch. 84). Dorothea's essential nature has deepened in its capacity for feeling, but she has had to submit to a conventional and inadequate expression of her love. The meaning of the book is nowhere more clear than here as we analyse the very words Dorothea uses. Her changing style *is* her changing self, and George Eliot allows it to speak for herself. She never tells us explicitly in what Dorothea's 'Sad sacrifice' consists—it is for us to hear the grass grow.

If George Eliot has this skill in characterization through individual speech, why then does she do so much of the work herself? Why is the inward reflection of her characters not presented in a brilliantly animated and individualized interior monologue? Is this at least not an artistic fault which we must regret—the sort of clumsy, uncoordinated fumbling we might expect from that 'osseous lengthy countenance' David Cecil discovers in the author's portrait? Or is there perhaps a good reason behind George Eliot's chosen method of presenting the inner life of her characters? I believe that there is.

In the treatment of her characters' thought, George Eliot has developed a technique which allows her to give both an internal and an external account of their experience. It is yet another example of the way in which George Eliot makes her point by zig-zagging. We oscillate between an emotional identification with a character and an obliquely judicious response to their situation.

The way in which George Eliot achieves this effect is principally by using what is called *erlebte Rede.* Professor Quirk has pointed out that English has 'no generally acknowledged term' for this device. In French it is known as *le style indirect libre.* It is a form of exposition readily available in German (which may be where George Eliot first became familiar with it), it approaches the immediacy of *oratio recta* whilst retaining the grammatical form of *oratio obliqua.* Thus, describing Dorothea's reaction to finding Ladislaw with Rosamond, George Eliot writes:

> The fire of Dorothea's anger was not easily spent, and it flamed out in fitful returns of spurning reproach. Why had he come obtruding his life into hers, hers that might have been whole enough without him? Why had he brought his cheap regard and his lip born words to her who had nothing paltry to give in exchange? He knew that he was deluding her—wished, in the very moment of farewell, to make her believe that he gave her the whole price of her heart, and knew that he had spent it half before. Why had he not stayed among the crowd of whom she asked nothing—but only prayed that they might be less contemptible? (Ch. 80)

The first sentence of this extract is straightforward author narrative. But then, without any warning, the reader is presented with a dramatization of the 'spurning reproach'. It is not of course pure dialogue that we hear: the verbs and pronouns are those of indirect speech. But indirect speech, made subordinate to an author's 'dixit', would have had much less immediacy of impact than is achieved by the use of the free indirect style. The questions are preserved as questions instead of being turned into the quasi-statement—'she asked why he had come . . .' George Eliot's form of speech reporting retains much more of the colloquial original. (pp. 73-82)

This seems to me the important achievement of the technique in the hands of George Eliot. The thoughts we hear do not come to us voiced in the actual idiom of the characters themselves. Translated into *oratio recta* they would sound slightly strange on the lips of their owners. It is partly a matter of decorum: in the first example given above, Dorothea could not herself say, 'Why did he not stay among the crowd of whom I ask nothing—but only pray that they might be less contemptible?' Partly it is a matter of tense, syntax and diction—Dorothea could not be responsible for the 'preconceived' of the following:

> The clear heights where she expected to walk in full communion had become difficult to see even in her imagination: the delicious repose of the soul on a complete superior had been shaken into uneasy effort and alarmed with dim presentiment. When would the days begin of that active wifely devotion which was to strengthen her husband's life and exalt her own? Never perhaps, as she had preconceived them: but somehow—still somehow. (Ch. 78)

The voice we hear has been distanced by *erlebte Rede*: the very presentation in this way is an implicit invitation to consider what is being said. George Eliot indicates that what we are hearing is a dramatic statement. She does not fully dramatize for fear perhaps that we would get carried away by the rhetoric of her character. 'This is the sort of way this character would represent it' is the effective message we get from the author.

In her survey of the novel, Lisa Glauser can find no use of *erlebte Rede* to express the central ideas of the novelists of the eighteenth and early nineteenth centuries. Only after the period of revolutionary romanticism was interest aroused in the inner life . . . 'but there was still lacking the balance, the distance, the muting which is the other premise of *erlebte Rede*'. She continues: 'In George Eliot's novels we find for the first time

all the conditions fulfilled for its complete development as the highly modern technique of expression we know.' To the qualities she discerns in this technique which I have already noted, the intuitive inward-looking element, she adds the 'other premise'—critical analysis. It is one more piece of evidence of George Eliot's two preoccupations in *Middlemarch*—the problem of the expression of the inner life and the problem of how to evaluate its quality from the outside—an outside that can never be wholly objective. It is even possible that it is this choice of the technique of *erlebte Rede* as opposed to straight dramatized reflection or interior monologue, which saves George Eliot and the reader from the trap of becoming uncritically identified with Dorothea's thoughts—a trap which Henry James for instance did not escape in his presentation of Maggie Verver. In other words *erlebte Rede* is yet one more variation on George Eliot's stylistic aim of combining emotional involvement and ironic criticism. She achieves this through her 'own' voice, through Dorothea's speech mannerisms, and finally through this oblique yet sympathetic presentation of Dorothea's thoughts. (pp. 83-4)

Derek Oldfield, "The Language of the Novel: The Character of Dorothea," in "Middlemarch": Critical Approaches to the Novel, *edited by Barbara Hardy, Oxford University Press, 1967, pp. 63-86.*

HILDA M. HULME (essay date 1967)

[Hulme studies Eliot's use of kinaesthetic imagery in a passage describing Lydgate.]

On 24 October 1871 George Eliot's publisher, John Blackwood, had his day's work destroyed by a visit from Alexander Main, a rhapsodic admirer of her novels ('the Gusher' as he was privately called), who was seeking permission to prepare a volume of extracts from George Eliot's writings. Blackwood describes with some enjoyment his talk with the 'little fellow': 'He is quite an enthusiast and told me he did "not read much but he read deep". He worships George Eliot as having done for the Novel what Shakespeare did for the Drama. When he wound up some glowing period by saying she was "Concrete" I was nearly upset.' (p. 87)

Many of George Eliot's readers would agree, I think, that Main's term 'Concrete' by which Blackwood's composure was nearly upset seems, now as then, precisely and totally appropriate. It has an obvious relation to the larger purposes of the novelist's art, the embodiment of general truth in a particular narrative example, and is probably also the best of single words to describe that quality on which Edith Simcox comments in an early review of *Middlemarch* (1 January 1873)—the author's gift, 'shared only, amongst contemporaries by Mr Browning, of choosing similes and illustrations, that do really illustrate the nature of the things compared' [see *NCLC*, Vol. 4]. Particularly striking to the present-day observer is her ability to select and control an accurate kinaesthetic imagery, through which, in a novel-world where little is static but the furniture, the reader's whole attention can be concentrated, for a few words' space, on just that emotional energy, narrowly limited and fully charged, which 'moves' or holds the novel-character. This kind of imagery is indeed so often and so effortlessly employed that, if we measure by George Eliot's standards, there is nothing remarkable in the following example, which tells of how Lydgate, after dining at Mr Vincy's and for the first time enjoying Rosamond's music, went home 'and read far into the smallest hour', bringing to a new book on fever 'a much more testing vision of details and relations . . . than he had ever thought it necessary to apply to the complexities of love and marriage' (Ch. 16).

> As he threw down his book, stretched his legs towards the embers in the grate, and clasped his hands at the back of his head, in that agreeable after-glow of excitement when thought lapses from examination of a specific object into a suffusive sense of its connections with all the rest of our existence—seems, as it were, to throw itself on its back after vigorous swimming and float with the repose of unexhausted strength—Lydgate felt a triumphal delight in his studies, and something like pity for those less lucky men who were not of his profession.

It is easy to see that this one sentence contains a three-fold series of coincident movement patterns: there is first the account of Lydgate's actual physical movement; then the change in the process of mental activity which is necessarily set out in abstract terms (mainly abstract nouns) and thirdly the imagined physical movement of swimmer turning floater. Through the simply organized interconnection of these three kinds of movement, abstract is made concrete and the double unity of body and mind, thinker and thought, is readily established. Lydgate the thinker changes his posture as he rests from reading; the swimmer, which is his thought, and which has been occupied in examining a specific object—driving forward, that is to say, in a given direction—changes its posture also, throwing itself on its back as Lydgate throws down his book. And as Lydgate lies back in his chair, his thought also 'lapses', the unexhausted thought-swimmer stretching out its body in the water, with its hands, no doubt, clasped at the back of its head in Lydgate's easy attitude. The language-base on which George Eliot has constructed the swimming-floating thought image is a part of ordinary speech; when work goes 'swimmingly' we all know what it is to feel 'buoyed up' with confidence. The 'as it were' phrase, we may notice, which introduces the image, is there not because the writer is working with an unusual image range, but so that she may carry the sentence more easily over the necessary pronoun changes; his book, our existence, to throw itself. And it is a true observation also, as all swimmers know, that in the effortless floating motion, as one looks up into 'illuminated space' (the 'inward light' of Lydgate's earlier 'fever' thoughts), consciousness of an urgent separate identity is lessened; there is the sense instead of belonging to an older, more instinctive, liquid world: 'thought lapses . . . into a suffusive sense of its connections with all the rest of our existence'.

It is interesting to note how the writer's exact economy of presentation enforces the abstract-concrete equivalence. Of Lydgate's three physical actions, 'threw down', 'stretched', 'clasped', only the first verb 'throw' is repeated in the metaphorical movement; it is left to the reader to complete the series. The only properties in the actual physical scene are Lydgate's book, which is discarded, and the 'embers in the grate'; there is not, for example, a chair in which he may lie back until my commentary provides it; all that the narrator requires him to have are what the reader is to supply for the swimmer, 'legs', 'hands' and the 'back of his head'. And even though the time is 'far into the smallest hour', no such adjective as 'dying' diminishes the embers; Lydgate's awareness of their agreeable glow after he finishes his reading is parallel, no doubt, to 'that agreeable after-glow of excitement' which follows vigorous thought and 'vigorous swimming'. As the reader, so to say, supplies the missing parts of such descriptions, he enters to some extent into the thoughts and feelings which are described. In this particular instance however we can see also that the novelist has quite deliberately set a limit to reader-character identification. Although Lydgate's existence becomes 'our' existence as thought takes on the 'sense of its connections with all the rest' of life, *we* are not grammatically present in the 'vigorous swimming'. It is clear, if we think about it, that the superlative energy of 'unexhausted strength' can belong only to part of our lives; for the rest of our existence we take our place with 'those less lucky men' (the Farebrothers of this world) for whom the vigorous swimmer feels 'something like pity'.

The placing of this incident within the narrative and the setting together of other swimming-floating images in the Lydgate context bring further correspondences and less clear cross-relations into the reader's own less active thought. Lydgate's throwing himself on his back after vigorous swimming to float with the repose of unexhausted strength seems, as a single unbroken movement, essentially a masculine and a sexual image; if, at the same time, the image is seen as two contrasted movements, such a contrast has an obvious relevance to the career-marriage opposition which is to break his intellectual strength. The reader has been warned in the previous chapter that 'that distinction of mind which belonged to his intellectual ardour did not penetrate his feeling and judgment about furniture or women'. Miss Brooke he has earlier found 'a little too earnest' (Ch. 10). 'The society of such women was about as relaxing as going from your work to teach the second form, instead of reclining in a paradise.' Yet although Lydgate had quite soon been conscious of being fascinated by Miss Vincy, 'he did not in the least suppose that he had lost his balance and fallen in love' (Ch. 11). At twenty-seven and with eight hundred pounds left him after buying his practice he was, we are told, 'at a starting point which makes many a man's career a fine subject for betting' if one could appreciate 'all the niceties of inward balance, by which a man swims and makes his point or else is carried headlong' (Ch. 15). Lydgate's first intention was to swim. As he walked home from Mr Vincy's on this particular night he thought 'of Rosamond and her music only in the second place; and though, when her turn came, he dwelt on the image of her for the rest of his walk, he . . . had no sense that any new current had set into his life'.

The verb 'dwelt on' here which follows more energetic thoughts of Mr Bulstrode and the new hospital, echoes back a little to the 'reclining in a paradise' which is Lydgate's idea of relaxing after his work; it leads on also to the repose which is to be enjoyed when the book is thrown down. The agreeableness of floating is mentioned once more before Lydgate's day closes. After his reading is finished and he thinks with satisfaction of how his profession calls forth 'the highest intellectual strain' (vigorous swimming) and yet keeps him in 'good warm contact' (embers, after-glow) with his neighbours, the thought of Mr Farebrother 'brought back the Vincys and all the pictures of the evening. They floated in his mind agreeably enough.' The intricacy of the image relations forbids more detailed comment; it is clear, at least, that the particular repetition on which attention has been concentrated is very delicately handled. Some sense of it still lingers perhaps towards the end of the story, when Lydgate hears from Dorothea 'the first assurance of belief in him' and gives himself up, 'for the first time in his life, to the exquisite sense of leaning entirely on a generous sympathy, without any check of proud reserve' (Ch. 76). And it is interesting here to see with what care and intuition the writer is selecting her image-language: 'leaning' is a manuscript correction for an earlier 'throwing himself'. It seems indeed that the more vigorous action is now out of context. As Lydgate says of his time in Middlemarch, 'I had some ambition . . . I thought I had more strength and mastery . . . I have lost all spirit about carrying on my life here.' (pp. 90-4)

> Hilda M. Hulme, "The Language of the Novel: Imagery," in "Middlemarch": Critical Approaches to the Novel, edited by Barbara Hardy, Oxford University Press, 1967, pp. 87-124.

KATE MILLETT (essay date 1970)

[*An important feminist writer, Millett came to the forefront of the women's movement with her* Sexual Politics, *in which she postulates that the oppression of women is essentially political and patriarchal. In her commentary on* Middlemarch, *which is drawn from* Sexual Politics, *Millett examines Eliot's contribution to the sexual revolution.*]

"Living in sin," George Eliot lived the revolution . . . , but she did not write of it. She is stuck with the Ruskinian service ethic and the pervasive Victorian fantasy of the good woman who goes down into Samaria and rescues the fallen man—nurse, guide, mother, adjunct of the race. Dorothea's predicament in **Middlemarch** is an eloquent plea that a fine mind be allowed an occupation; but it goes no further than petition. She marries Will Ladislaw and can expect no more of life than the discovery of a good companion whom she can serve as secretary. (p. 192)

> Kate Millett, "The Sexual Revolution, First Phase: 1830-1930," in her Sexual Politics, 1970. Reprint by Avon, 1971, pp. 91-214.*

U. C. KNOEPFLMACHER (essay date 1971)

[*Knoepflmacher studies how Eliot uses allusion and myth in* Middlemarch *to arrive at a "complex and multi-form" vision of reality that sharply contrasts with her characters' limited perceptions of truth. Knoepflmacher's comments were first delivered as a lecture in 1971.*]

In chapter 27 of **Middlemarch,** Tertius Lydgate and Rosamond Vincy thumb through the pages of the last issue of '"Keepsake," the gorgeous water-silk publication which marked modern progress at that time.' The journal has been given to Rosamond by her admirer Ned Plymdale, 'one of the good matches in Middlemarch, though not one of its leading minds.' Eager to show his mental superiority to poor Ned, Lydgate draws the magazine towards him and gives a 'short scornful laugh,' while tossing up 'his chin, as in wonderment at human folly.' He finds the writing as trite as the engravings; mockingly, he says to Rosamond: 'Do look at this bridegroom coming out of a church: did you ever see such a "sugared invention"—as the Elizabethans used to say?' (p. 43)

[What] about Lydgate's curious use of an Elizabethan phrase, 'sugared invention,' within the confines of the Vincys' drawing room? Does the phrase carry some meaning that he does not quite fathom? . . . To understand the import of the allusion, we will have to indulge in a little literary detective-work.

In 1868, after the publication of her long epic poem **The Spanish Gypsy,** George Eliot began to consider new themes for shorter poems, as well as for longer works, either of poetry or of prose. In the fall of 1868 she embarked on a rereading of English poetry from its beginnings, using both Thomas Warton's *The History of English Poetry* and Edwin Guest's *History of English Rhythms* as guides. Almost at the same time, she began to read George Grote's eight-volume *History of Greece.* (p. 44)

[Both Warton and Grote], in tracing sources, suggested that an intimate correlation between historical fact and mythical fable existed in early periods of poetry. Thus, Warton admits that it is impossible to distinguish between historical truth and fiction in the *Gesta Romanorum* because in an age of 'vision' in which every work 'was believed to contain a double or secondary meaning' no such distinctions had been made; similarly, Grote credits Theagenes of Rhegium for starting 'the idea of a double meaning in the Homeric and Hesiodic narratives' and refers his readers to Milton's own blurring of fable and history in *Paradise Lost,* a work which George Eliot dutifully reread around this time.

Her simultaneous readings in Greek subjects and in the literatures of the Middle Ages and the Renaissance also seems to have sharpened George Eliot's ever-ready eye for comparisons and analogies. For example, under the heading of 'Kinship of the Medieval and Classic,' she juxtaposes in her Notebook [of 1868-71, which contains her prose and poetry reading notes,] events taken from the myth of Theseus and their counterparts in Spanish chivalric romances. It is this same interest in comparisons and cross-references which therefore may have originally stimulated the entry recorded on page 14 of her Notebook: '"Sugared invention" (Frances Meres of Theagines + Chariclea).' She follows this citation with another: 'As Italy had Dante [etc.] . . . So England had Matthew Royden [etc.] . . .' and then gives the title of the work from which both of these citations are taken: 'A Comparative Discourse of our English Poets with the Greek, Latin & Italian Poets,' by Frances Meres, MA, 1598. She had obviously come across the work better known as *Palladis Tamia,* either in Grote or, more likely, in Warton. Clearly she wanted to remember the name of the man who had thought of exalting one Matthew Royden as England's Dante. But Meres himself must have been of considerably less interest to her than the context of the phrase, 'sugared invention.' In drawing up his analogies between English poets and their Greek, Latin, and Italian counterparts Meres was actually touching upon a subject of deep concern to George Eliot in 1868—namely, the relation between poetry and prose.

In the pertinent passage in *Palladis Tamia* in which the phrase 'sugared invention' occurs, Francis Meres slavishly copies the ideas expressed in a far more important Elizabethan critical manifesto, Sir Philip Sidney's 'Defence of Poesy' and renders these ideas in Sidney's exact wording. It was Sidney who had first asserted that verse was 'but an ornament and no cause to poetry, sith there have been many most excellent poets that never versified . . . For Xenophon, who did imitate so excellently as to give us *effigiem justi imperii*—the portraiture of a just empire, under the name of Cyrus (as Cicero saith of him) made therein an absolute heroical poem; so did Heliodorus in his sugared invention of that picture of love in Theagenes and Chariclea; and yet both of these writ in prose.' Meres repeats Sidney's argument and phrasing. He, too, asserts that Xenophon and Heliodorus, both 'excellent admired poets,' in the *Cyropaedia* and in *Theagenes and Chariclea,* respectively, achieved in prose what others achieved in poetry.... (pp. 45-7)

The phrase that Lydgate so casually tosses out in chapter 27 in **Middlemarch** thus turns out to have a rather venerable ancestry. Moreover, its use in George Eliot's novel is, I think, rather significant. . . . [The] fullest significance of the phrase lies in its relation to George Eliot's emerging views about the nature of poetic form and to her dissatisfaction with the imitative realism she had practiced in her earlier fiction. Let me explain.

The George Eliot who, in 1868, envisioned *Timoleon* as a long companion piece to **The Spanish Gypsy,** and who, in 1869 and 1870, worked on the shorter poems, **"Agatha," "Lisa," "Jubal," "Armgart,"** as well as the **"Brother and Sister"** sonnets, had turned to poetry because she regarded it as a form less restricted to a faithful reproduction of the outlines of the external world. Her readings in Warton and Grote and in Max Müller the linguist gradually allowed her to see that she could do in a work of prose fiction what in her **"Notes on Form in Art"** she suggested that poetry alone could do: transcend the limitations imposed on the natural historian. In that extraordinary essay . . . , George Eliot argues that poetry can convey truths higher than those attained by Harvey and Bichat (Lydgate, it ought to be remembered, is first stimulated by Harvey and then tries to model his career after the precedent of Bichat). Form, George Eliot asserts, must first depend on discriminations, on the recognition of unlikeness and difference. Only after smaller and smaller unlikenesses have been recognized, can a conception of wholes be gained—'wholes composed of parts more and more multiplied and highly differenced, yet more and more absolutely bound together by various conditions of common likeness or mutual dependence.'

In **Middlemarch**—a novel which originated in a fusion of unlike parts—George Eliot puts on trial Lydgate's empiricist view of reality. To the physician, words are vague, less trustworthy than the microscope. In a conversation with Bulstrode, Lydgate seizes on the banker's use of the phrase 'spiritual interests' by saying, 'those words are apt to cover different meanings to different minds.' Lydgate prefers to reduce reality to its smallest and—as he thinks—precisest, components by 'diligent application, not only of the scalpel, but of the microscope.' A votary of 'scientific culture' who adheres to 'the philosophy of medical evidence,' he is particularly distrustful of the vagueness of that 'sugared invention' which feigns or distorts. And yet, ironically enough, Lydgate has in the past already once been fooled by a fiction. The melodrama staged by the Provençale actress Laure appealed to his fancy. Relying on that fancy (rather than imagination), Lydgate was led to sentimentalize reality: 'all science had come to a stand-still while he imagined the unhappy Laure, stricken by ever-wandering sorrow, herself wandering, and finding no comforter.' His sentimentalization, the fiction he has concocted, comes to an abrupt halt when he discovers the truth; chastened, he returns to his laboratory, believing that 'illusions were at an end for him.' He is determined henceforth to take a 'strictly scientific view of woman'. (pp. 47-8)

Unlike the Ladislaw who defends language as a 'finer medium' for its ability to capture those essences or forms that a painting or sculpture can only represent through an external copy, Lydgate never learns to see beneath 'mere coloured superficies.' He mistakes copies for truth and confuses ornament for essence. On first listening to Dorothea speak, Lydgate dismisses her because he finds fault with her unclever words: 'It is troublesome to talk to such women.' By way of contrast, Ladislaw, who has met Dorothea in the previous chapter, is quick to separate her 'words' (which he finds *too* clever) from her musical voice: 'But what a voice! It was like the voice of a soul that had once lived in an Aeolian harp.' A similar separation is made by Caleb Garth much later. Reporting on his conversation with Dorothea to his wife, he says: 'You would like to hear her speak, Susan. She speaks in such plain words, and a voice like music.' Ladislaw and Caleb Garth recognize what Lydgate fails to see. Although the one is the cosmopolitan grandson of a man who could speak 'many languages—musical' and the other an ineloquent carpenter, both men revere music. Both identify Dorothea with the 'structure of tones' which George Eliot regards as the highest form of art and which in her **"Notes on Form"** she equates with the highest modes of poetry. Lydgate, however, lacks the ear to distinguish between the music of the senses and the music of the soul. His own 'sugared invention' leads him to falsify Rosamond into a water-nixie whose melodious sea-breezes will, he hopes, only strengthen his work at the microscope.

It is fitting that this scoffer at the imprecision of words should later be punished by Rosamond's willful silence. Although his private canary bird warbles back at him, there is neither soul nor understanding in her song. If Lydgate becomes the victim of his own, inferior 'sugared invention,' George Eliot, however, opposes her own powers of invention to his. Through the Elizabethan phrase she puts into his mouth, she creates what Sidney calls a 'speaking picture,' a 'figuring forth' of reality, that allows us to divine meanings which Lydgate the diagnostician cannot fathom. 'How often,' says Sidney in his 'Defence,' 'think you, do the physicians lie, when they aver things good for sickness . . . Now for the poet, he nothing affirmeth, and therefore he never lieth.' Years ago, in *Religious Humanism and the Victorian Novel,* I cited this passage to show how the views of reality figured forth by Lydgate and Ladislaw, physician and poet, are contrasted in **Middlemarch** [see Additional Bibliography]. And indeed, George Eliot seems to approve of Ladislaw's contention that language alone can render a fuller image, 'which is all the better for being vague.' Ladislaw's view that the 'true seeing is within' . . . , is in direct variance with Lydgate's too rigid perception of truth.

But my present object is not to contrast the imaginations of Lydgate and Ladislaw, but rather to look at some of the characteristics of the imagination that shaped **Middlemarch.** I have started out with Lydgate because he not only is the foil of Dorothea and Ladislaw, but is also very much the foil of George Eliot herself. And Lydgate is George Eliot's foil, because—like all those other characters in the novel who try to impose their mental structures on reality—he is engaged in the same quest as the novelist. Lydgate wants to demonstrate the 'more intimate relations of living structure, and help to define men's thought more accurately after the true order.' . . . George Eliot's aims in this work are identical: she wants to demonstrate more intimate relations within the reality she creates and so help define her readers' thoughts more accurately after a truer order—an order which partakes both of fact and of myth.

What I am saying, then, is this: in **Middlemarch** the artist is a participant in the very same process of ordering that her characters are engaged in. Yet whereas the structures erected by a Lydgate, a Casaubon, a Dorothea, or a Bulstrode prove to be too fixed, it is the richly allusive medium of language which the novelist employs that allows her to discover a more complex and multiform order of meaning. What George Eliot has to say about 'poetry' in her **"Notes on Form in Art"** thus very definitely applies to the mode she came to develop in **Middle-**

march: 'poetry, from being the fullest expression of the human soul, is starved into an ingenious pattern-work, in which tricks with vocables take the place of living words fed with the blood of relevant meaning, and [are] made musical by the continual intercommunication of sensibility and thought.' By fusing history and fiction, the prosaic and the poetic, the factual and the mythological, George Eliot blurs through the superiority of her own 'sugared invention' the fixities which her main characters adopt. Words, vocables, 'the old phrases,' asserts George Eliot toward the end of her essay, should not have to 'give way to scientific explanation.' Instead, they can carry meanings that defy empirical classification—whether that classification be Casaubon's pigeon-holing of myths he has emptied of their affective content or Lydgate's false separation of matter and essence. (pp. 48-50)

The fixity of Lydgate's and Casaubon's structures are at odds with the fluidity of the rhythms and images created by George Eliot. The novelist broadens the basis of our understanding—and constantly heightens our pleasure—by allowing us to discover connections unperceived by the characters, who remain limited by the conditions under which they labour. Gradually, the reader becomes trained to see universal 'wholes' where the characters see only particulars. Yet not only the vision of the characters comes under George Eliot's scrutiny. In the first paragraph of chapter 19, the chapter which introduces us to Dorothea's Roman honeymoon, we are told:

> In those days the world in general was more ignorant of good and evil by forty years than it is at present. Travellers did not often carry full information on Christian art either in their heads or in their pockets; and even the most brilliant English critic of the day mistook the flower-flushed tomb of the ascended Virgin for an ornamental vase due to the painter's fancy. Romanticism, which has helped to fill some dull blanks with love and knowledge, had not yet penetrated the times with its leaven and entered everybody's food.

Again, a cryptic allusion must be closely examined before its full meaning can be understood and its relation to other images and rhythms be appreciated. The brilliant critic of the day referred to is William Hazlitt. In his book, *A Journey Through France and Italy . . .* , Hazlitt assumed that the 'Popish' representations of the Virgin Mary were little more than a 'transposition of the Pagan Mythology' of Greek and Roman 'superstitions.' George Eliot corrects Hazlitt's anti-Catholic bias by showing that his statement is based on the mistaken supposition that the 'flowers and the urn' so often depicted in paintings of the Assumption are identical to the offerings to Flora and Ceres depicted in pagan art. His lapse is quickly explained: insufficiently aware of Christian iconographic tradition, too provincial to have sampled a sufficient number of representations of the ascending Virgin, Hazlitt failed to realize that the flowered urn in the foreground of paintings such as Filipino Lippi's is but a stylized version of the full-flowered sarcophagus found in more realistic representations of the Assumption.

But why is this pedantic emendation brought up by the narrator at this particular point in the novel? Why is a lack of 'information about Christian art' paired with the ironic assertion that, forty years ago, the world was 'more ignorant of good and evil'? Let us first look at what comes immediately before the passage from chapter 19 that I have cited. Chapter 18 ends

with a conversation between Mr Farebrother and Lydgate. Emulating the words of Mr Tulliver in *The Mill on the Floss,* Mr Farebrother first laments, 'The world has been too strong for *me,* I know.' He then adds, 'But then I am not a mighty man— I shall never be a man of renown. The choice of Hercules is a pretty fable; but Prodicus makes it easy work for the hero, as if the first resolves were enough. Another story says that he came to hold the distaff, and at last wore the Nessus shirt.' In depreciating his weaknesses Mr Farebrother distinguishes between two variant myths about the mighty Hercules. As narrated by the Sophist Prodicus, Hercules seems a grand and heroic figure because he has an absolute freedom of choice. As suggested by other accounts, however, Hercules seems puny, denigrated by his submission to Deianeira. Farebrother applies the latter parable to himself, although he is—and will remain— a single man. It will, however, become applicable to his interlocutor. Lydgate, the masculine hero of this novel without a hero, scorns Farebrother for his failings and tends to think of himself rather complacently as that 'mighty man' soon to gain a 'renown' that Farebrother admits he will never attain. But Lydgate does not yet know that marriage will be as fatal to him as to Hercules and that he will be forced to wear the Nessus shirt given to him by a new Deianeira.

If we now move from the end of chapter 18 to the description that opens chapter 19, we are invited to view first 'the reclining Ariadne, then called the Cleopatra' in the 'marble voluptuousness of her beauty' and, subsequently, 'another figure standing against a pedestal, whose form, not shamed by the Ariadne, was clad in Quakerish grey drapery.' . . . Here, too, myth is adapted so that it can yield new meanings. Just as there are two variants of the Hercules myth, so are there two variants of the story of Hercules' admirer and emulator, Theseus, and of his relationship to Ariadne. . . . [In the Homeric version] Theseus is innocent of Ariadne's death; in the version of Plutarch which George Eliot consulted Theseus is responsible for deserting Ariadne on the island of Naxos.

Let us now try to thread through a few of the patterns created through that 'process of grouping or association' to which George Eliot refers in her **"Notes on Form in Art."** The allusions to Hercules and his Nessus shirt, to Cleopatra, and to Ariadne refer to fictions about victims betrayed by a member of the opposite sex. If Lydgate is a Hercules or an Antony betrayed by his uxoriousness, Dorothea is an Ariadne betrayed by a man—by the sallow *Geistlicher* whom Adolf Neumann immediately confuses with 'her father.' The epigraph to chapter nineteen ratifies this interpretation: L'altra vedete ch'ha fatto alla guanca / Della sua palma, sospirando, letto' ('The other see, who, sighing, has made a bed for her cheek with the palm of her hand'). The quotation is taken from Dante's *Purgatory* and refers to still another victim, Charles Valois, a son sacrificed by the excessive ambitions of his father, Philip III of France. The change from Dante's masculine 'l'altro' to the feminine 'l'altra' is deliberate. We are meant to read in Charles' plight the suffering of Dorothea, another innocent confronting experience. In chapter 20, she, too, will be sobbing bitterly.

There are complications, however, which prevent us from seeing Dorothea as exclusively a victim of treachery. Can Mr Casaubon really be identified . . . with the treacherous young Theseus? Ought he not rather, as the images of labyrinths associated with him suggest, be identified with the Minotaur? And, if so, is Ladislaw then to be seen as a Theseus who will deliver a new Ariadne from a mythical monster? The fact that two alternate versions of the myth exist, like the fact that the statue of the Ariadne is not yet known as such to the tourists, prevents the reader from succumbing to any such straightforward allegorization. If Dorothea is an Ariadne who was never betrayed by Theseus, yet victimized nonetheless by fate, perhaps it is her own confusion which led her to see a delivering Theseus in a Minotaur that is to blame for her present predicament. The question of free will, raised by the Hercules myth, thus is raised again. But no answer needs to be given. Ladislaw's contention in chapter 22 that Dorothea has received a faulty education by being brought to embrace 'some of these horrible notions that choose the sweetest women to devour—like Minotaurs,' would place the blame on neither Casaubon nor Dorothea but on those same 'conditions of an imperfect social state' at which George Eliot herself lashes out in her Finale.

The allusions to Hercules, Dante, Cleopatra, and Ariadne thus complicate our responses to the literal fabric of the narrative. Taken together, they yoke the about-to-be-told story of Dorothea's unhappiness as a married woman to the still-deferred story of Lydgate's marriage to Rosamond. In addition, they alert us to the symbolic mode of beholding reality of a Naumann who sees 'Mistress Second-Cousin as antique form animated by Christian sentiment—a sort of Christian Antigone' and of a Will Ladislaw who, though less interested in the painter's *Plastik,* responds similarly to Dorothea. It is Will who now realizes that Dorothea is not 'coldly clever' but 'adorably simple and full of feeling.' His imagination allows Dorothea to rise above the ruins of classical and Christian art to which she has been brought by her dead and deadening husband. On meeting Dorothea for the second time in his life, Ladislaw canonizes her into the saint with a 'heart large enough for the Virgin Mary' that Tertius Lydgate will not come to recognize until near the end of his travails. . . . (pp. 59-62)

It is in Rome, the 'city of visible history' that Ladislaw, that unformed Romantic conscience, signifies his love for Dorothea by calling her the best part of a poet—'a poem.' Dorothea must be brought to Rome so that she can reject Mr Casaubon's sterile notions of reality. The pieces that Casaubon vainly tries to combine now stare at her in all their 'fragmentariness'; they remain unintegrated disparates: 'all that was living and warm-blooded seemed sunk in the deep degeneracy of a superstition divorced from reverence.' . . . By seeing only such a sundering, Dorothea sees what Hazlitt, that other Protestant visitor, perceived. In her innocence, she does not know that she, the Eve who wanted instruction from a debased archangel, is also that second Eve who brought love into the world. She has thirsted for knowledge, for the fruit of the forbidden tree, and yet she has, in her own person, all along possessed the key to all mythologies. The world of inert fixities, a universe of death, that spreads out before her eyes 'like a disease of the retina' is still seen by her through Casaubon's eyes. But Will . . . possesses the imagination required to thaw Casaubon's frozen landscape. Ladislaw is able to communicate to Dorothea 'the enjoyment he got out of the very miscellaneousness of Rome, which made the mind flexible with constant comparison'; he saves her from seeing human history as but 'a set of box-like partitions without vital connection.' . . . But it is the narrator and the artist who speaks through him who can combine Ladislaw's raw imagination with genuine knowledge. The narrator explains that the 'fragmentariness' that so depresses Dorothea could easily have been avoided: 'To those who have looked at Rome with the quickening power of a knowledge which breathes a growing soul into all historic shapes, and traces out the suppressed transitions which unite all contrasts, Rome may

still be the spiritual centre and interpreter of the world.' . . . (pp. 62-3)

Ladislaw is uninterested in literal 'sources'—be they of the Nile or of mythology; he wants to preserve some 'unknown regions' as 'grounds for the poetic imagination.' . . . For this sense, he is favourably contrasted to those misusers of knowledge, Lydgate and Casaubon. For all his imagination, however, Ladislaw lacks the supplementary knowledge and experience necessary for the formation of great art. 'You leave out the poems,' says Dorothea to him, 'I think they are wanted to complete the poet.' . . . She is right. Although she becomes his 'poem,' he remains subordinate to her. It is the novelist and not Ladislaw who can capture Dorothea's voice—'the voice of a soul' that becomes so incalculably diffusive.

And so we are left with Dorothea herself, a seeker who must renounce her quest for knowledge, a voice whose language remains simple and unadorned. She incarnates the 'idealistic in the real' and as such epitomizes the view of form adopted in the novel built around her. The opening paragraph of chapter 1 should not be taken lightly: 'Miss Brooke had the kind of beauty which seems to be thrown into relief by poor dress. Her hand and wrist were so finely formed that she could wear sleeves not less bare of style than those in which the Blessed Virgin appeared to Italian painters.'

We can now return to chapter 19. If it locates Dorothea in a necropolis, a city of tombs to which she has been taken by her musty husband, it also marks for us the point of her ascension in the novel. . . . Dorothea is forced to suffer in the City of Experience, forced to admit the imperfection of the constructs which she—like Lydgate and Casaubon—has tried to impose on the external world. To eyes which unduly magnified Casaubon and his aims, Rome must present a vision of nothingness; to such eyes, there can be no unity amidst its shards. But in Rome Dorothea also learns instinctively what Ladislaw the namer tries to put into hyperbolic words. Only the power of feeling can animate human life. And so, at the same time that she is brought to realize the futility of Casaubon's endeavours and the sterility of their marriage, her pity for this petty and unhappy man mounts and mounts. Innocent yet experienced, virginal yet maternal, she becomes like the Mother of Mercy. Her capacity for pity soothes Casaubon's last days; that same capacity later gains her a new convert in Lydgate, Casaubon's fellow rationalist. It is this pity also that makes Ladislaw finally admit his dependency on his best poem: '"You teach me better," said Will . . . There was a gentleness in his tone which came from the unutterable contentment of perceiving—what Dorothea was hardly conscious of—that she was travelling into the remoteness of pure pity and loyalty towards her husband.' . . . (pp. 63-4)

In chapter 19, the narrator of **Middlemarch** corrects Hazlitt, not out of scholarly scrupulosity, but because that so brilliant critic was unable to see a greater universality in the flower-flushed tomb of the ascended Virgin. The narrator praises Romanticism, in the next sentence, not only for its 'knowledge'—a knowledge which Hazlitt should have possessed before yoking 'Popish' representations to their presumed pagan counterparts—but also for its 'love.' The same attitude informs the other examples I have cited. Whether the myth of Cupid and Psyche is 'the romantic invention of a literary period,' as Mr Casaubon asserts, or not, what truly matters is its universal essence. Hazlitt should have seen that emotional essences can bind Christian and pagan art, that the dogmas of all religions have a common source in the ageless questions of 'good and evil.' Whether the reclining Ariadne is known as Cleopatra or by her true name, does not matter. The statue's 'voluptuousness' does make for the same 'fine bit of antithesis' that Naumann the artist is quick to spot. . . . That antithesis becomes enfleshed when, much later in the novel, an Ariadne wronged by Ladislaw nonetheless embraces and comforts her rival, Lydgate's voluptuous Cleopatra. The two women are united through the power of feeling. Again, whether this or that myth of Hercules or Theseus is employed, all myths, like history, are nothing more than the record of some very basic and simple human emotions. To change Dante's historical Charles of Valois into a fictitious Dorothea Brooke is therefore no sleight of hand: there are emotions that remain archetypal, despite the differences between men and women.

Thus it is that an 'ingenious pattern-work' which, like a Beethoven symphony, relies on the confluence of hundreds of smaller tributary motifs and movements, should nonetheless depend on the same earthly Madonna, the same creed of feeling, presented in George Eliot's earlier fictions. In a novel where 'tricks with vocables take the place of living words,' feeling remains a non-verbal state. Asked by Celia to describe the story of her infatuation with Ladislaw, Dorothea refuses: 'No, dear, you would have to feel with me, else you would never know.' . . . (pp. 64-5)

> *U. C. Knoepflmacher, "Fusing Fact and Myth: The New Reality of 'Middlemarch',"* in This Particular Web: Essays on "Middlemarch", *edited by Ian Adam, University of Toronto Press, 1975, pp. 43-72.*

LEE R. EDWARDS (essay date 1972)

[*Edwards details the evolution of her personal response to* Middlemarch. *Mentioning that she had once believed it to be an inspirational feminist work, Edwards here laments Eliot's failure to provide an outlet other than marriage for Dorothea's spiritual and social energies.*]

[When I was an undergraduate], *Middlemarch* became one of the "books of my life," to use the phrase Hugh Walpole used in describing his reaction to Virginia Woolf's *Jacob's Room*. . . . Like Dorothea, I was a cygnet among ducklings, passionately looking for the great river whose current would carry me to others of my kind. Like her, I had great, half-formed aspirations. Like her, I felt harrassed by pressures to marry some nice young man and abandon my private and no doubt weird ideas. In Rosamond, too, I thought I had found a heroine worthy of my hate, one who was condemned not for her sexuality, but for her weakness, vanity and evil, ethical categories which, in the book at least, superseded sexual definitions. I ignored Mary Garth, mentally sending her to stand at the end of the line of insipid, goody-goody heroines. And, while I noted Dorothea's second marriage, I failed to consider its implications, sanctified as it is by children and by Dorothea's reconciliation with her sister and with a world where the continuity of life is represented by the safe inheritance of entailed estates passing through the male line. . . . I saw in Dorothea an endorsement I had found in no other book I had read of energy and social commitment on the part of a woman in combination, as I believed, with the promise that these qualities did not render the possessor either a social misfit or a danger to herself or others. In the interests of finding what I badly needed to find in some imaginative work, I had reduced the novel to a comic homily on the possibility of combining marriage with intellectual aspiration.

Eliot's home from 1863 until her marriage to John Walter Cross.

I also misread the book. For, while *Middlemarch* is undoubtedly a work which devotes many pages to Dorothea, she is by no means the whole novel. And while energy illuminates the work, its light seems now neither so clear nor so powerful as I once thought, or hoped, it was. For *Middlemarch* is finally not an endorsement of this energy, but first an examination and finally a condemnation of it.

In this condemnation, however, George Eliot is by no means unambivalent, as we can see if we look briefly at the structure of the book. In these terms, *Middlemarch* is peculiarly divided. Both tragic and comic, it divorces its emotional centers—Dorothea and Lydgate and their foils Casaubon and Rosamond—from its ethical pivot. It is the Garths and the other permanent residents of the town who, guaranteeing the enduring life of Middlemarch itself, also provide the moral norms of the book. In this connection it is, I think, significant to note that the action of the book, excluding the Finale, stops before the Reform Bill becomes fact, and the characters who threaten Middlemarch's values are changed (Dorothea), defeated (Lydgate), killed (Casaubon), condemned (Rosamond), or sent away, perhaps into a wider world, or merely into exile.

George Eliot sacrifices energy and personality to place and to the conservative necessities which that place dictates. But her ambivalence toward this sacrifice can be seen and felt if we notice that the book's structural anomalies are reinforced by the treatment character receives as well. The weight of the book's tragic structure is carried by a quartet of characters whose complexity George Eliot both apprehends and renders and whose stories compose the bulk of the book. The book's comic structure, on the other hand, is carried by characters who are frequently little more than caricatures, fragments of identity left over from a Jane Austen or a Dickens novel. With the exception of Mary Garth and Fred Vincy and, if one is being generous, Sir James and Celia, these characters have no stories but only scenes which take up the space between the major narratives.

It is, of course, possible that what I have defined as structural ambivalence was in fact accounted for by George Eliot when she called the book not after one of her major figures but instead *Middlemarch: A Study of Provincial Life.* In other words, the book is neither tragic nor comic but simply realistic, and what in tragic terms is annihilation is for the author, and hence for the reader who would read the book correctly, merely a realistic assessment of the best that can be done in the world, both fictional and real. Even if this position is taken, however, the particular sense of reality which the novel as a whole engenders derives from a tension—implicit and covert, it is true, but nonetheless there—between truncated tragic and attenuated comic modes.

These modes are linked by the character of Dorothea who, it seems, participates in both and is, for this reason, as well as others more commonly noted, the center of the book. But the linkage is incomplete because for Dorothea to become a comic rather than a tragic heroine she must be transformed from one whose energy is so great as to constitute a threat to her society to one whose power can be contained by it. She is, in a very real sense, not the same character at the book's end that she was at its beginning. Although she leaves Middlemarch she still has a home there and, in claiming it, is herself diminished.

The image of Dorothea presented at the book's beginning is, to borrow a phrase from Simone de Beauvoir, apparently transcendent. To turn to her from Celia, Mary Garth, and Mrs. Garth is to turn from characters and women who are themselves both innately conservative and a cause of conservatism in others, who either have no energies—like Celia—or who ruthlessly suppress them—like Mrs. Garth—who function through stasis to inspire others to return to the fold, to one for whom radical upheaval, both personal and social, seems, at least initially, possible. With her ardent nature, her intelligence, her desire not simply to be good but to discover what might be good in order to use the fruits of this discovery to change the world, Dorothea seems to be a woman whose like had not been fictively recorded in 1871 and whose imaginary history still does not exist. Even today, women readers in particular, feel in the book's opening chapters the promise of a new spiritual incarnation, possibly even an entirely new creation. We wait, almost desperately, for the author's imagination to divine a world whose shadowy existence we have long suspected, but whose reality has been perpetually denied.

But, however much we may wish it otherwise, *Middlemarch* gives very little evidence that George Eliot wished to be the god in some new machine. From Prelude to Finale, and for 86 chapters in between, she tells us instead that in the early part of the nineteenth century in England, a woman whose "passionate ideal nature demanded an epic life," . . . whose inner "flame . . . soared after some illimitable satisfaction, some object which would never justify weariness, which would reconcile self-despair with the rapturous consciousness of life beyond self" . . . would be defeated or, at best, deflected. George Eliot is writing not the ultimate comedy of some new incarnation, but rather the record of its failure. Seeing a world which lacked "coherent social faith and order," . . . George Eliot

either would or could not choose to create an alternative universe in her fiction. Instead, she records the dislocation which is "offspring of a certain spiritual grandeur ill-matched with the meanness of opportunity," . . . the isolation of the cygnet who "never finds the living stream in fellowship with its own oary-footed kind." (pp. 230-33)

This failure could be tragic, however, and Dorothea a tragic character, if and only if her aspirations at the book's beginnings were taken entirely seriously by the author. And they are not. Nor are Dorothea's longings as unfettered by traditional assumptions about the kinds of fulfillment open to women as a cursory reading might seem to indicate. Throughout the book, George Eliot both pities and gently mocks Dorothea. This attitude of sorrowful amusement is not merely consequent upon her marrying Casaubon, but in fact precedes the marriage and exists precisely because Dorothea is the sort of woman who would marry Casaubon in the first place. Dorothea is shortsighted, a physical defect which in this book, as in many, has its psychic implications. Moreover, George Eliot or her narrative surrogate in the book continually addresses and identifies the elder Miss Brooke as "poor Dorothea" and ranges herself regretfully but unequivocally with Celia in her assessment of Dorothea's character. In Chapter 7, for example, it asserts that "Miss Brooke was certainly very naive with all her alleged cleverness. Celia, whose mind had never been thought too powerful, saw the emptiness of other people's pretensions much more readily." . . . This statement, however, is less simple than it seems. Apparently, the pretensions referred to belong to Casaubon, but it is equally possible that they may secondarily refer to Dorothea as well. For, the immediately preceding sentence states that Dorothea "had not reached that point of renunciation at which she would have been satisfied with having a wise husband: she wised, poor child, to be wise herself." . . . In other words, it is at least possible that it is not only Casaubon's knowledge which is empty pretense, but also Dorothea's desire for knowledge of her own.

If the possibility that Dorothea's quest for knowledge was, at best, misguided were raised only here, the passage would hardly be worth noting. But it is not. Indeed, George Eliot repeatedly insists on the futility and even foolishness of any desire to find an outlet for energy in the acquisition of wisdom defined narrowly as education and dissociates Dorothea from Casaubon by saying that "it would be a great mistake to suppose that Dorothea would have cared about any share in Casaubon's learning as mere accomplishment." . . . On the contrary, she seems to be saying that Dorothea's desire for knowledge is a confused expression of her true longing for a combined moral and intellectual guidance, an analogue in the nineteenth-century world and in her own life to the force which the Catholic faith provided for Saint Theresa. Unable to find her "ideal of life" in the "walled-in maze" which constitutes the usual occupations open to a woman of the leisured class, Dorothea sees knowledge as offering the only way out of the labyrinth. But the radical implications of this vision are tempered since both Dorothea and her creator see this knowledge in terms of a "union which . . . would . . . give her the freedom of voluntary submission to a guide who would take her along the grandest path." . . . This union is not a transcendent linking of the mind with abstract principles systematically combining wisdom and morality, but is instead mediated by physical reality and institutionalized.

Desiring to lead "a grand life here—now—in England," . . . neither Dorothea nor George Eliot can see a way to realize this desire directly. "Since the time was gone by for guiding visions and spiritual directors, since prayer heightened yearning but not instruction," . . . and more interestingly, since George Eliot does not even consider the possibility of educational reform as a way out of Dorothea's dilemma, marriage becomes the educating institution. In marrying Casaubon, Dorothea is mistaken merely about the contents of this knowledge, but not about the form through which such knowledge should come to her.

When Dorothea says that "people may really have in them some vocation which is not quite plain to themselves," . . . she is speaking to Casaubon about Will. We, however, may hear her words as unwittingly self-referential and, more significantly, as revealing as well George Eliot's own bafflement with certain aspects of Dorothea's character. For, at the book's beginning, Dorothea is like Will, a character in search of a vocation, a form in which her spiritual and social energies can be harmonized and through which they can be directed in order to affect the world at large. Since, however, George Eliot has drawn Dorothea as a character to whom "permanent rebellion, the disorder of a life without some loving reverent resolve" . . . was impossible, her search for a vocation is cut short almost before it begins. In contrast to Will, who has not only time but space in which to try on different roles, Dorothea does not. And where Will can attempt and reject a number of vocations before finding his niche as a member of Parliament, Dorothea can not. Unlike Will, Dorothea has only two alternatives: she can marry or she can remain a spinster. But even this choice is more apparent than real. Dorothea *must* marry. For unmarried and not endowed with the strength for permanent rebellion, there is no way for her even to begin to find for herself the wisdom she desires. Unmarried and untutored, she can only devise plans for cottages whose fireplaces may well interfere with their stairways. And even were her plans correct, she can not build the cottages in any case, having neither the money nor, more importantly, the courage to do so on her own. Like Kate Chopin's Edna Pontellier, she lacks the strong wings necessary for the artist: her wish for freedom is always checked by her equally strong desire to submit. And if, for whatever reasons, we ignore both sides of the equation George Eliot has set up throughout the book for defining Dorothea's character, the book's ending becomes as incomprehensible as many critics have found it to be.

Why, it is asked, does Dorothea marry Will? Because the answer to this question is most often given in terms which account for the marriage by opposing Will's presumed sensuality to Casaubon's sterility, even those posing this solution are unhappy with it and condemn the author for failing to make Dorothea's savior more sexually viable. Sexuality, however, does not provide the key to Will's significance, though the truth of this statement may indeed point to a gap in George Eliot's perceptions. Far from being an erotic radical, a pre-Lawrencian Mellors saving Dorothea by his phallic force, Will is instead a social reformer who finds a vocation which can use his romantic vision when, at the book's conclusion he is transformed into "an ardent public man," . . . and through Dorothea's adjective, into a version of Dorothea herself. Since wrongs exist and since Will is in the thick of a struggle against them, George Eliot establishes him as a husband for Dorothea, who can "give him wifely help" . . . of just the sort she wanted to give Casaubon but could not. What *Middlemarch* is missing then is a more powerful rendering of both Ladislaw's physical presence and his social vision. We know he would reform, but

what and how we know not. We know that Dorothea would help him, but don't know the exact nature of her help.

At this point, however, some real problems concerning Dorothea's second marriage do intrude themselves. The objection is not that Dorothea should have married Will but that she should have married anybody at all, that she should ultimately be denied the opportunity given Will to find her own paths and forge her energies into some new mold. Acknowledging that "many who know her, thought it a pity that so substantive and rare a creature should have been absorbed into the life of another, and be only known in a certain circle as a wife and mother," . . . George Eliot acknowledges the fact that Dorothea is a character who might have been fulfilled in a wider world than the one she as author finally provides. But she also claims that "no one stated exactly what else that was in her power she ought rather to have done" . . . ; looking outward, George Eliot simply could not find this new and bigger world. The religion which inspired Antigone and Saint Theresa to perform their heroic deeds alone is gone. And to fill this vacuum George Eliot found it necessary to impose tradition, widening it a bit to allow Mary Garth to write a book and Dorothea to go to London, but stopping short of a full exploration of a world which would have had its birth not in reality's mirror but in the artist's will. We could perhaps have had this vision if the author held the mirror to reflect not only the world both she and Dorothea knew and left behind but also that one she forced into existence when she stopped being Mary Ann Evans and became George Eliot instead. In *Middlemarch,* however, George Eliot refuses this option and accepts a safety not entirely celebrated but rather tinged with resignation, ambivalently regarded.

It is, however, only when we draw away from Dorothea to look instead at Rosamond that the reasons for George Eliot's ambivalent attitude toward Dorothea's energy become clear. In thus moving, we are not travelling so great a distance as it might at first appear. Although Rosamond is in many ways Dorothea's opposite, they are opposed as two sides of the same coin are opposed and are centrally bonded by the common metal of their energy. It is usual to see Rosamond as simply the typical nineteenth-century heroine exposed by the persistent hostility of George Eliot's vision. This view seems to me both distorted and reductive, for it fails to take note of precisely that facet of Rosamond's character which is most interesting: the strength of her will. Like Jay Gatsby, Rosamond would spring from her own Platonic image of herself. Formed like him out of a mixed romanticism and vulgarity, her reckless will is finally even stronger than Dorothea's because it is not tempered as Dorothea's was by either the cooling winds of self-effacement or the broadening channels of social concern. What she wants is simply her own way out of Middlemarch. But her way, like Dorothea's is defined throughout the book in society's terms, though Rosamond's society is, to be sure, more limited because more narrowly class and money conscious than Dorothea's. And, like Dorothea, Rosamond cannot get her way, cannot gain both the freedom from Middlemarch's constrictions and the material perquisites she feels are due her without a husband. (pp. 233-36)

George Eliot has a powerful awareness of the destructiveness of Rosamond's energy. And, as is the case with Dorothea, she can find nothing to do with it, no place to put it once the possibility of wifely submission is denied. Thus, what I have called George Eliot's conservatism is finally both the logical conclusion to the problem of female energy posed in her work and, less happily, the result of the failure of her own imagination to create [alternative outlets for this energy].... Middlemarch and its environs are a closed world whose survival depends on the continuing life of values cherished by the author. Her fidelity to these values, however, prevents George Eliot from arriving at a radical solution—or, indeed, any solution—to the problems of female energy the book proposes. She can only struggle to contain the energy, force the new wine back into the old bottles, as she does with Dorothea, or condemn its egotism as most hostile to the community she loves.

Only one small scene, Lydgate's memory of Madame Laure, points to the road George Eliot rejected. These passages, like no others in the book, leap from the page, demanding to be read symbolically. But as symbol of what? The traditional reading makes the scene reflect on Lydgate, showing us what he as yet can't see: that he would do well to stay unmarried. Obviously, too, Madame Laure herself reflects on Rosamond, a spiritual rather than a physical murderer. If, however, the general reading proposed here has any validity, if, that is, *Middlemarch* is significantly, even centrally, concerned with the problem that excess energy in combination with the world's conventions poses for George Eliot and her female characters, then certainly another reading is possible. When Madame Laure says, "You are a good young man. But I do not like husbands. I shall never have another," ... she is speaking as a woman who has literally killed a man to gain her freedom. By underscoring the violence of Laure's energy, the ruthlessness of her power, George Eliot shows clearly what she is most afraid of if she leaves her female characters generally unbridled. But we can only wonder—and perhaps regret—that this image was not pursued further and in another direction, that George Eliot did not finally create a woman who knew before the fact that she neither liked nor needed husbands since such liking would force her either to submit or to destroy. Had George Eliot been able to find some system of values by which such a woman could live, she might have succeeded in breathing life again into Saint Theresa's dessicated image.

It is illegitimate, I know, to condemn an author for what she did not choose to do. But as I have moved away from what I now believe was merely an adolescent fantasy concerning the contents and implications of *Middlemarch* to what I hope is a more true understanding of the text's attitudes toward woman, I see that it can no longer be one of the books of my life. In so seeing, I am alternately angered, puzzled, and finally depressed. Madame Laure's history without her husband, the story of Dorothea as a social force, the tale of Rosamond as a political novel, none of these have been written. If we can imagine a world or a vision that might write them, then perhaps this condition is not final and, creating our own futures, we may be consoled. (pp. 237-38)

Lee R. Edwards, "Women, Energy, and 'Middlemarch'," in The Massachusetts Review, *Vol. XIII, Nos. 1 & 2, Winter & Spring, 1972, pp. 223-38.*

J. HILLIS MILLER (essay date 1974)

[*Miller is associated with the "Yale critics," a group that includes Harold Bloom, Paul de Man, and Geoffrey Hartman. Throughout his career, Miller has successfully applied several critical methods to literature, including New Criticism, the existential phenomenology of Georges Poulet, and deconstructionism. Based on the thought of the French critic and philosopher Jacques Derrida, deconstructionism asserts that language can never express a* speaker's intended meaning and that in itself language can convey no objective meaning. Deconstructionists concentrate solely on the linguistic elements of a text, denying the representational function of words and delineating instead the way a work is constructed of verbal forms. In the excerpt below, Miller analyzes Middlemarch *from a deconstructionist point of view. He argues that the text of the novel "pulls the rug out from under itself" by demythologizing the basic assumptions on which it was built.*]

Middlemarch is solidly within the tradition of realistic fiction and in fact might be taken as the English masterpiece of the genre. *Middlemarch* places its events carefully in a particular historical time and place, English provincial life in the period just before the first reform bill. It builds up carefully the historical background of this time and place. In that sense it is an "historical novel." It presents its narrator explicitly as an "historian" and is overtly based on certain historical assumptions. These include the assumption that each historical period is unique and the assumption that "historical forces" determine the kind of life that can be lived at a certain time.... In *Middlemarch,* moreover, history is a theme within the story itself, in the historical researches of Casaubon, and in the relation of art and history as it is put in question in the discussions between Will Ladislaw and his German friend Naumann. History is also constantly kept before the reader as the basic analogy for the narrator's own enterprise. (pp. 462-63)

History takes its place in *Middlemarch* then as one theme parallel to a chain of other themes. Among these themes are religion (dramatized in Bulstrode's story), love (in the three love stories), science (Lydgate), art (Naumann and Ladislaw) and superstition (Fred Vincy). The treatment of each of these themes falls into the same pattern. In each case the character is shown to be mystified by a belief that all the details he confronts make a whole governed by a single center, origin, or end. In each case the narrator demystifies the illusion and shows it to be based on an error, the fundamental linguistic error of taking a figure of speech literally, of assuming that because two things are similar they are equivalent, sprung from the same source, or bound for the same end, explicable by the same principle. As the narrator says, in what might be taken as a diagnosis of the mental illness from which all of the characters in *Middlemarch* suffer, "we all of us, grave or light, get our thoughts entangled in metaphors, and act fatally on the strength of them." ... Casaubon is beguiled into wandering endlessly and fruitlessly in the labyrinthine complexity of ancient myth by his false assumption that there is a "Key to All Mythologies," his belief "that all the mythical systems or erratic mythical fragments in the world were corruptions of a tradition originally revealed." ... Lydgate searches for the "primitive tissue" of which all the bodily organs will be differentiations: "... have not these structures some common basis from which they have all started, as your sarsnet, gauze, net, satin and velvet from the raw cocoon?" ... Bulstrode thinks Providence justifies his deceptions and that his worldly success is proof that God is guiding his life toward his salvation. Poor Fred Vincy believes that because he is a good fellow luck will be on his side, "keeping up a joyously imaginative activity which fashions events according to desire" ...: "What can the fitness of things mean, if not their fitness to a man's expectations? Failing this, absurdity and atheism gape behind him." ... Rosamond's spinning of the "gossamer web" of love ... in her courtship by Lydgate falls into the same paradigm. It too is the construction of a fiction governed by an illusory beginning and end. In her case the model is literary. Like Emma Bovary she has read too many bad novels. "Rosamond," says the narrator, "had registered every look and word, and estimated them as the opening incidents of a preconceived romance—incidents which gather value from the foreseen development and climax.'' . . . Though the ''basis for her structure had the usual airy lightness'' and is, so to speak, a groundless ground, nevertheless she ''was of remarkably detailed and realistic imagination when the foundation had been once presupposed.'' . . . (pp. 464-65)

Dorothea's nearly fatal mistake in marrying Casaubon is only the most elaborately described version of this universal error. She is both ''ardent'' and ''theoretic.'' Her ardor takes the form of seeking some guide who will transfigure the details of her everyday life by justifying them in terms of some ideal end. Her error is generated by her ''exalted enthusiasm about the ends of life, an enthusiasm which was lit chiefly by its own fire.'' . . . It is an error of interpretation, once again the error of taking a figurative similarity as an identity. She thinks that because Casaubon reminds her of St. Augustine, of Pascal, of Bossuet, of Oberlin, of his seventeenth-century namesake, of Milton and ''the judicious Hooker,'' he must be the equivalent of those spiritual geniuses, ''a guide who would take her along the grandest path.'' . . . Casaubon is a text, a collection of signs which Dorothea misreads, according to that universal propensity for misinterpretation which infects all the characters in **Middlemarch**. ''The text, whether of prophet or of poet,'' says the narrator apropos of Dorothea's ''reading'' of Casaubon, ''expands for whatever we can put into it, and even his bad grammar is sublime,'' . . . and, in another place, ''signs are small measurable things, but interpretations are illimitable, and in girls of sweet, ardent nature, every sign is apt to conjure up wonder, hope, belief, vast as a sky, and coloured by a diffused thimbleful of matter in the shape of knowledge.'' . . . (pp. 465-66)

Exactly parallel to all these forms of mystification is the belief that history is progressive, teleological. This illusion is deconstructed along with the rest, perhaps even more explicitly . . . ; the example George Eliot gives is the Hegelian theory that art cooperates in the world process and assists in the self-development of the world spirit. Will Ladislaw is the spokesman for George Eliot's demolition of this particular version of the association between history and narrative. Unlike all the other characters, he has no desire to find out origins. Casaubon acidly reports him to have ''said he should prefer not to know the sources of the Nile, and that there should be some unknown regions preserved as hunting-grounds for the poetic imagination.'' . . . He makes fun of Naumann's Hegelian or ''Nazarene'' theory of art: ''the divinity passing into higher completeness and all but exhausted in the act of covering your bit of canvas. I am amateurish if you like: I do *not* think that all the universe is straining towards the obscure significance of your pictures,'' . . . and he presents Dorothea with a mocking parody of Naumann's theory in his description of his own painting: ''I take Tamburlaine in his chariot for the tremendous course of the world's physical history lashing on the harnessed dynasties. In my opinion, that is a good mythical interpretation.'' Dorothea asks, ''Do you intend Tamburlaine to represent earthquakes and volcanoes?'' To which Will answers, ''O yes, . . . and migrations of races and clearings of forests—and America and the steam-engine. Everything you can imagine!'' ''What a difficult kind of shorthand!'' says Dorothea. . . . (pp. 466-67)

The effort of demythologizing in **Middlemarch,** then, can be defined as a dismantling of various versions of the metaphysical system on which the traditional idea of history depends. In spite of its recourse to the conventional *locus standi* of defining itself as a displaced form of history, the novel, so to speak, pulls the rug out from under itself and deprives itself of that solid ground without which, if Henry James is right, it is ''nowhere.'' Her fiction deprives itself of its ground in history by demonstrating that ground to be a fiction too, a figure, a myth, a lie, like Dorothea's interpretation of Casaubon or Bulstrode's reading of his religious destiny.

George Eliot's effort in **Middlemarch** is not, however, wholly negative. The metaphysical notions of history, of story-telling, and of individual human lives are replaced by different notions. The concepts of origin, end, and continuity are replaced by the categories of repetition, of difference, of discontinuity, of openness, and of the free and contradictory struggle of individual human energies, each seen as a center of interpretation, which means misinterpretation, of the whole. History, for George Eliot, is not chaos, but it is governed by no ordering principle or aim. It is a set of acts, not a passive, inevitable process. It is the result of the unordered energies of those who have made it, as well as of the interpretations these energies have imposed on history. History, for her, is stratified, always in movement, always in the middle of a march, always open to the reordering of those who come later. Rome is the ''spiritual center'' not because it is an occult origin but because it is ''the interpreter of the world.'' Rome is the place where over the centuries has congregated the most intense activity of interpretation. As the narrator says in another place, ''souls live on in perpetual echoes, and to all fine expression there goes somewhere an originating activity if it be only that of an interpreter.'' . . . The only origin is an act of interpretation, that is, an act of the will to power imposed on a prior ''text,'' which may be the world itself seen as a text, a set of signs. Such signs are not inert. They are nothing but matter, like the ''stupendous fragmentariness'' of Rome. At the same time, however, they are always already heavy with a weight of previous interpretations. So Dorothea's response to Rome adds itself to the layer upon layer of interpretations of it which have been made before, ''the gigantic broken revelations of that Imperial and Papal city thrust abruptly on the notions of a girl who had been brought up in English and Swiss Puritanism'' forming ''one more historical contrast'' and taking a new meaning in her response to it. Though Dorothea's life does not have a given aim any more than it has an other than accidental origin, nevertheless she may give it an aim, as she ultimately does in her decision to marry Ladislaw. In the same way, though the past does not have a fixed ''meaning'' I may give it meaning in the way I appropriate it for the present, just as the narrator gives Dorothea's life a meaning by repeating it in her story, and just as the reader in his turn adds himself to the chain when he interprets the novel.

Against the notion of a work of art which is an organic unity and against the notion that a human life gradually reveals its destined meaning, George Eliot opposes the concepts of a text made of differences and of human lives which have no unitary meaning, for whom ''every limit is a beginning as well as an ending.'' . . . Such lives have meaning not in themselves but in terms of their influence on other people, that is to say, in the interpretation which other people make of them. In place of those errors which cause the characters in **Middlemarch** to suffer so, George Eliot presents each life in the novel as justifiable by no ideal origin or end. Each has such effect as it does have on those around, an influence not capable of being generalized or predicted, but ''incalculably diffusive,'' like Dorothea's ''full nature'' which ''had still its fine issues,'' though they were "like that river of which Cyrus broke the strength," so that it "spent itself in channels which had no great name on the earth." ... And in place of the concept of elaborate organic form, centered form, form organized around certain absolute generalizable themes, George Eliot presents a view of artistic form as inorganic, acentered, and discontinuous. Such a view sees form as based on unlikeness and difference. This view is expressed in her extraordinary little essay, **"Notes on Form in Art,"** ... and in the actual structure of *Middlemarch* (not least in its metaphorical texture), as well as in explicit statements in the novel.

"Fundamentally," says George Eliot in **"Notes on Form in Art,"** "form is unlikeness, ... and ... every difference is form." "I protest against any absolute conclusion," she affirms in one place in *Middlemarch.* ... In several passages in the novel she argues that all generalizations are falsifications because they derive from the amalgamation of specific instances which are all different. "But this," she says of the stimulation of imagination by emotion, "which happens to us all, happens to some with a wide difference." ... In another place she says, "all conceit is not the same conceit, but varies in correspondence with the minutiae of mental make in which one of us differs from another." ... A final example is the observation that "there are many wonderful mixtures in the world which are all alike called love, and claim the privileges of a sublime rage which is an apology for everything." ... In fact, it is "this power of generalising which gives men so much the superiority in mistake over the dumb animals." ... (pp. 467-69)

Middlemarch itself is an example of form arising from unlikeness and difference, a form governed by no absolute center, origin, or end. Its meaning is generated by the juxtaposition of its several plots. The three love stories, for example, are as much different from one another as they are similar. Even the styles in which they are written differ. The story of Dorothea, Casaubon, and Will employs an abstract, metaphysical vocabulary, as in the early descriptions of Dorothea as "ardent" and "theoretic," in search of the way to an "ideal end." This elevated style is supported by a carefully but somewhat covertly manipulated parallel with the myth of Ariadne and Dionysus. ... The story of Rosamond and Lydgate, on the other hand, is told in a middle style, the basic style of nineteenth-century realistic fiction. A lower, pastoral, comic, or ironic style is used for the courtship of Fred Vincy and Mary Garth. Critics have erred in expecting the novel to be in one homogeneous "realistic" style throughout. They have misunderstood and misjudged it as a consequence, for example in what they have sometimes said about Will Ladislaw.

Middlemarch itself, finally, is an example of form as difference in its effect on its readers. The novel, like Dorothea, is "incalculably diffusive." It has such effect on its readers as it does have, as they thread their ways through its labyrinth of words, making such interpretations of it as they can, none absolute, each a misreading in the sense that the text is expanded for what the reader can put into it. The reader of the novel, like Dorothea, Lydgate, or Casaubon, links similar elements and makes patterns out of diversity in an activity which is shown in the narrative as being both entirely human and also inevitably in error, the imposition of a will to mastery over the text. (pp. 469-70)

J. Hillis Miller, "Narrative and History," in ELH, *Vol. 41, No. 3, Fall, 1974, pp. 455-73.**

ALAN MINTZ   (essay date 1978)

[*Mintz first discusses a passage in* Middlemarch *in which Eliot comments on the themes of romantic love and vocation in contemporary literature. The critic then examines the extent to which* Middlemarch *may be termed a "novel of vocation." In contrast, however, Blake (1983) argues that Mintz ascribes too much importance to the theme of vocation in* Middlemarch.]

After describing the moment in which Lydgate first became conscious of a growing "intellectual passion" for medicine, George Eliot reflects on the treatment of vocation in literature.

> We are not afraid of telling over and over again how a man comes to fall in love with a woman and be wedded to her, or else be fatally parted from her. Is it due to excess of poetry or of stupidity that we are never weary of describing what King James called a woman's "makdom and her fairnesse," never weary of listening to the twanging of the old Troubadour strings, and are comparatively uninterested in that other kind of "makdom and fairnesse" which must be wooed with industrious thought and patient renunciation of small desires? In the story of this passion, too, the development varies: sometimes it is the glorious marriage, sometimes frustration and final parting. And not seldom the catastrophe is bound up with the other passion, sung by the Troubadours. For in the multitude of middle-aged men who go about their vocations in a daily course determined for them much in the same way as the tie of their cravats, there is always a good number who once meant to shape their own deeds and alter the world a little. The story of their coming to be shapen after the average and fit to be packed by the gross, is hardly ever told even in their consciousness; for perhaps their ardour in generous unpaid toil cooled as imperceptibly as the ardour of other youthful loves, till one day their earlier self walked like a ghost in its old home and made the new furniture ghastly. Nothing in the world more subtle than the process of their gradual change! In the beginning they inhaled it unknowingly: you and I may have sent some of our breath towards infecting them, when we uttered our conforming falsities or drew our silly conclusions: or perhaps it came with the vibrations from a woman's glance. (Ch. 15, p. 107)

Just prior to this passage, George Eliot describes how the inchoate intellectual energies of Lydgate's adolescence were suddenly catalyzed into a conscious passion for medicine, and presently she will proceed to describe how Lydgate managed to acquire a first-rate medical education by avoiding the English universities in favor of more progressive centers of knowledge. In the meantime, however, she interrupts the work of description in order to address the reader in one of those remarkable instances of authorial disclosure that give *Middlemarch* its particular texture. Like a scientist pausing over his experiment to reflect on the general state of his discipline, the novelist looks up from her narrative long enough to deliver a meditation on the state of her art.

Literature, she concludes, is in serious trouble. An excessive preoccupation with romantic love on the part of both producers and consumers of literature has threatened the institutions of "telling" and "listening" with the prospect of exhaustion. How, we are asked in a series of tedious questions that mock their own tediousness, are we able to abide such repetition? Do we never weary of hearing stories of beauty and love, marriage and separation? Is it simply stupidity, or is there, perhaps, a quality of entropy fundamental to literature that tends toward diffusive excess and refuses to let go of a theme even after the experience and its literary representation have been emptied of meaning?

The answers are not important. The true task at hand is to reinvigorate literature by detaching it from a moribund preoccupation with romantic love and reconnecting it to the new, generative experiences of the age. Since the meaning of man's life in modern society has shifted decidedly from his relation to woman to his relation to the world, literature must now be induced to focus on the experience of work and vocation. The nobility of man's capacity for "generous unpaid toil," the promise of his commitment "to alter the world"—these must now become the writer's true subjects.

If this reorientation can be managed, the narrator continues, it will not dry up the flow of gratifications we expect from fiction. The play of passion and desire will still be there, even if the theme is vocation and not romantic love; for in the new age, a man's heart goes out to the world with a passion equal to his former longing for feminine beauty. This is not an incidental similarity, but a complete correspondence of function. The prospect of vocational achievement can lure the aspirant on with the same endowment of "makedom and fairness" as any woman's. Although it is only with "industrious thought and patient renunciation" that vocation can be won, like a beautiful woman, it too must be wooed. Vocation and romance converge later: "sometimes it is the glorious marriage, sometimes frustration and final parting," sometimes the gradual cooling of the ardour of youthful love. A man can fall in love with his vocational destiny, court it, and, in the end, marry with the same uncertainty of outcome that marks flesh-and-blood marriages.

There is, however, one significant difference between love and vocation, a difference that will require the new theme to be treated with a new set of imaginative instruments. Whereas the older art dilated on the intense early stages of the life of a marriage—on magnificent attraction and glorious union—the new art must necessarily focus on the stages of disillusionment and breakdown. Even the nature of the separation is different. Although the union of a man and a woman comes asunder with the melodrama of fateful parting, a man's separation from his vocation is marked only by an imperceptible weakening of resistance to the forces that would shape him "after the average." "Nothing in the world more subtle than the process of their gradual change!" One day a man awakes to find that his passionate commitment to vocation has cooled and conformed, and he knows not how or when it happened. Since the new fiction will have to register the subtle processes of winding down and giving in, it will have to employ techniques capable of a finer concentration on the gradual changes that mark the movement from one stage of life to another. If in the past the grand moments of passion could comfortably be the writer's subject, the establishment of vocation as the modern theme will require closer measurement of more complex experiences.

In this text from an early section of *Middlemarch*, George Eliot reveals a program for the novel of the future, the novel of vocation. Living in one of the great moments of historical discontinuity (the Middle Ages of the Troubadours and the Renaissance of King James are conceived of as a vast, undifferentiated stretch of time that has given way to the modern period), the novelist stands before the necessity of appropriating for writing the central experiences of the new age: work, vocation, and the passion to improve the world. We need not read the manifesto of the novelist as a summary of the meaning of novel, or, for that matter, as an indication that an example of the new novel has been produced. Yet as a declaration of authorial intent, the text is important, for to read *Middlemarch* is to watch the writing itself both respond to and swerve away from the conscious will of the novelist. And at the very least, we are introduced to recurrent concerns that determine the shape of the novel.

To begin with, we can expect the constellation of experience that includes erotic love, marriage, children, and family to have an altered value in *Middlemarch*. Although the formation of new families was once a central event of the novel as a genre, here it has been decidedly moved to the margin; as for children, *Middlemarch* is a consummately adult world in which the experiences of childhood and youth barely figure. Although erotic love, that "passion sung by the Troubadours," continues to play a role in the novel, it persists chiefly as a demonic presence, a "catastrophe" that wrecks the more valuable marriages of men to their vocations.

In addition, we expect *Middlemarch* to be a world in which man's new means of realizing himself will be his own works. If in the past a man could realize himself by occupying a position in society that required him to do nothing in particular—a gentleman being a man who could afford not to work—the modern era will see men judged by the works, beyond land and children, they leave behind them. No longer merely a compromising struggle for livelihood, work has been transformed into an impassioned struggle to change the world.

Since value is so firmly rooted in significant work, the special anxieties of the novel's characters are for the success of their vocational projects: fears of incompletion, insignificance, interference, and incapacity. Since, moreover, the completion of his work is something for which the individual alone bears full responsibility, the attendant anxieties must also be endured alone, removed from the consolations of family and fellowship.

Finally, and perhaps most essential to the nature of *Middlemarch,* is the fateful intertwining of vocation with originality and negation. To work means to assert one's individuality, to mean to "shape [one's] own deeds," to strive to effect an original relationship to the world. Since the world with its routinizing and collectivizing pressures repels such efforts, vocation can proceed only through acts of resistance and negation. Furthermore, since the "world" is nothing other than the community we all inhabit, it is our own sense of security that is unhinged by our vocational assertion. And just as we find ourselves threatened, we also constitute a threat to others in the form of a series of temptations we present to young aspirants. "You and I may have sent some of our breath towards infecting them, when we uttered our conforming falsities or drew our silly conclusions." Communal opinion and that older passion, "the vibrations from a woman's glance," will dog the steps of the characters of *Middlemarch,* hampering the free and full exercise of vocational expression.

One of the hallmarks of *Middlemarch* is that its narrator, as a figure in the novel, is also touched by these contradictions.

For if narration counted for anything in the eyes of both the historical Marian Evans, the author of the novel, and George Eliot, its narrator, it was most certainly as a vocation. And like other vocations, narration realizes itself through negation: the delapidated stage props of romantic love have to be cleared away before the real drama of modern life can be portrayed. To write means to transform the world of literature, as other men transform the social world, by negating superseded forms and originating new fictions.

The problem of originality and community is imbedded in the rhetorical complexity of the text quoted above. The voice that speaks throughout speaks as a "we," presupposing a community of sentiment and an identity of condition. We *all* persist in tolerating endless stories of romantic love; we *all* decline interest in that other kind of "makdom and fairnesse;" it is the exhalations of *our* breath and the "conforming falsities" of *our* opinions that fatally infect that aspirant to vocation. Yet beneath the communalizing sweep of the "we," the voice that addresses us is essentially polemical, encouraging resistance to discredited ideas and soliciting approval for new undertakings. As readers, we cannot so easily be collapsed into the seamless solidarity of the speaker's "we," for we know that we are being spoken to, and spoken to for a purpose. The consciousness of being the object of a rhetorical strategy consequently makes us wonder whether the "we" is a sign of achieved community or, perhaps, enforced collectivization. The drama of *Middlemarch* unfolds in precisely these spaces that separate the questioning individuality of the reader (or character) from the generalizing will of the narrator (which is itself divided). Individuality and individuation are part of the idea of vocation, and in their resistance to the embrace of community we find the ironic pain that defines the world of the novel and animates its story. (pp. 53-9)

> *Alan Mintz, in his* George Eliot & the Novel of Vocation, *Cambridge, Mass.: Harvard University Press, 1978, 193 p.*

K. M. NEWTON (essay date 1981)

[*Newton analyzes* Middlemarch's *relationship to the Romantic tradition. In examining Dorothea's religious beliefs, Newton finds that Eliot implicitly rejects the Enlightenment approach to knowledge in favor of a Romantic approach. Newton also discusses the Romantic aspects of Ladislaw's character, focusing on his rebelliousness and egotism.*]

[*Middlemarch* is] a much more ambitious work than anything George Eliot had attempted previously. It reflects to a greater extent than any of her other novels the wide range of her intellectual interests, in sociology, psychology, philosophy, science, religion and art, to name only the most obvious, and it is arguable that no other nineteenth-century novel can compete with it in terms of the breadth and complexity of the intellectual issues with which it deals.... [It] is one of the great artistic merits of *Middlemarch* that its interest in a wide range of intellectual issues does not diminish the quality of its human and social presentation, since George Eliot is largely successful in integrating the intellectual and philosophical aspects of the novel with the human and social. (p. 123)

In *Middlemarch,* George Eliot is concerned with the same fundamental problems in her study of character, as regards both individual psychology and human and social relationships, as she is in her other novels, but her characters are placed in a much more intricate and dominant environment and involved in a more complex social life than the characters in her other fiction.... With society being more at the centre of the novel and dominating character, such problems as the moral dangers of Romantic egotism or the conflict between strong impulse and the need for a sense of continuity of self, are treated more in a social context with less detailed concentration on individual psychology.

Despite the greater prominence of society in *Middlemarch,* which results in less emphasis being given to the individual problems of the main characters, at least in comparison with earlier novels such as *The Mill on the Floss* or *Romola* and her later novel, *Daniel Deronda,* there are important continuities between the characters in *Middlemarch* and those in her other novels, and their Romantic connections are equally clear. The most obvious similarity is between Dorothea Brooke and George Eliot's previous heroines. Dorothea possesses the same strength of feeling and potentially dangerous egotistic energies as Maggie Tulliver, Romola and Esther Lyon. Her Romantic affinities are suggested by the frequent use of the word 'ardour' in connection with her. This suggests the kind of idealistic enthusiasm associated with a figure like Shelley. She is seen in a Romantic light by Ladislaw, who thinks of the Aeolean harp, a key Romantic image, when he first meets her and again in Rome, and Naumann, a Romantic painter, sees her as 'a sort of Christian Antigone—sensuous force controlled by spiritual passion' ..., a juxtaposition which again calls to mind Shelley. It seems clear that George Eliot intends Dorothea's ardent nature to be seen as Romantic.

The prime characteristic of Romantic feeling is that it operates as a means of spontaneous knowledge, prior to rational thought, and ... [in an important passage Dorothea] tells Ladislaw that, for her, knowledge passes directly into feeling. Feeling and thought are inseparable for her, and it is natural for her to respond to experience with a unified consciousness: 'But in Dorothea's mind there was a current into which all thought and feeling were apt sooner or later to flow—the reaching forward of the whole consciousness towards the fullest truth, the least partial good'.... The word 'current', which is used several times in connection with her, suggests, like 'ardour', a Romantic sensibility.

But while the main problem for Maggie and Romola is that their strong feelings make them vulnerable to impulsive acts which contradict their past lives and past selves, Dorothea is at first faced with a different danger. Her most serious temptation is that form of idealism which longs for belief in an external order and meaning which one can serve with complete devotion because one believes utterly in its truth and value. Though Dorothea possesses such strong feelings, she at first distrusts what they tell her. She desires a form of knowledge and sense of truth which will be superior to subjective feeling. This is why she is so upset when Casaubon regards her only as a creature of feeling: 'She was humiliated to find herself a mere victim of feeling, as if she could know nothing except through that medium'.... She fears that what her feelings communicate to her may be wrong, and believes she needs a standpoint based on objective knowledge:

> Those provinces of masculine knowledge seemed to her a standing-ground from which all truth could be seen more truly. As it was, she constantly doubted her own conclusions, because she felt her own ignorance: how could she be confident that one-roomed cottages were not for the glory of God, when men who knew the

classics appeared to conciliate indifference to the cottages with zeal for glory? . . .

Though this passage satirises her belief that knowledge is required to support feeling over the cottages, this does not solve the problem created by the over-subjective and unstable nature of feeling on its own. . . . Dorothea believes religion combined with knowledge will provide a sense of moral direction for the self which will be independent of subjective feeling.

Her desire to devote herself utterly to the service of a religious ideal is repeatedly stressed: 'Her mind was theoretic, and yearned by its nature after some lofty conception of the world which might frankly include the parish of Tipton and her own rule of conduct there'. . . . Dorothea longs 'for a binding theory which could bring her own life and doctrine into strict connection with that amazing past, and give the remotest sources of knowledge some bearing on her actions'. . . . This longing is not wrong in itself, but the form in which she hopes for its realisation is untenable. . . . Dorothea in her early idealistic stage desires a theory which will prove that there is a religious meaning in reality itself, and that knowledge will reveal this.

It is this religious longing that lies at the root of her attraction to Casaubon. It is his intellectual aim to provide the 'lofty conception of the world' and 'binding theory' which would create the basis for a unified Christian world-view similar to that which existed in the time of St Theresa, and which Dorothea could serve with certainty because knowledge had been used to establish in unquestionable terms the truth of Christianity. He says of himself: 'My mind is something like the ghost of an ancient, wandering about the world and trying mentally to construct it as it used to be, in spite of ruin and confusing changes'. . . . This grandiose aim immediately appeals to Dorothea's Christian idealism: 'To reconstruct a past world, doubtless with a view to the highest purposes of truth—what a work to be in any way present at, to assist in, though only as a lamp-holder!' The theoretic side of her nature seeks an explanation of the world which will reveal the existence of a religious meaning and order external to the mind, and which would in consequence provide an absolutely firm basis for moral and social values. In other words, she sets her hopes on the establishment of a pre-Romantic world-view, as her Enlightenment faith in knowledge indicates: 'something she yearned for by which her life might be filled with action at once rational and ardent; and since the time was gone by for guiding visions and spiritual directors, since prayer heightened yearning but not instruction, what lamp was there but knowledge?' . . . (pp. 124-27)

It is natural then that she should be attracted to Casaubon. The aim of his 'Key to All Mythologies' is to counteract the fragmentation of man's knowledge and to provide the foundation for 'the coherent social faith and order' which a new St Theresa would require to give direction and purpose to her life. He will accomplish this by revealing that all mythologies are really only transformations or corruptions of the events in the Bible, which embodied religious truth. . . . Casaubon's aim makes him for Dorothea 'a living Bossuet, whose work would reconcile complete knowledge with devoted piety; here was a modern Augustine who united the glories of doctor and saint'. . . . Here again we see Dorothea interpreting Casaubon in pre-Romantic terms as someone who could use knowledge to establish the existence of a spiritual order in the world which could be the beginning of a new age of faith. (p. 127)

George Eliot should be seen as an advanced Romantic who rejects the pre-Romantic view that reality possesses a mean-

ingful order and structure which exists independently of the mind. . . . For her, it was no longer possible to believe that there was an immanent order in the world identical in structure with human thought. Probably she believed that the key to all mythologies, if it existed, was to be found not by trying to find a coherent structure underlying the diversity of knowledge but by investigating the mind itself. The key that would unlock all mythologies and systems was to be discovered in psychology. This is implicit in the philosophies of Feuerbach and Lewes. Even if Casaubon had succeeded in finishing his 'Key to All Mythologies', he would only have created a closed system, incapable of being either proved or disproved, and so able to appeal only to the converted. This seems to be the point of the narrator's comment that his theory was based on 'a method of interpretation which was not tested by the necessity of forming anything which had sharper collisions than an elaborate notion of Gog and Magog: it was as free from interruption as a plan for threading the stars together'. . . . George Eliot is perhaps suggesting that such a theory could never establish the objective truth of Christianity, and indeed that religion cannot be proved in scientific terms. Dorothea's hope that knowledge could reveal the existence of a religious order in the world, which everyone would have to recognise and accept, is misconceived, and she eventually realises this.

Her disillusionment with Casaubon and his work leads to a reluctant acceptance that the world lacks an immanent order which knowledge would discover and which would support Christian values. Her religious idealism seemed to her to justify moral action in the world, to create the foundation for a larger social faith, and to give her own life direction and purpose. Its breakdown, then, is a crisis in her life. She must come to terms with the failure of her pre-Romantic belief in a coherent order in the world, which revealed the existence of divine purpose. It is her experience in Rome which does most to make her aware of a disorder in the world that cannot be reconciled with her narrow religious principles. There she discovers a complexity and sense of the contradictory in her experience which shatters the excess of order in her religious theories about the world, and causes severe disorientation. . . . (pp. 129-30)

It is implied that personal disenchantment with Casaubon is in part responsible for creating the frame of mind which makes her respond to Rome in this way, for George Eliot . . . brings together the philosophical and the human significance of Dorothea's experience. After discovering that the reality of marriage bears little resemblance to what she had expected, she 'found herself plunged into tumultuous preoccupation with her personal lot'. It is tempting to believe that George Eliot intends to suggest that Dorothea's experience of his physical impotence leads to an awareness of his intellectual impotence, though strictly speaking such an interpretation has to be read into the text. However, the crisis she suffers in Rome produces a state of mind in which she can see Casaubon's work critically instead of, as formerly, in the light of her religious hopes. Her loss of faith in him and his work undermines further her religious world-view; if her belief in him could have been sustained and he had been one of the wisest of men, 'In that case her tottering faith would have become firm again'. . . . But she eventually realises that the fragments he is trying to put together disintegrate again in his hands and can only support 'a theory which was already withered in the bud like an elfin child'. . . . She finally accepts that he will never be able to create a synthesis which will reconcile faith and knowledge, and it is implied that she believes it is impossible; after his death his notebooks resemble 'the mute memorial of a forgotten faith', and she must reject his request that she carry on his work: it would be 'working hopelessly at what I have no belief in'.... (p. 131)

Though it is not stated openly that she has lost her religious faith, these passages suggest that her belief that knowledge would reveal the presence of a Christian order in the world has gone. She does, however, preserve a religious world-view, even though she says she hardly ever prays. The following declaration she makes to Ladislaw suggests that she becomes a transcendentalist: 'That by desiring what is perfectly good, even when we don't quite know what it is and cannot do what we would, we are part of the divine power against evil—widening the skirts of light and making the struggle with darkness narrower'.... But her main problem now is how to confront life without the 'binding theory' she had hoped for. This creates for her the difficulty faced also by George Eliot's previous heroines, of supporting her sense of identity solely from her inner resources, without succumbing to negative egotistic forces in herself or to impulsive feeling. There are two important occasions in which the strongly egotistic side of her nature threatens to gain control: when she is nearly overcome by an impulse of the moment and when she almost lapses into selfish despair.

The first of these occurs after Casaubon has snubbed her, having learned from Lydgate that he might not live long. All through her married life with Casaubon, Dorothea has restrained the strong feeling which is natural to her, and such feeling becomes transformed into egotistic revolt against her lot: 'She was in the reaction of a rebellious anger stronger than any she had felt since her marriage'.... Impulsive, resentful feeling threatens to overcome her more stable, sympathetic emotions. She wants to tell Casaubon 'the truth about her feeling' and to hurt him. But gradually she becomes aware of the danger of allowing 'her resentment to govern her', and that such feeling is false to her more persistent sense of self. She has to struggle hard to find an alternative feeling which is truer to her sense of whole self and not the expression of pent-up resentment.... Despite the loss of her religious idealism, in a moment of crisis in which she can rely only on her own resources, she is able to overcome a strong impulse. Her sympathy with how Casaubon must feel on learning that he might not have long to live and her own sense of continuity of self allow her to overcome a crisis, even though she is no longer supported by an external framework of Christian belief.

Her second serious crisis takes place when she sees Rosamond and Ladislaw together, believes that they are lovers, and that she has lost all hope of personal happiness through love. Like Romola when she has been forced to give up all affectionate feeling for Tito and lost her faith in Savonarola, Dorothea feels a sense of despair. While for Romola it had been Savonarola and religion which had provided her with greatest support after her original disillusionment with Tito, with Dorothea this process is reversed; it is her relationship with Ladislaw, which has developed into love, that has sustained her after the breakdown of her Christian idealism. In each case disappointment leads to despair, but as with Romola, Dorothea overcomes this and finds through feeling the means of reconstituting her life. She must come to terms with the fact that the world is indifferent to her own hopes and desires, just as she has had to accept already that reality does not conform to the structure of her Christian ideals. But the underlying feelings which were the real basis of her former Christian idealism are still valid, though she must not expect the world to conform with human

ideals or take account of human hopes and desires. Her idealistic feelings remain valuable even if they must be projected onto an indifferent, unstructured world. This realisation comes to her when she recovers, after a night of conflict, the original sympathetic feelings which motivated her in the first place to visit Rosamond. These have not been shown to be false, despite what she thought she saw at Lydgate's house, and in her new self-knowledge she can use them to overcome the egotistic feelings of anger, resentment, and despair aroused by the disappointment of her hopes and expectations.... Sympathetic feeling, with its basis in the human and social aspect of the self, triumphs over animal egotism and becomes her source of knowledge.

Even though she can no longer accept that there is religious meaning immanent in the world, and believes, mistakenly as it turns out, that events have frustrated her own hopes of happiness, this sympathetic feeling remains to give her life moral direction and to discipline egotistic impulse. It can be the foundation of an ideal value which can 'rule her errant will' and shape human action in the world. Dorothea also resembles Romola in that this inner moral feeling leads to a larger, more social vision when she opens the curtains of her room and looks out at the world beyond her own ego: 'Far off in the bending sky was the pearly light; and she felt the largeness of the world and the manifold wakings of men to labour and endurance'. During her Christian phase she had hoped that knowledge would reveal religious meaning in external reality, but now she discovers that though there may be no such meaning objectively in the world, it is present in her intense human feeling and vision. Her earlier Christian beliefs and idealism were the projection into objective form of this feeling, and despite the breakdown of her projection, the underlying feeling remains valid. She can go on to create a new orientation which supports her sense of identity and directs her life. (pp. 131-34)

The relationship between Dorothea and Ladislaw has been generally regarded as one of the artistic weaknesses of *Middlemarch*, primarily on the grounds that Ladislaw is too idealised or too lightweight to be worthy of Dorothea. It is probable that Ladislaw had to perform too many functions in the plot for George Eliot to succeed fully in creating both a complex psychological portrait and a character who plays an important part in the novel's philosophical structure. But he seems to me to be much more central to the novel and more successfully characterised than most previous critics have tended to think. His importance is closely connected with the novel's Romantic concerns. He is the character most obviously associated with the Romantics. For example, he has been educated at Heidelberg, one of the most important centres of German Romanticism; he is twice compared to Shelley by Mr Brooke: 'he has the same sort of enthusiasm for liberty, freedom, emancipation' ...; and he is described by Mrs Cadwallader as 'A sort of Byronic hero'.... His flamboyant appearance, his experiments with opium and his general attitudes all contribute to building up a picture of a Romantic, and this seems clearly to be George Eliot's intention.

But it is the development of Ladislaw as a Romantic that is important. At the beginning of the novel he is attracted towards the egotistic side of Romanticism. He sees himself as 'Pegasus' and he regards 'every form of prescribed work' as 'harness'.... The words 'pride', 'defiance', and 'rebellion', all of which have a Byronic connotation, are frequently associated with him. He tells Dorothea proudly that he comes 'of rebellious blood on both sides'.... Casaubon's opinion of him is 'that he was capable of any design which could fascinate a rebellious temper and an undisciplined impulsiveness'. . . . He is also Byronic in being an outsider and an alien, a role he takes some pleasure in: 'he was a sort of gypsy, rather enjoying the sense of belonging to no class; he had a feeling of romance in his position, and a pleasant consciousness of creating a little surprise wherever he went'. . . . He feels little connection with any country or social group, nor at the beginning of the novel does he wish to have any. He is a rootless wanderer, associated with gypsies and Jews.

In the dominating social world of *Middlemarch,* however, Ladislaw's rebellious and egotistic tendencies present little threat to society. The common criticism that Ladislaw is an insubstantial character perhaps does not take sufficient account of the fact that in the world of the novel the Romantic rebel is inevitably a lightweight figure. His egotistic rebellion expresses itself only in aestheticism and dilettantism. When Dorothea asks him what his religion is, he replies: 'To love what is good and beautiful when I see it. . . . But I am a rebel: I don't feel bound, as you do, to submit to what I don't like'. . . . Naumann believes he is incapable of devoting his attention to any one subject: 'His walk must be *belles-lettres.* That is wi—ide' . . . , and Casaubon considers him to be 'a man with no other principle than transient caprice'. . . . But his aestheticism and dilettantism are sufficient to alienate him from society or from any chosen vocation. Without the influence of Dorothea on his life, it seems certain that he would have remained a rootless aesthete.

The change that takes place in Ladislaw is an important element in the novel's structure. Dorothea's influence encourages him to direct his Romantic energies into social channels. He had previously believed that genius was 'intolerant of fetters' . . . , but his feeling for Dorothea makes him accept the 'harness' he had formerly rejected, 'having settled in Middlemarch and harnessed himself with Mr Brooke'. . . . The same image is present in the following passage: 'Ladislaw had now accepted his bit of work, though it was not that indeterminate loftiest thing which he had once dreamed of as alone worthy of continuous effort. His nature warmed easily in the presence of subjects which were visibly mixed with life and action, and the easily stirred rebellion in him helped the glow of public spirit'. . . . The last part of this passage shows how his former rebellious energy is being socially directed. He no longer cuts himself off from society but devotes energies, once taken up by the study of art as a form of escape from society, to working for the social good: 'he studied the political situation with as ardent an interest as he had ever given to poetic metres or mediaevalism'. Dorothea has made him feel that Romantic ardour must be given a social expression. His transformation is shown in Dorothea's conversation with him when he is on the point of leaving Middlemarch: 'And you care that justice should be done to every one. I am so glad. When we were in Rome, I thought you only cared for poetry and art, and the things that adorn life for us who are well off. But now I know you think about the rest of the world'. . . . Significantly by the end of the novel this former Romantic rebel has become 'an ardent public man'. . . .

Dorothea's ardent desire to do some good in the world and her implied criticism of Ladislaw's attitudes are the most important factors in making him give up his rootless existence and involve himself in society. Her idealistic conception of him becomes part of his sense of self, and the need to earn her respect brings out tendencies in himself that might otherwise have been over-whelmed by his attraction to egotistic Romantic attitudes. . . . (pp. 136-37)

But though Ladislaw is able to play an active role in society and directs his energies in a socially responsible way, society is as little affected by this as it was by his period of rebellion and social alienation. The 'Finale' suggests that, like Dorothea, he is subject to the limitations that result from living in 'an imperfect social state'. Though he devotes himself energetically to trying to reform his society, this seems to lead to no obvious benefit: 'working well in those times when reforms were begun with a young hopefulness of immediate good which has been much checked in our days'.

It might be objected that despite Ladislaw's importance in the novel's philosophical structure, he is still an artistic failure. But in my view those who have criticised Ladislaw's characterisation have not sufficiently recognised that in *Middlemarch* George Eliot has made considerable progress in the dramatic presentation of what I have called sublimated egotism. In her previous novels, her positive characters often appeared to be idealised and one-dimensional in comparison with her negative egotists. In *Middlemarch* this artistic weakness is to a great extent overcome, particularly in the characterisation of Dorothea and Mary Garth. But even Ladislaw, though less convincing than Dorothea or Mary, is not the idealised figure many critics have seen him as being. Even after Dorothea's reforming influence on him, he remains strongly egotistic, and this is not merely stated but presented in dramatic terms. We see, for example, in a convincing and psychologically credible scene, how he succumbs to the egotistic temptation of going to church in Lowick to see Dorothea, realises his 'wretched blunder' when Casaubon and Dorothea enter, and feels 'utterly ridiculous, out of temper, and miserable' in the 'cage' he has created for himself. . . . We also see how his egotism shapes his interpretation of his relationship with Dorothea in their difficult meetings after Casaubon's death, and his vulnerability to a strong impulse of the moment in his cruel treatment of Rosamond when Dorothea surprises them together, an experience which makes him realise later that he is in danger of drifting into an affair with Rosamond and that he might not be capable of resisting this. To see Ladislaw as merely an idealisation of the Romantic, as 'sentimental because he lacks the adult energies that would make his freedom problematic', is to overlook George Eliot's dramatic presentation of the tension between the egotistic and the idealistic sides of his character, even if this tension is not consistently maintained. (pp. 138-39)

> *K. M. Newton, in his* George Eliot, Romantic Humanist: A Study of the Philosophical Structure of Her Novels, *Barnes & Noble Books, 1981, 215 p.*

KATHLEEN BLAKE (essay date 1983)

[*Blake contends that* Middlemarch *is a "great feminist work" because, through Dorothea's story, Eliot castigates societal conditions that prevent women from working and force them to rely on marriage as an outlet for their energies. Thus, in response to Mintz (1978), Blake argues that Eliot places equal emphasis on the themes of romance and vocation in* Middlemarch.]

Everybody finds *Middlemarch* a great work, and many of its original reviews found that it raises the woman question. Yet the body of criticism from then till now makes surprisingly little case for it as a great feminist work. I think it is. (p. 26)

A number of nineteenth-century reviewers questioned whether the indictment of society for its treatment of women in the

"Finale" receives convincing support in the novel's action. Specifically, the first edition of 1871-2 says that Dorothea's mistakes owe something to a society that "smiled on propositions of marriage from a sickly man to a girl less than half his own age". The reviewers pointed out that Middlemarch does *not* smile, certainly not Celia, Mrs Cadwallader, Sir James Chettam, not even Mr Brooke. In *The Fortnightly Review* Sidney Colvin responds aptly to this criticism, observing that Dorothea's whole education prepares her for the mistake of her marriage [see excerpt dated 1873]. However, Eliot did change the disputed paragraph. Specific criticism of social pressure toward marriage for women and of education that opens no other prospects to them gives way in the 1874 edition, now taken as the standard, to a general complaint against "the conditions of an imperfect social state" . . ., which does not mention women at all. Is Eliot backing off from the woman question? (p. 27)

I wish to argue that the deletion of the indictments of the "Finale" makes little difference to the novel's focus on the "postponement" by society of a woman's aspirations, causing her to fall back on love and marriage, which [often] become modes of self-postponement. . . . (p. 28)

The story begins and ends with Dorothea, and even in its revised state the "Finale" still completes what the "Prelude" launches, the study of the soul that aspires to epic life but finds no channel for "far-resonant action" and so achieves only a blundering life. Its aspirations "dispersed among hindrances", it becomes the accomplice to its own "lapse". This fate is specifically feminine. The ardour that appears extravagant because its object is vague alternates with the "common yearning of womanhood". If a woman tries to take her stand anywhere but at the level that defines her by sex, her character becomes liable to the odd condition of "indefiniteness", "inconsistency and formlessness". In preference to this she may choose the common womanly state. Several passages in the novel explain what makes up this state and makes it common. Eliot herself generalises on the bent of every sweet woman toward love, from her childhood passion for her dolls on, and she calls this "the ardent woman's need to rule beneficently by making the joy of another soul". . . . Casaubon expresses in a complacent commonplace the masculine expectation of feminine affection: "The great charm of your sex is its capability of an ardent self-sacrificing affection, and herein we see its fitness to round and complete the existence of our own". . . . Lydgate relies on womanly devotion, and this forms one of his "spots of commonness". . . . He believes all wives are devoted to their husbands, but finds out to his sorrow that while his own wife prettily declares this belief, she does not feel impelled to act on it. The tendency of women to love is strong but not as all-sufficing as it is presumed to be, and to presume upon it may mean the exploitation of the woman, or sometimes the disillusionment of the man. The "common yearning of womanhood" offers greater definiteness and hope of attainment than vague ideals, precisely because it is common, and so a would-be Saint Theresa, tired of external hindrances and her own indefiniteness, has little choice but to choose the common fate. This may be "condemned as a lapse", but *Middlemarch* takes more interest in understanding how it comes about than in condemning it.

The "Prelude" does not explain feminine nature as the fashioning of a supreme power, for it resists the scientific measurement that should be possible if it were a given of creation. Eliot turns, rather, to social forces for explanation. Hence she contrasts Dorothea's situation to that of Saint Theresa, who found the favourable medium for action that Dorothea lacks. Significantly, the "Prelude" pictures a Saint Theresa not of mystic beatitude but of very concrete accomplishment as a reformer of a religious order. But "no coherent social faith and order" aids later-born Theresas. A religious calling as a nun represents one of the few high vocations which have been open to women historically, but when religion weakens and convents become things of the past, the opportunities shrink. Society offers women, especially those of the middle and upper classes, little to do besides the exercise of their affections, it expects less, and it fails to imagine that they need work as much as men.

Thus Eliot, like Herodotus, thinks it well to take a woman's life as her starting point . . ., for this lot presents the extreme case of the human impulse toward vocation meeting frustration and becoming in the process dangerously entangled with the impulse toward love. If Eliot modified her conclusion to make it a less specific indictment of society for the problems it creates for women, the modification is minor. For there remain in the "Finale" strong reminders of the social conditions that break the force of women's striving and deflect it into domesticity, so that a full nature like Dorothea's "spent itself in channels which had no great name on the earth". . . . For instance, the "Finale" returns to Letty Garth, who seems to exist in *Middlemarch* to allow for occasional simple articulations of a feminist theme, lest it should be muffled in the massive orchestration. She, "whose life was much checkered by resistance to her depreciation as a girl" . . ., finds herself beleaguered in the "Finale" by brotherly arguments and parental pronouncements to the effect that girls are good for less than boys. She is Middlemarch's staunchest feminist, for she "took it ill, her feeling of superiority being stronger than her muscles". . . . But Letty is only a little girl. Her feeling of superiority could hardly survive in a society that gives no credit to women even when it is due, let alone expecting much from them and thereby giving them something to aim at and to be, beyond wives and mothers. (pp. 28-30)

Eliot may have been right to modify the final passage that blames Middlemarch for smiling on Dorothea's marriage to Casaubon. Her letters of the period show her desire to avoid polemical statements which could be extracted as messages and her preference for imbuing the whole with meaning. Furthermore, the social pressures actually depicted in the novel operate a good deal less directly, while none the less forcefully, than those summed up in the original "Finale". Let us look at a few instances among many of the subtle means by which Middlemarch delivers Dorothea into the arms of Casaubon. That it doesn't mean to only gives Eliot's analysis greater depth by avoiding the sentimentality of making out every victim the product of somebody's intention. (p. 30)

[Dorothea's] "mind was theoretic, and yearned by its nature after some lofty conception of the world which might frankly include the parish of Tipton". . . . It is possible to misread Dorothea's character to conclude that a quality blameably abstract attaches to her way of thinking and that her myopia symbolises her oversight of the tangible in favour of nebulous ideals. While she often doesn't see what is before her face, and this can give her apprehension a certain Dodo quality, to match her nickname, not all she overlooks is worth seeing— the Maltese puppy, for instance. Sometimes her blindness protects her—"her blindness to whatever did not lie in her own pure purpose carried her safely by the side of precipices where vision would have been perilous with fear''. . . . Her idealising vision is sometimes truer than the short view—her belief in Lydgate restores him in some measure to himself. And the carnally-minded do not see everything either—however well Celia sizes up Casaubon, she misses a great deal that matters. But most important to bear in mind is that Dorothea *wants* to include the parish of Tipton in her ideal. It is simply not true that she seeks intensity and greatness separate from the actual. She longs to realise them ''here—now—in England''. . . . (p. 31)

Dorothea does not abjure the concrete, but such concrete goals as society offers a woman in her position cramp her. To be satisfied with them she would need to combine ''girlish instruction comparable to the nibblings and judgments of a discursive mouse'' (which she has) with ''an endowment of stupidity and conceit'' (which she has not). Then

> she might have thought that a Christian young lady of fortune should find her ideal of life in village charities, patronage of the humbler clergy, the perusal of ''Female Scripture Characters,'' . . . and the care of her soul over her embroidery in her own boudoir—with a background of prospective marriage to a man who, if less strict than herself, as being involved in affairs religiously inexplicable, might be prayed for and reasonably exhorted. From such contentment poor Dorothea was shut out. . . .

Imagery of enclosure and compression often signals the cramping narrowness of such prospects, as seen in Dorothea's dissatisfaction with the ''walled-in maze of small paths that led no whither''. . . . She is weighed down and must bear ''dimness and pressure''. . . . (pp. 31-2)

But when she rejects the narrow prospects of the married lady's life in order to find room for her energies, her problem becomes the reverse of cramp—too much space. Her goals necessarily suffer from haziness of outline and lack the clear demarcation of those offered ready to hand by society. Far from complacent about her vague ideals, Dorothea faces this vagueness as a problem. ''For a long while she had been oppressed by the indefiniteness which hung in her mind, like a thick summer haze, over all her desire to make her life greatly effective. 'What could she do, what ought she do?' '' . . . Dorothea's confusion in viewing the wide vista of Rome deserves considering in this connection. Her inability to seize upon any single object leaves her strength scattered and diffuse. Eliot shows that such diffusion can prove as obstructive as simple narrowness of outlook.

Aims unrecognised by others often lack clarity for the self, and so energy is squelched, or diffused or redirected. When Dorothea speaks at her uncle's table with more energy than is expected of a young lady, Mr Brooke remarks that young ladies don't understand political economy, and this comes like ''an extinguisher over all her lights''. . . . But Dorothea possesses too much spark to be really extinguished, and she wants anything but the haze of undirected energy, so she grasps at the closest objects of enthusiasm, Mr Casaubon and his work. (p. 32)

Elderly, stiff and pedantic, Casaubon becomes the incongruous embodiment of the lover/saviour. For Dorothea he takes on the aspect of a ''winged messenger'' holding out his hand to aid her. . . . She thinks marriage to him will provide the room she needs while at the same time saving her from the haze of her own indefiniteness. He offers ''large yet definite duties''. He

also offers entry into the provinces of masculine knowledge—Latin and Greek. Dorothea believes that education will remove the doubt of her own conclusions that adds to their haziness. While she casts herself in prospect in a self-subdued role as a devoted wife, as her husband's lampbearer and so on, she is hardly so selfless as she thinks. ''She had not reached that point of renunciation at which she would have been satisfied with having a wise husband: she wished, poor child, to be wise herself''. . . . A husband promises to supply objects of action which are already decided and also the means for Dorothea herself to grow more decisive.

Middlemarch need not smile on this union to bring it about. Middlemarch has made, Middlemarch is, the conditions that make a poor, pedantic, mummified suitor appear to an ardent young woman barred from the vocation she seeks as a sort of enabling angel, though he turns out to be a disabling husband.

The question of vocation is central to **Middlemarch**. George Eliot says that her story does not simply present the often-rendered romance of man and woman, but also the romance of vocation, of those who mean ''to shape their own deeds and alter the world a little''. . . . This passage provides the launching point for Alan Mintz's *George Eliot and the Novel of Vocation*, an interesting study which suggests that vocation virtually supersedes the romance of the sexes as a fictional theme in **Middlemarch**, whereas I think the novel examines the intertwining of the two themes. Mintz treats the feminine situation secondarily. If we give it primacy as the ''Prelude'' invites us to do, then the role of love in relation to vocation gains importance. Indeed, the passage in question holds that the impulses toward vocation and love interact, and ''not seldom the catastrophe [in the case of the one] is bound up with the other passion''. This is true for both sexes because Middlemarch disallows vocation for women other than conjugal. We have seen that Dorothea marries to find work in her husband's scholarship and as mistress of his estate. In the course of her marriage the man himself becomes the only real work she can claim, at the price of self-postponement, as we shall see. Moreover, Lydgate becomes the victim of the vocational vacuum for women that makes a husband the most available instrument of a wife's ambitions.

It needs no long repeating that virtually all of the characters are engrossed by the desire for vocation. . . . The novel offers one of the most searching of literary investigations of the Victorian work ethic, for it shows that not to shape the world is to remain shapeless oneself, which for natures conscious of shaping energy means painful consciousness of their own dispersal.

Both Lydgate and Casaubon fail to muster energy sufficient for success, but each man's energy receives greater sustenance than Dorothea's. . . . Dorothea possesses only the most meagre work in which to acquit herself and the meagrest education to help her tred out her own path. Instead of being called forth and reinforced, her energy, which exceeds that of anyone else in the book, often fails of effect precisely because no one expects much energy from a woman.

Eliot analyses this failure with subtle penetration. She shows that energy begins to relax when no effort is elicited and no impact results from effort. This accounts for Lydgate's slackening of will in the face of the impervious Rosamond. ''Lydgate sat paralysed by opposing impulses: since no reasoning he could apply to Rosamond seemed likely to conquer her assent, he wanted to smash and grind some object on which he could at least produce an impression, or else tell her brutally that he was master'', but ''the very resolution to which he had wrought himself by dint of logic and honorable pride was beginning to relax . . .''. Any ''further overtures seemed blocked out by a sense of unsuccessful effort''. . . . Women more often suffer such paralysis of energy because their efforts are more often unwanted in the first place and received as null when made.

A passage on Dorothea's life at Lowick after her return from Rome examines the process of paralysis. The poor don't need her. Casaubon has discouraged her schemes. He shuts her out of his work, which Will has also discredited. The result is a blank that begins to invade her sense of herself. Crucial here is the energy supply, which is threatened in two related ways. Something not called for may cease to be forthcoming, and seeing no sign of one's own power, one may lose it. Again Dorothea encounters the indefiniteness that erodes enterprise. A ''dun vapour'' figures this hazy mental state. Liberty and oppression seem to be opposites, but when liberty merely consists of lack of anything definite to do, it makes the very width of the space into a hampering medium. The more one can do anything one pleases, the more difficult to please to do any one thing, or to please to do anything at all:

> Meanwhile there was the snow and the low arch of dun vapour—there was the stifling oppression of that gentlewoman's world, where everything was done for her and none asked for her aid—where the sense of connection with a manifold pregnant existence had to be kept up painfully as an inward vision, instead of coming from without in claims that would have shaped her energies—''What shall I do?'' ''Whatever you please, my dear'': that had been her brief history since she had left off learning morning lessons and practising silly rhythms on the hated piano. Marriage, which was to bring guidance into worthy and imperative occupation, had not yet freed her from the gentlewoman's oppressive liberty; it had not even filled her leisure with the ruminant joy of unchecked tenderness. Her blooming full-pulsed youth stood in moral imprisonment which made itself one with the chill, colourless, narrowed landscape, with the shrunken furniture, the never-read books, and the ghostly stag in a pale fantastic world that seemed to be vanishing from the daylight. . . .
>
> (pp. 33-7)

In her oppressive liberty the gentlewoman lacks impact, and her sense of powerlessness to make contact is conveyed by the odd image of the vanishing stag. The next paragraph develops the implications of such vanishing; it describes Dorothea's nightmarish struggle ''in which every object was withering and shrinking away from her''. Later Dorothea sees Will in the same terms, ''receding into the distant world of warm activity and fellowship''. . . . He literally recedes from her when she passes him in her carriage; she feels that they are moving further and further apart and yet that she cannot stop. (p. 37)

The existence from which Dorothea feels cut off includes a sense of her own existence, for Eliot insists on the shaping force of outward things for the energies that reach out to shape the world. Outward claims elicit energy as well as shape it. Outward effects confirm energy and keep it coming. Dorothea's life presents a prospect ''full of motiveless ease—motiveless,

if her own energy could not seek out reasons for ardent action''. . . . The worst danger of ease is that it might leave one motiveless. Worse than reaching out to touch things that shrink and wither away would be no longer reaching out to touch at all.

Everyone comments on George Eliot's celebration of duty and work and the renunciation of self in favour of some worthy object. Most concentrate on the content of that duty or work—what constitutes the worthy object? Answers can be found, but they skip over an important point, namely, Eliot's deep concern with the human need for duty, work or object, whose value lies as much in the sense of worth conferred by the act of striving as in objective content. (p. 38)

[Dorothea] and Will hold a conversation that brings the example of art to bear on an issue of life: whether value lies in potential or accomplishment. Will maintains that to be a poet means possessing a certain state of intellect and feeling. This fails to satisfy Dorothea. She maintains that poems ''are wanted to complete the poet''. Possessing a poetic state of mind does not suffice because ''I am sure I could never produce a poem''. . . . Dorothea's idea parallels Carlyle's ''produce, produce!'' or Mary Garth's ''might, could, would—they are contemptible auxiliaries''. . . . It epitomises the Victorian work ethic, understood without the crassness of the merely materialistic or utilitarian, for it locates in the results the motive for self-completion.

Will says that if Dorothea is no poet because she cannot produce a poem, she is herself a poem, and this pleases her, which at first seems surprising since it offers no fulfilment of that ''idea of some active good within her reach, [that] 'haunted her like a passion' ''. . . . It seems to deny the importance of active shaping for the shaping of the self. But Dorothea must find satisfaction where she can, and I think the satisfaction here rests in the thought of the difference she makes in the mind that might make the poem, in a word, the difference she makes to Will. She enjoys thinking she governs a little kingdom in him, that she can sway him, because she has generally found very little room in other people's minds for her thoughts. He proves to be the most receptive person she has ever known. Will does not please her only because his eyes give out light, but because his eyes tell her that not the smallest movement of her own passes unnoticed, which realisation ''came like a pleasant glow to Dorothea''. . . . (pp. 39-40)

John Halperin interprets this glow as a sign of Dorothea's discovery that ''she is a woman who needs a man'', which is true in a way that he pays very little attention to [see Additional Bibliography]. He doesn't consider what she needs him *for*. For one thing, and it is not a little thing, she needs him for the testament he gives her of her own power of impact. The glow signals a movement toward hope in that near-despairing meditation on the stifling oppression of a gentlewoman's life. It signals the returning sense of power which also carries a sense of life. It doesn't turn her away from her husband as one would ordinarily suppose that love for another man would do, and Halperin seems to have something very ordinary in mind. Rather, this feeling turns her toward him, with a hope that formulates itself in a reversal of the nightmare images of a world receding from her touch. That is, it gives her hope of impact: ''She felt as if all her morning's gloom would vanish if she could see her husband glad because of her presence''. . . . (pp. 40-1)

We have already observed the entanglement of love and vocation when Dorothea marries in hope of finding work through her husband. Here we encounter a yet more intimate meshing, as love *becomes* vocation for her and her work becomes the man himself. Failing everything else, Dorothea falls back on "the common yearning of womanhood", "the ardent woman's need to rule beneficently by making the joy of another soul". (p. 41)

That women's work is men is a tired old truism, but it fills with fine insight in Eliot's treatment. She shows how it follows from Middlemarch's easy assumption that as the world can pretty much do without the work of women, women can pretty much do without work. She shows that no one can do without it, so that men become women's work by default. Such a vocation is little enough for some energetic souls, while at the same time it may cost them, or sometimes their husbands, dearly.

In seeking some response from the unresponsive Casaubon, Dorothea must practise self-postponement. Why do anything that will only read back one's own incompetence—"What she dreaded was to exert herself in reading or anything else which left him as joyless as ever". . . . Eliot returns repeatedly to the idea of self-arrest by premonition of impotence, showing Dorothea's "nightmare of a life [with Casaubon] in which every energy was arrested by dread", "a perpetual struggle of energy with fear". "Her ardour, continually repulsed, served, with her intense memory, to heighten her dread, as thwarted energy subsides into a shudder". . . . This shudder perfectly figures the idea of energy defeated of outward impact, turning back upon itself. Another good instance of the effort involved in motionlessness appears in Dorothea's constraining herself to lie still in bed lest she should wake her husband. She learns to "shut her best soul in prison . . . that she might be petty enough to please him". . . . She learns "timidity", "self-repression", and "resolved submission". . . . Constraint of her best soul, which might otherwise have acted to the highest account, proves to be the only way to count at all.

Feminine self-postponement allows Dorothea to achieve something, which means to retain some initiative. Quelling her resentment of her husband, she produces a movement of human fellowship in him. She manages to get through to Rosamond after a struggle to subdue the claims of self, which if somewhat different in its occasion, is very similar in its psychological movement. She wrings motive out of despair: "She said to her own irremediable grief, that it should make her more helpful, instead of driving her back from effort". . . . (pp. 41-2)

Dorothea has learned to regard her power of active effort as a precious resource, one that can be lost, as many women lose it:

> I had no notion . . . of the unexpected way in
> which trouble comes, and ties our hands, and
> makes us silent when we long to speak. I used
> to despise women a little for not shaping their
> lives more, and doing better things. I was very
> fond of doing as I liked, but I have almost given
> it up.
>
> (p. 42)

Dorothea comes closest to giving up altogether when she decides to consent to Casaubon's request that she carry on his work after his death. This would truly condemn her to labour to no avail in that she finds meaningful work only in Casaubon himself, the living man. Significantly, the decision to accept this ultimate renunciation induces a "passivity which was unusual with her". . . . (p. 43)

[After Casaubon's death Dorothea] emerges only into "another sort of pinfold than that from which she had been released". . . . Does Dorothea escape from this pinfold when she takes the initiative and marries Will despite Middlemarch? I think not entirely, for the tone of regret sounds strongly in the "Finale", at the same time that the novel reconciles itself to what could hardly be helped. The end balances gains and losses. Dorothea and Will are dear to each other, and she finds some scope for achievement in her marriage, and yet their union represents some sacrifice too, only less sad than might have been. . . . Eliot says that "many . . . thought it a pity that so substantive and rare a creature should have been absorbed into the life of another . . . but no one stated exactly what else that was in her power she ought rather to have done". . . . (pp. 45-6)

Dorothea does not gain the stature of a nineteenth-century Saint Theresa. The blocking of the channels to deeds also diffuses or deflects the character which might have performed them, hence the "inconvenient indefiniteness" of even the most impressive women, or their lapse into "the common yearning of womanhood". Dorothea achieves the definite at the expense of her highest potential, which remains too vague to do much good to her or the world. In explaining her decision to marry Will she says, "I might have done something better, if I had been better. But this is what I am going to do". . . . *Middlemarch* shows that Dorothea would have *been* better if she had been in a position to *do* better. Eliot does not allow us the sentimental contemplation of great souls trapped in an indifferent universe; souls that do not contribute significantly lose some of their greatness. Lydgate apprehends this in his own case. . . . The same holds for Dorothea, though she bears less blame for her fate. In her essay on Margaret Fuller and Mary Wollstonecraft, Eliot commends the two feminists for refusing to idealise women. Indeed, women's standing below the level of their potential argues the need for emancipation.

While generally recognising that Dorothea hardly liberates herself from Middlemarch to the extent of undertaking epic action, opinion varies as to the scope of her pinfold and the amount of satisfaction we should feel in it. At the centre of this debate stands Will Ladislaw. Dorothea's marriage to Will disappointed many early reviewers. . . . (p. 46)

I place myself among the small number of critics for whom R. H. Hutton in the *British Quarterly Review* of 1873 may speak: "one feels, and is probably meant to feel acutely, that here too, it is the 'meanness of opportunity' and not intrinsic suitability, which determines Dorothea's second comparatively happy marriage". Will seems a slight creature beside her. Surely Eliot means us to sense this when she follows the climactic chapter on Dorothea's noble resolve in going to Rosamond by opening the next chapter with Will's flimsier kind of resolve—"a state of mind liable to melt into a minuet with other states of mind, and to find itself bowing, smiling, and giving place with polite facility". . . . (p. 47)

Will adds to his own limitations certain assumptions about women's limitations which create a sometimes uncomfortable resemblance to Mr Brooke, Sir James, Lydgate and Casaubon. He can be as put off by Dorothea's power and eloquence as any of them. Eliot says of him, "A man is seldom ashamed of feeling that he cannot love a woman so well when he sees a certain greatness in her: nature having intended greatness for men". . . . He cherishes Dorothea's innocent shortsightedness and her inaccessibility. He would almost rather do without her love than that she be sullied by recognising the obvious fact of his devotion and the implications of Casaubon's jealousy. Also, "what others might have called the futility of his passion, made an additional delight for his imagination". . . . His pedestal theory—Dorothea sits "enthroned in his soul" according to the dictates of the "higher love poetry" . . .—sometimes produces problems for her. In her carriage, passing him as he walks on foot, she "felt a pang at being seated there in a sort of exaltation, leaving him behind". . . . One wonders whether she might not lose a bit of her charm for him in delivering herself from the pedestal into his arms, just as she does in speaking with unfeminine greatness.

Will shares some of the attitudes that contribute to the meanness of a woman's opportunity, but at the same time, the very irresoluteness and flexibility that make him slight, make him impressionable. He can take the pressure of other people's thoughts. . . . And Dorothea certainly needs to make a mark somewhere. She will be able to find some vocation in influencing his work.

Any estimation of Dorothea's final lot should take account, not only of her husband's character, but of his work toward political reform, for we know that she gives him wifely help in it. The magnitude of the undertaking to which she contributes is too seldom considered. Eliot's readers had just witnessed the passage of the second Reform Bill, and though *Middlemarch* ends with the defeat of the first Reform Bill, they would have recognised this as a temporary setback. An historical perspective informs the novel. Setting the story in "ante-reform times" . . . locates it in relation to the ultimate passage of Reform. Helping a husband who works for this passage, Dorothea helps forward a movement that would eventually prevail and that bears comparison to Saint Theresa's reform of a religious order as a "far-resonant action". The importance of Reform is, I think, a given. To understand it forms part of the necessary equipment for reading the novel. . . . Whatever Eliot's reservations about some of the tactics for passing Reform, she surely judges it part of "the growing good of the world". . . . While our hopefulness in response to the end of *Middlemarch* should be somewhat dashed in contemplating Will, we may find something heartening in the prospect of Reform. (pp. 47-9)

Kathleen Blake, "'Middlemarch': Vocation, Love and the Woman Question," in her *Love and the Woman Question in Victorian Literature: The Art of Self-Postponement, Barnes & Noble Books, 1983, pp. 26-55.*

KAREN CHASE (essay date 1984)

[In this study of Middlemarch's *scientific underpinnings, Chase examines Eliot's perception of the relationhip between the mind and the body.]*

[What does George Eliot's evocation of the inner life have] to do with that other great current in her work—the attention to the constraints of circumstance? What does the portrayal of mind have to do with the depicting of mindless forces? Or, to place the question in the more manageable terms we will employ here: what is the relation of mind to that most immediate of circumstances, the body? (pp. 136-37)

A good deal is known about the scientific interests of George Eliot: the deep entanglement in the work of Lewes; the close association with Spencer; the careful reading of Darwin, Huxley, Tyndall, and their contemporaries; the arduous research into the medical history of the early nineteenth century. Unlike

John Walter Cross, whom Eliot married shortly before her death.

Dickens or Brontë, who were willing to forage among such highly speculative theories as phrenology, physiognomy, and mesmerism, George Eliot had her most important intellectual links to those who moved in the main current of nineteenth-century empiricism. The translator of Feuerbach, the admirer of Comte, had little tolerance for intuitive doctrines that prized metaphysical sweep over sound evidence. George Eliot frequently satirized medical charlatanism, and like her character Lydgate, she looked with great interest on the task of "enlarging the scientific, rational basis" of the medical profession. . . . It is not possible here, nor is it necessary, to follow the complex intellectual history with which George Eliot engaged, but one particular episode deserves attention, the Comtean assault on psychology.

For those in the empirical tradition, nineteenth-century psychology posed special problems. If science it were to be, then it must have precise data and a rigorous method; it must abandon its traditonal associations with metaphysics and join biology, chemistry, and physics on the firm ground of empirical investigation. Such a program encouraged the pursuit of a strict physiological basis for psychology, and through the nineteenth century there emerged a tendency to erect the discipline of psychology on biological foundations. This raised a vexing question. If psychology must look to biology for its grounds, then in what sense can it be regarded as an independent discipline? Why should we not assimilate psychology to biology and award it scientific status by refining it out of existence?

Auguste Comte, for one, contemplated this step with equanimity. Within the system of positive philosophy, psychology appeared as an entirely derivative body of thought, its contributions insignificant, its principles incoherent. Biology studies the human organism, and sociology the structure of human community. The two exhaust the field in which psychology has claimed a place. (pp. 145-46)

George Henry Lewes was very nearly the complete Comtean, but he hesitated before these uncompromising strictures against psychology. In *Comte's Philosophy of the Sciences* (1853), Lewes invokes John Stuart Mill ''as a balance against the authoritative weight of Auguste Comte,'' and with Mill, he charges ''that Positive Philosophy demands a modification of Comte's Classification [of sciences].'' Lewes argues that ''we must separate Mind from Life, not because there is any *essential* (noumenal) separation—(the former is but the outgrowth of the latter)—but because the phenomena of Thought are *special;* they are not the same as the phenomena of Life.'' . . .

Comte, of course, had not denied the distinctive character of human consciousness, but he had refused to grant it any theoretical priority. Since consciousness is only a derivative phenomenon, an introspective psychology can never lead us to origins. Moreover, a science that studies facts of consciousness remains mired in methodological incoherence. . . .

This argument must have told gradually on Lewes, for by the mid-sixties he had thoroughly reversed himself and now embraced the severe Comtean position. He conceived the difficulty as a false split between mind (psychology) and body (biology). According to Lewes, this dichotomy had been the plague of philosophy until the advent of Comtean positivism, which recognized the inter-relatedness of all sciences—indeed, of all phenomena. With these grand claims on Comte's behalf, Lewes placed himself at severe odds with Mill, who had sharply criticized Comte in a series of articles printed in the *Westminster Review* of 1865. (p. 147)

To show the bearing of this dispute on George Eliot's fiction, it is not necessary to rely on the merely probable influence of her intellectual context. Nor is it necessary to depend on her relation to Lewes. . . . *Middlemarch* itself broaches the issues. They are part of the fiction, not simply part of its context. Like Comte and Lewes, George Eliot contemplates a material basis for human character, and throughout the novel there occur moments when the mind meekly follows the reflexes of the body. The ''end of Mr. Brooke's pen'' provides a comic example, as ''a thinking organ, evolving sentences, especially of a benevolent kind, before the rest of his mind could well overtake them. It expressed regrets and proposed remedies, which, when Mr. Brooke read them, seemed felicitously worded.'' . . . When Ladislaw speaks hastily and ungenerously of Casaubon, the narrator remarks that ''our tongues are little triggers which have usually been pulled before general intentions can be brought to bear.'' . . . These are minor instances, but the priority of the body appears in other, and more significant, ways.

When Fred Vincy carelessly loses the money he owes to Caleb Garth, selling his own horse and laming another, he faces the disapproval of the Garths, his father's anger, Mary's disappointment, and his own guilt. He endures great anguish, falling ''into worse spirits than he had known in his life before'' . . . , and the reader expects serious repercussions. When he makes his confession to Mary, she notes ''how ill'' he looks, and, indeed, after his series of confessions, he becomes dangerously ill. Nevertheless, although the chain of circumstances invites a connection between the guilt and the ailment, the novel makes no such connection. As Fred rode home, the narrator observes, ''he began to be more conscious of being ill, than of being melancholy.'' . . . The illness is not connected, but opposed, to the melancholy. And the narrator goes further, specifying the source of the contagion: ''those visits to unsanitary Houndsley streets.'' . . . For a day or two the discomfort seems ''mere depression and headache,'' but when Mrs. Vincy calls in Lydgate, he quickly realizes that Fred is in ''the pink-skinned stage of typhoid fever.'' . . . The question of Fred's guilt no longer pertains. George Eliot lets the convergence of melancholy and illness remain coincidental, representing the disease in strictly organic terms. It is a small but revealing decision.

In a still more complicated fashion Bulstrode's anxieties also resolve into merely physical disorders. In the midst of his ''strange piteous conflict,'' he begins to worry about his health and summons Lydgate. We learn that

> A hypochondriacal tendency had shown itself in the banker's constitution of late; and a lack of sleep, which was really only a slight exaggeration of an habitual dyspeptic symptom, had been dwelt on by him as a sign of threatening insanity. . . .

Why should Bulstrode not fear insanity? Caught in a ''struggle of his longings and terrors'' he suffers from a morbid dread of exposure; his long-kept secret has become precarious; his social position has been jeopardized; his wife has begun to suspect him. Nevertheless, the novel treats the suspicion of insanity as utterly groundless. Bulstrode is merely ''hypochondriacal.'' Lydgate need only to repeat reassuring medical opinion in order to achieve the ''dissipation of his fears'' and provide Bulstrode ''with a sense of comfort.'' . . . The psychological aspect of the problem, the threat of insanity, disappears as soon as the physiological aspect, dyspepsia, is identified.

A certain irony colors the role of Lydgate in these episodes. When he is first introduced, George Eliot presents at some length his attraction to the medical profession. She brings forward the familiar appeals: the intellectual rigor, the professional challenge, and the sense of human solidarity. But there is more, and here George Eliot's own preoccupation with medicine becomes clearer. For she describes how from a medical standpoint Lydgate hopes to go further—following ''long pathways of necessary sequence''—and to achieve understanding of the deeper mysteries of the mind:

> he wanted to pierce the obscurity of those minute processes which prepare human misery and joy, those invisible thoroughfares which are the first lurking-places of anguish, mania, and crime, that delicate poise and transition which determine the growth of happy or unhappy consciousness. . . .

Neither Comte nor Lewes could have put the physiological thesis more concisely. What psychology had always claimed as its own—''anguish, mania, crime,'' ''happy or unhappy consciousness''—are to be traced to the ''minute processes'' which it is the province of medicine to determine. The grand project is to elaborate, in Lewes's phrase, the ''physiology of psychology.'' Still more interestingly, this passage puts Lydgate, and physicians generally, in the role of psychotherapists. If "anguish, mania, and crime" are at bottom minute cellular processes, then medicine stands to provide the cure for such disorders, by studying the "delicate poise and transition which determine the growth of happy or unhappy consciousness." In Bulstrode and Fred Vincy (as well as Casaubon and Raffles), Lydgate meets transitions of the most delicate kind. The dramatic background thus suggests a psychological convergence— Fred overwhelmed by remorse, Bulstrode wracked by anxiety, and Lydgate eager to relieve the "unhappy consciousness." But this aspect of the drama never appears; Lydgate remains an alienist *manqué*. Fred suffers from typhoid fever, not guilt; Bulstrode's fears of insanity prove groundless; and Lydgate offers medical advice where it once seemed that psychological counsel was in order.

One of the notable aspects of *Middlemarch* is the prominence of bodily illnesses, whose details George Eliot had so diligently researched. Not only Bulstrode and Fred Vincy, but Casaubon, Raffles, and Dorothea, all suffer illnesses which Lydgate treats. It is equally notable that great emotional anguish often accompanies the organic disease (as Mrs. Bulstrode recognizes, her husband is "not suffering from bodily illness merely, but from something that afflicted his mind" . . .). All through the novel Lydgate, in his role as doctor, finds himself confronting great emotional urgencies which he habitually ignores in favor of the physical debility. At psychologically suggestive moments, it is the body, not the mind, that is threatened, the body that demands treatment. Psychology gives way to physiology. Moreover, Lydgate willingly accepts this limitation. Despite his desire to relieve mania, misery, and anguish, he sees psychology as a temptation whose charms must be resisted. When he decides to inform Dorothea of Casaubon's illness, he

> said to himself that he was only doing right in telling her the truth about her husband's probable future, but he certainly thought also that it would be interesting to talk confidentially with her. A medical man likes to make psychological observations, and sometimes in the pursuit of such studies is too easily tempted into momentous prophecy which life and death easily set at nought. Lydgate had often been satirical on this gratuitous prediction, and he meant now to be guarded. . . .

Dorothea finds the news of her husband's condition shattering. . . . She appeals to the doctor for advice, and then, when he rises to leave, she speaks from "an impulse which if she had been alone would have turned into a prayer": "Oh, you are a wise man, are you not? You know all about life and death. Advise me. Think what I can do." . . . For years afterward, we learn, Lydgate would remember "the impression produced in him by this involuntary appeal—this cry from the soul to soul." But in the event he treats not soul but body: "what could he say now except that he should see Mr. Casaubon again to-morrow?" . . . (pp. 148-52)

The ambiguity of Lydgate's attitude—his fascination with "psychological observations" and his paralysis when confronted with emotional suffering—points to a deep ambiguity in the novel itself. . . . [In George Eliot's work there is] a resolute commitment to the rational structure of experience, an insistence on the intelligibility of human behavior which leads to a preoccupation with the motives, reasons, and grounds for action. But . . . a difficult question obtrudes. Must a rational understanding of human psychology halt where the psyche halts? Is our understanding of a consciousness limited to the way a consciousness understands itself? Comte, and after him Lewes, had answered with an uncompromising No. For them, a thorough understanding of the mind depended on a reduction of mental to physical facts. (p. 152)

The prospect of a rigorous scientific materialism held the same fascination for George Eliot that it held for Comte, Lewes, and so many of their contemporaries. In *Middlemarch* this appears not only in the "biological" theme of organic illness but also through that other term in the Comtean dyad, sociology. The force of social circumstance in the novel is obvious, and we need not dwell on it. We need only to recognize that emphasis on social causes, like the emphasis on biology, threatens to undermine moral autonomy. As Bulstrode realizes at the critical moment, "intention is everything in the question of right and wrong." . . . In order to sustain the ethical imperative *Middlemarch* must preserve human intention even as it demonstrates, to borrow Lewes's phrase, "the objective conditions of production." The presentation of both inward and outward perspectives might be seen as the attempt to maintain both moral force and scientific neutrality, and the novel often shifts violently from the one to the other. The most attentive recording of mental states can suddenly give way to a ruthlessly externalized point of view, which regards mental life as mechanical, insignificant, epiphenomenal. (pp. 152-53)

We come to the compelling duality in George Eliot's realism. On the one hand, she sets out to recover the common reasons of reasonable beings. She will arouse our sympathy by persuading us that even the most unusual act is the outcome of familiar motives. This task obliges her to assume the perspective of her characters; since, for instance, "Mr. Casaubon, too, was the centre of his own world," she must duly present his reasons from his standpoint. On the other hand, her commitment to the goals of science led her to rely on "objective" causal explanation, and this leads to that other distinctive aspect of her realism: the representation of forces that exceed individual will and often escape individual consciousness, the "conditions of existence."

George Eliot once described her subject-matter as "motives and influences," and the phrase neatly captures her dual commitment: on the one hand, a solicitous attention to the self as it regards itself, a faithful relating of its own motives, its own images, its own words; on the other hand, a casual disregard for the workings of private consciousness, a view of the self as a body among other physical bodies, an emphasis on the power of circumstance to direct human action. *Middlemarch* presents the self as mind and the self as body, the individual as a subjectivity irreducible to surrounding objects and as an object in the chain of causation. Comte, Mill, and Lewes had quarrelled over the competing claims of these rival principles. Was human subjectivity an independent datum? Or was it simply the complex product of physiological sources? But George Eliot, let us remember, was neither philosopher nor physiologist, and had no responsibility for resolving these questions. It was not for her to reduce psychology to physiology, not even for her to choose between them. Scientific issues inform her fiction; so much is obvious; but they exist as imaginative data, not as urgent questions demanding resolution. *Middlemarch* acknowledges motives *and* influences. It refuses to submit one to the priority of the other. Instead of a materialist reduction, the novel offers an addition, entertaining the lawful claims of both contending parties. (pp. 154-55)

Karen Chase, "Mind and Body in 'Middlemarch'," in her Eros & Psyche: The Representation of Personality in Charlotte Brontë, Charles Dickens, and George Eliot, *Methuen, 1984, pp. 136-62.*

ADDITIONAL BIBLIOGRAPHY

Allen, Walter. "Chapter Seven." In his *George Eliot*, pp. 147-61. Masters of World Literature Series, edited by Louis Kronenberger. New York: Macmillan Co., 1964.
     Investigates the theme of human aspiration in *Middlemarch*.

Armstrong, Isobel. "*Middlemarch*: A Note on George Eliot's 'Wisdom'." In *Critical Essays on George Eliot*, edited by Barbara Hardy, pp. 116-32. New York: Barnes & Noble, 1970.
     Defends Eliot's moral commentary in *Middlemarch* as an effective means of involving readers in the world of the novel.

Beaty, Jerome. "History by Indirection: The Era of Reform in *Middlemarch*." *Victorian Studies* 1, No. 2 (December 1957): 173-79.
     Praises Eliot's subtle incorporation in *Middlemarch* of historical details concerning the passage of the First Reform Bill of 1832.

———. "*Middlemarch*" *from Notebook to Novel: A Study of George Eliot's Creative Method*. Illinois Studies in Language and Literature, vol. 47. 1960. Reprint. Westport, Conn.: Greenwood Press, Publishers, 1981, 134 p.
     Closely examines the composition of *Middlemarch*. Beaty's study is based on Eliot's letters and journals, her *Quarry for "Middlemarch"* (see annotation below), and the *Middlemarch* manuscript.

Briggs, Asa. "*Middlemarch* and the Doctors." *The Cambridge Journal* I, No. 12 (September 1948): 749-62.
     Relates Lydgate's career to the Victorian concern with medical and public health reform. Briggs suggests that *Middlemarch* reflects a number of social issues from Eliot's era.

Bullett, Gerald. "*Middlemarch*." In his *George Eliot: Her Life and Books*, pp. 230-45. New Haven: Yale University Press, 1948.
     Cites the depth and breadth of Eliot's vision of humanity in labeling *Middlemarch* a masterpiece comparable to the works of Tolstoy. Bullett's work helped to revive critical interest in Eliot's fiction.

Carroll, David, ed. *George Eliot: The Critical Heritage*. The Critical Heritage Series, edited by B. C. Southam. New York: Barnes & Noble, 1971, 511 p.
     A collection of excerpted contemporary views of Eliot's works that includes seven essays on *Middlemarch*. Carroll provides an overview of Eliot criticism in his introduction.

Coles, Robert. "Maturity: George Eliot's *Middlemarch*." In his *Irony in the Mind's Life: Essays on Novels by James Agee, Elizabeth Bowen, and George Eliot*, pp. 154-204. Charlottesville: University Press of Virginia, 1974.
     A psychological reading of *Middlemarch*. Coles determines that the novel's controlling theme is "life's indefiniteness," or, the unlimited variations in human behavior.

Cross, J. W. *George Eliot's Life as Related in Her Letters and Journals*. 3 vols. Edinburgh: William Blackwood and Sons, 1885.
     A biography largely based on Eliot's letters and journals. Cross's work, in which Eliot emerges as a humorless Victorian sage, contributed to the marked downswing in her posthumous reputation.

Eliot, George. *Quarry for "Middlemarch."* Edited by Anna Theresa Kitchel. Berkeley and Los Angeles: University of California Press, 1950, 68 p.
     A notebook Eliot kept while writing *Middlemarch*. In the *Quarry*, Eliot worked out the structure of the novel and recorded information on medical subjects that forms the background for Lydgate's portrait. This notebook is considered an indispensable guide to the genesis of *Middlemarch*.

———. *George Eliot's "Middlemarch" Notebooks: A Transcription.* Edited by John Clark Pratt and Victor A. Neufeldt. Berkeley and Los Angeles: University of California Press, 1979, 305 p.
     Eliot's notes on her prose and poetry readings from 1868 to 1871. These notebooks shed light on *Middlemarch*'s intellectual background and, in conjunction with the *Quarry* (see annotation above), provide a guide to the evolution of the novel.

Fernando, Lloyd. "George Eliot, Feminism and Dorothea Brooke." *A Review of English Literature* 4, No. 1 (January 1963): 76-90.
     Discusses Dorothea as an incarnation of Eliot's views on feminism.

Fujita, Seiji. *Structure and Motif in "Middlemarch."* Tokyo: Hokuseido Press, 1969, 202 p.
     Documents the great care Eliot took in constructing *Middlemarch*.

Fulmer, Constance Marie. *George Eliot: A Reference Guide*. Reference Guides in Literature, edited by Joseph Katz. Boston: G. K. Hall & Co., 1977, 247 p.
     A comprehensive annotated bibliography of criticism on Eliot's works from 1858 to 1971.

Gilbert, Sandra M., and Gubar, Susan. "George Eliot as the Angel of Destruction." In their *The Madwoman in the Attic: The Woman Writer and the Nineteenth-Century Literary Imagination*, pp. 478-535. New Haven: Yale University Press, 1979.
     A feminist interpretation of *Middlemarch*. Gilbert and Gubar suggest that the novel should be read as an attempt on Eliot's part to resolve the conflict between two opposing sides of her personality, her "man's mind" and "woman's heart."

Graver, Suzanne. *George Eliot and Community: A Study in Social Theory and Fictional Form*. Berkeley and Los Angeles: University of California Press, 1984, 340 p.
     Places Eliot in the tradition of such nineteenth-century social theorists as David Friedrich Strauss, Ludwig Feuerbach, Auguste Comte, Herbert Spencer, John Stuart Mill, and George Henry Lewes, all of whom stressed the importance of recovering traditional communal values. In her commentary on *Middlemarch*, Graver discusses how the novel's structure reflects Eliot's concern with social regeneration.

Haight, Gordon S, Introduction to *Middlemarch*, by George Eliot, edited by Gordon S. Haight, pp. v-xx. Boston: Houghton Mifflin Co., Riverside Editions, 1956.
     A broad overview of *Middlemarch* covering the novel's characterization, genesis, autobiographical elements, imagery, and structure.

———. *George Eliot: A Biography*. New York: Oxford University Press, 1968, 616 p.
     The definitive biography.

———. "Poor Mr. Casaubon." In *Nineteenth-Century Literary Perspectives: Essays in Honor of Lionel Stevenson*, edited by Clyde de L. Ryals, pp. 255-70. Durham: Duke University Press, 1974.
     Details Casaubon's shortcomings as both a scholar and husband. Haight also discusses the character's genesis, rejecting the commonly held belief that Casaubon was patterned after Eliot's friend Mark Pattison.

———, and VanArsdel, Rosemary T., eds. *George Eliot: A Centenary Tribute*. Totowa, N.J.: Barnes & Noble Books, 1982, 174 p.
     A collection of essays on Eliot's works occasioned by the centenary of her death. The work includes discussions of *Middlemarch* by Ruth apRoberts, Robert B. Heilman, and John F. Hulcoop.

Halperin, John. "George Eliot." In his *Egoism and Self-Discovery in the Victorian Novel: Studies in the Ordeal of Knowledge in the Nineteenth Century*, pp. 125-92. New York: Burt Franklin, Publisher, 1974.
     Traces Dorothea's psychological development from egoism and self-absorption to objectivity and self-knowledge.

Hardy, Barbara. *Particularities: Readings in George Eliot*. Athens: Ohio University Press, 1983, 204 p.

Reprints most of the essays Hardy wrote on Eliot's novels between 1964 and 1980, including five that deal specifically with *Middlemarch*.

———; Miller, J. Hillis; and Poirier, Richard. "*Middlemarch*, Chapter Eighty-Five: Three Commentaries." *Nineteenth-Century Fiction* 35, No. 3 (December 1980): 432-53.

A three-part essay on *Middlemarch* in which Hardy, Miller, and Poirier offer separate interpretations of the headnote to chapter eighty-five.

Harvey, W. J. *The Art of George Eliot*. 1969. Reprint. Westport, Conn.: Greenwood Press, Publishers, 1978, 254 p.

A general study of narrative technique, structure, characterization, language, imagery, and symbolism in all of Eliot's novels. Harvey's work, which was first published in 1961, was influential in promoting the view of Eliot as a great formal artist.

Hornback, Bert G., ed. "*Middlemarch*": *An Authoritative Text, Backgrounds, Reviews, and Criticism*, by George Eliot and others. Norton Critical Editions. New York: W. W. Norton & Co., 1977, 770 p.

An annotated text of *Middlemarch*. Hornback appends a section on the novel's background, which includes Eliot's *Quarry* (see annotation above) in its entirety and extracts from her other writings. Also included is a selection of contemporary and modern critical response to the work.

Kermode, Frank. "D. H. Lawrence and the Apocalyptic Types." In his *Continuities*, pp. 122-51. New York: Random House, 1968.

Interprets the personal crises of *Middlemarch*'s characters as parables of a great historical crisis, the political upheaval surrounding the passage of the First Reform Bill of 1832.

Knoepflmacher, U. C. *Religious Humanism and the Victorian Novel: George Eliot, Walter Pater, and Samuel Butler*. Princeton: Princeton University Press, 1965, 315 p.

Analyzes the novels of Eliot, Walter Pater, and Samuel Butler as expressions of the Victorian attempt to reconcile religious longings with a belief in the evolutionary theories of Charles Darwin and T. H. Huxley. In his discussion on Eliot, Knoepflmacher studies *Middlemarch* in relation to three important aspects of her thought: "her scientific positivism, her 'humanization' of Christianity, and her Arnold-like belief in the force of tradition."

———. "*Middlemarch*: Affirmation through Compromise." In his *Laughter and Despair: Readings in Ten Novels of the Victorian Era*, pp. 168-201. Berkeley and Los Angeles: University of California Press, 1973.

States that in *Middlemarch* Eliot achieves a balanced compromise between the realism of William Makepeace Thackeray and the idealism of Charles Dickens.

———. "*Middlemarch*: An Avuncular View." *Nineteenth-Century Fiction* 30, No. 1 (June 1975): 53-81.

Argues that Eliot castigates patriarchal values through her portrayal of uncles and fathers in *Middlemarch*.

Lerner, Laurence. "George Eliot: Dorothea and the Theresa-Complex." In his *The Truthtellers: Jane Austen, George Eliot, D. H. Lawrence*, pp. 249-69. London: Chatto & Windus, 1967.

Uses the comments of F. R. Leavis on *Middlemarch* (see *NCLC*, Vol. 4) as the starting point for a discussion of Eliot's attitudes toward Dorothea.

Liddell, Robert. "*Middlemarch*." In his *The Novels of George Eliot*, pp. 123-61. New York: St. Martin's Press, 1977.

An in-depth analysis of *Middlemarch*'s characters and plot.

McSweeney, Kerry. "*Middlemarch*." Unwin Critical Library, edited by Claude Rawson. London: George Allen & Unwin, 1984, 167 p.

A critical study focusing on characterization, structure, and narration in *Middlemarch*. McSweeney also traces the novel's critical history and discusses Eliot's views on the art of fiction.

Paris, Bernard J. *Experiments in Life: George Eliot's Quest for Values*. Detroit: Wayne State University Press, 1965, 281 p.

Contends that for Eliot the creative process was a conscious attempt to discover a system of moral values that would ennoble human life in a godless universe. Paris devotes the first half of his book to examining the evolution of Eliot's moral beliefs. In the second half of the work, which contains a chapter on *Middlemarch*, Paris analyzes the moral development of the main characters in her novels.

Putzell-Korab, Sara M. *The Evolving Consciousness: An Hegelian Reading of the Novels of George Eliot*. Salzburg Studies in English Literature: Romantic Reassessment, edited by James Hogg, no. 29. Salzburg: Universität Salzburg, 1982, 140 p.

Demonstrates that Eliot's novels are colored by the philosophic theories of Georg Wilhelm Friedrich Hegel. Putzell-Korab analyzes the spiritual development of Dorothea, Lydgate, Casaubon, Bulstrode, Ladislaw, and Mr. Brooke in terms of Hegel's phenomenology of evolving consciousness.

Roberts, Neil. "*Middlemarch*." In his *George Eliot: Her Beliefs and Her Art*, pp. 145-82. Novelists and Their World, edited by Graham Hough. London: Paul Elek, 1975.

An examination of *Middlemarch* within the context of Eliot's moral, social, and religious ideas.

Sackville-West, Edward. "*Middlemarch*." In his *Inclinations*, pp. 27-32. London: Secker and Warburg, 1949.

Relies on the traditional distinction between Eliot's early "creative" novels and her later "analytical" ones. Sackville-West praises *Middlemarch*'s sympathetic characters, but faults its colorless style.

Shuttleworth, Sally. "Science and Social Thought: The Rise of Organic Theory" and "*Middlemarch*: An Experiment in Time." In her *George Eliot and Nineteenth-Century Science: The Make-Believe of a Beginning*, pp. 1-23, pp. 142-74. Cambridge: Cambridge University Press, 1984.

Discusses Eliot's interest in organic social theory and its impact on the development of *Middlemarch*. According to Shuttleworth, Lydgate's scientific methodology, which recognizes the interdependence of bodily organs, is a paradigm for the novel's structure and social model.

Smith, Anne, ed. *George Eliot: Centenary Essays and an Unpublished Fragment*. Barnes & Noble Critical Studies, edited by Anne Smith. Totowa, N.J.: Barnes & Noble, 1980, 221 p.

An anthology of essays on Eliot's novels commemorating the centenary of her death. Jan B. Gordon, George Levine, and Susan Meikle write on *Middlemarch*.

Stallknecht, Newton P. "Resolution and Independence: A Reading of *Middlemarch*." In *Twelve Original Essays on Great English Novels*, edited by Charles Shapiro, pp. 125-52. Detroit: Wayne State University Press, 1960.

Argues that *Middlemarch* can be read solely as an argument in favor of Dorothea's decision to marry Ladislaw.

Steiner, George F. "A Preface to *Middlemarch*." *Nineteenth-Century Fiction* 9, No. 4 (March 1955): 262-79.

Holds that *Middlemarch* is artistically weak in comparison with the classic French and Russian novels of the nineteenth century. Steiner faults the novel's uneven style, incoherent structure, and omniscient mode of narration.

Stoneman, Patsy. "G. Eliot: *Middlemarch* (1871-2)." In *The Monster in the Mirror: Studies in Nineteenth-Century Realism*, edited by D. A. Williams, pp. 102-30. Oxford: Oxford University Press, 1980.

Uses *Middlemarch* to illustrate Eliot's theory of literary realism.

Swinden, Patrick, ed. *George Eliot: "Middlemarch," a Casebook*. Casebook Series, edited by A. E. Dyson. London: Macmillan, 1972, 256 p.

A selection of *Middlemarch* criticism from 1872 to 1967. The collection also includes extracts from Eliot's journals and correspondence that contain information on the novel's composition, publication, and contemporary reception.

Thale, Jerome. "The Paradox of Individualism: *Middlemarch*." In his *The Novels of George Eliot*, pp. 106-20. New York: Columbia University Press, 1961.

Explores the relationship between the individual and society in *Middlemarch*.

Wagenknecht, Edward. "The 'New' Novel: George Eliot." In his *Cavalcade of the English Novel: From Elizabeth to George VI*, pp. 319-35. New York: Henry Holt and Co., 1943.

Briefly examines the histories of Dorothea and Lydgate, concluding that *Middlemarch* is "a study in frustration."

Wiesenfarth, Joseph. "*Middlemarch:* The Myth of the Hero." In his *George Eliot's Mythmaking*, pp. 186-209. Heidelberg: Carl Winter Universitätsverlag, 1977.

Maintains that Eliot underscores the heroic qualities of Dorothea, Lydgate, and Ladislaw by identifying them with mythic figures.

Witemeyer, Hugh. *George Eliot and the Visual Arts*. New Haven: Yale University Press, 1979, 238 p.

Examines Eliot's pictorialism. *Middlemarch* figures prominently in Witemeyer's discussion of how her novels reflect the Victorian attitude toward sacred and heroic history painting, genre painting, and landscape painting.

Novalis

1772-1801

(Pseudonym of Friedrich (Leopold Freiherr) von Hardenberg)
German poet, novelist, and essayist.

One of the most important writers of the early German Romantic period, Novalis is remembered today for his lyrical poetry in *Hymnen an die Nacht (Hymns to the Night),* his intricate use of symbols, and his imaginative experiments with the form of the novel. With his closest friends Ludwig Tieck and Friedrich von Schlegel, Novalis articulated and refined late eighteenth-century Romantic doctrine in Germany, and his works are valued for their embodiment of this doctrine, as well as for their literary merit. Critics continue to admire the originality, breadth, and intellectual depth of Novalis's theories, in which he sought to bring literature, philosophy, and science together into a comprehensive system of knowledge shaped by his belief in the unity of all things.

Novalis was born on his family's estate of Oberwiederstet in Thuringia, Germany. His father, a landed aristocrat, insisted on maintaining a strict religious atmosphere in the household. The Hardenberg children were privately educated, but it was not until 1781, when a serious illness confined Novalis to a lengthy period of bed rest, that he exhibited much intellectual curiosity. From then on he read voraciously, and by the time the family moved to Weissenfels in 1784 and he enrolled in the Eisleben Gymnasium, he had acquired a thorough education in the classics. The period between 1790 and 1794 was a time of ongoing development for Novalis: he studied philosophy, history, and law at Jena University, at the University of Leipzig, and at the University of Wittenberg, where he graduated with a degree in law. During his years as a student, Novalis was profoundly influenced by his contact with Friedrich von Schiller, then a history professor at Jena, the philosopher Johann Gottlieb Fichte, and his fellow-student Schlegel, who later became a key theoretician of German Romanticism.

Following his graduation, Novalis, who had chosen to pursue a career in public service, traveled to Tennstedt for further administrative training. There he fell deeply in love with Sophie von Kühn, the thirteen-year-old daughter of his landlord, and in 1795 they became secretly engaged. Novalis continued his training and also embarked on a rigorous self-directed course of study in science and philosophy. His diligence was rewarded when he won the position of assistant administrator of the Saxon Salt Works in 1796. However, the next year brought twofold tragedy into Novalis's life—the deaths of Sophie and his brother Erasmus. Devastated by grief, Novalis entered into a period of mourning that, in the view of many biographers, never ended. Yet he continued his studies, attempting to distract himself with the works of Immanuel Kant, Jakob Boehme, and Tiberius Hemsterhuis. In 1798, Novalis experienced the first symptoms of tuberculosis and was successfully treated in Teplitz. Later that year, he became engaged to Julie von Charpentier. He also began to write at this time, encouraged by the poet Christoph Martin Wieland. Two early collections of axioms and fragments, *Blütenstaub* and *Glauben und Liebe,* which grew out of his readings in poetry, philosophy, and science, appeared in 1798, although the majority of his writings were published posthumously. When symptoms of tuberculosis re-

Courtesy of the German Information Center

appeared in 1800, he traveled to Dresden to seek a cure; however, the disease could not be controlled this time, and he died in Weissenfels in 1801.

All of Novalis's works were published under his pseudonym—which in Latin means "new land"—as a symbol of the uncharted spiritual and intellectual territory he was exploring. Philosophical and theological speculation serves as the basis for two works: *Die Christenheit oder Europa (Christianity or Europe),* an essay in which Novalis celebrated the unified world view afforded by medieval Catholicism, and *Geistliche Lieder (Sacred Songs of Novalis),* a collection of poems marked by his concept of religion as a personal relationship with God. This individualistic view of religion and his lush, lyrical style are the main features of Novalis's Romanticism, which figures prominently in his best-known collection, *Hymns to the Night.* This work was acclaimed by his contemporaries and established the poet's reputation with its mystical philosophy, striking imagery, and blending of free verse with prose. Recounting his feelings about Sophie's death, Novalis described in the six poems that make up *Hymns to the Night* his newfound faith in a reunion with Sophie in the afterlife. "Life is the beginning of Death; Life is lived for the sake of Death," he proclaimed; thus these poems, vibrant rather than somber in mood, record his longing for death and his view of it as a joyful new beginning.

Critics have praised Novalis's two novels, *Heinrich von Of-terdingen (Henry of Ofterdingen)* and *Die Lehrlinge zu Saïs (The Disciples at Saïs)*, both incomplete at his death, for their experimental narrative style characterized by surrealistic plot elements and unusual shifts in time and place. Influenced by Johann Wolfgang von Goethe's *Wilhelm Meisters Lehrjahre*, *Henry of Ofterdingen* depicts a young medieval poet's initiation into the mysteries of his art. His search for knowledge is symbolized by his quest for an elusive blue flower, which thereafter became the universal image of longing in German Romantic poetry. Novalis also structured the novel around a central story-within-a-story, the fairy tale "Klingsohrs Märchen," in accordance with his belief that fairy tales, or Märchen, can convey a higher order of experience than realistic narratives. Novalis's second novel, *The Disciples at Saïs*, is also imbued with philosophy and mysticism. The work follows the experiences of a group of pupils in ancient Egypt and focuses on their mission to unite science and poetry through discovery of the symbolic meaning of natural objects. Like *Henry of Ofterdingen*, *The Disciples at Saïs* relies upon a Märchen, "Hyazinth and Rosenblüte," for its symbolic meaning.

Novalis's works were known to only a small circle of friends at the time of his death. In nineteenth-century Germany, E.T.A. Hoffmann and Henrik Steffens praised Novalis's profundity and melodious style, while at the same time members of Junges Deutschland, the Young Germany movement, condemned what they perceived as his turning away from reality. His reputation grew when Thomas Carlyle introduced Novalis to English-language readers, stressing his originality, spirituality, and subtlety of intellect; and Wilhelm Dilthey's positive assessment in German in the latter part of the nineteenth century contributed to a revival of critical interest in his works. Since that time, commentators have applauded Novalis's complicated system of imagery and symbols, his wide-ranging philosophical speculations, and his innovative narrative style. Other critics, however, have objected to what they view as abstruseness, prolixity, and passiveness in Novalis's work. Some particularly censured the poet's morbid self-absorption and the strongly erotic, almost decadent quality of his pieces.

Today, Novalis's prose and poetry are highly esteemed by many scholars. Critics confess to a fascination with the abstract themes, challenging style, and ethereal mood of his works: as August Wilhelm von Schlegel wrote, Novalis seemed to him "like a bird of passage, tired from its flights over immeasurable oceans, stopping on a green island, and forgetting there its former fatherland, and the vast regions of free thought." Novalis's influence on the American Transcendentalists, the French Surrealists, and on such writers as Richard Wagner, Hermann Hesse, Thomas Mann, and André Gide testifies to his enduring relevance to succeeding generations of readers. For his bold use of imagery, for the modernity of his narrative style, and for his vision of the unity of all life, Novalis is today regarded as one of the chief writers of early German Romanticism.

PRINCIPAL WORKS

Blütenstaub (axioms) 1798; published in journal *Das Athenäeum*
Glauben und Liebe (fragments) 1798; published in journal *Jahrbücher der preussichen Monarchie*
Hymnen an die Nacht (poetry and prose poetry) 1800; published in journal *Das Athenäeum*
[*Hymns to the Night*, 1948]

Die Christenheit oder Europa (essay) 1802; published in *Novalis Schriften*
[*Christianity or Europe*, 1844]
Geistliche Lieder (poetry) 1802; published in *Novalis Schriften*
[*Sacred Songs of Novalis*, 1956]
Heinrich von Ofterdingen (unfinished novel) 1802; published in *Novalis Schriften*
[*Henry of Ofterdingen*, 1842]
Die Lehrlinge zu Saïs (unfinished novel) 1802; published in *Novalis Schriften*
[*The Disciples at Saïs*, 1903]
Novalis Schriften. 2 vols. (poetry, prose poetry, unfinished novels, essays, letters, diaries, axioms, and fragments) 1802
Schriften. 4 vols. (poetry, prose poetry, unfinished novels, essays, letters, diaries, axioms, and fragments) 1960-75

E.T.A. HOFFMANN   (essay date 1814-15?)

[*Hoffmann was a German composer, music critic, fiction writer, and illustrator whose stories and novels are considered among the best works of the German Romantic movement. In this excerpt from his* Phantasiestücke, *written about 1814-15, Hoffmann commends Novalis's artistic and spiritual purity.*]

The blue flower reminds me of a dead poet, who belonged to the purest that ever lived. His childlike mind reflected the purest poetry and his pious life was a hymn dedicated to the highest Being and the wonders of Nature. In order to understand him it is necessary to descend with him into the deepest depth and to bring to light, as from an eternally productive mine, all the wonderful combinations by which Nature welds her appearances into one; a task for which, to be sure, most men lack inner strength and courage.

> E.T.A. Hoffmann, "German Estimates of Novalis from 1800 to 1850," edited by J. F. Haussmann, in Modern Philology, Vol. 9, No. 3, January, 1912, p. 407.

[THOMAS CARLYLE]   (essay date 1829)

[*A noted nineteenth-century essayist, historian, critic, and social commentator, Carlyle was a central figure of the Victorian age in England and Scotland. In his writings, Carlyle advocated a Christian work ethic and stressed the importance of order, piety, and spiritual fulfillment. Known to his contemporaries as the "Sage of Chelsea," Carlyle exerted a powerful moral influence in an era of rapidly shifting values. In the following excerpt from his review of the 1826 edition of Novalis's works, Carlyle offers a balanced assessment of the author's strengths and weaknesses. Carlyle's commentary proved extremely influential in introducing Novalis's works to English and American readers and is therefore considered one of the milestones in Novalis criticism.*]

[Novalis's **Writings** indicate] a mind of wonderful depth and originality; but at the same time, of a nature or habit so abstruse, and altogether different from anything we ourselves have notice or experience of, that to penetrate fairly into its essential character, much more to picture it forth in visual distinctness, would be an extremely difficult task. Nay perhaps, if attempted by the means familiar to us, an impossible task: for Novalis belongs to that class of persons, who do not recognise the 'syl-logistic method' as the chief organ for investigating truth, or feel themselves bound at all times to stop short where its light fails them. Many of his opinions he would despair of proving in the most patient Court of Law; and would remain well content that they should be disbelieved there. (p. 113)

Naturally a deep, religious contemplative spirit; purified also . . . by harsh Affliction, and familiar in the 'Sanctuary of Sorrow,' he comes before us as the most ideal of all Idealists. For him the material Creation is but an Appearance, a typical shadow in which the Deity manifests himself to Man. Not only has the unseen world a reality, but the only reality: the rest being not metaphorically, but literally and in scientific strictness, 'a show;' in the words of the Poet, *Schall und Rauch amnebelnd Himmels Gluth,* 'Sound and Smoke overclouding the splendour of Heaven.' The Invisible World is near us; or rather it is here, in us and about us; were the fleshly coil removed from our Soul, the glories of the Unseen were even now around us; as the Ancients fabled of the Spheral Music. Thus not in word only, but in truth and sober belief, he feels himself encompassed by the Godhead; feels in every thought, that 'in Him he lives, moves, and has his being.'

On his Philosophic and Poetic procedure, all this has its natural influence. The aim of Novalis' whole Philosophy, we might say, is to preach and establish the Majesty of Reason, in that stricter sense; to conquer for it all provinces of human thought, and everywhere reduce its vassal, Understanding, into fealty, the right and only useful relation for it. Mighty tasks in this sort lay before himself; of which, in these Writings of his, we trace only scattered indications. In fact, all that he has left is in the shape of Fragment; detached expositions and combinations, deep, brief glimpses: but such seems to be their general tendency. One character to be noted in many of these, often, too obscure, speculations, is his peculiar manner of viewing Nature: his habit, as it were, of considering Nature rather in the concrete, not analytically and as a divisible Aggregate, but as a self-subsistent universally connected Whole. This also is perhaps partly the fruit of his Idealism. (p. 118)

As a Poet, Novalis is no less Idealistic than as a Philosopher. His poems are breathings of a high devout soul, feeling always that here he has no home, but looking, as in clear vision, to a 'city that hath foundations.' He loves external Nature with a singular depth; nay we might say, he reverences her, and holds unspeakable communings with her: for Nature is no longer dead, hostile Matter, but the veil and mysterious Garment of the Unseen; as it were, the Voice with which the Deity proclaims himself to man. These two qualities—his pure religious temper, and heartfelt love of Nature, bring him into true poetic relation both with the spiritual and the material World, and perhaps constitute his chief worth as a Poet; for which art he seems to have originally a genuine, but no exclusive or even very decided endowment.

His moral persuasions, as evinced in his Writings and Life, derive themselves naturally enough from the same source. It is the morality of a man, to whom the Earth and all its glories are in truth a vapour and a Dream, and the Beauty of Goodness the *only* real possession. Poetry, Virtue, Religion, which for other men have but, as it were, a traditionary and imagined existence, are for him the everlasting basis of the Universe; and all earthly acquirements, all with which Ambition, Hope, Fear can tempt us, to toil and sin, are in very deed but a picture of the brain, some reflex shadowed on the mirror of the Infinite, but in themselves air and nothingness. Thus, to live in that

Light of Reason, to have, even while here, and encircled with this Vision of Existence, our abode in that Eternal City, is the highest and sole duty of man. These things Novalis figures to himself under various images: sometimes he seems to represent the Primeval essence of Being as Love; at other times, he speaks in emblems. . . . (p. 119)

In his professedly poetical compositions, there is an indubitable prolixity, a degree of languor, not weakness but sluggishness; the meaning is too much diluted; and diluted, we might say, not in a rich, lively, varying music, as we find in Tieck, for example; but rather in a low-voiced, not unmelodious monotony, the deep hum of which is broken only at rare intervals, though sometimes by tones of purest, and almost spiritual softness. We here allude chiefly to his unmetrical pieces, his prose fictions: indeed the metrical are few in number; for the most part on religious subjects; and in spite of a decided truthfulness both in feeling and word, seem to bespeak no great skill or practice in that form of composition. In his prose style he may be accounted happier; he aims in general at simplicity, and a certain familiar expressiveness; here and there, in his more elaborate passages, especially in his *Hymns to the Night,* he has reminded us of Herder. (pp. 131-32)

[His *Hymns to the Night*] are of a strange veiled, almost enigmatical character: nevertheless, more deeply examined, they appear nowise without true poetic worth; there is a vastness, an immensity of idea; a still solemnity reigns in them, a solitude almost as of extinct worlds. Here and there, too, some light-beam visits us in the void deep; and we cast a glance, clear and wondrous, into the secrets of that mysterious soul. A full commentary on the *Hymns to the Night* would be an exposition of Novalis' whole theological and moral creed; for it lies recorded there, though symbolically, and in lyric not in didactic language. (p. 132)

[But it would be giving the reader] a false impression of the Poet, did we leave him here; exhibited only under his more mystic aspects: as if his Poetry were exclusively a thing of Allegory, dwelling amid Darkness and Vacuity, far from all paths of ordinary mortals and their thoughts. Novalis can write in the most common style, as well as in this most uncommon one; and there too not without originality. . . . *Heinrich von Ofterdingen* [is] written, so far as it goes, much in the every-day manner. . . . (p. 133)

For the great body of readers, we are aware, there can be little profit in Novalis, who rather employs our time than helps us to kill it; for such any farther study of him would be unadvisable. To others again, who prize Truth as the end of all reading, especially to that class who cultivate moral science as the developement of purest and highest Truth, we can recommend the perusal and re-perusal of Novalis with almost perfect confidence. If they feel, with us, that the most profitable employment any book can give them is to study honestly some earnest, deep-minded, truth-loving Man, to work their way into his manner of thought, till they see the world with his eyes, feel as he felt, and judge as he judged, neither believing nor denying, till they can in some measure so feel and judge,—then we may assert, that few books known to us are more worthy of their attention than [Novalis's *Writings*]. They will find it, if we mistake not, an unfathomed mine of philosophical ideas, where the keenest intellect may have occupation enough; and in such occupation, without looking farther, reward enough. All this if the reader proceed on candid principles; if not it will be all otherwise. To no man, so much as to Novalis is that famous motto applicable:

> *Leser, wie gefall' ich Dir?*
> *Leser, wie gefälst Du mir?*
> Reader, how likest thou me?
> Reader, how like I thee?

For the rest it were but a false proceeding did we attempt any formal character of Novalis in this place; did we pretend with such means as ours to reduce that extraordinary nature under common formularies; and in few words sum up the net total of his worth and worthlessness. We have . . . expressed our own imperfect knowledge of the matter, and our entire despair of bringing even an approximate picture of it before readers so foreign to him. The kind words, 'amiable enthusiast,' 'poetic dreamer;' or the unkind ones, 'German mystic,' 'crackbrained rhapsodist,' are easily spoken and written; but would avail little in this instance. If we are not altogether mistaken, Novalis cannot be ranged under any one of these noted categories; but, belongs to a higher and much less known one, the significance of which is perhaps also worth studying, at all events, will not till after long study become clear to us.

Meanwhile let the reader accept some vague impressions of ours on this subject, since we have no fixed judgment to offer him. We might say that the chief excellence we have remarked in Novalis, is his to us truly wonderful subtlety of intellect; his power of intense abstraction, of pursuing the deepest and most evanescent ideas, through their thousand complexities, as it were, with lynx vision, and to the very limits of human Thought. He was well skilled in mathematics, and, as we can easily believe, fond of that science; but his is a far finer species of endowment than any required in mathematics, where the mind, from the very beginning of *Euclid* to the end of *Laplace*, is assisted with visible symbols, with safe *implements* for thinking; nay, at least in what is called the higher mathematics, has often little more than a mechanical superintendence to exercise over these. This power of abstract meditation, when it is so sure and clear as we sometimes find it with Novalis, is a much higher and rarer one; its element is not mathematics, but that *Mathesis*, of which it has been said many a Great Calculist has not even a notion. In this power, truly, so far as logical and not moral power is concerned, lies the summary of all Philosophic talent: which talent accordingly we imagine Novalis to have possessed in a very high degree: in a higher degree than almost any other modern writer we have met with.

His chief fault . . . figures itself to us as a certain undue softness, a want of rapid energy; something which we might term *passiveness* extending both over his mind and his character. There is a tenderness in Novalis, a purity, a clearness, almost as of a woman; but he has not, at least not at all in that degree, the emphasis and resolute force of a man. Thus, in his poetical delineations, . . . he is too diluted and diffuse; not verbose properly; not so much abounding in superfluous words, as in superfluous circumstances, which indeed is but a degree better. In his philosophical speculations, we feel as if, under a different form, the same fault were now and then manifested. Here again, he seems to us, in one sense, too languid, too passive. He *sits*, we might say, among the rich, fine, thousandfold combinations, which his mind almost of itself presents him; but, perhaps, he shows too little activity in the process, is too lax in separating the true from the doubtful, is not even at the trouble to express his truth with any laborious accuracy. With his stillness, with his deep love of Nature, his mild, lofty, spiritual tone of contemplation, he comes before us in a sort

of Asiatic character, almost like our ideal of some antique Gymnosophist, and with the weakness as well as the strength of an Oriental. However, it should be remembered that his works both poetical and philosophical, as we now see them, appear under many disadvantages; altogether immature, and not as doctrines and delineations, but as the rude draught of such; in which, had they been completed, much was to have changed its shape, and this fault with many others might have disappeared. It may be, therefore, that this is only a superficial fault, or even only the appearance of a fault, and has its origin in these circumstances, and in our imperfect understanding of him. (pp. 137-39)

Between Pascal and Novalis, a lover of . . . analogies might trace not a few points of resemblance. Both are of the purest, most affectionate moral nature; both of a high, fine, discursive intellect; both are mathematicians and naturalists yet occupy themselves chiefly with Religion: nay, the best writings of both are left in the shape of 'Thoughts,' materials of a grand scheme, which each of them, with the views peculiar to his age, had planned, we may say, for the furtherance of Religion, and which neither of them lived to execute. Nor in all this would it fail to be carefully remarked, that Novalis was not the French but the *German* Pascal. . . . (p. 140)

> [*Thomas Carlyle*], *"Novalis," in* The Foreign Review, *Vol. IV, No. VII, 1829, pp. 97-141.*

RALPH WALDO EMERSON　(journal date 1834)

[*Emerson was one of the most influential figures of the nineteenth century. An American essayist and poet, he founded the Transcendental movement and shaped a distinctly American philosophy that embraces optimism, individuality, and mysticism. In this excerpt from a journal entry, Emerson briefly addresses Novalis's stance toward morality.*]

Goethe & Carlyle & perhaps Novalis have an undisguised dislike or contempt for common virtue standing on common principles. Meantime they are dear lovers[,] steadfast maintainers of the pure ideal (of) Morality. But they worship it as the highest beauty; their love is artistic. Praise Socrates to them, or Fenelon, much more any inferior contemporary good man & they freeze at once into silence. It is to them sheer prose. (pp. 300-01)

> *Ralph Waldo Emerson, in a journal entry of June 26, 1834, in his* The Journals and Miscellaneous Notebooks of Ralph Waldo Emerson: 1832-1834, *Vol. IV, edited by Alfred R. Ferguson, Cambridge, Mass.: Belknap Press, 1964, pp. 300-02.*

HENRIK STEFFENS　(essay date 1840-44)

[*Steffens, a Norwegian-born German philosopher and scientist, was an influential member of the German Romantic movement as well as an acquaintance of Novalis. Steffens here comments on Novalis's special brand of mysticism, praising his innate versatility and stylistic "charm and melody." Steffens's comments are taken from his memoir,* Was Ich Erlebte, *published in 1840-44.*]

There was an ethereal glow in [Novalis's] deep eyes; he was a poet in the truest sense. His whole existence, the whole meaning of life, was to him a profound mythos. From the world of mythical existence in which he lived the images of our own world looked out, sometimes clearly, sometimes obscurely. He cannot be called a mystic in the ordinary sense of the word, for the common mystic believes himself imprisoned by the world of sense, seeking behind it a profound mystery which is to reveal to him his true spiritual being and liberty, but to Novalis this sacred realm beyond was not an unsolvable mystery, but his original home, clearly perceived by him; from here, he looked out upon the world of sense and judged its relations. This mythos, instinctively a part of his nature, opened to him the secret doors of philosophy, the sciences, the arts, and the minds of great men. The wonderful charm and melody of his style were not the result of study, but the natural expression of his being; therefore he was as much at home in the scientific world as in the world of poesy, and the profoundest thoughts could no more conceal their relationship with the fairy tale than the most fantastic fairy tale could conceal its hidden meanings.

Henrik Steffens, "German Estimates of Novalis from 1800 to 1850," edited by J. F. Haussmann, in Modern Philology, *Vol. 9, No. 3, January, 1912, p. 404.*

THE DUBLIN UNIVERSITY MAGAZINE   (essay date 1859)

[*The author of the following review surveys Novalis's works, expressing admiration for his "mystical insight," but noting that Novalis's ideas are often difficult to fathom.*]

Truly it is difficult to form a correct estimate [of the works of Novalis]. In Germany they have learnt to appreciate them, partly perhaps because they cannot altogether understand them. That which we, who boast not Novalis' mystical insight, can see, we love and admire. His aphorisms are often sparkling, nearly always profound. Many times a truth shines through them bright as the star of the Epiphany.

He is deeply reverential in an age of mocking unbelief. He cares not to rush in with fools, knowing that where such come the very Holy of Holies becomes a place all common and unclean. His is not the superficial gaze satisfied that it has comprehended the universe at one glance. Rather he will take up the meanest stone, too ugly for the little child to build into its fairy grotto, and seek to find a meaning there—a history and a prophecy.

In studying the works of Novalis, the reader is constantly reminded of Aubrey de Vere's noble "Hymn to the Meek"—

The single Eye alone can see
All truths around us thrown.

Novalis, we have been told, was a "genuine, true man." He was "free from vanity and hypocrisy." His was the "*Single Eye.*" But to descend to particulars.

The first volume of the *Schriften* contains *Heinrich von Ofterdingen.* . . . It is a tale of a somewhat rambling character, and was intended to be the "Apotheosis of Poetry." The *Hymns to the Night,* with which the second volume commences, are obscurely solemn, mystically grand. There is a wealth of words and power of expression in them which make us, as we read, believe that we are listening to some involved, but stately music. *The Disciples at Sais* are at present unfathomed—perhaps they are not unfathomable. The *Spiritual Songs* and the Fragments are special favourites. (p. 363)

The Fragments are probably little known to the reader. . . . They are very weighty, and full of meaning. It seems as though each contained materials enough for a dozen sermons of a very superior class to what we, poor *habitantes in sicco,* are fated to hear from Sunday to Sunday.

Tieck likens Novalis to Dante. Carlyle more justly calls him the German Pascal [see excerpt dated 1829]. He was not endowed with the dramatic power of the Italian, but he did possess all the depth, and what, for want of a better word, may be termed the *pensiveness* of the Frenchman. Pascal is often grand in his "Thoughts." Novalis, too, is grand when, like Pascal, he is most simple. It is difficult to mention any English writer who may compare with him. Shelley has some points of contact. Both Shelley and Novalis were deeply imbued with mysticism; each was gifted with a wonderful wealth of words, and dealt in the same impassioned language. But in other particulars the two are wide asunder as the poles. Shelley, it must be confessed, after all the allowances which Christian charity can make, was a blasphemer. Novalis was a most devout believer. We carefully withhold from the youthful reader many of the writings of the Englishman. There is not a line written by the German which may not be perused with perfect safety. The contrast may be summed up in a word. Shelley is the author of "Queen Mab." Novalis wrote that most touching hymn, **"Was wär' ich ohne dich gewesen?"** (**"What had I been if Thou were not?"**) (p. 364)

E. S., "Friedrich von Hardenberg," in The Dublin University Magazine, *Vol. LIV, No. CCCXXI, September, 1859, pp. 358-65.*

GEORGE BRANDES   (essay date 1873)

[*Brandes, a Danish literary critic and biographer, was the principal leader of the intellectual movement that helped to bring an end to Scandinavian cultural isolation. He believed that literature reflects the spirit and problems of its time and that it must be understood within its social and aesthetic context. Brandes's major critical work,* Hovedstrømninger i det 19de aarhundredes litteratur, *won him admiration for his ability to view literary movements within the broader context of all of European literature. In the following excerpt, Brandes criticizes Novalis's overreliance on "an inward world," his self-absorption, and his "lawless fancy." He also compares Novalis's* Henry of Ofterdingen *to Goethe's* Wilhelm Meister. *Brandes's comments were first published in 1873.*]

Novalis was seventeen when the French Revolution broke out. If one were asked to give a brief definition of the main idea of that great movement, one would say that it was the destruction of everything that was merely traditional, and the establishment of human existence upon a basis of pure reason, by means of a direct break with everything historic. The thinkers and heroes of the Revolution allow reason, as it were, to upset everything, in order that reason may put everything straight again. Although Novalis is deaf to all the social and political cries of the period, and blind to all its progressive movements, he is, nevertheless, not merely influenced, but, all unconsciously, completely penetrated by the spirit of his age. Between him—the quiet, introspective, loyal Saxon assessor—and the poor *sans-culottes* who rushed from Paris to the frontiers, singing the "Marseillaise" and waving the tricolour flag, there is this fundamental resemblance, that they both desire the destruction of the whole outward and the construction of an inward world. Only, their inward world is reason, his is soul: for them, reason with its demands and formulae—liberty, equality, and fraternity; for him, the soul, with its strange nocturnal gloom, in which he melts down everything, to find, at the bottom of the crucible, as the gold of the soul—night, disease, mysticism, and voluptuousness.

Thus, in spite of his violent animosity to his age, Novalis belongs to it; the direct opponent of all its enlightened and beautiful ideas, he is, despite himself, possessed by its spirit.

What in Fichte and the men of the Revolution is clear reason, comprehending and testing everything, is in Novalis an all-absorbing self-perception, which becomes actual voluptuousness; for the new spirit has taken such a hold upon him that it is, as it were, entwined round his nerves, causing a species of voluptuous excitement. What with them is abstract liberty, liberty to begin everything from the beginning again, with him is lawless fancy, which changes everything, which resolves nature and history into emblems and myths, in order to be able to play at will with all that is external, and to revel unrestrainedly in self-perception. (pp. 187-88)

Novalis is himself thoroughly conscious that, in spite of all its would-be spirituality, the hectic imagination inclines towards the sensual. (p. 188)

Tieck writes with enthusiasm of music, as teaching us to *feel feeling*. Novalis is a living interpretation of these words. He, whose aim is feeling, unrestrained, irresponsible feeling, desires to feel himself, and makes no secret of the fact that he seeks this self-enjoyment. Therefore to him sickness is preferable to health. For the sick man perpetually feels his own body, which the healthy man does not. Pascal, and our own Kierkegaard, contented themselves with defining sickness as the Christian's natural condition. Novalis goes much further. To him the highest, the only true life, is the life of the sick man. *"Leben ist eine Krankheit des Geistes"* ("Life is a disease of the spirit"). Why? Because only in living individuals does the world-spirit feel itself, attain to self-consciousness. And no less highly than disease does Novalis prize voluptuousness, sensual rapture. Why? Because it is simply an excited, and therefore in his eyes diseased, self-consciousness, a wavering struggle between pleasure and pain. "Could man," he says, "but begin to love sickness and suffering, he would perhaps in their arms experience the most delicious rapture, and feel the thrill of the highest positive pleasure. . . . Does not all that is best begin as illness? Half-illness is an evil; real illness is a pleasure, and one of the highest." And he writes elsewhere of a mystic power, "which seems to be the power of pleasure and pain, the enrapturing effect of which we observe so distinctly in the sensations of voluptuousness."

To Novalis's voluptuous feeling of sickness corresponds the pietist's conviction of sin, that spiritual sickness which is at the same time a voluptuous pleasure. Novalis himself is perfectly aware of this correspondence. (pp. 188-89)

And just as Novalis now prefers sickness to health, so he prefers night to day, with its "impudent light."

Aversion for day and daylight was general among the Romanticists. . . . Novalis simply gives expression to a heightened degree of the general feeling in his famous *Hymns to Night*. That he should love the night is easy to understand. By hiding the surrounding world from it, night drives the Ego in upon itself; hence the feeling of night, and self-consciousness, are one and the same thing. The rapture of the feeling of night lies in its terror; first comes the fear of the individual, when everything round him disappears in the darkness, that he will himself disappear from himself; then comes the pleasant shudder when, out of this fear, self-consciousness emerges stronger than before. (pp. 189-90)

Life and death are to Novalis only "relative ideas." The dead are half alive, the living half dead. It is this thought which in his case first gives zest to existence. (pp. 190-91)

Novalis relegated everything to the inner life, the inner world. It engulfed everything, the forces of the Revolution and of the counter-revolution; in it all the lions of the spirit lay bound; in it the Titanic powers of history were shut up and hypnotised. Night surrounded them; they felt the voluptuous joys of darkness and death; the life they lived was the life of a plant, and in the end they turned into stone. In the inner world lay all the wealth of the spirit, but it was dead treasure, inert masses, ingeniously crystallized according to mathematical laws. It was like the gold and silver in the inward parts of the earth, and the poet was the miner who was spirited down into the depths and rejoiced in all that he saw.

But while he stayed down below, things in the upper world pursued their usual course. The outer world was not in the least disturbed because the poet and the philosopher were employed in taking it to pieces in the inner world. For they did not go to work in the rough, material fashion of a Mirabeau or a Bonaparte; they only disintegrated it inwardly in an inner world. When the poet, released by the spirits, came up from the mine again, he found the outer world, which he supposed he had resolved into its elements, exactly as it had been before. All that he had melted in his heart stood there, hard and cold; and, since the outer world had never really interested him, and since it seemed to him almost as night-like, murky, and drowsy as his inner world, he gave it his blessing and let it stand. (pp. 201-02)

• • • • •

It was Novalis who gave to the object of Romantic longing the famous, mystic name of "the blue flower." The expression is, of course, not to be understood literally. The "blue flower" is a mysterious symbol, something of the nature of . . . the Fish of the early Christians. It is an abbreviation, a condensed formulation of all that infinitude of bliss for which a languishing human heart is capable of longing. Hence glimpses of it are caught long before it is reached; it is dreamed of long before it is seen; it is divined now here, now there, in what proves to be a delusion, is seen for a moment amongst other flowers, only to vanish immediately; but its fragrance is perceptible, at times only faint, at times strong, and the seeker is intoxicated by it. Though, like the butterfly, he flutters from flower to flower, settling now upon a violet, now upon some tropical plant, he is always seeking and longing for the one thing—perfect, ideal happiness.

It is with this longing and its object that Novalis's principal work [*Heinrich von Ofterdingen*] deals. It is a work which we must study, and, to understand it aright, we must first see how it came into existence.

Its germ is contained in Goethe's *Wilhelm Meister*, and we can clearly trace the mental processes by which *Wilhelm Meister* is slowly transmuted into *Heinrich von Ofterdingen*. Wilhelm does not act, he is acted upon. He does not strive, he longs. He pursues ideals, seeking them first on the stage, then in real life. Wilhelm too, is the offspring of "soul." The book is pervaded by soul. It is not only that the characters, like those of many modern English novels (some of Dickens's, for instance), are full of soul, but there is, as it were, soul in the peculiar, hazy atmosphere which surrounds them. No feature is realistically coarse or decided; the children of soul have soft contours. Heiberg once summed up Goethe's philosophy, of which he himself was a disciple, in the following sentence: "Goethe is neither immoral nor irreligious, in the general acceptation of the word, but he shows that there are no unconditional laws of duty, and that we must place our religion on the same level as our poetry and philosophy." We are struck in reading *Wilhelm Meister* by the manner in which rigid school or text-book ethics, the narrow-minded, conventional ideas of morality and equity, are so re-moulded that morality is no longer regarded as the absolute law of life, but simply as an important principle of life, one among others all equally legitimate and equally under control. . . . As the tale is not the offspring of the union of imagination and reality, but of imagination and "soul," there is something unreal in its whole character; much is veiled, much refined away; everything is so idealised that the material world stands, as it were, in the shadow of the spiritual. (pp. 207-09)

Poetry has to give way to reality, the poetic conception of life to the practical. Novalis could imagine nothing more shameful than this; it was sin against the holy spirit of poetry. In the novel, in fiction, poetry is not to be done away with, not even to be restricted, but to be exalted and glorified.

So he determines to write a novel which shall be the direct antithesis of *Wilhelm Meister*. He even takes thought of such small matters as type and size, and determines that in them *Heinrich von Ofterdingen* shall be the exact counterpart of the book, the worldly philosophy of which it is to refute by its magic mysticism. He writes to Tieck: "My novel is in full swing; it is to be a deification of poetry. In the first part Heinrich von Ofterdingen ripens into a poet; in the second he is the glorified poet. The story will have many points of resemblance with your *Sternbald,* but will lack its lightness. This want, however, may not be a disadvantage, considering the subject."

Goethe and *Wilhelm Meister* Novalis criticises thus: "Goethe is an altogether practical poet. His works are what English wares are—simple, neat, suitable to their purpose, and durable. . . . He has, like the Englishman, a natural sense of order and economy, and an acquired sense of what is fine and noble. . . . *Wilhelm Meister's Lehrjahre* is, in a way, altogether modern and prosaic. Romance perishes in it, and so does the poetry, the magic quality, of nature. The book only deals with everyday human affairs; nature, and the belief in her mysterious powers, are quite forgotten. It is a poetically written story of bourgeois domestic life, in which the marvellous is expressly treated as poetry and fancy. Artistic atheism is the spirit of the book. *Wilhelm Meister* is a *Candide* directed against poetry."

Novalis's aim, then, is to produce a work exactly the opposite of this, one in which everything is finally resolved into poetry, in which "the world becomes soul." For everything is soul. "Nature is to the soul what a solid body is to light. The solid substance stops light, breaks it up into wonderful colours, &c., &c. Human beings are soul prisms." (pp. 212-13)

[In] *Heinrich von Ofterdingen* Novalis succeeded in producing something as unlike *Wilhelm Meister* as possible. The "blue flower" was the emblem of the ideal. Here we have the real forgotten in the ideal, and the ideal in its emblem. Poetry is entirely separated from life. Novalis thinks that this is as it should be. In *Ofterdingen* he says of poets:

> Many and important events would only disturb them. A simple life is their lot, and they must make acquaintance with the varied and numberless phenomena of the outer world *only by*

means of tales and books. Only seldom during the course of their lives is it permissible for them to be drawn into the wild eddy of some great event, in order that they may acquire a more accurate knowledge of the position and character of men of action. Their receptive minds are quite sufficiently occupied with near and simple phenomena. . . . Here upon earth already in possession of the peace of heaven, untormented by vain desires, only inhaling the fragrance of earthly fruits, not devouring them, they are free guests, whose golden feet tread lightly, and whose presence causes all involuntarily to spread their wings. . . . If we compare the poet with the hero, we shall find that the poet's song has many a time awakened heroic courage in youthful hearts, but never that heroic deeds have called the spirit of poetry to life in any soul.

The fundamental error could not have been defined more clearly. According to this theory, poetry is not the expression of life and its deeds; no, life and its deeds have poetry as their *origin*. Poetry creates life. Undoubtedly there is poetry of which this may be true; but if there be any one kind of poetry of which it could never be true, it is the kind under consideration. To what possible deed could it incite? To the changing of one's self into a singing tree or a golden ram? There is no question of action in it at all, only of longing.

All the best of Novalis's work is simply an expression of this longing, which includes every desire, from the purely natural ones to the most transcendental aspiration. Perhaps the most beautiful things he has written are two songs—the one giving expression to the sensuous longings of the young girl, the other to the longing which is part and parcel of the enthusiastic friendship of young men.

The song in which the young girls complain of the hardships of their lot is charming. Here the "blue flower" is simply the forbidden fruit. But the longing is expressed with bewitching roguishness. In the poem **"To a Friend,"** again, we have it expressed with fervency and solemnity. . . . The longing here is almost that of the Crusader—a seeking in the far distance for something great and glorious. The "blue flower" melts into the blue of the horizon. Its very colour betokens distance. (pp. 218-20)

> George Brandes, "Romantic Soul: Novalis" and "Longing: 'The Blue Flower'," in his Main Currents in Nineteenth Century Literature: The Romantic School in Germany, Vol. II, translated by Diana White and Mary Morison, William Heinemann, 1902, pp. 181-206, 207-29.

HJALMAR HJORTH BOYESEN (essay date 1875)

[*Arguing that Novalis's poems "fascinate by their very strangeness," Boyesen discusses Novalis in the context of his time and comments on the inherent contradictions in his style. He concludes that while Novalis the philosopher is a "dilettante," his poetry will be remembered.*]

[Novalis's poetry] lacks that distinctly virile quality and that robust health which characterize the lyrical effusions of poets like Goethe, or even Schiller before he had drunk too deeply of Kantian philosophy. Nevertheless, the lyrics of Novalis have a vague, spiritual, not to say phantasmal beauty of their own;

they fascinate by their very strangeness; their fleeting perfume lures the sense by its very deftness in evading its grasp; they gleam with that "light that never was on sea or land;" they move onward with a delicious, subdued splendor of cadence that falls upon the ear like melodious whispers from distant fairy realms. (p. 689)

[In the midst of his grief after the death of his fiancée], when the violent emotion might be expected to banish all thought of self, [Novalis's] attitude is that of a true Romanticist. His self-consciousness never for a moment leaves him; his eye is constantly turned inward, and its keen sight penetrates into the darkest chambers of his mind. With a half psychological, half poetical interest he watches the *crescendos* and *diminuendos* of his emotions, records in his journal the results of his observations, and upbraids himself whenever a note of natural, worldly joy mingles in the transcendental harmonies of his soul. To an unprejudiced observer this appears very much like dallying with one's grief, in order, by artificial means, to keep it up to the proper pitch; and if Novalis had not from his earliest youth breathed the air of philosophical abstraction, and if he had not lived in an age which was universally afflicted with this habit of morbid introspection, we might be justified in regarding these delicately retouched negatives of his mental states as insincere and affected. But a deeper knowledge of Novalis's character excludes such a supposition; he was, in the truest sense of the word, a child of his time, and it is perhaps the best proof of his sincerity that he followed it in its extravagances, shared its infirmities, and unconsciously respected its limitations. (p. 691)

A mixture of sensuous pleasure and high religious raptures give a curious interest to [Novalis's *Hymns to the Night*]. It is as if this earthly body which he is resolved to renounce and to mortify, in spite of the poet, again and again asserted its rights; as if his spiritual nature struggled desperately to break loose from the trammels of the flesh, and in the ardor of the combat gathered strength to rise to ever loftier flights. But this forcible heightening of every sensation, these endless distorted attitudes of ecstasy and despair, indicate a state of mental disease. Novalis seems himself to have been aware that his was not the normal condition of humanity, but this does not, to the mind of a Romanticist, necessarily prove that his condition leaves anything to be desired. The Romantic poet, according to Friedrich Schlegel's manifesto, knows no law except his own sovereign will, and where he differs from the rest of humanity the presumption is that humanity is in the wrong. Thus Novalis also performs a series of philosophical somersaults, and ends with the conclusion that disease is preferable to health. For "life," he says, "is a disease of the spirit."

A volume of fragments, published under the title of *Flower-Dust (Blüthenstaub)* contains numerous abstruse speculations on these same subjects of life and death, health and disease, pain and pleasure, etc. There is no obscure region of the soul which the mystic poet has not attempted to explore, there is no human emotion so ethereal and fleeting as to evade his eye, and no object in heaven or on earth too mean or too exalted for his earnest interest and consideration. Here we find a striking aphorism embodying some homely truth, in the next paragraph a conjecture as to the nature of the divine trinity, and a few lines further on some mere personal item, a literary project, a sigh of regret and resignation, or a half-subdued sob for the death of the beloved. (pp. 691-92)

Without an acquaintance with the leading philosophical systems of Germany, and especially that of Fichte, the greater part of Novalis's prose writings will appear obscure and unintelligible. And their obscurity does not always, as Carlyle would have us believe [see excerpt dated 1829], prove that the thought which is struggling for utterance is too profound to be embodied in the common vernacular of cultivated men, but is as frequently the result of a confusion of ideas in the author's mind. It is truly to be regretted that a man in whom there dwelt so rich a fountain of song should have spent so great a portion of his life in unprofitable investigations regarding "the internal plural," or the relation of mathematics to the emotional life of man. It may be that occasionally he caught glimpses of truths too high for the comprehension of men of coarser fibre, but it is as certain that his speculations often lost themselves in vague abstractions and pedantic sophistries. (pp. 692-93)

No doubt Novalis was an ingenious *dilettante* in philosophy, and perhaps divined a profounder meaning in the systems of his day than even the founders themselves; but the world has outgrown many an elaborate philosophic structure in this century, and will doubtless outgrow many more. But of its true poets mankind can afford to forget none; and when the philosopher Novalis shall long have been forgotten, the poet Novalis will still survive. (p. 693)

Novalis's romance, *Heinrich von Ofterdingen,* being a true product of the Romantic soil, shares the extravagances and imperfections which characterize Tieck's early works, and indeed all works of a similar nature within the school. It teems with sub-plots and allegories within allegories, and at times, it must be confessed, tasks the reader's patience to the utmost; for the very moment he imagines that he has caught hold of a tangible thread and is determined to keep it, it somehow slips out of his fingers, and he is again lost in a huge, dimly lighted labyrinth, filled, it is true, with many beautiful things, but leading nowhere, without end and without beginning. . . . [The] book was written as a protest against *Wilhelm Meister,* and as the latter, according to Novalis, was a glorification of the prose of life, so *Heinrich von Ofterdingen* should be an apotheosis of its poetry. But poetry the Romanticists conceived to be of a vague, ethereal, and impalpable essence, which impressed the sense not through the grosser faculty of understanding, but according to some mysterious law appealing directly to the deepest emotions of the heart. This theory, which the author shared with his friends Schlegel and Tieck, is no doubt largely responsible for the hopeless confusion which reigns in this otherwise well-conceived and interesting work. Singular enough, and apparently conflicting with the above theory, is the fact that the lyrical poems which are found scattered through the story are by far the clearest and most intelligible part of it; but Novalis was primarily a lyric poet, and nature will not fail to assert itself in spite of all theories.

To unravel the many allegorical complications of the plot is no easy task. Novalis has, however, himself given us the key to the understanding of it. In the first part, he says, the hero is matured as a poet, and in the second (which was left incomplete at the author's death) he is glorified as a poet. In the very first chapter we meet with all the conventional machinery of Romantic fiction: night, moonlight, dreams, and the longing for the blue flower. This blue flower is the watchword and the sacred symbol of the school. What it is meant to symbolize it is difficult to tell, but judging from the *rôle* it plays in the present romance we should venture to say that it is an emblem of the deep and nameless longings of a poet's soul. Romantic poetry invariably deals with longing; not a definite, formulated desire for some attainable object, but a dim, mysterious aspiration, a trembling unrest, a vague sense of kinship with the infinite, and a consequent dissatisfaction with every form of happiness which the world has to offer. The object of the Romantic longing, therefore, so far as it has any object, is the ideal—the ideal of happiness, the ideal of a woman, the ideal of social perfection, etc. The blue flower, like the absolute ideal, is never found in this world; poets may at times dimly feel its nearness, and perhaps even catch a brief glimpse of it in some lonely forest glade far from the haunts of men, but it is vain to try to pluck it. If for a moment its perfume fills the air, the senses are intoxicated, and the soul swells with poetic rapture.

In *Heinrich von Ofterdingen* the presence of this wondrous flower is felt on every page, and quite unawares one may catch a glimpse of its fragile chalice. (p. 695)

Considered as a story, this romance of Novalis may have very little importance, but regarded as a phenomenon in literature, containing the germs of various tendencies of a school which during the present century has spread throughout Europe, it is well worthy of the attention we have given it. (p. 696)

> Hjalmar Hjorth Boyesen, "Novalis and the Blue Flower: The Romantic School in Germany," in The Atlantic Monthly, Vol. XXXVI, No. CCXVIII, December, 1875, pp. 689-98.

ALEXANDER HAY JAPP (essay date 1880)

[*Characterizing Novalis as "the most mystic and dreamy of later German thinkers," Japp analyzes the relation between Novalis's romanticism and his religious beliefs.*]

[Novalis was] a pietist in a new guise. Every pietist is a mystic; but every mystic is not a pietist. Therein lies the distinction between Novalis and those who have so persistently claimed him as a disciple or as a partizan. It is true, that like F. Schlegel, he came to regard the Roman Catholic Church as that which might under certain circumstances most efficiently represent the religious life of Europe, and ally it with everyday activity, art, science, and industry, thus finding the unity of which the brotherhood of German mystics were especially in search; but Novalis to the end remained a Lutheran, too wise to yield his ideal to the keeping of a very degenerate form of Catholicism. His interest for us will be found to lie in the impulse he has given to the religious life, by the infusion of deeper veins of sentiment, and the poetic atmosphere which he has thrown around the common dogmas of Christianity. (p. 442)

[Though] Novalis may well be cited as an example of the mystic, of the philosophic dreamer, penetrating by some finer instinct to the hidden relations of ideas and principles, this view of him by no means exhausts his character or his significance. Nay, rather his originality, his depth, his subtle insight, and his refined vein of pervading poetic mysticism can only be properly apprehended and understood when seen in strict relation to the daily devotion—the dutiful practicality by which his life was so informed and distinguished. He himself would have been the last to regard as faithful to him any analysis which magnified the one element at the expense of the other, because, critically, the problem was thus rendered more simple. He would have urged that, however hard it might be to detect the unity between his philosophy and his practical life, an essential unity there was; that the one was at every point dependent on the other; and that both in the directest fashion of which they were susceptible were expressive of the man. His

practical life, he would have urged, was in this respect more complete and connected than his philosophy.

Here, then, we have one of the very highest testimonies to the compatibility of mysticism and speculative endeavour of the most refined character, with the faithful performance of daily duties thoroughly commonplace and trying in themselves. From his more strictly scientific studies in view of his profession, from the most prosaic details of his mining experiences, we can perceive that he drew the richest suggestions for thought, and was thus enabled to fill up many *lacunae*, which else had in all probability been left. In his later fragments, and the *Scholars of Sais*, this is more especially discernible, for in them illustrations are more and more frequently drawn from the world of practical scientific order to the world of mind and spirit. It is not at all probable that, had he succeeded in his youthful desire to enter the army, these later *Fragments* could have been so suggestive as they are, so that his case presents in the most tangible and efficient form an illustration of the unexpected benefits that may arise to the philosophic aspirant from being compelled, at the call of duty, into lines of activity, from which, by inclination, he would at the moment have decisively retreated. The life of Novalis—the most mystic and dreamy of later German thinkers—has thus a lesson of the most valuable kind for the crowd of ambitious students whose ideal of success is the attainment of "lettered ease" and complete escape from the encroachments and vulgar interruptions of commonplace life.

And, further still, in Novalis we can see how the romantic idea in its purer form is practically a regenerating one. It may claim to set before the mind and heart an unselfish purpose—a noble self-sacrifice, which may fulfil itself in the narrowest circle of the family, thence expanding into wider and wider circles, bringing all, however, into complete harmony; and seeking, so far as it concerns itself with art, for the most expressive symbol of this relationship. Family, the Church, the State, the more expansive circle of human brotherhood, are thus held in relation in the mind of the true romanticist, who can only be said to have approached to success when his representation of life is disinterestedly inclusive of them all. The great errors of the romanticists, as we shall hereafter see, were excesses into which they were tempted by re-action against excesses of their rivals—the classicists; the one sought to make art directly interpretative of *ideas*, that in their abstractness froze and impeded the fluid movements of creative impulse; they, in fact, aimed at too much, and did injury to form by their determination to present too wide a surface; while again the other erred in subjecting matter to form, and initiating a series of false rules which they outraged in the very act of applying them. But romanticism, as truly conceived, is more fitted to adapt from classicism than classicism is fitted to adapt from it; and the great prevailing literatures of the present century are distinctly romantic. What Novalis so aptly said of Shakespeare may be said, without much modification, of all the literature which regards him as an originator and influence, and how inclusive that is those who know most of literature know best. Here are Novalis's words:—

> In Shakespeare throughout poetry interchanges with the unpoetical, harmony with disharmony, the common, low, and ugly with the romantic higher beauty, the actual with the invented, the pedantic and unnatural of poetry, and in the Greek drama the ruin is from an opposite cause. Shakespeare's works and poems, like all the

prose of Boccaccio and Cervantes, are well-founded, elegant, neat, unpedantic, and complete.

Novalis's idea of the relation of art to life is most admirably summed up in his axiom, ''The artist stands to the man as the statue to the pedestal.'' (pp. 458-60)

[Novalis is], more than any of his compeers, the efficient interpreter of romanticism, not in the field of art-product proper, but in the representation of the necessary unity and harmony that must exist between the man and his work, between the artist and the citizen, the individual and the nation in its various aspects. Classic art, especially as more lately exhibited, would divorce the artist from the man, just at the point where the ethical element is most assertive, and declare that there is really no dependence of the one upon the other. It would initiate and justify a kind of artificial exercise of the imaginative faculties upon a world that remains undisturbed, and even untouched by any of the strife and disorder of the real world in which we live and move; and would thus present us with an *art-pour-art*, which should supply all that might thus be held as lacking to the completeness of human nature. Novalis can have no value for such. His life is an abiding protest against such a theory of art and life. What I live and feel and create is in the last result of value only as I live and feel and create in harmony with what is most essential in the moral and spiritual being of man. He would have said with Kant, ''two things move me to wonder, the starry system without and the conscience within.'' Little dogmatic as Novalis was, it is this incessant recognition of the nexus between the wonders of the world without and the wonders of the world within, as being sealed in the moral nature of man, that gives him that strong hold upon the religious consciousness; and undoubtedly a strong hold he has there. The mystic borderland on which our instinctive feelings of worship and wonder dimly play, as they pass from the half-sensible perception of the grandeur and overwhelming greatness of the visible universe to the consciousness of the yet more ineffable greatness of man's soul, has never perhaps been uttered with more sincerity of refinement, more of artistic delicacy or unaffected comprehensiveness. In his hymns he sets into simple, fervid, yet familiar language the dim images that hover uncertainly before the religious sense, but refuse to take definite form, and are as little embodied in doctrinal hymns as they are in harshly-reasoned sermons. Novalis passes inward to the human and universal of religious experience, because he is faithfully recording his own sorrow, struggle, joy, and victory. (pp. 462-63)

> *Alexander Hay Japp, "Friedrich von Hardenberg (Novalis)," in his* German Life and Literature in a Series of Biographical Studies, *Marshall Japp & Company, 1880, pp. 439-66.*

KUNO FRANCKE (essay date 1895)

[*Francke, a German-born American historian and educator, here examines Novalis's work in relation to Romanticism and Classicism in German literature. In his scathing criticism of* Henry of Ofterdingen, *Francke condemns Novalis's "absolutely aimless contemplation" and characterizes him as "the highpriest of a capricious mysticism and supranaturalism."*]

How is it that a poet who had drunk so deeply from the well of life, who was endowed with such a profound instinct for the unity of existence, as the author of the incomparable **Hymns to Night**, should after all have ended as the highpriest of a

capricious mysticism and supranaturalism? The answer is not far to seek. Only the will bridges the gulf between the ideal and the real; only the moral command: Thou shalt! establishes the unity of matter and spirit. This homely truth, which in one form or another shines out from the whole lifework of Kant and Herder, of Goethe and Schiller, was something entirely hidden from the over-refined circles to which Novalis belonged. To him, as to the rest of the Romanticists, conscious activity was a sin against the Holy Ghost. What he called the highest life was at bottom something purely negative, a fathomless nothing, complete absence of endeavor, absolutely aimless contemplation. No wonder that the actual life with its manifold claims on will and self-consciousness should have appeared to him as ''a disease of the spirit;'' that the visible world should have seemed to him a chaotic dream, and dreams the only true reality. No wonder that his pantheistic inclinations should have led him, not to a firm faith in the supreme rule of an all-pervading and all-embracing moral law, but to a superstitious belief in the divineness of individual caprice and fantasy. No wonder that he should have found the true object of poetry in representing the miraculous and the irrational; that he should have reviled the Reformation and glorified the Jesuits; that he should have fled from what he was pleased to call the infidelity and frivolity of modern science to the fairyland of a phantastic Mediaevalism. (pp. 90-1)

[The scenery in Novalis's **Heinrich von Ofterdingen** is] but an idle play of fancy, a degradation of poetry to the role of a juggler, a wilful jumbling together of conceptions which have nothing in common with each other, a complete failure to give the impression of an organic and harmonious whole. It is a typical instance of the difference between the mediaeval and the romantic spirit.

The fanciful exterior of mediaeval life, its naive joy in the mysterious, its childlike belief in the impossible, rested on the solid foundation of an unbroken tradition, of an implicit faith in divine omnipotence and goodness. It was counter-balanced by an earnest devotion to common social tasks, by a strong sense of mutual dependence, of the moral obligation of each to all. The romantic predilection for mystery and wonder proceeded from the overwrought imagination of extreme individualists and free-thinkers. It had no moral background. It was devoid of true religious feeling. It was a literary symptom of social disintegration, a concomitant phenomenon of the final breakdown of the Holy Roman Empire. The mysterious ''blue flower,'' in the pursuit of which Heinrich von Ofterdingen consumes his life, was a fit symbol of the aimless and phantastic yearning in which not only Novalis, but the majority of the cultivated youth of his time squandered their intellectual energies, and which was to plunge the country into the disasters of Austerlitz and Jena.

It is instructive to compare **Heinrich von Ofterdingen,** the representative novel of Romanticism, with representative works of other ages or tendencies, such as Wolfram's *Parzival,* Grimmelshausen's *Simplicissimus, Wilhelm Meister.* In all three of these romances the hero enters into a conflict with the world and himself, in all three of them he is enriched and strengthened through this very conflict. Parzival wins the crown of life through earnest striving for self-mastery and through active work for the common weal. Simplicissimus, though tossed about in a sea of meanness and vice, maintains after all his moral nature and at last reaches the harbor of a tranquil indifference to outward circumstance. Wilhelm Meister, through the striving for self-culture, through contact with the most varied conditions of society, is led to a perfectly universal sympathy with actual life.

Nothing of all this do we find in *Heinrich von Ofterdingen*. "Die Welt wird Traum, der Traum wird Welt"—this is the ideal of existence held up to us here. In the whole novel not a single thing is done which may be called an act of free moral endeavor, nor a single character appears whose will-power would be equal to any decisive test. The book impresses us as a series of charming hallucinations; it is as though the subconscious self had emancipated itself from the will and was roaming about, in sweet intoxication, through the shadow-land of the incoherent and the incredible.

The air is filled with gentle music, a blue haze enshrouds the distance. Mediaeval merchants with faces of pre-Raphaelite saints ride on the highway, discussing in chorus questions of poetry and art. Hidden paths lead through rock and underbrush to subterraneous caverns where venerable hermits are poring over prophetic books. Voices are heard from beneath the ground; visions appear in the trees; spirits of the departed return in manifold reincarnations. In the midst of these phantastic surroundings we see Heinrich himself traveling in search of the wonderful flower at which he once has gazed in a dream, the symbol of ideal poetry; and the further he travels, the further is he removed from the life of reality, the more completely does he seem to loose his human identity. So that we are not surprised to hear that for a while he resides with the dead; that he lives through all the ages of history; that the various maidens in the love of whom he finds the same delight which the vision of the flower had given him, are in reality one; that he at length reaches a stage of existence where "men, beasts, plants, stones, stars, elements, sounds, colors, commune with each other like one family, act and talk like one race," and that he himself is transformed successively into a rock, a singing tree, and a golden wether.

In studying these phantastic ravings of an eccentric and uncontrolled imagination, one understands how a generation whose reason and will-power had been benumbed by their influence, should have become unfit for discharging the simple duties of the citizen and the patriot; one comprehends Napoleon's contempt for "ces idéologues Allemands;" and one sees the inner justice of the political humiliation of Germany in 1806. (pp. 93-6)

> Kuno Francke, "The Social Aspect of Early German Romanticism," in PMLA, 10, Vol. X, No. 1, 1895, pp. 83-96.*

UNA BIRCH (essay date 1903)

[*In the following excerpt from her introduction to* The Disciples at Saïs, *Birch briefly outlines the historical context of Novalis's philosophical ideas. She asserts that his theme of the search for unity embodies "the aspiration of his age," but adds that Novalis was more successful as a poet and dreamer than as a philosopher because "he lacked the power of consecutive, concentrated thought."*]

Novalis had come into the world at a critical moment. The years between 1772 and 1801, the term of his natural life, were some of the most vital in European history, for they witnessed the culmination of that great struggle of the Rights of the Individual, that mighty egoistic wave that enveloped Europe and even America in its advance towards Social Reconstruction. Surveying the world, we see England losing America, France emergent from the Feudal system, and men everywhere

systematising all things. In spite of social anarchy there was a deep, strong undercurrent of Order, a genius for investigation was abroad, all branches of knowledge were being classified and systematised into sciences. In the realm of Natural Philosophy there were many eager searchers, and it is not surprising that Novalis, with his fervid imagination, was captivated by their quest. Joseph Priestly was discovering that air parts with its oxygen to the blood as it passes through the lungs; Aloysius Galvani, who gave his name to the Force which he discovered, was working along the same lines as Ritter and Volta. Novalis was absorbed by the new galvanic theories, and said that "Thought must be galvanisation," while Schelling waxed enthusiastic about oxygen, and thought it the Philosopher's Stone. It was necessary for Novalis to know something of Mineralogy in his profession, and so he went to learn of Werner, the professor at Freyberg. Werner was a man of note who had first applied the term "Formations" to the groups of strata which are usually found associated, and the term "Transition" to the rocks lying between those called primitive and secondary, and he it was who led Novalis into the secrets of Nature and who greatly inspired him. *The Disciples at Saïs* was the natural outcome of the tumultuous yet ordered activity around him, that great Nature-Revelation which, with its strange analogies and nascent harmonies, is one of the greatest poems in the possession of men. . . . In this remarkable work we may learn that he conceived Nature as a vast self-existent universally related Whole, and his idea of the sciences was "that they should mutually elucidate, confirm and enforce each other." Here we find expressed the idea of Unity that possessed all the Romantics, the idea that made even the great Goethe rejoice more in the discovery of the "os intermaxillare" in man than in any other of his work.

There is no question but that the genius of Novalis lay in his capacity for Unification; and it is for this reason that he seems to be the embodiment of the aspiration of his age, though he had neither real mathematical nor philosophical training; yet an extraordinary intuition combined with a strong poetic faculty enabled him, like Emerson, whose mind more nearly resembles his than any other, to be a weaver of thoughts, a writer of theories, a mingler of discoveries. Like Coleridge he was fragmentary and unconsecutive in his work, and it is difficult to give in a few words an idea of the philosophy that is scattered up and down in the thought exercises and encyclopaedic fragments. He says: "Philosophy is the science of self-analysis, through philosophising we begin to perceive that Nature or the outer world is similar to a human being, we find out that we can only begin to comprehend things in the same way in which we know ourselves and those dearest to us. At last we realise the true bond of union between subject and object, and discover that even in our own selves there is an outer world, which stands in the same relation to our inner selves that our outer life bears to the outer world, that the latter are as closely connected as our outer and inner life, and, therefore, we can only comprehend the inner life and soul of Nature by reflection, even as it is only by sensation that our outer life comes in contact with material forces." "The road leads inwards, inwards to the depths of the Ego; the highest task of culture is self mastery of the inner life, so that it may become indeed the true Ego." "We are called to the cultivation of the Earth," he says, "she takes man's impression. Humanity is the higher sense of our planet, the nerve that connects this portion (of the Universe) with a higher world, the Eye that it lifts to Heaven." For Novalis Man is Mediator between God and Nature. "Nature shall become moral, we are her teachers, her moral tangents, her moral attraction." Novalis, in spite of his deep-seated monistic tendency, becomes a dualist in his view of Nature. Instead of making God and Nature the same, he places her in opposition to Him as her goal; God, endless Activity; Nature, endless object (theme or matter); *I* the Endless condition. God and Nature must be separated, God is the Goal of Nature, that with which she shall one day harmonise. He seems to represent God not as the moving Spirit with the cosmos, but as over against the world that He had thrown off in order that it might yield itself to Him. The Ego is that which binds the subjective and objective world, and it must be in its very essence Love, for the Ego is forever two who are yet one, and thus it is that the conception of an extra mundane God and of a temporal creation is evaded. For Novalis as for Fichte if there is Man there must be God, if there is God there must be Man.

There is no occasion to dwell much on the philosophy of Novalis; his system, if it can be called a system, was made up of monistic and dualistic ingredients on Fichtean lines. He was in reality a born Poet and Religionist, and it is as such, and not as a Philosopher, that he must live; and though his intense realisation of that dream of the ages, the Unity of the Universe, may appear philosophic, yet he was in truth no thinker but a dreamer, whose innate tendency was to regard phenomena as the everlasting breaking of waves on some shore, each wave disappearing only to reappear in some other, all alike being manifestations of the hidden Unity. He arrived at the same results as the thinker, but, as he said himself in *Sais,* there are many roads that lead to the Temple of the veiled Goddess, of Isis the Mystery. (pp. 41-6)

Novalis is such a beautiful dreamer that when we come to analyse his work we feel as if we were bruising the wings of some glorious blue butterfly, whose life has been a series of flights from mystery to mystery, and whose true home is the empyrean, the real Bird of Paradise, of which it is said that it has no feet, and so must hang hovering for ever. If we are going to brush the dust from the blue wings we must tell first what he said of himself: "Spinoza climbed to Nature, Fichte to the Ego or Personality, I to the thesis, God," and yet, in spite of his vaunt, as far as thought went, he remained in a far smaller circle than either. And why? Because he lacked the power of consecutive, concentrated thought, the really trained faculties; he was full of intuitions, enthusiasms, interests, originality; with a wide vision and a small grasp. But after all, perhaps the lustre of the blue wings is really enhanced by the removal of the philosophic dust; their true colour is shown to be the diviner cobalt of Poetry, and their owner as a magic Intuitionist in the Spiritual Kingdom. (pp. 48-9)

> *Una Birch, "Novalis: The Author," in* The Disciples at Saïs and Other Fragments *by Novalis, edited by Una Birch, translated by F.V.M.T. and U.C.B., Methuen & Co., 1903, pp. 34-49.*

MAURICE MAETERLINCK (essay date 1909)

[*Maeterlinck was a Belgian poet, dramatist, and essayist who was awarded the Nobel Prize for literature in 1911. In the following excerpt, he analyzes Novalis's writing style and philosophy, praising him as "a scientific mystic" who can "bind all worlds together." Maeterlinck's essay, first published in 1909 as an introduction to a French translation of* The Disciples at Saïs, *is historically important because it brought Novalis to the attention of French readers.*]

Novalis probably represents one of the most imponderable, one of the most subtle, and one of the most transparent aspects of

the superior being silent within the depths of us. . . . [He is a mystic], but his mysticism is of a special kind. "What is mysticism?" he asks himself in one of his fragments, "And what should be treated mystically? Religion, love, politics. All lofty things have some connection with mysticism. If all men were only a couple of lovers, the difference between mysticism and non-mysticism would be at an end." (pp. 72-3)

Novalis does not concern himself expressly with theosophy, with magic, with transcendental pneumatology, with metaphysical cosmology, or with all we find in the spacious circles of the mystic, properly speaking. He is an almost unconscious mystic who has no aim. He thinks mystically, since a thought which communicates in a certain fashion with the infinite is a mystic thought. We must everywhere seek for thoughts of this kind, for they are the only ones in which our soul truly lives. And as these thoughts are very rare, we must be contented with the slightest efforts and attempts. I do not mean to say that Novalis is a supremely admirable being. His teaching is very vague, and he does not advance any new solution to the great questions of being. But some of his thoughts are undoubtedly impregnated with the special odour of our soul, and you recognise without trouble this odour that no language can ever define. He has found a way to clothe a certain number of earthly things in mystic vestments; and these are the calmest, the most spontaneous, and the most virginal vestments one can encounter. His mysticism is even so natural and so essential that we do not see it at the outset.

In him, infinite communications are formed before you realise it, and extend over all with grace. He does not torture himself; he does not search in shadows or in tears, but he smiles at things with a gentle indifference, and regards the world with the attentive curiosity of an angel, unoccupied and distraught by long memories. He plays simply in the gardens of the soul, without suspecting that he has reached the extreme end of life, and that he often passes his hands between the branches to pluck the flowers from the other side of the burning hedge.

He is also very far from the exuberant and obscure joy of the ascetic mystic. He does not feel the intolerable flames that melt souls at the opposite poles of divine love. He is rather an astonished and sweet-voiced child who possesses the sense of unity. He is not sad and he is not restless. "There is not, properly speaking, any unhappiness in this world," he tells us; and yet he was as unhappy as any other man. But unhappiness could not sink into his soul, nor did it succeed in troubling his thoughts.

"Sorrow is a divine vocation," he says again; but one feels that he has not known sorrow, and that he speaks of it as a traveller who has not fathomed the language of a country through which he passes. (pp. 74-7)

[He] does not concern himself with anything that is certain. He lives in the domain of erratic intuitions, and nothing is more elusive than his philosophy. His mysticism, to use one of his expressions which he loves and which he often employs when he speaks of his science, is rather "a magic idealism." It seems to him that nothing is more within reach of the spirit than the infinite, and that is why he scarcely ever enters the ordinary field of human thoughts. He only wanders over the frontiers of this thought, but he goes over nearly all of them.

With the greater number of mystics known to us, mysticism is psychological; that is to say, it attaches itself to a species of transcendental psychology where the soul itself endeavours to study its own habits and passions, as our mind, in ordinary psychology, endeavours to study the passions and habits of our being, apart from mystery. The immovable soul falls back upon itself and concerns itself less with the unknown which lies about it than with the unknown which lies within; or rather, it perceives accidentally the exterior mystery only through and in relation to the inner mystery. In general, it is mystic only in respect to itself, whereas, in Novalis, the soul may be mystic in its relation to a chemical phenomena, a pathological law, or an arithmetical problem. (pp. 78-9)

If we must characterise Novalis by a word, we might say that he was a scientific mystic, though he only concerned himself with science at moments, and at places where it was on the point of being confounded with poetry. "There is a divining atmosphere," he says somewhere; and he is the one of those who come forth the most rarely out of his precious atmosphere. He catches a glimpse continually, on the extreme limits of the plausible, of many things of which there is no proof, but which we ourselves are nevertheless unable to refrain from recognising and admiring. He touches upon them only in passing; and before you have had time to recover from your astonishment, he awaits you, all smiles, on the most solitary cape of the other hemisphere.

Novalis has those eyes which for an instant bind all worlds together. Perhaps he is the one who has most profoundly penetrated intimate and mystic nature and the secret unity of the universe. He has the sense and the very sweet torment [meaning that he chafes under the thought] of unity. "He sees nothing isolated," and above all things he is the doctor who looks in amazement at the mysterious relations existing between all things. He gropes without cessation at the extremes of this world, where the sun only rarely shines, and on every side he suspects and touches lightly upon strange coincidences and astounding analogies, obscure, trembling, fugitive, and timid, which vanish before one has understood.

But he has caught a glimpse of a certain number of things one would never have suspicioned, had he not gone so far. He is the clock that has marked some of the most subtle hours of the human soul. It is evident that he has more than once been mistaken; but despite the winds of folly and of error whirling around him, he has been able to maintain himself a longer time than any other on the dangerous peaks where all is at the point of being lost. He seems to be the hesitant consciousness of unity, but the most vaguely complete that we have had thus far. And there are few human beings in whom our universe was more spiritualised and more divinely human. He is like the serene master of Saïs [in his *The Disciples at Saïs*]: "He hears, sees, touches, and thinks at the same time. Often, the stars seem to him like men; then again men seem to him like the stars, stones like animals, clouds like plants. He plays with forces and phenomena." (pp. 83-5)

Maurice Maeterlinck, "Novalis," in his On Emerson and Other Essays, *translated by Montrose J. Moses, Dodd, Mead and Company, 1912, pp. 53-118.*

ROBERT M. WERNAER (essay date 1910)

[*Wernaer discusses Novalis's contribution to the Romantic school of poetry. Describing his state of mind as "primordial" in its lack of affectation, Wernaer lauds Novalis's ability to unite the poetic and the mystic and the real and the ideal in his poetry.*]

Novalis lived in the world of the spirit while still on earth. This was the impression he made on all who came in contact with him. All loved him for that, all revered him for that. Through it, he exerted his influence as a poet. It was a state of mind absolutely primordial; no affectation, no artificial acquisitions, no intellectual convictions, no mannerism, it was as natural to him as the glow of colors to the setting sun. This was Novalis' fundamental trait, and is the key to his individual romanticism. Steffens, who met him at Jena and upon whom he made a profound impression, gives us an admirable characterization of Novalis' master passion: "There was an ethereal glow in his deep eyes," so he tells us; "he was a poet in the truest sense. His whole existence, the whole meaning of life, was to him a profound *mythos*. . . . The wonderful charm and melody of his style were not the result of study, but the natural expression of his being; therefore, he was as much at home in the scientific world as in the world of poesy, and the profoundest thoughts could no more conceal their relationship with the fairy tale than the most fantastic fairy tale could conceal its hidden meanings" [see excerpt dated 1840-44]. Fairy tales! We cannot characterize his literary products better than by putting them all into this class. Even his epigrams have a fairy tale quality. [Friedrich] Schlegel wrote epigrams, and [August Wilhelm] Schlegel and Schleiermacher and Caroline; but there is a distinguishing atmosphere about those of Novalis, a peculiar blending of the here and the beyond not found in the writings of the others. What he says is not doctrinal, not didactic, not polemic, rarely theoretically speculative, even not strictly metaphysical; but essentially poetic, prophetic, interpretative of spiritual things, revealing spiritual relationships, unfolding symbolic meanings of things seen and unseen. He was mystic because poetic, and poetic because mystic. "The sense of poetry," so reads one of his epigrams, "has much in common with the sense of mysticism. It is the sense of the unknown and the mysterious. The poet represents the subject-object: mind and world. The sense of poetry is closely related to the sense of prophecy, to the religious sense, the sense of the prophetic seer."

This is Novalis' personal contribution to the romanticism of the School. It gives a distinctive color to the School's poetic life which it would not possess otherwise. It gives a seriousness to it which is unquestionable; though we may sometimes miss it in the individual writings of the others. His individualism does not show itself in the form of revolt. It is never aggressive. It never assumes the attitude of superhumanity as in the case of Fried. Schlegel. It submits from the start to higher influences. Even when he rejoices in the magic powers of the imagination it is not for the sake of the mere enjoyment in that power, but for the sake of establishing, through that power, important relations between his own mind and the mind of the world. Irony, in the Schlegelian sense, is, therefore, excluded. He also rejoices, like Tieck, in individual, poetic moods, but he never uses them as mere playthings, as was so often done by his less serious friend. Tieck played with his moods, but Novalis attached to them a profound meaning. They were to him important messages sent from the distant background of his inner life. (pp. 78-80)

Robert M. Wernaer, "Romantic Leaders," in his Romanticism and the Romantic School in Germany, *1910. Reprint by Haskell House, 1966, pp. 55-82.**

GEORGE SAINTSBURY (essay date 1911)

[*Saintsbury was an English literary historian and critic of the late nineteenth and early twentieth centuries. A prolific writer, he composed several histories of English and European literature as*

A portrait of Novalis's fiancée, Sophie von Kühn.

well as numerous critical works on individual authors, styles, and
periods. Saintsbury here evaluates Novalis's critical writings,
according him a high place among the German Romantics and
praising his wit, perceptiveness, wide range, and "critical magic."]

The German "Romantic School" has been the occasion of
divers solid books (and famous booklets) all to itself. . . . In a
certain justifiable sense it may be said to have begun with
Klopstock and only died, if it died even then, with Heine. . . .
[It is usually considered] a period extending from the latest
years of the eighteenth century over about the first quarter (or
the first thirty or forty years) of the nineteenth, and dominated
by a remarkable quartette of friends—the two younger Schlegels, "Novalis," and Tieck. The work of all the four is saturated with literary criticism of the polemic and propagandist
kind, but it is rendered more troublesome to handle than it
need be by the pestilent habit (which the Germans took from
Rousseau, and from Goethe downwards indulged after the most
intemperate fashion) of throwing polemic and propagandist
thought into the forms of prose romance.

Of these four the *greatest* critic is, in my humble judgment,
Novalis—though he wrote the least criticism. Indeed, there is
a sense in which one might, without absurdity, call Novalis
the greatest critic of Germany. He is, in fact, the Shelley of
criticism; and it may be left to the Devil's Advocates to suggest
that, like Shelley, he had time to indicate, at least, all that was

of truth in him, and had no time to turn it into, or muddle it
with, error. He, very much more than Jean Paul, is *der Einzige:*
though his uniqueness is such that, while it does not adjust
itself to all times or temperaments, it will, when once apprehended, always re-present itself at some time or other with
some slight assistance of fortune.

It would hardly have assisted his critical position if he had
carried out the intention, which we are told he entertained . . . ,
of writing seven documents of the kind, on Poetry, Physics,
the Civic Life, Commerce, History, Politics, and Love! *Wilhelm Meister,* which . . . he judged so well, would have had
much to answer for if this had been done. As it is, the existing
but unfinished *Heinrich von Ofterdingen* represents the first of
these, and the not much more than begun *Lehrlinge zu Sais* is
believed to represent the second: but the rest remained bodiless
and in the gloom. It was much better so: for neither the partly
completed nor the hardly begun book approaches in value the
Fragmente which follow. In fact, even if the scheme were
really practicable (which, despite certain imposing instances,
may be very much doubted), it is pretty clear that Friedrich
von Hardenberg was not the man for it.

It can hardly, on the other hand, rejoice any reader of *Heinrich
von Ofterdingen,* whether he be philosopher, critic, or simple
reader for reading's sake, when the Quest of the Blue Flower,
and all the other agreeable Fouqué-like "swarmeries," are
interrupted by a discourse of three pages from the poet Klingsohr on the *Überschwenglichkeit* of certain subjects for poetry.
Even if you are a poet, and a Middle-High-German, and the
father of Matilda, you must not talk like that in a novel. And
your poetry, and your Middle-High-Germanship, and your fa-
therhood of Matilda are very distinctly *überschwenglich* for
you in your character as a critic. From *Heinrich,* therefore, we
shall chiefly get (though there are tempting *aperçus* in it here
and there) a somewhat vague notion of the *clair-de-lune* Poetic
of the central Romantic school. The *Disciples at Sais* hardly
concern us. But the *Fragments* that remain give much less
unsubstantial food. Here is that witty and appallingly accurate
judgment of Klopstock, which applies to a whole class of poets
as well, that "His works appear to be, for the most part, free
translations and workings up of an unknown Poet by a very
talented but unpoetical philologist." Here, too, is that remarkable judgment of Goethe's work in general, and of *Wilhelm Meister* in particular . . . , which remains almost a pattern
of independent and solid judgment, unspoilt by any petulance
or jealousy of youth, from a young man of letters on the living
leader of his country's literature. Here also are some almost
equally remarkable things on Shakespeare, not quite showing
the *adequacy* of those on Goethe, but very acute and especially
valuable because they enter a protest against the exaggeration—
a reaction, of course, from the opposite exaggeration of Voltaire & Co.—of Shakespeare's deliberate artistry. And these
individual judgments occur side by side, in the aesthetic and
literary division of these *Fragments,* with more general dicta
of astonishing profundity and beauty.

The most pregnant of all the sayings, as it seems to me, though
the aestheticians may not like it, is this, "Aesthetic is absolutely independent of Poetry"; and I should pair with it the
other, "May not poetry be nothing but *inner* painting and
music, freely modified by the nature of [the individual's?]
feeling (Gemüth)?" The further Shakespearian remarks on the
blending of contradictories in our poet, with the remarkable
approximation of his style to Boccaccio's and Cervantes' prose,
as "gründlich, elegant, nett, *pedantisch* und vollständig," may

puzzle some people, but they do not puzzle me. What a critical genius must a German have had who, about 1800 and before he himself was thirty, combined with the above-cited judgments of Klopstock and Goethe, recognition of the facts that Wieland and Richter sin from formlessness, and from having "not aesthetic or comic *spirit,* but only aesthetic or comic *moods,*" *and* that Schiller "starts from too definite a point, and draws in too sharp and hard an outline." "Man ist allein mit allem was man liebt" may be said, by any one who likes, to be mere "dropping into poetry" in feeling as in form. Again: it is not so to me. And the postil on a highly aggressive text, "Die Welt muss *romanticisirt* werden," is not so aggressive as it looks.

I am, however, inclined to think that there is still further improvement in the fragments and thoughts of the *third* volume. This was not published till nearly twenty years after Carlyle wrote the Essay by which, in all probability, most Englishmen know Novalis [see excerpt dated 1829]. But I should venture to recommend, to any one who wishes to understand him, the reading of it both first and last. (pp. 386-89)

How much more critical and more informing is the confession that "Shakespeare is darker to him than Greece"—that he is more at home with Aristophanes' jokes than with Shakespeare's—not merely than the old abuse, but than certain kinds of laudation! What a combination . . . of *giustizia, potestate, sapienzia, e amore* (not a bad definition, by the way, if I may dare to borrow it, of the qualifications of the critic) is there in the saying that Goethe is "der wahre *Statthalter* des Poetischen Geistes auf Erden"! The words—idle paradox as they may seem to some—"Moments may occur when A B C books and Compendia seem to us poetical," are a better text for a whole aesthetic—or, at least, for a whole theory of real criticism—than *oratio sensitiva perfecta* or any of its clan. So is this: "By industrious and intelligent study of the classics of the Ancients, there arises for us a classical literature which the Ancients themselves had not." How just the observation that "Lessing saw too clearly: and so missed the feeling of the *undefined* Whole"!

These are but specimens. But I shall venture to say of them that for awaking the critical power, and qualifying the critical taste where it exists—as examples of that critical unity of subject and object which has been so often spoken of—they are specimens of some significance. There is only one other person who can, I think, be yoked with Friedrich von Hardenberg. If you want critical system, range of actual critic examination, and the like, you must go elsewhere. But for critical *magic*—for the critical "Open sesame!"—go to the two contemporaries, Novalis and Joubert. (pp. 389-90)

> George Saintsbury, "Goethe and His Contemporaries," in his A History of Criticism and Literary Taste in Europe from the Earliest Texts to the Present Day: Modern Criticism, Vol. III, *1911. Reprint by William Blackwood & Sons Ltd., 1949, pp. 352-405.*

GEORG LUKÁCS   (essay date 1916)

[*Lukács, a Hungarian literary critic and philosopher, is acknowledged as a leading proponent of Marxist thought. His development of Marxist ideology was part of a broader system in which he sought to further the values of rationalism (peace and progress), humanism (Socialist politics), and traditionalism (Realist literature) over the countervalues of irrationalism (war), totalitarianism (reactionary politics), and modernism (post-Realist literature). In his major works Lukács explicated his belief that "unless art can be made creatively consonant with history and human needs, it will always offer a counterworld of escape and marvelous waste." In the excerpt below, Lukács examines Novalis's style from the perspective of his handling of reality. Lukács posits that Novalis failed in his attempt to recreate "the broken unity between reality and transcendence," which thus remain only tenuously connected in his works. This essay was first published in 1916.*]

[The ironic Romantic presentation of reality contains a great danger] which only Goethe—and not always he—succeeded in escaping. It is the danger of romanticising reality to a point where it becomes a sphere totally beyond reality or, still more dangerously from the point of view of artistic form-giving, a sphere completely free from problems, for which the forms of the novel are then no longer sufficient. Novalis, who rejected Goethe's work as prosaic and anti-poetic precisely on these grounds, sets the fairy-tale—transcendence realised in reality—as the goal and canon of epic poetry against the method used in *Wilhelm Meister.* 'Wilhelm Meister's Years of Apprenticeship,' he writes, 'is in a sense a completely prosaic and modern work. The Romantic element is absent from it, and so is the poetry of nature—the miraculous. It deals only with ordinary, human things; nature and mysticism are quite forgotten. It is a poeticised story of bourgeois domestic life. The miraculous is dismissed from it as mere poetry and exaltation. Artistic atheism is the spirit of this book . . . It is at bottom . . . unpoetic to the highest degree, however poetical the writing may be.' And again, Novalis' own harking back to the age of the chivalrous epics was not accidental but the result of that enigmatic and yet so deeply rational elective affinity between an author's fundamental intention and the matter of his works. Novalis, like the authors of those epics, wanted to create a totality of revealed transcendence within an earthly reality (although we can speak only of an *a priori* sharing of aims, not of any direct or indirect 'influence'). His stylisation, like that of the chivalrous epics, had therefore to be oriented towards the fairy-tale. But whereas the intention of the authors of the medieval epics was epic in a naïvely natural sense and consisted in giving form directly to real life (the glimpsed presence of the transcendent and, with it, the transfiguration of reality into a fairy-tale being, merely a gift they received from their historico-philosophical situation), for Novalis this fairy-tale reality as a re-creation of the broken unity between reality and transcendence became a conscious goal. And this is precisely why he could not achieve a decisive and complete synthesis. His reality is so much weighed down by the earthly gravity of idealessness, his transcendent world is so airy, so vapid, because it stems too directly from the philosophico-postulative sphere of pure abstraction, that the two are unable to unite in a living totality. And so the artistic fault which Novalis so penetratingly detected in Goethe is even greater—is irreparable—in his own work.

The triumph of poetry, its transfiguring and redeeming domination of the entire universe, has not the constitutive force to make all earthly and prosaic things follow it into paradise; the romanticising of reality merely gives reality a lyrical semblance of poetry, but this semblance cannot be translated into events—into epic terms; and so the genuinely epic in Novalis' work suffers from the same problematic as in Goethe's (but to a more acute degree) or is evaded altogether by lyrical reflexions and mood-pictures. Novalis' stylisation remains a purely reflexive one, superficially disguising the danger but in fact only intensifying it. Lyrical, mood-dominated romanticising of the structures of social reality cannot, given the fact that reality at the present stage of development lacks pre-stabilised harmony, relate to the essential life of the interiority. Since Novalis rejected Goethe's solution of seeking an ironical, fluctuating balance maintained from the point of view of the subject and touching as little as possible upon the actual structures of society, no other way was left open to him but to poeticise these structures in their objective existence and to create a world which was beautiful and harmonious but closed within itself and unrelated to anything outside: a world connected only reflexively, only by mood, not in any epic sense, with the ultimate realised transcendence or with the problematic interiority: a world which therefore could not become a true totality. (pp. 138-40)

> *Georg Lukács, "'Wilhelm Meister's Years of Apprenticeship' as an Attempted Synthesis," in his* The Theory of the Novel: A Historico-Philosophical Essay on the Forms of Great Epic Literature, *translated by Anna Bostock, The MIT Press, 1971, pp. 132-43.* *

HERMANN HESSE (essay date 1924)

> [*Hesse is considered one of the most important German novelists of the twentieth century. Lyrical in style, his novels are concerned with a search on the part of their protagonists for self-knowledge and for insight into the relationship between physical and spiritual realms.* Das Glasperlenspiel (Magister Ludi), *his last major work, is generally held to epitomize Hesse's achievement, delineating a complex vision that intermingles art and religion to convey a sense of harmony unifying the diverse elements of existence. This work, along with his earlier novels, established Hesse's reputation as an author who to many readers and critics approximates the role of a modern sage. In this brief excerpt from his* My Belief, *Hesse describes Novalis's style, noting that his influence on later writers derives from his "positive, magical, extraordinary relationship to death." Hesse's comments on Novalis were written in 1924.*]

Among the life stories of remarkable men of intellect the ones that have always aroused the deepest interest in later generations have been those which clearly expressed the fact that genius is not simply a matter of intellectual development but at the same time and principally a biological matter. In modern German intellectual history the noblest figures of this sort are Hölderlin, Novalis, and Nietzsche. While Hölderlin and Nietzsche, after life had become impossible for them, withdrew into madness, Novalis withdrew into death, and not into the form of it that intrudes so often in the case of genius, suicide; rather he died by consciously consuming himself from within, a magical, early blossoming followed by an enormously fruitful death.—It is precisely from this strange end of the poet, from his positive, magical, extraordinary relationship to death, that his strongest influence radiates. And this influence is far deeper than the surface of our intellectual life permits us to imagine. In his own time Novalis was understood by only a few, and even later, yes, even today, his readers have been small in number. But every serious reader has caught fire from that marvelous, almost dangerously animated spirit, from the blazing intensity of that life. Intimate acquaintance with Novalis means for any perceptive spirit a deep and magical experience, that is, the experience of initiation, of consecration into mystery. (pp. 130-31)

[Novalis] died of consumption, but what is the signficance of that? Others have died at an early age from consumption, Novalis's own siblings suffered that fate, but only from Novalis, only from his grave, radiates that magic attraction; only he, instead of suffering death, entered into it like a banished king returning to his palace out of the grayness of a foreign land.

He left behind the most marvelous and mysterious work in the intellectual history of Germany. Just as his short, externally uneventful life strangely gives the impression of great abundance and seems to have exhausted every sensuous and every spiritual experience, so the runes of his work reveal beneath the playful, enchantingly flowery surface all the abysses of the spirit, apotheosis through the spirit, and despair of the spirit. Novalis lived out his fate consciously and trustingly, aware of its tragic aspect and yet superior to it, since a creative piety allowed him to hold death of small account.

His poetry remains, still read by only a few, still signifying to those few a gate into the realm of magic, yes, almost the gift of a new dimension. (pp. 131-32)

> *Hermann Hesse, "Postscript to 'Novalis, Documents on His Life and Death'," in his* My Belief: Essays on Life and Art, *edited by Theodore Ziolkowski, translated by Denver Lindley, Farrar, Straus and Giroux, 1974, pp. 130-32.*

WALTER SILZ (essay date 1929)

> [*In his examination of the German Romantics, Silz discusses Novalis as "a composite of extraordinary contradictions," analyzing the interplay between asceticism and sensuality, reason and irrationality, and structure and chaos in his works.*]

Of Novalis it could be said, as Marie von Kleist said of her cousin, that he was a composite of extraordinary contradictions. He seemed to combine the qualities of a staid bourgeois and an eccentric genius. He was a poet of metaphysical craving and of attachment to mundane reality, of religious adoration and sensuous delight; a saint and an epicure; a dreamer and a reasoner; a devout child and a superior, penetrating critic; now lost in purely abstract mathematical speculation, and then again busied . . . with the project of a publishing establishment which should assure to him and his friends the profits of their literary labors. In his notebooks we find deep mystical intuitions side by side with such practical devices as double windows to keep rooms warm, or pious meditations followed by the remark that he has once again overeaten. In his poems, ascetic spirituality gives place at times to frank sensuality and even coarseness. (pp. 127-28)

Novalis could write ethereal lyrics and sober, matter-of-fact descriptions of travel; he required of the poet both inward and outward sense, introspective contemplation and sharp observation of external reality. . . . Far from being lost in "Romantic subjectivity," Kleist and Novalis strove in their poetry for the same union of the objective and subjective that Friedrich Schlegel desired in theory.

Novalis shares with Kleist and others of his generation a striking dualism of rational and irrational attributes. This dualism is . . . characteristic of the early Romanticists; it reaches a tragic intensity in them, but it is found, in a less critical stage, already in the older writers of this Classic-Romantic age: Goethe and Schiller wrote not only imaginative poetry but scientific and philosophical treatises, and the relation of reason and feeling was one of the chief problems of the period. . . . Novalis, like Friedrich Schlegel, dreamed of reconciling reason and feeling and fusing them into one intellectual power. (pp. 129-30)

Novalis himself believed fantasy to be the chief trait of his contradictory personality, but in the estimation of his friends it appeared counterbalanced by equally strong reason, and the uniting of reason and fantasy seemed to him to constitute religion. . . . Even during his most poignant grief at the death of Sophie and of his brother, his strong intellect never relinquished its supremacy. Yet the author of *Die Lehrlinge zu Sais* esteemed feeling as the most divine and most natural of all human powers, and believed that its cultivation would bring about the return of the golden age, when men understood and lived in harmony with nature. Thought was to him a less direct and less profound approach to the truth of nature than feeling. . . . It is related of Novalis that he planned to write a new hymnbook, because the religious songs of modern writers, even those of Gellert, seemed to him to contain too little fantasy, to be calculated for cold reason and not for warm and immediate emotion.

One does not readily imagine the keenness and power of intellect that lay behind the large, soulful, childlike eyes which look at us from the traditional portrait of Novalis. There was a period in his life, as in Kleist's and Schlegel's, when reason reigned supreme. . . . The author of the mystical *Hymnen an die Nacht* and the logical *Fragmente* considered it impossible and undesirable to divorce the poet and the philosopher, and it has been said that his whole poetry is the product of a rational process. His reason had the same inflexible tenacity as Kleist's in the pursuit of ideas. He was convinced, like Kleist, of the need of rigid self-training, of a rational "plan of life"; self-perfection, "Bildung," was his aim also. (pp. 130-32)

One fails to gain from the perusal of Novalis' writings the impression of formlessness, haziness, and confusion which is alleged to be so typical of Romantic literature. In his fragments and letters one finds lucidity and reason, and not only the flash but the steady glow of intellect. In the crystalline transparency of the *Hymnen an die Nacht* there is no playing with forms and moods, no jingling of pretty bells, no arbitrary vagueness. And *Heinrich von Ofterdingen* appears on closer view, even with Klingsohr's mystical "Märchen," to be not a work of wayward fancy, but a well-ordered and meaningful composition that corresponds closely to its author's intention. In other words, Novalis' works are remarkably free from those faults which can be so abundantly illustrated from the works of Tieck. (pp. 132-33)

In Novalis' library there were almost as many books on science as on literature, and his life, like Kleist's, can be divided into a rational-scientific and a poetic period. He studied physics, philosophy, and psychology for years, and his observations in these fields seem not to have been without scientific value; he was well versed in mathematics, chemistry, and mechanics, especially in mining. His writings, like Kleist's, bear traces of his extensive study of science. With a catholicity of intellect like Kleist's he excluded no field of human knowledge from his investigation; he wished to study all sciences and make one science of them. . . . (p. 134)

Novalis, like Kleist, found a metaphysical solace in the study of science. Kleist, in a mood of personal and public dejection in Königsberg, seeks comfort in scientific work, and Novalis in his bereavement experiences "the wondrous healing powers" of the sciences. . . . (p. 136)

Their remorseless rationality turned also upon itself: Kleist shares with Novalis and Friedrich Schlegel an unhappy bent toward self-analysis, of which his very earliest letters give evidence. . . . [Novalis' diary betrays a high] degree of morbid introspection: every thought, every emotion, every degree of emotion is here set down; every lapse from his purpose to die, every symptom of his recrudescent joy in living, is mercilessly

recorded; one must conceive Novalis' life at this time to have been self-conscious to the verge of insanity. He recognized, as sharply as the author of *Über das Marionettentheater*, the dangers of this excessive reflection upon himself. But it had become more or less habitual to this age of "intellektuelle Anschauung," and it is one of the causes of "Romantic irony." (pp. 137-38)

Novalis was, like Kleist, excessively preoccupied with problems of sexuality; even his cult of death, like Kleist's, contains a large erotic element. One need only compare the phraseology and imagery of Kleist's last letters with those of parts of the *Hymnen an die Nacht* or "Das Lied der Toten" to distinguish this peculiar blending of love and death. Novalis entertained the project of a novel which would have been strangely like Kleist's actual end, and Heinrich and Mathilde in *Ofterdingen* conceive the possibility that their love may become a door to death. (p. 139)

Kleist's and Novalis' conception of love, which reached such extremes of Romanticism, began, like Friedrich Schlegel's, in the Rationalism of the eighteenth century. They regarded women as indubitably secondary in the hierarchy of creation, addicted to the mediocre and trifling, and inferior to men in all mental capacities. The morality of women is based on feeling, that of men on reason; women resemble children, even plants; their sphere is very limited, and they are connected only through their husbands with the momentous life of the world. And yet on the other hand what idealization of womanhood in the poetic works of these men! They both were in love, not with their fiancées, but with a poetic ideal of them; they seemed attracted to these simple girls by their very simplicity; here was material with which the poets' creative powers could work. Kleist's sober reason did not deceive itself as to the mediocrity of Wilhelmine, and Novalis well knew, as his cool diagnosis shows, that Sophie was a crude, illiterate child with a mentality below her years. But what a transfigured being is Käthchen, or Alcmene, or the angelic love of Novalis' lyrics! Thus, even as lovers, these poets reveal their characteristic dualism of critical reason and emotional fantasy. (pp. 140-41)

Walter Silz, "Three Early Romanticists," in his Early German Romanticism: Its Founders and Heinrich von Kleist, *Cambridge, Mass.: Harvard University Press, 1929, pp. 106-41.**

R. PEACOCK (essay date 1938)

[*Peacock comments on theme, style, and imagery in several of Novalis's works, terming the "preoccupation with a metaphysical world" the fundamental trait of his poetry. Stressing Novalis's visionary qualities, Peacock also discusses the writer's unique and highly personal view of religion.*]

It is strange that the position of Novalis as the only creative genius of the older Romantic School in Germany should so long have been obscured. . . . Probably the speculative side of romanticism, that ferment of philosophical thinking they caused round about the year 1798, and Novalis's collaboration in it, have overshadowed his poetic work and its uniqueness. For Novalis had a philosophic and scientific mind equal to that of Friedrich Schlegel in its alertness, elasticity, adventurousness, and profundity, and superior in the diversity of sciences it embraced; so that a certain degree of congeniality made for a good understanding and enjoyable co-operation in literary tasks. But Novalis was, too, a visionary, with his own life, whilst Schlegel, though brilliant and suggestive, was a critic and historian. His chief faculty was a masterful intellect; he had no soul such as Novalis possessed, deep, full, and initiate. Novalis's poems, sprung from a genuine inspiration, have a life that the critical and philosophical work of the romanticists could never have; a life, moreover, that could only come from an individual spirit and not from the kind of collaborative literary production in which the romanticists, as a 'school', in indulged. The predominance of the critical spirit, and the preoccupation with a theory of poetry, might create, indeed, do create, amongst the unwary the impression that romantic critical theory produced romantic poetry; that the latter was composed according to a formula. The theories of the Schlegels, however, produced nothing whatever, unless it be the salonesque verse of August Wilhelm, or the spiritless disorder and undisciplined intellectual conceits of *Lucinde*. But they did throw light on poetry and literature that already existed and had existed for a long time before the work they all admired—*Wilhelm Meister*—appeared; and though this light may not have been pure, showing up everything in its completeness as the sun's light does, but one tinged by the colour of their own temperament, making some things stand out in relief at the cost of others, yet it did illumine much that had been obscure, and rendered critical service of a high order. There is, of course, a relationship between Novalis's poems and the criticism of the Schlegels; but it is the relationship of derived thought to the living spirit; his poems make Novalis not a mere collaborator, still less a follower, but rather the leader of the group.

An urgent disposition towards the transcendental is the common origin of those works that give Novalis a high rank as poet, though they are so few in number—two unfinished romances, one of them, indeed, only just begun, and a score of poems. The fundamental trait of them all is their preoccupation with a metaphysical world. It takes different forms in different works; or rather, Novalis finds his way to the transcendental by different approaches; now by way of nature, now through love of a woman, now by the mediation of Christ. But however unlike these various approaches may seem to be, his peculiar vision of a transcendental state remains constant; and the effect of this is to draw closer together those various media, nature, the loved woman, and Christ, since they are all the objects of the poet's longing, and since their names are used as symbols of the transcendental state. This process of *rapprochement* is a violent one for those who distinguish between God and nature, between love of a woman and love of Christ, however anxious they are to see an ordered relationship in things, de-pendent on a supreme Law-giver. But violence was one of the things Novalis, and his friends, enjoyed; they liked, on occasion, to be reckless, wilful and shameless, even impious; they then felt that absolute freedom of spirit they demanded and coveted. It is an element in all their activity, even in their religion, as we see here with Novalis. For in considering him we have to do with a trend of religious feeling, however unusual, capricious, or irreligious it might sometimes appear; the very paradox would please the romanticists.

There are the clearest indications of Novalis's nature philosophy in the early fragment *Die Lehrlinge zu Sais*. Its theme is the search for the meaning of nature and of human existence in its dependence on nature, and it consists of a series of conversations between an apprentice, his friends, and their master, in which various theories about man, nature, and life are discussed. For these theories Novalis draws on the thought of past and present, and from them emerge gradually his own principal ideas. The different, contradictory arguments confuse the apprentice, but they are suddenly broken off and the so-

called sprightly playfellow, freeing him from the criss-cross of opinions, tells him of feeling and love. He does this by means of a fairy-story. Tenderly and gracefully, and with a sweet flow of language all his own, Novalis tells the story of Hyazinth and Rosenblüt; how Hyazinth leaves his home and beloved playmate Rosenblüt and goes far away to seek Isis, the veiled maiden, the mother of things, the goddess of fertility. After a long time he reaches the dwelling-place of the goddess; in ecstasy he enters and then sinks into sleep—for dream alone gives access to the holy of holies. He wanders through many chambers, all earthly things are left behind, and at last he stands before the heavenly maiden; he raises the veil—and Rosenblüt sinks into his arms.

The teaching which is embodied in so pregnant and lively a manner in this delightful story is that the force of love stirring in one's own heart is the key to the true being of nature. Speculation is therewith put on one side, for final truths are communicated through other organs than reason. This lesson is the kernel of what is now said by a beautiful youth, in whom we hear the voice of the poet himself. Some thoughts are retained from the earlier conversations; they are, briefly, as follows: man and nature are really one, and the relation between them is of a religious kind. Nature is also intimately connected with poetry, and thus nature, religion, and poetry are very close together in the thought of the poet, a point to which we shall come back. There is, further, a gradual progress towards a new age of harmony between nature and man; and poets are the prophets of this new age. These ideas receive a new complexion and a more precise meaning by now being combined with three new ones: *Liebe Wollust, Genuss* (love, voluptuousness, pleasure) which recur again and again in Novalis, to the point of satiety. They are obviously three aspects of one thing. The beautiful youth reveals the true working of nature: incessant generation, and its energizing force, voluptuousness. The most evident symbol of this process is water, as the element infinitely capable of embracing and mingling. . . . (pp. 323-26)

In Novalis, however, the world of bodies and forms is dissipated; his aim is to shake off the forms of our consciousness and participate in the endless flux of universal life, to give up his own personality and sink into the voluptuous mingling process. It is not entirely clear what he really means, and that is probably because he is struggling to express himself in a medium which is inadequate. For the words he is obliged to use to describe his transcendental state are heavy with sensual, physiological, and organic associations, whereas he constantly hints at processes and organs far more refined and spiritual than earthly man knows or possesses. The mingling and embracing of fluids and essences which forms the transcendental is not an organic process, but seems to be a spiritual counterpart of the organic processes of nature. Moreover, being spiritual, it is conceived by Novalis as being conscious of itself; it is knowing. Thus Novalis seizes on the essential principle of nature, generation, and then makes it into an absolute, spiritual principle, that can be called divinity. He thinks it is possible for man to apprehend this by means of a delicate, inner organ. Here appears that element of magic in Novalis, who, by means of a mysterious power, strains beyond the ordinary experience of the human senses. The language of the fragment reflects the tendency: the prose of the first parts, although glowing with enthusiasm, is yet the language of thought, but gradually it passes into the most intense expression of an inspired vision of supra-sensuous mysteries. It is by this particular contribution that Novalis has enriched the general poetic experience of nature.

Now, an experience of this kind being religious in character, since it relates to the absolute, divine significance of things, that near connexion we have mentioned between poetry and religion in Novalis's work becomes clearer; poetry proclaims the mysteries of religion. Thus nature, religion, and poetry are bound up with one another in the most intimate manner. And this gives grounds for the belief that only poets are enabled to see and communicate such mysteries; they are therefore seers and educators. (pp. 328-29)

Thus we see Novalis as a man predisposed to religion and mysticism in a rare degree, and in *Die Lehrlinge zu Sais* we have had experience of it. But the most significant unfolding of spiritual life in him was occasioned by the death of the girl he loved, Sophie von Kühn. (p. 330)

In his attitude towards her there is combined love and reverence; both the feeling within himself of the voluptuous creative impulse, the longing for mingling, and at the same time the perception of a purer spiritual life.... [She gives him] that key to the knowledge of nature's true being that Hyazinth discovered; but she is also a force making for spiritual regeneration. The implications of *Die Lehrlinge zu Sais* are that death is the gateway to participation in nature's inmost being, to the dissolution which enables one to sink into the eternal flux of life. Moreover, some early fragments, in an apprehension of the truth, point to death as the real life, and affirm that the dark night of the grave is in reality the bright daylight. Sophie's death brings these half-perceived truths to maturity, as the sun opens the budding flower. The Night of death which holds Sophie is the transcendental sphere of love and true life; and whether Novalis speaks of descending into this night or of being united and mingling with Sophie in death, he means in both cases the same thing, participation in the eternal process of love, the transcendental life; he means quitting earthly life to be taken up into that true life, which he conceives as an eternal flux and as a spirit, as the eternal spiritual, from which flow lower forms of life. Night is understood, in the sense of the old Greek myth, as the pregnant sphere, the fertile chaos, the progenitress; but also, in a spiritual sense, as the absolute, all-embracing, everlasting; and in this respect the idea of the higher life embodied in Sophie helps us to understand more clearly the spiritual nature of the transcendental in Novalis's conception. The living Sophie is a sign for Novalis of a higher existence; the dead Sophie is identical with the transcendental.

Night, then, in all this complexity of meaning, is a homeland for which the poet longs; after Sophie's death his whole feeling is directed to night, in such a degree that he wished to follow her into death (though the method he contemplated—volition alone—introduces a touch of intellectual experimenting which, whilst entirely in keeping with his character, spoils the purity of his sentiment). Love and nostalgia combine and produce that state of emotional excitement in him from which sprang the *Hymnen an die Nacht.* (pp. 331-32)

Let us bring out the peculiar character of this poem by comparing it with others. In Young's *Night Thoughts* a cult is made of night and thoughts of death, but only out of a spirit of sentimentality, and the wish to indulge in melancholy moods; this sets a limit to Young's influence on Novalis. Again, the enthusiasm of later German romanticists for night and death springs rather from a childlike, primitive awe at the secret things of nature, or from the desire of the weary for the rest that liberates. To understand how deep a significance love has in the *Hymnen an die Nacht,* let us recall Lamartine's *Le Lac,* a well-known and typical product of French romanticism. It

represents a despairing and sorrowful attempt to cling to the memory of lost love in a beautiful landscape, such memory alone being a sure possession. Novalis goes deeper than all these; he seeks not the cessation and calming of life in death, but the renewal of life, he seeks regeneration, the essential life. He is similar only to Shelley in philosophy and visionary experience.

The fourth Hymn sings the praise of night as the spiritual sphere of fertile mingling, the theatre of voluptuous creative processes. But new conceptions are brought in, for in an unexpected but most significant way the Cross of Christ appears. (pp. 333-34)

This gives us the third principal element—a Christian tendency—of the background of Novalis's poems. We must be careful not to look upon this sudden turn as a straightforward confession of Christian faith. It is due to the fusion in Novalis's thought and feeling of two worlds: that of the night which holds Sophie, and the Christian beyond. For the significance of the latter dawns on him, now that Sophie, his own very life, is lost in night. It was Christ who unsealed the mystery of the grave. With that act a new era was born, a new life; it presented to Novalis, then, a parallel to his own experience, as the third Hymn records it. Sophie and Christ, and all they represent, thus blend in the imagination of the poet. This interpenetration of two originally separate spiritual spheres is seen especially clearly in the fourth of the *Geistliche Lieder....* (p. 334)

The connexion between nature, Sophie, and Christ, and the character of Novalis's religious feeling, can be made more explicit still by reference to his conception of 'mediation'. In a famous fragment in *Blütenstaub* Novalis asserts that nothing is more indispensable to true religiosity than a mediating member (*Mittelglied*), which connects us with the divinity. Each man must be free to choose his own mediator. That religion is the true one which takes the mediator simply as a mediator (not as the divinity itself), and considers it to be, as it were, the organ of the divinity, its sensuous form. Novalis distinguishes then between pantheistic and monotheistic mediators. Anything, he says, can be an organ of divinity, a mediator, by man raising it to that position; this is the pantheistic interpretation. On the other hand, there can be a single mediator, a God-man, for instance, like Jesus; and this according to the belief of each individual. These apparently incompatible ideas can be reconciled, in Novalis's opinion, by conceiving two degrees or levels of mediation; first, things—the pantheistic degree; secondly, a single God-man—the monotheistic degree. The God-man mediates between things and the divinity.... Religion is here translated into a completely personal sphere by the force, indeed, by the violence, of this one personality, Novalis. He creates a religion for himself. It consists of pantheistic, ideal-human, and Christian elements, which he chooses arbitrarily, and connects by means of this idea of mediation. One asks, what is the object of such mediation?—And the answer is: the 'divinity' (*Gottheit*), not a clear 'God'; Novalis avoids the word God in this connexion. By 'divinity' we have undoubtedly to understand the transcendental, that metaphysical state or existence which occasions in him all his nostalgia. Nature, Sophie, Christ are the mediators he chooses to link himself with that metaphysical life which is the true reality, that voluptuous and mysterious mingling of all things. And though these various mediators follow after each other in the course of his spiritual development, they do not replace each other, but indicate a gradual widening of the possibilities of religious experience for Novalis. Thus Sophie remains the 'sun' of night; she is not displaced by Christ, but their figures mingle.

Thus, too, Christ is seen pantheistically intermingled with all the fluid things of nature. . . . In this way he makes nature, his beloved, and Christ serve his purposes. They are a trinity which have a unity only in his consciousness, or in the use to which he puts them. It is extremely difficult to determine whether he imagined a personal reunion with Sophie, or Christ, in the flux and intermingling of the beyond. But he attributed such magic properties to the absolute spirit, such all-penetrating consciousness and all-powerful will, or caprice, that we can fairly believe he thought everything possible, both the most extreme and desirable degree of intermingling, and at the same time the ability to perceive persons at will. A related difficulty, already noticed in considering *Die Lehrlinge zu Sais,* is that of understanding the spirituality of the eternal flux he describes in such sensuous terms. For the refinement of sensuous vocabulary he uses emphasizes the sensuousness just as much as it hints at something supra-sensuous. We can conceive with ease an organic flux of things; we can grasp, too, the idea of a spiritual state; but a combination of both eludes us. And yet it is precisely the combination that is important, that is so unique; it is precisely the combination, we can be sure, that fascinated and held Novalis in its sway, as did, in a smaller way, the corresponding notion of 'thinking and feeling at once'.

The most comprehensive expression for the complex spiritual experience of Novalis and all the longing it induced in him is the so-called *Abendmahlshymne,* which, in consequence, is at the centre of his work. . . . This astonishing poem shows to the full extent how personal the religious feeling of Novalis was, to what extent he took material and symbols from a religion of wide appeal and used them to express feelings which only he had; and it shows, too, in the most striking manner, all the wildness of his transcendental thirst. Comparison with the Christian sacrament is scarcely possible, for there the believer participates by means of bread and wine in the Body and Blood of Christ to refresh his spirit. But in the poem, this act of cult is exploited by the poet in order to represent the mystic mingling not with Christ alone, but with nature, too, and Sophie, and all things. . . . Here is no celebration of Christ, the Redeemer from sin; Christian cult is used to reveal the transcendental condition of voluptuous intermingling, of endless flux, of chaos. The longing of the poet for eternal love and dissolution discharges itself here with such power of vision and force of emotion, that the very language, strained to the utmost, almost bursts the bounds of the possible and threatens itself to become chaotic.

All the motives we have mentioned recur again and again in the *Hymnen an die Nacht* and the *Geistliche Lieder* which follow them, recalling continually the spiritual core of Novalis's life. The same words and phrases, into which the utmost force and meaning are pressed, are used again and again in his poems, in varied combination, to express rapturous or consuming longing and love-desire, or the ecstatic urge beyond earthly bounds, or the drunken surrender of one who lets himself sink into the eternal flood. . . . In the *Geistliche Lieder,* it is true, there is, too, a simpler language, which lends to them a pious, child-like quality; it is one of their principal charms, and provides a strange contrast to the deep spiritual turmoil of their origin.

The *Hymnen an die Nacht* have a considerable narrative and even dramatic element in them, because they tell of the crisis which occurred in the life of Novalis. The *Geistliche Lieder* flow from the settled emotion that followed the crisis, from the constant nostalgia for the home beyond life. Characteristic for the difference between them is the transition from free rhythms to fixed metrical forms; the poet felt no restraint in the expressing of his own intense, violent personal experience, but now he feels and seeks a certain connexion with the Christian community, so that he is no longer entirely free. For the same reason further Christian motives are introduced. . . . But again we see how Novalis, in spite of his intention to write for a Christian congregation, really stands alone, how he expresses not what a congregation feels when at prayer and in communion with its God, but his own metaphysical needs. Hence his *Lieder* are far more independent as poetry, compared with the subservient position of ordinary religious songs or hymns. The religious feelings of the latter are general, though the poet, in the role of spokesman, may express them more delicately or forcibly than others could; the poems of Novalis are the result of the unique religious experience of a single man. Novalis owes the greater liveliness, intensity, fervour, and mysticism of these *Lieder* to his love experience. The fourth *Lied* and its connexion with the third hymn are a proof of this. Let us recall the kernel of the Christian faith, the redemption of sins, and ask where it is to be found in the work of Novalis. It is nowhere mentioned; neither are repentance, humility, charity, spiritual virtues without which Christianity is inconceivable. (pp. 335-40)

Finally, then, these *Lieder* fail as [pieces] . . . for congregational use. (p. 340)

A rapid glance at *Heinrich von Ofterdingen* will be enough to show how this romance, too, receives its substance from the same sources as the poems. The transcendental world, the vision of which is communicated by these poems, is called by Novalis 'poetic', and his conception of poetry is determined by it; poetry is simply the revelation of it by means of words. Poetic revelation communicates to earthly men the eternal life of the beyond. The poet, then, is a mediator (in the religious sense of Novalis), a seer and teacher, as we have already seen in considering the *Lehrlinge zu Sais.* The romance *Heinrich von Ofterdingen* represents the development of a poet, seer, teacher of this kind. We recognize Novalis himself. Time and milieu are provided by the Middle Ages, a poetic age in the imagination of Novalis, since they stand under the sign of Christian otherworldliness. . . . For Novalis, music is simply movement, spiritualized movement, a symbol, therefore, of the transcendental state of flux; it is, too, the most adequate, intense expression of infinite longing. For that reason he introduces *Lieder* into his romance; they are an approach to music, for the meaning of the words is less important than the *Stimmung* they provoke, than the longing they convey. Secondly, Heinrich's dream, that he is immersed with Mathilde in the flowing of those eternal waters he so often mentions. It is clear, from what has been said, how it comes about that love and Mathilde give Heinrich the key to the poetic world. Klingsohr, the poet, shows him this world, and in the form of a fairy-tale (*Märchen*). The fairy-tale is Novalis's ideal of poetry, because it gives free rein to fantasy, because all limits and restrictions are broken down, because chance reigns supreme; in other words, it is the image of chaos, of a state of flux. But Klingsohr's *Märchen* contains a moral which corresponds to the whole tendency of the book: that poetry liberates, or redeems, the world. We saw how in the *Lehrlinge zu Sais* the fairy-tale of Hyazinth and Rosenblüt was a revelation that liberated the apprentice from his doubts. The peculiarity of Klingsohr's *Märchen,* compared with this and others, is that it is poetic representation, and at the same time shows the will to poetry, the conviction and teaching that poetry is an instrument of revelation. The very point, wrapped up as it is in the most extraordinary and complicated trappings, is a demand it makes that poetry should fulfil a certain function; but, being poetry itself—according to the poet's own ideal of poetry—it is itself fulfilling that function whilst teaching it. Add to this that an author, a poet, within the larger framework of his romance, makes a mature poet use this *Märchen* to teach a young one what poetry should be:—in what folds of that notorious romantic irony we are being wrapped! In spite of his independence and his superior creative genius, there were elements in his temperament that Novalis had in common with his witty friends. The romance was thus in danger of the capricious play of sovereign and absolute mind; it shows a tendency to the chaos Novalis loved, the chaos which is conscious of itself; and Novalis himself says of *Ofterdingen,* it was gradually to become a *Märchen.* It reflects the transcendental of Novalis's conception.

What is our reaction to these poetic works, the unity of which we have tried to demonstrate and explain? Whatever graces **Heinrich von Ofterdingen** has, the poems, and especially the **Hymnen an die Nacht,** scarcely occasion the serene joy, or the warm and pleasurable excitement, or the still satisfaction that poetry generally gives; but they disturb profoundly, as everything must do that opens up, whether to enjoy or to conquer, recesses of life into which the good light of day never penetrates. One reads these poems with admiration, no doubt, still more with astonishment, and recoiling from the abysses they reveal. Only those who in themselves feel the same urge as Novalis will be able to surrender completely and really 'enjoy' them as Novalis might wish them to. But whoever adheres to an ideal of human and earthly life, will reject the fundamental tendency of Novalis to dissolution and chaos, in however spiritualized a form he may conceive it. And yet his poems are so significant, the poetic diction so compelling in its magic quality, that they must be considered by all who are concerned with poetry at all.

In the light of Goethe's work—and let Goethe be taken as representing the whole of humanist culture—that of Novalis with its mysticism, its emotionalism, its strange, 'magical' control of sensuous and spiritual experiences, its urge to dissolution, to eternal movement and chaos, is a reaction. For it offended Goethe's ideal of human mastery within the bounds of moderation, it destroyed the ideal of form. His work is the negation of the values and art-standards won by Goethe from the Greeks. But in spite of the fact that Novalis joined with his romantic friends, and, in a common intoxication of thought and feeling, nailed Christianity to his banner, his work indicates by no means a simple, clear reversion to Christianity, as is sometimes affirmed of him as well as of the whole romantic movement. It puts forward new values, in the formation of which old, Christian ones have been used; but the new values are of so peculiar and personal a kind, and the old Christian ones are so adapted to personal ends, and in consequence deprived of their significance for the general run of Christians, that Novalis appears in a solitary position. He is neither the Brutus of the old religion, nor the Christ of a new gospel.

His connexion with that general revival of the poetry of Christian chivalry, especially amongst his successors, is thus seen to be anything but direct and simple. For his work went much deeper; it was a poetry devoted to the transcendental and having roots in his own entirely personal spiritual experiences. And the romanticism of night and death in poems that followed cannot be compared in intensity with his feelings, whether or not one sees his influence, or a similar emotional tendency.

He was, too, far superior to his successors in breadth and force of intellect. Novalis as poet is as solitary as that contemporary of his who was of such different composition, Hölderlin, the representative of the Hellenic ideal. Judged by their inmost kernel, his poems seem to us to spring from such unique earthly and spiritual circumstances that they neither come from a past nor point to a future, but stand alone, with their strangeness and force, their fervent and fantastic vision. (pp. 340-44)

> R. Peacock, ''The Poetry of Novalis,'' in German Studies Presented to Professor H. G. Fiedler, M. V. O., by Pupils, Colleagues, and Friends, on His Seventy-fifth Birthday 28 April, 1937, *Oxford at the Clarendon Press, Oxford, 1938, pp. 323-44.*

AUGUST CLOSS   (essay date 1948)

[*Closs's comments, taken from his introduction to the first complete English translation of* Hymns to the Night, *center on Novalis's handling of style, imagery, symbolism, and theme. Closs deems Novalis's poetry in that work ''the finest product of German Romanticism.''*]

What is more sudden than lightning?—vengeance. What vanishes most swiftly from sight?—unrightful possessions. Who knows the world?—he who knows himself. What remains an eternal mystery?—love.

Such are the riddles of the sphinx as they appear in the fable at the end of the first part of the fragmentary novel, **Heinrich von Ofterdingen,** by Novalis. They are the ore of his own *Weltanschauung,* washed up by the limpid ripple of his rhythmic prose.

Novalis' writing possesses neither Hölderlin's tragic tension nor Schiller's divine pathos. None the less, it is unique in its graceful, almost childlike fervour and sincerity. In his sombre and magnificent **Hymns to the Night** (**Hymnen an die Nacht**) he can indeed rank with either poet in power of imagery and creative activity. These Hymns, written in rhythmic prose and free verse, represent not only the finest product of German Romanticism but belong with Hölderlin's and Goethe's works to the rarest treasures of European lyric poetry.

Immeasurably sad they may appear at first—Dilthey in *Das Erlebnis und die Dichtung,* called them an interminable lament drawn through the depths of night. Actually, however, they reveal themselves not only as the expression of Novalis' yearning for love and death but as the promise of a new and nobler world. Goethe rightly said that Novalis might have become the '*imperator*' of German literature. But it was his fate to die before he had completed his twenty-ninth year. Novalis is the true poet of the German Romantics. Untrammelled imagination is for him the essence of all reality. Soaring above the material, his poetry is yet not divorced from the earth. It is not disembodied flight but embraces everything. Only, the world of the spirit is as true to him as that of the senses. Herein lies the key to an understanding of his poetic personality. (p. 7)

Novalis' **Hymns to the Night** indeed belong in the main, together with Hölderlin's Odes and Hymns, to the mightiest of European lyrics. They are inspired by a vision in which the finite is reflected in infinity and the accidental becomes a symbol. For him the world of poetry is the real one. Mathematics becomes religion, the individual the universe. His poetry is more than seeing, hearing or tasting—it is the language of his innermost self: he is no sickly pervert hankering after death. His poetry is just as far removed from Catullus's *Vivamus,* *mea Lesbia*. In the *Fragmente*, **Blütenstaub** and *Aphorismen* he unfolds before us hitherto unknown treasures of deep worldly wisdom. They are rare seeds of poetic insight. He tries to give an 'encyclopaedia' of poetry and science which to him belong together. Like Herder and Hamann he sees in both a redeeming and ever-developing unity. The way to true knowledge is for him self-examination and this inwardness is only one step from mysticism. (p. 10)

Pain at the loss of the beloved awakens the poet's enthusiasm for the night and his readiness for death. Yet his sorrow is softened by the sight of the heavens and of the landscape that rises steeply. The dream disappears, yet the reality remains, namely the unshakable faith in the beloved. This dream-life is quite conscious. Sophie and Christ overcome death. They return to the light of day, in a new world.

We see that the poet's longing for death is not 'romantically' and morbidly confused, but full of delicacy of feeling and self-possessed. (p. 11)

When in his Hymns Novalis asks the dark night: 'Have you too a heart as mortals have?' Eros, Death and Night merge into one great conception. Night transforms all things again into a new conscious existence. Night is here more than a Romantic transfiguration with winged spirit and 'infinite' eye. Night flows cool and refreshing, she grants us joy and holy sleep, she is eternal, dark and inexpressible—Night is the path to inner being, the way to poetry, to creation. (pp. 12-13)

Novalis himself is the poet of Romantic yearning. His **Hymns to the Night** are . . . without question the most powerful lyrical product of the Jena circle and German Romanticism in general. Hölderlin's unique and solitary genius stands outside the movement. Novalis is its exponent.

The path he trod leads . . . ever more inward to a yet purer integration. Creative activity of the spirit, unalloyed and untrammelled by utilitarian purpose, is his goal. Everything he expresses must spring from the fountain of moral freedom. Everything aggressively loud or near offends him, till he has removed it to a rarefied plane. He sees only the symbol and desires a creative independence from material things, not, however, a complete divorce. The purpose, he feels, of all poetry is to raise man above himself to a vision of the universal. In a letter to August Wilhelm Schlegel his brother, Friedrich, says of his friend Novalis: 'Fate has laid into my hands a young man who may rise to anything . . . I never saw such serenity in youth. His emotion has a certain chastity which is rooted in spiritual integrity, not in lack of experience.'

For us today above all for the Germans, Novalis should have a special significance. No reconstruction plans from without can rescue them from chaos. They must be reborn out of themselves. Like the giant Antaeus they must re-discover their maternal earth and find the way to their true selves. Their best guides are their own great masters of the spirit, of music, of poetry and of art.

Unfortunately, we learn little from history, and facts are certainly not the essential influences. Science and education, through political abuse and a barbaric lust for over-specialization, have often enough proved themselves equally bankrupt. The ultimate truths of existence cannot be solved through evolution, scientific analysis or the rivalries of intellectual ambition. The only hope of re-birth lies in a recognition of the spiritual realities of beauty and a reverence for the mystery of nature, creative activity, the totality of life, and last, not least, in a full

understanding of the individual's right of freedom and responsibility towards society.

Herein lies the real significance of Novalis' work. His art touches the secret heart of our existence through the power of imagination and intuitive sensibility. We saw how he nevertheless always maintains the balance between nature and the ego, between phantasy and reason. His poetry is like a mighty tree whose roots plunge into the depths of his native soil, and whose crown reaches the heavens.

In him Hölderlin's words found their true realization:

> He who thinks deepest loves life most.

Novalis' song is at once individual and universal, born both of a chastening and fiery intoxication of the spirit. (pp. 18-19)

> *August Closs, in an introduction to* Hymns to the Night *by Novalis, translated by Mabel Cotterell, Phoenix Press, 1948, pp. 7-19.*

RALPH TYMMS (essay date 1955)

[*Characterizing Novalis as "a man possessed by art," Tymms comments upon his "morbid reversal of normal values" and "escapist" tendency. Tymms also discusses Novalis's attempt to combine the values of the Aufklärung and Sturm und Drang movements, his view of the artist as "magus," or "the unknowing instrument and property of a higher power," and his use of the Märchen form.*]

Oscar Wilde's dictum that 'Romantic Art begins with its climax' might be supported by the appearance of Novalis at the outset of the romantic age in Germany, since a great deal could be said for considering him the prototype of romantic poets, the nearest approach to a realization of Friedrich Schlegel's visionary ideal of the romantic artist, the creator of an ideal world of his own: probably no poet persisted more stubbornly in the romantic mood, refusing to face reality, and taking refuge instead in a fanciful dream-existence. He was also highly poetic in his exquisite sensibility, reacting to the buffets of the world of physical reality with practically a caricature of hypersensitivity; he was a man possessed by art, as by a dangerous, debilitating sickness, very much in the sense in which Wackenroder's literary self-portrait Berglinger, regards it: 'Art is a seductive, forbidden fruit; whoever has once tasted its inmost, sweetest juice is irrevocably lost for the active world of everyday life.' The addiction of Novalis to art does go hand in hand with a morbid reversal of normal values, an insistence that death is the higher potential of life. In various ways then he does exhibit exaggeratedly 'romantic' features: he is perhaps the most 'romantic' of them all (just as August Wilhelm Schlegel was the least 'romantic'), because he is most escapist and most poetic—though not necessarily the greatest German romantic poet: Brentano or Eichendorff dispute that claim. And it was this most emphatically romantic poet who was also the first in time, and indeed the only poet of the pioneer Jena group. (p. 147)

His intelligence links him with the intellectualism of the *Aufklärung,* and suits him for the age of Kant, of the theories of the French Revolution, and of revolutionary advances in natural sciences: and on this intellectual plane he seems to be prepared, at least to some extent, to cope with reality; but his intelligence is combined in the most bizarre fashion with an indulged imaginative sense, nourished by the contrasting, and more characteristic refusal to come to terms with the reality of the world of physical causality. The retreat into a world of fancy distinguished this romantic form of imaginative escapism ('*Phantasieromantik*') from the emotional escapism of the *Sturm und Drang* in the 'seventies and 'eighties of the eighteenth century (the 'pre-romantic romanticism' of feeling—'*Gefühlsromantik*'), with its noisy outbursts of moral indignation about the social injustice of the world.

The union of intellect and the imagination in Novalis is so striking just because it is an attempt to harmonize, or at any rate combine, these respective principles of the rival, and warring, movements of *Aufklärung* and *Sturm und Drang*. Goethe and Schiller, in their Weimar classicist phase, produced works in which a similar synthesis of reason and feeling is evident, but the Weimar poets give the primacy to reason, Novalis to the imagination, even when he is ostensibly indulging in intellectual speculation; the result is that his axioms are as often as not bizarre and inconsistent, and are more remarkable for invention than for good sense. Feeling, on the other hand, though it is overlaid by imagination, exists precariously in the writings of Novalis; it is the original reason for his agonized escape from intolerable experience, for the escape into fancy. In complete contrast to the hysterical emotionalism of the *Stürmer und Dränger*, Novalis has the heroic stoicism of a mature, aristocratic convention because, as he confesses in a maxim: 'feelings are positively deadly, like illnesses'. But this distaste for expressed emotion does not mean that he did not feel it, for his diaries suggest deep sensibility. With his combination of imagination, implied (but inexplicit) emotion, and a bewildering variety of intellectual interests—particularly in the later years of his short life—Novalis did then indeed combine many of the features of the *Athenäum* artist, a heterogeneous figure who depends on rational perception as well as on intuition and imagination.

But Novalis, though he was a great poet, was never even a moderately significant philosopher: he was not systematic or consistent enough for that. His virtuosity in devising axiomatic 'splinters' of semi-philosophical speculation is in fact rather the product of his poetic and imaginative ingenuity than of true philosophical capacity, so that there is in his works the interaction (though it is that of two unequal partners) of poetry and philosophy—just as Friedrich Schlegel had required: 'Poetry and philosophy should be united.' The two genres are not kept apart: Novalis writes poems and prose with some pretensions at least to deep meaning, and, on the other hand, his speculative writing has often an undeniable poetic cast. Schlegel on occasion insisted on the artist's ethical responsibility, and Novalis certainly had a serious belief in his own ethical vocation: as a poet he was not merely a minstrel but a potential seer and priest. The result is the curious, rapt gravity of his writing, imparting the sense of dedication to a mystical task, the 'pilgrimage to the holy grave'. Yet there is little that is portentous in all this: the awareness of dedication is too implicit, too self-explanatory, to need over-emphasizing, nor does it inhibit him from wild imaginative caprices. The sense of mission is as evident in his fairy-tales as when he drafts his philosophical paradoxes in axiomatic form; perhaps—and in itself this is an evident paradox—he is more of the teacher in his *Märchen* than in his speculative axioms. The apparently artless technique of the *Märchen* can hardly ever have been employed for a purpose more remote from that of simple entertainment, except perhaps in Goethe's 'model' *Märchen* . . . , for Novalis packs his tales with aesthetic and ethical dogmatism, apparently indifferent to the effect this has on the readability of the narrative. Indeed, he was reconciled to the fact that 'great' art (that is, the art which is most completely governed by dogmatic aesthetic and ethical principles) must necessarily lose in attractiveness what it gains in significance: 'The highest works of art are in the nature of things *unpleasing*. They are ideals which can and *should* only please to an approximate degree—aesthetic imperatives.' This is not to say that because Novalis is reconciled to the assumption that the highest works of art must lose in pleasing qualities what they gain in didactic emphasis, he renounces the classicist acknowledgement of beauty as the highest law of art. Still true to the Shaftesbury-Schiller mode of aesthetics of Friedrich's early essays on the Greeks, Novalis equates beauty with good and truth, so that aesthetic and ethical good are the same, or at any rate together form a higher synthesis, which is the essence of *Bildung*: 'beauty is objective goodness; truth is subjective goodness'. To Novalis, ethical responsibility is the supreme law of art, it imposes duties on the artist, but it is also the source of his divine creative powers in the first place.

The artist's powers are divine because (so Novalis believed) in the process of creating the work of art he becomes the instrument of a higher power than himself—the spirit of poetry, of that poetry which is 'the true Absolute Reality'. Once he has completed the creative act and produced the work of art, he loses his power over it, so that it then assumes an independent, even a superior, existence of its own, unattached to its maker: 'In the moment in which it [the work of art] came into being it became more than he, its creator—and he became the unknowing instrument and property of a higher power. The artist belongs to the work, and not the work to the artist.' This is then one of the 'mysteries' of Novalis's semi-mystical aesthetics: that the artist, though he is regarded as the most blessed of men, should yet fall into the role of a mere agent of a higher power. On the face of it there are difficulties in the way of reconciling this conception of the artist's inferiority to his own work of art with the apotheosis of the artist as a magus, a prodigy of ethical and aesthetic will-power: the two ideas do not seem to be entirely consistent. Yet perhaps Novalis had in mind the analogy of the priest, whose obedience to the divine service culminates (according to Catholic belief) in the transubstantiation of the mass: as an agent, an instrument of the divine will he brings into being something greater than himself, and effects a miraculous translation of the Deity. This is precisely what the artist does, according to Novalis: by the miraculous act of artistic creation he translates into words the divine spirit of poetry. The romantic artist is therefore a priest of sorts, who must justify by faith his marvellous vocation and immense powers: 'What reason is to the philosophers, faith, in the narrower sense, is to poets.' Faith is the world-creative force by which the divine inspiration becomes available to the poet, and thus it is the very basis of artistic creation. Faith expresses its power as will, working upon the intelligence, and will has no limits.

This apotheosis of faith and the subordination of the intellect to the will are the irrational, and even anti-rational, culmination to the protracted speculation in which Novalis indulged, his mind darting in many directions, though his main point of departure had been Fichte's fantastic, but (given the initial premise of solipsism) logically argued system into which Friedrich Schlegel had initiated him.

According to Fichte's formulation, the world is the product of the human imagination (*Einbildungskraft*), an involuntary, transcendental force; Novalis was in step with Friedrich Schlegel when he confused this transcendental imagination with another sort of imagination (*Phantasie*), which is voluntary and empirically based. Novalis, the bold young amateur philosopher, proceeds to expound this already confused interpretation of the imagination by asserting that *Einbildungskraft* is called *Phantasie* when it is applied to the memory, and *Denkkraft* (rational thought, or the power of rational perception) when it is applied to the reason. In this way he extends the usually accepted limits of imagination so as to include (ludicrously!) intellectual activity—as if imagination were the same thing as ingenuity; perhaps he considered that his own curious partnership of analytical reason (too often the sleeping partner!) and fantastic imaginativeness is more easily justified if the two partners are regarded as related conceptions, or even the same faculty seen from different points of view; but the absurdity of the suggestion is staggering. And at this point the magus makes a dramatic appearance: the poet-priest of his imagination, the mystically coloured counterpart to Friedrich Schlegel's visionary ideal of the romantic artist of the future, better world. The magus, or poetic seer, is the romantic artist—Novalis himself, as it might be—in his highest potentiality, and he will consequently combine in a higher degree both imagination and intellect.

Fichte's own conclusions are bizarre enough, but they were at least reached by predominantly systematic and logical stages of thought, however questionable the premise. The vague, rhapsodic and poetic modifications by Novalis of the *Wissenschaftslehre* are a very different matter: logic and consistency are impatiently thrown aside at a very early stage of the proceedings; and in their place Novalis offers scraps of mystical thought from various sources. (pp. 149-53)

Through all the erratic ingenuity of Novalis's ideas, particularly as they are recorded in his thousands of *Fragmente*, runs the recurring theme of salvation by faith—an aesthetic-cum-ethical faith which justifies the aesthetic priesthood of the magus. The romantic poet may become a magus, but only by means of an act of faith which in present circumstances must be a miracle, a visionary and ideal act, a magical extension of the ordinary laws of reality, a projection on to a higher, metaphysical plane of the potentially boundless powers of ethical will-power. In our present earthly state this visionary triumph of the ideal can only be revealed prophetically to us in the form of the dream or *Märchen* (in which the rational mind is in abeyance): it presents us with a prophetic and gloriously distorted vision—Novalis even calls it a 'caricature', though in an admiring way—of a wondrous future on a higher spiritual plane.

Because the ideal can only be achieved in the dream or *Märchen*, the magus therefore enters into his ideal kingdom by means of the dream or *Märchen*: consequently they both play an important part in the works of the aspirant magus Novalis himself. They are related phenomena (or so Novalis thinks, plausibly enough): indeed, the *Märchen* is a translation into words of the dream; it is 'really like a dream—without inner connection—an ensemble of wondrous things and events'; and in it is 'the true anarchy of nature. Abstract world, dream-world. . . .' In his novel *Heinrich von Ofterdingen*, for instance, Novalis was to show how everything was at the last to turn into a dream, and, in keeping with this, Novalis says in an aphorism that ultimately man's life should, and perhaps will, become a dream. It follows that in the dream we catch a glimpse of our future state, when all our potentialities are realized; and, because the world of the dream is equally the world of the *Märchen*, we are granted equally a glimpse of the future when we read a *Märchen*, and surrender to its vision of a world other than that of our own, dull, present-day existence. The author of the *Märchen* is therefore a visionary, a prophet.

There is practically no end to the aspects of the dream and *Märchen* which Novalis examines in his *Fragmente*: he is obsessed by them, as if they were twin gems which he holds up and twists about between his fingers, to catch the light on each facet. His obsession helps one to understand his mind, and in particular his attitude to the conventional artlessness of the *Märchen*—a central problem of romantic practice. To the romantic author the *Märchen* reproduces the artless narrative of the dreaming mind, and both are more sophisticated than they appear at first sight (for the dreaming mind can draw on resources of intellectual data from the experiences of the waking mind, though notoriously the conscious mind cannot easily reverse the process and have access to the subconscious). Practically everything that Novalis wrote, apart from his *Fragmente*, has a pronounced simplicity of formulation, even *Die Lehrlinge zu Sais*, in which he grapples with the superfluity of often abstruse theories about the relationship between man and nature, and the aesthetic-cum-metaphysical extravagances of Klingsohr's *Märchen*, interpolated in *Heinrich von Ofterdingen*. Now something he says in one of the *Fragmente* suggests that this *Märchen*-simplicity of expression is ironical, for though he maintains that the *Märchen* should represent the 'confessions of a . . . child'; he goes on to say that 'the child must be a thoroughly ironical child'. So far so good; this, one might think, is clear enough: it is the confession of a deliberate hoax, the assumption of a bogus artlessness to suit the preconceived convention that the *Märchen* must be artless and childish. But his meaning becomes less evident when one examines the epithets he gives to this *Märchen*-child, whose (almost Wordsworthian!) simplicity is the romantic counterblast to the middle-aged sophistication of the *Aufklärung*, and the subsequent reaction of adolescent noisiness in the 'hobbledehoy' years (*Flegeljahre*) of the *Sturm und Drang*. The *Märchen*, Novalis says, must be the confessions of 'a true, synthetic child—an ideal child'. This is a mysterious utterance, a magian pronouncement, and the non-magian modern reader can only hazard the guess that the synthesis referred to is that of intellect and imagination in the Schiller-Friedrich Schlegel sense of an ideal wedding of sense and soul, in the golden age of perfect harmony. Alternatively, perhaps the child is synthetic in the sense that it is a hypothetical, ideal being, symbolizing the quintessence of childlike naïveté and innocence, as abstract qualities. (pp. 154-56)

The ultimate marriage of allegory and *Märchen* is consummated by Novalis in its most rarefied form in *Heinrich von Ofterdingen*, for though it is a novel in scope, in almost every other way it is a long-drawn-out allegory clothed superficially in the *Märchen* conventions. It starts out, it is true, with a nucleus of what are supposed to be real people, but they become increasingly insubstantial, abstract figures, who were then (as the prolegomena show) to dissolve into their own prophetic visions of a higher, ideal world, as into Tieck's dream-vortices. The allegory is at times strangely suffused with mystical ideas borrowed from Jakob Böhme: for instance, the hero was to turn into a stone, a musical tree and a golden ram; then he was to resume his human form; the key to this multiple transformation is apparently the chance fact that Novalis happened to know of Böhme's similar allegory of man's mystical 'threefold birth', his successive stages of redemption from the bonds of earthly life.

In the *Märchen* of Hyazinth and Rosenblütchen, interpolated in *Die Lehrlinge zu Sais*, Novalis presents less of a disembodied, transparent allegory, for it has as its basis a not unpleasing, and comparatively substantial, fairy-tale anecdote; and the same can be said of the merchants' tale of the princess and the youth, in *Heinrich von Ofterdingen*. In both of these little tales love is more convincingly portrayed than it is in Klingsohr's lengthy *Märchen*, with which the first part of *Heinrich von Ofterdingen* closes, and which is meant to be the key to the whole novel: for Klingsohr's Eros, the fairy prince of tradition, is a colourless abstraction, overshadowed by his sister, *Fabel*, the symbol of poetry. Yet Eros should have played an emphatic part, for to Novalis (theoretically) love is an important, magical, element of the *Märchen*: true love is *Märchen*-like, a miracle, and 'all novels in which true love occurs are *Märchen*, magical events'.

The *Märchen* must have its roots in everyday reality, in ordinary human life, as well as in the supernatural, if it is not to wither away from sheer abstraction, and the virtue of the old *Volksmärchen* lay in its unforced combination of earthy and spiritual, realistic and fantastic, natural and supernatural. But Novalis feeds his allegories on air, on metaphysics, alone, and denied the health-giving nourishment of reality: his *Märchen*-figures and motifs never truly come into existence, so artificial and desiccated are they. Not the least of his many paradoxical characteristics is that it is in the *Märchen* (in which he should have been at his most artless) that he often shows his most sententious and unspontaneous sides: certainly this is true of the whole wearisome length of Klingsohr's *Märchen*. In his pseudo-philosophical aphorisms, his *Fragmente*, on the other hand, he sometimes reverses the process, so that here the truly inconsequential, capricious atmosphere prevails which he should have kept for his fairy-tales, and which might have lessened the tedium of even Klingsohr's story. In one *Fragment*, for example, he plays with the extravagant conceit that the interior of the earth is very likely to be a diamond!

Another grave weakness of his *Märchen* is their lack of humour: the examples of the later romantics Brentano, Arnim and Hoffmann show how helpful even a little sardonic temper can be in making a modern *Kunstmärchen* palatable, especially when there is aesthetic allegory to be swallowed, as there is in Hoffmann's stories *Der goldne Topf* and *Prinzessin Brambilla*. The only perceptible attempt at fun in Klingsohr's *Märchen* is a laboured incident when the tarantulas attack the Fates, and sting the malignant deities of mortality into a grotesque, agonized dance: the effect is embarrassingly unfunny, as it usually is when someone who has no natural comic gift tries to tell a joke. Though Novalis claimed to like Aristophanes, his confession that he could not see the point in Shakespeare's jokes— though by no means a proof of humourlessness in itself—does support the impression of an insensitivity to comic effects. (pp. 157-59)

Later romantics, on the other hand, often kept in touch with reality, even when they soared off into their escapist world of fancy from the tedious restrictions of everyday existence. To them the *Märchen* afforded precisely the opportunities for bringing out the effective contrast between the real and the ideal which Novalis failed to show; Brentano, Arnim and Hoffmann alike make much of this contrast, from a number of aspects....

Perhaps the trouble with Novalis was that instead of bringing out the contrast between real and ideal, with a sense of the relativity of achievement which Friedrich Schlegel shows in his aesthetic theories of irony, he tries to achieve a synthesis of the two—an ideal consummation which Friedrich seems to relegate to the distant future, when *Bildung* is reached.... (p. 160)

Novalis cannot bring out the humour of contrast because he underrates the extent of the contrast; reality means little to him, because it is merely an intermediary state, an interregnum between the first state of man (in a mythical, primal state of harmony, a primitive golden age) and man's arrival at a second golden age, when the ideal shall reign again, in a *Märchen*-kingdom: 'In time history must become *Märchen*, become again what it started as.' He subordinates the real almost entirely to the ideal, for in his eyes the links still holding man back, subject to the world of physical causality, are tenuous. (p. 161)

Ralph Tymms, "Novalis (Friedrich Leopold, Baron von Hardenberg)," in his German Romantic Literature, *Methuen & Co. Ltd, 1955, pp. 147-206.*

RENÉ WELLEK (essay date 1955)

[*Wellek's* A History of Modern Criticism *comprises a major, comprehensive study of the literary critics of the last three centuries. Wellek's critical method, as demonstrated in* A History *and outlined in his* Theory of Literature, *is one of describing, analyzing, and evaluating a work solely in terms of the problems it poses for itself and how the writer solves them. For Wellek, biographical, historical, and psychological information are incidental. Here Wellek briefly explores Novalis's ideas about the union between the conscious and the unconscious mind, the function of language, and the implications of those views for criticism.*]

[Novalis is] perfectly aware of the difference between "real, perfected, achieved art, working through outer organs, and imaginary art." He can say, and Croce would support him, "We know something only insofar as we can express, i.e. make, it." This emphasis on the union of the conscious and the unconscious and on the role of language and expression needs to be interpreted in the context of Novalis' general philosophy. Consciousness is certainly not Cartesian rationalism but rather a state which must have passed through the unconscious; it is in fact identical with "irony," which he defines as "genuine consciousness, true presence of mind." This highest consciousness is not reason, ratiocination, but illumination. Similarly, language is not merely the tool of the poet's craft which he must know and cherish but a world of signs and sounds, of hieroglyphics, which allows us to read the great book of nature, to decipher its mysteries. Words to Novalis are not general signs, but "magic words," "tones," "incantations." "As the garments of a saint still preserve miraculous powers, so many a word is hallowed by some sublime memory and has become almost in itself a poem. For the poet language is never too poor, but it is always too general. He needs frequently recurrent words, played out by use," presumably in order to revive them, to make them over into magic words. "The world is a universal metaphor of the spirit, its symbolic image." Thus Novalis can wish for a "tropology that comprises the laws of the symbolic construction of the transcendental world." Language is magic, just as poetry and science are magic; they are all to "raise man above himself," reconcile him again with nature, lead him back to the golden age, transform the world into paradise. "Through poetry arise the highest sympathy and cooperation, the most intimate union of the finite and infinite."

One can understand that in such a view of the world there is really no room for criticism. "Criticism of poetry is monstrous. The only possible decision (and that is difficult) is whether anything is poetry or not." This is a reasonable attitude if poetry is actually divine and revelatory. At most, Novalis would admit "productive criticism," the "ability to produce the very product to be criticized.'' But this makes the critic a poet and at the same time abolishes criticism. Actually, there is still some hope for criticism. Novalis concludes that we should

censure nothing that is human. Everything is good, but not everywhere, not always, not for everybody. In judging poems e.g. one must beware not to censure anything which, taken strictly, is not a real artistic mistake, a false tone in every connection. We should assign to every poem, as exactly as possible, its precinct, and that is enough criticism for the vanity of its author. For we must judge poems only in this respect, whether they should have a wide or narrow, near or distant, dark or bright, high or low place. Thus Schiller writes for the few, Goethe for the many. Today we have paid little attention to advising the reader how to read a poem—under what circumstances alone it can please. Every poem has its relations to all kinds of readers and diverse circumstances. It has its own environment, its own world, its own God.

Criticism thus seems a strategy of finding the place of a work of art, discovering its proper readers, defining its position in the world of poetry. A book, Novalis realizes, causes thousands of sensations and activities, some determined and defined, some free. An ideal review would be a complete extract or essence of everything that can be written or said about it. (pp. 85-7)

> *René Wellek, "The Early Romantics in Germany,"
> in his* A History of Modern Criticism, 1750-1950:
> The Romantic Age, *Vol. 2,* Yale University Press,
> *1955, pp. 74-109.**

BRUCE HAYWOOD (essay date 1959)

[*In this excerpt from his important full-length study of Novalis's imagery, Haywood lauds the writer's imaginative use of theme, technique, and figurative language. Haywood focuses, in addition, on the predominant symbols and images in Novalis's poetry, citing his influence on later writers and pronouncing him "indubitably the foremost poetic talent of the Early Romantic school."*]

The influence Novalis has exerted on succeeding generations of poets and the acclaim that has been his scarcely seem commensurate with the limited quantity of his poetry. Small as is the body of his work, it bears the stamp of decided originality. It is this individuality in both his themes and techniques that has given his poetry its lasting freshness. Novalis' development of an unconventional and personal mode of expression is the more remarkable when we recall the trite nature of most of his early verse. To be sure, there remain in his major works some conventional elements. Readily identifiable too are occasional faults of redundancy, exaggerated hyperbole, and digression that can equally be attributed to his relative immaturity as an artist. The emergence of Novalis' genius was comparatively sudden. He died before having reached full artistic maturity. His youthful faults are insignificant, however, when contrasted to the many positive qualities of his work. The imaginative nature of his themes, the lyric intensity of his language, his strikingly evocative metaphor, the rich color that permeates his poetry—these are but a few of the qualities which spring to mind when one thinks of Novalis. His efforts to explore the ultimate expressive powers of language have made his work a source of stimulation for later poets. Indubitably the foremost poetic talent of the Early Romantic school, Novalis ranks among

the most inventive of German poets. Few individuals have contributed as much to the growth of a literary movement as has Novalis. That the movement is in this case Romanticism, the longest lived and most important movement in German literature, makes Novalis' contribution the more significant. Novalis gave to German Romanticism its first great creative impulse and provided a model of Romantic style for those who came after. It is fitting that from his poetry should have come the symbol of that movement, the blue flower.

Important as Novalis is as a pioneer of Romantic poetic techniques, he is equally important in terms of his influence on the choice of subject matter of his successors. There are few themes in later Romantic literature that are not to be found in his work. Indeed, Novalis might well be called the prototype of the German Romantic poet. With him, too, begins that tendency for which critics, following Goethe's example, have most often castigated the German Romantics—the tendency to seek in Christianity the answers to the problems of life and death. It has often been claimed that underlying this tendency is an antagonism or a sense of revulsion toward this world and its life. The hero of Thomas Mann's *Tonio Kröger* tells his confidante: "People have said—they have even written and published it—that I hate or fear life, or despise or loathe it." The same words have, in effect, been used of Novalis. Yet such a characterization is unjust, failing, as it does, to take note of much that is expressed in his writings. Death, it is true, occupies a place in the forefront of Novalis' works. Indeed, virtually all his later works may be said to be concerned ultimately with the problem of death. Yet equally prominent in these works—and perhaps more important—is the poet's concern for the knowledge of life that is gained from the understanding of death's true meaning. Novalis' dream-vision, to which he alludes on several occasions in his writings, brought him a revelation of the relationship of life and death that transformed his existence. His conviction that death is but a door to a richer, fuller life in eternity persuaded him of the truths of the Christian doctrine. The poetic works of his last years are the fruits of this experience. In them Novalis seeks to show the meaning for mankind of his unique revelation. It is not only the conviction that man may in heaven attain to knowledge of the secrets of life that is the source of the joy so evident in these works. For Novalis there is the further promise that man may in this life have foretaste of the delights of heaven. With the acceptance of Christ as Saviour comes full understanding of life, an appreciation of its beauty and true value. Through Christ (and therefore in the full renunciation of all attempts to interpret life and death rationally), man may hope to recapture the blissful state of naive innocence in intimate communion with nature which, Novalis believes, mankind had once enjoyed. For through Him all can be understood, all can be meaningful and beauteous. Fear of the unknown, that fear which had destroyed the Golden Age of the childhood of man, disappears with the revelation of Christ's victory over death.

Two media other than religious inspiration itself, Novalis indicates, afford mankind direct knowledge of divine truth. Love and poetry, those flowers blooming in a foreign clime, are envoys on earth of the realm of the spirit. Love that has been purified by Christ binds together earth and heaven. Through its intoxicating and inspiring power the individual may grasp the mysteries of life and death. Poetry, the creation of a divinely inspired imagination, reveals knowledge to which rational thought cannot aspire. By its power to make known the transcendent through the immanent poetry can lead man to ultimate truth.

Through poetry and love, then, the individual may on earth recapture for himself the lost Golden Age.

The nonrational beliefs to which Novalis clung became the central themes of his later works. To present the nondemonstrable truths he grasped intuitively and to make palpable the inexpressible, Novalis turned to poetry rather than to philosophic treatise. In the language of metaphor he found the one medium appropriate to his visionary utterances. His work has the character of a brilliantly colorful tapestry, the individual pictures of which are brought into relationship through a skillfully woven pattern of recurrent imagery. Because of the frequency with which certain metaphors are encountered, they may be regarded as elements of a fixed system of private symbols. Conventional and traditional as some of these are, the poet has made them his own through his preferred, perhaps instinctive, use of them to express ideas or attitudes he cherishes. (pp. 145-47)

The image we meet most frequently in Novalis is, of course, that of a new Golden Age. This is, however, but one element of a threefold metaphorical representation of the growth of individual and mankind to full knowledge of the transcendent. To this broad image are related all the elements of the poet's private system of symbols. The first phase in man's history is depicted as an original Golden Age, the childhood of man. It is characterized by man's apprehension of the spiritual through representation. In the portrayal of this phase, therefore, we find spiritual values personified in the gods of ancient myth, or the worship of supernatural forces represented in the sun and the stars. This first period is invariably seen as an age of blissful naïveté, faith and fantasy. It came to an end, it is suggested, because of man's fear of death, the horrifying riddle to which he could find no satisfactory answer. The failure of myth and secular religions to interpret adequately the problem of death, Novalis implies, robbed man of his childlike faith and happiness, bringing this idyllic state to a close. The middle period is characterized by the growth into adulthood. Then man puts irrational emotionalism behind him and seeks through rational thought to master the secrets of life and death. Novalis represents this phase most poignantly in an image of a desolate waste, chilled by freezing winds and devoid of blossoming growth. Man moves from an Eden to a polar region. It is an age of discord, strife and barbarism. While man gropes blindly in a darkened universe, spiritual values—the "benevolent goddesses"—battle with the forces hostile to them. The final phase sees man's attainment to knowledge of the divine. Spiritual values triumph and are restored to their rightful place as the guiding powers of the universe. A variety of metaphor embodies the nature of this new Golden Age. Invariably it is depicted as a new spring, a time of sudden blossoming and of life springing from graves and the lifeless earth. Always, too, we find allusion to the flowing together of heaven and earth, of spiritual and physical realms. Associated with it, explicitly or implicitly, is the revelation of the true nature of death by Christ. Thus to the pagan concept of a Golden Age is joined the Christian heaven as well as the notion of paradise regained. Then a new poetic spirit, inspired by the revelation of Christ, recreates the myth of life. Through the new myth there is revitalized the myth that had given the first age meaning and beauty even as the gods of the first phase are reborn in Christ. Here, as in the Golden Age of his childhood, man enjoys intimate communion with nature, conversing with plants, rocks and animals. As the individual recaptures his lost innocence, he discovers the hidden secrets of life and the world.

Light and color images intensify this depiction of growth to knowledge of the divine. Physical light, represented variously as the sun, the day, or as lamps, symbolizes secularism and rationalism. With this image of physical light is invariably associated the belief that death marks the end of man's existence. Thus the destruction of this belief is frequently represented as the death of the sun. . . . One might expect that the antitheses of the powers represented by physical light would be portrayed as night or darkness. This is rarely the case. Instead, the power of the divine and the victory of life over death are seen as another form of light, greater than physical light. Only in the *Hymnen an die Nacht* does night have fixed symbolic value for Novalis. To this must be contrasted the "long night" of Klingsohr's "Märchen" and the images of night and darkness in the sacred songs, all of which represent, in effect, the middle phase of man's development. Even in the hymns to the night we find allusion to a "light of night's heaven" and to a "sun of night." Elsewhere we find metaphors of flame, sparks and fire that revitalize the lifeless middle period. Perhaps the most striking representation of this concept, however, is to be found in Klingsohr's fable in the rainbow-like source of new light which replaces that of the burned-out sun. Related to these last light images are those which portray the light emanating from precious stones. The quality of these images is to suggest subtly that such objects may reveal the sympathy existing between physical and spiritual realms. Similarly, color imagery reveals the presence or absence of spiritual values. The middle period is remarkable for its drabness, while the Golden Age, old and new, sparkles with brilliant colors. Specific symbolic value, of course, attaches to the color blue in *Ofterdingen,* where its presence invariably implies some manifestation of the divine.

Invariably joined with those images representing the attainment to the final state is bold erotic metaphor. Here again we may speak of fixed symbolic value, for eroticism is always identified with apprehension of the spiritual. Most frequently this imagery depicts the power of love to transform and to reveal. Thus, through such metaphor, Novalis identifies eroticism with the love of Christ as a mode of communication with the divine. It must be emphasized that at no point is erotic imagery subordinated to the Christian. The two are daringly juxtaposed. Death itself is experienced as erotic passion, while eternity is seen in images of an everlasting nuptial night. The dawn of eternity is heralded in Klingsohr's fable by the transformation of the throne into a bridal bed, as lover embraces beloved. From Novalis' early poetry to his last works water images are representative of eroticism. Water is identified explicitly by the intensely emotional youth in *Die Lehrlinge zu Sais* as the erotic element. Elsewhere we find thirst and sexual appetite equated. Like the explicitly erotic metaphors cited above, water imagery then depicts death and transfiguration, with the final *unio mystica* a vaporous commingling in the *Hymns to Night*. Eroticism is, then, implicit in the frequently met image of the flowing together of physical and spiritual realms. A similar value attaches to an equally constant image, that of twilight. Implicit in this representation is the flowing together of immanent and transcendent as physical light ends and the greater light of night approaches.

Two distinct values are found for the dream image in Novalis' poetry. On occasion we meet the "oppressive" dream or dream of pain, its nature always made known through epithet. In this case the dream graphically characterizes the "unreal" existence of the middle period. Otherwise the dream image symbolizes the rich, full life of the eternal Golden Age, whether in direct experience of it or as anticipatory enjoyment. Music images have established connotation after they are first met in *Die Lehrlinge zu Sais.* These represent the creative forces and ordered pattern of nature and the universe. Dissonance, as might be expected, then suggests man in his middle phase clumsily seeking to reproduce this harmony. Finding expression in music images too is the sympathetic bond between man and nature, while the relationship of the artist to the creative forces of the universe is suggested by his power to compose song. The image of the stringed instrument as a symbol of the poet's vocation and genius grows almost naturally from the original music images depicting nature's creative forces.

Certain metaphors of animistic projection develop unchanging values. Stones, stars, trees, and animals are invariably endowed with human attributes or spiritual qualities. Through these metaphors, particularly, Novalis reveals one of his most cherished beliefs—that all things exist in one another and that all are united by an indefinable bond. For Novalis, nature is understandable only as a living creature with emotional attributes analogous to those of man. (Thus he regards the farmer and the miner as curators of spiritual values equally with the artist and the musician.) It is somewhat surprising that in the poetry of the creator of the blue flower we meet few metaphors of animistic projection in the form of flower images. When these occur, however, they invariably symbolize the spiritual life attained to by man in his final phase as well as the gentle spirit, beauty and richness of that life.

Although the blue flower is the best known of Novalis' symbols, two other images are of ultimately greater significance for the understanding of his work. The images of the spiral and the veil recur as fixed symbols in the poetry of his last years. These are, I believe, the most important individual symbols in Novalis, for in them he has embodied his view of man's existence. The spiral image grows directly from the constant depiction of man's progress as the following of a path. The figure man describes on his road toward ultimate truth is that of a spiral, for he returns eventually to his point of origin but at a higher level. Through his efforts to recapture the lost Golden Age the individual attains to a state of conscious naïveté, a state fuller and richer than his original state of innocent naïveté. It is a requisite for the attainment to the final stage of communion with the divine. The idea of such a course of development is inherent in the concept of the Golden Age regained—a state both old and new, familiar and yet strange, the same and yet more than the original state. Into this figure of a spiral is compressed the course of action of both Novalis' novels, while in his recurrent metaphor of "going home" the concept is given poignantly simple expression. The veil image is invariably present, explicitly or implicitly, in Novalis' depiction of the middle phase, for then nature, truth, and spiritual values are always hidden from man by a veil of his own making. The image represents both the false culture that has divorced man from nature and the rational thought processes which constantly frustrate his efforts to recapture his lost happiness. Beneath the veil, obscured and yet occasionally glimpsed in moments of inspiration, are the beauty, mystery and wonder of the life that might be ours.

Novalis found in poetic imagery [a] special language within language. . . . It became for him a mode of communication with those he called the "initiated," those sympathetic to poetry and to himself. Through metaphor he has succeeded in creating a private language by which to impart his convictions to those responsive to figurative representation. His belief in

the metaphorical nature of life and the world about him finds appropriate expression in his work in the metaphorical representation of all that concerns him. His imagery is often bold and esoteric; always it has a highly imaginative quality. Through such metaphor he is able to burst the bonds of conventional language. His work, as a result, presents a challenge to the imagination of the reader. For those unresponsive to figurative language Novalis' poetry must remain a riddle. The veil of imagery he has cast over his poetry hides from those he called "the profane" his convictions, his faith and the truths he grasped intuitively. For those, however, who share Novalis' love of figurative representation and his belief in the power of metaphor to reveal hidden truths it is a veil that enhances, rather than conceals, the beauty of his art. (pp. 147-52)

> *Bruce Haywood, in his* Novalis, the Veil of Imagery: A Study of the Poetic Works of Friedrich von Hardenberg (1772-1801), *Cambridge, Mass.: Harvard University Press, 1959, 159 p.*

KARL BARTH   (essay date 1959)

[*Barth was a Swiss theologian and educator whose doctrine of dialectic theology has strongly influenced twentieth-century religious scholarship. In the following excerpt from an essay written in 1959, Barth situates Novalis in the history of Protestant theology by analyzing his views on poetry, art, philosophy, nature, history, love, religion, and the roles of Mary and Jesus. Barth emphasizes that "Novalis is the only Romantic whose work goes on seeming relevant and new."*]

[Novalis's] direct utterances concerning the problem of religion are few, and, outwardly at least, they carry no particular weight beside his much more emphatic and detailed remarks relating to every other conceivable 'province' of human intellectual life, as the favourite expression then was. Even his famous *Sacred Songs* would not in themselves be sufficient to secure him a place in a history of theology. But he does belong there

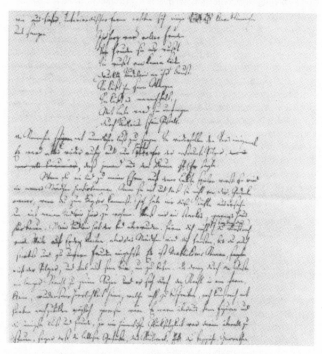

A manuscript page from Henry of Ofterdingen.

because he, and really he alone, of all his fellows, succeeded in exposing the meaning of Romanticism with a certain unequivocality and finality, and with a clarity that demands judgment. It is possible to master Friedrich Schlegel, Tieck, Brentano and Eichendorff, but with Novalis it is not so easy. He proclaimed the concern of Romanticism in a form in which it must at least be heard. We cannot dispose of Romanticism without disposing of Novalis.

But that is precisely what has not happened up to now. It has been rightly said of him, that he alone of all the Romantics has assured for himself, through all the numerous changes of outlook of the nineteenth century, 'a singularly certain *succès d'estime*'. We might well add that leaving Schleiermacher out for the moment, Novalis is the only Romantic whose work goes on seeming relevant and new. He is the poet whom we cannot silence by any historical relativizing, any more than we can silence Kant—who was so different—in that way. And it must further be said that we shall perhaps only be able to speak of a true Neo-romanticism for all time when Romanticism is once again seriously taken up in the sense that Novalis understood it and in his spirit.

The peculiar significance of Novalis is closely bound up with the fact that he can scarcely be said to have given the world a true lifework. Those of his works we do possess are a little book of poems, *The Apprentices of Sais*, a story of natural philosophy, a sketch in the philosophy of history entitled *Christendom or Europe*, the unrevised first part of a biographical novel, *Heinrich von Ofterdingen*, planned on a grand scale in the style of Wilhelm Meister, some attempts at a continuation of this work and finally a chaotic collection of *Fragments*, i.e. isolated thoughts set down at varying length for later use.

Fundamentally all these works are fragments. Novalis died of consumption in 1801 at the age of twenty-nine. The lament for the work which by his premature death he was forced to owe his time and all time is understandable. But it is at least open to question whether he has not precisely thereby, in this beginning, which remained a beginning—like Wackenroder, his older contemporary and sharer of the same fate—said everything he had to say in a way truer and more essential than that in which he would have said it in a long life, which would have brought him beyond this beginning. Another reason why he is the pure type of the Romantic is that the Romantic principle hardly achieved in him any length or breadth but remained almost a mathematical point. Perhaps Romanticism is something which should not achieve length and breadth, but which should flare up in this meteoric way if it is to bring forth its concern in a manner impressive and worthy of credence. Would it be possible for a Romanticism which acquired length and breadth to end anywhere but in the psychologism and historicism of Herder, or back again in the pure rationalism of Kant? (pp. 344-45)

The second feature about Novalis, which he reveals in a manner both relevant to the moment and decisive for an understanding of the time which came after him, is the uniquely exact way in which he stands between the ages and between the great problems of the two ages. W. Bölsche wrote of him: 'Of all the figures of the great epoch of Goethe, he is the one who most plainly stands upon the border between the eighteenth and the nineteenth centuries. He is bathed simultaneously in the light of the setting and of the rising sun. He stands in this magic dual splendour as if steeped in an artificial glow.... He is an immeasurably concentrated figure, crowned and sometimes also a little bowed by the richness of the hour'. But not only the eighteenth and nineteenth centuries are finely divided in him. Again and again we find ourselves compelled to ask, within the problem-complex of the old and the new age which moves him: Is it philosophy or is it art which is really his true sphere? And if it is both, if his particular problem is in fact the merging of the one with the other, is this philosophical art or artistic philosophy really directed towards nature or towards history? And if once again the answer should be that he is concerned with an attempt at a synthesis, is the personal expression of this synthesis love in the sense of the Platonic *eros,* or *agape* in the sense of the Christianity of Augustine and Roman Catholicism, the direct love for the distant object or the love emanating from this distant object being answered by love and loved again and therefore religion? And if yet again it should be a question of a synthesis, then will the word 'poesy', with which Novalis is in the habit of defining the creative centre and unity of all these antitheses, remain comprehensively and decisively valid here also? Will it be Mary or will it be Christ—Novalis sang the praise of both of them—who will keep the central position? It is possible to decide all these questions either way with equal degrees of probability. It is just the way these questions remain open which is typical of Novalis, and of him alone in this fashion, and which makes him in particular into the pure type of the Romantic. Pure Romanticism is truly the border: between the eighteenth and nineteenth centuries as it is the border between philosophy and art, between nature and history, and between love and religion. Their border? Romanticism imagines it to be their unity. But strangely enough it is only in actually revealing their borders that it can actually make it plain that it is their unity which it has in mind. It is pure Romanticism only in so far as it draws up its programme, and not by carrying it out.... Pure Romanticism must not wish to extend itself in such a way as to become a science or action, or—the science and action of which it is capable will signify its disloyalty to itself. Romanticism is pure as yearning, and only as yearning. That is why Novalis is a pure Romantic. That is why we can scarcely refute and dispose of him. And that is why he is scarcely to be imitated. That is why through him Romanticism became something which was perhaps unassailable, but which is perhaps also never to be recalled. Just in this way it became a word which continues to speak to us in an incomprehensibly real and relevant way. (pp. 346-47)

We shall in the first place consider the world of Novalis's thought, irrespective of its theological content. The form in which we find it in his literary remains and which in its incompleteness is its final and perhaps its most perfect form, is like a field of early corn in the spring: open to the view and yet with much that remains hidden from sight. This is also true because in its rather unfixed state of early development it delights, but can also confuse those who would know it at every step in its naturalness, in the apparent secret of a creative life which is reflected and represented there.... What is uniquely moving in Novalis is the state of early development, of first germination, in which all his thoughts are to be found and in which they speak all the more eloquently of the creative power which is indeed their true object. We find here no world-tree, with its roots, trunk and spreading branches; here there is truly only a blue flower—which, to be true, is in the process (but only in the process!) of developing into a world-tree, a pretentious lack of pretentiousness, against which we can say everything and nothing, which we should perhaps only look upon, and which perhaps, for all our doubts, we must simply like in order to understand it. I venture to speak in these unusual terms because we may be concerned here with the very heart of nineteenth-century theology, because it is perhaps just in Novalis that the question of the understanding of the entire age, and of the entire age of the Church, with which we are here concerned, is posed with an urgency which compels us to final decisions.

It is, I think, impossible to give an account of the world of Novalis's thought; only Novalis himself could do it if he returned among us. We can only make an attempt at a general survey, without claiming to present everything there is to be seen, much less interpret it all. We shall do this by attempting to see some of the systems of co-ordinates which, all at different levels, seem to weave a criss-cross pattern in Novalis's thought. I have already mentioned the antithetic unities which seem to me to be the most significant in that respect: art and philosophy, nature and history, love and religion. We shall finally come to speak of a last antithesis, which raises the problem as to whether it is likewise to be understood as an antithetic unity, or as a disjunctive antithesis, as an either—or: I should like to describe this last one as the Mary-Christ antithesis.

The first three antitheses are antithetic unities because each of them has an exact and therefore neutral and therefore superior centre. This neutral centre is common to all of them: the three systems of coordinates intersect, therefore, in such a manner that their points of intersection coincide. (pp. 347-49)

It should be clear that the fact that this neutral superior centre of these antitheses is a common one will give rise to an abundance of mutual relationships, and indeed of new antithetic unities between the antitheses themselves too, so that, strictly speaking, with each single antithesis it is not only its two poles and its centre which we have to reckon, but because this centre is also the centre of all the others, we have at once indirectly to take all the others into account.

1. *Poesy.* Novalis sometimes, in accord with Fichte, defined this centre as the ego, which is confronted by the non-ego, the universe, consisting in the unity of every object of sense, but in such a manner that the positing of the ego is to be understood as a positing of the universe, and the positing of the universe as a positing of the ego. . . . [Novalis], advancing beyond Fichte, defined this centre better and more peculiarly as the life which consists precisely in its defiance of the attempt to comprehend it, because it has its being beyond the ego and non-ego, being and non-being, composed of synthesis, thesis and antithesis and yet nothing of all three. Life is 'the stuff that truly and absolutely binds everything together'.

At the point where he defines the centre as poesy Novalis speaks in terms which are completely characteristic of him and quite original. 'Poesy is that which is truly and absolutely actual. That is the core of my philosophy. The more poetic a thing is the truer it is'. Novalis understood the concept of poesy primarily in its original sense of . . . work, creation. 'The poetic philosopher is *en état de créateur absolu*'. He posits subject, predicate and copula simultaneously. 'Transcendental poetics treats of the spirit before it becomes spirit'. 'The poet is *a priori* the inventor of symptoms'. 'The true poet is omniscient, he is a real world in miniature'. It is precisely for this reason that poetry is admittedly ultimately 'something completely personal and therefore indescribable and indefinable. Anyone who does not immediately know and feel what poesy is can never have any conception of it instilled into him'. The poet, the true poet, he of genius, and no other, is the true man: 'It is the poets, those rare nomadic men, who pass from time to time through our dwelling-places and everywhere renew the old and

venerable service of mankind and of its first gods, of the stars, spring, love, happiness, fertility, health and gladness; they who are in this life already the possessors of a heavenly peace and not driven hither and thither by any foolish desires, only breathe in the scent of earthly fruits without consuming them and thus becoming bound irrevocably to the underworld. They are free visitors, whose golden foot steps gently and whose presence causes all men to spread involuntary wings. A poet, like a good king, is to be discerned by the joy and clarity of his countenance, and he alone it is who rightly bears the name of a sage'.

Thus poetry by no means coincides with art and for this reason it would not be fitting in discussing Novalis to speak of 'aestheticism' in the customary meaning of the word. Poetry, according to Novalis, is certainly also art, but is at the same time distinct in principle from all other art, as the art of expression by means of the word. It distinguishes itself from painting on its right and music on its left by the fact that what it does is in no way produced with tools and hands. 'The eye and the ear perceive nothing of it . . . it is all achieved inwardly . . . through words and poet presents us with an unknown splendid world for our perception. Past and future times, countless human figures, wonderful regions and the strangest occasions rise up in us as if from deep caverns and tear us away from the known present. We hear unfamiliar words and are yet aware of what they should mean. The utterances of the poet exercise a magic power; the familiar words, too, appear in delightful assonance and bemuse the enchanted hearer'. This, according to Novalis, is in fact the essence of Romantic poetry: its way of 'pleasantly surprising art, of making an object strange, and yet familiar and attractive . . .'. But this is something only poetry can do of all the arts, or which all other arts can do only in so far as they, too, are poetic. Making the strange familiar by means of making the familiar strange: this is nothing else but the rhythm of ego and non-ego, the rhythm of life itself, in which Novalis imagines he has discovered the essential nature of poesy, and of the creative process in general. That is why poetry is the secret not only of this or that person, but the secret of man in general. (pp. 349-51)

To summarize, the concept of the ego or of life or, significantly, poesy, and, therefore, the concept of the neutral superior centre is, with Novalis, to be defined as the endless becoming outward of endless inwardness, or also as the endless becoming inward of endless outwardness, in the way that these processes both can and should and do in fact take place in the human act of living. It is a principle which is not only systematic, which does not only organize, but which is a creative principle that we have thereby come to know. All other principles are applications of this one creative principle, and are identical with it in substance. That is why it and it alone can stand neutral and superior as the centre of all of them. Novalis stated his notion of this principle in a manner entirely and uncannily characteristic of him, in describing it finally also as a magic principle, and the poet, and thus man in general, as a magician. (p. 352)

2. *Art.* There can be no mistaking the particular affinity of this poetic or magic principle with art. We have already heard that the two do not simply coincide. But the poet in whom Novalis perceives the true man is yet, primarily at any rate, also the poet in the narrower sense of the word, one identifying him also as one of various kinds of artist. . . . [In his doctrine of art], Novalis is very far from wishing to throw open the floodgates of an unrestrained immediacy. The poet cannot be cool and composed enough. . . . A poet must not idly wander about

all day and go hunting after images and states of feeling. That is the wrong way entirely. A pure and open state of mind, skill in reflection and observation, and an adroitness in transforming all his abilities into an activity which in its turn enlivens the mind, and keeping them there; such are the demands of our art'. It is only upon this condition that the identification of life with art, art with poesy, is valid. With this we have already cast a glance from art at the thing which makes it possible and orders it, the power of thought: without philosophy there can be no perfect poetry.

3. *Philosophy.* 'The division between the poet and the thinker is only an apparent one and is harmful to both. It is a sign of disease and a diseased constitution'. Philosophy is only feeling when it is dreaming. This statement is not meant in any derogatory sense. Dreaming, for the pure Romantic, is something to be treated in all earnestness. Philosophy is in its original form feeling. It treats of an object which cannot be learned, of no object, that is to say. That sets it apart from all the other sciences, which have as their objects things which can be learned. . . . And it is precisely because philosophy in its perfect form is nothing else but poesy that it must now come together with art in the narrower sense, must conceive of itself as art, the art of 'producing all our ideas in accordance with an absolute artistic idea and of evolving by way of thinking a world-system *a priori* from the depths of our spirit, of using the organ of thought actively for the representation of a world to be comprehended only in thought'. 'The poet closes the procession just as he opened it. If the task of the philosopher is only to order everything and put it in its place, the poet loosens every bond. . . . Poesy is the key to philosophy'. Thus we are directed back from the second pole of this antithesis to the first one again.

4. *Nature.* Corresponding to the antithesis of art and philosophy on the ontological there is the antithesis of nature and history on the ontic plane. Nature is 'the quintessence of that which moves us'. It is 'that wonderful community into which our body introduces us and which we come to know according to the body's facilities and capacities'. It is 'an Aeolian harp, it is a musical instrument whose sounds moreover are the keys to higher strings in ourselves'. '"Where is the man", cried the youth with sparkling eyes, "whose heart does not leap with delight when the inmost life of nature enters his mind in all its abundance, and when, at this, that mighty feeling, for which language has no other name but love and desire, expands within him, like a strong, all-releasing vapour, and he sinks trembling with sweet anguish into the dark, alluring womb of nature, his poor personality being consumed in the breaking waves of delight, and nothing remaining but a focal point in the immeasurable procreative power, a sucking whirlpool in the vast ocean"'. With Novalis, as his *Fragments* in particular show, such dithyrambs have as their background a true abundance of observations in natural science, drawn especially from the fields of biology, physics and chemistry, psychology and medicine. 'The essential qualities required of a true naturalist are a long and unrelenting association with the object of his study, free and ingenious observation, an attention to the slightest indications and tendencies, an inner poetic life, practised senses, and a simple and God-fearing mind'. The most significant of these requirements is, however, once again, the 'inner poetic life'. 'The spirit of nature has appeared at its purest in poems. Upon reading or hearing true poems one feels an inner understanding of nature moving there, and hovers like nature's heavenly body, at once in it and over it. The naturalist and the poet,

in that they speak a common language, have ever revealed themselves to be as one race and people'.

It is precisely at this point, however, that one is tempted to see the objectivity of that which is observed threatened, in spite of the realism which Novalis recommends here, too, by the stormy *eros* of the observing subject. And if this be in doubt then the balance of the rhythm of this entire system of thought is threatened also! There is a disturbing note in Novalis's proclamation: 'The secret path leads inwards. Eternity with its worlds, the past and the future, is within us, or nowhere'. 'What need have we of laboriously journeying through the muddy world of visible things? For the purer world lies within us within this fountain-head. It is here that the real meaning of the great, variegated, confused spectacle is revealed; and if, full of these sights, we step into the realm of nature, everything there is familiar to us, and we have a sure knowledge of every form. We have no need of any long research; a light comparison, a few lines traced in the sand, are enough to ensure our understanding. Thus all things are like a great book to us, for which we have the key, and nothing takes us by surprise, because we know in advance the way the great clock-work runs'. (pp. 352-55)

We do not know whether Novalis would have continued further along this course, which was not without its dangers, or whether he might have more nearly approached the great maturity of Goethe's outlook upon nature. What is certainly intended, even in such striking passages, is, however, the proclamation of the referring back of the perception which is directed outwards to the principle of the centre. This is achieved by the proclamation of the necessary counter-pole to this world of nature, which presses in upon man in an overwhelming way. This counter-pole of nature coincides, however, in Novalis, with history. For it is not enough to be able to improvise upon nature, as upon a great musical instrument. It is only the man who understands the history of nature, its dimension of depth in time, who understands nature. History, however, means mind, as it is opposed to nature in the 'counter-image of humanity'. Nature would not be divine if it did not also have a history, did not also have a spirit. (pp. 355-56)

5. *History.* . . . Nature and history are in very fact opposed to one another in an antithetic unity. In history, too, according to Novalis, in so far as it is now to be taken especially into account, man seeks and finds the ego in the non-ego, the familiar in the strange. It is characteristic of Novalis that with nature it is primarily a question of finding, and with history, of seeking the great ×, the × which is his subject the whole time. . . . [There] can be no mistaking the fact that the concept of a historical realism, which now truly seeks the familiar in the strange, is not unknown to Novalis. But far more important to him than an assessment of the significance of exact research into the details of history is here once again the polemic against its degeneration, against every study of history which is merely analytic, unphilosophic, unpoetic, and the canon that 'a student of history must also of necessity be a poet', and the assertion that there is more truth in the fanciful tales of the poets than in the learned chronicles. (p. 356)

[In *Christendom or Europe,* the sole example of historical art Novalis has left to us,] he draws a mighty circle from the boldly idealized, or perhaps imagined, picture of the peaceable and friendly single Church of the Middle Ages, through the Reformation, which declared a revolutionary government permanent, profanely identified the boundaries of the Church with those of the state, and introduced the highly alien secular science of philology into affairs of religion, on to the farthest point of the orbit, which in so far as it is the farthest point already heralds the return, the Enlightenment, with its hatred of the Church, the Bible, faith, enthusiasm and poesy, and finally back to the time just then coming, that of the resurrection, the conception of a new Messiah, in which one Brother in particular is described and lauded as the 'heart-beat of a new age', who has made for the Holy one, i.e. religion, 'a new veil', which 'clingingly betrays the divine mould of her limbs and yet veils her more chastely than any other'. Novalis awaits the revelation of this new age and with it the coming to life of Christianity, the bringing of awakenment and peace to Europe in every field, from the convocation of a 'venerable European council'. 'When?—and when most likely? That is not the question. Just be patient, the time will come, must come, the holy time of lasting peace, when the new Jerusalem shall be the capital city of the world; and until this day, be cheerful and courageous amid the dangers of the time, sharers of my faith; proclaim with word and deed the holy Gospel, and remain faithful unto death to the true eternal faith'. . . . [We] see the pure Romantic standing in affecting isolation, and ask ourselves whether it might not be that his need is sprung from a tragic guilt; whether a view which has so largely renounced the ability to see could in fact end anywhere but in this convulsive hope which simply does not speak in tones worthy of credence. And we ask ourselves . . . whether, if he had lived longer, Novalis would have proceeded further along these lines, or whether from this point he would have found his way forward or back to an ultimate historical wisdom. Suffice it to say that here the problem of history is at all events passionately felt to be a problem, and poesy, man's creative inward world, has shown itself to be the key to this book of mysteries as well.

6. *Love.* What art and philosophy are on the ontological plane, and nature and history on the ontic one, love and religion are on the personal or ethical plane. It becomes even more difficult than before to distinguish the antitheses to some extent, both among themselves, and from the creative centre.

It is part of the quality of Novalis as a phenomenon that his utterances concerning love in the most obvious sense have not the breadth which one might perhaps expect. . . . According to Novalis sexual love is the decisive event in human life because it is the revealed secret of reciprocal effect. Love is 'a mysterious flowing together of our most secret and most peculiar being'. It is a question in life, in all art and philosophy, in nature and history, of ego and non-ego. Novalis, however, advancing beyond Fichte, wished to have the non-ego understood as Thou. It is, he finds, precisely love which is lacking in Fichte. Love understands the non-ego as Thou in understanding it as beloved and loving Thou and consequently as the 'centre-point of a paradise', as the 'object of all objects'; consequently the propositions are valid that 'love is the most highly actual thing, the primal basis', 'the final goal of world history, the Amen of the universe'. 'I do not know what love is, but one thing I can tell you; I feel as if I were only now beginning to live.—My Matilda, for the first time I sense what it means to be immortal.—How deeply you shame me! For it is only through you that I am what I am. Without you I should be nothing. What is a spirit without a heaven, and you are the heaven which contains me and bears me up.—I can conceive nothing of eternity, but should think that must be eternity which I feel when I think of you.—Yes Matilda, we are immortal because we love each other'. Thus we hear the lovers speaking in *Heinrich von Ofterdingen*. But what is decisive in this representation of love is not, after all, the way the lovers find

each other for themselves, but the way in which, simultaneously looking at and beyond each other, they each discover in the object of their gaze the new secret world of poesy.

> A darkling pathway love did tread,
> Seen by the moon alone,
> The shadows realm, unfolded wide,
> Fantastically shone.
>
> An azure mist with golden edge
> Around her hung in play
> And eager Fancy bore her fast
> Oe'r stream and land away.
>
> Her full and teeming breast rose up
> In wondrous spirit-flow;
> A presagement of future bliss
> Bespoke the ardent glow.

The *eros* which is the subject of this poem has become the divine *Eros,* or is at any rate no longer merely that *eros* which unites two human beings. For when this *eros* reaches its goal the human couple, the man and the woman, have vanished in the eternally-human, that the one has found in the other, the romance is lost in the purely Romantic quality, for whose sake alone the romance shall and may exist, and the truth then, is that

> Love's kingdom now is opened full
> And Fable 'gins to ply her wheel;
> To primal play each nature turns,
> To speak with tongues each spirit burns.
> And thus the world's great feeling looms,
> Moves everywhere, forever blooms.
> For each thing to all else must strive,
> One through the other grow and thrive;
> Each one is shadowed forth in all
> While it itself with them is blending,
> Eager to their deeps doth fall,
> Its own peculiar being mending,
> And myriad thoughts to life doth call.—
> The world's a dream, and dream the world.

And therefore by virtue of this passage through the creative centre the counter-pole must always shine forth in love, too, in magical identity with love itself. That is why the lovers' conversation goes on as follows: 'O beloved, heaven has given you to me to worship. I pray to you, you are the saint who carries my wishes to the ear of God, through whom he reveals himself to me, through whom he declares to me the abundance of his love. What is religion but an unlimited understanding, an eternal union of loving hearts? Where two are gathered together he is there. It is through you that I have to draw breath forever; my breast will never cease to draw you in. You are the divine splendour, eternal life in most alluring guise . . . I swear to be yours eternally, Matilda, as truly as love, God's presence, is with us'. That is why Novalis himself was able to write in his diary: 'I feel religion for Sophie—not love. Absolute love, independent of the heart, based upon faith; such is religion'.

7. *Religion.* 'Through absolute will love can be transformed into religion'. We were already prepared for that sentence. Like art and philosophy, like the study of nature and history, and like love, religion for Novalis is without doubt in the first place a work of man, something to do with Romantic civilization. There is as yet no religion. First of all a lodge for training in true religion must be founded. Do you believe that

religion exists? Religion must be made and put forward by the union of a number of people'. The concept of God is achieved 'from the union of every capacity for feeling' ... 'by means of a moral revelation, a moral miracle of centralization'. For the finding of God an intermediate link is of course necessary. But this intermediate link must be chosen by ourselves, and this choice must be free. Regarding the intermediary as God himself is idolatry. The intermediary is the organ of the Godhead, its sensory manifestation, and Novalis declares himself a believer in Pantheism in the sense that he wishes to understand by it the idea that everything can be the organ of the Godhead, the intermediary, if I exalt it to that position. He rejects monotheism, which seeks to acknowledge only one such organ, but believes it possible to unite pantheism and monotheism by making the monotheist intermediary the intermediary of the intermediate world of pantheism, through it centring this world, as it were. ... Novalis furthermore thinks that the Bible is still in process of growing. 'The history of every man is intended to be a Bible; will be a Bible. ... A Bible is the highest task of authorship'. 'There is no religion that would not be Christianity'. 'Our whole life is service of God'. No wonder Novalis speaks of 'the infinite sadness of religion': 'If we are to love God he must be in need of succour'. No wonder he has given us, one might well say, an absurd philosophy of the Lord's Supper, the existence of which could not be well enough noted by the present-day adherents of symbolism. Its climax is contained in the sentence: 'Thus daily we enjoy the genius of nature, and thus each meal becomes a commemorative one, a meal which changes our soul just as it sustains our body, a mysterious means of transfiguration and deification on earth, of a quickening intercourse with that which lives absolutely'. (pp. 358-62)

If we are justified in speaking of a *hubris* of the Enlightenment, then it is here, in the magic religious teaching of pure Romanticism, that it broke out, and if perchance it was precisely the religious teaching of pure Romanticism which was to become the esoteric secret of nineteenth-century religious teaching, then it is just in this event that the uninterrupted connexion with eighteenth-century absolutism would stand revealed. It is surely clear, indeed Novalis says it himself, that his teaching of religion is the teaching of love, of heavenly love indeed, but of love nevertheless. For all this, however, we should not perhaps bear him ill-will, in the last assessment. ... (p. 363)

What is the nature of [Novalis's religious] insight? It can be described by a linking up with ... [his] definition of the concept o: it is a question of the insight into the 'positive non-determinate' of the ego, of life, of poesy. The Romantic doctrine of poesy proceeds, to begin with, from the point of determination 1: in poesy man posits himself as the ultimate reality. It is upon this basis that he dares to establish the Romantic doctrine of poesy. ... But the secret wisdom which Novalis acquired in 1797 [upon Sophie's death] says that beyond this point of determination 1 there takes place the positive non-determinate! Let it be noted: *positive* non-determinate; this border, this Beyond of the Romantic synthesis requires therefore to be construed not merely negatively, but positively. It seems as if a new field of at least equally serious problems were unfolding itself, above this synthesis and its problems. It seems! For it is precisely this which we do not know, and we must take good care not to feel tempted to decide positively (just as little as we can decide negatively) whether this new field of problems really disclosed itself to Novalis's thought; whether a shaking of the somnambulist feeling of security with which we see the pure Romantic going his purely Romantic

way, took place, therefore, or not. It may also be that as a result of this insight he felt himself yet again, all the more confirmed and strengthened in this security. It is also possible that he succeeded in relating the antithesis of life and death which revealed itself to him beyond the antithesis of love and religion, to the Romantic synthesis. He may have succeeded in dissolving death 'in a play of harmonies', in 'pointing to it as an arabesque in the poetry of each individual life' .... It may also be that the figure before whom he apparently desires to clasp his hands, having come up against this positive frontier, was after all only that of Mary and not of Christ. We must content ourselves with establishing the fact that it could, none the less, have been otherwise: it might also be (and judging by the nature of the matter there are no strong indications against this) that a perception of a radically different kind had announced itself, that the Romantic synthesis in the entire splendour of its self-given sense of security yet ultimately bore within it a great, fundamental and inescapable flaw, capable of shaking, challenging, and even of destroying it, and that, therefore, it was after all Christ and not Mary whom Novalis encountered at this frontier.

The facts of the matter are these: In the *Hymns to the Night* Novalis speaks of his discovery that in the conflict between the Daylight, the most beloved of all the miraculous manifestations of space by those living and endowed with sense—and the Night, the sacred, ineffable, mysterious Night, it is the latter which should be accorded pride of place and greater honour. (pp. 367-68)

Novalis did not then renounce the world of light as a result of this discovery and change of attitude. On the contrary: it is Platonic, doubly reflected negation which is in question here.

> Gladly will I move
> With busy hands,
> And ever look to see
> Where you need me,
> Praise the utter glory
> Of your splendour,
> Tirelessly pursue
> The wonderful contrivance
> Of your work.
> Gladly I observe
> The meaning course
> Of your great glowing
> Measurer of time,
> Plumb the regularity
> Of forces
> And the rules
> Of the fantastic play
> Of spaces numberless
> And all their periods.
> But my most inward heart
> Remains the thrall of night
> And of her daughter,
> Creative love.

For night is at once the secret, the true principle of the world of light. (pp. 369-70)

That the Night which the poet thus extols is the night of death ... is something which finds direct expression in that very artistic part of Novalis's poetry written in the form of a mythical history. Life was once:

> An endless feast
> Of gods and men.
> In childlike awe

Each race revered
The tender, precious flame
As the highest thing in the world.

But there is one thing which mars and irresistibly, irreparably interrupts this feast:

One thought alone was there,
Which, its dread form amid gay revels showing,
Did sudden fill their heart with horror wild;
Nor means had all the gods within their knowing
To still men's troubled mind with comfort mild;
Mysterious ill the spectre e'er went sowing;
Nor prayer subdued his rage, nor gift beguiled;
For Death it was who all their merry cheer
Suppressed, with pain and anguish and with tears.

      .   .   .

With daring spirit and impassioned breast
Man sought to beautify the mask of dying,
A pallid youth puts out the light and rests,
The end as gentle as a harp's low sighing—
And memory melts mid shadow-waves' cool crests,
The poet sang, to this sad need replying.
But still unfathomed was the endless Night,
The awful symbol of a far-off might.

Until the great reversal of death actually came about:

The night became
The fruitful womb
Of revelations

      .   .   .

The deep divining
Fertile wisdom
Of the East
Did first perceive
The new millennium's dawn.

Christ was born and lived, an event which Novalis describes as follows:

The heavenly heart
A lonely flower unfolding,
Turned towards
The glowing source of love,
The Father's countenance sublime—
Resting on the loving-earnest mother's
Breast, which dreamed of blessedness.
The growing child's prophetic gaze,
With fervour to ensure divinity,
Was turned towards the future,
To his loved ones, future
Bearers of his name,
Not caring for the earthly
Fate in store.
Around him soon,
Miraculously drawn by
Love all-powerful
The child-like hearts assembled.
A new and unknown life
Grew up like flowers
Where he was—
From his loving lips
Undying words
And tidings most rejoicing
Fell like sparks
Of a divine spirit.

And then Novalis causes this wondrous child to be addressed by a minstrel hailing from a far-off shore, and who then joyfully journeys onward to Hindustan, as follows:

The youth art thou who all these years hast stood
In thought inclined o'er graves of mortal beings;
A sign of comfort in dark solitude,
And of a higher manhood's glad beginning;
That which hath made our soul so long to pine
Now draws us hence, sweet aspirations winning.
In death eternal life hath been revealed,
And thou art Death, by thee we first are healed.

For while Christ is dying, while his holy mouth, drawn in dreadful anguish, is draining the dark cup of suffering, the birth hour of the new world is drawing near him.... [The *Hymns to the Night*] are balanced by the two songs to the Virgin Mary and the thirteen Sacred Songs. Their thought-content is apparently the same as that of the first two works, the only difference being that now, instead of the ideas, night and death, it is the ideas, Mary and Christ, which occurred in the mythical-historical turn of the first train of thought, which acquire central importance, so that, accordingly, the positive, affirmatory significance of the entire new insight is stressed even more strongly and one-sidedly, being indeed the sole subject of emphasis. It is, however, precisely at this particular point inevitable, in face of this specifically religious, and indeed Christian writing by Novalis, that this entire final problem which he raises should once again itself become highly problematical ...: problematical in its ultimate seriousness as regards the genuineness of the transcendence which, seemingly, makes itself noticeable here, and as regards the solidity of the ground upon which all the rest of his work, as a thinker and poet, is here seen to be standing. Has the 'awful symbol of a far-off might' in death become visible with such complete clarity ... that the thought of the overcoming of death does not have the significance of a renewed attempt to beautify the gruesome mask of dying, with daring spirit and impassioned breast? Be that as it may— it is now the faith in the love for Christ which overcomes death, which is declared loudly, and with spirit and persistence. (pp. 371-77)

In short: Novalis has suddenly become remarkably ripe for the hymn-book. This is not without its more doubtful aspects. For it is certainly the modern hymn-book he has become ripe for. The Christian song we hear him singing is certainly not the first person plural song of the Reformation, praising the great deeds of the Lord, but a species, and perhaps the most pronounced species, of the first person singular song which has advanced mightily since 1600, in which the congregation thinks to find edification by letting each individual say and sing that he has felt the hand of God in such and such a way, and how his works have been of benefit to him, to him, to him.

We wonder where death is now, a figure full of menace, warning and promise, who after all confronts too this entire Christian heaven, in so far as it is part of earthly experience. Can it perhaps be that the poet does not intend to express this opposition as something so dangerous, so critical, so full of promise, as he seems to portray it in several passages? Has not death, after all, been resolved in a play of harmonies? And can it be thus resolved? Can the 'positive non-determinate' be included in such a manner; can it, after all, carried away by a powerful 'enthusiasm for Night', be included in the point of determination? Was the poet's whole meaning no more serious than in this way when he spoke of the visitor, 'its dread form amid gay revels showing'? Can one dispose of him by simply, in the twinkling of an eye, giving him the name of Christ? And what has Christ become, if he is deemed just good enough to appear as a mythical symbol—or is the poet's meaning different?—at this point, where it is a question of replacing the negative by the positive sign? If it is possible to mention 'Jesus' and 'the sweet bride' in the same breath and sense? If the name Mary can simply be set down with equal meaning for the name Jesus? If he is omnipresent in this way and only seems to have been waiting for the inclination of our hearts, to become our own? ... Is there a knowledge here of the decision between Baal and Jehovah, or has not Baal been chosen unconsciously a long time previously—an act suppressing from the outset, perhaps, the question which flashed into the mind like lightning? Was Novalis in the *Hymns to the Night* and in the *Sacred Songs* singing another melody or was he not rather singing the same one as he usually sang an octave deeper: the song of the magic identity between the ego and the non-ego, with Night now additionally included, with death now additionally included, with Christ himself now additionally included? These things we can only ask. And we are not entitled to ask them as if perhaps we knew the answer. We do not know it. But in order to understand Novalis we must ask, sharply, remorselessly.

The question is concentrated with much symbolic force in the question concerning the meaning of the opposing of Christ and Mary. If the *Sacred Songs,* in spite of all the talk of Christ, are, in the final and decisive assessment, songs to the Virgin Mary, then that would mean that Novalis has in fact succeeded in understanding death . . . as a 'romanticizing principle', as he once said, as the ultimate principle of this great process of things growing more strange and more familiar, in making it part of the reality of this dancing god, and in including Christ too in the train of Dionysus. For if Mary is the final word— Mary in the sense of Roman Catholic Church doctrine, to which, upon this point, Novalis was receptive enough—then that means that the final word is the creature open to what is above, open to God, capable of participating in God. The creature thus described can at most be regarded with fervour, at most also with infinite sadness but by no means worshipped. In what concerns Mariology the Roman Catholic Church doctrine too in fact—whatever else may be said of it—is still confined within the frame of the ancient and ever new religion of immanence, which one hundred years ago was called Romanticism. The meaning of 'Star of the sea, I greet thee' may well be one of wondrous beauty, but is not sufficient to make plain the decision or the revelation.

Everything would be different if the *Sacred Songs* could really be referred to by the title they lay claim to, that, namely, of songs of Christ. . . . [However] there is a great deal which argues against this. But . . . we do not have the final right not to recognize them as what they claim to be. Behind them lies a life that might well have known, and seems to have known, enough of the 'dreadful anguish' to compel us at all events to respect its confession of faith, for all the doubts it might awaken in us. Thousands and thousands of people over the last hundred years have believed that in these poems they have heard a most genuine testimony. Who would argue that they have not really heard it? The fact that *our* confession and testimony, for serious reasons, perhaps, cannot be this one is another question. At all events the simple fact that Novalis wrote these *Sacred Songs* (and in such quantity, too, in relation to the sum-total of his output) is evidence that his gaze was in some way fixed upon the point which forms their subject, and fixed so strongly that it cannot be explained as the conduct of the pure Romantic,

for whom things Christian also became a symbol, as has often been said. Certainly that aspect is also part of the matter. But the emphasis with which here just things Christian become a symbol, and the proximity in which things Christian find themselves to the critical concept of death, would still remain striking and singular, even if our final judgment must be that in the last resort the riddle of death has been juggled away once more and that Christianity has yet again been interpreted in humanistic terms. In that event we should be compelled to say that pure Romanticism, in order to mark out the field containing its particular problem, had inevitably to approach extremely close to this other quite different field of problems. (pp. 380-82)

Karl Barth, "Novalis," translated by Brian Cozens, in his Protestant Theology in the Nineteenth Century: Its Background & History, *SCM Press Ltd, 1972, pp. 341-83.*

MARIANNE THALMANN (essay date 1964)

[*Thalmann theorizes about Novalis's poeticizing of reality in his fairy tales, focusing on narrative technique in "Hyazinth and Rosenblüte."*]

Novalis' views on the fairy tale are expressed in his journals in so many different interpretations and formulations that they cannot be summed up in one sentence. It is evident from them, however, that he considers the fairy-tale's "alogical" dream-like character, which to him represents experience on a higher level, and its mysterious linking of past and future the most

A depiction of Heinrich from Henry of Ofterdingen.

dependable source of a higher reality. He values the fairy tale more than any other narrative form because it poetizes reality and is, therefore, the "poetry of poetry." One can also read the sentence in reverse: "Everything poetic must be like a fairy tale." One might say, poetry is a fairy tale, history is a fairy tale, the evening is a fairy tale, love is a fairy tale—"everything is a fairy tale." . . . And as such it contains the deepest truth, far surpassing all the naturalistic transcriptions of the world and all the factual wealth of learned chronicles. The customary contrast between the fairy-tale world and the everyday world seems to be eliminated with one blow. The "higher" fairy tale, as Novalis calls it to distinguish it from the folk fairy tale, is, in short, the highest reality, for poetry is now the yardstick of the world. Novalis has shifted the physical world to the realm of the spirit in order to make it his own.

Here through his speculative thinking Novalis arrives at a concept which runs parallel to one developed by Tieck. With his imaginative vision Tieck sees the unusual emerge from the usual, and he transforms the unpoetic of life into something poetic. In doing this he casts a certain magic spell over the world, and extends the artist's domain to include even the commonplace things. (pp. 11-12)

We know the narrator of ["**Hyazinth and Rosenblüte.**"] The fellow is "a gay playmate whose temples are adorned with roses and bindweed," . . . in other words, it is not the author himself. This fairy tale is told for one of the apprentices, a thoughtful young man who is confused by the learned arguments of the master's pupils. And what is told is the story of just such a young man who runs to the end of the world, looks behind the veil of secrets, and finds the world within himself. The fairy-tale form is made to order for such a story since it is not dependent upon the things of the existing world and permits the problems of life to be solved on a different level without being tried by a psychological court. Like the dream, it can enlist the aid of "alogical" forms and imaginary figures, and it may combine philosophy with poetry. (pp. 16-17)

The narrator of "**Hyazinth and Rosenblüte**" remains in natural contact with his story, which keeps it from becoming dull and lifeless. He lives with it, he lets it come into being before our eyes. "Many years ago far to the West there lived a very young man." This is how he begins. It is not the same beginning as "once upon a time," where time and place are cautiously avoided for the child. We are approached in a different way: it was so, and everyone who is listening knows it is so and will be so, for "nothing is so poetic as memory and presentiment or an idea of the future." . . . It is told in the imperfect tense; in the fairy tale this is undoubtedly meant as past time, permitting us to enjoy the illusion in full. The introduction contains an enormously concentrated presentation of time and place—once and in the West. We respond immediately.

Novalis wrote the story without a break. It has the rapid breathing of storytelling and does not make allowances for visual pauses. Only an occasional remark by the narrator affords time for a breath. With the words, "Oh, how quickly the splendor was over," . . . the golden age of childhood comes to an end. The meeting with the stranger who awakens consciousness and speculation in Hyazinth is safely concealed by a short "as far as one heard later," . . . thereby eliminating endless destructive discussion of it. And the fairy tale closes with the comforting assurance that Hyazinth and Rosenblüte will live happily ever after and that the golden age of maturity has begun for them.

Hyazinth himself is seen from within. He is a strange sort of fellow who likes to be alone, converses with animals and trees, and can be entertained by a squirrel or a brook or a stone. On the surface he is the ideal fairy-tale prince: he "looked like a picture and danced like a dream." . . . The girl whom he left and found again is a little fairy-tale princess with cherry-red lips and hair like golden silk, and she is blindly in love. The names Hyazinth and Rosenblüte do not identify these figures with any bourgeois family circle but keep them on the same fairy-tale level as Snow White and Rose Red. Hyazinth's two decisive encounters are brought about with the air of familiar masks: the magician from distant lands who leaves the book behind and the old woman of the forest who burns the book and sends Hyazinth out from the West to the East in search of the "mother of all things."

If, in addition, we consider the beginning and end as a framework, it is clear that we are dealing here with a young man who is a stranger to himself and the world, who in forgetfulness, meetings, and memories has the ultimate experience of "the secret of loving reunion." . . . He discovers his ego in the nonego and then realizes that truth and the world are in man himself. The resulting vision of the world is a new synthesis. In between the beginning and end a life history unfolds which contains typical experiences presented in the rapid abstraction of different stages of life: books, love, travel, mountains, rivers, deserts, the secret of the temple, and the discovery of oneself. Hyazinth races through them all, overcoming dangers and obstacles as befits a fairy-tale character. It is not a question here of learning and progress, of casual necessity and reaching a sensible maturity. He is simply carried along by the stream. He matures like a plant toward his goal. The fairy tale has become an intellectual game which understandably grew to be more and more a necessity for the romantic generation which no longer depended on subjective experience. A poet is an artist, but also a thinker, a mathematician, and an architect. For that reason, too, the fairy tale must do more than merely entertain the mind and wit. Between dream and reality, freedom and exactness, this so-called "literary fairy tale" arrives at a sur-reality beyond time and space. This does not mean that it is an untruth; what is involved here is the first stage of a kind of "alienation" whereby a new level of reality is added, which may be considered modern without being an ism. It is not our intent to incorporate the sur-reality of the fairy tale into the usual discussion of sous-realism and sur-realism, but to point to the fact that it dared to advance toward the truth behind the existence of reality in the ontological sense, and thus discovered new degrees of reality beyond the realm of imitative realism. (pp. 17-19)

[The] action is contained and revealed in the verbs. There is seldom a direct reference to the lapse of a regular interval of time. Time is no longer measured by the clock. The stranger stays with Hyazinth for three days, a "three" which still has symbolic significance in the fairy tale. In the course of his journey the moment comes when Hyazinth is suddenly deeply conscious of distances. But space is expressed in terms of time: "It was as if many years lay behind him." His wanderings turn into an Odyssey. The last lap of his journey begins with "one day" and ends with "finally," when he steps out of time "into the dwelling place of the eternal seasons." . . . Timeless time is not murdered time, as has been said. Time is "inner space," space is "outer time"; here Novalis already experiments with the speculations which are so fundamental to his thinking. All his figures live in a time-world full of imagination, transitions, and metamorphoses which space tends to resist. The place is called Sais—a hieroglyph suffices. To connect Sais with the geographical location of Egypt as some have tried to do is out of the question and unthinkable. The romanticists relied more and more on the associations which a word itself evoked, not so much on the significance of the word's origins. Hyazinth's journey takes him past all the phenomena of the earth. It does not have a destination which would be given an asterisk in the Baedeker of occult sciences any more than the countries to the right and the left of his road are prettified by names. Not places and continents, that is to say, livable space with its restrictions, are wanted here. The world itself is what counts. Journeys are paths of life which bring us ever closer to ourselves. "We dream of journeys through the universe," Novalis says, "but is not the universe in us?" . . . (pp. 19-20)

The action itself unwinds with—he ran, asked, came, found, went. The phase-structure of life is implemented by adverbs of time: the frustrations of childhood by then, now, soon; the meeting with the stranger by now, then, finally; the frightening tempo of the journey by the emotional—time drags, how many years, time passed more quickly. And the last phase takes place within the repeated and enraptured there—there. And from then on, time and the seasons are actually dissolved, as was planned for the end of *Heinrich von Ofterdingen*.

There is virtually no connection between the duration of the action and the duration of the narration. The exceedingly swift compression of time effected by the verbs borders on an elimination of time and causes the events to rush past the listener in a continuous surge forward. Whereas Wackenroder tried to express human life as the agony of relentless motion in one spot, Novalis sees it as a condition which does not permit one to stand still. The flow of the narrative slows down only twice, both times in conversations. At the beginning of the fairy tale we hear how a rumor spreads through the garden and woods, turns up in the scoffing gossip of the violets, gooseberries, and strawberries, and is blurted out in the babbling song of the lizard. What is presented here in indirect speech is repeated toward the end of the story in Hyazinth's direct conversation with the spring and the flowers whom he asks about the home of Isis. In both cases the confrontation with the world becomes an integral part of the fairy tale, as does the surrounding space: the neighborhood, the mountains, valleys, rivers, and also the colors in the sky, which have the comforting effect of change.

A comparison with the classical treatment of this subject as it is found in Schiller's *The Veiled Image at Sais* (*Das verschleierte Bild zu Sais*) shows the position of the two generations. For the classicist the entry into the temple of Isis and the desire to look behind the veil fall under a moral law: whoever lifts the veil is guilty; we must wait until she, Truth herself, lifts it. But one of the priest's pupils lifts it in the night. From that moment on he is saddened, and he dies at an early age. "Woe unto him who goes to truth through guilt." Schiller develops his narrative in strict conformity to this concept of guilt and to an ethical principle. But not so Novalis. Hyazinth does not enter the temple as a rebel in search of knowledge but as a dreamer of countless dreams. He falls asleep because only a dream can lead him through "endless chambers full of strange things, sounds, modulating chords." Perhaps our concept of "consciousness which dreams" ("träumendes Bewusstsein") has become too loose. The romantic dream state has a very positive side: it penetrates what cannot be fathomed by the mind. The veil must be lifted so that we discern the world in ourselves. And dreams and love bring about the union of man and nature, a golden age. Truth for Novalis is something very different than for Schiller. Who knows truth? Who knows the world? "He who knows himself," says Fabel. "What is

the eternal secret?" the Sphinx asks. The answer in *Ofterdingen* is "Love." . . . (pp. 20-2)

Marianne Thalmann, "The Novalis Fairy Tale," in her The Romantic Fairy Tale: Seeds of Surrealism, *translated by Mary B. Corcoran, The University of Michigan Press, 1964, pp. 11-32.*

ROBERT MARTIN ADAMS (essay date 1966)

[*In this excerpt from his study of representations of the void in nineteenth-century literature, Adams explores Novalis's concept of death and observes that for the writer, death represents a "fulfillment" rather than a negation.*]

[One] would think Novalis's avid, open death wish more likely to bring him into the immediate presence of void; "suicide," he declared roundly, "is an eminently philosophic act," and no poet ever solicited non-being with more hungry anticipation. Yet, curiously, a reading of the *Hymnen an die Nacht* (1800) seems at first to yield no sense of the void, nor even very much of the terminology. The experience which Novalis describes under night-imagery is surpassingly sensual and ecstatic; it is a surrender of self and a discovery of self, the annihilation of the world and its reconstitution. As the world of sense falls away, serving no further function than to limit the expansion of the ego by reflecting it back on itself, the inner world recedes into infinite dimensions and perspectives:

> Abwärts wend'ich mich
> Zu der heiligen, unaussprechlichen
> Geheimnissvollen Nacht—
> Fernab liegt die Welt,
> Wie versenkt in eine tiefe Gruft,
> Wie wüst und einsam ihre Stelle!

Though essentially inward, Night is more than darkness, more than subjectivity; it is the creative unconscious, it is death and a world beyond death, thus an experience rich in joyous suggestions of erotic surrender; here the lover will be at last and forever reunited with his beloved:

> Du kommst, Geliebte—
> Die Nacht ist da.
> Entzückt ist meine Seele—
> Vorüber ist der irdische Weg
> Und du bist weider Mein.
> Ich schaue dir ins tiefe dunkle Auge
> Sehe nichts als Liebe und Seligkeit
> Wir sinken auf der Nacht Altar
> Aufs weiche Lager—
> Die Hülle fällt
> Und angezundet von dem warmen Druck
> Entglüht des süssen Opfers
> Reine Glut.

The world of Night, to which the poet's ultimate allegiance is given, does not altogether replace the world of garish day, but instead supports and enriches it with gleams from beyond the veil. Addressing the world of Light, the poet says,

> Sie trägt dich mutterlich
> Und ihr verdankst du
> All deine Herrlichkeit.

The transcendence of the dark world is taken for granted because the things the conscious mind can know are mere shadows and appearances; only the death-devoted, imagination-intoxicated ego is creative and ultimate. Thus Novalis plunges into this strange, illimitable ocean of the beyond, not as into destruction or self-annihilation, but with ecstasy and orgiastic delight. Death is almost entirely fulfillment, hardly at all negation. Evil is a mere illusion, like the world in which it occurs; neither Doctor Pangloss nor Mary Baker Eddy (and German idealism has streaks of both characters) could be more emphatic on this score. The "philosophic suicide" which Novalis advocated, and in effect practiced, was therefore an act of supreme confidence. It involved living in this world as if one's only intent were to die, making death a part of one's daily life. One might continue to inhabit the flesh for a while, and to incarnate one's intuitions in meager human words—but one would live only provisionally, while maintaining behind all one's human values an infinite, ironic reservation.

He envisaged a "cancellation of the distinction between life and death," and thanks to congenital tuberculosis, the timely death of an adored fiancée at fifteen, generous philosophical borrowings from Fichte, and a special gift of abstract imagination, this confusion was effectively accomplished. The world became a dream, and his dream a world. Under these circumstances Nothing (in the full sense of cosmic emptiness) was difficult and should in strict theory have been impossible for him to discover. For even if the nullity of the sensible world be assumed, the omnipotent imagination, the energetic will, the creative ego should be capable of filling quickly any temporary void. If, seeking the "*Unbedingte*," he found mere "*Dinge*" everywhere, his own philosophy might have assured him that it was only because he was creating them. Faith, for Novalis, is at the root of ordinary perception—how much more at the root of the visionary process by which the poetic-religious imagination is forever re-creating and reconstituting the world.

In this process, it is but natural that the perspectives are shortened and the outer world, the world of not-void (of history, for example, and ethical generalization) tends to sink from sight. Though it is infinite and opulent, the visionary world of Novalis looms before us immediate and continually present, a smothering rush of perceptions; experience goes on and on, the mind passing through it like a train through a tunnel, without panoramas or sweeping overviews. It is a little like the recessing frameworks of which Keats was so fond, as one vision opens endlessly into another. Immediacy counting for so much, it is not altogether surprising to find Novalis melding the pattern of one violent sensual absorption with another, and persistently thinking of sexual love as a covert form of eating. (pp. 29-32)

> *Robert Martin Adams, "Sénancour, Novalis, De-Quincey: Equivocal Romantics," in his* Episodes in the Literary Conquest of Void During the Nineteenth Century, *Oxford University Press, 1966, pp. 18-38.**

J. M. RITCHIE (essay date 1969)

[*Through a close reading of* Henry of Ofterdingen, *Ritchie discusses the novel's themes, structure, and technique and then analyzes the implications of those elements on Novalis's theories about poetry and the poet.*]

[Novalis' novel *Heinrich von Ofterdingen*] is a typically Romantic one in that it combines order and chaos, extreme aesthetic sophistication and naiveté; it is highly literary and intellectual, yet it preserves throughout the simplicity of the fairy-tale. It abounds not only in personal allusions but also in "lore derived from alchemy, geology, physics, the mystic writing of the Orient and of the Middle Ages, Böhme and Karl von

Eckarthausen (1752-1803), Hemsterhuis and the Bible, Homer, Apuleius, Horace, Ovid, Schiller, Goethe and Tieck".

The first sentence of the novel could not be simpler, more straightforward, or more down-to-earth. This is the normal "bürgerlich" world, the "Dürer-style":

> His parents were long since fast asleep in bed,
> the wall clock kept up its regular tic-toc, the
> howling wind kept the shutters banging. . . .

But very soon the action moves into a more Romantic realm, a world of night and moonlight. A mysterious stranger has filled a young man's head with tales of strange treasures and his heart with unspeakable longings. By the second sentence of the narrative we have moved from the sights and sounds of external reality to the inner world of the young hero's thoughts and emotions. He has an obsession, an *idée fixe*. Like the narrator in Heine's famous *Lorelei* who cannot get the strange tale of ancient times out of his head, Heinrich cannot forget the blue flower, and longs to see it. The stranger seems to have been telling Heinrich something along the lines of the old Thuringian legend concerning the treasure flower of the Kyffhäuser mountain, but now it is not the story itself, nor the idea of hidden treasure that obsesses him. The concept of the flower itself has somehow lifted him out of his normal sphere. He feels he has moved into a different realm, "for who worries about flowers in the normal world". And he is the only one who has been singled out for this deep inner turmoil, this strange kind of madness, a "madness", however, which makes everything seem clearer than ever before and nothing seem foreign to him. From these small beginnings of a young man's fascination with a flower Novalis builds up a motif which was to become the supreme Romantic symbol. Indeed from the use of this leitmotif of the blue flower and of the colour blue in general it soon becomes apparent that the whole novel is a *symbolic* one in which symbols and motifs are used "to link various worlds, combine experiences and mediate between disparate realms". . . . [The] world of myth is already conjured up by the young hero in the novel. He recalls another half-remembered story of ancient times when animals, trees and rocks could converse with men, and in the strange mental and emotional state in which he finds himself he feels this is about to happen any minute and that he can tell just by looking what they wish to express!

This marks another characteristic affecting the whole structure of Novalis' Romantic novel. Just as Heinrich's thoughts "tend towards music" consistent with the novel's ultimate goal of absolute harmony, so too the normal barriers of logical time are broken down leaving past, present and future to flow easily into one. The climax to the novel was to be a grand poem "The Marriage of the Seasons", closing the never-ending cycle of the novel structure by going back to the very first lines of the novel. . . . Where the novel has since the second or third sentence developed into a kind of interior monologue, now it moves deeper and deeper into the subconscious of Heinrich, who loses himself in sweet fantasies before he eventually falls asleep. What follows is a dream, and then a dream within a dream. For Heinrich's father, the realist and rationalist, "dreams are mere empty bubbles". According to him, there may have been some need for dreams once upon a time because they led to divine visions, as the Bible shows. But he denies that any such immediate exchange between heaven and earth is now possible. Hence he claims that ancient tales and sacred books are the only sources of information about any higher realm, in so far as we need any at all: now instead of direct revelations the holy spirit speaks to us through the medium of the *reason* of wise and right-thinking men. Heinrich cannot accept this realistic, rationalistic viewpoint. For him even the most confused dream is a "significant rent in the mysterious curtain falling with a thousand folds into our soul", and he continues, with a statement which is in a sense a Romantic defence of the dream as well as a pointer to the dream-like course of the narrative in *Heinrich von Ofterdingen:*

> As I see it the dream is a kind of bulwark against the regular and the commonplace in life, a free recreation for the captive imagination which is given a chance to jumble up all life's images and break into the grown-up's unceasing solemnity with some merry child's play. If it weren't for dreams we should certainly age sooner. Hence even if one does not accept the dream as sent directly from heaven one can take it as a divine gift, a friendly companion on the pilgrimage to the holy sepulchre. . . .

The advantages of the dream as a literary vehicle for the Romantic aesthetic can be seen here. In it all the barriers of normal existence crumble allowing Heinrich to move freely in space and time, over immeasurable distances and through wild unknown regions. He can walk across oceans, meet all manner of men, experience war and peace, and maintain what would otherwise be an unbelievably high emotional pitch. In this one dream, for example, he not only survives an infinitely varied life, he dies and is reborn, experiences the absolute limit of passion only to be eternally separated from his beloved. Clearly, as Heinrich realizes, this is not just any dream; this is his *fate.* In it he is living his own future life in extremely condensed form. And this is only the preliminary dream, for in the dream within a dream that comes to him just before dawn he penetrates even more mysteriously into the depths. After climbing upwards through the green net of a forest he finds an opening leading into a mountain. Everything he sees and experiences in his passage down the shaft into the cavern seems a symbolic revelation of the mysterious movements within his own soul—the experience is ecstasy but it is important to notice that more than mere feelings are conveyed. There is also delight for him in the countless *ideas* striving towards inner unity within him and in the new *images* which fuse together and assume visible shape. This ecstatic vision is like a small foretaste of the *visionary* quality the novel itself strives to achieve.

Nor must it be thought that these ecstatic heights leave the Romantic unaware of the erotic possibilities of dream language. Novalis' novel is in many ways far removed from the calculated eroticism of Schlegel's *Lucinde,* but it does contain some strange erotic fantasies like the passage here in which Heinrich, filled with an irresistible longing, undresses and climbs into the mysterious fountain:

> Every wave of the pleasing element snuggled close to him like a soft bosom. The waves seemed like a solution of delightful maidens assuming human form against the youth from second to second. . . .

As he follows the gleaming river in his dream state of ecstasy and hyper-awareness he falls into another slumber from which he awakens into yet another moment of illumination. In a strange blue light he sees the blue flower which this time is going through a mysterious transformation: in its leaves he sees a maiden's face. In this way the blue flower is early associated both with love and with his future beloved. Indeed it will be seen that when Heinrich's dream (or cycle of dreams) is studied in detail everything that is to happen to him in the novel is already foreshadowed or hinted at in them. Hence there are never any surprises for Heinrich in life: in his dreams he is offered, not only the key to his own future life, but, like his father who has experienced a similar dream, he has seen the "miracle of the world". If his father before him had kept his mind focused on the blue flower and asked God for the meaning of the dream, he too could have been the happiest man in the world and "the supreme mortal lot" could have been his.

The first chapter of the novel has revealed its inward direction and Heinrich's mother, noticing that he has become so quiet and turned in upon himself, decides on a journey to expose him to new people and new places. In other words, Novalis, who from the start has adopted the form of the historical novel, also exploits now the traditional device of the journey. His hero is to be a wanderer through the world with a girl waiting for him at the end of the journey as his prize. Later still Heinrich, when he loses this girl, becomes that even more Romantic figure, the religious wanderer—the pilgrim. It is apparent that the novel also follows the traditional German pattern of the *Bildungsroman.* Heinrich has no knowledge of the world except for what he has gathered from stories, hence his journey will be a voyage of discovery on which above all he will discover himself. At this point too it becomes clear how "romantic" is the view of the Middle Ages which the author finds so attractive, compared with the *modern* age of prosperity, uniformity and unrelated reality:

> Between the crude ages of barbarism and the aesthetic, scientific and prosperous age of the present (was) a profound and *romantic* age concealing a higher form under a simple cloak. Surely everybody likes to wander in the twilight when night fractures on light and light on night into higher shadows and colours. That's what makes us so ready to immerse ourselves in the age when Heinrich lived. . . .

(pp. 122-26)

Revealing at this point is the significance attached to Heinrich's feelings on parting from the known world of his house on the Wartburg for the unknown world which awaits him outside. Parting means sorrow, the first awareness of the transience of all temporal things, a first premonition of death. Such experience is seen as necessary, indeed essential, for the old world is never lost and even at this early stage the novel's cyclical form is indicated by the suggestion that the hero leaves only to return, his path into the world always leads him home, following "the dialectical principle of self-finding through self-expression". This time the miraculous blue flower which appears before him seems to mean home.

The narrative form employed also becomes readily apparent. There are, for example, no long or detailed descriptions of the country through which the travelling company passes. Hence just as it is difficult to tell exactly when in the Middle Ages this is all taking place, so too there is no precision of geographical detail. Instead of descriptions there are all sorts of *discussions, conversations* and *stories.* From the start the novel presents a passive and purely receptive hero listening to various voices. The first general conversation is essentially a hymn of praise to Suabia, the land in the south they are journeying towards, but it soon develops into a fundamental discussion of the true path through the labyrinth of confusion existing in the real world. Already Heinrich, like the boy Christ before the Elders, talks as from boyish dreams to defend "childish untrammelled innocence" and differentiates two paths leading to the knowledge of human society. One of these is laborious and endless with countless twists and bends. This is the way of experience. The other, "more like one quick leap", is the path of inner contemplation. Heinrich's fluency in the expression of his inner feelings, his mastery of appropriate analogies, and his natural bent for the marvellous, reveal to the merchants his true nature. He has the makings of a poet. Though he has no knowledge of the art of poetry and has never seen a poem, the seeds have been sown within him and his old teacher was obviously correct in his prophecy that he would dedicate his whole life to poetry once he discovered his true nature. In other words, *Heinrich von Ofterdingen* is a Romantic novel of the artist, and the first of many definitions of the nature of the poet then follows:

> In the old days, the story goes, poetry used to be far commoner and everybody had some knowledge of it, only some more than others. It was said to have been related to other marvellous lost arts. The singers were thought to be so constantly honoured with divine favour that inspired by this invisible communion they were able to proclaim divine wisdom on earth with pleasing song. . . .

This preliminary definition is significantly expanded by the merchants who point to the difference between poetry and the arts of music and painting. While these are mainly external in their effect on the senses poetry is entirely internal in that the poet fills the *inward* sanctuary of the mind with new, wonderful and pleasing thoughts. He knows how to rouse the secret forces within the reader and by his words reveals a marvellous unknown realm. He can summon great ages of the past and the future, countless beings, marvellous regions and strangest events out of the depths, and transport us out of the everyday existence we know so well. The words he uses are strange, yet meaningful, his utterances have a magic power and even the most commonplace words are made to sound so wonderful that the listener is entranced. With this Novalis has described not any poet in any age but the creative power of the Romantic *imagination* in particular.

At this point the merchants begin to tell stories which they have heard on their travels. The first of these takes us back to mythical times in ancient Greece when poets:

> were said to have been both soothsayer and priest, law-giver and physician, while even the higher beings, attracted to earth by their magic art, instructed them in the secrets of the future and revealed to them the symmetry and the natural order of all things, also the inner virtues and healing powers of cyphers, herbs and all creatures. . . .

Here again it is significant how much power is ascribed to the poet, for he not only brings peace into a warring universe, it is he who brings order out of chaos and it is he who is responsible for the peculiar traces of harmony and order still visible in nature.

The second story the merchants have to tell is taken from a later stage in history, by which time disharmony lived on only in the ancient tales of the poets:

> All hateful, ugly passions had been banished as discords from the mood of gentle harmony which prevailed in all minds. This wonderful age possessed the peace of soul and the blissful inward reflection of a contented self-created world. . . .

But even this earthly paradise, in which poetry rules supreme, is shown to be divorced from the true forces of nature and religion and exposed to pride and socially divisive forces. The tale is a Romantic one of a mysterious fate that disrupts a whole kingdom, a tale of love, hope, faith and dreams, in which the difficulties that separate lovers are overcome. Indeed love has the power to transport them out of this world:

> A higher power seemed anxious to unravel the knot more quickly and brought them under strange circumstances to this *romantic* place. The innocence of their hearts, the magical mood of their state of mind and the irresistible force of their sweet passion and of their youth made them immediately forget the world and everything associated with it and against a background of the storm's epithalamium and the lightning's wedding torches, cradled them in the sweetest intoxication ever to have transported a mortal couple. The dawn of the clear blue day was an awakening to a new blissful world for them. . . .

In a sense too the tale of Atlantis reflects the theme indicated by the title of the novel, namely the "Battle of the Poets," for in the same way that Heinrich was to give birth to a new poetry incorporating but surpassing the old, so here too the young man devoted to the science of nature is inspired to poetry which far surpasses the achievements of the court poets. His voice is extraordinarily beautiful and his song displays a strange and wonderful character. It deals with the origins of the world, the stars, plants, animals and men, the almighty harmony in nature, the Golden Age of ancient times and its rulers, Love and Poetry, with the appearance of hatred and barbarism and their struggles against those benevolent goddesses, and finally the song tells of the future triumph of the latter, of the end of misery, the rejuvenation of nature and the return of an eternal Golden Age. This ecstatic poet whose eyes are filled with a vision of a secret world, whose features reveal an unnatural childlike innocence and simplicity, is more than the archetypal poet, for in this little inserted narrative, which typically seems to sum up once again the purport of the whole novel, Novalis also reveals his conception of the Romantic poet.

However, Novalis does not allow his novel to become merely a discursive novel *about* poetry and the nature of the poet. The power of poetry is demonstrated directly by the songs and Romances which he includes in the novel. These songs have also a major rôle to play in the texture and structure of the novel, recapitulating in lyrical form the essence of the action, stressing particular motifs and marking the transition to a new stage in the development. They are also great works in themselves, so that all in all the novel contains a cycle of poems and songs equal to, if not better than, the *Spiritual Songs* and the *Hymns to the Night*.

Heinrich, it is clear by this time, is destined to become a poet, but though he may "inhabit a higher world" he is still "like a little bud which has not yet opened up to flower in fullest glory". He still has a growing period to go through. So the novel now passes from the celebration at the end of Chapter Three to the revelry of a feudal castle with talk of peace and war, a war of religion between Christian and Muslim in the Crusades, and conversations in which once more narrative is reinforced by song. Yet again Heinrich's whole soul is plunged into turmoil, his whole being is excited, he is in a state of inner unrest. And once more Heinrich's spirit is flung from one Romantic extreme to the other, from the dark stirrings of militant Christianity to gentle compassion with the sufferings of the captive Eastern Maiden Zulima. Once again the narrative flow is interrupted while she then tells Heinrich *her* story, starting with a kind of panegyric to nature and the romantic beauties of this exotic paradise on earth:

> There is a special charm to living on ground long populated and previously given lustre by diligence, activity and affection. There nature seems to have grown more human and comprehensible, a dark memory under the transparent present reflects the images of the world with sharply defined edges, and so one enjoys a twofold world which thereby loses everything heavy and insistent and becomes the magical fiction and fantasy of our senses. . . .

The interesting point here is the *romantic* vision of nature presented through the characteristic imagery of a magic mirror. Surface reality becomes transparent and the awareness of a twofold world stressed, the normal world of the senses and the other world revealed when one penetrates the accidental phenomena crowding in upon the senses. Here again Novalis is paraphrasing the aim of the Romantic poet, namely to pass beyond the real to the transcendental. While this chapter has introduced the poet Heinrich by story and song to the spirit of militant Christianity in the Crusades and the lure of the exotic East through the captive Zulima, the aim for Heinrich, as for Novalis in the novel, is ultimate harmony, the reconciliation of Christian and Muslim.

If Zulima the Muslim maiden can be taken as an example of Romantic love of the exotic, the treatment of the next person Heinrich meets in the novel is a perfect example of how Novalis the Romantic gives the normal a magical aura, the familiar the dignity of the unfamiliar. This man comes from strange lands, wears strange clothes, and his stories and songs bear the imprint of strangeness. He is a seeker after buried treasure, and he describes the work that leads him into the hidden bowels of the earth as a rare and secret art, characterized by secret signs and an unintelligible private language which only heightens the fascination of it. The practice of his art is something which offers complete satisfaction:

> It is impossible to explain and describe this complete fulfilment of an inherent wish, this wonderful delight in things which might have a closer connection with our secret being, that is with occupations for which one is fated and equipped from the cradle. . . .

All this sounds more like the absolute dedication of the artist to his art than a description of a miner's calling, for this is what he is! Like the poet's, the miner's art makes him happy and noble of spirit, it awakens in him faith in God's wisdom and the divine order and keeps him innocent and childlike at heart. Far removed from the claims of day-to-day existence he works underground in darkness and alone, free from the degrading lust for property and inspired only by the longing for

greater insight into the mysteries of the natural world and a love of harmony:

> In his loneliness he thinks in his inmost heart of his comrades and of his family with constantly renewed awareness of the mutual and indispensable ties of blood that bind all men together. . . .

The art of mining as treated here is in effect "a serious symbol of all human existence". Like the Welsh miners, German miners are famous for their songs and Novalis' character is no exception, though his second song in particular seems somewhat Romantic, being "almost as obscure and incomprehensible as the music itself, which is exactly what made it so strangely attractive and entertaining, like a waking dream". . . . (pp. 126-31)

If Romanticism is the poetry of night and moonlight then the power of the moon for the Romantic poet is particularly apparent in the description of evening which now follows:

> The moon hung in gentle radiance over the hills giving rise to wonderful dreams in all creatures. Itself looking like something dreamt by the sun, it lay turned in upon itself over the dream world and led a nature divided into countless parts back to that mythical age when every seed slumbered by itself and, lonely and intact, longed in vain to unfold the dark abundance of its incommensurable being. Heinrich's mind mirrored the fairy tale of the evening. He felt as if the world were lying opened up within him showing all its treasures and concealed delights as if to a welcome guest. The great simple spectacle struck him as so comprehensible. Nature seemed to him to be incomprehensible only because it heaped such a mass of close and familiar things with such an extravagance of multifarious forms round people. . . .

Here, as with Zulima's Romantic landscape, the significant thing is the sudden ability to see through the mass of natural phenomena which normally cloud the senses. This it is in the power of the moonlight to accomplish, leading divided nature back to a primeval state of unity and harmony. This the miner's words have also accomplished for Heinrich. They have opened a secret door within him:

> He saw his little room built on to a lofty cathedral, while from the cathedral's stone floor rose up the stern world of the past to be greeted by the clear happy future. . . . Suddenly now he sees all his relationships to the great world about him in proper perspective. . . .

From such reflections and inner musings which are such a feature of the novel, the narrative takes our hero into the strange underground realm of the miner, a world of its own beneath one's feet, teeming with traces of life dating back to the beginning of time. Here a distant voice rises out of the depths in song announcing the presence of a hermit, Friedrich von Hohenzollern. Like the miner's, his is a life of loneliness, dedication to piety and contemplation of the natural world. Though youthful fantasy had drawn him early in life to the contemplative life of a hermit, he had lacked the inner resources and it is only after a hectic period as a soldier that he has returned to it. In other words, he has travelled both paths described by Heinrich, namely the path of contemplation and the path of experience. Now living in the world of memories, what this recluse has developed, looking back over his own rich store of them, is a sense of their real inter-connection, the deeper significance in their sequence and the meaning of what they reveal. What follows is a statement of the Romantic view, not only of memory but of history. A true sense of history:

> develops late, and more with the quiet exercise of memory than under the pressure of present experience. Most recent events seem only loosely connected, but they sympathize all the more wonderfully with remoter events; and it is only when one is in a position to survey a long sequence, neither taking everything literally nor jumbling the real order with capricious dreams, that one can discern the secret concatenation of past and future and learn how to piece together history out of hope and memory. . . .

Like the Romantic landscape in which the poet can see the message of the past and the hieroglyphs of God, so too history must be like a beam of light from the dome of a church setting everything off in the most appropriate and attractive light and illuminating the ultimate meaning as with a divine spirit. The writer of history must also be something of a poet, for only the poet knows the art of revealing the proper relationship between events, hence there is more essential truth in the tales of the poets than in the learned compendia of disparate facts the chroniclers produce. In history, as in everything else, the goal is to break through the multiplicity of confusing trivia to the spirit of the age. If this is achieved then incidental details do not matter. Once again the scale of the novel opens up with reflections like these to embrace the infinites of geological time and the difference between the chaos that was the rule during the phases of creation and the peace and harmony that are the rule in nature at the present time is once again stressed. (pp. 131-33)

> *J. M. Ritchie, "Novalis' 'Heinrich von Ofterdingen' and the Romantic Novel," in* Periods in German Literature: Texts and Contexts, Vol. II, *edited by J. M. Ritchie, Oswald Wolff (Publishers) Ltd., 1969, pp. 117-44.*

MICHAEL HAMBURGER   (essay date 1970)

[*Starting with the premise that "Novalis' thought is remarkably consistent," Hamburger examines the interconnections between his ideas on art, religion, and philosophy, asserting that his doctrine is utopian rather than mystical.*]

In spite of its fragmentary character Novalis' thought is remarkably consistent. Since his philosophy is a dynamic one, a philosophy of becoming, we must allow for a certain measure of development; but though his later thoughts may add to the earlier ones, they rarely contradict them. "To philosophize," Novalis wrote, "is to dephlegmatize, to vivify"; and that is what his own thinking was designed to do. For that very reason, it is very difficult to give a summary of his thought, all I can do is to pick out a few representative ideas and indicate the spirit in which the reader himself should enlarge them to cover all the related spheres.

Novalis began with the extremely subjective idealism of Fichte on the one hand, the no less subjective religious emphasis of the *Herrenhuter* on the other; to this must be added the literary and personal influence of Friedrich Schlegel, with his theory

A depiction of Freya from Henry of Ofterdingen.

of "romantic irony" and his analytical finesse (which derives in part from the French school of aphorists, from La Rochefoucauld to Chamfort in Schlegel's own time). The subjective tendency of Novalis' thinking was confirmed by Schlegel's literary program for the Romantic School, his emphasis on fantasy, free association, and deliberately contrived illusion (which could be shattered by romantic irony or by other sophisticated devices). Other thinkers whose influence on Novalis is apparent in the *Fragments* include Plotinus, Jacob Boehme, Spinoza, Hemsterhuys, Lavater, Zinzendorf—the founder of the Herrenhut communion—Schleiermacher, and Schelling. Novalis' debt to Goethe, especially to his *Wilhelm Meister*, which he both admired and condemned as a "pilgrimage to the patent of nobility," is clearly acknowledged in the *Fragments*.

Novalis set out to "philosophize" literature and to "poeticize" philosophy. "The world must be romanticized. Only in that way can one rediscover its original significance. Romanticization is nothing other than qualitative potentialization. The baser self is identified with the better self in this operation. . . . By giving a lofty sense to what is vulgar, a mysterious aspect to what is commonplace, the dignity of the unknown to what is familiar, an infinite extension to what is finite, I romanticize them. This operation is reversed for what is sublime, unknown, mystical, infinite—these are turned into logarithms by the connection—they are expressed in familiar terms. (Romantic philosophy. *Lingua romana.* Reciprocal elevation and debasement.)"

The subjective basis of Novalis' thought can be seen in an early aphorism: "Inwards leads the mysterious way. Within us, or nowhere, is eternity with all its worlds, the past and the future. The external world is the world of shadows, it casts its shadows into the realm of light." Novalis' individual contribution to philosophy was to concentrate on the relation between these two worlds of light and shadow. By taking subjectivity even farther than mere philosophers had dared to do, he arrived at the point where subject and object are indistinguishable. "The proof of the realism is idealism, and vice versa," a later aphorism asserts; and again: "The world is a universal trope of the mind, a symbolic image of the same." The word "trope" is the operative one; for, like Rilke after him, Novalis evolved a philosophy based on the poetic process itself, on the freedom of the individual mind to re-create the world in its own image. The relation between world and mind becomes reciprocal; long before Rilke claimed that it is the business of men to transform the outward and visible world by the act of creative contemplation, Novalis wrote: "We are on a mission, our calling to fashion the earth." It is in the light of the same creative philosophy that we must interpret Novalis' maxim that "to become a human being is an art." But Novalis' doctrine is more extreme than Rilke's; his whole philosophy and literary practice are based on the belief that the perfectly developed man can turn thoughts into things and things into thoughts.

Rilke, too, was long regarded as a mystic. Perhaps one ought to distinguish the ascetic tradition in mysticism from the aesthetic or pantheistic. If an ascetic mystic denies the reality of the outward world, it is in favor of a reality that transcends the capacity of his senses. Novalis and Rilke, on the other hand, endow the senses with the power, if not to create, to re-create and to transform the outward world; their vision is the "unmediated vision" of modern poets, not the mediated vision of the traditional religious poet, who employs a symbolism that can be interpreted in terms of dogma. Where Novalis differs from Rilke is in directing his unmediated vision toward the plane of revealed religion; his magical philosophy was intended to open a new approach to Christian doctrine. For that reason, Novalis was careful to make a clear distinction between natural and revealed religion. His magical synthesis applied only to the natural sphere; but since he accepted the superiority of revealed religion to natural religion, there would come a point where "God must be separated from Nature. God has nothing to do with Nature. He is the aim of Nature; that with which Nature must one day harmonize. Nature must become moral. . . . The moral God is far superior to the magical God. . . ." But this point could be reached only when rational, scientific, and natural knowledge cease to conflict with the truths of revealed religion. That is why Novalis chose the way of a magical synthesis: "We must endeavour to become magicians in order to become truly moral. The more moral we are, the more God-like, the more closely united and in harmony with God. Only through the moral sense does God become perceptible to us." This vital distinction should be borne in mind by readers of Novalis; for in practice he never reached the point where "God is separated from Nature." All his work remained magical and animistic, even where it was dedicated to the "moral God" of Christianity. Novalis foreshadowed the three categories of Kierkegaard—aesthetic, ethical, and religious—when he wrote: "Every mathematical science aspires to become philosophical once more, to be animated or rationalized; then to become poetic; then ethical; lastly religious." But it is to the poetic or aesthetic category that nearly all his work belongs. (pp. 76-8)

In reading Novalis we have to try to clear our minds of certain deep-rooted prejudices; for instance of the prejudice that to understand the psychological mechanism by which we attain any particular state of mind detracts from the validity or the value of that state of mind. Novalis does not rate empirical knowledge lower than spiritual knowledge, for he does not accept the division. His psychological observations can be devastating; but he does not mean to disparage philosophy when he reduces it to a subjective craving, remarking that it is "really nostalgia, the urge to be at home everywhere." This psychological aperçu must be related to the very different one in **Heinrich von Ofterdingen:** "Where, then, are we going? Always to our home." Nor must we be too much disturbed by the positively Freudian penetration of his remark on the cult of Nature: "The reason why people are so attached to Nature is probably that, being spoilt children, they are afraid of the father and take refuge with the mother." Novalis himself was deeply attached to nature and studied it with indefatigable zest; for nature, to him, was also "an encyclopedic, systematic index or plan of our minds. Why content ourselves with a mere inventory of our treasures? Let us look at them ourselves, use them and work upon them in manifold ways." His analytical inquiries are all part of his great scheme; there could be no "syncretism" without "syncriticism." It was only by giving scope to his skepticism that Novalis attained certainty in his faith. In the *Fragments* he asks: "How does one avoid tediousness in representing perfection? The contemplation of God seems too monotonous as a means of religious enquiry; one has only to think of perfect characters in plays, of the dryness of genuine, pure, philosophical or mathematical systems etc. Thus even the contemplation of Jesus is wearying. Sermons should be pantheistic; they should contain individual religion, individualised theology." Novalis himself intended to write a series of sermons on this principle, as a complement to the hymns of his *Spiritual Songs*.

Although some of them did in fact find their way into a hymnbook, the *Spiritual Songs* are no less magical in origin than the rest of Novalis' work. It is the same process of magical substitution that enabled Novalis to translate his love for Sophie into poems devoted to the praise of the Virgin Mary. Novalis believed that the love between men and women could transcend its natural bounds, that *eros* could turn into *agape*. "By absolute willpower," he noted, "love can be gradually transmuted into religion. Of the highest being we become worthy only through death. (Expiatory death)." This belief . . . is familiar to readers of Rilke, with his cult of young lovers who exhausted the possibilities of human passion and looked to death or religion for its consummation. (pp. 81-2)

If we choose to remember its subjective origin in the case of Novalis, it is easy to condemn such love as "morbid"; but we should at least consider that Novalis would not have been unduly abashed by that word. He himself remarked that "Love is essentially an illness: hence the miraculous significance of Christianity." Illness too, both mental and physical had its place in his system; in fact he speculated whether "illness could not be a means to a higher synthesis" and went so far as to claim that "illness is one of our human pleasures, like death." True to the spirit of Paracelsus (and not unlike the more advanced medical theorists of our time), Novalis devoted special attention to the relation between physical and spiritual or mental disorders. He stressed the importance of dreams to the psychologist; but here had the precedent of a brilliant German aphorist of the pre-Romantic era, Georg Christian Lichtenberg, whose works he knew. Of organic illnesses he remarked that they should "be considered in part as physical madness or, to be more precise, as *idées fixes* of the body." He would have laughed at the idea that the morbid origin of a state of mind makes it incompatible with true spirituality; for illness is as much a part of our condition as any ideal norm of health that we may oppose to it. "It is their illnesses that distinguish men from animals and plants. Man is born in order to suffer. The more helpless a man, the more receptive he is to morality and religion." Against this necessary condition Novalis prescribed the "panacea of prayer," by which one "attains all things."

The importance of dreams is equally relevant to Novalis' practice as a poet and to his theories about art. . . . [His] whole magical and syncretic philosophy is an attempt to reconcile traditional beliefs with a mode of vision that is poetic rather than religious. The main distinction between the traditional religious artist and the modern artist lies in their different conceptions of artistic creation. The traditional religious artist assumes that the world has been created once and for all: his only freedom, therefore, can be one of rearrangement. The modern artist, on the other hand, accepts no such restriction; whether he is aware of it or not, his practice rests on the assumption that art, quite literally, is a creative process and that the product of this process is not subject to whatever laws may govern the universe as a whole.

Since these two views are not, in fact, compatible, it was almost inevitable that Novalis should come to consider the question of poetic creation. Very significantly, he concluded that "the poet borrows all his materials, with the exception of his imagery," for it is the gradual liberation of the poetic image from its traditional functions and associations that characterizes the progress of modern poetry.

The state in which we create images most freely, without need to borrow more than the rawest of material from the created world, is the state of dreaming. It can be argued that the mind, including that part of it which generates images in the dream state, is also a part of the created world; and that, as such, it is subject to universal laws of one kind or another. But one may still doubt that even the most devout of dreamers has ever succeeded in imposing the strictest orthodoxy on his dreams; and it is the issue of orthodoxy, not of religious belief in the widest sense, that divides the modern poet from the traditional religious poet.

Novalis believed that literature should aspire to the dream state. All his imaginative works tend toward a magical equilibrium in which "Die Welt wird Traum, der Traum wird Welt" (World becomes dream, dream becomes world). "Poetry is what is truly and absolutely real," Novalis wrote; "this is the kernel of my philosophy. The more poetic, the more true." It is clear from this statement alone that poetry, to Novalis, meant something quite different from the literary productions for which we commonly reserve that name. What Novalis meant by poetry is the magical mode of vision that some, but by no means all, of these literary productions embody. "Poetry" was a synonym for the creative imagination, that faculty which he described as an "extramechanical power"—a power exempt from the physical laws that govern the universe. This power he identified with the principle of freedom itself; for it enables us to fulfill his demand that "life should not be a romance given to us, but a romance that we have made."

On that basis, we can understand all Novalis' exorbitant claims for poetry and for poets; it is always in his own special sense of the words that he makes these claims. If poetry becomes "the basis of Society, as virtue is the basis of the State," and the poet becomes a "transcendental physician," we must not refer these statements to any poet other than Orpheus. Novalis' interest in the actual craft of verse was no greater than his interest in any other human skill; nor did he particularly like professional writers as such. "Writers are as one-sided as all artists in any particular medium, only still more stiff-necked. Indeed, among professional writers one finds few persons of large and liberal disposition, especially where such persons are wholly dependent on writing for their livelihood." This criticism is more than an aristocrat's comment on the professional classes; it comes from the heart of Novalis' philosophy. For genius, to Novalis, was "the capacity to deal with imagined objects as with real ones, and to accord them the same kind of treatment." This gift is not confined to artists and writers; in fact there are many good writers who have only "the talent to present something, to observe it exactly and to give a fitting account of the thing observed," a talent that Novalis thought "different from genius"; although he concedes that literary genius cannot do without it, Novalis' true concern was with genius itself, whether manifested in the arts or in any other field of activity.

For the talent itself, mere realism or verisimilitude, he had so little respect that in *Heinrich von Ofterdingen* he grants a long sequence of important dialogue to a kind of composite character or chorus whom he calls "the merchants"—and this in the most mundane part of the narrative. Heinrich himself and Mathilde have little more personality. Yet this lack of individual characterization does not strike one as more than faintly grotesque; for one knows from the start that, even where it deals with waking life, the logic of *Heinrich von Ofterdingen* is the logic of dreams. The highest form of art, in Novalis' system, is the *Märchen* or supernatural tale, a genre which in the classical era had been regarded as fit only for children and peasants. But of all literary genres, the *Märchen* permits the closest approximation to the dream state; and Novalis, like other Romantic writers, so greatly extended its traditional freedom that it became the one medium in which the creative imagination is very nearly autonomous. *Heinrich von Ofterdingen* progresses by logical stages to the *Märchen* that concludes Part I, a tale so freely imaginative that no traditional symbolism quite exhausts its meaning. It is supernatural to the point of surrealism.

Novalis' imaginative works are most original and most successful where they come closest to his ideal of creative autonomy; they are often commonplace where this ideal conflicted with his religious faith. The difference, again, lies in his choice of poetic media, but especially in his use of imagery. His proper medium was the prose poem or fantasy, like the unrhymed parts of the *Hymnen an die Nacht,* the whole of *Die Lehrlinge zu Sais* and the *Märchen* woven into the narrative of *Heinrich von Ofterdingen.* With few exceptions—the truly magical **"Lied der Toten"** written for Part II of the same novel is a splendid one—regular verse forms had the effect of inhibiting his imagination and of making his imagery both incongruous and bizarre. One reason, perhaps, is the very simple one that Novalis never lived to perfect his art; and that even in his lifetime the actual writing of poetry occupied only a small space in his larger "poeticizing" activities. But a more deep-rooted reason is that Novalis' magical practices conflicted with his theological commitment; and this commitment is much more apparent in his poems written in regular meters—poems that were intended to rise from the aesthetic plane to the strictly ethical or religious—than in his free verse and poetic prose. The **"Lied** der Toten'' again, is an exception, because it is not a devotional poem but an imaginative and idyllic account of domestic life among the dead. But the disparity is very striking in the **Hymnen an die Nacht,** a single sequence that combines poems in free verse, in rhythmical prose, and in regular stanza form. (pp. 83-7)

[The one major contradiction between his thought and practice] is that between Novalis' belief in the unlimited power of the creative imagination—as summed up in his aphorism: "Life should not be a romance given to us, but one that we have invented"—and his statement: "All that we call chance comes from God." If the very course and import of our lives can be determined by an act of creative choice, neither chance nor Providence can have any true significance; and the qualities of God Himself become subject to the requirements of the imagination. To a certain degree, this contradiction is inherent in idealism itself, at least in modern idealism from Descartes and Berkeley onward; but there is a vital difference between the *cogito, ergo sum* of Descartes and the *imaginor, ergo est* that is constantly implied by Novalis. It is only with Fichte that modern idealism reaches its logical and absurd conclusion; and Novalis, being inhibited neither by logic nor by the *logos* itself, was able to improve on Fichte's absurdities.

The former of the two aphorisms I have just quoted is part of the fragment that begins as follows: "Whoever looks upon life as anything but an illusion that destroys itself, is himself still caught up in life." This is the kind of statement to which Novalis owes his reputation as a mystic; and it might indeed be a mystical statement but for the corollary cited above, and a host of other statements that contradict it. No true mystic could have asserted, as Novalis did, that "when our intelligence and our world are in harmony, we are like God." It is clear enough from Novalis' writings that this very harmony between mind and world can be attained by allowing full play to the creative imagination; and the creative imagination usurps the place of God.

Novalis' philosophy, then, is not mystical, but utopian. That is why the imaginative works are almost wholly lacking in conflict. They are a perpetual idyll, an idyll in which evil does not exist and death is a rare sort of pleasure. The true religious mystic may reach conclusions not unlike those of Novalis: but he does not reach them so easily. Novalis' mysticism is a shortcut from the aesthetic plane to the religious; it leaves out the ethical, which is the plane of conflict. Thus Novalis asserts: "To the truly religious, nothing is sinful." But the truly religious man, to Novalis, is the truly imaginative man; the only sense in which his assertion is true is that the imagination is harmless as long as it functions *in vacuo*. His assertion becomes not only inept but dangerously misleading as soon as we extend its relevance from art to life. The imagination intrinsically may be harmless, but it is not innocent. Novalis' own imagination was no exception, as we can see when he passes on from his favorite idyllic themes to the bloody cannibalistic fantasies in No. XV of the *Geistliche Lieder;* his answer, in the same sequence, was that the coming of Christ caused sin to disappear:

> Da kam ein Heiland, ein Befreier . . .
> . . . Seitdem verschwand bei uns die Sünde.

> Then came a savior, a redeemer . . .
> Sin vanished from among us then.

The same poem dismisses sin as an "ancient burdensome delusion":

> Ein alter schwerer Wahn von Sünde
> War fest an unser Herz gebannt.

It was only by denying the existence of evil that Novalis was able to create his perpetual idyll; and to claim that "all absolute sensation is religious."

Novalis had no use for the whole range of experience that lies between pure sensation and universal truth; for the imagination deals in archetypes, not in particular phenomena or individual persons. Just as he leaps straight from the aesthetic plane to the religious, in the historical summary of the fifth **Hymn to Night** he leaps straight from classical antiquity to the Christian revelation, leaving out the ethical heritage of the Old Testament. The Old Testament era, perhaps, is intended to correspond to that phase of antiquity in which "strict measure and the arid number prevailed," the "flower of life disintegrated into dark words" and —most important of all—Imagination withdrew; his characterization of the Old Testament Jews as a people who "had grown estranged from the blessèd innocence of youth" would suggest as much. The "blessèd innocence of youth" is apt to be lost when a person or a people reaches moral maturity; but there is a different, much rarer, innocence that outlasts experience. This is not to be found in Novalis' works. The Romantic cult of innocence is the sentimental one of the very sophisticated; it is an escape from experience, not a renewal of innocence by the acceptance of experience and of guilt. Novalis' idealization of childhood—"Where there are children, there is a golden age," he wrote—is connected with his denial of sin; and the golden age of childhood corresponds to early antiquity in his historical vision. That vision itself is utopian, being directed only at an idealized past and an ideal future.

One of the fragments provides a comment on his vision of classical antiquity in the **Hymns to Night** and of medieval Christendom in the essay **Die Christenheit oder Europa:** "Absolute abstraction, annihilation of the present, apotheosis of the future, that essential and better world: this is at the root of the injunctions of Christianity, and at this point Christianity links up with the religion of the antiquaries, the divinity of the ancient religion, the institution of antiquity as the second main wing; these two wings together bear up the universe, the Angel's body, in an eternal state of hovering suspense, in the eternal enjoyment of space and time." In his imaginative works, Novalis far exceeds the bounds of even this highly synthetic interpretation of history; for the autonomous imagination has as little respect for historical restrictions as for ethical or physical ones. His projected continuation of **Heinrich von Ofterdingen** not only includes parts to be set in ancient Greece and the Orient, with corresponding excursions into Greek and Indian mythology, but culminates in a purely utopian realm in which "the Christian religion is reconciled with the pagan. The legends of Orpheus, Psyche, will be sung." Even this is not enough; the idyll is not complete, since even this realm is still subject to certain physical laws of the created universe. The seasons, therefore, must be abolished: "Heinrich destroys the dominion of the sun."

The triumph of the imagination over matter—and over the *logos*—can hardly go further than that. But in justice to Novalis it must be added that its apotheosis in Part II of *Ofterdingen* was to be followed by six other novels that would have embodied his views on physics, social life, action, history, politics, and love. *Ofterdingen* itself is concerned with the development of a poet; more than one of the projected novels would have required a very different sort of treatment. Novalis would have attempted to fill the gaps between desire and its fulfillment, just as he planned to fill these gaps in his projected philosophical work. In the case of a writer so ambitious as Novalis, one must consider the intention, as well as the achievement. This ambition itself one may censure as a form of *hubris*, . . . though Novalis' gentle nature and undisturbed piety seemed to appeal against such a judgment. As it stands, Novalis' work is rich in fragments that do not call for considerations of so general a kind; of visionary prose and verse that may take us well beyond our own experience, without trespassing on any truth that our own experience or beliefs may oppose to them. And perhaps Novalis was right in claiming that reality is indivisible, the quarrel between world and mind a mere historical misunderstanding. If so, the creative imagination itself may yet find its place in an order not of its creation. (pp. 96-100)

> *Michael Hamburger, "Novalis," in his* Contraries: Studies in German Literature, *E. P. Dutton & Co., Inc., 1970, pp. 66-100.*

JACK FORSTMAN (essay date 1977)

[*In the excerpt below, Forstman probes the connection between Novalis's literary and theological ideas, analyzing the poet's belief in the power of imagination and magic to achieve transcendence and immortality.*]

For Novalis the world is not, strictly speaking, an illusion, but it is a veil covering a more fundamental or higher order of reality. It is the realm of polarity, opposition, separation, and boundedness. In spite of its goodness and beauty, it is a fetter that binds us to penultimate reality and a prison that withholds us from the purer air of the spirit. Unlike fetters and prisons, however, it is the bearer of the spiritual realm, the veil that conceals a still more stunning beauty beneath itself, a world of enchantment barred to superficial eyes but transparent and visible to those who can penetrate the veil.

Who is able to lift the veil? How can it be lifted? What will the one who lifts the veil see? These are questions Novalis tried to answer in his fragmentary nature novel, *The Novices of Sais (Die Lehrlinge von Sais).* Sais was the ancient locus in Egypt of the Isis cult, the mystery goddess of the ancient Egyptian fertility cult who lived on into the Graeco-Roman period as the mistress of a mystery religion of personal salvation. Novalis' novel deals with the mysteries of nature and with probing nature for the secrets to the higher realm. The novices or disciples are all engaged in trying to decipher the holy language of nature, not as researchers (as a matter of fact in opposition to callous scientists who do violence to nature) but as listeners and observers, not as actors upon nature but as those who are open to the acting of nature upon them.

The search can be symbolized by the desire to gaze directly upon the face of the veiled goddess, Isis. It is no simple task. The poet and professor of history, Schiller, who had befriended Novalis in his student days at Jena, had reported in a short piece written in 1790 that a pyramid at Sais bore the following inscription: "I am everything, what was, what is, and what shall be. No mortal man has lifted my veil." Novalis had this awesome announcement in mind when his novice declares, "If, according to the inscription there, no mortal man lifts the veil, then we must seek to become immortal. He who does not want to lift it is no true apprentice of Sais." The way to unlock the mysteries, to enter the enchanted world, to lift the virgin's veil, is to become immortal.

The yearning for immortality in *The Novices of Sais* corresponds to a comment by Novalis in an unpublished fragment: "God is known only by a god." To lift the veil is to know God. Just as the first feat can be accomplished only by an immortal, so the second requires deification. Deification as salvation from the corruptible body was a theme in early Christian piety, especially in the East, from the end of the second century. The Christians, however, believed that only God can deify. So they insisted that Jesus as savior was both God and man. "God became man in order that man might become god," was the frequently repeated formula. In the mystery tradition and Neoplatonism there were other possibilities: deification could be accomplished through initiation and through the recognition and enhancement of the part of man and the world that is akin, if not identical, with God. The latter apparently is closer to the view of Novalis. "God wants gods," he stated, and "everyone who now lives from and through God shall himself become God." Somewhat milder: "When our intelligence and our world harmonize—then we are like God." But again more starkly: "We *are* God." (pp. 37-8)

The deification of man takes place, Novalis thought, through the imagination. As such it is both a gift and a task. In his philosophical studies and especially in his careful and sympathetic study of Fichte, Novalis came to the conclusion that philosophy is unable to unlock the doors blocking us from real knowledge. Philosophy can only order what is given to it. The over-view, the substance with which to work must be given. "Motto: we can know nothing by ourselves; all true knowledge must be given to us." Novalis was certainly not opposed to philosophical work. . . . To insist that philosophy must work with what is given is not an antiphilosophical position, nor does pointing to imagination as the source for the given necessarily lead a philosopher astray from his discipline. To be sure, imagination is a gift normally associated with poets, but Novalis wanted to unify poetry and philosophy for the momentous task of unlocking the mysteries. In this unification, however, imagination speaking through the medium of poetry supplies the materials to the faculty of judgment. To assure us that the materials are real and not figments they must be reasonable. This will be the case, however, to the degree that the imagination is pure. "The purer the power of imagination the truer it will be." Poetry, therefore, is "the hero of philosophy," and philosophy founds itself in poetry, provides its theory and demonstrates that poetry is "one and all." The unification of poetry and philosophy, however, is not understood merely by the juxtaposition of substance (provided by the poet through imagination) and method (provided by the philosopher). Novalis envisioned an organic unification issuing in "transcendental poetry." "Transcendental poetry is a mixture of philosophy and poetry. It grasps fundamentally all transcendental functions and embraces, in fact, the transcendental itself." By working out transcendental poetry a system of tropes may be expected—which comprehends the laws of the *symbolic construction* of the transcendental world (including its spiritual functions)."

Whether one describes the effect of the power of imagination as an elevation to deity or to a similitude with God, the effect is clearly the granting of the divine or transcendent perspective. (p. 39)

Like a seer among more primitive peoples, [the poet] is possessed by the deity. The result is revelation, and the agent is inspired (visited by the Spirit) or moved by enthusiasm (the presence of God in him). Thus Novalis praises "heavenly quietism'' as the mode by which the poet attains a direct line to the ''source, the mother of all reality, reality itself.''

To gain a direct line to the mother of all reality is to be deified, to be carried beyond oneself and one's own world. The power of the higher world takes possession of the poet and expresses itself in his work. He becomes, in his own consciousness, a medium and no longer controls what comes into being through himself. On the contrary, he feels controlled by it.

> With every impulse to perfection the work of the master flies away into more than spatial distances—and thus, with the final impulse of the master, his ostensible work appears separated from himself through a breach of thought—whose breadth he scarcely grasps—and beyond which only the power of imagination, like the shadow of the giant, intelligence, is able to find a place. In the moment in which it should become entirely his own, it becomes more than him, his creator—he becomes the unknowing organ and property of a higher power. The artist belongs to the work and not the work to the author.

If the veil of the virgin goddess cannot be lifted by any mortal man, then one must become immortal. But a man does not immortalize himself. The feat is accomplished by a higher power acting on the poet through his power of imagination or, what is similar, through his free play of fantasy or his dream life. (p. 40)

For Novalis, however, the process is not entirely passive. Without denying in any way the priority of the activity of the sublime realm upon the poet, he emphasizes also the work of the poet. . . . Novalis wants to emphasize that imagination is free from all external stimuli, that it can work without any of the normal senses that depend on the tangible world of arousal. Obviously this does not contradict what he says . . . about the necessity of stimulus from the other world. Still, imagination, in his thinking, is subject to one's power of will. If the poet is one who gives himself to ''heavenly quietism,'' we need to note that the verb is active and that the acting subject is the poet.

More significantly, imagination is a power that can be controlled by the will of the poet. Given the supposition that the imagination is the line to the other world, ''the mother of all reality,'' and noting the insistence that imagination is subject, in some degree at least, to the will, we are led to the conclusion that the poet may see himself as a builder of a new tower of Babel, that with his own words and under his own power he may successfully construct a tower that reaches into the heavens.

Magic is the craft by which this tower is built, and Novalis calls on poets especially but also philosophers and scientists of all varieties to become magicians. In a fragment entitled **''Theosophy''** he asserts:

> We must seek to become magicians in order to be able to be truly moral. The more moral, the more harmonious with God—the more divine—the more bound to God. Only through the moral sense does God become perceptible to us. The moral sense is the sense for existence, without external stimulation—the sense for covenant—the sense for freely chosen and found and thus common life—and being—the

sense for the thing-in-itself—the true sense for divining.

One must not suppose that the use of the word ''moral'' in this excerpt is in the sense of what one commonly takes to be moral virtues or morality or moralism. Certainly it has to do with the way a person lives, but for Novalis that means to live in such a way that the external becomes transparent to the internal, distinction to harmony, things to their essence, parts to the whole, the world to God. That is what it means to become a magician. In another place he states, ''Magic = the art of using the sense world arbitrarily.'' By an act of will the magician wrests from the sensible world its super-sensible truth. Insofar as he does this with words, an imaginative representation is necessary. Thus ''the magician is a poet.''

Novalis writes often about ''magic idealism.'' It is another term for the unification of poetry and philosophy that he sought. (pp. 41-2)

Magic, however, is not as stiff or steely as the repeated use of ''willful'' and ''arbitrary'' might imply. It is loose, unbounded, playful. The purpose of the magician is to find and free the spirit hidden behind the veil of the bodily world. Although willfulness is the *sine qua non* for the possibility, it is a willfulness that wins its object by seduction or enticement. Willfulness acts through playfulness. The secrets do not resist unveiling to the one who approaches their abode properly. The resistance is entirely in the one who is too wedded to visible reality and to an analytical mode of thought that measures and divides. Love, which combines playfulness, desire (will), and devotion, is ''the basis for the possibility of magic.'' Every novel in which true love occurs, is a fable—a magical event.''

Thus we begin to see the kinship between imagination and magic, between what is ''given'' and what is ''taken,'' between passivity and activity. But magic idealism, even though it is inseparably connected to imagination, is founded in the human will. Bruce Haywood defines Novalis' magic idealism as ''essentially nothing more than metaphorical representation—the representation of the abstract in terms of the concrete, and the seeing of the physical as a manifestation of the spiritual.'' The magician accomplishes this act of transformation by his own act of aggression against the concrete and physical. (p. 43)

In spite of the apparent contradiction between the emphasis on the active will in the exercise of magic and the emphasis on gift and passivity in the deification of the poet, no real contradiction was intended. Just as in medieval Christendom, of which Novalis was so enamored, human initiative on behalf of the good and divine grace moving a man toward the good were entirely harmonious, so the gift of immortality or the revelation of the higher world through the power of imagination and the pursuit of magic were one and the same event for Novalis. It would be inappropriate to assign priority to either the human will or the divine revelation. A single event takes place, the opening of spiritual realities in and through the physical world. . . . One who has tried to perform the simplest magic trick, such as the disengagement of two metal rings or the putting together of a group of cut blocks into a sphere or cube, learns, first of all, that forcing the material is wrong and, finally, that the solution is easy. One must work not against but with the conditions of the material. . . . The magician does not force the world to yield its secrets. The effort to do so would evoke impregnable resistance. Novalis' magic idealist deals, to be sure, arbitrarily with the world of sense, but this mode of treatment . . . is not a forceful subjugation but a unison of tonalities, a concert of forces. Thus the taking is, at the same time, a giving, and the work a poet does is at the same time the work given to the poet. It is his work, but it is also true that the work possesses him. He is an inspired creator, priest, and magician.

As in ancient times the magician-priest was elevated above his countrymen by virtue of his special connection with the gods, so for Novalis, the poet, the modern magician-priest, occupies a high place by virtue of his elevation above the boundaries that restrict and restrain the normal breed of men. "Poets and priests," he writes, "were one in the beginning and were separated only in subsequent times. But the true poet is always a priest just as the true priest always remained a poet. Should not the future reinstate the old condition of things?" The reinstatement begins with Novalis' experience of poetry. "I hover now and perhaps forever in lighter, stranger spheres," he wrote to August Wilhelm Schlegel in 1798. The place of this sphere is unearthly and represents an elevation beyond the boundedness of the earthly.... Just as the ancient magician-priest revealed and the mediated the truth from beyond by virtue of his special transport, so the poet "leaps beyond himself," "dissolves all the bounds," and is "thoroughly transcendental." "Poetry elevates every individual through a special connection with the remaining whole.... Through poetry originate the highest sympathy and coactivity, the most inward *community* of finite and infinite." To put it briefly, "The true poet *knows everything....*" Whether by magic or by revelation, by act or by gift, the poet speaks like the priest, from his "direct line to the source, the mother of all reality, reality itself." The veil yields to his touch because he has been led into the sanctuary of the gods. Having been made immortal and having become omniscient he is himself a god. (pp. 44-5)

> *Jack Forstman, "On Being Gods and Poets: Novalis," in his* A Romantic Triangle: Schleiermacher and Early German Romanticism, *Scholars Press, 1977, pp. 35-46.*

JOHN NEUBAUER (essay date 1980)

[*Neubauer discusses Novalis's poetic theory and its manifestations in his mature works. According to Neubauer, Novalis attempted to fuse poetry and prose into a language that "reveals the universal structure of the mind."*]

We may divide Novalis' mature poetry into three general categories, each of which is explored in his theoretical statements: (1) the prose poetry of the early *Hymnen,* (2) the simple religious poetry of the later *Hymnen* and most of the *Lieder,* and (3) some of the latest poems tending toward abstract symbolism.

Although the immediate reasons for the new form are not known, the prose poetry of the first *Hymnen* may be regarded as part of a larger effort to fuse poetry and prose in the spirit of Schlegel's *Universalpoesie.* Well before turning the verses into prose, Novalis had already considered the demands of prose poetry, though he came to conclusions he did not carry out. On January 12, 1798, he suggested to August Wilhelm Schlegel that prose poetry's looser organization and meter should be tied to a "more transparent and colorless expression." He did not adopt such an expression in the first *Hymnen,* perhaps because these prose poems were more object-oriented than the verse sections and therefore in need of more colorful expression.

"Transparent and colorless expression"—that is, a language that does not call attention to itself, is more typical of the second category, the *Lieder* and later *Hymnen,* because their sphere is further removed from the world into an interior space which has no physical equivalents: "I see you in thousand images, yet none of them can portray the way my soul beholds you." ... Most of these verses do not contain images but merely feelings, moods, and beliefs and their shifts (*Gemütsbewegung*) from dejection to hope, from loneliness to faith. Since this poetry wishes to elicit corresponding shifts in the reader, it also functions as *Gemütserregungskunst,* an art that stimulates the spirit. The *Hymnen* and *Lieder* should mediate religious experience to the reader. The poet assumes the roles of prophets and priests and becomes a leader of mankind: "Poets and priests were one at the beginning, and only later ages have separated them. But the true poet always remained a priest, just as the true priest always remained a poet. And shouldn't the future reestablish the old state of affairs?" ... However, if poetry becomes enigmatic, as in Novalis' last poems, universal symbols become private, and language acquires a plurality of meaning. The thoughts and feelings excited in the reader no longer need to correspond to those experienced by the poet, as reading becomes a second creation. This third category, that of abstract poetry, divides into two: in the first the poet is in complete control of his material, in the second the formative force is the universal structure of the mind embodied in language.

The first of the two abstract modes is theoretically supported by an extension of idealism. In obvious reference to Kant, Novalis notes in the *Brouillon*: "The poetic philosopher is in the position of an absolute creator. Even the circle, a triangle are created this way. Nothing is added to them except of what their producer allows to be added." ... This relies on Kant's notion that mathematical representations are "constructed" out of certain mental entities—namely, concepts. In poetry, these entities may also be emotions or changes in mood, in which case poetry becomes musical. Novalis' poetry is expressive primarily through its musical qualities: rhythm and meter overshadow metaphor and imagery; verbs, fortified by expressive adverbs, register states and changes of inwardness; nouns and adjectives are generally pale. This musicality of Novalis' language is the prime vehicle of his "auditory" eroticism, which portrays desire, lust, and yearning rather than the visual quality of objects responsible for them.

The tendency toward music suggests a nonrepresentative, logically incoherent poetic language: "Poems—merely sonorous and full of beautiful words—but also without sense and coherence—at most individual stanzas understandable—they must be like fragments from the most divergent things." ... Poetic words are, then, abstract musical notes which acquire meaning from the composition, the particular way in which the acoustic patterns of language are shaped into a poetic meaning. Novalis follows the eighteenth-century tradition which regained prominence with the linguistics of Saussure and contemporary semiotics, believing that linquistic signs are conventions which have no intrinsic relation to their referent. He goes beyond this view by envisioning and experimenting with a poetry which breaks convention, anticipating thereby the Symbolist theory and practice of Verlaine, Rimbaud, Mallarmé, Valéry, Hofmannsthal, Trakl, and others.

This new conception of poetry intends to reduce the semantic units of language (words) to the role of meaningless phonological units. The resultant poetic constructs are also like algebraic formulas containing arbitrarily chosen letters: algebraic letters perform certain functions and may acquire concrete meaning, just as concrete nouns, verbs, adjectives, and other parts of speech may be fitted into a syntactic structure. This "structuralist" conception of poetic language is the second version of Novalis' theory of abstract poetry. Conceiving of syntax as a general rule for combining the parts of speech and of language as a combinatorics of words, Novalis adopted the Leibnizian ideas on symbolic logic and combinatorial mathematics. Transposing them into poetry he came to think of poetic language as an abstract and general syntactic structure which imposed itself upon the poet's mind and subordinated semantic content to structural context. Poems could thus emerge not from ideas or words but from a "musical" sentence or phrase structure into which specific parts of speech would be "plugged" according to the demands of rhythm, sonority, and imagery. . . . According to this line in Novalis' poetics, language is a set of internalized rules in the mind capable of generating texts without rational control and guidance. Language imposes itself upon the speaker; the poet is not a divine creator but merely a powerless medium in which language articulates itself. Novalis' conception is related to surrealist notions on "automatic writing" and to T. S. Eliot's idea that the poet is a mere catalyst because according to all three theories the poet has no control over language. But in "automatic writing," that control is relinquished to the subconscious; in Eliot, to experience and tradition, and in Novalis, to the sovereign power of language itself. . . . In this view, poetic language is neither a mirror to nature nor a lamp radiating from the mind of a genius, but a set of rules whose application generates texts. In everyday language, these rules are used to allow communication and to achieve specific purposes; but poetic language serves its own end; it is, in Kant's sense, "purposive without [any specific] purpose." In this, Novalis anticipates important modes of modern poetry, although he is building on tenets of an idealism which most modern poets no longer hold. For Novalis, the formulaic structure of poetry is pivotal because here, freed from the service of everyday communication, language reveals the universal structure of the mind, a structure which he considers to exist in some kind of "preestablished harmony" with the structure of the universe. The more language is liberated, the more readily it will reveal the world. Free language plays "only with itself," but, doing so, it mirrors the "strange interplay of objects." (pp. 121-25)

John Neubauer, in his Novalis, *Twayne Publishers, 1980, 185 p.*

ADDITIONAL BIBLIOGRAPHY

Avni, Abraham A. "The Old Testament in Novalis' Poetry." *Monatshefte* LVI, No. 4 (April-May 1964): 160-66.
    Discusses Old Testament imagery and themes in Novalis's early poetry. Avni points out that the religious tone of the pieces is modified by Novalis's belief in the principles of the Enlightenment.

Barrack, Charles M. "Conscience in *Heinrich Von Ofterdingen*: Novalis' Metaphysic of the Poet." *Germanic Review* XLVI, No. 4 (November 1971): 257-84.
    Examines Novalis's treatment of the theme of conscience in *Henry of Ofterdingen*. Barrack argues that Heinrich comes to understand poetry as "a manifestation of conscience and God Himself" as a result of his initiation process.

Behler, Diana. "Novalis." In her *The Theory of the Novel in Early German Romanticism*, pp. 69-114. Utah Studies in Literature and Linguistics, edited by Andrée M.L. Barnett and others, vol. 11. Peter Lang: Berne, 1978.
    A study of Novalis's ideas regarding genre in the context of early German Romantic novel theory. Behler addresses such issues as Novalis's handling of the relationship between prose and poetry and his use of fairy-tale motifs.

Birrell, Gordon. *The Boundless Present: Space and Time in the Literary Fairy Tales of Novalis and Tieck.* University of North Carolina Studies in the Germanic Languages and Literatures, edited by Siegfried Mews, no. 95. Chapel Hill: University of North Carolina Press, 1979, 163 p.*
    A detailed analysis of Novalis's treatment of space and time in his Märchen. Birrell argues that Novalis's tales are "instructional parables on the ways and means of reconsolidating a broken universe."

Brennan, Christopher. "Writings on Philosophy and Aesthetics: Symbolism in Nineteenth Century Literature." In his *The Prose of Christopher Brennan*, pp. 48-172. Edited by A. R. Chisholm and J. J. Quinn. Sydney: Angus and Robertson, 1962.*
    Explores Novalis's poetic symbolism. Brennan also defends Novalis from the charge that he glorifies death and disease in his philosophy, stressing that for the poet they were "expressions of the perfect life that transcends this."

Calhoon, Kenneth S. "Language and Romantic Irony in Novalis' *Die Lehrlinge zu Sais.*" *Germanic Review* LVI, No. 2 (Spring 1981): 51-61.
    Focuses on *The Disciples at Saïs* as "the most paradigmatic" novel of German Romanticism. Calhoon proposes that the form and themes of the novel grow naturally out of the philosophical underpinnings of Novalis's thought.

Cardinal, Roger. "Werner, Novalis and the Signature of Stones." In *Deutung and Bedeutung: Studies in German and Comparative Literature Presented to Karl-Werner Maurer.* Edited by Brigitte Schludermann and others, pp. 118-33. The Hague: Mouton, 1973.*
    Explores the influence of Abraham Werner, a famous geologist with whom Novalis studied in Freiberg, on the development of the author's philosophy.

Dyck, Martin. *Novalis and Mathematics.* University of North Carolina Studies in the Germanic Languages and Literatures, edited by Frederic E. Coenen, no. 27. Chapel Hill: University of North Carolina Press, 1960, 109 p.
    Examines Novalis's writings on mathematics and their relation to his views on magic, music, religion, philosophy, language, and literature. According to Dyck, Novalis regarded mathematics as the "ideal science" that could encompass all other fields of knowledge.

Freedman, Ralph. "Eyesight and Vision: Forms of the Imagination in Coleridge and Novalis." In *The Rarer Action: Essays in Honor of Francis Fergusson*, edited by Alan Cheuse and Richard Koffler, pp. 202-17. New Brunswick: Rutgers University Press, 1970.*
    Compares Novalis's method of presenting experience as symbol and vision with that of Samuel Taylor Coleridge. Analyzing *The Rime of the Ancient Mariner* and *Hymns to the Night*, Freedman traces a progression in Novalis's philosophy from nature, to individual isolation, to the possibility of redemption.

Friedrichsmeyer, Sara. *The Androgyne in Early German Romanticism: Friedrich Schlegel, Novalis and the Metaphysics of Love.* Stanford German Studies, vol. 18. Peter Lang: Bern, 1983, 192 p.*
    Discusses the image of the androgyne as a symbol of wholeness in early German Romantic literature, especially in the works of Schlegel and Novalis.

Frye, Lawrence O. "Spatial Imagery in Novalis' *Hymnen an die Nacht.*" *Deutsche Vierteljahrsschrift für Literatur und Geistesgeschichte* 41, No. 4 (1967): 568-91.
    Suggests that in *Hymns to the Night* Novalis attempted to create a poetic "vessel" for transporting the soul from reality to cosmic

unity. This results, Frye maintains, in poetry that is both "oblivious to" and yet "firmly rooted" in nature.

———. "Prometheus under a Romantic Veil: Goethe and Novalis's *Hymnen an die Nacht.*" *Euphorion* 61, No. 3 (1967): 318-36.*
Traces the influence of Goethe's depiction of Prometheus in his poetry on Novalis's *Hymns to the Night.* Frye concentrates on the poetic form of the fourth hymn.

Furst, Lilian R. "The Structure of Romantic Agony." *Comparative Literature Studies* X, No. 2 (June 1973): 125-38.*
Contrasts the structure and theme of Novalis's *Henry of Ofterdingen* with those of Joris-Karl Huysmans's *À rebours.* Furst theorizes that Huysmans's and Novalis's treatment of the theme of "Romantic Agony" should be interpreted as "an inversion of romantic idealism."

Gilman, Sander L. "Friedrich von Hardenberg's Twelfth 'Geistliches Lied'." *Seminar* VI, No. 3 (October 1970): 225-36.
Discusses the influence of Baroque and early Romantic writers on Novalis's twelfth "Geistliches Lied."

Hannah, Richard W. *The Fichtean Dynamic of Novalis' Poetics.* Stanford German Studies, vol. 17. Bern: Peter Lang, 1981, 226 p.
Describes the influence of Fichte's philosophy on Novalis's attitude toward such topics as the imagination, time, space, mathematics, music, and language.

Harrold, Charles Frederick. "Carlyle and Novalis." *Studies in Philology* XXVII, No. 1 (January 1930): 47-63.*
Explores the similarities and differences between the ideas of Carlyle and Novalis and the special intellectual "kinship" that existed between them. Harrold points out that although Carlyle disagreed with many of Novalis's concepts, he sympathized with Novalis's admiration for Fichte.

Hiebel, Frederick. "Novalis." *Twice a Year,* No. 14-15 (Fall-Winter 1946-47): 178-80.
Briefly emphasizes Novalis's importance and calls for a revival of his work. Hiebel characterizes Novalis as the "purest lyrical poet" of the early German Romantic period and as "one of the greatest mystics of all time."

———. "Novalis and the Problem of Romanticism." *Monatshefte* XXXIX, No. 8 (December 1947): 515-23.
Focuses on Novalis in the context of Romanticism. Though he views Novalis as representative of the movement, Hiebel also stresses that his ideas diverged from Romantic theory.

———. *Novalis: German Poet, European Thinker, Christian Mystic.* University of North Carolina Studies in the Germanic Languages and Literatures, no. 10. Chapel Hill: University of North Carolina Press, 1954, 126 p.
A full-length critical study of Novalis's life and works. Hiebel also includes a list of editions of Novalis's works in English, a bibliography, and an index to persons and places associated with the poet.

Komar, Kathleen. "Fichte and the Structure of Novalis' *Hymnen an die Nacht.*" *Germanic Review* LIV, No. 4 (Fall 1979): 137-44.*
A detailed analysis of the interrelationships between the individual poems in *Hymns to the Night* and their collective relationship to Fichte's philosophy.

Lewis, Leta Jane. "Novalis and the Fichtean Absolute." *German Quarterly* XXXV, No. 4 (November 1962): 464-74.
Explores Novalis's reaction to Fichte's philosophy. Lewis attributes the poet's disenchantment with Fichte's ideas to his realization that mortality could not be overcome by means of the intellect.

———. "Fairy Tale Elements in Novalis' 'Kunstmärchen'." In *Folklore International: Essays in Traditional Literature, Belief, and Custom in Honor of Wayland Debs Hand,* pp. 131-38. Edited by D. K. Wilgus. Hatboro, Pa.: Folklore Associates, 1967.
Describes Novalis's use of the supernatural and of traditional fairy-tale elements in "Klingsohrs Märchen" and in "Hyazinth und

Rozenblüte." According to Lewis, Novalis combines these two kinds of imagery in the tales to give shape to his idealistic philosophy.

Malsch, Sara Ann. "Novalis." In her *The Image of Martin Luther in the Writings of Novalis and Friedrich Schlegel: The Speculative Vision of History and Religion,* pp. 23-70. European University Papers, series 1: German Language and Literature, vol. 103. Bern: Herbert Lang, 1974.
A discussion of the Romantic image of Martin Luther in Novalis's *Christianity or Europe.* The unity and continuity inherent in Luther's view of history fascinated Novalis, Malsch posits, and Luther became for him "a symbol for the Providential Man with a Mephistophelian function."

Middleton, Christopher. "Two Mountain Scenes in Novalis and the Question of Symbolic Style." In his *Bolshevism in Art and Other Expository Writings,* pp. 258-73. Manchester: Carcanet New Press, 1978.
Generalizes about Novalis's use of imagery by tracing the elements and antecedents of his representations of two mountain scenes in *Henry of Ofterdingen.*

Molnár, Géza von. "The Composition of Novalis' *Die Lehrlinge zu Saïs:* A Reevaluation." *PMLA* 85, No. 5 (October 1970): 1002-14.
Describes and evaluates Novalis's compositional scheme in *The Disciples at Saïs.* Molnár traces Novalis's use of Kantian principles in the novel and praises his poetical-philosophical exposition of the theme of humanity's relationship with nature.

———. *Novalis' "Fichte Studies": The Foundations of His Aesthetics.* Stanford Studies in Germanics and Slavics, edited by Edgar Lohner, C. H. van Schooneveld, and F. W. Strothmann, vol. VII. The Hague: Mouton, 1970, 117 p.
A detailed study of the influence of Fichte on Novalis's philosophy. Molnár devotes special attention to Novalis's concepts of the ego and of artistic representation.

Moser, Walter. "Fragment and Encyclopedia: From Borges to Novalis." In *Fragments: Incompletion and Discontinuity,* pp. 111-28. Edited by Lawrence D. Kritzman. New York Literary Forum, edited by Jeanine Parisier Plottel, vols. 8-9. New York: New York Literary Forum, 1981.*
Surveys the nature and scope of Novalis's *Brouillon* fragment.

Neubauer, John. *Bifocal Vision: Novalis' Philosophy of Nature and Disease.* University of North Carolina Studies in the Germanic Languages and Literatures, edited by Siegfried Mews, no. 68. Chapel Hill: University of North Carolina Press, 1971, 194 p.
Addresses Novalis's lifelong interest in science, particularly in medicine and anthropology. Neubauer includes Novalis's diagram of diseases as well as a list of scientific books read by him.

O'Brien, William Arctander. "Twilight in Atlantis." *MLN* 95, No. 5 (December 1980): 1292-1332.
Argues that *Henry of Ofterdingen* is Novalis's response to the attack upon poets in Plato's *Republic.*

Pickar, Gertrud Bauer. "Elements of the Enlightenment in Novalis' Poetics." *Rice University Studies* 55, No. 3 (Summer 1969): 185-95.
Contends that Novalis's philosophy of poetry and his conception of the poet are drawn from traditional Enlightenment ideas. Pickar focuses in particular on the influence of Johann Christoph Gottsched and Johann Georg Sulzer on Novalis's theories.

Prawer, S. S. "The Romantics: Novalis—'Sehnsucht nach dem Tode'." In his *German Lyric Poetry: A Critical Analysis of Selected Poems from Klopstock to Rilke,* pp. 112-20. London: Routledge & Kegan Paul, 1952.
Delineates the themes and images in Novalis's poetry through an in-depth reading of his "Sehnsucht nach dem Tode." Prawer concludes that Novalis is the "most dangerous, most fascinating, and most elusive of the Romantic poets of Germany."

Reiss, H. S. "The Concept of the Aesthetic State in the Works of Schiller and Novalis." *Publications of the English Goethe Society* n.s. XXVI (1957): 26-51.*

Discusses Novalis's concept of the "poetic" state as it is expressed in his political aphorisms in *Glauben und Liebe*. Reiss also compares Novalis's ideas about the ideal state with those of Schiller.

Rose, William. "The Romantic Symbol." In his *Men, Myths, and Movements in German Literature: A Volume of Historical and Critical Papers*, pp. 181-200. London: George Allen and Unwin, 1931.
Explores the relationship between Novalis's life and his art, emphasizing the way the poet reconciled his ideals with his environment.

Saul, Nicholas. *History and Poetry in Novalis and in the Tradition of the German Enlightenment*. Bithell Series of Dissertations, vol. 8. London: Institute of Germanic Studies, University of London, 1984, 208 p.
Focuses on Novalis's treatment of history and poetry. Saul also discusses Novalis's theories in the context of the German Enlightenment.

Schaber, Steven C. "Novalis' Theory of the Work of Art as Hieroglyph." *Germanic Review* XLVIII, No. 1 (January 1973): 35-43.
A reading of *Hymns to the Night* based on Novalis's view that poetry can be understood only by a small group of initiates with like interests and capabilities.

Scholz, Joachim J. *Blake and Novalis: A Comparison of Romanticism's High Arguments*. European University Papers, series 18: Comparative Literature, vol. 19. Peter Lang: Frankfurt am Main, 1978, 397 p.*
Compares the art of Novalis and William Blake and their ideas on such topics as politics, imagination, love, and the role of the poet.

Schueler, H. J. "Cosmology and Quest in Novalis's 'Klingsohrs Märchen'." *Germanic Review* XLIX, No. 4 (November 1974): 259-66.
Analyzes the mythic structure of the "Klingsohrs Märchen" in terms of its quest motif and its cosmological imagery.

Scrase, David A. "The Movable Feast: The Role and Relevance of the *Fest* Motif in Novalis' *Heinrich von Ofterdingen*." *New German Studies* 7, No. 1 (Spring 1979): 23-40.
Focuses on the *Fest* theme in *Henry of Ofterdingen*. Scrase stresses that through this theme Novalis succeeded in unifying such seemingly disparate elements as love, intoxication, music, poetry, and the Eucharist.

Spring, Powell. *Novalis, Pioneer of the Spirit*. Winter Park, Fla.: Orange Press, 1946, 174 p.
A full-length study of Novalis's philosophy, religion, mysticism, and poetry.

Stopp, Elisabeth. "'Übergang vom Roman zur Mythologie': Formal Aspects of the Opening Chapter of Hardenberg's *Heinrich von Ofterdingen, Part II*." *Deutsche Vierteljahrsschrift für Literatur und Geistesgeschichte* 48, No. 2 (May 1974): 318-41.
Argues that the unfinished opening chapter of the second part of *Henry of Ofterdingen* represents a significant development in Novalis's novelistic technique. Novalis, according to Stopp, showed "a possible way of making the transition from novel into myth."

Strauss, Walter A. "Novalis: Orpheus the Magician." In his *Descent and Return: The Orphic Theme in Modern Literature*, pp. 20-49. Cambridge: Harvard University Press, 1971.
Examines the Orphic theme in Novalis's works. Strauss concludes that although Novalis imagined himself in the role of the "unveiling prophet-priest," his attempt to present the world as it really is was undermined by his use of irony.

Wagner, Lydia Elizabeth. *The Scientific Interest of Friedrich von Hardenberg (Novalis)*. Ann Arbor, Mich.: Edwards Brothers, 1937, 117 p.
Chronicles Novalis's scientific studies from his childhood to his last years.

Walzel, Oskar. "The Programs of Romantic Ethics and Religion: The Establishment of a New Religion—Hardenberg's Religious Poetry." In his *German Romanticism*, pp. 84-91. Translated by Alma Elise Lussky. New York: G. P. Putnam's Sons, 1932.
Discusses the influence of such writers as Boehme and Friedrich Schleiermacher on Novalis's ideas about religion.

Wilson, A. Leslie. "The *Blaue Blume*: A New Dimension." *Germanic Review* XXXIV, No. 1 (February 1959): 50-8.
Explores the similarities between Novalis's use of the blue flower as a symbol for poetic growth and its similar function in Sanskrit literature.

Mercy Otis Warren

1728-1814

American historian, dramatist, and poet.

Warren was a foremost patriot during the revolutionary period and one of the United States' first women of letters. A prominent pamphleteer and historian, she is remembered for her anti-Loyalist dramas, which helped to stir patriotic fervor at a crucial time in American history. Critics value her *History of the Rise, Progress, and Termination of the American Revolution: Interspersed with Biographical and Moral Observations,* one of the first accounts of the revolutionary war, as an astute analysis and vivid firsthand description of the era. Through her works Warren was an outspoken champion of independence and Republican democracy at a time when few women were involved in politics. Many of the nation's leaders, including John Adams, Alexander Hamilton, George Washington, and Thomas Jefferson, were personal friends who respected her opinions and sought her advice. While modern critics find Warren's plays and poetry stilted and overly emotional, they praise her prose writings, particularly the *History,* and regard all her works as valuable social and historical documents.

Warren was the third of thirteen children of the prosperous, politically active Otis family of West Barnstable, Massachusetts. Her parents provided formal education only for their sons, but Mercy was occasionally permitted to join the lessons conducted by her uncle, the local parson. She was also allowed to use his library, where she discovered Walter Raleigh's *History of the World* and works by Alexander Pope, John Dryden, John Milton, William Shakespeare, and Molière, all of whom influenced her writing. Her intelligence and intellectual curiosity were shared by her elder brother James, who also became an ardent patriot and revolutionary. The two were extremely close, and he tutored his sister in Greek and Latin and continued to share his education with her after leaving for Harvard.

At James's college commencement in 1743, Mercy first met her brother's friend James Warren, whom she married in 1754. The son of an established merchant-farming family in Plymouth, he served in the Massachusetts legislature and eventually as Washington's paymaster during the revolutionary war. Throughout their long, loving marriage, James Warren prized his wife's intellect and encouraged her literary pursuits, which began with attempts at religious and sentimental verse. Warren gave birth to five sons between 1757 and 1766, but her rigorous domestic duties never deterred her from literature and, increasingly, politics, as her Plymouth home became a center of activity and discussion for the revolutionaries. The heightened anti-Tory feeling inspired by the Stamp Act of 1765 directed her toward political writing. Moreover, the brutal beating of her brother James by Tory soldiers in 1769, which resulted in long bouts of insanity, confirmed Warren's resolve to protest British tyranny.

Warren's first published work was *The Adulateur,* a verse drama which, like her subsequent two prewar plays, *The Defeat* and *The Group,* aimed its satire chiefly at Thomas Hutchinson, the Loyalist governor of Massachusetts. He is represented by the main character, Rapatio, a villainous tyrant who crushes the

rights of the good citizens of Servia, the fictional scene of the action. In *The Adulateur,* the citizens are murdered on Rapatio's orders, and Warren thus implicates Hutchinson in the Boston Massacre. *The Defeat,* a fragmentary work, utilized incriminating letters written by Hutchinson and his colleague Andrew Oliver, which were intercepted in England by Benjamin Franklin and revealed to the outraged colonists. *The Group,* in contrast, is not based on a specific historical event, but portrays in general the greed and dissolution of the Loyalist party. Each play was published initially in two newspaper installments, and *The Adulateur* and *The Group* were subsequently distributed as pamphlets to great popular response. According to critics, Warren's satires were so well known that patriots referred to the Tory leaders by the names of their fictional counterparts.

Two later anonymous dramas, *The Blockheads; or, The Affrighted Officers* and *The Motley Assembly,* are often attributed to Warren. Some critics assert that the satiric tone and political stance of these works are consistent with Warren's previous plays. Dissenters point out, however, that while the earlier pieces are verse dramas, these are prose works. They argue that the language and action of the later plays are often too crude for a woman with Warren's background and that, furthermore, nowhere in her letters or journal does Warren allude to these works. The controversy remains unresolved and the dramas, perhaps for lack of a better candidate, are most often assigned to Warren.

A political piece unquestionably penned by Warren is the poem "The Squabble of the Sea Nymphs," a witty spoof on the Boston Tea Party written in 1774 at John Adams's urging. This was later included in *Poems Dramatic and Miscellaneous,* Warren's first signed work. The collection also includes two verse dramas, *The Sack of Rome* and *The Ladies of Castile,* which in their depiction of strong female characters illustrate some of the feminist beliefs that Warren expressed most eloquently in her letters, particularly in those to Abigail Adams. Although Warren never espoused extreme feminist views, she continually decried the denial of education for women and asserted that women lacked not talent but opportunity for high achievement. She incorporated these convictions in some of her poetry, as in the lines from her poem praising the English writer Elizabeth Montagu: "A sister's hand may wrest a female pen / From the bold outrage of imperious men."

During the difficult war years (1775-1781) when her family and friends were fighting actively for independence, Warren contributed to the effort by recording the momentous events of the day. Though critics believe that she wrote most of her *History* at this time, it was not published until 1805. She continued to write poetry and to work on the *History* in the decades following the war, which proved to be traumatic for Warren. During the 1780s she lost her brother James and three of her sons to accident, illness, and war. In addition, the new government's Federalist leanings dismayed the Warrens, who were firm Republicans in the Jeffersonian tradition. Warren first expressed her dissatisfaction in an anonymous treatise, *Observations on the New Constitution and on the Federal Convention by a Columbian Patriot, Sic Transit Gloria Americana.* Printed in both Boston and Philadelphia, the pamphlet was controversial, and copies sent to Albany, New York, were returned with a stinging dismissal: "The style is too sublime and florid for the common people in this part of the country."

With the rise of Federalism, the Warrens became increasingly disenchanted with the current political climate, and their influence began to decline. James Warren lost his seat on the Massachusetts legislature, and former allies refused to intercede to obtain political positions for the Warrens' sons. With the publication of her anti-Federalist *History,* the rift widened between Warren and many of her Federalist friends, notably John Adams, who was offended by Warren's candid, somewhat critical commentary on him in the book. The two subsequently exchanged a series of well-known letters, later collected in *The Correspondence of John Adams and Mercy Warren,* in which Warren is considered to have defended herself ably against her friend's angry charges. Nonetheless Adams, formerly one of Warren's greatest admirers, felt justified in writing to a friend: "History is not the Province of the Ladies." The breach between the two families, who for years had been deeply attached, persisted until a mutual friend brought them together in 1813, a year before Warren's death.

Because her dramas were issued in pamphlet form and never staged, there is little early commentary on Warren's plays apart from the admiring remarks of friends. According to nineteenth- and twentieth-century critics, these dramas lack structure, metrical consistency, and successful characterization; yet they demonstrate the satirical bite and exhortatory language of the effective polemical pamphlet, and Warren is generally consid-

ered outstanding in that specialized genre. Critics acknowledge that Warren's plays were intended to be read rather than performed and therefore often exempt them from the standard criteria of drama criticism, stressing their topical and historical interest rather than their strictly literary merit. Warren's formal verse dramas, *The Sack of Rome* and *The Ladies of Castile,* which lack the revolutionary fire of the political satires, are often disparaged by critics as merely dull and prolix. Scholars value them, however, as further expressions of Warren's moral and political ideology. The same critical treatment is generally accorded to Warren's poetry, whose literary merit is still debated.

Warren's *History* has received the greatest share of modern critical consideration, although it was largely neglected at publication because of its anti-Federalist slant and overlooked in succeeding decades. Early critics discussed the work's style, which they generally termed stilted and artificial, and debated the relative accuracy and impartiality of Warren's judgments. Both nineteenth- and twentieth-century critics have concurred that her personal involvement with the participants allowed Warren to paint a particularly vivid and accurate portrait of the political leaders of the revolution. In the 1950s and 1960s, commentary on the *History* became more specialized, and critics focused on such issues as Warren's application of morality to history and the philosophical background of her works. Increasingly sophisticated elaborations of these issues have been published since the 1970s, with a particular emphasis on the latent feminist philosophy expressed in the *History.* This depth and variety of criticism assure Warren's reputation as an eminent historian and early American feminist.

While Warren's political dramas remain historically important, her most enduring work is the *History.* As critics point out, it stands as not only a fresh account and thoughtful analysis of a vital period in American history, but as a testimonial to its author, who ventured with confidence and success into areas outside the proscribed realm of women of her time. Warren is now counted among the most eloquent and independent thinkers in the early history of the United States.

(See also *Dictionary of Literary Biography,* Vol. 31: *American Colonial Writers, 1735-1781.*)

PRINCIPAL WORKS

The Adulateur [first publication] (verse drama) 1772
The Defeat [first publication] (verse drama) 1773
The Group [first publication] (verse drama) 1775
The Blockheads; or, The Affrighted Officers [first publication] (drama) 1776
The Motley Assembly [first publication] (drama) 1779
Observations on the New Constitution and on the Federal Convention by a Columbian Patriot, Sic Transit Gloria Americana (essay) 1788
*Poems Dramatic and Miscellaneous (poetry and dramas) 1790
History of the Rise, Progress, and Termination of the American Revolution: Interspersed with Biographical and Moral Observations (history) 1805
The Correspondence of John Adams and Mercy Warren (letters) 1878
The Plays and Poems of Mercy Otis Warren (poetry and dramas) 1980

*This work includes the dramas *The Sack of Rome* and *The Ladies of Castile*.

JOHN ADAMS   (letter date 1774)

[*Adams, the second president of the United States, was a lifelong friend of the Warrens. In the following excerpt from a letter to her husband, James, he praises Warren's poem "The Squabble of the Sea Nymphs" and likens it to Alexander Pope's *The Rape of the Lock*.]

I hope Mrs. Warren is in fine Health and Spirits—and that I have not incurred her Displeasure by making so free with the Skirmish of the Sea Deities—one of the most incontestible Evidences of real Genius, which has yet been exhibited—for to take the Clumsy, indigested Conception of another and work it into so elegant and classicall a Composition, requires Genius equall to that which wrought another most beautifull Poem, out of the little Incident of a Gentlemans clipping a Lock of a Ladys Hair, with a Pair of scissors. (pp. 106-07)

> *John Adams, in a letter to James Warren on April 9, 1774, in *Mercy Warren *by Alice Brown, Charles Scribner's Sons, 1896, pp. 106-07.*

JOHN ADAMS   (letter date 1775)

[*In response to a letter from Warren expressing doubts about her writing, Adams here assures her that satire, or "Satyr," is a worthy occupation and one for which she possesses much "Genius."*]

The Truth is, Madam, that, the best Gifts are liable to the worst uses & abuses, a Talent at Satyr, is commonly mixed with the choicest Powers of Genius and it has such irrisistable Charms, in the Eyes of the World, that the extravagant Praise, it never fails to extort, is apt to produce extravagant Vanity in the Satirist, and an exuberant Fondness for more Praise, untill he looses that cool Judgment which alone can justify him.

If we look into human Nature, and run through the various classes of Life, we shall find it is really a dread of Satyr that restrains our Speeches from exorbitances, more than Laws, human, moral or divine, indeed the Efficacy of civil Punishments is derived chiefly from the same source.—. . . But classical Satyr, such as flows so naturally & easily from the Pen of my excellent Friend, has all the Efficacy, and more, in Support of Virtue and in Discountenancing of Vice, without any of the Coarseness and Indelicacy of those other Species of Satyr, the civil and political ones. . . .

Of all the Genius's which have yet arisen in America, there has been none, superior to one, which now shines, in this happy, this exquisite Faculty,—indeed, altho there are many which have received more industrious Cultivation I know of none, ancient or modern, which has reached the tender the pathetic, the keen & severe, and at the same time, the soft, the sweet, the amiable and the pure in greater Perfection. (pp. 162-63)

> *John Adams, in a letter to Mercy Otis Warren on March 15, 1775, in *Mercy Warren *by Alice Brown, Charles Scribner's Sons, 1896, pp. 161-63.*

ELIZABETH F. ELLET   (essay date 1848)

[*An American translator and historian, Ellet chronicled the accomplishments of American women in several books, including *The Women of the American Revolution, *from which the following favorable survey of Warren is drawn.*]

The name of Mercy Warren belongs to American history. In the influence she exercised, she was perhaps the most remarkable woman who lived at the Revolutionary period. (p. 91)

How warmly Mrs. Warren espoused the cause of her country—how deeply her feelings were enlisted—appears in her letters. Her correspondence with the great spirits of that era, if published, would form a most valuable contribution to our historical literature. . . . It includes letters, besides those from members of her own family, from Samuel and John Adams, Jefferson, Dickinson, Gerry, Knox and others. These men asked her opinion in political matters, and acknowledged the excellence of her judgment. (pp. 93-4)

Every page from the pen of Mrs. Warren, is remarkable for clearness and vigor of thought. Thus her style was not vitiated by the artificial tastes of the day; yet her expression is often studiously elaborated, in accordance with the prevalent fashion. This is the case in her letters written with most care; while in others her ardent spirit pours out its feelings with irrepressible energy, portraying itself in the genuine and simple language of emotion. (pp. 100-01)

The Group [is] a satirical dramatic piece in two Acts, in which many of the leading tory characters of the day were humorously introduced. A strong political influence has been ascribed to this and other satirical poems from her pen. It is in allusion to this that Mrs. Adams speaks of "a Rapatio soul"—Governor Hutchinson being thus designated. The following description is applied to him:

> But mark the traitor—his high crime glossed o'er
> Conceals the tender feelings of the man,
> The social ties that bind the human heart;
> He strikes a bargain with his country's foes,
> And joins to wrap America in flames.
> Yet with feigned pity, and satanic grin,
> As if more deep to fix the keen insult,
> Or make his life a farce still more complete,
> He sends a groan across the broad Atlantic,
> And with a phiz of crocodilian stamp,
> Can weep, and wreathe, still hoping to deceive;
> He cries—the gathering clouds hang thick about her,
> But laughs within; then sobs—
> Alas, my country!
>
> (pp. 101-02)

Mrs. Warren employed much of her leisure with her pen. She kept a faithful record of occurrences during the dark days of her country's affliction, through times that engaged the attention both of the philosopher and the politician. She did this with the design of transmitting to posterity a faithful portraiture of the most distinguished characters of the day.

Her intention was fulfilled in her history of the war [*History of the Rise, Progress, and Termination of the American Revolution*]. Her poetical compositions, afterwards collected and dedicated to General Washington [*Poems Dramatic and Miscellaneous*], were the amusement of solitude, when many of her friends were actively engaged in the field or cabinet. Some of them contain allusions to bodily sufferings, her health being far from robust. The tragedies, *The Sack of Rome* and *The Ladies of Castile,* are more remarkable for patriotic sentiment than dramatic merit. The verse is smooth and flowing, and the language poetical, but often wanting in the simplicity essential to true pathos. An interest deeper than that of the story is awakened by the application of many passages to the circumstances of the times. (pp. 103-04)

"A Poetical Reverie" was published before the breaking out of the war. It gives a poetical view of the future greatness of America, and the punishment of her oppressors. "**The Squabble of the Sea Nymphs,**" celebrates the pouring of the tea into the sea, and is something in the Rape of the Lock style. The lines ["**Things Necessary to the Life of a Woman**"] to a friend, who on the American determination to suspend all commerce with Great Britain, except for the necessaries of life, requested a poetical list of the articles the ladies might comprise under that head, have some fine satire. (p. 105)

The powers of Mrs. Warren were devoted to nobler objects than chastising the follies of the day. She gave her tenderest sympathies to the sufferings of her friends, and poured the balm of consolation into many a wounded heart. The letters of Mrs. Adams show how much she leaned, amidst her heavy trials, on this faithful support. (p. 107)

Towards the close of her protracted life, her influence did not diminish; for her mental superiority was still unimpaired and acknowledged. Seldom has one woman in any age, acquired such an ascendency over the strongest, by the mere force of a powerful intellect. She is said to have supplied political parties with their arguments; and she was the first of her sex in America who taught the reading world in matters of state policy and history. (pp. 125-26)

> *Elizabeth F. Ellet, "Mercy Warren, Janet Montgomery, Hannah Winthrop, Catharine Livingston," in her* The Women of the American Revolution, *Vol. I, 1848. Reprint by George W. Jacobs & Co., 1900, pp. 91-126.**

RUFUS WILMOT GRISWOLD (essay date 1873)

[Griswold, a nineteenth-century American editor, critic, and anthologist, left a valuable store of information on the writers of his era in such collections as The Female Poets of America. *His critical judgment, however, is considered to be often limited by personal prejudice. He here states that Warren's writings have little poetical and dramatic merit, although he praises the humorous poem "Things Necessary to the Life of a Woman."]*

This woman, once so well known as a poet, and whose historical writings are still consulted as among the most valuable authorities relating to our revolutionary age, was . . . for many years honorably conspicuous in public affairs. . . .

The popular excitement which preceded the separation from England . . . had a quick and powerful influence upon her ardent and sympathetic spirit, and perhaps nothing would give us a more just impression of the feelings of the time than her eloquent and terse correspondence with the Adamses, with Jefferson, Dickinson, Gerry, Knox, and other leading characters, upon the aspects and prospects of affairs. Her intercourse with the remarkable women who seconded so earnestly the movements of the fathers of the republic, was more inti-

mate, and probably would admit us yet further into the secrets and passions of the youthful heart of the nation. . . .

There is certainly very little poetry in . . . [her satirical dramas]; but as reflexions of the common feeling her satires received the best applause of the day. (p. 21)

Her tragedies [published in *Poems, Dramatic and Miscellaneous*] were written for amusement, in the solitary hours in which her friends were abroad, and they are as deeply imbued with the general spirit as if their characters were acting in the daily experience of the country. They have little dramatic or poetic merit, but many passages are smoothly and some vigorously written—as the following, from *The Sack of Rome:*

SUSPICION.

> I think some latent mischief lies concealed
> Beneath the vizard of a fair pretence;
> My heart ill brooked the errand of the day,
> Yet I obeyed—though a strange horror seized
> My gloomy mind, and shook my frame
> As if the moment murdered all my joys.

(pp. 21-2)

The lines to the Hon. John Winthrop ["**Things Necessary to the Life of a Woman**"], who on the determination in 1774 to suspend all trade with England except for the real "necessaries of life," requested a list of articles the ladies might comprise under that head, are in the author's happiest vein of satire. . . . [*The History of the Rise, Progress, and Termination of the American Revolution, Interspersed with Biographical, Political, and Moral Observations*] will always be consulted as one of the most interesting original authorities upon the revolution. It is written with care, and in a spirit of independence which is illustrated by her notice of the character of her friend Mr. Adams, which was so unfavorable as to cause a temporary interruption of the relations between the two families. . . . (pp. 22-3)

> *Rufus Wilmot Griswold, "Mrs. Mercy Warren," in his* The Female Poets of America, *revised edition, James Miller, Publisher, 1873, pp. 21-3.*

ALICE BROWN (essay date 1896)

[In the following excerpt, drawn from two chapters of her biography of Warren, Brown surveys Warren's literary work, touching upon the artificial excesses of her style and emphasizing her role as pamphleteer.]

Of all [Mrs. Warren's] work, *The Group* is most incisive, most earnest, and was probably widest-reaching in its influence. (p. 164)

[It] is a boldly satirical piece of work, which we are forced to consider a farce because the titlepage bids us. (pp. 165-66)

To us, save as a literary curiosity, Mrs. Warren's farce is eminently dull; but we must not forget that its reason for existing has itself ceased to be. To an inflamed patriotism it must have been a vivid delight to find the enemies of peace held up bleeding under the eye of day, to hear some one voice the hot rancor of every heart and say what all patriots would fain have said themselves had they been clever enough. (p. 166)

Mrs. Warren was the voice of the time, but that this was a somewhat too ruthless voice is evident in her portraiture of Governor Hutchinson: a Tory to be sure, a man faithful rather to the crown than alive to this alarming fever of Colonial revolt, and a man who, like even the patriots, thought all fair in war, and thus succeeded in rousing against himself a sort of hydrophobic madness. (p. 167)

Never was there a more frankly partisan piece of work [than *The Group*], showing, according to the patriotic standpoint, vice "her own image." One overmastering joy of the performance lies in the fact that out of their own mouths are the public enemies condemned. (p. 169)

[*The Adulator*] had preceded **The Group,** and though far less harmonious in conception, [it was] equally incisive and pregnant of result. (p. 176)

[*Poems, Dramatic and Miscellaneous*] is chiefly occupied by two long and very dull tragedies: **The Sack of Rome** and **The Ladies of Castile**,—dull, yet truly significant in that they mirror the constant tendency of the author's mind. Throughout her life she was almost morbidly apprehensive over the danger which might befall the hardier virtues of a state by the enervating approaches of luxury. The old Spartan principles of toil and endurance were, in her mind, never too austere. (p. 181)

The rest of the poems are nearly all occasional: **"To Fidelio, Long absent on the great public Cause, which agitated all America, in 1776,"** **"To the Hon. J. Winthrop, Esq.,"** **"To a Young Gentleman Residing in France,"** and the like. Yet these were not all. To study the pile of yellowed manuscript in the obscure but painstaking chirography of that hand which seemed never to tire, is to find page after page of rhymed and metrical reflection. The wonder is, with this Revolutionary dame, that she found time for such an extraordinary amount of work. She owns once, in a comparative estimate of the status of men and women, that woman's mental labor is far harder to pursue because it must be interrupted by household cares; but she says it without complaint. Her own domestic life was full to the brim. She could have found little time for literature. She had five boys to educate and train. She had an enormous correspondence; and yet, ever welling into light, is this irrepressible desire to put the world into verse. She copies her own letters, and those of other people. Her clerical labors are enough to afflict a scribe. (pp. 184-85)

But Mercy Warren's place is not among the poets. She has left no line so inevitable, so perfect, as to have struck root into the soil of literature, to grow and flourish there. In form she is strained and artificial, like the greater of her day; and it is only her abiding earnestness which succeeds in loosening the shackles of too elaborate artifice and lets her breathe and speak. Her home is among those fighting souls who swayed the time through onslaught upon special abuses. That her work was thrown into poetical form does not debar her from taking her rightful stand among the pamphleteers. For this was the age of the political pamphlet. It flourished as the theological essay had done at an earlier date. When the political situation had become unbearable, and the air was heavy with thought, the lightning of words played hotly. (p. 187)

[Mrs. Warren] was one of the teachers of the time; she reiterated, she insisted and warned. Like John Adams in his quest for gunpowder, she was determined to think of nothing but liberty, and to repeat that splendid cry until the echo, at least, came back from other mouths.

Doubtless Mrs. Warren would have considered her *History of the Revolution* the crowning labor of her life, the evidence through which it should afterwards be weighed. (pp. 190-91)

Perhaps the chief drawback of the *History,* from a literary point of view, is that it proves to be what the titlepage honestly leads you to expect, "Interspersed with Biographical, Political, and Moral Observations." Mrs. Warren was, as we have been accustomed to find her, too abstract, too sparing of the red blood of life. She is a little dry and very verbose, and it perhaps seems to us now that she had not always a judicious discrimination as to the relative value of events. Her portraits are very bold, very trenchant, as those of an "incomparable satirist" must ever be; but they are not portraits after the Clarendon type,—warm, living, and dressed in English which could not have been imagined otherwise. When she wholly approves she is less graphic than when she recoils through moral aversion. Witness her characterization of George Washington, which is exceedingly dignified, but runs as sluggish as a fenland stream. . . . (pp. 203-04)

It is only when she approaches Thomas Hutchinson, the object of what seems to her a just detestation, that she becomes truly piquant and human; after remarking that "it is ever painful to a candid mind to exhibit the deformed features of its own species," she goes on to characterize him as "dark, intriguing, insinuating, haughty and ambitious, while the extreme of avarice marked each feature of his character. (p. 205)

This . . . is one of the judgments of the time which posterity has reversed. Mrs. Warren was no less enlightened, no less keen of vision than her associates; but they were all too near the object of their scrutiny, and too hot-headed with the rage born of oppression to judge justly. Thomas Hutchinson was not perhaps a martyr, but he was a most intelligent man, who tried conscientiously to perform the duties of an impossible situation, and failed, as any one would have failed who had not gone over, heart and soul, to the Colonists. (p. 206)

Hers was no light task,—to face her own contemporaries with what she intended for absolutely faithful portraits, drawn without fear or favor. There can be no doubt that she wrote her *History* with a religious fervor consecrated to the cause of truth and justice. When she erred it was through the natural fallibility of human eyes when they dare to scrutinize human motives. (pp. 207-08)

> *Alice Brown, in her* Mercy Warren, *Charles Scribner's Sons, 1896, 317 p.*

ANNIE RUSSELL MARBLE   (essay date 1903)

[*In the following excerpt from a biographical survey of Warren, Marble discusses Warren's treatment of Hutchinson in both the plays and in the* History *and identifies the historical figures that the characters in her dramas represent. In general, Marble disparages Warren's writing style.*]

Among [Mercy Warren's] sentimental stanzas are some **"To Honoria, on her Journey to Dover,"** and another **"To a Young Lady on Showing an Excellent Piece of Painting, much faded."** The latter theme afforded scope for moralizing, a faculty ever dear to the versifier of that age:

> As beauteous paintings lose their dye,
> Age sinks the lustre of your eye.
> Then seize the minutes as they pass;
> Behold how swift runs down the glass.

This scarcely seems fine poetry to our ears, yet its author was lauded as a genius in those days of ecstatic praise of mental tastes. Not alone in letters and inconsequent verses of friendship was she content to employ her literary faculty. Perhaps, as one reads the effusive adulation in friendly letters and her husband's proud encouragement, it does not seem so strange that she should have thought herself a poet, even of the dramatic scope. With opportunities almost unsurpassed for inside facts and predictions, with a fund of satire and deep personal interest in the leaders of Whig and Tory forces, she exercised her mental skill in the early years of imminent struggle by writing a tragedy, *The Adulator.* This was printed in 1772. The best portion from a literary standpoint is the text from **"Cato's Tragedy,"**—suggestive of her own resolute patriotism,—

> Then let us rise, my friends, and strive to fill
> This little interval, this pause of life
> (While yet our liberties and fates are doubtful)
> With resolution, friendship, Roman bravery,
> And all the virtues we can crowd into it;
> That Heaven may say it ought to be prolong'd.

The Adulator and its sequel, *The Retreat,* were in reality only dramatic sketches, full of vindictive rancor against Governor Hutchinson and his allies. One dislikes to believe the assertion that the author's bitterness towards the last Tory governor of her state was due to family pique at his appointment, since the office had been sought for her father. Whatever the cause, this woman, in all her writings from plays to history, never ceases to ridicule Hutchinson, crediting him with baser motives than a fairer mind would have done. Such, in general, was the contemporaneous sentiment against him, which time has mollified, joined, perchance, to a feminine tenacity of prejudice.

Despite her mental seriousness, Mistress Warren had the typical foibles as well as the merits of womanhood. While Governor Hutchinson is caricatured as the hated "Rapatio," "Brutus, Senator" is a portrait of her beloved brother James, while the attendant Roman statesmen are modelled after her husband and his friends, John and Samuel Adams, Hancock and others. The maintenance of rhythm and metre was often too great a tax upon the author's skill, yet these plays were widely read and were succeeded by the yet more famous satire-farce, *The Group.* To modern readers the merit of these dramas consists in their representation of Boston atmosphere during the years of mental strife from 1770 to 1773. The internal ferment as well as the pictorial features are well painted. The play was sent in parts to her husband while he was in camp, was loaned by him to John Adams, who divulged the authorship and urged the printing. His admiration for Mistress Warren's mental talent now became the most fulsome adulation. He entreats her to continue exercise of a genius, "superiour is none, ancient or modern, which has reached the tender, the pathetic, the keen and severe, and at the same time, the soft, the sweet, the amiable and the pure in greater perfection" [see excerpt dated 1775]. Again, he emphasizes her divinely entrusted powers, whose use "it would be criminal to neglect." In response to urgence from the same source, she wrote a **"Tea-Ballad,"** stifled with classical allusions and in limping measure, **"The Squabble of the Sea-Nymphs,"** which seemed to her admirer quite comparable to Pope's "Rape of the Lock" [see excerpt dated 1774].

After satiety of servile praise from John Adams it is a relief to turn directly to a copy of *The Group.* . . . The introductory stanza, or prologue, is apt and superior to the author's usual verse:

> What! arm'd for virtue, and not point the pen,
> Brand the bold front of shameless, guilty men,
> Dash the proud Gamester from his gilded car,
> Bare the mean heart which lurks beneath a star.

With this and similar stanzas she threw down the personal gauntlet and proceeded to enumerate her *dramatis personae,* with uncompromising emphasis bestowing hostile names upon such of her characters as represented the Tory leaders and prominent Loyalists. As in the previous farce, "Lord Chief Justice Hazelrod" is a malignant caricature of Peter Oliver, while Governor Hutchinson is lampooned as "Judge Meagre" and Sir William Pepperell as "Sir Sparrow Spendall." Other Loyalists are ridiculed as "Hum Humbus," "Brigadier Hateall," "Beau Trumps." The last was doubtless a satiric sketch of Daniel Leonard who deserted the patriot cause and entered the sparring discussion as "Massachusettensis," while as a fop with "broad gold lace around his hat" and kindred adornments he drove his coach and four from Taunton to Boston. This character gives opportunity for keen sarcasm, as he discusses the chances for victory and the spoils:

> But if by carnage we should win the game,
> Perhaps by my abilities and fame,
> I might attain a splendid glittering car,
> And mount aloft and sail in liquid air.
> Like Phaeton, I'd then outstrip the wind,—
> And leave my low competitors behind.

The most vigorous portion, the speech of the secretary, is near the close,—an antithesis of the opposing motives in Tory and patriot hearts:

> They fight for freedom while we stab the breast
> Of every man who is her friend profest,
> They fight in virtue's ever sacred cause,
> While we tread on divine and human laws.
> Glory and Victory and lasting Fame
> Will crown their arms and bless each Hero's name.

The scenes are enacted in a small "back-parlor," well guarded by soldiers, while *The Group* of sycophantic Tories drink their bumpers and discuss their prospects.

To comprehend, in any way, the plaudits which greeted these satires in dialogue, then called dramas, one must revert to the conditions of the age. In the first place, they were designed to foster patriotism by encouraging the already acrid feelings towards the Loyalists,—not a lofty motive, it is true, but a common mode of warfare. To establish the patriot's sense of injury and redress there was resort to a scoring of his enemies. Again, in her aspiration towards drama, Mrs. Warren was almost a pioneer among native writers, and this would bring her distinction. . . . Fired by her success with the war dramas, for they were widely read and praised, she later sought to add to her laurels by two other tragedies, *The Sack of Rome* and *The Ladies of Castile.* She even harbored a hope that these might be placed upon the stage. While they reveal some constructive skill and a broad grasp of the historical scenes chosen, they are too stilted and unimaginative to be considered as real drama. . . . That she was considered a fluent speaker and writer by her own generation, who admired her stately Johnsonese, is evidenced in letters and also in an amusing incident. It is stated that she wrote some speeches for the members of the Provincial Congress and that one of the orators—identity kindly hidden—stumbled so often over her long words and mispronounced so many of her classical allusions, that he was finally chagrined into a confession of the source of his eloquence. If, as a letter writer, she "lived upon stilts," as has been wittily said, one must remember the favorite style of the time and the natural reserve of her nature. Charming Abigail Adams, in her simple, piquant letters, deplores her uncouthness beside her "elegant friend, Marcia." In the metrical list of articles for a lady's toilet ["**Things Necessary to the Life of a Woman**"], written at request in view of closing importation of British goods, she is surprised into a semi-drollery and enumeration of trivialities which is truly refreshing. . . . (pp. 171-75)

Urged, perhaps unduly, by her family and friends, Mrs. Warren consented to write [*History of the Rise, Progress, and Termination of the American Revolution*], using her own data and journals assiduously kept during the years of stress, and having access to important state papers. Designing this as "a record for her children of their mother's mental life," she worked most faithfully, copying as well as creating the three large volumes. It was a monumental task and the style grew more ponderous as the pages accumulated. With a strong moral sense she presented public and personal incidents, yet it was inevitable that her prejudices should color her views, especially upon such close perspective to the events themselves. If her characterizations of many of the Tory statesmen, especially Hutchinson, show too much animosity to be authentic to-day, we must recall the change of sentiment during the last fifty years under the guidance of such wise historians as John Fiske and his compeers. (pp. 177-78)

> Annie Russell Marble, "Mistress Mercy Warren: Real Daughter of the American Revolution," in The New England Magazine, *n.s. Vol. XXVIII, No. 2, April, 1903, pp. 163-80.*

MICHAEL KRAUS (essay date 1937)

[*In a brief review of the* History, *Kraus states that Warren's account of events after the war is "practically valueless," but that the book provides a "vivid glimpse" of the leaders of the period.*]

Although [her *History of the Rise, Progress, and Termination of the American Revolution* was] published more than a score of years after the treaty of peace, Mrs. Warren said that she had been collecting materials "many years antecedent to any history since published," and it is probable that much of her work was written contemporaneously with the events they describe. (p. 144)

After some introductory remarks, Mrs. Warren begins her history with the Stamp Act. Halfway through the first volume she reaches the period of military hostilities, where the Warren bias is immediately apparent. A special object of vituperation is, of course, Thomas Hutchinson. In the eyes of the historian, Hutchinson was "dark, intriguing, insinuating, haughty and ambitious, while the extreme of avarice marked each feature of his character"; and his was a Machiavellian attitude toward government. In her second volume Mrs. Warren broadens her view of the war period to include references to discontent in Ireland and internal politics in England, which she relates, rather lamely, to the American Revolution. Some eighty pages in the third volume reveal the broader scope of the history of the Revolution, which now includes the naval history of these years—Rodney in the West Indies, events in Minorca, Gibraltar, and elsewhere. The following chapter refers to the

war's repercussions in Great Britain and in Ireland. In thus making more comprehensive her history Mrs. Warren was in accord with John Adams, who held that to write on the American Revolution one must write the history of mankind during that period. After her description of the war, said the author, her mind was "now at leisure for more general observations on the subsequent consequences, without confining it to time or place." The remarks that follow on the later history of the United States are practically valueless as historical writing. As honest John Adams bluntly wrote to Mrs. Warren: "After the termination of the Revolutionary war your subject was completed."

A long correspondence with Mrs. Warren initiated by John Adams, who felt himself aspersed by the historian, makes a valuable addition to the work because of the inclusion of many interesting items on our diplomatic history. The Warren family's leaning to Jeffersonianism was a cause of friction with Adams, although friendly relations between the families were maintained to the end. Adams remarked ungallantly that history was "not the Province of the Ladies." "It is my opinion . . . ," said Adams to Mrs. Warren, "that your History has been written to the taste of the nineteenth century, and accommodated to gratify the passions, prejudices, and feelings of the party who are now predominant." To which she replied by saying that her history had been under consideration long before the nineteenth century and had received encouragement from John Adams himself. The writing of Mrs. Warren was often diffuse and her rhetorical passages, especially on the Declaration of Independence, were of the stuff that makes typical patriotic orations. To read Mrs. Warren's history, however, is to get a vivid glimpse of the thoughts and feelings of the leaders during this period. (pp. 144-46)

> Michael Kraus, "Historiography 1750-1800, and the Growing National Spirit," in his A History of American History, *Farrar & Rinehart, Inc., 1937, pp. 105-62.**

ARTHUR HOBSON QUINN (essay date 1943)

[*An early twentieth-century American critic, editor, and biographer, Quinn was a strong advocate for his native literature before it gained widespread appreciation and critical acceptance. In the following excerpt, he provides an overview of Warren's dramas, stressing their social and historical significance.*]

While her husband and her friends were moulding the Revolution, [Mercy Warren] wished to do her share. In fact, we find her urged to the task by John Adams in a letter written to James Warren on December 22, 1773, in which he speaks of the destruction of the tea and hopes to see it "celebrated by a certain poetical pen which has no equal that I know of in this country." This praise was probably inspired by her first Satire, *The Adulateur.* . . .

The chief satire of the play is directed against Thomas Hutchinson, who had held at once the three offices of member of the Council, Chief Justice, and Lieutenant Governor, and who finally became Governor of the Colony. He is known as Rapatio. He was a native of Massachusetts, and for that reason his duplicity was more keenly resented by his fellow citizens. . . . Untrue even to his employers, he pretended to deny the right of Great Britain to tax America, and handed about patriotic letters to be read, which he never sent. The immediate inspiration for the satire was the publication of letters from Hutchinson, the Governor, and Andrew Oliver, the Lieutenant

Governor, to Thomas Whately and others, in England. These had come through the agency of a member of Parliament into the hands of Franklin in December, 1772, and by him had been transmitted to the speaker of the House of Assembly of Massachusetts, of which he was the agent. The letters, which urged the British Government to declare martial law in the colonies, to make the judges absolutely dependent upon the Crown, to suppress the charter of Rhode Island, and in many other ways to nullify the rights of the citizens, were published, with the natural result of fomenting hatred against the fellow countryman who had betrayed them. In the first scene, Brutus, Cassius, Junius and Portius, who represent James Otis, John Adams, Samuel Adams, and John Hancock, declare their intention to strike for liberty. Read superficially, it seems the characters are so united in their sentiments that they are hardly sufficiently characterized, but read with a better understanding of the various functions of the leading patriots of that early period, one notices first, the peculiar quality of enthusiasm that was Otis's great contribution, and which his sister here represents. Samuel Adams, as Junius, speaks as an older man:

> *Junius:* When Brutus speaks, old age grows young.
> Whatever right I've lost—I've still a dagger,
> And have a hand to wield it—'tis true it
> shakes—
> With age it shakes: Yet in the cause of
> freedom,
> It catches vigor. You shall find it strike
> The tyrant from his Throne.

Hutchinson is then represented as longing for the day when he shall, through the fall of his predecessor, Bernard, really be governor, in order that his revenge may be taken for the indignities he suffered during the Stamp Act agitation.

In Act II, the killing of a boy of eleven by an informer, Richardson, is described by Cassius. Then Governor Rapatio conspires with Bagshot, the chief of the Janizaries, who represents Captain Preston of His Majesty's Twenty-ninth Regiment of Infantry, to fire on the people and in consequence the Boston Massacre occurs. This is represented off the stage, but the author describes in vigorous language the killing of unarmed men and children by the troops. The language naturally is a bit bombastic, but such a speech as that of Junius rings with a real sincerity across the years.

> *Junius:* Her sighs?—and hear them tamely? never—
> never—
> Who knows the secrets of my soul,
> Knows 'tis on fire, and bursting for revenge.
> What tho' I totter with a weight of years,
> And palsied age relaxes every nerve,
> Yet such foul deeds have rouz'd the genial
> current,
> That long had lag'd—this life by nature's laws,
> Like an old garment must have soon been
> drop'd:
> And never could I, had I liv'd to ages,
> Have dy'd so well as now—to die at ease,
> And drop into the grave, unheard, unknown,
> This is but common fate—
> He, who bleeds in freedom's cause, expires
> illustrious.
> He falls, but catches immortality.
> While greatful millions croud around,
> And with a generous tear bedew his urn.

The scene in Faneuil Hall in which the town determined upon the withdrawal of the troops and the conference between Hutchinson and his Council are then given, but the most dramatic episode of all, that in which Samuel Adams told Hutchinson in no uncertain terms what he must do, is not used by the dramatist. Up to this point in the *Adulateur* there had been little real satire—it was mostly forcible and direct description, but with the introduction of the character of Meagre, under which name Foster Hutchinson, the Governor's brother appears, the satirical touch becomes evident. Meagre introduces himself thus:

> *Meagre:*   Bravely spoke!
> And here's a soul, like thine, that never
> linger'd,
> When prompted by revenge—If thirst of
> power;
> A spirit haughty, sour implacable,
> That bears a deadly enmity to freedom,
> But mean and base; who never had a notion
> Of generous and manly; who would stab,
> Stab in the dark, but what he'd get revenge;
> If such a soul is suitable to thy purpose,
> 'Tis here.

Rapatio does not seem to be altogether satisfied with the result of his efforts and there is almost a real note of tragedy in his last soliloquy in which he cries out,

> I dare not meet my naked heart alone.

The play ends with a speech of Brutus in which the author, through her brother, sounds a note of prophecy:

> *Brutus:* Yes, Marcus, poverty must be thy fate,
> If thou'rt thy country's friend—Think upon it
> When I'm gone, as soon perhaps I may be.
> Remember it—those men whose crimes now
> shock,
> May close their measures—Yes, the wish'd for
> period
> May soon arrive, when murders, blood and
> carnage,
> Shall crimson all these streets; when this poor
> country
> Shall loose her richest blood, forbid it heaven!
> And may these monsters find their glories fade,
> Crush'd in the ruins they themselves had made,
> While thou my country, shall again revive,
> Shake off misfortune, and thro' ages live,
> See thro' the waste a ray of virtue gleame,
> Dispell the shades and brighten all the scene,
> Wak'd into life, the blooming forest glows,
> And all the desert blossoms as the rose.
> From distant lands see virtuous millions fly
> To happier climates, and a milder sky.
> While on the mind successive pleasures pour,
> Till time expires, and ages are no more.

(pp. 34-7)

The Group is built around the abrogation of the charter of Massachusetts and the appointment by the King of a Council, the upper house of Massachusetts, through a royal mandamus instead of through election by the Assembly. This action was deeply resented by the people. Their charter was to them their most sacred possession, and the tradition of their resistance to its abrogation under Charles II and its triumphant recovery was a glorious spot in their annals. Everyone who accepted the appointment to the Council was by that fact an enemy of the people, and Mrs. Warren's satire needed no "key" when she pilloried the "group" which had sold their birthright for office.

In order to understand the satire of *The Group* it is necessary to visualize the situation in Massachusetts which the sharp logic of events was shaping, and to distinguish clearly the personalities of the actors and the reasons for their fidelity to the royal cause. Read without this interpretation the satire has little meaning, but read in the light of the intense feeling which separated the community into hostile classes and even broke up the ties of family, it becomes a vital document in the history of our national progress. The list of characters was printed, of course, without any interpretation, but is here given with what is believed to be the correct key.

Lord Chief Justice HALZEROD
    [Hazelrod]   [Peter Oliver]
Judge MEAGAE [Meagre]   [Foster Hutchinson]
Brigadier HATEALL   [Timothy Ruggles]
HUM HUMBUG, Esq.   [John Erving, Jr.]
SIR SPARROW SPENDALL   [William Pepperell]
HECTOR MUSHROOM   Col. (John) [Murray]
BEAU TRUMPS   [Daniel Leonard]
DICK, the Publican   [Richard Lechmere]
SIMPLE SAPLING, Esq.   [Nat(haniel) Ray Thomas]
Monsieur de FRANCOIS   [James Boutineau]
CRUSTY CROWBAR, Esq.   (Josiah) [Edson.]
DUPE,—Secretary of State,   [Thomas Flucker]
SCRIBLERIUS FRIBBLE,   [Harrison Gray]
COMMODORE BATTEAU   (Joshua) [Loring]
Collateralis, a new-made Judge (William) [Brown[e]
[Sylla]   [General Gage]

By the time *The Group* appeared, Governor Thomas Hutchinson had fled to England, but he still lives in the satire by the remarks of his former associates. The chief mantle of dislike fell upon his brother, Foster Hutchinson, who is represented as possessing a mean and timeserving disposition. He was a judge of the Supreme Court of the province, and a Mandamus Councillor until his flight to Halifax in 1776.

Certain characteristics all these gentlemen shared. They were believers in the royal prerogative, in the right of the King to take away the freedom of the people of Massachusetts. They were of a conservative tendency, usually had property, and most of them held office or wished to do so. All but Oliver and Loring were Mandamus Councillors. They were educated men and well bred, and nine were graduates of Harvard College. They represented the feudal system that was beginning to grow up in New England to a larger degree than is generally realized, and to which the Revolution put an end. They were by their very position natural leaders, and *The Group* voiced the resentment of the people against those who should have led rather than betrayed them.

But there were differences, also, which are represented in the degrees of dislike with which Mrs. Warren viewed them. Naturally those most hated were drawn best and become, from the dramatic point of view, most interesting. Some of the characters are but lightly touched. Joshua Loring, whose inhumanity as Commissioner for the Whig prisoners had not yet begun, does not even speak. Harrison Gray, whose daughter had married Mercy Warren's brother Samuel, is lightly flicked. For those who seem to have been rather genial gentlemen, living contentedly on their large estates and enjoying personal popularity, like Sir William Pepperell and Judge William

Browne, she shows no special rancor. Pepperell's name, through his grandfather's valiant services at the fall of Louisburg, was among the most respected in the commonwealth. He inherited great wealth from this source, and changed his own name of Sparhawk to his maternal grandfather's in consequence. Hence the name of "Sir Sparrow Spendall." His later career when, exiled in England and his estates confiscated, he shared his British pension with his less fortunate fellow loyalists, shows him to have been a man of feeling. He had the melancholy distinction of becoming the principal figure of another "group," that of the loyalists in Benjamin West's painting, "The Reception of the American Loyalists by Great Britain in 1783." Boutineau and Lechmere were representative of that class of men, who at first resented the encroachments of the ministry but later recanted when separation seemed the logical result of continued action. They had signed in 1760 the first memorial against the crown officers, and this relapse from grace is described in *The Group* by the words put into Boutineau's mouth:

Monsieur: Could I give up the dread of retribution,
          The awful reck'ning of some future day,
          Like surly Hateall I might curse mankind,
          And dare the threat'ned vengeance of the
            skies.
          Or like yon apostate—[*Pointing to Hazelrod,
            retired to
            a corner to read Massachusettensis.*]
                    Feel but slight remorse
          To sell my country for a grasp of Gold,
          But the impressions of my early youth,
          Infix'd by precepts of my pious sire,
          Are stings and scorpions in my goaded
            breast.

Mrs. Warren had a personal grudge against him also. His son-in-law John Robinson was found guilty in 1772 of a violent assault on her brother, James Otis, and Boutineau acted as his attorney.

She reserved her finest rage for a select few of the characters. For the office-holding class, which Peter Oliver, Foster Hutchinson, and Thomas Flucker represented, she had the most contempt. To Timothy Ruggles, on account of his rough and violent nature, and his action when as delegate from Massachusetts to the first American Congress in 1765 he refused to sign the resolution of union, she gives a large share of attention as Brigadier Hateall. The title refers to his rank in the French and Indian War, and he was later one of those Tory generals who led the "Loyal Militia" against their countrymen. His sentiments are thus represented in the play:

Hateall: Curse on their coward fears, and dastard
            souls,
          Their soft compunctions and relenting
            qualms,
          Compassion ne'er shall seize my stedfast
            breast
          Though blood and carnage spread thro' all
            the land;
          Till streaming purple tinge the verdant turf,
          Till ev'ry street shall float with human gore,
          I Nero like, the capital in flames,
          Could laugh to see her glotted sons expire,
          Tho' much too rough my soul to touch the
            lyre.

Simple: I fear the brave, the injur'd multitude;
Repeated wrongs arouse them to resent,
And every patriot like old Brutus stands,
The shining steal half drawn—its glitt'ring
   point
Scarce hid beneath the scabbard's friendly
   cell
Resolv'd to die, or see their country free.

Hateall: Then let them die—*The dogs; we will keep
   down*—
While N—'s my friend, and G— approves
   the deed,
Tho' hell and all its hell-hounds should unite,
I'll not recede to save from swift perdition
My wife, my country, family or friends.
G—'s mandamus I more highly prize
Than all the mandates of th' etherial king.

Peter Oliver, though not a lawyer, had been made Chief Justice of Massachusetts in 1756. As he describes himself in the first Act of *The Group:*

Hazelrod: Resolv'd more rapidly to gain my point;
I mounted high in justice's sacred seat,
With flowing robes, and head equip'd
   without;
A heart unfeeling, and a stubborn soul,
As qualify'd as e'er a *Jefferies* was;
Save in the knotty rudiments of law,
The smallest requisite for modern times,
When wisdom, law and justice, are supply'd
By swords, dragoons, and ministerial nods,
Sanctions most sacred in the pander's creed,
I sold my country for a splendid bribe.

In the first Act the characters reveal themselves. In the second, they gather in a scene whose stage directions are of interest:

> The scene changes to a large dining room. The table furnished with bowls, bottles, glasses, and cards. The group appear sitting around in a restless attitude. In one corner of the room is discovered a small cabinet of books, for the use of the studious and contemplative; containing Hobb[e]'s Leviathan, Sipthrop's Sermons, Hutchinson's History, Fable of the Bees, Philalethes on Philanthrop, with an appendix by Massachusettensis, Hoyle on Whist, Lives of the Stewarts, Statutes of Henry the eighth; and William the Conqueror, Wedderburn's speeches, and Acts of Parliament, for 1774.

In this Act the situation is further developed, the results of Governor Hutchinson's actions are outlined by Leonard, who speaks of the uselessness of patriotism:

> But 'twas a poor unprofitable path
> Nought to be gain'd, save solid peace of mind.

In the third scene the most dramatic quality of the play develops with the appearance of General Gage. He is drawn in quite a favorable light compared with the ''Group,'' and the keenness of Mrs. Warren's pen shows in the discussion about the quartering of troops upon the inhabitants. Dupe asks who will harbor them and Meagre replies:

> None but the very dregs of all mankind,
> The Stains of nature,—the blots of human race,
> Yet that's no matter, still they are our friends,
> 'Twill help our projects if we give them aid.

Simple Sapling: Though my paternal Acres are eat up,
My patrimony spent, I've yet an house
My lenient creditors let me improve,
Send up the Troops, 'twill serve them well
   for Barracks.
I somehow think, 'twould bear a noble
   sound,
To have my mansion guarded by the King.

Sylla: Hast thou no sons or blooming daughters
   there,
To call up all the feelings of a Father,
Least their young minds contaminate by
   vice,
Caught from such inmates, dangerous and
   vile,
Devoid of virtue, rectitude, or honour,
Save what accords with military fame?
Hast thou no wife who asks thy tender care,
To guard her from Belona's hardy sons?
Who when not toiling in the hostile field,
Are faithful votaries to the Cyprian Queen.
Or is her soul of such materials made,
Indelicate, and thoughtless of her fame:
So void of either sentiment or sense,
As makes her a companion fit for thee!

The moment nearest to real drama is occasioned by the struggle in Gage's breast between his realization of the justice of the colonial cause and his duty as a soldier, culminating in the words:

Sylla: And shall I rashly draw my guilty sword,
And dip its hungry hilt in the rich blood
Of the best subjects that a Brunswick boasts,
And for no cause, but that they nobly scorn
To wear the fetters of his venal slaves!
But swift time rolls, and on his rapid wheel
Bears the winged hours, and the circling years.
The cloud cap'd morn, the dark short wintry day,
And the keen blasts of rough[e]ned Boreas'
   breath,
Will soon evanish, and approaching spring
Opes with the fate of empires on her wing.

The rest of the play is anticlimax, but we close it with a sense of the strong feeling which it represents, the outcry of democracy against oligarchy, of liberty against prerogative, of the descendant of the Puritans against the upholders of kingcraft and oppression. From the dramatic point of view, both Mrs. Warren's satires are conversations rather than plays. There is no evidence that they were performed, although on the title page of *The Group* we read:

> As lately acted, and to be reacted to the wonder
> of all superior intelligences, nigh headquarters
> at Amboyne.

Mrs. Warren also wrote, some years after, two carefully constructed tragedies in verse, *The Sack of Rome* and *The Ladies of Castile,* which were published in 1790. She sent the former to John Adams while he was in London in 1787, asking him to find a producer for it, but there was no opportunity. Indeed, these tragedies could hardly have been played.

Two more of these early satires have been attributed to Mrs. Warren, due probably to that tendency in literary history to credit any anonymous work to an author already known to have composed a work of a like nature. One of these, *The Block-heads, or the Affrighted Officers* is a prose farce, published in 1776, vigorous but coarse in language, and consisting mainly of conversation between British officers and Tory refugees, lamenting their starvation in Boston. It was inspired by General Burgoyne's farce, *The Blockade*, which was performed in Boston in the winter of 1775-6 and was evidently a farce, ridiculing the patriot army then blockading the city. This was not printed. The coarseness of *The Blockheads,* especially the scene between Simple and his wife, indicates that the play is not by Mrs. Warren, for that element is not found in her known works. That the satire was prompted, however, by her work is certain, for some of the names used by her reappear. (pp. 40-6)

[A] satire published in Boston in 1779 [is also] attributed to Mrs. Warren, although the author speaks of himself as "he." *The Motley Assembly, a Farce. Published for the Entertainment of the Curious* ridicules that element in Boston which believed that hearty support of the Revolution was incompatible with secure social standing. The principal characters are Esq. Runt, "a short fat old fellow: fond of gallanting the Ladies;" Turn-coat, one of the managers of the Assembly; Mrs. Flourish, Mrs. Taxall, Mrs. Bubble, Miss Flourish, Miss Taxall, women of supposed fashion who preferred the scarlet coat to the blue, and, contrasted with them, Captain Aid, of the American Army and Captain Careless of the Navy. There is little plot, but the conversation is well done, especially in the scene in the house of Mrs. Flourish, when Captain Aid proposes a toast to General Washington and Mrs. Flourish says:

> "I believe Mr. Washington, or General Washington, if you please, is a very honest, good kind of a man, and has taken infinite pains to keep your army together, and I wish he may find his account in it. But doubtless there are his equals—so say no more,"

and Captain Aid replies:

> "If you meant that as a compliment, madam, it is really so cold a one, that it has made me shiver."

The satire is keen, and reflects the indignation of one who loved his country and had no apologies to make for that affection, at that half-hearted allegiance which animated a certain section of society in Boston.... (pp. 54-5)

Viewed from an absolute standard the artistic quality of these dramas of the Revolution [both Mercy Warren's and others'] may not be high, but it is noteworthy that the more closely they are studied in relation to their inner meaning, the greater their significance becomes. In them not figments of the fancy but real people live and move. Being drama they represent the feeling of the time in its most intense moods, and the hopes, fears, and agonies of that great period are mirrored in a glass that is most interesting when it reflects the nature of human beings who are emotionally under stress. The great strife that separated families, brought ruin to a few and liberty to all who believed in freedom, lives again in a peculiarly vigorous form in these few rare old volumes which preserve all that is left of the drama of the Revolution. Of their significance, therefore, as social history there can be no shadow of doubt. (p. 60)

Arthur Hobson Quinn, "The Drama of the Revolution," in his A History of the American Drama: From the Beginning to the Civil War, *second edition, 1943. Reprint by Appleton-Century-Crofts, Inc., 1951, pp. 33-60.**

MAUD MACDONALD HUTCHESON　(essay date 1953)

[*In the following excerpt from her highly regarded biographical essay on Warren, Hutcheson discusses her writings as "pamphleteering" and praises aspects of the* History.]

Why ... has the luster dimmed on the name of this *femme extraordinaire*? The answer is that much of her work belongs to pamphlet literature, the medium in which the eighteenth century expressed editorial or columnist opinion. Journalistic in essence, the appeal of the pamphlet is limited by time and topic. The success achieved by Mrs. Warren's plays and poems was ephemeral, and their place is with rare books. Those nearest and dearest to her played important roles in the Revolution, and while she wrote its *History* as events took place, the book lay in manuscript until 1805. When published, it encountered competition from Marshall's *Life of Washington,* and its tone was definitely Anti-Federalist.

Mrs. Warren conversed with charm and informality with her friends, but the reader of her works will find her style artificial and her expression abstract, for this was the prevailing mode. In her language, correspondence became "epistolary intercourse," a house was a "habitation," and when she spoke of her "wounded optics," she meant weak eyes. (p. 379)

[Mercy Warren] turned to playwriting in 1772.

The undertaking was not without courage, for in Massachusetts the theatre was still "the highway to hell," and public performances were forbidden by law. Mrs. Warren, however, held remarkably liberal views on the theatre. Lessons of morality, she argued, might be enforced as successfully from the stage "as by modes of instruction less censured by the severe." Although arranged in acts and scenes, her "plays" are lacking in plot, love interest, and women characters. They are rabid conversation pieces, propaganda, intended primarily for reading, as witness her directions. A stage manager would have been hard pressed to provide for abrupt changes of scene, great crowds of people, processions of coaches....

These polemical essays earned adulation of which even the echo has died long since, but they entitle Mercy Warren to distinction among America's political satirists. For Hopkinson, Trumbull, and Freneau, she blazed the trail. As native output replaced literary dependence, the cultural break between mother country and colonies was completed. (pp. 382-83)

As an excellent sample of partisan writing, [*The Group*] merits its place in the literature of the American Revolution. (p. 387)

In judging [Mercy Warren's plays and poems], timeliness is the important factor. They catered to the prevailing taste and reflected the feeling and temper of the period. (p. 389)

In *The Adulateur* and *The Group,* Mercy had limited herself to high-sounding declamation, uttered by male characters. [In] *The Ladies of Castille,* she brought women into the picture and all the elements of drama. The young soldier is torn between duty to his country and love for "the sister of my foe," while another character casts covetous eyes on his friend's wife. It was somewhat daring for the circumspect Mrs. Warren to experiment with such themes and motifs, but she pointed a moral, as she was wont to do. Against the background of blood and battle, plot and counterplot are played out, and just as all promises well, tragedy intervenes.

Action, suspense, and conflict enter again into the composition of *The Sack of Rome,* where the struggle between love and duty, honor and guile, is repeated. (p. 392)

History, for which each generation sets its own standard, is one of the most changing of literary types. Mercy Warren's work [*History of the Rise, Progress, and Termination of the American Revolution*] is a product of the eighteenth century, when the function of the historian was to record rather than interpret, and to trace the hand of God in events instead of the working of natural laws. To Mercy Warren, history was "the record of everything disgraceful or honorary to mankind."

Her opportunities as an observer of the American Revolution were exceptional. It was a source of pride to her that she was connected by "nature, friendship, and every social tie, with many of the first patriots and most influential characters on the continent," and she had kept her own account of events as they occurred. For background information, she made ample use of the *Annual Register,* as did other historians of the time. (It published serially an account of the American war attributed to Burke.) (pp. 397-98)

Mrs. Warren shows an awareness of significant factors—the importance of Canada, the Indian question, the evils of paper money, America's entry into the family of nations, the first feeble strivings towards international organization.

That she was a disciple of the natural rights theory, of which her brother had been a leading advocate, is obvious throughout, and she handles the Lockean doctrine with knowledge and competence. Political economy was a budding science, for which Adam Smith furnished the theory, but the inflation of the post-war period—when "the deranged state of American finances" threatened the very independence of the young United States—was a matter of first-hand knowledge. She recapitulated the arguments against the Constitution which she had expressed years earlier in letters to Mrs. Macaulay and in the pamphlet [*Observations on the New Constitution*] ascribed to *A Columbian Patriot.*

Bibliography was not demanded of the eighteenth-century historian, but the range of Mrs. Warren's reading is evident in her references—Hume's *History of England,* Gibbon's *Decline and Fall of the Roman Empire,* Prince's *Chronology,* Paley's *Moral Philosophy,* Parliamentary *Debates, Journals of Congress,* the *British Encyclopaedia,* and many other titles.

Footnotes were far from mandatory, but while Mrs. Warren's as a rule are vague and general, she sometimes quotes even volume and page.

Her style is impersonal and abstract to a fault. Various friends "verbally detailed" their experiences to her, but she scorned to exploit such information. To the current gossip or scandal, which she knew well, she permits herself only an occasional reference—Sir William Howe's engrossment with his bottle and his mistress, the dashing Tarleton's boast of the men he had killed and the women he had ravished in America.

In the matter of accuracy, she seems to measure up well. James Winthrop found only two minor errors in the "well digested and polished narrative" and mentioned them merely because she would not believe his praise unless he gave proof of critical reading. A few corrections can be found in a copy that evidently belonged to Peter Force, but for a work of more than twelve hundred pages, the percentage is small. (pp. 398-99)

For three quarters of a century after her death, the *History* was neglected by scholars, but as the century was closing, Winsor and Tyler commented generously on Mercy Warren's works. Since then, she has received increasing attention. Larned emphasized the importance of the *History* to the special student;

Bassett has assigned her a position between Washington Irving and Parson Weems; to Beard, she is "an active pamphleteer" in the intellectual defence of the American cause; Merle Curti dignifies her work as a "realistic history of the struggle for independence"; and from Michael Kraus, she merits three pages in his work on American historiography [see excerpt dated 1937]. Thus her *History,* while outmoded for the general reader, is respected by historians as the account of a contemporary witness and friend of the leading patriots, and the special student of the period cannot afford to pass it by. (pp. 399-400)

[The *History*] remains a notable one for an era that granted its women little formal education beyond a nodding acquaintance with the three R's. (p. 402)

> *Maud Macdonald Hutcheson, "Mercy Warren, 1728-1814," in* William and Mary Quarterly, *third series, Vol. X, July, 1953, pp. 378-402.*

WILLIAM RAYMOND SMITH (essay date 1966)

[*Smith outlines the philosophical precepts behind Warren's historical theory.*]

Mercy Otis Warren's method of writing history depended upon four interrelated concepts: human nature, human history, divine nature and divine history (Providence). She believed that all men are equal, not only in the sight of God, but in their nature. Endowed with a "restless" mind, man is discontented with his natural state. This produces a strong desire for personal distinction in every individual. Desire for distinction, the goad to human action, can take the forms of either love of fame or love of wealth. Of the two, the latter, avarice, is the stronger, for when his personal property is endangered, even though he may have allowed all his intangible possessions to be destroyed, a man will strike back with the force of a predator. Man's natural ferocity makes the state of nature one of war.

Human nature, however, is endowed with reason and a moral sense as well as emotions. Although too frequently submerged in passion, reason and the moral sense are capable of using the desire for distinction for the benefit of the individual and society. Reason and the moral sense place man a little above the beasts. Indeed, it is doubtful whether man can be considered to have evil in his nature when he is living in the "state of nature". However, once men begin to amass wealth the passion of avarice turns the love of distinction toward evil ends. Thus, man and his condition, though susceptible of improvement, never can achieve perfection because, once he possesses property, although it is necessary to life, it produces the passion of avarice, which breaks down his reason and moral sense.

As they advance along the scale of civilization, societies continually fall from liberty into despotism, because ambition and avarice destroy the natural equality of men and the few gain power over the many. Once a society begins to develop along one line, a change of direction is unusual because their inherent conservatism holds men to ancestral patterns of behavior. Therefore, although men are born free and equal, in advanced societies the majority are slaves and a minority hold power.

It is difficult to say whether Mrs. Warren intended the "state of nature" to mean a real condition of man in some remote past or an idealized condition of men in the present upon which political and social theories must be built. It is clear, however, that she bases her definition of man upon those characteristics that are essential and therefore unchanging: Man is by nature free and equal, created not only with a restless mind that seeks distinction, producing the passions of ambition and avarice, but also with reason and a moral sense. However, the predominance of any characteristic and the balance of all of them at any particular time in a society depends upon the historical circumstances. Thus, although an avaricious despotism is "natural", a society in which men live in harmonious equality is more in accord with the "better nature" of man.

Since Mrs. Warren based her concept of history upon her concept of human nature, analysis of individual character was very important in her history. Men, in essence the same through history, vary in their balance of characteristics according to historical circumstances. Therefore, men must study history in order to avoid errors of the past and to further the conditions for individual and social welfare. Since history contains useful lessons for men, the function of the historian is to teach. History teaches that some form of government is necessary to check the ambition, avarice, and the resulting ferocity of natural man. It also teaches that true religion holds society together and reveals proper forms of government.

Upon true religion depends the success or failure of men because the will of God determines human action. The nature of God, however, is beyond the grasp of human reason. God's will concerning any particular sequence of human action is only known when that sequence is finished. Only one aspect of divine nature is revealed to man: that God wills human happiness.

As man looks at his condition much appears the result of accident. However events may appear to his limited mind, the creature man is an instrument of divine history, the Providence that shapes the course of events in accordance with the will of God. The sudden rise and fall of individuals and the progress and decline of nations reveals the natural equality of men. Indeed, Providence uses the nature of man, the evil intermixed with the good, to bring about the final end of human happiness.

Human history, then, depends upon the nature of man as created by God. This nature is a mixture of what appears to man as both good and evil. However, both the good and the evil in human nature are instruments in the workings of Providence. Man, as he appears to himself, wills his own action; but as an instrument of Providence, human will fulfills the divine plan for man. Although on the human level man has the capacity to will his action, on the divine level, everything that he wills to do contributes to the aim of Providence. Thus, men in relation to each other act freely, while in relation to God they are acted upon. Since everything that they do contributes to the divine aim of good, Mrs. Warren concludes that even though they are naturally ferocious animals, it is doubtful that they are evil in their natural state.

Such then is the foundation of Mercy Otis Warren's history of the American Revolution: human history, as seen by men, is the result of their actions growing out of ambition. They are, however, capable of willing not only from passion but from reason and morality. On a higher level human action is the result of that superintending Providence that directs the fortunes of men in accordance with the final end of God. By watching the changes of human fortune men sometimes are able to direct their actions in accordance with Providence. Therefore, history serves the function of recording these changes so that men may direct their actions in the ways of God. (pp. 73-5)

To common sense, a theological—or, properly, teleological—interpretation of history is paradoxical. In this type of argument, all human experience is interpreted as means producing an end. Since the end is the only real fact, the means must be progress toward the end. Thus, the means assume significance beyond ordinary human experience, which, from a common sensical point of view, distorts experience, the facts. The theological argument depends upon belief in the primacy of the end, subordinating the means, which are important only in revealing the end. Since the end is still to be achieved and can only be known through revelation, not reason, this interpretation of history appears paradoxical to the commonsensical men.

Mrs. Warren based her interpretation of history upon an argument of this kind. In her argument, the concepts of human nature, human history, divine nature and divine history are central. God created men in a state of natural equality, endowing them with reason, a moral sense, and a love of distinction. As they amass property, passions of ambition and avarice are unleashed due to men's love of distinction, which overwhelms reason and the moral sense. As these passions subvert reason and morality, social distinctions develop that reduce men to misery under despotic government. God, however, wills human happiness and in Providence, God uses both the good and bad aspects of human nature to return men to natural equality, in which happiness lies.

The history of the American Revolution was, for Mrs. Warren, a prime example of the operations of Providence. It revealed a moral, reasonable people, whose social organization approaches the state of natural equality, throwing off despotic rule to set up a government that insured natural equality and, thereby, human happiness. Since this interpretation is based upon a theological argument, the means of the American Revolution—the decadence of the British and the reason and morality of the Americans—were made subservient to the end of the American Revolution, thereby appearing distorted to common sense. Again in the establishment of the Federal government, Mrs. Warren's argument necessitated what appears to the commonsensical man a distortion of the relative positions of the Federalist and Republican parties. For Mercy Warren, however, the facts of human experience faded away before the vision of "the closing scene, when the angel of his presence will stand upon the sea and upon the earth, lift up his hand to heaven, and swear by Him that liveth for ever and ever, that there shall be time no longer."

Mrs. Warren's use of a teleological argument reveals her inheritance from her New England ancestors. The New England Puritan was a peculiar mixture of an idealist and a pessimist. As an idealist, the Puritan believed that since God clearly revealed through the course of history what man ought to do, man could order his life according to God's will. However, in the Puritan concept of human nature, men have a strong tendency to throw away the gifts of God. Therefore, the Puritan idealism evinced in the attempt to establish a model community was tempered by the Puritan expectation that the base desires of men would destroy the project. Mrs. Warren had an expectant hope that the United States could maintain its model society and government because Providence clearly pointed out that this model ought to exist; but she also had an expectant fear that human passion would prevail over human morality and reason, dooming America to a future of despotic misery. In this simultaneous hope and fear, Mercy Otis Warren was a New England idealist. (pp. 117-19)

William Raymond Smith, "Mercy Otis Warren: New England Idealist," in his History as Argument: Three

Patriot Historians of the American Revolution, *Mouton & Co.*, 1966, pp. 73-119.

LAWRENCE J. FRIEDMAN and ARTHUR H. SHAFFER (essay date 1975)

[*In their review of the* History, *the critics propose that because Warren was reluctant to undermine national unity, she used the work neither to express fully her own Republican and feminist beliefs, nor to treat the issue of her role as a female historian.*]

In 1805, Mercy Otis Warren . . . published her *History of the Rise, Progress and Termination of the American Revolution.* Warren's interest in historical writing had extended over a number of years. She claimed to have begun recording the events of the Revolution during the conflict itself, "at a period when every manly arm was occupied . . . either in the cabinet or the field. . . . I have been induced to record as they passed . . . the new and unexperienced events. . . ." Though nearly finished by 1791, she laid her manuscript aside because, as she explained, "the virulence of party spirit shuts up the avenues of just information until *truth* has a chance for fair play. . . ." Warren probably had in mind the debate over the Federal Constitution—a document she had sharply criticized. Although she was already quarreling with John Adams in 1791 over the operations of the new national government, she could not have anticipated the depth of feeling during the course of the 1790's that would divide the nation into warring political camps. It was not until after 1800 that she was to complete her *History* with an account of the heated controversies of that decade.

The passage of time failed to quiet "the virulence of party spirit" or to open "the avenues of just information." Consequently, the publication of Warren's *History* . . . was regarded more as a political than a literary event. As a Republican enthusiast, her work was inevitably compared with John Marshall's *Life of Washington* (1804-1807). Books by two such noted partisans, one a devout Republican and the other a stanch Federalist, appearing at roughly the same time, could not fail to stimulate partisan comment. Indeed, Warren's *History* stirred a small tempest with her characterization of Alexander Hamilton as a "foreign venturer" with crackbrained financial schemes, and she shattered her already strained friendship with John Adams by accusing him of "a partiality for monarchy." (pp. 194-95)

Despite its partisan reception, Mercy Warren's *History* was a fairly circumspect document. If she was critical of the Federalists and even the "Great Washington," she refrained from slanting the bulk of her narrative—the years before 1789—to support the views of a particular faction. Indeed, Adams himself had only objected to her observations of the post-Revolutionary years and acknowledged that this was but a small portion of the three-volume work. He bluntly wrote that "after the termination of the Revolutionary War your subject was completed." Federalist Adams had not read Warren's closing chapters with sufficient care. The ardent Republican had actually muted her strong feelings on the factional warfare of the 1790's by refusing to single out parties. Instead, she had used euphemisms like "the friends of the administration" and "the opposition." She refrained from associating these terms with any particular class, section, or state; nor did she specifically endorse the Republican Party or spell out its specific views or policies. Thomas Jefferson's name was not mentioned. Clearly, Mercy Warren had been holding back, unwilling to underline her strong Republican sympathies.

What is more revealing about Warren's *History* than the muted "biases" of a stanch Republican in Federalist Plymouth is its similarity to the works of other American historians, Federalist as well as Republican. For all their partisan differences, the men and women attracted to the writing of American history at the end of the eighteenth century were united by an emotional and intellectual commitment to the Revolution derived from firsthand experience. (pp. 195-96)

[Warren's] *History* was devoted to a strongly patriotic theme that had become a staple of a new American nationalism—she celebrated the New Nation and the Revolution that produced it as major steps toward fulfilling God's plan for mankind. "Providence has clearly pointed out the duties of the present generation, particularly the paths which America ought to tread. . . . The world is now viewing America, as experimenting a new system of government, a Federal Republic . . . if she succeeds, it will refute the assertion, that none but small states are adapted to republican government. . . ." Even when she attacked the proposed Federal Constitution in a hard-hitting pamphlet, *Observations on the New Constitution* . . . , she did so because she feared that the document would subvert the libertarian precepts of the "promised land." (pp. 197-98)

The story that Mercy Warren told in her *History* of New World settlement and the Revolution was one of the emergence of the national character. She operated on the late eighteenth-century assumption of the constancy of human nature. Mankind is by nature free and equal, but whether that natural state is retained rests upon historical and physical circumstances. Warren contended that those circumstances had existed in America from the beginning of English settlement. The American colonists "seemed, previous to the rupture with Britain, to have acquired that just and happy medium between the ferocity of a state of nature, and those high stages of civilization and refinement, that at once corrupt the heart and sap the foundation of happiness." In such circumstances the colonists developed a strong sense of their rights; it was British encroachments against colonial liberties and their defense by the Colonies that produced the Revolution. Developing this theme in her narrative, Warren persistently interpreted the causes and nature of events in the context of national moral strength. She found the unity of the American people in the republicanism of the national character.

There was little in Warren's narrative on the emerging national character to distinguish her as a Republican historian. But she was no sycophant; she was merely reflecting the historian's concern with establishing a sense of common nationality on what seemed to be the only sensible basis. However, when it came to discussing the Constitution and the new national government, she broke with the pattern established by her predecessors. Until she published her *History,* no American historian had deviated from an uncritical support of the Constitution. None had used the discussion of the early national period to represent the views of any particular group. David Ramsay set the accepted pattern in his *History of the American Revolution* (1789), the first work published after ratification. For Ramsay, the Constitution represented nothing more than an administrative reorganization necessitated by the problems of conducting a war and of organizing a nation. Unlike Ramsay, who had published his *History* when the success of the new government was very much in doubt, Warren must have felt less constrained. Her version appeared when the Union, if not secure, had nonetheless survived the party battles of the 1790's and a transfer of political power from Federalists to Republicans. Whereas Ramsay had been a strong advocate of ratification,

Warren's feelings toward the Constitution were ambivalent. Actively opposed to ratification, once the Constitution had gone into effect she changed her tone and began to evidence a mixture of apprehension and pleasure: "We now seem to have verged to the entrance of a permanent and I hope peaceful Government, an object which has long been the wish of every good man and woman in America." Warren's ambivalence was also reflected in her rambling, sometimes contradictory narrative on the genesis of the national government.

On one point in her *History,* Warren agreed with her predecessors—the success of the Revolution had been endangered by the Confederation's inability to cope with the nation's problems. In particular, she was critical of the government's lack of "sufficient powers" to deal with problems like the funding of the debt, disputes between the states over the national domain, internal disorders such as Shays's Rebellion, and most important, a decline in private and public virtue. Faced with so dangerous a threat to "their internal felicity, the inhabitants of America were in general sensible, that the freedom of the people, the virtue of society, and the stability of their commonwealth, could only be preserved by the strictest union. . . ." Yet, if Warren conceded that the nation needed a new frame of government, she disagreed with Ramsay over the motives of the authors of the new Constitution: "The greatest happiness of the greatest number was not the principal object of their contemplations. . . ." For Ramsay the Constitutional Convention had been nonideological, a debate between the states and the central government over the redistribution of sovereignty. He emphasized the politics of self-interest. However, in Warren's account, economic self-interest played no conspicuous part. For her the issues were exclusively ideological—a struggle between republicans and monarchists.

There was a deceptive simplicity in Warren's analysis calculated to discredit the Federalists. She cast the post-Revolutionary War years of her *History* along the lines of a moral drama in which true republicans were pitted against thinly disguised monarchists. While not ignoring the difficult economic problems that plagued the nation, she commented on them only to illustrate that the question of reorganizing the national government had become inescapable. But when it came to determining what form the central authority should take, the issue was characterized as exclusively ideological. Just as the Revolution had been a struggle between republican America and monarchist England, "soon after the organization of the new Constitution a struggle began to take place between monarchists and republicans. . . ." The insinuations of an ideological *coup d'état* were unmistakable.

By monarchism, Warren meant political and social practices "that wore the appearance of regal forms and institutions." She singled out those members of the Society of Cincinnati who "panted for peerages in the shade of retirement," "ambassadors abroad, who had adopted a fondness for nominal distinctions, members of congress and of legislatures, and many others who had acquired a taste for the external superiority that wealth and titles bestow. . . ." By their actions these men "threatened the annihilation of the daring opinion, that the whole sovereignty in the republican system is in the people. . . ." Opposing the monarchists were the general body of citizens committed to "the ideals of a free and equal participation in the privileges of a pure and genuine republicanism." They objected to "being precipitated, without due consideration," into adopting "a system that might bind them and their posterity in the chains of despotism. . . ." (pp. 199-203)

Clearly, then, Warren used historical narrative as a vehicle for attacking Federalists. But it is crucial to note the self-imposed limitations of her attack. There was a restraint in her *History* that can only be understood in the context of the politics of historical writing in post-Revolutionary America. Her characterization of the new national government as a threat to American liberty, and the decade of the 1790's as a battleground between monarchists and true republicans, did not prevent her from praising the Constitution in extravagant terms: "Perhaps genius has never devised a system more congenial to their wishes, or better adapted to the condition of man, than the American Constitution. . . . On the principles of republicanism was this condition founded; on these it must stand." Many of her doubts had been relieved by the passage of a Bill of Rights. But Warren was also an ardent nationalist, and by the time she published her *History* . . . , the Constitution had become *the symbol* as well as the reality of union. By then the national government was in the hands of men she trusted. Moreover, fifteen years of observing the operations of the new federal system probably convinced her that her worst fears had not materialized, especially with the election and reelection of Thomas Jefferson.

Therefore, it is not surprising that Warren offered an ambiguous interpretation of the Constitution; she impugned the motives of its authors without repudiating the document itself. But if the men who seduced the nation into accepting so potentially dangerous a scheme of government held views inimical to liberty, how was it that the Constitution was founded "on the principles of republicanism"? Warren never answered this question; she simply intimated that the Bill of Rights had set things right. But why had the new frame of government worked despite the monarchist tendencies of its supporters? Warren replied that "the United States of America . . . may perhaps be possessed of more materials that promise success than have ever fallen to the lot of any other nation." The republicanism of the American character had made the Revolution possible. Even if the process of fighting a war and organizing a nation had led to a declension in republican morality, Americans still possessed enough virtue to overcome a challenge to their liberties and to insure the future of a republican society. Here was as optimistic an assessment of the nation's future as was possible for a latter-day Puritan from Plymouth who believed that "perfection in government is not to be expected from so imperfect a creature as man."

Notwithstanding the marked constraint of her partisan Republican proclivities, Warren's strictures against Adams and her more oblique criticism of Washington gave her *History* the appearance of a party tract. After all, she used the familiar Republican device of portraying the Federalists as monarchists who "creep under the mantle of federalism." But if Warren came out as an avowed Republican and an unquestioned foe of the Federalist Party, her more general distaste for political parties and her intense nationalism prevented her *History* from degenerating into overt party propaganda. . . . Warren avoided writing party history in the English tradition. She did not use the entire span of American history to demonstrate the correctness of her party's philosophy. More important, she did not argue that the divisions in American society were the result of deep-seated economic, class, ethnic, or sectional differences.

Instead, Warren's account of the years after 1789 is less an expression of support for the Republican Party than a critique of the (never specified) Federalist Party. She failed to support her arguments with a clear substantive program. Committed to a republican form of government, she expressed that republicanism so vaguely that it is difficult to tie it to the program of a party. (pp. 203-05)

[Though] restraint was a characteristic feature of Warren, the historian, it is significant that in her nonhistorical activities she was often exceedingly outspoken—much more so than Ramsay or even Marshall. She was a talented, egocentric woman, confident of her judgments. The author of numerous highly opinionated plays, essays, and poems, she was an outspoken but equal partner in the inner councils of the Revolutionary leadership. (p. 206)

Yet as an historian, Warren actually labored to soften her firm, vigorous personality. Indeed, in the introduction to her *History,* she even apologized for usurping the male prerogative of historical writing. "It is true," she conceded, that "there are certain appropriate duties assigned to each sex; and doubtless it is the more peculiar province of masculine strength . . . to describe the bloodstained field, and relate the story of slaughtered armies." Given her background, achievements, and undeniable frankness (no other historian of the period dared criticize the "Great Washington"), one wonders why Warren bothered, even in a patriotic national history, to apologize for being a woman historian.

The moderate tone of Warren's history and the apology in her introduction must have had some relationship to her participation in political affairs and to her rôle as the only woman in the Revolutionary generation of historians. Despite Warren's influence in public affairs, she denounced Mary Wollstonecraft—the most radical feminist of the day—and promoted a model of soft, retiring, malleable American womanhood as an alternative: "our weak and timid sex is generally but the echo of the other and like some pliant piece of clockwork the springs of our souls move slow or more rapid just as hope, fear, or fortitude give motion to the conducting wires, that govern all our actions. . . ." (pp. 206-07)

Mercy Warren's advice, then, did not comport with her conduct. Active, influential, and assertive in public affairs, she urged other women to discharge their patriotic obligation by being pliant domestic servants of their husbands and their sons. The disparity between doctrine and practice was substantial, and Warren was keenly aware of it. This may explain why she apologized for writing about public issues. Using what was to become a common device for female writers of the nineteenth century, she acknowledged that a woman was not properly an historian, a politician, or even a poet. Her own activities were merely spontaneous expressions born of chance circumstances that reflected no special skill or vocation. Warren's political poetry was purportedly "written as the amusement of solitude, at a period when every active member of society was engaged, either in the field, or the cabinet, to resist the strong hand of foreign domination." (p. 208)

Because her poems were not published until 1790 and her *History* was delayed until 1805, Warren could conceivably have given her wartime notes to a male author—one whose "peculiar province" it was to write about such matters. Instead, she published both works under her own name and used them to advance "manly" if restrained opinions about the conduct of the Revolutionary War, Washington's fallibilities, American tendencies to emulate European "corruptions," excessive anti-French feeling in the land, and similar controversial matters. The same pattern persisted in her correspondence. Although

she would apologize for going "so much out of the road of female attention" or into an area "not altogether consonant to Female Genius . . . ," she would comment at length on the specifics of current national questions. Clearly, these apologies, like the other references to retiring womanhood, seemed designed to disarm potential critics. She did not make herself malleable to male needs. But by defending the very theory that she violated, Warren may have been trying to make the violation less conspicuous or at least "understandable."

Indeed, Mercy Warren, the restrained Republican historian, was a constant practitioner of sexual politics. Writing her play, *The Sack of Rome,* she was apprehensive about her literary abilities and about American disdain for drama as an artistic form. If the play were distasteful, Warren urged her readers that she "be forgiven, as there have been instances of men of the best abilities who have fallen into the same error." *Because* she was a woman, she should not be condemned for poor artistry. (pp. 209-10)

Beneath the level of sexual politics, historian Warren had a distinct feminist philosophy. Occasionally she expressed it in public as when she dedicated her book of poetry to the English writer Elizabeth Montagu: "A Sister's hand may wrest a female pen, / From the bold outrage of imperious men." But Warren usually kept her views to herself. The important thing was to do as one wished—not to make a public display of one's sexual ideology. In random, guarded comments found almost exclusively in her private correspondence, one discovers a woman who could not accept the notion of retiring patriotic femininity that she had publicly espoused. "I ever considered human nature as the same in both sexes, nor perhaps is the soul very differently modified by the vehicle in which it is placed," she told her son Winslow. Men seemed more proficient than women because they were properly educated and allowed to learn from varied experiences, while women were "confined to the Narrow Circle of Domestic Care." Indeed, Catharine Macaulay, the English Whig historian-politician, was a living refutation of the charge "that women make but indifferent politicians." Even in the marital relationship, Warren insisted, women were entitled to full, creative lives transcending the domestic sphere. A "minute similarity of sentiment" between man and wife was not required for "a friendly union of hearts." A woman did not have to mold herself to meet man's changing needs; she had a life of her own to lead. But though woman was fully man's equal and was entitled to all male privileges, Warren contended, it was best for American females to play a "little game." Out of longstanding tradition, men wanted women to be subordinate, retiring, and pliant. Thus, for the sake of social stability, American women ought to offer the appearance of subordination and malleability but never the substance; "while we own the appointed Subordination (perhaps for the sake of order in families) let us by no means acknowledge such an inferiority as would check the ardour of our endeavors to equal in all mental accomplishments the most masculine heights. . . ." (pp. 210-11)

It seems clear, then, why Mercy Warren told all but her most confidential acquaintances that patriotic womanhood was soft and retiring, while she proceeded to live an active, partisan public life and to become one of the leading historians in the New Nation. Consciously, Warren seemed to be trying to offer men the appearance of traditional womanhood while denying them the substance. By all counts, she succeeded. . . .

Mercy Warren felt compelled to play a "little game." As it related to her *History,* that strategy reflected a larger concern.

Like other Patriot historians, Federalist and Republican, Warren was guided by certain basic considerations that exercised a controlling influence. These considerations—nationalist in nature—compelled the historian to emphasize what Americans had in common and to de-emphasize or even ignore what divided them. The problem was not simply a matter of closing political ranks; it reflected a larger fear that the stability of the union was in jeopardy. (p. 212)

Just as Mercy Warren emphasized those qualities that unified Americans, she was reluctant to arouse fears that might endanger the nation's all too fragile cohesiveness. She approached her *History* with the avowed purpose of helping to cement "a union of interests and affection." She gave the impression of a common national character formed in the ideal civil and physical environment of North America, or a unity of purpose prevailing against British tyranny. Even her criticisms of the Constitution and the Washington administration were cautious. For Mercy Warren was neither a radical social critic nor a moderate reformer. Like her male colleagues, she imagined herself as an insider, as an integral part of the established order, and as a leader of a society that had already gone far toward fulfilling the dream of reformers—a society to which she felt both personally and ideologically committed. (p. 214)

As a woman who functioned in the male world of establishment politics and Patriot history, Warren understood that no public figure of either sex could afford to be too critical of a weak and embryonic if promising New Nation or could openly challenge the existing "order in families" in the "promised land." The Revolution and the task of nation-building had been a trying experience and even with Jefferson in power, success was by no means assured. Thus, the historian had to restrain partisan political feelings in order to foster American pride in a mythically united, vigorous national past. Like partisan political history, partisan sexual commentary would be counterproductive, setting American against American. A woman of the established order, Mercy Warren doubtlessly felt that there would be more lost than gained by a public display of partisanship on either count. For a woman on the inside, national cohesiveness seems to have taken precedence over the more "provincial" interests of the Republican Party or the female sex. (pp. 214-15)

> *Lawrence J. Friedman and Arthur H. Shaffer, "Mercy Otis Warren and the Politics of Historical Nationalism," in* The New England Quarterly, *Vol. 48, No. 2, June, 1975, pp. 194-215.*

EDMUND M. HAYES (essay date 1976)

[*In a discussion focusing on* The Defeat, *Hayes posits that Warren's first three plays are linked by the portrayal of the villain Rapatio and theorizes that Warren used the metaphor of the theater within her dramas to emphasize the villainy of the Royalists.*]

As Mrs. Warren depicts him, Hutchinson is a stark, one-dimensional figure representing various types of evil. As the action of *The Adulateur* moves towards its climactic episode, the Boston Massacre, he evolves from a semicomic villain into a devilish master of policy grasping for power. In his betrayal of the patriot cause, he is Judas. When he promises to tempt others by whispering in their ears, he is Satan. When looking forward to the destruction of Boston on the eve of the massacre, he is portrayed as a mad-Nero anticipating the imminent ruin of the city and its people.

At the close of Warren's portions of *The Adulateur*, Rapatio has captured the high position he sought. In *The Defeat* he "falls" from power and his removal from the office of Governor of Massachusetts is assured. When we last see him in the May 23 installment, he is a lonely, tormented man—a Faust figure who is damned because of his over-reaching soul. His worldly ambition thwarted, his greed blunted, Rapatio hears the dogs at Hell's gates and gapes horrified at the yawning pit.... (pp. 440-41)

In spite of his hovering doom, Rapatio neither dies, nor descends into hell. He survives to reappear in the July 19 installment where he and his confederate in deception, Limpet (Andrew Oliver), plot to save themselves from an outraged and victorious public. Limpet proposes that they enlist the aid of their friend, the unprincipled scribbler, "Philalethes," whose "prostituted pen" has made him the "dangerous foe of liberty, of Truth, and of Mankind." In this last installment Rapatio and Limpet are quivering cowards, pretenders who have deceived themselves into thinking that a propagandist can save their hides, if not their souls. The scene is anticlimactic, yet it demonstrates how deception can re-coil ironically upon itself to destroy its practitioners.

The introduction of Philalethes, who sells his conscience for silver, planted the seed for Mercy Warren's third play in the series—*The Group*.... By the time it appeared in print, Hutchinson had been called to England and replaced by General Gage (Sylla of *The Group*). A significant theme in the little drama is how men loyal to Hutchinson are ready to sell their consciences for wealth and power.... Hutchinson, although an exile, still left his imprint upon the political events in America. One character in the play says of Rapatio,

> He sends his groan across the broad Atlantic
> And with a phiz of Crocodilian Stamp
> Can weep, and wreathe, still hoping to deceive.

Some of the Mandamus Councillors were relatives of Hutchinson. In the play, Lord Chief Justice Hazlerod (mentioned in *The Defeat*), represents his brother-in-law, Peter Oliver, and the hateful Judge Meagre, his brother, Foster Hutchinson. Nevertheless, it is not simply the blood ties that link Rapatio with the characters in *The Group*. As the drama goes forward it is obvious that for Mercy Warren he was the evil genius of the conspiratorial, self-seeking circle. No one in the play states his debt to Rapatio more effectively than Beau Trumps (Daniel Leonard):

> I saw Rapatio's arts had struck so deep
> And giv'n his country such a fatal wound
> None but its foes promotion could expect;
> I trim'd, and pimp'd, and veer'd, and wav'ring stood
> But half resolv'd to show myself a knave,
> Till the Arch Traitor prowling round for aid
> Saw my suspense and bid me doubt no more;—
> He gently bow'd, and smiling took my hand,
> And whispering softly in my listening ear,
> Shew'd me my name among his chosen band.

It is Warren's dramatic portrayal of the "Arch Traitor" and his political fortunes that ties the three plays so closely to one another. Because she saw Hutchinson as a peril to liberty, as the fallen angel despoiling the garden of America, she assailed him with her pen. Although her characterization of him as Rapatio is biased and narrow, she was not alone in thinking of Hutchinson as a hypocrite and a traitor. Her uniqueness is that she used the metaphor of the theatre in an attempt to destroy him.

While other patriots wrote blistering tracts against the machinations of the loyalists, Warren drew upon the "idea" of the play and put forth her vision that all the world's a stage. *The Defeat* illustrates the point effectively. Since she was writing primarily for the readers of the *Boston Gazette* and *The Massachusetts Spy,* Warren did not construct a long, well-made play for her audience. Because her purpose was to expose vice as pointedly as possible, she needed only dramatic "scenes" to reveal the truth about Rapatio. Consequently, she took the image of the stage villain, the Vice figure of the English morality plays, and applied it to Hutchinson. She chose the Vice because he traditionally represents the hypocrite who wears a mask in public and "plays" at virtue. Then she placed Rapatio in situations where he revealed himself to his confederates or in soliloquies spoken directly to the "audience." The playwright sacrificed developing action and complicated characterization for this direct form of exposure.

In the opening soliloquy, for example, Rapatio confesses, freely admitting his hypocrisy. During the speech he wonders aloud what will happen when the patriots discover "The traiterous purpose of my rankling mind, / That's hid behind a subtle meagre form." The meagre form he admits, is masked by "The soft smooth grimace of a pander's smile, / The oily droppings of a courtier's tongue." Rapatio, like the Vice, is thus a theatrical figure. Indeed, he and his followers are not only conscious of their theatrical posings, but are fond of seeing themselves as actors in the drama of life and politics.

A simple instance occurs at the outset of *The Adulateur.* When he first appears in the play, he expresses his joy that Brundo (Governor Bernard) has left office and that he is next in line for that post. "The Stage is clear," he gloats as he imagines his entrance to power. Later, when he and Bagshot confer on the threatening behavior of the patriots, he envisions a time when the British will have to fire upon the Americans:

> 'Tis well—a scene now opens to my mind.
> And hark'ee Bagshot—should these high swoln
>   wretches
> Again insult, remember you are soldiers.

The scene that opens to Rapatio's mind is one of violence. His grim, dramatic imaging is an insight into a man who equates reality with a theatrical "scene." This tendency is clearly reenforced when Rapatio is exposed in *The Defeat.* When he turns to Limpet for advice, the latter reminds him of the metaphor of the theatre:

> Few thought that we so black a Part could act,
> That we behind the Curtain play'd the wires,
> Push'd on our Engine to disturb the Peace,
> To make the Farce compleat, pretended Fear.

That Mercy Warren used the metaphor of the theatre to attack her political enemies by portraying them as stage villains, poseurs who mirrored the "role-playing" of Hutchinson and his circle, is confirmed by citations in the three plays. The title page of *The Adulateur* reads, "A Tragedy as it is now acted in Upper Servia." In the first installment of *The Defeat* the remarks to the reader boast that the play was "lately exhibited." Near the end of the May 23 installment there is a stage direction "After which several Tragical Scenes are exhibited, but we refer the curious to the whole Representation as acted at the Head Quarters of the Bashaw of Servia. . . ." The title page of *The Group* proclaims the play "As lately acted, and to be re-acted to the wonder of all superior intelligences, nigh headquarters at Amboyne."

A reading of these plays leaves no doubt that Servia is America and Upper Servia and Amboyne are Boston. Allusions to "public performances" are meant to reenforce the idea that the loyalists are acting out their pretense at public virtue. The scenes "lately exhibited" and those "acted at the Head Quarters of the Bashaw of Servia," are intended to suggest that the world of Boston was truly a stage.

One may or may not agree that Mercy Warren's Revolutionary war plays comprise the first American dramatic trilogy. But one can agree that the plays are not only linked by the creation of the hero-villain, Hutchinson, and the recurrent theme of treachery, but also by the fact that they constitute a persistent dramatic metaphor. One cannot separate *The Defeat* from the other two plays without doing injury to Warren's satiric vision, and to her perception of the dramatic continuity of the events in the calamitous times between 1772 and 1775. (pp. 441-45)

Edmund M. Hayes, "Mercy Otis Warren: 'The Defeat'," in The New England Quarterly, *Vol. LXIX, No. 3, September, 1976, pp. 440-58.*

CECELIA TICHI   (essay date 1977)

[*Tichi discusses Warren in the context of her relationship with John Adams and Benjamin Rush, suggesting that Warren wrote the* History *not only as a paean to the virtue of the American people, but also to express her own doubts about their ability to sustain their moral superiority.*]

Mercy Otis Warren needed to keep faith in the Revolution whose aftermath was fraught with ominous signs for America's future. Had she confined her *History . . . of the American Revolution . . .* to the war, Warren would have left us a hymn to the insuperable American character triumphant in the crucible of military affliction. She, however, had some twenty additional years against which to test the premises of the Revolution, for the Treaty of 1783 was but one benchmark on the revolutionary continuum. The war was finished, but the Revolution uncomplete.

In large part Warren's *History* is a hymn to a fixed American character and a hagiography of the revolutionary leaders. On the eve of war when, as she writes, "the people trembled for their liberties, the merchant for his interest, the tories for their places, the whigs for their country, and the virtuous for the manners of society," Warren insists that "the genius of America was bold, resolute, and enterprising." (pp. 286-87)

Writing her history after the war, Warren found in its campaigns, in its naval engagements, and even in local skirmishes a verification of an *a priori* American character she believed to be racially inbred since seventeenth-century settlement. Thus the war, which occupies some two-thirds of the work, is less a testing of the American will and public virtue than it is an exhibition of them. Her premises are verified deductively, and so it is no surprise to find at the close of the war a people whose spiritual biography points toward national election: "They had obtained their independence by a long and perilous struggle against a powerful nation. We now view them just emancipated from a foreign yoke, the blessings of peace restored upon honorable terms, with the liberty of forming their own governments, enacting their own laws, choosing their own magistrates, and adopting manners the most favorable to freedom and happiness.''

For all this, Warren's is no work of flatulent optimism. All three volumes of the *History* are riddled with qualifications, provisos, grim doubts, above all by her fear that military victory may end in revolutionary defeat. Like Rush and Adams, Warren bore the heavy backpack of current events portending destruction of the new nation. She too worried about "a spirit of avarice and peculation" which as of 1780 had, she felt, "taken deep hold of the majority of the people" and which made her fretful about future public "pursuit of the golden fleece." Too, she had particular postrevolutionary *bêtes noires*. While Adams feared that every descendant of Washington would be a genetically subversive neo-nobleman, Warren dreaded the power of militarism and aristocracy combined in the fraternity of veteran revolutionary war officers, the Order of the Cincinnati. While Rush saw in partisan politics a mortal national malignancy, Warren was most appalled at the anarchy she read in Shays's Rebellion that flouted the social compact.

Warren's anxieties about the so-called Whiskey Rebellion and about the Order of the Cincinnati reveal attitudes that set *her* American Revolution apart from those of Rush and Adams. She understood the war neither as culmination nor as inauguration of the Revolution, but as its premature birth made necessary when Britain twisted the colonial umbilical into a Gordian knot. This precipitate revolution and its consequent new nation troubled her deeply because she feared the results of America's political and social immaturity. On the one hand exultant that America was unfettered by centuries of serfdom and vassalage, Warren found little comfort in the potential for growth by a nation "untimely rip't."

This skepticism is consonant both with her belief in progressive evolution of human enlightenment, which William R. Smith has discussed at length [see excerpt dated 1966], and with her personal distaste and suspicion of a gullible, credulous public. Unswerving in faith that primitives (or dim yeomen) were capable of emerging through the years into socially responsible enlightenment, Warren nonetheless suspected there would not be time enough—or rather, that the necessary maturative years would be spoiled by political opportunists, corruptive foreigners, or a greedy public blind to its own higher interest. Thus, while she concedes that the people of the United States are better educated than "the common classes of men in most other countries," she regrets that "many of them ha[ve] but a superficial knowledge of mankind," being "ignorant of the intrigues of courts" and of the "nature or origin" of government. Accordingly, she thinks them susceptible to "problematic characters which come forward, the new-born offspring of confusion, and assume merit from the novelty of their projects and the inscrutability of their designs." Such demagogic "hot-bed plants . . . often hurry into irretrievable mischief, before time has ripened the systems of men of more principle and judgment." Looking back at the war she reflects that the folk "had generally supposed there was little to do, but to shake off the yoke of foreign dominion, and annihilate the name of *king*." At the same time she fears that liberty is but a semantic anodyne that "tickles the fond pride of man" and "is a jewel much oftener the play-thing of his imagination, than a possession of real stability."

Warren's class biases reinforced her fears. Despite professed Jeffersonian republicanism, her sympathies lie all with a cultivated respectable class. Throughout her *History* it is apparent that Warren highly values the decorum of officers on both sides,

because she finds the highest standards of civilization to be represented in their codified gentlemanly behavior. And though she consistently portrays the British as the Hun of the Enlightenment and carefully includes such supportive evidence as that of the East India Bubble, Warren does refer sincerely to the "usual valor of British troops." She is far more at ease reciting exemplary conduct (however sanguine) between honorable foes than reckoning with "the manners of the mountaineers and borderers of the Carolinas" who, though "descended from civilized ancestors" have sunk "into the habits of savages." Not motivated by snobbery, Warren's sense of need for social hierarchy is best revealed in her own observation that "it may be beyond the reach of human genius to construct a fabric so free as to release from subordination, nor in the present condition of mankind ought it ever to be wished. Authority and obedience are necessary to preserve social order, and to continue the prosperity or even the existence of nations."

The prosperity and the continued existence of the United States recur topically in Warren's *History* with that particular urgency of cosmic questions. Like Adams, she transcends nationalistic ardor to consider America's role as the redeemer nation of biblical prophesy. The Revolution has "awakened the attention and expectation of the millions among the nations beyond the Atlantic." It "may finally lead to the completion of prophetic predictions, and spread liberty and peace, as far at least as is compatible with the present state of human nature." She reminds skeptics that the world's confusion, begun with severance of the colonies from Britain, was divinely directed "in order finally to complete the beauty and harmony of the divine system." And she concludes her final volume with a millennial vision of the American West, "this last civilized quarter of the globe," which "may exhibit those striking traits of grandeur and magnificence, which the Divine Economist may have reserved to crown the closing scene."

For all the grandeur of possibility Warren cannot be assertive but only suggestive about America's destiny. The "prolific soil, abundant resources, commercial genius, and political principles" of America indicate a national rise "into eminence and consideration," but Warren is not confident of these indices. Her grammar becomes subjunctive and conditional as she ponders the future, and her grandest hopes rest upon a groundword of provisos. "From the accumulated blessings which are showered down on the United States," she writes, "there is reason to indulge the benign hope, that America may long stand a favored nation." Indulgence of "benign hope" is the extent of Warren's risk. She is a tenuous prophet.

Constrained empiricism and guarded optimism characterize Warren's work at the point of summation, which is itself protracted because, her story told, Warren was reluctant to stop. In efforts to be dignified and serious, she often became sententious and clumsy, her clauses as persistent and involuted as ground vines. Under the rubric of "Political and Moral Observations" she reviews endlessly her doubts and fears about America's future. This prolongation of the *History* suggests something other than Warren's uncertainties about literary pacing, namely her sense of political confinement in *belles lettres*. Unlike Adams or Rush, or the prolific Founding Fathers, Warren had only the printed page and the theater for her reformist political energies. She seems understandably reluctant to end the work whose directives and caveats, if heeded, could be instrumental in insuring the continuous success of the American Revolution. It seems that she too wished to be a Founder.

Mercy Warren's revolutionary aspirations dovetail with those of John Adams and Benjamin Rush because like them she shared passionately in the national vision of a redemptive America. In revolutionary context they all three revivified the visionary legacy of seventeenth-century Puritan thought by fitting it to a secular but fervid language of the Enlightenment and to a geography transcendent of, but specific to, the United States and the North American continent. Politically committed and unequivocating, at intervals self-pitying, baffled, or angry, these three figures year after year reassessed the Revolution compulsively in letters, diary, autobiography, and history. Conjointly over time they emerge as a chorus of worried celebrants, a troubled conscience of the Revolution afterward sullied in their interpretive doubt and fear, but embodying still their brightest hope for worldwide betterment of the human condition. (pp. 287-90)

> Cecelia Tichi, "Worried Celebrants of the American Revolution," in American Literature, 1764-1789: The Revolutionary Years, edited by Everett Emerson, The University of Wisconsin Press, 1977, pp. 275-91.*

WALTER J. MESERVE (essay date 1977)

[In an overview of the dramas, including The Ladies of Castile and The Sack of Rome, Meserve emphasizes Warren's role as "gadfly" propagandist and explores the question of authorship of The Blockheads and The Motley Assembly.]

Within the world of propaganda pamphlets [in America during the Revolution], the drama held a unique position. Stirring events call for dramatic expression. Despite religious condemnation and legal prohibition, the drama seemed both a natural and a logical means of communication. And communication is the proper word. Writers of plays and dialogues during the Revolution had something to say, and their primary objective was to persuade others to their points of view. Because they were protesting attacks on their sense of freedom or their means of livelihood, they showed anger, indignation, and defiance in plays which mocked, ridiculed, and assaulted adversaries in bitter terms. . . . [The] pamphlets of protest drama were, as an analysis of their structure reveals, intended more for reading than for performance. It was the idea that was important—the dramatic representation of a historical event as filtered through a certain political or philosophical persuasion. Personal feelings and morale were what mattered. Plays were read and perhaps acted, while spokesmen of opposing factions condemned or praised. (pp. 64-5)

In general, those who created plays for the War of Belles Lettres showed little interest in plot, no concern for character, and no knowledge of stage setting. They were writing emotionally biased protest plays, bitter satires for which they sought reactions as explosive as those generating their creations. The effect of their work is difficult to discover, but, in reading some of the plays two hundred years later, one can still feel their power. (p. 65)

[Mercy Otis Warren] rallied to the Patriot cause with a fury that distinguishes her writing during the Revolution. She was no middle-of-the-roader; what she thought, she spoke or wrote. Her effect as a gadfly during the early years of the Revolution cannot be underestimated. (pp. 66-7)

Mercy Warren herself never saw a play on stage, but she had read both Shakespeare's and Molière's plays with pleasure and understanding. Perhaps instinctively, she expressed her emotional reaction to current events in play form even if it was meant only for reading. . . .

As a satiric attack [The Adulateur] had a strong appeal for a people who easily identified the heroes and villains in the play although its stylized and exaggerated sentiment and verse do not give the modern reader the same pleasure. (p. 67)

As a play The Group must be described as merely a dialogue, as all of Mercy Warren's political farces should be described. It lacks action, character portrayal, and a good conflict although it shows the author's excellent touch for satire. For that time, however—and all satiric propaganda must be judged in terms of the event satirized—it truly represented a view which attracted an enthusiastic reading audience. (pp. 69-70)

Mercy Warren's authorship of [The Blockheads; or, The Affrighted Officers] has been seriously questioned, and despite both internal and external evidence which suggests that she could have been responsible, she remains an unlikely choice. While the social and political satire in the play is consistent with her usual attitude, the vindictive tone, though not out of character in her condemnation of Burgoyne, is absent in her other works. None of her propaganda plays, of course, carried her name, and she claimed only The Group late in her life. The argument that the language in The Blockheads is too crude and that the thought, too vulgar for Mrs. Warren is countered by her familiarity with all social levels in Barnstable and by the anonymity which she always chose. It is also noted that her publisher of The Group also printed The Blockheads and that several characters in the play, although with different names, appeared also in The Group. The differences from her other works that this play provides, however, are also noteworthy: the level of characters presented, female characters, the lack of subtlety throughout, an interest in plot, the use of prose rather than poetry, and an ending which included a popular flag-waving technique unused elsewhere by Mrs. Warren: "And let's conclude with huzza for America." Essentially, the authorship must remain something of a mystery. (p. 71)

Another satire that may well have come from the pen of Mercy Warren is a short sketch entitled The Motley Assembly: A Farce. Published for the Entertainment of the Curious. . . . Although basically farcical in structure, there is something of the comedy of manners in this one-act play where the satire is aimed mainly at fashionable society, in particular at Americans who placed social standing above support of the Revolution. As is The Blockheads, it is in prose, with some rather stiff lines but also with some speeches that foreshadow the wit in Royall Tyler's The Contrast. (p. 72)

[In the play, politics] has forced itself upon society, and the assembly, once a simple diversion and entertainment for young ladies, now has a new significance. Will the British return? Perhaps it is best to be a "turncoat," as Esq. Runt urges, or the "versatile man," which Mrs. Flourish praises. The Taxalls also fear that attendance at the Assembly will affect their social prestige. Because the Flourishes and the Taxalls think rather more of scarlet uniforms than of blue ones, the American serviceman has a problem: shall he take "a little damn'd paracidical viper to his bosom because it is pretty?" Obviously not; honor and patriotism forbid it. Meanwhile "whigs and tories joined by fashion 'meet' in mixed assembly to their sires' disgrace." It is all very slight, distinguished only by the dramatist's vivid disdain for people who have nothing more substantial to direct their lives than the frivolous breezes of social fashion.

If *The Motley Assembly* was written by Mrs. Warren, it was the last of her satirical farces. Five years earlier her thoughts had turned to a different style of drama. In a letter dated January 19, 1774, to her close friend Abigail Adams, Mercy Warren wrote that "the solemn strains of the tragic Muse have been generally more to my taste than the Lighter Representations of the Drama. Yet I think that the Follies and Absurdities of Human Nature Exposed to Ridicule in the Masterly Manner it is done by Molière may often have a greater tendency to reform Mankind than some graver Lessons of Morality." She was at this time, of course, deeply involved in writing plays that ridiculed particular activities of particular men and women. For historians of the drama, those efforts would certainly be classed as "lighter representations of the drama," and yet they were seriously written, not only to entertain, but to provoke thought. In fact, Mrs. Warren does not seem to have been a person with a great sense of humor. She had a good feeling for language, and she had a ready wit fired by strong opinions about life around her. She lacked the detached view of life that comedy demands, however, while personal sorrows and the solemn issues of the Revolution weighed on her. (p. 73)

In blank verse *The Ladies of Castile* . . . showed a knowledge of the elements of drama not associated with her farces—plot, character, action, and conflict—but it does not raise her work above the conventional historical tragedy of the period. Taking as her thesis the last heroic struggle for liberty in Spain before the "complete establishment of despotism by the family of Ferdinand," she was able to indulge her interest in revolution and in patriots rising against a tyrant. Central in her play, as the title suggests, are women: the daughter of the tyrant is loved by a patriot; the tyrant's son loves the wife of one of the rebels; Maria, the major figure, wife and sister to patriots, defies the tyrant with a passion that suggests Mercy Warren's earlier convictions. But the revolution fails, and the play ends conventionally.

The Sack of Rome was no better, another historical play which she started as soon as she completed *The Ladies of Castile.* This was a period of personal sadness for Mrs. Warren, and her suffering seems reflected in the play. "Debilitated by the habits of every species of luxury," she wrote in the preface, "man has sunk to his lowest depravity and wants a lesson in morality, valor, and virtue." Traditional conflicts of love-versus-duty and honor-opposed-by-venality control a plot in which innocence suffers from the violence of those dominated by evil passions. If that was her lesson, it lacked her customary optimism, which at the time was being countered by periods of gloom. In the final act the invading Vandals sack Rome with the impartiality of degenerate arrogance. (p. 74)

[Mercy Warren's] life focused on the Revolution, and the little farces which she wrote in support of her opinions not only provide a substantial reflection of her talents as a satirist and political gadfly but serve as the best illustration of the way in which drama was used during the revolutionary period. (p. 75)

Walter J. Meserve, "Drama and the 'War of Belles Lettres'," in his An Emerging Entertainment: The Drama of the American People to 1828, *Indiana University Press, 1977, pp. 60-91.**

EMILY STIPES WATTS (essay date 1977)

[*In a thorough discussion of Warren's nondramatic poetry, Watts uncovers its philosophical bases and asserts that it is "certainly*

not so weak as the current critical neglect suggests." Watts also examines Warren's portrayal of women in the plays.]

In whatever literary form Warren wrote, she had but one theme—liberty. In her farces and history, it was national and political freedom. In her poems, it was intellectual freedom. In her anti-Federalist pamphlet, it was individual freedom. Throughout all of these works, moreover, runs the thread of freedom (equal treatment) for women. Not "militant," she nevertheless urged men to educate their daughters and to treat their wives as equals. Her ideas concerning women were formed and had already been distributed to America long before Mary Wollstonecraft's *Vindication of the Rights of Women* (1792) appeared. In the midst of the male poetasters' abstract and personified panegyrics to Freedom and Liberty, Warren particularized freedom and, at the same time, gave it a scope and intellectual foundation simply not evident in the poetry of the men in her day. (pp. 39-40)

Warren's pen [in her farces] is certainly not gentle, but as sharp and quick as that of any man in her day. The farces themselves are no longer funny to us, partially because of the now obscure topical references and partially because the historical figures on whom the fictional characters are based are now shadowy to us. The farces have little action and much conversation, and the satire is built upon exaggeration.

Warren accuses the Tories of every kind of sin and corruption, but in *The Group* she adds one evil which does not appear in other political satires of the time: the Tory men are cruel to women. In act 2, scene 3, Hateall, who has married "nut brown Kate" for her dower, speaks:

> I broke her spirits when I'd won her purse;
> For which I'll give a recipe most sure
> To ev'ry hen peck'd husband round the board;
> If crabbed words or surly looks won't tame
> The haughty shrew, nor bend the stubborn mind,
> Then the green Hick'ry, or the willow twig,
> Will prove a curse for each rebellious dame
> Who dare oppose her lord's superior will.

Simple Sappling is equally cruel to Silvia, who, Publican admits, "descended to become thy wife." The colloquialism and direct dialogue of the farces are amazingly realistic. The high rhetoric, invocations, and neoclassical abstractions which abound in the verse of most of Warren's contemporaries are remarkably absent.

Warren apparently hoped that her two tragedies, *The Sack of Rome* and *The Ladies of Castile* . . . would surpass Shakespeare. They cannot rival Shakespeare, but they are better than most of the bombast created by her contemporaries. In five acts of blank verse, the plays feature noble women acting decisively in times of national crisis. *The Sack of Rome* is the better of the two tragedies and establishes the kind of woman ("Roman matron") Warren hoped would develop in America. The ideal woman for her is Edoxia, the empress of Rome. The mother of two adolescent girls and a loyal wife to her depraved husband, Edoxia spends most of the play trying to outwit Genseric, the King of the Vandals, whose troops are now at Rome's gate. Ardelia, another one of "th' illustrious matrons" and the wife of an honest but weak Roman nobleman, has been deceived and raped by Edoxia's husband, Emperor Valentinian (who appropriately dies before act 3).

The plays are, as Quinn says, "carefully constructed" [see excerpt dated 1943] and are by no means dull. Written as moral pieces, as Warren points out in a prefatory statement, they nevertheless contain some true poetry. Strangely enough, the best lines are spoken by men (most of whom are lecherous, selfish, and brutal). For example, in *The Sack of Rome,* Traulista, a barbarian prince, questions a young man in love:

> Why does my friend wear that soft April eye?
>
> . . . .
>
> Come, be thyself again; nor longer bask
> Upon the silken, downy lap of hope;
> Leave her to sigh, and whisper to the winds—
> Else snatch by force, and bear her o'er the wilds,
> Through growling forests—hideous, broken cliffs,
> And frozen seas—to Scythia's icy banks,
> Where rugged winds pour from the brindled north
> Adown the mountain's brow—a blast may cool
> The transports of thy love.
>
> (act 4, scene 5)

The young lover, Gaudentius, is a Roman noble in love with one of Edoxia's daughters. He is the model young Roman for whom only honorable marriage can provide relief from the "transports" of love. No double standard for Warren! I should note, however, that Warren provided more complexity in character motivation than my summary suggests. Indeed, Edoxia seeks God's help in solving such "complicated guilt."

The same general theme is repeated in *The Ladies of Castile.* The heroine is again a mother, Maria. She states to her condemned husband during their final interview:

> Maternal softness weakens my resolve,
> And wakes new fears—thou dearest, best of men,
> Torn from thy side, I'm level'd with my sex.
> The wife—the mother—made me less than woman.
>
> (act 4, scene 5)

Nevertheless, Maria is soon leading the troops, upon "the prancing steed."

Warren's high and optimistic estimation of woman's possibilities is undoubtedly based on her own capabilities and her own propagandistic accomplishments during the war. Warren's women can be as influential as men and are, in fact, wiser. They are capable of murder (justifiable, of course), trickery, and all kinds of male heroics. Her Roman matrons (under some influence from Joan of Arc) are Minervas, but Minervas who suckle the babe with one arm while wielding the sword with the other. This kind of woman will survive throughout the poetry of American women, but she will not, for the most part, emulate male heroics, nor will she be so active in the larger social or political scene. Warren's matrons represent an attempt to create a model for the American women of her day—a model who is by no means an Eve, nor a mystic, nor any kind of ideal woman espoused by the American men in the late eighteenth century. Warren, however, was not naïve; she was aware of the limited possibilities of success for this kind of woman: Edoxia's Rome and Maria's Castile fall to the forces of the barbarous Genseric and the vicious Charles V.

Warren's best poetry appears in her farces and plays, but her poems, generally occasional verse, reveal an analytic and educated mind attempting to solve the moral and social crisis of her day. As such, her poetry is no less poetically interesting than the later, discursive verse of T. S. Eliot, or W. H. Auden's political verse of the 1930's. Indeed, in terms of reason and logical analysis, her poems are more interesting. They are

imitations of English Augustan discursive verse, written in heroic couplets, but are intellectually independent.

In a 124-line poem, **"To Torrismond"** ("a young Gentleman educated in Europe"), Warren argues against both "superstitious" religion and Hobbesian materialism:

> Then the grey druid's grave, majestic air,
> The frantic priestess, with dishevell'd hair
> And flaming torch, spoke superstition's reign;
> While elfin damsels dancing o'er the plain,
> Allur'd the vulgar by the mystic scene,
> To keep long vigils on the sacred green.
>
> . . . .
>
> . . . artful politicians saw the jest,
> And laugh'd at virtue as a state machine,
> An engine fit the multitude to rein;
> With more facility to rule mankind,
> They lent their efforts to obscure the mind.

Her intellectual heroes are Boyle and Locke and, especially, Newton, whose authority she used to refute English Deism. We should remember that Franklin's *Autobiography,* which also refutes English Deism, was not published at this time, nor had Thomas Paine's Deistic *The Age of Reason* appeared. Warren understood the metaphysical side of Newton's work, although she appreciated his scientific discoveries and analytical methods as well. She is a traditional "Christian Deist," not a "Deist" or even a "methodical Deist" like Benjamin Franklin (if such distinctions can clearly be made). The Deists, she tells Torrismond, have "The depths of erudition just skim'd o'er; / Nurs'd in refinements of a skeptic age." Their out-of-hand rejection of "revelation" is condemned. For Warren, "revelation" can be found in the Bible and in writers such as Newton.

The Deistic theories, she saw, had two weaknesses. The first is that man is not wise enough to pursue the intellectually independent course suggested by the Deist. Ironically she comments, "They all things doubt but their superiour sense." Man's reason is too weak, and he must "grope his way." Her villains are Hobbes, Hume, Shaftesbury, and Voltaire. Perhaps most interesting is her objection to Voltaire (also an intellectual follower of Locke and Newton). I suspect that she was reacting against his consistent stand against organized religion (and perhaps, considering Warren's feminist tendencies, against his brutal burlesque of Joan of Arc in *La Pucelle,* which appeared in 1755 and, in final form, in 1762).

Dependence on "frail reason," Warren felt, had forced the Deists to two positions: The first is a moral vacuum, in which no firm standards exist. For Warren, the standards are evident in the Bible and in the works of the more traditionally religious philosophers, such as Newton. The Deists, however, based their ethical considerations on individual reason and individual conscience and thus as far as Warren could see, justified any kind of vice or any kind of "unreasonable action." The Deist had an "oscillating brain." For Warren, the various liberties she espoused could exist only in a society based on firm moral principles. (As we can see in Warren's later prose works, such moral principles were embodied at least in part in the Bill of Rights.)

Absolute dependence on "frail reason" also led the Deists, she felt, to a personal isolation and alienation from any ideas beyond their limited, individual minds and consciences. In short, Deism led to a vain and dangerous self-centeredness, an egocentrism: "They spurn . . . / The wish of man to be to God ally'd." Warren did not suggest a transcendence (no Emersonian "transparent eyeball" for her) but rather argued the necessity for man to find values outside of himself, to take history, "revelation," and religion into consideration.

She thus rejected what she saw as a morally dangerous and potentially self-destructive path. It is clear that she was not advocating Calvinism or simply "orthodox religion." She remained a Christian Deist throughout her life. In other poems, such as **"To Mr. ——,"** she rejects a system of fatalism and Hobbesian self-love; and in **"The Genius of America weeping the absurd follies of the Day,"** Warren's criticism of the Deists, one of whom she calls "a smooth romantic bard," produces some of her best verse:

> An *ignis fatuus* floats from lake to bog,
> The vapor plays in pestilential fogs,
> Sparkes and sinks in the dark marshy tomb,
> As modern wits in metaphysic fume.

Her poems are also political and social; **"The Squabble of the Sea-Nymphs; or the Sacrifice of the Tuscararoes"** concerns the Boston Tea Party. In the epilogue to a long poem, **"Simplicity,"** she mentions "The narrow bounds, prescribed to female life." And, although the "mother" is "kind," she acts a "little part." Another poem, **"To the Hon. J. Winthrop, Esq.,"** satirizes women who devote their lives to luxury and adornment, but the men who court such ladies are gently chastised too.

Warren was not without intelligence and humor. Her poetry is certainly not so weak as the current critical neglect suggests. Moreover, in light of the social and political history of America, her poems, farces, and plays are certainly more valuable and interesting than the poetry of the Connecticut Wits. She was a woman who refused to allow herself to be limited to woman's prescribed "narrow bounds" and, in her refusal, found an intellectual and artistic independence. (pp. 40-4)

> *Emily Stipes Watts, "1735-1804: Another Kind of Independence," in her* The Poetry of American Women from 1632 to 1945, *University of Texas Press, 1977, pp. 29-62.**

LESTER H. COHEN   (essay date 1980)

[*Cohen posits that in her* History, *Warren interpreted the American Revolution "in terms of a simple moral opposition between American virtue and British avarice." Therefore, the critic concludes, she used ideological and ethical bases not only to interpret the past, but also to exhort future generations to uphold their moral responsibility to the new nation.*]

In a crucial sense, the histories written in [America between 1785 and 1807] demonstrate a greater concern for America's present and future than for its past. For they reveal their authors' anxiety, as William Gordon put it as early as 1777, that "a horrid corruption hath spread itself so rapidly thro' the American States. . . ." (p. 200)

This fear of widespread corruption, which is especially emphatic in the historians' narratives of events from the late 1770s to (in most cases) the passage of the Constitution, is not surprising, for corruption had been a dominant patriot concern since the 1760s. But the historians' persistent focus on corruption in history reveals more than patriotic zeal. The anxiety it reflects also gave rise to a theory of history that was designed to unite ideology and ethics in a single interpretive framework. The historians presupposed a dialectic between ideology and ethics, such that republican principles and institutions and the ethical practices of the people mutually affected one another. They assumed, moreover, that the dialectic gained its impetus from the ethical side, that principles and institutions were predicated upon the people's practice of republican virtue. (p. 201)

Mercy Otis Warren's *History of the American Revolution* . . . reveals the same concerns and the same attempt to fuse ideology and ethics in historical interpretation. She, too, believed that the nation was already in trouble. Instead of showing that independence would solidify the people's commitment to republican values, events of the 1780s and '90s, when her *History* was taking shape, seemed to confirm her worst apprehensions about human character and about the people's unwillingness to practice political self-discipline. She wrote her *History* in a mood of profound concern. . . . She was anxious about the future of American republicanism because public virtue was yielding to private ambition, the rising generation "laying aside their simple habits, and . . . hankering after the modes, distinctions, and ranks of the servants of European despots." (pp. 201-02)

Warren's anxiety can be explained in part by her political attitudes and by events, particularly in the 1780s, that affected her personally. If, for example, Federalists like Ramsay and Marshall were comforted by the belief that the Constitution was likely to be an effective brake on corruption, the Antifederalist Warren had less sanguine expectations. Although for tactical purposes she softened her criticism of the Constitution in her *History,* in 1788 she feared that the Constitution represented a renunciation of popular sovereignty and that it might even prove to be a new way of enslaving the people. (p. 202)

At the same time, Warren was frustrated by what she saw as the neglect of her family in the new political order. . . . In Mercy Warren's view . . . [her husband] James had been abandoned in the '80s, his virtuous pursuit of republican simplicity having become an embarrassment to those—like the Warrens' bête noire, John Hancock—who would use political power to foster their private ambitions. As she crafted her *History* in the '80s and '90s, she saw crumbling around her the values to which she had long been committed. Antifederalism had failed and Massachusetts politics was in shambles; her husband had been repudiated, three of the five Warren sons were tragically dead, and she and James were reduced to pleading for a minor government position for their son Henry. Warren's *History* may thus be seen as a mirror reflecting both its troubled time and its troubled author. (pp. 202-03)

[Though Warren's] concerns and the categories she used to interpret history were similar to those of the other historians, her *History* illustrates more clearly than theirs how a commitment to republican ideology and a concern for its future generated an ethical theory of history. For Warren had the most systematic understanding of the relationship between ideology and ethics, the best-developed interpretation of how corruption operated in history, and the clearest insight into the historian's role as a social and political critic. Thus her *History* is not merely a reflection of her personal concerns and convictions; it is also a work of moral art: a self-consciously created instrument of ideology and ethics that simultaneously expressed the Revolutionaries' commitment to republicanism and served as a beacon shining back upon the exemplary forebears.

Warren perceived herself as a writer "who wishes only to cultivate the sentiments of public and private virtue in whatsoever falls from her pen." She thought it her central duty as a playwright, poet, and historian "to form the minds, to fix the principles [and] to correct the errors'' of ''the young members of society,'' and to encourage them to tread the path of true virtue ''instead of the hackneyed vulgar walks crowded with swarms of useless votaries, who worship at the pedestal of pleasure or bow before the shrine of wealth.'' As early as 1780 Warren called for ''the steady influence of all the old republicans, to keep the principles of the revolution in view,'' already concerned that the spirit of the Revolution was eroding. For the ''giddy multitude'' was destroying all the gains of independence, rather than adhering to ''the manners that would secure their freedom.'' With this end in mind, she presented her *History* as a work of partisan ideology that would ''justify the principles of the defection and final separation from the parent state,'' and at the same time as a work of moral suasion, a manual of republican ethics designed to exhort future generations of Americans to engage in the uncompleted struggle.

Although some contemporaries saw patriot history as polemics masquerading as objective narrative, Warren believed that she could both justify the Revolution and transcend partisan polemics. By insisting on the priority of ethical categories in historical and political interpretation, she attempted to generate a vision of an American future that would fulfill the promise of the Revolution. Thus if her proximate aim was to justify the Revolution, she saw that aim subserving the greater principle of which it was a part: that, as Lord Bolingbroke put it, ''history is philosophy teaching by examples,'' that it ''inculcates images of virtue and vice,'' and that its proper task is to train people, particularly young people, in ''public and private virtue.'' The fundamental requirement of this ''exemplary theory'' of history was that historical writing instruct in the principles of personal morality and public virtue; it enjoined the historian to suppress all personal biases in order to serve the higher end of providing models of virtue and deterrent images of vice.

Warren self-consciously wrote in this tradition of exemplary history both because she was convinced philosophically that historical models instructed youth and because the tradition provided a framework for developing her ideological commitments. In short, the exemplary theory was not only right but useful. . . . Warren joyfully embraced the exemplary theory as the perfect vehicle for uniting her ethical and ideological concerns, for the theory required her to write what she longed to write: that the Revolution originated in British avarice, against which the colonists responded with moral outrage and political and military resistance. The Revolution epitomized the exemplary theory itself, pitting the forces of virtue against the forces of avarice. By grounding her ethical and ideological convictions, the exemplary theory accomplished two related aims: it provided Warren's historical theory with its explanatory categories, and it laid the foundation for her use of history as a mode of social and political criticism. (pp. 203-05)

In Warren's version of the exemplary theory, ''virtue'' and ''avarice'' were the fundamental categories of historical explanation, the terms in which historians properly interpreted and shaped events, because they were the leading principles of human character. Believing that the study of history ''requires a just knowledge of character,'' Warren outlined the characterological terms that constituted history's ethical dynamic:

> The study of the human character opens at once
> a beautiful and deformed picture of the soul.
> We there find a noble principle implanted in
> the nature of man, that pants for distinction.

This principle operates in every bosom, and when kept under the control of reason, and the influence of humanity, it produces the most benevolent effects. But when the checks of conscience are thrown aside, or the moral sense [is] weakened by the sudden acquisition of wealth or power, humanity is obscured, and if a favorable coincidence of circumstances permits, this love of distinction often exhibits the most mortifying instances of profligacy, tyranny, and the wanton exercise of arbitrary sway.

It is not clear here whether Warren believed that human character is fundamentally virtuous and that evil is introduced when certain social conditions (notably the acquisition of wealth and power) operate against the ''noble principle,'' or whether she believed that virtue and avarice have equal status in character and that one or the other will be manifested to a greater degree given certain social conditions. Since she did not describe two ''plants''—one virtuous, the other avaricious—she apparently believed that, while avarice is as manifest in conduct as is virtue, social conditions exert a preponderance of determining power.

This view squares with Warren's environmentalism. Although she refers here to ''the nature of man,'' it is useful to distinguish her remarks on ''human character'' from whatever ideas about ''human nature'' we may wish to infer from them. For Warren was far less concerned with ''human nature,'' understood as a set of fundamental passions or appetites that determine people's conduct, than she was with ''human character,'' construed as the people's manifest social and political conduct itself. (pp. 205-06)

It was clear to her . . . that avarice was unavoidable in history because man is a social being who craves distinction from his fellows. Virtue and reason were, for Warren, inseparable, and both rested on the principle of self-discipline. (p. 206)

As a historian, Warren was less interested in virtue and avarice as traits of personal character than as principles of society and history. Unfortunately, in history avarice tended to get the better of virtue, for ''ambition and avarice are the *leading springs* which generally actuate the restless mind. From these *primary sources of corruption* have arisen all the rapine and confusion, the depredation and ruin, that have spread distress over the face of the earth from the days of Nimrod to Cesar [*sic*], and from Cesar to an arbitrary prince of the house of Brunswick.'' The historian had to recognize virtue when it appeared and applaud ''the many signal instances of disinterested merit'' among mankind. But the melancholy fact remained that ''virtue in the sublimest sense, has an influence only on a chosen few,'' for ''the guidance of reason . . . operates too little on the generality of mankind.''

Virtue and avarice were timeless and culturally universal because they were ontological facts of human character. But they were not, as Warren used them, vague abstractions like Good and Evil, for their observable manifestation in time constituted the ethical condition of people living in society. Since they were the basic terms of history's ethical dialectic, virtue and avarice provided Warren an explanatory schema for analyzing not only the American Revolution but all of human history. Like all the historians as well as others of their generation, she was preoccupied with the rise and fall of nations, particularly republics. Geneva represented ''a striking portrait of the means by which most republics have been subverted.'' Subversion was accomplished not by the lone tyrant, but by "the pride of a few families, the ambition of individuals, and the supineness of the people." The few exerted such "an undue authority" over "the middling-class of mankind" that "the mass of the people" was rendered "abject and servile." The "middling-class," of course, ought never to be supine and inattentive to their political condition, and it was the proper role of the republican historian to keep the people informed, to point out the danger of tyranny, and to call the people back to virtue and reason whenever their rights were threatened. But the problem persisted in history: in the face of an avaricious few, the people fall into a torpor of unconcern and irresponsibility, and their voice "seldom breathes universal murmur, but when the insolence or the oppression of their rulers extorts the bitter complaint." (pp. 207-08)

Warren's immediate aim was to explain the Revolution, and she did so in ethical terms. Upsetting the general harmony that had prevailed for a century and a half, George III and his ministers began in the 1760s to tie imperial policy to trade objectives, thereby strengthening colonial subordination both to the English merchants and to the crown and Parliament (and, she strongly hinted, making the colonists virtual slaves of Britain). In addition, George and his ministers were not content to let the colonists raise their own taxes by the voluntary consent of the people's representatives. Instead, "grown giddy with the lustre of their own power, in the plenitude of human grandeur," they pursued "such weak, impolitic and unjust measures . . . as soon threw the whole empire into the most violent convulsions."

The contrast between British avarice and American virtue grounded the theory that Britain (and Europe generally, until the French Revolution) was degenerating politically and culturally, whereas America was on the ascendant. As early as 1774 Warren wrote to Hannah Lincoln, who was unsympathetic to the patriot cause: "You ask why did we urge on this sudden display of ministerial power? In return let me ask by whose avarice and ambition the people were precipitated to take some rash and unjustifiable steps?" The answer was obvious, she pointed out a year later: Britain already was internally corrupt; its "venality and vice," "corruption and wickedness" were "nearly compleat." In the face of such corruption, Lexington and Concord were merely the signs of "the natural struggles which ensue when the genius of *liberty* arises to assert her rights in opposition to the ghost of Tyranny."

Precisely as earlier republics had fallen—Greece, the Achaean League, the Amphyctions, Rome, Venice, Geneva—so England's "republican opinions and the freedom of the nation have been in the wane" since the accession of the first Stuart. England had become "an ungrateful, dissipated nation," fallen into "barbarism," her people "the ensigns of cruelty." Britain's degeneration was at no time more apparent than during the war. Hiring foreign mercenaries was the most obvious sign. Another was British treatment of the colonial citizenry. The Bostonians, wrote Warren in 1775, "are exposed to daily insults of a foe, who seem not only to have lost that sense of honour, freedom, and valour once the characteristic of the British nation—but that generosity, and humanity, which has [*sic*] long been the boast of the most civilized parts of the world." (pp. 208-09)

If avarice and corruption signalled Britain's political and moral decline, the question remained whether the Americans would, like the Genevans, lie supine in the face of tyranny or whether they would discover the spirit of virtue and resist. . . .

Warren argued that the Americans manifested the kind of virtue only rarely witnessed in history. Although a common maxim held that "a state of war has ever been deemed unfavourable to virtue," the Americans, at least until the late 1770s, displayed the virtues of patriotism, self-denial, industry, and prudence to an astonishing degree. On the civil front, virtue reigned supreme. . . . From the Stamp Act to the introduction of a standing army in Massachusetts, from the nonimportation agreements to the Coercive Acts, despite threats to the very fabric of society and law, "it must be ascribed to the virtue of the people, however reluctant some may be to acknowledge this truth, that they did not feel the effects of anarchy in the extreme." (p. 209)

Warren's *History* thus easily explained the Revolution in terms of a simple moral opposition between American virtue and British avarice, an opposition that appears to subordinate ethical interpretation to ideological conviction. How else would a zealous patriot rationalize the Revolution in retrospect? That the ethical dimension of the *History* was more than a convenient rationale, however, is better understood by focusing on the anxiety the *History* betrays over two central and related issues: first, Warren's concern that America, too, was already showing signs of decline; second, the problem of distinguishing the American republic from all earlier ones, lest the logic of history hold true and America decline precisely as they had done. What was at stake in Warren's *History* was not British as much as American avarice and, therefore, the possibility of an American republican future. With respect to these issues, the historian of the Revolution asserted herself as a revolutionary historian, a writer who uses historical narrative as a tool of social and political criticism. For if the past was to be made comprehensible through the categories of virtue and avarice, the future still had to be lived in their terms—and the future was very much in doubt [as she expressed in her poem, **"The Genius of America, Weeping the Absurd Follies of the Day"**].

> Behold the schedule that unfolds the crimes
> And marks the manners of these modern times.
> [Freedom] sigh'd and wept—the folly of the age,
> The selfish passions, and the mad'ning rage
> For pleasure's soft debilitating charms,
> Running full riot in cold avarice' arms.

Thomas Jefferson revealed the same anxiety and urgency as he concluded his discussion of religion in *Notes on the State of Virginia* (1786) with a prophecy of America's future. Religious liberty was temporarily safe, he argued, because "the spirit of the times" secured the people against pernicious legislation. But "the spirit of the times may alter, will alter," he predicted. "Our rulers will become corrupt, our people careless. A single zealot may commence persecutor, and better men be his victims." . . . Warren's attitude toward the likelihood of American decline was even gloomier than Jefferson's, for she believed that the attempt to institutionalize the future by "fixing every essential right on a legal basis" would prove fruitless without the precondition of a virtuous people. For more than thirty years her writings reveal an impelling concern about internal American corruption, born of avarice. It was clear to her that an American decline was virtually inevitable—if decline were the natural phenomenon that most theorists assumed it was.

"Corruption," "decay," "degeneration," the words most frequently used to describe the fall of republics, were borrowed from the language of nature and were freighted with connotations of necessity. Characteristically of those eighteenth-century theorists who viewed history cyclically, the anonymous author of "Thoughts on the Decline of States" argued in 1791 that all nations inevitably decline and die, and "he must think little of the order of nature who sees not all of our efforts must be defeated at last, whether for the preservation of individuals, or the body politick." (pp. 210-11)

[Warren] attempted to abandon the language of nature altogether by employing an ethical and social language to account for decline. While traditional theory held that corruption acted like a cancer, metastasizing through the state, eating at its vitals until the state died, Warren sought a non-naturalistic explanation for decline, and thus for a way of liberating America's future from the teleology of nature. She centered her analysis in virtue and avarice because they were fundamentally societal, not natural, terms. Since avarice was the cause of corruption, the historian's proper task was to exhort her countrymen to virtue, even as she pointed to the pustulating signs of corruption and decay.

Warren, like the other historians, tended to emphasize the symptoms of decline in the decade after independence. The war, of course, played its insidious role in undermining American virtue, for war created opportunities for speculators and brought to America the influence of foreign manners. "[S]uch a total change of manners in so short a period I believe was never known in the history of man," she wrote to John Adams in 1778. The problem was that avarice, once introduced, led to systemic corruption, infecting not only the manners of individuals but the society's ethical and political order as well. (pp. 211-12)

With nothing less at stake than independence and the possibility of an American republican order, David Ramsay called upon "the Press, the pulpit & all the powers of Eloquence" to counteract the ruinous avarice and "to excite us to the long neglected virtues of industry & frugality." For Warren even more than for Ramsay, historical writing was just such an instrument of "Eloquence," and it was in this context that she expressed her anxiety over the rising generation and called for the vigor of "the old republicans." Indeed, apprehensive about the signs of imminent decline, Warren wrote of the social significance of the historian:

> It is an unpleasing part of history, when "corruption begins to prevail, when degeneracy marks the manners of the people, and weakens the sinews of the state." If this should ever become the deplorable situation of the United States, let some unborn historian, in a far distant day, detail the lapse, and hold up the contrast between a simple, virtuous, and free people, and a degenerate, servile race of beings, corrupted by wealth, effeminated by luxury, impoverished by licentiousness, and become the *automations* of intoxicated ambition.

That "far distant day," obviously, was now, and the "contrast" was clear, for the generation that had suffered English oppression, declared independence, and mobilized America's forces for war was being superseded by a younger generation that was sacrificing liberty and virtue at the shrine of private ambition. To this younger generation Warren addressed her *History,* mixing condemnation of their avarice with hope that moral suasion and the examples of the old republicans would turn their attention back to the virtues of their ancestors. Her *History* was thus a radically contemporary document, less con-

cerned with the past for its own sake than with the bearing of the past on the present and future.

Motivating Warren's statements about American decline was the zeal of the revolutionary-as-historian who believes that narrative history is an instrument of social and political criticism. History could be instructive only if it exhorted future generations not to forget, for the problem with avarice was that it led to "forgetfulness," a denial of history's lessons. Thus the younger generation "cease to look back with due gratitude and respect on the fortitude and virtue of their ancestors, who, through difficulties almost insurmountable, planted them in a happy soil."

There is no reason to think that Warren actually believed that the younger generation was altogether avaricious whereas her own had been filled with paragons of virtue. To think this is to depreciate her strategy of exhortation. Those who "lusted" for wealth, power, and distinction were always present in history, as apparent in America before the Declaration of Independence as afterwards. And, of course, Warren condemned the avaricious, like Thomas Hutchinson, and the timid, like those who capitulated to British policies rather than resisting them with "manly fortitude." But to portray a contrast between the generations was to rely on a theatrical convention, as useful to historical as to dramatic presentation, for creating among the characters a stark opposition that both simplified the moral drama and made its resolution more urgent. Indeed, she wrote of the rising generation more optimistically in her letters than in her *History,* and she wrote more optimistically of the Revolutionaries in her *History* than in her letters, revealing not so much a confusion in her beliefs as her notion that the creation of tense moral dichotomies was a valuable hortatory technique.

The use of this technique also reveals more of Warren's motivation as a historian. She contrasted the rising generation with the seventeenth-century settlers and the Revolutionaries in order to establish hegemony over the future. She sought not merely to influence how future Americans would interpret the Revolution but, more important, to establish the very categories in which interpretation was properly to be conducted. (pp. 212-14)

Warren's persistent emphasis on avarice in history strongly suggests that she refused to adopt the notions of historical progress then emerging in Enlightenment Europe. The suggestion is strengthened by her version of the exemplary theory, her view of her own ethical role as historian, and her sense of the imminent possibility of catastrophe, for the "faith" in historical progress, as J. B. Bury described it, was incompatible with her ethical commitments. Bury argued that the idea of progress is a theory "which involves a synthesis of the past and a prophecy of the future"; it is a theory "which regards men as slowly advancing . . . in a definite and desirable direction, and infers that this progress will continue indefinitely."

Although several aspects of Warren's historical theory led logically toward an idea of progress, they were effectively undermined by her repudiation of any notion that mankind was "destined" to advance gradually "in a definite and desirable direction." If anything, she believed that the reverse was true, that history contained no interior principle conducive to man's betterment, for all past republics had been eaten away from within by corruption caused by avarice, and no subsequent republic seemed capable of building upon the failures of earlier ones. America, it appeared, would be no exception if the early signs of avarice were genuine presages.

Equally important, perhaps more so, Warren had no interest in showing abstractly that history was progressive. For it was precisely such comfortable conceptions that lulled people into a false sense of security or, worse yet, provided them with an excuse for avarice, as if civilization would progress regardless of what they did. She repudiated any principle—call it providence or progress—that guaranteed the shape of the future at the expense of wresting responsibility from man's hands.

Yet despite her repudiation of progressive history, Warren wrote optimistically. Even a jeremiad could not be a story of unrelieved gloom lest it inculcate despair; exhortation demanded at least the possibility of a desirable future. Thus at the same time that she depicted a younger generation declining from the ethical and ideological standards of the Revolutionaries, she held out the hope of a resurgence of American virtue, painting the future as opportunity. Consistent with her philosophical commitment to human efficacy in history, she wrote of the promise of the Revolution even as she condemned the rising generation for leaving the path of political and ethical propriety. (pp. 214-15)

Warren wrote this optimism back in time, attributing it to the Revolutionaries throughout their efforts to secure independence. But, at the same time, she sought to chasten optimism because the nation's virtue still required protection. "Notwithstanding the advantages that may be derived, and the safety that may be felt, under so happy a constitution," she wrote, muting her Antifederalism in the interest of making her *History* useful as exhortation, "yet it is necessary to guard at every point, against the intrigues of artful or ambitious men, who may subvert the system." The people of America had every reason to congratulate themselves on the success of their Revolution and on the spirit in which independence had been won. But they had now to preserve their accomplishments "by a strict adherence to the principles of the revolution, and the practice of every public, social and domestic virtue." These statements have the style of the secular jeremiad, presenting both a challenge and a hope.

To conclude, however, that Warren wrote with "guarded optimism" is to depreciate her sense of threat. For even after hostilities had ended, she wrote, "it was yet uncertain" whether the union could be consolidated "under wise, energetic, and free modes of government." Indeed, it remained uncertain whether such government, "if established, would be administered agreeable to laws founded on the beautiful theory of republicanism." For although "the name of *liberty* delights the ear, and tickles the fond pride of man, it is a jewel much oftener the play-thing of his imagination, than a possession of real stability." Liberty "may be acquired to-day in all the triumph of independent feelings," but, she added, scarcely veiling the challenge to her readers, "perhaps to-morrow the world may be convinced, that mankind know not how to make a proper use of the prize, generally bartered in a short time, as a useless bauble, to the first officious master that will take the burden from the mind, by laying another on the shoulders of ten-fold weight." This, as Warren repeatedly pointed out, was what generally happened in history—it was "the usual course of human conduct. . . . The game of deception is played over and over to mislead the judgment of men, and work on their enthusiasm, until by their own consent, hereditary crowns and distinctions are fixed, and some scion of royal descent is entailed upon them forever."

The threat was clear enough as Warren outlined it. But what could be done to reverse the pernicious tendencies to which she pointed? Gordon S. Wood has argued that in the 1780s different solutions to America's ills came from two emerging schools of thought. One, eventually associated with Federalist political sociology, argued that the remedy for avarice and corruption was to arrange the institutions of government in a way that minimized the potential for social "viciousness." The other, more loosely identified with Antifederalist theory, argued that only a kind of education aimed at the moral regeneration of the people and their social institutions could reinfuse virtue into the republic. The former view held that America could avoid the failures of past republics by adopting a properly mixed mode of government, thereby overcoming institutional weaknesses by erecting more perfect institutions. This, in fact, was one means of avoiding the inexorable logic of nature, for it substituted a political framework and language for the then conventional natural ones. (pp. 215-17)

As a student of political philosophy, Warren was thoroughly imbued with enlightened social and political theories that recognized the importance of a properly mixed republican government. Indeed, she made plain to Adams that a properly constituted republic did more than merely guard the people against their own excesses. It actually produced "many excellent qualities, and heroic virtues in human nature—which often lie dormant for want of opportunities for exertion." "Yet," she added in a crucial qualifying statement that reasserted the priority of ethics over institutions, "I have my *fears,* that American virtue has not yet reached that sublime pitch which is necessary to baffle the designs of the artful, to counteract the weakness of the timid, or to resist the pecuniary temptations and ambitious wishes that will arise in the breast of many." Adams, of course, had the same fears, which was precisely why he turned to governmental form as a remedy. But implicit in Warren's statement is her belief that, while the form of government is of obvious importance, a republic is impossible without a virtuous people. She took Montesquieu's injunction seriously: "There is no great share of probity necessary to support a monarchical or despotic government. The force of laws in one, and the prince's arm in the other, are sufficient to direct and maintain the whole. But in a popular state, one spring more is necessary, namely, virtue." The ideal government was a republic in which the people were virtuous: thus the form would reflect and be strengthened by the people's virtue, and the virtue of the people would be enhanced and perpetuated by the form, people and institutions reflecting one another, as in parallel mirrors, to infinity. But, as Warren saw it, it was chimerical to believe that America could avoid the failures of past republics merely by creating a mixed form of government. While the politicians addressed themselves to matters of statecraft, the historian would use her writings to inculcate that virtue which she saw as the mainspring of the republic.

Warren's project is simplicity itself. Her fusion of ethical and ideological interpretation to make historical writing useful as explanation of the past and exhortation for the future reasserted the primacy of the people's responsibility for their future. This was the lesson of the Revolutionaries who, she insisted, "procured their own emancipation from foreign thraldom, by the sacrifice of their heroes and their friends." It was "the wise and patriotic" who had "by inconceivable labor and exertion obtained the prize." Warren sought no guarantees for the people's future conduct—not in nature (the logic of which pointed to decline and decay in any case), nor in overarching principles like progress, nor in government itself. There was, as she saw it, no way to institutionalize the future. It would have to be lived, as the Revolutionaries had lived it, as strenuous republicans in the face of contingency. (pp. 217-18)

Lester H. Cohen, "Explaining the Revolution: Ideology and Ethics in Mercy Otis Warren's Historical Theory," in William and Mary Quarterly, *third series*, *Vol. 37, No. 2, April, 1980, pp. 200-18.*

JOAN HOFF WILSON AND **SHARON L. BOLLINGER** (essay date 1980)

[*In their survey of Warren's works, excerpted from a study of female scholars, the critics discuss such issues as Warren's gender consciousness and political beliefs, while generally dismissing her literary merit.*]

A review of Mercy Otis Warren's circuitous career as a late eighteenth-century literary figure and historian represents a striking example of the high aspirations of the fettered female mind in the last quarter of the eighteenth century. (p. 162)

Her stultified, classical style, although highly regarded at the time, seems unduly artificial to the modern reader. Later her three-volume history was to read like a narrative prose version of [the] early poems. In retrospect, it is difficult to perceive any significant literary development in her writing. Her style has been described as a pseudo-elegant "flowery mode of expression." Only *The Blockheads,* renowned at the time for its "vulgarity," stands out from the rest because she used terms such as "prig," and "pimp," and described one character as having "shit his breeches." As a result, some scholars question her authorship of this play and of *The Motley Assembly.* However, the sentiments in both plays are surely hers. Their vocabulary and broad sexual humor afford a glimpse of a considerably less staid and protected homebody than her portraits and private correspondence would lead us to expect.

The Blockheads, interesting because of its sexual innuendos, is distinguished by unusual demographic insight. As in all her satires, she portrayed the British as more degenerate and avaricious than they were; however, she also depicted American Loyalists as stupid, pretentious, lower-class farmers mainly interested in rising socially among their new-found British friends. Until very recently, accounts of the Loyalists stressed their wealth, education, and cultural refinement. While she exaggerated both their social ambitions and uncouthness, she was demographically correct in describing the American Loyalists as primarily poor farmers, dissatisfied with their lot in life. For what it is worth, Warren's satire comes closer to the collective biographical truth about rank and file native American Loyalists than most standard accounts since that time. Thus, Mr. and Mrs. Simple and their daughter Tabitha leave their "filthy farm" because "it is all dirty stuff, only fit for Yankees," in response to false promises from the British (including the propositioning of their daughter by Lord Dapper). Their humiliation and suffering as refugees is approved by a woman in good radical Whig—later Jeffersonian Republican—fashion in the last soliloquy of the play.

Good enough for them, they have brought it upon themselves; they had better have minded their farms.... If I had a good farm, I would see government to the devil, before they should catch me here, to be froz'd, famish'd, ridiculed'd—curse them and their spiritless pro-

tectors, and let's conclude with huzzas for America.

(pp. 166-67)

[*The Ladies of Castile* and *The Sack of Rome*] focus upon the conflict between love and duty, virtue and corruption, responsibility and ambition. Both contain introductions which anticipate the rather gender-conscious, semi-apologetic way Warren would twenty years later introduce her history. *The Ladies of Castile,* the first of the two tragedies, concerns the tyrannical successors of Charles V in Spain; however, it begins with unadulterated praise of the uniqueness of the newly created United States:

America stands alone:—May she long stand, independent of every foreign policy; superior to the spirit of intrigue, or the corrupt principles of usurpation that may spring from successful exertions of her own sons ... whose valour completed a revolution that will be the wonder of the ages. What a field day for genius: What a difference of capacity ... in science, in business, and in politics does this revolution exhibit! Certain enough to fire the ambition, and light every noble spark in the bosoms of those who are in the morning of life....

In spite of these confident words, Warren apologized because *The Ladies of Castile* was a dramatic poem rather than an epic, saying that "the candor of the public will be exercised not so much for the sake of the sex, as the design of the writer, who wishes only to cultivate the sentiments of public and private virtue in whatsoever falls from her pen." ... *The Sack of Rome* begins more pessimistically, focusing on the intrigues of the Roman court under Petronius Maximus. Here, Warren claims that her aim is to improve morals in the United States "by an exhibition of the tumult and misery into which mankind are often plunged by an unwarrantable indulgence of the discordant passion of the human mind." She asks to be forgiven if the play is distasteful, and in an epilogue she describes herself as a "female bard" asking the public for a "candid eye." ...

Between the writing of these two dramatic poems Warren's evaluation of the American Revolution changed as did perhaps her estimation of herself. She seems more self-assertive and desirous of public approval in the second tragedy. Both poems have stronger female characters than her previous play, even though the most virtuous women are doomed to suffer and often die with their virtuous fathers, husbands, lovers, brothers, or sons. Nonetheless, strong women emerge in the two poems, and both end with either death scene statements by or about them. Thus, *The Ladies of Castile* concludes with the words: "To virtue bend the wayward mind of men," which *The Sack of Rome* echoes with "[v]irtue, sublim'd by piety and truth, now beckons to the skies." ... (pp. 169, 171)

The opinions expressed in *Observations* certainly correspond to the political and ideological stance taken by Warren in her previous literary works and in her unfinished *History.* The author calls the Constitution a degradation and views loss of liberty as the probable consequence of ratification. After reiterating the Lockian doctrines regarding sovereignty and inalienable rights, the author warns that the new document may promote tyranny and points out critical omissions from the Constitution.

The author noted the lack of provisions for direct annual elections, freedom of the press, clear separation of executive and legislative power as well as a bill of rights. Equally important, certain provisions in the document seemed dangerous. Included in the list of objectionable provisions are the power over a standing army given to the President, the elimination of state resources for taxation, the appellate jurisdiction given to the Supreme Court, the excessive length of the term of office for Senators, and the power of the Electoral College to take freedom of choice from the people. Finally, the author questions the practicality of the Constitution, arguing that the United States is too large to be governed by one legislative body. The legality of the Constitution is also questioned with the author charging that the Constitutional Convention went beyond its authorized duties. In conclusion, the author points out that the mode of ratification appeared to deny the people enough time for reasonable consideration of the new document and objects as well to the provision which stipulated ratification by only nine states before becoming effective. . . . (pp. 171-72)

From our vantage point it is easy to see in Warren a precursor of the late nineteenth-century historian Frederick Jackson Turner who developed the "Frontier Thesis." In 1779, long before she composed her *History,* she had written Abigail Adams about the United States with sentiments very similar to those made famous by Turner:

> America is a theatre just erected—the drama is here but begun, while the actors of the old world have run through every species of pride, luxury, venality, and vice—their characters will become less interesting, and the western wilds which for ages have been little known, may exhibit those striking traits of wisdom, and grandeur and magnificence, which the Divine economist may have reserved to crown the closing scene.

From this letter and her other writings it is clear that Warren, like Turner a century later, saw America as distinctly different from European society and attributed the democratic principles evident in the emerging American society to the equality of conditions which existed on this continent, especially on the frontier. She warned her readers that freedom may be lost as it was in other democratic experiments and urged them to oppose the Constitutional provision of a standing army. More idealistically, she called for the conquest of poverty, end of servility, and respect for the dignity of native Americans.

Although Warren concentrated upon the divine plan for humankind and the religious aspects surrounding both the Revolution and the formation of the new nation, she also emphasized a unifying patriotic theme. In this way, she thought she had provided the vehicle by which Americans could gain a sense of their nationality through a common history and tradition, despite her serious doubts about the conservative nature and undemocratic potential of the Constitution of 1787. She almost succeeded in synthesizing two basic ideas—republicanism in the national character and the special destiny of the nation—into a portrayal of not only a new nation, but a new society. She failed in this attempt because of her commitment to radical republicanism, natural rights, and the essential equality of human beings. This persistent commitment to individualism ultimately contradicted her patriotic appeal to national unity. (pp. 173-74)

Warren's insistence on the rights of individuals was out of step with the times, however in tune it may be with the present. She advocated individuality and humane treatment of native

Americans, for example, at the expense of western expansion. . . . No wonder her *History* so quickly became obsolete for those Anglos interested in conquering the continent. Thus, she prophetically wrote:

> But if the lust of domination, which takes hold of the ambitious and the powerful in all ages and nations, should be indulged by the authority of the United States, and those simple tribes of men, contented with the gifts of nature, that had filled their forests with game sufficient for their subsistence, should be invaded, it will probably be a source of most cruel warfare and bloodshed, until the extermination of the original possessors (III, 206).

Warren's *History of the Rise, Progress and Termination of the American Revolution* is the work of a keen mind and a painstaking scholar, but it is neither a brilliant nor an astute historical document. She never perceived the modern political system that evolved from the Revolution; nor did she accept the vision of a pluralist society developed by James Madison in *Federalist Papers,* Number 10, during the fight over the Constitution of 1787. It is ironic that John Adams was to accuse her of having written for the nineteenth century; if anything, her belief in virtue and conviction that God or Providence had used the American experiment to further His ultimate plan for humankind seems closer to that of the seventeenth century. Accepting the Lockian concept that men are created equal in nature as well as in the sight of God, she believed that each man must search his inner being, overcome selfishness and act in accordance with God's will. She viewed the Revolution as a defense of divinely inspired principles that Americans had discovered and practiced through their colonial experience. That other countries had learned from the American example and instigated their own revolutions was evidence of the success of God's plan. (pp. 174-75)

Fortunately, the letters which passed between John Adams and Warren have survived, for from them we get the full impact of her formidable and independent mind. (p. 175)

Her *History,* although of historical interest because it preserves an eighteenth-century critique of Federalism, is remarkable principally because it was written by a woman at a time when it was necessary to justify interest in politics and history on the part of a woman. It was in her private correspondence with John Adams that she revealed the wit and sense of self which make her of interest today. (p. 179)

> *Joan Hoff Wilson and Sharon L. Bollinger, "Mercy Otis Warren: Playwright, Poet, and Historian of the American Revolution,"* in Female Scholars: A Tradition of Learned Women before 1800, *edited by J. R. Brink, Eden Press Women's Publications, 1980, 161-82.*

ADDITIONAL BIBLIOGRAPHY

Anthony, Katharine. *First Lady of the Revolution: The Life of Mercy Otis Warren.* Garden City, N.Y.: Doubleday & Co., 1958, 258 p.
  A biography stressing Warren's public and political influence.

Anticaglia, Elizabeth. "Mercy Otis Warren." In her *Twelve American Women,* pp. 17-36. Chicago: Nelson-Hall, 1975.

A general biographical sketch. Anticaglia comments briefly on Warren's writings, noting the influence of Pope, Dryden, and Molière.

Cohen, Lester H. "Mercy Otis Warren: The Politics of Language and the Aesthetics of Self." *American Quarterly* 35, No. 25 (Winter 1983): 481-98.

Examines the notion of a "politics of language" through a close analysis of Warren's language and thought. Cohen suggests that the "republican idiom" ultimately restricted Warren because its outdated language accommodated neither her growing feminism nor what she saw as the failures of republicanism.

Franklin, Benjamin, V. Introduction to *The Plays and Poems of Mercy Otis Warren*, by Mercy Otis Warren, pp. vii-xxx. Edited by Benjamin Franklin V. Delmar, N.Y.: Scholars' Facsimiles & Reprints, 1980.

Includes individual sketches on Warren's five dramas and commentary on *Poems*. Franklin details publication histories and provides plot summaries for each of the plays. In addition, he comments on Warren's literary technique and accomplishments and argues for her authorship of *The Blockheads* and *The Motley Assembly*.

Fritz, Jean. *Cast for a Revolution: Some American Friends and Enemies, 1728-1814.* Boston: Houghton Mifflin Co., 1972, 400 p.*

A "collective biography" of Warren and her circle, including James Warren, James Otis, John Hancock, and John, Abigail, and Samuel Adams. Warren herself is the central figure, however, in this vivid portrayal of the patriots' lives and times.

Gardiner, C. Harvey, ed. *A Study in Dissent: The Warren-Gerry Correspondence, 1776-1792.* Carbondale and Edwardsville: Southern Illinois University Press, 1968, 269 p.

A collection of correspondence between James and Mercy Warren and Elbridge Gerry, the Massachusetts patriot and politician. The letters deal primarily with the establishment of the state of Massachusetts and the United States government. Gardiner provides a detailed introduction and extensive commentary.

Hayes, Edmund M. "The Private Poems of Mercy Otis Warren." *New England Quarterly* 54, No. 2 (June 1981): 199-224.

A brief discussion of the religious attitudes expressed in Warren's "private" poems, first published here.

Jensen, Merrill. "Historians and the Nature of the American Revolution." In *The Reinterpretation of Early American History: Essays in Honor of John Edwin Pomfret*, edited by Ray Allen Billington, pp. 101-27. San Marino, Calif.: Huntington Library, 1966.*

Compares Warren's historical approach and perceptions with those of other early American historians.

Philbrick, Norman, ed. *Trumpets Sounding: Propaganda Plays of the American Revolution.* New York: Benjamin Blom, 1972, 367 p.*

An anthology of seven propaganda plays of the American Revolution, including *The Blockheads* and *The Motley Assembly*. In separate introductions to the two plays, Philbrick presents extensive evidence that Warren indeed wrote them, although he concludes that authorship of *The Blockheads* must remain a matter of conjecture.

Smith, William Raymond. *History as Argument: Three Patriot Historians of the American Revolution*, Studies in American History, Vol. V. The Hague: Mouton & Co., 1966, 207 p.*

Explores the "extreme republicanism" of Warren's *History* and compares it with the works of her contemporaries, the historians David Ramsay and John Marshall.

Teunissen, John J. "Blockheadism and the Propaganda Plays of the American Revolution." *Early American Literature* VII, No. 2 (Fall 1972): 148-62.*

Discusses anti-Tory propaganda in Jonathan Sewall's *A Cure for the Spleen* and *The Blockheads*, which the critic fully accepts as Warren's work.

Warren, Charles. "Elbridge Gerry, James Warren, Mercy Warren, and the Ratification of the Federal Constitution in Massachusetts." In *Massachusetts Historical Society Proceedings: October, 1930-June, 1932*, Vol. LXIV, pp. 143-64. Boston: Massachusetts Historical Society, 1932.

Establishes Warren as the author of the pamphlet *Observations on the New Constitution*, which had been previously attributed to Elbridge Gerry. The critic also includes several letters by Warren on the subject of the constitution, notably a lengthy one to her friend, the English historian Catherine Macaulay.

Weales, Gerald. "The Quality of Mercy, or Mrs. Warren's Profession." *Georgia Review* 33, No. 4 (Winter 1979): 881-94.

An informative biographical essay emphasizing Warren's commitment to writing. Weales states that her most enduring works are the prose pieces: the *History, Observations on the New Constitution,* and her letters. But he asserts that in all her works one can glimpse beneath the artificial eighteenth-century style the "urgent intelligence, the passionate morality, the human vulnerability . . . behind the fine words and borrowed conceits."

———. "*The Adulateur* and How It Grew." *Library Chronicle* XLIII, No. 2 (Winter 1979): 103-33.

A detailed, nearly scene-by-scene reading of *The Adulateur*. Comparing the original newspaper version of the play with the expanded pamphlet version of 1773, Weales attempts to locate which scenes were written by Warren and which by her anonymous collaborator, concluding that the play is the "product of several hands." The critic also relates the characters and action of the play to contemporary figures and events.

Appendix

The following is a listing of all sources used in Volume 13 of *Nineteenth-Century Literature Criticism*. Included in this list are all copyright and reprint rights and acknowledgments for those essays for which permission was obtained. Every effort has been made to trace copyright, but if omissions have been made, please let us know.

THE EXCERPTS IN NCLC, VOLUME 13, WERE REPRINTED FROM THE FOLLOWING PERIODICALS:

The Academy, n.s. n. 135, December 5, 1874; v. LI, June 19, 1897.

Albion, v. 4, Spring, 1972. © Appalachian State University 1972. Reprinted by permission.

The American Literary Magazine, v. II, May, 1848.

The American Magazine, n. 4, March, 1788; n. 8, July, 1788.

American Quarterly Review, v. 22, September, 1837.

The Analytical Review, April, 1789.

The Anti-Jacobin Review and Magazine, v. XXXI, November, 1808.

The Athenaeum, n. 340, May 3, 1834; n. 626, October 26, 1839.

Atkinson's Casket, v. VII, October, 1832.

The Atlantic Monthly, v. XXXVI, December, 1875.

Blackwood's Edinburgh Magazine, v. CVII, March, 1870; v. CXII, December, 1872.

Blackwood's Magazine, v. LXXXVII, March, 1860.

The Bookman, New York, v. XVI, February, 1903; v. LXIX, May, 1929.

Brighton Guardian, November 14, 1855; November 28, 1855.

Brighton Herald, November 17, 1855.

The British Critic, v. XXVIII, September, 1806.

The British Quarterly Review, v. LVII, April 1, 1873.

The Christian Spectator, v. IV, March, 1822; v. IV, August, 1822.

Comparative Literature, v. XXX, Spring, 1978 for "City Life and the Novel: Hugo, Ainsworth, Dickens" by Richard Maxwell. © copyright 1978 by University of Oregon. Reprinted by permission of the author.

Contemporary Review, v. LXV, February, 1894; v. CLXXXVIII, August, 1955.

Critical Inquiry, v. 3, Spring, 1977 for "The Female as Metaphor in William Blake's Poetry" by Susan Fox. Copyright © 1977 by The University of Chicago. Reprinted by permission of the author.

The Critical Review, n.s. v. III, March, 1813.

The Dublin Magazine, n.s. v. XXI, July-September, 1946.

The Dublin University Magazine, v. LIV, September, 1859.

The Edinburgh Review, v. XLIII, February, 1826; v. LII, January, 1831; v. LXV, April, 1837.

Éire-Ireland, v. XVII, Spring, 1982. Copyright Irish American Cultural Institute. Reprinted by permission.

ELH, v. 41, Fall, 1974. Reprinted by permission.

Essays and Studies, v. II, 1911.

The European Magazine, and London Review, v. XIII, February and April, 1788.

The Examiner, n. 90, September 17, 1809; n. 1372, May 18, 1834; n. 1657, November 3, 1839; n. 1691, June 28, 1840; n. 1693, July 12, 1840.

The Foreign Review, v. IV, 1829.

The Fortnightly Review, n.s. v. XIII, January 1, 1873; v. LXXXIII, March 1, 1905.

Fraser's Magazine, v. IX, June, 1834; v. XIII, April, 1836; v. XIV, December, 1836; v. XXI, February, 1840.

The Gentleman's Magazine and Historical Chronicle, v. XCV, July, 1825.

Hampstead Annual, 1903.

The Irish Monthly, v. LVIII, July, 1930.

The Irish Quarterly Review, v. XV, December, 1854; v. V, March, 1855; v. V, June, 1855; v. V, December, 1855.

The Kenyon Review, v. XVIII, Winter, 1956 for "Pride Unprejudiced" by Mark Schorer. Copyright 1956 by Kenyon College. Renewed 1984 by Ruth Page Schorer. All rights reserved. Reprinted by permission of the Literary Estate of Mark Schorer.

The Library, n.s. v. V, July, 1914.

The Literary Gazette, London, n. 1187, October 19, 1839.

The Literary Journal, n.s. v. II, July, 1806.

The London Magazine, n.s. v. III, September, 1825; n.s. v. VII, January 1, 1827.

The London Quarterly Review, v. XLVII, January, 1877.

London University Magazine, v. II, March, 1830.

The Massachusetts Review, v. XIII, Winter & Spring, 1972. © 1972. Reprinted from *The Massachusetts Review,* The Massachusetts Review, Inc. by permission.

Modern Philology, v. 9, January, 1912.

The Monthly Chronicle, v. V, January, 1840.

The Monthly Review, London, v. VI, December, 1791; v. IV, January, 1827; v. 1, January, 1837.

The Nation, v. XVI, January 30, 1873.

The New England Magazine, n.s. v. XXVIII, April, 1903.

The New England Quarterly, v. 48, June, 1975 for "Mercy Otis Warren and the Politics of Historical Nationalism" by Lawrence J. Friedman and Arthur H. Shaffer; v. LXIX, September, 1976 for "Mercy Otis Warren: 'The Defeat'" by Edmund M. Hayes. Copyright 1975, 1976 by *The New England Quarterly*. Both reprinted by permission of the publisher and the respective authors.

The New Statesman & Nation, v. XXXVI, November 27, 1943.

Nineteenth-Century Fiction, v. 15, June, 1960 for "Narrative Perspective in 'Pride and Prejudice'" by E. M. Halliday; v. 16, December, 1961 for "A Major Thematic Pattern in 'Pride and Prejudice'" by Mordecai Marcus; v. 19, June, 1964 for "Setting and Character in 'Pride and Prejudice'" by Charles J. McCann; v. 35, September, 1980 for a review of "Tales by the O'Hara Family" and others by Robert Tracy. © 1960, 1961, 1964, 1980 by The Regents of the University of California. All reprinted by permission of The Regents and the respective authors.

The North American Review, v. VII, September, 1818.

Once a Week, n.s. v. X, November 30, 1872.

The Papers of the Bibliographical Society of America, v. 67, fourth quarter, 1973 for "The Imitators and the Imitated: Scott, Ainsworth, and the Critics" by Llewellyn Ligocki. Copyright 1973 by the Bibliographical Society of America. Reprinted by permission of the publisher and the author.

PMLA 10, v. X, 1895.

Research Studies, v. 43, September, 1975 for "William Harrison Ainsworth as Novelist-Historian" by Llewellyn Ligocki. Reprinted by permission of the author.

The Saturday Review, London, v. 34, December 7, 1872.

The Sewanee Review, v. LXIV, Autumn, 1956. © 1956, renewed 1984, by The University of the South. Reprinted by permission of the editor of *The Sewanee Review*.

The Spectator, v. 63, November 21, 1863.

Tait's Edinburgh Magazine, v. IX, July, 1842.

The Times, London, September 2, 1840.

University of Toronto Quarterly, v. XVI, July, 1947.

William and Mary Quarterly, third series, v. 37, April, 1980 for "Explaining the Revolution: Ideology and Ethics in Mercy Otis Warren's Historical Theory" by Lester H. Cohen. Copyright, 1980, by the Institute of Early American History and Culture. Reprinted by permission of the author./ third series, v. X, July, 1953. Copyright, 1953, renewed 1981, by the Institute of Early American History and Culture. Reprinted by permission of the Institute.

Women & Literature, n.s. v. 3, 1983. Copyright © 1983 by Holmes & Meiers Publishers, Inc. All rights reserved. Reprinted by permission.

THE EXCERPTS IN NCLC, VOLUME 13, WERE REPRINTED FROM THE FOLLOWING BOOKS.

Adams, Hazard. From *William Blake: A Reading of the Shorter Poems*. University of Washington Press, 1963. Copyright © 1963 by the University of Washington Press. Reprinted by permission.

Adams, John. From a letter in *Mercy Warren*. By Alice Brown. Charles Scribner's Sons, 1896.

Adams, Robert Martin. From *Nil: Episodes in the Literary Conquest of Void During the Nineteenth Century*. Oxford University Press, 1966. Copyright © 1966 by Robert Martin Adams. Reprinted by permission of Oxford University Press, Inc.

Addison, Daniel Dulany. From *The Clergy in American Life and Letters*. The Macmillan Company, 1900.

Ainsworth, William Harrison. From *Rookwood*. G. Routledge & Co., 1853.

Anderson, Quentin. From ''George Eliot in 'Middlemarch','' in *From Dickens to Hardy*. Edited by Boris Ford. Revised edition. Penguin Books, 1960. Copyright © Penguin Books Ltd., 1958. Reproduced by permission of Penguin Books Ltd.

Arner, Robert D. From ''The Connecticut Wits,'' in *American Literature, 1764-1789: The Revolutionary Years*. Edited by Everett Emerson. The University of Wisconsin Press, 1977. Copyright © 1977 The Regents of the University of Wisconsin System. All rights reserved. Reprinted by permission.

Austen, Jane. From *Letters of Jane Austen*. Edited by Lord Edward Brabourne. R. Bentley & Son, 1884.

Austen, Jane. From a letter in *A Memoir of Jane Austen*. By James Edward Austen-Leigh. N.p., 1870.

Baldwin, James, Frank O'Connor, and Lyman Bryson. From ''Jane Austen, 'Pride and Prejudice','' in *The Invitation to Learning Reader: The Individual & Society*. Edited by Ralph Backlund. Herbert Muschel, 1955.

Barth, Karl. From *Protestant Theology in the Nineteenth Century: Its Background & History*. Judson Press, 1972, SCM Press, 1972. © SCM Press Ltd 1959, 1972. Reprinted by permission of Judson Press. In Canada by SCM Press Ltd.

Bennett, Joan. From *George Eliot: Her Mind and Her Art*. Cambridge University Press, 1948.

Bentzon, Thérèse. From ''Contemporary Reviews: 'Middlemarch' '' in *George Eliot, Middlemarch: A Casebook*. Edited by Patrick Swinden. Macmillan, 1972. Selection and editorial matter © Patrick Swinden 1972. All rights reserved. Reprinted by permission of Macmillan, London and Basingstoke.

Birch, Una. From ''Novalis: The Author,'' in *The Disciples at Saïs and Other Fragments*. By Novalis, edited by Una Birch, translated by F.V.M.T. and U.C.B. Methuen & Co., 1903.

Blackstone, Bernard. From *English Blake*. Cambridge at the University Press, 1949.

Blackwood, John. From a letter in *The George Eliot Letters, 1869-1873, Vol. V*. Edited by Gordon S. Haight. Yale University Press, 1955. Copyright, 1955, by Yale University Press. Renewed 1983 by Gordon S. Haight. All rights reserved. Reprinted by permission of the Literary Estate of Gordon S. Haight.

Blake, Kathleen. From *Love and the Woman Question in Victorian Literature: The Art of Self-Postponement*. Barnes & Noble, 1983. © Kathleen Blake, 1983. All rights reserved. By permission of Barnes & Noble Books, a Division of Littlefield, Adams & Co., Inc.

Blake, William. From *A Descriptive Catalogue of Pictures: Poetical and Historical Inventions*. J. Blake, 1809.

Blake, William. From *Jerusalem: The Emanation of The Great Albion*. W. Blake, 1804-1820?

Blake, William. From a letter in *Life of William Blake*. By Alexander Gilchrist. Revised edition. Macmillan and Co., 1880.

Blake, William. From marginalia comments in *The Works of Sir Joshua Reynolds, Knight*. By Sir Joshua Reynolds, edited by Edmond Malone. N.p., 1808?

Bloom, Harold. From *Blake's Apocalypse: A Study in Poetic Argument*. Doubleday, 1963. Copyright © 1963 by Harold Bloom. All rights reserved. Reprinted by permission of Doubleday & Company, Inc.

Bottrall, Margaret. From *The Divine Image: A Study of Blake's Interpretation of Christianity*. Edizioni di Storia e Letteratura, 1950.

Brandes, George. From *Main Currents in Nineteenth Century Literature: The Romantic School in Germany, Vol. II*. Translated by Diana White and Mary Morison. William Heinemann, 1902.

Brontë, Charlotte. From a letter in *The Brontës: Life and Letters, Vol. I*. By Clement Shorter. Hodder and Stoughton, 1908.

Brown, Alice. From *Mercy Warren*. Charles Scribner's Sons, 1896.

Butler, Marilyn. From *Jane Austen and the War of Ideas*. Oxford at the Clarendon Press, Oxford, 1975. © Oxford University Press, 1975. All rights reserved. Reprinted by permission of Oxford University Press.

Butler, Samuel. From *Letters between Samuel Butler and Miss E.M.A. Savage, 1871-1885*. Edited by Geoffrey Keynes and Brian Hill. Jonathan Cape, 1935.

Cahalan, James M. From *Great Hatred, Little Room: The Irish Historical Novel*. Syracuse University Press, 1983. Copyright © 1983 by James M. Cahalan. All rights reserved. Reprinted by permission.

Chase, Karen. From *Eros & Psyche: The Representation of Personality in Charlotte Brontë, Charles Dickens, and George Eliot*. Methuen, 1984. © 1984 Karen Chase. All rights reserved. Reprinted by permission of Methuen & Co. Ltd.

Closs, August. From an introduction to *Hymns to the Night*. By Novalis, translated by Mabel Cotterell. Phoenix Press, 1948. Reprinted by permission.

Coleridge, Samuel Taylor. From *Collected Letters of Samuel Taylor Coleridge: 1815-1819, Vol. V*. Edited by Earl Leslie Griggs. Oxford at the Clarendon Press, Oxford, 1959. © Oxford University Press 1959. Reprinted by permission of Oxford University Press.

Cronin, John. From *The Anglo-Irish Novel: The Nineteenth Century, Vol. 1*. Barnes & Noble, 1980. Copyright © John Cronin, 1980. All rights reserved. By permission of Barnes & Noble Books, a Division of Littlefield, Adams & Co., Inc.

Cross, J. W. *George Eliot's Life as Related in Her Letters and Journals: Sunset, Vol. III*. William Blackwood and Sons, 1885.

Cunningham, Allan. From *Biographical and Critical History of the British Literature of the Last Fifty Years*. Baudry's Foreign Library, 1834.

Daiches, David. From *George Eliot: "Middlemarch."* Edward Arnold (Publishers) Ltd., 1963. © David Daiches 1963. Reprinted by permission of the author.

Damon, S. Foster. From *William Blake: His Philosophy and Symbols*. Houghton Mifflin Company, 1924.

Damrosch, Leopold, Jr. From *Symbol and Truth in Blake's Myth*. Princeton University Press, 1980. Copyright © 1980 by Princeton University Press. All rights reserved. Excerpts reprinted with permission of Princeton University Press.

Duckworth, Alistair M. From *The Improvement of the Estate: A Study of Jane Austen's Novels*. The Johns Hopkins University Press, 1971. Copyright © 1971 by The Johns Hopkins Press. All rights reserved. Reprinted by permission.

Dwight, Timothy. From *The Conquest of Canäan: A Poem*. N.p., 1785.

Dwight, Timothy. From *Greenfield Hill: A Poem*. N.p., 1794.

Dwight, Timothy. From *Travels in New England and New York, Vol. I*. Timothy Dwight, 1821.

Eliot, George. From *Middlemarch: A Study of Provincial Life, Vol. I*. William Blackwood and Sons, 1871.

Ellet, Elizabeth F. From *The Women of the American Revolution, Vol. I*. Second edition. Baker and Scribner, 1848.

Ellis, Edwin John, and William Butler Yeats. From *The Works of William Blake, Vols. I and II*. By William Blake, edited by Edwin John Ellis and William Butler Yeats. Bernard Quaritch, 1893.

Elton, Oliver. From *A Survey of English Literature: 1830-1880, Vol. II*. Edward Arnold, 1920.

Elwin, Malcolm. From *Victorian Wallflowers: A Panoramic Survey of the Popular Literary Periodicals*. Jonathan Cape, 1934.

Emerson, Ralph Waldo. From *The Journals and Miscellaneous Notebooks of Ralph Waldo Emerson: 1832-1834, Vol. IV*. Edited by Alfred R. Ferguson. Cambridge, Mass.: Belknap Press, 1964. Copyright © 1964 by the President and Fellows of Harvard College. All rights reserved. Excerpted by permission.

Erdman, David V. From *Blake, Prophet against Empire: A Poet's Interpretation of the History of His Own Times.* Revised edition. Princeton University Press, 1969. Copyright © 1954, 1969 by Princeton University Press. All rights reserved. Excerpts reprinted by permission of the publisher.

Fitzgerald, Edward. From *Letters and Literary Remains of Edward Fitzgerald, Vol. I.* Edited by William Aldis Wright. Macmillan and Co., 1889.

Flanagan, Thomas. From *The Irish Novelists, 1800-1850.* Columbia University Press, 1959. Copyright © 1958, Columbia University Press. Reprinted by permission of the author.

Forstman, Jack. From *A Romantic Triangle: Schleiermacher and Early German Romanticism.* Scholars Press, 1977. Copyright © 1977 by The American Academy of Religion. Reprinted by permission.

Friswell, J. Hain. From *Modern Men of Letters Honestly Criticised.* Hodder and Stoughton, 1870.

Frye, Northrop. From *Fearful Symmetry: A Study of William Blake.* Princeton University Press, 1947. Copyright 1947, © 1975 renewed by Princeton University Press. Excerpts reprinted with permission of Princeton University Press.

Gifford, William. From an extract of a letter in *A Publisher and His Friends: Memoir and Correspondence of the Late John Murray, Vol. I.* By Samuel Smiles. Charles Scribner's Sons, 1891.

Gilchrist, Alexander. From *Life of William Blake, "Pictor Ignotus."* Macmillan and Company, 1863.

Gleckner, Robert F. From *The Piper & the Bard: A Study of William Blake.* Wayne State University Press, 1959. Copyright © 1959 by Wayne State University Press. All rights reserved. Reprinted by permission of the Wayne State University Press and the author.

Gosse, Edmund. From *Aspects and Impressions.* Cassell and Company, Ltd, 1922.

Griswold, Rufus Wilmot. From *The Female Poets of America.* Revised edition. James Miller, Publisher, 1873.

Hamburger, Michael. From *Contraries: Studies in German Literature.* E. P. Dutton & Co., Inc., 1970. Copyright © 1957, 1965, 1970 by Michael Hamburger. All rights reserved. Reprinted by permission of the author. Published in Britain as *Reason and Energy: Studies in German Literature.* Revised edition. Weidenfeld & Nicolson, 1970.

Hardy, Barbara. From *The Appropriate Form: An Essay on the Novel.* The Athlone Press, 1964. © Barbara Hardy, 1964. Reprinted by permission.

Hardy, Barbara. From *The Novels of George Eliot: A Study in Form.* The Athlone Press, 1959. © Barbara Hardy, 1959, 1963. Reprinted by permission.

Harvey, W. J. From *Middlemarch.* By George Eliot, edited by W. J. Harvey. Penguin Books, 1965. Introduction and notes copyright © the Estate of W. J. Harvey, 1965. All rights reserved. Reproduced by permission of Penguin Books Ltd.

Hawthorne, Mark D. From *John and Michael Banim (The "O'Hara Brothers"): A Study in the Early Development of the Anglo-Irish Novel.* Institut für Englische Sprache und Literatur, Universität Salzburg, 1975. Reprinted by permission.

Haywood, Bruce. From *Novalis, the Veil of Imagery: A Study of the Poetic Works of Friedrich von Hardenberg (1772-1801).* Cambridge, Mass.: Harvard University Press, 1959. Copyright © 1959 by the President and Fellows of Harvard College. Excerpted by permission.

Hesse, Hermann. From *My Belief: Essays on Life and Art.* Edited by Theodore Ziolkowski, translated by Denver Lindley. Farrar, Straus and Giroux, 1974. Translation copyright © 1974 by Farrar, Straus and Giroux, Inc. All rights reserved. Reprinted by permission of Farrar, Straus and Giroux, Inc.

Hollingsworth, Keith. From *The Newgate Novel, 1830-1847: Bulwer, Ainsworth, Dickens, & Thackeray.* Wayne State University Press, 1963. Copyright © 1963 by Wayne State University Press, Detroit 2, MI. All rights reserved. Reprinted by permission of the Wayne State University Press and the Literary Estate of Keith Hollingsworth.

Holloway, John. From *Blake: The Lyric Poetry.* Edward Arnold (Publishers) Ltd., 1968. © John Holloway 1968. Reprinted by permission of the author.

Horne, R. H. From *A New Spirit of the Age, Vol. II.* Smith, Elder and Co., 1844.

Howard, Leon. From *The Connecticut Wits.* University of Chicago Press, 1943. Copyright 1943 by The University of Chicago. Renewed 1971 by Leon Howard. All rights reserved.

Howells, W. D. From *Heroines of Fiction, Vol. II*. Harper & Brothers Publishers, 1901.

Hulme, Hilda M. From "The Language of the Novel: Imagery," in *"Middlemarch": Critical Approaches to the Novel*. Edited by Barbara Hardy. Athlone Press, 1967. © 1967 University of London The Athlone Press 1967. Reprinted by permission.

Japp, Alexander Hay. From *German Life and Literature in a Series of Biographical Studies*. Marshall Japp & Company, 1880.

Jenkins, Elizabeth. From *Jane Austen: A Biography*. Victor Gollancz Ltd., 1938.

Joline, Adrian Hoffman. From *At the Library Table*. The Gorham Press, 1910.

Kettle, Arnold. From *An Introduction to the English Novel: To George Eliot, Vol. I*. Hutchinson's University Library, 1951.

Knoepflmacher, U. C. From "Fusing Fact and Myth: The New Reality of 'Middlemarch'," in *This Particular Web: Essays on "Middlemarch."* Edited by Ian Adam. University of Toronto Press, 1975. © University of Toronto Press 1975. Reprinted by permission.

Krans, Horatio Sheafe. From *Irish Life in Irish Fiction*. The Columbia University Press, 1903.

Kraus, Michael. From *A History of American History*. Farrar & Rinehart, Inc., 1937. Copyright, 1937, renewed 1964, by Michael Kraus. All rights reserved. Reprinted by permission of the author.

Lamb, Charles. From *The Letters of Charles Lamb, Vol. II*. Edited by Alfred Ainger. A. C. Armstrong & Son, 1888.

Landor, Walter Savage. From *Walter Savage Landor, a Biography: 1821-1864, Vol. 2*. By John Forster. Chapman & Hall, 1869.

Lascelles, Mary. From *Jane Austen and Her Art*. Oxford University Press, London, 1939.

Lewes, M. E. From a letter in *George Eliot's Life as Related in Her Letters and Journals*. Edited by J. W. Cross. Revised edition. W. Blackwood and Sons, 1886.

Lewes, M. E. From a letter in *George Eliot's Life as Related in Her Letters and Journals, Vol. III*. Edited by J. W. Cross. W. Blackwood and Sons, 1885.

Litz, A. Walton. From *Jane Austen: A Study of Her Artistic Development*. Oxford University Press, 1965. Copyright © 1965 by A. Walton Litz. Reprinted by permission of Oxford University Press, Inc.

Lukács, Georg. From *The Theory of the Novel: A Historico-Philosophical Essay on the Forms of Great Epic Literature*. Translated by Anna Bostock. MIT Press, 1971. © Hermann Luchterhand Verlag GmbH, 1963. Translation © The Merlin Press, 1971. Reprinted by permission of The MIT Press, Cambridge, MA.

Maeterlinck, Maurice. From *On Emerson and Other Essays*. Translated by Montrose J. Moses. Dodd, Mead and Company, 1912.

Maugham, W. Somerset. From *The Art of Fiction: An Introduction to Ten Novels and Their Authors*. Doubleday, 1955. Copyright, 1948, 1954, by W. Somerset Maugham. All rights reserved. Reprinted by permission of Doubleday & Company, Inc. In Canada by A. P. Watt Ltd. on behalf of The Royal Literary Fund.

McGann, Jerome J. From "The Aim of Blake's Prophecies and the Uses of Blake Criticism," in *Blake's Sublime Allegory: Essays on the Four Zoas, Milton, Jerusalem*. Edited by Stuart Curran and Joseph Anthony Wittreich, Jr. The University of Wisconsin Press, 1973. Copyright © 1973 the Regents of the University of Wisconsin System. All rights reserved. Reprinted by permission.

Meserve, Walter J. From *An Emerging Entertainment: The Drama of the American People to 1828*. Indiana University Press, 1977. Copyright © 1977 by Indiana University Press. All rights reserved. Reprinted by permission.

Milbanke, Anne Isabella. From an extract of a letter in *Lord Byron's Wife*. By Malcolm Elwin. Harcourt, Brace & World, 1963. © Malcolm Elwin 1962. Reprinted by permission of the Literary Estate of Malcolm Elwin.

Millett, Kate. From *Sexual Politics*. Doubleday, 1970. Copyright © 1969, 1970 by Kate Millett. All rights reserved. Reprinted by permission of Doubleday & Company, Inc.

Mintz, Alan. From *George Eliot & the Novel of Vocation*. Cambridge, Mass.: Harvard University Press, 1978. Copyright © 1978 by the President and Fellows of Harvard College. All rights reserved. Excerpted by permission.

Mitford, Mary Russell. From *The Life of Mary Russell Mitford, Told by Herself in Letters to Her Friends, Vol. I*. Edited by Rev. A.G.K. L'Estrange. Harper & Brothers, Publishers, 1870.

Mitford, Mary Russell. From *Recollections of a Literary Life; or, Books, Places, and People*. Harper & Brothers, Publishers, 1855.

Mudrick, Marvin. From *Jane Austen: Irony as Defense and Discovery*. Princeton University Press, 1952. Copyright, 1952, by Princeton University Press. Renewed 1980 by Marvin Mudrick. Reprinted by permission of the author.

Murry, John Middleton. From *William Blake*. Jonathan Cape, 1933.

Neubauer, John. From *Novalis*. Twayne, 1980. Copyright 1980 by Twayne Publishers. All rights reserved. Reprinted with the permission of Twayne Publishers, a division of G. K. Hall & Co., Boston.

Newton, K. M. From *George Eliot, Romantic Humanist: A Study of the Philosophical Structure of Her Novels*. Barnes & Noble, 1981. © K. M. Newton 1981. All rights reserved. By permission of Barnes & Noble Books, a Division of Littlefield, Adams & Co., Inc.

Oldfield, Derek. From "The Language of the Novel: The Character of Dorothea," in *"Middlemarch": Critical Approaches to the Novel*. Edited by Barbara Hardy. Athlone Press, 1967. © University of London The Athlone Press 1967. Reprinted by permission.

Onderdonk, James L. From *History of American Verse (1610-1897)*. A. C. McClurg & Co., 1901.

Ostriker, Alicia. From *Vision and Verse in William Blake*. The University of Wisconsin Press, 1965. Copyright © 1965 by the Regents of the University of Wisconsin. Reprinted by permission.

Page, Norman. From *The Language of Jane Austen*. Basil Blackwell, 1972. © Basil Blackwell, 1972. All rights reserved. Reprinted by permission.

Parrington, Vernon Louis. From an introduction to *The Connecticut Wits*. Edited by Vernon Louis Parrington. Harcourt Brace Jovanovich, 1926. Copyright, 1926, Harcourt Brace Jovanovich. Copyright renewed, 1954, by Vernon L. Parrington, Louise P. Tucker, Elizabeth P. Thomas.

Peacock, R. From "The Poetry of Novalis," in *German Studies Presented to Professor H. G. Fiedler, M.V.O., by Pupils, Colleagues, and Friends, on His Seventy-fifth Birthday 28 April, 1937*. Oxford at the Clarendon Press, Oxford, 1938.

Quinn, Arthur Hobson. From *A History of the American Drama: From the Beginning to the Civil War*. Second edition. F. S. Crofts & Co., 1943. Copyright 1923, 1943, 1951 by Arthur Hobson Quinn. Copyright renewed © 1970 by Arthur Hobson Quinn, Jr. All rights reserved. Reprinted by permission of Irvington Publishers, Inc. and the Literary Estate of Arthur Hobson Quinn.

Raleigh, Sir Walter. From *The Letters of Sir Walter Raleigh (1879-1922), Vol. II*. Edited by Lady Raleigh. Macmillan Publishing Company, 1926.

Ritchie, J. M. From *Periods in German Literature: Texts and Contexts, Vol. II*. Edited by J. M. Ritchie. Oswald Wolff (Publishers) Ltd, 1969. © 1969 Oswald Wolff (Publishers) Ltd. Reprinted by permission of Berg Publishers Ltd.

Robinson, Henry Crabb. From *Henry Crabb Robinson on Books and Their Writers, Vol. I*. Edited by Edith J. Morley. J. M. Dent and Sons Limited, 1938.

Rossetti, William Michael. From *The Poetical Works of William Blake, Lyrical and Miscellaneous*. By William Blake. Edited by William Michael Rossetti. G. Bell & Sons, 1874.

Saintsbury, George. From *A History of Criticism and Literary Taste in Europe from the Earliest Texts to the Present Day: Modern Criticism, Vol. III*. William Blackwood & Sons Ltd., 1911.

Saintsbury, George. From *A History of English Criticism: Being the English Chapters of a History of Criticism and Literary Taste in Europe*. Revised edition. Dodd, Mead and Company, 1911.

Saintsbury, George. From *A History of Nineteenth Century Literature (1780-1895)*. The Macmillan Company, 1896.

Saintsbury, George. From a preface to *Pride and Prejudice*. By Jane Austen. George Allen, 1894.

Sala, George Augustus. From *The Life and Adventures of George Augustus Sala, Vol. I*. Charles Scribner's Sons, 1895.

Sanders, Andrew. From *The Victorian Historical Novel, 1840-1880*. Macmillan, 1978, St. Martin's Press, 1979. © Andrew Leonard Sanders 1979. All rights reserved. Reprinted by permission of St. Martin's Press, Inc. In Canada by Macmillan, London and Basingstoke.

Schorer, Mark. From *William Blake: The Politics of Vision*. Holt, 1946. Copyright, 1946, by Henry Holt and Company, Inc. Renewed 1974 by Mark Schorer. Reprinted by permission of the Literary Estate of Mark Schorer.

Scott, Sir Walter. From *The Journal of Sir Walter Scott*. Edited by John Guthrie Tait. Revised edition. Oliver and Boyd, 1950.

Scudder, Vida D. From *Social Ideals in English Letters*. Houghton, Mifflin and Company, 1898.

Sensabaugh, George F. From *Milton in Early America*. Princeton University Press, 1964. Copyright © 1964 by Princeton University Press. All rights reserved. Excerpts reprinted with permission of Princeton University Press.

Shaw, Bernard. From *Back to Methuselah: A Metabiological Pentateuch*. Revised edition. Oxford University Press, London, 1946. Copyright 1946 by Oxford University Press, London. Renewed 1974 by The Literary Estate of Bernard Shaw. All rights reserved. Reprinted by permission of the Society of Authors on behalf of the Bernard Shaw Estate.

Silverman, Kenneth. From *Timothy Dwight*. Twayne, 1969. Copyright 1969 by Twayne Publishers. All rights reserved. Reprinted with the permission of Twayne Publishers, a division of G. K. Hall & Co., Boston.

Silz, Walter. From *Early German Romanticism: Its Founders and Henrich von Kleist*. Cambridge, Mass.: Harvard University Press, 1929. Copyright 1929 by the President and Fellows of Harvard College. Renewed 1957 by Walter Silz. Excerpted by permission.

Smith, William Raymond. From *History as Argument: Three Patriot Historians of the American Revolution*. Mouton, 1966. © copyright 1966 Mouton & Co., Publishers. Reprinted by permission of the author.

Southey, Robert. From *Henry Crabb Robinson on Books and Their Writers, Vol. I*. By Henry Crabb Robinson, edited by Edith J. Morley. J. M. Dent and Sons Limited, 1938.

Sprague, William B. From "Life of Timothy Dwight," in *The Library of American Biography: Lives of Roger Williams, Timothy Dwight, and Count Pulaski, Vol. IV, second series*. Edited by Jared Sparks. Charles C. Little and James Brown, 1847.

Stauffer, Donald Barlow. From *A Short History of American Poetry*. Dutton, 1974. Copyright © 1974 by Donald Barlow Stauffer. All rights reserved. Reprinted by permission of the publisher, E. P. Dutton, a division of New American Library.

Stephen, Leslie. From *George Eliot*. Macmillan & Co., Ltd., 1902.

Stump, Reva. From *Movement and Vision in George Eliot's Novels*. University of Washington Press, 1959. © 1959 by the University of Washington Press. Reprinted by permission.

Sutherland, J. A. From *Victorian Novelists and Publishers*. University of Chicago Press, 1976. © 1976 by J. A. Sutherland. All rights reserved. Reprinted by permission of The University of Chicago Press and the author.

Swinburne, Algernon Charles. From *William Blake: A Critical Essay*. J. C. Hotten, 1868.

Swinnerton, Frank. From an introduction to *Rookwood*. By William Harrison Ainsworth. E. P. Dutton & Co., 1931.

Thalmann, Marianne. From *The Romantic Fairy Tale: Seeds of Surrealism*. Translated by Mary B. Corcoran. University of Michigan Press, 1964. Copyright © by The University of Michigan 1964. All rights reserved. Reprinted by permission.

Tichi, Cecelia. From "Worried Celebrants of the American Revolution," in *American Literature, 1764-1789: The Revolutionary Years*. Edited by Everett Emerson. The University of Wisconsin Press, 1977. Copyright © 1977 the Regents of the University of Wisconsin System. All rights reserved. Reprinted by permission.

Twain, Mark. From *Mark Twain, a Biography: The Personal and Literary Remains of Samuel Langhorne Clemens, Vol. III*. By Albert Bigelow Paine. Harper & Brothers Publishers, 1912. Copyright, 1912, by Harper & Brothers. Renewed 1939 by Dora L. Paine. Reprinted by permission of Harper & Row, Publishers, Inc.

Tyler, Moses Coit. From *Three Men of Letters*. G. P. Putnam's Sons, 1895.

Tymms, Ralph. From *German Romantic Literature*. Methuen & Co. Ltd., 1955.

Van Ghent, Dorothy. From *The English Novel: Form and Function*. Holt, Rinehart and Winston, 1953. Copyright 1953, renewed 1981, by Dorothy Van Ghent. Reprinted by permission of the Literary Estate of Dorothy Van Ghent.

Walker, Hugh. From *The Literature of the Victorian Era*. Cambridge at the University Press, 1910.

Washington, George. From a letter to Reverend Timothy Dwight, Junior on March 18, 1778, in *The Writings of George Washington from the Original Manuscript Sources, 1745-1799: March 1, 1778-May 31, 1778, Vol. 11*. By George Washington. Edited by John C. Fitzpatrick. United States Government Printing Office, 1934.

Watts, Emily Stipes. From *The Poetry of American Women from 1632 to 1945*. University of Texas Press, 1977. Copyright © 1977 by University of Texas Press. All rights reserved. Reprinted by permission of the publisher and the author.

Wellek, René. From *A History of Modern Criticism, 1750-1950: The Romantic Age, Vol. 2*. Yale University Press, 1955. Copyright, 1955, by Yale University Press. Renewed 1983 by René Wellek. All rights reserved. Reprinted by permission.

Wernaer, Robert M. From *Romanticism and the Romantic School in Germany*. D. Appleton and Company, 1910.

White, Helen C. From *The Mysticism of William Blake*. University of Wisconsin, 1927.

Wicksteed, Joseph H. From *Blake's Innocence and Experience: A Study of the Songs and Manuscripts*. E. P. Dutton & Co., 1928.

Wilkinson, James J. G. From *Songs of Innocence and of Experience*. By William Blake, edited by James J. G. Wilkinson. W. Pickering; W. Newbury, 1839.

Williams, Alfred M. From *The Poets and Poetry of Ireland*. James R. Osgood and Company, 1881.

Wilson, Joan Hoff, and Sharon L. Bollinger. From ''Mercy Otis Warren: Playwright, Poet, and Historian of the American Revolution,'' in *Female Scholars: A Tradition of Learned Women before 1800*. Edited by J. R. Brink. Eden Press Women's Publications, 1980. © 1980 Eden Press Women's Publications. Reprinted by permission.

Woolf, Virginia. From *A Room of One's Own*. Harcourt Brace Jovanovich, 1929, Hogarth Press, 1929. Copyright 1929 by Harcourt Brace Jovanovich, Inc. Renewed 1957 by Leonard Woolf. Reprinted by permission of Harcourt Brace Jovanovich, Inc. In Canada by the Literary Estate of Virginia Woolf and the Hogarth Press.

Wordsworth, William. From *Blake Records*. Edited by G. E. Bentley, Jr. Oxford at the Clarendon Press, Oxford, 1969. © Oxford University Press 1969. Reprinted by permission of Oxford University Press.

Worth, George J. From ''Early Victorian Criticism of the Novel and Its Limitations: 'Jack Sheppard', a Test Case,'' in *The Nineteenth-Century Writer and His Audience: Selected Problems in Theory, Form, and Content*. Edited by Harold Orel and George J. Worth. University of Kansas Publications, 1969. Copyright 1969 by The University of Kansas. Reprinted by permission of the author.

Worth, George J. From *William Harrison Ainsworth*. Twayne, 1972. Copyright 1972 by Twayne Publishers. All rights reserved. Reprinted with the permission of Twayne Publishers, a division of G. K. Hall & Co., Boston.

Yeats, W. B. From *Representative Irish Tales*. Edited by W. B. Yeats. N.p., 1891.

Cumulative Index to Authors

This index lists all author entries in the Gale Literary Criticism Series and includes cross-references to other Gale sources. For the convenience of the reader, references to the *Yearbook* in the *Contemporary Literary Criticism* series include the page number (in parentheses) after the volume number. References in the index are identified as follows:

AITN:	*Authors in the News*, Volumes 1-2
CAAS:	*Contemporary Authors Autobiography Series*, Volumes 1-3
CA:	*Contemporary Authors* (original series), Volumes 1-118
CANR:	*Contemporary Authors New Revision Series*, Volumes 1-18
CAP:	*Contemporary Authors Permanent Series*, Volumes 1-2
CA-R:	*Contemporary Authors* (revised editions), Volumes 1-44
CLC:	*Contemporary Literary Criticism*, Volumes 1-40
CLR:	*Children's Literature Review*, Volumes 1-10
DLB:	*Dictionary of Literary Biography*, Volumes 1-48
DLB-DS:	*Dictionary of Literary Biography Documentary Series*, Volumes 1-4
DLB-Y:	*Dictionary of Literary Biography Yearbook*, Volumes 1980-1985
LC:	*Literature Criticism from 1400 to 1800*, Volumes 1-4
NCLC:	*Nineteenth-Century Literature Criticism*, Volumes 1-13
SAAS:	*Something about the Author Autobiography Series*, Volumes 1-2
SATA:	*Something about the Author*, Volumes 1-44
TCLC:	*Twentieth-Century Literary Criticism*, Volumes 1-21
YABC:	*Yesterday's Authors of Books for Children*, Volumes 1-2

Aiken, Conrad (Potter)
  1889-1973............CLC 1, 3, 5, 10
  See also CANR 4
  See also CA 5-8R
  See also obituary CA 45-48
  See also SATA 3, 30
  See also DLB 9, 45

Aiken, Joan (Delano) 1924-........CLC 35
  See also CLR 1
  See also CANR 4
  See also CA 9-12R
  See also SAAS 1
  See also SATA 2, 30

Ainsworth, William Harrison
  1805-1882.................NCLC 13
  See also SATA 24
  See also DLB 21

Ajar, Emile 1914-1980
  See Gary, Romain

Akhmatova, Anna
  1888-1966...............CLC 11, 25
  See also CAP 1
  See also CA 19-20
  See also obituary CA 25-28R

Aksakov, Sergei Timofeyvich
  1791-1859.................NCLC 2

Aksenov, Vassily (Pavlovich) 1932-
  See Aksyonor, Vasily (Pavlovich)

Aksyonov, Vasily (Pavlovich)
  1932-...................CLC 22, 37
  See also CANR 12
  See also CA 53-56

Akutagawa Ryūnosuke
  1892-1927.................TCLC 16

Alain-Fournier 1886-1914........TCLC 6
  See also Fournier, Henri Alban

Alarcón, Pedro Antonio de
  1833-1891.................NCLC 1

Albee, Edward (Franklin III)
  1928-..... CLC 1, 2, 3, 5, 9, 11, 13, 25
  See also CANR 8
  See also CA 5-8R
  See also DLB 7
  See also AITN 1

Alberti, Rafael 1902-...............CLC 7
  See also CA 85-88

Alcott, Amos Bronson
  1799-1888.................NCLC 1
  See also DLB 1

Alcott, Louisa May 1832-1888.....NCLC 6
  See also CLR 1
  See also YABC 1
  See also DLB 1, 42

Aldiss, Brian W(ilson)
  1925-.................CLC 5, 14, 40
  See also CAAS 2
  See also CANR 5
  See also CA 5-8R
  See also SATA 34
  See also DLB 14

Aleichem, Sholom 1859-1916......TCLC 1
  See also Rabinovitch, Sholem

Aleixandre, Vicente
  1898-1984................ CLC 9, 36
  See also CA 85-88
  See also obituary CA 114

Alepoudelis, Odysseus 1911-
  See Elytis, Odysseus

Alexander, Lloyd (Chudley)
  1924-......................CLC 35
  See also CLR 1, 5
  See also CANR 1
  See also CA 1-4R
  See also SATA 3

Alger, Horatio, Jr. 1832-1899.....NCLC 8
  See also SATA 16
  See also DLB 42

Algren, Nelson
  1909-1981..............CLC 4, 10, 33
  See also CA 13-16R
  See also obituary CA 103
  See also DLB 9
  See also DLB-Y 81, 82

Allen, Heywood 1935-
  See Allen, Woody
  See also CA 33-36R

Allen, Roland 1939-
  See Ayckbourn, Alan

Allen, Woody 1935-..............CLC 16
  See also Allen, Heywood
  See also DLB 44

Allende, Isabel 1942-........ CLC 39 (27)

Allingham, Margery (Louise)
  1904-1966..................CLC 19
  See also CANR 4
  See also CA 5-8R
  See also obituary CA 25-28R

Allston, Washington
  1779-1843.................NCLC 2
  See also DLB 1

Almedingen, E. M. 1898-1971......CLC 12
  See also Almedingen, Martha Edith von
  See also SATA 3

Almedingen, Martha Edith von 1898-1971
  See Almedingen, E. M.
  See also CANR 1
  See also CA 1-4R

Alonso, Dámaso 1898-............CLC 14
  See also CA 110

Alta 1942-......................CLC 19
  See also CA 57-60

Alter, Robert 1935-......... CLC 34 (515)
  See also CANR 1
  See also CA 49-52

Alther, Lisa 1944-.................CLC 7
  See also CANR 12
  See also CA 65-68

Altman, Robert 1925-.............CLC 16
  See also CA 73-76

Alvarez, A(lfred) 1929-......... CLC 5, 13
  See also CANR 3
  See also CA 1-4R
  See also DLB 14, 40

Amado, Jorge 1912- .... CLC 13, 40
  See also CA 77-80

Ambler, Eric 1909-...........CLC 4, 6, 9
  See also CANR 7
  See also CA 9-12R

Amichai, Yehuda 1924- .... CLC 9, 22
  See also CA 85-88

Amiel, Henri Frédéric
  1821-1881..................NCLC 4

Amis, Kingsley (William)
  1922-.........CLC 1, 2, 3, 5, 8, 13, 40
  See also CANR 8
  See also CA 9-12R
  See also DLB 15, 27
  See also AITN 2

Amis, Martin 1949-..........CLC 4, 9, 38
  See also CANR 8
  See also CA 65-68
  See also DLB 14

Ammons, A(rchie) R(andolph)
  1926-............CLC 2, 3, 5, 8, 9, 25
  See also CANR 6
  See also CA 9-12R
  See also DLB 5
  See also AITN 1

Anand, Mulk Raj 1905-...........CLC 23
  See also CA 65-68

Anaya, Rudolfo A(lfonso)
  1937-......................CLC 23
  See also CANR 1
  See also CA 45-48

Andersen, Hans Christian
  1805-1875.................NCLC 7
  See also CLR 6
  See also YABC 1

Anderson, Jessica (Margaret Queale)
  19??-......................CLC 37
  See also CANR 4
  See also CA 9-12R

Anderson, Jon (Victor) 1940- ....CLC 9
  See also CA 25-28R

Anderson, Lindsay 1923- ....CLC 20

Anderson, Maxwell 1888-1959 .... TCLC 2
  See also CA 105
  See also DLB 7

Anderson, Poul (William)
  1926-......................CLC 15
  See also CAAS 2
  See also CANR 2, 15
  See also CA 1-4R
  See also SATA 39
  See also DLB 8

Anderson, Robert (Woodruff)
  1917-......................CLC 23
  See also CA 21-24R
  See also DLB 7
  See also AITN 1

Anderson, Roberta Joan 1943-
  See Mitchell, Joni

Anderson, Sherwood
  1876-1941...............TCLC 1, 10
  See also CA 104
  See also DLB 4, 9
  See also DLB-DS 1

Andrade, Carlos Drummond de
  1902-......................CLC 18

Andrews, Cicily Fairfield 1892-1983
  See West, Rebecca

Andreyev, Leonid (Nikolaevich)
  1871-1919.................TCLC 3
  See also CA 104

Andrézel, Pierre 1885-1962
  See Dinesen, Isak
  See also Blixen, Karen (Christentze
    Dinesen)

Author Index

Author Index

Author Index

Author Index

Author Index

Howard, Richard 1929- .... CLC 7, 10
See also CA 85-88
See also DLB 5
See also AITN 1

Howard, Robert E(rvin)
1906-1936.................. TCLC 8
See also CA 105

Howe, Julia Ward 1819-1910 .... TCLC 21
See also CA 117
See also DLB 1

Howells, William Dean
1837-1920............... TCLC 7, 17
See also CA 104
See also DLB 12

Howes, Barbara 1914- .... CLC 15
See also CAAS 3
See also CA 9-12R
See also SATA 5

Hrabal, Bohumil 1914-........... CLC 13
See also CA 106

Huch, Ricarda (Octavia)
1864-1947.................. TCLC 13
See also CA 111

Hueffer, Ford Madox 1873-1939
See Ford, Ford Madox

Hughart, Barry 1934-....... CLC 39 (155)

Hughes, Edward James 1930-
See Hughes, Ted

Hughes, (James) Langston
1902-1967....... CLC 1, 5, 10, 15, 35
See also CANR 1
See also CA 1-4R
See also obituary CA 25-28R
See also SATA 4, 33
See also DLB 4, 7, 48

Hughes, Richard (Arthur Warren)
1900-1976................ CLC 1, 11
See also CANR 4
See also CA 5-8R
See also obituary CA 65-68
See also SATA 8
See also obituary SATA 25
See also DLB 15

Hughes, Ted 1930-..... CLC 2, 4, 9, 14, 37
See also CLR 3
See also CANR 1
See also CA 1-4R
See also SATA 27
See also DLB 40

Hugo, Richard F(ranklin)
1923-1982............. CLC 6, 18, 32
See also CANR 3
See also CA 49-52
See also obituary CA 108
See also DLB 5

Hugo, Victor Marie
1802-1885............... NCLC 3, 10

Hulme, Keri 1947-......... CLC 39 (158)

Hulme, T. E. 1883-1917........ TCLC 21
See also CA 117
See also DLB 19

Humphreys, Josephine
1945-.................. CLC 34 (63)

Hunt, E(verette) Howard (Jr.)
1918-........................CLC 3
See also CANR 2
See also CA 45-48
See also AITN 1

Hunt, (James Henry) Leigh
1784-1859.................. NCLC 1

Hunter, Evan 1926-......... CLC 1, 11, 31
See also CANR 5
See also CA 5-8R
See also SATA 25
See also DLB-Y 82

Hunter, Kristin (Eggleston)
1931-......................CLC 35
See also CLR 3
See also CANR 13
See also CA 13-16R
See also SATA 12
See also DLB 33
See also AITN 1

Hunter, Mollie (Maureen McIlwraith)
1922-......................CLC 21
See also McIlwraith, Maureen Mollie
Hunter

Hurston, Zora Neale
1901?-1960............... CLC 7, 30
See also CA 85-88

Huston, John (Marcellus)
1906-......................CLC 20
See also CA 73-76
See also DLB 26

Huxley, Aldous (Leonard)
1894-1963...... CLC 1, 3, 4, 5, 8, 11,
18, 35
See also CA 85-88
See also DLB 36

Huysmans, Charles Marie Georges
1848-1907
See also Huysmans, Joris-Karl
See also CA 104

Huysmans, Joris-Karl
1848-1907.................. TCLC 7
See also Huysmans, Charles Marie Georges

Hyde, Margaret O(ldroyd)
1917-......................CLC 21
See also CANR 1
See also CA 1-4R
See also SATA 1, 42

Ian, Janis 1951-.................CLC 21
See also CA 105

Ibargüengoitia, Jorge
1928-1983...................CLC 37
See also obituary CA 113

Ibsen, Henrik (Johan)
1828-1906.............TCLC 2, 8, 16
See also CA 104

Ibuse, Masuji 1898-...............CLC 22

Ichikawa, Kon 1915-..............CLC 20

Idle, Eric 1943-
See Monty Python
See also CA 116

Ignatow, David 1914- .....CLC 4, 7, 14, 40
See also CAAS 3
See also CA 9-12R
See also DLB 5

Ilf, Ilya 1897-1937 and Petrov, Evgeny
1902-1942................. TCLC 21

Immermann, Karl (Lebrecht)
1796-1840................... NCLC 4

Inge, William (Motter)
1913-1973............... CLC 1, 8, 19
See also CA 9-12R
See also DLB 7

Innaurato, Albert 1948-...........CLC 21
See also CA 115

Innes, Michael 1906-
See Stewart, J(ohn) I(nnes) M(ackintosh)

Ionesco, Eugène
1912-.......... CLC 1, 4, 6, 9, 11, 15
See also CA 9-12R
See also SATA 7

Irving, John (Winslow)
1942-................. CLC 13, 23, 38
See also CA 25-28R
See also DLB 6
See also DLB-Y 82

Irving, Washington 1783-1859 .... NCLC 2
See also YABC 2
See also DLB 3, 11, 30

Isaacs, Susan 1943-...............CLC 32
See also CA 89-92

Isherwood, Christopher (William Bradshaw)
1904-.................CLC 1, 9, 11, 14
See also CA 13-16R
See also DLB 15

Ishiguro, Kazuo 1954?-............CLC 27

Ishikawa Takuboku
1885-1912.................. TCLC 15

Ivask, Ivar (Vidrik) 1927- ....CLC 14
See also CA 37-40R

Jackson, Jesse 1908-1983..........CLC 12
See also CA 25-28R
See also obituary CA 109
See also SATA 2, 29

Jackson, Laura (Riding) 1901-
See Riding, Laura
See also CA 65-68
See also DLB 48

Jackson, Shirley 1919-1965........CLC 11
See also CANR 4
See also CA 1-4R
See also obituary CA 25-28R
See also SATA 2
See also DLB 6

Jacob, (Cyprien) Max
1876-1944.................. TCLC 6
See also CA 104

Jacob, Piers A(nthony) D(illingham) 1934-
See Anthony (Jacob), Piers
See also CA 21-24R

Jacobs, Jim 1942-
See Jacobs, Jim and Casey, Warren
See also CA 97-100

Jacobs, Jim 1942- and
Casey, Warren 1935-.........CLC 12

Jacobson, Dan 1929-........... CLC 4, 14
See also CANR 2
See also CA 1-4R
See also DLB 14

Jagger, Mick 1944-
See Jagger, Mick and Richard, Keith

Jagger, Mick 1944- and
Richard, Keith 1943-........CLC 17

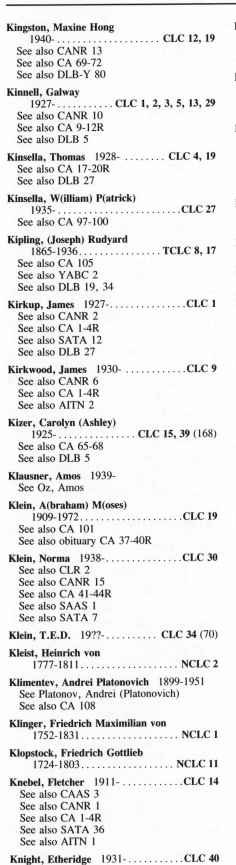

Author Index

Author Index

Author Index

Author Index

Moravia, Alberto
    1907- . . . . CLC **2, 7, 11, 18, 27**
    See also Pincherle, Alberto

Moréas, Jean 1856-1910 . . . . TCLC **18**

Morgan, Berry 1919- . . . . .CLC **6**
    See also CA 49-52
    See also DLB 6

Morgan, Edwin (George)
    1920- . . . . .CLC **31**
    See also CANR 3
    See also CA 7-8R
    See also DLB 27

Morgan, Frederick 1922- . . . . .CLC **23**
    See also CA 17-20R

Morgan, Janet 1945- . . . . CLC **39** (436)
    See also CA 65-68

Morgan, Robin 1941- . . . . .CLC **2**
    See also CA 69-72

Morgenstern, Christian (Otto Josef Wolfgang)
    1871-1914 . . . . TCLC **8**
    See also CA 105

Mori Ōgai 1862-1922 . . . . TCLC **14**
    See also Mori Rintaro

Mori Rintaro 1862-1922
    See Mori Ōgai
    See also CA 110

Mörike, Eduard (Friedrich)
    1804-1875 . . . . NCLC **10**

Moritz, Karl Philipp 1756-1793 . . . . . . LC **2**

Morris, Julian 1916-
    See West, Morris L.

Morris, Steveland Judkins 1950-
    See Wonder, Stevie
    See also CA 111

Morris, William 1834-1896 . . . . NCLC **4**
    See also DLB 18, 35

Morris, Wright
    1910- . . . . CLC **1, 3, 7, 18, 37**
    See also CA 9-12R
    See also DLB 2
    See also DLB-Y 81

Morrison, James Douglas 1943-1971
    See Morrison, Jim
    See also CA 73-76

Morrison, Jim 1943-1971 . . . . .CLC **17**
    See also Morrison, James Douglas

Morrison, Toni 1931- . . . . CLC **4, 10, 22**
    See also CA 29-32R
    See also DLB 6, 33
    See also DLB-Y 81

Morrison, Van 1945- . . . . .CLC **21**
    See also CA 116

Mortimer, John (Clifford)
    1923- . . . . .CLC **28**
    See also CA 13-16R
    See also DLB 13

Mortimer, Penelope (Ruth)
    1918- . . . . .CLC **5**
    See also CA 57-60

Moss, Howard 1922- . . . . CLC **7, 14**
    See also CANR 1
    See also CA 1-4R
    See also DLB 5

Motley, Willard (Francis)
    1912-1965 . . . . .CLC **18**
    See also obituary CA 106

Mott, Michael (Charles Alston)
    1930- . . . . CLC **15, 34** (460)
    See also CANR 7
    See also CA 5-8R

Mowat, Farley (McGill) 1921- . . . . . .CLC **26**
    See also CANR 4
    See also CA 1-4R
    See also SATA 3

Mphahlele, Es'kia 1919-
    See Mphahlele, Ezekiel

Mphahlele, Ezekiel 1919- . . . . .CLC **25**
    See also CA 81-84

Mrożek, Sławomir 1930- . . . . CLC **3, 13**
    See also CA 13-16R

Mueller, Lisel 1924- . . . . .CLC **13**
    See also CA 93-96

Muir, Edwin 1887-1959 . . . . TCLC **2**
    See also CA 104
    See also DLB 20

Mujica Láinez, Manuel
    1910-1984 . . . . .CLC **31**
    See also CA 81-84
    See also obituary CA 112

Muldoon, Paul 1951- . . . . .CLC **32**
    See also CA 113
    See also DLB 40

Mull, Martin 1943- . . . . .CLC **17**
    See also CA 105

Munro, Alice 1931- . . . . CLC **6, 10, 19**
    See also CA 33-36R
    See also SATA 29
    See also AITN 2

Munro, H(ector) H(ugh) 1870-1916
    See Saki
    See also CA 104
    See also DLB 34

Murdoch, (Jean) Iris
    1919- . . . . . . CLC **1, 2, 3, 4, 6, 8, 11, 15,**
                            22, 31
    See also CANR 8
    See also CA 13-16R
    See also DLB 14

Murphy, Sylvia 19??- . . . . CLC **34** (91)

Murray, Les(lie) A(llan) 1938- . . . . . .CLC **40**
    See also CANR 11
    See also CA 21-24R

Murry, John Middleton
    1889-1957 . . . . TCLC **16**
    See also CA 118

Musgrave, Susan 1951- . . . . .CLC **13**
    See also CA 69-72

Musil, Robert (Edler von)
    1880-1942 . . . . TCLC **12**
    See also CA 109

Musset, (Louis Charles) Alfred de
    1810-1857 . . . . NCLC **7**

Myers, Walter Dean 1937- . . . . .CLC **35**
    See also CLR 4
    See also CA 33-36R
    See also SAAS 2
    See also SATA 27, 41
    See also DLB 33

Nabokov, Vladimir (Vladimirovich)
    1899-1977 . . . . . . CLC **1, 2, 3, 6, 8, 11,**
                            15, 23
    See also CA 5-8R
    See also obituary CA 69-72
    See also DLB 2
    See also DLB-Y 80
    See also DLB-DS 3

Nagy, László 1925-1978 . . . . .CLC **7**
    See also obituary CA 112

Naipaul, Shiva(dhar Srinivasa)
    1945-1985 . . . . CLC **32, 39** (355)
    See also CA 110, 112
    See also obituary CA 116
    See also DLB-Y 85

Naipaul, V(idiadhar) S(urajprasad)
    1932- . . . . CLC **4, 7, 9, 13, 18, 37**
    See also CANR 1
    See also CA 1-4R
    See also DLB-Y 85

Nakos, Ioulia 1899?-
    See Nakos, Lilika

Nakos, Lilika 1899?- . . . . .CLC **29**

Nakou, Lilika 1899?-
    See Nakos, Lilika

Narayan, R(asipuram) K(rishnaswami)
    1906- . . . . CLC **7, 28**
    See also CA 81-84

Nash, (Frediric) Ogden
    1902-1971 . . . . .CLC **23**
    See also CAP 1
    See also CA 13-14
    See also obituary CA 29-32R
    See also SATA 2
    See also DLB 11

Nathan, George Jean
    1882-1958 . . . . TCLC **18**
    See also CA 114

Natsume, Kinnosuke 1867-1916
    See Natsume, Sōseki
    See also CA 104

Natsume, Sōseki
    1867-1916 . . . . TCLC **2, 10**
    See also Natsume, Kinnosuke

Natti, (Mary) Lee 1919-
    See Kingman, (Mary) Lee
    See also CANR 2

Naylor, Gloria 1950- . . . . .CLC **28**
    See also CA 107

Neihardt, John G(neisenau)
    1881-1973 . . . . .CLC **32**
    See also CAP 1
    See also CA 13-14
    See also DLB 9

Nekrasov, Nikolai Alekseevich
    1821-1878 . . . . NCLC **11**

Nelligan, Émile 1879-1941 . . . . TCLC **14**
    See also CA 114

Nelson, Willie 1933- . . . . .CLC **17**
    See also CA 107

Nemerov, Howard
    1920- . . . . .CLC **2, 6, 9, 36**
    See also CANR 1
    See also CA 1-4R
    See also DLB 5, 6
    See also DLB-Y 83

Author Index

Author Index

Sisson, C(harles) H(ubert) 1914-.....CLC 8
  See also CAAS 3
  See also CANR 3
  See also CA 1-4R
  See also DLB 27

Sitwell, (Dame) Edith
  1887-1964................. CLC 2, 9
  See also CA 9-12R
  See also DLB 20

Sjoewall, Maj 1935-
  See Wahlöö, Per
  See also CA 65-68

Sjöwall, Maj 1935-
  See Wahlöö, Per

Skelton, Robin 1925-.............CLC 13
  See also CA 5-8R
  See also AITN 2
  See also DLB 27

Skolimowski, Jerzy 1938-.........CLC 20

Skolimowski, Yurek 1938-
  See Skolimowski, Jerzy

Skrine, Mary Nesta 1904-
  See Keane, Molly

Škvorecký, Josef (Vaclav)
  1924-.............. CLC 15, 39 (220)
  See also CAAS 1
  See also CANR 10
  See also CA 61-64

Slade, Bernard 1930- ....CLC 11
  See also Newbound, Bernard Slade

Slaughter, Frank G(ill) 1908- ......CLC 29
  See also CANR 5
  See also CA 5-8R
  See also AITN 2

Slavitt, David (R.) 1935-........ CLC 5, 14
  See also CAAS 3
  See also CA 21-24R
  See also DLB 5, 6

Slesinger, Tess 1905-1945....... TCLC 10
  See also CA 107

Slessor, Kenneth 1901-1971.......CLC 14
  See also CA 102
  See also obituary CA 89-92

Smart, Christopher 1722-1771 .... LC 3

Smith, A(rthur) J(ames) M(arshall)
  1902-1980...................CLC 15
  See also CANR 4
  See also CA 1-4R
  See also obituary CA 102

Smith, Betty (Wehner)
  1896-1972...................CLC 19
  See also CA 5-8R
  See also obituary CA 33-36R
  See also SATA 6
  See also DLB-Y 82

Smith, Cecil Lewis Troughton 1899-1966
  See Forester, C(ecil) S(cott)

Smith, Dave 1942-...............CLC 22
  See also Smith, David (Jeddie)
  See also DLB 5

Smith, David (Jeddie) 1942-
  See Smith, Dave
  See also CANR 1
  See also CA 49-52

Smith, Florence Margaret 1902-1971
  See Smith, Stevie
  See also CAP 2
  See also CA 17-18
  See also obituary CA 29-32R

Smith, Lee 1944-.................CLC 25
  See also CA 114
  See also DLB-Y 83

Smith, Martin Cruz 1942- ....CLC 25
  See also CANR 6
  See also CA 85-88

Smith, Martin William 1942-
  See Smith, Martin Cruz

Smith, Mary-Ann Tirone
  1944-................... CLC 39 (97)
  See also CA 118

Smith, Patti 1946-................CLC 12
  See also CA 93-96

Smith, Sara Mahala Redway 1900-1972
  See Benson, Sally

Smith, Stevie 1902-1971 ..... CLC 3, 8, 25
  See also Smith, Florence Margaret
  See also DLB 20

Smith, Wilbur (Addison) 1933-.....CLC 33
  See also CANR 7
  See also CA 13-16R

Smith, William Jay 1918-...........CLC 6
  See also CA 5-8R
  See also SATA 2
  See also DLB 5

Smollett, Tobias (George)
  1721-1771..................... LC 2
  See also DLB 39

Snodgrass, W(illiam) D(e Witt)
  1926-................CLC 2, 6, 10, 18
  See also CANR 6
  See also CA 1-4R
  See also DLB 5

Snow, C(harles) P(ercy)
  1905-1980....... CLC 1, 4, 6, 9, 13, 19
  See also CA 5-8R
  See also obituary CA 101
  See also DLB 15

Snyder, Gary 1930-..... CLC 1, 2, 5, 9, 32
  See also CA 17-20R
  See also DLB 5, 16

Snyder, Zilpha Keatley 1927- ......CLC 17
  See also CA 9-12R
  See also SAAS 2
  See also SATA 1, 28

Sokolov, Raymond 1941-...........CLC 7
  See also CA 85-88

Sologub, Fyodor 1863-1927 .... TCLC 9
  See also Teternikov, Fyodor Kuzmich

Solwoska, Mara 1929-
  See French, Marilyn

Solzhenitsyn, Aleksandr I(sayevich)
  1918-.....CLC 1, 2, 4, 7, 9, 10, 18, 26,
                  34 (480)
  See also CA 69-72
  See also AITN 1

Somers, Jane 1919-
  See Lessing, Doris (May)

Sommer, Scott 1951-.............CLC 25
  See also CA 106

Sondheim, Stephen (Joshua)
  1930-.............. CLC 33, 39 (172)
  See also CA 103

Sontag, Susan
  1933-............ CLC 1, 2, 10, 13, 31
  See also CA 17-20R
  See also DLB 2

Sorrentino, Gilbert
  1929-............ CLC 3, 7, 14, 22, 40
  See also CANR 14
  See also CA 77-80
  See also DLB 5
  See also DLB-Y 80

Soto, Gary 1952-.................CLC 32

Souster, (Holmes) Raymond
  1921-..................... CLC 5, 14
  See also CANR 13
  See also CA 13-16R

Southern, Terry 1926- ....CLC 7
  See also CANR 1
  See also CA 1-4R
  See also DLB 2

Southey, Robert 1774-1843 .... NCLC 8

Soyinka, Akin-wande Oluwole 1934-
  See Soyinka, Wole

Soyinka, Wole 1934-......CLC 3, 5, 14, 36
  See also CA 13-16R

Spacks, Barry 1931-..............CLC 14
  See also CA 29-32R

Spark, Muriel (Sarah)
  1918-........CLC 2, 3, 5, 8, 13, 18, 40
  See also CANR 12
  See also CA 5-8R
  See also DLB 15

Spencer, Elizabeth 1921- ....CLC 22
  See also CA 13-16R
  See also SATA 14
  See also DLB 6

Spencer, Scott 1945-...............CLC 30
  See also CA 113

Spender, Stephen (Harold)
  1909-..................CLC 1, 2, 5, 10
  See also CA 9-12R
  See also DLB 20

Spicer, Jack 1925-1965........ CLC 8, 18
  See also CA 85-88
  See also DLB 5, 16

Spielberg, Peter 1929-..............CLC 6
  See also CANR 4
  See also CA 5-8R
  See also DLB-Y 81

Spielberg, Steven 1947-............CLC 20
  See also CA 77-80
  See also SATA 32

Spillane, Frank Morrison 1918-
  See Spillane, Mickey
  See also CA 25-28R

Spillane, Mickey 1918- .... CLC 3, 13
  See also Spillane, Frank Morrison

Spitteler, Carl (Friedrich Georg)
  1845-1924.................. TCLC 12
  See also CA 109

Spivack, Kathleen (Romola Drucker)
  1938-........................CLC 6
  See also CA 49-52

Sturgeon, Theodore (Hamilton)
    1918-1985.......... CLC 22, 39 (360)
    See also CA 81-84
    See also obituary CA 116
    See also DLB 8
    See also DLB-Y 85

Styron, William
    1925-............. CLC 1, 3, 5, 11, 15
    See also CANR 6
    See also CA 5-8R
    See also DLB 2
    See also DLB-Y 80

Sudermann, Hermann
    1857-1928.................. TCLC 15
    See also CA 107

Sue, Eugène   1804-1857........... NCLC 1

Sukenick, Ronald   1932-...... CLC 3, 4, 6
    See also CA 25-28R
    See also DLB-Y 81

Suknaski, Andrew   1942-...........CLC 19
    See also CA 101

Summers, Andrew James   1942-
    See The Police

Summers, Andy   1942-
    See The Police

Summers, Hollis (Spurgeon, Jr.)
    1916-........................CLC 10
    See also CANR 3
    See also CA 5-8R
    See also DLB 6

Summers, (Alphonsus Joseph-Mary Augustus)
    Montague   1880-1948 .... TCLC 16

Sumner, Gordon Matthew   1951-
    See The Police

Susann, Jacqueline   1921-1974.......CLC 3
    See also CA 65-68
    See also obituary CA 53-56
    See also AITN 1

Sutcliff, Rosemary   1920- ....CLC 26
    See also CLR 1
    See also CA 5-8R
    See also SATA 6, 44

Sutro, Alfred   1863-1933.......... TCLC 6
    See also CA 105
    See also DLB 10

Sutton, Henry   1935-
    See Slavitt, David (R.)

Svevo, Italo   1861-1928 .... TCLC 2
    See also Schmitz, Ettore

Swados, Elizabeth   1951-...........CLC 12
    See also CA 97-100

Swados, Harvey   1920-1972 ....CLC 5
    See also CANR 6
    See also CA 5-8R
    See also obituary CA 37-40R
    See also DLB 2

Swarthout, Glendon (Fred)
    1918-........................CLC 35
    See also CANR 1
    See also CA 1-4R
    See also SATA 26

Swenson, May   1919-........... CLC 4, 14
    See also CA 5-8R
    See also SATA 15
    See also DLB 5

Swift, Jonathan   1667-1745.......... LC 1
    See also SATA 19
    See also DLB 39

Swinburne, Algernon Charles
    1837-1909.................. TCLC 8
    See also CA 105
    See also DLB 35

Swinfen, Ann   19??-........ CLC 34 (576)

Swinnerton, Frank (Arthur)
    1884-1982...................CLC 31
    See also obituary CA 108
    See also DLB 34

Symons, Arthur (William)
    1865-1945.................. TCLC 11
    See also CA 107
    See also DLB 19

Symons, Julian (Gustave)
    1912-.................. CLC 2, 14, 32
    See also CAAS 3
    See also CANR 3
    See also CA 49-52

Synge, (Edmund) John Millington
    1871-1909.................. TCLC 6
    See also CA 104
    See also DLB 10, 19

Syruc, J.   1911-
    See Miłosz, Czesław

Tabori, George   1914- ....CLC 19
    See also CANR 4
    See also CA 49-52

Tagore, (Sir) Rabindranath
    1861-1941.................. TCLC 3
    See also Thakura, Ravindranatha

Talese, Gaetano   1932-
    See Talese, Gay

Talese, Gay   1932- ....CLC 37
    See also CANR 9
    See also CA 1-4R
    See also AITN 1

Tamayo y Baus, Manuel
    1829-1898.................. NCLC 1

Tanizaki, Jun'ichirō
    1886-1965........... CLC 8, 14, 28
    See also CA 93-96
    See also obituary CA 25-28R

Tarkington, (Newton) Booth
    1869-1946.................. TCLC 9
    See also CA 110
    See also SATA 17
    See also DLB 9

Tate, (John Orley) Allen
    1899-1979...... CLC 2, 4, 6, 9, 11, 14,
                                        24
    See also CA 5-8R
    See also obituary CA 85-88
    See also DLB 4, 45

Tate, James   1943-........... CLC 2, 6, 25
    See also CA 21-24R
    See also DLB 5

Tavel, Ronald   1940- ....CLC 6
    See also CA 21-24R

Taylor, C(ecil) P(hillip)
    1929-1981...................CLC 27
    See also CA 25-28R
    See also obituary CA 105

Taylor, Eleanor Ross   1920- ....CLC 5
    See also CA 81-84

Taylor, Elizabeth
    1912-1975............... CLC 2, 4, 29
    See also CANR 9
    See also CA 13-16R
    See also SATA 13

Taylor, Kamala (Purnaiya)   1924-
    See Markandaya, Kamala
    See also CA 77-80

Taylor, Mildred D(elois)   19??-......CLC 21
    See also CA 85-88
    See also SATA 15

Taylor, Peter (Hillsman)
    1917-................CLC 1, 4, 18, 37
    See also CANR 9
    See also CA 13-16R
    See also DLB-Y 81

Taylor, Robert Lewis   1912-........CLC 14
    See also CANR 3
    See also CA 1-4R
    See also SATA 10

Teasdale, Sara   1884-1933........ TCLC 4
    See also CA 104
    See also DLB 45
    See also SATA 32

Tegnér, Esaias   1782-1846........ NCLC 2

Teilhard de Chardin, (Marie Joseph) Pierre
    1881-1955.................. TCLC 9
    See also CA 105

Tennant, Emma   1937- ....CLC 13
    See also CANR 10
    See also CA 65-68
    See also DLB 14

Teran, Lisa St. Aubin de   19??-.....CLC 36

Terkel, Louis   1912-
    See Terkel, Studs
    See also CANR 18
    See also CA 57-60

Terkel, Studs   1912-...............CLC 38
    See also Terkel, Louis
    See also AITN 1

Terry, Megan   1932- ....CLC 19
    See also CA 77-80
    See also DLB 7

Tesich, Steve   1943?- ....CLC 40
    See also CA 105
    See also DLB-Y 83

Tesich, Stoyan   1943?-
    See Tesich, Steve

Tertz, Abram   1925-
    See Sinyavsky, Andrei (Donatevich)

Teternikov, Fyodor Kuzmich   1863-1927
    See Sologub, Fyodor
    See also CA 104

Tey, Josephine   1897-1952 .... TCLC 14
    See also Mackintosh, Elizabeth

Thackeray, William Makepeace
    1811-1863.................. NCLC 5
    See also SATA 23
    See also DLB 21

Thakura, Ravindranatha   1861-1941
    See Tagore, (Sir) Rabindranath
    See also CA 104

Thelwell, Michael (Miles)
    1939-........................CLC 22
    See also CA 101

Author Index

Tyler, Anne 1941- ....CLC 7, 11, 18, 28
See also CANR 11
See also CA 9-12R
See also SATA 7
See also DLB 6
See also DLB-Y 82

Tyler, Royall 1757-1826 .... NCLC 3
See also DLB 37

Tynan (Hinkson), Katharine
1861-1931 .... TCLC 3
See also CA 104

Unamuno (y Jugo), Miguel de
1864-1936 .... TCLC 2, 9
See also CA 104

Underwood, Miles 1909-1981
See Glassco, John

Undset, Sigrid 1882-1949 .... TCLC 3
See also CA 104

Ungaretti, Giuseppe
1888-1970 .... CLC 7, 11, 15
See also CAP 2
See also CA 19-20
See also obituary CA 25-28R

Unger, Douglas 1952- .... CLC 34 (114)

Unger, Eva 1932-
See Figes, Eva

Updike, John (Hoyer)
1932- ......CLC 1, 2, 3, 5, 7, 9, 13, 15,
23, 34 (283)
See also CANR 4
See also CA 1-4R
See also DLB 2, 5
See also DLB-Y 80, 82
See also DLB-DS 3

Uris, Leon (Marcus) 1924- ...... CLC 7, 32
See also CANR 1
See also CA 1-4R
See also AITN 1, 2

Ustinov, Peter (Alexander)
1921- ....CLC 1
See also CA 13-16R
See also DLB 13
See also AITN 1

Vaculík, Ludvík 1926- ....CLC 7
See also CA 53-56

Valenzuela, Luisa 1938- ....CLC 31
See also CA 101

Valera (y Acalá-Galiano), Juan
1824-1905 .... TCLC 10
See also CA 106

Valéry, Paul (Ambroise Toussaint Jules)
1871-1945 .... TCLC 4, 15
See also CA 104

Valle-Inclán (y Montenegro), Ramón (María)
del 1866-1936 .... TCLC 5
See also CA 106

Vallejo, César (Abraham)
1892-1938 .... TCLC 3
See also CA 105

Van Ash, Cay 1918- .... CLC 34 (118)

Vance, Jack 1916?- ....CLC 35
See also DLB 8

Vance, John Holbrook 1916?-
See Vance, Jack
See also CANR 17
See also CA 29-32R

Van Den Bogarde, Derek (Jules Gaspard Ulric) Niven 1921-
See Bogarde, Dirk
See also CA 77-80

Van der Post, Laurens (Jan)
1906- ....CLC 5
See also CA 5-8R

Van Doren, Carl (Clinton)
1885-1950 .... TCLC 18
See also CA 111

Van Doren, Mark
1894-1972 .... CLC 6, 10
See also CANR 3
See also CA 1-4R
See also obituary CA 37-40R
See also DLB 45

Van Druten, John (William)
1901-1957 .... TCLC 2
See also CA 104
See also DLB 10

Van Duyn, Mona 1921- .... CLC 3, 7
See also CANR 7
See also CA 9-12R
See also DLB 5

Van Itallie, Jean-Claude 1936- ......CLC 3
See also CAAS 2
See also CANR 1
See also CA 45-48
See also DLB 7

Van Peebles, Melvin 1932- ...... CLC 2, 20
See also CA 85-88

Van Vechten, Carl 1880-1964 ......CLC 33
See also obituary CA 89-92
See also DLB 4, 9

Van Vogt, A(lfred) E(lton)
1912- ....CLC 1
See also CA 21-24R
See also SATA 14
See also DLB 8

Varda, Agnès 1928- ....CLC 16
See also CA 116

Vargas Llosa, (Jorge) Mario (Pedro)
1936- .... CLC 3, 6, 9, 10, 15, 31
See also CANR 18
See also CA 73-76

Vassilikos, Vassilis 1933- .... CLC 4, 8
See also CA 81-84

Verga, Giovanni 1840-1922 ...... TCLC 3
See also CA 104

Verhaeren, Émile (Adolphe Gustave)
1855-1916 .... TCLC 12
See also CA 109

Verlaine, Paul (Marie)
1844-1896 .... NCLC 2

Verne, Jules (Gabriel)
1828-1905 .... TCLC 6
See also CA 110
See also SATA 21

Very, Jones 1813-1880 .... NCLC 9
See also DLB 1

Vian, Boris 1920-1959 .... TCLC 9
See also CA 106

Viaud, (Louis Marie) Julien 1850-1923
See Loti, Pierre
See also CA 107

Vicker, Angus 1916-
See Felsen, Henry Gregor

Vidal, Eugene Luther, Jr. 1925-
See Vidal, Gore

Vidal, Gore
1925- ....CLC 2, 4, 6, 8, 10, 22, 33
See also CANR 13
See also CA 5-8R
See also DLB 6
See also AITN 1

Viereck, Peter (Robert Edwin)
1916- ....CLC 4
See also CANR 1
See also CA 1-4R
See also DLB 5

Vigny, Alfred (Victor) de
1797-1863 .... NCLC 7

Villiers de l'Isle Adam, Jean Marie Mathias Philippe Auguste, Comte de,
1838-1889 .... NCLC 3

Vinge, Joan (Carol) D(ennison)
1948- ....CLC 30
See also CA 93-96
See also SATA 36

Visconti, Luchino 1906-1976 ....CLC 16
See also CA 81-84
See also obituary CA 65-68

Vittorini, Elio 1908-1966 ..... CLC 6, 9, 14
See also obituary CA 25-28R

Vizinczey, Stephen 1933- ....CLC 40

Vliet, R(ussell) G. 1929- ....CLC 22
See also CANR 18
See also CA 37-40R

Voigt, Cynthia 1942- ....CLC 30
See also CANR 18
See also CA 106
See also SATA 33

Voinovich, Vladimir (Nikolaevich)
1932- ....CLC 10
See also CA 81-84

Von Daeniken, Erich 1935-
See Von Däniken, Erich
See also CANR 17
See also CA 37-40R
See also AITN 1

Von Däniken, Erich 1935- ....CLC 30
See also Von Daeniken, Erich

Vonnegut, Kurt, Jr.
1922- ......CLC 1, 2, 3, 4, 5, 8, 12, 22,
40
See also CANR 1
See also CA 1-4R
See also DLB 2, 8
See also DLB-Y 80
See also DLB-DS 3
See also AITN 1

Vorster, Gordon 1924- ...... CLC 34 (121)

Voznesensky, Andrei 1933- ..... CLC 1, 15
See also CA 89-92

Waddington, Miriam 1917- ....CLC 28
See also CANR 12
See also CA 21-24R

Wagman, Fredrica 1937- ....CLC 7
See also CA 97-100

Wagner, Richard 1813-1883 ...... NCLC 9

Author Index

Williams, Jonathan (Chamberlain)
1929-..........................CLC 13
See also CANR 8
See also CA 9-12R
See also DLB 5

Williams, Joy 1944-..............CLC 31
See also CA 41-44R

Williams, Norman 1952-..... CLC 39 (100)

Williams, Paulette 1948-
See Shange, Ntozake

Williams, Tennessee
1911-1983....... CLC 1, 2, 5, 7, 8, 11,
 15, 19, 30, 39 (444)
See also CA 5-8R
See also obituary CA 108
See also DLB 7
See also DLB-Y 83
See also DLB-DS 4
See also AITN 1, 2

Williams, Thomas (Alonzo)
1926-...........................CLC 14
See also CANR 2
See also CA 1-4R

Williams, Thomas Lanier 1911-1983
See Williams, Tennessee

Williams, William Carlos
1883-1963....... CLC 1, 2, 5, 9, 13, 22
See also CA 89-92
See also DLB 4, 16

Williamson, Jack 1908-...........CLC 29
See also Williamson, John Stewart
See also DLB 8

Williamson, John Stewart 1908-
See Williamson, Jack
See also CA 17-20R

Willingham, Calder (Baynard, Jr.)
1922-...........................CLC 5
See also CANR 3
See also CA 5-8R
See also DLB 2, 44

Wilson, A(ndrew) N(orman)
1950-...........................CLC 33
See also CA 112
See also DLB 14

Wilson, Andrew 1948-
See Wilson, Snoo

Wilson, Angus (Frank Johnstone)
1913-........ CLC 2, 3, 5, 25, 34 (579)
See also CA 5-8R
See also DLB 15

Wilson, August 1945-....... CLC 39 (275)
See also CA 115

Wilson, Brian 1942- ....CLC 12

Wilson, Colin 1931-............ CLC 3, 14
See also CANR 1
See also CA 1-4R
See also DLB 14

Wilson, Edmund
1895-1972......... CLC 1, 2, 3, 8, 24
See also CANR 1
See also CA 1-4R
See also obituary CA 37-40R

Wilson, Ethel Davis (Bryant)
1888-1980....................CLC 13
See also CA 102

Wilson, John 1785-1854......... NCLC 5

Wilson, John (Anthony) Burgess 1917-
See Burgess, Anthony
See also CANR 2
See also CA 1-4R

Wilson, Lanford 1937- ..... CLC 7, 14, 36
See also CA 17-20R
See also DLB 7

Wilson, Robert (M.) 1944-....... CLC 7, 9
See also CANR 2
See also CA 49-52

Wilson, Sloan 1920-...............CLC 32
See also CANR 1
See also CA 1-4R

Wilson, Snoo 1948-...............CLC 33
See also CA 69-72

Winchilsea, Anne (Kingsmill) Finch, Countess
of 1661-1720 .... LC 3

Winters, (Arthur) Yvor
1900-1968............... CLC 4, 8, 32
See also CAP 1
See also CA 11-12
See also obituary CA 25-28R
See also DLB 48

Wiseman, Frederick 1930-.........CLC 20

Wister, Owen 1860-1938 .... TCLC 21
See also CA 108
See also DLB 9

Witkiewicz, Stanislaw Ignacy
1885-1939.................. TCLC 8
See also CA 105

Wittig, Monique 1935?- ....CLC 22
See also CA 116

Wittlin, Joseph 1896-1976 ....CLC 25
See also Wittlin, Józef

Wittlin, Józef 1896-1976
See Wittlin, Joseph
See also CANR 3
See also CA 49-52
See also obituary CA 65-68

Wodehouse, P(elham) G(renville)
1881-1975........ CLC 1, 2, 5, 10, 22
See also CANR 3
See also CA 45-48
See also obituary CA 57-60
See also SATA 22
See also DLB 34
See also AITN 2

Woiwode, Larry (Alfred)
1941-...................... CLC 6, 10
See also CANR 16
See also CA 73-76
See also DLB 6

Wojciechowska, Maia (Teresa)
1927-...........................CLC 26
See also CLR 1
See also CANR 4
See also CA 9-12R
See also SAAS 1
See also SATA 1, 28

Wolf, Christa 1929-........... CLC 14, 29
See also CA 85-88

Wolfe, Gene (Rodman) 1931- ......CLC 25
See also CANR 6
See also CA 57-60
See also DLB 8

Wolfe, Thomas (Clayton)
1900-1938............... TCLC 4, 13
See also CA 104
See also DLB 9
See also DLB-Y 85
See also DLB-DS 2

Wolfe, Thomas Kennerly, Jr. 1931-
See Wolfe, Tom
See also CANR 9
See also CA 13-16R

Wolfe, Tom 1931- ..... CLC 1, 2, 9, 15, 35
See also Wolfe, Thomas Kennerly, Jr.
See also AITN 2

Wolff, Tobias (Jonathan Ansell)
1945-................... CLC 39 (283)
See also CA 117

Wolitzer, Hilma 1930-.............CLC 17
See also CANR 18
See also CA 65-68
See also SATA 31

Wonder, Stevie 1950- ....CLC 12
See also Morris, Steveland Judkins

Wong, Jade Snow 1922-...........CLC 17
See also CA 109

Woodcott, Keith 1934-
See Brunner, John (Kilian Houston)

Woolf, (Adeline) Virginia
1882-1941...............TCLC 1, 5, 20
See also CA 104
See also DLB 36

Woollcott, Alexander (Humphreys)
1887-1943................... TCLC 5
See also CA 105
See also DLB 29

Wordsworth, William
1770-1850.................. NCLC 12

Wouk, Herman 1915-........ CLC 1, 9, 38
See also CANR 6
See also CA 5-8R
See also DLB-Y 82

Wright, Charles 1935- ...... CLC 6, 13, 28
See also CA 29-32R
See also DLB-Y 82

Wright, James (Arlington)
1927-1980............CLC 3, 5, 10, 28
See also CANR 4
See also CA 49-52
See also obituary CA 97-100
See also DLB 5
See also AITN 2

Wright, Judith 1915-..............CLC 11
See also CA 13-16R
See also SATA 14

Wright, Richard (Nathaniel)
1908-1960....... CLC 1, 3, 4, 9, 14, 21
See also CA 108
See also DLB-DS 2

Wright, Richard B(ruce) 1937-......CLC 6
See also CA 85-88

Wright, Rick 1945-
See Pink Floyd

Wright, Stephen 1946- ....CLC 33

Wu Ching-tzu 1701-1754 .... LC 2

Wurlitzer, Rudolph
1938?-..................... CLC 2, 4, 15
See also CA 85-88

Wylie (Benét), Elinor (Morton Hoyt)
  1885-1928................... **TCLC 8**
  See also CA 105
  See also DLB 9, 45

Wyndham, John 1903-1969........**CLC 19**
  See also Harris, John (Wyndham Parkes
    Lucas) Beynon

Wyss, Johann David
  1743-1818................. **NCLC 10**
  See also SATA 27, 29

Yanovsky, Vassily S(emenovich)
  1906-..................... **CLC 2, 18**
  See also CA 97-100

Yates, Richard 1926-........ **CLC 7, 8, 23**
  See also CANR 10
  See also CA 5-8R
  See also DLB 2
  See also DLB-Y 81

Yeats, William Butler
  1865-1939.............**TCLC 1, 11, 18**
  See also CANR 10
  See also CA 104
  See also DLB 10, 19

Yehoshua, Abraham B.
  1936-.................... **CLC 13, 31**
  See also CA 33-36R

Yep, Laurence (Michael) 1948-.....**CLC 35**
  See also CLR 3
  See also CANR 1
  See also CA 49-52
  See also SATA 7

Yerby, Frank G(arvin)
  1916-.................. **CLC 1, 7, 22**
  See also CANR 16
  See also CA 9-12R

Yevtushenko, Yevgeny (Aleksandrovich)
  1933-.................**CLC 1, 3, 13, 26**
  See also CA 81-84

Yglesias, Helen 1915-.......... **CLC 7, 22**
  See also CANR 15
  See also CA 37-40R

Yorke, Henry Vincent 1905-1974
  See Green, Henry
  See also CA 85-88
  See also obituary CA 49-52

Young, Al 1939-.................**CLC 19**
  See also CA 29-32R
  See also DLB 33

Young, Andrew 1885-1971.........**CLC 5**
  See also CANR 7
  See also CA 5-8R

Young, Edward 1683-1765.......... **LC 3**

Young, Neil 1945- ....**CLC 17**
  See also CA 110

Yourcenar, Marguerite
  1903-................... **CLC 19, 38**
  See also CA 69-72

Yurick, Sol 1925-.................**CLC 6**
  See also CA 13-16R

Zamyatin, Yevgeny Ivanovich
  1884-1937.................. **TCLC 8**
  See also CA 105

Zangwill, Israel 1864-1926....... **TCLC 16**
  See also CA 109
  See also DLB 10

Zappa, Francis Vincent, Jr. 1940-
  See Zappa, Frank
  See also CA 108

Zappa, Frank 1940- ....**CLC 17**
  See also Zappa, Francis Vincent, Jr.

Zaturenska, Marya
  1902-1982................. **CLC 6, 11**
  See also CA 13-16R
  See also obituary CA 105

Zelazny, Roger 1937- ....**CLC 21**
  See also CA 21-24R
  See also SATA 39
  See also DLB 8

Zhdanov, Andrei A(lexandrovich)
  1896-1948................. **TCLC 18**

Zimmerman, Robert 1941-
  See Dylan, Bob

Zindel, Paul 1936-............. **CLC 6, 26**
  See also CLR 3
  See also CA 73-76
  See also SATA 16
  See also DLB 7

Zinoviev, Alexander 1922-.........**CLC 19**
  See also CA 116

Zola, Émile 1840-1902 ......**TCLC 1, 6, 21**
  See also CA 104

Zorrilla y Moral, José
  1817-1893................... **NCLC 6**

Zoshchenko, Mikhail (Mikhailovich)
  1895-1958................. **TCLC 15**
  See also CA 115

Zuckmayer, Carl 1896-1977 ....**CLC 18**
  See also CA 69-72

Zukofsky, Louis
  1904-1978....... **CLC 1, 2, 4, 7, 11, 18**
  See also CA 9-12R
  See also obituary CA 77-80
  See also DLB 5

Zweig, Paul 1935-1984 ...... **CLC 34 (378)**
  See also CA 85-88
  See also obituary CA 113

Zweig, Stefan 1881-1942 .... **TCLC 17**
  See also CA 112

Cumulative Index to Nationalities

Vigny, Alfred de 7
Villiers de l'Isle Adam, Jean
 Marie Mathias Philippe
 Auguste, Comte de 3

GERMAN
Arnim, Achim von 5
Brentano, Clemens 1
Droste-Hülshoff, Annette Freiin
 von 3
Eichendorff, Joseph Freiherr
 von 8
Fouqué, Friedrich de La
 Motte 2
Goethe, Johann Wolfgang
 von 4
Grabbe, Christian Dietrich 2
Grimm, Jakob Ludwig Karl 3
Grimm, Wilhelm Karl 3
Heine, Heinrich 4
Herder, Johann Gottfried
 von 8
Hoffmann, Ernst Theodor
 Amadeus 2
Immermann, Karl 4
Jean Paul 7
Kleist, Heinrich von 2

Klinger, Friedrich Maximilian
 von 1
Klopstock, Friedrich 11
Ludwig, Otto 4
Mörike, Eduard 10
Novalis 13
Storm, Theodor 1
Tieck, Ludwig 5
Wagner, Richard 9

IRISH
Banim, John 13
Banim, Michael 13
Carleton, William 3
Croker, John Wilson 10
Darley, George 2
Edgeworth, Maria 1
Griffin, Gerald 7
Le Fanu, Joseph Sheridan 9
Maginn, William 8
Maturin, Charles Robert 6
Moore, Thomas 6
Sheridan, Richard Brinsley 5

ITALIAN
Foscolo, Ugo 8

NORWEGIAN
Wergeland, Henrik Arnold 5

POLISH
Fredro, Aleksander 8
Krasicki, Ignacy 8
Krasiński, Zygmunt 4
Mickiewicz, Adam 3

RUSSIAN
Aksakov, Sergei
 Timofeyvich 2
Belinski, Vissarion
 Grigoryevich 5
Chernyshevsky, Nikolay
 Gavrilovich 1
Dobrolyubov, Nikolai
 Alexandrovich 5
Dostoevski, Fedor
 Mikhailovich 2, 7
Gogol, Nikolai 5
Goncharov, Ivan
 Alexandrovich 1
Herzen, Aleksandr
 Ivanovich 10
Karamzin, Nikolai
 Mikhailovich 3
Krylov, Ivan Andreevich 1
Lermontov, Mikhail
 Yuryevich 5
Nekrasov, Nikolai 11

Pushkin, Alexander 3

SCOTTISH
Baillie, Joanna 2
Ferrier, Susan 8
Galt, John 1
Hogg, James 4
Lockhart, John Gibson 6
Oliphant, Margaret 11
Stevenson, Robert Louis 5
Wilson, John 5

SPANISH
Alarcón, Pedro Antonio de 1
Caballero, Fernán 10
Castro, Rosalía de 3
Tamayo y Baus, Manuel 1
Zorrilla y Moral, José 6

SWEDISH
Bremer, Fredrika 11
Tegnér, Esias 2

SWISS
Amiel, Henri Frédéric 4
Keller, Gottfried 2
Wyss, Johann David 10

Cumulative Index to Critics

Critic Index

Critic Index

Hall, Donald
Walt Whitman 4:602

Hall, Evelyn Beatrice
See **Tallentyre, S. G.**

Hall, James
Robert Montgomery Bird 1:84

Halliday, E. M.
Jane Austen 13:90

Halliday, R. J.
John Stuart Mill 11:391

Halline, Allen Gates
William Dunlap 2:213
Royall Tyler 3:572

Hamburger, Michael
Heinrich Heine 4:268
Heinrich von Kleist 2:457
Novalis 13:399

Hamilton, Catherine J.
Joanna Baillie 2:42

Hamilton, Clayton M.
Alexandre Dumas (fils) 9:235
Victor Hugo 3:268

Hamley, E. B.
George Eliot 4:102

Hammell, G. M.
Jones Very 9:372

Hammond, Muriel E.
Charles Robert Maturin 6:333

Hamsun, Knut
Walt Whitman 4:554

Handschin, Charles H.
Gottfried Keller 2:412

Hannay, J.
Douglas Jerrold 2:403

Hanska, Madame
See **L'Étrangère**

Hanslick, Eduard
Richard Wagner 9:401, 408

Hapgood, Norman
Eugène Fromentin 10:229

Harap, Louis
Emma Lazarus 8:428

Harbison, Robert
Jakob Grimm and Wilhelm
Grimm 3:230

Hardiman, Milton G.
Alphonse de Lamartine 11:275

Harding, D. W.
Jane Austen 1:48
Samuel Taylor Coleridge 9:176

Hardman, Frederick
Prosper Mérimée 6:352

Hardy, Barbara
Charlotte Brontë 8:66
George Eliot 4:133; 13:312,
322
William Makepeace Thackeray
5:503

Harmon, Maurice
William Carleton 3:95

Harms, Alvin
Théodore de Banville 9:29

Harpham, Geoffrey
Aubrey Beardsley 6:150

Harris, Edward
Sidney Lanier 6:265

Harris, Frank
Eugène Fromentin 10:232
Edmond de Goncourt and Jules
de Goncourt 7:175

Harris, May
Edward FitzGerald 9:275

Harris, William T.
Amos Bronson Alcott 1:22
Edward Bellamy 4:24

Harrison, Frederic
Anthony Trollope 6:468

Harrison, Jane Ellen
Ivan Alexandrovich Goncharov
1:364

Hart, Francis Russell
Susan Ferrier 8:254
James Hogg 4:287
John Gibson Lockhart 6:307,
310
Charles Robert Maturin 6:336
John Wilson 5:569

Hart, Pierre R.
Ivan Andreevich Krylov 1:437

Harte, Bret
Ralph Waldo Emerson 1:280
James Russell Lowell 2:510

Hartman, Geoffrey
John Keats 8:379
Gérard de Nerval 1:487
William Wordsworth 12:462

Harvey, W. J.
George Eliot 13:325

Hassan, Ihab
Donatien Alphonse François,
Comte de Sade 3:487

Hathaway, E. J.
Isabella Valancy Crawford
12:152

Hauck, Richard Boyd
David Crockett 8:153

Haugaard, Erik
Hans Christian Andersen 7:37

Havard, Robert G.
Rosalía de Castro 3:101

Havens, Raymond Dexter
William Wordsworth 12:444

Hawk, Affable
See also **Squire, J. C.**
Edward Lear 3:299

Hawthorne, Julian
Eugene Field 3:204

Hawthorne, Mark D.
John Banim and Michael
Banim 13:138

Hawthorne, Nathaniel
Nathaniel Hawthorne 2:297,
299, 304; 10:269
Henry Wadsworth Longfellow
2:473
Herman Melville 3:325
Henry David Thoreau 7:351
Anthony Trollope 6:454
John Greenleaf Whittier 8:487

Hay, John
Edward FitzGerald 9:267

Hayden, Robert E.
Frederick Douglass 7:132

Hayes, E. N.
Jane Austen 1:54

Hayes, Edmund M.
Mercy Otis Warren 13:425

Hayley, William
Elizabeth Montagu 7:250

Hayman, Ronald
Donatien Alphonse François,
Comte de Sade 3:493

Hayne, Paul Hamilton
William Gilmore Simms 3:502
John Greenleaf Whittier 8:497

Hays, H. R.
Jules Laforgue 5:271

Hayter, Alethea
Elizabeth Barrett Browning
1:129

Hayward, Abraham
Alexandre Dumas (père) 11:62
William Makepeace Thackeray
5:444

Haywood, Bruce
Novalis 13:383

Hazard, Lucy Lockwood
David Crockett 8:146

Hazlitt, William
William Blake 13:158
Fanny Burney 12:22
George Gordon Byron, Lord
Byron 2:65, 69
Samuel Taylor Coleridge 9:135,
138, 141
William Cowper 8:104
Leigh Hunt 1:410
Washington Irving 2:371
Charles Lamb 10:388, 389
Matthew Gregory Lewis 11:298
Charles Robert Maturin 6:318
Thomas Moore 6:382, 383
Richard Brinsley Sheridan
5:358
Robert Southey 8:460
William Wordsworth 12:409

Hearn, Lafcadio
Matthew Arnold 6:50
George Borrow 9:51
George Gordon Byron, Lord
Byron 2:83
Fedor Mikhailovich Dostoevski
2:159
Matthew Gregory Lewis 11:300
Henry Wadsworth Longfellow
2:484
Guy de Maupassant 1:442
William Morris 4:422
Dante Gabriel Rossetti 4:505
Robert Louis Stevenson 5:422

Heath-Stubbs, John
Thomas Lovell Beddoes 3:37
George Darley 2:132
Dante Gabriel Rossetti 4:516

Heber, Reginald
George Gordon Byron, Lord
Byron 12:94

Hedges, William L.
Washington Irving 2:385

Heermance, J. Noel
William Wells Brown 2:460

Heilman, Robert B.
Charlotte Brontë 3:69

Heine, Heinrich
Heinrich Heine 4:234
Ludwig Tieck 5:513

Heller, Erich
Johann Wolfgang von Goethe
4:207

Hemenway, Robert
Hugh Henry Brackenridge 7:57

Hemingway, Ernest
Herman Melville 12:261

Hemmings, F.W.J.
Honoré de Balzac 5:82
Alexandre Dumas (père) 11:88

Henderson, Arnold
Charles Lamb 10:431

Henderson, C. R.
Edward Bellamy 4:25

Henley, William Ernest
Théodore de Banville 9:17
Robert Louis Stevenson 5:388,
390, 397, 408

Henrotin, Ellen M.
Alphonse Daudet 1:233

Heraud, John Abraham
Friedrich Gottlieb Klopstock
11:223

Herbold, Anthony
Jones Very 9:386

Herder, Johann Gottfried von
Friedrich Gottlieb Klopstock
11:219, 220, 222

Herold, Amos L.
James Kirke Paulding 2:527

Herrnstadt, Richard L.
Amos Bronson Alcott 1:27

Herzberg, Max J.
Thomas Jefferson 11:171

Herzen, Alexander Ivanovich
Aleksandr Ivanovich Herzen
10:323
Alexander Pushkin 3:422

Hesse, Hermann
Jean Paul 7:234
Novalis 13:373

Hewitt-Thayer, Harvey W.
Eduard Mörike 10:450

Hewitt, John Hill
Edgar Allan Poe 1:492

Hewlett, Henry G.
William Morris 4:417

Hewlett, Maurice
Leigh Hunt 1:415
John Wilson 5:567

Hicks, Granville
Edward Bellamy 4:26
James Russell Lowell 2:519
Herman Melville 3:345
Walt Whitman 4:569

Critic Index

Critic Index

Critic Index

Critic Index

Critic Index